EISENHOWER
PORTRAIT OF THE HERO

EISENHOWER
PORTRAIT OF THE HERO

Peter Lyon

Little, Brown and Company—Boston—Toronto

The author is grateful to the following for permission to reprint previously copyrighted material:

Columbia Broadcasting System, Inc. for material from C.B.S. news broadcasts. Copyright © 1973 by Columbia Broadcasting System, Inc. All rights reserved.

Doubleday & Company, Inc. for excerpts from the following books: *Crusade in Europe* by Dwight D. Eisenhower, Copyright 1948 by Doubleday & Company, Inc.; *The White House Years: Mandate for Change 1953–1956* by Dwight D. Eisenhower, Copyright © 1963 by Dwight D. Eisenhower; *The White House Years: Waging Peace 1956–1961* by Dwight D. Eisenhower, Copyright © 1965 by Dwight D. Eisenhower; *At Ease* by Dwight D. Eisenhower, Copyright © 1967 by Dwight D. Eisenhower; *Diplomat Among Warriors* by Robert Murphy, Copyright © 1964 by Robert Murphy; *Six Crises* by Richard M. Nixon, Copyright © 1962 by Richard M. Nixon.

Harper & Row, Publishers, Inc. for excerpts from: *First-Hand Report* by Sherman Adams, Copyright © 1961 by Sherman Adams, and *Blast of War* by Harold Macmillan. Copyright © 1967 by Thomson Newspapers Limited.

The Johns Hopkins Press for excerpts from *Collected Papers of Dwight David Eisenhower* (Five Volumes). Copyright © 1970 by The Johns Hopkins Press.

Houghton Mifflin Company for excerpts from *Full Circle* by Anthony Eden. Copyright © 1960 by The Times Publishing Co. Ltd.

Simon & Schuster, Inc. for excerpts from *My Three Years with Eisenhower* by Harry C. Butcher, Copyright 1946 by Harry C. Butcher, and with Weidenfeld (Publishers) Ltd., London, for excerpts from *Unity* (Volume 2 of *Complete War Memories of Charles De Gaulle*) by Charles De Gaulle, Copyright © 1956 by Librairie Plon; Copyright © 1959 by Simon and Schuster, Inc.

Published simultaneously in Canada by Little, Brown & Company (Canada) Limited
PRINTED IN THE UNITED STATES OF AMERICA

Contents

Illustrations

General Eisenhower presides at a meeting of his senior commanders (U.S. Army Signal Corps Photo)

Eisenhower with Air Marshal Arthur Tedder and General Montgomery inspecting armored unit (U.S. Army Signal Corps Photo)

Eisenhower in London with Churchill three weeks before D-Day (U.S. Army Signal Corps Photo)

Eisenhower with U.S. Joint Chiefs on inspection of Normandy beachheads (U.S. Army Signal Corps Photo)

Eisenhower with Generals Bradley, Gerow, and J. Lawton Collins after awarding them decorations (U.S. Army Photograph)

Eisenhower with Tedder, broadcasting victory message (U.S. Army Signal Corps Photo)

Eisenhower with Columbia University football team and Coach Lou Little (Photo by Manny Warman. Courtesy of Columbia University)

As supreme commander of Allied Powers in Europe, Eisenhower addresses NATO Council in Rome (United Press International Photo)

Between pages 710 *and* 711

Eisenhower with Robert A. Taft at the Republican convention, July 1952 (United Press International Photo)

Eisenhower considers his running mate, Richard M. Nixon (United Press International Photo)

Eisenhower with Senator Joe McCarthy (Wide World Photo)

Eisenhower takes the oath of office, January 20, 1953 (United Press International Photo)

Eisenhower with Attorney General Herbert Brownell, Secretary of Agriculture Ezra Taft Benson, Secretary of HEW Mrs. Oveta Culp Hobby, and Secretary of the Treasury George Humphrey (National Park Service, Washington, D.C., courtesy of the Dwight D. Eisenhower Library, Abilene, Kansas)

Churchill and Anthony Eden confer with Eisenhower and John Foster Dulles, June 1954 (National Park Service, Washington, D.C., courtesy of the Dwight D. Eisenhower Library, Abilene, Kansas)

Nikolai Bulganin, Eisenhower, Edgar Faure, and Anthony Eden at Geneva summit, summer 1955 (Eastfoto)

Eisenhower at Fitzsimons Army Hospital, October 1955 (U.S. Army Signal Corps Photo)

Eisenhower off for a turkey shoot with George Humphrey (United Press International Photo)

The President and Mrs. Eisenhower at their home in Gettysburg, September 1956 (National Park Service, Washington, D.C., courtesy of the Dwight D. Eisenhower Library, Abilene, Kansas)

Foster Dulles confers with the President, October 30, 1956 (National Park Service, Washington, D.C., courtesy of the Dwight D. Eisenhower Library, Abilene, Kansas)

The President holds a press conference, June 1957 (National Park Service, Washington, D.C., courtesy of the Dwight D. Eisenhower Library, Abilene, Kansas)

Eisenhower at NATO conference with Macmillan and Paul-Henri Spaak, November 1957 (United Press International Photo)

The President playing golf at Newport (U.S. Naval Photo Center, Washington, D.C. Courtesy of the Dwight D. Eisenhower Library, Abilene, Kansas)

Eisenhower with Negro leaders (National Park Service, Washington, D.C., courtesy of the Dwight D. Eisenhower Library, Abilene, Kansas)

The President meets with congressional leaders over the Berlin crisis, March 1959 (National Park Service, Washington, D.C., courtesy of the Dwight D. Eisenhower Library, Abilene, Kansas)

Eisenhower and Winston Churchill visit Foster Dulles at Walter Reed Hospital (National Park Service, Washington, D.C., courtesy of the Dwight D. Eisenhower Library, Abilene, Kansas)

Eisenhower with Khrushchev at Camp David (U.S. Naval Photo Center, Washington, D.C. Courtesy of the Dwight D. Eisenhower Library, Abilene, Kansas)

The summit in collapse—de Gaulle, Macmillan, Eisenhower (United Press International Photo)

Eisenhower and President-elect Kennedy confer (United Press International Photo)

Generals Eisenhower and Bradley before the television cameras, November 1967 (United Press International Photo)

Funeral services for Dwight Eisenhower, April 1, 1969 (Wide World Photo)

The funeral cortege at Abilene, Kansas, April 2, 1969 (Wide World Photo)

Cartoons

PART ONE

APOTHEOSIS

CHAPTER ONE

Victory

VERY EARLY ON MONDAY, MAY 7, 1945—only a few minutes after midnight—General of the Army Dwight D. Eisenhower, supreme commander of the Allied Expeditionary Force in Europe, stepped from his command car and strode into the École Professionelle et Technique des Garçons, a red brick building in Rheims, France, which had been converted into his advance headquarters and designated SHAEF Forward. At the entrance there was a gaggle of correspondents, British and American, clamoring to be admitted. General Eisenhower pressed his way through them; inside, in the large entrance hall, he acknowledged the salutes of the MPs on guard and turned up the private stairs that led to his small office on the floor above. He had come here because the final instrument of surrender, of unconditional capitulation, was after many delays about to be signed by the appropriate German officer, Colonel General Gustave Jodl.

General Eisenhower and his aides had planned carefully, if imperfectly, for this ceremony. His V-E Day speech had long since been drafted, thrice redrafted, rehearsed, and substantially committed to memory. The large square SHAEF war room, customarily a most secret and closely guarded chamber, on whose walls were mounted maps of all the battle fronts, maps of railways and communications systems, weather charts, tables showing air force operations, and estimates of Allied casualties and of German prisoners, was now a tangle of radio microphones, cables, newsreel camera equipment, and floodlights. The big conference table had been shoved into a corner for a better camera angle; here the documents of surrender would be ratified.

With the actual signing General Eisenhower was not concerned; that would be supervised by his chief of staff, Lieutenant General Walter Bedell (Beetle) Smith, and his chief of intelligence, British Major General Kenneth W. D. Strong. These two men had negotiated the Italian surrender in September 1943; moreover, thanks to a prewar tour of duty as military attaché in Berlin, Strong spoke fluent German.

As for the terms of the surrender, a European Advisory Commission consisting of delegates from the United States, the United Kingdom, and the Soviet Union had toiled for months to draft a detailed document (and also to divide Germany into three zones of occupation), but on May 4 Beetle Smith had told John Winant, the American ambassador to the Court of St. James's, who was also the American representative on the European Advisory Commission, that no copy of this document had been transmitted to SHAEF. Winant was incredulous, but Smith's denial was firm. In consequence, Eisenhower had instructed his staff to draft at once two documents, an "Act of Military Surrender" and an "Undertaking Given by Certain Emissaries to the Allied High Command." The first of these required unconditional surrender of all German land, sea, and air forces on both eastern and western fronts simultaneously; the second required the chief of the German High Command and the commanders of the German army, navy, and air force to appear when and where ordered to do so by General Eisenhower and the Soviet Supreme Command, to ratify the "Act of Military Surrender."

The ranking German official was Grossadmiral Karl Dönitz, appointed by Hitler on April 30 to succeed him. Dönitz had established an ersatz government in Flensburg, a town in northern Germany near the Danish border, as far from the oncoming Russians as he could get, and he had made his policies both clear and public: "to save German territory and the German race from Bolshevism" by "continuing to resist in the west only for so long as [is] required for the implementation of my plans in the east." Dönitz hoped for "a separate and partial capitulation" to the British and Americans so that they and the Germans might unite and turn on the Russians. With this scheme in mind, he had dispatched his emissaries to Rheims.

The first of these, Admiral Hans-Georg von Friedeburg, had arrived in Rheims on the evening of May 5 and contrived to stall and haggle and argue—quite obviously so that more Nazis might successfully elude the Red Army by slipping through the Allied lines to the west—for a full twenty-four hours. The second spokesman, General Jodl, had arrived on the evening of May 6 and managed to temporize yet further. Jodl had still hoped to split his western enemies from his eastern: since, as he insisted, the British and Americans would soon be warring with the Russians, why should they not allow as many Nazi troops as possible to escape to the west, there to be freshly equipped as allies in the upcoming battle against the savage hordes from the east?

Jodl had argued this point with such assurance and conviction that Beetle Smith and Strong at length deemed it necessary to consult with the supreme commander. Eisenhower's reaction was tart and abrupt: unless the surrender terms were promptly accepted, he would order the western

4

front sealed forthwith. Still Jodl persisted, pleading for a forty-eight-hour delay in executing the terms, contending that immediate submission would be technically impossible. Even Strong, who as Eisenhower's G–2 was aware of the utter confusion of German communications, was inclined to support Jodl's request. Eisenhower had been reluctant, as he reported to the War Department in Washington, to place "the decision as to when fighting would cease in the hands of the Germans." Moreover, he had understood that the Germans' motive was "to continue to make a front against the Russians as long as they possibly can in order to evacuate maximum numbers of Germans into our lines." Impatient to have it over with, however, he decided that the surrender, if signed at once, might be dated to take effect from midnight of May 8. (The implication—if Dönitz would swiftly accommodate, his countrymen would in turn be more swiftly accommodated—was presumably not lost on the Soviets.) In the event, a little before midnight on May 6 Eisenhower had been told that Jodl had at last agreed to sign.

Except in one crucial respect, the moment of triumph seemed to most of those at SHAEF a thundering anticlimax, and the lengthy palaver at Rheims, already protracted from Friday until Monday, had done nothing to improve the supreme commander's disposition. He was impatient and irritable. For more than a month he had perceived that he was witnessing the final convulsions of Hitler's Germany and the collapse of the Nazi dream of world dominion. Back in March had come the desperate Nazi attempts to conclude a separate peace with the western allies and so permit a last-ditch struggle against the implacable Russian advance from the east. After the first week of April it was clear that few German commanders on the western front knew how their troops were disposed; their orders, intercepted by Allied intelligence officers, were irrational. By April 16 General H. H. (Hap) Arnold, commander of the U.S. Air Force, had considered the time ripe to announce that the air war in Europe was won. On April 25 reconnaissance patrols of the American First Army, under the command of Lieutenant General Courtney Hodges, had joined on the Elbe with elements of the 1st Ukrainian Army Group knifing west beyond the Oder, and presently the troops of both armies, American and Russian, were happily carousing together. By the end of April both Mussolini and Hitler were violently dead, the one executed by Italian partisans, the other a suicide. Nazi generals had hastened to surrender their armies: in Italy to Field Marshal Harold Alexander; in northwest Germany, Holland, and Denmark to Field Marshal Bernard Montgomery; and three more to Lieutenant General Jacob L. Devers's 6th Army Group. Berlin had fallen to the Red Army. What was left for the supreme commander? Apparently nothing but the formality of making official the final surrender of the Nazi hierarchy.

Moreover, as the evidence of imminent victory had become more obvious, the grand alliance which Eisenhower had been at such pains to construct had been subjected to greater and growing stresses. The grit in the gears was ideological, as had been so clearly foreseen by, among others, the brilliant propagandist Paul Josef Goebbels: it was the inherent conflict, once Hitlerism and fascism had been squashed, between the Anglo-American alliance and the Soviet Union. British Prime Minister Winston S. Churchill had some time before resumed with relish his long-time antipathy to the Soviets. In the spring of 1944, indeed even before D-Day (June 6), he had assembled in London an Imperial Conference to consider the possibilities of Soviet expansion; he had instructed the Foreign Office to prepare a memorandum that would define "the brute issues between us and the Soviet Government which are developing in Italy, in Roumania, in Bulgaria, in Yugoslavia and, above all, in Greece." On the same day he had complained to his foreign secretary, Sir Anthony Eden, of "Communist intrigues in Italy, Yugoslavia and Greece," and he had grumbled that the Russian "attitude becomes more difficult every day."

Quite naturally, then, Churchill and the British Chiefs of Staff had opposed, with every determined and emotional argument at their command, Eisenhower's decision not to race the Red Army to capture Berlin.* The quarrel had been taken to the highest level, but in Washington there had been no disposition to shift the emphasis of the directive given the supreme commander. Churchill and the British Chiefs had been even more vexed with Eisenhower when he acquainted the Soviets with his strategic plans for penetrations north and south of Berlin. The chief of the Imperial General Staff, Field Marshal Sir Alan Brooke (later Viscount Alanbrooke), wrote petulantly in his diary that Eisenhower "has no business to address Stalin direct," and for two or three days at the end of March the British leaders had spent hours of their time fretting over what they considered a most grievous political blunder. For substantially the same reasons, the British had also been growling about Eisenhower's refusal to compete with the Russians as to who should liberate Prague. Finally, General Charles de Gaulle, ever cantankerous in defense of what he conceived to be France's national interests, had suddenly got sticky about American rights to use the city of Stuttgart as a traffic center in support of their advanced armies; as a quid pro quo he had demanded of Eisenhower that the Anglo-American allies concede to the French a zone of occupation in Germany.

---

* The reasons for Eisenhower's decision, and the British objections to it, are discussed later (pages 350–354).

To Eisenhower, moreover, it seemed that his increasingly contentious allies had not sufficiently appreciated the fact that after V-E Day the armed forces of the United States—and of Great Britain and France—would still be facing a determined foe in the Pacific. All hands, he felt, should be more concerned with the swift deployment of troops and supplies halfway around the world and less distracted by European haute-politique.

Little wonder the supreme commander's patience was wearing thin.

Even a festive party planned early in May by Lieutenant Kay Summersby, the supreme commander's comely aide and confidential secretary, to celebrate the impending V-E Day had fallen flat. She had set the evening of May 6 for the revels; at the time the date had seemed comfortably fixed in the future, but when her guests had gathered there was still nothing to celebrate. General Eisenhower, tense and preoccupied, stayed only a few minutes at this cheerless frolic. "Keep in touch with the office," he told her as he left. "Let me know what's happening."

In the event, he was summoned to SHAEF Forward before she was. When she arrived, bringing with her Telek, Eisenhower's Scottish terrier, he was prowling back and forth between his empty office and hers, restless and fretful. She found the rooms "lonely and pathetic," and the silence oppressive. Thus the supreme commander, as the last minutes wore on before his ultimate military triumph.

Those last minutes were to bring in their train something else, by no means anticlimactic: the apotheosis of Dwight D. Eisenhower into the most admired, the most beloved, and the most extravagantly praised of all men of his time. This was the culmination of a process that had begun nearly three years before, a process at first gradual and almost imperceptible, but since D-Day, eleven months before, racing like a mountain torrent in spring flood, uncontrollable, inevitable, smashing to bits old friendships and warm intimacies, sweeping everything before it to clear the way for an unknown but predictable future. The man who had been so little known in September 1941 that he had been labeled "D. D. Ersenbeing" in a caption for a newspaper picture was now a world hero, about to be saluted as "the principal architect of victory in the West," "the greatest military strategist of our time," and "the most brilliant strategist of war since Napoleon."

Swift emergence from almost complete obscurity to worldwide adulation is bound to unsettle the most surefooted. The best evidence, however, indicates that General Eisenhower was still, on this May 7, 1945, largely unaware of the full-throated acclaim that was waiting for him wherever he might go. Admittedly, it seems incredible. He had been surrounded by able and articulate correspondents almost from the day in June 1942 when he arrived in England as the commanding general of American forces in Europe; to a man they had shouted his hosannas for home consumption. Later the writers sent overseas to do feature pieces had filled the American magazines with paeans in praise of him. Even before D-Day he had afforded the time for interviews by his prospective biographers; they had all been at once transformed into his hagiographers. His mobile, expressive face had converted every photographer into his votary. His fan mail had multiplied astronomically; admirers from every Allied nation had showered him with gifts of food, liquor, clothing, keepsakes, good luck charms, and the like. Politicians, publishers, industrialists, and movie stars had for twenty months deemed access to his headquarters to be worth more than much fine gold. For more than a year a zealous, ever mushrooming corps of volunteers at home and abroad had been clamorously urging that he should be nominated for the presidency of the United States. The temptation is to conclude that if General Eisenhower was truly unaware of this concerto, scored for brasses and timpani crescendo, he was a remarkably stupid man. The skilled craftsmen who have woven the lustrous Eisenhower legend would have it that his astonishment at the acclamation that was to be his lot was proof of his modesty and humility. The trouble with this view is that Eisenhower was never particularly modest, much less humble, about an accomplishment which he believed deserving of praise. The reason he failed to anticipate the future fanfares was that, in sharp contrast to some of his field commanders, General Eisenhower was lacking in arrogance and theatricality. He was a tough-minded professional soldier; as such, he quite understood that the commanding general of a victorious army is no more praiseworthy, and perhaps less, than the footslogger in a platoon of infantry. He was self-conscious, he was self-confident, but he was not cursed with any overweening sense of self-importance.

On this night, as he walked impatiently back and forth through his office and that of Kay Summersby, when he thought of the future he thought of what he would like to do and of what he would have to do— and of the conflict between them. What did he most want to do? At least part of his dream was to resign his commission and go to some peaceful place, some private place, where he could sit beside a lazy stream and hang a lazy hook for fish. He yearned for the irresponsibilities of total privacy.

This dream, he knew, could never come true. He had known for some time that he was slated to take military command of the American zone of occupied Germany; he knew he was spoken of as the man who would succeed General of the Army George C. Marshall as chief of staff of the United States Army. He knew he would take these posts when he was asked to do so. He knew he was condemned to a life of public responsibility.

The general and his aide were together in their adjoining offices for two hours or more while they awaited the conclusion of the formalities in the war room down the corridor.

A little before 3 A.M. Beetle Smith, the chief of staff, reported that the surrender had been signed and that the Germans were on their way to the supreme commander's office. They were marched in, Colonel General Jodl, Admiral von Friedeburg, and an aide; they halted before the supreme commander's desk and saluted smartly. General Eisenhower stood straight and still. Lieutenant Summersby, her pencil poised, sat waiting next door to record the dialogue.

General Eisenhower's voice was hard. "Do you understand the terms of the document of surrender you have just signed?"

A swift translation by General Strong. Two voices in assent: "Ja."

"You will get details of instructions at a later date. And you will be expected to carry them out faithfully."

A nod from Jodl. A silent stare from Eisenhower. A bow, a salute, an about-face, a march out of the office.

Then a rush of photographers for more pictures. A group picture: all the top people of SHAEF. Where were the pens that had been used for the signing? General Ike, a big grin, held two pens in a V-for-victory. The flashbulbs popped, and popped again; a cheer; smiles all around. Back to the war room for newsreels and radio recordings; a goof, a wrong word used, a retake, tempers stretched and thin. Then back to the supreme commander's office so that he might jot down a characteristically unadorned message for transmission to his superiors, the Combined Chiefs of Staff of the United States of America and the United Kingdom of Great Britain. The message, in its entirety, ran:

CC/S.
The mission of this Allied Force was fulfilled at 3 A.M. local time, May 7, 1945. Eisenhower.

This message was dispatched. He scribbled another, using the careless shorthand of extreme weariness:

To CC/S.
A detailed report on signing of armistice and my recommendations respecting govermtal ~~pron~~ annoucmnts follow immediately. ~~I believe earliest~~ Although hostilities do not officially cease until one minute after midnight on ~~the~~ night of May 8/9, I believe, as explained in longer telegram to follow, that ancment should be at earliest hour that cordination can be achieved. Eisenhower

Coordination of action, of purpose, of strategy and tactics—coordination of all the conflicting nationalist impulses into one irresistible drive to victory—this had been General Eisenhower's overriding concern since he had taken command of American troops in the European theater, back in June, 1942. "From the outset," as Major General H. L. (later Lord) Ismay, who was Churchill's staff officer and personal representative on the British Chiefs of Staff Committee, has noted, "he regarded Anglo-American friendship almost as a religion," and his determination to win the friendship and trust of the Soviets was equally firm. Coordination in every detail, whether ceremonial or substantive. Thus, even as the photographers crowded around him at Rheims to record his moment of final triumph, he had reached out to make sure Air Chief Marshal Sir Arthur (later Lord) Tedder, his deputy, would appear beside him in the pictures and newsreels.

But coordination of jealous and competitive efforts, as who could know better than General Eisenhower, is an elusive thing. The coordination he mentioned in his telegram to the Combined Chiefs was relatively trivial: a matter of agreement among the leaders of the three principal Allied powers—Truman, Churchill, and Stalin—on the hour of their simultaneous announcement of the victory over Hitler and Nazi Germany. Behind this trifle, however, there loomed the awesome task of making a stable, enduring peace, and the hopes of unity in seeking that peace were already prejudiced, perhaps irreparably.

With some of the rumbles of discord General Eisenhower was familiar; with others he was not. There was no compelling reason for him to have been informed, after the death on April 12 of his commander in chief Franklin Roosevelt and the accession to that post of Harry S. Truman, about the hostility that had crept into the diplomatic exchanges between the United States and the Soviet Union. Nor was he acquainted with the wrangle that had developed over differing interpretations of the imprecise agreements on the new government and boundaries of Poland reached at the Yalta Conference in February. He did not know that Truman, after only eleven days as President, had subjected the Soviet foreign minister, V. M. Molotov, to unprecedented hectoring, an episode that shocked the Russians the more because Stalin had dispatched Molotov to the United States (to head the Soviet delegation at the San Francisco conference convened to establish the United Nations) at the particular behest of W. Averell Harriman, American ambassador to the Soviet Union. (Stalin had told Harriman he was anxious "to give some immediate assurance to the American people [of] his desire to continue on a cooperative basis" with the United States.) Moreover, while Eisenhower had been told of the project to devise the atomic bomb, the weapon that would so balefully affect American foreign policy, especially toward the Soviet Union, he did not know how far that project had been advanced. On the other hand, Eisenhower was fully aware of the mistrust aroused in Moscow when Allen Dulles, as chief of the U.S. Office of Strategic Services in Switzerland, had maneuvered in late February and March to contrive a surrender of the German armies in Italy, while denying the Russians the right to attend the negotiations. That venture had provoked more than a half-dozen lengthy cables at the highest level.* It had also moved the supreme commander to resolve that he would, in his dealings with the defeated enemy, be most meticulous to avoid any difficulty with his Russian allies, most careful to abort any suspicion.

Indeed, General Eisenhower had at all times acted toward the Soviets in circumspect fashion. When Heinrich Himmler, chief of the Gestapo and the Schutzstaffel (the infamous SS, the elite Nazi security guard), made an offer via Sweden in late April to surrender Germany to the British and Americans, Eisenhower had promptly sent a signal to Moscow, disavowing the offer. His army group commanders—Montgomery, Devers, and others—had, by his orders, accepted German surrenders only locally; he had made it clear that no wholesale surrender was permissible unless made simultaneously on eastern and western fronts. He had at once notified General A. E. Antonov, chief of staff of the Red Army, when von Friedeburg and Jodl were about to arrive in Rheims; he had invited the Soviets to send a plenipotentiary to his headquarters if they did not consider Major General Ivan Suslaparov, chief Russian liaison officer at SHAEF, of sufficient rank to represent them; he had apprised the Soviets of his views at each stage of the negotiations. He had teletyped the terms of his two surrender documents to Major General John R. Deane, head of the American military mission in Moscow, and Deane had casually transmitted them on Sunday, May 6, to General Antonov.

Antonov acted more swiftly. His letter, handed to Deane early on the

* The exchange included Roosevelt's last message to Stalin, sent April 12, in which he said: "In any event, there must not be mutual distrust, and minor misunderstandings of this character should not arise in the future." Stalin did not consider the attempt to conclude a separate peace a minor misunderstanding. At one point in the exchange (April 7), he showed that he was bothered by something else. "The Germans have 147 divisions on the eastern front," he said. "They could safely withdraw from 15 to 20 divisions from the eastern front to aid their forces on the western front. Yet they have not done so, nor are they doing so. They are fighting desperately against the Russians for Zemlenice, an obscure station in Czechoslovakia, which they need just as much as a dead man needs a poultice, but they surrender without any resistance such important towns in the heart of Germany as Osnabrück, Mannheim and Kassel. You will admit that this behavior on the part of the Germans is more than strange and unaccountable." While Stalin characterized the behavior as "unaccountable," it is likely that without unduly exerting himself he could with fair accuracy have accounted for it.

morning of May 7, desired changes in the surrender document, expressed apprehension that the Nazis would not surrender on the eastern front (indeed the fighting persisted, bloody and savage, until Friday, May 11), and demanded that a treaty of surrender, the only proper such treaty, be signed in Berlin, where Marshal Georgi Zhukov would represent the Soviet Union. Deane, much disconcerted, at once sent a TWX (teletypewriter exchange) to Eisenhower at Rheims.

The supreme commander was still comfortably absorbed with his TWX messages to the Combined Chiefs in Washington, with his telephone calls to Churchill, Ismay, and General Omar Bradley to share with them the satisfaction of victory and an end to the slaughter, with his notification of the surrender to Moscow. Then he was handed Deane's message.

What had gone wrong? Even as Eisenhower was framing the answer for Moscow, saying that the surrender had already been signed but that he would be happy to fly to Berlin to countersign a formal ratification, the responsibility for the blunder was coming to light, down the corridor in the office of General Bedell Smith, where Eisenhower's chief of staff was talking with Robert Murphy.

Murphy, Eisenhower's political adviser both in North Africa and now in Germany, had not attended the surrender ceremony (it was "strictly military," and Murphy was habituated by many years in the American foreign service to the precise observance of protocol), but directly the formalities were completed he had picked up the documents and glanced at the texts. Strange texts, he reflected; unrecognizable documents. And this was odd, for Murphy had studied and then personally delivered to Beetle Smith the surrender instruments hammered out by the European Advisory Commission and thereafter formally approved by the governments of the United States, the United Kingdom, and the Soviet Union. Murphy was at once gravely concerned. Smith, exhausted by the protracted negotiations, had gone to bed, but Murphy telephoned him to ask what had become of the documents from the EAC. As he had done a few days before to Winant, Smith irritably denied knowledge of any such documents.

"But the big blue folder I gave you a month ago," Murphy insisted, "when I told you these were the terms everybody had approved. Don't you remember?"

General Smith hurriedly dressed and rushed back to his office. There, in his locked file, was the big blue folder. And there, a few moments later, came a TWX message from Washington reporting the protest from Moscow that the wrong surrender documents had been signed—a confirmation of the earlier message received from Deane. Other messages presently told of the announcement by the Nazi radio station in the so-called capital at Flensburg that a separate peace had been signed with the Anglo-American allies, but none with the Soviets.

In short, the surrender ceremony, so carefully planned, so eagerly anticipated, was a spectacular botch.

Murphy later dismissed Smith's contribution to the mess as "a rare lapse of memory." At the least, it was atrocious staffwork by a man whom Eisenhower called "a godsend." Routine procedure, in the great military tradition, required that the whole business be swept under the rug. The supreme commander decided on a tactical withdrawal. He observed—"without," as Kay Summersby noted, "the slightest sign of exuberance" —that some champagne would be appropriate to the occasion, and went off with her and two or three others to his residence, a handsome manor taken over from a wealthy champagne vintner. The party—"no gaiety, no joking, no laughing . . . absolutely no buoyancy"—lasted till dawn.

Before eight o'clock that morning Eisenhower was busy at his bedside telephone, drafting more cables and TWX messages, trying to resurrect order from the chaos of the night before. To Captain Harry Butcher, his close friend and naval aide, who wandered into his room a little after nine, the supreme commander looked drawn and worn. "The last four days," Butcher noted in his diary, "have taken more out of him than have the past eleven months of the campaign"—all the months since D-Day on the beaches of Normandy.

But if Eisenhower thought he could pick up the pieces and fit them together again, he had set himself an impossible task. In his bedroom and later that day in his office he could find only evidence of worse confusion and more bitter conflict.

There was first the matter of his generous, instinctive offer to fly to Berlin to share in the official surrender together with Marshal Zhukov of the Red Army. (He was anxious to see Berlin, smashed into ruins, and he wanted to meet the Soviet commanders.) Suddenly all his advisers were against the idea. Churchill, who called him eight times from London during the day, exerted every effort to dissuade him from the trip. Beetle Smith added his negative counsel and got other staff officers to weigh in with their objections. They all urged that his presence in Berlin would damage the prestige of the western allies; after all, he was a General of the Army, outranking Zhukov, who was a mere army group commander; protocol required that he ignore this "encore," which was being staged by the Russians as a propaganda circus to entertain their people at home; to give in to the Russians would be demeaning; western pride would suffer, et cetera, et cetera. So, with Eisenhower's reluctant compliance, a gesture that might have compensated for the follies of the surrender at Rheims was scotched.

And all day reports continued to come in of Nazi radio broadcasts that referred only to a surrender of German arms to the western allies.

Even the simple matter of coordinating the announcement of victory from the capitals of the three great powers fell apart. There had been tentative agreement on the hour—3 P.M. Greenwich mean time on the afternoon of Tuesday, May 8— but suddenly Churchill demanded that V-E Day be proclaimed at once, while the Soviets, still battling on the eastern front, urged that any announcement be postponed another twenty-four hours.

Then, the final indignity, word came that a correspondent of the Associated Press had disobeyed SHAEF's orders and filed a story of the surrender from Paris a full twenty-four hours ahead of time. From the AP wire the news had been picked up by the U.S. Office of War Information, for short wave radio transmission, and thence broadcast by Radio Luxembourg, which was operated by SHAEF's own Psychological Warfare Division. The supreme commander was white with anger, but his loss of temper was an exercise in futility. What matter the hour they heard about it? People the world over wanted only the good news.

It was, in Churchill's words, "the signal for the greatest outburst of joy in the history of mankind."

CHAPTER TWO

The Victors Measure Each Other

FOR MUCH OF THE WORLD the joy focused, quite naturally, on the supreme commander. His was the picture on the front pages of the newspapers, set two or three columns wide beneath the big black headlines proclaiming V-E Day; to him came the flood of congratulatory cablegrams and the insistent invitations to be guest of honor at all manner of celebrations, private, civic, and national; to him the glasses were raised and the toasts offered; when his image flashed on the screen in motion picture theaters the audiences burst into applause; his name was murmured in the prayers of thanksgiving offered up in churches and synagogues on both sides of the Atlantic. He was Ike, and he could do no wrong. His apotheosis was complete.

Along with the glory come the duties, and Eisenhower knew it. A cable from George Marshall was at hand telling of the scheme in Washington to bring back groups of officers and enlisted men so that the folks at home would have a chance to rejoice over a few flesh-and-blood heroes. Generals Bradley, Devers, George S. Patton, Leonard Gerow, William Simpson—each would head a party, each would be sent to a different city to be cheered and make a speech or two. Most in demand would be the supreme commander himself; for him would be reserved the celebrations in Washington and New York City; but, not to keep the residents of those cities too long in suspense, he should start at once to plan his victorious return home.

Triumphal tours cannot be arranged overnight. Committees of dignitaries must be formed, banquet halls reserved, and schedules synchronized. Personages all the way up to the President himself must be consulted and their consent to the preparations obtained. At length it was agreed that General Eisenhower would fly home in mid-June.

During the intervening five weeks the supreme commander would be preoccupied with some notably explosive issues, ranging from the behavior of American politicians as they junketed through western Europe to policies for conquered Germany that would later shape tactics and strategy in the Cold War. Captain Butcher, who was wise in the ways of public relations, reckoned that "General Ike and his entire command are in for a rough time." He predicted "critical stories of General Ike and his policies in handling displaced persons, repatriated prisoners, and the occupation of Germany." But in truth much of what Eisenhower did and said was, for reasons of supposed security, shielded from public scrutiny.

Most of the headaches of that May and June were provoked, one way or another, by fears or suspicions of the Russians. Churchill was bent on preserving German arms for possible use against the Soviets, and he kept a steady pressure on Eisenhower to see that this was done. Further, the prime minister counseled the supreme commander that "German problems should be handled by Germans and some of the German generals now held by us might be employed for this purpose since they would be obeyed by the German people." Such a posture was implicit in the lenient British attitude toward the Nazi government still functioning in Flensburg.* But Eisenhower, whose loathing of the Nazis was undiminished,

---

* Flensburg was in the British zone of occupation, where also the British maintained, under command of Field Marshal Bernard (later Viscount) Montgomery (of Alamein), some seven hundred thousand German troops, organized in military formations including one corps of one hundred thousand veterans of the Wehrmacht. These units were not disbanded, despite the Potsdam protocols forbidding them, until after a formal Russian protest had been filed in November 1945.

believed that Flensburg called for prompt and radical surgery. He dispatched Robert Murphy and Major General Lowell Rooks, a SHAEF staff officer, to take the measure of Grossadmiral Dönitz. Their report confirmed Eisenhower's suspicions that the Nazis "were trying to create a rift between Anglo-Americans and Russians"; indeed, Dönitz's remarks, as Murphy wrote later, "could be interpreted only as an offer to join us in a crusade against the Bolsheviks." Eisenhower sent orders to arrest Dönitz and everybody connected with his so-called government.

There was also the matter of organizing the Allied Control Council, arranging for access by the three western powers (United States, United Kingdom, and France) to Berlin, which was in the Soviet zone of occupation, and settling the vexatious question of Anglo-American withdrawal from German territory that was, by agreement, part of the Soviet zone. Nothing exasperated Churchill more in the last days of May and early days of June than the "abandonment," as he put it, "of this enormous area —400 miles long and 120 at its greatest depth." He did his best to persuade Eisenhower, the American Joint Chiefs of Staff, and President Truman to hold their ground against the encroachment into western Europe of those whom Field Marshal Montgomery characterized as "barbarous Asiatics." On June 4 Churchill cabled to Truman: "I view with profound misgivings the retreat [sic] of the American Army to our line of occupation in the central sector, thus bringing Soviet power into the heart of Western Europe and the descent of an iron curtain between us and everything to the eastward."* But Truman, largely influenced by Eisenhower, had already made up his mind that the urgent need was to get the Allied

---

* This was not the first use of the Churchillian phrase "iron curtain." On May 12 the prime minister had cabled to Truman his misgivings that too many Americans were quitting Europe, leaving it to too many Russians. "An iron curtain is drawn down upon their front," Churchill complained. "We do not know what is going on behind." Still in the future was his first public use of the phrase, in a speech at Fulton, Missouri, on March 5, 1946, after which every western politician and journalist would drub it into the most tiresome of clichés.

The phrase, however, was not originally coined by Churchill. In its contemporary sense, as the demarcation of Soviet hegemony in Europe, it was first spread abroad by Paul Josef Goebbels in an editorial in the newspaper *Das Reich*, dated February 25, 1945, but published some days earlier. Goebbels wrote: "If the German people lay down their arms, the whole of eastern and southeastern Europe, together with the Reich, would come under Russian occupation. Behind the iron curtain, mass butcheries of people would begin, and all that would remain would be a crude automation, a daily fermenting mass of thousands of proletarians and despairing slave animals knowing nothing of the outside world."

This paragraph was republished in the *Times* of London and in the *Manchester Guardian* on February 23, 1945, where it would lie ready to be read and later unconsciously plagiarized by Churchill. There it was also noted by the well-known British Marxist R. Palme Dutt, who has observed that the phrase "should be recognized as part of the legacy of Goebbels."

Control Council in working order to avert the total collapse of Germany's social and economic structure. The formal declaration of Germany's defeat had by May 22 been approved by the four powers concerned; it remained only for the military commanders to sign it and set up shop in Berlin.

As for the imperative political issues involved, Truman hoped his special emissary Harry Hopkins might, in face-to-face conversations with Stalin, be able to establish not only an understanding about the Allied Control Council and its future operations but also a solution of the Polish question, the time and place for a summit meeting of Truman with Stalin and Churchill, and the date when the Soviet Union would enter the war against Japan. Hopkins was selected for this delicate mission to Moscow, despite the precarious state of his health, because he had been President Roosevelt's trusted and intimate adviser in all the complex wartime negotiations. On his way from Washington to Moscow, Hopkins stopped off in Paris, on May 24, and met briefly with Eisenhower, whose interest in how the Russians would conduct themselves on the Allied Control Council was naturally quite lively.

Everything about this governing body represented a departure from Eisenhower's accustomed procedures. He was used to dealing with political questions in substantive fashion, relying upon General Marshall, the American Joint Chiefs, and the American commander in chief to back him up as they had wholeheartedly done during the past three years in Great Britain, in North Africa, and in Europe. Now he suspected, and with good reason, that he would more and more be serving only as an agent for the Joint Chiefs and the President, taking their orders and obeying them like any other soldier in the chain of command. Heretofore he had been the supreme commander, expecting and getting (soon or late) obedience from every other officer in the Western Alliance. Nominally he would continue as supreme commander for a few more weeks, but time was running out on this exalted rank. Already, on May 22, Field Marshal Montgomery had been posted as commander of the British forces of occupation and British delegate to the Allied Control Council, which elevated him from Eisenhower's subordinate officer to his peer. The French commander was to be General Jean de Lattre de Tassigny, who had led the French First Army in ANVIL-DRAGOON, the invasion of southern France; now he too was to be Eisenhower's equal in rank.

But it was the Russian representative to the Control Council in whom Eisenhower was most interested. Would it be Marshal Zhukov? Eisenhower was impatient for the council to get to work. Would Zhukov (or whoever) be empowered to act decisively? Or would every last minutia have to be scrutinized and approved by the Kremlin? Eisenhower asked Hopkins to explore these matters in Moscow.

The Russians were much on the supreme commander's mind. The night of Hopkins's visit he talked about them at length with Captain Butcher, who noted Eisenhower's comments in his diary the next morning (May 25):

> Ike said he felt that the American and British relationship with Russia was about at the same stage of arms-length dealing that marked the early contacts between Americans and British when we first got into the war. As we dealt with each other, we learned the British ways and they learned ours. A common understanding developed and eventually we became Allies in spirit as well as on paper. Now the Russians, who have had relatively little contact, even during the war, with the Americans and British, do not understand us, nor do we them. The more contact we have with the Russians, the more they will understand us and the greater will be the cooperation. The Russians are blunt and forthright in their dealings, and any evasiveness arouses their suspicions. It should be possible to work with Russia if we will follow the same pattern of friendly cooperation that has resulted in the great record of Allied unity demonstrated first by AFHQ [Eisenhower's North African command] and subsequently by SHAEF. Only now, in peace, the motive for cooperation is the betterment of the lot in life of the common man. If we can create singleness of purpose on this theme, as we did to win the war, then peace should be assured.

These generous and hopeful sentiments, while probably representative of a majority of American citizens during the postwar flush of European victory, were in sharp conflict with the opinions of some politicians, militarists, and powerful newspaper publishers. Early in June a pair of influential senators, Burton K. Wheeler (Democrat, Montana) and Albert Hawkes (Republican, New Jersey), speaking to an audience of GIs in Rome, suggested that rather than go home the U.S. troops might better stay in Europe and "finish the job"; that is, pick a fight against the Russians and wallop them at once. In private, General Patton was saying much the same thing. And during his conversations with Stalin, Harry Hopkins twice saw fit to urge the Russian leaders to judge American policy by the actions of the government itself rather than by "the public expressions of the Hearst newspapers and the *Chicago Tribune*." It was a prophetic warning. Less than a week later *Red Star,* the newspaper of the Red Army, would charge the American press with trying to stir up an anti-Soviet war; the journal would single out Hearst's *New York Journal-American* for having said, "A Red wave threatens to drown Christian civilization," and the *Chicago Tribune* for having said, "The Soviet Union is the only aggressor in the world." Meanwhile the *New York*

Daily News, the *Tribune's* younger sob sister, was warning of a Russian invasion by way of Alaska and the Aleutian Islands.

But Eisenhower persisted in his faith that Soviet-American cooperation would prevail if Americans were willing and friendly. By the end of May his headquarters had been moved north from Rheims to Frankfurt-am-Main, to the immense, pretentious structure (unscathed by bomb or shell) that had housed the central offices of Interessen Gemeinschaft Farbenindustrie (I. G. Farben), where his chief concern was still the redeploying from Europe to the Pacific theater of war of some four hundred thousand troops a month, along with the vast tonnage of arms and supplies needed to sustain their military efforts. His daily round, however, was not all work. There were pleasant hours spent horseback riding with Lieutenant Kay Summersby. Once, with Lieutenant Summersby, General Bradley, his military assistant Colonel (later Brigadier Sir) James Gault, and a few others, he flew to London for an evening at the theater and later a champagne supper and an hour or two of dancing at Ciro's, a nightclub. Early in June he spent a day and a night on the Riviera with twenty of his West Point classmates (one of whom was General Bradley), celebrating the thirtieth anniversary of their graduation.

On May 30 word reached Frankfurt from Hopkins in Moscow: Stalin had appointed Marshal Zhukov to the Allied Control Council; moreover, he had proved conciliatory on most of the other matters up for discussion. To Eisenhower and his advisers, the prospects for the joint military government to be based in Berlin at once seemed more encouraging. Still impending, however, was the question of when the British and American troops should withdraw from the Russian zone.

The first gathering of the Allied Control Council on June 5 was a curious occasion, compounded of frustration, friendliness, and ritual in about equal parts. As usual, Eisenhower had required that a precise schedule be arranged in advance and endorsed by all concerned; as usual, he expected that all concerned would stick to that schedule faithfully. His airplane touched down at Tempelhof airport on the tick. He was accompanied by his political adviser, Robert Murphy, and his deputy, Lieutenant General Lucius Clay; a large party of aides, journalists, broadcasters, and privileged sightseers came in other airplanes. He was welcomed by General Vassily Sokolovsky, Zhukov's deputy, and an impressive formation of Soviet troops, who looked fit and well disciplined. He spoke briefly: "It is a tremendous honor for me to be here and to greet commanders of the great Red Army which did so much to bring the German to his knees." Then a swift drive through the desolate, silent capital, over which hung "the odor of death," arriving promptly at noon at Zhukov's headquarters in Karlhorst, a suburb of East Berlin. Russian hero greeted

American hero with great cordiality. Eisenhower formed a favorable impression of his "affable and soldierly-appearing" host. He presented the marshal with the Legion of Merit, chief commander grade. Later, in the pleasant villa assigned them, the Americans were served an excellent lunch.

So far, at least for the Americans, all had gone according to plan. Not so with the British. Montgomery had got to Berlin late and almost at once had begun to behave in ill-mannered, pompous, and self-righteous fashion. As he later told the story: "I asked to see Marshal Zhukov but was told he was busy. I then became very insistent and said that if I was not taken to see the Marshal I would leave Berlin and return to the British zone—which, of course, I could hardly have done!" This display of petulance "did the trick," and Montgomery was taken to Zhukov's headquarters. In the course of their conversation, Zhukov suggested that the proclamations requiring their attention* be signed at four o'clock. That, said Montgomery, suited him, and presently he went off to discuss with Eisenhower "the divergent views of our two governments."

Churchill wanted no withdrawal of American troops until after the summit meeting, now scheduled to begin in Potsdam on July 15 or thereabouts; Truman, acting on Eisenhower's advice, was quite prepared to proceed with the withdrawal without delay, should the Russians insist upon it. To Montgomery, "All this looked a bit awkward." But Eisenhower proved to be accommodating. Montgomery later wrote that Eisenhower's "view was that we could not challenge the pledged word of our respective governments; to do so would wreck any possibility there might be of working in friendly cooperation with the Russians. I agreed with him . . . But I was of course bound by the instructions I had received from my government; if the question was raised I was to say it was a matter for intergovernmental decision. Eisenhower agreed to adopt the same line."

Eisenhower now began to get annoyed because they had not been called for the scheduled signing ceremony. To him the delay "began to look deliberate." General Clay likewise chafed at "the unexplained lack of courtesy," and so did Montgomery and the French commander, General de Lattre de Tassigny, who had joined the group. (Montgomery apparently never told the others that he had agreed to Zhukov's suggestion that the documents be signed at four o'clock.) "What's going on here?" Eisenhower asked Murphy. "Do you think these people are giving us a runaround?" Murphy applied to Andrei Vishinsky, Zhukov's political adviser, who at

---

* "Declaration [on] the Assumption of Supreme Authority [in] Germany by the Allies," "Statement . . . on Control Machinery in Germany," and "Statement . . . on Zones of Occupation in Germany." The signing of these three proclamations was what had brought the Allied commanders together in Berlin.

once explained: in one of the three proclamations was a clause requiring the Allies to intern any Japanese in their respective zones, but since the Russians had not yet declared war against Japan, they obviously could not agree to such a clause. Everybody involved—Eisenhower, Clay, Montgomery, and others—urged that the offensive clause be stricken forthwith, but Vishinsky said only that he must hear from the Kremlin. As the afternoon waned, Eisenhower grew more impatient. But promptly at four o'clock word came that the principals were to assemble in the conference hall of the same big building where the Germans had surrendered to the Russians and their allies, and by four-thirty the papers had at last been signed.

Zhukov then called to order the first meeting of the military governors of Berlin. Eisenhower at once proposed that the Allied Control Council be established, adding that for that purpose he would like to have Murphy and General Clay remain in Berlin. Zhukov, after conferring with Vishinsky, rejected the proposal, arguing that each power must first withdraw its troops into its own zone before the Allied Control Council could function.

There ensued a brief skirmish over the elaborate banquet and entertainment the Russians had laid on for their guests. Eisenhower maintained that he had already tarried too long in Berlin, that he must return to Frankfurt, as scheduled, at six o'clock. Zhukov at first refused to believe him and then, with quick jocularity, exclaimed, "I shall arrest you and *make* you stay!" This jest thawed the supreme commander a trifle. He climbed down off his dignity long enough to come to the banquet hall for an exchange of toasts and to hear a Red Army chorus sing a group of songs. The banquet tables were heaped with Russian delicacies, the Russians were at their friendliest, Zhukov and Eisenhower exchanged warm, cordial toasts and hopes that the four allies, so successfully linked in war, would remain side by side in peace. But Eisenhower cut these amiabilities short. At his behest, Zhukov and Montgomery piled with him into a car that raced them back through the city to Tempelhof. On the way Zhukov remarked that he had been instructed by Stalin to decorate both Eisenhower and Montgomery with the Order of Victory, a Soviet honor that had never before been conferred upon a foreigner. Eisenhower, who was already uncomfortable because of his chilliness in the face of the exuberant Russian hospitality, now felt even more remorseful. He invited Zhukov to Frankfurt for the ceremony, "to stay as long as he pleased, with the assurance of a warm welcome."

Back in Frankfurt, the Americans were uneasy. Had they been pushed around? Had they been too standoffish? What had they gained? Perhaps most ominous was the fact that not Zhukov, not even Vishinsky, had been able to settle on the spot a matter of no great importance; it suggested that the Soviets were not prepared to let their representative on the Allied Control Council take responsibility for political affairs in Germany. A few days later, when Harry Hopkins stopped in Frankfurt on his way home from Moscow, he confirmed Eisenhower's apprehension that Zhukov would have little power. Indeed, Hopkins warned that the British Foreign Office would be calling the shots for Montgomery as well, and that Eisenhower himself would soon find, if he had not already, that he had many masters in Washington. Eisenhower gloomily acknowledged he was aware of that. War had been fought by the generals, but peace would now be disputed by the politicians.

As for the question of American troops in the Russian zone, Eisenhower was more than ever for pulling them back. Murphy had reported as much to the State Department and added that he agreed with the recommendation. So, when they told him of it, did Hopkins. (President Truman subsequently informed Stalin he was ordering the withdrawal of American troops to begin on June 21. At Stalin's request, this date was postponed to July 1.)

Curiously, while all the documents signed in Berlin assumed the joint occupation of the capital by the four powers, in none of them were there provisions for access to the city by rail, highway, or air corridor. Right of presence in Berlin, it was assumed, surely implied right of access to Berlin. Eisenhower, Murphy, and Clay were all conscious of the omission, but no one considered it more than a technicality; when the matter was discussed with the Russians, no one even troubled to enter it in the minutes.*

On Sunday morning, June 10, Marshal Zhukov and his entourage arrived at Frankfurt in two airplanes. Montgomery had flown in an hour or so before. In Eisenhower's office, with a minimum of fuss, Zhukov presented the two men with the Order of Victory, a jagged star-shaped platinum plaque studded with dozens of diamonds and rubies. (Estimates of its intrinsic value ranged from eighteen thousand to one hundred thousand dollars; at her first opportunity Lieutenant Summersby nervously popped it into the general's safe.) The Russian commander also presented lesser medals to twenty-four British and American officers attached to SHAEF. Eisenhower had arranged to have seventeen hundred American and British pursuit planes and medium and heavy bombers fly overhead in what Zhukov could take either as a stirring welcome or as a mighty warning; the party then gathered in the mess hall for an elaborate lunch, accompanied by the obligatory exchange of gracious compliments. Marshal

---

* Much later General Clay would argue that the guarantee of free access to Berlin should have been formally negotiated as a condition of American withdrawal from the Soviet zone, and would confess that the American authorities had erred in not doing so.

Zhukov wished to "raise a glass to General of the Army Eisenhower, due to whose abilities and talents the Allied armies attained their great and brilliant successes," saluted the "genius and talent" of the American general, and hoped for "the same cooperation . . . in peace" that they had achieved in war. General Eisenhower raised his glass in a similar hope: the Allied "soldiers, sailors, airmen" all were "going to have peace if we have to fight for it," and "high officials of the Soviet Union . . . are one with us." The war had been a "holy war," an "array of the forces of evil against those of righteousness," and for the victory, "to no man do the United Nations owe a greater debt than to Marshal Zhukov."

It was a fine occasion, a warm and pleasant moment, one that, in Eisenhower's own retrospective words, "held nothing but bright promise for the establishment of cordial and close relations with the Russians." What happened to that promise was something that General Eisenhower would himself be much concerned with in the next fifteen years.

On that Sunday afternoon, though, General Eisenhower could think only of his more immediate future. He was now called upon to step forward, front and center on the world stage, in his public role as The Hero.

CHAPTER THREE

Adoration

FIRST STOP, LONDON. At the airport, the full treatment. General Eisenhower was fair game for the reporters. Germany, he told them, would never again be able to compete with the other highly industrialized nations. "Britain, the United States, and Russia," he went on, "are aiming to make it impossible for Germany to wage war again—at least in our time." It sounded like a replay of the celebrated Morgenthau Plan.* As for the Russians, they "are very friendly" and "want peace and a chance to develop themselves the same as anyone else." All his relations with them, he said, had been "heartwarming." Then he was whisked away to the Dorchester Hotel, across the street from Hyde Park.

* The Morgenthau Plan, so called, and Eisenhower's part in its inception, is discussed at pages 316–317.

The next day, Tuesday, June 12, was filled with ceremony. In its early hours Eisenhower was understandably tense. Attempting to relax with a solitary stroll in Hyde Park, he got a foretaste of the indiscriminate adulation that would be his portion all the rest of his life. As he crossed Park Lane a cabby spied him, called out, "Ike! Good old Ike," stopped his taxi, got out, and begged his autograph. So did his passengers. So, in a matter of minutes, did a swelling crowd of dozens, scores, more than a hundred. Happily, a pair of bobbies on point duty rescued him and escorted him back to the Dorchester. On the way a British general crossed his path, saluted, and said, quite deadpan, "Good morning, sir. I see you are being brought home by the police."

With more decorum General Eisenhower and his deputy, Air Chief Marshal Arthur Tedder, were driven to the City of London, where they were carried, in a landau drawn by six white horses, through cheering crowds that spilled over the narrow sidewalks into the roadway, to the Guildhall, an ancient and honorable structure scorched and scarred by the blitz. Inside, before a packed audience of dignitaries and nobility, Eisenhower, bronzed and smiling, six rows of ribbons a splash of color on his tunic, was given the freedom of the City and, as a token of the sword he was later to receive, the Wellington Sword, a bejeweled scimitar.* He then addressed the assemblage.

The speech was a triumph, not because of any novel ideas in it—its intellectual content was well within the range of any high school commencement orator—but because it was graceful, simple, delivered with a crystalline sincerity, and above all because the British people were in a postwar euphoria of thanksgiving and bonhomie. Eisenhower sounded a strain of sadness that his acclaim had been "earned in blood of his followers and sacrifices of his friends," one of praise for the British, who had stood against Hitler "alone but unconquered, almost naked but unafraid," one of pride in the "smooth-working" unity of the Allied team, and one of hope for peace. "Immortal words," a London newspaper proclaimed above the text of his speech.

He was honored at a lunch in the Mansion House, received by the dowager Queen Mary, and had tea with the king, the queen, and Princess Elizabeth at Buckingham Palace, where the king conferred on him the Order of Merit, an honor never before given an American; that night he dined as the prime minister's guest of honor at Number 10 Downing

* Freedom of the City of London (the most ancient part of Greater London and now its financial and commercial center, with its own lord mayor) had been previously given to only four Americans: George Peabody, Ulysses S. Grant, Theodore Roosevelt, and John J. Pershing. Work on the great ceremonial sword later presented to Eisenhower had not, by June 12, been completed by the armorer.

Street. In short, June 12 was a day on which England and General Eisenhower conducted a love affair with each other, for all the world to see.

After a day of rest back in Frankfurt, Eisenhower flew to Paris, the second stop on his triumphal tour. As supreme commander, he had never got along so well with his French allies as with his British. During his North African campaign the rivalries among Admiral Jean Louis François Darlan, General Henri Honoré Giraud, and General Charles de Gaulle had led him to refer irritably to "those damn Frogs," a type of epithet which if applied to the British (e.g., "those damn Limeys") would have led to the swift recall, on a slow, unescorted freighter, of any offending American officer attached to AFHQ or later to SHAEF. Moreover, Eisenhower, after a year of dispirited study of the French language, still found it hopelessly foreign. Nevertheless, he approached the celebrations in Paris with the high hope that every ceremony would fit into place.

Alas, from the outset nothing was comme il faut. The military band at Orly airport, as the first airplane taxied to the appointed apron, at once burst into "The Star-Spangled Banner" and then "La Marseillaise," but from the plane there dismounted British Air Chief Marshal Tedder, without so much as a bar of "God Save the King" to accompany him.

Had Tedder's earlier arrival been deliberate? At all events, when Eisenhower's plane taxied to the same apron, the French musicians, now well rehearsed, repeated their performance, after which the supreme commander was whisked off to the Arc de Triomphe by General Joseph Koenig, the military governor of Paris. A few minutes later de Gaulle arrived and presented Eisenhower with a decoration which was, in the new France, of high honor: he was made Compagnon de la Libération. After he had lifted the ribbon over Eisenhower's head, de Gaulle bent slightly and bestowed the two ceremonial kisses, one to each cheek, a ritual that Eisenhower abhorred. Eisenhower then placed a wreath on the Tomb of the Unknown Soldier, taps were sounded, and together with de Gaulle he reviewed an honor guard of French troops. A drive down the Champs Élysées through cheering crowds, across the Seine to the Invalides for the obligatory visit to the tomb of Napoleon and that of Marshal Foch, and then a tour of the city during which once again he was warmly applauded by the city's millions. When he spoke (in English, with a translation) at the Hôtel de Ville, he was careful to acknowledge the gallantry of the Resistance and the help it gave to the armies he led into France:

"We know very well that through the forces of Resistance the FFI sustained a tremendous effort during the years of the occupation. The full worth and importance of the effort of the French Forces of the Interior have not yet been revealed. . . . Later, when we landed, your aid was always of the greatest importance. You blew up bridges, telephone lines.

You even subdued entire garrisons, and here at Paris in the very heart of France, the regeneration of the city came from within itself." These pieties fell short of the mark, but his audience, like those in London, nonetheless applauded him heartily.

That evening Eisenhower was to be tendered a state dinner at the Élysée Palace. As the supreme commander of the Allied Expeditionary Forces he was careful to come to Paris accompanied by his deputy, Tedder, and by the deputy chief of staff, British Lieutenant General Frederick E. Morgan, among others. But de Gaulle, because of a tiff with the British over spheres of influence in the Middle East, had decreed that Eisenhower had been invited as an American general of the army and that in consequence only American officers should be invited to the dinner. When he learned of this protocolary crisis Eisenhower was furious; he even threatened to decline his invitation unless his senior staff officers were invited. After many telephone conversations by junior officers he was assured that the oversight had been corrected. Before the dinner came a cocktail reception at which de Gaulle presented the American people (Eisenhower being their representative) with one of Napoleon's swords, a symbol of the friendship of the French people. Tedder and Morgan were both present for this ceremony, but after it they withdrew, graciously insisting that they were expected elsewhere. Eisenhower, withholding comment, marched in to dinner.

At the Hôtel Scribe the next day, the supreme commander held a farewell press conference with many of the newspaper correspondents who had reported his more public activities over the previous three years. Captain Butcher, his adviser on press and public relations, considered the conference "satisfactory but not spectacular, perhaps because most of the topics covered were things I had heard him talk about and therefore they did not seem new." Butcher, himself still unaware of the emotional intensity building up in the United States over the hero's return, was astonished to learn that the Associated Press wanted the complete text of Eisenhower's remarks to the press. At home his compatriots were hungry for any scraps that might help them decide what sort of ideas their hero held, what sort of man he was. Actually, the press conference had produced only one moment of tension.

Q: There has been a considerable campaign recently . . . to talk about a "Russo-American war." There is nothing in your experience with the Russians that leads you to feel we can't cooperate with them perfectly?

EISENHOWER (*after a pause, sharply*): On my level, none. I have found the individual Russian one of the friendliest persons in the world. He likes to talk with us, laugh with us. He loves to laugh, and I have talked to many British officers and they find him the same way. He likes to see the humor of life, and I am sure they like the Allies and were darn glad to see us. . . .

The peace lies, when you get down to it, with all the peoples of the world, not just for the moment with some political leader who is trying to direct the destiny of a country along a certain line. If all the peoples are friendly, we are going to have peace.

I think the Russians are friendly. I know all the officers I have met are.

The next day General Eisenhower was at last bound for home. It should be remembered that he was, as always, under the orders of the War Department. Those orders had denied him a visit to Moscow, which he had very much wanted to undertake; Harry Hopkins had told him several days earlier how urgently Stalin had requested that he come to Moscow for the great victory celebration scheduled for June 24; Eisenhower could answer only that in view of the pressing need for closer ties with the Soviet Union, he "thought it a mistake" that he did not go when he was asked.

Official Washington also had a lively interest in some politically explosive issues that a homecoming hero like Eisenhower could best advocate: unification of the armed services was one such, and universal military training was another. Indeed, even before getting home General Eisenhower had begun to speak his piece. In a letter mailed from Frankfurt to a committee of the House of Representatives on postwar military policy, he had testified that the Congress should legislate to ensure universal military training in peacetime. To have peace, he argued, we must be strong; "the quicker the maximum potential can be converted into tactical war, the surer the victory and the less the cost." The best that can be said for this policy of peace through strength, of preserving peace by training bigger armies and devising more terrible weapons, is that some day, despite all past experience, it may yet work; but the fact that Eisenhower spoke up for it unquestionably helped to deodorize it.

As the hero flew home in a C–54—the presidential airplane, the *Sacred Cow*, dispatched for his convenience to Frankfurt by Truman—he was, so to say, adjusting his official mask and making sure it fitted well in place. Very few Americans in the next week or so would glimpse the private Eisenhower; the millions would see only the public persona of the hero, who would be careful to utter only what was proper to the occasion. No doubt much of what he was to say would be sincerely and deeply believed by the private Eisenhower too, but it would be the martial hero, home on official leave granted by the War Department, who would be on public display.

There was a warm, sunny day in Bermuda, deliberately planned so that the supreme commander might restore his tissues against the ordeal of his triumphal tour. The *Sacred Cow*, after circling over the estuary of the Chesapeake to avoid a too early arrival, was put down at Washington National Airport at 11:07 A.M. General Marshall and the hero's wife Mamie were on hand to greet him as he stepped down the portable stairway. Reporters duly transcribed his first words: "Oh God, it's swell to be back!"

He climbed into a jeep. As it started off, the thousands jamming the airport screamed for Ike, and General Marshall said crisply from the back seat, "Stand up so they can see you." Presently, as the driver shifted gears and moved the jeep forward, the supreme commander, standing, swayed unsteadily, but General Marshall's commands came calm, steady, and authoritative: "Drive slowly. Avoid fast starts and stops. Be careful when you shift gear."

Ike stood firm, his wonderful lopsided grin turned on full, his arms upspread in a victory salute. The jeep moved him forward, aiming straight into the heart of America.

Washington, New York City, West Point, Kansas City, Abilene. On a triumphal tour one day is very like another, but each place has its distinctive flavor. In New York City he proclaimed himself "a Kansas farmer boy," but in Kansas City, "I'm only a simple soldier," he said; at West Point, after suggesting a moderate reform of the armed services, he added, "but I don't suppose that Congress and the big brass would ever agree to that."

Washington sees men and events chiefly in terms of politics: Will it cost votes? Can he be elected? As to Eisenhower there was never any doubt. The crowds that lined Constitution Avenue that hot June day included federal employees in civil service, lobbyists, staff workers from the congressional offices up on the Hill, reporters, Republicans, Democrats, cynics, idealists, voters from the towns around the capital, and citizens disfranchised because of residence in the District of Columbia; it is likely that every one of them had the same thought. Standing in that throng was a professor of economics from George Washington University, Arthur Burns. When General Ike drove past, waving and smiling happily, Dr. Burns turned to his wife and voiced the universal thought: "This man is absolutely a natural for the Presidency."

Speaking a few minutes later to a joint session of the Congress, Eisenhower could scarcely have been unaware of the charged political atmosphere. "I stand before the elected Federal lawmakers of our great Republic," he said, "the very core of our political life and a symbol of those things we call the American heritage." And when he left the House chamber to a standing ovation, those elected lawmakers could only have been wondering wistfully if he was a Democrat or a Republican.

In New York City the immediate concern was whether the turnout in the streets had been four million persons or six million. At all events the crowds were the biggest in the city's history, and the General Electric Company, which had developed a new device for measuring sound, reported that the cheer given General Ike at City Hall was as loud as three thousand thunderclaps. On that day in the metropolis some men were measuring him for other than political preferment. A vice chairman of the mayor's reception committee, Thomas J. Watson of International Business Machines, was also a trustee of Columbia University, which would soon require a new president; Watson had a special interest in Eisenhower.

When the hero came to Kansas City he was getting close, not to home, for as a professional soldier he had, properly speaking, no home, but at least to the town where he had spent his boyhood. His four brothers—Arthur, Edgar, Earl, and Milton—were on hand to meet him, and so was his eighty-three-year-old mother, Ida Elizabeth Stover Eisenhower.

"Hello, Mother. How are you?"

"Hello, Dwight."

The midwestern heartland had traditionally been regarded, as he acknowledged in his speech to seventy-five thousand midwesterners, as the hotbed of isolationism. "I do not believe it," he said, and went on to urge the blossoming foreign policy that envisioned the U.S. necessarily and rightfully concerned with international affairs all over the globe. "In our future conduct with the world," he said, "we must understand that the problems of Europe and the world are our problems, whether we like it or not."

Prairie politicos buzzed hopefully about him as he climbed aboard the ten-car special train that was to take him, his family, and the party of officers, soldiers, correspondents, and broadcasters west to Abilene. "Oh boy, I'm glad to be back here!" he said when he had ended the journey. "When I get out of this uniform, this is the country I'm coming back to!" Once again he had said precisely what his audience wanted to hear.

Another great crowd, the next morning another parade, that afternoon another speech (in a pasture which had been hastily dubbed Eisenhower Park), and that evening General Ike met once again with the press. The day before, President Truman had told reporters in Olympia, Washington, that Eisenhower deserved to have whatever he wanted and that he, the President, would see to it that what Eisenhower wanted Eisenhower would get. Now, in Abilene, every correspondent was curious as to whether what Eisenhower wanted was a political plum, and whether perhaps he wanted the juiciest political plum of all. His answer seemed plain, precise, and definite; and yet in truth it was none of these.

"I am in the federal service and I take orders from my commander in chief," he said. "All I want is to be a citizen of the United States, and when the War Department turns me out to pasture that's all I want to be. I want nothing else.

"It is silly to talk about me in politics, and so for once I'll talk about that, but only to settle this thing once and for all. I should like to make this as emphatic as possible. There's no use my denying I'll fly to the moon, because no one has suggested it and I couldn't if I wanted to. The same goes for politics.

"I'm a soldier, and I am positive that no one thinks of me as a politician. In the strongest language you can command you can state that I have no political ambitions at all. Make it even stronger than that if you can. I'd like to go even further than Sherman did in expressing myself on this subject."*

But of course General Ike did not go further than Sherman, nor even come close to matching him. This first expression of Eisenhoverian distaste over the idea of a political career had no effect at all after the many professional and ambitious politicians across the country had had the chance to read the statement more than once.

On Monday, June 25, General Eisenhower returned to Washington for conferences at the War Department. On Wednesday he traveled with his wife Mamie and their son John to White Sulphur Springs for a rest—some golf, some horseback riding, some fly-fishing. He was back in Washington again on Monday, July 9, then left the next day for Stewart Field, near West Point, whence he would be driven to Hyde Park to lay a wreath on the grave of his former commander in chief. Later he would fly back to Frankfurt-am-Main and the perplexing problems of a commander in charge of occupied Germany.

He left behind him a populace which, without knowing much about him, nevertheless adored him.

* On June 5, 1884, General William Tecumseh Sherman sent his classic message to a Republican national convention: "I will not accept if nominated and will not serve if elected."

PART TWO

OBSCURITY

CHAPTER ONE

The Background

PERHAPS THE MOST REMARKABLE ASPECT of Dwight D. Eisenhower's life before he became a world hero is that there was nothing remarkable about it. This violates every canon. Heroes, whether legendary or historical, are required by long-established convention to have led lives filled with wonderful events and, if possible, with miracles. Certainly researchers, whether academic or journalistic, have been at pains to turn up at least one wonderful incident in Eisenhower's boyhood, at least one strange portent of future greatness, at least one auspicious manifestation among his antecedents. Alas! they have drawn a blank. Perhaps in a half-century or so this lamentable deficiency will have been imaginatively remedied, but for the present we must be satisfied with a recital of commonplace facts about an essentially commonplace existence.

He was the third of seven sons born to David and Ida Eisenhower. His parents were members of the River Brethren, a small sect of fundamentalist Christians of the Baptist persuasion, an offshoot of the Mennonites. The River Brethren were mostly of German and Swiss stock, farmers in the valley of the Susquehanna River in southeastern Pennsylvania when the sect was first formed sometime in the 1770s, and for them religion was a stern and exacting way of life. They worshiped in their homes or in a meetinghouse; they rejected the frills of ecclesiastic ritual; they believed the Bible to be indisputably the word of God; they were a closely knit community, conservative, pacifist, self-reliant, thrifty, abstinent, exclusive, plain in their dress, strict in their behavior, severe in rearing their children.

David Eisenhower was fourteen years old when in 1878, with his grandfather, father, mother, older sister, two younger brothers, two uncles and aunts, a swarm of small cousins, and at least four other River Brethren families, he traveled west from Pennsylvania to Kansas. The journey was not undertaken of necessity. David's father Jacob was not only a preacher to the Brethren but also a farmer of substance, worth several thousand dollars when he moved to Kansas. Jacob Eisenhower bought a stretch of farmland in southern Dickinson County, built a house, a barn, and a windmill, and settled down to wrest a living from the prairie.

It was Jacob's custom when his children married to give to each two thousand dollars in cash and one hundred and sixty acres of farmland. David, however, was stubbornly set against a lifetime as a farmer. Instead he insisted on attending Lane University, an obscure temple of learning situated on the plains in a village called Lecompton. Lane was meagerly supported by the United Brethren in Christ, another small evangelical fundamentalist sect, this one, however, more nearly allied with the Methodists than with the Baptists. Here it was not possible to learn much, but at least it was possible to meet other youngsters who, like David, were groping for some sort of existence away from the farm. Here David Eisenhower met Ida Elizabeth Stover.

Less is known of Ida Stover's antecedents than of David Eisenhower's, but enough to indicate that the families were very similar. Stovers, like Eisenhowers, had moved from Germany to Switzerland to America; in this country they had embraced the same strait religious beliefs, and the Stovers, in the valley of the Shenandoah River in Virginia, had likewise been farmers. In 1874, when she was twelve, Ida was orphaned. Two of her older brothers journeyed to Kansas when she was still a child; when she was twenty-one she used part of her inheritance to follow them west. In the fall of 1883 she entered Lane University. She was an attractive young woman, endowed with a boundless vital energy. She married David Eisenhower in September 1885, on his twenty-second birthday.

David was duly given the two thousand dollars and the quarter-section of farmland by his father. He mortgaged his land for another two thousand and risked his capital to open a general store in the small village of Hope, a few miles south of Abilene. His partner in this enterprise, chosen because he was presumed to have the necessary business experience, was Milton Good, a young man who had for some time clerked in an Abilene clothing store.

There was every reason for optimism. The young Eisenhowers and the young Goods were popular in the community, which at the time seemed to be flourishing; Jacob, a notably cautious man, had invested in the local bank, a circumstance that lent to David's store an appearance of health and permanence; moreover, the store's custom was quite lively not only for the first fortnight but for two years or so. To cap their contentment, David and Ida could rejoice in their first son (Arthur) in November 1886, and two years later Ida would be heavy with their second child. It was then that David's store went bankrupt.

Stores go bankrupt when they are not properly managed. In this case, since the store was owned and operated by the father of a future world hero, there has been a scramble to retouch the picture, to load the blame on other shoulders or, even better, on natural calamities over which no mortal could have had control. The authorized account of the matter is that a severe drought, coupled with a plague of grasshoppers, desolated the crops of Dickinson County; young David Eisenhower, generous to a fault, extended the farmers credit, but young Milton Good, "too weak" to shoulder the responsibility of his commercial debts, fled town one night with "what little cash was left."

This account may well be true. At all events, David Eisenhower likewise left town. Behind him he left his pregnant wife and infant son. A lawyer was charged with settling his affairs. The store was sold, the mortgage on his farmland was foreclosed, his debts were paid, his assets were wiped out. Four hundred miles away, in Denison, Texas, he found a job as an engine wiper in a roundhouse of the Missouri-Kansas-Texas Railroad. His wage was about ten dollars a week. He rented a room in a frame house close to the railroad tracks.

Back in Hope, Ida Eisenhower gave birth in January 1889 to their second son (Edgar), and a couple of months later she went south with her two small children to rejoin her husband in Texas.

There followed an uneventful period of hard times on the flat Texas plain, while David Eisenhower labored obscurely, somewhere near the bottom of the American heap, without any discernible future, uncomfortably conscious that his past was marked by a shattering failure, and rarely cheered by what happened in his day-after-day present. In the spring of 1890 he learned that his wife Ida was once again pregnant, and he was forced to reflect that soon, at the age of twenty-seven, he would have to support a wife and three small children, all less than four years old, on some forty dollars a month. Early that summer a letter came that told him his mother had died, back in Kansas, and his grief was the more bitter for his being far from home.

When his third son was born, in the night hours of October 14, 1890, the circumstances were those of any birth in a very poor family in the working-class district of a small city. Neighboring wives had gathered in Ida Eisenhower's room on the ground floor to help as they could; the one available male was pressed into service to summon a physician; the night was cold and dark; the physician was late in coming. The infant was named David Dwight Eisenhower, but his mother, to avoid confusion with his father, took to calling him Dwight, and so before long his given names were shuffled about.

But this third son was not to stay long in Texas. Back in Kansas the River Brethren were about to open in Abilene a new plant of their Belle

Springs Creamery, and the foreman was to be young Chris Musser, who was not only David Eisenhower's brother-in-law but was also the man who had foreclosed the mortgage on his farmland two years before. Musser wrote to David to offer him a job "as a mechanic-engineer" with a starting wage of "less than fifty dollars a month." It was not much more money than David had been making as a railroad worker, but he would be at home, among his own. In the spring of 1891 he and Ida carried their children to a train, rode a day and a night and a day, and so came again to Abilene. David had only twenty-four dollars in his pocket, but he was home, and he breathed deep.

CHAPTER TWO

Abilene

FOR ALMOST THE NEXT TWENTY YEARS, young Dwight Eisenhower, who would be known to his schoolmates as Little Ike or Ugly Ike, was to be in or near Abilene. There are far worse places for a boy to grow up. The town itself—its name was inspired by Holy Writ (Luke III, 1)—has changed very little in size or character since Ike came to live there. The countryside roundabout is not of the sort that sells picture postcards; still, it has an agreeable serenity, with the gentle roll of upland prairie and the broad shallow bottomland along a small muddy river, the Smoky Hill. It is farmland. Most of its people are content to be tranquil, to shun the violent commotions and perplexities of the anarchic cities, to grow up and to grow old among the simple verities and pieties honored by their fathers and grandfathers. Of those who speed east or west through Kansas on Interstate 70 bound for St. Louis or Denver, how many wonder about Abilene? To some, surely, it is an isolated backwater, a hick town, a Bible Belt settlement where a stranger can't buy a drink unless, perchance, he is taken in hand by some compassionate member of the local lodge of the BPOE. Others may occasionally slow the pace of their automobiles, vaguely aware that they are passing through the heartland of America. In the neighborhood of Abilene, such a presentiment is smack on the mark. Not far southwest of Abilene is Kinsley, a town which boasts that it stands 1,561 miles from New York City and 1,561 miles from San Francisco;

quite close to Abilene and northeast of it is Fort Riley, which is generally accepted as the nation's geographic center; off to the northwest of Abilene is the geodetic center of the country.

To all appearances, Abilene is Dullsville, but time was, about a century ago, when it had the reputation of being the wildest and wickedest town in the country; perhaps indeed in the world. The man who put Abilene on the map was a tall, lanky young zealot named Joseph McCoy, the first to make a market for, on the one hand, the Texas cattlemen and, on the other, the big butchers of Kansas City and Chicago. To be sure, when first he glimpsed Abilene, in the spring of 1867, McCoy considered it "a very small, dead place," but his energy and enterprise transformed it into the first of the cowtowns to spring from the prairie after the Civil War, so that by July 1868 a journalist could note in a Topeka newspaper: "At this writing, Hell is now in session in Abilene." Such an alarming (and titillating) judgment was possible because the town had attracted the gamy throng of cardsharps, madams, whores, gunslingers, saloonkeepers, and associated riffraff that traditionally gathered to relieve the Texas cowboys of their trail's-end wages. These scruffy folk would be chiefly responsible for the preposterous legends of the so-called Wild West; because of them, Abilene would be for five or six years the peerless capital of that never-never land.

To assimilate such a lurid past into the tame present is a hard task, perhaps one that can be accomplished only by small boys. Who else can look upon a humdrum freight depot where farm tractors have been unloaded near a filling station and, by an act of imagination, transmute it into a Front Street lined with gaudy saloons and dance halls and gambling dens, ablaze with gaslights, raucous with drunken cowboys, and patrolled by no less a bravo than Wild Bill Hickok, a six-gun swinging at either hip? Back around the turn of the century the task may have been a little simpler, but not much. When he was eight or nine years old, young Dwight Eisenhower used to listen to the talk of an Abilene neighbor, a man named Dudley, who claimed he had been a deputy during the brief time (April to November 1871) when Hickok served as marshal of Abilene, and the boy found the tall tales of Wild Bill's marksmanship "entrancing."

But Wild Bill is a hero suitable only for small boys. A careful consideration of his career shows that he was a thoroughpaced scoundrel, the killer of dozens of men, several of whom he shot down from behind. Only a Chamber of Commerce could without a blush boast of association with such a one. No matter, for Abilene was nurturing its own authentic hero, matchless in his lifetime for the affection and respect accorded by his countrymen, glittering more brightly in the American firmament than

Robert E. Lee or Ulysses S. Grant, approaching even the stellar magnitude of the archetypal American father figure George Washington. At the time, of course, the townspeople saw only a boy who was much like every other boy in town. The word that would later most often come to their lips is "average." "He was just another average chap," Orin Snider, coach of his high school football team, said later. "He was a capable player . . . but was just another player." "In his schoolwork Dwight was not outstanding," his schoolmates recalled. "He made about average marks." And the editor of an Abilene newspaper, having searched his memory, said: "We found him going along the average road."

They all seem to have had some difficulty in remembering any salient anecdotes, characteristics, facts about him. "He was just a jolly good friend." "I do not recall his ever being in any serious trouble." "I was with him in high school. He was always a natty dresser." "He was a real boy, associated with real boys, did the usual boyish pranks." Like other boys, he got into fights; like other boys, he yearned from afar for pretty young classmates not yet nubile. He was a "tough cooky," he was a "terrible dancer," he was careless of his appearance, he was a "regular guy." It scarcely seems the stuff of heroes.

The conventional view—the consensus of his first half-dozen biographers—is that young Eisenhower's superior character was tempered within the circle of his family; what would lift him so far above the average was the "religious teaching" of his parents, the "strict family discipline," and the "stern instruction in the need for hard work and thrift." Unimpeachable doctrines like these, which have come to be described rather pejoratively as old-fashioned, are, to be sure, indispensable to the rearing of any future hero, but it can scarcely be argued that they were the exclusive property of the Eisenhower family. One must look further.

There is no question about the regimen of religious instruction. The boys were steeped in it. They got prayers with every meal; before breakfast they got Bible readings from their father; after supper they all sat around and read from the Bible again, passing it from hand to hand.* Often their house was used for religious services, the mother playing the piano to accompany the singing of hymns. The specific nature of the religion is uncertain. The parents appear to have left the River Brethren for a more primitive and austere sect, something referred to as the Bible Students, and they would later gravitate to the evangelical sect known as Jehovah's Witnesses. The most singular of the father's religious beliefs materialized in the form of an impressive (five or six feet high, ten feet long) wall chart

---

* "This was a good way to get us to read the Bible mechanically," Milton Eisenhower, the youngest of the family, has recalled. "I am not sure it was a good way to help us understand it."

of the Egyptian pyramids, by means of which he proved to his own satisfaction that the lines of the pyramids—outer dimensions, inner passageways, angles of chambers, and so on—prophesied later Biblical events and other events still in the future. As might be expected, this demonstration fascinated his children; the chart came to be one of the family's most prized possessions.

As for the strict family discipline, it was the iron fist grasping a maple switch or a leather strap. "We never dared to stay out after nine o'clock at night," the oldest son later recalled, and when the boys were summoned in the morning by their father a little after five o'clock, they knew they had best get up at once, no matter how cold it might be. Any delinquency in his chores brought a boy instant punishment, and there were chores aplenty: milking the cow, mucking out her stall, finding kindling for the morning fire, feeding the chickens and gathering eggs, cultivating the vegetable garden, helping to cook or bake, washing the dishes, doing the laundry, caring for the youngest brothers, taking their father his midday dinner, and so on and on.

The need for all this hard work was that the Eisenhower family was desperately poor. When David and Ida Eisenhower came with their three small children to live in Abilene, the only dwelling they could afford was a very small house—little more than a shack—in a very small yard just south of the railroad tracks. Kerosene lamps, no indoor plumbing, no amenities; merely subsistence. Here they were obliged to stay for nearly seven years while three more sons were born: Roy in 1892, Paul in 1894 (he died of diphtheria in infancy), and Earl in 1898. Later that year David's brother Abraham, a self-taught veterinarian, decided he would be an itinerant preacher of the Gospel; he offered to rent David his two-story frame house which, with a big barn, was set in a three-acre plot on the southern edge of Abilene. To David and Ida the offer seemed heaven-sent, and they snapped it up.*

The house, which to Dwight Eisenhower "seemed a mansion, with its upstairs bedrooms," and the barn and land enabled the family to exist fairly comfortably, at one or two removes from penury. They were still packed in together so tight as never to know privacy: four boys in two double beds

* Around this house, now a shrine, has been built the Eisenhower Center, comprising the Dwight D. Eisenhower Library; the Eisenhower Museum, a treasure-house where are displayed the trophies, medals, honors, and mementos of the conquering captain; and the Place of Meditation, which is also the hero's sepulcher. If local maps can be trusted (see, for example, the map at page 32 in *Cowtown Abilene: The Story of Abilene, Kansas, 1867–1875*, by Stewart P. Verckler, privately printed, 1967) the three-acre tract on which the Eisenhower boys grew up was the same tract as, or very close to, the one on which a generation earlier the whores had been sequestered during Abilene's brief but vivid career as a cowtown. At that time the area was known as the Devil's Addition.

jammed into one small room, mother and father in another bedroom, with the smallest son sleeping in a crib instead of (as in their earlier house) a bureau drawer, and grandfather Jacob, who had lost his savings when the little bank in Hope failed in 1891, tucked away in a small bedroom on the ground floor. When Jacob died in 1906, everyone could expand a bit; when a high school girl was hired at minuscule wages to live with them and help with the housework, everyone had to contract a bit. On the other hand, now they could keep the horse, one or two cows, and some chickens and pigs; now they could grow their own fruits and vegetables; now, as well, the boys' chores would multiply.

But cash was still woefully short. Lack of cash meant that the boys all had to wear hand-me-downs, and in turn hand-me-downs meant jeers and ridicule from their schoolmates. When Dwight was the only one in his grade to wear overalls, when he or Edgar came to school wearing their mother's battered old button shoes, they could expect derision. They were ready for it, and met it with their fists. "It made us scrappers," Edgar said later. "Any time anybody walked on us they heard from us. It didn't make any difference how big or how little he was, if he did something that infringed on our rights, he got a punch right then and there." And thus the Eisenhower boys won a deserved reputation as those tough little roughnecks from the wrong side of the railroad tracks.

To raise more cash, wanted more than ever after the seventh son, Milton, was born in 1899, the older boys all worked at odd jobs around town. In addition, Edgar and Dwight used to fill a little wagon with vegetables from their garden and peddle their produce among the more prosperous families on the north side. "They'd make us feel like beggars," Edgar was to recall. Dwight insisted later that he "never suffered this way," but there is no question that poverty steeled young Dwight's ambition and his determination to excel, to succeed.*

But ambition to succeed how? Excel at what? When he graduated from the Abilene High School in the spring of 1909 he had no idea of his future course.

At eighteen Dwight Eisenhower was a rawboned youngster, with only about one hundred and fifty pounds distributed over a frame nearly six feet tall, but an active life out-of-doors and a willingness to tackle hard work had given him big hands, a deep chest, wide, sloping shoulders, and hard muscles. (One year, to help his family in the incessant search for more cash, he had dropped out of high school to work at various jobs, in-

---

* One proof that his family's poverty provided much of his impetus lies—this is only apparently a paradox—in the denials he would later make of that poverty; for example: "If we were poor—and I'm not sure that we were by the standards of the day —we were unaware of it."

cluding hauling ice and heaving coal for the Belle Springs Creamery.) He had also picked up an assortment of useful knockabout skills and, in the process, formed a temperament that would stand him in excellent stead over the next few years. He had, for example, learned to camp, to fish, to shoot well enough to bring home quail or rabbits or other small game, to cook and bake, to figure the odds against drawing to a pair, filling an inside straight, or improving a bobtail flush, and to apply himself with discipline and cheerfulness to the jobs that were open to a youngster on the Kansas plains. In his schoolwork he had shown an interest in history (he absorbed the facts—the dates, the events, the battles, the leading personages—without overly troubling himself about the reasons why history had taken shape as it had) and in plane geometry (it was logical), but he vastly preferred the opportunity that school gave him to play football and baseball.

Growing up in this small town, in this farming country, had bred in him an ample self-confidence and a readiness to assume responsibility. He was sure of himself and of what he could do; nearly the only test that had consistently proved to be too much for him was that of licking his brother Edgar, who was twenty-one months older than he, and even that struggle, after a thousand failures, he was always ready to try again to win. His physical energy, his vitality, seemed inexhaustible. How to use it?

The oldest brother, Arthur, had gone to Kansas City after only two years of high school to take a job first as messenger boy, then as clerk in a bank. Edgar, ambitious to be a lawyer, went off in the fall of 1909 to the University of Michigan. Dwight stayed in Abilene, working at the creamery to help pay Edgar's bills. (The notion was that after a year or two Edgar would drop out of Michigan for a year to help Dwight get started there, in his footsteps.) He worked first as iceman, then as fireman, and finally as second engineer (which was another way of saying night foreman) from 6 P.M. to 6 A.M. seven days a week for a wage, after his last promotion, of ninety dollars a month. So for several months.

In this fashion the nascent hero contrived to duck his destiny for more than a year, but neither brotherly altruism nor procrastination could enable him to elude it indefinitely. It finally caught up with him in the summer of 1910 when a friend, Everett (Swede) Hazlett, son of a well-to-do Abilene physician, first told him about the service academies. Young Hazlett had a congressional appointment to Annapolis; he urged Ike to request another one for himself from either of the Kansas senators. The suggestion confronted young Eisenhower with a very real dilemma: on the one hand, if he could somehow wangle an appointment and pass the entrance examination, he would be guaranteed a free college education, which was by no means to be sneezed at, least of all by an Eisenhower; on the other hand, since his parents detested war and those who waged it, how painfully would they receive the news that he proposed to train himself in the profession of warfare? They both took the Ten Commandments quite literally as imperatives; the Sixth Commandment is brief and unequivocal: Thou shalt not kill. But still, an education, without placing any burden on the family . . .

Dwight Eisenhower struggled with this dilemma for almost two months, then he opted for the financial benefit over the religious or ethical injunction. He dispatched a letter to Senator Joseph L. Bristow on August 20, 1910, praying the favor of his appointment to "either the school at Annapolis, or the one at West Point." His own preference—for he was still dodging his destiny—was for Annapolis, since there he would be Swede Hazlett's classmate, but the regulations for entrance into the Naval Academy stipulated an age from sixteen to twenty. Nevertheless, he was so anxious to get into Annapolis that he wrote Senator Bristow that he would be "nineteen years of age this fall," an extraordinary error (error?) for a youth whose nineteenth birthday had been celebrated ten months earlier.

No matter. There followed on September 3 a second letter to Bristow, a response from Bristow notifying him of competitive examinations for the appointment, his success in that competition, his appointment to West Point, his entrance examinations, and at last, in March 1911, his orders to report to the United States Military Academy on June 14, 1911. Early in June he made his farewells and left on the train that would take him to Kansas City, then to Chicago, then to Ann Arbor (to visit his brother Edgar), and at last to West Point.

After he had bid his mother goodbye, she went to her room and wept.

CHAPTER THREE

West Point

THE FIRMLY ESTABLISHED ASSUMPTION about the United States Military Academy—a comforting one in a democracy—is that its undergraduates, the corps of cadets, constitute a fair and representative sample of American society. How can it be otherwise, when the cadets are selected equally from each state of the union, often after a competitive examination? Since the corps of cadets continually merges into the officer corps, it follows that, as one student of the matter has put it, "the officer corps became the mirror of the nation. . . . Both those entering the officer corps and those reaching its highest ranks in the years after the Civil War [i.e., through 1902] were a cross-section of middle-class America." For the first forty years of this century the officer corps was, to be sure, withdrawn and isolated from the mainstream of civilian society (except briefly during the War of 1914–1918), but still the corps was assumed to be typical of that society; bone of its bone; alienated, but essentially the same. As the officer corps, so also the corps of cadets. A pleasing pair of notions.

Since both notions are so patently absurd, it is hard to understand how either the complacent assumption or its corollary could have got much currency, except perhaps within the officer corps itself. Not, however, until after the officer corps had been monstrously swollen—from an average of 7,000 officers in the first decade of the century to 188,000 in the years just before the Korean War, a growth of more than 2,500 percent—was the validity of assumption and corollary subjected to any thoroughgoing sociological analysis. Without inordinate effort it was shown that, so far from being a "mirror of the nation," the general officers of the American army from 1910 to 1950 had been white, native-born, Anglo-Saxon (of pioneer and predominantly English and German stock), and Protestant (predominantly Episcopalian). Further, these general officers have been and still are drawn more from the South, and from such southerly regions of Illinois, Indiana, and Ohio as are drained by the Ohio and Mississippi rivers, than could be the case if they were truly representative, geographically, of the republic. Still further, these officers have come appreciably more often from small towns or farm country than from the big cities, and far more often than is warranted by the urban-rural imbalance of the national population. Yet still further, these officers seem to spring suspiciously often from upper-class or upper middle-class origins. In short, they appear to have been the scions of landed gentry, of the WASPs most WASPish, and with a southern accent.

For the moment, this analysis is of interest solely as it indicates the sort of youngsters with whom Dwight Eisenhower would be associated at West Point. At first encounter, the United States Military Academy afforded him the experience of Abilene all over again, but on a more extravagant scale: he was once again the boy from the wrong side of the tracks who would have to prove himself, if not with his fists, at least with his physical superiority, with his athletic prowess; but he would be testing himself against, and with, an abler, more experienced, and much more knowing assortment of contemporaries.

He was able to weather his initiation into academy life—the hazing of the plebes that goes on during their first few weeks while they are still beasts, so called—better than most of his classmates because he was older and tougher than most of them, because during his boyhood as one of six brothers he had had the unnecessary vanities knocked out of him, and because he had worked hard at a variety of jobs under a variety of ornery taskmasters. Whether or not it was deliberately designed to do so, that hazing, often apparently aimless and brutal, serves to transform a youngster from indifferent civilian to disciplined soldier—to make him obey orders alertly and instantly, despite unceasing pressure, without panic. Whenever the hazing threatened to upset the quick-tempered Eisenhower he would remember to warn himself, "Where else can I get a college education without cost?"

In his time West Point was a military monastery in which the cadets were isolated from the outside diseases of commercialism and money-grubbing, and the officer corps approved of this sequestration. For four years the cadets were confined to their post except for one ten-week furlough after their second year and a brief Christmas leave awarded to those who had done well in their studies and had kept out of trouble; they were allowed no cash, not even pocket money; and they were constantly subjected to exacting discipline and to detailed, intimate, incessant inspections of their property and their persons. But for Eisenhower such a regime was not very different from his life at home in Abilene; once again he found it easier to endure than did most of his classmates.*

Moreover, as had been the case in Abilene, he was encouraged at West Point to devote a great deal of his energy to athletics. This was so from his very first day when, because of his height, he was automatically assigned to F Company, traditionally the company of the roughnecks, the jocks, the men who were proud of their muscles and contemptuous alike of the "runts" in other companies and of those who sought to do well in their studies, the "tenth-boners," the "hivey" ones. Eisenhower fitted well into F Company. He himself later recalled: "It would be difficult to over-emphasize the importance that I attached to participation in sports." At his second summer camp he swaggered down F Company Street as he had swaggered across the railroad tracks on his way to high school in Abilene: self-confident, truculent, game for anything.

As a yearling (which is to say, in his second year at the academy), his athletic prowess had already won him the respect of his peers. He would later recall that he weighed one hundred and seventy-five pounds. Thanks

---

* In 1922, seven years after Eisenhower had been graduated, General Douglas MacArthur, then superintendent of the academy, announced that the cadets would be given five dollars a month for spending money and an occasional six-hour pass. "They are no longer walled up within the academy for two years at a time," MacArthur reported. "These few privileges . . . will go far to break down the walls of isolation and broaden their experience."

to the hyperbole customarily employed by eager college publicists, his weight was advertised in the press as one hundred and ninety pounds. At all events, he was a slashing halfback on offense, running with more power than quickness, and a savage tackler on defense. In five or six games he proved himself to have been, as he was described by one sportswriter, "one of the most promising backs in Eastern football." Whereupon, just before the traditional Army–Navy game, he sustained severe injury to a knee, and with that his auspicious athletic career was finished.

"It was a bitter blow," one of his biographers has written, "perhaps the heaviest of his life." "No disappointment in his later life," another biographer agreed, "was bitterer than this." Is it possible? Since his later bitter blows and disappointments would include his failure to be posted for combat duty overseas in the War of 1914–1918 and the death of his first son in 1920, one is tempted to dismiss these judgments as absurd; but Eisenhower himself later wrote that the "end of my career as an active football player had a profound effect on me." "I was almost despondent," he recalled, "and several times had to be prevented from resigning by the persuasive efforts of classmates. Life seemed to have little meaning; a need to excel was almost gone."

His scholastic standing fell off sharply. As a plebe he had stood fifty-seventh of 212 cadets; as a yearling he stood eighty-first of 177. Thereafter matters improved somewhat: as a second classman he was sixty-fifth of about 170 cadets, and he graduated sixty-first of 164. With no chance to excel in athletics, he gave rein instead to a rebellion against discipline: began to smoke cigarettes (which were forbidden; he had to roll his own) and to gamble at poker (which was likewise forbidden, but he profited handsomely), and the number of his demerits for misconduct began to climb. During his last year his one hundred demerits meant that he stood one-hundred-and-twenty-fifth in conduct among 164 cadets, and he was ninety-fifth for his four-year tour of duty. In short, he was a far from model cadet.

And yet his instincts were sound. He had no way of knowing it—the sociologists had not yet got round to fixing the professional soldier under their glass—but "to have been outstanding in athletics at West Point was the best indicator that a cadet would become a general," and Ike had been awarded his big A for skill in a major sport. Moreover, as he could not know, intellectual attainments count for very little in an officer's future career. (General Douglas MacArthur's unusually excellent academic record is the notable exception to this rule.) Even Eisenhower's wretched record of indecorum would prove no particular roadblock to his later promotions and might even be said to have worked to his advantage. For, while there is no question that in the gradual process of his absorption into the officer corps the cadet must learn to conform both in small ways (how to button the blouse of his uniform) and in weighty ones (how to adapt himself to the code of military honor), there is a middle ground within which challenge to authority may even win a cadet a reputation for audacity, self-confidence, ingenuity—all good qualities in a commander.

In Eisenhower's case, the record of extracurricular achievement was maintained despite his injury. He filled in as cheerleader, as a maker of speeches at pep rallies before big games. Army's football coach, appreciating his passionate involvement in the game, asked him to serve as coach of the junior varsity squad, the scrubs, the cadets with desire but not enough speed or heft to make the varsity squad. At this task he proved himself a true leader.

His game knee also very nearly cost him his commission; a medical officer warned him as much. Eisenhower had, at twenty-four, so little sense of mission that he began at once to dream of a journey to the Argentine— the frontier! Just like the Old West! Why not—maybe he could become a gaucho!—and even wrote away for travel literature. This romantic fever was abruptly chilled when the medical officer once again summoned him to say that he had gone over Eisenhower's record and was prepared to recommend a commission so long as Eisenhower did not request service in the cavalry. The medical officer's decision, it would seem, was collective: it embraced various judgments, like that of an officer charged with maintaining cadet discipline ("We saw in Eisenhower a not uncommon type, a man who would thoroughly enjoy his army life. . . . We did not see in him a man who would throw himself into his job so completely that nothing else would matter") and that of a more perceptive officer (that Eisenhower was "born to command"). At once more heedful of his destiny, Eisenhower told the medical officer that he would choose, of the army services, only the infantry.

Before his graduation, each cadet was also asked to indicate his own preference for duty station. In the spring of 1915, with Europe at war, did young Eisenhower foresee that "ultimately the United States would be drawn into the conflict"? No. Was he, after the sinking of the *Lusitania*, in "a terrible rage against this barbarity"? No. Had he "eagerly expressed his own desire to get into action" against the Huns, and did it seem to him that "such a war would be righteous"? No, and again no. In the spring of 1915, with Europe at war, Eisenhower had, despite his more enthusiastic biographers, no such gaudy and flatulent ideas. He chiefly desired to celebrate his leave by parading up and down the streets of Abilene in his new lieutenant's uniform, by occasionally getting drunk, and by having as good a time as his funds would permit. Thereafter he hoped to be ordered to an army post halfway round the world from the European carnage, in the

Philippines. Not only did he set this down as his preference for duty station, but he was so confident he would be posted to Manila that he bought only tropical uniforms. It may be doubted that he gave the war in Europe more than cursory attention. Europe was Europe, far away, none of America's business, and, to a soldier, of interest merely as its conflicts were described in textbooks.

If Cadet Eisenhower had not learned to assess the probabilities of political economy at West Point, what had he been taught? In his time the United States Military Academy had, in fact, a better than good reputation as a technical school. Unfortunately, its docents essayed instruction both in the liberal arts and in military science. "The four-year course, however, simply was not long enough to permit achievement of both these purposes." As a first classman Eisenhower studied drill regulations and horsemanship, law, practical military engineering, civil and military engineering, ordnance and the science of gunnery, and Spanish. While one may fairly conclude that he had, at best, only a loose grasp of most of these matters, he fared best at his technical and engineering courses.

More important to Eisenhower's education, to be sure, was his indoctrination in the articles of any army officer's faith, circa 1915, for only that would lubricate his absorption into the officer corps, only that would open the way to his future advancement.

As has been indicated above, the army officer was not truly representative of the society from which he had come and, to his own private satisfaction, his ideology was quite different from that of civilian society. (In 1915, it should be noted, he was temporarily less alienated from civilian society than he had been earlier and would be again.) He was, above all, a dedicated professional, whose code demanded that he submit his will, his individuality, and his ambition to his sense of duty, that he always conduct himself as would an honorable gentleman, and that he faithfully serve his country. Duty, honor, country: these become holy to the cadet as (it is presumed) they are to the officer. But such sacramental obligations can create, in human clay, extraordinary tensions. To take one instance: what, exactly, is "a gentleman"? And how the devil can conduct "unbecoming the character of an officer and a gentleman" be defined with any precision?* To take another instance: fealty to one's country implies

---

* The quoted phrase is from an early formulation of military law which equates "officer" and "gentleman": "Whatsoever commissioned officer shall be convicted, before a general courts martial, of behaving in a scandalous, infamous manner, such as is unbecoming the character of an officer and a gentleman, shall be discharged from the service." But as Professor Morris Janowitz has observed, the law has been revised in the 1951 Uniform Military Code of Justice, Article 133: "Any officer, cadet or midshipman who is convicted of conduct unbecoming an officer and a gentleman shall be punished as the courts martial may direct." Thus, since the behavior of a gentleman resists defi-

wholehearted support of the status quo, which is to say, a conservative stance. What, then, if one's country veers violently to the left? Or, to put the matter more within likelihood, what if one thinks one's country is veering to the left? Where, in that hour, stand duty and honor? Do they clash with sworn fealty to country?

Another foundation stone for the officer's faith was (and still is) military tradition. At West Point, in Eisenhower's time, tradition was already as tangible as granite. Here were the rooms where once Lee studied, and Grant; there was the chapel where were furled the regimental British colors captured in the Revolution; these palisades above the Hudson, these same hills on which the cadets marched back and forth, were the linked chain that had held the colonies together against the redcoats. Tradition works into the grain of every cadet; tradition is the backbone of the officer corps. Yet a reliance on traditionalism can lead to moss-backed thinking and a stubborn resistance to innovation; "military traditionalism," Professor Janowitz has remarked, "implies a rigid commitment to the political status quo, a belief in the inevitability of violence in the relation between states, and a lack of concern with the social and political consequences of warfare."

Furthermore, the sense of conserving a tradition imbues the officer corps with pride of mission and encourages them to a secret belief in their superiority to the commonalty. They end by conceiving of themselves as the champions and protectors of our nation's good and ancient virtues —"integrity, courage, self-confidence, and unshakable belief in [the] Bible," as Eisenhower would later define them—against the corrosive influences of a contemporary environment.

Professionalism, duty, honor, fealty to country, military tradition, political conservatism, belief in the inevitability of war and in the need for national armed might, and a readiness to fight and to die—these were the chief tenets of the army officer's creed, these were the concepts which Eisenhower embraced in June 1915.

In that month he was formally denoted, by act of Congress, an officer and a gentleman.

---

nition, conduct unbecoming a gentleman no longer is cause for peremptory dismissal, and it is left to the courts-martial to make judgments.

CHAPTER FOUR

Need to Excel

SECOND LIEUTENANT DWIGHT D. EISENHOWER was now at the disposition of the War Department, an impersonal bureaucratic force the ways of which were always inscrutable and usually incomprehensible. After a little experience of it, Eisenhower was to think of the War Department as "that nebulous region," as if it were an uncharted waste from which issued orders as abrupt and perplexing as whirlwinds up from the Gobi Desert. Thus he was astonished (and dismayed, too, for it meant going into debt to purchase an entire set of uniforms, olive drabs for garrison duty and blues for dress) to find that he had been ordered to report not to the Philippines but to the 19th Infantry, which he joined at Fort Sam Houston, near San Antonio, Texas.

Ever resilient, the young lieutenant promptly formed several lasting friendships—with, among others, Leonard Gerow, Wade Haislip, and Walton Walker—and a strong regimental loyalty, for "in those days the man stayed with a regiment as long as possible." In those days, moreover, Fort Sam Houston was a large and lively center of social activities for the military; near it senior officers, upon their retirement, hoped to buy land for a ranch, and around it as well there had grown up military academies for the schooling of the sons of army officers. The headmaster of one of these, the Peacock Military Academy, had been told of Eisenhower's talent for football and offered him one hundred and fifty dollars to coach the school's team. Hesitant under the burden of his new responsibilities, Eisenhower decided he should renounce such irrelevancies as football and declined the offer. Wonderful to relate, this refusal brought the second lieutenant to the august attention of no less a personage than the commanding officer of the Southwest Department, Major General Frederick Funston.* With studied informality, General Funston contrived to send

* General Funston was indeed an officer of intimidating eminence. In a year or so he would be conditionally nominated by the general staff to command the American Expeditionary Force in Europe; that is, if all had gone well, he would have been Eisenhower's predecessor. But General Funston dropped dead in San Antonio in February 1917, and so to General John J. Pershing went the honor of leading the AEF.

for Lieutenant Eisenhower in the Officers Club, bought him a drink, and then said, of the invitation to coach football: "It would please me and it would be good for the Army if you accept this offer." Somewhat mystified, Eisenhower said, "Yes, sir," perceived that the general had no more to say, saluted, and withdrew. Before very long he got the message: one of the fixed notions the War Department had about Lieutenant (and later Captain, even Major) Eisenhower was that he was a dependable football coach; orders to coach army football teams would follow him for years, all over the continental United States.

One of the benign aspects of Fort Sam as a military post was that San Antonio attracted a number of families wealthy enough to while away the winter months relaxing in the warm sunny weather, and thus pretty young women were always in the neighborhood. One of these families, the Douds, was from Denver, Colorado; in 1915 there were three daughters, of whom the eldest was Mamie Geneva Doud. At eighteen she was a well-formed, slender young woman, whose dark brown hair was combed to fall in a wave down and back over her rather high forehead. She had many friends among the younger officers at Fort Sam, and they found her attractive and full of fun. So did Eisenhower, when he was introduced to her in October 1915. Quite a few fanciful tales have been told about their first meeting, all of them designed to enhance the incident in relentlessly romantic fashion, but none of these yarns needs to detain us; what is important is how she appeared to Eisenhower. He saw "a vivacious and attractive girl, smaller than average, saucy in the look about her face and in her whole attitude." She is said by others to have looked like the actress Lillian Gish and to have been something of a flirt.

No matter; he at once began to pay court to her, confidently and persistently, and in short order found that he quite liked her parents too. Her father, John Sheldon Doud, had all but retired after amassing a generous competence from the operation of a packinghouse in Iowa; her mother, Elivera Carlson Doud (whom everybody called Min after a character in the Andy Gump comic strip), had been only eighteen years old when she gave birth to Mamie, and was quite as full of fun as her daughter. They were a close-knit family, like his own; they were affable, gregarious midwesterners, like himself. As he liked them, so they liked him; more, he won their respect as a responsible and trustworthy young man, healthy, vigorous, resolute, obviously able to take care of himself and of others; and so they approved when he and Mamie became engaged on Valentine's Day, 1916. After the alarums and excursions along the Mexican border had made Mamie nervous about what might happen to her Ike if he were to join the punitive expedition into that exotic land, the rising tensions over the submarine warfare waged by Germany against American shipping bound for Great Britain convinced her that her fiancé would be ordered into perilous service at any moment if not sooner; in consequence she insisted that their wedding, planned for November, take place much earlier. They were married in Denver on July 1, 1916, and the War Department, ever unpredictable, added its mite to the merry-making by promoting the bridegroom, on that same day, to first lieutenant. Everything about the occasion enchanted its principals, so durably, indeed, that a bit of the wedding cake was preserved over the years to be enshrined at last, under glass, in the Eisenhower Museum.

Back at Fort Sam and sharing with Mamie his old bachelor quarters—two rooms and a bath—Eisenhower experienced once again, more strongly than at any time since the injury to his knee, his "need to excel." In the summer and fall of 1916, when the United States Army (if not the United States) was getting ready for war as fast and as intensively as possible, how could an obscure lieutenant excel? Perhaps by volunteering for more hazardous duties, in consonance with the officers' code? Some months before his marriage Eisenhower had applied for transfer to the aviation section of the Signal Corps (this was the larval stage of what would become, more than thirty years later, the U.S. Air Force), but Mamie's parents had deemed the notion reckless to the point of insanity and threatened, if he persevered in his course, to revoke their consent to his marrying Mamie. Glumly, he had reconsidered. At length, in the process of concluding that he would abandon aviation, he had come to a decision that warrants citation: "The decision was to perform every duty given me in the Army to the best of my ability and to do the best I could to make a creditable record, no matter what the nature of the duty."

On the face of it, the decision seems scarcely momentous. Even if every officer does not instinctively act in this way, why should Eisenhower have needed a "couple of days" to resolve upon such a thundering platitude? Yet that decision, taken and put into practice, was responsible for his having no combat experience in the War of 1914–1918, a fact that would fill him with a bitter frustration and haunt him throughout his subsequent spectacular career. Acting on his decision, he tackled the most cheerless tasks with such zest and energy that his commanding officers filled his 201 file—the official record of a soldier's career that is automatically consulted before promotions and assignments—with impressive reports of his efficiency at what he had been ordered to do, which was to train others to fight. He was good at it—it called for some of the same skills as coaching a squad of indifferent football players—and so he was stuck with it. For several months he was on detached duty as inspector instructor of a National Guard regiment, the 7th Illinois Infantry, charged with administration and the supervision of training. In April 1917 he was one of the officers separated from the 19th Infantry (an unhappy rupture of his regimental loyalty) in order to form and thereafter train the new wartime 57th Infantry. He did well: on May 15 he was promoted to the rank of captain. After less than six months with the 57th, he got special orders to report to Fort Oglethorpe in Georgia as an instructor of prospective officers, taking them into the field and preparing them for trench warfare, and, as if the assignment were not galling enough for a man who yearned to be in those trenches himself, it took him away from his wife just when she was about to give birth to their first child. Two months later fresh orders posted him to Fort Leavenworth, in Kansas, to instruct a company of provisional second lieutenants and to supervise the physical training of an entire regiment of them.

Periodically Eisenhower had applied for duty with units that were being organized for duty overseas; each time he had been promptly rebuffed, and in December 1917 he actually got an official reprimand from the War Department for his repeated requests. He was angry and resentful: the tradition he had absorbed as a cadet and now honored as an officer demanded that he be given the chance to lead men in battle, as some of his West Point classmates were already in France to do. What of glory? What of promotion? What of his "need to excel"? As he led his squads of shavetails through their calisthenics on the wintry Kansas plains, for the first time he began to think seriously of resigning his commission when the war was over.

Worse was to come. Late in February 1918 Captain Eisenhower got orders to report to Camp Meade, in Maryland, where he was to join the 65th Engineers which, he learned to his huge delight, had as its chief function the organization of the 301st Tank Battalion, Heavy, for duty on the western front. At Camp Meade everything went lickety-split, everybody was excited. The tank, the new weapon, the thing that would win the war! (There was none on hand, of course, but a soldier could dream.) In mid-March Eisenhower was in an ecstasy of exhilaration: word had come that the tank battalion was to be got ready to take ship in New York City, and that he would be sailing, too, and in command. At once apprehensive lest something go wrong, he hurried to New York City to investigate beforehand every detail of the imminent embarkation and voyage. Back again at Camp Meade he was congratulated on his splendid "organizational ability" and told that the War Department had a new plan for him: instead of going to France with the 301st, he was to collect all the troops of the 65th Engineers who were not going overseas and take them for further training to Camp Colt, near Gettysburg, Pennsylvania. These troops, he was told, were no longer to be called the 65th Engineers; they were instead the nucleus of the brand-new Tank Corps, and Captain Eisenhower, as the only regular army officer in command at Colt, would have the responsibility of training, equipping, and organizing those soldiers who volunteered to join the new corps, and of having them ready to be shipped overseas whenever the War Department so decreed.

"My mood was black," Eisenhower would recall years later, and the statement can be believed.

The job was a nightmare. No precedents existed for the training; no tanks were available; Camp Colt had been envisaged as a depot for the mobilization and embarkation of volunteers, but all at once the War Department decided that only selected troops were to be carried overseas, a decision that transformed Camp Colt into a bottleneck;* by the end of July, thanks to the willingness of American troops to volunteer for combat with a new weapon, Major Eisenhower (he had been temporarily promoted one rank on June 17) commanded ten thousand men and six hundred officers, and the grave danger was that morale would collapse like an unpegged tent. But morale stayed taut and trim. Young Major Eisenhower ran the camp with enthusiasm, a willingness to innovate, and a soldierly snap.

Never, however, did he relax his pressure to be assigned for duty overseas. Assurances given him by his commanding officers in the War Department were invariably flouted. He would be considered for such duty when Camp Colt was properly organized and running smoothly; no, not till the end of summer; no, not till after the tank training center had been moved to its winter quarters—but to keep him in cheery spirits he would be temporarily promoted to lieutenant colonel. (Notification of this new rank came on his twenty-eighth birthday, October 14, 1918.) At length, the provisions of the Abbeville Agreement having been fulfilled, he was told he would go to France in command of the troops scheduled to sail in November. Even then an effort was made to keep him stateside by offering him temporary promotion to full colonel if only he would renounce his dreams of glory; he refused the offer. Then came the Armistice, one week before his scheduled departure.

The war was over. Soon, as the army shrank back to peacetime size, Lieutenant Colonel Eisenhower would lose his rank,† and only after

---

* The Abbeville Agreement was an agreement of convenience between the United States and Great Britain that the British would furnish all necessary ocean transport if the United States would move to the ports of embarkation only infantry and machine gun battalions. The agreement, clearly, excluded tank troops.

† In the summer of 1920 Eisenhower was reduced to his permanent rank of captain; in December of that year he was promoted to a permanent majority, with his new rank to take effect from July 2, 1920. He fared a great deal better than some army officers in the postwar diminution of the military establishment. George C. Marshall, for example, who was commissioned a second lieutenant as of February 2, 1901, served on

nearly four years had passed would he belatedly be awarded the Distinguished Service Medal for what he had done during wartime. The need to excel was still present, but it had been all but stifled.

CHAPTER FIVE

Between Wars

FOR THE AMERICAN PROFESSIONAL SOLDIER the period between the great wars—roughly 1920 to 1940—was a vexatious passage over uncharted shallows, through narrow rocky channels, with the winds baffling. He considered himself ill-used by a society of which, nevertheless, he was the guardian and protector. He was spurned by that society, ridiculed by it, relegated by it to a status somewhat below that of a street cleaner or garbage collector (who after all, it was acknowledged, performed a socially useful function), scorned by it as vainglorious and oafish, as a creature of savage impulses and antiquated pursuits, a clod of no taste, no sensibility, and limited intelligence; in short, as an obsolete and dangerous pest. For his part, the professional soldier more and more mistrusted the society which he had dedicated himself to defend. His spokesmen, often spluttering with rage, more and more often filled his professional publications with harsh criticisms of that society. They saw the republic as morally bankrupt; sometimes they blamed its ills on too much freedom of speech and expression, sometimes on too much equality and democracy, but the "insidious doctrines" that incessantly outraged them were bolshevism (i.e., communism) and pacifism.

These two hobgoblins obsessed the army officer throughout the 1920s and well into the 1930s. At times it was hard to tell which was considered more pernicious; indeed, in June 1932 General Douglas MacArthur, then chief of staff, coupled the two in intimate equation. "Pacifism and its bedfellow, Communism, are all about us," the general proclaimed in a speech

General Pershing's staff as a full colonel but, in that same summer of 1920, was likewise reduced to his permanent rank of captain and on the next day promoted to major. That spread of seniority—from Marshall's commissioning in 1901 to Eisenhower's in 1915—and their reduction to the same grade in 1920 gives an idea of how glacial would be the rate of Eisenhower's promotions from 1920 to 1940.

at the University of Pittsburgh. "In the theaters, newspapers and magazines, pulpits and lecture halls, schools and colleges, it hangs like a mist before the face of America, organizing the forces of unrest and undermining the morals of the working man. Day by day this canker eats deeper into the body politic."

Hair-raising as was the specter of bolshevism, pacifism loomed as more ominous to all that was adored by the professional army officer. First and last, to the army, pacifism was the murrain of the 1920s and early 1930s, blinding patriotic citizens to the desperate national need to arm, to prepare, to train, to be disciplined, to levy troops, to expend more of the national wealth for the invention, development, and production of machines designed to deal death and destruction—always and only, it was to be understood, in the interest of the national defense.

Although pacifism was blamed for the collapse of military preparedness, there were more culpable forces at work: the postwar slump in commerce and industry; the temptation to cut taxes, which the Congress found impossible to resist; the haste with which capital turned for investment to fields other than the military. At all events, after legislating the National Defense Act of 1920, which authorized an army of just a shade under three hundred thousand officers and men, the Congress faced about and sliced both taxes and appropriations so shrewdly that the army was reduced by the end of the fiscal year 1923 to less than half its authorized strength. The army brass was appalled. An attempt was made to frighten the Congress into a more generous appropriation by warning of nationwide strikes, of race rioting, of anarchist upheavals to control which a strong army would be essential. To no avail; in 1922 the Congress would rise only to the bait of economy.

While these grave matters were in train, Colonel (then Captain, then Major) Eisenhower, too insignificant an officer to be concerned with the War Department's campaign on behalf of preparedness, too sensible an officer to have got himself involved in any public squabble over bolshevism or pacifism, was preoccupied, as a professional soldier should have been, with whatever lessons could be learned from the old war about new weapons and new techniques for the next war. After the fiasco of his non-assignment overseas he had been sent here and there in the erratic, disjointed fashion of the War Department—to Camp Dix in New Jersey, to Fort Benning in Georgia, and at length back again to Camp Meade in Maryland, where it had been decided the Tank Corps would make its home base and where, too, there would be established an Infantry Tank School. For most of the next three years Eisenhower would be stationed at Meade, in command of tank battalions, testing new models of tanks, exploring in a primitive way the tactics of tanks in support of infantry, attending the Infantry Tank School.

At Meade, Eisenhower met for the first time the officers who had commanded the men he had sent to fight in the American tank corps at St. Mihiel and in the Meuse-Argonne offensive. By all odds the most dashing of them was Major (late Colonel) George Patton. Florid tales of Patton abounded: he was a cavalry officer who was reported to have ridden into battle astride one of the small tanks under his command as though it were a high-spirited polo pony; he was said to have breached the Hindenburg Line single-handed, leaving his tank battalion and the supporting infantry far in the rear. Which would come to him first, a Medal of Honor or a court-martial, no one dared guess. In appearance he was tall, tight-lipped, and stiff; in manner, melodramatic, swaggering about with flashy guns at his hips ("Goddammit, my guns are ivory-handled. Nobody but a pimp for a cheap New Orleans whorehouse would carry one with pearl grips"), but upon confrontation disillusioning, for his voice was high-pitched and squeaky.

Together with Patton and a few other officers Eisenhower tentatively fussed about, through the woods and along the ravines of the Camp Meade reservation, with tactical ideas for tank warfare. They had some light two-man Renaults; they had some big, clumsy American-built Mark VIIIs; they even had an experimental model, the M.1919, built by Walter Christie, an automobile mechanic and pioneer racing car driver. They elaborated the tactical problems posed by the instructors at the Command and General Staff School in Leavenworth, Kansas, and they found that those theoretical troops which were supported by a theoretical complement of tanks always "won."

Having convinced themselves, Patton and Eisenhower naturally set about convincing others. Both men prepared articles for *Infantry Journal*, Patton's characteristically a trifle overblown, Eisenhower's more judicious. Patton commanded a battalion of light tanks, Eisenhower one of heavy tanks, but Eisenhower liked neither. The Mark VIII was "too weighty, unwieldy and cumbersome," the little Renault "too short, underpowered, and deficient in firepower." What was needed was a tank "of sufficient length to cross a 9-foot trench, a maximum weight of 15 tons, a firepower of one 6-pounder and two Browning machine guns, sufficient power to run cross-country at a speed of 12 miles per hour, and on good roads, with treads dismounted, at a rate of 20 miles per hour." Eisenhower concluded: "The clumsy, awkward and snail-like progress of the old tanks must be forgotten, and in their place we must picture this speedy, reliable and efficient engine of destruction." Here was surely a modest proposal, but Eisenhower went further: he presumed to suggest the reorganization of the infantry division to include one tank company (twenty-six motor vehicles, of which sixteen would be tanks) as a useful force in the hands of any divisional commander. No question about the value of the idea, but for an officer scarcely five years out of West Point to dare to tinker with an infantry division was of heresy and wickedness all compact.* He was summoned before the chief of infantry and told the facts of life. As he later recalled: "I was told that my ideas were not only wrong but dangerous and that henceforth I would keep them to myself. Particularly, I was not to publish anything incompatible with solid infantry doctrine. If I did, I would be hauled before a court-martial."

This was his second invaluable postgraduate lesson in the ways of soldiering. The first he had begun to learn during the war: that he should never importune for desirable duty, that the proper post for a soldier is where he is ordered by his superior officers. Now the second lesson: that he should shut up. Neither lesson can be said to have damped his short-fused temper.

During his first year at Meade, Eisenhower had to endure separation from his young wife and baby son (David Dwight, born in September 1916), for the camp afforded few houses for family residence. He lived in Bachelor Officers Quarters; Mamie and the child stayed with her family in Denver or San Antonio; occasionally she would leave the child with an aunt in Iowa while she came east to be with her husband for a short time. In 1920 permission was given to convert some wartime barracks at Meade into residential quarters for officers, and that spring the family was reunited. Major Patton had quarters nearby and the two men continued to ride together, study war together, and discuss tank tactics together; their friendship took firm root. This was as well, for it enabled Patton to play a modest part in one of the most important developments of Eisenhower's career, a true turning point. The Pattons invited the Eisenhowers to Sunday dinner, and there the young officer was introduced to Brigadier General Fox Conner.

Conner was an officer of high reputation and considerable influence. During the war he had been chief of operations at General Pershing's GHQ (where one of his assistants had been Colonel George G. Marshall); at the moment he was chief of staff of the AEF in Washington, a command which had been given separate status so that General Pershing would not fall under the command of Major General Peyton March, the army's chief of staff (these two gallant officers hated each other's guts).

* The U.S. infantry division as constituted in 1944 still had no tank company as part of its strength. An army corps, however, had as many as three armored divisions, and each of these comprised three tank battalions, with a total complement of 269 tanks.

Conner spoke fluent French, he was well and widely read, he was accounted one of the army's "brains." He was a tall and handsome man, self-possessed and quiet-spoken. He was Mississippi-born, of a wealthy family; he had graduated from West Point in 1898 and had soon afterward married an heiress. In short, he was a valuable man to know.

He proved to be most interested in whatever ideas Patton and Eisenhower had about the possible uses of tanks in warfare. After dinner he asked to be shown about the Infantry Tank School. Once in the shops, he sat down and began asking questions, directing most of them to Eisenhower. Hours passed. The day faded. At length he stood up, thanked his hosts, and went away.

But Eisenhower had made his mark. Before very long he heard again from General Conner, who had been ordered to Panama to command a brigade of infantry at Camp Gaillard: would Major Eisenhower care to come along as his executive officer? Nothing could have better suited Major Eisenhower; at once he applied to the commandant of the Tank Corps, Brigadier General Samuel D. Rockenbach, for his transfer. General Rockenbach had earlier directed Eisenhower to coach Camp Meade's football team; now he rejected Eisenhower's request. When Eisenhower pressed the point, Rockenbach agreed to pass his application on up to the War Department. He did, and it was at once rejected. In the summer of 1921, however, when General Pershing took over as chief of staff, a proposal from Fox Conner was more likely to meet with a favorable response. Sure enough, orders were drafted and (after the football season of 1921) issued, assigning Major Eisenhower to Camp Gaillard. He and Mamie arrived there early in January 1922.

By that time, in addition to his eagerness to serve a tour of duty with Conner, Eisenhower had another reason for wanting to get away from Meade. Both for him and for Mamie the camp was forever stained by the most dismal of memories. A day or so before Christmas in 1920, when their small son was three years old, he had come down with scarlet fever, and despite the best efforts of the physicians at the camp hospital, just after the turn of the new year he was dead.

This event, so sudden, so shocking, put the Eisenhowers' marriage to a strain. Predictably, each parent shouldered a self-imposed burden of guilt. Had they taken their child too much for granted? Should they have left him with relatives in Iowa? Why had they hired a nursemaid for him? Should they have inquired about the state of her recent health? (They were later told by the camp medicine men that the girl they had hired as their son's nursemaid had not long before been sick of the same streptococcus that infected their boy.) Was there nothing more they could have done for him? No gifted specialist they could have summoned to his bedside? Self-reproach is the inevitable concomitant of these sad occurrences, and unfortunately such censures are sometimes turned from one self toward another.

Despite their constraint, however, Mamie Eisenhower had conceived another baby before they arrived in Panama.

Gaillard was not an exacting post; in fact quite a pleasant one for those who could come to terms with the tropics. Conner's command, the 20th Brigade, had been dehydrated by congressional economy—it was only one regiment, the 42nd Infantry—and duty involved little more than making sure that officers and men stayed up to the mark, and maintaining a network of trails for the use of troops and their pack animals in the unlikely event of any hostile action near the Culebra Cut. In his ample spare time Major Eisenhower could pursue his education in military history, an interest reawakened by Conner. Before long Eisenhower's curriculum had been expanded to include all kinds of military affairs and some philosophy and English literature as well, for Fox Conner was, among other things, a natural teacher. Under Conner's tutelage, and drawing freely on Conner's copious library, Eisenhower undertook with relish a kind of "Great Books" program, proceeding from historical fiction to military history to memoirs to military doctrine to dramatic poetry to philosophy—from the American novelist to Winston Churchill to Clausewitz to Plato and Nietzsche. He fitted a screened porch at his quarters with shelves and tables and drawing boards; here he mapped the campaigns he had been studying, for he knew that when he returned a text to Conner he would be searchingly cross-examined on every command decision: why it had been made, what had been the alternatives, what might have happened under altered circumstances, how it could be justified and how criticized. And if for some reason that catechism was interrupted, Conner would prosecute it when next they took horse to go out on two or three days of reconnaissance. Eisenhower learned to do his homework.

This master-pupil association endured and deepened for nearly three years while Eisenhower served at Gaillard, and the pupil was properly appreciative of the master; "life with General Conner," he said later, "was a sort of graduate school in military affairs and the humanities, leavened by the comments and discourses of a man who was experienced in his knowledge of men and their conduct." Eisenhower kept busy, administering the camp and the regiment under Conner's satisfied gaze, and finding, to his astonishment, that his horizons were steadily opening out.

For Mamie Eisenhower the case was different. From the first day, when she had to walk under the blazing tropical sun for more than a quarter-mile across the canal on one of the gates, she detested Panama. Camp

Gaillard was removed from any sizable town; the only convenient shops were the camp commissary or the post exchange; she lived in an old house, damp, mildewed, verminous, infested by roaches and bats; no rooms in Panama were frigerated in the 1920s; the only amusements were a once-a-week game of bridge and a once-a-week dance about which her husband was less than enthusiastic. Unlike him, she had no pleasure in horseback riding or other out-of-door sports. When he took to spending much of his time with General Conner, she began to find reasons to visit Mrs. Conner, and what she had to say was querulous and fretful. "I never knew exactly how Ike felt," Mrs. Conner said later, "as he knew Mamie was wearing down a path to my front porch." There was still an uneasy coolness between the Eisenhowers. Mrs. Eisenhower sought advice and Mrs. Conner gave it. "You mean I should vamp him?" Mrs. Eisenhower asked. "That's just what I mean," said Mrs. Conner fiercely. "Vamp him!" Mrs. Conner felt at the time that she was watching Mamie grow from a girl into a woman.

In the summer of 1922 Mrs. Eisenhower went home to Denver to give birth to her second son. Major Eisenhower was given leave to be with her on August 3 when John was born. After that, when they had come together again in Panama, all between them was almost as it had been before their first child's death. And when the Eisenhowers left the Canal Zone, at the end of his tour of duty in September 1924, she said to Mrs. Conner: "You bawled me out and I thank you for it."

Actually, Eisenhower had been ordered back to Meade three months before his tour of duty at Gaillard would have run, and why? To coach another football team. When the football season was done, he asked the military bureaucrat who was then chief of infantry if he might be assigned to the Infantry School at Fort Benning. No, he was told; no, he was to go to Benning, but only as commander of a tank battalion. It appeared that he was off on another of the aimless, mindless peregrinations dictated by the War Department, but once again Fox Conner intervened. Eisenhower's tutelary guardian was also back from Gaillard, scheming now from a lofty command post smack in the tripes of the military establishment, as deputy chief of staff. Having at once learned of his protégé's disappointment at his failure to be posted to the Infantry School, Conner at once contrived some expert complications. If the chief of infantry blocked the path, clearly the way to circumvent Bumbledom was to place Major Eisenhower in some service over which the chief of infantry would be impotent. All swift guile, Conner had orders issued that transferred Major Eisenhower to the adjutant general's office and assigned him as recruiting officer to Fort Logan, outside Denver, Colorado, comfortably proximate to his wife's family. But he knew his man would be outraged by such orders, which he would take to be a rebuke deliberately intended to humiliate him, so Conner also dispatched a telegram to Eisenhower:

No matter what orders you receive from the war department make no protest accept them without question. CONNER

Conner then persuaded the adjutant general to nominate Major Eisenhower, "an exceptionally efficient officer," as one of those he was empowered to send to the Command and General Staff School at Fort Leavenworth. Thus Eisenhower, an officer now in his middle thirties, approached what he later called "a watershed in my life."

In the army's postgraduate educational system, the Command and General Staff School is the second stage of a successful professional career. First comes the specialized service school (in Eisenhower's case the Infantry School at Fort Benning, which he had been denied), next comes Leavenworth, and finally the Army War College in Washington. There are still other schools, like the Industrial College, also in Washington, where the problems of economic mobilizations are stressed, and the National War College, established in Washington in 1947, at which are explored such stately matters as foreign policy and national security, but these schools are operated collectively by all the armed forces. If he follows the conventional routine, the qualified army officer will attend his service school some five or ten years after having been commissioned; if he has a superior rating he will be invited to attend Leavenworth ten or fifteen years after having been commissioned; and, depending on his record, if he is regarded as a prospective general officer, he will later be given the chance to attend the Army War College. The entire process is designed "to identify and train those officers who have the capacity to become military managers, rather than just 'military mechanics.'"

In Eisenhower's time, Leavenworth was crucial. "Graduation there was thought to be a passport to better assignments in the Army and graduation high in the class was said to mark a man for future advancement." In consequence, competition for a high ranking was fierce, so fierce indeed as to be deleterious to more than a few officers. (Some were said to have committed suicide when they failed to measure up to their own high hopes. At all events, the system of grading the graduates by ranked numbers was abolished not long after Eisenhower's class was graduated.) One of Eisenhower's acquaintances who worked in the office of the chief of infantry was ready with his cheery encouragement. "You will probably fail," this man wrote Eisenhower, and added that his failure would end his usefulness as an infantry officer.

Eisenhower had two invaluable assets: his self-confidence, always full to the brim or overflowing, and his need to excel, which Fox Conner had revived and which had always responded to competition. In a letter to Conner, Eisenhower indicated that nevertheless he was troubled, since so many of his classmates would have the advantage of having graduated from their service schools. Conner was peremptory in his reply: ". . . you are far better trained and ready for Leavenworth than anybody I know. . . . You will feel no sense of inferiority."

And yet . . .

When Eisenhower arrived at Leavenworth in August 1925, he found the technique of the school to be uncommonly sensible—no examinations, no learning by rote, no cramming of facts—with an emphasis on the solution of problems. A theoretical enemy force, so-and-so strong, equipped with such-and-such, and located in this-and-that sort of territory; the student was given command of another theoretical force and told its mission. First, what to do? Second, when told what one should have done, how to plan to do it? And how to order the reserves and supply forces to support it? In short, at Leavenworth in 1925–1926 the students played war games and were asked only to excel at them. But this was precisely what Fox Conner had asked of Eisenhower for nearly three years and on a far more exacting and rigorous level. Of a surety he was "far better trained and ready for Leavenworth" than most of his classmates.

And yet . . .

Most of Eisenhower's classmates joined together in study groups of four or six or eight, pooling their experience and their ideas. He was asked to join such a group, but declined. How could one of a pool excel?

And yet . . .

One of his classmates was Major Leonard (Gee) Gerow, whom he had known years before in Fort Sam Houston, when they were both lieutenants with the 19th Infantry. Gerow had graduated from Virginia Military Institute in 1911, four years before Eisenhower had graduated from West Point, so he was four years senior in grade, but the two men were about the same age. Moreover, Gerow had only the previous spring graduated top of his class from the Infantry School at Fort Benning. (The second man in that class had been Major Omar Bradley.) Eisenhower thought that perhaps it might be helpful if he and Gerow were to study together. Gerow agreed.

They worked in a room on the third floor of Eisenhower's quarters, a room outfitted like his screened porch in Panama, with maps on the walls, textbooks on the shelves, and a long wide worktable. They worked well together at night and did well, each on his own, when they reported to the war game sessions in the afternoon.

Major Eisenhower graduated top of his class of some two hundred and seventy-five superior officers. Major Gerow trailed him by two-tenths of one percent. It is hard to conceive of an event in June 1926 that the people of the United States would have considered less relevant to their immediate concerns and their future welfare.

"A watershed in my life." Metaphorically it was the divide in Eisenhower's life between mediocrity and frustration on one side and on the other the excellencies for which he had striven and the rewards that would attend them. Little wonder that Eisenhower later acknowledged that Fox Conner was "the one more or less invisible figure to whom I owe an incalculable debt."

But rewards for his excellence did not at once tumble into Major Eisenhower's lap. Indeed, even before graduating from Leavenworth he had been transferred back into the infantry, whose chief had promptly ordered him to report to Benning as executive officer of the 24th Infantry. When he arrived to take up his duties he was told that he was once again to coach a football team. This instruction, so exasperating, so dismally recurrent, showed only that the War Department, once heedful of a fatuous suggestion, could never untrack, could never perceive that what was already antiquated ten years before was now hopelessly obsolete. Meanwhile Eisenhower's name had been added to the General Staff Eligible List and Fox Conner, who had General Pershing's ear, was still deputy chief of staff; so before long Major Eisenhower was ordered to Washington, D.C., to report for duty at the Battle Monuments Commission, a new agency under Pershing's command.

This commission was charged with designing, landscaping, and greening the fields in France where were scattered the American dead of the armies that had fought in the War of 1914–1918; also with commissioning and setting up suitable memorials to those dead; also with preparing a guidebook to the battlefields where Americans had fallen. It was the sort of task that might more effectively have been done by civilians, but could in fit and seemly fashion be done only by soldiers. It was a trust, a matter of military honor, like being selected as one of the guard at the bier of a once and future hero; and so appointment to the commission was much prized and was reserved for the most promising of officers.

Eisenhower was assigned the writing of the small guidebook. A vast deal of matter was turned over to him—maps, pictures, statistical data, historical data, chronologies and so on, most of it superfluous—and he whipped it into coherent shape and produced a creditable typescript within four or five months. To a simple soldier like Pershing this feat seemed little short of miraculous. He had a letter drafted to the chief of infantry extolling Major Dwight D. Eisenhower's "splendid service," "superior ability," and "unusual intelligence and constant devotion to duty."

The task completed, Eisenhower could have stayed on to revise his own work lazily and comfortably. In fact, he was urged to do so by Pershing's executive officer, Colonel Xenophon Price. "Every officer attached to the commission is going to be known as a man of special merit," he reminded Eisenhower. But Eisenhower had been offered the chance to study at the Army War College. "For once the Department has given me a choice," he said, "and for once I'm going to say yes to something I'm anxious to do."

In 1927–1928 the Army War College was in Washington at the post now known as Fort McNair. To anyone subjected to the pressures at Leavenworth, the War College seemed by contrast to be pleasurably contrived for a leisurely respite. The Eisenhowers lived across town at the Wyoming Apartments, an old-fashioned building with generous, high-ceilinged rooms, on Connecticut Avenue not far from Rock Creek Park. Both the Wyoming and the War College were filled with old friends. There was Gee Gerow, for example, and Wade Haislip, who had also served with the 19th Infantry at Fort Sam Houston, and Everett Hughes, who had been one of Eisenhower's instructors at Leavenworth and was now his classmate at the War College, and several others, men whose paths had crossed and recrossed a half-dozen times or more since graduation from their military academy, at camp or fort or school, in the withdrawn and exclusive brotherhood of the professional soldier. These men worked together, studied together, played golf with each other, dined at each other's apartments, and spent the evenings at parties together.

Such close associations were crucial in molding and advancing an officer's career, for they became in effect a process of continuous judgment, what the sociologists call a "system of peer rating," in the course of which a man either adapted to the group or was eliminated from it without compunction—and elimination, of course, carried with it the implicit threat of an end to promotions, an end to a career. "The officer had to establish his individuality, but within the confines of narrow and acceptable limits. The result was to reinforce conformity in social behavior, for excessive individuality would injure one's reputation." Inevitably these associations would persist over the years and, in time of war, be a sure source of supply for the senior commander in search of staff officers or junior commanders. In the period between the wars, moreover, these intimate and exclusive patterns of behavior helped the professional soldiers maintain their esprit de corps—indeed, to maintain the officer corps itself during a time when the army officer was, to civilian society, a figure of fun.*

* Contrary to popular belief, very few West Pointers resigned their commissions during

Quite evidently, in such a sequestered segment of society, the officer's wife is of absolute importance. An unfortunate marriage, by effectively precluding an officer from his fellows, has more than once snuffed out his chances of promotion. In these circumstances Mamie Eisenhower was unexceptionable. Like her husband, she loved having people around; like him she was gay and vivacious; at a party she could play the piano for the group that wanted to harmonize, and if the tune was unfamiliar, no matter, for she could quickly pick it up by ear, and if the tune had to be repeated again and again and again and again, no matter, for she was always enjoying herself.*All her friends of this time remember her with an unstinting affection. Kate Hughes, who was married to Everett Hughes, is only representative in her recollection of the Eisenhowers during the late 1920s:

> Most of the time people were at their house. We'd gather there after the men had played their golf, or when they'd finished for the day at the War College. The men would stop at the Eisenhowers for a drink and get to talking and then call their wives and we'd all go over. . . . Sometimes we'd go out to a Chinese or Italian restaurant, but mostly we'd stay at the Eisenhowers. Mamie would have food for us, or sometimes each of us would bring something.

Close-knit and withdrawn. But Major Eisenhower had, as well, fairly good connections with the civilian society around and about the military. His youngest brother, Milton, was in Washington, launched on a career in government; he was an assistant to the secretary of agriculture; before long he would be appointed director of information for the Department of Agriculture; himself once briefly a journalist (he had been able to help his older brother outline and write the guidebook for the Battle Monuments Commission), he had many friends among the Washington correspondents. One man whom Milton had come to know, first professionally and later as a close friend, was a tall, affable young midwesterner, Harry Butcher, who was editor of a trade magazine, the *Fertilizer Review*. Butcher and his wife Ruth were brought by Milton to the Eisenhowers' apartment in the Wyoming, and before long the Butchers were as close to Ike and Mamie as they were to Milton and his recent bride, Helen Eakin. Before long, too, Butcher's considerable charm had transported him far

---

the years between the wars: the rate was not more than 5 percent during the period from 1923 to 1933. For a more detailed analysis see Janowitz, *The Professional Soldier*, pages 15, 136, and 149.
* Of her husband, Mrs. Eisenhower has said: "His favorite song is 'Abdul the Bulbul Amir,' to which he can sing about fifty verses."

from fertilizer to the infant Columbia Broadcasting System, a corporate organization in which he was destined to rise like a rocketing pheasant.

Milton insisted on taking his older brother to parties in Washington where the major might meet the men Milton imagined could be helpful to a soldier's career, but unhappily the young assistant to a secretary of agriculture was not likely to be plugged into the circuit of cocktail parties frequented by any very puissant kingmakers. Once a reporter who had been invited to an affair informally pasted together by a bunch of his pals was about to leave when Milton stopped him, saying: "Please don't go until you've met my brother; he's a major in the army and I know he's going places." The reporter shook hands with an officer he had never before seen nor heard of; as he did so he thought casually, If he's going far he'd better start soon; in truth the major looked a little long in the tooth for his rank. But the handshake was firm, the crooked smile was already a principal asset of its copyright owner, the charm was remarkable even when taken in small doses, and the departing reporter was powerfully impressed.

After his graduation from the War College in June 1928, Major Eisenhower accepted another tour of duty with the Battle Monuments Commission because this second one afforded him the chance to spend a year in France. (His wife was anxious to travel in Europe, and anxious, too, that their small son, who would be six that summer, might begin his education at a school in Paris.) They took an apartment in Paris on the Quai d'Auteuil, on the right bank of the Seine, and that summer, while the city swarmed with American tourists, their apartment was nicknamed le Club Eisenhower, for it was always an open house for army friends and always seemed, at least at certain hours, to be filled with music and gaiety.

The major's duties were not onerous. With a chauffeur-interpreter he drove from the Vosges, the wooded, mountainous region between the Moselle and the Rhine, north and west to the English Channel, crossing back and forth over country which ten years before had been trenches and no-man's-land, pocked by shellholes and fouled by the stench of death. His military training automatically converted countryside into terrain, and he automatically registered on some level of memory the rivers and railroads, the gaps and plains and massifs, the approaches and objectives, but it would be footling to suppose that this year in France was in any sense a preliminary study for campaigns still unconceived, much less enwombed.

The tour of duty was, rather, honorific, giving the major and his wife the chance to junket through Belgium, Germany, and Switzerland, and, when young John had finished his year at the MacJannet School in Paris, enabling the family to sojourn for a month in Italy.

On November 8, 1929 (and the date is of some relevance; it was ten days after the Black Tuesday when the great bull market on the stock exchange shuddered and collapsed and so ushered in the Great Depression), Major Eisenhower took a desk as assistant executive in the office of the assistant secretary of war.

This functionary's chief task, a statutory responsibility under the National Defense Act of 1920, was "the supervision of the procurement of all military supplies and other business of the War Department pertaining thereto and the assurance of adequate provision for the mobilization of matériel and industrial organizations essential to wartime needs." In short, it was to figure out how American industry would, in wartime, be smoothly harnessed to the military establishment. Major General George Van Horn Moseley, who had been Pershing's chief of supply (G–4), was the army officer charged with keeping this problem quiescent, but he who wears two stars on his shoulder loops has long since learned how to delegate, and so in practice such work as there was devolved on two majors—Eisenhower of the Infantry and Wilkes of the Engineers.

On the face of it, there was every reason to suppose that Major Eisenhower had landed in another well-cushioned berth. In the years between the wars a representative officer's workday ended around noon so that he might enjoy the country club life of an army post—the swimming pools, golf courses, tennis courts, polo and horseback riding, the officers' clubs— which was deemed a reasonable compensation for the spartan rigors of army life. The staff officer assigned to duty in Washington might, depending on his superior, have to observe longer office hours, but it would be absurd to say that he was ever worked to the point of fatigue. And a study of the war potential of American industry, at a time when captains of industry were off in dark corners licking their wounds, factories were being shut down on every hand, and the only army under discussion was that of the unemployed, seemed the sort of study that could be ingeniously spun out over years, perhaps over a decade, before anyone would ask for a look at it. Moreover, when Eisenhower first came to his desk, even the study itself appeared to have been torpedoed. There was a feud going on between the assistant secretary and chief of staff, General Charles Summerall, as a result of which orders were issued forbidding any officer on the general staff to enter the offices of the assistant secretary.

And yet, because of an odd and yeasty brew of personalities and political pressures, Eisenhower was soon hard at work surveying the plants that had manufactured supplies for the army in 1915–1918, investigating the supply of raw materials and the feasibility of synthetic substitutes in case the sources of supply were cut off, trying to grasp such thorny matters as procurement, priorities, price controls, the divided wartime responsibilities of executive and legislative branches, determination of fair profit, excess-profits taxation, plant expansion, manpower controls, administrative organization, and rationalizations of power and transportation for wartime emergency, and finally drafting a comprehensive Plan for Industrial Mobilization, no less, which inevitably came to be reported in the press in terms of something vague but ominous called M-Day.

In this way Major Eisenhower found himself involved with that bugbear of the professional soldier, pacifism.

His unwonted activity, or at least the urgency with which it was tackled, was owing to Public Resolution Number 98 (H.J. Res. 251), a "Joint Resolution to promote peace and to equalize the burdens and to minimize the profits of war," approved by the Seventy-first Congress on June 27, 1930, after more than eight years of unremitting agitation by a handful of congressmen. What most exercised the legislators (who were led by southern and western populists and by big-city insurgents like Fiorello La Guardia) was that while some men were drafted into the armed forces and asked to make considerable sacrifices, even that of their lives, other men were permitted—nay, encouraged—to make unconscionable profits from the operation of wartime industries. They pointed, for example, to the ten steel companies which had cleared, on the average, a profit of less than 5 percent over the four years 1912–1915 but had averaged a profit of more than 107 percent in 1917; for another example they pointed to the manufacturers of shells and explosives, whose profits zoomed 1500 percent in three years.* United in their belief that such scandalous inequities were intolerable in a democracy, so called, they were divided as to how to correct them. By statute? But they could never rally enough votes to pass the Capper-Johnson bill. By constitutional amendment? At last they agreed upon the resolution, which created a commission "to study and consider amending the Constitution" to make war unprofitable and require everyone to bear its burdens equally. The War Department of course had seen that commission coming way down the road. When General MacArthur replaced General Summerall as chief of staff in November 1930, there was also a new assistant secretary, Frederick H. Payne. All hands agreed that the War Department had better get humping on a plan for industrial mobilization, and the two majors, Eisenhower and Wilkes, began to work up a little sweat.

Speaking generally, if this sort of commission is to do its work properly, its leading members must have a clear idea of their conclusions before they begin to receive witnesses at public hearings, and the principal witnesses must have been prudently selected and their testimony rehearsed in a can-

* Both examples, and others of like character, lose some of their impact under a close examination. But they had the power to agitate in the 1920s.

did and cordial atmosphere. This particular commission—it comprised four senators, four representatives, the secretaries of war, navy, agriculture, commerce, and labor, and the attorney general—chose Patrick J. Hurley, secretary of war, as chairman, and it was swiftly apparent that the commission's accomplishments would be largely negative. No promotion of peace; instead it would be known as the War Policies Commission. No constitutional amendment, since the goal of equalizing the burdens of war, however desirable in the abstract, could never in fact be legislated. No stipulation against excessive profits; the War Department's plan for industrial mobilization, which was already being drafted by Wilkes and Eisenhower, would have to be a sufficient curb. (The plan proposed that manufacturers be paid a profit of 6 percent on "what it is claimed is the investment.") The key witnesses were duly lined up and given the treat of discussing their testimony in advance with an officer who for candor and cordiality was unrivaled in the American military establishment, viz., Major Dwight D. Eisenhower.

Thus Eisenhower got a chance to meet and chat with some American operators of impressive amperage, such as Bernard Baruch, Walter S. Gifford of American Telephone & Telegraph, and Daniel Willard of the Baltimore & Ohio; and thus, incidentally, a congressional effort to fix constitutional restraints on war profiteering was shunted off on a siding.

What Eisenhower himself thought of this venture into the alien world of civilian politics is suggested by an article he wrote in 1931 for *Infantry Journal*. A large part of his space was given over to scrutinizing the pacifists who had, with gallant futility, testified before the commission. The dispassionate tone of his article is rather like that of a biochemist describing what swims into the field of his microscope, and is the more admirable when one reflects on the conflicting emotions that must have tugged at the author: on the one hand the memory of his own pacifist upbringing, and on the other his awareness that he would be read almost exclusively by army officers, many of whom believed that pacifism was a subversive doctrine fomented by those civilians whom they labeled, with detestation, the "liberal intelligentsia." Eisenhower wrote that the witnesses against war were "a retired admiral of the Navy, two ministers of the Gospel, a leader of the Socialist party, an oculist, editors of magazines of so-called 'pacifist' leanings, and officials of various peace associations." The list was disingenuous. It conveniently ignored a half-dozen congressmen (of both parties, and including one Republican senator) who were militantly against drafting men if capital were not also conscripted, and it characterized as an oculist a physician who had earned a perfectly adequate degree as Medicinae Doctor. "A listener gained the distinct impression," Eisenhower wrote, "that the members of this group, with possibly one or two exceptions, were earnestly and unselfishly laboring for the promotion of an idea which they implicitly believed." Supercilious, but on the whole fair-minded. Quite gratuitously, however, the whole caboodle of them were tarred with a guilt-by-association smear that would characterize them indelibly as sinister radicals to those who regularly read *Infantry Journal*: "most of" them, Eisenhower wrote, were also advocates of the World Court and the League of Nations, opposed the dispatch of U.S. Marines to Nicaragua, urged independence for the Philippines and recognition of the Soviet Union, and desired a revision of U.S. policy in respect to Latin America. Some even argued that the war debts should be canceled.

What was the root of all this pacifist evil? Eisenhower was too circumspect to make any blunt charges, but the close reader could find at least a clue. The Democratic party in its national platforms of both 1924 and 1928, he wrote, had included a plank that read: "In the event of war in which the manpower of the nation is drafted, all other resources should likewise be drafted. *This will tend to discourage war by depriving it of its profits.*" (The emphasis was added by Eisenhower or, as it may be, by the editor of *Infantry Journal.*)

The implication was that the resolution creating the commission, the pacifist congressmen who had pressed for passage of the resolution, and the pacifist witnesses who had testified before the commission were alike inspired by a persistent Democratic campaign waged against war and more especially against those industrialists who manufactured the machines of war. Yet the passage in Eisenhower's article was full of error, evidently deliberate, for it was taken in distorted form from the record of the commission's hearings. The record shows that the Democrats included the plank only in their platform for 1924, while the Republicans, unmentioned by Eisenhower, used substantially the same plank both in 1924 and in 1928 ("in time of war the nation should draft for its defense not only its citizens but also every resource which may contribute to success").

The balance of Eisenhower's article was taken up with a becoming appreciation of the Plan for Industrial Mobilization which had been presented to the commission by the chief of staff, General Douglas MacArthur—the plan which Major Eisenhower had himself worked so hard to prepare.

Once he had attracted General MacArthur's favorable attention, it followed that Major Eisenhower would swing closer into the orbit of that resplendent figure. Although still formally attached to the office of the assistant secretary of war, where he busied himself with improving the standards, the faculty, and the quality of the officer-students selected to attend the Army Industrial College, Eisenhower was more and more considered an aide to the chief of staff. (General Moseley, his nominal superior, was now deputy chief of staff.) General MacArthur came increasingly to depend on Eisenhower "to draft statements, reports, and letters for his signature."

More often than not, Eisenhower relished the relationship. MacArthur's idiosyncrasies, such as his habit of referring to himself in the third person, tickled him ("He was a peculiar fellow"), as did MacArthur's grandiloquent style ("With that dramatic voice, he could have been a *great* actor") and his vanity ("MacArthur could never see another sun, or even a moon, for that matter, in the heavens as long as *he* was the sun"), but he had a solid respect, approaching awe, for MacArthur's store of knowledge ("largely accurate") and his mental caliber ("He did have a hell of an intellect! My God, but he was smart. He had a *brain*"). On the other hand, MacArthur's readiness to mix it in the bearpit of partisan politics distressed him and embarrassed him. Despite his own recent lapse into political hanky-panky, Eisenhower honored the tradition of the officer corps that required the army to stay out of politics, at least when on duty. Both General MacArthur and General Moseley—and Major Eisenhower, too—held strong right-wing views on politics, traditionalist views, but Major Eisenhower felt that army officers should keep those views bottled up except when they were alone together far from civilians, or at least from civilians they could not thoroughly trust. The Bonus March of 1932 afforded an instance of MacArthur's predilection for grandstanding on an essentially political issue. And willy-nilly, Eisenhower was caught up in the shaming affair as MacArthur's aide.

The bonus marchers—they called themselves the Bonus Expeditionary Force, or BEF—were some twenty thousand jobless veterans of the War of 1914–1918 who flocked into Washington from all parts of the country in the early summer of 1932, when the Great Depression was hotting up to a hellish roast. There were then some fifteen (or seventeen, or twenty—the statistics of the time are unusually unreliable) million unemployed Americans, hungry and wretched and desperate, but President Hoover was impaled, inert and impotent, on a Tory dilemma: the idea of soup kitchen handouts was accursed in America, yet the alternative of a make-work program, building roads or amphitheaters or post offices or whatnot, seemed to ape Mussolini's fascism or, worse, Russian bolshevism. In the event, Hoover did nothing except to urge that the Reconstruction Finance Corporation extend inadequate funds, at 3 percent interest, to the states for direct relief.

So the BEF thought to exert pressure for some swift action. A bill before the Congress offered by Wright Patman of Texas would have provided immediate payment of the veterans' adjusted compensation certificates—

the bonus—voted by the Congress in 1924, payable in 1945, worth one dollar for each day's war service in the U.S. and one dollar and twenty-five cents for each day's service overseas. In those days such sums looked like the big rock candy mountain. The destitute veterans flocked into Washington on foot, on the rods of freight trains, in every way imaginable. Many came with their wives and children. Some squatted in abandoned buildings and vacant lots near the Capitol; most were settled in an impromptu camp on the alluvial flats of the Anacostia River southeast of the Capitol. The ragged army was notable for "rigid discipline, flag-waving, and militant anti-radicalism." Friendly merchants and a compassionate superintendent of metropolitan police, Pelham D. Glassford (a West Pointer and a retired brigadier general), contributed to their support; but the secretary of war, the self-infatuated Patrick J. Hurley, refused any help to what he termed an "invasion."

The BEF's success in winning over the Congress was nil. Hastening to adjourn and so escape from these scarecrow reminders of the national agony, House and Senate alike rejected the Patman bill and fled from the city on July 16.

What was to be done with the BEF? Most of its members had no homes to return to, no money, no prospects, no hopes, nothing but hunger and misery. Since they had nothing to do and nowhere to go, why not stay? They hunkered down.

Established authority abhors such a rabble and at once begins to manufacture the rationalizations that lead to its removal by force and violence. The rabble was "aggressive . . . lawless . . . an ever-present [threat] of disease and epidemic . . . subversive . . . incited by radicals and hotheads."

On July 28 the Treasury Department ordered the veterans to vacate the Treasury-owned buildings near Pennsylvania Avenue and 4½ Street. Then the hour by which they were to be gone was abruptly put forward by the department, Treasury agents with police bodyguards appeared, and a confused brawl ensued. The police fired, wounding several men, two mortally. Within a very few minutes Glassford had restored order, but the commissioners of the District of Columbia had already asked the President for federal troops to quell the "riot"; the President, fully prepared, at once issued a statement alleging that "a considerable part" of the BEF were not veterans at all but "communists and persons with criminal records"; from Hoover to Hurley to MacArthur, like a bolt of lightning, went the pre-arranged order to clear the "affected area" without delay.

From Fort Washington came a battalion of the 12th Infantry, from Fort Myer came a squadron of the 3rd Cavalry and a platoon of tanks, from the State, War and Navy Building came a headquarters company of military police. Also from headquarters came General MacArthur himself —in full fig, booted, spurred, and adorned with seven strips of ribbons across his left breast, a glorious burst of color—with his two aides, Major Eisenhower and Captain T. J. Davis, likewise in uniform but more subdued, by comparison almost funereal, marching obediently at his heels.

It is quite certain that Major Eisenhower was unhappy. Indeed, in one of the pictures taken of him later that day, standing beside MacArthur, the look on his face is like that of a dog caught sucking eggs. He knew something of the issues involved, and for a time had served as liaison to keep MacArthur informed about the metropolitan police operations in connection with the bonus marchers. Reporters covering the District of Columbia Building were used to seeing him sitting in the press room, smiling, friendly, reading pulp magazines, steering clear of trouble. When the trouble got to be too much, on July 28, Major Eisenhower was confident enough of his ties to General MacArthur—and of his own independence—to feel "free to object" to his chief's taking active command of this ignoble mission. Eisenhower had urged that the chief of staff of the United States Army should be off the streets, removed from anything so vulgar as a riot. But MacArthur had been in epic mood. There was, he had said, "incipient revolution in the air." The mob "down there" was "animated by the essence of revolution." He had paced back and forth. They were, he had said, "insurrectionists," and their riot was "the focus of the world today." Where the attention of the world was focused MacArthur proposed to be. He had ordered Eisenhower to get into uniform and follow him into the fray.

So that afternoon the major glumly marched to the Ellipse, then east along the Mall with MacArthur and the troops to the disputed area near the Capitol. It was later officially alleged that here "a few brickbats, stones and clubs were thrown" at the troops, but competent reporters at the scene saw no signs of resistance. What they saw, and reported, was a charge by a troop of cavalry, with drawn sabers, into the crowd of veterans.*

For the rest of that dispiriting day and into the night the troops, using tear gas grenades, slowly herded the veterans and their families south and east toward the Anacostia flats. Here the miserable shacks were fired (by their former occupants, MacArthur later insisted; by the soldiers, said reporters on the spot), the encampment leveled, and the BEF dispersed

---

* Major George Patton was one of the officers commanding the cavalry. It was later reported that one of the veterans injured during the subsequent melee was Joseph Angelo, late Sergeant Angelo, who had been Patton's orderly in the AEF and in September 1918 had stanched a wound that Patton sustained when he led a charge during the fighting in the Argonne Forest.

from the District of Columbia. Late that night, the dirty job done, the major advised the general to avoid any further encounters with newspapermen. Since the whole affair had been political, not military, the major suggested that any press conference would be best left to the politicians. But to the general a press conference was irresistible and, flushed with victory, he hastened away to face the reporters, on whom, as it turned out, he made a most lamentable impression.

Early in 1933 Major Eisenhower was formally appointed MacArthur's aide and took the office next to his in the State, War and Navy Building. To an officer who was by training and tradition committed to preserving and cherishing the status quo, the next few months were to be a bizarre experience. Franklin Roosevelt had replaced Herbert Hoover in the White House; innovation had replaced passivity. With the advent of the New Deal, the status quo was apparently pulverized, and all the familiar landmarks seemed to have been switched about. The trade union had become respectable, forsooth, and Wall Street was a hissing and a byword; instead of attempting to strike a thrifty balance between its receipts and its expenditures, the federal government was sluicing out more than twice as much money as it took in, quite as though the nation were at war (which, of course, it was: against hunger and misery and despair); before long old people began to get pensions, and jobless people checks, and the gangs of homeless kids who had been wandering about all over the country were being given a chance to join something called the Civilian Conservation Corps—two hundred and fifty thousand young men, President Roosevelt predicted, could be usefully at work in the CCC by the summer of 1933—and who knew how to mobilize them, organize them, build the camps, and administer them? Only the United States Army.

It was an unexpected development, and because of it we have the chance to reflect on a most provocative juxtaposition—two men at least superficially much like each other who suddenly found themselves engaged, more or less, in the same sort of work: Major Dwight D. Eisenhower and Harry L. Hopkins.

They were of an age, both born late in 1890; they had grown up in neighboring states, Kansas and Iowa; both had been raised in poverty, both reared in a strict Gospel faith. Eisenhower was the third of seven children, Hopkins the fourth of five. Eisenhower's father was a storekeeper, an engine wiper, and the janitor-engineer for a small dairy; Hopkins's father was a harnessmaker, a traveling salesman, and a storekeeper. Eisenhower loved to play football and baseball; Hopkins, who was sick as a boy, stuck to basketball, at which he excelled. Both were unimpressive scholars. Each had been aimless, vague as to his future; each had drifted into a career of service, the one social, the other military, but each with a growing sense of commitment. Early in 1933 they were temporarily engaged in similar work, but on the basis of quite different postulates and to quite different effect.

While Eisenhower as cadet and officer had been maturing into the mold of a professional soldier, self-confident, self-controlled, authoritarian, conventional, gregarious within severely exclusive limits, vigorous, financially secure, politically conservative, and atypically optimistic, Hopkins was being toughened in a very different way. He slipped into social work by accident and stuck with it out of conviction, living among the poor in the slums of the lower East Side of Manhattan, running an employment bureau for the derelicts and transients, then making a study of health conditions, then building the Tuberculosis Association into what amounted to a statewide health association concerned with a dozen ailments, and in 1930, as the Great Depression deepened, once again operating a volunteer employment bureau. In the process, Hopkins was shaped in another sort of mold, to be libertarian, unconventional, innovative, experimental, so financially insecure as to be a standing joke, politically impatient, boundlessly energetic, impetuous, and always self-confident, gregarious, and optimistic after his own sardonic fashion. (Like Eisenhower, Hopkins had his wise mentor who widened his intellectual extravagations: he was Dr. John Kingsbury, a gentle, cultivated, and serene man who, like Fox Conner, had an ample library which, however, contained more volumes of poetry than of military annals. Hopkins read more Keats than he did Clausewitz.) By 1931 Hopkins was administering relief for the state of New York, under Governor Franklin D. Roosevelt, and when the New Deal exploded in Washington in 1933 it was only a matter of months before the President summoned Hopkins to administer relief for the entire nation.

No figure of the New Deal would be more reviled by the press and by the brass-collar Republicans than Hopkins. A later generation can agree that Eisenhower and Hopkins, wildly contrary though their methods were, were identical in their will to preserve and defend the basic status quo.

In the event, Major Eisenhower was at work on these, for him, unwonted tasks a few days before Hopkins even got to Washington. On May 10, 1933, President Roosevelt bade the War Department prepare to receive two hundred and fifty thousand young men into CCC work camps by July 1. A plan had to be prepared and orders for corps area commanders drafted. "All that night, lights burned in the War Department as the staff went to work as if for war." Before long field commanders and reserve officers called up for training in the emergency were hard at work organizing an army of "approximately three hundred thousand men— more than were enlisted during the Spanish-American War—establishing them in a series of small camps in various and often isolated regions throughout the United States, and making therein adequate provision for health, welfare, and maintenance." As was pointed out in General Mac-Arthur's annual report (drafted by Eisenhower), the job gave officers of army and reserve "valuable training in mobilization procedures and leadership."

If they were alert and imaginative soldiers, the CCC gave some few field commanders a great deal more than that. George C. Marshall was a lieutenant colonel commanding a battalion of the 8th Infantry at Fort Screven, Georgia, when the advent of the CCC at once enormously added to the load of his work. He loved it. In speeches at Savannah and later, when he was assigned to Fort Moultrie, near Charleston, South Carolina, he praised the CCC as "the greatest social experiment outside of Russia." There could have been few better ways for a wartime commander to come to know his future civilian-soldiers. As late as 1938 Marshall was still enthusiastic about the CCC and the chance it offered to make men out of unemployed youngsters. "The best antidote for mental stagnation that an Army officer in my position can have," he called it; it had brought him "the most instructive service I have ever had, and the most interesting."

But in spite of the bang-up job it did with the CCC, the army was still on short rations when it came to slicing the national pie. On May 22, 1933, Harry Hopkins arrived in Washington to run the Federal Emergency Relief Administration and at once commenced to put five hundred millions of dollars to work; later that year, through the Civil Works Administration, he put another nine hundred and thirty-three millions to work in just four months. ("Gross waste," wailed the Republican National Committee, and "downright corruption.") In the office of the chief of staff sums like those could provoke only bitter jealousy. Appropriations for the army (which included the Air Corps) were comparatively slim:

Fiscal 1933 $304,000,000
       1934   277,000,000
       1935   284,000,000

In fiscal 1936, however, and for the next few years, the situation was altered. Not only was the Congress able to appropriate more money directly for the army, but two of the hated New Deal agencies—the Public Works Administration and Works Progress Administration—would be spending more hundreds of millions on airfields, airplanes, ammunition, trucks, tanks, barracks, and coastal defenses for the army, and a great deal of construction for the navy, including two aircraft carriers, the *Enterprise* and *Yorktown*. When General George Marshall was appointed deputy chief of staff in October 1938, he was able to judge how substantially WPA and PWA between them had helped the army* and he grieved over the failure of the War Department to take further advantage of these remarkable subventions, "but it seemed that some of the aging generals had been too afraid of the Congressional criticism they might incur if they became involved in dealings with such vulgar, radical fellows as Hopkins."

Major Eisenhower did not meet Hopkins during this period, and it may be doubted that he would have walked around the corner to do so. Hopkins was one of those New Deal "visionaries" (i.e., crackpots), no man for a self-respecting army officer to consort with. In this time Major Eisenhower could be found at parties in Washington wondering about the health of the republic. At one party there was present an undergraduate from George Washington University who was taking a course in communism, and Eisenhower reacted sharply: he didn't think students should be subjected to that sort of thing. (The course was in economics and under the safe tutelage of Arthur E. Burns, who was later conscripted to serve on President Eisenhower's White House staff.)

For the professional soldier it was not a happy time. Tradition obliged him to stand mute on political issues that gravely disturbed him; he had to wait for retirement to speak his mind. Thus not until 1938 would Eisenhower's friend General George Van Horn Moseley begin to attract a good deal of attention, first as an outspoken critic of the New Deal and its foreign policies, later as an advocate of action by vigilantes to protect and defend the republic, and as an alleged associate of such noisome citizens as Gerald L. K. Smith, the Christian Fronter, and William Dudley Pelley, the popgun fascist. (Many years later Eisenhower would loyally say of Moseley that "he was a patriotic American unafraid to disagree with a consensus.")

It was not hard to see what dismayed the professional soldier about the New Deal's new look at foreign affairs. Of the items on the list Eisenhower had used to stigmatize the pacifist witnesses before the War Policies Commission, nearly all had been disposed as the pacifists had desired: the last

---

* A contributor to *Army & Navy Register* wrote in the issue of May 16, 1942: "In the years 1935 to 1939, when regular appropriations for the armed forces were so meager, it was the WPA worker who saved many Army posts and Naval stations from literal obsolescence."

American marines had been withdrawn from the Caribbean, legislation that would bring de jure independence to the Philippines in 1946 had been approved by the Congress, the Soviet Union had been accorded diplomatic recognition, and the United States had formally adopted a policy of nonintervention in Latin-American affairs and had assured the hemisphere of its good-neighborly intentions. It was almost a clean sweep. Even the question of the war debts had been shelved and forgotten.

Perhaps never had the military and civilians been so removed from each other as in 1935. An army officer writing for *Infantry Journal* during this melancholy period articulated the bitter sense of alienation:

> If a man cannot find satisfaction in living a purely military life, he should get out of the Army. The superimposition of any semicivilian system will reduce the military consciousness and should not be tolerated. The soldier and the civilian belong to separate classes of society. The code of the soldier can never be the same as that of the civilian; why try to mingle them?

It was in 1935 that MacArthur's tour as chief of staff was to end. The Tydings-McDuffie Act, which transformed the Philippines into a commonwealth and guaranteed the islands their independence after ten years, had recently been signed, and Manuel Quezon, the president-elect of the prospective commonwealth, invited MacArthur to come to Manila as military adviser to the new government. MacArthur, who knew the Far East of old (this would be his fifth tour of duty there), accepted the post with alacrity. He also urged Major Eisenhower to come as his assistant.

Eisenhower had served with troops only four months in nearly eleven years, a shocking indolence for a professional soldier, and he knew it was high time he got back to active duty, but there were a number of considerations that beckoned to Manila. One: servants were cheap, accommodations were luxurious, the tour of duty promised to be a snap. Two: he would go on detached service and would draw generous extra pay from the Philippine government. Three: he would be issuing orders and advice to a government that held him in high regard rather than taking orders from a government that gave no sign of wanting him. Four: General MacArthur showed in every way that he both wanted and needed him.

It was twenty years since he had first thought he would go to the Philippines. Twenty years, presumably the most active and productive years of his life, but he hadn't much to show for them. He was forty-five years old, still only a major; no hope of a lieutenant-colonelcy for another year or so; disaffected, uncharacteristically dispirited, in need of a change.

In September 1935 Major Eisenhower took ship for Manila. He went alone, because Mamie had decided to stay in Washington another year, until their son John finished primary school.

General MacArthur had assured President-elect Quezon that the Philippines could be defended "if sufficient men, munitions, and money were available, and above all sufficient time to train the men, to provide the munitions, and to raise the money." The timetable of these assurances is not clear: when was President-elect Quezon told how much money would be needed, and how quickly? At all events, in a reversal of the proverbial procedure, generals blithely propose, after which majors must dispose, as best they can.

The first plan for the defense of the Philippines was drafted by Major James Ord, a classmate of Eisenhower's at West Point and an instructor at the Army War College. He had the assistance of other members of the faculty at the War College and the supervision of MacArthur and Eisenhower. The plan "set a meager pay scale for [a] conscript army," would have cost twenty-five million dollars a year, and sent Quezon into a tizzy when he first heard of it. Ord and Eisenhower thereupon slashed pay, reduced armaments, shrank training time, and emerged with a plan that would have cost eleven million dollars a year. MacArthur now told them that Quezon would not hold still for more than eight million annually. Back at their drawing board, the two majors shriveled their paper army from some twenty thousand officers and men to less than eight thousand, they spread the cost of purchasing munitions over twenty years instead of ten, they canceled an artillery corps, and at last they fetched up within MacArthur's budget. No navy. No air force.

All these revisions were accomplished before Ord and Eisenhower had left the War Department. When they reached Manila they found that MacArthur was once again dreaming of "an army of 30 divisions, supported by 250 planes and 60 torpedo boats."

This was fey enough, but quite soon Major Eisenhower learned that Quezon's chief need was a constabulary, "a military adequate to deal with domestic revolt," as Eisenhower himself put the matter. (There is no evidence that he troubled, then or later, to determine why the countryside, especially in central Luzon, sporadically seethed with agrarian revolt.)

Legislation providing for the national defense of the Philippines took effect in December 1935, but nothing much ever came of it. In various parts of the archipelago, ground was cleared and rude barracks were built for small training stations. These were so remote and inaccessible that a tiny air force had to be created simply to permit instructors to reach the conscripts they were supposed to train. (Thanks to this air force, and some instructors borrowed from the U.S. Army Air Corps, Major Eisenhower learned to pilot a plane and was issued his license. Because of this air force, on the other hand, Major Ord was killed when his Philippine pilot crashed his plane.) Funds were exhausted before the first batch of conscripts had been trained, even before their first weapons—obsolescent Enfield rifles from the War of 1914–1918—had been purchased on the cheap in the United States. In short, the defense program was a shambles.

In 1938 the Philippine National Assembly voted an additional two million dollars for the military budget and almost as much again for military construction, but even these temporary increases were far from enough. Morale sagged. Corruption thrived. In those days Manila and the islands were administered by a Philippine clique closely associated with the dominant commercial interests, which were of course American-owned. These parasitic politicos cared about national defense only as they could make money out of it; when war came in December 1941 they cheerfully collaborated with the Japanese invaders and remained in titular power; indeed, they were maintained in that nominal power when MacArthur later reconquered the Philippines in 1944 and 1945. In the art of survival they were incomparable, but that did not make Eisenhower's work any easier.

Meanwhile, Eisenhower enjoyed compensations. For one thing, in July 1936 he was at last promoted to lieutenant colonel. For another, he was on velvet: he and Mamie (recently arrived with John) occupied a spacious suite, air-conditioned, in the Manila Hotel; they hobnobbed with the wealthy American businessmen who had been attracted to the city by cheap and plentiful labor; often he would be invited to spend the weekend on the presidential yacht, playing bridge with Quezon and lounging in the sun. Quezon liked him and outfitted him with a private office in the presidential palace in Malacañan; they passed many hours together idly talking of this and that, taxes, corruption, government, public affairs generally. Certainly Eisenhower saw more of Quezon than did MacArthur, for that proud-spirited officer kept singular office hours. "He never reached his desk until eleven," Eisenhower has noted. "After a late lunch hour, he went home again."

By 1939 the plan for defending the Philippines had collapsed, and the friendly warmth between MacArthur and Eisenhower had appreciably cooled. In 1935, when the general was anxious that Eisenhower accompany him to the Philippines, he had sent a letter (a copy went into Eisenhower's 201 file) packed with praise:

> . . . your success in performing difficult tasks . . . comprehensive grasp of the military profession in all its principal phases . . . analytical thought and forceful expression. . . . I have been impressed by the cheer-

ful and efficient devotion of your best efforts to confining, difficult and often strenuous duties, in spite of the fact that your own personal desires involved a return to troop command and other physically active phases of Army life, for which your characteristics so well qualify you.

. . . convincing proof of the reputation you have established as an outstanding soldier. . . . this reputation coincides exactly with my own judgment.

But in the Philippines the two men quarreled more and more often. Later Eisenhower would recall the crescent antagonism and the incident that irrevocably disrupted their intimacy. "Probably no one has had more, tougher fights with a senior than I had with MacArthur," Eisenhower said. "I told him time and again, 'Why in the *hell* don't you *fire* me?' I said, 'Goddammit, you do things I don't agree with and you know damn well I don't.' For example, he wanted to be a field marshal, and I said, 'General, you have been a four-star general. . . . This is a *proud* thing. There's only been a few who had it. Why in the *hell* do you want a *banana* country giving you a field-marshalship? This . . . this looks like you're trying for some kind of . . .' Oh, Jesus! He just gave me hell!"

The incident that cooled the MacArthur-Eisenhower relationship began with a typically MacArthurian desire for show, a demonstration of the new Philippine armed strength, units brought from all over the archipelago and then marched through the streets of the capital in a big parade. "I didn't like it, but it was an order, and Ord and I said, 'All right, we'll try to do it.'"

"Jimmy [Ord] and I estimated the cost. We told the General that it was impossible to do the thing within our budget. . . . But following the General's orders, we began to do the necessary staff work.

"Somewhere along the way [someone]—and I don't know who, I think it must have been Jimmy Ord, who was a great friend of Quezon's—let Quezon know what was going on and when I came into my office that morning in Malacañan (in which I stayed an hour, two hours a day) he called me in and asked about this, and I told him about the order. And he in the meantime had called MacArthur.

". . . I returned to my other office in the Walled City within the hour. General MacArthur was exceedingly unhappy with his entire staff. By the time I saw him, he was visibly upset. You know what his defense was? He never gave such an order.

"Here we were, we were flabbergasted, didn't know what to say. And finally I said to him, I said, 'General, all you're saying is that I'm a liar, and I am *not* a liar, and so I'd like to go back to the United States right away.' Well, he came back . . . and he said, 'Ike, it's just fun to see that

81

damn Dutch temper'—he put his arm right over my shoulder—he said, 'It's just fun to see that Dutch temper take you over,' and he was just sweetness and light. He said, 'It's just a misunderstanding, and let's let it go at that.'"

But Eisenhower never liked being called a liar, or being in a position where he seemed to have told a lie (although, of course, he told his full quota of lies during his lifetime), and so he cared little for MacArthur's belated sweetness and light. "Now *that's* the time," he said later. "From there on our relationships were never really close."

On the evening of September 3, 1939, Colonel Eisenhower and his wife visited friends, Colonel and Mrs. Howard Smith. The Smiths owned an old shortwave radio. While their wives chatted, the two colonels listened with earphones to the broadcast from London: "It is the evil things that we shall be fighting against—brute force, bad faith, injustice, oppression, and persecution—and against them I am certain that the right will prevail."

Later Colonel Eisenhower wrote his brother Milton that "we have been listening to broadcasts of Chamberlain's speech stating that Great Britain was at war with Germany. After months and months of feverish effort to appease . . . a sad day for Europe and for the whole civilized world . . . Communism and anarchy . . . crime and disorder . . . abject poverty . . . privations and starvation . . . power-drunk egocentric . . . the final result will be that Germany will have to be dismembered."

This time he was determined that he would be actively involved, if possible as a fighting commander. He applied for immediate reassignment in the United States. MacArthur argued against it: what could be more important than his duty in the Philippines? Quezon insisted that he remain, handing him a blank contract and telling him he might himself fix his salary for staying. Eisenhower was adamant. Only the War Department, bureaucratic as ever, let time slip by before his new orders were cut. Three months passed before Colonel Eisenhower and his wife and son took ship from Manila for San Francisco. General and Mrs. MacArthur came down to see them off and stood waving on the pier as the steamship was drawn away.

CHAPTER SIX

With Troops

NOBODY WAS MORE AWARE than Dwight Eisenhower of how scant was the time he had served with troops: six months in the last eighteen years, none in the last nine. Moreover, he was uncomfortably conscious of "the War Department policy that requires a certain proportion of troop duty in order for a man to be considered a capable and rounded officer." But the gap in his record was not entirely nor even chiefly his fault. He had "earnestly tried for many years to get an assignment to troops and to serve at least a normal tour with them." Unfortunately, he had earned a reputation as a most superior staff officer: the general whose staff he adorned did all he could to hang on to him, and other generals all over the country tried unsuccessfully to prize him loose, each for his own staff. General MacArthur had gone so far, in trying to hold Eisenhower firmly in his grip, as to keep all Eisenhower's requests for assignment to troops unrecorded.

It was, then, to be expected that when Colonel Eisenhower stopped off in San Francisco on his way to report to the 15th Infantry at Fort Lewis, on Puget Sound in the state of Washington, he would be, so to say, kidnaped by Lieutenant General John L. DeWitt, commander of the Fourth Army, and ordered to remain on temporary duty at his headquarters, doing work in a planning section (G–3).

The task was to plan the movement of all the troops, including the National Guard, in the Fourth Army area (the entire west coast and northeast into the interior as far as Minnesota) down into southern California for a training exercise. While he was engaged in this tedious donkeywork, Eisenhower had a chance to go south to Monterey Bay to observe a field exercise involving an amphibious landing against simulated opposition. The exercise had been planned by Major Mark Clark, USMA 1917, an old friend of Eisenhower's, and it involved the 15th Infantry, the regiment to which Eisenhower had been assigned before his orders were changed. As he walked along the beach, reflecting on his aborted opportunity, he ran into General DeWitt and the chief of staff, General Marshall. (This was Eisenhower's second encounter with Marshall; the first had come when he was on the Battle Monuments Commission and had resulted in Marshall's asking Eisenhower to join his staff of the Infantry School at Fort Benning.) Now Marshall, indicating that he knew Eisenhower was fresh back from the Philippines, said: "Have you learned to tie your own shoes again since coming back, Eisenhower?" And Eisenhower, flashing his grin, said, "Yes, sir, I am capable of that chore, anyhow."

In February 1940, his job of planning done, Eisenhower joined the 15th Infantry at Fort Ord, California; was named the regiment's executive officer; asked for and was given, in addition, command of a brigade; and with his new command moved north to Fort Lewis.

Within the army he was by no means an obscure lieutenant colonel but rather a man who was widely assumed to be marked for enviable advancement. He had been officially informed that among field officers he was rated at or close to the top, and at various times he got word from well-placed friends in the War Department that various corps and division commanders had sought him for their staffs. The chief of infantry, however, rejected all such requests on the ground that Eisenhower needed duty with troops. Eisenhower enthusiastically agreed. He was enjoying himself hugely. When his regiment went on midsummer maneuvers with the 3rd Division he "never had in any one stretch more than one and three-quarters hours' sleep, and at times was really fagged out," but "had a lot of fun." He was strong and healthy, bursting with physical vigor and reveling in the chance to use it.

By the end of June the Battle of Britain was raging, eight hundred Royal Air Force fighters against twenty-five hundred bombers and fighters of the Luftwaffe. France had fallen as had Norway and the Low Countries, Hitler had declared that "the war in the West is won," and the British were on guard against expected invasion. Eisenhower's keenest ambition was to get command of a fighting force, and in October a letter came from George Patton saying that he anticipated being given command of an armored division and that he meant to ask for Eisenhower as a regimental commander under him. Eisenhower was elate. He could think of no more splendid future. But in mid-November there came a wire from Leonard Gerow, now a brigadier general and chief of the War Plans Division in the War Department:

I need you in War Plans Division do you seriously object to being detailed on the War Dept General Staff and assigned here please reply immediately.

Assignment to War Plans was considered one of the choicest in the army, a broad highway leading straight to high command. General Marshall, for example, had been chief of War Plans before he was nominated as deputy chief of staff. Eisenhower was torn. If he accepted he would never get the field command that he coveted more than gold, yea, than much fine gold; but he was modest enough to fear that if he refused he might be sidetracked to no higher a post than staff officer at Fort Lewis. What to do? He sweated over a long letter that he thought the most important he had ever written. After walking the edge of the blade for more than one thousand words, he contrived to duck the decision and leave it in Gerow's lap. All this effort was, as so often, for naught— back at the War Department the decision as to his destiny had already been taken. It was, like most War Department decisions, an adroit compromise. He was detailed to the General Staff Corps and assigned to duty as chief of staff, 3rd Division, Fort Lewis: back on staff, which was bad, but on staff with troops rather than in the War Department, which was good.

(Meanwhile the RAF had won the Battle of Britain and so made implausible any Nazi cross-Channel invasion of Great Britain; selective service was under way in the United States; and the concept of lend-lease as a means of buttressing the valiant British effort was being converted into legal jargon. Before long President Roosevelt, newly elected to an unprecedented third term, would summon his countrymen to make America an "arsenal of democracy.")

For Lieutenant Colonel Eisenhower the path was now prescribed, as precisely as in a formal garden. He would be bounced higher and ever higher, not by accident but because he had satisfactorily demonstrated that he was, in every sense of the phrase, an accomplished professional soldier.

In early March 1941 he was named chief of staff to IX Army Corps. Still stationed at Fort Lewis, he got a promotion to colonel (temporary), and his responsibilities reached out to every fort, camp, station, and post in the northwestern quarter of the nation. Before he had even time to count his responsibilities, he would bounce up again.

On June 11 Lieutenant General Walter Krueger wrote to his old friend and comrade General Marshall. He wanted a chief of staff for his Third Army. Further, he knew just the kind of man he wanted: "a man possessing broad vision, progressive ideas, a thorough grasp of the magnitude of the problems involved in handling an army, and lots of initiative and resourcefulness." Yet further, he knew his man's name: Dwight D. Eisenhower. He wanted him. On June 13 Marshall wrote back saying that Krueger should have him. On June 24 (the speed of lightning in those days) Eisenhower had his orders to proceed to headquarters, Third Army, San Antonio, Texas. He arrived at Fort Sam Houston with his wife Mamie on July 1, their twenty-fifth wedding anniversary. The next day he was named deputy chief of staff, Third Army. A month later he was designated chief of staff.

He had been plunged into the biggest peacetime war exercise in the country's history; had to help plan it, organize it, and execute it; more than two hundred thousand officers and men of the Third (Blue) Army against almost that many of the Second (Red) Army, commanded by Lieutenant General Ben Lear; a "war" waged in Louisiana, where all hands had to "live with mud, malaria, mosquitoes and misery," getting drenched by the tail end of a hurricane into the bargain.

The rest of the chapter is well known: "the brilliant planning" of Third Army's chief of staff, which almost resulted in the capture of Second Army's hapless commander; the accolade in a nationally syndicated newspaper column, "Washington Merry-Go-Round," in which it was written that "Colonel Eisenhower . . . conceived and directed the strategy that routed the Second Army"; and Eisenhower's promotion on September 29 to brigadier general (temporary). Less well known, perhaps, is the fact that before, during, and after the maneuvers Colonel Eisenhower displayed his talent for press relations, converting his tent into a home-away-from-home for civilian correspondents who were the rawest of cubs on this bizarre new assignment, charming them with his warm friendliness, and amusing them with unprintable stories about the New Orleans whores with whom some of his troops had consorted. He may have been still unknown to the American public, but more than a handful of the best journalists in the country had already a strong affection for him.

Then came Pearl Harbor, and the celebrated nap from which he was wakened, and the urgent telephone call a few days later from Colonel Walter Bedell Smith, then secretary to the Joint Chiefs of Staff: "The chief [Marshall] says for you to hop a plane and get up here right away. Tell your boss that formal orders will come through later."

Brigadier General Eisenhower's foot was on the threshold of fame.

PART THREE

THE
GROWING BURDEN
OF COMMAND

CHAPTER ONE

To the War Department

If Brigadier General Eisenhower was at all astonished when the call came bidding him to Washington, it can have been only because it had been so slow in coming. After all, five days had passed since the stunning and lethally effective attack on Pearl Harbor, on Sunday, December 7, 1941, five days since the later but equally disastrous blow to the Philippines, and Eisenhower was confident there were few if any officers in the continental United States who were as intimately familiar as he with the martial strength of the defenders of the Philippines, their recuperative ability after an attack, their experience, training, planning, battle readiness, and not least consequential, their commander.

On the Friday morning when at last he was summoned, rain clouds were heavy over east Texas, the valley of the Mississippi was drenched by steady downpours, and all commercial flights to the East were grounded. He thumbed a ride on an army transport plane north from San Antonio to Dallas, where he found accommodation on a train that would bring him to Washington early on the morning of Sunday, December 14.*

As he traveled north and east, General Eisenhower had ample time to reflect on how imposing must be the problems that lay ahead on Constitution Avenue, in the building that then housed the War Department. He had "no clear idea of the progress of the fighting in the Philippines," the reports that had come to Fort Sam Houston had been "fragmentary and obscure," but General Eisenhower, more surely than most, was able to appreciate the unenviable responsibility of relieving that Pacific outpost that had now been dumped in the lap of the chief of staff, General George Marshall.

More than eight thousand miles to the west, in Manila, was Douglas

---

* Brigadier generals travel as best they can, hitchhiking if necessary. On this trip Eisenhower would share a compartment thanks to an amiable official of the Lend-Lease Administration, William Kittrell. This trip would be the last in his life on which his way would not be smoothed by prestige, priority, private airplane, special train, or other such perquisites of the well-Established.

MacArthur, the imperious soldier who had himself been chief of staff, and for a longer time than any of his predecessors. Now Marshall held the office. MacArthur, as Eisenhower knew, held Marshall in contempt. He knew MacArthur had hoped that Lieutenant General Hugh Drum would be named chief of staff in 1939, and he knew what MacArthur thought when Marshall won the appointment instead. He had been one of the guests at a dinner party in the Philippines soon after the news of Marshall's accession was made public and he had listened as MacArthur had suavely ripped into the new chief, deprecating Marshall's achievements and insisting upon Marshall's lack of experience, always with his customary elegance of expression. Now MacArthur was in a position where he would have to take orders from a man he despised, a man who had been only a colonel while he had been a four-star general. It was an association that, on the face of it, held little promise of success.

There was another, more personal aspect of this prickly relationship. In the officer corps of peacetime, field officers quite naturally gravitated into the field dominated by one or another influential general officer: promotion could follow from such an attraction if the general officer were so fortunate as to move into a position of command. Thus, as we have seen, Eisenhower had benefited from his association with Fox Conner. Thus, later, he had been drawn into the electromagnetic field of which MacArthur was the compelling force. In his own more modest fashion, Marshall too had attracted a following: the officers he had taught when he was an instructor at Leavenworth, the officers who taught or studied at the Infantry School at Benning during the five years he ran the school as assistant commandant—Stilwell, Bradley, Lightning Joe Collins, Ridgway, Van Fleet, Bedell Smith, Bull, Terry Allen, John R. Deane, and a dozen others who rose to high command in the army after 1941. Perhaps foolishly, perhaps wrongly, it was nevertheless the fact that an officer could come to be labeled MacArthur's man or Marshall's man. Loyalty played its part in such an identification, and so did respect, and ambition, and pragmatism, and dependence, and army politics, and hope for preferment, and other considerations both lofty and ignoble. Now General Eisenhower, for so long regarded as one of MacArthur's men, was to report to Marshall for emergency duty, and he was sensible of the fact that one of his likely tasks would be to bridge the chasm between the new chief and the old. The way was open for Eisenhower to move confidently into the new field of influence and so become known as another of Marshall's men.

His train reached Union Station early on Sunday, December 14. His brother Milton, responsive to a telegram, was on hand to greet him and tell him something of what it was like in the capital of a country suddenly at war. No reliable memorandum of their conversation was, of course, ever recorded, and even if one had been preserved for posterity it could not, in the haste of those crowded moments, have done justice to the confusions, the tensions, the antagonisms and rivalries that already threatened to sunder the national resolution so piously professed only a week before, nor to the predictable welter of rumors that had, as if from an open sewer, befouled the capital. The rumors alone could fill a selective volume of history, and later helped to fill several volumes of testimony in hearings before various congressional committees or commissions. These dealt with alleged dereliction of duty in high places, paving the way to the disaster at Pearl Harbor; with the extent of that disaster, whispered to have been far worse than any official would ever dare reveal; and even with a conspiracy that had deliberately provoked and invited the disaster, a conspiracy alleged to have involved General Marshall and Admiral Harold R. Stark, chief of naval operations, and to have been concocted by the commander in chief, no less, President Franklin D. Roosevelt.

Far more serious were the delays and confusions that had blocked—were still blocking—the mobilization of industrial resources for what had been called the national defense but had suddenly become the war. Eisenhower was the more dismayed by these confusions inasmuch as, eleven years before, he had himself helped to formulate the War Department's plan for industrial mobilization, and that plan had won the approval of the illustrious sage Bernard Baruch. What could have gone wrong?

No time on this Sunday morning to wonder why. No time to speculate about the series of agencies—among others, the War Resources Board, the Advisory Commission to the Council of National Defense, the Supply Priorities and Allocations Board, the Office of Production Management—that had come and gone in the previous two years or so. Each had been established to harness the nation's industrial strength; each had somehow tripped and tumbled: because of bungling New Deal bureaucrats, the industrialists complained; because of commercial greed and complacency, retorted the New Dealers. For whatever reason or complex of reasons, each agency had failed, and this bitter fact would in the next few weeks stalk through General Eisenhower's long working days and nights, a grim reminder of lost opportunities, a harsh memento of lives lost or about to be lost needlessly.

The successive failures of these agencies would lead in a month or so to the establishment of the War Production Board and to decisions by its director, Donald Nelson, that would in turn make possible the military-industrial complex, so called, the great Gog of Magog against which, in later years, Eisenhower himself would feel obliged to set his face. Nelson's two salient decisions would be, first, to leave military procurement in military hands, that is, to permit the War Department or the Army and Navy Munitions Board to continue to negotiate and sign the contracts for war goods, despite the fact that the "War Department had given no faintest sign, up to the beginning of 1942, that it comprehended the size of the job that was to be done"; and, second, to maintain the system of hiring dollar-a-year men, that is, men who would work for the government but would be paid their fat peacetime salaries while they retained their corporate connections and financial interests. This latter decision would vex the members of the prestigious Special Senate Committee to Investigate the National Defense Program and especially its chairman, Harry S. Truman. The Truman committee's inquiries had persuaded them that the dollar-a-year executives were a deadweight loss, and they were disagreeably astonished when Nelson later informed them he meant to retain the dollar-a-year men, and on their own terms—in effect to create and nurture a special class of patriots, secure as to life and fortune, armed against any peradventure, and privileged in the prospective division of postwar spoils. "I don't think there should be any special class," Senator Truman would tell Nelson, thinking of the young men who had been earning salaries of twenty-five thousand dollars a year or more and who had nevertheless gone into the armed services without complaint. Why should it be true of the dollar-a-year men that "their morale won't stand" the same treatment? But Nelson would insist that the job of production could not be done unless their special privileges were guaranteed them, and the Truman committee would reluctantly concur in his judgment. Under these dubious circumstances a great many of Eisenhower's future friends, trusted advisers, golfing companions, and bridge partners would make their contributions, favored and immune, to the war effort.

So, at last, would go glimmering the dream of those who after the War of 1914–1918 had struggled to ensure that the burdens of any future war would be evenly loaded upon the shoulders of all alike. Instead, the citizenry went off to the training camps; and the practical men took over, the longheaded men of business, the men who plucked at their lower lip and considered, the men with cost-plus-fixed-fee contracts who earned, at government risk, in three months, profits "nearly fifteen times as great" as they had been able to earn in a year at their own risk, the men who subsequently testified, "If it hadn't been for taxes, we couldn't have handled our profits with a steam shovel," the smiling, compliant dollar-a-year men who between June 1, 1940, and April 30, 1941, had collared army and navy contracts worth almost three billion dollars and divided them among the sixty-six corporations of which they were officers.

And Brigadier General Dwight D. Eisenhower, author of the War Department's obsolete M-Day plan and all unaware of these recent and more voluptuous developments, reported on that same Sunday morning, December 14, to the chief of staff in his office in the Munitions Building.

George Marshall was, as nearly always, self-possessed and even-tempered, despite the burden of his awful responsibilities. In 1939 he had assumed command of an army of one hundred and seventy-four thousand trained troops; he now commanded an army of one and one-half million troops who were, for the most part, woefully untrained. The Selective Service Acts of 1940 and (more especially) of 1941 under which this army had been mustered had been legislated, most knowledgeable persons agreed, thanks to Marshall's patient, reasonable, candid intercession with a Congress more fractious than usual because of Franklin Roosevelt's campaign for an extraordinary third term as President.

Here was a solid achievement, one of inestimable benefit to the nation, but it was now behind him, as were other matters—such as the War Department's wretched mismanagement of the construction of army camps and army ordnance plants—of which the less said the better. Also fully a year behind him was the most momentous strategic decision of the war: that if the United States were to be drawn into a war with Japan, military operations in the Pacific should nonetheless be restricted "so as to permit use of forces for a major offensive in the Atlantic"; i.e., in Europe. George Marshall had the estimable ability to make a decision and at once turn to the next problem with no energy wasted on compunction or on subsequent self-debate.

Marshall's immediate problem was with this brigadier general, Eisenhower, about whom he had heard so much but knew so little at first hand. Was he as able as he was reputed to be? When Marshall fixed his steady gaze upon the officer, what he saw was a man of (as he knew) about fifty years, but who looked younger; who seemed quite self-confident, even cheerfully optimistic; who was brimming with physical vitality; with thinning reddish-blond hair, artless blue eyes, and a friendly expression; who was quite evidently fit and ready. Marshall decided to test him with an exercise in strategy.

In fifteen or twenty minutes the chief of staff sketched in the data: the navy's carriers, having by chance been at sea when the Japanese attacked Pearl Harbor, were whole, but warships to protect and support them were so scarce that months would pass before the Pacific Fleet could take part in any offensive operations; if Hawaii's air and ground strength were not at once reinforced there was danger the islands might once again be attacked, perhaps even captured and converted into a Japanese naval base;

93

the defense of the Philippines, never very stout, had been seriously impaired when many of MacArthur's airplanes, bombers and fighters alike, had been caught flatfooted and either destroyed or badly damaged. (The Japanese had got seventeen of MacArthur's thirty-five B–17s on the ground, on the second day of the war.)

Quite naturally Eisenhower was anxious to learn what he could of the Philippines, since he had left so many close friends there, both in the American colony and among the army officers and their wives. Now he was told that MacArthur had estimated that a garrison of 200,000 troops would be adequate for a defense of the islands, but that a considerably smaller number was actually on hand and under arms: some 30,000 U.S. Army troops (including 10,000 American soldiers, 8,000 American airmen, and 12,000 Philippine scouts earlier absorbed into the U.S. Army) and 80,000 troops of the Philippine Army, poorly trained and poorly equipped as few could know better than Eisenhower himself. Another 27,000 American troops, chiefly regiments of field artillery and air corps personnel, had set out in troopships from San Francisco between November 21 and December 6, but the attack on Pearl Harbor had caught them sitting like ducks on a pond, so some of them had already been recalled to San Francisco and the others would soon be diverted to Hawaii or to Australia.

The effective defenders of the Philippines, then, numbered some 30,000 troops, and the stocks of some of their essential supplies were critically low. The Japanese, moreover, had given unmistakable signs that they proposed to invade and overwhelm the islands with all possible dispatch.

After Marshall had described this bleak situation in some detail he abruptly asked: "What should be our general line of action?" For a moment Eisenhower hesitated. It was like the hypothetical war games at Leavenworth all over again, or, from an even earlier time, like the war games he had contested with Fox Conner at Gaillard in the Canal Zone —except that now there was the deadly difference of reality. In both those times past, he had been goaded by his need to excel; now the incentive was much greater. He asked for a few hours to study the matter. Marshall at once nodded assent and dismissed him. The few hours would make no difference. The chief of staff had already considered the problem and made up his mind as to its solution. Eisenhower, as he himself realized, was being measured and his analytic ability put to the test. He was in Marshall's crucible, precipitate. Now he would drop to the bottom, be suspended in mediocrity, or rise to the top.

Eisenhower strode down the corridor through the swing doors that led to the War Plans Division of the War Department, and into the office that went with his new assignment as deputy chief for the Pacific and Far

94

East. (His old friend Leonard Gerow was still the chief.) At his designated desk he sat down and began to concentrate on his task.

Whatever he found confirmed the desperate plight of the Philippines. Plainly, both Marshall and Stark had made every belated effort to reinforce the outpost. Ten days before the attack on Pearl Harbor they had urged the President that "the most essential thing now, from the United States viewpoint, is to gain time." They had reminded him of the troopships scheduled to sail for Manila in early December, and had argued that it was "important that this troop reinforcement reach the Philippines before hostilities commence." Events had been unmistakably taking the country toward what seemed unavoidable conflict, but Marshall and Stark had yet advocated every possible delay, at least until the Philippines were defensible. "Precipitance of military action on our part," they had warned, having in mind the diplomatic negotiations then in progress, "should be avoided so long as consistent with national policy."

On December 7, five troopships bound for Manila—guarded by the USS *Pensacola* and carrying 4,500 troops and a substantial cargo of guns, ammunition, bombs, trucks, aviation gasoline, and airplanes—had been in the South Pacific. On Tuesday, December 9, the Joint Army and Navy Board had decided to order the convoy back to Hawaii. The next day, after pressure from Marshall, the Joint Board had reconsidered, and on Friday, December 12, the convoy had been ordered to proceed to Brisbane, Australia, and its senior officer had been directed to do what he could to get the planes unloaded, assembled, and flown north to the Philippines. On that same Friday, MacArthur had reported that he had only twelve bombers and twenty-seven pursuit planes still fit to fly.

For some time General Eisenhower stared at a map of the Pacific, gloomily pondering the imponderables and reckoning the immense distances: seventy-eight hundred miles by air from San Francisco to Sydney, eight thousand miles by ship from San Francisco to Melbourne. At length he inserted a sheet of yellow paper in a typewriter and set to work:

Assistance to the Far East
Steps to be Taken
    Build up in Australia a base of operations from which supplies and personnel (air and ground types) can be moved into the Philippines. Speed is essential.
    Influence Russia to enter the war . . .

With two quick fingers Eisenhower clattered busily on, setting forth his suggestions as to how pursuit planes, heavy bombers, transport planes, and bombs and ammunition might be ferried first to Australia and thence to the Philippines. His hasty memorandum would be the first official suggestion that Australia should be used as the base for the defense of the Southwest Pacific; it would also be one of the first two or three War Department papers to urge Soviet intervention in the war against Japan— a preposterous notion, in view of the heavy German blows sustained by the Red Army since June 22, 1941.

While Eisenhower still typed, Marshall learned from Henry Stimson, the secretary of war, that the President agreed with the army (and disagreed with the navy) on the importance of giving all possible support to the Philippines. Marshall was much relieved.

Presently Eisenhower reported back to Marshall's office with his answer. "General," he later said that he said, "it will be a long time before major reinforcements can go to the Philippines, longer than the garrison can hold out with any driblet assistance, if the enemy commits major forces to their reduction. But we must do everything for them that is humanly possible. The people of China, of the Philippines, of the Dutch East Indies will be watching us. They may excuse failure but they will not excuse abandonment. Their trust and friendship are important to us. Our base must be Australia, and we must start at once to expand it and to secure our communications to it. In this last we dare not fail. We must take great risks and spend any amount of money required."

If the formulation of this advice about the Philippines seems considerably more stilted and sententious than General Eisenhower's customary mode of expression, the burden of it coincided precisely with what Marshall had already decided should be done. "I agree with you," Marshall said. "Do your best to save them."

On his first day in Washington, Eisenhower had passed his first test with high marks.

CHAPTER TWO

An Eye to the East

FOR THE NEXT SIX MONTHS Eisenhower would stick to his job in War Plans, steadily shouldering more responsibility, steadily rising in Marshall's good opinion, regularly earning promotions—to chief of the War

Plans Division when his friend Gee Gerow left to take command of the 29th Division, to assistant chief of staff in charge of the Operations Division when the War Department was reorganized, to major general—working long hours under hectic and arduous conditions, maintaining his cheerful confidence despite the bewildering complexities of his daily agenda, and consistently demonstrating the range of his abilities as a professional soldier. In later years, after he had shot up from the obscurity reserved by civilians for most military men to the glittering eminence of commanding general, European Theater of Operations, there would be a good deal of conjecture, much of it mischievous, as to how this nobody, this Kansas cornball, could have been lofted over the heads of three hundred and sixty-six general officers who were his seniors. It is a measure of the civilian ignorance about military matters that so few people supposed the reason for Eisenhower's appointment might have been, quite simply, that he had proved he was the logical man for the job.

His first assignment was the impossible one of trying to succor the beleaguered Philippines. His first recommendation—to establish a base in Australia from which the Philippines and all Asia could be liberated from the Japanese—was relatively simple and began fortuitously to be acted upon as early as December 22, when the convoy of ships protected by the USS *Pensacola* reached Brisbane. His second recommendation—that Russia be persuaded to enter the war and thereafter to provide the Americans with airfields at Vladivostok and in the Maritime Territory from which long-range bombers could attack Japan—was, to put the matter most kindly, quixotic. How could anyone seriously expect that the Russians, already staggering under the most savage assaults of the entire war, would undertake to engage a second enemy on a second front four thousand miles away? At all events, when President Roosevelt invited Marshal Stalin to discuss the possibility, the suggestion was diplomatically shelved, and the British likewise argued against any step that might weaken Russian resistance to the Nazi armies on the most important, indeed, almost the only front.

In practice, Eisenhower's doleful task of helping the defenders of the Philippines boiled down to devising methods of getting planes, ammunition, and supplies through the Japanese blockade to Manila, and of somehow placating the toplofty commander of those defenders. The blockade, MacArthur insisted, was of no consequence. The navy could bring in the necessary reinforcements; navy carriers could bring planes. But first the commander of the Asiatic Fleet and later the chief of naval operations flatly refused to risk running the blockade with precious carriers. Almost every day Eisenhower sent radio messages (signed by Marshall) to MacArthur acquainting him with the current efforts to support him. Ships laden with supplies were being sped to Australia. Transport planes were flying east by way of Brazil, Africa, and India, as were heavy bombers. Smaller planes, it was hoped, might fly north from Australia by way of the Netherlands East Indies. Vital supplies were being carried to Corregidor by submarine. Plans were afoot to charter Australian steamships to run the blockade.

But these brave schemes were, for one reason or another, unavailing. Foul weather held the big planes back until the airfields in the Philippines had been overrun by the Japanese. (The first Japanese landings on Luzon came on December 10; two weeks later MacArthur was obliged to pull back to the Bataan Peninsula across the bay from Manila.) The way north for the smaller planes likewise fell to the enemy's swift offensive. Submarines could haul only a pathetic fraction of what was needed. And despite offers of fantastic sums, few freebooters could be found in Australia who dared to run north through the blockade.*

All efforts—Eisenhower's included—to aid the garrison were undertaken within the context of the governing strategic concept that the chief war effort should be directed against Germany and Italy. The basic American war plan, known as RAINBOW 5 and adopted in April 1941, called for the defense of the Western Hemisphere and the dispatch of American armed forces to either or both of the continents of Europe and Africa "as rapidly as possible . . . to effect the decisive defeat of Germany, or Italy, or both." Although it was never officially stated in so many words, the Philippines had never been regarded as an essential bastion, to be defended at all hazards. According to RAINBOW 5, "the Army would defend the Philippines coastal frontier, but no Army reinforcements would be sent to that area"; while the CINCUSAF (commander in chief of the United States Asiatic Fleet) would assist in the defense of the Philippines and later in the defense of the Malay Barrier, but would neither expect nor plan for naval reinforcements in the Far East.†

MacArthur, who was of course aware of this plan, on January 1, 1942, sent a lengthy radio message to Marshall urging that the basic strategy

* The man who volunteered to recruit blockade runners was MacArthur's old friend the former secretary of war, Patrick J. Hurley. He was commissioned a brigadier general ("For Christ's sake," Major General Joseph W. Stilwell exploded when he was told of this development), got a star apiece from Eisenhower and Gerow for his uniform, and was tucked aboard a plane bound for Australia. He was able to find only six ship's masters with the gumption to venture the voyage to the islands. Of these, only three slipped through the blockade. Some ten thousand tons of supplies were landed either on Mindanao or on Cebu; only one thousand tons reached the defenders on Luzon.

† For the purposes of RAINBOW 5, the Malay Barrier comprised the "Malay Peninsula, Sumatra, Java, and the chain of islands extending in an easterly direction from Java to Bathurst Island, Australia."

98

be revised and the Philippines made secure. "The yielding of the Philippines by default and without a major effort would mark the end of white prestige and influence in the East," he warned, and cautioned against American withdrawal "in shame from the Orient."

To Eisenhower fell the task of writing Marshall's reply to this plea. As it happened, a good deal of hard thinking had been done for him on the matter quite recently, for the British chiefs of staff had been meeting in Washington with their American counterparts for the first time since Pearl Harbor, at the conference known under the code name ARCADIA. After gloomily examining the inadequacy of the shipping available for transport of troops and their necessary equipment, the Combined Chiefs (a title they took for themselves at this conference) had concluded that any dreams of swift Anglo-American landings at Dakar in West Africa, or at Casablanca and Oran and Algiers in North Africa, must regretfully be postponed for some months.

It was aggravating. There could be no question about the eventual victory of Allied arms. After all, as Prime Minister Churchill had reminded the Parliament on December 8, 1941, "We have at least four-fifths of the population of the globe upon our side." More to the point, the Anglo-American alliance (leaving aside China and the Soviet Union) was four times as rich in natural resources as all its enemies combined, and it controlled a far greater share of the earth's territory. On one side a group of powers who dominated the world's markets and had, as their ally, a huge country (the Soviet Union) which had removed itself from competition in the world's markets; all these had wanted only peace and a preservation of the status quo. On the other side another group of powers who were hungry and aggressive, who demanded a bigger slice of the world's resources and markets, and who would go to any desperate lengths to seize them. In short, the haves against the have-nots.

Surely the haves would prevail in the end, but just now, in the early winter of 1941–1942, they had not got enough ships. "Ships!" Eisenhower was to scribble on his desk pad a few days later. "Ships! All we need is ships!"

Ships. With six U.S. battleships destroyed or badly damaged at Pearl Harbor and two British battleships sunk by torpedo planes in the South China Sea on December 10, the Japanese were the undisputed masters of the Pacific, and months would pass before their sovereignty could be challenged.

Ships. If the U.S. Navy had had more warships, if the U.S. government could somehow have commandeered more transports, it might have been possible to relieve the garrison on the Bataan Peninsula. But as matters stood, the thing was impossible. Eisenhower had helped Gerow draft a memorandum for the chief of staff which characterized the diversion to the Far East of the forces needed to secure the islands as "entirely unjustifiable." (The study had been undertaken in response to a specific request by the President.) In his memorandum Gerow spelled out in detail what strength would be needed for such a mission, and which bases would have to be stripped if that strength were to be made available: 1,464 airplanes, half of which would have to be taken from Hawaii, the Canal Zone, and the continental United States; new airfields to be built all across the Pacific, with a commensurate demand for supply ships; seven to nine capital warships, five to seven carriers, some fifty destroyers, several dozen submarines, and a vast flotilla of smaller vessels—and so the supply of armaments to England would be cut off, the oilfields of the Middle East would be jeopardized, all supply lines to the Soviet Union would be forgotten, and the defense of the Western Hemisphere itself would be put in question. Even if all this were worth saving the Philippines, the ships to do the job simply did not exist.

Nevertheless, Eisenhower addressed himself to the composition of a radiogram that would convey only encouragement:

. . . there is here a keen appreciation of your situation [but there is] a marked insufficiency of forces for any powerful naval concentration in the Western Pacific at this time. Our great hope is that the rapid development of an overwhelming air power on the Malay Barrier will cut the Japanese communications south of Borneo and permit an assault in the southern Philippines. A stream of four-engine bombers . . . is enroute [across] Africa. Another stream of . . . bombers started today . . . from Hawaii . . . Two groups of powerful medium bombers . . . leave next week. Pursuit planes are coming on every ship we can use. . . . should give us an early superiority in the Southwestern Pacific . . . exert a decisive effect on Japanese shipping and force a withdrawal northward. These measures provide the only speedy intervention now possible unless naval carrier raids may be managed. We are searching our resources . . . Every day of time you gain is vital . . . accelerating speed of ultimate success. Marshall

It was not much, but there was nothing else that could be done; indeed, even as this message was being encoded and dispatched, the Japanese advance, well planned and well executed, was threatening to crush the Malay Barrier like an eggshell.

A few days later, in another of the messages to MacArthur which he drafted for Marshall's signature, Eisenhower added a personal touch: "Incidentally General Eisenhower in WPD who is familiar with your situation and naturally keenly interested in your success has been handling all Far Eastern business since December 14th. He becomes head of WPD this month." A little later he sent a personal message of greetings on the occasion of MacArthur's sixty-second birthday. If these amiable gestures were suggested because of some apprehension that MacArthur had less than perfect confidence in the chief of staff and his strategic competence, they failed in their purpose. (War Department files fail to show that the messages were even acknowledged.) MacArthur continued to pepper the War Department with lectures on strategy, and specifically to disparage the notion that consolidating a base in Australia would halt the Japanese advance. What was wanted, he instructed Marshall, was prompt attacks on the Japanese lines of communications. Always thoughtful of the desperate plight of the defenders, always patient, Eisenhower and Marshall again and again explained that MacArthur's strategic approach had long since been considered but regretfully discarded, and why. (The Japanese had never advanced before securing their flanks by capturing airfields and furnishing them with long-range bombers, poised to assault any hostile naval forces.)

As the final tragedy of Bataan and Corregidor crept to its climax, Eisenhower still drafted the orders sent from Washington to MacArthur and still advised as to what those orders should say, but the final decision about them was being taken on the highest level, in the White House, and the name Eisenhower signed to his messages was that of the President.

President Quezon, in pain from tuberculosis, in emotional anguish as the Japanese marched into the capital city of what he had hoped would be, by 1946, an independent republic, on February 8 sent a message to President Roosevelt urging unconditional independence for the Philippines and their immediate neutralization by agreement between the governments of Japan and the United States.

Francis B. Sayre, U.S. High Commissioner for the Philippines, concurred with this proposal if "American help cannot or will not arrive here in time to be availing."

General MacArthur seemed also to concur. "Since I have no air or sea protection," he warned, "you must prepare at any time to figure on the complete destruction of this command. . . . The temper of the Filipinos is one of almost violent resentment against the United States. Every one of them expected help and when it has not been forthcoming they believe they have been betrayed in favor of others. . . . the problem presents itself as to whether the plan of President Quezon might offer the best possible solution of what is about to be a disastrous debacle. . . . Please instruct me."

Neutralize the Philippines, as though the United States and Japan were equally guilty of its agony? As though the Philippine people had no interest in who should win the war? As though the American presence in the islands over the last forty years (what was described without irony as a "historic friendship") counted for nothing? Quezon's proposal was disturbing enough, but what was worse was the apparent approval of it by Sayre and MacArthur. When Secretary Stimson and General Marshall showed the Quezon message to the President, Roosevelt at once declared: "We can't do this at all."

After careful discussion and a drafting of replies in which Stimson, Marshall, Eisenhower, Undersecretary of State Sumner Welles, Admiral Stark, Admiral Ernest J. King, and the President all took a hand, Eisenhower composed the message that was sent to MacArthur on February 9. Quezon's proposal was emphatically rejected. Over the President's signature, MacArthur was authorized, if he chose, "to arrange for the capitulation of the Filipino elements of the defending forces," but was further instructed:

> American forces will continue to keep our flag flying in the Philippines so long as there remains any possibility of resistance. I have made these decisions in complete understanding of your military estimate that accompanied President Quezon's message to me. The duty and the necessity of resisting Japanese aggression to the last transcends in importance any other obligation now facing us in the Philippines. . . .
>
> I therefore give you this most difficult mission in full understanding of the desperate situation to which you may shortly be reduced. The service that you and the American members of your command can render to your country in the titanic struggle now developing is beyond all possibility of appraisement.

To be reminded by this Roosevelt-Eisenhower-Marshall message of the obligations of military honor was, to a man of MacArthur's stripe, scarcely tolerable. He retorted next day that he would, with both Filipino and American troops, fight without question of surrender to the last possible inch of ground.

The tragedy was now in danger of being transformed into a farce of military one-upmanship. Official Washington was dismayed by the possibility that MacArthur, the symbol of defiance in the Far East, the only commander who had been able in any way to stem the Japanese advance, seriously planned to go down fighting with his ill-equipped and battered comrades; and indeed that was precisely what he seemed determined to do. Sundry politicians began to clamor that he must be summoned to some sort of supreme command over all American armed forces. While the Japanese were nailing down their conquest of the oil-rich Netherlands East Indies, thereby justifying their attack on Pearl Harbor, the U.S.

press was focusing the attention of its readers on the gallant defenders of Bataan.

On February 22 General Eisenhower sent a radio, again signed by Marshall, ordering MacArthur to Mindanao and then on to Australia, where he was to take command of all American troops. This directive, he made clear, was issued by the President, and he added: "You are directed to make this change as quickly as possible."

To bid a commander leave his men in the midst of their last battles would, as Marshall and Eisenhower were both aware, do grievous damage to the morale of the garrison and so of the American people. But Roosevelt was constrained to take the cruel decision by the need to stifle the wildfire of alarm in Australia and New Zealand, spreading fast since the fall of Singapore and the defeat sustained by the Allied naval forces in the Battle of the Java Sea. Only MacArthur's imposing leadership in Australia, it was thought, would stiffen Australasian sinews and again summon up their martial blood.

The question was, would MacArthur obey the order? At the War Department late that Sunday night, Eisenhower had personally taken the message to the encoding clerk and had waited to make certain of its arrival in the Philippines at 10:57 P.M. (EST) and its delivery into the hands of MacArthur at 12:30 A.M. (EST) on February 23. Back in his office he jotted a note: "Message to MacA was approved by Pres. and dispatched. . . . It's a back breaking job to get a single battle order out—and then it can't be executed for from 3–4 months!!!"

Would MacArthur execute the order? At first he thought not. The courageous last stand, embattled, against overwhelming odds; the ultimate pentecostal flame; the enduring legend—that, for MacArthur, was the way to go. But his senior staff officers, less romantic, hardened in a less heroic mold, were able to persuade him that his greater service to the garrison on Luzon and elsewhere in the Philippines lay in his leading a triumphant and vengeful force north from Australia. At length he agreed, nevertheless insisting to Washington that he be granted permission to choose the moment for his departure.

He set forth by PT boat on March 11, taking with him his wife, his son, and seventeen officers and men of his staff. (These last were later known, in Australia, as "the Bataan crowd"; officers subsequently attached to the Southwest Pacific command would learn that the assent of one of these loyalists was a prerequisite to favorable action on any request, no matter how petty.) Behind him he left Major General Jonathan Wainwright, upon whom would devolve the sad responsibility of withdrawing from Bataan on April 9 and, acting upon advice sent him by General Eisenhower, General Joseph T. McNarney, and Secretary Stimson, of surrendering Corregidor on May 6. (American forces in the other Philippine Islands would all consequently surrender, the last by May 10.)

CHAPTER THREE

An Eye to the West

IF THE ASSIGNMENT of nursing the Philippines along to defeat was a bitter one, and frustrating, Eisenhower was so busy with so many other, farther-reaching tasks as to be effectively insulated against despondency. His long days were crammed with problems that demanded his full concentration; he thrived in this season. Lunch or dinner away from his desk was an exceptional event; he wolfed his hot dogs and ham sandwiches as eagerly as if they had been oysters and tenderloin. For some weeks—until his wife could pack or store their things in San Antonio and make a home at Fort Myer, outside Washington—he lived with his brother Milton in Falls Church, a Virginia suburb, and never once did he see that house by daylight. He was doing what he had been trained to do—make war—and he was proving to be very good at it.

In the winter of 1941–1942, at General Eisenhower's level, making war was like making a large, cumbersome, unpleasant commodity intractable as to design, ungovernable as to manufacture, difficult to distribute, and uncertain of acceptance by its consumers. The War Department and the Navy Department, to pursue the figure, were like two rapidly expanding industrial corporations which, although they were engaged in a cooperative venture, too often competed with each other in petty, vexatious ways. They shared with industry a bureaucratic involution; they were prone to get snarled in administrative procedures and organizational red tape, the more so as they grew bigger; and so they made inviting targets for the witticisms of individuals lost in their toils ("The War Department is just like the alimentary canal. You feed it at one end, and nothing comes out at the other but crap"). Moreover, few officers on the executive level had any experience of their business (i.e., of making war), so that special skills and adaptations were instantly needed.

What General Marshall wanted most, what he sought constantly, were senior officers who would take the responsibility for action in their own areas of competence without coming to him for the final decision; officers who in their turn would have enough sense to delegate the details of their decisions to their subordinates. "It's hard as hell to find anybody in our high command who's worth a damn," Marshall complained to an old friend late in January. "There are plenty of good young ones, but you have to reach too far down." By that time, however, he had confirmed his own first good opinion of Dwight Eisenhower.

Before Eisenhower had been a week at his new desk, Marshall had plunged him into the preparations for ARCADIA. The British chiefs of staff arrived in Washington on the evening of Monday, December 22, anxious to discuss the possibility of quick, uncontested landings, preferably at the invitation of the French authorities, at Dakar in West Africa or at Casablanca and Agadir in North Africa. Eisenhower helped prepare the planning papers Marshall would need at his first session with the British, and then at once began to draft for Marshall a memorandum entitled "Methods of Co-operation between U.S. Air and Allied Forces in the Southwestern Pacific," in which for the first time unity of command was projected for an entire theater of war. American, Australian, Dutch, and British forces, each independent of all the others, were operating along the Malay Barrier, and Eisenhower urged: "The strength of the allied defenses in the entire theater would be greatly increased through single, intelligent command."

He and Marshall were both aware, of course, that involved in the concept of a single command was the ticklish idea that one nation might have to cede to another some part of its rights, its potentially competitive interests, its precious sovereignty, its prerogatives, its operational autonomy, not to speak of the traditional interservice rivalries that would be inflamed by such a suggestion. Moreover, reverses suffered under, say, a British supreme commander would inevitably provoke recriminations by Americans, Australians, and Dutch, and consequently subject the fabric of the alliance to severe strains.

There were other difficulties, but to Marshall and Eisenhower they all seemed trivial when juxtaposed with the advantages. Both men appreciated that a supreme commander in the southwest Pacific would constitute an invaluable precedent for the appointment of a supreme commander elsewhere, in some far more vital theater of war. And so when the Combined Chiefs met for their second session, on Christmas Day, Marshall insisted: "There must be one man in command of the entire theater—air, ground, and ships. We cannot manage by cooperation. Human frailties are such that there would be emphatic unwillingness to place portions of troops under another service. If we make a plan for unified command now, it will solve nine-tenths of our troubles. . . . I am willing to go the limit to accomplish this."

To General Eisenhower, sitting behind General Marshall and removed from the conference table, with all the other officers in view, it was clear that despite his chief's fervent conviction he was not persuading them. For one thing, he had not prepared any of them for this far-reaching proposal. Admiral King, who would in a few days assume command of the U.S. Fleet, seemed the least opposed, but Admiral Stark was noncommittal and the British Chiefs, especially Air Marshal Sir Charles Portal, were quick to voice objections.

Realizing that he had spoken too hastily, Marshall at once moved to rectify his oversight. As the conference broke up, he took Eisenhower aside and instructed him to prepare a letter to "a supreme commander" in the southwestern Pacific, "giving him his mission, defining his authority and placing upon his authority specific limitations so as to exclude his interference from anything that was strictly the business of any particular government." Eisenhower observed: "The purpose of these rigid restrictions was to convince the other members of the conference that no real risk would be involved to the interests of any of the Associated Powers, while on the other hand great profits should result."

Eisenhower's draft of the letter of instructions was ready for Marshall on the morning of December 27, and the chief of staff nursed it along carefully, winning approval of it first from Secretary Stimson, then from President Roosevelt, then from the Navy Department, then from the hesitant British Chiefs, and finally, after a heated discussion with Churchill in his White House bedroom, which was interrupted by Churchill's taking his bath, from the exceedingly reluctant prime minister.

In this way the Australian-British-Dutch-American command (ABDA) was established, and a fortnight later Lieutenant General Sir Archibald Wavell was appointed its supreme commander, with headquarters near Batavia, in Java. As a functioning command, ABDA survived only forty-six days—January 10, 1942, to February 25—while "the Japanese machine was working with speed and precision" to reduce and capture every worthwhile objective within it. "Wavell never had a chance," Eisenhower said later.

The British had feared as much from the outset. Churchill told his Chiefs of Staff on December 26 he was by no means convinced that ABDA was either workable or desirable, but he concluded that he had to meet the American view. "We are no longer single, but married," Churchill later explained to Clement Attlee, who was serving in the War Cabinet as lord privy seal. On December 28, Field Marshal Sir John Dill, who had just been relieved as chief of the Imperial General Staff but who represented the British Army at ARCADIA, wrote his successor, General Alan Brooke: "It would, I think, be fatal to have a British commander responsible for the disasters that are coming to the Americans as well as ourselves. . . . It is of the first importance that we should not be blamed for the bloody noses that are coming to them." General Brooke, who had been left behind in London by Churchill to measure the immensity of his new responsibilities, learned of ABDA from the prime minister's cables and he despaired. "The whole scheme," he wrote in his diary on December 29, was "wild and half-baked." Brooke's chief objection to ABDA was to its perimeter: why should Burma have been included, and so separated from its supply base, India? and why should Australia have been excluded, when that great island-continent was a natural supply base for New Guinea, the Philippines, and the Netherlands East Indies?*

ABDA was a disaster, and that fact has tempted some chroniclers to downgrade all the achievements of ARCADIA. At least one historian has taken the view that the only decision of significance at the Washington conference was the confirmation of the earlier agreement to press first for the defeat of the Axis powers in Europe, leaving the war in the Pacific to be mopped up later. As to that fundamental strategy, however, there was never any slightest disagreement among those at the conference.

ABDA was a disaster, but the decision to put it under the command of one officer obliged the British and American chiefs of staff to consider very carefully just how such a supreme commander was to be charged with his mission. How would his directives be formulated, and by whom? These questions raised others: How were the British and American chiefs of staff to function together? And how, at the same time, were they severally to subserve the President (who was the American commander in chief) and the prime minister (who was also first lord of the treasury and minister of defence)?

The device finally agreed upon was the committee, called the Combined Chiefs of Staff and having headquarters in Washington, that was to supervise Anglo-American strategy throughout the war. The British Chiefs of Staff† sat on this committee only during international conferences; otherwise they were represented in Washington by a Joint Staff Mission, headed

* In General Eisenhower's original draft, the theater was defined as "the region Malaya-Australia-Philippine Islands, all inclusive." Only when the size and shape of ABDA were debated by the Combined Chiefs (and by Roosevelt and Churchill) was it considered advisable to include Burma and remove Australia.
† The four British chiefs were: General Sir Alan Brooke, chief of the Imperial General Staff; Air Chief Marshal Sir Charles Portal, chief of the air staff; Admiral of the Fleet Sir Dudley Pound, chief of naval staff; and Lieutenant General Sir Hastings (Pug) Ismay, chief of staff to the minister of defence (Churchill). Pound retired in October 1943 and was succeeded by Admiral Andrew Cunningham; the others served till the end of the war.

by Field Marshal Sir John Dill. The American Chiefs of Staff, who had no organization analogous to that of the British, had now to create, despite the lack of empowering legislation, their own Joint Chiefs of Staff; in practice this required only that Lieutenant General H. H. (Hap) Arnold, chief of the Air Corps, be formally denoted one of the chiefs of staff. A few months later Admiral William D. Leahy, home from Vichy, where he had served as U.S. Ambassador, would be designated chief of staff to the commander in chief and would thereafter meet regularly with the Joint Chiefs and the Combined Chiefs.

Once this structure of command had been firmly established and the precedent of a unified command set, the way was clear for a single officer to lead the Anglo-American armies in an invasion of Europe. With this in mind, it may be doubted that General Eisenhower ever tended to downgrade the achievements of ARCADIA. The decisions of that conference, which he had helped to formulate, had transcendent consequences for him.

General Eisenhower's chief concern, even before February 16, 1942, when he succeeded General Gerow as chief of the War Plans Division, was with the strategy of attack, with the need for pressing an assault on Festung Europa, for stabbing at the heart of Nazi Germany. Although he was still primarily preoccupied with the conduct of the war in the Pacific and the Far East, as an accomplished professional soldier he was fully aware that the two-front war could best be won by first crushing Hitler's power. On January 22 he scribbled an entry on his calendar pad: "We've got to go to Europe and fight—and we've got to quit wasting resources all over the world—and still worse—wasting time. If we're to keep Russia in, save the Middle East, India and Burma, we've got to begin slugging with air at West Europe; to be followed by a land attack as soon *as possible.*"

On that same wintry January 22, the messages flashed from all over the world to the War Department were almost uniformly bleak: the defense of Singapore was collapsing; the Japanese were landing in force on the islands of Bougainville and New Britain; MacArthur was retreating on the Bataan Peninsula; and in North Africa, General Erwin Rommel was cutting through the British lines near El Agheila, precipitating a British flight and presaging the capture of Benghazi. The only cheerful news was coming from Russia, where the Red Army's winter offensive continued to crunch the Nazis back. Nevertheless, the sanguine General Eisenhower kept arguing that the Allies should counterattack, and as speedily as might be. On January 24 he noted on his calendar pad: "Went to Bill Somervell this A.M. to find out what he knows about this landing craft business. He has known nothing of it to date—but is having matter looked up."*

General Eisenhower was one of the few—very few at first—who kept his attention nailed, in spite of the myriad bewildering distractions, on the pressing need for an Allied invasion of Europe. Few officers—very few until too late in 1942—gave thought to the question of landing craft, which were, of course, essential to any invasion. In the last weeks of January, the duties that distracted Eisenhower were only representative of his agenda for years to come. He was loaded down with problems of strategy and leadership in the Far East, quite apart from his attempts to get help to the Philippines. He had been involved in the decision to reject General Hugh Drum and in his stead to appoint General Stilwell as chief of staff to Generalissimo Chiang Kai-shek and officer commanding the U.S. Army forces in China (and later in Burma and India); in this connection he had represented Secretary Stimson and Assistant Secretary John J. McCloy in the exceedingly delicate negotiations with T. V. Soong, the generalissimo's brother-in-law.† He had undertaken to speak for General Marshall about the posture of the South American governments toward the Axis powers, and so had involved himself in a fragrant olla-podrida of diplomacy, psychological warfare, espionage, financial subventions, franchises to operate present and future airlines, supplies of armaments, and the political stability of those South American countries regarded by the War Department as essential to the U.S. war effort. He was also hip-deep in discussions among officials of the State and War departments concerning the political and diplomatic repercussions in Vichy France should the Chinese armies invade French Indochina. In most of these stately affairs he operated on his own, free-wheeling, guided only by his own common sense and General Marshall's dictum, delivered on December 14: "Eisenhower, I must have assistants who will solve their own problems and tell me later what they have done."

Of course Eisenhower's counsel was not always sound (his advice as to South America, for example, was opposed by Brigadier General Matthew Ridgway, who was then chief of WPD's Latin-American section, and

* Brigadier General Brehon B. Somervell, who was in the class ahead of Eisenhower's at West Point, was at this time supply and procurement chief (G–4) in the War Department. He was soon to be promoted and to command the Services of Supply.
† To be Chiang Kai-shek's chief of staff was not an enviable post. The British and the Chinese had conceived for each other an enduring enmity and matters between them would not be quickly improved. Stilwell's own comment on his appointment to the post was characteristically sardonic. "The old gag about 'they shall offer up a goat for a burnt sacrifice' is about to apply to my own case," he wrote in his journal. "The Chief of Staff called me in and said that I appeared to be 'it,' and . . . Eisenhower took me down to Drum's office and I moved in. . . . and then went down . . . and told the staff the news. They were sort of stunned and took it in silence."

General Marshall later sustained Ridgway's objections), but the staggering scope and character of his responsibilities showed clearly how, beginning in 1941, the military had become the prepotent force in the conduct of the nation's affairs. What an officer of the War Plans Division of the War Department wanted was far more likely to get a respectful hearing in the White House or in the Congress than what was sought by, say, an assistant secretary of the State Department. After all, wasn't there a war on? And even the most unassuming of men can come to wear easily the habit of command.

Meanwhile, General Eisenhower held out stubbornly for his central concern. On January 27 he jotted another note:

> Tom Handy and I stick to our ideas that we must win in Europe. Joe McNarney not only agrees—but was the first one to state that the French coast *could* be successfully attacked.
>
> It's going to be one h—— of a job—but, so what? We can't win by sitting on our fannies giving our stuff in driblets all over the world—with no theater getting enough. Already we're probably too late in Burma—and we'll have to hurry like hell in Ceylon.*

Mamie Eisenhower, having emptied the house at Fort Sam Houston, arrived in Washington on Friday, February 6. (She had made one brief earlier visit on her way to West Point to spend Christmas with their son John, who was in his plebe year at the military academy.) Now she faced the task of settling their things in another house on another army post, this time at Fort Myer; how long they would live in it before this house in its turn would have to be vacated she could not know; until the new house was ready she and General Eisenhower would share a suite in a hotel, the Wardman Park. Private Michael J. (Mickey) McKeogh, the general's orderly, reported the next day, having driven their Chrysler east from Texas. McKeogh was shocked when he first saw the general: he was "more tired-looking than I'd ever seen him; all of his face was tired. . . . His voice was tired, like his face."

After the arrival of his wife, however, General Eisenhower began to work on a more reasonable schedule—only twelve or fifteen hours a day —and even to take a rare half-day off once in a while to rest. Mrs. Eisenhower saw to it that on occasion some old friends—perhaps Ruth and Harry Butcher—or Helen and Milton Eisenhower would drop in of an

* Colonel Thomas T. Handy would be promoted and, in June, succeed Eisenhower as chief of the Operations Division. Major General Joseph T. McNarney, one of Eisenhower's classmates at West Point, a man "of analytical mind and a certain ruthlessness in execution," was at the time reorganizing the War Department with buzz saw and bulldozer.

evening, and sometimes the general would shuffle a pack of cards in his big hands and enjoy a couple of hours of bridge.

But his preoccupation with the enemy in Europe was constant. On February 17 he noted:

> The Navy wants to take all the islands in the Pacific—have them held by Army troops, to become bases for Army pursuit and bombers. Then! the Navy will have a safe place to sail its vessels. But they will not go farther forward than our air (Army) can assure superiority.
>
> The amount of time required for this slow, laborious and indecisive type of warfare is going to be something that will keep us from going to Russia's aid in time!!

And two days later the unwonted note of alarm was still evident:

> We've got to go on a harassing defensive west of Hawaii; hold India and Ceylon; build up air and land forces in England, and when we're strong enough, go after Germany's vitals. And we've got to do it while Russia is still in the war—in fact, only by doing it soon can we keep Russia in. The trickle of supplies we can send through Basra [in the Persian Gulf] and Archangel [in the Barents Sea northeast of Norway] is too small to help her much.

Eisenhower's tendency to be fearful for the Red Army as against the German aggressor was not unusual; it was, to be sure, a trifle behindhand, but it was fairly typical of the consensus of British and American military leaders (and also of the German militarists) from the first moment of the Nazi invasion of Russia. It is instructive to recall some of the predictions soberly proffered just after June 22, 1941. According to Secretary Stimson, General Marshall and the officers then attached to War Plans (who did not of course include Eisenhower) estimated it would take Germany "a minimum of one month and a possible maximum of three months" to conquer Russia. (According to his biographer Forrest Pogue, however, General Marshall hedged on this estimate.) Sir John Dill, then still chief of the Imperial General Staff, "was not alone in thinking that the 'Germans would go through [the Red Army] like a hot knife through butter,'" but the British Chiefs were a trifle more cautious in their predictions: "the first phase, involving the occupation of Ukraine and Moscow, might take as little as three or as long as six weeks, or more." Colonel General Franz Halder, chief of the German Army general staff, surveying with satisfaction the havoc his armies had wrought in less than two weeks, noted in his diary on July 3, 1941: "It is . . . no exaggeration to claim that the Russian campaign had been won in a fortnight." To Count Galeazzo Ciano,

the Italian foreign minister, his German counterpart Joachim von Ribbentrop boasted that "the Russia of Stalin will be erased from the map
within eight weeks." The minimum estimated for the Nazi conquest of
Soviet Russia, then, was two weeks; the maximum three months. Yet thus
far the Red Army had successfully resisted for eight months.

There is no question but that the strategic ideas subsequently formulated by American and British planners were affected by their various
estimates of the Red Army's ability to resist and counterattack. All the
British plans, Eisenhower noted, were based on such assumptions, most
of them involving the Red Army's ability to draw German divisions away
from the invasion coast in western Europe. Whether Eisenhower agreed
with these assumptions is not clear, but it is quite evident that any suggestion the Red Army do all the fighting for the Allies was abhorrent to
him.

By late February, when General Eisenhower had been promoted to
chief of the War Plans Division, he was able to urge his ideas more pro-
grammatically and at a higher level. One of his earliest papers as chief of
WPD was a memorandum to General Marshall arguing that "maximum
promise of defeating the Axis" lay in an "attack through Western Europe," and "speed in preparation is important," since one of the "vital
tasks" was "to assist Russia." This early argument was supported by another, handed in on February 28, in which he iterated that "*we must*" keep
on sending arms to Russia as fast as possible, and "should at once develop, in conjunction with the British, a definite plan for operations
against Northwest Europe." That plan, moreover, "should be sufficiently
extensive in scale as to engage from the middle of May onward, an increasing portion of the German Air Force, and by late summer an increasing amount of his ground forces."

These propositions were put forward at a time when a public clamor
—much of it from the same citizens who had not long before advocated
pacifism from every platform—was loud all over the country to "Open up
the second front!" To witness the astonishment of these zealots, had they
known that their slogans were being cogently asserted by the War Department's chief planner, would have been an unalloyed delight.

Eisenhower was the leader in pressing this view of global strategy and,
at least in the upper echelons of the War Department, he had no considerable opposition. Marshall encouraged him; Hap Arnold agreed with
him; so also did Secretary Stimson. Indeed, the notion of a second front
against the Germans in Europe had been advanced by army planners as
long before as August 1941. Since then, however, the Japanese attack and
sweeping advance had changed some minds: navy planners and, more
especially, the articulate MacArthur were urging that additional Ameri-

can troops be deployed into the Southwest Pacific Theater; they were supported by a vocal and sizable slice of American public opinion. Moreover, the idea of landing a force of invaders somewhere along the Mediterranean coast of North Africa (the operation known by the code name of GYMNAST) or of landing at Casablanca on the Atlantic coast of North Africa as well (this was SUPER-GYMNAST) still powerfully tempted the commander in chief, President Roosevelt, despite the fact that all his military advisers were obstinately set against it and had even succeeded in spiking it during the ARCADIA deliberations. But the President had never utterly discarded the idea. (Churchill knew this, and of course he was also quite aware that the interests of the British Empire required safety of the sea-going traffic through the Mediterranean.) Away back in September 1940, Roosevelt had recalled Robert Murphy, then U.S. chargé d'affaires in Vichy, the capital of the French collaborationist government, and had instructed him to familiarize himself thoroughly with conditions in Algeria, Tunisia, French West Africa, and French Morocco, always bearing in mind that North Africa "was the most likely place where French troops might be brought back into the war against Nazi Germany." Murphy had been told to bypass the Department of State and to make his reports directly to the President. Thus, as Murphy later observed, the French African policy of the U.S. government became the President's personal policy. "He initiated it, he kept it going, and he resisted pressures against it." That policy was Roosevelt's ewe lamb, and he would cherish it even against the best advice of the War and Navy departments.

To rebut those who sought additional troops for the Southwest Pacific was comparatively simple. Some of these warriors, citing the military axiom that faced with a divided foe, a commander should first attack and destroy the weaker of the two, had argued that the U.S. should first concentrate its force against Japan. "The reasoning is without validity," Eisenhower wrote, like an instructor correcting an errant scholar. "Military estimates are based upon *relative power at a particular point* of actual or possible contact," and since Japan was far away, to war against her would require "at least three, possibly four, times the shipping" needed to wage war in Europe. Japan, therefore, "is relatively stronger in East Asia . . . than is Germany-Italy in Europe. This is particularly true as long as Russia is in the war." Further, Eisenhower pointed out that with the collapse of the Malay Barrier one big reason for support of the Southwest Pacific—to deny to the Japanese the rich natural resources of the region—had vanished.*

* The editors of *The Papers of Dwight David Eisenhower* (see Bibliography) estimate that by conquering Malaya and the Netherlands East Indies, Japan had taken control

To rebut the strategical whims of one's commander in chief was a trifle stickier. Eisenhower relied on studies of GYMNAST and SUPER-GYMNAST made in WPD and referred on up to the Combined Chiefs. The conclusion at this level was that planning for an invasion of North Africa was "an academic study and should be treated as such." On March 3 SUPER-GYMNAST was dismissed as not feasible at that time. Weighting the scales against any operation in North Africa, moreover, was the intelligence freshly received both from Ambassador Leahy in Vichy and from the astute operatives of the Office of Strategic Services (OSS) that Vichy was supplying Field Marshal Rommel's Nazi troops in Libya not only with food but also with trucks, guns, and thousands of tons of gasoline—half of it high-octane aviation fuel.* Roosevelt was quite cross when he was informed of these developments, and sent some sharp notes of complaint to Admiral Jean François Darlan, vice president of the Vichy Council of State under Marshal Henri Philippe Pétain. Darlan was also the official chiefly responsible for providing the Nazis with war matériel, in direct violation of the terms of the armistice signed by the French and the Germans. The record does not show that Darlan paid much attention to Roosevelt's reproofs; it *does* show that he lied to Ambassador Leahy and was generally evasive, rude, and contemptuous of American efforts, diplomatic, military, or other. It must be assumed that General Eisenhower, as chief of WPD, was apprised of these developments and of Admiral Darlan's role in shaping them to the satisfaction of the Nazis.

At all events, the voices calling for more troops in the Southwest Pacific were temporarily stilled, and the diversionary notions of Roosevelt and Churchill seemed likewise to have been forestalled. General Eisenhower could note:

Gradually some of the people with whom I have to deal are coming to agree with me that there are just three "musts" for the Allies this year— hold open the line to England and support her as necessary; keep Russia in the war as an active participant; hold the India–Middle East buttress be-

---

of 2.8 percent of the world's petroleum, 64.6 percent of its tin, and 89.5 percent of its rubber.
* The OSS was typical of U.S. government agencies established by Roosevelt in that it began in one way and ended in quite another. In July 1941 Roosevelt had authorized Colonel (later Major General) William J. (Wild Bill) Donovan, a hero of the War of 1914–1918, to organize the Office of Coordinator of Information. Like an amoeba, this agency split and became (1) the Office of War Information, devoted to propaganda, and (2) the Office of Strategic Services, concentrating on subversion, espionage, and other cloak-and-dagger pursuits. When the War of 1939–1945, after a shift of gears, was transformed into the Cold War, the OSS was transformed into the Central Intelligence Agency (CIA).

tween Japs and Germans. . . . We lost 8 cargo ships yesterday. That we must stop, because any effort we make depends upon sea communications.

That was on March 10. The way seemed to have been cleared for the decision to mount a cross-Channel invasion of Europe, and Eisenhower could now devote all his energies to prompting that decision. Later that same day he learned that his father had died.

When his father dies, every man is in some way diminished, in some way exalted. He may have to stand in his father's stead; he may had "rather/Have a turnip than his father"; he may keep his grief private, or be at pains to make it known, paying it out in the coin of awe, or affection, or contempt, or mockery, or great joy; whatever he does he cuts his own measure.

General Eisenhower was, mercifully, quite busy. On the next day, a Wednesday, he was driven to the White House to confer with President Roosevelt about a radio message to Generalissimo Chiang Kai-shek which Eisenhower had drafted for the President's signature. Roosevelt approved the draft but warned Eisenhower not to show it to T. V. Soong, the generalissimo's brother-in-law, who was also the Chinese envoy to Washington; he was merely to telephone a paraphrase of the message to Soong. Eisenhower had also to send a message to Stilwell over Marshall's signature, about the same business—a squabble over supreme command of the British and Chinese troops in the China-Burma-India theater. There were other featherweight crises and routine conferences to be handled, other appointments, other headaches. At seven-thirty that night he pulled toward him his calendar pad, many of the notes from which would, as he knew, become part of the public record. He wrote:

I have felt terribly. I should like so much to be with my Mother these few days. But we're at war! And war is not soft—it has no time to indulge even the deepest and most sacred emotions. I loved my Dad. I think my Mother the finest person I've ever known. She has been the inspiration for Dad's life, and a true helpmate in every sense of the word.

I'm quitting work now—7:30 P.M. I haven't the heart to go on tonight.

The next morning he jotted down an obituary note:

My Father was buried today. I've shut off all business and visitors for thirty minutes—to have that much time, by myself, to think of him. He had a full life. He left six boys and, most fortunately for him, Mother survives him. He was not quite 79 years old . . . a just man, well liked, well educated, a thinker. He was undemonstrative, quiet, modest, and of exemplary habits—he never used alcohol or tobacco. He was an uncomplaining person in the face of adversity, and such plaudits as were accorded him did not inflate his ego.

. . . I'm proud he was my father! My only regret is that it was always so difficult to let him know the great depth of my affection for him. David J. Eisenhower 1863–1942.

For the next few days he buried himself once again in his work—dispatching orders to MacArthur and Wainwright, sending memoranda to Roosevelt and messages (signed by Roosevelt) to Churchill, worrying about strategy in the Middle East, command in the Far East, production of pursuit planes, and unity of coastal command, attending a meeting of the Standing Liaison Committee (of State, War, and Navy) at which most of his ideas about a proposed joint defense agreement with Brazil were approved, and in general comporting himself like an aggressive, confident warrior-statesman. But his father's death had sharpened his awareness of his family, and late in March he took a full weekend away from his duties at the War Department (the first such respite in four months) so that he and his wife could visit their son at the U.S. Military Academy at West Point.

A father dead; a son growing into manhood.

Back in Washington, matters were impending that would once again empty his mind of anything but concentration on his job.

The first was personal. A week or so before his trip to West Point he had been in conference with General Marshall in the chief's office when, their talk turning to the promotion of some group of officers, Marshall had said, "I want you to know that in this war the commanders are going to be promoted and not the staff officers." Eisenhower had sat silent while Marshall had cited examples of superior leadership of combat troops in the War of 1914–1918, of men who had nevertheless been passed over, the promotions having gone instead to staff officers. This practice, he had insisted, would be reversed. "The field commanders carry the responsibility and I'm going to see to it that they're properly rewarded, so far as promotion can provide a reward." Abruptly he had turned to confront Eisenhower. "Take your case," he had said. "General Joyce [then the commander of the IX Army Corps] wanted you for a division commander and General McNair [commanding general of Army Ground Forces] said you should have a corps command. Eisenhower," Marshall said emphatically, "you're not going to get any promotion. You're going to stay right here on this job and you'll probably never move." After a pause for effect he added, "While this may seem a sacrifice to you, that's the way it must be."

Eisenhower, the old poker player, had sat for a long moment immobile, recalling the bitter frustrations of 1917 and 1918, digesting the unpleasant news that once again he was stuck, this time behind a desk, deprived of the professional soldier's exhilaration for conflict, and perhaps, as well, listening to an echo of the resolution he had taken as a young officer a quarter-century before at Fort Sam Houston, "to perform every duty given me in the Army to the best of my ability." Finally he had told Marshall: "General, I don't give a damn about your promotion. I was brought in here to do a duty. I am doing that duty to the best of my ability and I am just trying to do my part in winning the war." He had then got up to leave.

The chief of staff's office was a big one, ten strides from his desk to the door, affording ample time for second thoughts by officers whose tempers reached high voltage. Eisenhower had quickly regretted his outburst and, at the door, turned to flash his remarkable grin in sheepish acknowledgment of his regret for his vehemence. In that instant he noticed that a little smile lifted a corner of Marshall's mouth.

Now, after his return from West Point, Eisenhower found on his desk a copy of a memorandum from Marshall to the secretary of war (who had passed it on to the President for his approval) recommending that Eisenhower be promoted to major general and that his two deputies, Colonel Handy for the ground forces and Colonel St. Clair Streett for the air forces, be promoted to brigadier general. "I was startled," Eisenhower said later; "I looked at it in bewilderment." Marshall's memo offered some clues for his seeming reversal of policy: he had avoided any mention of staff duties as such, emphasizing instead that the three officers were charged with operations and were "involved with orderly organization for the control . . . of theaters of operations."*

At all events, he was now Major General (temporary) Eisenhower, bumped up three grades in little more than a year, now at the rank which,

---

* Eisenhower's own account of this promotion (see *At Ease*, pages 249–250) makes a much better story. He wrote that Marshall, in his memorandum, referred to Eisenhower as his *subordinate commander* (Eisenhower's emphasis), and that Marshall rebuked the officer who, in the course of the memo's having been "routed through normal channels," had presumed to correct this description of Eisenhower's status. The phrase, however, does not appear in the memorandum Marshall wrote in recommendation of Eisenhower's promotion, and I have found no evidence to buttress the tale of Marshall's rebuke.

Incidentally, the nomenclature used by Marshall to describe Handy and Streett was not strictly accurate. Eisenhower had one deputy chief of the Operations Division, Brigadier General Robert W. Crawford. Handy was chief of the Strategy and Policy Group, Streett chief of the Operations Group, which supervised theater operations.

for most officers before 1940, was the highest they could reasonably expect to attain, and soon to be named assistant chief of staff in charge of the Operations Division (OPD). Apart from its chief function as General Marshall's command post, charged with planning and supervising the strategy, tactics, and operations of global warfare, OPD had to cope with psychological warfare, economic warfare, allocation of matériel, coordination of political warfare with the State Department and with the scattered officials of the infant United Nations, and a myriad other matters. The remarkably expanded scope of OPD's responsibilities following the reorganization of the War Department is best reflected in the altered allocation of officers to the department's various divisions:

Division	Number of officers March 1, 1942	Number of officers April 1, 1942
WPD (April 1, OPD)	80	107
G–1	62	13
G–2	425	16*
G–3	81	14
G–4	174	12

The other matter, far more absorbing, was professional. Before his weekend at West Point, Eisenhower had discussed with his deputy, General Crawford, the need for pressing the Combined Chiefs of Staff to a decision as to where and how soon the Anglo-American forces would mount their first major offensive action against the Axis. The need was becoming urgent, for it was clear that the British and American planners disagreed as to timing, quantity and quality of forces ready for battle, and availability of such necessary matériel as shipping and landing craft. If the Combined Chiefs could not agree, Eisenhower foresaw an interminable set of piecemeal demands for American troops to minister to small crises—what Secretary Stimson called the plugging of "urgent ratholes" —in the Far East, in Africa, in the Middle East, in southeastern Europe, wherever there was fear of Axis tactical superiority.

What Eisenhower and Crawford (and the other OPD officers concerned with strategy) wanted was agreement that Germany was the target, to be attacked from England across the Channel and through western Europe. A memorandum for Marshall was drafted by Crawford, thoroughly studied and revised by Eisenhower on his return from West Point, and submitted to Marshall on Wednesday, March 25.

The plan proposed "to attack our principal enemy while he is engaged

* Not included in this figure was the ample personnel of the independent Military Intelligence Service, which was dissociated from the general staff.

on several fronts; hence speed in preparation is important." Eisenhower acknowledged that "success of the plan" depended on complete agreement among the Combined Chiefs that this second front was the essential task, overwhelming air support, ample landing craft, ample shipping to bring American reinforcements rapidly into the theater, and "husbanding of combat power—to acquire the necessary strength, and avoid the evils of unjustified dispersion." Recognizing that the British Chiefs were likely to demur, Eisenhower recommended further that "unless this plan is adopted as the eventual aim of all our efforts, we must turn our *backs* upon the eastern Atlantic and go, full out, as quickly as possible, against Japan!"

Marshall read this memorandum on the Wednesday morning. He clipped to it a bit of notepaper on which he had scribbled, "Hold for me. GCM," and went off to lunch in the cabinet room of the White House with the President, Secretary Stimson, Secretary Knox, Admiral King, General Arnold, and Harry Hopkins.

At lunch the President seemed, as Stimson noted later in his diary, to be "off on the wildest kind of dispersion debauch; but, after he had toyed a while with the Middle East and the Mediterranean basin, which last he seemed to be quite charmed with," Marshall and Stimson drew him back to the Atlantic, and Marshall, using the arguments from Eisenhower's memorandum, held him there. At length persuaded, the President was about to direct that the War Department's plan be referred to the Combined Chiefs; but Harry Hopkins interposed to urge that as soon as it had been carefully considered and finally detailed, the plan should be taken straight to London so that "someone" (Hopkins meant Marshall) could solicit prompt approval of it from Churchill and the British Chiefs. Roosevelt agreed.

The planners of OPD at once set intensively to work to draft what was subsequently known as the Marshall Memorandum—the basis of three operations, one actual and two hypothetical. They were called BOLERO, ROUNDUP, and SLEDGEHAMMER, code names that were often later confused and erroneously interchanged.* Suddenly the plan that Eisenhower had been advocating for two months was at hand, within grasp, and rousingly specific. It called for all energies to be directed to the "single end" of "an attack, by combined forces of approximately 5,800 combat airplanes and

---

* BOLERO was the operation by which the enormous military might of the United States was to be organized, shipped across the Atlantic, and poised for action in the British Isles. ROUNDUP was to have been the cross-Channel invasion, in April 1943, of western Europe. SLEDGEHAMMER denoted a hastier, more desperate invasion, tentatively scheduled for September 1942, to have been undertaken only if it appeared (1) that the Red Army was about to collapse and the Soviet Union to sue for peace, or, contrariwise, (2) that the strength of the Nazi grip on western Europe was suddenly and unexpectedly rendered impotent.

48 divisions [18 British, 30 American] against western Europe as soon as the necessary means can be accumulated in England—estimated at April 1, 1943." The assault was to be made over beachheads between Le Havre and Boulogne and would then aim toward the Belgian port of Antwerp.

On April 1 Marshall presented to the President the plan developed by Eisenhower and his OPD associates. Roosevelt still hankered for GYMNAST, the Mediterranean operation, but Stimson and Hopkins added their counsel to Marshall's and at length the President gave his approval. He instructed Hopkins and Marshall to take plane for London and win British concurrence.

On April 8 Marshall and Hopkins reached London, and that afternoon Marshall sketched the broad outlines of the plan to Churchill, who seemed to offer much less resistance than he had expected. Later Marshall sized up his opposite number, the chief of the Imperial General Staff, General Sir Alan Brooke, and it was as though a pair of stiff-legged dogs were circling about each other, hackles up. "A pleasant and easy man to get on with," Brooke confided, of Marshall, to his diary, "rather overfilled with his own importance. But I should not put him down as a great man." Marshall told Hopkins that Brooke "may be a good fighting man," but "he hasn't got Dill's brains." These first impressions were later somewhat revised on both sides.

On April 15 Marshall was able to report to Secretary Stimson that the British government had, after several days of discussion, formally accepted the plan. Approval had come in the early hours of the morning at a momentous meeting of the Defence Committee of the British war cabinet at No. 10 Downing Street. Not only the meeting was momentous; so also, said the prime minister, was the proposal Marshall had brought to London, a proposal that, Churchill added, he had "no hesitation in cordially accepting." Except that there was just this one reservation. Churchill's "entire agreement . . . with all" that had been proposed was an agreement "in principle," and the difficulty with an agreement in principle is that it is no agreement at all; and all talk of how "our two nations are resolved to march forward into Europe together in a noble brotherhood of arms on a great crusade for the liberation of the tormented peoples," while affording a characteristic example of Churchillian rhetoric, was still only talk. Agreements in principle can lead to quite bitter disagreements in fact and as to fact, and that is what happened to the Anglo-American alliance in this case. Neither Marshall nor Hopkins was, like the simple-minded Yankee of the cliché, gulled by any of this artful snake oil. Marshall was fully aware that while everyone had agreed "in principle," "many if not most" of the British clung to "reservations regarding this or that." But still he hoped. And the truth seems to be, in human affairs, that hope seduces everyone into remembering only what he chooses to remember of an agreement.

In the meantime, during this fortnight, Eisenhower had bent himself to push forward the business of BOLERO and SLEDGEHAMMER and ROUNDUP quite as if the agreement had already been made and not only in principle. (Naturally, he also hoped.) From his desk in Washington he pressed the U.S. Navy on its schemes for training troops for amphibious landings; he was "much disturbed" by evidence under his hand that the navy was seriously derelict in various aspects of this specialized essential training. He studied the latest available facts about landing craft. He outlined smoother functions within the War Department to maintain consistent planning for BOLERO. Constantly he fed advice and information to Marshall in London, to help him convince the British about the need for a speedy cross-Channel operation.

He must have been in an intolerable itch of anxiety and ardor as to what was being decided about his plan, far away across the Atlantic, but he appears to have maintained an admirable address. There is a glowing account of his conduct at this time, attested by Colonel (later Lieutenant General) Lucian K. Truscott, Jr., who first met Eisenhower in 1941 when they were both staff officers of the IX Army Corps under General Joyce. Eisenhower, aware that some British doubt about an early cross-Channel invasion arose from qualms as to the Americans' readiness for battle, was arranging for a small group of officers to join the staff of Admiral Lord Louis Mountbatten, chief of Combined Operations, the still relatively hush-hush organization that had developed the glamorous commandos for special hazardous missions against the enemy's European coast. Truscott was to be the senior officer of the first American group to join Mountbatten; awaiting his assignment, he sat for long hours in Eisenhower's office, and later wrote:

> I spent much time listening to the discussions of problems and studies brought to him by officers of the Operations Division, by other sections of the War Department, by naval officers, Congressmen, committees, and by the endless chain of visitors that passed through his office during his long days. . . . Every view was considered. Each problem was carefully analyzed. . . . the same extraordinary ability to place his finger at once upon the crucial fact in any problem or the weak point in any proposition . . . the same ability to arrive at quick and confident decisions. And the same charming manner and unfailing good temper.

On Friday, April 17, General Marshall was back in Washington. ("He looks fine," Eisenhower noted. "I hope that—at long last, and after months of struggle by this Div—we are all definitely committed to one concept of fighting!") The next Monday morning Marshall summoned Eisenhower to his office. Over the weekend the newspapers had been full of stories about how Colonel James Doolittle had led sixteen B–25s from the carrier *Hornet* on a bombing mission over Tokyo, Kobe, Yokohama, and Nagoya —a great lift for American morale, "the first good news for the United Nations that had come from any non-Russian sector of war in many awful months." But to Marshall and Eisenhower, who had helped to plan the raid, this was old stuff. They were looking ahead to BOLERO.

Who was to command U.S. forces in the British Isles? What was to be the structure of organization? A planning group would have to be organized at once, and a corps commander selected for the troops ordered to Great Britain.

In the next few days even tougher problems, relating to the availability of troopships and cargo ships and the allocation of airplanes of all types, served to put in question Eisenhower's cherished OPD plan for BOLERO itself. To be sure, the plan had been drafted in great haste and in an irregular manner: it was "at variance with the long-standing plans and expectations of the British Chiefs of Staff" and was neither preceded by nor based upon "a full and explicit analysis" of the differences between British and American planning. Now it devolved upon the Allied planners in Washington to make BOLERO work; plans for SLEDGEHAMMER and ROUNDUP were to be devised by the Allied planners in London.

To make BOLERO work, it was swiftly apparent, would entail revising established policy in no less than four theaters: in the Middle East the position of the British became "very precarious" when plans to send groups of airplanes to Cairo had to be canceled; in China, as a result of BOLERO, "nothing but token forces" could be made available to General Stilwell; in the Soviet Union, lend-lease aid had to be "drastically reduced," despite President Roosevelt's emphasis on "the simple fact that the Russian armies are killing more Axis personnel and destroying more Axis matériel than all the other twenty-five United Nations put together";* and in the Southwest Pacific, General MacArthur's theater, that doughty strategist was calling for three first class divisions, two aircraft carriers, and as many as one thousand more airplanes, along with the personnel and matériel needed to keep his air units constantly at full strength—all this only for adequate defense of his theater—and demanding as well that grand strategy be switched in order to open up a second front which "would have the en-

---

* The President hammered away at "this simple fact" on a number of occasions: in a Fireside Chat (April 28, 1942) to the nation, in a radio message (May 6) to MacArthur, and in a memorandum to his ranking military advisers on the same day.

thusiastic psychological support of the entire American nation," a second front not in Europe but against the Japanese in the Pacific.

Was the concept of BOLERO grander than its performance could be? Had Eisenhower and the OPD planners been too ambitious and ignored a prudent schedule of priorities? A second severe shortage had appeared besides the shortage of seagoing ships: there were not nearly enough airplanes—transport planes, heavy bombers, medium bombers, or pursuit planes—to satisfy the anxious demands of Chinese, Russians, British, and Americans. Nor should this astonish, for in the spring of 1942 the arsenal of democracy was far from being tooled up. How could it have been when on January 5—a month after Pearl Harbor and eighteen months after inauguration of the defense program—representatives of the biggest mass production industry in the country, the automotive industry, were rather casually discussing who should make what, and government officials were expressing the modest hope that "negotiations . . . which may lead to contracts later will be opened soon"? The industry's executives were then still supervising the manufacture of automobiles, would continue so to do until January 31, and had valiantly if vainly argued that they should be allowed to keep on producing automobiles until February 28. Matters were rather more sensible in the aircraft industry, but even there production would not be really satisfactory until well into 1943. And so in the spring of 1942 there was still an appreciable shortage of airplanes and other tools of war.

However much all this may have dismayed Eisenhower in January, by April his buoyant optimism had persuaded him otherwise. He was convinced that BOLERO would prove to be its own justification, even if it deprived other theaters of equipment. If BOLERO were pressed as vigorously as possible, and ROUNDUP (if not SLEDGEHAMMER) thereafter mounted and prosecuted with all will and all dispatch, the need for airplanes in other theaters would be automatically relaxed: in Russia because German forces would be pulled west; in the Middle East because German forces would be drawn back into Europe; in China and the Southwest Pacific because the success of BOLERO and ROUNDUP (if not SLEDGEHAMMER) would enable the United Nations to turn upon Japan more swiftly and destroy her militarism more terribly.

Still, in early May, Eisenhower was persuaded that what would hobble BOLERO and any consequent cross-Channel invasion was not lack of men or ships but only faltering leadership by civilians at the highest level. On May 5 he scribbled a bitter note on his calendar pad:

Bolero is *supposed* to have the approval of the Pres and Prime Minister. But the struggle to get everyone behind it, and to keep the highest authority from wrecking it by making additional commitments of air-ship-troops elsewhere is never ending.

The actual fact is that not 1 man in 20 in the Govt. (including the W. and N. Depts) realizes what a grisly, dirty, tough business we are in! They think we can buy victory!

Apart from the vexatious proclivity of such civilian politicians as the President and the prime minister to meddle in what the soldiers regarded as an exclusively military preserve, another difficulty appeared in the form of still another critical shortage, one which would again and again upset the timetable of offensive operations against Germany: the shortage of landing craft. Who was responsible? After the war, one segment of the official bureaucracy would exculpate industry and the government agencies supervising production and would blame "the failure of top officials responsible for strategic planning"; viz., Major General Dwight D. Eisenhower. The record shows that Eisenhower was concerned earlier than most about the production of landing craft, but presumably because of the press of other business failed to follow through with any diligence. In early April, at a conference in the White House, a production schedule had been fixed under which so many craft were to be built and shipped to the United Kingdom in time for SLEDGEHAMMER and so many more in time for ROUNDUP. This schedule did not allow for enough craft to haul the American troops and armor assigned to SLEDGEHAMMER, but Eisenhower had dismissed the paucity. If SLEDGEHAMMER were to be mounted at all, he wrote, "it will be carried out with whatever personnel and equipment is actually available at the time." In the British view, the number of craft available was not nearly so important as their size. The British wanted craft big enough to cross the Atlantic under their own power, so that valuable shipping space would not be assigned to smaller craft. The dispute led to another White House conference in early May, and to a decision to build only the bigger craft—by which time "a good many craft of the smallest types were scheduled for delivery." As the GI phrase had it: SNAFU.

The next day Eisenhower attended a meeting of the Special Committee on Landing Craft for the Continent. Little was accomplished except to acknowledge the contradictory decisions of the day before. What was needed, clearly, was a gilt-edged priority, but unhappily the construction of landing craft depended upon matériel and facilities controlled by the navy, and the navy was in no hurry to approve the construction of vessels designed primarily for army business. The navy had a Shipbuilding Precedence List: in March 1942 landing craft stood tenth on this list; in October, just before the landings in North Africa, they would soar to second, yielding place only to aircraft carriers; but in November they would plummet again, to twelfth.

On May 6 Eisenhower showed his temper on the subject:

> This morning I attended a committee meeting on "Landing Craft" at which were discussed questions on which I begged the answers last February.
>
> Who is responsible for bldg. landing craft?
>
> What types are they bldg?
>
> Are they suitable for cross-Channel work?
>
> Will the number of each type be sufficient? etc?
>
> How in hell can we win this war unless we can crack some heads?

It would seem to be the case that everybody involved—the President, his advisers, the strategic planners, the War Department, the Navy Department, the British, the government agencies, and industry—were alike culpable for the shortage of landing craft. In short, in vital matters its System will always entangle the Establishment.

There remained the question of the commander of U.S. forces in Britain. BOLERO might be facing difficulties because of a shortage of transport, there might not be enough landing craft for SLEDGEHAMMER, the British might be showing signs that they were dubious even about ROUNDUP—to Eisenhower all this only underlined the need for a firm and aggressive commander in London. But who? In mid-May he described to Marshall the *"type of officer to serve as Commanding General, United States Forces"*:

> . . . he must enjoy the fullest confidence of the Chief of Staff in order that he may efficiently, and in accordance with the basic ideas of the Chief of Staff, conduct all the preliminary work essential to the successful initiation of Bolero. [Eisenhower meant the cross-Channel assault, probably ROUNDUP.]
>
> . . . if Bolero develops as planned, there will come a time when United States Forces' activity and interest in that region will be so great as to make it, for an indefinite period, the critical point in all our war effort. When this comes about, it is easily possible that the President may direct the Chief of Staff, himself, to proceed to London and take over command. The officer previously serving as Commander should be one who could fit in (and would be acceptable to the new Commander) as a Deputy or as a

Chief of Staff. This will insure continuity in planning and execution, and in understanding.

And the next day, in another memorandum, Eisenhower urged again that a theater of operations for BOLERO should be established and a commander designated.

Who would this commander be? Who best fitted the qualifications that Eisenhower had laid down? Who had most energetically pressed the strategic concepts of BOLERO-SLEDGEHAMMER-ROUNDUP? Who obviously enjoyed the fullest confidence of the chief of staff? Who was himself already an assistant chief of staff? Eisenhower had described himself, but he had discreetly nominated no officer for the post.

A few days later, however, Colonel Albert C. Wedemeyer of the OPD Strategy and Policy Group recommended to Marshall that, assuming Marshall himself would in time take command of the prospective invasion, he name Eisenhower as his chief of staff. As it happened, General Marshall had already concluded that Eisenhower was in all likelihood the best man for the job. The chief of staff had only one reservation: Eisenhower had never been stationed in England and he was relatively unknown to the British. To remedy this deficiency was simplicity itself: he sent Eisenhower to London with instructions to inspect the American headquarters and recommend what changes if any should be made to expedite BOLERO. Further, Marshall directed him to extend the best wishes of the chief of staff to Brooke, to Major General Archibald Nye (Brooke's vice chief), and to Portal, Pound, and Mountbatten, thereby ensuring that Marshall would be able to arrive at a British consensus about Eisenhower, either directly or through his good friend Sir John Dill, to whom reports from London on this American officer would inevitably be made.

Being no fool, Eisenhower was alive to the challenge. Unquestionably he knew why he was being sent on this mission; he had of course already confided his high hopes to his wife; even his orderly, Mickey McKeogh, had been tipped off that his boss might turn out to be "the Pershing of this war." Should one attempt to weigh the hero in the scales of this incident, testing whether he was motivated by an intelligent and highminded ambition or by something meaner, an opportunism perhaps? Or, blessed with the hindsight of victory over the Nazi evil, should one simply rejoice that the right man was being groomed for the right job at the right time?

At all events, General Eisenhower took off in a C–54 from Bolling Field early on Saturday morning, May 23, accompanied by General Hap Arnold; Major General Mark Clark, then chief of staff to the general commanding army ground forces; Admiral John Towers, chief of navy aviation; Air Marshal Douglas C. S. Evill, the RAF officer attached to the

British Joint Staff Mission in Washington; and a cluster of aides and secretaries.

Bolling Field, Montreal, Goose Bay; out across the Atlantic, then driven back to Gander by foul weather. A day of skeet shooting, then east again, on a flight that, much more in 1942 than today, was calculated to unsettle the passenger and throw his biological clock out of whack.

Prestwick, Glasgow, London. . . . A whirl of impressions, the scars left by the blitz, the patient queues of people, new voices shaping strange new sounds, new faces appearing, abrupt and indistinct as in a dream. . . . A round of conferences, a dinner given by Air Marshal Portal.

A day in the countryside southeast of London, observing a training exercise being conducted by a peppery little lieutenant general named Montgomery; "a decisive type," Eisenhower reflects, "who appears to be extremely energetic and professionally able." A briefing by Montgomery in his small map-lined headquarters, thronged with attentive officers. Eisenhower lights a cigarette. Without turning from his map Montgomery stops in mid-sentence, sniffs, and raps out: "Who's smoking?" Eisenhower: "I am." Montgomery: "I don't permit smoking in my office." Eisenhower pinches out his cigarette.

More conferences. A meeting of the British Chiefs of Staff at which the question of command of Bolero-Roundup is discussed. Eisenhower urges the American position, that unified command is "essential," and suggests further that the assault echelon should be under a single commander directly responsible to a supreme commander. General Brooke disagrees, then asks, "Who would you name as commander of this expedition?" Eisenhower: "In America, I have heard much of a man . . . I think his name is Mountbatten . . . I have heard that he is vigorous, intelligent, and courageous, and . . . I assume he could do the job." General Brooke stares at Eisenhower for a moment and says, "General, possibly you have not met Admiral Mountbatten. This is he sitting directly across the table from you." Eisenhower is flustered, but he maintains his position.

A meeting with Mountbatten to talk of commandos and assault tactics and landing craft. Further conferences, one with General Brooke, to talk of attack and command and organization. Late one night, in a room in Claridges, Hap Arnold, Mark Clark, and Eisenhower sit about exchanging views of "conditions in England and the need for a theater commander who could meet the British senior officers on even terms." Who should it be? They agree it must be a man with the "experience and knowledge of our ways of doing things," and "fully acquainted with our War Department plans. He must have the confidence of General Marshall and the secretary of war." This description is a familiar one, and once it is reached Eisenhower leaves. Clark and Arnold talk further, and come to the conclusion that the commander "should be Ike." Clark asks Arnold to tell Marshall of their recommendation.

It is Saturday. Eisenhower and Clark ask Kay Summersby, the driver assigned them, to drive them down Bomb Alley (so called because during the blitz Nazi bombers too closely beset by RAF fighters would dump their bombs along the Dover road as they fled back to France) to Dover Castle, so that they may inspect the Channel defenses against the invasion that never came. Eisenhower and Clark stand on the battlements of the castle and stare east across the water, toward Festung Europa.

During their last two days, Eisenhower and Clark are sightseers, with Mrs. Summersby as their guide. Then to Northholt, to Prestwick, and back to the United States.

On Wednesday morning, June 3, Eisenhower reported again to Marshall. Later he dictated a memorandum to the chief of staff about the command of BOLERO. In his first paragraph he recommended that General Clark be immediately sent to England to command the first corps of American troops to take part in the cross-Channel assault. In his second paragraph he was at last ready to nominate an officer to command all U.S. forces in England: he recommended General McNarney, his classmate at West Point, whom Marshall had just promoted to deputy chief of staff.

But Marshall had already made his decision. Reports on Eisenhower from the senior officers in England had been uniformly good. One of them, Mountbatten, had arrived in Washington a day ahead of Eisenhower; he had been particularly impressed by Eisenhower, perhaps because of the latter's inadvertence (if it was indeed an inadvertence) at the meeting of the British Chiefs of Staff; he had been ready with his praise of Eisenhower both to President Roosevelt and later to Marshall. Eisenhower had cleared the last barrier to his appointment.

On Saturday, still on the subject of a commander for BOLERO, Eisenhower sent another memorandum to Marshall: "I believe it highly desirable to promote the individual concerned," whoever it might be, to lieutenant general.

On Monday, June 8, Eisenhower handed Marshall a directive he had drafted for the commanding general, European Theater of Operations, and advised Marshall that it should be studied with some care before it was sent overseas, since it was likely to be of importance in the further waging of the war. As Marshall took it he said: "I certainly do want to read it. You may be the man who executes it. If that's the case, when can you leave?"

A big moment. Not, as matters were to develop, the biggest moment of his career, but certainly the most exhilarating yet to come his way. Should he send up rockets? Phone all his friends? Start at once to celebrate? Not Eisenhower. Always wary, playing his cards always close to his blouse, he marched down the corridor to his office, put in a day's hard work, and at length, late in the evening, jotted a note on his calendar pad:

> The C/S told me this A.M. that its *possible* I may go to England in command. It's a big job—if U.S.-U.K. stay squarely behind Bolero and go after it tooth and nail, it will be the biggest American job of the war. Of course command now does not necessarily mean command in the operation—but the job before the battle begins will still be the biggest outside of that of C/S himself.

On Thursday, June 11, another note, this one scribbled in quiet satisfaction:

> The C/S says I'm the guy. He also approves Clark for Corps C.G. in England and gives us the II Corps.* Now we really go to work. Hope to leave here by plane on 22nd.

The command was Eisenhower's, but what was he to command? Almost as soon as they had agreed "in principle" to the possibility, under certain conditions, of mounting an assault in the fall of 1942, and assuredly to a cross-Channel invasion in 1943, the British had set about a planned withdrawal from their agreement. Indeed, it is evident that Churchill, his gorgeous speech of April 14 to the contrary notwithstanding, had never for a moment entertained the idea that SLEDGEHAMMER would be launched in 1942, and further that he was determined to engage in operations which in all likelihood would rule out any chance for ROUNDUP in 1943 as well. His subsequent justification of his duplicity was this: "I had to work by influence and diplomacy in order to secure agreed and harmonious action with our cherished Ally, without whose aid nothing but ruin faced the world."

Churchill's "influence and diplomacy" functioned smoothly. In late May the Soviet commissar for foreign affairs, Vyacheslav M. Molotov, flew from Moscow, across a Europe subjugated by the Nazis, to London; his mission was to beseech a second front in western Europe, an invasion stout enough to force the withdrawal of forty German divisions from the Russian front. Forty divisions! If it accomplished nothing else, the Soviet

---

* Eisenhower had nominated Clark for the job he got on June 3. Clark had urged Marshall to appoint Eisenhower the commanding general, European Theater of Operations, a day or two later. Marshall, considering these crosscurrents, told Clark, "It looks to me as if you boys got together."

entreaty served to set in bloody relief the enormity of the struggle that was being fought from Leningrad south through the vast spaces of Russia to the Crimea. In response, Churchill tendered Molotov a lecture on military strategy as conditioned by modern technology (cold comfort), and a reminder that an estimated forty-four Axis divisions were in one way or another already committed against British troops in Africa or against the threat of an Anglo-American offensive. Churchill, moreover, "had faith in the power of the Russian armies and nation fighting in defence of their native soil." But if the Red Army were to be defeated in 1942, no matter, for ultimately "the power of Great Britain and the United States would prevail."

No doubt shivering within the shroud of these assurances, Molotov flew on to Washington. Before he landed there came a radiogram from Churchill to Roosevelt reporting that "all preparations are proceeding ceaselessly on the largest scale"; announcing that Mountbatten was also flying to Washington "to explain to you the difficulties of 1942" (i.e., to undermine SLEDGEHAMMER); hinting at the desirability of another diversionary attack, this one against the northern cape of Norway (an operation called JUPITER); and adding, "We must never let GYMNAST [the landings in North Africa] pass from our minds."

Since General Marshall was still, in late May, persuaded that a cross-Channel invasion was "inevitable sometime in 1942 merely by the force of circumstance," Molotov must have been much better satisfied by his conversations in Washington than by those in London. When he bluntly asked Roosevelt if a second front in 1942 were being planned, the President referred the question to Marshall, who said, "Yes." This led to the sentence in the public statement issued from the White House a few days later: "In the course of the conversations full understanding was reached with regard to the urgent tasks of creating a Second Front in Europe in 1942."

By that time, however, Mountbatten had arrived in Washington for talks with the President; already he had dwelt upon the acute shortage of landing craft and upon the British conviction that an Allied invasion of France would draw from Russia no Nazi troops at all, since the German High Command was believed by the British to have disposed some twenty-five divisions in France anyway; already he had attracted the President's eye to the inviting coasts of North Africa.

It was against this background of high-toned strategic palaver that Eisenhower was named to his new command, but while he was still savoring his triumph, that command was dwindling from the biggest of the war to something that could scarcely be seen by the naked eye.

The fact was that any notion of a second front in Europe during 1942 was dead. On June 11, the same day that Eisenhower was formally told he was to be commander of U.S. forces in the European theater, Churchill proposed to his war cabinet that there be no substantial landing in France unless the Allies were prepared to stay there and that there be no invasion in 1942 unless the Germans had suffered such serious setbacks in Russia that their armies were demoralized. The cabinet approved the prime minister's proposition. The agreement "in principle" was finally shown to be no agreement at all.

This decision of the war cabinet was still unknown to the Americans. In Washington Eisenhower still worked overtime on plans for BOLERO and contingency plans for SLEDGEHAMMER. In London a joint intelligence committee, working on an assessment of the situation on the Russian fronts, had on June 9 offered this as part of its considered opinion: "Margin between success or failure very narrow, and it may be touch and go which adversary collapses first. If Germans realize they cannot avoid further winter campaign in Russia and faced with threat of Anglo-American invasion in the West, collapse may, as in 1918, ensue with startling rapidity."

The validity of this opinion was questionable, the more so in view of the serious defeat sustained by the Russians west of Kharkov late in May (the Russians announced a loss of 5,000 dead and 70,000 missing; the Germans claimed 240,000 prisoners) and the investment of Sevastopol, which would fall on July 2. When the Germans late in June launched their offensive south and east across the Don, it would seem that they would surely seize the oilfields of the Caucasus. The battle of Stalingrad was months in the future. But the British Chiefs of Staff had concurred in the opinion of the Joint Intelligence Committee, "though they think it may be slightly *over optimistic* from the Russian point of view."

At all events, the estimate precisely suited Eisenhower's case. In the margin next to the paragraph quoted above, he wrote: "Time for us to do something—whatever we can!" and asked Colonel John R. Deane, then on Marshall's staff, to send the paper on to Roosevelt. (It never reached the White House.)

At this time the American Chiefs were still determined to attack cross-Channel in 1942, but the British Chiefs were dead set against it. Since the major share and weight of any such early thrust would fall upon the British, theirs would be the determining voice in any combined council. It is for this reason, even disregarding the earlier decision of the British war cabinet, that SLEDGEHAMMER was dead and all efforts to revive it vain. Was there now to be only an impasse? No, for Churchill was ready to apply his "influence and diplomacy."

Here he is, on the night of June 17, as he prepares to fly to Washington, accompanied by the CIGS, General Brooke. In General Brooke's words: "He was dressed in his zip-suit and zip-shoes, with a black Homburg hat on the side of his head and his small gold-topped malacca cane in his hand. Suddenly, almost like Pooh-Bear [General Brooke apparently could not bring himself to refer to the prime minister as Winnie-the-Pooh], he started humming, 'We're here because we're here—We're here because we're here!' "

Churchill and Brooke landed in Washington in the evening on June 18. Early next morning Churchill was flown to Hyde Park to confer with Roosevelt at his home on the Hudson. Generals Brooke, Ismay, and Dill at once began a series of meetings with American officers. Apart from the disagreement over Sledgehammer, their accord was remarkable. Eisenhower wrote the minutes of the informal conference held that afternoon; these show that "there was general agreement . . . that Gymnast should not be undertaken [under the existing situation*]," that Bolero should be pushed "with all possible speed and energy," and that "any 1942 attack on western Europe should be studied further" but in any event "should be undertaken only in case of necessity."

The next morning, at a formal meeting of the Combined Chiefs which Eisenhower attended, his minutes of the earlier meeting were the basis of further discussion. Once again there was near unanimity of opinion, especially on the question of Gymnast. Soldiers, sailors, and airmen alike expressed their opposition to it. General Brooke spoke also against any "so-called 'sacrifice' operation on the Continent" in 1942 to help the Russians (this was, of course, Sledgehammer), since, as he argued, even if a bridgehead were to be won it could not be followed up and expanded.

Eisenhower disagreed. He maintained there was a "possibility at least of securing a bridgehead and holding it as Malta or Tobruk had been held. If the air forces in Great Britain were concentrated for the operation, the Germans would certainly have to bring back air forces to deal with the situation." He added that "we must be ready to seize immediately any favorable opportunity."

But while the professionals talked and agreed to reject any suggestion of Gymnast, they were uncomfortably "doubtful as to what P.M. and President [might] be brewing up together" in Hyde Park.

P.M. and President were experimentally sipping a brew cooked from a recipe quite different from the one the Combined Chiefs had elaborated,

---

* The words within square brackets were later added by General Bedell Smith, who was then the secretary to the Combined Chiefs. The Chiefs had five reasons for rejecting Gymnast, among them that "its favorable effect on the Russian situation would probably be very slight" and, most important, its "marked effect in slowing up Bolero"; i.e., its threat to any chance for a cross-Channel assault in 1943.

a recipe that called for assaults on the shores of Africa, most of them from the Mediterranean; in short, a recipe that called precisely for GYMNAST or some such operation under another code name. Churchill was the master chef. He had confronted Roosevelt with a note that he supported with all his considerable forensic skill:

. . . We hold strongly to the view that there should be no substantial landing in France this year unless we are going to stay.

. . . No responsible British military authority has so far been able to make a plan for September 1942 which had any chance of success unless the Germans have become utterly demoralized, of which there is no likelihood. Have the American Staffs a plan? At what points would they strike? What landing craft and shipping are available? Who is the officer prepared to command the enterprise? What British forces and assistance are required? If a plan can be found which offers a reasonable prospect of success, His Majesty's Government will cordially welcome it, and will share to the full with their American comrades the risks and sacrifices. This remains our settled and agreed policy.

. . . But in case no plan can be made in which any responsible authority has good confidence, and consequently no engagement on a substantial scale in France is possible in September 1942, what else are we going to do? Can we afford to stand idle in the Atlantic theatre during the whole of 1942? Ought we not to be preparing within the general structure of Bolero some other operation by which we may gain positions of advantage, and also directly or indirectly to take some of the weight off Russia? It is in this setting and on this background that the French Northwest Africa operation should be studied.

A masterful performance. No operation in France could avail; but some operation was necessary in 1942, if only to help the Russians, to whom Roosevelt had already all but promised a second front; hence, the Allied armies should land in North Africa. Q.E.D.

P.M. and President at once returned to Washington, where Churchill was "very upset" to find that after his considerable effort to promote GYMNAST, the Combined Chiefs had perversely and unanimously decided against it. Signals off. He summoned Brooke, the CIGS, who found him "a bit peevish, but not too bad and, after an hour's talk with him, had him quiet again." Signals on. Brooke was now committed once again to the North African landings.

Here was a major strategic decision, one of the most momentous of the war, one which would play a part in provoking the Cold War after the War of 1939–1945 had been fought to a finish, and one of the very few instances when the politicians believed it necessary to overrule the generals. Which were the more nearly right—the statesmen or their military advisers? the amateurs or the professionals? Was Clemenceau correct when he pronounced his celebrated aphorism, "War is much too serious a matter to be entrusted to the military"? To be sure, politicians find it easier to impose their will on their professional military advisers after victory has become a certainty; but in June 1942, while the issue was still very much in doubt, the politicians had nevertheless intervened. To what effect?

All questions about a mortal conflict can more comfortably be answered by the victors. In 1956, eleven years after the war had been won, General Marshall would wave a tolerant hand and say of his political chieftain, "The leader in a democracy has to keep the people entertained. . . . The people demand action. We [the military] couldn't wait to be completely ready. Churchill was always getting into sideshows. If we had gone as far as he did we never would have gotten out. But I could see why he had to have something."

To the victor the indulgent reminiscence. In June 1942, however, Marshall was hopping mad at Churchill, and so were all the American military professionals. As to Churchill's series of hard questions beginning "Have the American Staffs a plan?" the answers were: No, they had no detailed plan; were not sure at what points in France to strike; did not know about landing craft, or shipping, or the extent of necessary British assistance; and had not formally nominated an officer to command the enterprise—all this for the excellent reason that they had agreed with the British more than two months before that detailed planning for SLEDGE-HAMMER and ROUNDUP should go forward in London, not in Washington. If, then, no plans for SLEDGEHAMMER had been worked out in detail, the onus for the lack was on the British alone.

The "American Staffs" did, however, consider themselves a "responsible authority" quite able to formulate the framework of a plan for a cross-Channel invasion in September 1942; and by Tuesday, June 23, the OPD had prepared such a framework for Marshall to hand to the President. The OPD argument stood on three legs:

(1) Since SLEDGEHAMMER had always been considered a desperate operation, to be launched against heavy odds, and had been accepted as such, it was mischievous now, belatedly, to make likelihood of success a precondition for proceeding with it.

(2) "If disaster is to be expected in an operation supported by the entire British Air Force based in the U.K. and a large increment from the United States Army Air Force, what chance can any other operation without such support have?"

(3) No other operation was more likely "to directly or indirectly take some of the weight off Russia." In this connection, the staff of OPD again

insisted that one of the greatest disadvantages of GYMNAST was that it probably would "not result in removing one German soldier, tank, or plane from the Russian front."

Another aspect of Churchill's proposition warrants comment. In his view, no cross-Channel invasion in 1942 could succeed "unless the Germans have become utterly demoralized, *of which there is no likelihood*" (emphasis added). Now the Americans had always regarded SLEDGE-HAMMER as an emergency operation, to be undertaken in September or October *if* the Red Army were in desperate straits or *if* the German position were "critically weakened." But they had insisted that the operation should, in any event, be planned and prepared so that the moment could be seized *if* it should prove necessary or propitious. With the advantage of hindsight, it is instructive to survey the situation on the Russian front as it did actually develop by September 1942.

During its summer offensive the German Wehrmacht was to roll to its uttermost limit, extending the sway of the Reich, by late August and early September, as far as to a few footholds on the western bank of the Volga, deep within Russia. But there the Nazi supermen were stopped at last, and scores of thousands of them were stopped dead. While what Goebbels's Propaganda Ministry called the "greatest battle of attrition that the world has ever seen" was being ferociously fought in the rubble and around the barricades of Stalingrad, demoralization did indeed set in, and from the lowest German ranks to the highest. (Contrariwise, the morale of the Soviet troops, poor in August and early September, lifted steadily during the battle for Stalingrad.)

Excerpts from the diary of a German soldier, Wilhelm Hoffman, of the 267th Regiment, 94th Division, trace the stages of that demoralization from arrogance through abusive contempt to fear and despair:

September 1: Are the Russians really going to fight on the very banks of the Volga? It's madness.
September 8: . . . insane stubbornness.
September 11: . . . fanatics.
September 13: . . . wild beasts.
September 16: Barbarism . . . [they are] not men but devils.
September 26: . . . barbarians, they use gangster methods.

Then for a month the diarist recorded only his gloom and terror.

October 27: The Russians are not men, but some kind of cast-iron creatures; they never get tired and are not afraid of fire.
October 28: Every [German] soldier sees himself as a condemned man.

In the meantime, German senior officers had been ignominiously dismissed one after another: first a pair of commanders of panzer divisions, Generals von Wietersheim and von Schwedler, the former of whom would end his career in 1945 as a private in Pomerania with the Volkssturm; next Colonel General Sigmund List, commander of Army Group A, whose advance southeast toward the Caucasus stumbled and ground to a halt; then, as demoralization reached still higher, Colonel General Alfred Jodl, chief of staff of OKW, the German Armed Forces High Command, who was in disgrace for a time in September, threatened with dismissal and assignment to other duties; and finally Colonel General Franz Halder, chief of staff of OKH, the German Army High Command, who was dismissed from office on September 24 after a quarrel with Hitler provoked, if remotely, by the lagging battle for Stalingrad.

Thus, though of course Churchill had no way of foreseeing it on June 20, demoralization would encompass the Wehrmacht by September and October, from lowly private all the way to commander in chief. There would still be plenty of fight left in it; but the black magic would have gone: a world that had trembled at the tread of the Nazi boots and the scream of the Nazi Stukas would know that the fearsome Übermensch could be driven back to defeat. And it was with precisely the possibility of such a deterioration that Eisenhower and Marshall had been concerned when they urged the preparations for SLEDGEHAMMER with all speed and energy.

Who was right in June 1942—the statesmen or the generals? the amateurs or the professionals? It is at least arguable that a cross-Channel invasion in 1942, pursued with the determination and sacrifice displayed by the Russians at Stalingrad, would have tumbled the Third Reich far sooner than June 1945 and would have saved the world much treasure and many lives.

As events came to pass, while the war in Europe was reaching and passing its turning point on the steppe west of the Volga, the Americans and the British were absorbed in Mediterranean operations that would postpone any possibility of a cross-Channel invasion until 1944.*

Gravest of all the repercussions of this strategic decision, however, would be the suspicion bred in the Soviets of their Anglo-American allies; the ugly suspicion that their allies chose not or dared not commit the men,

* Goebbels wrote in his diary on March 2, 1943, that Goering was "somewhat worried about our having pretty much stripped the West in order to bring things to a standstill in the East. One dreads to think what would happen if the English and the Americans were suddenly to attempt a landing." And on May 9, 1943: "[Our soldiers in North Africa] retarded developments for half a year, thereby enabling us to complete the construction of the Atlantic Wall and to prepare ourselves all over Europe so that an invasion is out of the question."

sacrifice the lives required to defeat Hitlerism; that the second front in Europe would always be postponed, for one excellent reason or another, for months, perhaps for years, perhaps forever; that their allies secretly hoped the Russian communists and German Nazis would contrive to kill each other off and so leave the world safe for what the Soviets described as bourgeois democracy, but the Anglo-Americans preferred to think of as the free world of the western democracies.*

Later, during the years of the Cold War, the leaders of the "free world" would wonder why the Soviets had conceived such a paranoid suspicion of every overture, every friendly gesture. The seeds of that suspicion were surely planted when the second front in Europe never materialized during the years when the Soviet Union was most sorely pressed by the Nazi invader.

On the day late in June when Roosevelt and Churchill returned to Washington to reverse the strategic decisions reached by the Combined Chiefs, Major General Dwight Eisenhower was busy with the last-minute details of his imminent flight to England.

He had originally planned to spend his last weekend in the States at West Point with his wife, visiting their son. When this proved not feasible, John was allowed to come to Washington; he arrived late Saturday morning, June 20, and was due back at West Point late Sunday. Eisenhower spent Sunday at home in Fort Myer with his family, somewhat feverish and uncomfortable after all the inoculations required of a man bound overseas. There were affairs to be attended to: a memorandum to Hap Arnold, another to Somervell; instructions to his orderly, Sergeant Mickey McKeogh, who would be traveling with him, and to Captain Ernest (Tex) Lee, a tall, mournful-looking man, formerly an automobile salesman, who had been Eisenhower's executive officer at Fort Sam Houston in 1941 and his aide in Washington since March 1942, and who would also be in the group traveling to England. Two other officers—Colonel Thomas Jefferson (T.J.) Davis and Lieutenant Commander Harry (Butch) Butcher, USNR—were to leave a day later and had also to be given final instructions. Davis was to be Eisenhower's adjutant general, charged with administering his headquarters; he was an easygoing, roly-poly South Carolinian who had been an aide to General MacArthur in

---

* On June 23, 1941, the day after the Nazi armies invaded Russia, Senator Harry S. Truman (Democrat, of Missouri), later to be Vice President and still later to be President of the United States, said: "If we see that Germany is winning we ought to help Russia, and if Russia is winning we ought to help Germany, and that way let them kill as many as possible, although I don't want to see Hitler victorious under any circumstances. Neither of them think anything of their pledged word." For some reason the Soviets found it difficult to forget or to forgive that honest opinion.

the 1930s and had served with Eisenhower in the Philippines. Butcher, a close friend of Eisenhower's since the late 1920s, had as vice president of the Columbia Broadcasting System in Washington been on affable terms with the politicians, journalists, tufthunters, and tagtails who throng that curious city, and was now in the unprecedented and anomalous post of naval aide to an army officer. Eisenhower had pulled strings to effect this assignment because, as he confided to friends, "I've got to have someone I can relax with," and Butcher was perfectly qualified.

These men were at the core of what was to be celebrated as Eisenhower's "official family"; in England they would be joined by his two drivers, Albert (Lord Gilbey) Gilbey, an English veteran of the War of 1914–1918, and Kay (Skib) Summersby, and by his American chief of staff, General Walter Bedell (Beetle) Smith. Mickey and Tex, T.J. and Butch, Lord Gilbey and Skib, Beetle and Ike—the nicknames sound like those of a bomber crew or a squad of embattled GIs in one of those banal radio playlets that infested the night air of the U.S. during the early 1940s, when every commercial sponsor strove somehow to link his product to the war effort.

On Monday, June 22, Eisenhower had some ceremonial duties to perform: the dictation of a few letters of farewell to general officers with whom he had been associated during his rapid rise; a last session with General Handy, his successor as chief of OPD; an appointment with Secretary of War Stimson, who still imagined that a cross-Channel invasion would be executed in 1942; a brief talk with Admiral King, who assured him of the U.S. Navy's full support in this "first deliberate attempt by the American fighting services to set up a unified command in the field for a campaign of indefinite length"; a formal visit to the White House to bid farewell to his commander in chief and to meet for the first time Prime Minister Churchill; and a leavetaking of General Marshall.

The chief of staff was an embattled man. The day before, during a stormy session at the White House, Marshall had stood alone against Churchill's scheme for landings in North Africa; he had ruefully noted that the two British chiefs present, Ismay and Brooke, had overnight shifted their ground on the subject; he had had to contend as well with Roosevelt, who was once again powerfully attracted to the Mediterranean. His task had been the harder because the news had arrived of the fall of Tobruk, a disaster that not only threatened the collapse of the entire Middle East but also kept everyone's attention riveted on the southern rim of the Mediterranean. Now at last it had come clear that Churchill's agreement "in principle" of two months before was worthless. Now had come what the official British war historian was later to call the "Day of the Dupes," and Marshall had not been cheered to find that his allotted role was that of chump. Ismay had undertaken the delicate task of writing, for the consideration of the American Chiefs, a memorandum of agreement on Allied offensive operations in 1942–1943. "Operations in Western Europe in 1942," he had written, "would, if successful, yield greater political and strategic gains," but if "examination shows that despite all efforts, success is improbable, we must be ready with an alternative . . . Operation Gymnast."

But Marshall had not yielded. A battle still impended when the Combined Chiefs met on Wednesday, June 24. What Marshall hoped would be the final decision was to be reached after Eisenhower had landed in England. The chief of staff was confident. Like Polonius, he offered Eisenhower one last word of counsel, "Persuade by accomplishment rather than by eloquence," bade him farewell, and dismissed him.

At 8 A.M. on Tuesday, June 23, General Eisenhower was driven to Bolling Field. His companions were there to snap him salutes and acknowledge his big happy grin. Mark Clark was there; his wife and children were on hand to see him off. That was not Eisenhower's way: he was unattended by family, undisturbed by tug at heart or tearful kiss or last lingering clasp. He shook a few hands in his big hand, smiled with confidence, bounced into the plane, spoke a few words to the pilot, nodded, found the seat he wanted, and composed himself for the journey.

At length, after the inevitable delays, the plane taxied to the head of its runway, paused as its four propellers whirled faster, moved, gathered speed, lifted, and was borne by air up and then in a slow bank first south, then west, then north, still lifting, while constantly Eisenhower gazed down from his seat by the window. As the plane passed over Fort Myer, down below, by the flagstaff on the parade ground, a slight feminine figure stood, clearly perceptible, waving. General Eisenhower smiled. He watched the figure as long as he could and then sat back and fetched a deep breath. The plane lifted steadily up, up, up, heading northeast toward Gander, toward Europe and the war.

CHAPTER FOUR

Second Front in 1942?

To ASSUME A NEW COMMAND in a strange country and to give it Snap, and Grip, is not the easiest thing in the world under the best of circumstances. For a few days Major General Dwight D. Eisenhower chafed fretfully despite having the command he had desired above all others, the command for which he had, indeed, himself drafted the directive just as he had drafted the orders relieving his predecessor. His task at first proved irksome because many of the officers in his new command were victims of either Anglophilia or Anglophobia, both being crippling ailments; because he was plunked down in an elegant hotel in London and then ignored by the most important of the British leaders with whom he had business; because he, who had worked in almost complete obscurity in the United States, was all at once a celebrity and a cynosure in the United Kingdom; and, not least, because his trunk had been mislaid in transit.

A suite had been engaged for him at Claridges, but neither the suite nor the smart and exclusive hotel fitted his style. Instead of a lobby with shops and bright lights and newspaper stalls and a buzz of friendly chatter, Claridges had only a quiet foyer with liveried footmen; and as for the suite, Mickey McKeogh, his orderly, who before the war had been a bellhop at the Plaza in New York, knew at once that it was not a place where his boss could take off his shoes, stretch out his legs, and relax. The sitting room was done in black and gold, the bedroom in pink. "Mickey," Eisenhower said, "this looks exactly like a funeral parlor." To Butcher he complained, "I feel as though I'm living in sin," and after a week or so he removed to the big shiny noisy Dorchester in Park Lane, where he shared a suite of rooms with Butcher.*

His headquarters were in Grosvenor Square, also in Mayfair, and so his life—his comings and his goings, his luncheons and dinners in the public rooms of nearby hotels, his visitors and his appointments, his attendance at receptions, his weekends in the country—became approximately as pri-

---

* This arrangement was appropriate; back in Washington Mrs. Eisenhower and Mrs. Butcher took an apartment together in the Wardman Park.

vate as that of a rare and exotic creature newly come to the zoo. His way was accompanied by nudges and stares. He inspired such an intense curiosity that inevitably he fell under the constant surveillance of the ladies and gentlemen of the press and finally, despite his becoming protests, was obliged to hold a press conference and to submit to an hour of picture-taking in his office.

In this fashion the remarkable public personality of Dwight Eisenhower —buoyant, cheerful, seemingly modest, seemingly simple, sunny, and utterly beguiling—was for the first time unveiled for international inspection. The result was the first of an unending series of stunning triumphs. His friendly informality, his disarming manner of confiding in the correspondents, his careful flattery, his making them part of his team (he called them "quasi-members of my staff"), his apparent candor, and his shrewd appeal for their cooperation ensnared them all. Ray Daniell of the *New York Times* had perhaps the coolest reaction; Eisenhower gave, he reported, "an excellent demonstration of the art of being jovially outspoken without saying much of anything." But later, after a similar occasion, Ed Murrow, then chief of the CBS European news service, phoned Butcher that "Ike had made a grand impression." Butcher himself noted, "After watching Ike deal with the press, I don't think he needs a public relations adviser. He is tops." And with the photographers, "no one but a Sunday school teacher with a class of nice girls could have been as obliging as Ike."

"It is a rather lonely life I lead," Eisenhower confided in a letter to his brother Milton; "every move I make is under someone's observation and, as a result, a sense of strain develops that is entirely aside from the job itself." To other officers he professed himself "quite astonished" at the flurries of journalistic interest in him, and he modestly deprecated them; but when it came to what was truly astonishing about his appointment, that is, the diminution of his influence in Allied war councils, he was curiously silent. In Washington he had been Marshall's "subordinate commander" and chief adviser on all strategical matters; in London he was a theater commander charged with a mission, given orders to obey. The outward and visible signs of his mission betokened greater rank and authority: he got his third star and became a lieutenant general (temporary) on July 7, and his titles (to peep into the future a bit) would soon swell to include such magnificences as supreme commander; and yet, the afflatus of his prestige and all its perquisites to the contrary notwithstanding, Eisenhower in stubborn fact was further from the mastery and control of power in London than he had been in Washington.

This aspect of the hero's gorgeous career warrants further inspection before we have been blinded by the brilliance of its future progress. Quite soon now his claque will have gathered about him, showering him with epithets that will obscure and distort his wartime role just as he was obscured by the tons of torn paper, confetti, and ticker tape that fluttered down about him as he rode on his triumphal tour through the stony gorges of New York City. An attempt must be made to define his wartime role with some precision.

Perhaps the most fashionable of the epithets with which he was garlanded has been "chairman of the board." We have been invited to suppose that General Eisenhower was a kind of managing director who, with emollient diplomacy, reconciled the prickly and contrary opinions of Washington and London; who smoothed the ruffled feathers of sundry British and American military cocks, persuading them to fight not each other but their common foe; who patiently mediated differences, coordinated opposites, soothed the bellicose children squabbling in the nursery, and so emerged as the chief architect of victory. Not to put too fine a point on it, this notion is nonsense.

General Eisenhower was never the "chairman of the board." Never did he determine Anglo-American strategy. He was, to pursue the inept metaphor a trifle further, no more than the chairman of an executive committee, a position that did not, however, confer upon him membership on the board of directors, let alone chairmanship of it. On the contrary, his mission kept him decidedly subordinate to those directors. The directors were the Combined Chiefs of Staff, of whom Eisenhower was never one. Occasionally the British Chiefs would invite him (or summon him) to meet with them and answer questions; less often the American Chiefs would find themselves in his neighborhood and make room for him at their deliberations. Whatever the case, Eisenhower was the creature of the Combined Chiefs, never their chairman.

Once on the battlefield and commanding the Allied armies in war, Eisenhower would be granted considerable latitude to act as he chose so long as he stayed within the bounds of his specific mission, and to make decisions even of a paramilitary nature—that is, political decisions—for this was standard American procedure. Such a procedure was, on the other hand, entirely foreign to British practice, and in consequence, since he was answerable to two sets of masters, Eisenhower would often find himself bedeviled, the more bitterly inasmuch as the governments of the United States of America and of the United Kingdom had two quite different conceptions of the postwar world.

Eisenhower himself was not always happy to be characterized as chairman of the board, for he perceived a slur in the phrase—a suggestion that he was only a figurehead, a political general who had been kicked upstairs out of the way, but who was never a true commander in chief of embattled armies, bleeding and dying. He recognized, however, that there was little more in this sense of the phrase than the sneers ever reserved for a man in a position of high trust. Neither sense of the term—neither the laudatory nor the derisive—fitted Eisenhower even approximately. But he would strive, as time went on, to assume the heroic stature appropriate to the first sense, and taking one thing with another, his effort would be entirely comprehensible.

In the summer of 1942, however, there were precious few signs of the future hero and none whatever of any chairman of the board. For Eisenhower there was, instead, first an illusion, then a profound gloom, and finally a protracted shambles. Not a happy summer.

During his first two or three weeks in London, Eisenhower still fancied he was on hand to command whatever American troops might be available for a cross-Channel invasion in 1942. (So, quite naturally, did most of the war correspondents in London; so also did a great many other folk.) He did not know, and was not told, of the shaky status of SLEDGEHAMMER, nor of the ambiguous decisions that had been reached after he left Washington.* Nor were the British leaders, on their return from Washington, at any pains to acquaint Eisenhower with what had happened in his absence; after all, he was only a Yank theater commander, and a very junior general at that. General Brooke ignored him totally, remaining "practically incommunicado." The prime minister, absorbed in domestic politics (following the calamitous defeats in the desert west of Egypt, he faced a vote of censure in the House of Commons), sent word he would not be able to see Eisenhower for some little time.

Eisenhower was troubled. Why, with a war on, did his allies not strive for greater dispatch? What of the imminent cross-Channel assault? His growing puzzlement, all at once become dismay, can be charted in excerpts from three communications he sent to Marshall:

June 30: There seems to be some confusion of thought as to the extent of the British commitment toward a 1942 operation.
July 7: Am somewhat uncertain as to existing agreements, if any, concerning 1942 operation but request information as to whether . . . British

---

* The latter decisions were merely imprecise verbal inflections of the former ones agreed to by Roosevelt and Churchill. Of GYMNAST, earlier described as "the best alternative in 1942" to SLEDGEHAMMER, plans for which "should be completed in all details as soon as possible," it was said later: "The possibilities . . . will be explored carefully and conscientiously, and plans will be completed . . . as soon as possible."

The British were content with these meaningless changes because they were confident that Allied operations would be shifted from cross-Channel to Mediterranean no matter what language was used. Marshall was content because he imagined he had forced the British to leave the way clear for a revival of SLEDGEHAMMER.

and U.S. forces . . . should now begin concrete preparations including assembly of shipping and landing craft so as to make possible an
operation no later than September 15 in the hope that it will prove
feasible.

July 11: The British Staff and Prime Minister have decided that Sledgehammer can not repeat not be successfully executed this year under
the proposition that the invading force must be able to remain permanently on the continent.

At last Eisenhower had got the message.

Marshall had known of the most recent British verdict for several days,
and he was at the end of his patience, "very stirred up," according to Secretary Stimson, ready to take any step to save the strategy of a swift cross-
Channel operation. In the event, Roosevelt sent him to London together
with Hopkins and Admiral King, to determine whether, for once and
finally, the Allies could reach an agreement for action in 1942 that would
not, a fortnight later, come unstuck. The President's instructions were
that they should press for SLEDGEHAMMER, but that in any event, if
SLEDGEHAMMER were "finally and definitely" rejected by the British, U.S.
ground troops should "be brought into action against the enemy in 1942."
Clearly, if the British stood firm against the cross-Channel invasion, the
Americans would be forced to an operation their military leaders detested,
the one against French North Africa. Nor had Marshall yet measured the
tenacity of the British, and especially of Churchill, on the question.
Churchill believed that SLEDGEHAMMER had been dead for some time and
should now be buried, while General Brooke on July 17 wrote in his diary:
"In my mind [an invasion of France in] 1942 is dead off and without the
slightest hope. 1943 must depend on what happens to Russia. If she breaks
and is overrun, there can be no invasion and we should . . . go into North
Africa instead."

Confronted with what he feared would be another long wrangle over
the risks of smiting the coast of France, Marshall wholly relied on Eisenhower and his subordinates to conjure for him a persuasive analysis of
SLEDGEHAMMER and a sanguine argument on its behalf. Why not? After
all, Eisenhower had been the principal architect of the original plan—
BOLERO, SLEDGEHAMMER, and ROUNDUP—for stabbing at Germany's vitals;
who could more cogently defend the plan against those who wished to
spike it?

Eisenhower on July 16 summoned into council his chief aides—Mark
Clark; Major General John C. H. Lee, who commanded his Services of
Supply; Major General Carl A. (Tooey) Spaatz, commander of the Eighth
Air Force; and other officers responsible for plans—and set to work. Time

was short. Naval experts were agreed that any cross-Channel invasion should be mounted before September 15 if it were to avoid the wicked autumnal weather, but British staff officers had warned that sixty days would be needed to put an attack like SLEDGEHAMMER under way.

"The belief of this headquarters"—it is Eisenhower dictating—"and of the principal subordinate commanders is that the Russian situation is at least sufficiently critical to justify any action on our part that would clearly be of definite assistance."

He recommended landings at and near Le Havre; in the next few days he would come to favor landings on the Cotentin peninsula near Cherbourg. "I personally estimate that, favored by surprise, the chances of a fairly successful landing by the leading division are about 1 in 2; of finally establishing a force of 6 divisions in the area with supporting air and other arms, about 1 in 5 . . . But we should not forget that the prize we seek is to keep 8,000,000 Russians in the war."

Portrait of a man in conflict: on the one hand, the belligerent strategist fighting for the plan he had conceived and for his own role in its execution, and on the other hand the professional soldier, professionally assessing a desperate operation.

Marshall, King, Hopkins, Beetle Smith, and their party reached London by train from Scotland on Saturday morning, July 18. (The train had been provided them by the prime minister, who had expected them to stop at Chequers, his country house, and spend the weekend with him. When, instead, they went straight to London to confer with Eisenhower and the other American officers, Churchill detonated into one of his celebrated tempers, commenced hopping up and down, and used such intemperate language that Hopkins felt obliged to go to Chequers to soothe the prime minister's choleric humor.) Meanwhile, at Claridges, Eisenhower, Clark, and Spaatz spent the day closeted with Marshall and King. The next day, Sunday, Eisenhower dictated to two stenographers the memorandum that Marshall would use on Monday at a meeting with Churchill and the British Chiefs.

Russia is the great question mark of the war. . . .

Defeat of the Russian armies would compel a complete reorientation of Allied strategy. It would practically eliminate all opportunity of defeating Germany by direct action, and would throw the Allies permanently on the defensive throughout Europe. Except for bombardment by aircraft, in which Germany would have the advantage of geographical position, there would be little that the Allies could undertake, of a positive nature, to bring the war to a successful conclusion.

The bleakness of this picture needs no emphasizing. . . .

. . . the fate of the rest of the Allied world is largely bound up in the endurance and efficiency of the Russian army. . . .

SLEDGEHAMMER was . . . conceived in the idea that circumstances in 1942 might be such as to require definite action. . . .

With respect to the Russian situation, there are three possible conditions that could develop . . .

(a) Progressive deterioration of Russian strength . . .

(b) A gradual turn for the better . . . with progressive absorption of German strength . . .

(c) A continuance of the struggle on the Russian front with the battle progressively approaching the crisis, with a consequent effort on both sides to bring to bear every available ounce of strength in order to clinch the victory or to avoid defeat. This is the particular situation in which it was considered that SLEDGEHAMMER might constitute effective intervention on the part of Great Britain and the United States.*

If a situation comparable to the one last described above should arise this year, with German defending forces in Western Europe reduced to a mere shell, we would be guilty of one of the grossest military blunders of all history, if Germany should be permitted to eliminate an Allied army of 8,000,000 men when some stroke of ours might have saved the situation. To be unready for this particular eventuality constitutes a grave risk. The stakes are high, the possible rewards are great. We maintain that we cannot afford unreadiness for this eventuality. . . .

There were still the shortages—of landing craft, of supporting warships, of pursuit aircraft, of trained troops—that always plague those who are less than audacious, and SLEDGEHAMMER would doubtless have been a costly operation. Nevertheless, with the acuity of hindsight, it is hard to fault this view of Anglo-American strategy. Yet the senior British leaders were adamantly opposed. On Sunday evening, while Marshall and King were reviewing what Eisenhower had dictated, Churchill summoned the British Chiefs to Chequers and, that night, came to a firm and unanimous agreement with them: SLEDGEHAMMER was finally, formally, to be declared extinct; GYMNAST was, for 1942, the only feasible Allied operation. It remained only to dose the Americans with this purgative pill.†

* This was precisely the particular situation that obtained along the Volga in mid-September.
† British opinion of SLEDGEHAMMER only seemed to be unanimous. Over the weekend Marshall had made it his business to talk with Brigadier General Lucian Truscott, who for three months had been attached to Mountbatten's staff at Combined Operations Command. Here Truscott had been in intimate professional association with the younger officers responsible for planning the commando raids against the French littoral—men like Major Robert D. Q. Henriques, Lieutenant Commander Ackroyd N. P. Costabadie, and Wing Commander Robert D. Homer. These planners, Truscott

Shortly after noon on Monday, July 20, General Marshall, Admiral King, and Harry Hopkins arrived in Downing Street for their first conference with the British. The American Chiefs had originally been invited to meet with the British Chiefs for a private talk at 10 A.M., but Churchill, "very suspicious," had vetoed the notion, explaining to Brooke, "that Marshall was trying to assume powers of commander in chief of American troops, which was the President's prerogative." With this mischief poisoning the atmosphere, statesmen and Combined Chiefs began seven hours of discussions, protracted over three days.

Eisenhower, excluded, was edgy. "There is an atmosphere of tension," he observed on Monday morning, and two days later he would again affirm, "The last few days have been tense and wearing." The British, who had theretofore held that an operation on the order of SLEDGEHAMMER might be mounted within sixty days, were now insisting on "four months, with an absolute minimum of three." Eisenhower, supported by Clark, finally told Marshall that if he considered a cross-Channel attack would help the Russians, "we should attempt the job at the earliest possible date—regardless." They did not promise that such an attack would be a tactical success; they *did* urge that with "whole-hearted cooperation all the way round we have a fighting chance." None of this was of any use. The British were not concerned with help for the Russians. In Brooke's view, Marshall "missed the point that after September the Russians might be past requiring assistance." British Chiefs, prime minister, and War Cabinet all stood firm against any cross-Channel operation.

If for Marshall it was a hard blow, for Eisenhower it was devastating. At once exploded were the strategic plans he had formulated and advocated for many long months and his personal dreams of professional glory. On Thursday morning, at breakfast with Clark and Butcher, he was notably glum. "Well," he said, "I hardly know where to start the day. I'm right back to December fifteenth" (his first full day at work in the War Plans Division of the War Department). Clark was also deeply disappointed; he too had had his dreams. They spoke of how the growing American might would now be dispersed in theaters where its best effect would be wasted. They spoke of the dispatches from the Russian fronts, where the Red Armies were reeling back under the savage Nazi assault. Eisenhower warned that Wednesday, July 22, the day when the decision was taken against SLEDGEHAMMER, could well go down as "the blackest day in history."

---

had assured Marshall, "believed that an operation to seize the Cherbourg peninsula was not only practicable and within our means, but that it would be a desirable operation to undertake during the fall in preparation for Roundup the following spring."

As has already been demonstrated, the decision taken on Wednesday, July 22, was not a determination reached for the first time so much as a reaffirmation of one that had been formed, at least by Churchill, more than a month before. Since the decision would impose an irreversible change of strategy, affecting Allied operations in 1943 as well as 1942, it provoked a good deal of puzzled speculation and has in later years become a subject of some controversy among historians and military memoirists. A few further comments may help to keep the controversy warm.

Naturally enough, since his was the decisive voice in the quarrelsome chorus, most of the controversy has swirled and eddied about the stumpy, bouncy figure of the prime minister, a personage at once implausible and inevitable, absurd and inspiring, who managed to consolidate a number of brilliant eccentricities—zippered siren-suit, cigars and brandy, truculent growl, talent for buoyant oratory, singular working schedule (much of the day in bed, much of the night hard at it), two fingers upthrust in a V-for-victory—into one idiosyncratic symbol of indomitability.

Did Churchill shirk a cross-Channel invasion? Robert Sherwood believed so: he wrote of "Churchill's warnings that the Channel would be a 'river of blood.'" Stimson thought so: he spoke of Churchill's "repeated assertions . . . as to the disastrous effect of having the Channel full of corpses of defeated allies." Churchill himself vigorously denied the charge: "So many tales have been published of my rooted aversion from large-scale operations on the Continent that it is important that the truth should be emphasized. I always considered that a decisive assault upon the German-occupied countries on the largest possible scale was the only way in which the war could be won, and that the summer of 1943 should be chosen as the target date." But close analysis of his recommended strategy shows that in fact he urged assaults by "adequate and suitably equipped forces" against "three or four" targets selected from among "Norway, Denmark, Holland, Belgium, the French Channel coasts and the French Atlantic coasts, as well as in Italy and possibly the Balkans." In the event, Churchill opposed a cross-Channel invasion in 1942, seemed unaware that the operation in French North Africa would entail cancellation of a cross-Channel assault in 1943,* and would argue most resourcefully for Mediterranean diversions that, if approved, would have forced cancellation of the cross-Channel invasion in 1944. How these procrastinations aroused Soviet suspicions has already been touched upon.

* Marshall patiently explained again and again that GYMNAST—later TORCH—would eliminate ROUNDUP in 1943, but Churchill apparently was not listening. Not until September 21 did he "for the first time" express himself to Eisenhower as "very much astonished" to learn how costly the less important operation would prove for the more important. "Discouraging, discouraging," Eisenhower muttered to Butcher, just after the prime minister had first voiced this astonishment.

Was the disagreement between the American and British Chiefs a nationalistic one? In retrospect, Eisenhower spurned any suggestion of such a thing. The apostle of Allied cooperation would insist, in 1948, that no argument "was based upon nationalistic lines. The conferees [the Combined Chiefs, meeting in July 1942] were merely searching for the most profitable line of combined action to be undertaken in 1942." Students of the Allies and their impulses disagree. J. M. A. Gwyer, one of the authors of *Grand Strategy,* the official British history of the war, perceived a salient difference between the Americans and the British in their approach to strategy: the Americans inclined toward "the crash program, the head-on collision, the quick victory . . . the single massive thrust at the center," while the British preferred a "more supple type of strategy," one which "by the skilful employment of limited means . . . relies on maneuver rather than frontal attack." Churchill put the matter in much the same way: "In the military as in the commercial or production spheres the American mind runs naturally to broad, sweeping, logical conclusions on the largest scale. . . . The British mind does not work quite in this way. . . . In war particularly we assign a larger importance to opportunism and innovation, seeking rather to live and conquer in accordance with the unfolding event than to aspire to dominate it by fundamental decisions."

There were other differences as well, some deeply ingrained by history and culture, some shaped by more recent events, that led to acrimony between the Allies. There was the Channel itself. To the Americans it was a narrow sea, a natural barrier to be hurdled by the Allied armies like any other natural barrier that intervened between them and their objective. Brisk, practical, pragmatic; no nonsense. The English were moved by historical imagination. Their island, after all, was

> *This fortress built by Nature for herself*
> *Against infection and the hand of war . . .*
> *This precious stone set in the silver sea,*
> *Which serves it in the office of a wall,*
> *Or as a moat, defensive to a house . . .*

and they never forgot that for nearly nine hundred years no invader had been able to hurdle that moat from east to west; why should it be any easier from west to east, the more especially since the coast to the east had been "elaborately fortified" and was defended by what they considered—*pace* the Red Army—"the finest soldiery in Europe"? Further, the British Chiefs were of the generation that had been grievously decimated on the Somme and at Passchendaele in the War of 1914–1918, that had essayed a landing at Gallipoli (one of Churchill's earlier and less well advised diversionary expeditions) only to be repulsed, leaving the sea "absolutely red with blood for a full fifty yards from the shore," and that had started off the present war with a defeat of which the climax was the remarkable evacuation from the beaches of Dunkerque. The Americans, having shared none of these bitter experiences, were still governed by a limitless optimism that must have seemed, at times, an insufferable arrogance.

All these subjective considerations combined, in one way or another, to shape the decision of July 22; but to Eisenhower, the professional soldier, excluded from the conference chamber, obliged to wait a few miles away for his eventual orders, the paramount consideration controlling the decision must have seemed a political one: the politicians, who for their own political reasons required what they supposed would be the easier, surer, swifter victory, had overruled their expert advisers and commanded that their armies make war far from the main theater of that war. And even when his training tells him the chosen course will cost time, treasure, and lives, the professional soldier must needs do the bidding of the politician.

In theory, every soldier has grasped this concept in his youth, at West Point or elsewhere; it is old stuff, not worth a second thought. In practice, the concept can give a thoughtful soldier pause to ponder. What may happen when the time comes to take his uniform off?

His illusions had been punctured, gloom had briefly enveloped him, but General Eisenhower was above all else a professional soldier with admirable resiliency. On that same Thursday morning he prepared for General Marshall a "Survey of Strategic Situation" in which he recommended, after hedging it about with several careful qualifications, the idea of GYMNAST "as a combined U.K.-U.S. operation" in the fall. Marshall himself had already glumly concluded that the North African expedition would be "the least harmful diversion." Churchill, who was for his part filled with "a great joy" by the prospect of the Mediterranean operation, now hastened to rechristen his darling. GYMNAST became TORCH, which was considered a more exhilarating monicker.

There remained the question of a commander for the venture, and this problem, like so many others arising from TORCH, was necessarily political. To sketch the background of the problem will entail a brief parenthesis.

The root of the political difficulty, or confusion, or mess, lay in the ambiguous character of France in 1942, and in the doubts entertained by the governments of the United States and the United Kingdom as to how France—or the French people, or the French army, navy, and air force, or the great dead weight of French fonctionnaires—would react to the sudden and uninvited arrival of large numbers of American and British troops, heavily armed and organized to shoot and kill. Such an advent is customarily considered an invasion, and the traditional response is to rise up and, if possible, fling back the invaders. Since the collapse of France in 1940, the British had thrice deemed it necessary to launch such armed attacks on their former allies: in July 1940 the British navy had destroyed or disabled the better part of a French naval squadron at Mers-el-Kebir in Algeria, killing more than one thousand French sailors in the process; two months later there had been a vain three-day attempt to capture Dakar in French West Africa; in June–July 1941 British troops had invaded and occupied Syria and Lebanon, killing or wounding more than six thousand French defenders. These three affairs had inspired the French Army and Navy with a bitter enmity for the British. In consequence the British were all but formally at war with the so-called government of France—the government headed by the aged Marshal Pétain—which had concluded an armistice in June 1940 with Hitler, which lay docile under his thumb, which cheerfully collaborated with the Nazis, which eagerly promulgated laws against the Jews, the trade unions, and all of its citizens who resisted the Nazi oppressor, which generously cooperated in dispatching French slave labor into German factories and concentration camps, and which, because its capital had been established in Vichy, a small city in central France celebrated for its mineral springs, had become internationally infamous as Vichy France. (The Nazis had occupied the larger, northern part of France, including Paris; they had left to the French the smaller, southern part, requiring of them that they make Vichy their capital.) Was this Pétain government the true France, or was it a puppet, existing only at the sufferance of Hitler? The British refused to recognize it. They had chosen instead to espouse the cause of the very junior and relatively obscure French general, Charles de Gaulle, who had managed on the morning of June 17, 1940, when the Republic of France was shuddering in its final humiliation, to leap aboard an airplane bound for London. Not many hours later he would be on the British radio, broadcasting his exhortation to the French people: "La France a perdu une bataille! Mais la France n'a pas perdu la guerre! . . . Vive la France!" In the next two years this haughty, intransigent figure would have infuriated most of his allies, antagonized many of his devoted followers, but nevertheless become the acknowledged leader of the Free French and the political leader of much of the French empire, at arms against the men of Vichy. The British had supported him with enormous subsidies, amounting, it was said, to as much as seventy million pounds sterling. He had personally commanded the futile attack on Dakar; his Free French had marched with the British against Syria. For this reason alone those officers of the French Army and

Navy who had vowed loyalty to Pétain despised de Gaulle even more than they did the British. Yet earlier, when Eisenhower had toiled in the War Department to organize supply lines to Australia and the Southwest Pacific, he had had occasion to rejoice that the commanders of French Oceania and New Caledonia had seen fit to shift their allegiance from Pétain to the Free French and de Gaulle.

The government of the United States, despite the impassioned complaints of an articulate segment of the American press, still recognized the men of Vichy as the de facto and de jure government of France and regarded de Gaulle with considerable mistrust, professing to suspect that he harbored visions of seizing autocratic power in postwar France. There was a sentimental aspect of American policy toward France: President Roosevelt thought of himself (and occasionally referred to himself) as the best friend the French ever had; from this amiable notion it was a very short step to the belief that Frenchmen held Americans in particularly fond esteem, and only another short step to the illusory hope that American soldiers would be warmly welcomed as liberators by the French military and naval officers in North Africa. This line of reasoning, while fatuous, was fuzzy and pleasant, permitting one to lave one's ego in equal parts of self-complacency and idealism; but there was also a less benign aspect to American policy, one that had to do with markets and commerce and profit, one to which the British and de Gaulle were alike sensitively attuned. The struggle over this aspect of American policy was disguised; it would seem before long to be a clash over personalities, with the Americans backing General Henri Giraud and the British sticking with de Gaulle. But in truth what was involved was power in the postwar world. To that end, as the British were aware, the chief American aim was to keep France weak and rudderless, lacking a strong central authority able to deal with the United States and Great Britain as an equal partner. Roosevelt was entirely persuaded that the French empire was "visibly withering on the vine," and he was to make it clear that he proposed to encourage American economic penetration wherever feasible in that tottery edifice.* For their part, the British were anxious to help the French

---

* Indeed, he had already done so. At his suggestion Robert Murphy, his personal representative in North Africa, had in February 1941 concluded an economic agreement with General Maxime Weygand, then Vichy's chief official in French Africa, by the terms of which all kinds of commodities—petroleum, cotton goods, coal, tea, sugar, tobacco—were dispatched from the United States to Algeria, Tunisia, and French Morocco. Both in the United States and in Great Britain this Murphy-Weygand accord was denounced as "appeasement"—a counterword that had even more fearsome an impact then than it has today—but, more important, the British viewed it as a breach of the blockade and were chary of the navicerts required to pass the blockade unchallenged.

The real value, at the time, of the Murphy-Weygand accord was that Vichy agreed

establish the strong central authority that could successfully confront the United States, particularly on colonial questions but also for the sake of constructing a strong bloc of postwar European nations that might vie economically with the United States. Simply stated, a strong France would favor British designs, a weak France would better suit the United States. De Gaulle likewise grasped, and was vexed by, President Roosevelt's evident intentions. He wrote later: "The United States, delighting in her resources, feeling that she no longer had within herself sufficient scope for her energies and wishing to help those who were in misery or bondage anywhere, yielded in her turn to that taste for intervention which concealed the instinct for domination. It was precisely this tendency that President Roosevelt espoused."

To snarl still further the political tangle that the commander of TORCH would be obliged to cope with, it should be noted that while Tunisia and Morocco were French protectorates, Algeria had by a legal fiction been incorporated into metropolitan France. The vast majority of the people of the region were pauperized Arabs, Berbers, and Negroes, most of them Muslims, but tribally divided beyond comprehension. There was also a small indigenous Jewish population, chiefly urban. The ruling class—wealthy African-born French landowners, called colons—had traditionally made certain of their power by fomenting among the Arabs a hatred of the Jews. Since the outbreak of war the population of the region had been swollen by an estimated two hundred thousand fugitives from Europe—a few very, very rich, but most very, very poor—of every nationality and every political passion from ultraviolet to infrared.

The region was, at best, a snake pit.

On Saturday, July 25, the British Chiefs met with General Marshall and Admiral King to select a commander for TORCH. Bearing in mind the predictable animosity of the French for the British, they all agreed that an American should be named the supreme commander and given a British deputy, and that the first waves of assault troops at each landing should be exclusively American. Since the command was to go to an American, in effect it was left to Marshall and King to name the man. That afternoon Marshall summoned Eisenhower to his suite at Claridges. When Eisenhower walked in, Marshall was in the bathroom, washing; the men talked through the bathroom door. Marshall told him that TORCH, née GYMNAST, was now definite, that he would be named supreme commander of the expedition, and that he would also serve as a deputy to the com-

---

to authorize a number of American observers to act as control officers and so make sure that none of these goods should be transshipped for use by the Axis. The so-called control officers swiftly became intelligence agents.

mander, yet to be named, of the eventual cross-Channel invasion. Eisenhower was to get right to work on the planning for TORCH, Marshall told him, without awaiting his formal orders.

The command would later be described as typical Eisenhower luck.

CHAPTER FIVE

Torch

LIEUTENANT GENERAL DWIGHT D. EISENHOWER knew next to nothing of the political complexities muddling TORCH and would give them next to none of his attention for several weeks. The politics of postwar power and the conjectural malignities of North Africa were both far down on the list of his priorities. First he had to forge an Anglo-American staff utterly without precedent in its unity of purpose and its refusal to engage in chauvinist squabbles. Next he had to lead that staff in the swift, smooth planning and preparation of an expedition which, as he well knew, few if any of his masters, the Combined Chiefs, wholeheartedly favored.

He had simply no time to fret over the politics of the operation or the underlying clash of national policies. All Allied planning had been suddenly, radically, wrenched out of shape. Instead of a concentrated assault over twenty or thirty miles of water against a limited and familiar target that had been microscopically analyzed, an armada must be hastily assembled and sent variously from the Clydeside and from the U.S. hundreds of miles across ocean water infested by packs of U-boats, and the troops landed on unfamiliar beaches to face they knew not what. (Allied intelligence estimated that French North Africa was guarded by perhaps as many as two hundred thousand troops, indifferently equipped, "not a first-class fighting force"; by an air force of five hundred airplanes; and by some powerful warships.) Instead of massed air power protecting beachheads from nearby airfields, there would be only one cramped air base, Gibraltar, which was too far removed for comfort and which lay exposed to Spanish spies and Spanish guns—or perhaps to German guns rushed south in cahoots with the Spanish. Instead of one short straight supply line to maintain the beachheads, there must now be two—one from Britain, the other from the U.S.—both long, both subject to constant attack, both requiring protective convoys of warships.

Worse, Eisenhower was for some time unable to determine precisely what ground, air, and naval strength was to be made available to him. On this score, the service most laggard was the United States Navy: one of its officers, sent to London to assist the planners, said bleakly, "We are here only to listen." How can one intelligently plan a complex military operation when one does not know precisely how many warships, aircraft, and assault troops are assigned to the mission?

Yet worse, the character of this complex operation was ill defined and, indeed, resisted definition. It was not an invasion; not, it was hoped, an armed assault upon an enemy; rather, it was a "liberation," to be conducted by one armed force against another, a "liberation" that might at any moment explode into a series of pitched battles and even, if enough men should be killed on either side, into a protracted war.

Yet still worse, since the Combined Chiefs of Staff were in general unhappy about TORCH and since they disagreed among themselves as to its ultimate purpose, they could not agree for several weeks even as to where Allied troops should be landed. The British urged assaults as far to the east as possible, as far as Bizerte and Tunis. The Americans, fearful that the Axis might entrap a vast Allied armada within the Mediterranean by slamming shut the Strait of Gibraltar, insisted on landings in the neighborhood of Casablanca on the Atlantic coast, so that at least the expedition's southern flank might be protected. Both Tunis and Casablanca could not be simultaneously "liberated"; there were not enough warships to support landings so far apart. Therefore the British opposed any effort toward Casablanca. An attempt at landing from the open Atlantic was mad, they argued; the long, deep swells of the ocean against the African coast made a violent surf that would surely founder any landing craft and drown the soldiers in them. In Washington, as late as August 19, General Marshall was dubious about a commitment to TORCH entirely. "Whether or not we should discuss this phase of the matter with General Eisenhower I do not know," Marshall confided to his staff, but he was quite sure that once American troops had been committed to TORCH, some of them were going to be landed outside the Mediterranean, near Casablanca.

Meanwhile, heedless of the military exigencies, President and prime minister were alike clamoring for landings as early as possible, certainly in October, preferably before October 15.

The result of all this for Eisenhower was a shambles that lasted six weeks, a time that sorely tested his patience and his good humor. Those six weeks, he said later, were "the most trying of my life." Not until August 14 did orders arrive appointing him commander in chief of TORCH, and although the officers in charge of planning the operation had for some time been at work under the direction of Brigadier General Alfred M. Gruenther, not until August 24 was the command structure for Torch officially approved by the Combined Chiefs and named Allied Force Headquarters (AFHQ).

The more the planners studied the unwholesome affair, the clearer it became that the Allies could not call upon a force strong enough to ensure the success of Torch on solely military grounds. The operation depended instead, as Eisenhower explained to Butcher, "entirely upon political factors—that is, upon the accuracy with which our political leaders could foresee the reactions of the French and Spanish armies in North Africa to this landing." On September 2 Eisenhower set down for the record his own opinion of Torch. It was that "the risks of the projected operation were so great as to condemn it if military factors alone were considered."

And still the Combined Chiefs disagreed, the British calling for landings at Oran and Algiers and farther east, the Americans insisting on landings only at Casablanca and Oran. The paperwork soared to impressive heights of complexity. Cablegrams were dispatched back and forth—between the British Chiefs and the American, between AFHQ and the War Department in Washington, between Churchill and Roosevelt—always without reaching agreement on a firm, sure policy.

Eisenhower's day became a grind: ten or twelve hours of appointments, conferences, dictation of cablegrams, study of reports, and briefings, spread among the Dorchester, Grosvenor Square, the War Office, and the prime minister's bomb shelter or residence. Tuesday luncheon with Churchill at Number 10 became a weekly function and Eisenhower grew used, as well, to the summons that might come at any hour of the night for another session of war-gaming with Churchill, perhaps in London, perhaps at Chequers, his frigid country residence. By his own choice Eisenhower was always on call, always concentrated on the tasks at hand, never relaxed. The suite at the Dorchester began to close in upon him. He was going stir crazy.

Obedient to Eisenhower's distress, Butcher canvassed the countryside outside London and, with the help of an experienced British billeting officer, hired a small house, the sort that might have been described by an agent as "Bijou rsdnce, cmftbl, 5 brs, 1 bth; pvt, 10 As, lwn, rose gdn, nr glf links, £8 wk." This was Telegraph Cottage—so called for obscure reasons by an earlier owner—a pleasant, unpretentious suburban villa hidden by fence and hedge, set in wooded grounds in Surrey, southwest of the city. Its advantages included an unlisted telephone (which was only an extension of the telephone in Eisenhower's office in Grosvenor Square), proximity to a golf course so that the general might occasionally slip out and play two or three holes in privacy, and the priceless opportunity to lounge at his ease, in old clothes, with nothing around to read except his beloved cheap western magazines. This place was his weekend hideaway, run by Mickey McKeogh and two Negro soldiers, John Moaney and John Hunt, who functioned as cook and waiter. Here he could play bridge with Clark, Beetle Smith, Butcher, Kay Summersby, and others. Here he could enjoy his creature comforts and briefly escape from his conviction that with TORCH, he was undertaking "something of a quite desperate nature" and "sailing a dangerous political sea . . . one in which military skill and ability can do little in charting a safe course."

At length, on September 3, President Roosevelt cabled Prime Minister Churchill to suggest a compromise: three simultaneous landings at Casablanca, Oran, and Algiers. After some minor modifications of the strength of the forces proposed for each assault, on September 5 the two statesmen and their military advisers reached a weary decision on the size and the targets of the landings—"Hurrah!" Roosevelt cabled to Churchill, who grimly responded, "O.K., full blast"—and it remained only to fix the date of the invasion, or "liberation." This decision was delegated to the commander in chief, Eisenhower.

On Tuesday, September 8, Eisenhower and Clark dined with Churchill at Number 10. The prime minister had that day reported to the House of Commons on his journey to Moscow to see Stalin, an awkward mission, since he had had to tell Stalin, even as the Nazi armies were cutting their way to the western bank of the Volga, that the Allies had determined not to attempt a cross-Channel invasion in 1942 but on the contrary would undertake landings in North Africa, far from the Nazi jugular. Stalin had appeared "very glum" as he listened to Churchill tell the tale, and later he had said "a great many disagreeable things" concerning what he quite naturally conceived to be his allies' promises to open a second front in Europe, promises now broken. For his part, Churchill had denied that any such promises had ever been made. He had drawn a picture of a crocodile and had explained "how it was our intention to attack the soft belly of the crocodile as we attacked his hard snout." Stalin, by Churchill's account, had been powerfully interested by this exposition of TORCH and had then said, "May God prosper this undertaking." Some of this story Eisenhower had heard before; now he listened to it again, for Churchill insisted on reading aloud most of the speech he had delivered that day to the Commons. But concern for TORCH at last pushed from Churchill's mind even his triumphant appearance before the House. By what date did the commander in chief reckon the landings could go forward? Eisenhower had been waiting for the question. "November 8," he said; "sixty days from today."

Churchill was disappointed; he had hoped to get things cracking more quickly. Contrariwise, Eisenhower's optimism that TORCH could be so swiftly put in gear touched no responsive chord among those officers who had the awesome responsibilities of outfitting, transporting, supplying, arming, feeding, tending, housing, nursing, burying, replacing, and retraining the scores of thousands of American troops aimed toward the North African beaches. One of Eisenhower's oldest and best friends, Colonel Everett Hughes, a senior officer assigned to cope with the logistical headaches provoked by TORCH, argued as early as September 14 that the monstrous problems of supply and administration could never be solved by November 8. Events proved him right, but the intractable demands of statecraft obliterated his warnings.

Gradually the plans took specific shape. The Western Task Force, assigned to attack Casablanca and other cities along the Atlantic coast, was to be exclusively American, would sail from American ports, and would be commanded by Major General George S. Patton. This dashing officer, who had assured Eisenhower some months before that "you are about my oldest friend," had been Eisenhower's first choice to command American armor in North Africa and one of his top choices to command all American troops in TORCH. The Center Task Force, objective Oran, was so organized that American troops would lead the assault with British troops in support; Eisenhower had selected Major General Russell P. (Scrappy) Hartle as its commander, but at Marshall's suggestion Hartle was later replaced by Major General Lloyd P. Fredendall. The Eastern Task Force, aimed against Algiers, would be led by the U.S. 34th Infantry Division commanded by Major General Charles W. (Doc) Ryder, a West Point classmate of Eisenhower's; once the force was established ashore, however, the British First Army under Lieutenant General Kenneth Anderson, a Scot, would assume responsibility for the advance on Tunis.*

By mid-September the time for supply of necessary equipment was past. The formula was: what was needed for the TORCH assault on November 8 must be sent forward for loading in cargo ships on September 26 and so must have been shipped from the United States to the United Kingdom no later than September 12.

* Anderson was the third British officer assigned to command the First Army. The first choice had been General Sir Harold Alexander, the second Lieutenant General Bernard Montgomery, but both these officers had been almost at once ordered to commands in the Middle East. To Eisenhower these sudden changes of his senior British commander, as through a revolving door, seemed still another intolerable grievance of this misbegotten operation. When Ismay informed him that Anderson was now his man, he snapped, "Are the British really taking TORCH seriously?"

The time had come when Eisenhower felt himself obliged to remind all the principal officers of the theater that they faced "a major crisis" and further that they should "impress this idea on all subordinates." Officers not coming up to standard must be relieved. "The time has passed for dilly-dallying," the commander in chief warned. "We must demand satisfactory performance." These admonitions, it must be admitted, are oddly lacking in fire. They seem less the clarion notes of a great captain rallying his officers for martial struggle than the pep talk of a district sales manager exhorting the boys to boost their sales record in a dull season. But this was ever General Eisenhower's way.

The time had also come to explore the murky politics of the land they proposed to "liberate." Eisenhower's guide and mentor as he peered into these ambiguities and perplexities was of course Robert Murphy, the foreign service officer who had for two years busied himself with mysterious, conspiratorial affairs throughout French North Africa, always acting as President Roosevelt's personal representative. Murphy's primary mission, aboveground and quite evident to the dozens of other operatives—Axis, Soviet, British, Vichy French, Gaullist, or uneasily neutral—who thronged the northern rim of the African continent, had been to reaffirm the historic, traditional, apodictic friendship of Americans for Frenchmen ("Lafayette, we are here") in such fashion that the Vichy French would be encouraged to refuse the Germans any access to African bases. He had also two nether, more furtive concerns: to identify the members of the French Resistance in North Africa and stitch them together into an underground organization that could help clear the way for any Allied landings that might be decided upon, and to find some Frenchman of irreproachable stature whom the United States might confidently back as a Resistance leader to rival de Gaulle.

The efforts to build an underground were duly reported to de Gaulle, who viewed them with a tolerant eye. To him, Murphy was "skillful and determined, long familiar with the smart world and apparently rather inclined to believe that France consisted of the people he dined with in town." In truth, the underground that Murphy had organized embraced men of the Right and of the Left, Jews and anti-Semites, idealistic young and cynical old, former Cagoulards (French fascists) and Communists, militarists, royalists, intellectuals—in brief, anyone who had decided, late or soon, that the Nazis should be trounced.

The search for a satisfactory rival to de Gaulle was harder. For some time Murphy had conducted a discreet flirtation with General Maxime Weygand, but that officer, despite President Roosevelt's high hopes, flatly rejected all overtures. Other possibilities were mooted in Washington. Then, in April 1942, General Henri Giraud, a soldier of good if somewhat faded repute, escaped from German imprisonment and surfaced a few days later in Vichy, where he amicably took lunch with Marshal Pétain. Murphy, operating through some of the less appetizing right-wing members of his North African underground, succeeded in opening pourparlers with Giraud as early as June. The quest was over. At last the United States had found the man to oppose to de Gaulle.

Murphy came to London to confer with Eisenhower in mid-September. His journey from Washington was so shrouded in secrecy as to seem ludicrous: he wore the uniform of a lieutenant colonel ("Nobody ever pays any attention to a lieutenant colonel," General Marshall had assured him); he carried no passport but had papers declaring him to be one Robert MacGowan; when at Prestwick an acquaintance hailed him, the unlucky man was at once arrested and rushed off, to be held incommunicado for seven weeks, or until the Allied armadas had landed the troops in North Africa. Murphy himself was flown to a military airport near London and then told to sit back out of sight during his journey by automobile to Telegraph Cottage. This entire hocus-pocus was staged in order to keep the plans for Torch secret from de Gaulle and the Free French, who had in any case known in a general way what was up before the end of July.

The elaborate subterfuges were the more curious since the Americans, and specifically General Eisenhower, had been forcefully instructed less than a week before that de Gaulle was without question the acknowledged leader of the French people, the French Resistance, and the entire French nation. The witnesses on his behalf could not be snubbed or doubted: they were the leaders of the most powerful Resistance groups within France, who had been smuggled out of France and brought to London to negotiate with representatives of the Office of Strategic Services the urgent question of military aid for the French underground. Should such assistance be funneled through de Gaulle's Free French? Certainly the Resistance leaders thought so. They estimated that fully 90 percent of the French population now supported de Gaulle; "all resistance movements within France have accepted de Gaulle as their leader"; and as for Giraud, they dismissed him as "a pure fascist," lumping him with Pétain, Laval, and the other leaders of the Vichy regime.

What did Eisenhower know of these conversations? He knew all he needed to know. He had been represented at the conferences by his chief of staff, Brigadier General John E. Dahlquist, who indeed approved an agreement between OSS and the French Resistance leaders calling for a regular supply of military equipment to the French fighters of the Resistance through de Gaulle's organization in London.*

* Dahlquist was Eisenhower's acting chief of staff until Beetle Smith arrived in London on Monday, September 7. The OSS conferences with the French Resistance

Nevertheless, when Eisenhower and Murphy gathered with staff officers and political advisers on the lawn behind Telegraph Cottage to talk North African politics, de Gaulle was by common consent ruled out of any participation in Torch, and the only French officers of high rank considered as possible confederates were General Giraud and Admiral Darlan. This was, however, not a political decision but an exclusively military one—insofar as political matters can ever be distinct from military ones. Above all else, Eisenhower desired that any opposition to the Anglo-American landings by the French armed forces be as brief and ineffectual as possible, and Murphy was able to convince him that only the intercession of a hero like Giraud would rally the salient commanders of French North African troops to his standard. (Darlan, who was commander in chief of all French armed forces, was likewise mentioned in this connection for the first time, but inconclusively.)

As to Giraud, events proved Murphy egregiously wrong, but his estimate of the ranking French officers in North Africa was reasonably sound. The military governors and most of the senior military officers and administrative officials in North Africa had been appointed by Vichy and were in accord with the ideas of Vichy; that is, they stood ready to collaborate with the Nazis, they despised de Gaulle, and they would recognize as a figure of authority only an officer congenial to Vichy. Moreover, the lower ranks of the French armed forces and of the French civil administration were—or, more accurately, were assumed by the Americans and the British to be—submissive to the forms of legality; it was supposed that they would obey the dictates of their superiors inasmuch as those superiors were in turn obedient to the dictates of the venerable Marshal Pétain, the proper documents having been properly stamped at each level of command. An American historian of these times has set it down that "the French as a people had a well-known 'complexe de légalité.'" Winston Churchill, in his speech to a secret session of the House of Commons on December 10, would remark "a peculiar form of French mentality . . . a highly legalistic habit of mind [which values] a direct, unbroken chain of lawful command." These sweeping generalizations, like all of their kind, were nonsense; but nonsense has many ways of creeping into national policy, and even becoming its foundation.

If, then, armed opposition to the Torch landings were to be summarily checked from within, the assumption was that it would require orders from Pétain or someone close to that ancient to check it. The only alternative would be an immaculate performance by Murphy's underground

leaders were held September 3–10. The military equipment promised the French underground seems never to have materialized.

organization, and such a recourse would involve pitting Frenchmen (many of them Gaullists, although Murphy never said so) against Frenchmen, in a brief, untidy civil war.

In short, the entire operation promised to be a mess.

As Murphy traced the complexities of French African factional politics, as he identified those officers who would welcome American troops and those who would contest their landings to the bitter end, as he assessed the size and capabilities of his underground force, as he warned that Giraud would ally himself with TORCH only if assured that command of the operation would be French, Eisenhower listened, he noticed, "with a kind of horrified intentness."

And yet Eisenhower reported to Marshall that he had been very favorably impressed with Murphy. The only urgent matters on which the two men could not reach agreement were that Murphy wanted more time for his underground agents to prepare for their tasks than Eisenhower would allow (they could not be told of TORCH until ninety-six hours before the landings, which seemed to Murphy "fantastically inadequate" advance notice); and Murphy wanted assurances for Giraud on the question of the TORCH command, but Eisenhower brushed this aside, saying only that the question of command must be postponed. Their failure to come to terms on these two matters would work serious mischief with both the commander in chief's reputation for good judgment and the swift success of his mission in North Africa, but at least Eisenhower had learned how little he knew of the land he was about to "liberate" and of its ways.

Next morning Murphy was flown west to Washington on his roundabout way back to North Africa, and Eisenhower could return to the more familiar routines of soldiering. He presided over conferences of planners, made his regular visits to the prime minister, exchanged cables with General Marshall in respect of Murphy's future status on his staff, drove into the countryside to inspect airfields, supply depots, and troop encampments. Early in October he took a full day off—his first since he had come to England—and spent it happily lounging, slouching, around Telegraph Cottage with Butch. He expressed the desire to buy a dog for his driver Kay Summersby, and since his own birthday was imminent his official family understood him to be pining for a dog of his own; out of this rich confusion there emerged, scrambling on wobbly legs, the Scottish terrier Telek, then a puppy six weeks old, whose name was a graceless combination of Telegraph Cottage. Though well advertised as Eisenhower's property, Telek was actually owned and tended by Mrs. Summersby.

Meanwhile, task force staffs were gathering, and American soldiers were thronging into England by the scores of thousands; from the first their presence was acutely noticeable. To Charles de Gaulle they seemed "good-natured, bad-mannered." To Evelyn Waugh they were "tall, slouching, friendly, woefully homesick young men" with faces "the color of putty." Harold Nicolson noticed how "they slouched, chewing gum," and to him it seemed they were "conscious of their inferiority in training, equipment, breeding, culture, experience and history." Englishmen less secure and less self-conscious were struck by the GIs' efficiency, by their smart uniforms, and "by the unending procession of American military equipment." (And everyone was aware of the litter of contraceptive devices the GIs everywhere left behind them.)

As the days wore on, in Grosvenor Square the commander in chief of all these young men seemed content with his business. By October 13—less than one month before the scheduled landings—General Eisenhower was satisfied that TORCH was moving "almost perfectly" ahead to the point of departure.

Still the "personal representative of the President" but soon to be the "Operating Executive Head of the Civil Affairs Section and Adviser for Civil Affairs under General Eisenhower," Murphy had arrived in French Morocco on October 11. He conferred in Casablanca with two or three leading members of his underground organization and, a day or two later, paid a call on the resident general of Morocco, Auguste Noguès, at his palatial headquarters in Rabat. Noguès, a five-star general who wore corsets under his tunic, was the man to reckon with in Morocco. In Murphy's view he was a "capable and intelligent officer and administrator" who could be "of incalculable assistance" if he chose to permit the Western Task Force to land unimpeded. He was also stubbornly devoted to Vichy, a virulent anti-Semite, and a warm friend of the Nazi officers attached to the German Armistice Commission in Morocco. His response to Murphy's circumspect suggestion that vast American armies might one day arrive on his shores was prompt and predictable. "Do not try that!" he snapped. "If you do, I will meet you with all the firepower I possess!"

Murphy regretfully withdrew. If Noguès were lost to the Allied cause, so also was Admiral François Michelier, commander of French naval forces in Morocco; and thus it seemed certain that Patton's Western Task Force would face a determined and ugly opposition. Yet Murphy had another small stack of chips to venture: General Marie-Émile Béthouart, the divisional commander at Casablanca, had pledged himself to support the American landings; that courageous officer now engaged to sequester Noguès, his commanding officer, and to hold him impotent until the Americans had secured the Atlantic ports and coastline.

Back in Algiers on October 16, Murphy plunged into excited discussions with his underground leaders. They could, he told them, expect far more than they had ever hoped for—intervention by a half-million men, two thousand airplanes, and scores of supporting warships, battleships, aircraft carriers; in brief, a major operation. (Eisenhower had authorized him to make these powerful promises.) Murphy had also been outfitted with an official rationale for the intervention, and this had come as a directive straight from the White House: "Information having been received from a reliable source that the Germans and Italians are planning an intervention in French North Africa, the United States contemplates sending at an early date a sufficient number of American troops to land in that area. . . . No change in the existing French civil administration is contemplated. . . . The proposed expedition will be American, under American command, and it will not include any of the forces of General de Gaulle." This directive, as Murphy later observed, "involved a certain amount of deception." In fact, there was scarcely a word of truth in it, and it included a gratuitous cuff at the Gaullists, many of whom would be charged with the most perilous tasks on the night of November 7/8.

To be sure, one no longer expects the verities to appear in a wartime announcement from official sources, and indeed Eisenhower had himself only a fortnight before acknowledged to a press conference that he would lie, cheat, or steal to vanquish his country's enemies. But as the day of TORCH drew closer, the American use of sophistries and deceptions to mislead their prospective allies the French got coarser, more impudent, and more likely later to entangle the Americans in their own web.

The chief difficulty arose because Murphy, on his return to Algiers, found himself confronted by two French officers, one representing General Giraud, the other representing Admiral Darlan, and each anxious for different reasons to get his principal mobilized under the forthcoming American banners. Did the Americans wish to enroll both these exalted officers? If so, how were their differences to be reconciled?

Giraud, through his agent General Charles Mast, chief of staff of the XIX Army Corps at Algiers, set a high price on his cooperation. He demanded that he alone be considered the leader of the French, urging that Darlan was at best untrustworthy and opportunist; that five officers from AFHQ, including one general officer, be secretly dispatched to confer with French officers at a designated place near Algiers, there to settle details of a military character; that the proposed operation be expanded to include the establishment of a beachhead in southern France; and that supreme unified command of the entire operation be his, with Eisenhower his subordinate.

Darlan, by reason of his high rank in the Vichy hierarchy, was at once invaluable and sinister as a potential recruit to the Allied cause. If he chose, as the commander in chief of the Vichy armed forces he presumably could issue orders that would ensure Allied occupation of their three objectives without a shot being fired. And yet, of the Vichy government, only Marshal Pétain himself and the contemptible Pierre Laval had more enthusiastically collaborated with the Nazis. Darlan had negotiated and signed the so-called Paris Protocols of May 1941, under the terms of which France would have given the Nazis an air base at Aleppo, assisted Nazi aviation in and over Syria, permitted the use of Syrian ports, roads, and railroads for Nazi transport, authorized the use of the Tunisian port of Bizerte and the railroad from Bizerte to Gabès by the Nazis against the British, and declared herself ready, in principle, to permit the use of Dakar as an air and supply base for Nazi warships and submarines. Thanks to the rapid intervention of the British and the Free French in Syria, and the determined opposition of Weygand in respect of Africa, the Paris Protocols never became operative; but a few months later Darlan had, as we have already seen (page 114), authorized shipments of aviation fuel, trucks, guns, and food in French freighters to Tunisia, to be used by Rommel's Afrika Korps against the British in Libya. In brief, Darlan's complicitous hands were red with the blood of British soldiers fallen in North Africa. Could such a man now be welcomed into Allied partnership?

The officer who represented Darlan, Admiral Raymond Fenard, indicated to Murphy that Darlan would cooperate fully, would even fetch the warships of the French navy from Toulon to Africa, if the Americans could and would supply him with abundant war matériel and economic assistance. That he would retain his rank of commander in chief of French forces was taken as granted.

What to do? Again and again the Allies had made clear they were not simply fighting a war against certain hostile and aggressive powers known as Germany, Italy, and Japan, but rather were launched on a crusade against an evil thing—Nazism, fascism—that had come into the world and must be crushed. Could the Allies in good conscience embrace Darlan, the sordid exemplar of what they were fighting? These considerations do not appear to have weighed much with Murphy. On October 16 he sent several long coded messages to the President and to General Marshall apprising them of the possibilities and recommending that the United States undertake to cooperate with Darlan. Admiral Leahy, acting for the President as his personal chief of staff, promptly cabled Murphy authorizing him to make any arrangement with Darlan that would smooth the way for TORCH. General Marshall sent Murphy's messages on to Eisenhower, adding his own comment that he was dubious of Darlan.

General Eisenhower reacted to Murphy's recommendations objectively, like a professional soldier. For others to dispute why the war was being fought; for him, as commander in chief of Torch, only to accomplish his mission at the least possible cost of human lives. He busied himself with devising a formula under which Giraud and Darlan might together work to help the Allies. On the morning of Saturday, October 17, he cabled to Marshall:

> . . . we are suggesting the following [formula] and will ask the British to comment: Initially, the Allied expedition to be commanded exactly as now contemplated. Giraud to be recognized as our principal collaborator on the French side, with the proposal that he accept the position immediately of French Governor of all French North Africa, responsible for all French civil and military affairs, and whose position will be supported and protected by the Allied Forces. Giraud to be requested to make proper contacts with Darlan and to accept him as Commander in Chief of French military and/or naval forces in North Africa or in some similar position that will be attractive to Darlan. . . .
>
> Obviously, if we should receive the extensive collaboration implied in [Murphy's] messages, the various American contingents can be concentrated . . . and prepared for . . . action much more rapidly than we have anticipated. An immediate solution . . . would be for me to organize an American Fifth Army and assign Clark as Commanding General. This would make it possible to designate either Giraud or Darlan as Deputy Allied Commander. . . .

Aside from his unfortunate choice of the word "collaborator," with all its dubious connotations (he used the word in one form or another five times in his first five hundred words), Eisenhower's memorandum compels other reflections.

Painfully obvious is that venerable brand of hardheaded, realistic, unprincipled mental behavior which is customarily epitomized by the phrase "The ends justify the means." Clearly Eisenhower was motivated in October, as he would be in November, exclusively by military considerations; whether he made a good bargain on this score can better be estimated when we come to the decisions of November and their inevitable repercussions.

It is quite as plain that when Eisenhower cabled Marshall, "I believe tentatively that, while we must decide as to which one of these two individuals [Giraud and Darlan] we should make our chief collaborator, we should at the same time attempt to secure the advantage accruing to us if both are absolutely honest in their proposals for assistance," he stood on the brink of a calamitous political blunder and stood, as well, in direct need of lucid, sagacious, prescient counsel, the sort of advice, one likes to believe, that would have been instantly forthcoming from the President of the United States or the prime minister of Great Britain, each of whom had for decades trafficked in the cunning treacheries of politics. Yet see what happened:

President Roosevelt, after authorizing Murphy through Admiral Leahy to make any arrangement with Darlan which in his judgment would help the military intervention, interfered in no way with Eisenhower's suggested formula.

Prime Minister Churchill presided over a conference at Number 10 Downing Street hastily assembled to hear from Eisenhower about the cables from Murphy and his proposed responses to them. Present were the foreign minister, Anthony Eden; Field Marshal Jan Christiaan Smuts, prime minister of South Africa, the officer commanding the Union Defence Forces, a Nestor much admired by Churchill for his wise judgment; Clement Attlee, the deputy prime minister; other members of the War Cabinet; and the British Chiefs of Staff. Churchill was "in full and complete accord" with Eisenhower's formula. More, he was gleeful. "This is great," he kept saying as Eisenhower read the cable he had sent to Marshall. Churchill and his advisers suggested only that the post of deputy allied commander not be offered to Giraud, on the grounds that "this would be incompatible with his position as military and civil governor general." Churchill further pronounced himself hugely happy with the plans Eisenhower had made for the secret mission of five officers from AFHQ—Clark was to be their leader—to meet with General Mast, Giraud's representative, near Algiers.

Clark's mission momentarily captured everyone's imagination. Was it a trap? Would he be captured by Vichy French police? How much of the British share of TORCH should he divulge to the French? Would the venture prove to be of any value to TORCH? But the question of Darlan's possible cooperation with AFHQ was still an urgent one. Clark was ordered to stress that TORCH, while necessarily involving the British, was under American control and command; he was not to reveal the date of the operation; he was not to mention Darlan. By airplane and submarine Clark and his party were taken to meet General Mast. Apparently that officer was fretted by the question of Darlan's participation, for on October 29, after Clark had returned to London and dined out for several nights on the strength of his adventure, Eisenhower reported to Marshall: "The opportunity that we had hoped for of getting Giraud and Darlan together . . . went glimmering, at least so far as General Mast is concerned. He believes that Darlan is not to be trusted and that Giraud will have nothing to do with Darlan."

But apart from the doubts earlier expressed by Marshall, no American or British chief or captain was yet on record as having the slightest qualm about the advisability of inviting Darlan's good offices.

By this time the troop transports had already begun to crawl across the Atlantic, east from America, north and west and south again from the Clydeside, pitching and wallowing, heavily guarded by convoys of warships, moving steadily toward their rendezvous near Casablanca, Oran, and Algiers. All was presumably cloaked in darkest secrecy.

Everyone in Europe whose business it was to know about such things knew about this vast troop movement, at least in a general way.

The Germans knew something of it, and so did the Italians; even the Japanese were aware of it. (The Germans, perhaps assuming that no soldier in his right mind would elect to land troops in North Africa, had sent a pack of submarines south to intercept landings at Dakar, or perhaps on the Canary Islands.) Vichy France knew about it but guessed wrong about the targets. Charles de Gaulle had been suspicious of it for some time and now withdrew into a lofty imperturbability, brooding over "the evil genius that inspired foreign powers to make use of [French] dissensions."

Darlan knew about it. One way and another he had pieced together a fairly accurate picture of what was about to happen. Earlier in October he had traveled through the French African territories, alert and wary, on what was called an inspection trip, and no doubt he had learned much from the reports of the talks Murphy had held with his agent, Admiral Fenard, and his son Alain, a naval officer on duty in Algiers. Nor, of course, should it be forgotten that Murphy, acting on his instructions from Admiral Leahy, was anxious to involve Darlan so as to minimize any armed resistance to the American landings. Early in November Darlan returned to Algiers. His son Alain had been stricken with poliomyelitis, which gave the turncoat admiral a sufficient excuse to turn up, but he needed no excuse. He knew he must be in Algiers, and why.

Only those French who had already risked their freedom and their fortunes to help the Allies with TORCH still knew next to nothing of what was imminent, for Murphy had been instructed by Eisenhower, for reasons of security, to keep the time and place of the landings secret even from the most important of his underground leaders. As late as October 27 Giraud, secluded in his villa near Lyon, still fancied that the Allies would intervene in southern France as well as in North Africa; he still imagined he would command this suppositious operation. In Algiers General Mast and in Casablanca General Béthouart likewise proceeded comfortably from day to day in the fond belief that the Allies planned no landings before the end of November at the earliest. Yet the Allies were counting on these three men to accomplish hazardous, crucially important tasks—in less than a fortnight.

There was worse to come. It is scarcely credible, but Murphy still assumed that TORCH would include landings at Tunis, a phase of the operation that had been canceled long before he had met with Eisenhower at Telegraph Cottage in mid-September. In consequence, some brave pro-Allied French conspirators in Tunis would soon find themselves in desperate case.

Murphy, as the American closest to this explosive situation, was easily the most apprehensive. On October 27 he besought of Eisenhower and was given permission to tell Mast that the expedition would arrive "early in November." Understandably, Mast was horrified: "he was distressed by American lack of confidence in their French allies, and by what he described as a form of political blackmail so far as he and his fellow conspirators were concerned." But there was nothing he could do about it, and before long Murphy had mollified him enough so that he would send word to Giraud of the abrupt change of plans.

Giraud's reply was categorical: he flatly declared that he would be unable to leave France before November 20.

No longer simply apprehensive, Murphy was now close to panic. The weeks of deception were taking their inevitable toll. Late on Sunday, November 1, Murphy dispatched a cable to Eisenhower urging that the expedition be delayed for two weeks: "I am convinced that the invasion of North Africa without favorable French High Command will be a catastrophe. The delay of two weeks, unpleasant as it may be, involving technical considerations of which I am ignorant, is insignificant compared with the result involving serious opposition of the French Army to our landing."

Eisenhower impatiently shrugged off this plea. It was, he said, "inconceivable," and he mentioned Murphy's "intimate knowledge of the operation and the present location of troops and convoys afloat." But the unfortunate Murphy, as he was at pains to point out later, had no such intimate knowledge: "Everybody assumed that somebody else had 'briefed' me thoroughly, but nobody had."

This particular patch of chaos might seem to suggest that politics and warfare are not always intimately intermingled; in fact, it demonstrates only how disheveled was AFHQ's control—i.e., Eisenhower's control—over the preliminaries to TORCH. Yet Eisenhower was supremely confident. He expected little opposition to the landings. "Everything for Torch is well in hand," he had assured Marshall on October 29.

Well in hand? Nobody in Murphy's underground organization in Africa, Murphy included, knew for certain what was going to happen, or when, or where; nevertheless, the first convoy of cargo ships and troop-ships had already swung eastward toward the Strait of Gibraltar.

Well in hand? In truth, there was a grave question whether Giraud, so far from engaging to lead a revived France against the Axis, would even leave his headquarters near Lyon to talk to his American allies. Murphy's messenger to Giraud, bearing his letter of ambiguous reassurance, was met by "an avalanche of reproaches." Giraud, like Mast, had been dismayed to learn that his schedule had been so precipitately advanced, and he would have none of it.

Well in hand? In Algiers, in the early afternoon of Monday, November 2, Murphy was under such tension that any physician measuring his blood pressure would have ordered the patient home for an extended period of bed rest. In fact, the man at Murphy's breakfast table that morning was Kenneth Pendar, one of the youngest and most inexperienced of the assistants imported to Africa as vice consuls ostensibly to check on the traffic of commodities under the Murphy-Weygand agreement. Pendar, easily perceiving Murphy's distraught manner, promptly catechized him, and learned in next to no time precisely what Murphy knew of where and when the American troops were to land early the following Sunday morning.*

Delayed by dirty weather, General Eisenhower and his staff flew to Gibraltar on Thursday, November 5, in a squadron of Flying Fortresses. There, with Eisenhower in command of that solid chunk of Empire, AFHQ was established. (Churchill sent him a message: "I feel that Rock of Gibraltar will be safe in your hands.") His chief concern was, of course, Giraud: how to get him to Algiers well ahead of H-hour—1 A.M. on Sunday, November 8? According to the fantasy proposed by Murphy and approved by Eisenhower, Giraud was to have been picked up in the Gulf of the Lion on Wednesday evening by a British submarine deceptively disguised as an American one and, after transfer to an airplane on Friday or Saturday, to have been taken to Algiers, where he would issue a ringing call to arms over the radio, after which the entire French North African army would close ranks behind him and join the Allies (under the supreme command of General Eisenhower) in pummeling the whey out of the Axis forces in Africa.

In fact, Giraud had finally elected to join in what he still presumed was

* And a good thing, too, that Pendar knew so early. The breach of security enabled him to alert the underground in French Morocco to what might be expected. In the event, the French commanders were still able to order opposition to Patton's landings and so were guilty of a wickedly needless loss of life, but this mischance was not Pendar's fault, and things would have been much worse snarled without his last-minute initiatives.

an American expedition. He still imagined he would command it. He still planned to shift the weight of its thrust against southern France. But he missed his Wednesday night tryst with the submarine and was not picked up until Thursday evening.

Time was getting scant. To deception Eisenhower now added presumption: he had Giraud's proclamation drafted for him. He planned to radio the text to the submarine, let Giraud approve it, and then have copies of it printed and dropped from airplanes over Morocco and Algeria. He drafted a letter to be handed to Giraud saying that he, Eisenhower, had been detained in London by bad weather, and urging Giraud to proceed at once to Algiers and read his proclamation over the radio. In this way, he told the Combined Chiefs, he hoped "to prevent interminable conference here [at Gibraltar] revolving around inconsequential details." Such inconsequential details as command of the Allied forces soon to be landing on French soil—a detail that had been pushed aside since mid-September but could no longer be ignored.

Friday dragged by, Friday night, Saturday morning, and still no word from Giraud. Was he aboard the submarine? Had it perhaps been sunk? No word; only frenzied cables from Murphy that showed, Eisenhower observed, "that he has a case of jitters." One cable demanded a landing in southern France by fifty thousand troops, together with diversionary attacks in Norway and western France; another predicted calamity for TORCH if Giraud were not in Algiers by Friday night.

During luncheon on Saturday a garbled radio message was received suggesting that perhaps Giraud had been transferred from submarine to flying boat. Eisenhower concluded he had better pay a visit to the tribes of monkeys that gambol atop the Rock and are reputed to bring good luck. He and Butcher were driven to their scampering grounds. Eisenhower patted one of the monkeys on the head. Regrettably, Butcher had no camera with him to record the event.

Back in his office at headquarters, one of several small rooms hewn off a long tunnel that was carved nearly a mile into the solid rock, Eisenhower presently learned that Giraud had indeed arrived and was demanding to see him personally. The deceitful letter was tossed aside. Giraud was at once invited to sit down in conference.

Thus the two soldiers met at last, in the worst possible atmosphere—one of suspicion, mutual irritation, ignorance of each other's aims, urgency, and haste—American and Frenchman in a British fortress, to talk at cross-purposes through interpreters about matters that should have been settled weeks before.

In about eight hours the invasion, or "liberation," was scheduled to begin. Some six of those eight hours Eisenhower spent in sterile argument with Giraud. Mark Clark was on hand to support Eisenhower's arguments, but to say that he was helpful would be imprecise. The Americans were wholly sensitive to the fact that Giraud had been for some time elaborating with other French officers a strategic plan to be used against the Germans; they ignored the duplicity of the letter Murphy had sent Giraud only a week before; they underestimated the significance to Giraud of the fact that they were about to invade French soil. To them Giraud was only a tool, pure and simple; pure, they hoped, and simple, they were quite sure.

Poor Giraud: he was among the first to face the impatient legions of the Pax Americana, and he had never been briefed as to how to act.

Since Giraud would not willingly and gladly offer to become their tool, Eisenhower and Clark grew angry. Clark completely lost his temper. At one point, addressing the interpreter, he said coldly: "We would like for the honorable general to know that the time of his usefulness to the Americans and for the restoration of the glory that once was France is *now*. We do not need you after tonight." At the end of the long unfriendly conference of allies, Clark instructed his aide to note in his diary that his last remark (through the interpreter) to Giraud had been: "Old gentleman, I hope you know that from now on your ass is out in the snow."

Eisenhower was more civil, but even his warm charm shone pale and ineffectual on Giraud's icy reserve. Yet the French soldier never lost his temper. In private, Eisenhower stormed about "these Frogs" and complained that Giraud (a five-star general) had even pulled rank on him. In a letter to Beetle Smith he exclaimed, "Can you beat it?" To the Combined Chiefs, Eisenhower reported just before midnight, just before H-hour, that Giraud "refused to issue any statement that could be broadcast tonight," that "there was no possibility of his guaranteeing nonresistance in our attacks tonight," and that he "would not make any attempt to do so."

At length, after having been insulted for the last time, Giraud stated "that he would be a spectator in the affair. He would not . . . interfere with our plans . . . but would not . . . take part in them and would not . . . authorize the use of his name in any way in connection therewith." Giraud insisted that word to this effect be cabled to General Mast in Algiers, so that any proclamation to be issued by the Allies over his name might be withdrawn. Eisenhower agreed. He hand-printed the message to Algiers himself. Giraud signed it. Butcher noted in Eisenhower's diary the commander in chief's ultimate deception: "Transmission [of the cable to Algiers] may be somewhat slow—perhaps publication [of the proclamations] will have already occurred."

CHAPTER SIX

Collaboration

EVENTS NOW MOVED toward an accommodation with Darlan.

In his cave dug deep inside Gibraltar, in the fetid gloom, where the walls were damp and the stone overhead dripped monotonously, General Eisenhower sat, outwardly relaxed, apparently quite controlled, awaiting messages over an inadequate signals system for word, any word, of how his three task forces were faring. Clark was near at hand, and Butcher, and the rest of the skeleton staff, all moving restlessly about, occasionally sipping spirits or twiddling the dials of shortwave radio amplifiers, anxiously waiting, their imaginations far away, seeking to conjure up starlit beaches most of them had never seen.

Messages were few, and those few trickled in late. Even the radio broadcasts addressed to North Africa—the messages in French from President Roosevelt and (his words spoken by another officer) from General Eisenhower, designed to reassure the French about what was to happen on their soil—were late in getting on the air. As always happens in a great sprawling enterprise like a war, time was passed in boredom, waiting.

How obstinately would the French oppose the landings, and for how long? It was clear that General Giraud's overrated leadership was worthless; much therefore depended on the energy and skill of Murphy's underground organization. But even these amateur combatants were soon to find that AFHQ (i.e., General Eisenhower) held them so cheap that orders had long since been given that would frustrate the most stouthearted Resistance.

To the south and east, across the sea in Algiers, the conspirators had gathered after dinner on Saturday night in the large apartment of Dr. Henri Aboulker, an elderly Jewish physician and professor of medicine on the faculty of the university. The apartment was centrally located on the main street of the city; its rooms had gradually filled with resolute young men who had for months been preparing for the insurrection they would launch on this night.* They were armed with an absurd collection of weapons scrounged from all sorts of dubious sources; "inadequate weapons," Murphy would later recall, adding, "their military capabilities were largely symbolic." They had been promised proper arms by the OSS and by the British SOE (Special Operations Executive); messages had come from Gibraltar assuring delivery of modern weapons, and night after night chosen Frenchmen had kept the rendezvous at the appointed lonely beaches only to be disappointed. "Evidently the American command [viz., General Eisenhower] felt that there was a risk that . . . the arms might be used against [American] forces." In short, AFHQ suffered from a fatal surfeit of security, one that would cost lives at sea, on beach, and on land.

In a bathroom off one of the bedrooms of Dr. Aboulker's apartment had been established a clandestine shortwave radio. Over this apparatus, shortly before midnight, came the coded message from London: "Allo, Robert; Franklin arrive." Murphy, listening, estimated the time left before H-hour: seventy-five—perhaps one hundred—minutes and the Americans would be riding up to the beaches in their landing craft. He turned and gave orders. Most of the young Frenchmen hitched their belts, clattered downstairs to the Rue Michelet, and slipped away to seize the most critical points of the city—telephone exchange, power station, police headquarters, and the like. A few minutes later others left, along with three American vice consuls, for the designated beaches to serve as guides for the landing troops. All went smoothly.

Murphy, accompanied by Vice Consul Pendar, now removed to an apartment nearby, where were gathered a few of the more respectable conspirators—military officers, industrialists; the right-wing leaders of Murphy's carefully compartmentalized underground—and here he joined Lieutenant Colonel Chrétien, who was head of G–2 (Intelligence) for General Alphonse Juin, commander in chief of all army and air forces in French North Africa. Escorted by Chrétien and followed in another automobile (in case anything should go amiss) by Pendar, Murphy drove up to the heights overlooking Algiers, to the suburb of El-Biar, to Les Oliviers, the big yellow palace where Juin lived, quite close to Fort L'Empereur, the military citadel that dominated the city.

Juin was roused from sleep and informed that an American expedition-

* These men were civilians of every conceivable occupation—even a couturier, a professor of philosophy, a jeweler—the shock troops, as it were, of the anti-Nazi Resistance. Some were drawn from the Chantier de la Jeunesse (youth camps organized by the Vichy government), of which the commissioner, Colonel Vanhecke, was a Gaullist. Most were Jews. One careful American reporter, A. J. Liebling of the *New Yorker,* was told a few weeks later that of the 540 young men involved in the Algiers uprising on the night of November 7/8, 450 were Jews.

ary force of half a million men was about to land all along the coasts of French North Africa. He expressed his vexation that he had not earlier been told of American plans, observed that if the matter were in his hands there would be no French opposition, but pointed out that Admiral Darlan, as his superior officer, could at once countermand his orders.

"Very well," said Murphy, promptly; "let us talk to Darlan."

Darlan was fetched by Pendar, arriving in less than twenty minutes, and as he entered the building it was silently surrounded by some three dozen armed men of the Resistance. The telephone wires leading into the palace were cut. Although he was not yet aware of it, Darlan was a prisoner. Elsewhere throughout the city the young Frenchmen of the Resistance had been equally efficient: post office, radio station, telegraph station, prefecture of police—every key point had been skillfully overcome. From the clandestine radio word went to the armada offshore informing the Eastern Task Force that their path was clear. (But the armada, observing radio silence, made no reply.)

Inside Les Oliviers, Darlan was in turn told of the imminent invasion. By Murphy's account, Darlan turned purple, exclaiming, "I have known for a long time that the British are stupid, but I always believed Americans were more intelligent. Apparently you have the same genius as the British for making massive blunders."

This charge was unfair, at least at the time it was made. To be sure, there had already been blunders, but the first truly massive one Darlan would not be able to appreciate for several hours, and even then, if blunder it was, it was British. What happened was that the Eastern Task Force was landed several miles away from the prearranged stations where the guides waited.* If this came about because of a miscalculation by the British navigators, it was inexcusable; if, on the other hand, it was no error but a deliberate betrayal of the French underground by AFHQ (i.e., by General Eisenhower) it was tragic folly, based on scandalous intelligence work by AFHQ G–2.

"It was impossible," Murphy noted later, "for the small group of badly armed young men to hold the city indefinitely." The first American troops did not reach Algiers until late Sunday morning, and did not arrive in

* Murphy says, "Ryder's troops [34th Division, U.S. Army] landed on a beach four miles distant." Pendar, whose account of the affair is generally more circumstantial if less exalted than Murphy's, says, "Later we were told that the transports had missed the landing spots near Algiers and hit some 25 to 30 kilometers [15.5 to 18.6 miles] away." Both men quote Royal Navy spokesmen as explaining "that an error of navigation occurred in the darkness." Both men suggest that the error was deliberate: "to guard against possible treachery in the French underground," says Murphy; because "British and American authorities . . . simply did not trust [the French underground] not to betray the exact point of the landings," says Pendar.

force until late Sunday afternoon. The delay was fatal for the men of the Resistance. By sunrise they had been routed from most of their key positions; some had been killed, some arrested, some driven into hiding. The city, the military barracks, Fort L'Empereur—all that the underground had hoped to turn over to their "liberators" without a shot being fired— were now alert and bristling with Vichy-inspired rancors: Vichy's military police were vengefully ranging the city, Vichy airplanes were off the ground, Vichy naval batteries were shelling a troopship loaded with American soldiers that had forced entry into the port. The needless, useless battle was raging.

Meanwhile, through the long watches of the night, Murphy, already exhausted beyond endurance, had been in parley with Darlan, urging him to turn his coat forthwith and accept the Allies as liberators. Murphy acknowledged the British share of the invasion, although he realized that Darlan most particularly detested the British. He further acknowledged that Giraud was the United States candidate for leader of a revitalized France. (At this, Darlan had gestured impatiently. "He is not your man," he had said, "for politically he is a child. He is a good divisional commander, nothing more.") As they talked, Darlan had perceptibly relaxed and, in Murphy's view, had begun to consider the possibilities offered by this abrupt if not unexpected development. As they talked further, the wheel of fortune suddenly whirled about: the young men of the underground who had been holding Darlan prisoner were themselves overwhelmed by a well-armed detachment of gardes mobiles, and all at once Darlan and Juin were free whereas Murphy and Pendar were seized, hustled into a porter's lodge, offered the cigarette that traditionally precedes summary execution, and stripped of their papers by angry police who jabbed them about with submachine guns. Juin arrived to rescue them. Pendar was released, but Murphy was obliged to remain in custody at Les Oliviers. It was then anywhere from two to four hours after the time American troops had been scheduled to arrive on the scene.

Darlan was free: free to proceed to Fort L'Empereur, to study the messages from Oran and Casablanca that testified to the scope of the Allied expedition, to telephone to the other Vichyite commanders scattered throughout French North Africa, to weigh the advantages of switching his allegiance. By midafternoon he was approaching a decision. General Juin, angered by the needless bombing, shelling, and strafing, pushed him to a final resolution. The little admiral returned to Les Oliviers at about 3 P.M. and asked Murphy to find the commanding general of the Eastern Task Force for the purpose of arranging an immediate cease-fire in and around Algiers. Another couple of hours and Murphy had located General Ryder and was accompanying him back to Fort L'Empereur (they arrived just as the American artillery was drawing a bead on the fort). There ensued a brief conference among Murphy, Ryder, Darlan, and Juin. Ryder was concerned as to whether he should accept a cease-fire from Darlan and insisted on authorization from Eisenhower. The message of approval was radioed from Gibraltar, and not long after the sun had set the shooting was finally stopped.

And Darlan, as the officer who had empowered the cease-fire, was now unmistakably the principal French personage, the man with whom General Eisenhower would be obliged to treat.

To General Eisenhower in his cave in the Rock, the news of Darlan's interposition signified nothing much, for he was still elated by the arrangement he had managed to work out with Giraud. That officer had at last agreed to fly to Algiers, do all he could to end French opposition, and start to rally French forces to battle against the Axis. This arrangement was, Eisenhower considered, a solid achievement, no matter how belated, and Giraud's airplane was scarcely on its way to Algiers before he had issued an incautiously sanguine statement:

> General Henri Giraud has arrived in Algiers from France. It can be expected that his presence there will bring about a cessation of scattered resistance. . . . General Giraud has assumed the leadership of the French movement. . . . The Allied Commander-in-Chief has agreed to support General Giraud in this theater with the strong forces under his command. . . .

General de Gaulle? And the Fighting French? They were not mentioned.

Eisenhower likewise dispatched his deputy commander in chief Mark Clark to Algiers in a separate airplane to interview Darlan and work out some sort of agreement with him. Belatedly he began to have second thoughts. Would the two Frenchmen cooperate? "Giraud hates and distrusts Darlan," he lamented to Beetle Smith, who was still in London, "while Darlan's message to me, via Ryder, says, 'I will *not* meet with any Frenchman.'" Eisenhower knew this meant "To hell with Giraud." His political problems, then, were undiminished. It was a relief to turn to a study of the landings.

Algiers. The city was quiet and controlled by the Allies. No details were yet at hand, but before long it would be clear that the success was due rather less to Darlan's acquiescence in a cease-fire than to the fact that General Mast, in command of the Algiers division, and General de Monsabert, in command of the Blida subdivision, had ordered several regiments south for maneuvers a few days before the landings. The principal airfields—Blida to the south and Maison Blanche to the east—had been seized and held secure for the Allies.

Oran. A brisk battle was in train, with most of the opposition coming from Vichy French warships and Vichy French onshore naval batteries. Whatever orders Darlan may have sent to the Oranais had been ignored. "The Frogs," Eisenhower observed, "seem to have some good tanks or armored cars in that area." The city and its harbors would not be surrendered until Tuesday midday. General Fredendall's Center Task Force "was the only one which could subsequently claim to have won a decision wholly by force of arms."

Casablanca. Allied hopes had been high that hereabouts and all along the Atlantic coast of Morocco the opposition would be minimal. David King, one of Murphy's vice consuls, had reported on November 5: "French General Staff at Casablanca entirely in agreement with [TORCH] operation, and are preparing landing between Safi and Port Lyautey. They propose landing north and south of Casablanca and auxiliary landing at Safi. There would be no resistance."

Sure enough, General Béthouart had gathered some chosen officers at his headquarters on Saturday night and had informed them the Americans would be landing at 5 A.M. the next morning. By 2 A.M. these officers had ordered soldiers to Rabat, the capital, to seize the headquarters and also the telephone exchanges of the general staff and the post office. A company of colonial infantry surrounded the residency of the relaxed and uncorseted General Noguès, the telephone lines were cut, and Béthouart's aide-de-camp Captain de Verthamon was sent to invite Noguès to join in liberating France. De Verthamon was, as it happened, Noguès's nephew, but that did not save him. Unknown to the conspirators, Noguès had a private telephone wire, and using the excuse that he wished to get dressed, he retired to his bedroom, picked up his hidden telephone, and was soon in touch with Admiral François Michelier, a diehard advocate of Vichy collaboration, and General Erich von Wulisch, commander of the Nazi Armistice Commission. Within a very few minutes French defenses all along the coast had been alerted; another few minutes and General Béthouart, together with Colonel Magnan, Captain de Verthamon, and a number of other officers, had been arrested, charged with treason, and ordered held for trial by court-martial.

Before long the fighting on the western beaches was fierce, and hundreds of French and American soldiers were dead.

"I am so impatient to get eastward and seize the ground in the Tunisian area," Eisenhower wrote to General Marshall on the afternoon of Monday, November 9, "that I find myself getting absolutely furious with these stupid Frogs."

The Allied commander in chief was learning that for him as for the least of his followers, much of the time was spent in waiting. Eisenhower used a good bit of that time in thinking of himself as a man who would leave his mark on the pages of history, and in modest efforts aimed at creating a properly laundered image of himself as commander for the assistance of the historians and biographers who would before long be assessing his record. He jotted down memoranda, entitled them "Worries of a Commander" or "Inconsequential thoughts of a commander . . ." and handed them to Butcher to be included in his diary. He also held a couple of press conferences with the one British and three American correspondents who were with him at Gibraltar, for, as he told Marshall, "I am keenly sensible of [the] importance [of public relations]." He dwelt on the military aspects of the operation. One journalist wanted to know how exactly Admiral Darlan fitted into the picture. The question was brushed off. Politics, said General Eisenhower, have "no place at present in the important military developments."

Meanwhile, in Algiers, the deputy commander in chief, the ineffable Mark Clark, was over his handsome head in politics.

Clark proposed to guide events in Algiers, or else to control them, or else, by God, to dictate them. His policy was: "Who is in power and who will be in power will be decided by the Allied forces," and he announced it in firm, loud tones. Behind him, Eisenhower gave every ounce of support he could. Their justification, then and later, was that of military expediency: We are fighting a war, everything for the war effort, it is a desperate venture, we have no choice; we are the commanders in the field, and we know best. Clark's method of conducting a negotiation was to gather the principal French fascists in a room, pound his fist on the table, and liberally sprinkle his orders with profanities and obscenities. These bulldozer tactics would have been unexceptionable if his ultimate purpose had been to arrest them, jail them, and leave them to be dealt with according to the processes of French jurisprudence, but Clark was seeking their cooperation. He wanted them to order an immediate cease-fire in Morocco and see that it stuck. Further, the Americans supposed (and so did several British officials) that these French fascists would and could persuade Admiral Jean Estéva, the governor general of Tunisia, to resist the Nazis, and would and could persuade Admiral Jean de la Borde to order the French fleet from Toulon to French Africa. These men of Vichy were top-drawer Frenchmen, the embodiment of the Vichy establishment.

In Murphy's view they were the men to administer the country, and Clark agreed, and so, back in Gibraltar, did Eisenhower.

By Thursday, November 12, most of the fighting around Casablanca having at last been stopped, Clark radioed Eisenhower that his plan was to put Darlan in charge of French North African political affairs, to name Giraud the commander of a volunteer French army to be equipped by the Allies, and to retain Noguès as resident general in Morocco and Yves Chatel as governor general of Algeria. Eisenhower responded that the plan was a good one and that he approved Clark's idea of "a public announcement about the consolidation of interests." Eisenhower deplored the way "these Frenchmen . . . are jockeying for personal power." He considered briefly, then added to the radio he was dictating to Clark: "Give them some money if it will help."*

What last reluctance the French fascists in North Africa may have fancied they had to an agreement with the Allies was overcome when Nazi armored troops, in violation of the armistice of 1940, abruptly rumbled over the line of demarcation into that part of France which had not before been occupied. This event, so long dreaded, permitted the fiction that Marshal Pétain was suddenly become a prisoner of the Nazis and that Darlan, as the only political heir available who was privy to the marshal's secret thoughts, might rightfully rule in his stead. Darlan's first proclamation was broadcast by the Algiers radio: "Every governor or resident . . . is to take care of the administration of his territory according to the laws in force, as in the past. Frenchmen and Muslims, I rely on your complete discipline. Everybody at his post. Long live the marshal! Long live France!"

The Vichy status quo had been assured, grace to the Allied armies of "liberation."

Pursuant to Eisenhower's advice, General Clark, newly invested with his third star by special request of the commander in chief, called a press conference at the Hotel St. Georges in Algiers. He was rarely disposed to mute his achievements, and on this occasion he had reason to be quite pleased, for he had in fact concluded an agreement with a pack of exceedingly slippery characters about whom none of his superiors, civilian

* In connection with this mercenary proposal, it is refreshing to turn to something General de Gaulle later revealed he had said, on the same subject and at about the same time, to Churchill and Eden: "You invoke strategic reasons [to justify the use of Darlan], but it is a strategic error to place oneself in a situation contradictory to the moral character of this war. We are no longer in the eighteenth century when Frederick the Great paid the courtiers of Vienna in order to be able to take Silesia, nor in the Italian Renaissance when one hired the myrmidons of Milan or the mercenaries of Florence. In any case we do not put them at the head of a liberated people afterwards. Today we make war with our own blood and souls and the suffering of nations."

or military, had yet offered a word of warning. Happily he expatiated on his negotiations, proudly he announced that Admiral Jean Darlan, late of Vichy, was now charged by the Allies with the administration of all internal affairs in French North Africa.

When the correspondents began to put their questions, Clark was quick to sense danger ahead. "We are being realistic," he said. He spoke of bases and lines of communication. The profound conflict between those who had collaborated with fascism and those who had resisted it he dismissed as "a political squabble." "All of you must understand," he said, "that Admiral Darlan was the one man in power here who controlled the land, sea, and air forces. . . . Whatever you may think of him, he was the only man who could issue the proper order to bring all factions together. He was the only man the armed forces would obey, and I had to play along with him."

"The only man who could . . . bring all factions together." In truth, few men could have been found who would more violently sunder those factions.

Word of the so-called Darlan deal went out from Algiers, but the immediate impact of it was felt at Gibraltar.

Eisenhower now found himself in a most peculiar position. Ostensibly he was in jeopardy. Under attack for his want of judgment, for maintaining in power a fascist, a collaborationist, a turncoat, a man despised by the Allies and even more by the French, it could be reasonably assumed (and was assumed, even by such perspicacious and knowledgeable observers as Robert Sherwood) that he was in danger of being relieved of his command. Eisenhower himself, writing later of this episode, would say: "If . . . political repercussions became so serious as to call for a sacrifice, logic and tradition demanded that the man in the field should take complete responsibility for the matter, with his later relief from command becoming the symbol of correction. I might be fired." But at the time Eisenhower never worried. In point of fact, his position was as unassailable as any professional soldier's can ever be in a democracy; and the longer he kept his mouth shut and tended strictly to his business, the more secure he would be and the more gratefully honored by his commander in chief in the White House. For as Eisenhower knew well, any error in assessing public disgust and dismay over the Darlan affair had to be scored against Roosevelt and Churchill, both of whom, as we have seen, had approved the formula of October 17, which had envisaged making either Darlan or Giraud "our chief collaborator." Since the time when Eisenhower had made that recommendation, nearly four weeks had passed without any note of caution having been sounded by either President or prime minister; Eisenhower could have assumed only that Clark's plan for clinching the cooperation of the Vichy fascists in administering North and West Africa was beyond cavil. Later Eisenhower would write, "I well knew that any dealing with a Vichyite would create great revulsion," but if he entertained any such notion prior to November 12, 1942, he kept it well concealed. Even his faithful diarist Butcher neglects to note any Eisenhoverian distaste for dealing with Darlan before that date.

The public outrage over the deal was, of course, so intense that Eisenhower recognized he must go at once to Algiers to confer with Clark and Murphy and to be forthrightly visible in the line of fire. It was a triumphant gesture, and one that cost him nothing. Once again his public manner was his surest strength. To an admiring observer, "He was a living dynamo of energy, good humor, amazing memory for details, and amazing courage for the future." In short, he was a hero. Genial, relaxed, confident as a sure-thing gambler, he put his stamp of approval on the Darlan deal, warned Clark to refrain from any further press conferences, smiled, shook hands all around, and swept Murphy into his airplane to fly back to Gibraltar and help draft the explanatory message to London and Washington.

This remarkable document was an essay in self-justification, running to about twelve hundred words, repetitious, loosely reasoned, false in its premises and misleading in the evidence adduced to support it. It was quite clear that Eisenhower had, rather late in the day, begun to appreciate how monstrous had been his (and the President's and the prime minister's) political blunder. Yet he chose not to correct it, but rather to defend it.

Eisenhower's estimate of the politics of French North Africa—and that of his advisers—was prejudiced by their readiness to deal gladly with the fascist rulers of Algeria and Morocco. (Murphy customarily chose to operate at the top level, and Eisenhower too found that procedure congenial.) Because a few Vichyite officers held certain beliefs, Murphy and Eisenhower concluded, in the face of contrary evidence, that so also did all the armed forces; because the fascist upper crust venerated Marshal Pétain, the Americans assumed that so also did the entire populace. Thus Eisenhower would say in his message to the Combined Chiefs: "Everyone from highest to lowest attempts to create the impression that he lives and acts under the shadow of the marshal's figure," a statement effectively refuted by the hundreds of North African patriots who had joined the underground Resistance to overthrow the marshal, and the thousands who supported that Resistance. A handful of Vichyite generals, admirals, and governors general protested that they would obey only Darlan, and this was transformed by Eisenhower to: "All concerned profess themselves to be ready to go along with us provided Darlan tells them to do so," and in evidence Eisenhower offered: "Admiral Estéva in Tunis says he will obey Darlan, while Noguès stopped fighting in Morocco by Darlan's order." Yet in fact Estéva persistently refused to obey Darlan, and as for Noguès, it is by no means certain that his decision to seek a cease-fire in Morocco came in response to any order from Darlan. On November 10, when Darlan issued his order for a general cease-fire, Marshal Pétain countermanded the order from Vichy and named Noguès to replace Darlan as commander in chief in North Africa. On the next day Noguès reported to Vichy, "I have lost all our fighting ships and aircraft after three days of violent combat," and only then did he send an officer to General Patton's headquarters to sue for peace. (He also helped General von Wulisch and most of the German Armistice Commission escape across the border into Spanish Morocco.)

This Noguès was, at least as Eisenhower depicted him in his radiogram, a figure of chilling menace, for he was reputed to exercise an uncanny control over those whom Eisenhower darkly alluded to as "the tribes." AFHQ knew little about "the tribes"; for all that was known of them they might have been like those encountered by another professional soldier, himself a Moor—"The Anthropophagi, and men whose heads / Do grow beneath their shoulders"—and because they were little known, "the tribes" were much feared. "In Morocco alone General Patton calculates that it would require 60,000 Allied troops to hold the tribes quiet," Eisenhower warned the Combined Chiefs, and added that trouble could be expected "particularly if Noguès, who will obey no one but Darlan, chooses to influence tribes."

But what seemed an elegant demonstration of the need for dumping Noguès forthwith was merely a plea for approval of Darlan's appointment.

As for Darlan's alleged duplicity, Eisenhower envisaged no difficulty. "The Kingpin [code name for Giraud] is honest and will watch Darlan," Eisenhower noted. In a wonderfully maladroit phrase, he added that Murphy, "who has done a grand job, will . . . practically live in Darlan's pocket," which was of course precisely what had most alarmed the critics of the Darlan deal.

To cap the fatuity of his radiogram, Eisenhower gravely reported: ". . . you may assure any of the Free French to whom it is necessary to impart this information that the Kingpin [Giraud] is an enthusiastic participant in this arrangement. . . . This should mollify the de Gaullists."

And yet, as if to emphasize his cheerful pliability in dealing with these fascists, Eisenhower deferred to their insistence that Giraud not be named as part of the Darlan group "for a period of several days." Thus it would seem to the world that Eisenhower had approved an exclusively Vichyite administration, as indeed, for all practical purposes, he had.

As might be expected, the President and the prime minister swallowed this special pleading whole and subsequently drew upon it for their own further justifications of the shameful policy. Sherwood has told how he heard Roosevelt read it aloud to Hopkins, with a "superb distribution of emphasis . . . as if he were making an eloquent plea for Eisenhower before the bar of history." Churchill, who belatedly recognized that the deal with Darlan had raised issues of what he was pleased to call "a moral and sentimental character," cabled Eisenhower a brief pat on the back: "Anything for the battle, but the politics will have to be sorted out later on."

Now when the Allied armies of "liberation" succeeded in sustaining in positions of power all the scoundrels, great and small, who had originally been appointed by Vichy, various unpleasant things inevitably followed in train. The calendar of these woes can be briefly summarized:

Frenchmen who had rejoiced at the "liberation" were impartially denounced as Gaullists, communists, or dissidents and were imprisoned.

Editors of newspapers found themselves still subject to the old Vichy censorship. Editorials welcoming the Allies to North Africa were expurgated.

Concentration camps, filled with political prisoners before the Allied landings, were jammed to bursting after those landings.

The Vichy laws against Jews remained in full force.

Members of such Vichy fascist organizations as the Légion des Anciens Combattants and the Service d'Ordre Légionnaire (familiarly known as the SOL), who had hidden their uniforms when the Allies arrived, were once again encouraged to parade about in public. The Compagnons de France, a carbon copy of the Hitlerjugend, began again to tramp through the streets in the early morning, chanting their theme song "Maréchal, Nous Voilà."

Those French officers who had undertaken to assist the Allied landings found themselves stripped of their commands. Those who were not jailed were in disgrace and in hiding. (General Clark had assured Admiral Darlan, "I do understand your resentment against their not obeying orders.") General Mast, who had ventured to meet with General Clark before the landings and had so disposed his troops as to keep the killing around Algiers at a minimum, had been obliged to find refuge in the Levant. General Béthouart and his principal associates, jailed in Morocco, were saved from summary execution only at the last minute and were thereafter with great difficulty extricated from prison and transferred by General Eisenhower to Gibraltar.

In Casablanca, General Patton's heart had been won by "displays of French military style and gold braid, Arab horsemanship, French cooking and general colonial razzle-dazzle," all laid on by General Noguès, who had been able without difficulty to persuade Patton that Morocco was, if it were not for the Jews, a paradise.

In Oran, General Fredendall assured an American correspondent that the SOL was nothing to be concerned about, since the fascist organization's secret intelligence section was working amicably with his own intelligence officers.

In Algiers, AFHQ's psychological warfare branch was, as may be imagined, stunned by the turn of events. Their whole carefully developed propaganda line had become, to use the word later chosen by two scholars who studied the affair, "unfeasible." The skills of the branch "had to be turned to moderating the damaging psychological warfare effects of the collaboration with Darlan."

In London, the more sophisticated British psychological warfare adepts were equally aghast. Bruce Lockhart, director general of Political Warfare Executive, noted later: "The resistance movements in all the occupied countries . . . were horrified by Allied collaboration with Frenchmen whom they regarded as little better than Quislings. [The Darlan deal] affected PWE acutely and made our propaganda exceedingly difficult. How were we to explain Darlan and his regime to our friends in France and in the occupied countries?"

General Eisenhower himself found that much of his time was required to sort out the politics of the Darlan deal. During the immediate aftermath, the six weeks when Admiral Darlan was in political control of French North Africa while the Allied troops were vainly trying to seize and establish dominion over Tunisia, the protests against the deal somewhat subsided, following the earnest efforts of President and prime minister to quiet them. President Roosevelt on November 17 gave out a statement at a press conference; in it he emphasized at least six times the "temporary" character of the arrangement with Darlan, adding:

> I have requested the liberation of all persons in North Africa who have been imprisoned because they opposed the efforts of the Nazis to dominate the world, and I have asked for the abrogation of all laws and decrees inspired by Nazi governments or Nazi ideologists. Reports indicate that the French of North Africa are subordinating all political questions to the formation of a common front against the common enemy.

These were brave words, and if they had been followed by any brave deeds the work of AFHQ's psychological warfare branch would have been much simplified. But they were most conspicuously not so followed. Wallace Carroll, the American OWI representative in London, later recalled the despair of the psychological warfare experts in November and December of 1942:

> So we who tried to defend America stood naked to the blast with only the words of the President to warm us. And when we had said these words a hundred times, they sounded thin and unreal and brought no comfort. Oh, for one little act to give meaning to those words! Just the name of one patriot released from jail, one honest man restored to his post, one fascist put out of the way. Or just one photograph of a Jewish schoolboy returning to his classroom, or of a refugee eating the bread of the liberators.

Did General Eisenhower know anything of these torments so far below him in the chain of command? If not, it was not for lack of attention. To be sure, he tried to concentrate on military rather than political affairs. Nevertheless, "Since this operation started," Eisenhower radioed his chief of staff Beetle Smith on November 18, "three-quarters of my time, both night and day, has been necessarily occupied in difficult political maneuver," and before long this proportion was increased. On November 30 he wrote General Marshall: "The sooner I can get rid of all these questions that are outside the military in scope, the happier I will be! Sometimes I think I live ten years each week, of which at least nine are absorbed in political and economic matters."

A growing political concern—one to which Eisenhower appears to have given at least as much of his attention as he did to the plight of those victimized by the Vichy fascists—was the protection of his own good name in respect of the decision to put Darlan in power. He never doubted the necessity of that decision, considered solely as a military expedient, but more and more it seemed advisable to find legal and moral grounds for it. Fairly quickly he assumed the position that he had "not set up any government," he had "merely required the dominating officials to get together with [Giraud] and decide upon the composition of a commission that could control the region." At length, when he came to write his memoir *Crusade in Europe*, he would declare that "we had no legal or other right arbitrarily to establish, in the Nazi style, a puppet government of our own choosing. . . . Such a resort to Nazi methods would have been a far more serious violation of the principles for which we were fighting than would the mere temporary acceptance of some individual whose past record was, from our viewpoint, distasteful." This would make for pleasant reading in 1948, but there is no question that, Nazi methods or no, in 1942 the Allied commander in chief did in fact attempt to force the establishment of a government headed by General Giraud, settled on Admiral Darlan instead to run that government when a half-dozen top-ranking Vichyites insisted they preferred Darlan, and, as we shall presently see, dictated the accession to power of Giraud after Darlan was assassinated on Christmas Eve.*

The British and American correspondents were not likely to be overwhelmed by any semantic niceties as to how a government might be merely a commission, established not by an official protocol but by an unofficial announcement, nor by whether Darlan was temporary or not. They had expected to see the armies of "liberation" toss the rascals out, and what they saw with their own eyes was that the rascals had been carefully preserved, en gelée, and they proceeded to tell the folks at home all about what they had seen—and smelled. Since he knew little of their dispatches and broadcasts General Eisenhower was not upset, but his brother Milton, who was then associate director of OWI, was most disturbed. Milton Eisenhower found a reason for flying to Algiers and arrived there December 11. (The general had removed his headquarters to the Hotel St. Georges in Algiers on November 23.) Together the brothers examined an OWI analysis of press reports, editorials, commentary, and popular reactions to the Darlan deal. The general was hurt and angered.

Milton Eisenhower went off to talk with Murphy, the adviser for civil affairs. Murphy imagined that the subject of discussion was to be the glacial pace at which political prisoners were being released from the Vichy concentration camps. Among these were twenty-seven communist members of the Chamber of Deputies, the French national legislature; and Murphy knew, from the many protests referred to him by the OWI mission in Algiers, how preposterous the continued imprisonment of these men was held to be, especially in France, where the Resistance was more often than not led by communists. Nevertheless, the Vichy fascists were in no hurry to release the twenty-seven deputies or, indeed, anybody else, contending that since they were destitute and had no place to go, all the many thousand political prisoners should stay where they were.

Murphy agreed. AFHQ, prodded by Murphy, likewise agreed.

Milton Eisenhower seemed to care less for these prisoners than for his brother's reputation. Murphy has described how Milton Eisenhower feared the general's career was in grave jeopardy. "Heads must roll, Murphy!" Milton Eisenhower is said to have exclaimed. "Heads must

* The best witness that General Eisenhower tried to force the acceptance of Giraud as head of a North African government is General Eisenhower. On November 19 he cabled General Marshall: "I attempted to force Giraud upon [the existing officials] as head but he collapsed under me."

roll!" He wanted some of the most prominent fascists dismissed from office—the name that jumped to his mind was that of Noguès—but Murphy persuaded him that no such drastic action could or should be taken.

Meanwhile General Eisenhower had already ordered a half-dozen officers trained as censors to be flown at once from London to Algiers. Brigadier General Robert McClure arrived on December 14, and the lid of censorship was slammed shut on all cabled dispatches or radio broadcasts that dealt with politics. No reporter could write about or comment upon the curious events that took place under the fascist dispensation. Some American reporters, like Ernie Pyle, stayed away from Algiers and so were able to sneak through the censorship their own striking epithets. (Pyle wrote from Oran of the "soft-gloving snakes in our midst.")

Murphy, the political adviser, later denied responsibility for the censorship of political matters. He thought it "a mistake." He blamed it on a "command decision" taken by Eisenhower. Eisenhower also thought the censorship a mistake, but he did not confess to that conclusion until 1948. In the winter of 1942–1943, by his order the censorship was tight and complete.

The political tangle persisted, more snarled than ever. Much of the commander in chief's time was spent in reaching an understanding (no more definite term was possible, for Roosevelt, with the memory of the Darlan deal still green, had forbidden Eisenhower "to enter into any 'protocol,' 'agreement,' or 'arrangement,' with any government officials in French Africa") with General Pierre Boisson, the Vichyite governor general of French West Africa, by which the Allies got the use of Dakar as a naval and an air base. More of his time had been taken up by the continuing enmity between Darlan and de Gaulle. A high-ranking emissary of de Gaulle, invited to fly from London to Algiers as an observer for the Gaullist French National Committee, was not met at the airport (Murphy's oversight); subsequently Darlan's fascist police tried to arrest him (Murphy had forgotten to tell Darlan he was coming). Both Darlan and Giraud promptly urged Eisenhower to have him ordered out of Africa at once, and Eisenhower eventually had to argue with both the emissary and Darlan just to get the two together for a brief, hostile conference.

By this time Eisenhower was beginning to fancy himself "a cagier diplomat" than his newspaper critics gave him credit for. But his bosses—General Marshall in Washington and General Brooke in London—were both unhappy that the commander in chief of TORCH was not wholly absorbed in his martial business. "Eisenhower," Brooke complained, "was far too much immersed in the political aspects of the situation. . . . I had little confidence in his having the ability to handle the military situation confronting him, and he caused me great anxiety." Late in December, Marshall instructed Eisenhower to delegate "international diplomatic problems to your subordinates and give your complete attention to the battle in Tunisia." Eisenhower at once concluded he had better visit the front.

In truth, the battle for Tunisia was going poorly. The hope had been that, by achieving surprise and holding the initiative, Allied troops could race east along the Mediterranean coast and seize Bizerte and Tunis while the Nazis were still giving ground under the buffets delivered them by the British Eighth Army in Egypt and Libya. On the heels of the landings around Algiers had come other landings to the east—at Bougie on November 11, by parachute troops at Bône on November 12— but these quick and daring forays, while they brought the Allies more than halfway from Algiers to Tunis, were accomplished by forces so absurdly small that a battalion seemed an army. The airfields in eastern Algeria had been captured but the entire advance was still, in mid-November, little more than a reconnaissance in force. To reinforce was a slow, frustrating, and onerous task. Shipping was scant. Roads were frightful. The only railroad, single track, was in disrepair. Nevertheless, in late November a brigade of British infantry, supported by American armor, had moved deep into Tunisia and captured Medjez. In Rome, Count Ciano, the Italian minister for foreign affairs, had noted in his diary on November 26, "Last night forty American tanks arrived at the gates of Tunis," and he expected that "within a month" the Axis armies would be driven from all of Africa. The Nazis had not been so precipitate. They had busily flown in first-rate troops in impressive numbers: fifteen thousand combat infantry by the end of November, along with a good deal of artillery and one hundred tanks, including a few of the brand-new Mark VI monsters, better than any Allied machine. Hermann Goering, in Rome to put some starch in the wilting Italian morale, had assured everyone within sound of his voice that Nazi panzer divisions would be in Morocco within ninety days and would have dumped the Americans into the sea. On November 28 General Anderson's Allied troops had got to within twelve miles of Tunis: so close! and in the city, as they knew, the Gaullists were waiting, ready to stage a coup de main at the first glimpse of the Stars and Stripes.

And then had come the heavy, steady rains, turning the Allied airfields into swamps and the roads into bogs. The Luftwaffe, operating from all-weather fields, had blunted the Allied advance and the Nazi armor had thrown it back. Painfully, arduously, supplies had been pushed forward to fuel a last determined attack on Tunis, scheduled to begin on Christmas

Eve. It was to check on the last-minute plans for this campaign that General Eisenhower, at 6 A.M. Wednesday morning, December 23, set out from Algiers.

His caravan—a Cadillac, a Packard, and two jeeps—drove east over the muddy winding roads through rough mountainous country, east to Constantine and on into Tunisia, fetching up in a torrential rain at the headquarters of the British V Corps in Souk-el-Khemis on Thursday afternoon, December 24. Behind him the commander in chief had left Darlan, whom he had several times characterized as indispensable to his chance for the swift accomplishment of his mission.

When Eisenhower reached corps headquarters, the word from his front-line commanders was uniformly doleful. The attack planned for Christmas Eve had already been put off for at least forty-eight hours, the most recent in a series of such postponements; now General Anderson reported that his best information—gathered from the local inhabitants—led him to believe that the rains would persist through January and much of February. Later Eisenhower would put it about that Anderson had been too cautious; just now no argument could avail against the deep mud. For the sanguine commander in chief there could have been no more bitter disappointment, but since it was quite certain that no wheeled vehicle could roll in mud over its axles, no attack on Tunis could be contemplated for six, perhaps for eight weeks. Torch had failed to achieve its optimum objective.

Even as the commander in chief was recommending the glum alternative of an aggressive defense he was called to the telephone for a message from General Clark. It was ambiguous and obscure. Something had happened, Eisenhower wasn't sure what, but he gathered that Darlan had been shot. At all events, Clark wanted him back in Algiers at once.

The caravan was back on the road to Algiers on Christmas Eve. Eisenhower and his party drove all night through rain and sleet; when he was not dozing, the commander in chief was puzzling over the problems raised by this sudden, still only partly explained message from Clark. All Darlan's intimates had apparently urged that Noguès should be summoned to replace Darlan, but Clark had refused, instead asking Eisenhower to have Giraud sent at once to Algiers. On the way, at Constantine, the news of Darlan's assassination was confirmed, and Eisenhower radioed Clark:

Kingpin notified and will arrive sometime Christmas. I will arrive Algiers about 1600 ZED Christmas. You were quite right in absolutely rejecting prime YBSOB repeat Yoke Baker Sail Option Baker [the prime yellow-bellied son of a bitch; viz., General Noguès]. Consider Kingpin only possibility.

Darlan's death ended one problem, Eisenhower remarked to Butcher as they resumed their journey, but no doubt it created many more.

Back in Algiers late in the afternoon of Christmas Day, Eisenhower at once called the staff officers concerned to the Hotel St. Georges and listened to their report: how twenty-year-old Fernand Bonnier de la Chapelle, son of a substantial Algerian family, had fired three or four bullets into Darlan at pointblank range; that he was a member of a small group of like-minded youths who, it was believed, wished Darlan removed so that the way might be clear for a restoration of the French monarchy; how the boy had been arrested and, by order of General Jean Marie Bergeret, the deputy high commissioner under Darlan, had been swiftly executed with no questions asked or encouraged.*

The assassination, at the very least, served to define just how "temporary" was the arrangement with Darlan: it lasted forty-two days, from November 12 to December 24. If there had been no assassination, there is no telling how long "temporary" would have been stretched. Only a week before Darlan died, General Eisenhower had indicated his belief that the Allied governments should continue to support Darlan and to cooperate with him "during the period of active hostilities" involved in the liberation of France; in short, until V-E Day.

In the rank atmosphere of North African politics, the assassination stirred no fresh breeze. Giraud was installed in Darlan's place. Despite all his obvious liabilities, he possessed one surpassing asset: he had been handpicked by Roosevelt and approved by Churchill. Giraud it would be. Early on December 26 Eisenhower made his intentions known to the War Department. Later in the day he was sent his authorization: Giraud was to be appointed high commissioner, in charge of both military and civil affairs, under Eisenhower.

Since he had neither taste nor talent for the political responsibilities of his lofty new office, Giraud was content to relinquish them to the deputy high commissioner General Bergeret, whom he had inherited from Darlan. Bergeret, a thorough reactionary, seized the opportunity to have his fascist police arrest all the Gaullists who had escaped the earlier dragnets. The haul this time was impressive. Nearly everyone taken was a leader of the Resistance which had paved the way for the Allied landings in November: Henri d'Astier de la Vigerie, a brother of the man de Gaulle had sent as emissary to North Africa; the Abbé Cordier; Pierre Alexandre; Dr. Henri

---

* According to French sources, young Bonnier de la Chapelle was one of the members of the Resistance who had, on the night of November 7/8, surrounded Les Oliviers and held Darlan a prisoner for several hours. Those men could of course have killed Darlan that night. "It would have been easy to finish him if killing had been part of our plan," one of them later told an American correspondent, "but we lacked the habit of ruthlessness."

Aboulker, in whose apartment the conspirators had gathered on the eve of the landings; even M. Muscatelli, the director of Algiers police. At least two of these men were held in prison for months.

AFHQ did nothing about these arrests. General Eisenhower looked the other way. If he was troubled by what had happened, he gave no sign.

There were at the time in Algiers about thirty British and American correspondents, "and not one of them accepted the official French version of the arrests—that the motive had really been the safety of General Giraud—or the far more disturbing official American efforts to play down the whole affair." They set up such a howl of protest at the flagrantly un-just arrests that AFHQ deemed it necessary to arrange two separate press briefings. The first, conducted in military style by General Giraud, was wintry; the second, supervised over cocktails in front of a pleasant crack-ling fire by Robert Murphy, was suave; neither succeeded in hushing the complaints. The correspondents could not forget that AFHQ was sitting comfortably in its offices while AFHQ's most loyal friends were hunkered down in jail cells; that Vichy's laws against the Jews, which outraged every instinct of decent behavior, were still in force; that the fascist lickspits strutted up and down the streets of the city in their SOL uniforms. Eisen-hower would later explain: "One complication . . . was the age-old antagonism existing between the Arab and the Jew. . . . Remembering that for years the uneducated population had been subjected to intensive Nazi propaganda calculated to fan these prejudices, it is easy to under-stand that the situation called for more caution and evolution than it did for precipitate action and possible revolution."

The time has come to balance accounts on the Darlan deal. To begin with, it is evident that Darlan was not, as advertised, essential to the maintenance of peace and order in the Allied armies' rear areas. Further, the several advantages claimed for Darlan's cooperation never came to pass: Estéva, the governor general of Tunisia, never submitted to his orders; the French fleet was never coaxed south from Toulon; the cease-fire in the cities where the first waves of troops landed was in no case ex-clusively the result of intervention by Darlan. Eisenhower would later ascribe to Darlan's influence the agreement the Allies made with Boisson, the one that brought Dakar and French West Africa into the Allied camp; but in fact, once the Allied armies were established in Algeria and Mo-rocco athwart Boisson's line of communication with Vichy, Boisson had little choice in the matter. The most forceful argument offered in defense of the Darlan deal was General Marshall's contention that while the Combined Chiefs had estimated the possible cost of the TORCH landings at eighteen thousand Allied casualties, in the event there were only eighteen hundred such casualties; but to credit the difference between gloomiest foreboding and actuality to the accommodation with Darlan is disingenuous.

As against the dubious benefits accruing from the deal, there was a substantial debit. To the antifascist men and women of the resistance movements in Europe and especially in France, the use of Darlan by the Americans would be hard to forget. To them, as to many in Britain and the United States, the deal sullied a noble cause, a cause for which they were ready to die.

The rumpus over the Darlan deal was inescapable, and arose from a natural confusion over the character of the war. To the antifascist ideologues the war was a crusade to crush the authoritarian, racist, reactionary Axis powers; to the average American the war was our side, the Good Guys, against their side, the Bad Guys; to the American or Britisher vitally concerned with what has been called free enterprise the war was a contest for economic supremacy, for continued and if possible improved commercial profits, hence for national wealth and health. To wage this war there had been formed an alliance of the United Nations, which yoked parliamentary democracies together with an authoritarian Soviet Union and an impossibly corrupt and backward China. Stated another way, the democracies, capitalist and imperialist, were ranged with a socialist dictatorship (Stalinist bolshevism) and a client dependency (Generalissimo Chiang Kai-shek's China) against the fascist dictatorships. In simplistic terms, the Left and the Center were pitted against the Right. But Left and Center made very uneasy allies; they were by no means agreed as to the shape and complexion of the world once the Right had been crushed; each was skittish about the other's presumed ambitions or sinister designs; the center was exceedingly nervous lest the peoples of the occupied countries arise in revolt and gravitate naturally to the Left. In consequence, unfurling banners that displayed the rightist device Law and Order, the captains of the armies of the Center found it convenient, or expedient, to form alliances with officials of the Right as they surged forward to "liberate" the occupied countries; contrariwise, the captains of the armies of the Left marched under Red banners that invited revolution and a dictatorship of the proletariat.

In these terms, an analysis of the power structure of French North Africa shows that the colons, the rich French predators of the country, were thoroughpaced reactionaries who had counted on a Nazi triumph over bolshevism; that with their approval Vichy had installed a handful of like-minded men to administer the country; that this handful had in turn appointed a larger number of fascist petty fonctionnaires—mayors, postmasters, and the like—who were easily able to restrain their enthusiasm for an Allied victory; that nevertheless, a much larger number of the French were ready to go to great lengths for a chance somehow to fight the Germans, but were dismayed and confused by the American eagerness to exalt the local fascists; and, finally, that the vast majority of the population—the native Algerians, Tunisians, and Moroccans—regarded the war as a conflict between two rivalrous sets of exploiters and conserved their energies against the day when they might struggle to win their own independence. The deal with Darlan propitiated the Right, which was presumed competent to hold in check the native population; the French Left and Center might go whistle.

To return now to Eisenhower, his crusade in Europe was never antifascist. He spoke rarely of the Nazis and often of the Boche or the Hun. To make the deal with Darlan was entirely natural; that it should be questioned so loudly and so long puzzled him. The circumstances of that deal have been taken up in some detail because they afford striking evidence of the sort of political animal Eisenhower was and would be: fundamentally right of center, fundamentally decent, indifferent to civil liberties, intolerant of abstract concepts, perfunctory rather than thorough in matters foreign to his experience, prone to repose confidence in men of wealth and temporal power, tending too easily to accept advice of doubtful value, anxious to be liked by others, and, when he chose to be, well-nigh irresistible.

A man of moods. When, for example, Harold Macmillan first arrived in Algiers, on January 2, 1943, to replace Henry Mack as the principal British political adviser at AFHQ, General Eisenhower knew nothing of his appointment and was openly peevish when Macmillan came to meet him. "Pleased to see you," said Eisenhower, "but what have you come for?" Macmillan attempted to explain, but Eisenhower was curt until Macmillan luckily thought to mention that his mother had been born in Indiana. "So," added this very representative British Tory, "I am a Hoosier." At this Eisenhower perceptibly brightened and before long was chattering away about his political difficulties and of course about Darlan and of course about the protests provoked by the Darlan deal.

"I can't understand," he complained, "why these long-haired, starry-eyed guys keep gunning for me. I'm no reactionary. Christ on the Mountain! I'm as idealistic as hell."

Macmillan warmed to Eisenhower, finding that he was "naturally openhearted and generous," and sensing "the inherent goodness and firmness of his character."

The general pursued his subject: "Now that poor Darlan has been killed we've got this Giraud, and no one can attack his record. We have made Giraud the boss. Of course we're going to make changes. We are going to get a new governor for Algeria. It's a guy called Pie-row-ton. They tell me he's a fine guy."

"They tell me . . ." Macmillan, whose specific responsibility was to tell Eisenhower about such men, went away without saying anything. When he learned that the new governor was Marcel Peyrouton, too late he realized he had been guilty of "a grave error." Peyrouton had served the Vichy government as minister of the interior, which is to say, as the boss cop, the man responsible for the arrest and detention and too often the torture and execution of those who resisted the Nazi occupation. During his term of office, moreover, the Vichy government had published its first set of decrees aimed at the Jewish citizens of France; he had enforced them.

". . . he's a fine guy." Peyrouton had been nominated as governor general of Algeria by Darlan; Murphy had passed the recommendation along to AFHQ with "no objections"; Eisenhower had passed it along to Washington; the State Department had approved it over the strong objections of Undersecretary Sumner Welles; the White House had likewise approved it. Peyrouton's appointment was announced on January 19, and once again the outcry of protest went up, almost as stormy as that over Darlan. Eisenhower scribbled a memorandum for his diary: "Peyrouton's [appointment] . . . has been received with howls of anguish at home. Who *do* they want? He is an experienced administrator and God knows it's hard to find many of them among the French in Africa."

Good administrators would not have been so hard to find if AFHQ had looked in the right places—such as the jails and internment camps of North Africa, in which some of them had been imprisoned by the Vichyites, or in the countries nearby, to which others had fled to escape the same fate. After several weeks, as de Gaulle's influence in North Africa increased and gradually became dominant, AFHQ at last began to discover these men who had been there all along. For example, Muscatelli, formerly the director of police, who had been jailed, was named prefect of Algiers; and later General Mast returned from the Levant and in time was appointed the governor general of Tunisia.

But it was a long, slow process.

CHAPTER SEVEN

Victory in Africa

WITH THE TURN OF THE YEAR General Eisenhower learned that his political chieftains and his military commanders were to be his guests within
his own theater, and the impending formalities promised to permit him,
even if transiently, to hold at arm's length the squabbles of the importunate French. Late in December a British officer, Brigadier (later Lieutenant General Sir) Ian Jacob, arrived in Algiers to select a proper place
for Anglo-American conferences on strategy. Jacob was satisfied with the
Anfa Hotel, set amid a group of pleasant villas in a suburb of Casablanca;
General Patton issued the necessary orders for requisition of the hotel
and all the villas; rolls of barbed wire were uncurled around the area; and
all was scrubbed and furbished for what would later be known as the
Casablanca Conference, held January 13–23, 1943.*

Once he had been assured that every step had been taken for the
security and comfort of his guests, Eisenhower could again concentrate on
his work as a professional soldier.

His peculiar position, subordinate to a few and in command of many,
invested him with peculiar responsibilities. One of the most exacting of
these was to fashion, with a kind of ruthless wisdom, the command structure of the vast war machine that had been placed at his disposal. American officers had to be found who could lead their troops in battle; British
officers, more experienced, more knowledgeable, had to fit smoothly into a
perplexing staff system. The staff was Anglo-American, but the system
was perforce American, since commander in chief, chief of staff, and
secretary, general staff, were all Americans and naturally established the
system they were used to.

Eisenhower's masters, the Combined Chiefs, had their own watchful

---

* All was furbished, that is, save the villa claimed from its owners for the use of the
officers in charge of strategic planning. This house was found to contain a large library of superior pornography, all in French (alas!) but many of the books were
profusely illustrated. "For some time we despaired of any work being done in that
villa," Jacob noted in his diary, "but after a bit the excitement died down, and . . .
generally speaking the work was not impeded."

concerns with the command structure in the North African theater of operations. They had to select replacements for the officers dismissed by Eisenhower; they had to supervise Eisenhower as well. Incessantly they peered over his shoulder, and second-guessed, and formed a fluctuating judgment of their man. Naturally enough, their appraisals tended to be nationalist. In brief, Marshall backed Eisenhower in every respect, while Brooke, the British CIGS, often found Eisenhower deplorably lacking in the qualities of a great captain.

Much of Eisenhower's energy as a theater commander was addressed precisely to the elimination of such nationalist differences. If he could mark up one superlative achievement, he believed, it would be to forge a truly Allied command, one in which American and British officers would mesh like gears tooled to highest tolerance, as though all had been educated in the same academies, trained in the same procedures, and born to the same traditions. This was in fact the achievement for which Eisenhower would later be lauded by, among others, Churchill; but in the winter of 1942–1943 there was still an appreciable gap between aim and act.

Brigadier Jacob must be accounted an informed observer; at the time of his trip to Algiers he was General Ismay's assistant as military secretary to the War Cabinet, and he was well acquainted with all the British officers on the staff of AFHQ. The chief impression Jacob got of Eisenhower's headquarters

> . . . was of a general air of restless confusion, with everyone trying [his] best in unnatural conditions. I was assured on all sides that there was no Anglo-American friction at all. But the simple fact of having a mixed staff is quite enough to reduce the overall efficiency by at least a half. . . . The British . . . have to work with U.S. officers who are often entirely ignorant and inexperienced, and have to operate on a system which is quite different from the one to which they are accustomed. They find their task harassing and irritating in the extreme . . . doubt whether a combined Allied Staff is a practical arrangement, and think the experiment should not be repeated. . . .
>
> A most disturbing factor . . . is the existence of General Clark as Deputy Commander-in-Chief. [He] is a most ambitious man, able and active, with a strong personality. He imposes himself in the most extraordinary way on the Commander-in-Chief. . . . Most U.S. officers are terrified of him, and he has all along been the evil genius of the Force. . . . When, if ever, he goes to take command of the Fifth Army, a great improvement may be found, and it won't be only the British officers who will heave a sigh of relief.

The fact that General Clark has been allowed to occupy the position he has made for himself and to create such havoc is a reflexion on the Commander-in-Chief.

These observations, especially as they touched upon General Clark, would not have particularly astonished General Eisenhower. More than a month before, he had had occasion to caution Clark for being overly ambitious; he had perceived the abrasive aspects of Clark's strong personality and warned him of their dangers. Less than a week after Jacob made this entry in his diary Eisenhower relieved Clark of his post as deputy commander in chief and sent him a warm, friendly note about his future usefulness as commander of the Fifth Army.

But who now would serve as his deputy? The need was acute, for troops of three nations were disposed along a rugged range of Tunisian hills and desert outcroppings, the so-called Eastern Dorsal, which slanted north-south-southwest for perhaps one hundred and forty miles; yet there was only one single line of communications leading eastward from Algiers. The situation demanded one single command of the battlefront. Only the British First Army, under Anderson, had a signals system adequate for control of the long, thinly held front, but Giraud and Juin flatly refused to put French soldiers under the orders of a British officer. The alternative was to place an American in command. When the American force in Tunisia had been designated a corps rather than an army, Clark had indicated his preference for command of the Fifth Army back in Morocco, and so it was left to Eisenhower to take command himself—or rather, since his duties kept him regularly in Algiers, to appoint some officer as his deputy.

The choice fell upon Major General Lucian Truscott, who was named deputy chief of staff, Allied Force, and sent to Constantine in eastern Algeria, there to operate Eisenhower's advanced command post. Truscott took this post in hand on January 14. It was a confusing solution of the problem, and Eisenhower knew it (later he would acknowledge that confusion in the structure of command was a factor in the subsequent tactical defeat in the Kasserine Pass). This confusion was much on his mind when, the next day, he traveled to Casablanca to report to the Combined Chiefs on the progress of his mission.

On arrival, Eisenhower went at once to confer with General Marshall and to tell him of his command problems. Marshall suggested that he might use General Patton "as a sort of deputy," and Eisenhower filed the idea away for future consideration. After lunching with Marshall and Admiral King he attended a session of the Combined Chiefs. He had come without notes or papers, feeling, as he told Marshall, "so confident of my complete familiarity with all major factors that I think [staff officers and records] would be a mere hindrance." He reported on the past and he also outlined a plan—earlier approved by AFHQ—which involved a thrust to be launched within eight days by American troops through southern Tunisia to the Mediterranean port of Sfax. General Brooke thought this plan "a real bad one" and criticized it sharply, since he considered that it was "in no way coordinated with either First Army [Anderson] or Eighth Army [Montgomery] operations." General Alexander, lately arrived from Cairo, agreed that the scheduled American attack seemed premature in view of Montgomery's progress with the Eighth Army. The attack which Eisenhower "had so laboriously planned" was canceled.

To find his American troops "held on a very short lead" was a bitter disappointment. Hard on this rebuff, Eisenhower was sent word that the President wished to talk with him privately. The two men were alone together for a short time: later they were joined by Churchill, Harry Hopkins, and several officers of exalted rank.

Roosevelt said to Hopkins: "Ike seems jittery."

Still later Harold Macmillan was summoned; he found Roosevelt resting, with Churchill sitting on one side of his bed and Eisenhower "standing to attention like a Roman centurion on the other side."

Eisenhower had reason to be jittery. He had suffered an attack of influenza from which he was not yet fully recovered; his hopes for a swift victory in Tunisia had been dashed; he was entangled in a bewildering political mess, some of which derived from the President's own improvisations toward a French policy. Only twelve days before, one of these improvisations had outraged Eisenhower. On Sunday, January 3, Beetle Smith had handed Eisenhower a cable which was a paraphrase of a message Roosevelt had sent to Churchill:

> I feel very strongly that, in view of the fact in North Africa we have a military occupation, our commanding general has complete control of all affairs, both civil and military. Our French friends must not be permitted to forget this for a moment. . . . I am not yet certain whether Eisenhower can hold Giraud in line, but I shall soon find out.

Eisenhower had taken this to be an unequivocal threat, one which was founded, moreover, on a fatuous misconception. To his mind, the Allied Force in North Africa was not a powerful army of occupation; he was convinced that any successful military operations in Tunisia required the active cooperation of the French, not their sullen obedience to his orders. He had concluded that if the President obliged him to issue orders to Giraud which would, in his view, provoke French antagonism, he would, as he had told Butcher, "of course carry out the order, but would then ask to be relieved." Such a course, as both he and Butcher realized, "would no doubt mean reversion to the rank of lieutenant colonel, and retirement."

It is doubtful that Eisenhower would have committed himself to such an intractable course, more likely that these terminal thoughts were only a reflection of what Butcher described as "Ike's foul frame of mind." In the event, as was his custom, Eisenhower had poured his alarm and indignation into a cable dispatched to Marshall, and it was left to the chief of staff to pass Eisenhower's cable, carefully edited, on to the secretary of war and to the President.

All of this, coupled with the suspicion and deep-seated horror with which the professional soldier traditionally regarded the politician, contributed to Eisenhower's jitters. He listened as Roosevelt expatiated on the probable disintegration of the French empire and the desirability of "controlling certain strategic points" of that empire—Indochina, Syria and Lebanon, Dakar—and as Roosevelt counseled that the military supplies the French needed so desperately were to be furnished only in exchange for the use of French bases and a French compliance with American strategic goals in Europe. Eisenhower, more intimately acquainted with the bloody and tedious burdens of warfare than his commander in chief, noted Roosevelt's "optimism and buoyancy, amounting almost to lightheartedness," and when pressed by Roosevelt to fix a date for the final collapse of Axis resistance in North Africa, "blurted out [his] most miraculous guess of the war"—May 15. (That hit the moment as precisely as is possible with an inchoate entity like modern warfare. Axis resistance ended on May 13.)

The President had not been alone in noticing Eisenhower's jitters, so uncharacteristic; and so a rumor was born and, given the nature and circumstances of the conference at Anfa, it quickly spread. General Eisenhower's head, it was whispered, was on the block. Since there had been a grievous political blunder, and since the first Allied military advance had fallen short of Tunis and Bizerte, someone had to go; precedent demanded that it be the commander who had blundered and failed. At the time, even Eisenhower's intimate friend Butcher put stock in these whispers. "I told him his neck is in a noose," Butcher wrote, adding, "and he knows it." Years later even such a well-placed observer as Robert Sherwood would write that Eisenhower's position was for a time insecure, with General Alexander the most likely candidate to supersede him as supreme commander in North Africa and later for the invasion of Sicily. After all, Alexander outranked Eisenhower and was far more experienced as a battle commander; he was, moreover, about to order the victorious British Eighth Army into southern Tunisia under the field command of General

Montgomery, and this would give the theater an overwhelming British preponderance.

If there had been any substance to this rumor, all Eisenhower's troubles about his command structure would have been magically packed up in some other officer's kit bag, but it was not to be. On his return to his headquarters in Algiers, Eisenhower sent a telegram to Marshall: "I have tentatively come to the conclusion that I am going to name [General Patton] as 'Deputy Commander for Ground Forces.' This . . . will avoid the difficulties that might be involved should I call him 'Deputy Commander-in-Chief.'" That was on Sunday, January 17. In the evening of the same day Churchill, with the prior approval of General Brooke, suggested to Roosevelt that "at the right time Alexander should fill the vacancy of Deputy C. in C. to Eisenhower which has been created by the appointment of Clark to the Fifth U.S. Army." As Churchill was aware, to put a British officer in command of the theater would subject the French to intolerable tensions. An American was essential. Eisenhower was not merely the logical choice; he was the only choice. And who knew better than Churchill and Roosevelt about the provenance of, and responsibility for, the lamentable political blunder over Darlan? Since everybody in sight was by now vigorously denying that the selection of Darlan to be high commissioner of French North Africa ever was or had been a political blunder, there was very little mileage to be got by now belatedly blaming it all on a busy and quite useful military commander.

Besides, there were other accounts to be drawn. As the CIGS, Brooke, observed, Churchill's suggestion:

. . . could not help flattering and pleasing the Americans in so far as we were placing our senior and experienced commander to function under their commander who had no war experience. . . . We were pushing Eisenhower up into the stratosphere and rarefied atmosphere of a supreme commander, where he would be free to devote his time to the political and inter-Allied problems, whilst we inserted under him one of our own commanders to deal with the military situations and to restore the necessary drive and coordination which had been so seriously lacking.

Roosevelt accepted the suggestion. Next day Marshall cabled Eisenhower: "Delay action on Patton until you see or hear from me. Alexander will be your man when British Eighth Army joins you after [capturing] Tripoli."

Eisenhower was delighted by this news. Before long the Combined Chiefs formally approved a structure of the high command that would give him three deputies—Alexander for ground forces, Air Chief Marshal

Arthur Tedder for air forces, and Admiral of the Fleet Sir Andrew Cunningham for sea forces—all of whom outranked him.* Alexander was still something of an unknown quantity, but Eisenhower had worked with the other two and had a thoroughgoing respect for both of them. In a memorandum (for Butcher, for his diary, for history) dictated several weeks before, he had rather cloudily tried to define the qualities he believed an officer commanding a modern army, navy, or air force must have:

> . . . rich organizational experience and an orderly, logical mind are absolutely essential to success. . . . In addition . . . an inexhaustible fund of nervous energy [for he must be able] to absorb the disappointments, the discouragements and the doubts of his subordinates and to force them on to accomplishments, which they regard as impossible. . . . Two British officers that I have met have these qualifications to a marked degree—Admiral Cunningham and Air Marshal Tedder. I regard them both as top-flight leaders.

Three deputies charged with taking much of the load off the supreme commander's shoulders, and all of them first-rate officers. They were to assume their responsibilities just as Eisenhower's authority was expanded by the inclusion under AFHQ of the oncoming British Eighth Army; they were to maintain their positions under Eisenhower in the next operation, the one fixed upon a few days before by the Combined Chiefs, the assault on Sicily, known by the code name HUSKY. Could Eisenhower have any further worries about the structure of his high command?

Well, yes. All unaware, he had walked smack into a snare baited and set not by human hands but by the inevitable consequences of the Anglo-American alliance. Quite soon he began to appreciate what had already been smugly noted by the CIGS, General Brooke, what seemed obvious to everybody else as soon as Alexander was named deputy c. in c., what would permanently strain his military reputation; to wit, that he had been kicked upstairs, that the British were running the military aspects of the war, that his business was solely with such joyless distractions as the contest between Giraud and de Gaulle, and that he stood in proximate danger of being branded a mere political general.

All this was generally supposed; how much was reality, how much only appearance would be sorted out in the months to come and eventually be relegated to the confident judgment of historians. At the time, however,

---

* Eisenhower was not disconcerted by this anomaly, for he had been assured by Marshall that he would soon be promoted to full general. So he was: his fourth star was given him as of February 11, 1943. By an unhappy irony, his promotion was announced only a day or two before the news of the tactical defeat at Kasserine occasioned a spate of doleful headlines in American newspapers.

Eisenhower formed the impression that the matter could best be handled by some adroit public relations. When he learned that Churchill proposed to announce the transfer of Eighth Army to AFHQ and the appointment of Alexander and Tedder as his deputies, he cabled Marshall:

> . . . there will probably be innocently created through these announcements a popular impression of an overriding British control of this great area and operation. This impression is likely to be strengthened if the British announcement follows their normal practice of specifying duties of subordinates. . . . I believe that such publicity as is given in the U.S. should stress the American grip on the whole affair. . . . I have the feeling that it would be unfortunate at home, as well as in the African and European theaters, to permit the growth of an impression that an undue share of the control of this great affair is slipping out of the hands of the Americans. . . .

From Eisenhower to Marshall; from Marshall to Roosevelt; from Roosevelt to Churchill: "best if the American Supreme Command is stressed . . . inadvisable to release . . . details of the duties of Alexander or Tedder." Churchill faithfully acquiesced, but warned that British press and public were alike critical of the American conduct of the North African campaign, and that they would be naturally resentful of any effort to aggrandize Eisenhower's role while slighting Alexander's, especially in view of the inevitable comparison of the military experience and qualifications of the two officers.

As is almost always the case, public relations—adroit or maladroit—was no substitute for achievement.

And now came the episode at Kasserine.

The tactical reverse suffered by the Americans when Field Marshal Rommel committed several battalions of veteran troops, infantry and armor, supported by several more battalions of artillery, to the thrust through Kasserine Pass was to become almost as celebrated as the later setback, on a much larger scale, in the Ardennes. It is a striking phenomenon, and one presumably responsive to the excessive patriotism that endemically afflicts the USA, that whole books must be written to rationalize and explain away any defeat, however slight, which has been visited on American arms. These books will subsequently be widely sold. Only so, perhaps, can the national self-esteem be kept properly inflated.

The action at Kasserine Pass followed hard upon an enforced withdrawal from one range of hills (the Eastern Dorsal) across a valley to another range (the Grande Dorsale). A recommendation that this retreat be undertaken was made on February 15 by the British General Anderson to the commander in chief, General Eisenhower, and was by him approved. There followed a disorderly skirmishing of men and weapons in the course of which the Americans proved to be considerably more confused than the experienced Germans attacking them. After a week (February 15–22) of bloody and inconclusive blunders, the Axis troops, having successfully forced the pass, hastily and timidly withdrew, thereby demonstrating that the German military bogeymen were little if any more effective than the apple-green American troops.

The Nazis and their Italian allies had desired two things: to kill enough Allied troops and destroy enough Allied matériel to forestall any Allied attack, and to force a retreat from Tunisia of the British First Army by slashing deep punctures in its southern flank. As to the first, they partially succeeded; as to the second, they flopped.

It happened that on the night before Rommel launched his attack, General Eisenhower inspected the exact spot through which it was to come, and thus was in excellent position to assess Allied errors and thereafter lower the boom on those in the high command whom he found to have been responsible. The first to go went quickly. AFHQ's G–2, Brigadier Eric Mockler-Ferryman, provoked Eisenhower by placing too much reliance on "particular types of intelligence" while ignoring general instructions. (In plainer words, Mockler-Ferryman guessed wrong on the point chosen by the Germans for their attack.) He was presently relieved by Brigadier (later Major General Sir) Kenneth Strong. Other heads in the high command would roll just as they should have done in the Axis high command. Before particularizing, though, there must be reported an assignment that seemed at the time almost an afterthought but would prove in retrospect to be among the most important of the war in Europe.

Not long after Alexander's appointment as Eisenhower's deputy, General Marshall suggested to Eisenhower that he might find it useful to have a general officer who could act as his "eyes and ears," undertaking inspection trips in Tunisia, visiting forward command posts, checking with officers from corps headquarters all the way down the line to platoon leaders in the field; in short, keeping the supreme commander intimately acquainted with the fluid situation along the battlefront. Since AFHQ in Algiers had already swollen to nearly six thousand persons, of whom more than a thousand were officers and many of these general officers, to add still another would seem to have been less than urgent. Nevertheless, on February 11, a day before he left to make his own inspection trip, Eisenhower cabled Marshall a baker's dozen of names of officers who he believed had the necessary "brains, tact, and imagination" for the task. From this list Marshall had selected the third name: Major General O. N. Bradley.

Although Eisenhower and Bradley had been classmates at West Point, in the years that followed they had rarely seen each other and were no more than casual acquaintances. Now they would be closely associated for the rest of the war, and Bradley would come to be recognized as the ablest field commander in western Europe. Eisenhower's share in Bradley's original appointment can be defined with a precision rare in such matters: he deserves one-thirteenth of the credit. But Eisenhower's appreciation of Bradley's talents was almost instantaneous. "What a godsend it was to me to get that man!" he wrote a friend on March 20. Bradley's subsequent rise was of course intimately supervised by the supreme commander.

Bradley reported to Eisenhower at the Hotel St. Georges on February 24. Three days later, with a brief letter of introduction in his pocket, he was bound for the Tunisian front. It was a delicate mission, the more so coming as it did in the days just after the Kasserine defeat, for he was sure to be suspected by II Corps headquarters as Eisenhower's spy, deputed to carry "tales home to the boss outside the chain of command." Eisenhower had told him he was to look not for a scapegoat on whom the defeat could be blamed, but only for the lessons that could be learned from the defeat, lessons that would be helpful in the combat training of troops still at home. It proved, however, impossible to ignore the question of command, for nearly every divisional commander in II Corps had lost confidence in General Fredendall. Eisenhower had to move with circumspection, for Fredendall had been Marshall's own choice to command the Central Task Force of Torch; nothing is to be gained by crossing wires with one's superior officer. Eisenhower made a careful canvass: with Major General Ernest Harmon, commander of the 2nd Armored Division, whom Eisenhower had ordered to Kasserine to give leadership when things seemed to have come unstuck; with General Alexander, who had assumed command of the front early on February 20; and finally with his "eyes and ears," General Bradley. Every judgment was the same. On March 5 Eisenhower relieved Fredendall and ordered Patton east from Morocco to take command of II Corps at once.

On his arrival Patton promptly requested Bradley as his deputy commander, and it was so ordered. Patton wanted no "goddam spies running around" in his headquarters. But Bradley continued, on Eisenhower's orders, to serve as his "eyes and ears."

The structure of the high command in North Africa now appeared to be stable, and soon the ground forces were to be rehabilitated, reorganized, re-equipped, and regrouped, mostly according to their nationalities. General Alexander commanded the 18th Army Group, which had two large components, First Army and Eighth Army—both British—and one small one, the U.S. II Corps. The French XIX Corps was part of First Army, there was a division of Gaullist French troops attached to Eighth Army, and finally there was the Corps Franc d'Afrique, which fitted in wherever it could.*

Now that affairs were better organized and all units were functioning in more orderly fashion, the supreme commander might have expected to enjoy a brief period of merely routine pressure. Certainly he needed such a respite. He was, after all, also a son, a brother, a father, and a husband. He found time to write now and again to his mother in Abilene; rather less often to his brothers, who were sensible enough to realize that he was too busy to answer their letters with scrupulous regularity; quite often to his son John, with whose maturing growth and progress at West Point he was naturally concerned; and most often to his wife, whom he sorely missed. There were other distractions: a man whose name is often printed in the newspapers can expect to find a swarm of friends who knew him before he achieved celebrity, and another swarm who insist upon writing to him simply because they can imagine nothing better to do; it is to handle the demands of both these swarms that a supreme commander must acquire aides. General Eisenhower saw to it that every letter was duly answered.

General Marshall, on his visit to AFHQ after the Casablanca Conference, had been sensibly concerned about Eisenhower's health and about what he was doing to make sure that he did not go stale from overwork. He recommended a masseur and a regular regime of horseback riding, and lectured Butcher at some length on the need for keeping Eisenhower out of the office as much as possible. "He is too valuable an officer to overwork

* The Corps Franc was a motley assemblage acceptable to neither Darlan nor Giraud for inclusion in the regular French Army. Its personnel could in fact be assimilated under no known military table of organization, but they nevertheless fought with great gallantry and singular efficiency right into Bizerte. Aged sixteen to sixty, in the main the rejects of Darlan's brief fascist regime, they were of all kinds—Gaullists, European antifascists from Vichy concentration camps, French communists, Jews, Spanish Loyalist refugees, and two battalions of Moroccan goumiers who had volunteered for the high wages and for the pure joy of fighting Germans—but as one in their simple desire to kill Nazis. The corps had been organized by General Joseph de Monsabert, who had helped plan the Allied landings at Algiers and had subsequently been cashiered by his collaborationist superiors. Later it was commanded by Colonel Pierre Magnan, who had helped clear the way for Patton at Casablanca and had therefore been jailed by Noguès. The corps was always undermanned and wretchedly equipped; it was first attached to the British First Army and later to General Manton Eddy's U.S. 9th Division.

Monsabert commanded a corps and Magnan a division of French troops before the war ended, so the schemes of their Vichy fascist superiors were unavailing.

himself," Marshall told Butcher. "You must keep him refreshed." Butcher got the impression that Marshall was discussing Eisenhower with him as a father would a son. "After all," Marshall said, "four or four and a half hours with the staff ought to be enough." Butcher produced an experienced masseur, and for two or three days Eisenhower slept later and reached the office later, but then the new system collapsed. The supreme commander assured Marshall that he was making a practice of dawdling over a two-hour luncheon, during which discussion of business was forbidden, but even this modest attempt in the direction of indolence was erratic and short-lived. When it came to the horseback riding, however, Marshall's "orders" were more easily obeyed: Butcher got the use of a run-down farm on a bluff overlooking the sea about fifteen miles from Algiers; another officer scrounged four splendid Arab stallions; by the end of March Eisenhower was finding it possible to go riding as often as two or three times a week with those of his friends or aides who knew anything of horses, usually with Kay Summersby, who was an experienced horsewoman from the days of her childhood in Ireland.

The nature of Eisenhower's job was such that relaxation was impossible. Problems were incessant; only their character changed. The pressure came impartially from above and below. No sooner had the structure of command been defined and firmly established, for example, than the issue of Anglo-American unity—or rather, disunity—arose to bedevil and drive him, for the second time within three months, to the verge of resigning his high commission.

The crisis first arose because General Alexander and his staff officers had a rather snubbing opinion of American troops. Patton's orders from Alexander kept II Corps limited in its objectives and, Patton therefore believed, in its effectiveness. The task assigned it was wholly supporting of and subsidiary to the northward advance of Montgomery's Eighth Army; Patton yearned to hammer through to the Mediterranean and so trap the Axis forces retreating before Montgomery, but he was specifically bidden to go slow and then to stop. Late on March 19 he was handed orders to detach the 9th Division from II Corps and transfer it north to Anderson's First Army, where it would fight on the British left flank in the drive for Bizerte. The rest of II Corps was to attack in the south at Fondouk, between First and Eighth armies; as the net closed on the Axis forces in the northeast corner of Tunisia, II Corps would inevitably be pinched out of the line.

Bradley was "alarmed" by this directive. Patton "exploded" with indignation. After having mounted the three TORCH landing assaults and supported the British in the long winter campaigns, the American combat command was to be frozen out of its share in the final victory.

A soldier's complaints must properly be passed up along the chain of command. Bradley went to Alexander's headquarters, where he was assured by the staff officers that no slight was intended, that it was simply a question of logistics, that II Corps could not be properly supplied and supported over the poor roads of Tunisia. Bradley and Patton thereupon decided to appeal over Alexander's head to Eisenhower, for, as Bradley later wrote, "I could not believe that Eisenhower knew of Alexander's plan or that he would willingly agree to it. With Patton's permission I flew back to Algiers to point out my objections."

Eisenhower listened attentively but did not at once commit himself. He was constrained, as Bradley was aware, to walk a chalk line "to avoid being branded pro-American by the British command." The net effect was that he attempted to strike a balance, satisfying neither British nor Americans and often paying dearly for what was called indecision but in fact was compromise. In this case he waited a day and then sent Alexander a lengthy letter in which he touched on various matters—the altered plans for HUSKY, the lack of shipping needed for HUSKY, a telegram from Churchill urging speed for the victory in Tunisia—and finally got round to the "future employment of the II Corps," but only in such a way as to leave Alexander able to deny what Bradley and Patton demanded. "I desire," Eisenhower wrote Alexander, "that you make a real effort to use the II U.S. Corps right up to the bitter end of the campaign, even if maintenance reasons compel it to be stripped down eventually to a total of two divisions and supporting Corps troops." This course, if followed, would have reduced II Corps to half strength and left it unable to prove, either to itself or to the American people, that it was battleworthy. "I would consider it unfortunate," Eisenhower added, "if the developments of the campaign were such that participation by American troops, in an American sector, was deliberately eliminated as the crisis of the campaign approaches."

Anglo-American tension was thus frigerated, but only temporarily. Under the surface the rancors festered.

For a man of Patton's martial impetuosity, the cautious restraint to which he was subjected by Alexander was a torture; from March 19 to April 1, moreover, II Corps's orders from 18th Army Group were altered no less than five times, with Alexander stipulating in detail each time exactly what should be done. "All I have is actual conduct of the operations prescribed," Patton wrote Marshall. Yet he did not complain, but only noted.

Early in April the crisis came to an abrupt boil. In his sitrep (situation report) for April 1, II Corps's G-3 wrote: "Forward troops have been continuously bombed all morning. Total lack of air cover . . . has allowed

German air force to operate almost at will." The commander of the Tactical Air Force was a New Zealander, Air Vice Marshal Sir Arthur (Mary) Coningham. He promptly sent a radio message to Patton pointing out that the total number of casualties during the period of the report was six, and adding:

It is . . . assumed that there was no intention to adopt discredited practice of using air force as an alibi for lack of success on ground. If sitrep is in earnest and balanced against . . . facts it can only be assumed that II Corps personnel concerned are not battleworthy in terms of present operations.

. . . such inaccurate and exaggerated reports should cease.

Copies of this signal were sent by Coningham to every senior commander in the Mediterranean. These officers were of course familiar with Eisenhower's zeal on behalf of Anglo-American unity. Eyebrows went up. Breaths were sharply drawn. The atmosphere was one of strained expectancy.

Patton's outrage was seismic. Not battleworthy? He reached for his field telephone, called Eisenhower, and decanted his wrath in high, squeaky decibels.

Tedder was at Constantine having his airplane refueled when he was handed a copy of Coningham's signal. He wagged his head and at once hastened to telephone orders to Coningham to withdraw his message and make immediate apology. Next he called Eisenhower, whom he found "deeply concerned," a phrase which nicely illustrates what is meant by British understatement. But for Coningham simply to cancel his earlier message did not suit Patton's book; he was still, as he wrote Eisenhower, "quite mad and very disgusted" on behalf of his "United States troops, many of whom have marched and fought over hostile country since the 17th [of March]."

So Tedder got Coningham to come to Patton with a personal apology and a gracious salute and a smile. Tedder was able to report to Eisenhower that peace, of a sort, had been restored.

The report came opportunely. Eisenhower had already drafted a cable to Washington saying that inasmuch as he could not control his commanders, it was evident he should be relieved. The cable was not dispatched.

But Allied unity was to suffer still another buffet. The 34th Division had been detached from II Corps and assigned to a makeshift British corps for the purpose of driving east toward the sea and thus trapping those Axis forces in retreat before the triumphant advance of Montgomery's Eighth Army. The officer commanding this British corps, Lieutenant General John Crocker, ordered the 34th Division to an assault in which its left flank was unprotected and during which, to the Americans' dismay and confusion, a British armored brigade passed through the area. The division's objective, a low but steep hill that dominated a gap in the Eastern Dorsal, was strongly defended by a small force of Germans who were, during the course of the battle, reinforced. The Americans failed to capture the hill; by the time the British took it the retreating Axis troops had escaped entrapment. In his frustration General Crocker had some hard words to add to what had already been said about the 34th,* and he said them bluntly to some correspondents gathered in his headquarters. Crocker placed the blame for the failure of his plan plump on the 34th. The division should be withdrawn, he said, and its junior officers retrained by British instructors somewhere in the rear.

This was red meat for the correspondents. They filed their copy and the military censors, to Eisenhower's subsequent discomfort, passed it all along to the English and American newspapers. In Washington those officers concerned with the prestige of American troops winced and noted a sharp dip in public approval.

Ripples of the public reaction to still another American failure (so soon after Kasserine) were recorded throughout the Pentagon and reached, with some force, even to the chief of staff. General Marshall leafed back through the reports of II Corps's combat record and through the file of letters and cables sent him by General Eisenhower. At Eisenhower's lengthy letter to Alexander of March 29 he paused, noting the suggestion that reasons of maintenance might compel II Corps "to be stripped down eventually to a total of two divisions and supporting Corps troops." On reflection, Marshall strongly disapproved. On April 14 he cabled Eisenhower warning him that his letter had "aroused a fear in my mind that in this vital matter you might give way too much to logistical reasons with unfortunate results as to national prestige."

This was about as close as General Marshall had yet come to censuring Eisenhower, and it fits pat that the one soldier should seek to inspire the other by invoking the now brave, now tinsel, always illusory notion of national prestige.

But of course Eisenhower had already thought most earnestly of national prestige. It is, indeed, symbolic of the close communion of the two

---

* A German officer, after an earlier attack by the 34th Division in the same area, had reported: "The American gives up the fight as soon as he is attacked. Our men feel superior to the enemy in every respect." In defense of the much maligned 34th it should be noted that its orders in this earlier attack were to make what amounted to a noisy large-scale demonstration, but not to occupy advanced ground at the expense of men and matériel.

soldiers' ways of thinking that at the same moment Marshall was dispatching his cablegram to Eisenhower, Eisenhower was at General Alexander's headquarters bidding him to deploy II Corps at its full strength and in its own sector, no matter how impossible might seem the problems of supply. (The British, inured to coping with troops in desperately short supply, were never able to accustom themselves to the rich profusion of American motor transport nor to the cheerful ability of American drivers and mechanics to push their machines over no matter what obstacle.) Alexander, with Eisenhower's approval, had previously planned to have only two American divisions—the 1st and the 9th—in the sector to the north next to the Mediterranean, and those two were to revert to the command of the British First Army. But now he agreeably fell in with the supreme commander's demands: II Corps would remain at full strength and under American command. Coincidentally, Eisenhower sent Patton back to Rabat, in Morocco, to resume working on the plans for Husky; Bradley succeeded him as corps commander at midnight on April 15.

By April 15 the situation in North Africa was manifestly terminal. A week earlier, when Patton's tanks had ranged southeast and joined with advance units of the Eighth Army, the Allies had closed an arc around the Axis forces and were in position to tighten that arc steadily and mortally. Only the Axis leaders refused to perceive the inevitable. Hitler and Mussolini had both decreed a stubborn, ceaseless resistance; Mussolini hoped to hold out until winter, Hitler imagined the Axis could hang on indefinitely. Nearly three hundred thousand Axis soldiers were hemmed into the northeastern quadrant of Tunisia; less than half of these were combat troops, but in mid-April the decision was taken that all these men would be ordered either to fight or to build field fortifications. The enemy was still formidable, but he was trapped.

When the first thirty thousand combat troops of the U.S. II Corps—the 1st and 9th divisions—took up their positions at the northern end of the Allied arc, they were opposed by an estimated twenty thousand Germans who had the advantage of rough terrain superbly suited to defense and the disadvantages of far less artillery, almost no air force, a sharply dwindling supply of fuel and ammunition, and the prospect of limited reinforcements. The advantage at first outweighed the disadvantages. For many months the enemy had buttressed his naturally defensive surroundings: he had drilled deep into the rocky hills to carve dugouts and gun emplacements, and he had braced these pits with concrete; he had thickly mined every approach, defile, draw, and pathway. To the south of the American sector lay a seductive valley through two parallel ridges of hills that seemed to beckon toward the first of II Corps's objectives. This approach caught the attention of the supreme commander and on April 16 he dutifully pointed out to Bradley that "the southern portion of your sector appears to be reasonably suited for tank employment and it is in that area that you will be expected to make your main effort, at least in the initial stages."

These instructions of Eisenhower's afford a very fair example of how useless a supreme commander can be, and usually is, in the tactical deployment of troops. Bradley's G–2 had of course noticed the inviting approach through the hills, had investigated it, had heeded the counsel of the British troops who had previously occupied that part of the line, had promptly nicknamed the approach Mousetrap Valley, and had advised against any commitment of tanks until after the hills commanding the valley should have been seized.

On April 23, when the general Allied attack was launched all along the semicircular arc, the 9th Division (Major General Manton Eddy) jumped off in the north, together with the Corps Franc d'Afrique, and the 1st Division (Major General Terry Allen) moved in on the hills farther south, alongside Mousetrap Valley. A few days later Bradley was able to send a third infantry division, the 34th (Major General Doc Ryder), against the nastiest obstacle in the sector, Hill 609. After five days of hard and bloody fighting, the 34th won the hill and also won its self-respect as a first-rate military outfit. The 2nd Armored Division (Major General Ernest Harmon), which had also come in for some severe criticism by the British, was then unlimbered and aimed east into the Mousetrap and through the gap forced by the infantry.

The Americans, still stung by the criticisms leveled at them in Africa and then relayed back to the U.S., were determined to prove those criticisms wrong. They had got to know something of their enemy and his ways in battle, such as his trick of approaching under a white flag of surrender only as a ruse so that he could open fire at point-blank range; they had learned the brutal rules of this insane and savage game; to use the phrase fancied by professional soldiers, they had been blooded. By now, moreover, they were led by able officers. Their mission, assigned them by 18th Army Group, was to capture a pass in the last range of the Eastern Dorsal, the Chouigui Pass,* and then to join with the British First Army to capture Bizerte. In the event, the 9th Division, pausing only to equip the Corps Franc d'Afrique with motor transport so that French soldiers might have the honor of being the first to roll into the city, took Bizerte by the late afternoon of May 7, fifteen days after II Corps had begun its attack.

* At once and inevitably known to II Corps as Chewy-gooey Pass.

At noon on May 9 all Axis forces in II Corps's sector formally surrendered to General Harmon.

On May 13 all Axis forces in North Africa surrendered—nearly two hundred and seventy-five thousand troops, more than half of them Germans—such a huge haul that Eisenhower complained to Marshall he had never been taught in any of his army colleges how to treat such a sudden and splitting headache.

On May 20 a monster celebration and victory parade was staged in Tunis. General Eisenhower abhorred the idea of a celebration; he wanted rather a commemoration of those who had been killed to achieve the victory, but celebration and victory parade was what the British craved and would have after so many long and difficult years of dispiriting defeat. "At no time, perhaps, in the whole of the Second World War," Harold Macmillan would observe later, "did the prestige and power of Britain stand so high." A warm sunny day; "the happiest kind of parade": a few French—Zouaves, Tirailleurs, native troops, the Foreign Legion—then a battalion of the 34th Division, very well received, and last the British, led by Highland bagpipers, regiment after regiment, fourteen thousand men in all. "A goddam waste of time," General Patton rasped to General Bradley. Neither man had been invited to stand on the platform to take the salutes of the passing soldiers; that honor had been reserved for Eisenhower and his chief subordinates, Giraud, Cunningham, Tedder, and Alexander.

There followed a feast at the palace of the newly installed French resident general and a call upon the newly installed Bey of Tunis. The latter dignitary gratefully passed out gauds, medals, decorations, and hideous insignia to all hands. As quickly as possible Eisenhower and his party left for the airport and the flight back to Algiers.

From his Flying Fortress the supreme commander gazed down at the sea and the coastline beneath him. His mind was almost wholly occupied, as it had been for some weeks past, with the task that lay immediately ahead; nevertheless, the mission so recently (and so belatedly) accomplished had its lessons that clamored for his attention. And the ceremonies of the day were like a memento mori, reminding him of what he had done, what he had failed to do, and how many had fallen in the effort.

Nine months before, the Combined Chiefs of Staff had instructed him to clear the enemy out of all northwest Africa, including Tunisia, so as to make possible further offensive operations into Libya against the Afrika Corps in the Libyan Desert. In the timetable of this he had failed, but he had eventually accomplished more than had been asked of him. The victory in Africa would come to be spoken of, at least among the Americans and the British, as a turning point in the great war; and certainly it would be true, after Stalingrad and Tunisia, that the Axis armies would never again find it possible to seize the initiative except briefly and locally. (Which ally deserved more credit for forcing the turning point would become a matter of dispute and of national prestige, to be converted at last into a minor polemic of the Cold War.)

General Eisenhower recognized—if only from the hordes of Axis prisoners and the mountains of Axis booty—the measure of the victory. He could smile as he recalled the message he had received from some West Point classmates then on duty in faraway India, congratulating him and dubbing him Ikus Africanus. He knew his military history. Whether he dared compare himself with Scipio was moot, for he had always admired Hannibal.

At all events, he could now look down below him on a sea that was safe for the passage of Allied ships, an enormous strategic advantage; on a sea over which Allied armies could now be transported to any of a half-dozen tempting objectives—Sicily, Sardinia, Corsica, Italy, southern France, Greece, the Dodecanese islands—to assault any one of which would conceivably wound the Axis. Which the most grievously? These were matters of high strategy, over which he no longer exercised any sway. He had a month ago sent General Marshall a lengthy cable in which, most tentatively, he had suggested the "many attractive features" of "a shifting of our weight further eastward to bring Turkey into the war and attack through that region." In the same breath he had protested his firm allegiance to the strategy of a cross-Channel attack, "but the time and assets required . . . we could not possibly undertake it. . . . The coastal defenses of western Europe are too formidable to attack except with over-whelming strength and with reserves piled up to make good our position as rapidly as those defenses have been penetrated."

This was scarcely the bold and bellicose Eisenhower who had advocated immediate cross-Channel invasion in the late summer of 1942. What had happened to the hero in a year's time? A growth of wisdom? Surely not an access of timidity? Or, as seems more plausible, had his daily association with British officers, whose conspectus of world affairs was a good deal more sophisticated than his own, gradually dissuaded him from the advisability of American strategy—the short, massive knockout punch, delivered with all force to the enemy's vitals?

However that may be, the victory won by the armies he commanded had given the Allies an unaccustomed assortment of options. It felt good. The victory had cost the Allies; Eisenhower did not yet know how dearly—the estimates had not yet been processed by the military bureaucracy—but surely as many as ten thousand men had been killed.* It did not bear thinking about.

He gazed down again. The airplane was passing over Bizerte. Below, crawling eastward toward Alexandria, was a vast convoy, the first to attempt the Mediterranean passage since 1941. Here was proof that the Mediterranean was once again controlled by the Allies. Harold Macmillan touched his arm. "There, General," he said, "are the fruits of your victory." Eisenhower turned to Macmillan, smiling, tears standing in his eyes. "Ours, you mean; ours," he said; "the victory that we have all won together."

CHAPTER EIGHT

Soldier in Politics

GENERAL EISENHOWER'S PERFORMANCE as supreme commander in the spring of 1943 suggests that of a juggler extraordinary: he was obliged to keep four vividly colored balls in the air at once, occasionally adding two or three smaller ones to the display. First sphere, the Tunisian campaign; second, the planning of HUSKY, the invasion of Sicily; third, an adjudicature of the contention among the French leaders, an act of pacification constantly embarrassed by orders from the White House; and fourth, the responsibility dumped on him by the Combined Chiefs, when they could not agree among themselves, to recommend which military operation might best be mounted to exploit the expected success of HUSKY. Should it be a swift attack on the toe of the Italian boot? An assault farther north, say at Naples? The capture of Sardinia? Of Corsica? Or a retirement from the Mediterranean in order to prepare for the cross-Channel invasion of France? Eisenhower was asked to judge.

In planning HUSKY, Eisenhower's initial notion had been to direct the assault forces against the southeastern corner of Sicily, a course designed to capture the port of Siracusa and the most highly developed airfields. His planners, however, were convinced that the forces required to hold a

---

* The TORCH landings and the Tunisian campaign together resulted in 10,820 Allied dead, 39,575 wounded, 21,415 captured or missing; a total of 71,810 casualties.

firm bridgehead could not be maintained over the beaches, and they feared Siracusa might be left a shambles; they fixed covetous eyes on the port of Palermo, up in the northwest, and set about drafting a series of plans, each of them for one reason or another found wanting.

The planners also had something else to worry about: the strength of the garrison defending the island. Nine Allied divisions were to make the assault (five British under Montgomery, four American under Patton), and G–2 estimated enemy strength at eight divisions. Of these, how many were German? If more than two "well-armed and fully organized" German divisions were in Sicily, Eisenhower cabled the Combined Chiefs on April 7, "the operation [Husky] offers scant promise of success." Eisenhower associated Alexander with him in this opinion.

Churchill found the message repugnant, and its content in striking contrast with the confidence Eisenhower had showed about a cross-Channel invasion of France, which would have been met by a great many more than two German divisions. "It is perfectly clear," Churchill told the British Chiefs of Staff, "that the operations must either be entrusted to someone who believes in them, or abandoned. I trust the Chiefs of Staff will not accept these pusillanimous and defeatist doctrines from whoever they come." He remarked "the total absence of one directing mind and commanding will power." "I regard the matter as serious in the last degree," he added. "We have told the Russians that they cannot have their supplies by the northern convoy for the sake of Husky, and now Husky is to be abandoned if there are two German divisions (strength unspecified) in the neighborhood. What Stalin would think of this when he has one hundred and eighty-five German divisions on his front, I cannot imagine."

The British Chiefs agreed; so did the American Chiefs. A temperate version of Churchill's view was dispatched to AFHQ. "Operation Husky will be prosecuted with all the means at our disposal," Eisenhower responded, more stiffly than usual; "there is no thought here except to carry out our orders to the ultimate limit [of] our ability."

Work was resumed on the most recent—it was the seventh or eighth—plan for Husky, but with growing acrimony. The views of the British Army, on the one hand, and of the RAF and Royal Navy on the other, were in sharp conflict, and mostly because of Montgomery. Some weeks before, he had given an earlier plan a cursory look and approved it on the condition that his Eastern Task Force be enforced by another division. This had been done. On April 24 for the first time he examined the plan in detail and "quickly decided that it would not do." He sent a signal to Alexander saying as much and recommended radical changes, observing that he must "be allowed to make [his] own Army plan." Cunningham and

Tedder were both thoroughly vexed by these proceedings, and because Alexander did not promptly call Montgomery to order.

At issue was the disposition of the attacking forces. The planners had assigned to Montgomery's Eastern Task Force a stretch of coast that reached some one hundred miles from the Gulf of Catania on Sicily's eastern shore around to the Gulf of Gela on the southern shore. As Montgomery complained to Brooke, the plan involved dispersing his army in "little brigade-groups all over the place." He preferred a massive assault over a coastline only some thirty miles long, from Siracusa down around the tip of the Pachino peninsula. To concentrate his troops in this fashion would mean that the complex of airfields near Gela was no longer among his objectives. Since those airfields were crucial to the success of HUSKY, both Cunningham and Tedder jibbed violently, protesting Montgomery's exclusive, individual approach to a problem that involved so many other services.

Up to now the supreme commander had kept clear of the wrangle, declining to compel a decision, but by May 1 it was unmistakable that he must intervene. His reluctance was deliberate, stemming in part from his conviction that he should when possible permit his subordinates to mend their own fractures, and in part from his singular notions about leadership. These notions invite scrutiny, if only because he was faithful to them as soldier and later as statesman and because he would be assailed on account of them as woefully vague, irresolute, pliable, dim, bewildered, lacking in authority, indifferent, and disposed to strike a compromise.

Essential to leadership, in Eisenhower's view, was the team. First the members of the team must be carefully selected and trained to work together, each man doing his own job; then all pull together, shoulder to shoulder, with a team spirit, an esprit de corps, a high morale, able to accomplish anything together, to fight together, to win. The captain of such a team need only have their respect and affection: the team would follow him anywhere.*

In any case, Eisenhower's senior commanders were summoned to confer in Algiers on May 2. When bad weather grounded Alexander at his Tunisian headquarters, Montgomery suggested instead an AFHQ staff conference at which he would present his plan for HUSKY. That plan had been notably elaborated to meet the earlier objections to it: Montgomery now recommended that Patton's Western Task Force be shifted from the

---

* In this spring of 1943, when his affairs were so tangled and cluttered, he nevertheless found time to write his son John some advice on leadership. The leader, he believed, was made, not born: "The one quality that can be developed by studious reflection and practice is the leadership of men. The idea is to get people working together, not only because you tell them to do so and enforce your orders but because they instinctively want to do it for you."

Palermo area to the Gela area and be charged with capturing the vital airfields in that direction. The two task forces would thus be concentrated side by side in the southeast.

Montgomery was gratified to find that Eisenhower and Beetle Smith alike supported his plan—Eisenhower saw no reason to tell him that it was substantially similar to his own first plan—and went away very much pleased with himself, imagining that his military perspicacity had saved Husky from disaster. (The supply officers, in the interval since their rejection of Eisenhower's version of the plan, had been promised a considerably larger number of LSTs, and the DUKW, the dual-drive amphibious truck nicknamed "the duck," had gone into quantity production; these two developments assured the landing forces of ample maintenance over their beaches.)

Next day, May 3, Eisenhower's senior commanders approved the plan. The supreme commander had satisfactorily demonstrated his leadership. No one was unhappy; Montgomery was purring; Tedder, Cunningham, and Alexander, as they came to think about the affair, were bound to admire Eisenhower's method; and Husky was at last on the road.

The Combined Chiefs approved the final outline plan for Husky on May 12, the first day of a two-week conference in Washington, known by the code name Trident.* But they were unable to agree as to how the expected swift capture of Sicily might be exploited and at length decided to refer the matter to Eisenhower for his recommendation. Churchill at once determined to travel to Algiers, accompanied by General Brooke and General Ismay, to personally press his opinions on the Allied commander in chief. But lest it be thought that his eloquent presence might intolerably weight the scales, Churchill besought Roosevelt to send Gen-

---

* The main business of Trident was the persistent effort of the Americans to get agreement on a cross-Channel invasion of France, and the opposed attempts of Prime Minister Churchill to have more sizable Anglo-American forces committed to the Mediterranean theater. President Roosevelt, gradually more magnetized by the forceful ideas of General Marshall, now said that he had "always shrunk from the thought of putting large armies into Italy." In response, Churchill still insisted that the "first objective," the "great prize," was to get Italy out of the war. The cross-Channel invasion, he added, might be undertaken "as soon as a plan offering reasonable prospects of success could be made." General Sir Alan Brooke picked up these threads and embroidered upon them. The invasion waited upon favorable conditions, he argued, and those necessary conditions could be brought about only by the Russian armies. General Marshall once again urged that there be definite agreement on a date for the cross-Channel invasion, and on the last day of Trident he finally got what he had been seeking for more than a year: British acquiescence on a plan to concentrate maximum resources as soon as feasible in order to mount "a decisive invasion of the Axis citadel." Target date for the cross-Channel invasion was fixed at May 1, 1944; twenty-nine divisions were to be ready in Britain by that date.

eral Marshall to Algiers as well, to act as counsel for the loyal opposition.

Thus, four days after TRIDENT had been adjourned sine die, Churchill bobbed up at Eisenhower's AFHQ along with a large party of eminent persons.

Now it happened that during TRIDENT there had been a chilly specter sitting at the conference table—uninvited, reproachful, tutelary, constantly remindful of principle and therefore the more vexatious—the specter of General de Gaulle. As the Allied commander in chief, North Africa, Eisenhower controlled the French territory in that theater; the difficult business of harnessing de Gaulle consequently was his responsibility. For some months he had been able to ignore what the British and Americans were pleased to call the French political mess, pleading that the Axis aggressor must first be flung out of Africa, but after the victory in Tunisia de Gaulle could be put off no longer.

Various silly ruses—unworthy of Eisenhower's advisers—were fabricated, such as demanding that de Gaulle meet privily with Giraud at Biskra or Marrakesh, far from the centers of Gaullist enthusiasm and from the watchful attention of American and British war correspondents in Algiers. These schemes were brushed aside by de Gaulle and the French National Committee in London. De Gaulle insisted that the work of restoring the glory of France was of too high and honorable a character to be relegated to some "remote oasis"; he demanded that he be invited to Algiers. In mid-May he was given conclusive support. A message transmitted from the French underground announced the formation of a National Council of the Resistance and proclaimed:

> Every movement, every part of the Resistance, from both northern and southern zones, on the eve of General de Gaulle's departure for Algeria, pledges anew its total adherence to the principles he and the National Committee embody and uncompromisingly uphold. . . .
>
> They further declare: (1) that political problems cannot be excluded from these [Algerian] talks; (2) that the French people will never tolerate the subordination of General de Gaulle to General Giraud . . . (3) that General de Gaulle will remain sole leader of the French Resistance whatever the result of the negotiations [in Algiers].

This message was broadcast by Algerian radio stations and published in Algerian newspapers.

On May 30, in the middle of the night, General de Gaulle and a half-dozen of the French National Committee were landed at a small airfield remote from Algiers. Everything was done by AFHQ to keep their arrival confidential if not actually secret. But de Gaulle had arrived, and nothing would ever be quite the same in "liberated" Africa.

First, however, Churchill was at hand, a guest in Admiral Cunningham's Algerian villa next door to that of General Eisenhower, and the king's first minister had weighty business to conclude before time could be spared to worry about de Gaulle. Of course de Gaulle knew Churchill was nearby, but not officially, not yet to talk to. Nor could de Gaulle call upon General Eisenhower; he had not as yet been formally introduced, he had no liaison officer at AFHQ through whom such an appointment might be made.

Churchill began to woo Eisenhower over to his view of Mediterranean strategy long before their first formal conference on future operations. The prime minister's airplane landed at Maison Blanche, the big airfield near Algiers, in the late afternoon of Friday, May 28, bringing Generals Marshall and Brooke as well. Eisenhower was there to greet them, as was Admiral Cunningham; the plan was for Churchill to ride with the admiral to his villa while Marshall rode with Eisenhower to his, next door. Churchill decreed otherwise. He climbed into Eisenhower's automobile and got out only to take a comfortable chair on the front terrace of Eisenhower's house. There he stayed, talking strategy, until time to dress for dinner. The large party of high-ranking officers dined with Churchill in Cunningham's house. After dinner there was a lengthy informal discussion of future action in the Mediterranean basin. Churchill told his tale "three different times in three different ways." "He talks persistently," Butcher noted, "until he has worn down the last shred of opposition." General Brooke joined in trying to convince Eisenhower of the rich dividends to be gained by knocking Italy out of the war. "I am quite certain," Brooke noted in his diary that night, "that Eisenhower does not begin to realize the possibilities that lie ahead of us in this theatre."

Brooke was a guest in Eisenhower's house; next day the two men had ample opportunity for extended talks. Brooke learned how much the Americans disliked Montgomery, and how furious Eisenhower was because Montgomery had taken seriously a joking offer of Beetle Smith's, that he might call upon Eisenhower for anything if only the Eighth Army should capture Sfax by April 15. When Sfax fell, Montgomery had promptly demanded an American heavy bomber for his personal use; Smith, dismayed to find that his frivolous proposal had been taken in earnest, had been obliged to refer it to his chief; Eisenhower had been outraged that Montgomery would so capriciously appropriate a valuable weapon in short supply, but for the sake of Allied unity had sent him a Flying Fortress complete with the American crew to fly it. The transaction rankled.

Brooke also undertook to urge his ideas on European strategy. He told Eisenhower he would be "glad" to eliminate the cross-Channel assault from accepted Allied strategy. "He said that he favored a policy of applying our naval and air strength toward the blockading of Germany and the destruction of its industry but avoiding great land battles on the main fronts. He held the belief that in ground conflict in a large theater we should be at a great disadvantage and would suffer tremendous and useless losses. He wanted to open no larger front than one we could sustain in Italy." He emphasized that the Red Army "was the only land force that could produce decisive results."*

The formal meetings were held in Eisenhower's house, with Eisenhower presiding. Churchill and Marshall told Eisenhower of the decisions taken at TRIDENT, which included elimination of Italy from the war without precisely specifying the methods to be used to that end. Eisenhower observed that if the Allies wanted to knock Italy out, they should do so at once after Sicily had fallen, and with all available means. If HUSKY proved to be an easy operation, he said, the Allies should invade Italy at once, without troubling about such other islands as Sardinia and Corsica.

If this sounded sweet to Churchill, surely Marshall must have been tapping his spectacles irritably on the table before him.

The prime minister reaffirmed that he had no wish to interfere with the cross-Channel assault projected for next spring, but he declared that his "heart lay in an invasion of southern Italy." To compare an attack on southern Italy with the capture of Sardinia, he said, was to contrast "a glorious campaign and a mere convenience."

General Marshall was not so sure. He worried about the exacting demands that would be put on Allied shipping in maintaining a major operation in Italy; and the effect of those strains on preparations for the cross-Channel invasion next year. He advised against any decision before the first phases of HUSKY had been encompassed; only then, he argued, would the Allies know how the Germans proposed to react: how tenaciously they might oppose landings in southern Italy, where they intended to make their stand, whether any troops would be redeployed from the Russian front. He suggested that until the time was come to take a decision, Eisenhower should prepare two forces, each with its own staff—one

---

* Eisenhower reported this conversation at the first formal conference held late that same afternoon. Churchill adverted to the talk in his account of the conference, but he added to the last sentence, the one dealing with the Red Army, a date—"[in 1943]" —putting it in square brackets to indicate that it was his, Churchill's, gloss.

Brooke's and Eisenhower's recollections of their talk did not touch precisely at all points. Brooke would later assert that either Eisenhower had misunderstood him or his memory was at fault. If Eisenhower's memory betrayed him, it was one of the very few instances on record.

to plan and prepare for operations against Sardinia and Corsica, the other for an invasion of Italy.

Churchill "very passionately" pleaded for the invasion of Italy and the capture of Rome. The people of Britain were, God knows, on short rations, but Churchill declared he would "gladly" cut their rations still further "rather than throw away a campaign which had possibilities of great success."* This ardent appeal was followed by General Marshall's cool rejoinder that he wished only to emphasize the need for prudence and discretion in selecting the target after the conquest of Sicily. General Alexander and Admiral Cunningham both seconded the prime minister, asserting that the Allies should push as far as they could "on the momentum" of Husky.

Eisenhower, as a result of General Marshall's suggestions, tempered his views. If Sicily collapsed quickly, he was for crossing the Strait of Messina and establishing a bridgehead on the Italian mainland; meanwhile he would appoint two separate commands, each with its own staff, to plan alternative operations, one against Sardinia and Corsica, the other against Italy.

Marshall's counsel had prevailed. Churchill recapitulated the conference by observing that "post-Husky would be in General Eisenhower's hands." This was exactly the state of affairs a week before, when Trident had been adjourned. Eisenhower had shown himself to be a cautious and pliable commander, heedful of his superior officer, sanguine about the future, skilled in compromise.

General Eisenhower did not turn his attention to the questions raised by General de Gaulle's arrival in Algiers: his attention was forcibly yanked from other matters and focused on what he called "the local political mess" by events and by several clamorous persons, chief among them President Roosevelt.

The "mess" was the struggle to achieve a unified government that could administer French affairs and speak for France—the nation and the empire—until after the country had been liberated and its people could re-establish the republic. What made the struggle difficult was that the

* At the peak of rationing, which came around August 1942, every British citizen was entitled to a trifle less than one pound of meat (beef, veal, mutton, pork) per week. Each was also entitled to four ounces of bacon and ham per week; eight ounces of fats, of which two might be butter; and eight ounces of cheese (which fell to only two ounces per week in April 1944). Over a period of four weeks each consumer might buy sixteen ounces of hard soap, eight ounces of candy, and sixteen ounces of jam or marmalade. Over eight weeks each adult could get one packet of dried eggs, the equivalent of twelve eggs in the shell. As for eggs in the shell, most people got no more than thirty a year, and no more than about two pints of milk a week in winter.

determination of the Americans and the more considerate desire of the English to guide, control, and shape—even, if possible, to dictate—the destiny of France, faced head on the implacable resolution of Charles de Gaulle that the destiny of France must be the sole prerogative of the French.

De Gaulle's performance in Algiers was impressive. Within thirty days he had re-established the sovereignty of France, thwarted the express designs of the United States, and managed his affairs in such adroit and politic fashion that his apprehensive adversaries, and conspicuously General Eisenhower, believed that his strength and influence were waning even as they were waxing. Yet de Gaulle neither gloated nor dismissed his opponents as incompetents but regarded them as capable men who were busily engaged in tasks that prevented their appreciating the noble claims of France.

A word about American policy toward France. President Roosevelt— and Secretary of State Cordell Hull too, although his will was never so decisive—had a carefree way with what belonged to France. Both men rejected the concept of one single strong French authority; they preferred to deal with individuals and "keep the position fluid." As early as January 1943 Roosevelt was talking of cutting up the French empire like a child's birthday cake. In March he told Anthony Eden, the British foreign secretary, that Dakar in French West Africa and Bizerte in Tunisia should be held after the war by the United Nations; British troops, he remarked casually, would occupy Bizerte, while American troops would take over Dakar. These were, to be sure, colonial possessions, and an excellent case could be made against the legitimacy of French control. But Roosevelt had already gone further. He had undertaken at Casablanca to supply General Giraud with American munitions and other military assistance, and he had proposed that this be done unilaterally, without reference to his British ally. In return Giraud was to serve as the instrument of American policy: he would be recognized as having "the right and duty of preserving all French interests" until the French people were able "to designate their regular Government"; his would be the sole authority under whom all the French fighting against Germany might reunite; his precise functions would be defined by General Eisenhower and his AFHQ political adviser Robert Murphy. Documents setting forth these and other terms were actually signed by Roosevelt and Giraud. What was worse, the documents named Churchill as a party to the agreement, although he knew nothing of it.

The arrangement was of course "completely unacceptable" to the British, "quite impossible"; and the use of Churchill's name was, as Macmillan has said, "unpardonable." Precisely how and why the President could have signed these documents has never been elucidated and may never be. Those closest to the affair incline to believe that the deal was struck without thought, without consideration, by a lighthearted man in holiday mood, a man of great confidence in Allied and more particularly American power and in his own control of that power.

Some exceedingly deft and tactful diplomacy was at once required, chiefly of Churchill and Macmillan, to make Murphy and Giraud accept the changes which, when they were ratified in Washington some months later, would decontaminate the agreement. Giraud's authority as a trustee of French interests was restricted to French North and West Africa; most important, it was stipulated that responsibility for achieving the unity of all Frenchmen under a single authority would be shared by Giraud and the French National Committee headed by de Gaulle.

Word of this agreement of course reached de Gaulle. He considered it both foolish and wicked; it confirmed him in his gloomy suspicions of what Roosevelt was up to, and it made the work of achieving French unity far more difficult—postponed that work, indeed, from January to June. Now the moment for unity had come, if the Americans and English would only keep their hands off. But de Gaulle knew that was too much to hope for.

On May 31 seven Frenchmen met to constitute themselves a government committee.* Robert Murphy and Harold Macmillan stood nervously in the wings, awaiting word of this first meeting. (General Eisenhower, as we have seen, was engrossed in another meeting in another part of town.) For his part, de Gaulle at once made his views clear. "The military command," he said, "will . . . be appointed by the government and will remain subordinate to it. If it is thought that this army chief should be placed during operations under the strategic command of a foreign general, this can be done only by order of the French authority." Giraud began to lose his temper. "Further," said de Gaulle, "so as to indicate clearly that France . . . repudiates Vichy entirely, it is necessary that we relieve General Noguès, Governor-General Boisson, and Governor-General Peyrouton of their duties." Since these Vichyite officers represented Giraud's chief if not only French support, he flatly refused to

* General Giraud had two associates: General Alphonse Georges, an elderly booby nominated to the committee at the suggestion of Churchill; and the unassuming, sagacious financier, Jean Monnet, who had come to Algiers at the request of the White House. General de Gaulle had brought with him two members of the French National Committee: André Philip and René Massigli. The seventh, Georges Catroux, was a five-star general whose long friendship with Giraud was balanced by his measured sympathy with the Gaullist cause; it was hoped his calm, reasonable presence would serve to bridge the predictable chasms.

yield their protection. As for subordination of the military command to the government, that was impossible. It could not even be discussed.

The two points raised by de Gaulle were precisely the two most certain to infuriate President Roosevelt. At issue was French sovereignty, the right of Frenchmen to decide how French affairs would be conducted; but Roosevelt took a longer view, perceiving ahead the peace table, the division of the booty, the new utopia, and the hope for blessed peace eternal. He imagined that France, poor Marianne, was sensitive about her defeat by the Germans and wanted only his strong friendship to revive her. What he and most other Allied statesmen failed to appreciate was that within metropolitan France there was in process a revolution. De Gaulle knew this, and knew also that most Frenchmen blamed the English-speaking nations for presiding over the renascence of Germany during the 1920s and 1930s and then leaving France to defend herself alone in 1939.

President Roosevelt was not at once apprised of de Gaulle's insistence that only Frenchmen might decide such matters as the subordination of French soldiers to the commands of foreign officers, or the propriety of the appointment of Vichyites to high office in French colonies, but he very swiftly made his views as clear as those of de Gaulle. "I want to give you," he cabled Churchill on June 5, "the thought that North Africa is in last analysis under British-American military rule, and that for this reason Eisenhower can be used on what you and I want."

Used. In this way Eisenhower was to be placed between the upper and nether millstones, in a splendid position to judge which ground the harder.

Was North Africa in fact under military rule? Certainly General Eisenhower had acted as if it were when he swiftly dictated the elevation of Giraud to civil and military commander in chief of North Africa under his own thumb; just as certainly he had ever since by emollient word and deed sought to persuade the French otherwise. The Americans and British, he had argued, were devoted allies of the French, if not indeed their blood brothers. Had not all three fought together in Tunisia against the Axis invaders? But his commander in chief had other ideas.

By June 3 the seven had declared themselves the French Committee of National Liberation, with Giraud and de Gaulle as co-presidents. They proclaimed: "The committee . . . is the central French power. . . . It exercises French sovereignty. . . . It assumes authority over the territories and the military forces hitherto under the French National Committee [de Gaulle] and the Civil and Military Commander in Chief [Giraud]."

Recognizing the inevitable, Peyrouton had already submitted his resignation. The seven appointed Catroux to replace him and agreed that

Noguès and Boisson would be relieved as soon as a minister had been found to take charge of the colonies.

AFHQ did not acknowledge these developments, and suppressed news of them for several hours, until after de Gaulle had personally made them public.

Giraud was resigned to the loss of his Vichyite proconsuls—his American support was in any case what mattered—but when on June 8 the seven undertook to settle the question of military command, he would consider only a proposal that put all French forces, including de Gaulle's Free French, under his sole authority, independent of the new French government. De Gaulle, in what he termed a "calculated outburst," thereupon withdrew from the committee and secluded himself in his residence, "shrouded in sorrow."

General Eisenhower could be forgiven for allowing these preliminaries to develop unheeded. King George VI was expected in Algiers on a most secret visit that would require much of his time; after a protracted bombardment the Allies were about to attack the small but important Italian island of Pantelleria, halfway between Tunisia and Sicily; and only a month remained before D-day for HUSKY, the greatest amphibious operation in all history. Nevertheless, word of de Gaulle's resignation was flashed from Eisenhower to the Combined Chiefs and on to Roosevelt.

The President, one gathered, was not inconsolable. He began to pepper Eisenhower with cables, as many as three in a day; once, when the commander was gone for three days on an inspection trip in Morocco, he found seven peremptory cables, all dealing with de Gaulle, waiting for him on his return. Instructions were crisp and concise. Control by de Gaulle of French forces in North and West Africa would "seriously jeopardize the safety of British and American operations." Giraud must retain complete authority over French troops in North Africa. De Gaulle must not be permitted to gain a foothold in Dakar. Eisenhower must speak personally with de Gaulle; he was to express concern over the rumors that Boisson was to be dismissed from his post at Dakar and to request reassurances that the rumors were groundless.*

For a few days Eisenhower enjoyed a respite from the "mess." Pantelleria fell without a shot, yielding eleven thousand prisoners, a valuable

---

* Roosevelt had given Boisson his written promise that the Allies would not penalize him for having cooperated with Vichy.

Since Eisenhower's French was far from fluent, Roosevelt's message was delivered by Murphy. He found de Gaulle "in a most amiable state of mind," but not disposed to yield to what was manifestly interference in French internal affairs. Boisson, he told Murphy, was entirely unacceptable; his replacement could not possibly affect the security of Allied operations. Boisson unexpectedly removed himself as an issue of contention by resigning at the end of June.

radar station, and an invaluable airbase. On June 12 he was invited to dine with His Britannic Majesty, who was traveling in the Mediterranean theater under the happily chosen nom de guerre of General Lyon. The king, Macmillan wrote his wife that night:

> . . . was in excellent form. He was very good with Eisenhower, who was himself in excellent shape—interesting, amusing, not too shy or too much at ease—in fact, the real natural simple gentleman which he is.
>
> After dinner, in the chief sitting room of the villa, the little ceremony took place to which Eisenhower had looked forward with great and genuine pleasure. The King took the general a little apart . . . and presented him with the G.C.B. [Grand Cross of the Most Honourable Order of the Bath] with a few very well chosen phrases.

And then it was back to the upper and nether millstones. "We will not tolerate," the President cabled Eisenhower on June 17, "control of the French army by any agency not subject to the direction of the Allied Supreme Commander." "Nor are we interested," Roosevelt added, "in the formation of any committee or government that in any way presumes to indicate that it will govern in France until such time as the French people select a government for themselves. . . . finally, it must be perfectly clear that we have a military occupation in North and West Africa and, therefore, no independent civil decision can be made without your full approval." A few hours later another cable, telling Eisenhower that "for your very secret information . . . we may possibly break with de Gaulle in the next few days." "It is an intolerable situation," Roosevelt cabled Churchill, at about the same time. "We must divorce ourselves from de Gaulle." Early the next day still another cable came for Eisenhower: "I want it distinctly understood that under no circumstances will we approve the removal of Boisson from Dakar or any changes in his command unless they are approved by you." The warning would prove to be gratuitous.

D-day for HUSKY was now twenty-two days away. The supreme commander had three or four things to attend to.

Fortunately for Eisenhower's equanimity, some of his advisers were dependable, shrewd, and cheerful.* At this juncture he sent for Harold Macmillan. They showed each other the strong admonitory cables each had received, the one from the President, the other from the prime minister. Eisenhower asked for advice. Macmillan showed him the cables Churchill had sent, instructing him to give Eisenhower absolute support

---

* "My two strongest and ablest assistants in this matter," Eisenhower wrote Marshall, "are General Smith and Mr. Macmillan. They are both sound, respected by everybody, and are not hysterical." Elsewhere he paid his respects to Jean Monnet. He was occasionally also grateful to Robert Murphy.

in carrying out Roosevelt's bidding. "Oh, yes," said Eisenhower. "But, as a friend, what would you advise me to do?" That was of course a quite different question; Macmillan suggested that they interpret their instructions in their own way. At length Eisenhower dictated a reply to Roosevelt, Macmillan occasionally interposing an amendment. Difficulties, Eisenhower assured the President, had been exaggerated "in the public press," that convenient whipping boy of all fair-minded statesmen. Much of the apparent acrimony was no more than the celebrated Gallic talent for tossing tantrums. He, Eisenhower, was arranging for a private meeting with Giraud and de Gaulle; he respectfully urged the President to take "no definite action regarding the local situation"—in short, not to break with de Gaulle—until Eisenhower could attempt to untangle all snarls.

In fact, Eisenhower had begun to despair that Giraud would ever become the powerful figure needed to lead the French, much less to oppose de Gaulle. He confided to Marshall that even within the French Army Giraud was dismissed as "reactionary, old-fashioned, [and unable] to modernize the forces already organized. It must be admitted," Eisenhower added, "that he moves with ponderous slowness. He has no . . . political acumen whatsoever." In Macmillan's view Giraud was "stupid and vacillating," and he noticed that Beetle Smith and Murphy were inclined to agree with Eisenhower that Giraud was a spent force.

On Saturday morning, June 19, General Giraud arrived at Eisenhower's villa promptly at 10 A.M. for what had been billed as the climactic confrontation with General de Gaulle to decide once and for all the question of French military command. Outside, on the veranda, Macmillan and Murphy sat with René Massigli, who had been designated commissioner for foreign affairs in the French Committee for National Liberation (FCNL). Inside were Eisenhower, Beetle Smith, an interpreter, and Giraud.

General de Gaulle deliberately arrived last and spoke first. He was very grand. "I am here," he told Eisenhower, "in my capacity as president of the French government. For it is customary that during operations the chiefs of state and of the government should come in person to the headquarters of the officer in command of the armies they have entrusted to him. If you wish to address a request to me concerning your province, be assured that I am disposed beforehand to give you satisfaction, on condition, of course, that it is compatible with the interests in my charge."

A quarter-century later the natural response to such a speech would have been, "Are you putting me on?" but this was 1943, this was de Gaulle at his most stately, and Eisenhower had not before been vouchsafed a glimpse of this powerful personality when it was operating at full amperage. He was, no doubt about it, impressed. Yet between the two men there was, quite apart from President Roosevelt's roughshod policy, a very real difference. Within twenty days Allied troopships would be steaming toward the invasion beaches of Sicily. To this end Eisenhower needed the use of railways, of docks and cranes and port facilities, of airfields, of every harbor on the southern littoral of the Mediterranean. He had to have them, and so, he maintained, he had to have Giraud as commander of the forces that would carry out the existing military agreements covering the use of all these facilities. He implied that only Giraud could be trusted. This approach, as Macmillan acknowledged, "was almost insulting to the French, and could only be justified by fundamental distrust."

The interview was, in consequence, chilly and hostile. Eisenhower outlined his demands and warned that if they were not met the shipments of American arms to French forces would be halted. De Gaulle frostily requested that these demands be put in writing and forwarded to the FCNL, since "the organization of the French command is the province of the French Government, not of yours," made his excuses to Eisenhower, and strode out.

Eisenhower was prepared to face "the necessity of dictatorial action," but on the whole he preferred to avoid the antagonism such an action would surely provoke. His memorandum went forward, as requested, to the FCNL. Three days later that committee, by this time expanded to a membership of fourteen, unanimously approved a decree describing the organization of the French High Command: Giraud retained control of North African forces, de Gaulle of all the rest, including the secret army of the Resistance within France; a military committee was given authority over the unification, recruitment, and training of the armed forces; de Gaulle and Giraud were at first co-chairmen of this committee, but de Gaulle swiftly assumed control of it; all major decisions were reserved to the FCNL.

Eisenhower and his AFHQ advisers imagined that this compromise represented "a definite victory" over de Gaulle. The supreme commander cabled Marshall: "De Gaulle has definitely lost ground and is not . . . in position to control anything here. . . . within a matter of weeks de Gaulle will, in the opinion of all our people and of the conservative French . . . have declined to a position of practical impotency." And four days later, on June 26: "I am quite sure that de Gaulle is losing ground."

Thanks to estimates like these, General de Gaulle steadily consolidated and extended his influence over French affairs.

General Eisenhower turned again, with relish, to his military tasks.

He watched the 1st Division practice an assault landing not far from Algiers. He inspected the 3rd Division in Tunisia. For seven hours he traveled about, inspecting seven airfields and the units based at each of them. He spoke happily to Butcher, his aide, about the competency of the three American admirals assigned him for HUSKY. As the moment for invasion crept closer, the strain mounted. "I feel as if my stomach were a clenched fist," he told Butcher. Outwardly he was cheerful, buoyant, brimful of confidence, his bright blue eyes gazing steady and direct at the imminent adventure, only his habit of consuming sixty or seventy cigarettes a day betraying his tension.

And yet HUSKY was for Eisenhower quite different from TORCH. Then he had controlled every operation, every important decision had been his. Now responsibility for all operations was vested in Alexander, Cunningham, and Tedder; by July 8 the only major decision left to Eisenhower was one he would never choose to take: to postpone the invasion, or even to call if off.

At 5 P.M. on Thursday, July 8, the supreme commander's airplane settled on an airfield at Malta, where his command headquarters would be during the first day or two of HUSKY. He was met by Alexander, Cunningham, Tedder, and other officers of exalted rank.

He was, Butcher noted, "like a football coach who is pleased that his team is keyed up for a big game."

CHAPTER NINE

The "Soft" Underbelly

THE EXCEEDINGLY COMPLEX OPERATION had begun some days before, when the troopships left first from the U.S., then from Britain, and then from every African port in the Mediterranean from Oran to Alexandria; but the thirty-five hundred vessels appeared to be moving reasonably close to their meticulously specific schedule throughout the early daylight of Friday, July 9. The ships had been committed to reach their points of rendezvous in the morning and to turn north in the late afternoon. In darkness they were to move through carefully appointed areas, sea-lanes that had been cleared by minesweepers for their passage. All seemed well.

There then arose a fresh westerly breeze, quite unseasonable in these parts, and before long it was blowing a gale. The sea got rough. Ships rolled; smaller vessels were bobbed and tossed about. Soldiers who had been brought to fighting pitch were now sunk in misery.

For General Montgomery's Eighth Army this weather was not too bad. His troops were ferried close to shore in oceangoing ships and their landing craft were sheltered from the high seas by the Pachino peninsula. Their landings would be largely unopposed. The men of General Patton's Seventh Army, unhappily, crossed the water and approached their beaches in smaller craft—LCIs and LSTs—which were broadside to the weather, unprotected, buffeted about by wind and wave, knocked off balance, off course, off schedule.

On Malta, General Eisenhower knew something of these difficulties. With the wind at forty knots, Royal Navy meteorologists were predicting that it would abate after dark. Eisenhower had in hand a cable from General Marshall inquiring as to whether HUSKY was on or off. Some of his staff officers advised postponement, which would have entailed a delay of two or three weeks, maybe more. What the high winds would do to the airborne troops, approaching by glider or dropping in parachutes, gave the commander in chief pause. On balance, delay seemed to promise greater confusion. He answered Marshall late in the evening of July 9: "The operation will proceed as scheduled in spite of an unfortunate westerly wind that may interfere somewhat with the landings of U.S. troops." In one pocket Eisenhower kept some lucky coins; he devoutly rubbed them and then retired.

On D plus 2 the commander in chief, a couple of aides, a couple of war correspondents, and a half-dozen other officers cruised from Malta to Sicily on a British destroyer, H.M.S. *Petard*. Off Gela they visited General Patton aboard his command ship. (Eisenhower scolded Patton for not keeping the headquarters at Malta more fully informed of his progress and his needs. Patton retorted that his signal apparatus was already so overloaded that even his operational orders were delayed.) Eisenhower wanted to land at Gela, but Patton refused him permission.

Back aboard the *Petard* they sped swiftly eastward, once coming under fire from a battery hidden in some woods beyond the beach. Someone brought Eisenhower a helmet several sizes too small. "If I use this," he said sharply, "I'll need two men to hold it on." He walked forward followed by John Gunther, the correspondent representing American press and radio. "They treat me like a bird in a gilded cage," Eisenhower complained to Gunther; then, lapsing into dialect, he added, "I'se a valuable fellow, that's what I is."

For an hour or so, as the *Petard* steamed steadily along the coast, Eisenhower sat chatting with Gunther, reminiscing, gossiping, submitting to an easygoing interview. He dwelt on the notion that any commander had to believe "above all" in his own luck. On came his grin. "Of course," he said, "anybody can draw a bad card sometimes." He spoke of tension and loneliness and the burden of responsibility. The general commanding a division or even a corps or an army could find some time to relax, he said, but he, as Allied commander in chief, was never for an instant free of his burden. (Even this relaxed chat, as Eisenhower was quite aware if Gunther was not, was one of his duties: creating a good image of a commander and helping in the process of transmitting that image to the folks back home. The process is necessary in wartime, and can do the commander no harm in the years of peace that will follow.)

Eisenhower was anxious to greet an officer, any officer, of the 1st Canadian Division, the first Canadian troops to come under his command; he wanted to land on their beaches at Cape Passero on the southernmost tip of the island. Gunther was of course delighted at the prospect. In his imagination he had already written his lead sentence: "The American commander-in-chief of the allied forces of liberation set foot for the first time on the soil of occupied Europe today." The *Petard* slowed to a stop; a DUKW was lowered alongside; soon the commander and his party were riding among a swarm of naked soldiers who were bathing in the shallows. Gunther said: "General, to go down into folklore forever, all you have to do is greet the first man we meet, and say, 'My name is Eisenhower.'"*

The general transferred to a jeep and was driven inland for a mile or so, but the Canadians had moved on. The visit ashore was of use only in giving the two correspondents some good copy for their dispatches. All hands returned to the *Petard*, and by 2:30 P.M. they were back at Malta.

For some time now, creaking ponderously, the vast, inert bureaucracy of the War Department had been processing a detail of consequence only to Dwight D. Eisenhower and his immediate family. Somewhere in the Pentagon a clerk, perhaps a corporal, had routinely scanned a list of names, checked a table of dates, typed a memorandum, and put it in his out basket. It was taken up and passed along. A stencil was cut; copies were made in quintuplicate and distributed to offices in different departments; officers with more urgent matters in hand pushed their copies to one side. After some days one of these copies would catch the attention of a secretary in the uniform of the Women's Army Corps and would be placed once again on its proper route. At length a junior officer in the Medical Corps would take it from a pile of others like it and duly cut another order:

* Did Gunther in fact make such a suggestion? First he said he did; later he was not so sure he had "actually dared" to be so presumptuous. It makes no difference; the incident has gone into folklore forever and is now widely accepted as a revealed truth.

Lieutenant Colonel Dwight D. Eisenhower was sent notice to appear for a physical examination, testing whether he were fit for promotion to colonel in the United States Army.

It should not be thought that this administrative detail had escaped Lieutenant Colonel Eisenhower's notice. Fully a month before, on June 11, when he had occasion to cable news of a victory to General Marshall, he added: "I am particularly pleased that the operation turned out as it did because . . . today marks the completion of my twenty-eighth year of commissioned service and I believe that I am now legally eligible for promotion to colonel."

The victory, the capture of Pantelleria, was followed shortly by the fall of the smaller islands of Lampedusa, Linoso, and Lampione. Now the isle was Sicily, and there it was soon apparent that the Germans were the Allies' only determined enemy. AFHQ learned of this in several ways—including the reaction of Sicilian civilians, the mettle of the forces opposing invasion—yet General Eisenhower would surely have been astonished to find how widespread was the Italian disaffection and how far it reached into the highest circles of the fascist state. On July 14—D-day plus 4—General Vittorio Ambrosio, the sixty-four-year-old chief of general staff of the Italian armed forces, an officer of higher rank in Italy even than General Marshall in the U.S., met with Benito Mussolini, told him there was no longer any military justification for continuing the war, recommended that Italy be severed from further combat, and handed him a formal minute from the comando supremo which argued that: "The fate of Sicily must be considered sealed. . . . It is useless to search for the causes of this state of affairs: they are the result of three years of war begun with scanty means and during which the few resources have been burned up in Africa, in Russia, in the Balkans."

Hitler and the Nazis had been aware of these defeatist views at least two months before; in mid-May the German general staff had, using the code names ALARIC and KONSTANTIN, begun to draft plans for the occupation of Italy and the assumption of military responsibility for the Balkan peninsula. The erosion of Mussolini's power had begun even earlier. The intrigues to encompass his overthrow had begun at least as early as January, and by May 15 King Victor Emmanuel was busily conspiring with the duke of Acquarone, his personal adviser, and with others, including General Ambrosio. The king had summoned politicians from the prefascist era to discuss a possible new government. He had also summoned the venerable maresciallo d'Italia, Pietro Badoglio, still accounted a hero in Italy for his triumphs in the war of 1935 against Abyssinia (as a result of which he was also the duke of Addis Ababa). Badoglio had retired from active duty after the disastrous defeats suffered by the Italians at the hands of the Greeks in 1940, and he was now once again conspicuously available for a job as figurehead. By June the plotters need wait only for events to provide them with the proper circumstance. The 15th Army Group, General Alexander commanding, cheerfully obliged by bringing about the events.

Against this background it is scarcely astonishing that when Mussolini fell from power the Germans had emergency measures fully prepared and were able to take over swiftly. The Americans and British were woefully behindhand.

At 5 P.M. on Sunday, July 25, an oppressively sultry day, Mussolini had an audience with the little king in the Villa Savoia in Rome. He was informed that he must resign and that Badoglio had already been appointed to head a new government. The Duce was curiously docile. On his departure he was taken in hand by two carabinieri officers who, explaining that the king desired his protection, ushered him into an ambulance by the back door. He was driven away at top speed under armed guard. At the carabinieri barracks to which he was taken, some hours passed before the Duce realized he was under arrest.

At 10:45 P.M. the Italian radio broadcast the news of Mussolini's resignation, Badoglio's appointment, and the king's determination to continue the war alongside the Germans. The news was at once picked up by the BBC and flashed all over the world. The first of the Axis dictators had been toppled: surely this wonderful event would galvanize the leaders of the United Nations to action?

President Roosevelt was closeted with Robert Sherwood in his retreat in the Catoctin Mountains,* at work on a speech he was to deliver a few days later, a speech that dealt in the main with domestic issues. It was a quiet summer Sunday afternoon. The telephone rang. An aide gave him the tremendous news. He was "not tremendously excited." A few minutes later, after a futile attempt to verify the item, "Oh," said the President, "we'll find out about it later." A draft of the speech completed, a leisurely dinner, the sixty-mile drive back to Washington, an unavailing effort to reach Churchill on the telephone, and so to bed.

The prime minister was at Chequers, his country residence, watching a French film, *Sous les Toits de Paris,* when the news was brought him. He hurried away to confer with Anthony Eden and so was not at home when the telephone call came from Washington. He cabled the President next day but had nothing more urgent to say than, "Let us consult together so as to take joint action."

General Eisenhower's reaction was far more jubilant. He had come to

---

* This was the woodland camp he and President Truman called Shangri-La. Later President Eisenhower, exercising his prerogative, would rename it Camp David.

Tunis on Sunday for a conference of his senior commanders, but as soon as he was told of Mussolini's fall he telephoned Harold Macmillan and asked him to come at once. Eisenhower "was in a state of considerable excitement," Macmillan has recalled, "and full of plans and ideas for exploiting the situation." Unfortunately AFHQ had neither instructions on what to do nor responsibility for doing it. The situation had not been anticipated. The need of the hour was to drive a wedge between Italy and Germany: any crack in the Axis should if possible be immediately forced wider. An obvious first step should be a broadcast to the Italian people by General Eisenhower. AFHQ needed at once to know if terms of surrender might be offered the Italians and, if so, what those terms should be. To be sure, President Roosevelt had proclaimed at Casablanca the doctrine of unconditional surrender, but it was one thing to announce a general policy and quite another to negotiate a specific cease-fire, armistice, surrender, or other instrument with an enemy who might suddenly indicate a disposition to quit the war.

The Allied commander in chief would have liked to act at once and on his own. He deplored the modern communications which obliged him to solicit the approval of Washington and London before he could make a move. He knew, too, how jealously hostile were the two Allied governments over their respective policies toward Italy and their respective ideas as to how Italy would fit into any postwar world. While plans for HUSKY were first being drawn, back in February and March, Eisenhower had witnessed the courteous wrangle between prime minister and President as to whether the U.S. or Britain should control the political and economic administration of an occupied Sicily and later an occupied Italy. Eisenhower had recommended "a firm policy of joint Anglo-American responsibility and joint conduct of military government," and as the wrangle persisted he had felt it necessary to interpose a caveat. "For either government to assume primary responsibility," he had warned, "would invite undesirable speculation with regard to imperialistic intentions." This consideration, together with the joint Anglo-American concern that the Italian people, in an explosive reaction from the repressions of fascism, might suddenly swerve to the Left, had brought about an uneasy truce; Churchill had consented to Roosevelt's dictum that "there should be no senior partner" in the administration of conquered Italian territory.

As if this Anglo-American rivalry would not make it difficult enough to get quick agreement on how to exploit the fall of Mussolini, there was also the problem of dealing with a government headed by such as Badoglio. Neither Roosevelt nor Churchill cared a rap that King Victor Emmanuel had from the outset given Mussolini's fascism his cordial blessing, nor that Badoglio had been Mussolini's tool in his war to win a colonial empire in Abyssinia; but both statesmen were uncomfortably reminded of the arrangement with Darlan, which they had approved and which had provoked such protest on both sides of the Atlantic.

For Eisenhower the case was simpler. He was a soldier with a mission to perform. He must recommend a course. If it was not, for political reasons, a feasible course, then there were politicians whose business it was to veto his recommendation: no blood spilled. Meanwhile he had no time to fret over nice distinctions between fascist and antifascist. What he wanted was authority to act and to act quickly. He set Macmillan to work drafting two papers: a declaration by General Eisenhower to the Italian people, and a summary of ten conditions to be imposed "only in the event that the Italian government asks for a general armistice before . . . any actual invasion of Italian mainland takes place." The draft of the declaration was cabled to the Combined Chiefs for approval on Monday, July 26; the armistice terms went to them the next day along with the suggestion that the terms were so brief and simple "that they could be immediately broadcast to the Italian population and, together with message previously recommended [the declaration], would present to the Italian population such a promise of peace under honorable conditions that no Italian government could remain in power if it refused to request an armistice."

President and prime minister alike regarded these proposals with a cold and suspicious eye. Might they not fetch up in another Darlan deal? "In no event," Roosevelt cabled Churchill, "should our officers in the field fix on any general terms without your approval and mine." Both statesmen disparaged the idea of General Eisenhower's issuing declarations for the purpose of propaganda. "Speaking broadly," Churchill observed in a telegram to Harry Hopkins, Roosevelt's trusted adviser, "it is quite right that politicians should do the talking and generals the fighting."

The declaration was approved, however, and broadcast on July 29. But the armistice terms were still moot, and German divisions were hurriedly being deployed in Italy while the chances for a quick and uncontested surrender grew daily dimmer.

On that same Thursday Macmillan noted: "Poor Eisenhower is getting pretty harassed." Cabled messages, all most urgent, most secret, most immediate, most personal, streamed steadily in upon him from the Combined Chiefs, General Marshall, the President, Secretary of State Cordell Hull, and Prime Minister Churchill. Frequently to his office came Macmillan, bearing still other messages from Churchill and from Foreign Secretary Anthony Eden. In the heat of the North African midsummer Eisenhower, Beetle Smith, and Macmillan, occasionally assisted by Murphy, would attempt to correlate and compose these contradictory instructions. Eisenhower appealed to General Marshall: "What has me worried . . . is the possibility that there might occur a vast but possibly fleeting opportunity to accomplish all that we are seeking in the Italian peninsula. . . . Actually of course [that opportunity] may never occur. However I deem it of the utmost importance that the two governments authorize me . . . to act decisively."

To no avail. President and prime minister were still unwilling to extend him that authority. "There are some contentious people here," Roosevelt lamented to Churchill, "who are getting ready to make a row if we seem to recognize the House of Savoy or Badoglio. They are the same element which made such a fuss over North Africa." "My position," Churchill responded, "is that once Mussolini and the Fascists are gone, I will deal with any Italian authority which can deliver the goods. . . . [Our war] purposes would certainly be hindered by chaos, Bolshevization, or civil war."

At the end of July General Eisenhower made a quick trip to Sicily to confer with Patton in his palace near Palermo, and with Alexander in his walled olive orchard at Cassabile, near Siracusa. Back in Algiers he found that he had at last been authorized, under certain conditions, to propose terms if asked for them by the Italians. More cablegrams arrived, revising the conditions, specifying the circumstances. By August 4 Eisenhower was "beginning to get rather rattled" by the "constant pressure of telegraphic advice on every conceivable point"; finally he sent Macmillan to London so that he might get a really clear idea of what Churchill was after.

The prime minister was gone, bound for Ottawa and another top-level conference with the President and the Combined Chiefs. Already—in utmost secrecy, for fear of what the Germans might do if they found out —the Badoglio government was putting out feelers, baited with tales of how Italy had "turned Red overnight," of Communist demonstrations in Turin and Milan "which had to be put down by armed force." (On the other hand, Churchill assured Roosevelt, "Fascism in Italy is extinct." Presumably the Allies could now safely treat with Badoglio and the little king. Furthermore, the Allies should forthwith proceed with plans to assault the Italian mainland.) A first overture was made in Lisbon, a second in Tangier. A third, in Barcelona, which came from the various renascent political parties of the Left, was never seriously considered.

The events of July had made inevitable an Allied invasion of Italy. Obedient to this inevitability, on Monday, August 9, General Eisenhower convened his three British senior commanders at Tunis and won their formal agreement to the strategy of an assault by Montgomery's Eighth Army across the Strait of Messina and the seizure of a bridgehead in Calabria (this operation was known as BAYTOWN), and the subsequent invasion of the peninsula rather farther north, at Salerno, by the Fifth Army, General Mark Clark commanding (this operation was AVALANCHE).

A date for BAYTOWN awaited completion of the Sicilian campaign; AVALANCHE was tentatively scheduled for September 7. Eisenhower had hoped that all Axis resistance in Sicily would be crushed by August 5 (he had indeed been so rash as to predict that date, off the record, at a press conference), but the Germans had conducted a superior delaying action. Their commander, Colonel General Hans Hube, had as his mission to gain time, to fight stubbornly, and, when necessary, to withdraw as many German soldiers as possible across the strait and into Italy. On August 9 he was succeeding admirably in the first two parts of this mission, and he would find his chances for bringing off the third part, the withdrawal into Italy, good beyond his fondest expectations.

Meanwhile General Eisenhower, most of whose days had been devoted to the fruitless effort to pry from the Allied governments a clear directive by which he might seek a swift Italian surrender, flew back to Algiers with no hope that the Italians could be offered terms more inviting than unconditional surrender and no assurance that the several overtures proffered by the Badoglio government would be usefully pursued. And all the reports from his intelligence officers indicated that deployment of veteran German divisions in Italy was proceeding apace.

When he returned to his headquarters at the Hotel St. Georges he found that the War Department, in its dull, thorough fashion, had at length caught up with him. He was handed orders to appear for a physical examination, pending his promotion to colonel in the regular army.

The army doctors found that the general had a tendency to be hypertensive, and they were not entirely happy about his blood pressure. They ordered the Allied commander in chief to bed for a rest. For how long? A week if possible, at least two or three days.

It was now Tuesday, August 10. The 15th Army Group had smashed the German defenses based on Mount Etna; the British had captured Catania on August 5, Troina had fallen to the Americans on August 6; the Germans were now jammed back into the northeast corner of the island, struggling to defend the Tortorici line, which was less a line than a linked chain of mountain redoubts that reached from the eastern slopes of Mount Etna northwest along the Tortorici River to the Tyrrhenian Sea. Throughout the long, difficult frontal assault over mountainous country the British and the Americans had fought valiantly and well, under brave and resourceful officers, but they had not been so well served by their senior commanders. In part this was because of the physical dispersal of command headquarters—Eisenhower either in Algiers or at his advanced headquarters at Amilcar in Tunisia; Cunningham in Malta;

Tedder at La Marsa in Tunisia; Alexander at Cassibile in Sicily. In part it was because all the senior commanders gave their thoughts too much to the strategic future in Italy and not enough to the tactical present in Sicily. But the chief fault lay in the excessively timorous approach toward Husky itself. Ever since May 2, when General Montgomery had insisted at an AFHQ staff conference in Algiers that "enemy resistance will be very great; it will be a hard and bitter fight; we must go prepared for a real killing match," the senior commanders of Husky had pursued a cautious and conservative plan, abjuring risk, daring little and seldom. AFHQ's G–2, Brigadier Kenneth Strong, reported to Eisenhower on August 5 that only one regimental combat team had opposed the British Eighth Army landing in July, and that a more mettlesome commander than Montgomery could have plunged ahead and captured Messina within the first week of Husky, and so trapped the entire Axis force. Eisenhower had passed a bowdlerized version of this estimate along to the Combined Chiefs, not mentioning Montgomery's name and commenting only: "If this was so I did not sufficiently appreciate the situation."

In these circumstances the commander in chief may be excused for being a trifle hypertensive.

He did not, however, go straight to bed. On Wednesday night, August 11, he entertained at dinner a group of American senators who had arrived in his theater to study postwar problems, with a particular emphasis on air bases. (Of the six senators on this junket, the two most important were Richard B. Russell of Georgia, a power in the Senate Committee on Military Affairs, and Henry Cabot Lodge of Massachusetts.) Eisenhower would quite soon again have occasion to reflect on the purposes of this senatorial expedition, this peek into the postwar world.

On Friday, August 13, he finally undertook to stay away from the office and to stay in bed—or at any rate to rest occasionally but more often to stride back and forth in his bedroom, talking spiritedly with Butcher, worrying about the progress of the troops toward Messina, wondering when next he would hear some talk of surrender from Badoglio. On Saturday he was still in bed "as much as his nervous temperament [would] permit," and still prowling around, pajama-clad, fretting about the affairs of his command and seeking to define the gravest errors for which he might be held responsible by "history."

The two mistakes that most vexed him were alike in that each had come about because the enemy's capabilities had been overestimated; each was due to excessive caution. With the benefit of hindsight he now perceived that the Torch landings had been too circumspect: if the Allies had ventured farther east, to Tunis, ignoring the imagined dangers at their rear, they might have cut several months off the time required to clear North Africa of Axis armies. Similarly, he wished now that the HUSKY landings had been staged on both sides of the Strait of Messina, cutting off all the enemy in Sicily at a stroke, leaving them to be subdued later or captured in wholesale lots, permitting a swift onslaught up the mainland and conserving precious landing craft for further rapid amphibious assaults toward Rome.

Too late, too late.

Quite early on Tuesday morning, August 17, General Eisenhower reported again to the dispensary for the tests to determine whether his brief rest had reversed his symptoms. He was told he was considerably improved. In due course the medical records would cross the ocean bound for the War Department's capacious files and for appropriate action.

It was as well that the Allied commander in chief had reported to the physicians early, for the developments of the day were calculated to demolish serenity and aggravate tension.

He had known—and had reported the day before to the Combined Chiefs—that the "Sicilian phase of the campaign" was "drawing rapidly to a close," and also that the Germans were "succeeding in evacuating considerable numbers of personnel and light equipment." This was tolerably depressing, for it showed that the Germans—outnumbered, outgunned, lacking naval forces, and at a serious disadvantage in the air—had nevertheless won what amounted to a psychological victory. Now Eisenhower was to learn that troops of Patton's army and Montgomery's army had simultaneously burst into Messina only to find that the last rearguard Germans had already escaped them. The end of the Sicilian phase turned up fresh problems: How soon could BAYTOWN be scheduled? Could AVALANCHE be mounted by September 9? And could Eisenhower persuade Marshall to let AFHQ keep the three groups of B-24s on loan from England and sorely needed for the success of AVALANCHE?

But before he could address himself to these questions, Eisenhower was handed copies of several cablegrams from Eden in London to Churchill in Ottawa; all dealt with the latest and most positive Italian appeal for peace, proffered by the Badoglio government to the British ambassador at Madrid. Eisenhower at once sent for Macmillan and his G-2, Brigadier Strong, and began to study Eden's cablegrams.

As if this were not enough to fill his day, his aides insisted that he clear time for an emergency appointment with Brigadier General Frederick Blessé, the ranking medical officer at AFHQ, to receive a report that charged his old friend General Patton with having so far lost control of himself as to strike and otherwise brutally abuse two of his own soldiers, in hospital.*

Eisenhower, distracted by his other concerns, did not at once comprehend the gravity of the charges. To him Patton was a valued friend and valuable leader whose army was at this very moment celebrating its victory—too long in coming, to be sure, but that was not Seventh Army's fault —after a hard-fought campaign. He said something offhand about the need for "giving Patton a jacking up." He and Blessé agreed there were no laggards in the Army of the United States. Blessé told him that many GIs had kept slogging in pursuit of Germans so doggedly over the mountainous terrain that they had marched the skin right off the soles of their feet. At the end of their chat Eisenhower ordered Blessé to fly to Sicily and conduct his own investigation of the allegations against Patton, but to do so with all discretion. "If this thing ever gets out," he said, "they'll be howling for Patton's scalp, and that will be the end of Georgie's service in this war. I simply cannot let that happen. Patton is *indispensable* to the war effort—one of the guarantors of our victory."

With Blessé gone, Eisenhower dictated a cablegram to Marshall urging "that no move be made to take the three B–24 groups out of this theater at this time. If our present heavy bombing strength," he argued, "should suffer this reduction we would be skating on very thin ice in Avalanche." But the bombers would be ordered back to Britain, and this refusal of Eisenhower's request was symptomatic: AFHQ, so long the dominant

---

* On August 3 Patton had visited a forward hospital under canvas, the 15th Evacuation Hospital. Here he spotted a private who had been diagnosed by physicians as suffering from "psychoneurosis anxiety state, moderately severe." Patton called him a coward, cuffed him across the face, grabbed him by the scruff of the neck, and kicked him out of the tent. "Don't admit this son of a bitch," Patton screamed at a medical officer. "Send him back to his unit at once!" He whirled to glare down at the private. "You hear me, you gutless bastard? You're going back to the front, *at once!*" Medical corpsmen carried the private to another ward. His temperature was 102.2°. He had, it was found, been suffering from a chronic diarrhea for some weeks. He also had malaria.

On August 10 Patton visited another such hospital, the 93rd Evacuation Hospital. Here he found a patient who sat huddled, shivering and sobbing. This soldier, who had begged not to be sent to hospital because he did not want to leave his unit, was suffering from a condition diagnosed as "an anxiety neurosis." "You are just a goddam coward, you yellow son of a bitch," Patton yelled. He struck the soldier. "Shut up that goddam crying!" He struck the soldier again. "You're going back to the front lines and you may get shot and killed, but you're going to fight. If you don't, I'll stand you up against a wall and have a firing squad kill you on purpose. In fact," and here Patton reached for one of his ivory-handled pistols, "I ought to shoot you myself, you goddam whimpering coward!"

This spare account of the two celebrated slapping incidents, so called, leans heavily on the painstaking researches of Ladislas Farago, author of *Patton: Ordeal and Triumph*, pages 324–327, 330–332, 341–344. The account is no more explicit and detailed than that reported to Eisenhower on August 17.

factor in Allied strategy east of the Atlantic, was now waning in importance and would soon be subsidiary to the massive aggregation of men and weapons gathering for the climactic cross-Channel invasion scheduled for launching in less than nine months. Next came a cablegram to Churchill, who was still skittish about the public reaction to any deal with Italian fascists. Churchill had to be reassured that "we never for a single instant forget the very difficult problems you have at home and [recognize] we are merely fighting one segment of the war directed by the governments of the United Nations."

Eisenhower could then resume his discussions with Macmillan and Strong on the peace proposals from Italy. Eden's messages told how Brigadier General Giuseppe Castellano, chief of staff to General Ambrosio, had proposed to the British ambassador in Madrid that the Italian Army be allowed to join in the war against the Germans. He was, he had said, authorized to negotiate only the military arrangements by which Italian forces would join the Allies once the latter had set foot on the Italian mainland. For this purpose Castellano wanted a senior staff officer from AFHQ to be sent to confer with him in Lisbon. Eden mistrusted this apparently tempting offer, fearing that "it will land us in all sorts of difficulties both military and political with few if any corresponding advantages." Churchill, while agreeing with Eden that the Allies should strike no bargain and make no common plans with the Badoglio government, nevertheless perceived the possibility of a new situation if serious fighting were to break out between Italians and Germans; he hoped somehow to encourage such a development. Eisenhower, unaware of Churchill's ideas, wished to go still further. He hoped to be authorized to send a staff officer to Lisbon, as Castellano had requested. He proposed to send his G-2, Brigadier Strong, an officer who numbered among his accomplishments a reasonable familiarity with Italian. Strong was to collect what information he could from Castellano, checking it against what he already knew; make no promises for the future but hold out the bait that sabotage of communications, airfields, and public utilities useful to the Germans would be gratefully remembered by the Allies; and remind the Badoglio government that it must "depend upon the decency and sense of justice of the Allied governments when once we have arrived in Italy." In essence, Eisenhower wanted a minimal military agreement, with no political complications.

Once this suggestion had been cabled to the Combined Chiefs, meeting in Ottawa, Eisenhower could pause to reconsider his nearer, more intimate problem. He must write a letter to Patton, he decided; he could give it to Blessé to be handed to Patton personally; he had better write the letter himself than dictate it. He reached for a sheet of notepaper and uncapped his fountain pen. This would not be easy.

> Dear General Patton:
> This personal and secret letter will be delivered to you by General Blessé . . .
> I am attaching a report which is shocking in its allegations against your personal conduct. I hope you can assure me that none of them is true, but . . .

The report, drafted by the commanding officer of the 93rd Evacuation Hospital, had gone through the various channels of military bureaucracy. One copy reached General Bradley as commander of II Corps. He sealed it up in his safe. Another copy reached General Alexander as commander of 15th Army Group. He took the view that this was a family affair, to be handled by Americans if at all, and took no action. A third copy had come to AFHQ. Eisenhower could not duck the responsibility.

> . . . I clearly understand that firm and drastic measures are at times necessary in order to secure desired objectives. But this does not excuse brutality, abuse of the sick, nor exhibition of uncontrollable temper in front of subordinates.
> . . . it is *not* my present intention to institute any formal investigation. . . .

No formal investigation, but besides sending Blessé to Sicily, Eisenhower would dispatch Dr. Perrin H. Long, the theater medical consultant attached to AFHQ with the assimilated rank of lieutenant colonel, and Major General John Lucas, who was asked to inspect the divisions of Patton's army "to determine . . . the extent to which the story had spread among the troops and to determine their reaction."

> Moreover, it is acutely distressing to me to have such charges as those made against you at the very moment when an American Army under your leadership has attained a success of which I am extremely proud. . . .

No doubt about it, Patton's dereliction had made Eisenhower sick at heart. One of the commander in chief's principal tasks had been to single out those officers who could best lead men in battle and, by giving them experience of their responsibilities, train them for ever more demanding commands. Patton had always been high on Eisenhower's list of such officers.

. . . but nevertheless if there is a very considerable element of truth in the allegations accompanying this letter, I must so seriously question your good judgment and your self-discipline as to raise serious doubt in my mind as to your future usefulness. . . .

Patton was his ancient friend and comrade. Patton had introduced him to General Fox Conner, who had in turn set his feet on the path to military preferment. Patton loved and trusted him.

No letter that I have been called upon to write in my military career has caused me the mental anguish of this one, not only because of my long and deep personal friendship for you but because of my admiration for your military qualities; but I assure you that conduct such as described in the accompanying report will *not* be tolerated in this theater no matter who the offender may be.

Signed, sealed, and handed to General Blessé to be delivered to General Patton. And then—it had been a moderately busy day—General Eisenhower was driven to his villa. Dinner prepared by his servants; maybe a rubber of bridge to help him unwind; early to bed. Beside him, on the night table, a pile of cheap western magazines, his anodyne for the heavyweight perplexities of his daylight hours. And when he had switched off his light, no time to waste on compunction or self-doubt, for tomorrow might be crowded with as many painful decisions as today had been. But the commander slept little that night, or the next, or the next.

To negotiate the surrender of Italy and to plan the successful invasion of the Italian mainland were collateral tasks and clearly far more important to Eisenhower's mission than the chastisement of a wayward general; yet while the more important affairs might suitably be managed by capable subordinates, there was no officer whom he could delegate to handle the disciplinary problem; he must do it himself.

On Wednesday morning, August 18, coded instructions bearing on the Italian surrender began to arrive from the Combined Chiefs in Ottawa. Eisenhower was to send not one but two staff officers—one British, one American—to Lisbon to talk with Castellano. These envoys were to hand Castellano the terms of armistice drafted earlier by Eisenhower's staff and later revised by Roosevelt and Churchill, what were called the "short terms" as distinguished from a harsh set of forty-some articles, the so-called "long terms," which had been drafted by the State Department in Washington and the Foreign Office in London, and which spelled out in great detail the political, economic, and financial capitulation of Italy to the Allies. (The "long terms" had not yet been transmitted to Algiers.

Despite the fact that several Italian divisions had warred against Russians on Soviet soil, the Soviet Union had not shared in the drafting of these terms; Stalin, however, had as yet raised no objections to the exclusion of the Soviets. The French, to their indignation, had also been ignored.) The envoys were to tell Castellano nothing of Allied military plans. They were not to negotiate. They were to demand surrender of a man who they knew wished to offer, instead, his nation's readiness to unite with the Allies against Germany. The exchange of views in Lisbon did not, on the face of it, promise to be very fruitful. Nevertheless, clad in some rather ludicrous civilian garments, the best that could be found in Algiers at short notice, Beetle Smith and Kenneth Strong flew to Gibraltar on Wednesday evening, were there supplied with spurious British passports, and flew on to Lisbon on August 19.

In Algiers, General Eisenhower acknowledged congratulations for the "brilliant success" of his Sicilian campaign, dictated letters to son, father-in-law, and old friends, scribbled a note to his wife, and bided his time. Meanwhile, in Sicily, word of General Patton's outbursts had got around among his troops and had reached the war correspondents. By nightfall at least a dozen reporters knew of what had happened. And so it came about that, even as General Eisenhower was troubled for the safety of Smith and Strong yet hopefully awaiting what word they might bring back of an enemy's surrender, he was confronted by a deputation of journalists who would be content with nothing less than General Patton's head in a charger.

The deputation included Demaree Bess of the *Saturday Evening Post*, Quentin Reynolds of *Collier's*, and Merrill (Red) Mueller of the National Broadcasting Company. They waited first upon Butcher. Bess, the author of a recent and flattering piece in the *Post* about Eisenhower, handed Butcher a report of the journalists' combined investigation of the affair; Butcher noticed one sentence particularly: "If I am correctly informed, General Patton has subjected himself to general court-martial by striking an enlisted man under his command." Bess told Butcher that he and the other correspondents had so far agreed not to file any accounts of the episode but observed that it would be impossible to keep stories of such a lurid event out of print indefinitely. Reynolds remarked that there were at least fifty thousand American soldiers who, if accorded the slightest chance, would at once shoot Patton. Butcher listened and at length ushered the correspondents into Eisenhower's office.

The Allied commander in chief, dismayed to find that the episode was already so widely known, was nonetheless determined to hush it up if he could. He had learned from experience that if he talked off the record to journalists with his transparent candor and honesty, they would usually honor his requests. This time he wanted nothing less than their pledge that they and the other correspondents, whether in Sicily or in Africa, would agree to suppress the story during the time that Patton could still be valuable in fighting the great battles that lay ahead in Europe. Eisenhower urged that Patton could indeed be valuable, even invaluable, to the war effort. In exchange he told them of the stern letter he had written to Patton, of the unofficial reprimand explicit in the letter, and of the requirement he had laid on Patton that he apologize to the enlisted men and to the doctors, nurses, and other hospital personnel involved in the two incidents. He dwelt on the mortification this would visit upon a proud and fiery man like Patton. The force of Eisenhower's personality, his evident sincerity, his passionate conviction that Patton was indispensable in the bloody business that faced the Allies—these persuaded the deputation and, in turn, the other correspondents. The story was dead, or at least moribund.

On their return from Lisbon, Smith and Strong reported that Castellano had consented to take the "short terms" for an Italian surrender to Rome to be studied by the Badoglio government. He had also agreed to transmit the Italian answer to Algiers no later than August 30.

In the meantime, from Ottawa, where Roosevelt and Churchill were conferring, there issued distracting instructions, of which potentially the most damaging was the text of the so-called "long terms" of the surrender —"a formidable document," as Macmillan characterized it, "a planner's dream and a general's nightmare." Despite the fact that negotiations had already been opened on the basis of the "short terms," Eisenhower was ordered to use this longer and more exigent instrument in all future discussions. He protested this procedure; he considered it "a crooked deal." Besides, to put forward the "long terms" would necessarily delay a quick surrender and, since two assaults on the mainland had been planned for the immediate future, Eisenhower wanted no time lost in haggling over conditions to which the Italians would surely object. Already the Germans had at least eighteen, maybe twenty divisions in Italy. The Italians had another sixteen divisions; they might have no more fight left in them, but AFHQ could not bank on that. Two Allied divisions were scheduled to cross the strait from Sicily; four more divisions were due to make the landings at Salerno; still another four had been got ready for reinforcement during the two weeks following the landings. In these risky circumstances Eisenhower needed some assurance that the Italians would not be fighting against his armies, that they would be giving at least "passive assistance," even that they might be willing to immobilize a few German divisions. "It is these factors," he cabled the Combined Chiefs on August

28, "which make me so very anxious to get something done now." Specifically, to sign a surrender document.

On the next day, a Sunday, General Eisenhower was flown to Montgomery's headquarters at Catania, in Sicily, and was driven with him over the winding road along the sea to Messina. Here, standing on a rung of the iron fence along the boardwalk, they studied through field glasses the Italian mainland, two miles away. In a little more than one hundred hours Montgomery was to lead the Eighth Army across that water in the first Allied invasion of the continent.

Back in Algiers on Monday, General Eisenhower found among his staff at the Hotel St. Georges a palpable tension. It was now August 30, and at midnight the time limit proposed by Castellano for the Italian answer to the "short terms" for a surrender would expire. Castellano had been sent a message inviting him to meet once again with Beetle Smith and Kenneth Strong, this time at Cassibile, in Sicily. To Eisenhower the tension was so much excess baggage, the more so since President Roosevelt had cabled his permission to use the "short terms" as the instrument of surrender. Now Eisenhower saw only one course: to assume that all would go forward as expected. He bid Smith and Strong fly at once to Cassibile, taking Macmillan and Murphy along. Castellano would join them. No need to worry.

Castellano did indeed appear, but with an unexpected response. He announced that his government desired the Allies, as a condition of the surrender, to land in force, preferably north of Rome. It was soon apparent that the Italians would be satisfied with nothing less than fifteen Allied divisions and that they were, as Eisenhower would presently report to the Combined Chiefs, "far more frightened of the German strength and reprisals within their country than they are of our threat of invasion or even of our bombing operations." Moreover, the chances of their signing any surrender document whatever seemed to depend on AFHQ's readiness to help defend Rome against a German occupation. In consequence Smith recommended to Eisenhower that an airborne division be landed at an airfield near Rome to join and support the several Italian divisions in the neighborhood. Eisenhower, believing this a good gamble, determined to have the 82nd Airborne flown to Rome on the eve of the Salerno landings. And Badoglio, encouraged by these developments, notified AFHQ late on the night of Wednesday, September 1, that Castellano would be back in Sicily the next day to resume the surrender negotiations.

The routine procedures of the War Department had meanwhile been slowly grinding through their fixed courses. The medical report on the state of Lieutenant Colonel Dwight D. Eisenhower's health having reached Washington and been noted and approved, a recommendation that the officer be promoted to colonel in the regular army had been duly drafted and on August 26 started through channels. Suddenly it was whisked out of channels and, at his particular request, handed to the chief of staff. Marshall regarded the form thoughtfully. It would not do. It would have to be substantially altered. General Marshall had in mind something that had already happened and something closely akin that would happen in the near future.

What had already happened was that at Ottawa Marshall had wrung from the prime minister and the British Chiefs of Staff a firm acknowledgment of the cross-Channel invasion, now known as OVERLORD, the chief Anglo-American effort in Europe, with the target date of May 1, 1944. It had not been simple. On the same day, August 24, that the Combined Chiefs had agreed that all available means were to be disposed with the "main object" of ensuring the success of OVERLORD, Brigadier General Albert C. Wedemeyer, chief of the Strategy and Policy Group in the OPD, who had spent several days in London conferring with the officers planning OVERLORD, reported to Marshall that the British planners appeared divided in their opinions of the operation, while Churchill seemed to be "seeking every honorable avenue" of escape from it. Nevertheless, despite the persistent British attempts to keep the Mediterranean theater dominant in Allied strategy and despite the several conditions imposed by the British before they would vote their approval, OVERLORD was now more certain than ever of execution.

This being the case, an officer would very soon have to be named to command the invasion. Churchill had thrice promised General Sir Alan Brooke that the coveted appointment would be his, yet at Ottawa on August 15 the prime minister had rather casually informed Brooke that his mind had been changed: he agreed with the Americans that Marshall should be named supreme commander of OVERLORD; Eisenhower, he added, was to replace Marshall as the American chief of staff. None of these appointments had as yet been finally decided upon, but Marshall was quite aware of what was afoot. He presumed, then, that Eisenhower's permanent rank in the regular army would have to be considerably higher than colonel. He summoned a stenographer and dictated a memorandum to the President recommending that Eisenhower be jumped two grades and appointed a permanent major general. Roosevelt announced the promotion at his press conference on August 31.*

---

* A few days later an acquaintance in the War Department wrote to congratulate Eisenhower and to tell him that he had been advanced to major general (one of twelve regular officers of that rank on active duty) "over 32 Brigadier Generals and approximately 778 Colonels of the regular army, or a total of 810 files. General

Eisenhower promptly cabled his thanks to the President and also to Marshall, since he was "well aware that no one except [Marshall] could have initiated this action." In response (September 1) Marshall warned his protégé that his had been a recess appointment (made by the President when the Senate, whose consent was constitutionally required, was in recess); this being the case, Eisenhower should not be upset if "a small political attack" were mounted against his promotion, an attack occasioned by the opportunity vouchsafed certain senators to complain that the European theater was once again being favored at the expense of the southwest Pacific.

For Eisenhower, this cable was a tidy reminder that the great mass of Americans were much more emotionally involved in the war against the Japanese than in the war against the Germans and Italians. Douglas MacArthur, as Eisenhower never needed to be reminded, was a heroic figure of mythic proportions to many, if not most, Americans, and in the view of a group of irreconcilable Republican senators, any arms or troops sent across the Atlantic were arms and troops of which gallant MacArthur, the imperishable hero of Corregidor, was being wantonly deprived by a power-hungry President who before long might be signing treaties with, or at the very least sitting down to make secret agreements with, godless communism.

For Marshall, the cablegram was a way of recalling to his trusted officer that wars are waged in a political world and that he must be always wary of the treacherous snares and deadfalls cunningly prepared by politicians for honest soldiers. It was as though the chief of staff were putting the theater commander through a cram course against the day when he would be back again in Washington, in the Pentagon, faced with the dismal perplexities of the soldier who must every day patiently and faithfully treat with the impatient and faithless.

Eisenhower showed himself an apt pupil. When he acknowledged Marshall's warning of a possible "small political attack" on his promotion he ventured to suggest that "two of your least trained divisions or old divisions of whose eventual battle efficiency you might have some doubt" might be splendidly trained in Morocco. Such a force, he pointed out, "would establish a firm and continuing American occupation along the west coast of Africa that seems so important, particularly in political circles." Eisenhower was the more sensitive on this point since, as he knew, he had only a few days before been criticized by the party of American senators who had come junketing through North Africa. They had formed the impres-

Pershing," this acquaintance added, "was advanced over approximately 700 officers in World War I."

sion that Eisenhower intended to turn over the airfields at Marrakesh, Port Lyautey, and Casablanca to the French or British, and the State Department, urging that possession was nine-tenths of the law, had cautioned that such concessions would gravely prejudice American postwar interests. Eisenhower had retorted that he had "long ago" realized there would be "conflicting commercial and economic interests" in North Africa, that he had no intention of turning over the airfields in question "to anyone other than the United States forces," and that "nothing will be done to jeopardize national interests."

There were other ways by which Marshall could accustom Eisenhower to the sort of decisions that confront a chief of staff. In this same cablegram, Marshall said he was preparing a list of recommendations for promotion to permanent grade and he solicited Eisenhower's advice, an extraordinary request. Of the twelve officers on the list only four (Patton, Bradley, Beetle Smith, and Spaatz) had served with AFHQ, three (Somervell, McNarney, and Handy) Eisenhower had not worked closely with for fifteen months, and most of the others (Stilwell, George Kenney, Ira Eaker, Millard Harmon, and Robert Eichelberger) were fighting their war halfway around the world from Algiers. But Eisenhower, as requested, gave his "honest opinion for what it may be worth." On Patton, he made one guarded comment. He had not yet told Marshall of the so-called slapping incidents; now he observed:

I do not see how you could possibly submit a list for permanent Major Generals, on combat performance to date, and omit his name. . . . It is possible that in the future some ill-advised action of his, might cause you to regret his promotion. You know his weaknesses as well as his strength, but I am confident that I have eliminated some of the former. His intense loyalty to you and to me makes it possible for me to treat him much more roughly than I could any other senior commander, unless my action were followed immediately by the individual's relief. In the last campaign he, under stress it is true, indulged his temper in certain instances toward individual subordinates who, in General Patton's opinion of the moment, were guilty of malingering. I took immediate and drastic measures, and I am quite certain this sort of thing will never happen again.

Eisenhower dictated this message to Marshall on September 6. Already he knew something of the decisions half taken at Ottawa as to the command of OVERLORD. He assumed, as did Marshall, that the supreme commander would be Marshall. But that he imagined he would be ordered back to Washington as chief of staff may be doubted. In any case, during the first days of September his attention was wholly concentrated on the landings in Italy and the negotiations looking toward an Italian surrender.

True to Badoglio's commitment, General Castellano and his associates arrived at Cassibile on the morning of September 2, and Beetle Smith recommenced negotiations. Once again there was a hitch. The Italians now announced they had no authority to sign any armistice; they could discuss only military arrangements for the landings of the 82nd Airborne. Smith coldly withdrew. It seemed to Harold Macmillan that "in this emergency" some amateur theatricals might prove helpful. He sent a message to General Alexander at his headquarters nearby, and presently the English were subjecting Castellano to something like a country house rag: Alexander in full-dress uniform, accompanied by a train of officers in parade order, appeared, sent for the Italians, rated them for their shocking breach of faith in having arrived without authority to sign the surrender terms, warned them of the baleful consequences, and retired with icy dignity.

Eisenhower had meanwhile cabled Smith that he would come "any place any time" to sign a formal armistice agreement but urged Smith to sign any preliminary documents himself. Under pressure the Italians agreed to ask for authority to sign, and off went a message by radio. More confusion, more delay, with atmospheric disturbances impeding and garbling the exchange of messages; more idiocy from the Allied governments, whose premier officials had conceived the daft notion that these exceedingly secret negotiations should be climaxed by a public ceremony and celebration. At length at 4:30 P.M. on September 3 the Italians were sent the authority they needed. (Just twelve hours earlier two divisions of Montgomery's Eighth Army had crossed the Strait of Messina and landed in Calabria, where they had met, as Eisenhower had predicted, no very determined German opposition.)

When radio communication between Algiers and Cassibile proved to be wretched, Eisenhower decided on a flight to Sicily. He arrived in time to witness the signing, at 5:20 P.M., in a small tent in an olive grove next to the airfield. American, British, and Italian officers ceremoniously broke twigs from the olive trees to keep as symbolic remembrances of the occasion. But peace, for all three nations, was still only a symbol.

It remained to decide on when, and how, the armistice should be proclaimed, and Eisenhower left this detail to his staff. Smith and Castellano presently agreed that Eisenhower and Badoglio should variously announce the armistice on the evening before the landings at Salerno. The Italians were still not told where or when those landings would come; instead they were told to listen each day to the BBC for the prearranged signal that would indicate they might join in proclaiming the armistice that evening. Smith was also stuck with the unpleasant task of having to present Castellano with the "long terms," of which the first sentence was: "The Italian

Land, Sea and Air Forces wherever located, hereby surrender unconditionally." The unpalatable phrase "unconditional surrender" had been avoided in the "short terms" that Castellano had already signed, and he had assumed it would be precluded by the status of co-belligerency offered by Badoglio. He was very disagreeably affected not only by that phrase but by the measures embodied in the terms that followed. How would Badoglio and the king react to these harsh and heretofore unknown conditions of capitulation? The deception that Eisenhower had earlier condemned now stood exposed.

Nevertheless, because he was anxious to cooperate with the Allies as best he might, Castellano undertook to keep these "long terms" in his inside pocket until after the king and Badoglio were publicly committed to the "short terms" he had signed. On such turncoat principles were founded the limited and belated successes of Allied arms in Italy.

Castellano, moreover, plunged into detailed discussions with Smith and Kenneth Strong as to how the Italians might further cooperate against their erstwhile allies, the Nazis. After two days of this careful staffwork, Eisenhower sent off a cablegram to the Combined Chiefs informing them that four airfields near Rome had been designated by the Italians to be protected by them during the landings by the 82nd Airborne, that "ammunition, supplies and a few heavy weapons [were to] be sent up the Tiber" to a rendezvous to be arranged, that a senior officer of the 82nd Airborne was then on his way to Rome to settle the details of the operation, and that the southerly Italian ports of Taranto and Brindisi were to be made free to the Allies and the 1st British Airborne Division was to be transported to Taranto as soon as the Italian Navy, in accordance with the terms of the armistice, had come under control of the British Mediterranean fleet.

If all these had dropped as the ripe fruits of the armistice with the Italians, the Allied commander in chief could have been well satisfied with a good job of work and might reasonably have assumed that the Germans would find it prudent to retire to defensive positions north of Rome. Allied prospects were beguiling. They included the British Eighth Army moving north from Calabria, British paratroopers in Taranto, American paratroopers at Rome and encouraging five or six Italian divisions near that city, and the Fifth Army at Salerno. But things did not work out quite that way.

The chief difficulty was that too many of the Italian military leaders were terrified of the Germans and convinced that the Allies would never be able to protect them from German vengeance. These officers were determined to have the Allied air landings canceled; even, if possible, to have the Salerno landings postponed. What could such assaults achieve except to enrage the Germans to more furious frenzies of retaliation?

On Monday, September 6, Brigadier General Maxwell Taylor, artillery commander of the 82nd Airborne, and Colonel William Gardiner of the Troop Carrier Command were given an intensive briefing by Eisenhower's G–2, Brigadier Strong, on the strength and disposition of the German forces in the countryside around Rome. At two the next morning (September 7) Taylor and Gardiner left Palermo in a British PT boat bound for Rome. In great secrecy they were landed on the Italian coast, transferred to a Red Cross ambulance, and smuggled into the capital, reaching it late in the evening. Thereupon they conferred with a number of Italian army officers, all of whom made it clear they had no stomach for a fight with the Germans. The Americans were beseeched to cancel their scheduled air drop. At length, around midnight, Taylor and Gardiner were taken to see Marshal Badoglio. He was as frightened as all the others, impervious to Taylor's arguments; panic had bereft him even of ability to honor his own agreements. With Taylor and Gardiner as dismayed witnesses, Badoglio at 1 A.M. Wednesday dispatched a radio message to Eisenhower:

> Due to changes in the situation brought about by the disposition and strength of the German forces in the Rome area, it is no longer possible to accept an immediate armistice as this could provoke the occupation of the capital and the violent assumption of the government by the Germans. [The air drop of the 82nd Airborne] is no longer possible because of lack of forces to guarantee the airfields.

Taylor sent a message of his own recommending that the operation be canceled.

The procedure for a secret radio message to be encoded, transmitted, and decoded is a lengthy one. Not until 8 A.M. on Wednesday, September 8, was Badoglio's message comprehensible, but by that hour the Allied commander in chief had left Algiers for Amilcar, his advance headquarters near Tunis. Badoglio's message went instead to Eisenhower's chief of staff, Beetle Smith. Some three hours later it finally caught up with Eisenhower, together with word that Smith had also sent a copy of it to the Combined Chiefs and had at the same time, over Eisenhower's name, asked the Chiefs "whether or not . . . we should proceed with the armistice announcement."

General Eisenhower had arrived at Amilcar with his mind focused on the last-minute concerns of General Clark's invasion fleet, which was already loaded and poised to start across the sea to Salerno. As he read the papers handed him—Badoglio's message, Smith's referral of it, in his name, to the Combined Chiefs, and Taylor's message—his expressive face was remarkably transformed. The wide, generous mouth tightened, the bright blue eyes hardened and glinted, the fair skin was suffused and empurpled, the veins in the high forehead swelled and thickened. The commander was struggling to master his temper, always volatile. It is a question which more enraged him, Badoglio's craven turnabout or Smith's bemused submission of it to Washington and London for advice.

His senior officers were with him, met for the final coordination of their plans for AVALANCHE; they promptly concurred in his own prompt, angry decision. He dictated first a message to Badoglio:

> I intend to broadcast the existence of the armistice at the hour originally planned. If you or any part of your armed forces fail to cooperate as previously agreed I will publish to the world full record of this affair. Today is X-day and I expect you to do your part.
>
> I do not accept your message . . . postponing the armistice. Your accredited representative has signed an agreement with me and the sole hope of Italy is bound up in your adherence. . . . On your earnest representation the airborne operations are temporarily suspended. . . .
>
> Plans have been made on the assumption that you were acting in good faith. . . . Failure now on your part to carry out the full obligations of the signed agreement will have most serious consequences for your country. No future action of yours could then restore any confidence whatever in your good faith and consequently the dissolution of your government and nation would ensue.

Much of this was only blather. It was based on the assumption that Badoglio and the king, ardent fascists both, were somehow capable of acting with more honor than the deposed Duce. The "serious consequences" for Italy were inevitable no matter which way old Badoglio jumped. Equally inevitable was the dissolution of his government and of the monarchy, for already an underground Committee of National Liberation had been formed in Rome and its members, allied with the popular resistance, would in the end push both into the dustbin.

Next came a cablegram to the Combined Chiefs: "I . . . have determined not repeat not to accept the Italian change of attitude. We intend to proceed . . . with . . . announcement of the armistice and with subsequent propaganda and other measures. . . . [We] will not repeat not recognize any deviation from our original agreement."

Further to relieve his outraged feelings, Eisenhower and his senior commanders indulged in some more amateur theatricals, with the unfortunate Castellano once again impressed as the victim. He was brought to Amilcar, forced to wait, ignored, and presently marched under armed guard to Eisenhower's office, where he stood at attention before a long table behind which sat Eisenhower, Alexander, Cunningham, and several other officers, all grim of visage. Eisenhower read the message he had drafted for transmission to Badoglio, now and then glaring imperiously at the forlorn Castellano, who was, after all, the Allies' most ardent advocate among the Italians. Following this performance, Castellano was sent back to Tunis, presumably so that he might somehow convince Badoglio to honor the armistice.

But brave words and playacting, Eisenhower knew, were of no value to the men who would be storming the beaches around Salerno in a few hours. His anger had spent itself: now he was worried. Brigadier Strong telephoned him from Tunis to urge that there was no new military information in the messages from Badoglio and Maxwell Taylor, that the chances for the airborne operation were quite as bright as ever. But Eisenhower answered only that "he could not overlook the recommendations of a commander who had seen things for himself on the spot." He was dispirited. He was to lunch with Bradley, who was, by contrast, in excellent spirits. After his successes in Tunisia and Sicily, Bradley had been picked by Marshall to go to England to take command of the American First Army and to form the staff for a fledgling U.S. Army Group, both earmarked for OVERLORD; now he was on his way, and Eisenhower envied him.

The Allied commander did not return to his villa for luncheon until almost two. To Bradley he looked drawn and worried. "Badoglio has gummed up the works," he said. "We've just had to call off Ridgway's air drop on Rome."*

At 6:30 P.M. Eisenhower's proclamation, which had been previously recorded, was broadcast via Radio Algiers, as had been arranged:

This is General Dwight D. Eisenhower, Commander in Chief Allied Forces. The Italian government has surrendered its armed forces unconditionally. As Allied Commander in Chief I have granted a military armistice, the terms of which have been approved by the governments of the United Kingdom, the United States, and the Union of Soviet Socialist Re-

* Major General Matthew Ridgway was commander of the 82nd Airborne. For Eisenhower to call off the operation was more easily said to Bradley than done. He realized that to send a radio message (encode, dispatch, decode) would take too long, so he ordered Brigadier General Lyman Lemnitzer, then deputy chief of staff of Alexander's 15th Army Group, to fly to the airfield in Sicily from which the 82nd Airborne was to take off for Rome and personally order the cancellation. Lemnitzer's pilot lost his way, nearly piled up on a slope of Mount Etna, and landed at the right spot only after sixty-two of the 82nd's one hundred and fifty transport airplanes were already aloft and maneuvering into formation for their flight to Rome.

publics. . . . The Italian government has bound itself to abide by these terms without reservation. The armistice . . . becomes effective this instant. . . . All Italians who now act to help eject the German aggressor from Italian soil will have the assistance and support of the United Nations.

In Amilcar, AFHQ radio technicians had adjusted their devices to monitor Radio Rome. The transmission in progress proceeded without interruption for any proclamation by Badoglio. Eisenhower sat waiting. Psychological warfare experts had mooted the possibility that if Badoglio did not declare an armistice, the Germans might seize Radio Rome to charge that Eisenhower's statement was a hoax. Still no interruption. The minutes crawled. Or of course Badoglio might come on the air to exhort the Italian armed forces to repel the Allied invaders, due this very night at Salerno, as he now knew. After ten minutes had passed, the order was given for the text of Badoglio's proclamation to be broadcast, again over Radio Algiers: it included the command to all Italian soldiers to avoid further hostility toward the Allies but urged them to resist attacks by any other forces.

With a few members of his staff Eisenhower continued to wait patiently by the radio. He had decided, as he wrote a friend a week later, "to play a little poker," and he was gambling that Badoglio—soon, not late; in fact, on that same night—would declare the armistice. At stake was the Italian Navy. He had been advised by friendly Italians that unless he allowed Badoglio to wait five or six days after the Salerno landings before declaring the armistice, he would wind up with nothing, and especially without the fleet. Yet he knew that to wait five or six days would enable the Italians and Germans to learn how limited was the strength of the Allied assault.

He needed Italian consent to an effective armistice, and he needed it at once. With the surrender of the Italian fleet, the naval base at Taranto, within the heel of the Italian boot, would fall to the Allies without a fight. The first elements of the British 1st Airborne Division were already aboard light cruisers of the Royal Navy, ready to start for Taranto at a word. The 8th Indian Division was being loaded into other warships at Alexandria and would soon start for Brindisi, on the coast of the Adriatic. These southern harbors, Eisenhower knew, were relatively free of German troops; once the Allied troops were ashore, they could move swiftly north to capture the vital airfields at Foggia, one hundred miles away. Eisenhower's tactical objective was "to keep the enemy upset and worried in the southern end of the boot so that he will be discouraged from making too heavy a counterattack on" the beachheads around Salerno. He hoped that "by exploiting to the full our sea and air power, we will control the southern end of the boot to include the line Naples-Foggia within a reasonable time."

As the minutes ticked by, then, the Italian fleet was Eisenhower's "big worry." If Badoglio did not on this night proclaim the armistice, Eisenhower could and unquestionably would let loose a barrage of propaganda that would leave the old marshal wholly vulnerable to the Germans. On the other hand, if Badoglio did proclaim the armistice, the seizure by the Germans of Rome and of the machinery of Italian government was a certainty. The old man was in an impossible position. At the end, it was the little king who made the decision: Badoglio must proclaim the armistice. Seventy minutes late, at 7:45 P.M., Badoglio was in front of a microphone broadcasting his proclamation over Radio Rome.

In Amilcar, much relieved, General Eisenhower went early to bed.

On balance, the armistice must be accounted a favorable accomplishment; no triumph, certainly, but a reasonably successful achievement. The Italian Navy duly steamed out of Genoa, La Spezia, and Taranto, heading as ordered for Malta. The pride of the navy, the modern battleship *Roma*, was torpedoed and sunk by the Luftwaffe, and a cruiser of the Royal Navy was sunk by a mine at Taranto, but a splendid prize had been won. Eisenhower and Cunningham went out on a destroyer to watch as the Italian fleet steamed past on its way to surrender at Malta, and before long Cunningham could grandly cable the Admiralty in London: "Be pleased to inform their lordships that the Italian battle fleet is now anchored under the fortress guns of Malta."

The Italian Army and Air Force did nothing, because they were given no orders. Rather than stay to issue the instructions that would have given substance to his request for the status of co-belligerency, Marshal Badoglio scuttled out of Rome before dawn on the morning of September 9, along with the woefully unmajestic king, his queen, and a couple of carloads of courtiers. Most of the Italian army units in the field, few of which were up to strength and none of which had an adequate supply of ammunition or fuel, were contemptuously disarmed by the Germans. In military terms, Italy had temporarily ceased to exist, a fact that gave its wretched people at least one reason to rejoice.

The political aspects of the armistice were quite another matter. For Eisenhower, it was maddening that an instrument—the "short terms" armistice—which had been deliberately drafted to exclude all political considerations was nevertheless highly political and politically damaging. The difficulty, of course, was that he who eats with the devil must have a long spoon. Despite the fact that on July 26 President Roosevelt had assured the nation, "We will have no truck with fascism in any way, shape or manner," Eisenhower had trafficked with fascists, as indeed he had to do, to make an armistice. But Roosevelt had also said, "We will permit no vestige of fascism to remain," yet here was Eisenhower, his officer, carefully propping up fascist monarch and fascist marshal as the rump government of that part of Italy that was not occupied by the Germans. The psychological warriors were once again dismayed. "The Italian campaign showed that the United States had learned little or nothing from the mistakes of North Africa," Wallace Carroll wrote. "Once again the long-term political interests of the United States had been sacrificed to military expediency. To men of good will around the world it seemed even clearer than before that the United States was linked to the forces of reaction."

General Eisenhower took a different view. After he had at last met Badoglio, at Malta on September 29, he was pleased to report to his masters that the old marshal, so far from being a fascist himself, "hates fascism and the Germans intensely." The reason for Badoglio's accommodating change of heart was not hard to find: the Germans, having on September 12 freed Mussolini from his temporary and rather insecure imprisonment in a ski resort atop a mountain in the Abruzzi, northeast of Rome, had obliged the weary, shrunken Duce to become the figurehead of something called the Fascist Republican party, which established an eggshell government on the shores of Lake Garda; from behind this façade the Nazi propagandists took delight in tormenting the equally absurd Badoglio government which was sheltered by the Allies at Brindisi.

If Badoglio and the king were struggling to shuck the outward and visible label of fascism, they went about it in very odd fashion. After Badoglio had signed the surrender document (the "long terms") at a ceremony aboard H.M.S. *Nelson* at Malta, General Eisenhower inquired whether it was the marshal's purpose to seek out some antifascist Italians and invite them to participate in his government. Badoglio answered by reading a letter from the king, who requested Eisenhower's approval of his wish to invite Count Dino Grandi to join in his government. Grandi? Who was Count Grandi? While Badoglio was arguing that the inclusion of Grandi in his government would deal a severe jolt to the Republican fascist government up at Lake Garda, Eisenhower's advisers engaged him in urgent, whispered consultation to remind him that Grandi had been one of the original Squadristi, the black-shirted hooligans who slugged and booted into insensibility the early opponents of fascism; that he had himself survived as one of the most obnoxious of the fascist hierarchy; and that for AFHQ to sanction his appointment would be diastrous. Smoothly Eisenhower told Badoglio that he would refer the question of Grandi's appointment to the Allied governments.

In truth, Eisenhower found this plenary conference with the Italian officers exceedingly distasteful. It was political work; he hated it. In his every waking hour he was obliged to recognize the fact that politics was the chief business of a conqueror, but never did he relish it. Now, with Italy very gradually and painfully coming under his command, the prospect was that politics, like some horrible weed, would extravagate all about AFHQ, constantly making more demands on his time, constantly requiring more officers to be added to his staff, constantly interfering with his business, which he liked to think was to make war. New officers on his staff concerned with politics meant politicians in uniform. For months now he had had to shunt the politicians wished on him by the White House. In April there had been the imminent menace of Fiorello La Guardia, mayor of New York City. He had been the worst of the lot. Apparently La Guardia had been promised a commission as Eisenhower's deputy chief of staff by Roosevelt himself. Eisenhower remembered La Guardia well: he had been one of the most articulate of the congressmen at those pacifist hearings he had managed back in 1930: an absolutely impossible man. After he had contrived to keep La Guardia off his staff, there had come a New York Democrat called Poletti, Charles Poletti; he had heard from Patton that Poletti was "electioneering for Roosevelt among the Sicilians." He could believe it.

He could believe, too, that the military politicians would multiply like guinea pigs. Already there was the Allied Military Government of Occupied Territories—AMGOT—and there was the military mission he had appointed, which would presently be superseded by something called the Allied Control Commission—ACC—and both these had to be supervised and kept in order by the appropriate section of AFHQ, which would itself inevitably expand, as Macmillan would later observe, "with Parkinsonian proliferation." None of these reflections was calculated to improve Eisenhower's disposition.

Badoglio was still talking about his government, assuring Eisenhower that he would give it a liberal character. The king, he said, knew the best men available and would select them. (Like Grandi?) Here Eisenhower interposed to suggest that the names of any such men should first be informally submitted to the military mission he had appointed. He had no wish, he explained, to interfere in internal Italian affairs, but such cooperation would facilitate matters. He added that his government had expressed the desire that Count Sforza visit Brindisi in the near future. With some delicacy Badoglio suggested that a man who, like Count Sforza, had antimonarchical sentiments might not be viewed with sympathy by the king, but he would attempt to persuade the king of the value of Count Sforza's credentials.*

Here was the nub of the difficulty with any armistice or surrender that kept a Badoglio–Victor Emmanuel government in power. Antifascist leaders abounded, some of them, like the philosopher Benedetto Croce, of international reputation; but if one could be found who would serve under Badoglio, he would refuse to have anything to do with the king, or the other way round. And so the Badoglio rump government staggered along, a cripple tenderly supported by the swarm of Anglo-American political officers, to its predictable collapse. And Eisenhower, as Allied commander in chief, was stuck with responsibility for the ugly, misshapen, neofascist botch.

Another damaging political effect of the capitulation was the decision by AFHQ—i.e., Eisenhower—that armistice and surrender should be transacted without any particular reference to the French Committee of National Liberation. Since the exclusion seemed to de Gaulle to have been deliberate (as indeed it was), French sensibilities, always apprehensive of any slight, were once again wounded. De Gaulle believed that France should be a full partner in any settlement with Italy, the more so since the French had never ceased to fight the Italians, the Italians had occupied part of France, and France alone among the western Allies was Italy's geographical neighbor. Yet, as he was obliged to conclude:

There could be no doubt: our Allies were in agreement to keep us at as great a distance as they could from decisions concerning Italy. We could expect that tomorrow they would make still greater efforts to determine the destiny of Europe without France. But they had to be made to realize that France would not tolerate this exclusion, and that they could not count on her in the future if they disregarded her now.

Thus in 1943 Eisenhower sowed the seeds for the disagreeable harvest he would reap ten and twelve years later.

On any value scale of the problems he faced in this new theater of war, Eisenhower ranked the matter of the surrender and its attendant po-

* Count Carlo Sforza very neatly embodied the Anglo-American conflict over the wartime management of Italian affairs and the postwar influence over Italian destiny. He had been the foreign minister in the government replaced by Mussolini's fascist state; he had lived in exile for many years in the U.S., where his repute in the Italian-American community lent him luster in the eyes of American politicians and so led to his being sponsored by Roosevelt as a leading Italian antifascist spokesman. On the other hand, since he was strongly opposed to giving the royal family houseroom in postwar Italy, Churchill was increasingly exasperated by him, until indeed he "was like a red rag to a bull to Churchill."

litical blunders very low. Far more important, especially in mid-September, was the battle for the Salerno beachheads, a struggle that for a time looked as if it might become the first real disaster for Allied arms under his command.

The Fifth Army, General Mark Clark commanding, had begun its assaults on beaches to the north and south of Salerno at 3 A.M. on Thursday, September 9. The British X Corps had three separate beachheads; the American VI Corps had one, twenty miles away. Their immediate objective was to link up. Little surprise attended the landings. Since the Germans could assume, from evidence of earlier operations, that the Allies would attack only within range of land-based fighter aircraft, they could predict with some assurance that the attacks would come around Salerno, and could dig in to defend and prepare their counterattacks on that coastline. AFHQ knew the Nazis had sent a panzer division to defend the region, that strong reinforcements could be deployed there within four to six days, and that from Sunday, September 12, onward Clark could expect very strong opposition. Events turned out almost exactly as predicted. At daybreak on Sunday, Feldmarschall Albert Kesselring ordered the German troops to attack, confident that the beachheads could be overrun before Montgomery's Eighth Army, driving north from Calabria but still a hundred miles away, could arrive to reinforce them. Kesselring's plan was to flatten the beachheads and then split them at the juncture of British X Corps and American VI Corps; he very nearly succeeded. The most critical hours came on Monday afternoon, when German troops badly mauled the U.S. 36th Division, sending it, according to the Nazi communiqué, into "headlong flight," and smashed the U.S. 45th Division, driving it back across the Sele River and threatening to knife through behind the Americans, seize their beaches, and cut them off from supply and reinforcement. At AFHQ there was consternation when a message from Clark announced a tentative plan to re-embark his headquarters so that he might continue the battle in whichever beachhead seemed to promise the better chance of success. Privately, Eisenhower was dismayed. He wondered why Clark did not emulate the spirit of Stalingrad, and stand and fight. (The message had been garbled; Clark never withdrew.) Officially, Eisenhower put up a cool front. The situation, he reported to the Combined Chiefs on Monday evening, was "tense but not unexpected."

American artillery held the perilously narrow position. That night and all next day Allied aircraft, fighters and bombers alike, worked overtime on the enemy and his communications; Allied warships moved close to shore and exploded more than eleven thousand tons of shell in direct support of the weary soldiers on the beaches. All German counterattacks were beaten back. That day Eisenhower dictated a memorandum for the record. He could not resist pointing out that "the situation has arisen which we so earnestly tried to make the Combined Chiefs of Staff see in advance as a definite possibility"—to wit, the need for more bombers and more landing craft, both of which had been refused him. (He had wanted bombers to deny Kesselring any opportunity to reinforce, landing craft to ensure his own capability to reinforce.) When his requests had been disapproved, "doubts were frequently expressed in this headquarters as to the wisdom of going on with AVALANCHE." (The most dubious of his senior commanders had been Alexander and Montgomery.) "I felt . . . we should go ahead. . . . This decision was solely my own, and if things go wrong there is no one to blame except myself." But by the time Eisenhower had revised and amended this memorandum he knew the situation had improved, at least temporarily. The Combined Chiefs, moreover, alarmed by the hazardous battle for the beachheads, belatedly turned over to him the landing craft and bombers he had earlier requested.

On Thursday leading elements of the Eighth Army reached the most advanced patrols of the Fifth Army. On Friday Eisenhower visited Clark's headquarters on the beachhead, found things "in reasonably good shape," but had the painful duty of relieving the commander of the VI Corps (an old friend) and the assistant division commander of the 36th Infantry. On Saturday, recognizing how wrong had been his confident predictions of victory, Kesselring began to disengage his troops and withdraw them to the north, toward Naples. The Allied beachheads were secure. Eisenhower and his deputy Alexander, in their turn overconfident, both imagined they would be in Rome within a month or so.

During these painful days, Eisenhower found time to gossip about the juiciest topic available to officers in the high command, to wit, the prospective shift of officers in that high command. He had few hard facts on which to flesh out his speculations, but any surmise was, God knows, more entertaining than interminable chatter about the hopeless Italian government at Brindisi or gloomy forebodings about what might happen at Salerno. At breakfast on Thursday, September 16, with Smith and Butcher, Eisenhower relaxed long enough to indulge in some conjecture.

The mandatory guess had to do, of course, with the supreme command of OVERLORD, the assignment that every Allied commander coveted, the plumpest plum of the war. Clearly it would go to George Marshall. No? Or maybe to the CIGS, Alan Brooke? Butcher insisted that Eisenhower was "the logical and inevitable choice," but Eisenhower said no: it must be either Marshall or Brooke, and more likely Marshall. (He did not yet know that Churchill had agreed with Roosevelt to nominate an American.) For himself, Eisenhower hoped only that he would not be recalled for a staff job in London or Washington; after his relative independence in the Mediterranean theater, a step down to serve on the staff in some other commander's headquarters would be dispiriting. By this time the scuttlebutt brought back to Algiers by AFHQ officers recently returned from the conference at Ottawa had been published in the American press: Eisenhower was to take Marshall's place as acting chief of staff. The thought of it depressed him. To be stuck in wartime Washington, surrounded by a swarm of politicians—the seventh circle of hell. He wondered whether perhaps Marshall might not be named supreme commander globally, and then depute Eisenhower to be field commander of OVERLORD. Or might he not at least be an army group commander, serving under Marshall?

Butcher stubbornly persisted in his nomination. There was more than simple loyalty to it. OVERLORD was to be an amphibious operation. Who among the Allied commanders had experience of such an operation? Only Eisenhower, and he had commanded no less than three of them—in North Africa, Sicily, and Italy—each giving him a different and invaluable layer of military accomplishment. But this aspect of the matter did not weigh very heavily in the judgment of the man who had to make the ultimate choice. Franklin Roosevelt would have other factors to take into consideration.

Foggia fell on September 27 and Naples on October 1. Across the southern end of the Italian peninsula (the impoverished end, the one lacking industry and commerce and political allure) General Eisenhower's armies had established a connected battlefront. He and his officers had confidently expected that Allied troops would sweep triumphantly up the peninsula, past Rome and Florence and Genoa, up to the valley of the Po River and the plain of Lombardy; they had suddenly appreciated the disagreeable fact that Kesselring was digging in behind the Gustav line, and was determined to contest every meter of Italian soil.

Faced with a stalemate, General Eisenhower was not consoled by his guests from overseas, the Very Important Personages who, for their own reasons, itched to gossip about impending changes in the high command. On Friday, October 1, it was luncheon at El Alouina with Colonel Frank Knox, the big florid friendly secretary of the navy. Knox had it on the highest authority: Marshall had been appointed supreme commander for OVERLORD, and Eisenhower was the "probable" choice to be ordered to Washington as chief of staff.

The "probable" choice. Eisenhower was not cheered by the news. To be sure, he would be once again with Mamie, but for a professional soldier that was the only consolation. Besides his reluctance to get involved with politicians in Washington, as chief of staff he would be required to issue orders to General Douglas MacArthur, and that was not a prospect of unalloyed delight.

On Sunday evening his guest at Amilcar was Admiral Lord Louis (Dickie) Mountbatten, who was bound for India to take up his duties as supreme Allied commander, Southeast Asia theater. This appointment, as it happened, had come in exchange for giving an American the command of OVERLORD, so Mountbatten presumed to have an insider's knowledge of the solemn and slippery proceedings required to make the final selection. Brooke had been promised the job, Mountbatten said, but Harry Hopkins had insisted on Marshall; in view of the proposed American share in the operation, surely the larger, Brooke had gracefully withdrawn himself from consideration for preferment. A pretty tale.

To Eisenhower the picture was gradually coming into focus, but some crucial details were still fuzzy. Nor was the situation improved when, next day, a batch of newspaper clippings arrived from the States, some backing Marshall's appointment, some opposing it. The editorials and commentaries reflected a controversy over the matter that involved even the Joint Chiefs of Staff. Admiral King and General Arnold both believed Marshall "should have the job" of commanding OVERLORD, but both "recognized the disadvantages of losing him from the Combined and Joint Chiefs of Staff." The chief disadvantage, recognized most clearly by the Operations Division of the War Department, was that Marshall's was the strongest and stubbornest voice raised at meetings of the Combined Chiefs in opposition to Churchill's persistent efforts to have men and munitions assigned for diversionary operations in the Mediterranean theater. In Marshall's absence, who would fight for his strategy? The officers of OPD feared that Eisenhower, as chief of staff, would be readier to compromise for the sake of unity; in short, less effective.

Fortuitously, during this same period, Churchill was eloquently pleading for still another Mediterranean diversion—just one more, just a little one—and Eisenhower was stoutly refusing him, thus precipitating what Churchill would later term "the most acute difference I ever had with General Eisenhower." What he had set his heart on this time was the Dodecanese Islands in the Aegean Sea, just south and west of the Turkish seacoast. To capture Rhodes, Kos, Leros, and Samos would mean that Crete would fall, Turkey would come into the war against Germany, a short and safe maritime route to the Soviet Union would be secured, the entire southern Nazi flank would be exposed and threatened, the Balkans would seethe to overthrow their conquerors, and all the world would dance to the music of the spheres. When he could find no Allied soldier or statesman to share his enthusiasm, Churchill "worked himself into a frenzy of excitement," as it seemed to General Brooke, and "magnified its importance so that he [could] no longer see anything else." But Roosevelt said no, the Combined Chiefs said no, and Eisenhower, backed by his three British senior subordinates, likewise said no. "It is personally distressing to me," Eisenhower said in his cable to the prime minister on October 9, "to have to advise against a project in which you believe so earnestly."

Meanwhile, in an effort to clarify those details about the impending shuffle in the high command that would affect his own immediate future, Eisenhower had decided to send Beetle Smith back to Washington to confer with Marshall. He gave Smith a list of seven specific matters on which he wished Marshall's advice (or on which he wished to advise Marshall, against the day when Marshall would be assuming command of OVERLORD), but more important, he urged Smith to try, with utmost discretion, to implant in Marshall's mind the idea that he, Eisenhower, would much prefer to serve as an army group commander in OVERLORD than as chief of staff in the Pentagon.

When Smith got to Washington he was distracted by the customary welter of rumors, so various, so contradictory; his first guarded cables back to AFHQ indicated that Eisenhower might retain his command in the Mediterranean theater, but later he was of the opposite opinion.

When Averell Harriman passed through Algiers on October 14, on his way to Moscow to take up his duties as American ambassador to the Soviet Union, he managed to contribute his mite to the confusion. Yes, he said, Marshall would command OVERLORD, and yes, Eisenhower was to be chief of staff. But on the other hand, he said, he was not so sure. Admiral King, he said, was trying to convince the President to keep Marshall in Washington. As for Marshall, said Harriman, that austere soldier "remained aloof."

To remain aloof was more than Eisenhower found possible. Another American on his way through Algiers to Moscow was Major General John R. Deane, who had served as secretary of the Joint Chiefs and as U.S. secretary of the Combined Chiefs, and who was now to head the first U.S. military mission to the USSR. Deane was an old friend and comrade; Eisenhower talked to him freely about the imminent switches of command. Presumably Eisenhower was aware that Deane would report the conversation to General Marshall. At all events, Deane did write Marshall that Eisenhower "expressed a great hope that you would not leave Washington. His view is that the whole Army regardless of theater looks on you as its commander."

Marshall himself, while maintaining his characteristic reserve about his own future role, could yet betray a curious inconsistency when it came to Eisenhower. Almost simultaneously he recommended that Eisenhower be designated an army group commander in OVERLORD, yet told Smith that to designate Eisenhower an army group commander would be a mistake since it would be generally regarded as a demotion.

Quite evidently, Roosevelt's procrastination in announcing that Marshall was his choice was discomposing some officers of notable composure.

And, no question about it, Marshall was the President's choice. On November 15 for the *n*th time he assured the Joint Chiefs on this point. The occasion was a meeting of the staff with the President and Harry Hopkins on board the big new battleship U.S.S. *Iowa*; they were all on their way to still another international conference, the one to be held variously with Generalissimo Chiang Kai-shek in Cairo and Marshal Stalin in Teheran. The American Chiefs were determined that at this conference the cross-Channel invasion, so long promised, so often postponed, so hedged about with arbitrary conditions, would suffer no further from Churchill's diversionary schemes. Hence the urgency of nominating a commander for OVERLORD and publicly announcing the appointment. To his officers aboard the *Iowa* Roosevelt said that "it was his idea that General Marshall should be the commander in chief against Germany and command all the British, French, Italian and U.S. troops involved in this effort."

As the U.S.S. *Iowa* steamed eastward, the commander for OVERLORD still unannounced but still presumed to be Marshall,* General Eisenhower and General Smith flew to Malta to confer with Churchill and the British Chiefs, who were also on their way to Cairo. The suspicions of the American Chiefs—that Churchill still hoped to avoid the hazards of OVERLORD and still hankered to attack Germany through the "soft underbelly" of Europe—would have been amply confirmed if they had heard Churchill's conversations with Eisenhower and Smith. Smith predicted that the Cairo-Teheran conference would be "the hottest one yet," since what he had heard convinced him that the British were once again bent on postponing the cross-Channel invasion.

Churchill spoke also of the command of OVERLORD: he felt, Eisenhower noted privately, "that the original proposal would go through as first approved; namely, that General Marshall would take command of OVERLORD in England and I would possibly go to Washington."

Two days later General Eisenhower met President Roosevelt and his other distinguished guests at Oran; he had them flown in a group of C-54s to El Alouina, in Tunisia. A big white villa overlooking the Bay

---

* General Marshall's wife has written how, beginning in September, she secretly had their furniture moved from the chief of staff's official quarters at Fort Myer south to Leesburg, and how, after Christmas, all that furniture was moved once again to Fort Myer.

of Tunis for the President, and rooms in Eisenhower's smaller house at Carthage for General Marshall and Admiral King.

On this Saturday night, November 20, Eisenhower had the social duty of dining with the President. His own guests, Marshall and King, were delighted with the prospect of a quiet evening free from protocol and formal festivity; they would stay in Eisenhower's cottage with Butcher. Before Eisenhower left for dinner the four men chatted quietly for a time, but all at once, when Admiral King raised the subject of a commander for OVERLORD, a constraint fell over the room. "Ike was embarrassed," Butcher observed. While King talked, "General Marshall remained completely silent," Eisenhower noticed; "he seemed embarrassed." What King said was familiar enough by now: that the President had tentatively decided to appoint Marshall commander of OVERLORD; that King and others were dead set against the appointment, since it would remove Marshall from the Combined Chiefs; that the return of Eisenhower to Washington in Marshall's stead was all that kept King from viewing the plan with anything less than consternation. "I hate to lose General Marshall as chief of staff," said King, "but my loss is consoled by the knowledge that I will have you to work with in his job." He added that he deplored the idea of breaking up a winning team. He would, he promised, continue to press his arguments on the President.

The next day, by appointment, Eisenhower guided the President on a tour of Tunisian battlefields, ancient and recent. They talked of many things—of Hannibal and elephants, of Kasserine and the king of Italy, of Darlan and Giraud, and of OVERLORD and who would command the great invasion. Roosevelt said: "You and I know the name of the chief of staff in the Civil War, but few Americans outside the professional services do. I hate to think that fifty years from now practically nobody will know who George Marshall was. That is one of the reasons why I want George to have the big command—he is entitled to establish his place in history as a great general."

That night, checking his impressions with Butcher, Eisenhower concluded that he had all but been given official notice that he would soon be exchanging his field command for a tour of duty in Washington. It was discouraging, but he was, first and last, a good soldier and would of course comply cheerfully with his orders.

His eminent visitors flew on to Cairo for their conference, and before long he too was summoned east to meet with the Combined Chiefs and report to them the prospects in his theater. Back in Algiers after an unwonted holiday—Marshall had ordered him to take a couple of days off, and he had gone sightseeing in Luxor, Jerusalem, and Bethlehem—he found himself on dead center, waiting.

It was an awkward and uncomfortable time. He could make no plans to speed the frustrating warfare in Italy, for his successor would want to make his own. Aside from a scheme to journey to Washington by way of Australia and the Pacific, so that he might better comprehend the problems on that side of the world, there was nothing he could do to prepare himself for his expected appointment. He was uncertain even as to which of his staff he would be able to take with him: their morale also suffered in this season. He consoled himself by reflecting on the sudden turns in his career over the last two years, always gratifyingly higher, always "lucky," as he observed to Butcher. The summons to the War Department, the promotion to direct the Operations Division, the posting to London, the command of TORCH, then of HUSKY, then of AVALANCHE—he saw himself as "a fortunate beneficiary of circumstances." Butcher, measuring his frustration, saw him rather as "a football quarterback who has been playing an excellent game but who rebels when the coach orders him to the sidelines while the game is at fever pitch."

The biggest moment of his life was at hand, but he knew nothing of what it would bring.

Meanwhile Franklin Roosevelt was at Teheran, three thousand miles from Eisenhower's headquarters at Algiers, conferring with Churchill and Marshal Stalin on the grand strategy of the war still to be fought. Much the larger part of that war was still being waged on Russian soil, but under conditions quite different from those of the year before. Enormous hosts had grappled with each other across the vast steppes, and the Red Army—or rather, some sixty Red armies—had triumphantly smashed the Nazi Wehrmacht to a halt and sent it reeling back a hundred miles, two hundred, then three hundred, along a front that curved north and south for more than a thousand miles from Leningrad to Sevastopol. In the process the morale of the entire Nazi war machine, from top to bottom, had undergone a wonderful change. The Übermensch had been taught a long-deserved lesson, that the Untermensch was braver, better armed, and more resolute than he.

The end had come, perhaps, in the German attack against the Kursk salient in July 1943, the greatest battle of tanks in history, with more than three thousand steel-clad monsters in action at one time, slugging shells at each other. The Red armies had, besides parity in tanks, a clear superiority in artillery. The invader had been everywhere repulsed. By July 14 the Wehrmacht had withdrawn and the Soviet armies were being marshaled for another triumphant counterattack. The German front had crumbled. Orel, Kharkov, Smolensk, and Kiev were recaptured before the first freeze of autumn, and the Red Army had kept moving west, faster now than ever thanks to American trucks and half-tracks.

When Stalin sat down at Teheran with Roosevelt and Churchill, he was assured that OVERLORD, the second front in France, was scheduled for the spring. He inquired, "Who will command it?" and, when Roosevelt replied that the commander had not yet been selected, Stalin at once said, "Then nothing will come out of these operations." Churchill assured him the appointment would be made within a fortnight. The next day, Tuesday, November 30, when the Combined Chiefs reported on their plans for OVERLORD, to be supported by another invasion (ANVIL) of southern France, Stalin professed great satisfaction but again asked: "When will the commander in chief be named?" Roosevelt answered he would need three or four days to consider the matter and consult with his advisers. He added that the Combined Chiefs had agreed, earlier that day, to assign one commander to OVERLORD, a second to the Mediterranean theater, and probably a third for the invasion of southern France. Stalin nodded.

The procedure all but ruled out George Marshall as commander of OVERLORD, and for the irrational reason that the appointment might to some people seem a step down. Roosevelt wanted all three commands rolled into one for his chief of staff, the British refused to roll the three into one, and so Marshall would not be given the one of three commands he wanted. The final decision came, as Roosevelt had told Stalin it would, three or four days later, on Sunday, December 5. Robert Sherwood's often quoted comment on the decision is still the best and only one: "He [Roosevelt] made it against the almost impassioned advice of Hopkins and Stimson, against the known preference of both Stalin and Churchill, against his own proclaimed inclination to give to George Marshall the historic opportunity which he so greatly desired and so amply deserved." But Marshall, offered the prize, refused to request it. He remained austerely aloof. He would not attempt to estimate his capabilities; his commander in chief would have to do that. Later he recalled only the President's cautionary remark: "I feel I could not sleep at night with you out of the country."

Whereupon Roosevelt dictated to Marshall his decision:

From the President to Marshal Stalin:
    The immediate appointment of General Eisenhower to command of Overlord operation has been decided upon.

Marshall handed his scrawl to Roosevelt. The President signed it.

And the Hero was once again set on his prescribed path.

CHAPTER TEN

Command of Overlord

THE PRESIDENT APPOINTED GENERAL EISENHOWER to his supreme command on Sunday, December 5, 1943. Other men had learned of the decision earlier—Churchill, General Brooke, Harry Hopkins—and by Monday all the Combined Chiefs knew of it, as of course did Stalin and a small group of Soviet leaders. Since information of this kind leaks easily, it is safe to assume that several dozen men and women of the Allies knew of it by Monday night, and similarly it is reasonable to suppose that word of the decision had trickled to some level of the Nazi superstructure at about the same time. Eisenhower himself first got the word in vague and rather garbled terms early on the morning of Tuesday, December 7, and even then he was not entirely sure of it. Beetle Smith was so sure that his voice almost trilled over the telephone, but Eisenhower, the cautious gambler, refused to believe it until the moment when the President, having left his homeward-bound airplane on Tuesday afternoon for a stopover at El Alouina, settled back in Eisenhower's automobile, turned to him with a smile, and said, "Well, Ike, you are going to command OVERLORD."

At AFHQ the news was electrifying. "For the first time," Butcher noted, "we now feel that we have a definite and concrete mission. This adds zest to living. . . . It has already made a remarkable difference in Ike. Now he is back to his old system of incessant planning and thinking out loud of qualifications of this or that man for certain jobs."

A new horizon; new problems. Some of these—such as what to call the commander, and the time when his appointment should be publicly announced—could be decided only at the highest level. Presently it was agreed that he would be the Supreme Commander, Allied Expeditionary Force, and the President made known his selection in a radio broadcast on Christmas Eve. Meanwhile Roosevelt thoughtfully suggested that perhaps Eisenhower might prefer to delay the transfer of his command until after he had captured Rome. "I am deeply appreciative of your consideration," Eisenhower told the President; "however . . ." It was as well he declined the offer. The Allies would not, in the event, enter Rome until June 4, 1944, two days before D-day of OVERLORD.

Problems of organization. Eisenhower would need officers to staff his supreme headquarters (SHAEF) and to command the armies, air forces, and navies of what was universally regarded as the sternest Allied test of the war. Churchill wanted him to leave his chief of staff, Beetle Smith, in the Mediterranean theater as deputy for General Sir Henry Maitland Wilson, the British officer who was to succeed Eisenhower as commander of that theater, and Marshall agreed that Smith should stay in Algiers at least till February 1944 to help Wilson settle into his new command. But Eisenhower flatly insisted that Smith must remain at his side, and he prevailed. On the other hand, to command the assault phase of OVER-LORD and to lead the British and Canadian armies after the beachhead had been secured, Eisenhower wanted Alexander; but Brooke, the CIGS, was determined that Montgomery should be appointed. The two men discussed the matter on December 11. Later Brooke noted: "I discovered, as I had expected, that he [Eisenhower] would sooner have Alex with him for OVERLORD than Monty. He also knew that he could handle Alex, but was not fond of Monty and certainly did not know how to handle him." Montgomery got the appointment. Brooke was apparently content to saddle the supreme commander of a crucial enterprise with a chief subordinate whom he neither liked nor could easily direct—a most curious method of ensuring success.

The British Chiefs of Staff also nominated Eisenhower's other two senior operational officers, Air Chief Marshal Sir Trafford Leigh-Mallory and Admiral Sir Bertram Ramsay, once again suggesting to Eisenhower's critics that he was an amiable figurehead who presided over committees while the British ran the war. These gibes would not unduly disturb him. What was more important was that in time he would come to regard Leigh-Mallory and Ramsay as men who, "although extremely able, are somewhat ritualistic in outlook and require a great deal more of inoculation" than had their counterparts in AFHQ, Tedder and Andrew Cunningham. Tedder was to come to SHAEF with Eisenhower as his deputy supreme commander, but because he was thought by the British Chiefs to be too easily influenced by the supreme commander, he was without portfolio, given no jurisdiction over Allied air power.

As to his American officers, Eisenhower fared better. Bradley was already in England, in command of the First U.S. Army. He conjectured that, as American strength grew in England or on the continent, Bradley would take command of an army group; one of his army commanders, Eisenhower suggested to Marshall, should be "somebody like [Lieutenant General Courtney] Hodges or [Lieutenant General William] Simpson," and as for the other Eisenhower was terse and explicit: "I would want Patton as one of my Army commanders." These recommendations were tolerably prescient. All three officers—Hodges, Simpson, and Patton—would indeed become army commanders in Bradley's 12th Army Group. The choice of Patton was extraordinary; for Eisenhower made his unequivocal request for Patton's appointment on December 17, which was only twenty-six days after that officer had become as cordially detested by the American public as any officer since Benedict Arnold.

The instant cause for Patton's name being submerged in obloquy was a radio broadcast on November 21 by a Washington journalist, Drew Pearson, whose syndicated gossip enjoyed the reputation of being confidential information. Pearson, who was not restricted by the gentleman's agreement to hush up the affair, gave a sensational account of the so-called slapping incidents, italicizing the allegation that Eisenhower had not reprimanded Patton. The broadcast, transmitted over a nationwide radio network, and the consequent front-page newspaper stories provoked a hurricane of protest. On Capitol Hill politicians sensitive to letters from scores of outraged constituents went so far as to demand that Patton be summarily court-martialed. In Marshall's absence overseas (he was attending the Cairo and Teheran conferences) the War Department sent Eisenhower aggrieved queries: what had happened? what were the facts about the alleged slappings? what had Eisenhower done about it? Nor were the correspondents in Algiers happy. Responsive to Eisenhower's request they had dutifully shushed, but nevertheless the story had inevitably erupted. Now each correspondent was being blistered by his home office (BADLY BEATEN PATTON STOP UPFOLLOW FULLEST SPEEDLIEST ETCHECK IKES UNCENSURE) and could be satisfied only by the frankest sort of press conference. Beetle Smith undertook the chore and promptly botched it. He was so ill advised as to confirm Pearson's charge that Eisenhower had not reprimanded Patton. (Eisenhower's rebuke, though sharp, had been personal and unofficial; hence Smith may be presumed not to have seen it.) Now Eisenhower was in a plight almost as prickly as Patton's.

The commander in chief reacted calmly. He had already cabled the War Department that he stood by his original decision about Patton. Now he reported to Marshall that "a bad mistake" had been made "by my ablest and finest officer, and there is nothing for me to do except to keep still and take the brunt of the affair [since] I have no intention of throwing valuable men to the wolves because of one mistake." As he had already advised Patton, so now he reminded Marshall that the public would soon find something more scandalous or more amusing to chatter about. It was a safe prediction. After sweating out his disgrace for a few more days in his penitential palace at Palermo, Patton would get his orders to proceed to England for further assignment and the slapping affair would vanish into limbo.

Problems of high strategy. Two days after Roosevelt's departure for Washington on December 9, Churchill arrived at Tunis from Cairo, full of pneumococcal bacteria and gloom because of the stagnation of the campaign in Italy. The pneumococci, having priority, distracted him from the war for a week or so, but by December 19 he was busily conjuring up schemes for striking around the enemy's flank to capture Rome. On that sunny Friday, convalescent at Carthage, Churchill learned that Brooke, the CIGS, "had by a separate route of thought arrived at the same conclusion as I had," to wit, the desirability of an amphibious assault on the Roman coast. There was nothing novel about this notion. It had been routinely explored by AFHQ planners during the first nine months of the year; Fifth Army planners had canvassed the idea exhaustively; in early November General Alexander had ordered specific plans to be drawn; on November 25 General Clark had tentatively approved a small amphibious landing at Anzio, an operation code-named SHINGLE, to be mounted as soon as the Fifth Army could fight its way close enough to support the troops in the beachhead. But Clark's troops were then still fifty difficult, mountainous miles from Anzio, stuck fast in front of the Gustav line.

The feasibility of any assault had turned, as always, on the availability of landing ships and crafts. As Eisenhower well remembered, the landings at Salerno had been the riskier because of a lack of LSTs when they were most needed. Yet of those LSTs still in the Mediterranean at the end of October, AFHQ had agreed to send more than a hundred to Britain before mid-December for use in OVERLORD. With his eye on the possibility of a small (one-division) assault on the beaches at Anzio, Eisenhower had on October 31 besought the Combined Chiefs to let him keep five or six dozen of these LSTs until January 5, a delay of three weeks. The British Chiefs had fervently concurred, but the U.S. Chiefs had demurred, stipulating that AFHQ might retain sixty-eight LSTs, but no later than December 15. "The situation appears to me to hang in the balance," Eisenhower had argued on November 4, in an appeal for an extension of his control over the vital landing ships. "Naturally I do *not* wish to interfere with the preparations for OVERLORD but . . ." But Italy had become a secondary theater. Before long Eisenhower had learned that the Combined Chiefs would be in Cairo within a fortnight and decided to wait till then before pressing the question of an amphibious attack near Rome.

At Teheran the political and military leaders of the three chief Allied powers—"friends in fact, in spirit, and in purpose"—had confirmed the strategy of OVERLORD, ratified its target date of May 1, and scheduled the concurrent amphibious assault on the southern coast of France

(Anvil). "Overlord and Anvil are the supreme operations for 1944," the Combined Chiefs had agreed on December 6. "They must be carried out during May 1944. Nothing must be undertaken in any other part of the world which hazards the success of these two operations." With their next breath the Chiefs had given deliberate emphasis to this proposition: "Overlord, as at present planned, is on too narrow a margin. Everything practicable should be done to increase its strength." In short, even more landing ships than available in the December inventory would be vitally needed in May. The Chiefs had presented these conclusions to the President and the prime minister; they had been approved.

Nevertheless, within two weeks Churchill was zestfully setting out to correct what he characterized as the "disastrous" failure to strike an amphibious blow toward Rome—a course that would, to be sure, require a raid on the inventory of Overlord's precious landing ships. The British Chiefs heartily agreed with him. More, they proposed that the earlier plan for Shingle (one division) be beefed up ("at least two divisions") so that the attacking force could hold its beachhead without requiring immediate support by the Fifth Army; an even sharper raid on the commitment to Overlord and Anvil was foreshadowed. The British Chiefs spoke of an assault "designed to enable Rome to be captured and the armies to advance to the Pisa-Rimini line." Churchill cabled Roosevelt that he had held a conference on Christmas Day "with Eisenhower and all his high officers" and it had "seemed to those present that every effort should be made" to land at Anzio around January 20. "This should decide the battle of Rome," Churchill confidently asserted. "If this opportunity is not grasped we must expect the ruin of the Mediterranean campaign of 1944." He desired to delay the departure of fifty-six LSTs promised to Overlord. He desired "a hazardous enterprise on the Italian coast," one that entailed, as he knew, four weeks' postponement of Overlord. He desired it despite the pledge he had given at Teheran less than a month before. Roosevelt cabled his approval of both requests on December 28.

To anticipate events: The assault forces, hastily organized and sketchily trained, swollen to twice their original size, arrived at Anzio on January 22, 1944; after a deceptively easy landing they were contained, very nearly forced back into the sea, and isolated for four long agonizing months. The demands Shingle made on assault shipping served to postpone Anvil from May until August. So far from deciding the battle of Rome, the operation cost the Allies much treasure and many lives; Churchill himself, faced with the consequences of the folly for which he was chiefly responsible, would lament: "I had hoped that we were hurling a wildcat onto the shore, but all we had got was a stranded whale."

For Eisenhower the whole bitter business of Anzio—from the early plans through the bloody and desperate combat to the eventual disruption of the encircling German forces late in May—had a special cursed pertinence. As commander in the Mediterranean theater he had sweated to retain assault shipping for the Anzio landings, but in December, as supreme commander of OVERLORD, he was compelled to keep in mind the precise and tyrannical timetables for assembling and refitting his landing ships and using them in training exercises for the climactic cross-Channel invasion. Now he was anxious to have every possible LST sent forthwith to Britain. The Combined Chiefs had assigned to him, moreover, the responsibility of producing a plan for ANVIL, the assault on the French Riviera; by December 24 his staff had completed an outline plan calling for a three-division landing. Where was the assault shipping to come from? And how would General Eisenhower apply his unique prestige—as retiring commander in the Mediterranean and prospective supreme commander in northwest Europe—to influence the debate over the feasibility of SHINGLE and the availability of landing craft? No question but that his favorable opinion was essential; his firm and energetic opposition to SHINGLE would have utterly stymied the operation.

Churchill of course appreciated the weight given in Washington to Eisenhower's good opinion and so was careful, in his cablegram to Roosevelt, to create the impression of unanimity on the part of "Eisenhower and all his high officers." This impression, not to put too fine a point on it, was false. Not for the first or last time, Churchill's passionate advocacy of a beloved strategy led him to palter with the truth. Eisenhower thought a landing at Anzio would be "a risky affair" and that "the attack would not by itself compel the withdrawal of the German front." He urged "careful consideration"; he argued that "a force of several strong divisions would have to be established in Anzio before significant results could be achieved"; he reminded everyone that "landing craft would be needed long after the agreed-upon date for their release." His chief of staff, Beetle Smith, praised by Churchill for his "active, knowledgeable, fact-armed diplomacy" on behalf of the Anzio landings, in fact was wary of them, and by January 5 would be in agreement with Eisenhower that because of the acute shortage of armored landing craft, SHINGLE should be canceled.[*] Furthermore, Eisenhower's G-2, General Kenneth Strong, expressed his grave doubts of the wisdom of the operation; not only at Carthage on Christmas Day, but again at Marrakesh two weeks later.

But although he disparaged the landing at Anzio, although he feared the operation would tend to prejudice the chances of OVERLOAD, Eisen-

---

[*] At that time, January 5, 1944, Eisenhower would maintain that "entirely aside from Overlord-Anvil considerations, [the Anzio landing] is open to grave objections under present conditions."

hower did not make clear and unmistakable his opposition to it. Later he would tell General Marshall that he had muted his opposition because he knew he would be leaving the theater before the operation was carried out and hence regarded it as outside his jurisdiction. In short, Eisenhower did not make any wrong decision about Anzio; he made no decision at all. In the next four months, as the controversies raged over ANVIL and over the proper priorities assigned to assault shipping, he would have ample occasion to regret his unwonted diffidence.

In the midst of these new problems, an old one suddenly backfired: the one precipitated by Anglo-American insistence on intervening in what the French were quite sure were their exclusive concerns. Specifically the French Committee of National Liberation (which had by now eased Giraud to the sidelines and installed de Gaulle as its president) had convened in Algiers a consultative assembly, and most of the members of this body, leaders of the underground Resistance who had somehow contrived to elude the formidable Sicherheitsdienst and slip out of France, demanded swift and condign punishment for those men of Vichy who had collaborated with the Nazis and were still at large in North Africa. So insistent was the call for "épuration" that late in December the FCNL ordered the arrest of several of the most hated Vichyites. About some of them—Pierre Pucheu, who had delivered up thousands of Frenchmen to the Nazis; General Bergeret, who as Darlan's second in command in Algeria had jailed scores of resistants; and Admiral Derrien, who had fought the Allies in Bizerte—there could be no question, but Churchill was furious over the arrest of Peyrouton, Boisson, and Pierre-Étienne Flandin. He sent cablegrams of protest to Roosevelt in Washington and Eisenhower at his advanced headquarters in Naples, and in no time he had stirred up a resounding row. "I am profoundly disturbed," Eisenhower acknowledged to Roosevelt, "particularly in the case of Boisson." This officer, who had recommended himself to Eisenhower and Roosevelt by making Dakar available to the Allies as a base for their aviation and their navies, was a cruel and brutal man, responsible for "unprintable" tortures suffered by, among others, British merchant seamen. Peyrouton and Flandin had both willingly collaborated with the Nazis in ways that brought misery and death to many of their countrymen. Yet now, faithful to the folly of their deal with Darlan, Churchill and Roosevelt—and Eisenhower—chose to interfere with French justice. Churchill even suggested that the three collaborateurs be offered asylum by the Allies. Roosevelt was more presumptuous. He wanted to have the FCNL "directed to take no action" against the three.

At this juncture Eisenhower suddenly reconsidered, which is to say, he began listening to his most trusted advisers, Macmillan and Beetle Smith.

This was no time for provocation: the Allies would need the cooperation of the French Resistance when they attacked Normandy, the assistance of French troops when they attacked the Riviera. Macmillan undertook to soothe Churchill; Beetle Smith sent a cable to Marshall explaining why Roosevelt's peremptory order should be modified; and Edwin C. Wilson, who had replaced Murphy as American representative to the FCNL, added pressure by way of the State Department. The President accepted the advice. Eisenhower's orders were sensibly tempered. On the face of this welcome telegram he scribbled a relieved "Good."

On December 30 the commander in chief paid a call on General de Gaulle. Butcher would later characterize this visit as "a love fest," a phrase presumably suggested to him by Eisenhower, but the reasons for the friendliness of the encounter differ. De Gaulle perceived their interview as an occasion for Eisenhower to confess that the Allies had stupidly misjudged de Gaulle but that he now saw the error of their ways. "I must have your help," said Eisenhower, according to de Gaulle's later recollection, "and I have come to ask you for it." To which de Gaulle replied: "Splendid! You are a man! For you know how to say, 'I was wrong.'" But were the triumphant Gaullist policies real or only apparent? Certainly de Gaulle was the salient symbol of opposition to the Nazis and, because he had been condemned to death by the Vichy regime, he was also able to articulate the contempt most Frenchmen had for that shabby collaborationist gang; but was he more than symbol? The most numerous, most aggressive, most skillful resistants were the Communists; after many wrangles they had reluctantly accepted de Gaulle's authority; yet he was apprehensive, sensing that his control over the Resistance was insecure. He recognized that France was in a ferment of revolutionary ardor. Macmillan appreciated the growing acuity of his dilemma, and so, after talking with him, did Eisenhower. De Gaulle, Eisenhower told Butcher, had become frightened of the radical and communistic elements which he had gathered in his coterie of supporters, both in the Resistance element in France and in Algiers, and had been sobered by their extreme views.

Thus, if the politicians in Washington could be persuaded, the opportunity dangled, ready for the grasping, to make an arrangement by which the U.S. would support de Gaulle against the Left while jostling him back to the reassuring Center and Right. For his part de Gaulle had given every indication that he would delight to be so jostled. Meanwhile, as an augury of this hopeful future, Eisenhower undertook that the first Allied troops to enter Paris would be French, and de Gaulle thereupon promised to postpone the trial of Boisson, Flandin, and Peyrouton until after a national assembly had been elected in France to supersede the FCNL. Roosevelt was content with this solution.

Through all these December days, Eisenhower's overriding concern had been with the command he would soon be taking up in London. On Christmas Day he had been formally notified that Montgomery would be commander of the 21st Army Group in England and his commander of ground forces for the invasion itself. On December 27 Montgomery arrived in Algiers to confer with him about their future tasks. The plans for OVERLORD, drawn during June and July under the direction of the British Lieutenant General Frederick E. Morgan,* had been circumscribed by the amount of assault shipping available and by other complex factors as well; they contemplated an attack over three beaches of the Cotentin peninsula by three divisions, supported by two airborne divisions, with another two divisions in floating reserve. On October 27 one of Morgan's American staff officers, Brigadier General William E. Chambers, had been sent to Algiers with an outline of these plans and orders to solicit Eisenhower's opinion of them. After studying the outline carefully, Eisenhower had warned that the front was too narrow, that it should be expanded from a three-division assault to one of five or six divisions. Now, in December, he told Montgomery of his misgivings and directed him to serve, pending his own arrival in London, as his representative in analyzing and revising the plans. On December 28 Eisenhower sent Beetle Smith off to London on much the same mission.

Meanwhile General Marshall, home from the Pacific, had been pressing Eisenhower to quit his Mediterranean duties and fly home for a brief rest before shouldering the new and awful responsibilities of OVERLORD. Eisenhower, dogged by the need to get at those responsibilities in a hurry, had resisted the pressure, but at last on December 29 Marshall cabled him what amounted to an order:

> You will be under terrific strain from now on. I am interested that you are fully prepared to bear the strain and I am not interested in the usual rejoinder that you can take it. It is of vast importance that you be fresh mentally and you certainly will not be if you go straight from one great problem to another. Now come on home and see your wife and trust somebody else for twenty minutes in England.

Accompanied by Butcher and Mickey McKeogh, Eisenhower flew west from Algiers on Friday, the last day of the year. An overnight stop at Marrakesh to talk with the convalescent Churchill; a stop in the Azores and another at Bermuda for refueling; and his C–54 put down at Wash-

* Morgan's title was Chief of Staff to the Supreme Allied Commander (designate), a mouthful which was usefully compressed into Cossac. He was later appointed deputy chief of staff of SHAEF.

Dwight Eisenhower (second from left, front row) was the only child in the fifth grade of his Abilene school who wore overalls.

Cadet Eisenhower (third from left) was at twenty-three one of the USMA's color guard.

At twenty, he was muscular, big-boned, and self-reliant — ready to tackle any job of work.

The young second lieutenant met Mamie Doud at Fort Sam Houston in Texas, and before long they were engaged.

They were married in her family's house in Denver on July 1, 1916. On the same day he was promoted to first lieutenant.

Major Eisenhower had a reunion with his family in Abilene in 1925. On the porch (from left): Roy, Arthur, Earl, Edgar, their father David, Milton, and their mother Ida.

General MacArthur, ablaze with decorations, and his aide Major Eisenhower, less festive, turned out to supervise the rout of the Bonus Army in the summer of 1932.

Christmas in Manila, 1938, when a tour of duty in the Philippines was a leisurely sojourn in the sun. From left, Major Eisenhower, Mrs. MacArthur, U.S. Commissioner Paul McNutt, Mrs. Eisenhower, and General MacArthur.

In June 1941, when the Nazi armies held all Europe in thrall, Colonel Eisenhower was chief of staff of IX Army Corps. Here he confers with Lieutenant Colonel James Bradley in a California encampment.

Summoned to Washington a few days after the attack on Pearl Harbor, Brigadier General Eisenhower joined his old friend Leonard T. Gerow and before long succeeded him as chief of the War Plans Division.

Fifteen months later General Eisenhower had his fourth star. Here, at the headquarters of Lieutenant General George S. Patton, another old friend, he checks on the progress of the fighting in Tunisia.

Eisenhower's grin is natural. The day before, President Roosevelt had officially
informed him that he was to command OVERLORD, the Allied invasion of Festung
Europa.

General Eisenhower presides at a meeting of his senior commanders. From left, General Omar N. Bradley, Admiral Bertram Ramsey, Air Marshal Arthur Tedder, Eisenhower, General Bernard Montgomery, Air Marshal Trafford Leigh-Mallory, and General Walter Bedell (Beetle) Smith.

The supreme commander, accompanied by Tedder, Montgomery, and others, inspects an armored unit one hundred days before D-Day.

Eisenhower is relaxed and confident as he rides in London with Prime Minister Churchill. The invasion is to be launched in three weeks.

On D-Day plus six, the supreme commander takes the U.S. Joint Chiefs on their first inspection of the Normandy beachheads. In the foreground, Admiral Ernest King; next, General George Marshall; behind him, General Henry H. (Hap) Arnold. Eisenhower is clambering aboard.

Eisenhower has just awarded decorations to these officers — Generals Bradley, Gerow, and J. Lawton (Lightning Joe) Collins — following the breakout from Normandy.

With Air Chief Marshal Tedder beside him, the supreme commander broadcasts his message of victory. A few minutes before, officers of the Nazi High Command had signed the instrument of surrender.

One of Eisenhower's less onerous duties as president of Columbia was to drop in on a practice session of the university's football team and exchange pleasantries with Lou Little, the coach.

Once again a supreme commander, this time of the Allied Powers in Europe, General Eisenhower here addresses the NATO Council in Rome. Here he is facing Secretary of Defense Robert Lovett and Secretary of State Dean Acheson. whose backs are to the camera.

ington at 1:30 A.M. on Sunday, January 2, 1944. He and Butcher (each leading a Scottish terrier puppy sired by Telek) simultaneously greeted their wives in the hall between their neighboring apartments of the Wardman Park Hotel.

During his twelve days in the United States, General Eisenhower was a military secret, traveling about in military airplanes or private railroad cars or automobiles with curtains drawn. For the most part this was to suit his personal convenience and protect him from masses of dear old friends; in some small part, however, the secrecy of his movements had military significance, for Nazi propaganda at this time showed that the Germans were beginning to get rattled about the possibility of an imminent cross-Channel invasion. To be sure, for any clamorous interest in his visit to have been manifested, the ground would have had to be cunningly prepared by the experts in public relations, for the national imagination was still transfixed by the war against the Japanese and the gallant exploits of General Douglas MacArthur, the Marine Corps, and the U.S. Navy. Pending OVERLORD, General Eisenhower was still a spearholder.

Of his twelve days he was able to spend five privately with his wife in a cottage at White Sulphur Springs, West Virginia, thanks to the thoughtful consideration of General Marshall; a sixth day he and Mrs. Eisenhower spent with their son John at West Point; a seventh he shared with his mother, his brothers Arthur and Milton and their families, and his wife's parents on the campus of Kansas State College, to which Milton Eisenhower had returned the autumn before as president. (Because she detested air travel, his wife did not keep him company on the trip to Kansas.) The other five days were crowded with official business—conferences with General Marshall and various officers in the Pentagon, a dinner with ranking members of the Military Affairs Committees of the Senate and House of Representatives, a meeting with the directors of the Office of War Information, and two lengthy conferences with President Roosevelt at the White House. At these, each of which lasted nearly an hour, the two men were alone and no record was kept of their discourse. On Wednesday, January 5, Roosevelt showed Eisenhower a cablegram from Churchill; the prime minister wanted command in the Mediterranean transferred three days later. Eisenhower, who had at first planned to return to Algiers for a formal transmission of the command, was now impatient to go to London directly: he recommended that Roosevelt approve Churchill's request. A week later they spoke of postwar plans for the occupation of Germany, Eisenhower urging a joint arrangement under one Allied commander and Roosevelt indicating that his decision to carve the occupation into national zones had already been taken.

On the evening of the next day General Eisenhower and his party left unobtrusively from National Airport in Washington on their way—Bermuda, the Azores, Prestwick, London—back once again to the old headquarters in Grosvenor Square.

"It is obvious," Eisenhower wrote Marshall from London, "that strong and positive action is needed here in several directions." It was the same sort of comment he had made when first he took up his command in London in June 1942, but he was by no means the same man.

In January 1944 Dwight Eisenhower was in his fifty-fourth year, a man likely to compel attention in a concourse of senior officers less because of his commanding physical presence than because of his sunny confidence, the warmth of his manner, and the vitality that surged within him like an electromagnetic wave. Parts of him were big—his hands, his mouth—and his head seemed large partly because it was by now so little hidden by his sparse grizzled hair, but he was not of imposing stature. He was a trifle thicker through the middle than he had been a couple of years before, but this was the only mark his long sedentary hours behind a desk had left on him.

The significant changes in the supreme commander, no less ponderable for not being readily apparent, had come with the experience of the past fifteen months. When the Allied troops forced their landings in Morocco and Algeria, their commander had never been tested in battle; had never led, indeed, so much as a platoon in hostile action. In North Africa, Sicily, and Italy he had bossed (and he *had* bossed) seasoned officers, veterans of a dozen campaigns, and, if his armies had not always scored swift, brilliant triumphs, at least they had accomplished the missions set for them in convincing fashion. They had steamrollered some accomplished and well-trained foes. Their commander had shown himself to be firm and steady under pressure, resilient in the face of temporary setbacks, an excellent judge of his officers but an indifferent judge of his political advisers, adroit in his conduct with the press but maladroit in his interpretation of the larger political concepts that had come his way, reasonable, clearheaded, matter-of-fact, usually even-tempered, and—except when the weather had sometimes betrayed him—phenomenally lucky. On balance, the past fifteen months had made him surer of himself. He had never lacked self-confidence, but now, looking back, he could reckon his sanguine disposition to have been justified; more than ever he had grounds for his unflagging optimism. He was also in greater control of himself: able to keep his fiery temper on a shorter leash, better able to lead men to the decisions he wished them to take, more careless than ever of credit for his accomplishments, readier than ever to push his senior commanders forward so that they might accept praise in his stead. In short, he had learned something of the wellsprings of power.

Further, his experience had been in the tricky and exasperating province of Allied command, where a man must serve two masters and govern several hundred officers of inimical background, conflicting modes and habits of work, and fierce, intractable pride in their contrarieties. In proof that he had united these immiscible elements, his counsel had been solicited by at least one high-ranking English officer eager to match his record—Admiral Mountbatten, who, as soon as he was named to the supreme command in the Southeast Asia theater, had at once written Eisenhower to ask if he would dictate some notes "on the pitfalls to avoid and the line you consider one should take up" when assuming a supreme Allied command. Eisenhower's response to this request had been dictated over a ten-day period in September while his attention was powerfully distracted by the Allied landings at Salerno and the bitter struggle to achieve a secure position on that well-defended coastline. In consequence much of his memorandum, casually skimmed today, has the ring of boy scout law (a scout is trustworthy, loyal, helpful, friendly, courteous, etc., etc.). Thus, in discussing the "true basis" for unity of allied command, Eisenhower listed "selflessness, devotion to a common cause, generosity . . . Patience, tolerance, frankness, absolute honesty . . . and firmness" as "absolutely essential" traits of the commander. There were, of course, other important considerations. The senior commanders for ground, air, and sea "must each have a great degree of independence," for "without a great degree of decentralization no allied command can be made to work." Yet a supreme commander is, "in no sense of the word, a figurehead or a non-entity." He has much to do, what with guarding the channels to and from the Combined Chiefs for his exclusive use; coordinating public relations, censorship, civil affairs, and the like; controlling supply, priorities, and shipping; riding herd on the enormous swarm of political and economic experts who cluster about and become such a curse for a modern captain; and keeping his staff happy, objective, and impartial. In the end, all problems came back to the happiness of the mixed staff and to striving for *"the utmost in mutual respect and confidence among the group of seniors making up the allied command."* In turn this came back to the supreme commander himself, requiring that he be "self-effacing, quick to give credit, ready to meet the other fellow more than halfway," that he "seek and absorb advice and . . . learn to decentralize," and finally that he "take the blame for anything that goes wrong . . . whether or not it results from his mistake or from an error on the part of a subordinate."

The formula ensures a leader the loyal devotion of his subordinates and, as well, assists him to soar gently into the empyrean of power. Simple to say, hard to do; for as Eisenhower recognized, "All of us are human and we like to be favorably noticed by those above us and even by the public" (note that disdainful word "even"), yet the Allied commander "must more sternly than any other individual repress such notions." How many can behave so? Very few. Eisenhower was paramount among those few. Curiously, he went on to describe himself in precisely the terms that would later come back to haunt him: the Allied commander in chief, he observed, "is in a very definite sense the chairman of the board, a chairman that has very definite executive responsibilities."

Having achieved an insight into the sources of power, General Eisenhower was no longer under any illusions about the dominion of such as the President and the prime minister. He understood it. He was a well-disciplined soldier, trained in the tradition of civilian control of the military, and he thoroughly respected it. At the same time he had contemplated both those great leaders in the commission of egregious blunders, for some of which, indeed, he had, standing erect and silent, taken the blame. This too was part of the experience that enabled him to approach his awesome responsibilities completely confident, completely relaxed.

The capacity for relaxation was always part of Eisenhower's affable, gregarious personality, and one that was sure to be favorably regarded by the troops in his theater. He recommended himself to the GIs in a number of ways, some synthetic, such as his way of talking about "big shots" and "the big brass" quite as though he were not one of them, but others genuine, such as his habit of cussing, his unpretentious bearing, and his very real concern for the well-being and creature comforts of the least of his soldiers. When, back in the Mediterranean, he had learned that General Spaatz had ordered the island of Capri reserved as a playground for air force officers, he at once gave sharp and vivid tongue; moreover, he sent an order winging off to Spaatz that scorched that officer's complacency to a crisp: ". . . must cease at once . . . all British and American personnel in this area, particularly from combat units," must have the freedom of such pleasant places. Word of actions like that one was bound to spread, even if the editors of the GI publications—*Yank* and *Stars and Stripes*—had not troubled to publish the glad tidings. Indeed, the good deeds might have been taken for granted, for the general's outward semblance, the impression he conveyed to the troops, could never be faulted. He was a man among men, judged by them, and approved. He was okay. GIs had their own precise and delicate instruments for detecting the pompous or the counterfeit; Ike passed their inspection. His nickname was proof. No derisive labels like Flash Gordon or the Green Hornet were ever pasted on him, as they were on MacArthur and Patton; he was never anything but Ike, and as he later told Carl Sandburg, his nickname "was one of the luckiest things that could have happened" to him. "A soldier always likes a good name for his officers," Eisenhower explained. "Ike was a good name. When they called me Uncle Ike, or during the war just plain Ike, I knew that everything was going well."

He was trusted by his soldiers, and he had won the endorsement of his chiefs. He recognized that a supreme Allied commander had at least to be "rather well acquainted" with the men who met together as the Combined Chiefs of Staff, and he had far more than their mere acquaintance. The American Chiefs all had respect for him, professionally and personally; of the British Chiefs at least two, Ismay and his good friend Andrew Cunningham (who had been named first sea lord to succeed the ailing Sir Dudley Pound), held him in high esteem, and even the CIGS, now Field Marshal Brooke, who was never his great admirer, believed that "the selection of Eisenhower instead of Marshall was a good one."

Hindsight does nothing to diminish the conviction that the purposes of the Grand Alliance were well served by choosing Eisenhower rather than Marshall as commander of OVERLORD. (There can be no question that Marshall was better qualified than Eisenhower to direct and control the waging of the global war as chief of staff in the Pentagon.) The evidence is that Marshall would have been more willing to dare, to risk, to innovate; and it is impossible to imagine Marshall suffering a senior commander to chop and change as later would Montgomery, or to seek to grab for glory as would Patton, just as it is difficult to imagine that either of those generals would have presumed to act so had Marshall been the supreme commander. And yet the weight of the argument in Eisenhower's scale is impressive. His experience of amphibious operations—planning and bringing them off—was invaluable; his day-to-day experience of the difficulties involved in administering an Anglo-American command was without parallel; his warmth, as contrasted with Marshall's austerity, suggests his flexibility when faced with a task about which his senior commanders or the Combined Chiefs were in serious disagreement. Marshall's superior attainments might not, paradoxically, have been so effective in cementing the unity of the Grand Alliance and winning the war as the qualities in Eisenhower that were widely criticized as his weaknesses.

At all events, Eisenhower undertook his new mission well prepared and superbly confident.

On his arrival in London, the supreme commander had a few more than one hundred days to prepare the climactic invasion, if the timetable originally pledged at Teheran was to be met. The agreed date—May 1—had, however, long since become any day "during May," and Churchill, when he decided the Anzio landing would be a useful operation, had also conjectured that OVERLORD would have to be postponed until sometime in June; for this and other reasons Eisenhower would actually have one hundred and forty-three days to get ready. He would need nearly all of them.

First there was the need to get the approval of the Combined Chiefs to an appreciably stronger assault force for OVERLORD. In Eisenhower's absence his chief of staff Beetle Smith had conferred with Montgomery and Montgomery's chief of staff Major General Francis (Freddy) de Guingand; all three officers reacted to the plans as Eisenhower had earlier, and Montgomery had particularly objected to the narrow front of the projected assault. Revisions of the original plan were now drafted: five divisions instead of three in the first assault, the front expanded from three beaches along a stretch of thirty-five miles to five beaches encompassing more than fifty miles, two hundred and seventy-one additional landing craft, eight additional fighter squadrons to afford cover for the extended front—a set of demands at least some of which seemed impossible of fulfillment. But Eisenhower prefaced his recommendations with hortatory resolution: "Every obstacle must be overcome, every inconvenience suffered and every risk run to ensure that our blow is decisive. We cannot afford to fail."

Since resolution alone cannot produce landing ships, the shortage of these precious craft remained acute. Many of them were reserved for two operations in the Mediterranean—SHINGLE, the Anzio landings; and ANVIL, the landings in southern France conceived to be simultaneous with OVERLORD—so a possible solution might have been to eliminate one or both of these. But by mid-January any notion of canceling SHINGLE was academic (the assault on the Anzio beaches was on January 22), and the pressure grew to abandon ANVIL. Montgomery argued that to free landing craft for OVERLORD, ANVIL should be jettisoned or, at most, maintained only as a threat. Smith agreed. Eisenhower, dreaming of how a concurrent attack in southern France would draw German defenders from OVERLORD, fought stubbornly for a three-division ANVIL but was gradually forced to the gloomy conclusion that if there were no assault shipping available, he would be obliged to keep ANVIL alive only as a threat. On January 24 he attended a meeting of the British Chiefs to discuss his recommendations for a stronger OVERLORD. Later Field Marshal Brooke entered an acerb comment in his diary: "I entirely agree with the proposal, but it is certainly not his [Eisenhower's] idea and is one of Monty's. Eisenhower has got absolutely no strategic outlook. He makes up, however, by the way he works for good cooperation between allies."

Anyway, the Combined Chiefs agreed that OVERLORD should be strengthened as Eisenhower requested, but thereafter disagreed among themselves at nearly every point, on strategy and tactics alike. So was touched off another prolonged and tiresome transatlantic debate having to do with the size, character, and timing of ANVIL, the glacial progress of the fighting in Italy, the casualty rate of assault shipping and the rate at which damaged ships could be refitted and once again made available, the advisability of postponing OVERLORD, the pledges made to the Russians at Teheran, the phases of springtime moon and tide in the Channel, and a hundred other matters of more or less importance, all of which seemed in the end to come back to the question of landing craft, a topic which led Churchill to snort that "the destinies of two great empires . . . seem to be tied up in some Goddamned things called LSTs."

The heart of the debate was strategy: whether, as the British wished, to press the war in Italy and perhaps exploit any success with an amphibious operation in the Adriatic, toward Istria and eventually Hungary, or, as the Americans preferred, to drive with all power against the Nazi legions as directly as possible, through France. Its relevance to this narrative lies in the way Eisenhower reacted to it, and in the estimate his commanders formed of his behavior. As was his custom, he struggled valiantly to reconcile the irreconcilable. For his pains, Marshall diagnosed a case of "localitis," by which he meant to suggest that British pressure "had warped" his judgment; Brooke believed that "Eisenhower sees the situation a little more clearly [than Marshall], but he is too frightened of disagreeing with Marshall to be able to express his views freely." Both comments were wrong. Their harshness may be attributed to the choler which any two battlers may feel toward one who would mediate their quarrel.

In sum, while the debate won for OVERLORD a substantial increase in assault shipping and an extended front, the corollary landings in the south of France were indefinitely postponed and everyone was more rancorous than before. Eisenhower, striving always for Allied amity, looked about for a convenient scapegoat and found the U.S. Navy: what was needed, he told Butcher, was a presidential order to the navy "to allot enough landing craft so the Mediterranean could be kept boiling throughout the summer." But to search for a scapegoat was idle. The United States was fighting two major wars at once, each of them against a skillful, determined foe. The task was an enormous one, and in the spring of 1944 simply required more resources than could be mustered to meet all the deserving demands.

Even as Eisenhower's staff officers were drafting detailed plans for the expanded OVERLORD, the supreme commander was engaged in brisk skirmishing with Churchill, the war cabinet, the British Chiefs, and the commanders of various Allied air forces to win control by SHAEF of all aviation—bombers and fighters alike, of whatever nationality—so that all would be operating at SHAEF's bidding, according to SHAEF's plans, to accomplish SHAEF's goals. It was not easy. The RAF Bomber Command and the U.S. Strategic Air Forces, operating under a directive* given them by the Combined Chiefs at the Casablanca Conference, were bombing targets deep within Germany according to their own schedule of priorities, and these busy airmen wanted no interference with their conduct of what they considered "the really important war against Germany." (Some of the American airmen in particular were known to believe that given twenty or thirty clear operational days, they could bring the war to a triumphant conclusion all by themselves.) On the other hand, his experience, especially of Salerno, had imbued Eisenhower with the urgent need of coordinating all the services to help invading troops get ashore and stay there; his authority over the heavy bombers must, he insisted, be absolute. Ready to exercise that authority on his behalf stood his deputy Arthur Tedder, an officer versed in all aspects of tactical and strategic air warfare. But Arthur Harris of RAF Bomber Command and Spaatz of the U.S. Strategic Air Force resisted any curtailment of their independence, and the British Chiefs and Churchill backed them up.

Tedder, moreover, had a definite bombing policy in view—to disrupt the railway networks of northern France and Belgium by systematically destroying switchyards, freight yards, repair shops, roundhouses, locomotives, and rolling stock in ninety-three key railroad centers, and so immobilize the Germans in the weeks just before and after D-day—a policy which Harris and Spaatz regarded as of very limited value if not indeed potentially diastrous for OVERLORD. Nor did Brooke think much of the idea; nor did Sir Charles Portal, chief of air staff; nor, when they speculated on the scores of thousands of French casualties they expected would be a likely result of the bombings, would Churchill or Eden approve it.

Before the disagreement on air strategy could be settled the structure of air command had to be firmly established.

Tedder—never, as he has written, a man "to take alarm easily"—was nevertheless now "really worried." He knew Eisenhower well, and he knew how strongly Eisenhower felt on the matter of a unified command. "I very much fear," he reported to his chief Portal, "that if the British Chiefs of Staff and the P.M. are going to take up a position regarding Bomber Command which prevents that unified control, very serious issues will arise affecting Anglo-American cooperation in OVERLORD. A split . . . might well . . . precipitate a quite irremediable cleavage." On February 28 Eisenhower dined with Churchill and was quite explicit as to how

* Bomber Command by night and the U.S. 8th Air Force by day were "to secure the progressive destruction and dislocation of the German military, industrial, and economic system, and the undermining of the morale of the German people to a point where their capacity for armed resistance is fatally weakened."

seriously he viewed the matter. If Bomber Command were not put under the control of SHAEF, he said, he would interpret it as something less than an all-out British commitment to OVERLORD and he would "simply have to go home." This plain talk served to shake up some settled opinions. On March 3 the British Chiefs met in a room cleared of secretaries so that Portal might further stir up those opinions. Six days later the British Chiefs wired the American Chiefs their recommendation that Tedder supervise all air operations for OVERLORD and that "the responsibility for supervision of air operations . . . of all the forces . . . should pass to the supreme commander." The Americans pounced on the word "supervision": why was it not "command"? Curiously, the British now refused to give Eisenhower command, although that, as he told Marshall, was precisely what he and Portal had had in mind when they weighed the word "supervision." It was clear the Combined Chiefs now required the good offices of a professor of linguistics, or perhaps of a poet who could unlimber a few supple, flexible nouns.

The debate persisted. Eisenhower, his patience slipping, finally on March 22 exploded at the end of a long secret memorandum for his private record in which he had given tongue to many grievances: "If a satisfactory answer is not reached I am going to take drastic action and inform the Combined Chiefs of Staff that unless the matter is settled at once I will request relief from this Command." He was then driven to Whitehall to attend a meeting of the British Chiefs. Here he was told that after another exchange of cablegrams the word "direction" was satisfactory to all the Combined Chiefs: he might "direct" the big bombers to do as he chose. "Amen," he murmured, and he grinned.

Within three days the supreme commander presided over a conference of his chief air officers, together with officials from various interested ministries. Should the weight of Allied bombing fall on the railway system or, as Spaatz preferred, on the dwindling stocks of Nazi oil? Eisenhower decided for Tedder and his transportation plan and the air offensive against the railways began at last. Ten days later Churchill informed Eisenhower that his cabinet "took rather a grave and on the whole an adverse view" of the offensive, "in view of the fact that scores of thousands of French civilians . . . would lose their lives or be injured." Eisenhower remained convinced that "our chances for success in the critical battle" would be enhanced by the bombings. "I personally believe," he added, "that estimates of probable casualties have been grossly exaggerated." (In this he was proved right: casualties from the air offensive were an estimated ten thousand as opposed to the fearful predictions of one hundred thousand or more.) Inasmuch as the cabinet was still reluctant, the matter was finally referred to President Roosevelt. When he refused on April 11 to intervene, the issue was settled.

Unquestionably the French people understood the need for the policy. Men and women of the Resistance zestfully joined in, to accomplish by sabotage whatever the bombers had missed. Railway traffic by early June was only a trifle more than a third of what it had been in January. On May 23 a commentator broadcasting over Radio Paris observed, "The French railway system is in complete chaos." Gordon Harrison, the official American historian of the invasion, agreed; by D-day, he wrote, the "transportation system was on the point of total collapse." How much this damage was due to the bombers and how much to sabotage by the Resistance is impossible to say; Michael Foot, the British historian of SOE in France, wrote that "the bonus from resistance was of a size and importance comparable with the air forces' achievement," and this seems a reasonable judgment. In any case, much of the credit for the success of the transportation plan must go to Eisenhower, who throughout had stubbornly insisted on a clear-cut system of command and throughout had firmly seconded the counsel of his senior air commanders. If, as Harrison suggests, the transportation plan was "to prove critical in the battle for Normandy," the supreme commander had done much to assure the outcome of OVERLORD long before the battle was joined.

As plans had to be elaborated to make the Cotentin difficult of access for the German defender and his reinforcements, so other plans, daring and ingenious, were hatched to ensure the maintenance and supply of the beachheads. Since the port of Cherbourg could not be captured overnight and would in any event be a shambles, its harbor mined, it was evident that the invaders would for some time have to be supplied over their beaches, a chancy undertaking under the best of circumstances and potentially disastrous in the Channel, a strait notoriously buffeted by heavy weather in all seasons of the year. Apart from the troops, ammunition, tanks, trucks, and supplies needed to muster the reserves for any prolonged offensives, more than three thousand tons of matériel would have to be hauled over the beaches every day. The imaginative solution, as Admiral Mountbatten had observed two years before, was to fabricate ports in sections, tow them across, and assemble them as needed on the Normandy coast. At the time his suggestion had been greeted with merry laughter, but by the winter of 1943–1944 the project (MULBERRY) was well in hand, as was another (PLUTO) to lay pipeline from England to Normandy and so assure delivery of oil and petroleum. MULBERRY involved enormous concrete caissons, two hundred feet long, fifty-six feet wide, sixty feet high, dozens of them. In theory they were highly secret, as were the big sections of pipe for PLUTO, but since they could scarcely be constructed in someone's back room they roused perplexed speculation as they gradually took shape on the Kentish marshes near London, the Merseyside at Liverpool, and the low-lying country near Portsmouth and Southampton.

A breach of secrecy was everyone's bugbear, yet how could the painfully obvious be kept secret? Throughout the first five months of 1944, on every road and railway military stores rumbled south; the moors and downs were first littered, then jam-packed, with ammunition dumps and depots for tanks, trucks, and jeeps; on every airfield the fighters and bombers were parked wingtip to wingtip: only the dead could ignore this martial encampment, swollen and bristling. Eisenhower did what he could to preserve the fragile secrecy. On February 23 he enjoined his field commanders and the chiefs of the various Allied military missions to "the most stringent observance of security" to deny the enemy the truly vital information as to where the Allies proposed to attack, and when. On March 25 he repeated his warning to all major U.S. units.* Meantime he had requested and got from the war cabinet a ban on all unauthorized travel to and from the coastal region of England from the Wash on the east all the way round to Land's End at the tip of Cornwall in the southwest, and also to and from a part of Scotland near the Firth of Forth; the interdiction began on March 10. Further, he ordered the movement of Allied troops restricted from the first weeks of April onward. (This step was taken as much to relieve the overloaded railway system as for any other reason.) Finally, he made the extraordinary request that the British government forbid the personnel of the various allied or neutral embassies and legations (apart from those of the British dominions, the U.S., and the USSR) to send or receive uncensored messages by cable or diplomatic pouch, or to leave the country. After this request had been much debated in February and March, Eisenhower finally appealed directly to the CIGS, Field Marshal Brooke. He was not concerned with diplomatic precedent, nor convenience, nor personal liberty, nor privacy. He simply wanted all leaks sealed "as soon after the 15th of April as possible," for "I regard this source of leakage as the gravest risk to the security of our operations and to the lives of our sailors, soldiers and airmen." The Foreign Office and the war cabinet, albeit with many grave reservations, bowed to the weight of Eisenhower's urgent demand: the repressive policy was instituted on April 17 on the supposition that it would be lifted on D-day or very soon thereafter, but Eisenhower successfully contrived its retention until D plus 13. Nearly

* So obsessed was SHAEF with the need for secrecy that this latter admonition was itself stamped Secret, a classification which of course narrowly confined its circulation. Four days later someone in G–2 with a firmer grip on reality redesignated it as Restricted, and off it went at last to those for whom it had been intended.

all the governments affected protested the policy; the French, as we shall see, went further than mere protest. Nor was the ban on visitors to the southeast coast of England and to the smaller Scottish area relaxed until well into July.

These latter two measures—the visitors' ban and diplomatic censorship—were alike instituted to enhance the credibility of an elaborate swindle code-named FORTITUDE and designed to make the Germans believe the major Allied assault was aimed first at Norway and then at Pas-de-Calais, the slice of northern France nearest England. To this end an imaginary British army was bivouacked in Scotland and an imaginary American army, ostensibly commanded by Patton, in East Anglia. These "armies" of dummy troops, who rehearsed their invasions with dummy landing craft so that they could be observed by German reconnaissance aircraft, also conducted a gradually heavier radio traffic, carefully indiscreet, cunningly illusory.

The swindle would owe much of its success to the respect in which Patton was held by OKH, the High Command of the German Army. Any force reputedly led by him was bound to attract their watchful eye. Patton himself chafed. He resented the notion that he could be used only as a stalking-horse. He had landed in England on January 26 under a cloud both real and metaphorical. The countryside had been blanketed in fog; news of his arrival was almost as obscured because Eisenhower was apprehensive of a critical reaction from the press not only in the United States but in the United Kingdom as well. Patton had established his headquarters in the Midlands at a place called Peover Hall; he had launched upon a series of conferences with the corps and division commanders of what would eventually become the Third Army; he had pledged his word to Eisenhower that he would keep out of mischief. During the third week in April his presence in England was officially confirmed. On April 25 he spoke his mind in public and once again plunged himself and the War Department into controversy. The occasion was the opening by some Englishwomen of a Welcome Club for American servicemen. The topic of Patton's remarks was Anglo-American unity, and the remark emblazoned on the front pages of American newspapers was that "since it is the evident destiny of the British and Americans to rule the world, the better we know each other the better job we will do." A silly and offensive thing to say, and it loosed a torrent of protests from Left and Right alike. General Marshall was the more vexed because he had been deftly steering through Congress a list of nominations for permanent promotion; Patton's name was on it, so now the entire list was threatened. "I have grown so weary of the trouble he constantly causes," Eisenhower cabled Marshall, "that I am seriously contemplating the most drastic action." To Patton he wrote:

". . . you simply will not guard your tongue in spite of the most drastic instructions and orders. . . . If you are again guilty of any indiscretion . . . I will relieve you instantly from command." But four days later, after Patton had staged some rather slobbery histrionics, Eisenhower relented and notified his old friend that he would be retained in command. (It was "the work of God," Patton wrote in his diary; "His will be done.")

To win agreement to all the strategies, plans, and deceptions, to soothe the rancors and pacify the disputants, to reinforce the superegos and stifle the ids, kept the supreme commander scurrying—with all dignity, of course—on an interminable go-round of conferences, conclaves, and committee meetings. He was never alone but, in his eminence, was often lonely.

His status tantalized several citizens of our acquisitive society: how, they wondered, might he be exploited to their profit? The most plausible of them recognized that if it were done, then 'twere well it were done honorably, and they made their pitch accordingly—book publishers, magazine editors, Hollywood film producers, and the like. At least three biographies were in the works. Less scrupulous journalists were laying hands on and causing to be printed his private letters to his mother or to old friends in Abilene. What part of this attention did not infuriate him whetted still further his already acute instinct for publicity; he came to be increasingly aware that he was, as they say, a valuable property, and if he was to be exploited he wished to make sure it would be done deftly, with the profits channeled in the proper direction.

His own tastes continued simple. His British military assistant, Lieutenant Colonel James Gault, an aide who had come to his staff from the Scots Guards in July 1943, had found him a town house in Mayfair a few minutes' stroll from his headquarters in Grosvenor Square, but when some overzealous supply officers furnished it with what Eisenhower termed "an unnecessary luxuriousness" he permitted himself a brief, volcanic outburst. By the time the lava had cooled the offending items had been returned, an investigation into the purchasing methods of ETO Headquarters Command was in train, the town house had been vacated, and the supreme commander had contentedly removed to Telegraph Cottage, the unpretentious little suburban villa he had rented in the days before the invasion of North Africa. To make the living room of this house more comfortable Butcher authorized the purchase of four sofa pillows that cost ten dollars each. These too were returned, and Butcher was scathingly reminded of the rich possibilities of a congressional investigation into the expenditure of forty dollars of the taxpayers' money so that a four-star general might coddle his sit-upon in sofa pillows.

To get out of London, to abjure metropolitan distractions—it seemed more than advisable to Eisenhower, it seemed essential. A country boy, perforce celibate for the duration, he preferred to think of his officers as being in like case. Early in March he had SHAEF moved from Grosvenor Square and the neighborhood into which it had overflowed to Bushy Park, a camouflaged common in the outskirts of London; here, he hoped, the Anglo-American staff could work together in cenobitic harmony, sharing coffee breaks in the morning and teatime in the afternoon.

His own office at this place was severely plain. A dark brown carpet; chairs and couches along the walls; three flags in a standard—American, British, and his own four-star flag—providing the only touch of color; a big desk, blank and ordered, bearing framed photographs of his mother, his wife, and his son; and two telephones, one of them a scrambler for conversations judged to be of extraordinary import. Near at hand was a leatherbound logbook in which was inserted the daily file of telegrams, digests of intelligence reports, correspondence, summaries of staff activities, and the like. Also near was a strip of buzzers by which he could variously summon Butcher or Gault or Tex Lee or Captain Mattie Pinette, his WAC secretary, or Kay Summersby, who now guarded his office as his appointment secretary.

Yet while SHAEF was to become a happy and close-knit community, its commander was nevertheless still lonely. "I think, at times, I get a bit homesick," he confessed to General Marshall on March 15, "and the ordinary diversions of the theater and other public places are denied me." What he wanted was "an opportunity to become acquainted again with my son." He recognized that John, who would be graduating from West Point in June, "should not, for his own good, stay in my theater too long," and he promised Marshall he would send him home after, say, sixty days in the ETO. He hesitated to ask, but he hankered. Marshall replied promptly that all would be arranged as Eisenhower requested, "as soon after June 6 [graduation day] as possible."

During the one hundred and forty-three days available to him before the cross-Channel invasion, General Eisenhower had, in common with his senior commanders, one enduring responsibility: to visit the troops, mingle with them, inspect and be inspected, win their trust and confidence. Bradley did a good deal of this and did it well; Montgomery did much more of it, and he was very good indeed. Eisenhower did as much of it as his tight schedule would permit: in four months (February–May) he visited twenty-six divisions, twenty-four airfields, five warships, and a great many depots, hospitals, ports, and other military installations. It was work he enjoyed. He always liked being with troops, talking with them, listening to their talk, signing autographs, effortlessly winning their trust and affection. "I've seen him sit in the shade, leaning up against a tree," General Bradley would recall, "and sign autographs for three-quarters of an hour."

This vital task of molding morale was the more important for Eisenhower since he was an American and the stickout spokesman of the United States of America. In truth, neither the U.S. nor Americans were particularly fancied in Britain during these months, and unless Eisenhower's informants were off hiding in euphoria he must have realized how deep was the British resentment of both his country and his countrymen. The GIs were, as the quip had it, "overpaid, oversexed, and over here," and that was bad enough, but on the whole the political thrust of the government in Washington stirred up livelier apprehensions. The British Right mistrusted Roosevelt quite as much as did the American Right; moreover, they had indignantly noted that the U.S. had already assumed Britain's leadership in world finance: the dollar had superseded the pound sterling. For much the same reason the British Left was hostile toward the U.S.: Wall Street if not Washington was now the prepotent master of an aggressive world capitalism. Various polls of British public opinion at about this time revealed that only a third of those questioned held favorable views of Americans. (After Mussolini's tumble from power, Americans were actually held in lower esteem than Italians.) Yet nine of ten Britishers thought well of Russia and the Russians.

As supreme commander, Eisenhower could do little more than deplore these disagreeable facts. But he also wore another hat as American commander of the European Theater of Operations, and in this guise he could at least go through the motions. On February 19 he instructed his deputy commander of ETO, the pompous and pious Lieutenant General John C. H. Lee, to ask every American in the theater to be "especially careful" about:

> Improper use of motor transportation;
> Drinking in public places;
> Excessive drinking, at any time . . . ;
> Loud, profane or indecent language, especially in public;
> Slovenliness in appearance;
> Any discourtesy to civilians.

These parental admonitions might have been more effective if they had come through any other officer than J. C. H. (Jesus Christ Himself) Lee, who justifiably or no was cordially detested by all ranks in and out of his own command, which was the Service of Supply. In any case, a week later Eisenhower issued similar instructions, emphasizing the need to avoid "statements derogatory to any troops of the United Nations," and ordered that they "be read by all officers and to all enlisted men at the first formation after receipt and at least once a month thereafter." Manifestly, Anglo-American unity was proving even harder to win in the public house than in the council chambers of the Combined Chiefs of Staff. Still later, acknowledging the large, loud, carefree way of an American when abroad with a fat wallet, Eisenhower bid Lee be "especially watchful to see that extravagance does not characterize the American Army in this Theater." But all those capital letters notwithstanding, the GI and his officers still swaggered about the big cities and the small towns, and "their attitude to women, their proneness to spoil a girl, to build up, exaggerate, talk big, and to act with generosity and flamboyance, helped to make them the most attractive boyfriends. In addition, they 'picked up' easily, and even a comparatively plain and unattractive girl stood a chance."

And so they made few friends among the British soldiers.

Eisenhower was less concerned about obedience to his deputy theater commander than about the battle-readiness of the troops. Each inspection had showed that the men were fit, in good heart, and, as the day approached, spoiling for a fight. The weapon was tempered and set. Eisenhower had chosen the commanders of corps and divisions and chosen well.

The day approached with the vexatious problem of association with the French still unresolved. This resulted from the fundamental disagreement, mentioned earlier, on the destiny of France as nation and world power. General de Gaulle, who by 1944 stood unchallenged as head of the French Committee of National Liberation (FCNL), envisioned a resurgent France, once and always a great world power, which must of necessity be warmly welcomed to the company of other great powers by its allies the United States, the United Kingdom, and the Soviet Union. Anthony Eden, His Majesty's secretary of state for foreign affairs, pursued a related policy, one which, as he wrote late in 1943, "must aim at the restoration of the independence of the smaller European allies and of the greatness of France." To that end he set the Foreign Office to work to build an association—perhaps later to be a confederation? an alliance? a military and economic union?—of the British Commonwealth with Britain's near neighbors of western Europe, and especially with France. Such a course, as he would tell the House of Commons in September 1944, "will give us more authority with the other great powers." President Roosevelt took a quite different view. He foresaw—and American policy was directed toward—a dissolution of the French colonial empire, second in extent only to Britain's, and the diminution of French influence in world affairs. The prospect, although of course this phase of the matter had not occurred to the

President, was of an uncontested American financial penetration into the oil-rich Middle East and of American financial domination of postwar Europe. The Soviets at this time were alertly aware of the British project of an alliance of western European countries (and suspicious of its purposes), but they were content to observe, to wait, to postpone any political debates with their Anglo-American allies pending the final defeat of Hitler.

These various policies dictated the contradictory approaches toward de Gaulle and the FCNL and effectively hamstrung SHAEF. Indeed, Eisenhower was never given instructions from the Combined Chiefs as to how he should manage affairs with the French. He faced an intolerable confusion.

De Gaulle saw the thing simply, proudly, and intransigently. The war against the common foe was to be fought over his country, with his countrymen giving invaluable assistance not only as resistants but also as soldiers of the French Army; he should therefore at once be invited to join the highest war councils of the Allies, his advice and support should be solicited, the FCNL recognized as the provisional government of France, and his own uphill path to establish a peaceful jurisdiction over France made smooth and straight by the military force of Allied arms.

Eisenhower was sometimes tempted to agree. From the Resistance within France, by way of the British SOE, he had been informed of plans for several operations designed to mesh precisely with the invasion, and one or two of those (Plan Vert to attack the railways and Plan Grenouille to sabotage railway turntables) had been approved in London and would be put into effect with notable success. As he remarked in an "ultra-secret" memorandum on March 22, "we are going to need very badly the support of the Resistance groups in France, and it is our general opinion that these can be brought into full play only through the agency and leadership of the French Committee."

But Roosevelt still shunned de Gaulle. He refused to permit any action that might constitute recognition of the FCNL as the government of France. On March 15 he had sent Eisenhower a unilateral directive empowering him to decide "where, when and how" a civil administration might be exercised in France; he might "consult" with the FCNL, but he must require of it assurances that it did not propose to take power for any considerable period of time and that it would assist in the restoration of France's traditional liberties. (Upon being apprised of these stipulations, de Gaulle observed: "France, who brought freedom to the world and who has been, and still remains, its champion, does not need to consult outside opinions to reach a decision on how she will reconstitute liberty at home.")

Eager as always to arrive at a compromise, the supreme commander was delighted when de Gaulle sent General Pierre Koenig to London as head of the French military mission and commander of the French forces in the United Kingdom. Conversations were opened in the third week of April "strictly on a military basis" and Koenig was "thoroughly co-operative." Eisenhower had reason to hope the conversations would slide smoothly into discussions of such necessarily related matters as civilian labor, public safety and health, displaced persons, monetary exchange, transfer of property, treatment of banks, and the like—all civil and political questions. But the conversations with Koenig were abruptly broken off on orders from the FCNL in Algiers.

The instant cause of those orders was the censorship on all traffic in diplomatic messages (save those of the Commonwealth, U.S., and USSR) which, fortuitously, was imposed just at this time. To the French, whose forces were to play an essential part in the invasion and whose territory would be the theater of the battle, the censorship seemed a "calculated insult." Despite appearances, however, there seems little doubt that the censorship was imposed on the French for reasons of security, an object of worship whose votaries are often moved by the most extravagant absurdities. Churchill was suspicious of the FCNL because two of its subordinate members were Communists. In any event, the censorship was clear evidence that the Allies refused to welcome the French as comrades, even for a venture so near to French hearts as the liberation of France. It is difficult to imagine a more wounding decision.

As D-day edged closer, Eisenhower once again called the attention of the Combined Chiefs to his urgent military needs:

> In order that arrangements can be made for the coordinated action by French resistance groups, it has become imperative that General Koenig, head of the French Mission here, be given certain general information [about] forthcoming operations.
>
> It is, therefore, my intention to give to him . . . under pledge of secrecy, the name of the country in which the main attack will take place and the month for which it is scheduled.

When the British Chiefs protested that the security of OVERLORD might be compromised by even these vague intimations, Eisenhower retorted with some heat:

> The limitations under which we are operating in dealing with the French are becoming very embarrassing and are producing a situation which is potentially dangerous. . . .
> . . . General Koenig feels very keenly the fact that he is denied even

the most general knowledge of forthcoming operations although French naval, air and airborne units are to be employed, and much is expected from French resistance, both active and passive. The sum total of these delays and resentments is, in my opinion, likely to result in acute embarrassment to the Allied forces, and it will be too late, after the event, to correct them all.

This was dispatched to the Combined Chiefs, together with Eisenhower's suggestion that he be allowed to tell Koenig what was afoot so that Koenig might in turn report to de Gaulle, "in French cipher, if necessary, so as to remove the present block to our plans and preparations." Or, perhaps better, de Gaulle himself might be invited to London so that Eisenhower might "deal with him direct on the most immediate and pressing problem of the initial approach to the French people and their organized resistance groups." This was on May 11; it lacked a trifle more than three weeks until D-day. "I request," Eisenhower insisted, "that this matter be treated as of the utmost urgency, and that it be considered, as far as possible, on its military aspects."

To the soldier the salient consideration is the success of the military operation, in this case a sure and expanding beachhead at an insignificant cost in human lives—if the loss of any lives at all is ever insignificant. (During the war under discussion such loss of life was referred to by the professional soldiers as "wastage.") The statesman, on the other hand, must take the longer view, one embracing the "national interest," and founded on such toplofty considerations as the "free determination" by liberated peoples of their own governors. In this case, some historians have found it useful to write of Roosevelt's idealism, and that would seem to have been, as well, the President's own most convenient self-justification.

At all events, President Roosevelt did not find it possible to consider General Eisenhower's request solely "on its military aspects." He had no objection to inviting de Gaulle to London, on the condition that he stay in England until after the invasion; such a condition obviously transformed invitation into insult. Roosevelt also cabled Churchill: "I do *not* desire that Eisenhower shall become involved with the Committee [FCNL] on a political level."

This deplorable mess was not, of course, the supreme commander's sole preoccupation as the days dwindled before the ultimate day; it was merely the most exasperating. Commander Butcher thought he looked worn and tired. "The strain is telling on him," Butcher noted. "He looks older now than at any time since I have been with him." On Monday, May 15, he presided over a general and final review of plans for OVERLORD; the conclave was held at St. Paul's School, headquarters of 21st Army Group in

West Kensington; the king was there, the prime minister, Field Marshal Smuts, the British Chiefs, and more than one hundred and fifty senior officers from all the commands that would take part in the invasion; the big lecture hall was ablaze with gold braid, gleaming brass, red tabs, and splendid blobs of color from medal ribbons commemorating every feat of arms of two generations past; Alan Brooke surveyed the supreme commander sourly and concluded he was "no real director of thought, plans, energy or direction, [just] a coordinator, a good mixer . . . but no real commander."

Next day Eisenhower was to sign agreements governing the conditions under which various European countries would be liberated: representatives of Holland, Belgium, and Norway appeared, but there was none from France. Later, in a cablegram to be transmitted to Roosevelt, Eisenhower assured the President he would confine himself, when treating with the French, "to military matters and related civil administration," and he then undertook to acquaint the President with the facts of life in wartime France: "I think I should tell you that so far as I am able to determine from information given to me through agents and through escaped prisoners of war, there exist in France today only two major groups, of which one is the Vichy gang, and the other characterized by unreasoning admiration for de Gaulle." As analysis this was inaccurate, for the French Communist party was both powerful and at this time articulately opposed, if not to de Gaulle, to the more obviously rightist of his followers; unreasoning admiration for de Gaulle was ebbing fast. As argument Eisenhower's message was useless, for the day before he sent it the FCNL in Algiers had voted to reconstitute itself the provisional government of the French Republic and had at the same time formally repudiated the Clark-Darlan agreements of November 1942. As president of the FCNL, de Gaulle was thus provisional president of France. Nothing could have more displeased Roosevelt.

It was now quite clear that any rapprochement between SHAEF and the French provisional government would wait upon the logic of OVERLORD itself.

Already the soldiers, having completed their training maneuvers, had begun to move in a steady stream of trucks and lorries, choking the roads by day and by night, to their camouflaged encampments along the southern coast. Their jeeps and trucks and tanks and artillery were waterproofed with wax; they were issued the special equipment they would need for their assault; they were given their briefing, their succinct preparatory instructions. Now they would be sealed off from the rest of England. From these assembly areas they would move to what G-3, the planning officers, called the hards, the concrete ramps from which they would board their landing craft. By May 31 more than a quarter-million troops—trained, tough, and ready—were waiting for orders in their embarkation areas.

June 1 was Y-day, so denoted by the planners as the day by which every detail of the whole great armada of invasion must be in place—every ship, vehicle, airplane; every gun, shell, bullet; every nurse, dressing, salve; every soldier, sailor, airman. So it was.

All waited, wondering what would happen across the water.

Across the water the Germans were waiting too, as they had been for some time, and with a degree of confidence that did not seem justified in the circumstances. They were protecting Festung Europa, well advertised by their superb propagandists as being impregnable. Belatedly recognizing that he would need more than boasts to protect his Reich against an invasion from England, in the early fall of 1943 Hitler had begun to give his western defenses closer attention. On September 29—while the Nazi legions were still recovering from the battering they had taken in the first Soviet summer offensive, while they were frantically attempting to make a stable front on the western bank of the Dnieper River, while they were scrambling to pull back from Naples, while they were apprehensively eying Tito's partisans south of Trieste—the Führer spoke to Goering, Speer, Rundstedt, and other Nazi leaders. "I must freely admit," he said, "that a major landing of the enemy in the west would bring us to a generally critical position." A handsome admission. Generalfeldmarschall Gerd von Rundstedt was instructed to inspect the defenses along the Channel and the western coast of France, report on their strength, and reinforce them as necessary.

Rundstedt's report on October 25 cannot have been reassuring. Divisions guarding the coast were spread thin and were under strength (many had only two regiments); they suffered from an almost total lack of transport and were short of artillery; the troops were on the average over thirty-one years old (six years older than the U.S. troops in Britain) and conspicuously without Ost-Härte, the East-toughness needed to fight the Russians. This report gave rise to Führer Directive 51, only the second such directive to deal with conduct of the war in the west. In this Weisung 51, issued November 3, Hitler ordered the western defenses fortified and invigorated "in preparing for the decisive battle." In conclusion, he said: "I can no longer take the responsibility for allowing the western front to be weakened for the benefit of other theaters of war."

In January 1944 the German defender had disposed fifty-three divisions in France and the Low Countries, thirty-five of them north of the

Loire. By June the number of divisions was fifty-nine, with all the increase in the north. To a great extent, however, this added strength was deceptive, for the complement of a German division had shrunk from an authorized fifteen thousand (infantry) and seventeen thousand (panzer) to twelve or thirteen thousand. Though some armor was shifted from Russia to France, the overwhelming bulk of the German forces in France lacked mobility. Indeed, more than half the divisions were labeled by G–2 as "static," and even most of the "mobile" units depended on bicycles and horse transport to get about. Moreover, the best troops available for defense were rooted in position in the Pas-de-Calais, owing to their touching faith in the fraudulent FORTITUDE.

In the general area of Normandy selected for the invasion there were six German divisions: one panzer; three static, assigned for coastal defense; and two infantry, one of which, the 352nd, had not long before D-day taken its position back of Omaha beach, one of the American landing places, where it would prove to be a most disagreeable surprise. The 352nd almost certainly was ordered to Normandy because Hitler himself in late April took an unusual interest in the feasibility of an Allied assault on the Cotentin and "began to insist strongly on the need to reinforce the defense there."

The defenders' command was imprecise and consequently tactics suffered. Rundstedt, recalled from a voluntary retirement, was in titular control, but Rommel was the active force and closer to the impending battle. Rundstedt, without experience of an adversary who absolutely controlled the air, desired to hold in reserve a strong armored force which could be swiftly dispatched (he imagined) to obliterate any Allied threat. Rommel, fearful that Allied bombers could intercept and destroy any armored column, wanted all reserves dug in near the coast to meet and at once repulse any assault. Rommel was nearer right, but Rundstedt called the turn. Both were confident any attack could be enveloped on the beaches.

As the Day approached, the U.S. Fifth Army at last burst out of the beachhead at Anzio, linked up with Alexander's main forces, and turned on Rome. In Byelorussia an apparent lull in the fighting persuaded German intelligence officers that the unstable eastern front would lie quiet, but the Soviet command was methodically assembling a host of tanks, artillery, and combat troops, one which would explode on June 22 in a vast offensive that would send the Nazis staggering back more than two hundred and fifty miles in twenty-five days.

Meanwhile, on either side of the Channel the men waited. The imminence of the invasion was no secret. The whole world waited.

Thursday, June 1. The supreme commander, the man whose word everyone awaited, was thinking most about the weather. He had, God knows, other matters on his mind—Leigh-Mallory, his commander in chief of air forces, feared the 82nd and 101st Airborne Divisions would suffer such severe losses that the plan for their drop should be changed or even canceled, and the supreme commander, while agreeing that the hazards were agonizing, had to decide that the airborne attack "must go on"; the prime minister had suddenly announced his intention of witnessing the invasion from a cruiser, H.M.S. *Belfast,* and the supreme commander had to cope with this caprice; intelligence reports had warned for a year and more of some frightful new German weapon, a long-range rocket that might kill one thousand Londoners at a whack; Eisenhower had also been privily informed of American efforts to develop an atomic bomb, and he had been simultaneously advised that since the Nazis might be close to perfecting the same awful device, perhaps his invading army would be repulsed by some ghastly radioactive poison—but despite all these nightmarish fantasies, weather was necessarily his chief preoccupation. "Weather forecasts," he cabled Marshall, "while still indefinite are generally favorable. I will keep you informed." On this morning there was a drizzle in London; later the sun came out; by midafternoon there was low cloud.

Friday, June 2. Accompanied by his British aide Colonel Gault, Eisenhower traveled to his advance command post in a wood near Southwick, a few miles north of Portsmouth. His headquarters was under canvas, his office in a caravan, but his most important hours were passed in Southwick House, an unsightly pile which was now operational headquarters for his senior commanders. Some time past, the invasion had been scheduled for Monday, June 5; so it was still. Eisenhower was entirely confident. As long ago as May 15 he had sensed "the smell of victory . . . in the air." From intelligence reports he and his senior commanders were pleasantly aware that a sizable proportion of the troops opposing them were either half-trained youths or middle-aged men; they appreciated the scarcity of Nazi transport and artillery; they knew how severely the Allied air forces had punished the Luftwaffe in the air battle of the past two months. They controlled sea; they controlled air; they were sanguine about control of an expanding beachhead, barring some unforeseen disaster, barring an unexpected turn in the weather.

On this night Eisenhower dined with Montgomery. Later they went to Southwick House to hear the latest report from the team of meteorologists. The weather charts seemed reasonably good, but the chief meteorologist, Group Captain J. M. Stagg, and his associates didn't like the look of a region of low barometric pressure over Iceland. Nevertheless, the plan to attack on Monday was not altered.

Saturday, June 3. Eisenhower was early up for a quick trip back to Bushy Park. Here he dictated a cablegram to Marshall: "Weather prospects . . . are rather favorable . . . almost an even chance of having pretty fair conditions. . . . I should say that only marked deterioration . . . would disarrange our plans." He kept appointments with two or three of his officers. He dictated a memorandum for his official diary, listing his complaints. On coordination with the French: "the whole thing [is] a rather sorry mess. . . . De Gaulle has failed to accept the prime minister's invitation to come to England." On the underwater obstacles the Germans had strewn over the tidal beaches: "a very considerable hazard." On his most vexing present concern, the weather: "The weather in this country is practically unpredictable." This reflection led him to luxuriate briefly and uncharacteristically in self-pity: "Probably no one that does not have to bear the specific and direct responsibility . . . can understand the intensity of these burdens. The Supreme Commander, much more than any of his subordinates, is kept informed of the political issues involved, particularly the anticipated effect of delay upon the Russians. . . . My tentative thought is," he concluded, "that we must go unless there is a real and very serious deterioration in the weather."

He was driven back to his advance command post, with a brief stop at Southwick House to check the latest weather reports, now ominous. As his automobile turned into his camp, an unexpected procession of limousines with a motorcycle escort roared in behind him—the prime minister, accompanied by sundry dignitaries, ready for a drink or two of whisky, and ebullient with word that de Gaulle would arrive in England next day.

After a quick supper the supreme commander met at Southwick House with his commanders in chief to hear Stagg's report. It was bad. The high-pressure system covering southern England and part of the continent was being shoved out by the low-pressure area moving eastward from Iceland. Already Bradley's westernmost task force was at sea, wallowing in the choppy Channel, headed for the scheduled June 5 assault. Clouds were low. Waves were breaking five feet high. Fresh winds were predicted for June 4 and 5, blowing from 19 to 24 mph, gusting higher. Sloppy weather; stormy, overcast. A decision to postpone meant recalling the American troops to their western harbors, and worse, halting the whole complex mechanism of invasion—bombers, airborne troops, warships, assault landing craft—at the moment all were poised to spring, at the moment each man had his set edge of anticipation. The supreme commander could duck a final decision until the small hours of Sunday. He bid his officers reassemble early the next day.

Sunday, June 4. Coffee was served at 4 A.M. in what had been the library of Southwick House. The commanders in chief and their ranking staff officers sat uneasily in the overstuffed chairs ranged round the edges of the room. Group Captain Stagg came in. They hushed. He said the seas were abating but the cloud cover was still low and thick. Eisenhower glanced round the room and put the question. Admiral Ramsay? A pause. Difficult but possible. Air Chief Marshal Leigh-Mallory? Not a chance. General Montgomery? He was for going. Tedder was for postponement. Eisenhower observed that the Allied assault forces were not preponderantly superior to the defenders, that the operation was feasible only if the vast Allied air superiority could be counted upon. Without air, he suggested, the operation should be postponed. Did anyone disagree? He glanced round the room. None did. The prearranged code words—HORNPIPE and BOWSPRIT—were flashed, and all along the southern coast the brakes of the mechanism complained as it was ponderously ground to a halt.

The supreme commander went back to bed. He lay, dozing fretfully, surrounded by paperback whoppers about the Wild West and by early editions of the Sunday newspapers, half his mind fully awake and preoccupied, the other half torpid.

Later, in midafternoon, Churchill arrived, hasty and urgent, to talk with the supreme commander before de Gaulle should arrive. The prime minister had entertained the president of the provisional government of France at luncheon, but they had not got along well together. The difficulty was that Churchill quite sincerely imagined he was being generous by inviting de Gaulle to be his guest on this momentous occasion, while de Gaulle perceived that he had been cheapened in the eyes of his allies. He was not a partner, not the chief of an equal state, but merely a symbol. Churchill had earlier urged de Gaulle to send a public message to France as soon as the invasion was under way, and de Gaulle had said he would, but thereafter the two gentlemen had lost their tempers and commenced to raise their voices. Churchill hurried first to Eisenhower's camp to advise that if the supreme commander wished de Gaulle to broadcast a message to the French people, now if ever was the time for him to play the emollient diplomat.

De Gaulle's arrival served at least to distract Eisenhower from the weather, which was foul. The Frenchman was received most ceremoniously and conducted into the supreme commander's war room, where Eisenhower explained the plan for the assault and the state of preparations at the moment. All went well until the matter of messages to be broadcast to France was broached. Eisenhower's speech had of course long since been prepared, vetted by the Foreign Office and the State Department, and recorded; printed versions of it were already packed in the bomb bays of Allied aircraft ready to be scattered over France; no change could possibly be made in it. Yet now, reading it, de Gaulle at once found it insupportable. It called on the French people to carry out Eisenhower's orders; it declared that the local (Vichyiste) administrations would continue in power until instructed otherwise; it ignored de Gaulle and the provisional government of which he was president; it ignored "the French authority which . . . had done Eisenhower the honor of placing under his command a great part of the French Army." Worse, de Gaulle knew that SHAEF had been provided with so-called invasion currency—franc notes issued without the authority of the French. The U.S. refused to ask de Gaulle to sanction these notes, since to do so would grant him de facto recognition, a step that Roosevelt could not take. Since de Gaulle considered that as president of the provisional government he alone had the right to issue French currency, he regarded the invasion francs as so much counterfeit. ("C'est de la fausse monnaie," he told Harold Nicolson.) At all events, coming down to the immediate difficulty, de Gaulle would not speak to his countrymen over the BBC on any program that included Eisenhower's speech, since to do so would give the impression that he approved what Eisenhower was to say. If de Gaulle were to speak to the French, he would do so at a different hour and in such terms as would contradict the supreme commander. (And so he did.)

De Gaulle left. The weather was getting worse.

Later the commanders gathered at Southwick House. At 9:30 P.M. Stagg came in with his weather report and, as the officers fell silent, they could hear the wind driving the rain against the tall windows. It was blowing harder now, at more than 30 mph. Nevertheless, Stagg was cautiously cheerful. The weather front was passing by, he said; the skies would clear in a few hours, the wind would abate, fair weather should hold through Monday night and into Tuesday. Better weather for aviation. Leigh-Mallory was dubious. Ramsay pointed out that if the American task forces sailed again from their West Country harbors but later had to be recalled again, it would mean postponement until the next day when the tides were right—June 19. Tedder agreed the operation was "chancy." Montgomery itched to go. Smith indicated that he would take the gamble. All this was merely advice. One man only had to risk the invaluable pile of chips. The order had to be given or OVERLORD could not be launched on June 6. At about 9:45 P.M. Eisenhower said: "I am quite positive that the order must be given."

Admiral Ramsay hurried out to send the signal to the waiting fleets.

Still the order could be revoked.

The supreme commander was driven back to his trailer, where he would undress, climb into pajamas, lower himself into his bunk, listen to the rain pounding against the metal roof above him, toss, turn about, and presently doze. His old friend Butcher had twenty-four hours earlier diagnosed a case of preinvasion jitters. He had himself protested there was no cause for unease: when the time came, someone would have to take the decision and he was that one and so he would do the job without hesitation. Yet he had hesitated and would again. He woke, turned over, and dozed once more.

Monday, June 5. He woke finally at 3:30 A.M. and at once arose. It is an evil hour: it seemed to him the wind was blowing a hurricane (it was less than half that strong) and the rain "seemed to be traveling in horizontal streaks." All this would make a splendid story in the years to come, but in truth the storm, as Stagg had predicted, had passed to the east and was now spending its fury on the French coast and so lulling the German defenders into a fine want of caution.

Having dressed, the supreme commander was driven the mile or so over muddy lanes to Southwick House. He was wretched. It seemed impossible that an invasion could be launched in such conditions.

But hot black coffee was served in the library. Gathered together, the officers no longer felt so sorry. Stagg appeared with another weather chart; he seemed actually cheery. The storm he had forecast was, he said, right where he had said it would be; lucky that the operation had been postponed, it would have been a disaster. But now there was promise of good weather for thirty-six hours. Indeed, even as he spoke the rain gentled and the skies began to clear.

Out in the wet darkness over the Channel the plan for OVERLORD had already begun to elbow indecision into oblivion. The ships creaked and plunged steadily forward. Soldiers were miserably sick.

In Southwick House the commanders and their officers each gave an opinion and then looked to the supreme commander.

Eisenhower considered very briefly. "Okay," he said. "Let's go."

It was then 4:15 A.M.

CHAPTER ELEVEN

Victory in Europe

AT THIS STAGE OF HIS CAREER the supreme commander suggests the male of *Apis mellifera*, which has one lively and essential function to perform, after which—curtains. Having given one indispensable three-word order, Eisenhower was no more useful than a squails board or a Welsbach mantle, and might reasonably have been tucked away in the attic for a week or so for all the good he could do the Allied invaders. Now it was up to Ramsay and Leigh-Mallory and Montgomery; to a lesser extent to Bradley and Major General Miles (Bimbo) Dempsey; to a greater extent to the platoon commanders and the noncommissioned officers of the U.S. 1st, 4th, and 29th, the Canadian 3rd, and the British 3rd and 50th divisions; also to the 6th British and the 82nd and 101st U.S. airborne divisions; most of all to the privates who would have to swarm across the beaches and up the bluffs and through the fields beyond.

Meanwhile the supreme commander talked to press and radio correspondents, fingered his lucky coins, witnessed the loading of some LCIs, talked with American paratroopers just before they took off, played checkers with Butcher, worried about de Gaulle and the French Resistance, swapped yarns about American politicians, grabbed a bite, napped, read and reread his Wild West fictions, smoked cigarettes incessantly, gossiped with his staff officers, stared at maps of the Cotentin, went to bed, woke early, received the first reports of the airdrop from Leigh-Mallory and of the landings from Ramsay, washed, shaved, dressed, sauntered to the war tent, at 8 A.M. dictated a brief cablegram to Marshall ("I have as yet no information concerning the actual landings nor of our progress through beach obstacles. . . . All preliminary reports are satisfactory. . . . I will keep you informed"), fretted that he knew so little of what was going on across the water, called on Montgomery and then on Ramsay at their headquarters, made plans to go to France on the morrow so that he might see for himself the progress of the lodgment, paced back and forth in his war tent while awaiting reports, dined early and, soon after dinner, exhausted, went to bed for a sound sleep.

By that time, one hundred and fifty-six thousand Allied troops were in France. Their number would swiftly grow in the next few days. The Atlantic Wall had been irrevocably sundered.

Military operations would now proceed through various phases familiar to all students of the history of warfare as the invasion, battle for the beachheads, stalemate, breakout, pursuit, single thrust versus broad front, bulge, battles of the Rhineland, crossing the Rhine, double envelopment of the Ruhr, and victory. All these (save of course the stalemate and bulge) were part of SHAEF's "general plan," according to Eisenhower, "carefully outlined at staff meetings before D-day [and] never abandoned, even momentarily, throughout the campaign." Beetle Smith loyally bore witness to the same notion: "I doubt that there has ever been a campaign in history where actual operations fitted so closely the initial plan of a commander, adopted so far in advance. Long before we set foot in Europe and tested the enemy's strength in battle, we had decided on the blueprint for his defeat."

This almost wholly fanciful conspectus has the virtue of making tidy a chaotic and confused campaign, one that was hammered out amid controversy when it was not improvised in response to the enemy's desperate convulsions. It would have been more accurate to say that the story of the campaign could best be summed up by describing the persistent conflict between the supreme commander and his foremost British lieutenant, Bernard Montgomery. But this conspectus too is far from the whole truth; it is only the most seductive, since to dwell upon it satisfies the natural desire of the British to score off the arrogant Americans, and the equally mischievous impulse of the Americans to disparage the timid British.

Allied troops by the scores of thousands continued to land on the beaches and push inward through the breach in the Atlantic Wall. Eisenhower himself toured the beachheads aboard a speedy warship on Wednesday, June 7; the next Monday he escorted the American Joint Chiefs—Marshall, King, and Arnold—on another inspection, this time going ashore. By that time sixteen divisions had been unloaded in Normandy. The Allied forces were linked together in a beachhead nearly sixty miles wide and were pressing steadily south and west, threatening to cut off Cherbourg.

The successful landings and their swift reinforcement made bitter fare for Hitler. He was obliged briefly to turn his attention from east to west. On June 17 he traveled to Margival, near Soissons. Here, some years earlier, a bunker had been built for him from which he had proposed personally to direct SEA LION, the invasion of England; here he now met with Rundstedt and Rommel because of another invasion, this one realized. To Rommel's chief of staff, Generaleutnant Hans Speidel, the Führer "looked sick and tired out. . . . His old personal magnetism seemed to have gone." Rundstedt and Rommel urged that the German forces in Normandy be withdrawn, linked with those guarding the Pas-de-Calais, and deployed north of the Seine in a suitably mobile defensive position. But as Speidel recalled: "Hitler, raising his voice, first expressed sharp dissatisfaction with the successful Allied landings, found fault with the local commanders, and then ordered that fortress Cherbourg be held at any cost."*

No withdrawal, no retreat. Indeed, there was no reason to retreat, for the secret Nazi weapon designed to bring England to her knees had already been experimentally launched—what in official English circles was called the flying bomb and was known elsewhere as the V-1, the buzz bomb, the doodlebug, and by other less amiable epithets—and would soon be raining its impersonal horror, more agonizing than the blitz, on London and most of southeast England.

The accursed buzz bombs did serious damage: in less than two months they injured some thirty-five thousand persons, killed more than five thousand, destroyed some thirty thousand dwellings; their impact on the morale of a war-weary people was too dolorous to be counted in statistics. Yet efforts to interfere with the bloody things were useless: to shoot them down did no good, they simply exploded on impact; to bomb launching sites did no good, the sites were easily repaired. Britain was so sorely hurt and the authorities so frustrated that early in July the British Chiefs briefly entertained the idea of attacking the launching sites with poison gas. They promptly rejected the idea, as they did also the suggestion that retaliatory bombing raids be mounted against the German civilian population, but the fact that the item had got on the agenda says much. When he heard that poison gas was being considered, Eisenhower was horrified. "Let's, for God's sake, keep our eyes on the ball and use some sense," he argued in a minute to Tedder. Clearly the only sure way to stop the bombs was to overrun the coast of the Low Countries whence they were loosed.

But at that time the armies of liberation were still penned in Normandy. Cherbourg had fallen to the U.S. VII Corps, more than one million Allied troops had landed, but OVERLORD was stuck, far behind schedule. The difficulty was on the left flank, the eastern end of the lodgment.

According to the timetable, Caen was to have been captured by the

---

* The concept of labeling a city a "fortress" or a "fortified place" first arose on the eastern front. Troops in cities so designated had one mission: to fight to the last man. They were given Himmelfahrtskommandos (missions to Heaven); the notion fitted Hitler's apocalyptic vision.

British and Canadians on D-day. It was an important town, a center of roads and railways; whoever controlled it could control the flow of reinforcements westward to Cherbourg. Beyond it, to the east, the countryside was open and rolling: ideal terrain for the superior Allied mobility. Montgomery had been confident of the town's swift capture. Indeed, at the final review of plans for OVERLORD—back on May 15 at St. Paul's School—Montgomery had rashly talked of a quick armored breakthrough to the south and east of Caen; he had pointed toward Falaise, some thirty miles inland, and had talked of how his tanks might "knock about a bit down there." Such speculative chatter had unduly raised the hopes of the airmen, who dreamed of establishing airfields for fighter bombers in the countryside east of Caen. The stage was thus set for rancorous bickering between ground and air, a dispute that would come to seem Anglo-American (although it was not) and would eventually focus on the cloudy, imprecise messages exchanged by Eisenhower and Montgomery. At first the supreme commander had tried the device of encouragement ("I thoroughly believe you are going to crack the enemy a good one") and Montgomery had issued stern orders to his Second Army ("The immediate task of this Army will be to capture Caen"), but the attacks had gone forward cautiously and had been called off at the first sign of stiff resistance.* At SHAEF there was growing inpatience with Montgomery's laggard tactics. By June 25 Eisenhower's tone with Montgomery had somewhat sharpened ("Whenever there is any legitimate opportunity we must blast the enemy with everything we have") and Montgomery had growled with greater pugnacity than ever ("Blitz attack of VIII Corps goes in tomorrow at 0730 hours and once it starts I will continue battle on eastern flank till one of us cracks and it will not be us"), but that attack too was halted after it got involved in close and heavy fighting. Caen was still securely held by the Germans, and the longer they held it the more strongly they reinforced it.

Meanwhile the summer weather—best for any Allied offensive—was slipping past, the buzz bombs still rained down on London, and just around the corner was the fearful V–2, the long-range rocket equipped with powerful warhead which Germany was known to have developed. If the Allies were not to break out on the left (and by now Montgomery was insisting he had never contemplated such a thing), then they would have to break out on the right, from the American sector, the so-called bocage country,

---

* The Germans had been quick to perceive the extreme prudence of Second Army's commanders. "The enemy," said a captured German report, "is extraordinarily nervous of close combat. Whenever the enemy infantry [that of Second Army] is energetically engaged, they mostly retreat or surrender."

which was crisscrossed with deep ditches, sunken roads, and impenetrable hedgerows of earth, hedge, and tree.

When Eisenhower visited Bradley's headquarters on June 24, the two officers agreed that the stalemate in Normandy would be broken only by the Americans. Tedder, the deputy supreme commander, who had despaired of Montgomery's ever undertaking decisive, energetic action, got word of the Eisenhower-Bradley conference and took heart. "It was refreshing," he observed later, "to hear of at least a possibility of breaking the deadlock." Still, could it be done through the bocage? Tedder found an occasion to ask Alan Brooke for his personal opinion of the prospects. "I know the bocage country well from my boyhood days," said the CIGS, "and they will never get through it."

"Ike is considerably less exuberant these days," Butcher commented toward the end of June, adding, "Just now he is concerned about slowness of Monty's attack." Smith and Tedder convinced him he must "tell Montgomery tactfully to get moving." The supreme commander edged closer to a command. ". . . we must use all possible energy in a determined effort to prevent a stalemate," he urged Montgomery on July 7. Stung by the mounting criticism of his tactics, Montgomery responded with some more bellicose language. He had decided, he told Eisenhower, after handing out a free lecture on how to organize for a battle, "to set my eastern flank alight, and to put the wind up the enemy by seizing Caen and getting bridgeheads over the Orne." Next day he promised that his broad attack "will continue without a halt." But on July 10 he halted his troops west of the Orne, the river that bisects Caen. Two days later he pledged Eisenhower a new attack. "My whole eastern front will burst into flames," he wrote. "The operation . . . may have far-reaching results." Eisenhower, eternal optimist, assumed that at last Montgomery was to deliver what SHAEF had so often been led to expect, the "brilliant stroke which will knock loose our present shackles." Did Montgomery require a massive bombardment? It would be laid on: seventy-seven hundred tons of bombs to be loosed from more than two thousand bombers—"the heaviest and most concentrated air attack in support of ground troops ever attempted." Everyone at SHAEF supposed that Montgomery meant precisely what he said and now planned a decisive battle. Montgomery, isolate and, like all very grand officers, absolutely persuaded of his rectitude, did nothing to correct SHAEF's misconceptions.

The seventy-seven hundred tons of bombs rained down. Second Army broke through for several miles beyond Caen. German resistance stiffened. Montgomery then called a halt.

At Portsmouth, in his forward headquarters, Eisenhower steamed. The most elaborate bombardment in support of ground troops in the history of warfare—for what? Seven miles? Must the Allies expend a thousand tons of bombs per mile through France?

Montgomery contended then and later that he knew precisely what he was up to, had succeeded admirably, and was satisfied with Second Army's achievements: they had obliged the enemy to commit his dwindling reserves on the eastern flank, thereby permitting Bradley, and subsequently Patton, to explode through the German defenses on the western flank. (This occurred at the end of July, after a delay occasioned by dirty weather.) Moreover, Bradley knew precisely what Montgomery was up to, and he heartily approved. Montgomery, he wrote later:

> . . . was spending his reputation in a bitter siege against . . . Caen. For three weeks he had rammed his troops against those panzer divisions he had deliberately drawn toward that city as part of our Allied strategy of diversion. . . . Monty was more than successful. . . . With the Allied world crying for blitzkrieg . . . the British endured their passive role with patience and forbearing. . . . The intense rivalry that afterward strained relations between the British and American commands might be said to have sunk its psychological roots into that passive mission of the British on the beachhead.

Montgomery later blamed his troubles on "the feeling that existed against me among [the] staff at Supreme Headquarters," and he rarely disguised his disdain for his supreme commander: "It was always very clear to me that Ike and I were poles apart when it came to the conduct of war." Brooke courteously encouraged Montgomery's misgivings about his supreme commander. "It is quite clear," the CIGS wrote Montgomery on July 28, "that Ike has the very vaguest conception of war!"

What is equally clear is that the two officers were temperamentally incompatible. Montgomery liked to work in monkish solitude; Eisenhower preferred the give-and-take of the committee, from which he could arrive at a consensus or even, perhaps, be impressed by a singular opinion. At SHAEF the members of his customary committee had no particular fondness for Montgomery, and little that Montgomery wrote or telegraphed to Eisenhower ever truly conveyed his ideas. If they had talked with each other more, matters might have improved, but since they disliked each other they seldom sought each other out for the conversation that each dreaded would be cramped and hostile. Brooke recognized the difficulty; indeed, he had anticipated it when first he assigned Montgomery as Eisenhower's commander of ground forces. At dinner on July 27 with Churchill, Eisenhower, and Smith, Brooke advised Eisenhower to tell Montgomery exactly what he thought, "to put all his cards on the table."

But, Brooke later wrote Montgomery, "He is evidently a little shy of doing so."

Eisenhower wanted to like people; he wanted people to like him; he was distressed when it failed to happen so. His need for a friendly rapport was one reason for his reluctance, so often remarked by journalists, to speak ill of anyone. Even when it came to Montgomery, whom he plainly disliked, he preferred to put his animus in someone else's words. Thus, speaking of Montgomery in 1967, Eisenhower said, "Well, I'll tell you. Montgomery—he was best described during the war by [General Harold] Alexander. Alexander says, 'He's just a little man, he's just as little inside as he is outside, Period.' He had a—he carried with him an inferiority complex." Eisenhower then changed the subject.

The business of making war is one in which men stand in constant peril of death, and if those in charge of the business disagree among themselves as to how it should be managed the peril grows. The fault for any collapse of communication between Eisenhower and Montgomery in the summer of 1944 lay with the supreme commander, if only because he was the supreme commander. Eisenhower knew this, and devoted his every best effort to reach a congenial understanding with Montgomery. The two men remained incompatible.

The supreme commander perforce must look beyond the battle to the shape of the campaign that lies ahead. During the latter half of June —while the artificial harbors of Mulberry were being towed across the Channel, assembled, put into operation, severely mauled by the worst June gale of forty years, and thereafter partly repaired—and during the whole of July—while Montgomery concentrated on keeping his forces balanced and the enemy unbalanced, while Bradley maneuvered U.S. First Army into position for its assault on the line St. Lô–Coutances, while Patton chafed to take command of U.S. Third Army—General Eisenhower was worrying about ports, supplies, reinforcements, and most of all the danger that Overlord had been and would continue to be stalemated in Normandy. When weather grounded the air forces, when Montgomery halted another of the attacks so confidently prepared and so enthusiastically anticipated, the gossip at SHAEF was of the possibility that Overlord might be mired for the winter in trench warfare of the kind that had butchered a generation back in 1915 and 1916.

And meanwhile the buzz bombs dropped on England.

"The line that we actually held when the breakout began on D plus 50," Eisenhower would point out later, "was approximately that planned for D plus 5." A depressing situation. To rectify it, Tedder pressed Eisenhower to open a tactical headquarters in France and himself assume command of the ground forces in Normandy. Only so, Tedder believed, could Eisenhower rebut the growing criticism (by Americans) that he was "too 'soft' in his relations with the British."

But by the end of June, Eisenhower was paying less heed to Tedder's advice, chiefly because he was embroiled in a debate on higher levels. He believed the favorable outcome of that debate would remove any threat of stalemate in Normandy. Once again the controversy was over the advisability of invading southern France; once again the Americans wanted ANVIL, once again the British preferred some other operation, perhaps one to the east, through the Ljubljana Gap, with a consequent drive toward Vienna—a variation on the familiar Churchillian theme of "the soft underbelly." Eisenhower at first played only a supporting role in the dispute, sounding a loyal Amen! to whatever Marshall had already maintained; occasionally he would privately cable Marshall an argument he thought the American Chiefs might be slighting. When the American and British Chiefs reached their predictable deadlock, Churchill appealed over their heads to Roosevelt: ANVIL was "bleak and sterile"; it would have little or no effect on OVERLORD; on the other hand, by taking troops from Alexander's armies in Italy, it would rob those armies of their offensive power and so "wreck one great campaign for the sake of winning the other." But the President, coached by Marshall, was resolute: "I am impressed by Eisenhower's statement that ANVIL is of transcendent importance. . . . [We must not] lose precious time and lives in indecision and debate." Churchill, "deeply grieved" by the "casting aside" of the Italian campaign, "with all its dazzling possibilities," made one last appeal, shrewdly inserting the dreadful suggestion that Stalin would rejoice over the American strategy, since as a result of it "east, middle and southern Europe" would "fall naturally into his control." This argument, so imperious in the years to come, moved neither Marshall nor Roosevelt. "I always think of my early geometry," the President replied: "'A straight line is the shortest distance between two points.'"

And so, on July 2, orders were dispatched to launch ANVIL "at the earliest possible date." August 15 was the target date.

Churchill was more than grieved, he was possessed by wrath. Useless for his advisers to remind him that the Americans had in years past invariably deferred to the British on matters of strategy in the Mediterranean; nor could the prime minister relieve his feelings by composing angry protests to Washington, since he knew better than actually to send them; he had to seek solace by privily informing his Chiefs of Staff that "an impression must be made upon the Americans that we have been ill-treated and are furious." How best to make such an impression?

Suddenly events made the question irrelevant and offered the prime minister a fresh vantage for his attack on ANVIL—which he had re-christened DRAGOON because, some said, he felt he had been dragooned into giving it his approval. U.S. First Army burst south of St. Lô and, Patton having at last been unleashed, U.S. Third Army slashed deep into Brittany. Not only was the stalemate in Normandy broken but a number of Atlantic ports—Brest, Lorient, St. Nazaire—were cut off and, it seemed, might soon drop into Allied hands. Who now needed Marseille and Toulon? Who now could care deeply about any invasion of the French Riviera?

On August 4—only eleven days before the carefully planned ANVIL landings—Churchill cabled Roosevelt to suggest that the invasion be abruptly switched to "some point or other . . . along the Brittany peninsula"—to a coast that had never been thoroughly examined, beyond the reach of fighter airplanes, and straight into the nests of Nazi submarines. The prime minister assured the CIGS, among others, that Eisenhower also believed the assault should be transferred to Brittany; soon the CIGS learned that Eisenhower strongly opposed any such thing.

To Churchill it seemed that if only he could persuade Eisenhower, perhaps DRAGOON could yet be abandoned. He traveled to Eisenhower's headquarters at Portsmouth on Saturday, August 5, to lunch with the supreme commander and to unlimber his most beguiling rhetoric. Three days before, Eisenhower had been all grins over the news from France. "If the intercepts are right," he had told Butcher, "we are to hell and gone in Brittany and slicing 'em up in Normandy." Now he was obliged to entertain with seemly gravity all Churchill's arguments for six long hours, saying no "in every form of the English language at his command," and ending "practically limp" when at last Churchill departed.

And still the prime minister's bulldog tenacity—or what the American military would have termed his mulish obstinacy—was not exhausted. On August 9, DRAGOON being then less than one week from its D-day, Churchill summoned Eisenhower to Number 10 Downing Street, to make his final appeal to divert the operation. It was an emotional interview. The ancient arguments were once again trotted out: Marseille was no longer an essential port, to land in southern France would be of no help to OVERLORD; the troops assigned for the invasion were better employed in a drive north through Italy and thence eastward into the Balkans, all southeastern Europe would flame in revolt against Hitler, and so on. Worst of all, why did the Americans cold-bloodedly abandon the British to pursue alone what had been a joint undertaking? Why did they persist in using their growing strength as a bludgeon in discussions of Allied strategy? Why were they lately become the "big, strong, and dominating partner"? Eisenhower had never seen Churchill "so obviously stirred, upset, and even despondent." Tears stood in his eyes. If things did not improve, the prime minister warned, in his most thrilling tones, he might have to wait upon the king to "lay down the mantle of my high office." What can have stirred him so powerfully, made him so obdurate about ANVIL-DRAGOON?

Eisenhower later maintained that he shunned political discussion during this interview, that he confined himself to military arguments in replying to Churchill. This was disingenuous. The supreme commander knew that military strategy and politics are inseparable, and in any case he himself invoked a political argument—the desirability of using French troops in the liberation of France—to defend the strategy of DRAGOON. Neither Churchill nor Eisenhower, it may be presumed, was entirely candid in later reporting the political difficulties that lay at the root of the strategic debate over ANVIL-DRAGOON.

For his part, Churchill was energetically concerned with Britain's strategic position throughout the Balkans and the Middle East, and at this time he was most apprehensive about the course of affairs in Greece. There was a Greek monarch in exile; it was the policy of the British government to restore him to his throne, but in his absence a coalition of republican, socialist, and communist groupings called the National Liberation Front (EAM) had organized a National Liberation Army (ELAS). During the Nazi occupation this coalition had administered much of the country, acting as a kind of de facto underground government. In March the EAM had won sufficient popular support to step forward and proclaim a provisional government. Since the British government considered political hegemony in Greece vital in order to dominate the eastern Mediterranean and so ensure control of Suez, they viewed the EAM and its sway over Greece with utmost gravity. Quite evidently the pressing need for troops in Greece was much on Churchill's mind when he spoke with Eisenhower.

General Eisenhower's need was ports, however, and Marseille would meet his need splendidly: through Marseille and the other southern French ports liberated by DRAGOON would come more tonnage in the last three months of 1944 than through any other ports available to SHAEF. And the part played by French troops and the men of the Maquis during that operation and later, north through the valley of the Rhône and into Germany, would help France regain its self-respect, no small consideration.

In the days of the Cold War to come, the decision to send three American and seven French divisions to invade southern France would be much censured, with the critics making sport of American naïveté and respectfully genuflecting to the superior grasp of the British on the realities of world politics. If only the western allies had marched east they "might have altered the whole political destinies of the Balkans and eastern

Europe." The voice is that of Harold Macmillan, who added: "Thus were sown the seeds of the partition of Europe, and the tragic divisions which were destined to dominate all political and strategic thinking for a generation." Thus, too, are statesmen locked into their postulates.

Still, Eisenhower did not forget Churchill's eloquent plea, for a supreme commander must also look beyond the campaign to the shape of the postwar world ahead. Early in September, responsive to a request from the British Chiefs, General Eisenhower agreed to make available one hundred transport airplanes for what he termed "a most important operation in Greece . . . throwing some forces and the Greek government back into Greece." This initiative somewhat puzzled General Marshall, who reminded Eisenhower that the U.S. had "scraped everything available . . . to give you 100 more transport planes" and so meet his appeal for help in maintaining his onrushing armies. Yet now Eisenhower wished to release them for an operation in Greece? (It turned out that the operation was postponed until October, when the aircraft were assigned by an American command based in the Mediterranean; in time EAM and ELAS, so long in arms against the Nazi invaders, would be embattled with their Allied liberators.)

By early September, when the supreme commander briefly turned his attention to counterrevolution in Greece, it was already evident that he would be more and more preoccupied with the slippery question of bringing to the postwar world—or imposing upon it—a semblance of law and order, or what he would later felicitously term "peace with justice." He had, indeed, already considered in programmatic fashion what was to be done about postwar Germany, and already taken specific military action to ensure that law and order would prevail in liberated France—the liberation of Paris would oblige him to close his mailed fist over the whole country.

The question of Germany arose on August 7 when the supreme commander entertained Secretary of the Treasury Henry Morgenthau, Jr., and two other Treasury officials at his mess near Portsmouth. As he gathered his luncheon party together Eisenhower cannot have been entirely happy. He was in the midst of his wearing, emotional debate with Churchill over Anvil-Dragoon, he was itching to fly back across the Channel to spur his officers on to more valiant efforts against the enemy, yet he was bound to break bread with this well-placed figure of the New Deal and his two understrappers. Who were they? He could scarcely get their names straight as they were introduced. A Mr. White? A Mr. Smith? The four men sat down together under canvas, unfolded their napkins, and composed themselves for conversation. Gradually, in the warmth of

Eisenhower's natural amiability, the ill-assorted quartet began to talk with animation, finding common ground where none would have been surmised, and in the course of an hour or so managing to construct a monstrous edifice of misunderstanding. Under the circumstances, it could hardly have been otherwise.

Morgenthau, tall, shy, professorial of aspect, was ostensibly concerned with the rate of monetary exchange in postwar Germany and anxious to deny that country any comfortable advantage. Harry Dexter White, his loyal and skillful assistant secretary, had just lately made an impressive contribution to postwar polity by helping Maynard Keynes and others design the International Monetary Fund. Fred Smith was an assistant to the secretary, a humbler fellow, a man whose experience was of advertising and public relations and the manipulation of mass audiences.

They talked of military government in Germany. White said: "What I think is that we should give the entire German economy an opportunity to settle down before we do anything with it." Eisenhower said he had been too busy to worry about the German economy but that he had an able staff section working on the problem. They spoke of guilt and punishment. Like many other soldiers, Eisenhower had pondered the fact that the German defeat in the War of 1914–1918 had not led to the occupation of Germany and hence had not forced on the German nation the bitter experience of being vanquished. Now he said: "There must be no room for doubt as to who won the war. Germany must be occupied. The German people must not be allowed to escape a sense of guilt." He indicated that he would like to "see things made good and hard for them for a while," that reparations should be made to Russia, France, Holland, Belgium, and the other occupied countries that were not Nazi satellites. "The war-making power of the country should be eliminated," he said, and spoke of strict controls on heavy industry and a ban on the manufacture of airplanes. The Germans, he insisted, "should not be supported by America." One of the others asked if what he had said might be attributed to him. Eisenhower saw no reason why not.

Some more pleasantries, and then the supreme commander made his excuses and was flown back to Normandy while Morgenthau and his party returned to London to talk further with Churchill, Eden, Winant, and others. The process of incubation had begun and presently the Morgenthau Plan was hatched, the plan whereby the war industries of the Ruhr and the Saar would be dismantled and Germany would revert to an agricultural or perhaps a pastoral economy. And Fred Smith, aglow with memories of having been witness to great affairs, would carefully file his notes of all the conversations he had heard, together with his notion that the Morgenthau Plan had been inspired by the supreme commander.

When it came to the liberation of Paris, General Eisenhower's role was thrust upon him; with what misgivings he accepted it none can yet say with confidence. His own professed preference was to bypass the city (or "the place," as he called it), advancing around it to get on with the business of killing and capturing Germans. To fight for Paris would entail destruction of the city, loss of lives, and use of precious fuel and ammunition; even to capture the city without a fight would mean the responsibility of feeding its people and its power plants, and so would put an added strain on supply lines already heroically burdened. Unquestionably Eisenhower wished he could pretend that Paris was not there.

But if Paris was only a fluster and a fret to Eisenhower, to de Gaulle it was "the center of strategy and the stake of political maneuvers," and Frenchmen of every political persuasion agreed with him. So much can be stated with certainty, but a good deal of the rest of the tangled story must rest on conjecture, for the principals in the drama, Eisenhower included, took one position in public and quite another in private, and they all harbored fears and assumptions wholly divorced from the objective realities.

Following D-day, the United States government had reluctantly inched toward an accommodation with de Gaulle, and after he had briefly visited Washington and talked with the President and Secretary of State Cordell Hull, the U.S. had at last acknowledged that the FCNL (but not the provisional government) was "qualified to exercise the administration of France." However belated, however graceless, this was a halfway de facto recognition, what Eisenhower had been hoping for since January. Meanwhile, SHAEF and the supreme commander had been steadily working out other forms of cooperation: the French general Pierre Koenig, whom de Gaulle had appointed to command the French Forces of the Interior (FFI, the armed and organized Resistance) had taken his place as a senior Allied commander, and with Koenig's approval Allied invasion currency was now accepted for use in France.

But an agreement covering the administration of civil affairs was yet to be signed when the American armies burst out of Normandy and began their lickety-split sweep across France. Why so? Approval of the agreement was obstructed somewhere in Washington. In the White House? In the State Department? Who could say?

As the American armies approached the Seine, carefully steering clear of Paris, de Gaulle, now back in Algiers, took alarm. Recalling that the U.S. had given its qualified recognition only to the FCNL and not to his provisional government, aware from his intelligence reports that Pierre Laval, of the collaborationist Vichy government, was in touch with Allen Dulles of the OSS in nearby Berne, de Gaulle began to suspect that snares were being laid by American operatives to have reconvened in Paris the French National Assembly of 1940 and, under a cloak of spurious legality, form a new government of "national unity." By relegating de Gaulle to an innocuous post and so greasing the skids for his eventual ejection, this government might be accorded immediate recognition by Washington and London—or so at least de Gaulle now began to imagine. Such a coup would be simple to deliver: the Allied armies were already in France to give it muscle, and the supreme commander was, after all, only the agent of Roosevelt's will and Churchill's concurrence. And even if the French people, now infused with patriotic ardor, were to repudiate such a coup from the Right, what about the odds on a coup from the Left, with barricades thrown up in the streets of Paris, and a Commune declared, as in 1792 and again in 1871, to infect France with a revolutionary fever?

The odds on a leftist coup were, as de Gaulle very well knew, prohibitive. His representatives were already in Paris and ready to take power "without," as he would later acknowledge, "a trace of difficulty." On the morning of Friday, August 18, de Gaulle had a conversation in Algiers with Secretary of the Navy James Forrestal, a man with an overpowering apprehension of communists and communist influences. Forrestal questioned de Gaulle about the "Russian menace" and about communist influence in France. The general asked that his answer be considered private. For some time, he had been aware that the French Communist Party's agitation and propaganda were directed toward achieving a unity of all Frenchmen to aid the Allies win a swift victory over Nazism. Now he told Forrestal there were no French communists preaching the rule of the proletariat and so on, there was only "a group of individuals who call themselves communists . . . and who are talking about the war, the peace, justice and liberty."

Still, to warn of communists might be useful later, especially when talking to Americans, who could, after all, help restore to France her ancient grandeur.

The danger of a rightist coup, clandestinely abetted by the Americans, seemed to de Gaulle far more ominous. At all events, it was clear that Paris was seething—the railwaymen were on strike, and so were the police— and de Gaulle was determined he should be there when the city freed itself. He was flown from Algiers to Casablanca the same day he met with Forrestal.

In his advance headquarters at Tournières, the supreme commander was informed that de Gaulle was on his way. Eisenhower complained to the Combined Chiefs that it was a "rather premature arrival." Why should he have thought it was premature? For his part, de Gaulle noticed efforts to delay his homecoming, efforts he attributed to the Americans. An airplane the Americans insisted on lending his party suddenly developed mechanical difficulties, he was instructed he must land at Gibraltar, he was urged to postpone his trip. Too dangerous, he was told. As well ask Atropos to postpone her snipping of the vital thread. De Gaulle landed in Normandy on Sunday, August 20, intent on his appointment with destiny, and was at once driven to the apple orchard where, under canvas, Eisenhower had established his command post. (Forrestal's airplane from North Africa landed a few hours later; he arrived at Tournières at about the same time as did Anthony Eden, who was flown from London. If there was any plot, and if now it was thickening, the supreme commander was in a good way to be kept in the picture.)

Whether or not there was a scheme "to silence or set aside de Gaulle," as de Gaulle suspected, the Resistance in Paris believed there was. They had observed Laval and other French politicians of the Right arrive suddenly in Paris and plunge into urgent conference. Despite SHAEF's refusal to smuggle arms to the FFI—an inventory in mid-August showed that the FFI in Paris could muster less than two thousand rifles, pistols, and other firearms, apart from what might be contributed by sympathetic policemen—on August 19 their commander had issued a call for a general uprising "to open the route to Paris to the victorious Allied armies and to welcome them there." The Resistance seized the mayor's office and the police station in one arrondissement after another; they seized the national ministries and the newspaper buildings; they seized the Hôtel de Ville. These actions were anti-Nazi, but their timing was anti-Vichy.

Whether or not Eisenhower knew of any such scheme, de Gaulle was sure he did. Eisenhower had been instructed by the Combined Chiefs to receive de Gaulle not as a head of state but as the commander of the French Army. Under either title de Gaulle was in a position of some authority, able to ask Eisenhower to do his bidding, at least in respect of the French soldiers now at SHAEF's disposal. And so, having tendered Eisenhower his congratulations on the whirlwind pace of the Allied armies, de Gaulle expressed his pained astonishment that no troops were marching on Paris. Normally, de Gaulle conceded, "the conduct of operations is your responsibility. But," he went on, "the fate of Paris is of fundamental concern to the French government. Which is why I find myself obliged to intervene and to ask you to send French troops there."

Eisenhower gave de Gaulle the impression that he was embarrassed, that if it were not for political considerations he would already have dispatched a French armored division to Paris. (Eisenhower himself never adverted to this meeting with de Gaulle in any of his memoirs; a pity, for his account might have afforded a hint of the spread between what was actually said and what each wished the world to think had been said.) At length, according to de Gaulle, after complaining that the Resistance had too hastily taken up arms against the Germans, Eisenhower assured de Gaulle he would assign General Leclerc's 2nd French Armored to march on Paris.

Nothing happened except that Leclerc's division was transferred from one U.S. corps to another and ordered to stay put one hundred miles from Paris. De Gaulle grew more suspicious, more impatient; he and Koenig now added to their earlier arguments the need for swift action to thwart an imminent communist seizure of power. Apparently they had found the magic formula: late on Tuesday, August 22, Eisenhower told Beetle Smith, "It looks now as if we'd be compelled to go into Paris." By that time Leclerc had already, without waiting for authorization from his American corps commander, dispatched a small column east to Paris; the first French tanks clattered to a halt in front of the Hôtel de Ville in the late evening of August 24 while church bells rang out all over the city; and by early light the next day the balance of Leclerc's division was fighting its way through the Porte d'Orléans, the Porte de Gentilly, and the Porte de St. Cloud to find that the city was encumbered with barricades and all but liberated by the Resistance. One or two regiments of American troops entered Paris too, but when the German commander, Dietrich von Choltitz, surrendered, it was to Leclerc and the commander of the Paris FFI, Colonel Rol, and they accepted the surrender not on behalf of the supreme commander but of the French nation.*

De Gaulle named General Koenig military governor of the city. Eisenhower named his old friend General Gerow, commander of V Corps, to the same job. De Gaulle ordered Leclerc to arrange for a parade through the city on August 26; Gerow told Leclerc to disregard the orders; the parade went off on schedule, led by de Gaulle, who firmly relegated the Resistance leaders to ranks well back in the parade formation. Gerow was not pleased to have his orders disobeyed. He informed Eisenhower, who reported to Marshall: "I rushed in there Sunday morning for an hour to back him up."

On that sunny Sunday the supreme commander was driven into the city together with Bradley (Montgomery had said he was too busy to join them). They were met by Gerow, they called on de Gaulle at the Prefecture of Police on the Île de la Cité. Eisenhower had some tardy but nonetheless agreeable news to offer: the compact governing the administration of civil affairs in France had at last been signed; hence all control over such matters was transferred from SHAEF to the French. De Gaulle bowed ironically. In his view, "the Allies transferred nothing because

---

* Both Leclerc and Rol were noms de guerre; Leclerc was the Marquis de Hautecloque, and Rol was Henri Georges René Tanguy, a prewar trade union leader and Communist party functionary.

they held nothing: they could hardly give away what they had never had."
It is not clear how the supreme commander backed up Gerow; de Gaulle
has noted that he "did not hide" from Eisenhower "how dissatisfied" he
was with Gerow's attitude. Later Eisenhower would recall that de Gaulle
had asked for the temporary loan of two American divisions "as a show of
force and to establish his position firmly" in Paris. For de Gaulle to ask
for help to maintain himself in liberated Paris seemed "sardonic" to
Eisenhower. When he was later questioned about Eisenhower's account of
this moment, de Gaulle emphatically denied he had either needed or
asked for such a display. Elements of two American divisions were in fact
marched through Paris, prompting jeers and catcalls from the British
press (since no British units were included in the display). Whether or not
de Gaulle requested the two American divisions, it is certain that he asked
for and got permission to keep Leclerc's division in Paris for a week or so;
a little later, when he asked for two French divisions to assert and establish his authority in southwest France, Eisenhower promised him the
troops as soon as they could be spared from duty elsewhere and told him
that SHAEF was "all in favor of maintaining order" and wanted "the
French to do it, not ourselves."

The justification for sending troops into a liberated region was always
to maintain "order" or to assure "security." American support came
quickly in response to a French request, provided de Gaulle had remembered to invoke the magic formula: he must warn of communists "so
strong and so well armed that there was no control over them whatsoever." Then the supreme commander was likely to react.

It was a rehearsal for the postwar world.

In truth, by early September the postwar world was at hand. The war
against Germany had been decided during the last month; it remained
only to stuff the carcass into its coffin and slam down the lid. That this
effort would require another eight months, the loss of many lives, and the
expenditure of much treasure does not alter the fundamental fact: the war
in Europe had been won.

The certainty of the Nazi defeat was acknowledged on nearly every
hand. A glance at the map proved it. The armies of OVERLORD had swung
through France, using Caen-Falaise as a hinge, inflicting the worst defeat on German arms since Stalingrad, driving the survivors in panic
ahead of them, and clearing all the country north of the Loire and west
of the Meuse; Montgomery's armies had pushed farther north and east,
into Belgium, until they held the port of Antwerp (but not the estuary of
the river Scheldt, where it flowed northwest past Antwerp to the sea).
Meanwhile, with the help of the French Resistance, the armies of DRAGOON

had come sprinting up the valley of the Rhône, the Americans on the right bank, the French on the left, reducing their phased schedules to absurdity, accomplishing in a fortnight what it had been gloomily predicted would take ninety days. In northern Italy, Alexander's armies had captured Firenze and Livorno, and were poised to swoop down on the valley of the Po. In the east the Red Army had forced the capitulation first of Finland, then of Rumania, then of Bulgaria; by the first week of September they had overrun the Carpathians and stormed west to the border of Yugoslavia.

On September 4 General Eisenhower telegraphed his senior commanders: "Enemy resistance on the entire front shows signs of collapse . . . disorganized, in full retreat, and unlikely to offer any appreciable resistance if given no respite."

On September 5 the British Joint Intelligence Committee reported to the British Chiefs: "In France, the German front has virtually ceased to exist. . . . In Italy, the German defenses based on the Gothic Line have been breached. . . . In the Balkans, the whole German position is crumbling."

On September 6 the CIGS told his colleagues that while he regarded this report as slightly optimistic, he was inclined to agree with it.

On September 7 General Beetle Smith, chief of staff to the supreme commander, told a press conference: "Militarily the war is won." He personally passed his remark through the censorship.

The plight of the Nazis was reflected in the continuing confusion at the highest levels of command. On July 1 Rundstedt had been removed from command of the west when, upon being asked by his superiors what he thought should be done, he had retorted, "Make peace, you fools." He had been replaced by Feldmarschall Gunther von Kluge, who was implicated in the attempt to assassinate Hitler on July 20 and was in turn relieved by Feldmarschall Walther Model on August 16. Kluge killed himself a few days later. Rommel had been badly wounded in the fighting near Caen; he too was suspected of complicity in the attentat against Hitler; he too killed himself. Rundstedt was reappointed commander in chief west on September 4, with Model under him as army group commander; thanks to their efforts some stability was forged in the German lines, especially in the north, where they apprehended the greatest danger. The flank east of Antwerp was consolidated and troops were dug in along both banks of the Scheldt so as to deny the Allies the use of that port.

The want of port accommodations was, indeed, the reason for Churchill's refusal to share the optimism that had spread from SHAEF and the army commands down through the armies and back to the people at home in Britain, France, and the U.S. The prime minister reminded the British

Chiefs on September 8 that Antwerp was of no use, Brest was not captured, nor Lorient, nor St. Nazaire; moreover, the Germans still held Le Havre, Boulogne, and Calais. "One can already foresee," Churchill warned, "the probability of a lull in the magnificent advances we have made," and he put his finger precisely on "supply conditions and the lack of ports" as the reasons for such a lull. Another reason, of course, was the very magnificence of the advances: the plans for OVERLORD had assumed that on D plus 90 (September 4) twelve U.S. divisions would be on the south bank of the Seine, but in fact on that day sixteen U.S. divisions were already one hundred and fifty miles beyond the Seine. From being forty-five days behind schedule before the breakout of Normandy, the Allied armies had in little more than a month raced about two hundred and fifty days ahead of schedule. The service forces simply could not keep up such a pace.

By this time a change had been made in the hierarchy of OVERLORD. On September 1 Eisenhower had assumed operational command of ground forces, which were divided into two army groups: 21st Army Group under Montgomery and 12th Army Group under Bradley. (After September 15 the armies of DRAGOON would become 6th Army Group under Devers, and would also operate at the direction of SHAEF.) Despite the fact that this shift had been contemplated ever since February 11, when the Combined Chiefs had issued their directive to Eisenhower, Montgomery was distressed by it and so was Brooke, who described it as "Eisenhower's new plan." Montgomery had sought to change the supreme commander's mind. He had asked for a conference with Eisenhower—at his own headquarters, naturally; Montgomery never troubled to travel to Eisenhower's headquarters—and when Eisenhower arrived on August 23 with Beetle Smith, Montgomery insisted on excluding Smith from the meeting. Thereupon he lectured the supreme commander on the strategic situation: he explained the administrative and logistical difficulties; warned that if Eisenhower insisted on adopting "a broad front strategy, with the whole line advancing and everyone fighting all the time," the Allied advance would inevitably sputter to a stop and the war would be protracted well into 1945; and told Eisenhower he "should not descend into the land battle" but "must sit on a very lofty perch" so as to achieve a dispassionate view of all his crushing responsibilities. What Montgomery wanted was overall control of the land battle, his own 21st Army Group reinforced by U.S. First Army and First Allied Airborne Army, a mission to clear the coast as far as Antwerp and advance into the Ruhr, and all available supplies to do the job. Patton's Third Army should sit tight, shut up, and be given only enough supplies for their bare subsistence. To all this Eisenhower listened quietly.

Even before Eisenhower made a decision on these extraordinary suggestions, rumors of the impending change in OVERLORD's command structure had provoked a mischievous clamor in newspapers on both sides of the Atlantic. The London journals wailed that Montgomery, after having conceived and directed a brilliant victory, was now to be demoted; the American press hotly demanded apologies for the suggestion that it was a demotion for Montgomery to be ranked equally with Bradley; there seemed to be a general disposition to agree that Eisenhower was only a symbol, a totem of Allied unity, having limited value as a commander.

When he was apprised by Marshall of the clatter in the American newspapers, the supreme commander retorted with unusual asperity. "In the first place," he cabled Marshall, "I have always been directly responsible for approving major operational policies and principal features of all plans of every kind." Montgomery had been placed "in temporary charge," to be sure, "but always under plans of campaign approved by me." He closed by requesting Marshall to inform the officer in charge of press and public relations for the War Department that "no major effort takes place in this theater by ground, sea, or air except with my approval and that no one in this Allied command presumes to question my supreme authority and responsibility for the whole campaign."

Clearly the supreme commander had decided it was time to have heed for the record of his leadership as he saw it. He was so weary of being dismissed as a figurehead that he had staked a claim to credit for the smashing Allied victories, but in the nature of things that claim encompassed something more: the errors of cautious preinvasion planning that were now shriveling the Allied supply lines, the decision that had permitted much of the trapped Seventh German Army to slip out of the pocket and through the narrow gap between Argentan and Falaise, the indifferent leadership that would bumble while the capture of adequate port facilities was critically postponed, and other miscalculations of more or less importance.

Of all the decisions taken by the supreme commander during his tour of duty with OVERLORD, the one most widely impugned—and without cease for at least the next quarter-century—was the one that resolved the debate between the concept of a "powerful and full-blooded thrust" in one sector, preferably a swift concentrated assault in the north across the Rhine against the Ruhr, and the concept of an advance on a broad front toward and then across the Rhine, at a pace to be dictated by the administrative and logistical facts—the debate that has come to be known rather simplistically as "single thrust versus broad front." This controversy, initiated by Montgomery on August 19, was determined by Eisenhower ten days later and clinched by him on September 5, although

Montgomery made every effort to protract it throughout September. In sum, the supreme commander rejected Montgomery's arguments and reaffirmed his own plan to "exploit our success by . . . crossing the Rhine on a wide front and seizing the Saar and the Ruhr . . . with all possible speed." As if to reassure himself, Eisenhower then dictated a memorandum for the record, reminding himself that "from the beginning of this campaign I have always visualized" an advance north and south of the Ardennes, that this approach "takes advantage of all existing lines of communication," and adding, "I see no reason to change this conception."

In fact he had already appreciably changed his conception. Acknowledging the importance of overrunning the V-1 and V-2 bomb sites in the Low Countries, seizing the airfields in Belgium, and capturing the estuary of the Scheldt northwest of Antwerp, and fearful lest Montgomery's "usual caution" would cause him to slow down unless he had an overwhelming preponderance of strength to use against the enemy, Eisenhower had given Montgomery's armies a priority for supplies and had ordered the U.S. First Army to advance in close support of Montgomery's right flank. As he noted in his memorandum, "This forced Patton, to the southeast of Paris, to stand still with his main bodies pushing only reconnaissance to the front." By partly acceding to Montgomery's concept, then, Eisenhower managed to anger nearly every one of his senior commanders: Montgomery because Eisenhower had done only part of what he wanted; Bradley because Eisenhower had temporarily diverted part of 12th Army Group to aid Montgomery; and Patton because Eisenhower had not allocated to his Third Army the supplies that would, as he believed, have enabled him to smash into Germany and win the war singlehanded.

The most striking aspect of the supreme commander's decision is that no matter which of the options before him he grasped, he was sure to be assailed for it. If he elected to seek a compromise between two of his options—as he did—he was sure to be further labored. In the event, his most confident critics have condemned his decision as "the most momentous error of the war" (Patton) and one that prolonged the war, cost tens of thousands of lives, and set at hazard the political balance of the postwar world (Montgomery).

Both sets of critics were wrong, having scrutinized the strategic problem through only one distorting lens, not clearly and wholly as did the supreme commander. The weight of the evidence and the cogency of the military authorities both in and out of SHAEF, both British and American, alike give Eisenhower's decision conclusive support.

The nub of the matter was supply capability, at best a humdrum subject. Examination in early September showed that less than thirty-five thousand tons of supplies a day were being unloaded in ports for American troops. This was several thousand tons less than needed, but even so it was more than could be hauled overland to the armies beyond the Seine. The result was inevitable: fewer divisions had the resources to go on fighting. Already three U.S. divisions had been immobilized; of the twenty-nine U.S. divisions scheduled to be in the line by October 1, it was estimated that nine would lack combat supplies. In mid-September Eisenhower wrote Marshall:

> . . . we are stretched to the absolute limit in maintenance both as to intake and as to distribution after supplies are landed. From the start we have always known that we would have to choose . . . some line which would mark a relative slackening in offensive operations while we improved maintenance facilities . . . but due to the decisiveness of our victory below the Seine I determined . . . to continue the drive . . . up to . . . the Rhine before we began the process of regrouping and refitting.

Montgomery's scheme Eisenhower dismissed out of hand as "a fantastic idea . . . based merely on wishful thinking." He pointed out that any attack mounted by Montgomery, nourished as it would be by the few ports then in Allied hands, "would be on such a narrow front that flanking threats would be particularly effective and no other troops in the whole region would be capable of going to its support." For Patton's Third Army, even farther from the Normandy ports and shorn of tactical air support, the case would have been even more desperate. Until the vast unwieldy apparatus of supply could be got to function properly, the Allied armies would be forced to slow down, seize advantageous positions along the German frontier, regroup, build advance airfields, equip the troops and their mechanical gear for the winter, and build up their stores for another advance. To accomplish so much, pressure would have to be applied along the entire front in a succession of assaults, delivered first by 21st Army Group, then by First Army, and last by Third Army, with priorities of supply being shifted as necessary.

Meanwhile, to shorten lines of communication and ensure a steady flow of supplies, the imperative need was for port facilities. Specifically, the need was for Antwerp.

The debate over single thrust versus broad front has served to obscure the supreme commander's gravest error: his failure to issue unmistakable orders to open the port of Antwerp; worse, his orders authorizing a delay in freeing the vital port so that an airborne attack might be mounted in a fruitless attempt to win a crossing of the Rhine. Here was the salient blunder in the Allied campaign of 1944.

Every officer, Allied or Nazi, had always appreciated the crucial importance of Antwerp. A week before the OVERLORD D-day, indeed, SHAEF planners had observed that "until after the development of Antwerp, the availability of port capacity will . . . limit the forces which can be maintained." On August 19 Montgomery had told the foreign secretary, Anthony Eden, that the Channel ports "had not the capacity he needed, and that if the battle unrolled as he planned, he must have the use of Antwerp." On September 5 Eisenhower had cabled Montgomery a reminder that as the Allied armies advanced, "we will be opening the ports of Havre and Antwerp, which are essential to sustain a powerful thrust deep into Germany," but he had said little more to distract Montgomery's fascinated gaze from the east, where lay Berlin. Up to this time, the first week of September, the Germans had prepared only very sketchily their defense of the Scheldt estuary, but when the Allies were laggard in that direction they set to work in careful haste, building fortifications across the narrow peninsula of South Beveland and laying mines around Walcheren Island, which controlled the approaches to the port. Some fifty-seven thousand Germans were mustered to contest those approaches, and by the end of September they were set to contest them implacably.

At some point, for some reason, Eisenhower began to wobble on the need to get Antwerp operating with all dispatch. How to account for this lapse? The causes were various, but the governing reason was Eisenhower's patient readiness to reach a compromise.

As noted above, Montgomery had stubbornly resisted Eisenhower's rejection of his thesis for a full-blooded thrust into Germany. On September 7 he asked that the supreme commander come to his headquarters at Brussels so that he might renew his arguments. Eisenhower's knee had got badly wrenched in a recent accident; it was encased in a plaster cast; nevertheless he emplaned for Brussels on September 10 and Montgomery considerately clambered aboard his airplane for their conference. Eisenhower had brought with him his deputy, Tedder, and his chief administrative officer, Major General Humfrey Gale. Montgomery requested that Gale leave and thereupon gave tongue to an impassioned denunciation of Eisenhower's recent directives. When he approached the extreme limits of stricture, Eisenhower reached out a big hand to grip Montgomery's knee and said: "Steady, Monty! You can't speak to me like that. I'm your boss." Briefly abashed, Montgomery apologized.

The British field marshal (he had been promoted on September 1, the day Eisenhower took over command of all ground forces) still spoke of a thrust to Berlin, but neither Tedder nor Eisenhower was disposed to take this talk very seriously. Eisenhower emphasized the need to capture Antwerp, but in truth the moment had come, not to discuss a vital task in the rear, but to settle upon a compromise assault forward, into Germany.

If it could not be a massive attack toward Berlin, at least it could aim at a crossing of the Rhine, a turning of the German flank to the north. The Allies had available a force—the First Allied Airborne Army, comprising two British and three American airborne divisions—for which no less than eighteen separate plans had been considered but, one after another, regretfully returned to file. Back in Washington, as Eisenhower knew, both General Marshall and General Hap Arnold were anxious to stage an airborne operation; they hankered for a combat experiment using airborne troops; what better occasion to test this new device of warfare than during pursuit of an off-balance enemy? Another occasion, equally suitable, might never bob up. The war might be won, and still the First Airborne Army would be impatiently waiting in Britain. To be sure, their airplanes might better be used to haul supplies to the advancing infantry (this was Bradley's preference) or to carry British troops to Greece (it was at this time that Eisenhower was momentarily toying with the procedural problems of counterrevolution in Greece), but an airborne assault was powerfully seductive.

The supreme commander succumbed to the temptation. Only three divisions—the British 1st Airborne and the U.S. 101st and 82nd Airborne—would be dropped along a narrow corridor into Holland, from Eindhoven north to Arnhem, while simultaneously the British Second Army would fight northeastward in an effort to link up with the British paratroopers near Arnhem. The twofold operation, code-named MARKET GARDEN, was scheduled first for September 26, then pushed forward to September 17.

And there went the chance for swift utilization of Antwerp.

Eisenhower wrote later that he "explained to Montgomery . . . our need for early use of Antwerp." He "instructed" Montgomery that what he wanted was "Antwerp working, and . . . a line covering that port." For his part, Montgomery specifically denied that "this point [the capture of Antwerp's approaches] was . . . ever mentioned at our conference on the 10th September." Tedder, who was present and taking notes, recalled that Eisenhower stressed "the need to gain the use of Antwerp promptly." Obviously Montgomery chose not to pay the matter much heed, which is perhaps why Eisenhower would note in his office diary next day that "Monty seems unimpressed by necessity for taking Antwerp approaches."

MARKET GARDEN narrowly failed of its objective. Montgomery persisted in devoting most of his attention and most of his necessarily limited supplies to his Second Army in the hope for the linkup at Arnhem, but in the process he scanted the Canadian First Army, which had been assigned the formidable task of clearing the Scheldt estuary. Not until October 16 did Montgomery at last decide to accord an unequivocal priority to getting

Antwerp into operation. Not until November 8 was the estuary clear. Not until November 28 did the first Allied convoy dock at Antwerp. At least one month had been lost.

The blame can be distributed. Even the CIGS observed on October 5, "I feel that Monty's strategy for once is at fault. Instead of carrying out the advance on Arnhem he ought to have made certain of Antwerp in the first place." Brooke added: "Ike nobly took all blame on himself as he had approved Monty's suggestion to operate on Arnhem."

Eisenhower was right to take the blame. When he authorized MARKET GARDEN he not only stopped Patton cold but also fatally postponed the capture of Antwerp's port facilities. When the decision was taken to launch MARKET GARDEN, any chance for winning the war in 1944 was wiped out.

The gambler had wagered his stake and lost. Now, throughout a long autumn of wretched weather, while the morale of the soldiers in the line slowly ebbed, while his senior commanders from Montgomery on the left clear round to Patton on the right grumbled that the supreme commander had not given them the tools to win the war, Eisenhower was reduced to such joyless chores as housekeeping, paperwork, entertainment of visitors from overseas, inspection of outfits along the front (during which he had constantly to keep his grin ready for all ranks), politics both military and international, and the incessant goading of his supply services. Trivia afflicted him. Should the still scarce drug penicillin be furnished to French brothels? (It was not.) What was he to do with all the hominy grits sent him from the States in response to a casual remark made by the entertainer Bing Crosby to a vast radio audience to the effect that Eisenhower yearned for a plate of that food? (His secretary Kay Summersby had it all sent to hospitals and staff messes.) The officer more and more often demanding his time was the judge advocate general, come to discuss courts-martial. How to dispose of the allegations that GIs had robbed a bank at Nijmegen and engaged in other acts of pillage? (The charges were dismissed as exaggerated or false.) What action to take about the lively black market in gasoline and cigarettes by which a number of officers and men were enriching themselves in Paris? (The officers were severely punished, the men given a chance to redeem themselves by volunteering for service in the front lines.)

Late in September he moved his supreme headquarters from Granville to the Trianon Palace Hotel at Versailles. By his orders a partition was installed to reduce his office in size; he preferred cozy enclosure to grandeur. An advance headquarters had been established near Rheims, and place for his caravan and tent secured alongside a golf course. Meanwhile a third U.S. army, the Ninth, Lieutenant General William Simpson commanding, had been formed and moved into the line.

While all these administrative measures were in train, almost imperceptibly gloom began to settle over and corrode Eisenhower's natural buoyancy. On September 18 he had written Marshall that "we have succeeded even beyond our best expectations" with the airborne operation (MARKET GARDEN), but a week later he could say only, "It is heavy going," and in the days that followed he avoided any mention of the matter. It would seem that Marshall recognized that something was amiss, for in early October he came over the ocean to confer with the supreme commander and his senior officers.

Meanwhile the troops of First, Third, and Ninth armies were, whenever they had the fuel and ammunition, stubbornly slogging forward, grinding out gains by the furlong where First and Third had earlier sliced them off at fifty miles a clip. Eisenhower told Marshall that "we have facing us now one of our most difficult periods of the entire European war," and late in October, when Marshall cabled him that the Combined Chiefs were thinking of issuing him a directive demanding extraordinary efforts to crush the enemy in 1944, Eisenhower had heart only to respond, "I am quite sure that the Combined Chiefs of Staff are no more anxious to wind this thing up quickly than are we," and to point bleakly to the logistical problem, now "so acute that all our plans have made Antwerp a *sine qua non* to the waging of our final all-out battle."

Aside from clearing the port of Antwerp, there was another vexing problem in Belgium for the supreme commander, a problem of the nation's internal politics. The government in exile had returned to the liberated country from London in early September to find a strong (estimated at more than eighty thousand) and armed Resistance, led by communists, organized into a Front de l'Indépendance (FI), which regarded the homecoming ministers with considerable repugnance and suspicion. Those ministers wished to restore the monarchy and dreaded the prospect of revolution. To replace Leopold III on his throne was quite impossible—he had collaborated with the Nazis—so the scheme of choice was to install his son Charles as regent and, more to the point, disarm the Resistance. Minor posts in the cabinet were tendered the communists and the FI, but members of the Resistance held on to their guns. Thereafter the sequence of events was predictable. On September 29 the supreme commander thanked the Belgians for their help, congratulated them on their anti-Nazi resistance, and warmly urged them to turn their arms over to the authorities. Nothing happened. By the end of October the supreme commander was weighing the idea of issuing a mandatory order. Some sort of public show of Allied support of the unpopular government was obligatory; so was an expression of Allied readiness to disarm the Resistance forcibly if necessary. Eisenhower told Montgomery that he planned to address the Belgian Parliament on November 9; Tedder, Bradley, Smith, Ramsay, and Coningham were to accompany him; he was personally anxious to have Montgomery join them in Brussels. Montgomery made his apologies: he had an appointment with his dentist in London, and meant also to discuss with the CIGS the possibility of more troops for 21st Army Group. The supreme commander traveled to Brussels, made his ceremonial speech, appeared twice or thrice in public panoply, a symbol of Allied might arrayed against any tendency toward republican revolution, and withdrew with thanks all around to U.S. Ninth Army headquarters. Eisenhower's intervention, being merely a gesture, was not particularly effective; sterner measures would be required and taken by the head of SHAEF's mission to Belgium, British Major General G. W. E. J. Erskine. A demonstration two weeks later in a spacious square of Brussels was met by a volley of shots from the police; the FI then called for a general strike; amid much tension, which Churchill subsequently informed the House of Commons might have led to "a bloody revolution," the communist leaders were able to reassert their authority over their more impetuous followers, invoke unity to win the war, and abort the general strike. The episode affords an instructive example of Eisenhower's way with a nasty situation when public passions are inflamed: first the public performance to apply the lenitive balm, then the departure, leaving for others the dirty work, and finally the cloud of confusion cast over the whole affair so as to make it seem that the forces of freedom have triumphed over a malevolent and violent conspiracy. Indeed, his agenda permitted the supreme commander little time for counterrevolution; he had battles to supervise over a front that stretched from the North Sea to Switzerland.

In London, Montgomery had meanwhile been busily brewing a pot of mischief. He had twice called on the CIGS to complain of Eisenhower and he had also seen fit to acquaint the military correspondent of the *Times* (if not other journalists) with his peevish discontent about the command structure of the AEF. There was nothing unusual about this display of anxiety; indeed, it might have been expected, and Eisenhower, when Montgomery told him of his dentist's appointment, might have glanced at a calendar and at once divined what his chief British lieutenant was really up to. Montgomery, it appears, was constitutionally incapable of letting more than three weeks go by without trying to get himself promoted commander of Allied ground forces. Observe the chronology:

On September 1 Eisenhower assumed that command. (Actually, Montgomery tried to dissuade him from the step a trifle earlier, on August 23.)

On September 21 Montgomery wrote a note to Beetle Smith. The structure of command, he explained, was all wrong. "To achieve success," he wrote, "the tactical battle will require very tight control and very careful handling. I recommend that the supreme commander hands the job over to me, and gives me operational control over First U.S. Army." But Eisenhower gave him permission only to communicate directly with Hodges, and only then in an emergency.

On October 10 Montgomery suggested, once again in a letter to Smith, that he take over from Bradley the command of 12th Army Group. (He had two days earlier suggested much the same inflation of his authority to General Marshall, on the occasion of that officer's visit to his command post at Eindhoven. "Marshall listened, but said little," no doubt because he reckoned the Grand Alliance would go up in smoke if he permitted himself to ventilate his reactions to the suggestion.) Eisenhower rejected the request on October 13; Montgomery replied on October 16: "You will hear no more on the subject of command from me. . . . Your very devoted and loyal subordinate Monty."

On November 7, twenty-two days later, Montgomery was in London unburdening himself to the CIGS, as Eisenhower might have conjectured if in fact he did not. Brooke and Montgomery saw the matter of command precisely alike: "Eisenhower completely fails as commander," said Brooke, and Montgomery echoed, "He has never commanded anything before in his whole career; now, for the first time, he has elected to take direct command of very large-scale operations and he does not know how to do it." During the next fortnight the two men conferred by letter and in person on the best method of ousting Eisenhower. They concluded that Bradley should supersede Eisenhower, since "in view of the American preponderance in strength" the ground commander had to be an American, with Montgomery commanding a northern group of armies (where "the major effort must be directed and at the expense of the southern front") and Devers commanding a southern group. It would also be necessary to keep a firm grip on Patton, so his Third Army was to be transferred to Montgomery's northern group. Montgomery, it was agreed, should talk to Eisenhower and "begin putting forward the above proposals."

On November 28—it was his fifth triweekly effort, and smack on schedule—Montgomery greeted Eisenhower at his tactical headquarters, then at Zonhoven. They talked long that night and further the next morning. It may be doubted that either understood much of what the other said. Certainly neither understood what the other was thinking. On cue, Montgomery raised the matter of command and, he imagined, finally got Eisenhower's approval of his fondest scheme. "There is no doubt he [Eisenhower] is now very anxious," Montgomery reported to

Brooke, "to put Bradley under my operational command . . . In fact, he now definitely wants me to handle main business. . . . I shall in reality be in operational charge and be able to influence whole land battle by direct approach to Ike myself." So Montgomery imagined. As for Eisenhower, to put it as moderately as possible, he planned nothing whatever of the kind. It has been remarked that the two men were incompatible, but on this occasion so profound was the chasm between them it seemed they might never again find common ground.

Montgomery's persistence, which had been accompanied by a swelling growl of demands from the London newspapers that Eisenhower get himself a deputy ground commander, had scarcely gone unnoticed at SHAEF, but Eisenhower's patience had been a match for it. Even if the supreme commander was likely to forget the fact, Montgomery stood ready to remind him that he, Montgomery, commanded the armed forces of one of the principal allies and as such was duty-bound to say what he thought about the conduct of the campaign; hence Eisenhower's exceeding restraint. But at last Montgomery tried Eisenhower's patience too far, and the cork blew out. He wrote in a letter to Eisenhower what he imagined his commander, made "worried and ill at ease" by his homiletics, had agreed upon during their talks on November 28–29. His "main points," listed merely for Eisenhower's confirmation, were:

> We have . . . failed; and we have suffered a strategic reverse.
> We require a new plan. And this time *we must not fail*.
> The need to get the German war finished early is vital, in view of other factors. The new plan MUST NOT FAIL.
> . . . we must get away from the doctrine of attacking in so many places that nowhere are we strong enough to get decisive results. We must concentrate such strength on the main selected thrust that success will be certain . . .
> . . . Bradley and I together are a good team. . . . I believe to be certain of success you want to bring us together again; and one of us should have the full operational control north of the Ardennes; and if you decide that I should do that work—that is O.K. by me . . .

Montgomery added that he was keeping two days free for a meeting with Eisenhower and Bradley, and noted that "we want no one else at the meeting except chiefs of staff, who must not speak."

It would have been hard to write a letter better calculated to enrage the soldier to whom it was addressed.

Point by point Eisenhower rejected Montgomery's notions. He did not believe the campaigns of November had failed ("There can be no question of the value of our present operations," he wrote Marshall on December

5), for all his reports showed his armies were inflicting a much higher casualty rate than they were sustaining; he believed his strategy of bringing all his armies up to the Rhine was sound; he had never dreamed of putting Bradley's army group under Montgomery's command, nor of making the Ardennes the boundary between the two army groups; finally, he considered offensive the proposal that he bid Beetle Smith stand mute at any conference he might attend.

At their next meeting—with Bradley and Tedder also present—Eisenhower gave Montgomery ample time to be heard and then firmly set forth his doctrine for the coming weeks: a principal assault north of the Ruhr, a secondary attack by Third Army in the south against the Saar; no alteration of the command structure. The decision sustained Bradley's conception and dashed Montgomery's hopes. "I personally regard the whole thing as quite dreadful," Montgomery wrote to Brooke. "We shall split our resources and our strength, and we shall fail."

In London, Brooke had meanwhile carried the struggle against Eisenhower's authority to the prime minister. Here he met with opposition. Churchill, as Brooke noted in his diary, "did not want anybody between Ike and the Army Groups, as Ike was a good fellow who was amenable and whom he could influence," whereas Bradley might prove to be of sterner stuff. Brooke retorted there was little point in a commander's being amenable if he was "unfit to win the war," but Churchill was unmoved. On Tuesday, December 12, when Eisenhower and Tedder came to London to brief Churchill and the British Chiefs on SHAEF's strategic plans, Brooke was scathing in his criticism. As he noted later, he "accused Ike of violating principles of concentration of force, which had resulted in his present failures." But Churchill cut in to side with Eisenhower, so disconcerting Brooke that he thought seriously of handing the prime minister his resignation.

Four days later, on Saturday, December 16, all rancors among the Allies were momentarily shelved when the Nazis burst out of the Ardennes in their last desperate counterattack.

The operative word in the previous sentence is "momentarily."

In mid-December the U.S. 12th Army Group was attacking north and south of the Ardennes. In the north, the First U.S. Army was pushing east of Aachen toward the Roer River; in the south the Third U.S. Army was slugging toward the Saar. Between them, defending a front that stretched about seventy-five miles across wooded, hilly country, were three divisions of the U.S. VIII Corps. At dawn of December 16 two panzer armies of twenty-two divisions, supported by two other armies of fifteen divisions, stabbed into this lightly defended region. The attack achieved complete tactical surprise, routed two divisions, disrupted communications, caused widespread local confusion, thrust a salient some fifty miles deep within Allied lines, cost the AEF some seventy-five thousand casualties, and forced a delay of two months in the Allied offensives toward the Rhine. It also failed utterly to achieve its objectives, which were to recapture Antwerp and split the Allied armies. It cost the Germans about one hundred thousand men, eight hundred tanks, and one thousand aircraft— gone, irreplaceable. In brief, once the Allies had contained the counteroffensive, the backbone of resistance on the western front would be snapped.

The counteroffensive did, however, almost achieve one success not deliberately intended: it very nearly disrupted the high command of the Allied armies, and along with it the Grand Alliance itself.

Eisenhower had for several weeks been aware, as he had told Montgomery, that "we are getting fearfully stretched south of Aachen and may get a nasty little 'Kasserine' if the enemy chooses at any place to concentrate a bit of strength." When word of the German counterattack was brought to Kenneth Strong, Eisenhower's G–2, the supreme commander was presiding over a meeting of senior officers in the map room of his headquarters at Versailles; the others present were Bradley, Tedder, Smith, Spaatz, and the G–3, Major General Harold R. (Pink) Bull. The circumstance was convenient. Strong could at once present an appreciation: that the Germans might well try to cross the Meuse, raid the Allied petroleum dumps, and proceed to recapture Brussels and Antwerp. Eisenhower could at once sense that here was "more than a mere local attack." Bradley could announce that he had two divisions ready to intervene in precisely such an emergency and ask to be excused while he telephoned the orders that would get them on the move. At no time was there undue concern, much less panic.

By Sunday the intelligence reports indicated that the attack was indeed formidable. Eisenhower, Smith, Strong, and Major General John F. M. (Jock) Whiteley, the deputy G–3, gathered in the map room to assess the reports and deduce the enemy's intentions. Whiteley, stooped over a map, put a finger on Bastogne and declared that here was the key, the hub of the countryside's network of roads; if it could be denied the Germans, they would find it hard to drive to the Meuse. Strong and Smith agreed. Eisenhower decided to order the 101st Airborne to join elements of the 10th and 11th Armored in Bastogne as soon as possible.

On Tuesday Eisenhower met at Verdun with Bradley, Patton, Devers, and a score of other senior officers. (Montgomery was of course not present, but he had sent Freddy de Guingand, his chief of staff.) The day was raw and cold. The British officers, recalling an earlier battle of the Bulge in 1940, when a German onslaught had erupted from these same Ardennes, were apprehensive; they had heard tales of disorganized American units flying away in panic, of American headquarters abandoned, of artillery and secret ciphers falling into enemy hands. Eisenhower, unruffled, began by remarking: "The present situation is to be regarded as one of opportunity for us and not of disaster. There will be only cheerful faces at this conference table." The tension abated. Patton cracked a joke. Everybody hitched up his chair. Plans were fomented for attacks on both flanks of the salient. All officers took notes. Patton was instructed to suspend his offensive and wheel Third Army north to reinforce Bastogne. Eisenhower asked how long it would take him to start moving north instead of east. "Forty-eight hours," said Patton, and there were audible snickers, especially from the British officers.

Eisenhower and the other SHAEF officers drove back to Versailles that night. The news from the Ardennes was worse. Too many German units had pressed well beyond Bastogne, driving too close to the Meuse; they had ripped far enough into Bradley's armies to make difficult his command of First Army, farther north. Whiteley told Strong that direct communications were already disrupted. A temporary change in the command structure seemed essential. Montgomery was the obvious choice to take command of the U.S. First and Ninth armies. Quite aware they were walking on eggshells, Whiteley and Strong went to Beetle Smith's quarters, roused him out of bed, and told him of their proposal.

"It was," as Strong has recalled, "a difficult moment for us all." Whiteley had been Smith's deputy in North Africa and had come with him to SHAEF; Strong had of course also served at AFHQ, and the refusal of the War Office to reassign him promptly to SHAEF had provoked Smith into a violent quarrel with Brooke. The three men were firm friends. Naturally Strong and Whiteley realized the misgivings many Americans had about Montgomery; they knew, too, with what tenacity Montgomery had sought to be named commander of all SHAEF's ground forces. Still, they judged the situation in the Ardennes warranted charging Montgomery with control over the two U.S. armies north of the salient.

Smith listened to their proposal and, in their presence, telephoned Bradley to tell him of it. "I'd question whether such a change-over's necessary," Bradley said, and considered. "Bedell, it's hard for me to object," he said, after a moment. "Certainly if Monty's were an American command, I would agree with you entirely. It would be the logical thing to do." Smith said a decision would be taken in the morning, rang off, and turned to the two British officers with a hard set to his jaw. Whenever any real trouble came along, he growled, the British never figured the Americans would be able to handle it efficiently. He questioned the further value of either of them as officers at SHAEF. Next day, he said, orders would be issued relieving them both of their appointments and returning them both to the United Kingdom. He wished them good night.

This was, it should be noted, the night of December 19, three weeks to the day since last Montgomery had officially raised the question of expanding his command.

On this night Montgomery was savoring what seemed his vindication. Everything was happening as he had warned it would. He was shown to have been right. Eisenhower was shown to have been incompetent. Perhaps he might preen himself upon his sapience? After listening to his officers, he dispatched a telegram to Brooke:

> . . . great confusion and all signs of a full-scale withdrawal. . . . a definite lack of grip . . . an atmosphere of great pessimism in First and Ninth [U.S.] Armies. . . . My own opinion is that . . . the American forces have been cut clean in half and the Germans can reach the Meuse at Namur without any opposition. The command set-up has always been very faulty and now is quite futile. . . . I have told Whiteley that Ike ought to place me in operational command of all troops on the northern half of the front. . . . This situation needs to be handled very firmly and with a tight grip.

Needless to say, Brooke warmly agreed. Needless to add, the American forces had not been cut clean in half, nor would they ever allow the Germans to reach the Meuse.

At SHAEF, General Strong and General Whiteley arose early for the daily briefing, scheduled for 8 A.M. Strong expected a telephone call about his relief; so did Whiteley. But they were asked to attend. Smith, who presided, "was glum and scarcely spoke." Later, as Whiteley and Strong started to march to Eisenhower's office, Smith intercepted them. He said he would put to Eisenhower their recommendation that Montgomery command the northern attack against the salient; better that it should come from an American; they should sit silent.

Eisenhower listened to Smith's proposal without comment. At length he telephoned Bradley. A long conversation followed, ending when Eisenhower said, "Well, Brad, those are my orders."

The supreme commander then placed a call to Montgomery. The connection was imperfect and, after impatiently shouting into the instrument for a minute or two, Eisenhower shrugged and sent his orders by wireless. Montgomery, elate at having got what he had so long yearned for, in his turn telephoned the CIGS. "He was very excited," Montgomery reported, of Eisenhower, "and it was difficult to understand what he was talking about; he roared into the telephone, speaking very fast. The only point I really grasped was that 'it seems to me we now have two fronts' and that I was to assume command of the northern front. This was all I wanted to know. He then went on talking wildly about other things; I could not hear and said so; at last the line cut out before he finished."

At SHAEF Smith apologized to Whiteley and Strong. "What made me really mad," he said, "was that I knew you were right. But my American feelings got the better of me . . . I knew of the outcry there would be in the United States."

Nationalist fervor, chauvinism, pride in flag and country, all the parochial articles of faith routinely instilled in the professional soldier—in this exigent time these familiar devotions arose to bedevil the supreme commander, whose overriding task was to sustain and to fortify the Grand Alliance. To this end he had labored while still in Washington; earlier, had studied how to do so, when in Panama with Fox Conner. Throughout his service overseas he had founded his leadership upon it, and now it verged on collapse. If victory was to be wrung from the Axis, the Grand Alliance must survive. If the Grand Alliance crumbled, Dwight D. Eisenhower's leadership would have failed.

At this time Eisenhower was sent notice of an extraordinary promotion: he was one of four officers named to a new rank, General of the Army, just authorized by the Congress. (The other three were Marshall, Arnold, and MacArthur.) Promotion was sweet, but Allied unity would be sweeter. Perhaps, to placate Bradley for the temporary loss of two-thirds of his command, Eisenhower might be able to wangle him a fourth star. (He tried, but not for another three months would Bradley become a full general.)

The weather continued foul. Clouds were low and heavy over northern France, Belgium, and Luxembourg, negating the Allied air superiority. (It was this weather, coupled with the pervasive mood of overconfidence, that had led to the failure of intelligence to learn of and warn of the impending German strike.) Inability to fly reconnaissance cut both ways, of course, and so the supreme commander coolly busied himself with the implementation of the orders issued the day before at Verdun, making sure that strong forces were being got ready for the attacks from north and south of the German salient. He proclaimed to all troops one of his rare orders of the day: ". . . By rushing out from his fixed defenses the enemy has given us the chance to turn his great gamble into his worst defeat. So I call upon every man, of all the Allies, to . . . destroy the enemy on the ground, in the air, everywhere—destroy him! United . . . we will, with God's help, go forward to our greatest victory."

United: it was time to extend further the alliance. He cabled the Combined Chiefs to say that in view of the German divisions recently shifted from eastern to western front, it was "essential" to "obtain from the Russians at the earliest possible moment some indication of their strategical and tactical intentions." In return, he stood "quite ready" to tell the Russians of his plans. United: in the supreme commander's view, it was wise to caution the commanders of First and Ninth U.S. armies, so suddenly switched to the control of a British officer. Identical telegrams went off to Hodges and Simpson: ". . . Now that you have been placed under the Field Marshal's operational command I know that you will respond cheerfully and efficiently to every instruction he gives. The slogan is 'chins up.'"

The encouragement was needed.

Neither Hodges nor Simpson was happy to have Montgomery become their immediate superior. Nor were matters improved when, two hours after his garbled telephone conversation with Eisenhower, Montgomery bounced into Hodges's headquarters looking, in the words of a British officer who was present, "like Christ come to cleanse the temple." Bradley, who was so furious that he could scarcely speak to Montgomery when later their paths crossed, saw the field marshal as unable to "resist this chance to tweak our Yankee noses," and Montgomery's complacent reports to Brooke would seem to justify Bradley's misgivings. "There were no reserves anywhere behind front," Montgomery telegraphed to the CIGS. "Morale was very low. They seemed delighted to have someone to give them firm orders." Hodges and Simpson were, no doubt, both cordial and polite, but they were also men who knew their business. Hodges knew how his troops were disposed. The 7th Armored was dug in at St. Vith, satisfactorily contesting the progress of a corps of Sixth Panzer Army, and on the shoulder of the salient were three veteran divisions, the 1st, 2nd, and 9th, whose officers and men were alike familiar with sticky situations and admirably capable of taking care of themselves. The VII Corps, Lightning Joe Collins commanding, had been withdrawn to prepare for counterattack. (Simpson's army, farther north, was not immediately affected.)

Montgomery saw things differently. He found Hodges wanting in grip. He telephoned SHAEF to tell Beetle Smith that some changes in command might have to be made, but since he was British he was reluctant to relieve American commanders personally. Smith fetched a deep, slow breath and answered that if any such step were necessary Eisenhower would take it. Eisenhower at once radioed Montgomery: "Hodges is the quiet reticent type and does not appear as aggressive as he really is. Unless he becomes exhausted he will always wage a good fight. . . . keep in touch . . . inform me instantly if any change needs to be made." Montgomery replied that Hodges seemed now to be in better shape.

If SHAEF was a target of derision and exasperation among the officers at the various Army Group headquarters—and it was—Eisenhower knew that Bradley at 12th Army Group was impatient to mount an attack on the southern flank of the German salient; his only concern would be to keep Patton from undue impetuosity. Montgomery, with his obsession for a "tidy" front, might on the other hand choose to hold back too long, and Eisenhower was determined to punish the enemy as severely as possible before he could withdraw again behind his fixed defenses. In consequence, he concluded he had better visit Montgomery at his headquarters in Belgium to administer a massive dose of git-up-and-go. The time was propitious. Affairs had improved. The skies had cleared on December 23, enabling the tactical air forces to buzz into action; the 7th Armored had disengaged from St. Vith, but the 101st Airborne, although surrounded at Bastogne, still and defiantly held; on December 26 Patton was able to thrust a column into the town; and on that same day Eisenhower was informed that Marshal Stalin agreed with him that a conference "to discuss the western front . . . and its relationship to the Russian front" would be a useful thing. Late on December 27, then, surrounded by zealous military police,* Eisenhower traveled by special train to Hasselt, some fifty miles removed from the fighting. Here, once again, the two incompatible officers sat down to one of their long muddled chats, from which each, quite evidently, took away his own interpretation.

A word about this confusion is in order. It is odd, since both men had rich and varied experience of their inability to communicate clearly with each other, that neither of them insisted on having at their conversations some officer competent at shorthand who could keep his mouth shut, note their speech verbatim, and thereafter present each of them with a fair copy of the entire colloquy. This was never done. Indeed, at Montgomery's insistence, his own chief of staff, Freddy de Guingand, and Eisenhower's deputy G-3, Jock Whiteley, were expressly excluded from the talks at Hasselt. Montgomery several times complained that Eisenhower was prone to agree with others and especially with the last person to speak with him, and it may be that Montgomery hoped, by getting Eisenhower alone and pounding away at him, to impress indelibly upon him the Montgomery view of things. As for the supreme commander, he may have refrained from ordering a third officer to stay in the room as a delicate con-

---

* A rumor was abroad that the Nazis had handpicked a special unit of English-speaking Germans, garbed them in American battle dress, found them American jeeps for transport, and ordered them to infiltrate Allied lines with the aim of assassinating Eisenhower and other senior Allied commanders. It was the sort of rumor that brought security officers to the top of their bent for alarming everyone bound on his customary round of duties. Eisenhower found the efforts on his behalf particularly irksome, but he fell in with all the dubious vaporings.

cession to Montgomery's wishes and hence to Allied unity. Whatever the reason, the two commanders were conspicuously unable to talk clearly to each other or later to agree on what each other had said.

Their recent differences had been, moreover, revived and exacerbated by the German counteroffensive. Eisenhower was suspicious, because of a great outcry in the London newspapers, that Montgomery believed he himself had saved the Allies from disaster and was once again seeking to be named commander of all Allied ground forces—and Eisenhower was right. Montgomery was fearful that Eisenhower might persist in what Montgomery considered the folly of pressing two or three attacks against the Germans rather than just one glorious assault to be led by Montgomery—and Montgomery was right, too.

When these two floundered in misunderstanding, others were bound to suffer. Most vulnerable was Omar Bradley. The London newspapers, copiously available to GIs of the First, Third, and Ninth U.S. armies, were trumpeting hosannas to Montgomery and making much of what they described as Bradley's failures. The fear grew at SHAEF that these mischievous stories would cause Bradley's soldiers to lose confidence in him and so end his usefulness as a commander. In Bradley's 12th Army Group headquarters every staff officer was sure the stories had been inspired by Montgomery himself.

In Montgomery's headquarters the even-tempered Freddy de Guingand was likewise disturbed. Better than most he appreciated how Montgomery's chosen sequestration from the outside world had blinded him to the dangers threatening the Grand Alliance. By early morning of December 30 he had a report from a liaison officer at 12th Army Group that confirmed his worst fears: Allied unity was indeed gravely threatened. At once he telephoned Beetle Smith at SHAEF in Versailles. Smith was irascible, a sure reflection of the supreme commander's own icy anger. Eisenhower had returned from his conference with Montgomery under the impression that an agreement had been struck between them that Montgomery would launch his attack on the northern wing of the salient, to coordinate with Bradley's attack from the south, on January 1. Instead, a letter had arrived from the field marshal again prescribing (and in terms that were tactless if not insulting) that he be given operational control of all ground forces. He even presumed to set forth the language the supreme commander should use in assigning him control over Bradley's army group.

Eisenhower was very angry, and he was also depressed. Montgomery's stubborn and unruly attempts to dictate administration and strategy meant that his own patient efforts to achieve Allied teamwork had failed. He read again a cablegram just received from General Marshall:

[About the] articles in certain London papers proposing a British deputy commander for all your ground forces . . . My feeling is this: under no circumstances make any concessions of any kind whatsoever. I am not assuming that you had in mind such a concession. I just wish you to be certain of our attitude. You are doing a grand job, and go on and give them hell.

The supreme commander called a staff conference. A message to the Combined Chiefs was drafted. Eisenhower went over the draft carefully, making occasional changes. This cablegram had to be precise. In it he proposed to make it quite clear that the protracted tug-of-war with Montgomery must end: either he or Montgomery must be relieved. Not a happy moment, but a necessary one.

Meanwhile, in Brussels, de Guingand was thoroughly alarmed. He had decided to fly to Versailles as soon as he rang off from his talk with Beetle Smith, but fog had closed in; the pilot shook his head: impossible. Around midday the pilot was ready to risk the weather, and the airplane lifted into fog and squalls of snow, with visibility a matter of a few feet. Over Paris the weather was no better, but flying low, they were able to follow the Seine and land at Orly between snow flurries. At Smith's office, de Guingand was told that since Eisenhower, Montgomery, and Bradley could "no longer work in essential harmony," the matter was being referred to the Combined Chiefs. De Guingand knew what that meant: "Since the Americans were the stronger ally, it really meant that Monty would be the one to go." He appealed to Smith. Could nothing be done? "I think we had better go right over and see Ike," Smith said; "otherwise it will certainly be too late."

Night had fallen when they walked across the grounds to the small house which contained Eisenhower's private office and living quarters. To de Guingand the supreme commander seemed "really tired and worried." He was, he said, thoroughly sick of the whole business. Bradley's position had become intolerable; did Montgomery realize how serious was the crisis he had created by his campaign to be appointed commander of all ground forces? Did he realize how he had affected public opinion in America—making it difficult, if not impossible, for Eisenhower to allocate American forces to a British commander; in short, putting the supreme commander in a nationalist straitjacket so that he could not group his forces with respect only to the military requirements? This aspect of the matter had not occurred to de Guingand. Eisenhower showed him the cablegram from Marshall.

Eisenhower told him that an answering cablegram to the Chiefs of Staff had already been prepared; was, as a matter of fact, being encoded at the moment; would go overseas at any moment. He handed a draft of the message to de Guingand.

De Guingand was "stunned" by what he read, but he made the speech he had flown to Versailles to make: that he was sure Montgomery had no idea things were so serious, that he would surely cooperate once he understood, and "several other things which I felt might ease the tension"; and then he begged a delay of twenty-four hours to enable him to fly back to Brussels and attempt to repair the damage. Eisenhower thought the damage was already too great, but Beetle Smith advised the delay, and after much painful discussion a delay was granted.

"What an incredibly lucky piece of timing," de Guingand later reflected—"if I had not decided to fly to SHAEF, or had arrived a few minutes later, the consequences might have been disastrous."

Weather again postponed de Guingand's flight back to Brussels; it was not until after teatime next day, December 31, that he was able to tell Montgomery: "I've just come from SHAEF and seen Ike, and it's on the cards that you might have to go." Quickly he explained why. Montgomery was "completely nonplussed"; de Guingand had never seen him "so deflated." He could only ask, "What shall I do, Freddy?" In his airplane flying north, de Guingand had thoughtfully prepared the kind of telegram he thought might do the job. Montgomery gratefully accepted it as a basis for a message that was marked Top Secret, Eyes Only, and Most Immediate:

Dear Ike . . . understand you are greatly worried . . . I am sure there are many factors . . . quite beyond anything I realize . . . you can rely on me one hundred percent . . . Very distressed that my letter may have upset you and I would ask you to tear it up. Your very devoted subordinate, Monty.

Eisenhower responded graciously. Montgomery's attack against the northern flank of the salient was finally launched on January 3, 1945, only two days late.

If this was not complete capitulation, at least it was a forthright acknowledgment that henceforth Eisenhower would indeed be the supreme commander insofar as his immediate subordinates were concerned. The episode left in its wake some distressing flotsam: Montgomery was so ill-advised as to hold a press conference on January 7 during which he said some exceedingly tactless things, but at least his intentions were honorable; in mid-January Bradley lost his temper with Eisenhower when told that only First Army, and not Ninth as well, would return to his command; he announced that he would resign, but as quickly recovered his sense of proportion. The one essential, Allied amity, had been preserved, even strengthened, and that was what mattered most.

The CIGS, however, still considered Eisenhower poorly suited to his position. He came with Churchill to visit the supreme commander at SHAEF on January 3; he found Eisenhower depressed, not only because Admiral Ramsay, a good friend, had been killed the day before in an airplane accident, but also because "of the serious reverse he had just suffered and which," Brooke fancied, "he did not even then seem quite to understand." Brooke obviously mistrusted Eisenhower's competence to end the war quickly; he saw the war dragging on while Britain's reserves of manpower dwindled, her imperial power waned, and the power of her mighty ally and commercial rival waxed insufferably. As if that prospect were not sufficiently dismaying, here from the east came the Red hordes. Brooke had, to be sure, long hoped that the great European land battles would be bloodily fought between Russians and Germans, anticipating that so Britain might dominate an exhausted Europe, but what had long been a vague hope, fixed in some indefinite, always receding future, was now suddenly at hand: out of the eastern mists tramped the triumphant Red armies, across Poland and Hungary and Austria, piercing into Germany itself.

The Russian offensive was, indeed, launched ahead of schedule in response to an appeal from Eisenhower, an appeal sped to Stalin by Churchill. After Stalin had approved the suggestion that SHAEF send officers to Moscow to arrange coordination of eastern and western fronts, Eisenhower had dispatched his deputy, Tedder; his G–3, Pink Bull; and his deputy G–2, Brigadier General Thomas J. Betts; when their journey was delayed by bad weather, Churchill cabled to Stalin:

> The battle in the west is very heavy . . . It is Eisenhower's great desire and need to know in outline what you plan to do . . . I shall be grateful if you can tell me whether we can count on a major Russian offensive . . . during January . . . I regard the matter as urgent.

Stalin at once replied:

> . . . the weather is at present unfavorable. Nevertheless, taking into account the position of our Allies . . . [we have] decided . . . to commence large-scale offensive operations . . . along the whole central front not later than the second half of January. . . . we shall do everything possible to render assistance to the glorious forces of our Allies.

Four days later, on January 16, the U.S. First Army met the U.S. Third Army in the rubble of Houffalize and so closed the breach in the Allied lines one month to the day after the Nazis had opened it. On the night of January 17 the First Army was returned to 12th Army Group and Bradley's command.

Meanwhile the British and American Chiefs had been preparing to meet each other on January 30 at Malta and later, with the Russians, at Yalta. To make ready, the British Chiefs had got up what amounted to a brief against Eisenhower's strategy and structure of command. What the British Chiefs wanted was one single commander of all ground forces and "one major thrust" into Germany, with "overwhelming strength [allocated] to this thrust to keep up the momentum." Once again the long encoded cablegrams sped back and forth across the Atlantic, once again the ancient arguments were resurrected, refurbished, and trotted out to do their familiar duty. Behind the British contention that only a strong thrust led by a British commander would win the war quickly lay the real issue: the U.S., once junior in the partnership between U.S. and U.K., was now decisively senior and no longer disposed to waste too much time in argument.

Eisenhower chose not even to travel to Malta to confer with the Combined Chiefs. Instead he flew to Marseille to talk with Marshall before the conference began; Beetle Smith went to Malta as his representative. During the three days (January 30–31, February 1) the Combined Chiefs met at Malta, Marshall turned a frosty stare on any discussion of saddling Eisenhower with a commander of ground forces, and at length Brooke was reduced to entering sullen comments in his diary. As for Eisenhower's strategic plans, the British had to be satisfied with some trumpery alterations in the wording of his memorandum of intention. Eisenhower cabled Smith: "You may assure the Combined Chiefs of Staff that I will seize the Rhine crossings in the north immediately this is a feasible operation and without waiting to close the Rhine throughout its length," but he added a caveat: "I will advance across the Rhine in the north with maximum strength and complete determination as soon as the situation in the south allows me to collect the necessary forces and do this without incurring unnecessary risks." Which left matters precisely as they had been before the meetings at Malta.

Brooke's semifinal effort to replace the supreme commander, or at least to jack him up with a properly qualified British officer, was made in a private conversation with Beetle Smith late at night on January 31. The CIGS told Smith he doubted if Eisenhower were "strong enough" for his job. Smith's threshold of irritation was always notably low, and Brooke had already overstepped it. "Goddammit," Smith snapped, "let's have it out here and now." What had Brooke against Eisenhower? Brooke, recalling Montgomery's peevish criticisms, came up with the charge that Eisenhower was too easily influenced by the last man to talk to him, that he paid too much heed to the wishes of his field commanders and so wobbled and wavered, acting on the advice first of Devers, then of Patton, then of Bradley, giving a little to each and dissipating Allied forces away from the indispensable operations in the north. Smith retorted that the supreme commander's cordial relations with his field commanders were the surest guaranty of Allied unity of purpose, the best way of dominating such a tempermental set of subordinates. If Brooke harbored any misgivings about Eisenhower, Smith growled in challenge, he should next day raise the matter candidly with the Combined Chiefs. But of course Brooke knew better than that. Smith was able to report to Eisenhower that the talk "had cleared the air."

Brooke's last stab came at Yalta on February 2, when the CIGS and Churchill raised with Marshall and Roosevelt the notion of replacing Tedder with Alexander. It got nowhere. When he heard of it later, even Montgomery thought it a bad idea.

By February it had become obvious even to Brooke that for the Allied armies to advance along a wide front toward the Rhine was not only feasible but positively valuable. The "double attack," Brooke belatedly observed, "might soon become a pursuit and as such [was] fully justified."

The warfare had been going on for so long and the technique for waging it was so elaborate that to deflect a SHAEF decision would have required something akin to a cataclysm. SHAEF itself was as big as a fair-sized city, numbering more than sixteen thousand souls of whom nearly three thousand were officers. This vast and topheavy bureaucracy, having once taken a decision, was well-nigh immovable. It ran the war. It supervised the administration of it, the planning of it, the operation of it, the supplying of its combat soldiers, the intelligence and counterintelligence activities that governed its decisions, the promotion and decoration of its valorous, the trial and punishment of its delinquent, the nursing and care of its wounded, the replacement of its effective troops, and the burial of its dead. Its finger was on every action and the publicity accorded every action. No GI moved without SHAEF's eye eventually fixing upon him, nor did any other Allied soldier. In theory, all SHAEF's actions moved up the chain of command to the supreme commander, but only in theory. In theory, all decisions were taken by the supreme commander and issued over his signature, but only in theory. In fact, perhaps one in a hundred decisions reached Eisenhower and perhaps one in a thousand of the messages bearing his name had been read and signed by him.

Was this the best way to run a war? It is tempting to imagine Caesar's response, or Napoleon's or Wellington's, most of all that of Clausewitz. But whether or not Eisenhower's was the best way to run a war, in 1944 and 1945 there was no other way, and his was working. It was the inexorable, cumbersome, bureaucratic way, the way dictated by crushing industrial power, with recommendations cautiously voted on by committees, passed along through departments, rough edges smoothed off, angles figured, options weighed and balanced, loose ends tied off, daring and imagination scuttled in the search for consensus; the triumph of rationalization, organization, compromise. Whatever one man could do well, a hundred men tampered with. Once SHAEF's plan had been painstakingly formulated—the careful expression of thousands of careful staff officers, themselves carefully selected for the particular skills they could contribute—who could interfere with it? presume to improve on it? gainsay it?

Answer: a few bold, resourceful American combat troops.

SHAEF's plan at the end of January 1945 was to close to the Rhine and then throw the weight of Allied strength behind Montgomery's elaborately prepared crossings in the north. By early March the men of the three Allied army groups had taken scores of thousands of prisoners, killed or wounded a great many more, destroyed more than twenty enemy divisions, and closed to the Rhine from Coblenz northward. Montgomery, his 21st Army Group reinforced by U.S. Ninth Army and First Airborne Army, was meticulously fixing to assault the Rhine on March 24. All according to plan.

On Wednesday evening, March 7, Bradley was at his command post in a palace at Namur talking with Pink Bull, the G-3 from SHAEF, when the telephone rang. It was Hodges, calling to report that a combat command of the 9th Armored had just captured intact a railroad bridge over the Rhine at Remagen. "Hot dog, Courtney," Bradley yelled. "Shove everything you can across it and button the bridgehead up tightly." He hung up, grinning, and wheeled around to Bull. "There goes your ball game, Pink," he crowed. "Courtney's gotten across the Rhine on a bridge." Bull shrugged. "What good's it going to do you?" he asked. "You're not going anywhere down there at Remagen. It just doesn't fit into *the* plan." "Plan—hell," Bradley retorted. Bull wagged his head. "Ike's heart is in your sector," he explained, "but right now his mind is up north." Bradley answered by putting in a call to Eisenhower. The supreme commander was at Rheims just sitting down to dinner with his commanders of airborne troops. Butcher was there too, ready to note what he could hear of the telephone conversation. From the next room he heard: "Brad, that's wonderful. . . . Sure, get right on across with everything you've got. . . . To hell with the planners. Sure, go on, Brad, and I'll give you everything we got to get to hold that bridgehead."

The soup tasted better when Eisenhower sat down again. Butcher, re-calling how the correspondents in Paris spent much of their time specu-lating about the capture of Berlin, asked Eisenhower if he proposed to take the city. Eisenhower discounted the value of Berlin. The Ruhr was far more important, he said, since without that industrial basin the Ger-mans would be unable to wage war.

To cross the Rhine ahead of Montgomery filled the Americans with a wicked delight—first Bradley and Hodges, and later Patton, who got ele-ments of his Third Army across the river several days before (officially, only the day before) the tremendous operation staged by 21st Army Group. But the supreme commander had the task not only of swiftly win-ning the war but also of keeping his chief warriors tractable and congenial. On the Thursday morning, then, having delayed long enough to give Hodges ample time to beef up his bridgehead, Eisenhower telephoned Montgomery to tell him not of an operation sensationally completed but of one hazardously undertaken. Montgomery at once reported the conver-sation to the CIGS: "I was consulted by Eisenhower . . . as to my opinion on this matter and said I considered it to be an excellent move, as it would be an unpleasant threat to the enemy and would undoubtedly draw enemy strength on to it and away from the business in the north."

Trifling, really; not to be compared with Montgomery's own majestic overture at Wesel; merely the first prong of what would later become a pincers "cutting off the Ruhr and a large area to the south," as General Marshall would later put it, "in the largest pocket of envelopment in the history of warfare."* By the end of March, troops of First and Ninth U.S. armies had closed the ring around the Ruhr, had captured three hundred and fifty thousand prisoners, and were sportively looking around for more.

And so the stage was cleared for the mopping up of the Nazis and the completion of the supreme commander's mission. The enemy's forces had been defeated west of the Rhine; the Rhine had been crossed; the Ruhr had been captured. Because the triumph was at hand, however, wait-ing only to be plucked, the Allied coalition was coming unstuck. The enemy had been torn apart and disorganized, his mines and mills overrun, his factories demolished, his treasures destroyed or buried, his reserves dissi-pated, his armies smashed, his will to resist reduced to furious spasms re-

---

* Eisenhower later wrote, in his *Crusade in Europe* (p. 229), that the double envel-opment of the Ruhr was part of a "general plan, carefully outlined at staff meetings before D-day." While it is probable that a plan for enveloping the Ruhr had been worked out by SHAEF before D-day—there were hundreds of such plans—it is quite certain that the double envelopment of the Ruhr, as it was executed, was conceived and planned by the staff of 12th Army Group. As late as March 15, Eisenhower was still wondering whether to authorize the operation.

quiring only a coup de grâce. In consequence, the politicians of Britain, the United States, and the Soviet Union, no longer sensing so sharply the need for unity, began to measure each other and each other's aspirations for the postwar world. Since Britain, so long a dominant world power, would surely be the weakest of the three postwar victors, her ministers—and in particular her prime minister—recognized that she could raise her voice with erstwhile authority only if she were an influential partner of one of her great wartime allies—against the other. No need to hesitate between the choices offered. Churchill must seek to enlist Roosevelt as an ally against the Soviet Union. But Roosevelt's vision of a durable peace was predicated upon a United Nations Organization already in the making in which the Soviet Union would be a full and cooperative partner. Of the Soviet Union's postwar policy there could only be surmise and, at first cautiously suggested, dread. Would Stalin, as Roosevelt evidently hoped, prove as mighty a confederate in peace as in war? Or would he, as Churchill evidently feared, guide the Soviet Union into a quest for world dominion? In the early spring of 1945 the answers to these questions were already being cramped into the harsh and confining strictures of the Cold War, but it is important to remember that the options still lay free for the taking when the western allies enveloped the Ruhr and turned their faces east, toward Berlin.

For Eisenhower, the supreme commander, the options were fewer. He led his troops pursuant to a directive given him a year before by the Combined Chiefs: "You will enter the continent of Europe, and . . . undertake operations aimed at the heart of Germany and the destruction of her armed forces." He was the agent of two governments—no, of three; for he was obliged also to heed the counsels of France and de Gaulle—and so had to conduct his military affairs according to their policies. And when their policies clashed? Conflict was resolved on the highest level. Eisenhower was an Allied commander who hoped always that he would serve an Allied will and never be forced to choose. When, however, power over policy shifted from Britain to the United States, Eisenhower happened to be confronted by a decision: should he or should he not set his armies to capture Berlin before the Russians could? The British, for reasons of military prestige, yearned to have Montgomery's army group, reinforced by at least one American army, sent north and east to take Berlin. The Americans, more concerned with the war in the Pacific, wanted only a swift end to fighting in Germany.

In this way Eisenhower was landed in the middle of another venomous political controversy.

His policy, a military one and, as he believed, untainted by political considerations, was always clear, straightforward, and sensible. Later, owing to the Cold War and his own political ambitions, the clarity of his policy would be deliberately fuzzed by Republican rhetors and so would afford the discriminating a good deal of innocent amusement, but in the spring of 1945 all was plain and fitted snugly into the supreme commander's view of Allied amity.

For example, at a press conference at the Hotel Scribe in Paris on November 21, 1944, he had shared in this exchange:

QUESTION: I believe on November 7 Marshal Stalin in paying tribute to the Allies in the west said that the Red Army will be in Berlin soon. That was a quotation I saw.

ANSWER: Good for him. He will do a good job there, I think.

That was before the Germans had thrust a salient into the Ardennes. Much later, after the Red Army had driven to the banks of the Oder and the Neisse, thirty-odd miles east of Berlin, and the western allies were closing the circle around the Ruhr, Eisenhower came back to the Scribe for another press conference (March 27, 1945):

QUESTION: To what extent did the previous Russian offensive make our rapid advance possible?

ANSWER: The Russians attacked on January 12. By that time Rundstedt was in complete retreat out of his bulge . . . and was going out as fast as he could. When they saw the weight of the Russian blows they got out the battered remnants of the Sixth Panzer Army and rushed it to the east. . . . Had [they] not been forced to take out the Sixth Panzer Army our task would have been more difficult definitely. So there is no question about the two attacks each having a good effect upon the other.

And a few minutes later:

QUESTION: Who do you think will be into Berlin first, the Russians or us?

ANSWER: Well, I think mileage alone ought to make them do it. After all, they are thirty-three miles and we are two hundred and fifty. I wouldn't want to make any prediction. They have a shorter race to run, although they are faced by the bulk of the German forces.

Nothing devious. Such candor was customary when the supreme commander spoke with journalists, and was the chief reason he enjoyed such an excellent press and had so many warm friends among the correspondents assigned to SHAEF.

But these remarks should not suggest that the supreme commander had never proposed to capture Berlin. On the contrary, back in September 1944, when the Allied armies were coursing across France and Belgium and all signs pointed to a speedy conquest of Germany, SHAEF planners had specifically singled out Berlin as the principal objective, and throughout the fall Eisenhower had often agreed with Montgomery that Berlin was the matchless prize. What changed everything about was, first, the rampaging Red Army, which had driven so hard and come so close to Berlin while the western allies were still recovering the positions they had lost during the desperate German counterattack, and second, the band of GIs who had seized the chance to take the bridge at Remagen. As any sensible commander would have done, Eisenhower perceived that Bradley's venturesome troops were more likely to accomplish his mission for him than those under Montgomery's more cautious leadership. He shifted the weight of the AEF assault from Montgomery, who was aimed toward Berlin to the north, to Bradley, who was aimed toward Leipzig and Dresden in the center.

Eisenhower had reached this tactical decision during an unpublicized five-day holiday on the French Riviera, near Cannes. The idyll had been arranged through the good offices of Major Alexis Lichine, a peacetime wine merchant who had been able to requisition a handsome villa, Sous le Vent, for a party that included the supreme commander; Bradley and an aide; Colonel Tex Lee; Ethel Westermann, a nurse; Ruth Briggs, Beetle Smith's WAC secretary; Nana Rae, Eisenhower's WAC stenographer; and Kay Summersby, recently appointed a first lieutenant in the WAC and now officially an aide to Eisenhower. In these opulent surroundings ("Never have I seen such wonderful bathrooms," Lieutenant Summersby noted in the supreme commander's war diary) Eisenhower had discussed with Bradley the exploitation of the Remagen bridgehead. What the supreme commander had first regarded as a diversion gradually grew to an operation rivaling and then outstripping Montgomery's offensive. While still at Cannes, Eisenhower talked by telephone with Pink Bull, his G-3, and had him issue the directive instructing Bradley to strike north "in strength" toward Kassel. Thus came the approval of the envelopment of the Ruhr; thus also, without troubling to state it in so many words, the decision not to race the Russians for Berlin. Why bother about Berlin? The supreme commander's mission in Germany was "the destruction of her armed forces," and the soldier's way to accomplish such a thing was to split those forces by joining hands with the Russians where they were closest, near Dresden. Moreover, Bradley had estimated it would cost one hundred thousand casualties to storm and take Berlin (the Russians were to lose at least that number) and, as he observed, that was a "pretty stiff price to pay for a prestige objective, especially when we've got to fall back and let the other fellow take over." (Berlin was within the occupation zone assigned the Soviet Union.)

At all events, Eisenhower was then flown north to witness Montgomery's crossing of the Rhine, told him he proposed to reinforce Bradley's earlier successes, returned to Paris for his press conference on March 27, and next day sent cabled messages from his headquarters at Versailles which effectively altered the tactical pursuit of the defeated Germans and, at the same time, outraged the British. To Stalin went a message to coordinate his plans with those of the Russians, to suggest a meeting of Allied armies near Dresden, and to inquire about Russian intentions. To Montgomery went a message instructing him that Ninth U.S. Army was to revert to Bradley's command. To Marshall went a cablegram explaining what he was up to, and why.

The British reacted angrily. Eisenhower had no business dealing directly with a head of state like Stalin; he should have sent the message through the Combined Chiefs. Eisenhower had changed his plans, Brooke complained, "from all that had been previously agreed on." Worst of all, said Churchill, Eisenhower was condemning the British 21st Army Group to "an almost static role in the north" when it should by rights have been careering triumphantly down the autobahn to Berlin. Montgomery considered the whole thing "a terrible mistake."

For once an Anglo-American controversy had been joined in which there was no misunderstanding. The British perfectly comprehended Eisenhower's intentions and stoutly denounced them. If Churchill disapproved of Eisenhower's directly addressing a chief of state, he felt no embarrassment in bypassing the Combined Chiefs and himself directly addressing Eisenhower. On March 30 he telephoned Eisenhower to inquire hotly about SHAEF's change of plans. On March 31 he cabled Eisenhower:

> . . . why should we not cross the Elbe and advance as far eastward as possible? This has an important political bearing, as the Russian armies of the south seem certain to enter Vienna and overrun Austria. If we deliberately leave Berlin to them, even if it should be in our grasp, the double event may strengthen their conviction, already apparent, that they have done everything.
>
> Further, I do not consider myself that Berlin has yet lost its military and certainly not its political significance. . . . The idea that . . . junction with the Russians . . . would be a superior gain does not commend itself to me. . . . But while Berlin remains under the German flag it cannot, in my opinion, fail to be the most decisive point in Germany.

This message "upset Eisenhower quite a bit," according to the tactful SHAEF office diary, and it is not hard to see why. The rapid crossings of the Rhine, the successful envelopment of the Ruhr, and the almost unopposed pursuit of the disorganized enemy—all this had lifted Eisenhower's normally buoyant spirits to elation; his grasp of the mighty forces under his command had never been firmer, his self-confidence never sunnier. Yet once again he was under a drumfire of criticism, once again the Grand Alliance was being wrenched apart, once again—most galling of all for a successful supreme commander—his judgment was being called in question.

To Montgomery, who had objected to Eisenhower's plans because they disturbed his own administrative procedures and exploded his dreams of taking Berlin, the supreme commander wired a crisp signal. "My plan is simple and aims at dividing and destroying the German forces and joining hands with the Red Army," Eisenhower began, and went on to explain why the U.S. Ninth Army would stay under Bradley's command. "You will note that in none of this do I mention Berlin," the message continued. "That place has become, so far as I am concerned, nothing but a geographical location, and I have never been interested in these. My purpose is to destroy the enemy's forces and his powers to resist."

To Churchill, Eisenhower's retort was almost as cross. "I have not changed any plan," he insisted, a statement that was not strictly accurate. What was "new," he argued, was Churchill's "idea respecting the political importance . . . of particular objectives," that is, of Berlin. "I clearly see your point in this matter," he went on. "The only difference between your suggestions and my plan is one of timing." What Eisenhower was suggesting to the prime minister was the obvious: first things come first. To strike across northern Germany to Lübeck, at the mouth of the Elbe, as he had ordered Montgomery to do, and so seal off the peninsula of Denmark and the North Sea ports from the onrushing Red Army, he deemed far more important than, as he would write later, "to expend military resources in striving to capture and hold a region [Berlin] which we were obligated . . . to evacuate once the fighting was over."

Churchill continued to urge "the importance of entering Berlin" and the need to "shake hands with the Russians as far to the east as possible," but he sensed that the rumpus between British and Americans must be quickly composed. Further bickering was in any case futile, since the American Chiefs so firmly seconded Eisenhower's chosen strategy; but Churchill was anxious to hush the Anglo-American wrangle for a more urgent reason: the time had come to present a common front to their formidable ally, the Soviet Union.

Quite fortuitously, that need was becoming most acute at precisely the time Eisenhower was forming—and the British were resisting—his decision to ignore Berlin and move in strength on his central front toward a quick junction with the Red Army. A number of critical issues had cropped up to impair the alliance with the Soviet Union—the question of who would govern Poland; the posture of other eastern European nations; the organization of the United Nations, with all the attendant procedural and parliamentary controversies; the method of accepting a Nazi surrender and the terms of such a surrender—and debate over each of these issues tended to exacerbate the others. If none of these problems had arisen, there would have been no want of volunteers in Washington or London or Moscow to find others, for by April the will to stick together had wholly collapsed. Given the nature of the three major allies against Hitler, so much was inevitable. The wonder is that the coalition had survived so long. Certainly its vigor and longevity dismayed and astonished Hitler, for all his hopes of somehow snatching a Nazi ascendancy from the impending cataclysm had been based upon his conviction that the Americans and the British would belatedly turn against the Russians. His desperate last energies had been harnessed and whipped toward that end. In December 1944 Hitler had reminded his generals:

> In all history there has never been a coalition composed of such hetero-geneous partners with such totally divergent objectives as that of our enemies. The states which are now our enemies are the greatest opposites which exist on earth: ultra-capitalist states on one side and ultra-Marxist states on the other . . . states whose objectives diverge daily. . . . In other words one day—it can happen any moment, for on the other side history is being made merely by mortal men—this coalition may dissolve.

But the Nazi counteroffensive in the Ardennes had failed, and so Hitler had cast the dice again: he had begun to transfer troops from the western to the eastern front until by the end of March less than thirty German divisions were left to face the British and Americans while more than one hundred and fifty divisions opposed the Russians. Would his western enemies not perceive the design? Perhaps, perhaps; for in Berne Allen Dulles of the American OSS, acting, as he would later observe, on "our own initiative," was already in touch with SS-Obergruppenführer Karl Wolff and had launched discussions looking toward a surrender of the German armies in northern Italy. Apparently Dulles and General Wolff, who commanded the SS and Nazi police forces in Italy, were apprehensive lest the Resistance, led by communists, would capture the industrial north before the Allies could do so, but Wolff later justified his negotiations to his chief, Heinrich Himmler, on the grounds that he had sought to drive a wedge between the Anglo-American allies and the Russians. However that may be, the Dulles-Wolff talks did in fact do much to sour relations between the western allies and the Soviet Union. The Russians were told of the talks but invited to participate only as observers; naturally they considered such a proposition offensive; when the British sought to suggest that the growing ill will was based on a misunderstanding, Molotov's retort was blunt. "In this instance," he wrote, "the Soviet Government sees not a misunderstanding, but something worse."

Churchill had chosen to regard this note as "insulting." On March 25 he had shown Molotov's letter to Eisenhower, simultaneously grumping and scowling. By Churchill's later account, Eisenhower was "much upset, and seemed deeply stirred with anger at what he considered most unjust and unfounded charges about our good faith." He may have been. How much of Eisenhower's anger was untrammeled emotion and how much a careful reaction to Churchill's political indignation can never be accurately assessed, but the supreme commander continued to turn toward the Russians the expression of amiable candor to be expected from a confident and trustful ally. In this regard he was only following the lead of his commander in chief and of General Marshall, who from Washington cabled Stalin assurances that the Dulles-Wolff talks had "no political implications" and insisted that the whole misunderstanding should be attributed to mischievous German sources, "which have made persistent efforts to create dissension between us."

But there was a less congenial aspect of the supreme commander's activities. Long months before, in October 1944, Eisenhower had cabled Marshall his recommendation that a strong force of heavy bombers be kept in Germany during the postwar occupation. He had deemed this advisable because so long as Europe was "in a state of almost violent unrest, any American contingent . . . should be a powerful one"; moreover, a force of big bombers "would place the U.S. . . . on a substantial basis of equality" with the Soviet Union, since "in the heavy bomber field we are far ahead of the Russians." In a prefiguration of the chief justification of the U.S. foreign policy of later years, Eisenhower had added: "We prefer to be too strong rather than too weak."

Now, as Churchill still disputed with Eisenhower the need for pushing east as far as possible, Eisenhower found himself in agreement with the policy laid down by the War Department in respect of the Ruhr: that it should not be further bombed or blasted by artillery fire, but rather spared as a guaranty of "the economic future of Europe." This phrase, which is quoted from the army historian, was understood by official Washington to mean "the economic barrier against communism." In the spring of 1945 this policy flourished in Washington. Secretary of the Navy Forrestal supported it; so also did Secretary of State Edward R. Stettinius, recently appointed; but it was pressed most vigorously by Averell Harriman, the railroad financier whom Roosevelt had appointed ambassador to Moscow. To Harriman the salient postwar task was to block Soviet penetration of Europe, and since Forrestal agreed he kept a record of Harriman's cablegrams from Moscow. The wartime alliance, Harriman argued, was to be regarded as a thing of the past. The huge Russian share in the defeat of Nazism must be thrust aside; ". . . now we should begin," Harriman cabled, "to establish a new relationship," one built "on a quid pro quo basis." He feared the use by the USSR of national Communist parties throughout western Europe. "The only hope of stopping Soviet penetration," he warned, "is the development of sound economic conditions." With all this Eisenhower could concur. He had already notified Marshall that reduction of the Ruhr would proceed with circumspection.

Other ways of achieving a premature alienation from the USSR would occur to the supreme commander. As the troops of U.S. First and Third armies drove eastward into the zone of Germany assigned to the Soviet Union they stumbled upon, were led to, or quite purposefully sought out and seized certain sensitive installations which, strictly considered, lay properly within Soviet jurisdiction. Of these, the first to come to light was the cache of gold bullion, a reserve of the Reichsbank, hidden more than two thousand feet deep in a salt mine. In reporting this find to Marshall, Eisenhower cabled, "May I suggest that information concerning location of this treasure be kept very secret."

Next day—it was April 12—Eisenhower joined Bradley and Patton for an inspection of the trove. They were told it was worth two hundred and fifty million dollars, a grossly inflated estimate. Besides the bullion there were enormous bundles of reichsmarks, crates of paintings (some evacuated from the Kaiser Friedrich Museum in Berlin, some stolen from art collections all over Europe), gold and silver plate hammered flat for more efficient packing, gold bridges prised from the teeth of corpses in the Nazi gas chambers, minted gold from a dozen European countries and even the U.S.; in short, loot amassed during six years of methodical brigandage and rapine. Fittingly, the three American generals were on the same day taken to inspect for the first time that other hallmark of Nazi culture, a concentration camp. The camp in question, Ohrdruf Nord near Gotha, was not one of the spectacular pestholes, no showplace: just the routine stink of death emanating from three thousand or more corpses that lay, some buried in shallow graves, some exposed, lice crawling over them, scabbed black where they had been gutted to provide a meal for the famished survivors. Bradley was revolted. Patton withdrew to vomit in a corner. Eisenhower, his face frozen white, forced himself to examine every last corner of the camp so that he might later be able "to testify at first hand about these things," in case ever the assumption might take hold that the tales of Nazi atrocities were only propaganda.*

The day before, fifty miles due north, a pair of First Army armored task forces had closed in on Nordhausen in the southeastern foothills of the Harz Mountains. The commanders had been forewarned by G–2 of something unusual in the area—was it the neighborhood concentration camp? the five thousand corpses of labor slaves that lay rotting in the barracks? No: rather it was the ingenious manufactory tunneled deep into the mountain rock where, under the direction of young Wernher von Braun, Nazi engineers and rocketry specialists supervised the assembly of the V–2s that had been loosed against Britain. More than a hundred of the missiles, ready for use, lay on freight cars in a rock-hewn siding. American ordnance officers at once set to work to "appropriate" one hundred of the weapons and have them cleared for transport to the White Sands Proving Ground in New Mexico; they were removed only hours before the Russians arrived to assert their authority. Several tons of working papers—designs, blueprints, all the arcane wizardry of rocket technology—had already been safely buried and sealed off by Braun's orders in another mine shaft; they would be recovered only when Braun accepted the American invitation to enlist his talents in the service of Pax Americana.

The supreme commander had still other plans afoot, one of them of sufficient importance to warrant a discussion with Churchill. On April 17 he took plane for London. His avowed motive for the journey was to explain again his refusal to press his troops against Berlin. Earlier, on April 11, advance columns of Simpson's Ninth Army had reached the Elbe at Magdeburg and had forced two bridgeheads across the river. One had been forced back, but on April 14 the other still held. With Berlin only fifty miles away, Simpson had naturally hankered to slash ahead, but when Bradley sent his request up through channels, Eisenhower had said no. As Eisenhower had explained to Marshall, "only our spearheads are up to that river; our center of gravity is well back of there." The Russians were closer, better prepared, better equipped, and far more numerous. Still, when they heard of Eisenhower's decision, the British Chiefs grumbled. They desired that Eisenhower be instructed to seize any chance of an assault on Berlin, and Churchill agreed. Hence Eisenhower's flight to

* That night Eisenhower learned that President Roosevelt was dead. "With some of Mr. Roosevelt's political acts I could never possibly agree," Eisenhower would write in 1947. "But I knew him solely in his capacity as leader of a nation at war—and in that capacity he seemed to me to fulfill all that could possibly be expected of him." The date of this gracious tribute is of interest: Roosevelt was two years dead, Eisenhower on the threshold of his own political career.

London. Prime minister and supreme commander settled down to a friendly chat about present priorities and postwar politics.

Eisenhower still proposed to send First Army ahead to link up with the Russians as it would do, northeast of Leipzig, in a week or so. He still proposed to secure his flanks: to the north using Montgomery's 21st Army Group to take Lübeck and thus deny the Russians any further advance into regions not previously adjudicated by the tripartite European Advisory Commission; to the south using Patton's Third Army and Devers's 6th Army Group to ensure that the Germans could not, as they had threatened to do, withdraw into a rumored national redoubt, an impenetrable fastness in the rugged Bavarian Alps. He had yet another argument for an encircling movement to the south, an argument of such moment and shrouded in such secrecy that he preferred not to confide it to his scrambler telephone or to his most secure telegraphic cipher. SHAEF's intelligence officers had deduced that south of Stuttgart, perhaps somewhere in the Black Forest, the Nazis had established a group of atomic scientists and set them to work with a small pile of uranium. In consequence, Eisenhower had the delicate task of investing the region (so far part of what was proposed as the American zone of occupation, but soon to be turned over to the French) without arousing the suspicions of the French, whose army held Stuttgart, or the Russians, whose armies were not too far to the east.

Supreme commander convinced prime minister. Presently Churchill cabled a minute "for your eyes alone" to Eden, who was in Washington:

. . . It would seem that the western Allies are not immediately in a position to force their way into Berlin. The Russians have two and a half million troops [this estimate, whether Churchill's or Eisenhower's, inflated Soviet strength by about one hundred percent] opposite that city. The Americans have only their spearheads . . . covering an immense front and . . . at many points engaged with the Germans. . . .

. . . Our arrival at Lübeck before our Russian friends from Stettin would save a lot of argument later on. . . .

Thereafter . . . it is thought well . . . by an American encircling movement to gain the region south of Stuttgart. In this region are the main German installations connected with their atomic research, and we had better get hold of these in the interest of the special secrecy attaching to this topic.

The special secrecy attaching to this topic. Here was the poison that would taint the victory over Germany and corrode the efforts to build a lasting and amicable peace among the victors. Before long the dreadful fruit of this topic, which would so closely affect the behavior and the life style of future generations the world around, coloring their dreams, work-ing its way with every fall of rain into their bloodstream and the marrow of their bones, would have extended its malign influence universally and eternally. And the special secrecy attaching to it would hold every states-man and soldier in its thrall.

On his flight to London, Eisenhower had been accompanied by three aides—Butcher, Gault, and Lieutenant Summersby. He had hoped to leave early on the morning of April 18, but Churchill wanted him to con-sult further with the British Chiefs, "to discuss action to be taken when we join forces with the Russians prior to our withdrawing into our re-spective occupation areas," as Brooke put it, and further to make sure SHAEF no longer communicated directly with Marshal Stalin. As to the latter point, the supreme commander jibbed. When it came to purely mili-tary matters, he insisted on his right to communicate directly with the Russians. After lunching at his beloved Telegraph Cottage, he was flown back to Versailles.

He had another two or three weeks of anxious waiting before his mis-sion would be accomplished. His temper was cautious: let no unforeseen calamity or egregious blunder intervene to botch the triumph that lay within his grasp. Lest there be any unfortunate incident as his troops closed in to meet the Russians along the line of the Elbe, on April 21 he sent to the Soviet High Command a précis of his tactical plans; four days later he was informed of the Russian plans, which were to occupy Berlin and sweep clear the eastern bank of the Elbe north and south of Berlin. Between SHAEF and the Soviet High Command there would be no unseemly competition, no race for objectives, no clash.

Caution. When the French chose to disobey his order that Stuttgart be turned over to General Patch's U.S. Seventh Army, ostensibly so that U.S. lines of communication and supply might be more directly provided, Eisenhower regretted the disobedience but chose to accept the situation.

Caution. On April 25 the U.S. Third Army was on the western border of Czechoslovakia. Nothing opposed an armored advance to Prague, and once again the British Chiefs urged that Eisenhower be instructed to lib-erate as much of the country as possible for the "remarkable political ad-vantages" that would accrue. Marshall duly passed the request along to Eisenhower, adding a comment that illuminates with blinding clarity how far the national policy of the United States would swing after 1945. "Per-sonally," the Chief of Staff observed, "and aside from all logistic, tactical or strategical implications I would be loath to hazard American lives for purely political purposes." Sundry historians have entered hasty disclaimers on Marshall's behalf, pointing out that Marshall had powerful political reasons (for example, the need for swift redeployment of American troops to the Pacific theater to war against Japan, and the desire to bring the Soviet Union into that war as an active fighting partner) for counseling Eisenhower to think twice before committing the Third Army to the liberation of Prague, but none of this can rid the remark of its quaint, even archaic flavor. At all events Eisenhower was able to assure Marshall that he would not move precipitately. "I shall *not* attempt any move I deem militarily unwise merely to gain a political prize," he cabled Marshall, "unless I receive specific orders from the Combined Chiefs of Staff." By May 4, when Eisenhower saw his way clear to unleashing Patton and aiming him toward Prague, he reconsidered after Red Army officers in Moscow urged the possible danger of a confusion of soldiery and a regrettable armed clash. Even when the embattled citizens of Prague begged for help over a captured radio transmitter, even when Churchill added his entreaties on May 7, the supreme commander was ruled by caution.

By then, moreover, the war in Europe was finished and General Dwight Eisenhower, as was his custom, was projecting his mind into the future. What did it hold for him—a professional soldier, aged fifty-four years, who had already tasted the headiest wines ever decanted? The stage was clear of its old principals; Roosevelt was gone, and Hitler, and Mussolini; the curtain had fallen. There was a new drama waiting to be played. An ambitious player, if he gave heed, might at any moment hear the tap at his dressing room door summoning him to take his place front and center. Eisenhower knew his lines already, or thought he did: God knows he had rehearsed them long and often enough. They had to do with peace, a peace built upon the warm and close-knit unity of the victorious Allies, a peace won by the blood and suffering of millions of men and women, by an anguish that made kin of Russians, British, Americans, French, Australians, Canadians, and a dozen other peoples the world around, now fused together in an organization of the United Nations. Was it not so? And would it not be?

The supreme commander closed his paperback Wild West fiction (it was called *Cartridge Carnival*), dropped it on his night table, turned out the light, and went to sleep.

PART FOUR

WILL HE? WON'T HE?

CHAPTER ONE

Military Governor

WHEN GENERAL EISENHOWER was flown back from his triumphal tour of the U.S. to Frankfurt in mid-July 1945 to preside over the dissolution of SHAEF, to take command of United States Forces in the European Theater (USFET), to govern the American zone of occupation, and perforce to speculate about what the future held for him and how he best might help to shape events to his own ultimate satisfaction, one consideration dwarfed all others. Remind himself as he might that he was a soldier and that his duty was service to his country, assure himself as he might that he had done more than his duty and was now free to relax and take his pleasure in the leisurely pursuits he fancied, at golf or bridge, shooting birds or catching fish, the brute fact was that his countrymen were inundating him with their limitless affection. It was unexpected, it was unsolicited, it was unprecedented. Somehow it had to be fitted into the equation.

No guidelines are provided a man suddenly become a National Hero. How shall he behave who overnight is endowed with some of the aspects of divinity? What shall he say who has been taken up into an exceeding high mountain, and shewn all the kingdoms of the world, and the glory of them, and has been told, All these things will be yours if only you do thus and so? If he seem to falter, now accepting the proffered gifts, now denying them, he can be forgiven his calculated indecision. Even such a glittering prize might prove an anticlimax.

It has been remarked that the American populace, while not knowing much about him, fiercely adored General Eisenhower. What they knew of him so far was that he was a victorious supreme commander who had cared about the welfare of their sons and their husbands, who was compassionate, honest, charming, modest, simple, sanguine of temperament, self-confident, and blessed with God's greatest grin. When he spoke of peace he spoke straight to their hearts. He had made friends of everybody —British, French, Russian, Polish, all those people over there, whoever they were—and not only did they all trust him, but evidently he could also make them do his will. He was a warrior and a most able one, yet he hated war, who knew more about it than most. He could be trusted. In short, the prayer of most Americans was: God bless him, sustain him, and return him safely to God's country.

Thus the public Eisenhower. If the private Eisenhower was not so easy to decipher, he was a good deal more interesting. The private Eisenhower was a complicated person. Of his considerable share of inner tensions and contradictions, perhaps the most consequential was the interplay between his public self and his private self, a relationship that enabled him to play hide-and-seek with the curious for a quarter-century.

In a society devoted to gossip and titillated by intimate glimpses into the lives of celebrated persons, the common experience of public figures so tormented is to grow callous to the incessant and ghastly invasion of their privacy, to come to expect it, even to recognize from its abatement that their prestige is fading and they are once again subsiding into obscurity. Notable in national politics, star of cinema, champion of athletic commerce, each has served his public apprenticeship, each has toiled to achieve the limelight, each bravely welcomes its attendant horrors. Not so Eisenhower. His celebrity had been thrust upon him while he was preoccupied with his martial affairs. This is not to say that he had wholly ignored the distasteful change. From the moment of his elevation from nullity to cynosure—say, when he was appointed commanding general, European theater, in June 1942—he had cheerfully accommodated the correspondents of press and radio, but only as he was able to make them serve the interests of AFHQ and later of SHAEF. He had shown himself a master of adroit management of those correspondents by (another contradiction) evidently behaving with the most transparent candor. As their dispatches and broadcasts showed, they had trusted him utterly. And yet he had revealed only a few of his professional secrets, nothing of himself, nothing private or personal, only what he deemed his countrymen had a right to be told.

Even on this last point he had contrived to maintain a professional pianissimo, always without prejudicing his own credibility and reputation for honest open discourse. Surely it was not advisable, two months before the landings in North Africa, to tell any but the Combined Chiefs that he planned to use Darlan as an ally, or later to tell anyone but General Marshall how he proposed to keep the airfields of postwar Morocco under close American military supervision. Need his countrymen know all about the arrangements entered into with Badoglio? or American schemes to delay de Gaulle's "premature" return to France? or the one hundred American airplanes to be diverted for counterrevolutionary purposes in Greece? or intervention in the domestic politics of Belgium? These matters were political, and he had always guilelessly assured the war correspondents that he had no concern with politics.

So, in truth, he had not, except as an agent. The chief difference between the British and the Americans in their conduct of war was this: the British required their ranking officers to report daily to the War Office or Admiralty on what they were up to, and thereafter they would be instructed in their future duties; the Americans were given widest latitude, their seniors in the War or Navy Department being confident that they would always manage their affairs in the national interest, whatever that might be at the time. As agent of the national interest, no officer, and certainly not Dwight Eisenhower, would ever venture an initiative calculated to unsettle the status quo. And if not as theater commander, then as Allied commander? as supreme commander? The thing was unthinkable.

Indeed, a remarkable aspect of General Eisenhower's tour of duty as a military executive was his instant ability to adapt to the wishes of his immediate superiors even as they were dictating those wishes to him from the Pentagon. As often as not he was able to respond that he had, before he had received his instructions, executed them. This was nothing so wonderful as extrasensory perception, it was merely deep calling unto establishmentarian deep.

An agent who can lie back in the weeds and accomplish the ends desired by the Pentagon while persuading a corps of able war correspondents that he loathed the deceptions and wiles of politics needs no instruction in the advantages to be gained from swift makeup changes. The sleight of hand involved in concealing the private Eisenhower behind the mask of the public Eisenhower was child's play. The sole essentials were the loyalty and discretion of his immediate circle, his "family" of aides and orderlies and secretaries, and these were accorded him without question.

His official family was somewhat diminished since V-E Day—Butcher had stayed in the States, Gault was due to return to London in August, there were other departures—but it was still big enough to shield him from the cares that lesser mortals must cope with. His official family tended his bank account, made his purchases when necessary, folded his clothes, shined his shoes, answered his mail, put through his telephone calls, filled the tanks of his various automobiles with gasoline, provided him with partners for bridge or companions for horseback riding, arranged his frequent holidays at Sous le Vent on the Riviera, had films screened for his private pleasure (he particularly liked those starring Betty Grable), cooked and served his meals; in short, provided him with both the necessities and the amenities of life, permitting him to concentrate his attention on such large matters as his own future and how elective politics might play a part in it.

This business of politics had necessarily absorbed Eisenhower's meditation ever since the extraordinary homage tendered him throughout his triumphal American tour. It was inescapable. It precipitated him into another of the tensions that tugged at him, one that did not bear talking about save with his closest associates. On the one hand his driving ambition made very alluring the siren voices that sang of a short sweet journey to the White House; Beetle Smith, when asked by a discreet British officer whether Eisenhower truly wanted the presidency would growl: "Want it! He wants it so bad he can taste it!" On the other hand, all Eisenhower's military training had taught him that the professional soldier must abjure any venture into domestic politics, and he knew how strongly his chief, General Marshall, felt on the matter.

The tempters kept dangling the prize before him. Soon after he returned to Frankfurt he had to go to Antwerp to greet President Truman, who had crossed the Atlantic aboard the cruiser *Augusta*, bound for the summit conference at Potsdam. Truman was in Germany a fortnight, and naturally found time to confer privately with Eisenhower. One day, touring with Eisenhower in a command car, he said: "General, there is nothing that you may want that I won't try to help you get. That definitely and specifically includes the Presidency in 1948." As Eisenhower later recalled, his reaction to this "astounding" proposition was to laugh and laugh, and to reply: "Mr. President, I don't know who will be your opponent for the Presidency, but it will not be I."*

Beyond identifying himself as a Republican and removing himself from the 1948 campaign, this remark of Eisenhower's left him free to maneuver as he might choose. At this point the private Eisenhower submerged, disappearing behind the public Eisenhower, whose broad grin was as infectious as ever.

The public Eisenhower would be, for the next few months, marking time. He was at his post—as commander of U.S. forces and American member of the Allied Control Council—more for the prestige his presence conferred on the post than for any efforts he exerted on behalf of the occupation. Most of the work was done by men like Brigadier

* This exchange was first publicly reported by Eisenhower in 1948 in his *Crusade in Europe* (page 444). Ten years later, during a televised interview conducted by Edward R. Murrow, Truman definitely and specifically denied having made such an offer to Eisenhower. Another five years and Eisenhower firmly repeated his account of the incident in his *Mandate for Change* (page 5). Truman's denial, coming as it did during an election year, may be presumed to have been one of those statements made by politicians during an election year.

General Cornelius Wickersham, in peacetime a New York attorney, who acted as Eisenhower's deputy in organizing the staff that conducted U.S. business within the Control Council; Robert Murphy, once again assigned to Eisenhower's headquarters, this time as his political adviser on German affairs; and particularly Lieutenant General Lucius DuBignon Clay, Eisenhower's deputy as military governor of the American occupation zone. Clay had known Eisenhower since their days at West Point; they had served together in the Philippines; Eisenhower had a high regard for Clay's administrative abilities and was delighted to delegate the economic, financial, and political problems of the occupation to him. Clay was, moreover, invaluable for another reason: he had a wide and intimate experience of Washington politics. His father had been a senator from Georgia, he had himself served as a page in the U.S. Senate, and during wartime he had been a deputy director of the Office of War Mobilization; such a man could steer the military governor safely past the cunning snares set about on Capitol Hill.

Eisenhower had not wanted to be the military governor—"Thank the Lord that will not be my job!" he had told Murphy ten months before—and at his first opportunity he had urged President Truman to give a civilian authority the responsibility of running the U.S. zone; but since he was stuck with it, he took comfort from the quality of the men who would actually be doing the work.

The policy these men were charged with administering was set forth in a document known as JCS 1067/7, which, being interpreted, meant it was the seventh draft of a paper produced by the Joint Chiefs of Staff. An earlier draft had been sent Eisenhower ages ago—on September 22, 1944—but only to be used in the event of Germany's sudden collapse; it had been filed away and forgotten. The common denominator of all drafts of JCS 1067 was that none of them could be made to work. Moreover, since the last draft, like all its predecessors, was classified as top secret, attempts to implement it could not be explained to curious and skeptical journalists. The final version forbade fraternization with the Germans, ordered the dissolution of all Nazi organizations, proscribed former Nazis from positions of influence in public or private life, barred all political activity including parades, and decreed the seizure and destruction of all arms and armaments. Attempts to legislate against friendly overtures to the former foe were laughable, and doomed to failure where cigarettes or chocolate could so easily be bartered for sexual satisfaction. The black market, too, involved a good deal of fraternization, and in the Berlin area alone black market transactions yielded American troops more than six times as much as their total pay—and cost the U.S. Treasury (the American taxpayers) an estimated $271 million before at length the military police put a stop to them. The process dubbed denazification likewise sputtered to an ignoble stop. General Patton, in command of the occupation in Bavaria, was heard to say it was "silly" to dismiss from their jobs "the most intelligent" people in Germany. His lead was followed elsewhere.

The economic provisions of JCS 1067 were yet worse: vague when they were not contradictory, reflecting the U.S. policy toward Germany, which was apparently to anesthetize German industrial power until the Allies could agree on what was to be done with it. After studying the directive, Clay professed himself shocked by the "failure to grasp the realities of the financial and economic conditions." His financial adviser, Lewis H. Douglas, an Arizona businessman of some importance, exploded, "This thing was assembled by economic idiots!" and presently he resigned. Clay's economic adviser, Brigadier General William H. Draper, was in peacetime a partner of Dillon, Read & Company, investment bankers with a sizable interest in the prewar German economy; he deplored JCS 1067 but soon found that application of it to German industry could proceed according to his indulgent and kindly judgment.

It is evident that General Eisenhower preferred a happy ship to a tight one.

Meanwhile, in the Cecilienhof at Potsdam, the leaders of the victorious Allies were once again met at the summit: Truman, new come to the world stage and a trifle uncertain of himself; Churchill, never suspecting that in a startling upset the Labour party had trounced the Conservatives and soon he would have to lay down "the charge which was placed upon me in darker times"; and Stalin, tenacious, enduring, confident that time was his sturdy confederate: three statesmen, each desirous of binding the world's wounds so as to benefit his own nation, each largely unaware of how the forces let loose by the war would willy-nilly scuttle empires, threaten societies whether capitalist or socialist, and put at hazard all life on the planet.

The statesmen were preoccupied with lesser matters. They wrangled fiercely over reparations; they fenced delicately as to whether the Soviet Union would join in the war against Japan; they debated the borders of Poland; they exchanged views on freedom of access to canals and inland waterways; they mooted the "open door" in China; Stalin attacked while Truman and Churchill defended Franco's fascist dictatorship of Spain; and they self-righteously assumed the rigid postures of hostility that would lead inevitably to the partition of Germany.

And over their conference table there impended, a grim memento mori, the awful shadow of the nuclear bomb.

A plausible case has been argued that President Truman deliberately postponed the meeting at Potsdam until after the first atomic bomb could be tested. The weapon, so it was supposed, would give the U.S. an imperious voice in the confrontation of Stalin. James F. Byrnes, whom Truman had appointed his secretary of state, had assured the President in mid-April that the bomb "might well put us in a position to dictate our own terms at the end of the war." To Stimson, the secretary of war, who had followed the development of the bomb project more closely than any other in Washington, the bomb was the "master card," essential to hold when gambling "with such big stakes in diplomacy." It is quite certain that Churchill and most of Truman's advisers anxiously importuned the President to meet with Stalin soon, not late—"at the earliest possible moment," Churchill pleaded—and Truman's only stated reason for postponing the meeting, the difficulty of his leaving Washington before the end of the fiscal year (June 30), was less than convincing. Eden, in the U.S. to help found the United Nations, was privily told of the strategy that dictated postponement, but Churchill still protested. The director of the project, J. Robert Oppenheimer, would later recall the "incredible pressure" from Washington that a bomb be completed and tested before the Potsdam meeting, but technical difficulties constrained Truman to postpone the conference once again, from June 30 to July 15. More dismayed than ever, Churchill went so far as to appeal to Stalin for an earlier rendezvous, but Stalin merely noted that Truman had set the date.

On July 15 the President disembarked from the cruiser *Augusta* at Antwerp.

On July 16 at 5:30 A.M., in a wild desert of New Mexico, Dr. Oppenheimer gave the order "Now!" in a strong voice, and as the officers and scientists of the project stood alert in a respectfully wide ring around the steel tower to watch the terrific blaze of flame through their darkened glasses, he recalled the two lapidary verses from the Bhagavad-Gita. First: "If the radiance of a thousand suns were to burst into the sky, that would be the splendor of the Mighty One." And second: "I am become Death, the shatterer of worlds."

On July 17 the Potsdam Conference began. Secretary Stimson had already told the President of the coded message, "Babies satisfactorily born."

On July 20 there came a U.S. Army courier with "vivid detailed accounts which showed," as Robert Murphy noted, "how greatly the power of the bomb exceeded expectations." This "exhilarating" report made "a decided change in the President's manner." On July 21 he "seemed much more sure of himself, more inclined to participate vigorously in the discussions, to challenge some of Stalin's statements." Churchill was likewise inspired with a new and explosive enthusiasm. Pushing out his chin and scowling, he told the British Chiefs that the bomb had re-dressed the diplomatic equilibrium; now the Americans and the British could say to the Russians, "If you insist on doing this or that, well . . . And then where are the Russians!" Brooke, listening, perceived that Churchill already imagined himself "capable of eliminating all the Rus-sian centers of industry and population," without, however, having taken into consideration all the attendant problems, which Brooke listed com-prehensively as "delivery of the bomb, production of bombs, possibility of Russians also possessing such bombs, etc."

On July 24, after the plenary session, when the statesmen had ad-journed from their big round conference table, Truman nodded to his interpreter Charles E. (Chip) Bohlen and sauntered over to Stalin. With elaborate nonchalance he remarked that the United States had developed a new weapon, one of extraordinarily destructive capability. Stalin seemed delighted. He expressed polite interest, as if Truman had observed that his daughter had earned excellent marks in her last term at school. Stalin said he hoped good use of the weapon would be made against the Japanese. A smile, a nod, a leavetaking. "He never asked a question," Truman told Churchill a moment later. It has since been widely assumed that Stalin knew of the bomb thanks to reports from his intelligence agents. While that is probably true, it is also quite likely that Soviet scientists had already set feverishly to work to the same end. If American politicians and military leaders were still complacently disposed to believe the Russians a rabble of illiterate peasants with none of the technical or scientific subtlety re-quired to develop nuclear weaponry, American scientists were under no such illusion. Indeed, a group of physicists attached to the Manhattan project had in June filed a report (named for Professor James Franck, who drafted it) pointing out that Soviet scientists had since 1940 known the basic facts about nuclear power and were well able to duplicate the Ameri-can achievement "in a few years." In any case, Stalin could deduce a great deal about the new American weapon from the striking change in Tru-man's comportment at conference sessions after word of the successful test reached Potsdam.

While those amiable festivities were in train, Eisenhower was only peripherally involved, only occasionally given informal opportunity to voice an opinion of the issues under discussion within the Cecilienhof. He duly paid his respects to George Marshall, he several times visited various members of the American delegation, but his headquarters and his temporary home were back in Frankfurt. In general, the opinions he ventured to express can without too much difficulty be traced back to others. Thus, when it came to reparations, he was content to present the consensus of his deputy Clay and his economic adviser Draper, urging the President to settle the problem of reparations "in such a way as to insure Germans an opportunity to make a living." The Russians, having in mind how the Germans had twice desolated their cities and ravaged their countryside, as they attacked and as they retreated, had at Yalta proposed "that the total sum of reparations should be twenty billions [of dollars] and that fifty percent of it should go to the Soviet Union." This formulation, as phrased by President Roosevelt and later incorporated in the Yalta protocol, gave rise to bitter controversy, the Americans insisting the proposal was merely "a basis for discussion," the Russians contending the sum of reparations had been settled and that it remained only to discuss how the reparations would be paid. They envisaged confiscation of factories, machinery, machine tools, and the like, but the bulk of such capital goods was in the zones controlled by the Anglo-Americans.

On an agreement about reparations, it was soon clear, depended the future effectiveness of the Allied Control Council, international control of the Ruhr, and the ability of the Allied powers to administer the German economy as a unified whole. The Russians urged international control of the Ruhr; the Americans opposed it, fearing an extension of the Soviet power into western Europe; and so Eisenhower presently joined his voice with all the others who counseled rehabilitation of the Ruhr and its reintegration into the world markets of capitalism. In line with this policy, Byrnes proposed that each country take reparations from its own zone, with the clear implication that economic control carried with it political control. So slipped away the concept of unified four-power control over Germany.

Eisenhower also suggested to Truman that he be flexible "in the termination of lend-lease arrangements with the French and British," but on behalf of the Russians he was silent. Pursuant to his policy of attempting to coerce the Russians, Truman had long since (on May 8) peremptorily issued an order halting all further shipments of lend-lease goods and recalling those cargoes already at sea. The order had hurt the British quite as much as the Russians, perhaps more, and had provoked instant outcries of public protest. In consequence, Truman had somewhat modified the order, permitting various categories of goods to go forward, including those that could be used by the Soviets when they joined in the war against Japan.*

* The cutoff of lend-lease goods by no means completed the transformation of the Soviet Union from wartime ally to Cold War enemy, but it speeded the process. The manner of the cancellation, Stalin told Harry Hopkins on May 27, had been "unfortunate and even brutal. . . . If the refusal to continue lend-lease," Stalin added, "was designed as pressure on the Russians in order to soften them up then it was a fundamental mistake." The fundamental mistake would be repeated because of mis-

The question of Soviet entry into the war against Japan was another matter on which Eisenhower later reported he undertook to counsel Truman. Stalin had promised Roosevelt at Yalta that the Red Army would be ready to engage the Japanese in Manchuria ninety days after V-E Day, and the promise would be precisely honored; but as the date crept closer soldiers and statesmen alike grew cool toward Russian participation. Eisenhower would later recall that he too "deprecated the Red Army's engaging in that war," and told the President as much, though there is no corroborative evidence that he ever gave Truman any such advice. The advice would seem to have been an act of pluperfect supererogation, for the list of those who, then or later, put themselves on record as having despised the notion of Russian help in the defeat of the Japanese is nearly endless—Churchill, Harriman, McCloy, Grew, Forrestal, Stimson, Byrnes, Leahy, King, Arnold, Ismay, and even Truman himself (sometimes)—and yet the odd fact is that on July 24, with Stimson's hearty approval, Truman and Churchill met with their Combined Chiefs of Staff and again agreed to encourage Russian entry into the war. Before the bomb had actually exploded over Hiroshima the professional military men still believed that an invasion of the Japanese islands might be necessary, and therefore that the Russians might play a useful role in the war by holding a Japanese army in Manchuria while the invasion went forward. Only after Hiroshima had been demolished did second thoughts about the advisability of urging the Soviets to join in the war begin to flood in. (Meanwhile, since American cryptographers had broken the Japanese ciphers, the approach of the Japanese ruling circles toward unconditional surrender could be plotted with some accuracy; the Americans cherished the hope that the bomb might supply the deciding motive before the Red Army got too far into Manchuria.)

In sum, Eisenhower's suggestions from backstage during the course of the Potsdam talks were those of the prudent man—circumspect, cautious, careful to vote with the majority of the committee—except in one instance. Almost alone among all the Americans and British who were privy to the awful secret, Eisenhower was opposed to use of the nuclear bomb. Others deplored the weapon after it had been exploded; Eisenhower's revulsion anticipated the horror.

Word of the successful test at Los Alamos was brought to Eisenhower at his Frankfurt headquarters by Stimson. As the secretary of war detailed the startling facts and went on to speak with animation of the plan to use the bomb against Japan, Eisenhower was "conscious of a feeling of

placed confidence in the atomic bomb, and so would freeze the two powers in the hostile postures of the Cold War. "Force," said Truman, "is the only thing the Russians understand."

depression" in contrast to Stimson, who was relieved and excited and evidently expected Eisenhower to feel the same way. It was not so. This time Eisenhower had not been prepared for the news by briefings and group studies and committee analyses, all weighed, balanced, and hammered into a consensus. This time his were "merely personal and immediate reactions," and he was appalled. He said he hoped the United States would never have to use anything "as horrible and destructive" as this weapon. Stimson was "deeply perturbed" by Eisenhower's attitude and "almost angrily" attempted to rebut his hasty arguments (for example, that Japan was already defeated, that American use of the indiscriminate bomb would shock world opinion).

But by that time the decision had already been taken. On July 24 the President had issued the order, and down through the chain of command it had sped, for delivery of the first "special bomb"—it was nicknamed "Little Boy" and was ten feet long, a little more than two feet in diameter, weighed nine thousand pounds, and had the kick of twenty thousand tons of TNT—"as soon as weather will permit visual bombing after about 3 August 1945."

Truman was in a hurry to get home. The presidential party left Germany on Thursday, August 2. On Sunday, August 5, the *Augusta* was in mid-Atlantic and the President and his secretary of state both attended divine service aboard the warship. Attentive journalists noticed that Truman seemed to enjoy the hymns. He and Byrnes joined in vigorously singing such favorites as "Come, Thou Almighty King" and "The Old Rugged Cross."

At about that same time "Little Boy" was being tenderly trundled across an airfield on an island in the western Pacific, on the next to last stage of its trip to final delivery.

At lunchtime on Monday, August 6, Truman was handed a message about the destruction of Hiroshima. He was greatly moved. "This is the greatest thing in history," he said. "It's time for us to get home."

In the meantime, while the statesmen had been coping with the future, the soldiers of the Allied Control Council had been dealing with the present in remarkably pacific fashion. To seek and achieve Allied unity was, for Eisenhower, to do what came most naturally: to attain, as he put it, "a common understanding and common purpose—our mutual good." He even entertained the notion that if in Berlin a friendly and cooperative spirit could be fostered, perhaps it might reach out from Germany to pervade Washington and London and Moscow. So inspired, he glimpsed world partnership.

There followed Eisenhower's second invitation to visit Russia, and this time Washington smiled on his acceptance of it. The day was set, the party formed, and the general's C–54, the *Sunflower,* made ready. Marshal Grigori Zhukov was of the party, accompanying Eisenhower as his official host; General Clay came too, and as Eisenhower's aides his son John and his old friend T. J. Davis were included; there was one servant, Master Sergeant Leonard Day. On the flight east Eisenhower and Zhukov chatted amiably, two professionals swapping yarns about the war they had fought and won. It was clear to Eisenhower that Zhukov was an accomplished soldier.

His five days in Russia were another easy triumph, an object lesson to show that when Americans and Russians set out to enjoy each other's friendly company, every barrier melts. Eisenhower was able to surmount even such obligatory obstacles of tourism as the inspection of the collective farm and the visit to the Moscow subway. Everything he touched was warmed by his sunny affability, wherever he turned precedents tumbled. In Red Square to watch a vast pageant of acrobatics, folk dancing, gymnastics, and massed calisthenic drills, he was invited by Stalin to survey the festivities from the marble podium atop Lenin's tomb—and so become the first foreigner ever to stand in those hallowed premises. After the visit to the state farm, when Zhukov accepted Eisenhower's informal suggestion that he drop in at the American embassy for a snack and a couple of drinks, Ambassador Harriman's eyes widened; never before during his tour of duty in Moscow had a ranking Soviet official so casually appeared, and at a moment's notice. (Perhaps none had ever been so casually invited?) When Zhukov escorted Eisenhower to the vast Dynamo Stadium to watch a football game, eighty thousand spectators roared the two soldiers their greeting, and when Eisenhower spontaneously slipped an arm around Zhukov's shoulders in a cordial embrace, the crowd roared again—could Allied amity have found a more vivid symbol?

To the journalists who trailed his steps, Eisenhower was as buoyant and congenial as ever. He told Brooks Atkinson, formerly the drama critic and now the Moscow correspondent of the *New York Times,* that he felt he was in the hands of friends, he sensed "a genuine atmosphere of hospitality." He had been pleasantly astonished by Stalin, finding him "benign and fatherly." He said he was "convinced that Russia and the United States must work together in the future in a spirit of amity," and he professed himself eager to promote friendship. At a press conference on August 14 he said: "I see nothing in the future that would prevent Russia and the United States from being the closest possible friends. If we are really going to be friends, we really must understand each other a bit." Here he paused, reflecting on American newspapers and the disposition of their publishers to criticize the Russians. "They will give you the devil," he said wryly to the Russian correspondents present. "All I suggest is," he resumed, once again the sunny optimist, "that we all keep our sense of values and not be upset by the lies or propaganda of a few crackpots."

The friendliness so evident wherever the public Eisenhower moved was not an accurate reflection of the temper at highest levels. After the first "special" bomb had dropped on Hiroshima on August 6 the world had changed, and Eisenhower, a great deal better informed and far wiser than most of his contemporaries, was saddened by the change. "Before the atom bomb was used," he answered a private question privately, "I would have said yes, I was sure we could keep the peace with Russia. Now, I don't know. I had hoped the bomb wouldn't figure in this war. Until now I would have said that we three, Britain with her mighty fleet, America with the strongest air force, and Russia with the strongest land force on the continent, we three could have guaranteed the peace of the world for a long, long time to come. But now, I don't know. People are frightened and disturbed all over. Everyone feels insecure again."

The world had changed. The Russians had quickly decided they must declare war on Japan at once: their armies had moved against Manchuria from three directions, slashing toward Harbin and Hsinking. On August 9 the Americans loosed another nuclear bomb, this time over Nagasaki, without waiting to assess the effect on Japanese leadership of the first bomb or of Russian entry into the war. On August 10 Washington learned that the Japanese were more anxious than ever to conclude a peace. Still, they refused to surrender unconditionally; they insisted their emperor must remain in power. On August 11 Truman answered that Hirohito might keep his throne but would have to obey the orders of an American supreme commander. In Tokyo there was reluctance to accept Truman's ultimatum. Meanwhile, the Red Army had already pushed into Korea and in Washington Truman was noticeably irked; from Moscow Harriman cabled a recommendation that Truman order American troops into Korea.

The end came while Eisenhower was still in Moscow, on the last night of his visit, during a reception and buffet supper tendered by Harriman at the embassy. Early in the morning of Wednesday, August 15, Harriman took the floor to announce news of the Japanese surrender. Eisenhower later recalled that the Americans present gave "a joyous shout of approval," while at least one Russian officer present showed no great enthusiasm. But the party became very gay, Russians and Americans joining to harmonize on the "Song of the Volga Boatmen" and "I've Been Working on the Railroad," and Lucius Clay perceived a "mutual desire for friendship between our countries."

The world had changed. "During the months of August, September, and October," Eisenhower would recollect, "there prevailed [in Berlin] a general attitude that encouraged us to believe that eventual full success [in cooperation with the Russians] was possible." But whereas Eisenhower was still animated by his tested and resolute principle—Allied unity to win the war and to establish and maintain the peace—in Washington the President and his secretary of state, placing their reliance in the growing American arsenal of nuclear weapons, were determined to force the Soviet Union into acceptance of the American schema for a lasting world peace.

Unquestionably the muscular foreign policy initiated by Truman and Byrnes induced the Russians to be more acquiescent, to yield to American demands in the Far East and in eastern Europe, demands that in some respects contravened the agreements struck at Yalta. Just as surely the threat of the awful power to destroy that underlay American diplomacy in the first postwar years led to worldwide fear, tension, and hostility. "There is widespread anxiety," Prime Minister Clement Attlee cabled Truman on August 8, "as to whether the new power will be used to serve or to destroy civilization." Truman's response, after a perfunctory reference to the atom bomb as "a weapon for peace," was to clamp more security, intensified vigilance, deeper secrecy around anything that had to do with nuclear fission. And the President noted with satisfaction that "our possession of the secret of harnessing atomic energy already had far-reaching effects on our relations with other nations." Stimson, who as the world had changed had himself changed his mind about using the menace of atomic weapons as a substitute for diplomacy, in mid-September was ready to resign as secretary of war, but before doing so he handed to Truman a long and thoughtful memorandum "about our relations with Russia in respect to the atomic bomb." Stimson argued that "unless the Soviets are voluntarily invited into partnership" in the development of this weapon "upon a basis of cooperation and trust, we . . . will almost certainly" provoke "a secret armament race of a rather desperate character." Stimson went on:

> The chief lesson I have learned in a long life is that the only way you can make a man trustworthy is to trust him; and the surest way to make him untrustworthy is to distrust him and show your distrust. . . .
>
> My idea of an approach to the Soviets would be a direct proposal . . . that we would be prepared in effect to enter an arrangement with the Russians, the general purpose of which would be to control and limit the use of the atomic bomb as an instrument of war and so far as possible to direct

and encourage the development of atomic power for peaceful and humanitarian purposes.

But Stimson's urgent suggestion was misunderstood, distorted, and kicked about until it was no longer recognizable. The easiest thing to do with it was to postpone action on it; this was done. It made little difference how long action was delayed, for the most powerful of Truman's advisers—Byrnes, Forrestal, and Robert Patterson, who succeeded Stimson as secretary of war—were all against even conferring with the Russians on the subject. The exorbitant and perilous arms race would begin and would inevitably hold the great powers in thrall.

Eisenhower, his bailiwick limited to a small fraction of a conquered nation, as yet did little more than observe these momentous events from his privileged perch.

Four months earlier, Harry Butcher had predicted that Eisenhower would take a pounding in the newspapers for his policies in administering the American occupation zone; "his standing in the near future," Butcher wrote on May 14, "is likely to slump." Now in mid-September the military governor was to appreciate how perceptive had been the prophecy.

The plight of the hundreds of thousands of people who had been caught up by the whirlwind of war and left destitute, homeless, impoverished, scattered over central Europe, had been much on Secretary Morgenthau's mind. At his suggestion and with Truman's approval, the State Department had selected Earl G. Harrison, formerly the U.S. Commissioner of Immigration and at the time dean of the Law School of the University of Pennsylvania, to be the American representative on an Intergovernmental Committee on Refugees. Harrison was charged with inquiring into the needs and despairs of these folk, soon to be described in chilly bureaucratic jargon as displaced persons or simply DPs; he was told to look especially into the condition of those German Jews who had somehow survived Hitler's "final solution," and those Jews from Poland and the Baltic states whose repatriation was for political reasons distasteful. Harrison's inspection was thorough and his report, submitted to Truman in August, was shocking. Jews were confined in camps behind barbed wire; the displaced persons, many of them sick, were obliged to wear prison garb or hand-me-downs from Nazi SS storm troopers; their diet was bread and ersatz coffee. These "desperate people," Harrison reported, were unable to get an audience with officers of the American military government, for the reason that AMGOT had staffed its offices with Germans and the Germans coolly ignored all pleas made by the DPs. As matters stood, Harrison disclosed:

> . . . we appear to be treating the Jews as the Nazis treated them except that we do not exterminate them. They are in concentration camps in large numbers under our military guard instead of SS troops. One is led to wonder whether the German people, seeing this, are not supposing that we are following or at least condoning Nazi policy.

Truman did not at once make public Harrison's report. After all, he was keenly aware of Eisenhower's value as a political property, still hoped despite the rebuff Eisenhower had given him that perhaps the general might reconsider and become the candidate of the Democratic party in 1948, and therefore was interested in keeping Eisenhower's name sweet in the public prints. The President had long since assured Joseph E. Davies, the wealthy Democratic lawyer who had been Roosevelt's ambassador to Moscow, that he agreed Eisenhower's political usefulness should not be impaired by protracted service as military governor in Germany. Truman was careful, then, to let Eisenhower know of the Harrison report well in advance of its release to the press.

Eisenhower learned of the report from a message sent him by Truman on August 31. At once he recognized that here was another ugly problem, comparable to the onerous chore of denazification, a policy he was finding exceedingly hard to enforce. He ordered a prompt investigation of the DP camps. Next he sent a sharp letter to George Patton, his proconsul in Bavaria, who had countenanced the retention of dozens of Nazi officials in positions of authority in the Bavarian government. Patton had disregarded Eisenhower's order to oust the Nazis, and "opposition to the faithful execution of the order," Eisenhower now warned Patton, "cannot be regarded leniently by me."

Eisenhower then left on a scheduled trip to Rome and Venice, fetching up on Friday, September 14, at Sous le Vent, the comfortable villa on the Cap d'Antibes where he was wont to loll and swim in the sun. He brought with him his old friend Mark Clark and had as other guests Averell Harriman and his daughter Kathy, who were on their way to the meeting of foreign ministers at London. Harriman rarely left Moscow without a generous supply of fresh caviar; moreover, thanks to the attentive ministrations of Major Alexis Lichine, a quite tolerable stock of wines had been laid down in the cellar of Sous le Vent; a pleasant holiday seemed assured.* But word came from Frankfurt that the President was

---

* The wines were no particular magnet for Eisenhower. He had little interest in, and no taste for, the great wines of France. His own preference was for the sweeter white wines of the Bordelais, especially the Barsac.

impatient to hear about the DP camps, and so on Saturday morning Eisenhower had to hurry back to Germany to look into the damned complaints. It was vexing.

The reporters who routinely kept an eye on Eisenhower's travels were vexed, too, to be robbed of an all-expenses-paid sojourn on the Riviera. They speculated that his abrupt departure meant the time had come for the Hero to report to the Pentagon and take up his duties as chief of staff. Their guesses were well founded but premature.

Eisenhower's vexation would stay with him for at least thirty months, or until he had finished the dictation of his memoir, *Crusade in Europe.* In that book, without mentioning the Harrison report, he spoke of "lies" and of "some so-called investigators [who] saw a golden chance for personal publicity." It seems likely that Eisenhower's irritation persisted because the chain of events that began with the Harrison report and included the laggard program of denazification was to end with the dismissal from his command of his old friend Georgie Patton. It was just one damned thing after another.

On his return to Germany, Eisenhower was driven to Munich, where he was met by Patton. Together the two men made the rounds of a couple of DP camps. What they found was deplorable. On their way back to his headquarters Patton ordered the automobile stopped so that he might vomit by the roadside. More cheerful, he then suggested that they go fishing in a nearby lake—"to get the smell of shit out of our lungs"—and he accepted with true penitence Eisenhower's scolding and his stern injunction that all the DP camps within his jurisdiction be cleaned up and made properly habitable forthwith. An officer who accompanied them during part of the afternoon reflected that Eisenhower treated Patton as though he were his "beloved naughty boy." Whatever he was, Patton during these weeks seemed determined to tighten the noose around his own neck. In every way he could imagine he delighted to insult the Red Army officers with whom he occasionally consorted; time and again he urged his superiors to let him provoke a war with the Russians and drive them back east out of Europe. His Third Army could do the job handily by itself, he boasted; sometimes, when he was feeling cockier than usual, he would vow to do it in six weeks, but usually he estimated it would take him three months. On this occasion he once again angered and embarrassed Eisenhower by entreating his permission to start another war immediately and send the Red Army scampering back into Russia. None of this swagger owed anything to the atomic bomb. To Patton nuclear fission was "no more revolutionary than the first throwing stick or javelin, or the first cannon, or the first submarine. It [was] simply . . . a new instrument added to the orchestration of death, which is war." Patton was a warrior who lusted after war, a man who could write his wife: "I love war and responsibility and excitement. Peace is going to be Hell on me."

To attempt to make a military governor out of Patton, especially after his disastrous experience with the ineffable Noguès in Morocco, was an egregious blunder, one that must be charged against the highest levels of the War Department. Patton himself, in his unstable fashion, was able to curtail his tour of duty with finality. A day or two after Eisenhower's visit Patton called a press conference at his headquarters in Bad Tölz. The correspondents knew that Murphy was in Bavaria, sent to inquire into the laxity in the enforcement of denazification; they knew of Patton's slowpoke responses to Eisenhower's orders on the matter; one of them mentioned the obvious fact that Bavaria was still being administered by reactionaries. "Reactionaries!" Patton exploded. "Do you want a lot of communists?" For a moment he seemed to be prudent, thinking before he spoke. "I don't know anything about parties," he said. A few moments later he proved how little he knew. "The Nazi thing," he said, "is just like a Democratic and Republican election fight." He said a good deal more, but that much was more than enough.*

If the decision to designate Patton the military governor of Bavaria had been taken in the Pentagon, the decision to remove him lay with the commander of USFET. Throughout Germany, and especially in the American zone, the affair was closely watched as affording one insight into the trend of American policy: unswerving resolution as to denazification would suggest that the U.S. still relied for future peace on the Anglo-Russian-American alliance, but anything less would hint that the Americans were salvaging the managers of German industrial might as a bulwark against some putative Soviet threat. The matter could be put more succinctly: Had General Eisenhower changed his mind?

On September 24, after discussion with Eisenhower, Beetle Smith telephoned Patton and instructed him that he was to call another press conference, during which he was to read aloud to the assembled correspondents the paragraphs from Eisenhower's letter to him, now twelve days old, wherein he had been unequivocally ordered to speed the process of denazification, or else.

On September 25 Eisenhower issued an order that all German industry and commerce must be purged of Nazi managers and supervisors, that

---

* Later it would be charged that Patton had been entrapped into these foolish remarks by a correspondent seeking to foment a provocative newspaper story. Evidence in support of such a charge is wholly lacking. A State Department representative attended the press conference, listened, but never spoke. The correspondents present were responsible and experienced journalists. The account here is based principally on dispatches sent to the *New York Times* by Raymond Daniell, Tania Long, and Kathleen McLaughlin, from September 20 to September 30, 1945.

former Nazis could be employed only as common laborers. From Eisenhower's deputy General Clay came word that the order was the law in the American zone and was effective immediately. The new order supplemented an earlier one, of July 20, which had required that no business or industry could be reconstituted until all Nazis associated with it had been discharged. (This was the order that in Bavaria had been ignored, evaded, or otherwise circumvented.) As he had been bidden, Patton held his second press conference, manfully gulping crow but still stubbornly insisting that he had sacked quite a few Nazis.

On September 26 Beetle Smith instructed Patton to report to Eisenhower's headquarters at Frankfurt. To correspondents Smith acknowledged that Murphy had been sent to Bavaria to investigate the disturbing "ultraconservatism" of that state's government.

On September 27 bad weather interfered with airplane travel. Patton arrived in Frankfurt late, and on Friday, September 28, was closeted with Eisenhower for a long and stormy confrontation. Outside, aides and WAC secretaries walked softly, with wide eyes. "It was the first time," Kay Summersby would recall, "I ever heard General Eisenhower really raise his voice." At the end, his old friend knew that he would be relieved of command of the Third Army and assigned instead to command of the Fifteenth Army, a paper outfit of officers and service troops established to study the experiences of the war and determine how the "science of warfare" might be refined as a result of them.*

If denazification was the only test, it was manifest that General Eisenhower was still firmly committed to Allied unity as the best way to win the peace. Dismissal of his ancient friend Patton had been exceedingly unpleasant, and on top of it came the release to the newspapers of the Harrison report. The public Eisenhower disappeared. Correspondents who sought his comments on the allegations of mistreatment by the Americans of the DPs had to be content instead with an officer described in their dispatches as "official Army circles." This faceless spokesman belittled the charges. They were based, he said, on "old information" about conditions that had existed before Eisenhower had ordered Patton to clean up the camps—ten days before. Less than a week ago, the spokesman continued, Eisenhower had ordered the DPs to be properly housed even if German civilians had to be ousted from their homes to make room. Other army officers insisted there was "nothing to apologize for" in the American zone; "our Jewish camps," they emphasized, "are in splendid shape now as compared with a few months ago." Before long,

---

* Two months after taking leave of his Third Army, Patton was involved in a freak automobile accident on a highway in Germany. His neck was broken. Twelve days later, as he was lying in hospital, his heart failed.

here came Harvey D. Gibson, the New York banker who was then commissioner of the American Red Cross, to report that the DP camps looked fine to him. Meanwhile Eisenhower himself had sent to Truman the fruit of his own investigations: the Harrison report, he said, was most misleading since the conditions described in it had been corrected by the time the report was handed the President. Harrison, offered an opportunity to comment on Eisenhower's reply, spoke gently. Eisenhower had doubtless issued proper orders, he said, but his subordinates had not executed them. The Jews and others uprooted by the war were still billeted in camps while their erstwhile oppressors, the Germans, lived comfortably at home; such a situation, he argued, was regrettable. By this time the commotion was running out of steam. Those who on September 30 had been outraged to learn that the victims of Nazism were being little better treated by the American army of occupation had after three weeks either forgotten the whole thing or found another indignity to upset them. As if to wipe the slate clean, Harvey Gibson issued a statement designed to explode the Harrison report into dust.

The DPs, who had survived worse horrors, still subsisted.

By mid-October it was sufficiently clear to those who make major policy decisions that General Eisenhower was no longer useful as military governor in Germany. His post was, for a man with a lustrous past as a supreme commander, demeaning. It could prove, for a man with a valuable future as a national political leader, positively dangerous. The man was too big for the job. Moreover, like Patton, he was beginning to evince alarming signs that he was not particularly well fitted for the job. In any event, to require him to stay in Frankfurt was insupportable.

Then what to do with him?

General Eisenhower himself had expressed a wish to retire, but it was difficult to determine whether the wish had been expressed by the public Eisenhower or the private Eisenhower. General Marshall was due to step down as chief of staff; General Eisenhower was his logical successor. Yet in the fall of 1945 Eisenhower was not anxious to take the job, or at least professed not to be. For one reason, the chief of staff would have to preside over the demobilization of the vast Army of the United States, but Eisenhower deemed a hasty demobilization unwise and so, by dragging his feet, was likely to provoke the wrath of the wives and families of all those soldiers. For another, a chief of staff was always caught up by politics, was at the beck of at least six congressional committees on Capitol Hill, was obliged to nod and smile and be affable to dozens of politicians whom Eisenhower considered to be no better than so many specimens of the family Hyaenidae. For a third, he was already uncomfortably aware that, as the world had changed, the duties of a chief of staff would no longer include what he had long preached and practiced, to wit, Allied unity.

There was, however, no easy way for Eisenhower to sidestep the appointment, even if his sense of duty had permitted him to try. Most of his classified chores were behind him. The eighty-eight Nazi scientists and specialists in rocketry had been rounded up, questioned, processed in various discreet ways, and packed off to the U.S. aboard a transatlantic steamer that was shrouded in deepest secrecy. A few ceremonial tasks remained: excursions to Amsterdam and to Prague, to receive the honors and gauds due the liberator; a trip to Berlin, to celebrate with Zhukov the twenty-eighth anniversary of the bolshevik revolution and to exchange toasts to Allied friendship. On Sunday, November 11, a curiously appropriate anniversary, General Eisenhower took plane for home, his duties in Europe at last behind him. He had written General Marshall that three things concerned him: unification of the armed forces, the need for universal military training, and the need for international cooperation, and those were three things that would inevitably and properly concern a professional soldier who had risen to the summit of Allied command.

But his greatest concern, whether he wanted it so or not, continued to be politics.

CHAPTER TWO

Chief of Staff

An EFFORT MUST BE MADE, as General Eisenhower assumes the rank, style, and quality of chief of staff, to define, or rather to delimit, the often expressed Eisenhoverian distaste for politics. What was it about politics that he professed to dislike? Which were those politicians who particularly inflamed him? Why were his own statements about politics so obviously contradictory? How could one able political analyst call him "a political genius" while so many others insisted that politically he was a boob? The confusion arises, as so often, from ambiguities of meaning.

Politics is the mechanics of government; the word is also used to suggest a technique of managing without friction the affairs of social groups; in the U.S. it connotes the partisan rivalries of the two dominant political parties; it is also a career, sometimes undertaken for noble and selfless reasons but more often for mean and commercial ones; finally, politics is used to signify ideology, in the sense of a set of opinions, beliefs, and broad sympathies or antipathies. These five uses (or misuses) of the word suffice to show how slippery it can be and how deceptive in its application. Thus, fishing among these five meanings, one can appreciate that while his training as a professional soldier made Eisenhower detest and shun politics, in the course of his military career and particularly in the previous four years he had proved himself a consummate politician; it is equally clear that while he knew very little about politics in one sense, in another he could give most practicing politicians cards and spades and trounce them handily at their own game. His own politics, in still another sense of the word, were carefully concealed, the better to fascinate professional politicians and excite speculation by the press.

During the twenty-six months he served as chief of staff, the capstone of an American soldier's career, General Eisenhower was constantly groping into the murk of politics, warily experimenting with the thing, exploring it, adjusting himself to new aspects of it, turning his back on it, cursing it, but always returning to it as—sometimes reluctantly, sometimes confidently—he measured it, hefted it, and sought to fathom its various uses.

The curious, ambivalent process began even before his appointment had been unanimously approved by the Senate. He appeared before the House Military Affairs Committee to speak on behalf of universal military training; he argued that such a precaution was necessary to "the preservation of our way of life—our American way of life," since it was likely that in any future war "the United States will be the first strategic target for attack." On the committee was a plump, bombastic politician, J. Parnell Thomas, who would later attract a certain notoriety for chasing alleged Reds through the great black headlines of the nation's newspapers, and a rather more fragrant notoriety for illegally padding his congressional payroll. (A man does what he can; Thomas fetched up in federal prison.) On November 15, 1945, this Thomas, tempted by talk of an attack on the United States, wondered if he might lure Eisenhower into indiscreet speculation and so prove himself the eagle-eyed patriot. The republic was threatened by potential aggressors, was it? We seem to be perilously close to another Pearl Harbor.

THOMAS: Let us name a couple of names.

EISENHOWER: You name them.

THOMAS: All right; I'll name them, and I'd like to have your views on them. What about Great Britain as a potential aggressor?

EISENHOWER: There will never be a war between Great Britain and the United States. (*Applause.*)

THOMAS: What about Russia as a potential aggressor?

EISENHOWER: Russia has not the slightest thing to gain by a struggle with the United States. There is no one thing, I believe, that guides the policy of Russia more today than to keep friendship with the United States.

Having failed to make any mischief with this line of questioning, Thomas tried asking Eisenhower about the nuclear bomb.

EISENHOWER: . . . I am sure of this, that if we could establish, through the United Nations Organization, a complete interchange of knowledge and a free access of every government to every other, you would at least inspire confidence, and thereby you could give such secrets to all nations and it would make no difference. (*Applause.*)

He was pressed on this question: Could, or should, the United States attempt to maintain its monopoly of atomic secrets during the brief period —estimated at two to five years—before some other nation might contrive the same scientific and technical success?

EISENHOWER: Let's be realistic. The scientists say other nations will get the secret anyway. There is some point in making a virtue out of necessity.

To many watchful ideologues in Washington and elsewhere, this testimony was evidence of a lamentable naïveté. Plainly the new chief of staff still harbored ideas which, while reasonable enough during wartime, were now hopelessly obsolete. He seemed to be saying, Russia is our friend and ally, and since the Russians will soon develop a nuclear bomb anyway why not cement our friendship by saving them the trouble of working out the details by themselves? In a not too distant future such talk would be regarded as either insane or positively treasonable, and even Eisenhower's eminence as a National Hero might commence to crumble if he persisted in it. Correct policy was already clear enough: the Soviets were potential enemies, and the secret of atomic weaponry was and should remain the exclusive property of the United States. The new chief of staff required immediate indoctrination.

The process could not, however, be undertaken with undue haste. One does not lightly set about telling a chief of staff that his ideas are all wet, especially when, as their foremost exponent, he has used those ideas to forge a Grand Alliance and lead it to victory. He is likely to persevere in the notion that peace may best be achieved by the warm and continuing alliance of the victors. Moreover, this particular chief of staff was, especially during his first weeks in office, an exceedingly busy one, obliged to supervise the dispersal of the mighty host assembled by his predecessor and eager to advocate his two pet projects, universal military training and unification of the armed services. Yet further, the common decencies required that General Eisenhower be afforded a few days of relative serenity so that he might rejoin his wife and renew, after more than four years' separation, their long and reasonably happy marriage. Mamie Eisenhower had already directed the work of redecorating Quarters Number One at Fort Myer, so recently vacated by General and Mrs. Marshall, but before the new chief of staff could take up residence he was ordered to hospital at White Sulphur Springs so that he might shake off a particularly nasty cold.

At the Pentagon there awaited him a new official family, one which would prove as devoted and loyal as the one he had left in Germany. Major C. Craig Cannon, boyish in appearance and imperturbable in nature, was now responsible for the administration of his office; Major Robert L. Schulz, a short-spoken man with experience of traffic and transportation, was to supervise his travels, his personal finances, and a good deal of his personal correspondence; Major Kevin McCann, a tall spare man with some experience of journalism, would advise him on his public relations, work on a good many of his speeches, and gradually move into the innermost circle of those whom the general most trusted. These officers were alike in their conviction that Dwight D. Eisenhower would make a superlative President of the United States. Nevertheless, they moved with gingerly circumspection, for they knew—without need of reminder by their boss—of the paragraph in Army Regulations then denoted AR 600-10.6b(1), wherein it was stated that "members of the Regular Army, while on active duty, may accept nomination for public office, *provided such nomination is tendered without direct or indirect activity or solicitation on their part.*" (The emphasis is added.)

Another member of Eisenhower's official family, a man who said of him, "I love that man . . . the sun rises and sets in him for me," was Beetle Smith, his wartime chief of staff. Smith had followed Eisenhower back to Washington, and in January 1946 was assigned to head the Operations

Division of the War Department, Eisenhower's old job. Before he could settle to his new tasks, however, he was reassigned by Truman as the American ambassador to Moscow, and the intimacy between the two men, a close bond that lapped the forty most momentous months of Eisenhower's career to date, would be reduced to the exchange of long, rather perfunctory letters about the press of their respective duties. Meanwhile Truman had dispatched General Marshall to China as his personal ambassador, charging him with the responsibility of obtaining a truce between the Nationalists of Chiang Kai-shek and the Communists, led by Mao Tse-tung, and of arranging the unification of all disputing factions in China under the leadership of Chiang so that the result would be a strong government friendly to the U.S.

As he took up his new duties, then, General Eisenhower was without the counsel of the two officers who had been throughout the war his surest reliance.

Considering the enormity of the task, the chronic shortage of ships, and the glut of valuable military stores in depots all over the world, demobilization had gone forward remarkably well, but not fast enough for the families at home and therefore not fast enough for the Congress. In September 1945, assurances had been broadcast that every soldier with two years of overseas service would be home by March 1946; but on January 8, 1946, President Truman, mindful of the nation's strategic posture amid rising tensions, reduced the rate of discharge from seven hundred thousand to three hundred thousand a month, and the pledge to release those with two years of service by March was scuttled. The squawks were instantaneous and worldwide. Ten thousand GIs massed to demonstrate in Manila, five thousand in Calcutta, four thousand in Frankfurt, and other mass protests were staged in Paris, Vienna, London, Yokohama, Tokyo, Seoul, Honolulu—even at Andrews Air Base outside Washington.

Overseas or stateside, the GIs were, no doubt about it, bored, impatient, and demoralized: their job was done, they wanted home. To some in the Pentagon it seemed shocking that the citizen-soldiers of the world's mightiest nation should behave so; disgusted officers used the word mutiny; attempts were made to blame the unseemly protests on—who else?—the communists, but these efforts died of inanition.

The chief of staff was in Canada. Eisenhower had arrived in good cheer for a ceremonial appearance, a speech, an investiture. On January 9 he issued an order by which he smoothly underhanded responsibility to the theater commanders overseas: all troops "for whom there is no military need" were to be shipped home "without delay." A few days later he addressed the nation by radio, renewing the assurance of a speedier rate of discharge and exhorting the soldiers to cease their demonstrations. But the whole affair had been most awkward.

Nor was his tour of duty marked by the enactment of legislation providing for universal military service, although never before or since had circumstances offered a better opportunity to slip that unpopular item through the Congress. Unification of the services was achieved while he was still in office, but only in a form that represented a triumph for the navy and a defeat for the army; a unification which, as Eisenhower himself ruefully acknowledged, was "too much form and too little substance." The army plan proposed a single consolidated Department of Armed Forces under a single civilian secretary; each of the three services (army, navy, and air force) would be commanded by a military officer who at least in military operations would be autonomous. The status of the marines was not clear (it was whispered that Eisenhower would not be unhappy if the corps were to be abolished) and the navy feared its aviation would be appropriated by the air force. The navy plan envisaged coordination of the services rather than their consolidation. Forrestal had done his homework well. He had got an old friend, Ferdinand Eberstadt, like himself a Wall Street investment banker, to draft a comprehensive report that advocated a civilian secretary of defense supervising three civilian secretaries who would exercise administrative control over the three services; further, the Eberstadt plan called for a National Security Council, a Central Intelligence Agency, a National Security Resources Board, and a Central Research and Development Agency. These were lollipops to titillate the Congress, but Forrestal had even more cunning inducements. The War Department, he warned the Senate Committee on Military Affairs, proposed a staggering concentration of power "which I believe is beyond the capacity of any one man to use." This comment was relayed to Eisenhower, who retorted that if Forrestal were correct, then no one man had the capacity to assume the presidency of the United States.

The exchange may have won Eisenhower points with the public and with reporters facing a deadline, but at best the chief of staff was being cute. For as Eisenhower would in time discover, the presidency of the United States is indeed too big a job for one man. In fairness to both men, Forrestal's remarks before the Senate committee had been inadequately reported to Eisenhower. Forrestal had spoken of a burden of power "which I believe is beyond the capacity of any one man to use, and [it is] certainly beyond his capacity to obtain and digest the knowledge [upon which] its use could be based." Since a single secretary of the armed services could never master his job and, in consequence, would be obliged to yield much of his authority to his military advisers, Forrestal warned that such a man "would have authority without knowledge, and authority without knowledge must inevitably become impotent." To clinch his argument, he pointed out that this path would lead to the end of civilian control over the military.

It would be hard to find in such precise form a better prediction of what was to happen when more power was generated in the Pentagon. Since even under Forrestal's more cautious plan the influence of the military would too soon be monstrously swollen and the generals and admirals would be able to bloat their tax-supported enterprise until it had outstripped America's five largest corporations combined, able to prescribe exorbitant weapon systems, able to recommend and persevere in a calamitous foreign policy, it is as well the republic was never saddled with the potentially more dangerous proposal advocated by the army and its chief of staff.

Judged by his control over his own concerns, then, General Eisenhower was plainly not an unqualified success as chief of staff. Most of the time he was away from the Pentagon—making speeches or ceremonial journeys, inspecting army bases here and abroad, testifying before committees of the Congress—in short, behaving like a politician. Hanson Baldwin of the *New York Times*, reviewing Eisenhower's tour of duty after six months, was able to report that he had delivered no less than twenty-six speeches since his appointment. Moreover, he had been out of Washington for one reason or another more than half the time he had been nominally in command of the army; nor would his pace abate in the months to come. A story circulated in Washington, finally appearing in print, that soon after Forrestal had taken office as the first secretary of defense he called a meeting of the War Council—the three service secretaries and the three chiefs of staff—which began like this:

FORRESTAL: I expect each of you gentlemen to attend every meeting of this body.

EISENHOWER: I presume if we are out of town we can send our deputies. (*A pause. Everyone looks at Forrestal.*)

FORRESTAL: I expect each of you gentlemen to attend every meeting of this body.

EISENHOWER: I had to break a very important engagement to get here this morning. (*A pause.*)

FORRESTAL: I expect each of you gentlemen to attend every meeting of this body. (*The meeting proceeds.*)

Whether or not the tale was true—and it almost certainly was not— it truthfully suggested an attitude, a set of mind about Eisenhower that was common enough among the senior officials in Washington during the late 1940s. Eisenhower could easily afford to shrug the gossip off. After all, the senior officials in Washington at the time were all Democrats, and since he had in mind his candidature as a Republican when the time was propitious, he regarded most of them with an icy distaste.

Eisenhower's third major concern as he entered upon this stage of his career, his transformation from evangel of international cooperation to cold warrior, was essential to his future. There were volunteers aplenty quite prepared to take at face value his claim that he was only "a simple soldier" and therefore zealous to set him straight about Russia. Forrestal never lost an opportunity to acquaint the chief of staff with the new postwar policy. Indeed Eisenhower would later acknowledge Forrestal's primacy as his augur of hidden Soviet dangers.

Of all his doctrinal texts, Forrestal's prize was an eight-thousand-word telegram sent to the State Department on February 22, 1946, by George Kennan, the minister-counselor at the American embassy in Moscow. The dispatch came quickly to Forrestal's attention. He pasted a copy of it in his diary—"it was exactly the kind of [analysis]," wrote Walter Millis, "for which Forrestal had looked vainly elsewhere in the government"— and made other copies of it, as Kennan learned later, "required reading for hundreds, if not thousands, of higher officers in the armed services." To Forrestal, Kennan was an unknown cog in the vast federal bureaucracy, but an Office of Naval Intelligence sleuth presently informed him that Kennan was a hard-liner who had for too long been muffled by the American ambassador, Harriman, whose opinions of the Soviet Union were considered, at least by the ONI, to be too gentle. A hard-liner Kennan certainly was at that time; he was on record as having strongly opposed any American "moral support to the Russian cause" in June 1941, just after the Germans attacked Russia. The long telegram that so delighted Forrestal was, as Kennan himself would later acknowledge, "exactly like one of those primers put out by alarmed congressional committees or by the Daughters of the American Revolution, designed to arouse the citizenry to the dangers of the Communist conspiracy."

This bugaboo made Kennan's reputation. It aroused official Washington. It aroused the journalists to whom it was accommodatingly leaked. But if it aroused the chief of staff he gave no sign.

Already on February 9, in an election speech which, Brooks Atkinson had reported to the *New York Times,* was "spoken in a conversational tone," Premier Stalin had declared that the Soviet Union must rebuild the areas devastated by war and must undertake "three more five-year plans, I should think, if not more," in order to build the kind of industrial plant that could annually produce sixty million tons of steel. Only by such a "mighty upsurge of the national economy," he had argued, could the USSR be secure when, as he expected would occur, the capitalist world would split into "two hostile camps" and a war break out between them. This speech, in which it was hard to find any suggestion of Soviet aggression, nevertheless had alarmed many officials in Washington. William O. Douglas, justice of the Supreme Court, had told Forrestal the speech seemed to him "the declaration of World War III." The next day, February 10, a Sunday, Winston Churchill had interrupted his holiday in Florida to fly to Washington for a conference with President Truman about the speech he had been invited to deliver at Fulton, Missouri. That address of March 5 is remembered today chiefly because it was the occasion for the first widely broadcast use in the English tongue of Dr. Goebbels's helpful term "iron curtain." There were, however, more interesting aspects of the talk. There was the lofty tone with which Churchill reminded his audience that "God has willed" that the United States, not some "Communist or neo-Fascist state," be lord of the atomic bomb, and that the "English-speaking peoples" were the ones to put the world in order again. There was also the more ominous passage in which he remarked that it was not "our duty *at this time* [emphasis added], when difficulties are so numerous, to interfere forcibly in the internal affairs of countries whom we have not conquered in war"—and there was the Anglo-American threat of war against the Soviet Union, the declaration of Cold War. (In London, the Labour government hastily dissociated itself from Churchill's speech.)

But still General Eisenhower, chief of staff of the U.S. Army, maintained his composure. Still he kept hammering away at the thesis that progress toward lasting peace could be achieved only through "organized international cooperation, mutual international understanding, and progressive international disarmament." A perverse and lonely voice. On June 2 Eisenhower told a press conference in Chicago that American relations with the Soviet Union were improving. It was odd.

To be sure, up to this point Eisenhower's own concerns had been paramount. He had been speculating about politics, selecting his speaking engagements with care (most of them had been on the campuses of colleges or universities), and managing to include in his extensive travels a trip to the Far East. It would be imprecise to say that the question of politics intruded itself during this journey, for in one way or another politics was the salient consideration from start to finish. In the President's view the most important reason for the trip was political: he was vexed with Secretary of State Byrnes, wished to know if General Marshall would accept the post in Byrnes's stead, and used the chief of staff as his courier to convey the request with maximum secrecy. Truman's vexation was likewise political: he judged that Byrnes, during the conference of foreign ministers at Moscow in December 1945, had not kept the President sufficiently informed of his transactions and had, moreover, too easily reached agreement on some of the points at issue between the U.S. and USSR. "I'm tired of babying the Soviets," Truman snapped to Byrnes. The word went out that Byrnes was appeasing the Russians, and *appeaser* was, of course, one of the most fearful counterwords of that fearful era; Byrnes's tenure as secretary of state was plainly approaching its end.

On May 9, 1946, General Eisenhower arrived at Nanking. He lunched with Generalissimo and Madame Chiang, he conferred privately with General Marshall. The answer was yes, Marshall would serve as the President wished.

Next day General Eisenhower flew to Tokyo, where he was greeted by the resident supreme commander, his old friend Douglas MacArthur. The two men had not seen each other in more than six years. Then one had been the other's aide, with rank as lieutenant colonel; now both held permanent rank as General of the Army. To witness this remarkable reunion of the nation's two most celebrated heroes the reporters pressed forward, eager to overhear an exchange that might warrant inclusion in the history books.

Eisenhower said, "Well, Mac, how are you?"

"It's good to see you again," said MacArthur.

That evening it was politics again, and for long into the night. The MacArthurs laid on a dinner party for the chief of staff—General MacArthur at one end of a long table, his lady at the other end, General Eisenhower at his right, and two or three dozen senior officers filling the spaces in between. "Quick as dinner was over," Eisenhower later told an acquaintance, "he just said, 'Good night, gentlemen,' and took me and we sat in his library till about one o'clock." They were two heroes with a single thought. You must run for President, MacArthur told Eisenhower. Not me, retorted Eisenhower; why don't *you* do it? Oh, I'm too old, MacArthur answered, and once again pressed Eisenhower to run. So it went, Eisenhower recalled, "from about ten-thirty till about one o'clock." What did it all mean? "I told the story to two or three political friends," Eisenhower remarked later, "and they said, 'Look, here was a man that just wanted *you* to come out flatly to run MacArthur for the presidency." If such was indeed MacArthur's motive, he had woefully misjudged his man.

While he was still chief of staff, Eisenhower spoke publicly of his own political availability in ways that reflected the inner conflict he had yet to resolve. On September 28, 1946, he was back at Frankfurt for a brief visit to his old headquarters. Slowly and emphatically he said: "There is no possibility of my ever being connected with any political office." Yet on July 4, 1947, speaking to a group of reporters at Vicksburg, Mississippi, he said: "I haven't the effrontery to say I wouldn't be President. No one has asked me to. I do say flatly, completely, and with all the force I've got, I haven't a political ambition in the world. I want nothing to do with politics."

Ten days earlier, announcement had been made that the trustees of Columbia University had offered him, and he had accepted, an appointment as president of the university, to take effect as soon as his successor as chief of staff could be named.

Here, from any point of view, was a most peculiar decision. For Dwight Eisenhower to be offered an important post in the academic community was so improbable that at once a delectable rumor sprang up, took root, and flourished like a weed. The trustees of Columbia, so ran the tale, had hilariously blundered. One member of the committee appointed to select a president had remarked, toward the end of a long and fruitless discussion, "What about Eisenhower?" Amid general if weary enthusiasm, another trustee had volunteered to send a letter of invitation next day. Off went the letter to General Eisenhower, to be promptly accepted, while all the time the other trustees had imagined the invitation was intended for Milton Eisenhower, the president of Kansas State College.

The facts of the matter are more interesting. The trustees of the university, like most such directorates, were men of substance who had made their mark as financiers or industrialists. The need of the hour, as they saw it, was a man of executive ability who would be able to raise funds for the big sprawling educational plant for which they were responsible. Intellectual distinction concerned them not a whit. Thomas J. Watson, the chief executive officer of International Business Machines, was chairman of the committee charged with finding a successor to Nicholas Murray Butler, the aging ornament of the Republican party—he had been its candidate for Vice President in 1912—who had presided over Columbia for more than half a century. Watson wanted Eisenhower—Dwight Eisenhower, no mistake—and back in March 1946 he had invited the chief of staff to speak at the seventy-fifth anniversary celebration of the Metropolitan Museum of Art. It was the sort of public appearance Eisenhower and his advisers favored, one that enabled the soldier to drape himself in the robes of peace and its seemlier pursuits. Watson reserved several rooms at the Waldorf-Astoria for the chief of staff and his considerable retinue. The ceremonies at the Metropolitan took place on April 2. That night, back at the hotel, Watson unveiled his proposition.

Eisenhower was inured to such offers. Even before his return from Germany they had flooded in upon him, most of them commercial, many of them honeyed with huge salaries and other financial inducements, none of them fit for a man who took very seriously his role as a world figure. This one he was inclined to reject out of hand. It entailed residence in New York City, which both he and his wife hated; he knew nothing of universities in general or of Columbia in particular; better Watson should consider his younger brother Milton for the job.

Watson did not repine. His committee agreed that another committee should be formed, of faculty members, to press the search for a president, for the faculty should always be led to suppose that its opinions were eagerly solicited and carried much weight in such a matter, but for his part he maintained the pressure on Eisenhower. Soon they were Ike and Tom. A little later, and Watson had discovered that the magic word to use in bringing Eisenhower round was duty. After that it was all downhill. Early in June 1947 Watson met Eisenhower at West Point to apply the decisive leverage. By that time the general had already discussed the matter with Truman; he was able to tell Watson that he could report to Columbia by March 1 next.

After the thing had been announced Eisenhower was constrained, somewhat sheepishly, to justify his conduct to old friends. Yes, he wrote Swede Hazlett, he and Mamie loathed New York, but he assumed they could find "a country place somewhere up in the Connecticut area" and they confidently expected to live at a comfortable remove from Morningside Heights throughout the year—"except possibly for the deep winter months," when presumably they could hire a suite in some midtown hotel. "I know nothing about the workings of a great university," he confessed, "and am certainly far from being an 'educator,'"—so far, indeed, that, in dictating the phrase he himself put the self-conscious quotation marks around the word educator—yet he fancied that Columbia would afford him a convenient platform from which he could exhort the nation. "From my viewpoint," he confided to Hazlett, "going to Columbia is merely to change the location of my headquarters."

It should be added that money was never a particular consideration in Eisenhower's choice of Columbia. By special legislation he held permanent rank as General of the Army and so was assured an annual income of nearly nineteen thousand dollars, the full-time services of an aide, and other such pleasant perquisites as free medical care and free hospitalization. To be president of Columbia commanded another twenty-five thousand a year. This was good money for the time and the place, but there was more to come, a great deal more.

As Eisenhower's tour of duty at the Pentagon drew to a close, book and periodical publishers began to lust after his memoirs of the war. There were at least two offers of half a million dollars, but as Eisenhower would later put it rather primly, "money alone had no temptation." Still, it must have been useful to know what the market would bear. Of the book publishers, Douglas M. Black, president of Doubleday, may be said to have had the pole position, for he was also one of Columbia's trustees and had met the general in that connection. He and William Robinson, a business officer of the *New York Herald Tribune,* joined forces to approach Eisenhower with the argument that he owed to history an authentic account of his campaigns, the more so since so many books filled with error had been written about the war in Europe by lesser folk for catchpenny purposes. This reasoning had perhaps more force than the two publishers realized: Eisenhower had been sorely nettled by some of the war memoirs, particularly by Harry Butcher's *My Three Years with Eisenhower* because in so many passages it provided glimpses of the private Eisenhower and therefore amounted to disloyalty by a member of his official family. In consequence, Eisenhower was easily persuaded, but on what terms was he to undertake the job? Most conveniently there now appeared the wealthy Joseph E. Davies, who was, among other things, senior partner of Davies, Richberg, Beebe, Busick & Richardson, a Washington law firm of impressive amperage. Davies was anxious to do whatever he could for his old friend Ike—about whose political future he still harbored vain Democratic hopes—and so from his commodious yacht, anchored off Palm Beach, he sent instructions to Donald Richberg to smooth all wrinkles from Eisenhower's brow. Richberg, formerly a powerful figure of the New Deal, moved with confidence through the bureaucratic wilderness of the federal government; before long Eisenhower could write Davies that "Don is collaborating with the Treasury Department and with the Doubleday people to see how a tentative instrument can be drawn up that can in no wise be interpreted either as a bona fide sale or as a 'contract for services.'"

What Richberg emerged with was less an instrument than a spacious loophole through the tax laws, whereby Eisenhower's memoir could be defined as a capital asset, and any moneys received by him taxed only as the profit from the sale of such capital goods. Of this remarkable device, which operated almost exclusively on his behalf, Eisenhower would later remark blandly that he was informed "this had been common practice" and was "approved procedure by the Treasury and the Internal Revenue Service," in which case every other general who wrote his account of the war was unconscionably gouged by the tax assessors, and so were at least two Presidents. The arithmetic of Eisenhower's first commercial literary effort was this:

Fee received	$635,000
Net, after 25% capital gains taxes	476,250

In theory, such tender treatment by the Internal Revenue Service was possible only because Eisenhower was a nonprofessional writer whose book was the end product of experiences accumulated, as in a piggy bank, over a lifetime. Yet the three volumes that later appeared under his name would be taxed according to normal procedures.

At all events, Eisenhower did not accept the presidency of Columbia University because he needed the money. He was a reasonably wealthy man.

Nevertheless, as the day came near when he would take over at Columbia, Eisenhower grew fretful over the cost of a university president's wardrobe. Watson had arranged for him to be outfitted by a custom tailor, and Eisenhower was consternated by the rich variety of gent's fancy clothes in which he was apparently expected to garb himself. A pearl-gray waistcoat! "Could you imagine me in such a thing?" he complained to Watson. He flatly refused to invest in a cutaway coat. Watson percipiently offered to foot the expense of Eisenhower's entire wardrobe. Eisenhower said he would accept only the formal evening wear as a gift, but in the end Watson paid out the full sum ($1,550.40) for evening clothes and overcoat, dinner clothes, three sack suits, a sack coat, and a pair of trousers.

But before he could savor the relative freedom of mufti at Columbia, Eisenhower had to serve out his time as chief of staff, and in one way or another politics continued to intrude. He inched closer to a consentient and respectable political position in regard to the Soviet Union. At first his tone was reproachful, as though he were more hurt than angered by the Russians, but before long he was plainly attacking the Soviets and being roundly applauded for it. To political observers the shift of ground and the cheers seemed clear enough: Eisenhower was taking aim on the next Republican national convention.

There were, however, annoyances. First came a flurry over the Morgenthau Plan, which everyone assumed had long since been given a decent burial. Yet the corpse had been exhumed for a belated autopsy. Fred Smith, the man who during the war had been a kind of press agent for Secretary Morgenthau, published an article on the origins of the plan in which he wrote: "Actually, it was General Dwight D. Eisenhower who launched the project." In a time when the Cold War was inflaming partisan passions, the sense of this revelation was that Eisenhower was a muttonhead too dense to foresee that the fearless, sturdy Germans were the first line of defense against the godless hordes of bolshevism, and that German industrial might must at all pains be maintained as a bulwark to protect western civilization. The foul imputation had to be nailed at once. Eisenhower denied it, to an audience of journalists at the National Press Club, but still it survived, a whisper circulating in the subterranean caverns of right-wing Republican obduracy. Late in 1947 General Lucius Clay, in Washington for a brief visit from Germany, loyally added the weight of his authority to stifle the rumor, but was it dead? Only the months ahead would tell.

Without doubt the old guard of brass-collar Republicans viewed Eisenhower's tentative progress toward politics with dismay. What kind of a Republican was he, anyway? Was he a rock-ribbed conservative or was he some kind of a meaching, so-called liberal Republican? For that matter, was he a Republican entirely? And whatever he was, where did he get the gall to assume he could casually saunter up and snatch the presidential nomination from professionals who had spent their adult years proving their Republican mettle in fierce sectarian struggle?

The question of Eisenhower's political affiliation remained obscure; the general himself managed to keep it more secret even than the time and place of the cross-Channel invasion of Europe. The President knew nothing of this momentous matter: as late as the fall of 1947 Truman authorized his secretary of the army, Kenneth B. Royall, to tell Eisenhower that should he wish to be the Democratic party's candidate for President, he had only to lift a finger and Truman would work for his nomination and would himself agree to run as Vice President if Eisenhower wanted him on the ticket. The proposal surpassed mere humility. It was abject, almost inconceivably so, and it provided a startling measure of Truman's own estimate of Democratic chances in the election of 1948, while it was still a year in the future. The whole affair would be incredible save for the unimpeachable testimony of Royall, a disinterested witness. Or was it a cunning Democratic snare set to entrap a "simple soldier"? At all events, Eisenhower promptly moved to extricate himself. He wanted no part of politics, he told Royall, but would appreciate some advice as to how he might get the politicians to believe him.

That took care of overtures from the Democrats, at least temporarily. There remained the entrenched Republicans. In December 1947 came evidence of their powerful opposition, and also of Eisenhower's artless candor when approaching, unbriefed, a prickly political question.

The occasion was a dinner at the 1925 F Street Club, one of the most expensive and exclusive resorts in Washington, given by a pair of rich

Pennsylvanians who had invited the governor of Pennsylvania, the state's congressmen, and a number of its most influential industrialists to meet some of the party's national spokesmen—and General Eisenhower. The company included some exceedingly hard-boiled eggs—men like Joseph R. Grundy, a coal and oil magnate who was the state's Republican boss, and G. Mason Owlett, head of the Pennsylvania Manufacturers Association and a Republican national committeeman; executives from the big Pennsylvania steel mills and railway companies; and a clutch of senators —Edward Martin of Pennsylvania, Styles Bridges of New Hampshire, Warren Austin of Vermont, and the two most substantial Senate leaders of all, Arthur Vandenberg of Michigan, the party's leader in building, with the Democrats, a bipartisan foreign policy, and Robert A. Taft of Ohio, the darling of party stalwarts all over the country, Mr. Republican himself, son of a Republican President and determined to take his own place in the White House. This was solely and exclusively a political occasion. Eisenhower was on strange turf; a wise man would have listened and grinned and listened; not Eisenhower.

Eisenhower ventured to preach a little homily, complete with moral uplift. The ladies having withdrawn after dinner and left the gentlemen to their coffee, tobacco, and spirits, the talk turned to the postwar inflation, one of the many formidable woes afflicting the Truman administration at the time. What to do about it? Eisenhower deplored it. Personal sacrifices, he argued, were demanded of everyone if the spiral of inflation were to be reversed.

Taft wondered if he had more specific counsel.

Well, yes, Eisenhower had a suggestion. Industry, because it was more cohesive than labor and less wracked by politics than the government, should set the standard. Let one leading industrialist—say, Benjamin Fairless, president of United States Steel—announce that for the next year his company would raise no prices, risk a year in the red if necessary, and let him bid other corporations to follow his lead. A wonderful example! Labor, the politicians, the general public—all would do likewise.

Arthur Krock, Washington correspondent of the *New York Times*, who was present and listening with intense interest, observed that the senators "were not impressed" and that the Pennsylvania businessmen and politicians "were hostile . . . and thoroughly approved the heckling" to which Eisenhower was subjected, especially by Taft and Vandenberg.

Next day someone made it his business to tattle a highly colored account of the incident, and someone saw to it that the tale reached Fulton Lewis, Jr., a radio gossip. This Lewis had no particular passion for accuracy, but over the years he had pieced together an audience—never very numerous but warmly devoted—made up mostly of the entrenched right wing but including quite a few who treasured his polemics as they treasured W. C. Fields. Lewis painted Eisenhower red. He had Eisenhower proposing that the government "put the pressure" on "the big industrial leaders . . . to reduce all prices for a period of two or three years, so as to eliminate all profits whatsoever," and, if the industrialists jibbed, that a confiscatory tax be levied on all corporation profits and the proceeds used to subsidize a reduction of prices "by force of government."

Considering how quickly such mischief would permeate the business community, it was superb psychological warfare. Had Eisenhower repudiated the Democrats? So now had the Republican right wing repudiated Eisenhower. The newspaper clatter that followed the Lewis broadcast— What had Eisenhower really said? Is he a candidate? How did Taft tell him off? Was it a technical knockout? Who was bleeding at the bell?— found Eisenhower in a cold fury over what he regarded as a flagrant breach of good manners. The private Eisenhower, in relaxed palaver over the brandy with friends, is all at once publicly pilloried. Politics! To hell with it!

A week or two later Eisenhower was presented with a splendid opportunity to declare himself. An admirer in New Hampshire, Leonard Finder, publisher of the *Manchester* (N.H.) *Union-Leader,* wrote to tell the general that a slate of delegates pledged to him would be entered in the presidential primary to be held in New Hampshire on March 9, 1948. Finder enclosed a front page of his newspaper, on which was spread an editorial urging election of the Eisenhower delegates. Presumably he regarded all this as helpful to Eisenhower, since the political weathercocks are most sensitive to the New Hampshire primaries, believing the winner of them to have shown early foot and good promise of going all the way.

Eisenhower studied his answer for nine days.

Long since he had (by his own account) told Truman he would not oppose him in 1948; more recently he had told Truman he would not stand in his stead in 1948; apparently 1948 was not to be his year. In January all signs pointed to a Republican victory in the fall, and of the two leading candidates for the Republican nomination, Taft would be fifty-nine years old and Thomas E. Dewey, the party's nominee in 1944, would be forty-six: each of an age to stand for a second term after he had won a first. In eight years Eisenhower would himself be sixty-six, too old, most politicians would agree, for a man to make his first campaign for the presidency, especially a man who had no experience of practical politics. It seemed, then, that to declare himself unavailable in 1948 meant to foreclose all possibility of ever being President. And yet . . .

A National Draft Eisenhower League was in business and boasting a popular strength that owed nothing to the professional politicians. Eisenhower for President offices were operating in several states and money was flowing in to them. The mail daily unloaded at the Pentagon post office bore witness to a widespread public demand for the general's name on the ballot, some ballot. Every month in the newspapers there appeared the results of one poll or another—those of Elmo Roper and Dr. George Gallup were most frequently cited—to demonstrate that Eisenhower was first choice of the voters, whether Democratic or Republican. And yet . . .

Precisely what the private Eisenhower privately thought may never be known, having in all likelihood never been committed to paper, or if so, quickly destroyed. The terms of the debate he carried on with himself on a more public level are defined in letters he wrote to Beetle Smith, his brother Milton, and others, and in the writings of such close cronies as Kevin McCann. All such evidence must, however, be discounted as having been quite consciously spread on the record for history. On that basis, it is of some interest. Eisenhower wished posterity to believe that he was utterly without political ambition, that he neither desired to be President nor considered himself particularly fitted for the office, and that he would hearken to a summons to the White House only if it came as a clear call of duty. How clear a call? To his brother Milton he had characterized it as "a terrific popular pressure" which would cause the professional politicians instantly to cease their politicking and "respond to such a general sentiment." In short, if he could be President by popular acclamation, all well and good, but he recognized that "under the political party system of this country" such an advent to the White House "would certainly be nothing less than a miracle."

Putting the possibility of a miracle to one side, General Eisenhower buckled down to the task of drafting an answer to Finder. Several revisions incorporated the suggestions of several advisers. At length on January 22, 1948, it was ready and Eisenhower, if not satisfied, had resigned himself to his decision. "I still don't believe that many people want a soldier for President," he told McCann. "I'm trying to be honest and realistic about it." The final draft was shown to Forrestal, who urged a bit more flattery of the professional politicians. A sentence was added: "Politics is a profession; a serious, complicated and, in its true sense, a noble one." The letter was retyped and mailed. It was long and diffuse, showing unmistakably how Eisenhower had agonized over his internal debate, but embedded in the dense verbiage were a few lucid, mortuary phrases: "I am not available for and could not accept nomination to high political office. . . . my decision to remove myself completely from the political scene is definite and positive. . . . I could not accept nomination even under the remote circumstances that it were tendered me."

Another letter, unpublicized, went to William H. Burnham, a Wall

Street investment banker in his forties who was an officer and leading spirit of the National Draft Eisenhower League. He was told in cordial terms to suspend his efforts. Burnham and his associates regretfully switched to the support of Harold Stassen, a former governor of Minnesota who was young (thirty-nine), regarded as progressive, and a refreshing new personality on the national scene. The Eisenhower boom of 1948 was finished.

Journalists and cynics settled down to see how long it would take for another boom to be organized and put into marching order.

On Saturday, February 7, General of the Army Dwight D. Eisenhower, having completed his tour of duty as chief of staff, turned the responsibilities of the office over to Omar Bradley. At once he went on terminal leave and was soon intensively at work on his book, *Crusade in Europe.*

The Eisenhoverian method of writing a book was unusual, if not unique. He began by dictating a chapter to one secretary; while this was being transcribed he dictated a second chapter to a second secretary; the first chapter was in time handed to an army historian at the Pentagon to be checked as to its facts; Eisenhower would meanwhile have turned to a third secretary to dictate a third chapter; before long he would be revising in longhand the corrected first chapter; and so the work proceeded, twelve or more hours a day, five or six days a week, while the machinery of the assembly line thumped and pounded, and at least four persons besides the author labored overtime, and several others labored part time. Of these others the two most important were his two remarkably competent editors, Kenneth McCormick, editor-in-chief at Doubleday, and Joseph Barnes, foreign news editor at the *Herald Tribune.*

Eisenhower had had some experience, during his years as MacArthur's aide, in the composition of cadenced fustian, and unquestionably could, had he chosen, have perpetrated a volume of shimmering prose studded with eye-popping exposures of celebrated soldiers and statesmen. To the contrary, he modeled his style on that of General Grant, whose memoirs have been too little read in this century but which stand as an enviable example of simplicity and straightforward vigor. Eisenhower could have chosen no better master. Objectivity and understatement have great force; plain words do well. Whenever Eisenhower was disposed to question these truths, McCormick and Barnes were at hand to reassure him and later, as required, to curry his tangled syntax.

The author could well be proud of his work.

CHAPTER THREE

In Mufti

ON SUNDAY, MAY 2, Dwight and Mamie Eisenhower left Quarters Number One at Fort Myer and were driven in an open automobile past the troops of the ceremonial Third Infantry Regiment, an outfit originally mustered by the First Continental Congress. The general took a salute and snapped his own in acknowledgment. At the gates of the fort a band played "Ruffles and Flourishes." A few hundred yards beyond Fort Myer the Eisenhowers alighted from the army automobile, climbed into their own, a closed sedan, and were driven away, away from the regular army, away from thirty-seven years of army life, away from all that a professional soldier can ever dream of having accomplished.

There must have been a sense of relief, and there must have been a wrench. For more than six years General Eisenhower had been at or very close to the point of greatest tension, the focus of the decisions that governed the history of the world. To be sure, he had not as chief of staff taken a leading part in the strategic thrust and parry of the Cold War, nor even so much of a part as he has since been credited with.* He had

* Most of the accounts that deal at first or second hand with the formulation of policy during that time are agreed that a conference of great moment took place around President Truman's desk on August 15, 1946. Present were Undersecretary of State Dean Acheson, Secretary of the Navy Forrestal, Undersecretary of War Kenneth Royall, the Chiefs of Staff, and several lesser figures. At issue was the response by the government of the U.S. to a proposal of the Soviet government made to Turkey, with copies to Britain and the U.S., that the USSR assume a share of the responsibility for defense of the Dardanelles, the straits between the Black Sea and the Aegean Sea. In Washington this suggestion was viewed as a demand, a Soviet threat to seize the Dardanelles, to dominate both Turkey and Greece, and finally to assume hegemony over all the Middle East, with its vast reserves of petroleum. As a consequence, Acheson urged that the Russian initiative be resisted "at all costs," even though it might take the country on a course that "could lead to war."

In his own memoir, Acheson places Eisenhower as sitting beside him during this conference. Joseph M. Jones, in his authoritative account, does likewise. Cabell Phillips, author of a study of the Truman presidency, also includes Eisenhower in the group sitting by the President's desk and quotes an admiring remark Eisenhower had next to nothing to do with the formulation of the Truman Doctrine, or with the conception or elaboration of the European Recovery Program, more familiarly known as the Marshall Plan. Still, he had shared in the moving and the shaking of the world, and now he was bound for a neo-classic mansion of stuffy propriety adjoining a grimy campus on Morning-side Heights. It was a long step down from the dizzy summit to which he was accustomed and, if it brought him more relief than regret, General Eisenhower was indeed unique.

A party of reporters and photographers awaiting his arrival attracted a throng of the idle and curious who stroll a city's streets on a Sunday in springtime. The Eisenhower automobile rolled up at 4:35 P.M. The general shook hands with an embarrassed small boy, the son of a professor of history at Columbia College. He spoke to a small girl, who was also shy. He strode across the pavement and into the house of the president of Columbia, recently vacated by Nicholas Murray Butler. He was, so to speak, home.

For how long?

Now began the most unsuitable of Eisenhower's lifetime tasks. For him to attempt to be a university president was absurd. It was wrong all around: wrong for the trustees to have selected him, wrong for him to have accepted, wrong for the faculties and staff of the university to have to abide him, wrong for the graduate and undergraduate scholars to have the atmosphere of their academic community unsettled, wrong even for those alumni who were proud that their school was associated with a cele-brated world figure. It was worse than wrong, it was cruel. It forced a national hero of stature and integrity to labor in ill-fitting harness; it sub-jected him to the pitiless sarcastic barbs of sharpshooters all across the country; on the campus of Columbia he was reduced to a standing joke. Perhaps the mildest of the gibes had one dean advising another to send Eisenhower no memorandum longer than one page since if he was obliged to read more his lips would get tired.

The most compassionate judgment of Eisenhower at Columbia is that he was not a bad president because he was no president at all.

During his first month on campus Eisenhower spent some of his time

---

made to Truman after a "masterful" dissertation by the President on the strategic significance of the area.

All these reports—and very likely there are others—are vivid and circumstantial. They share one fault. General Eisenhower was not there. On August 14 he was in Panama. He dined there, spent the night there, and on August 15 was carried by air-plane to Mexico City. After a parade under triumphal arches decorated in his honor he was taken to the U.S. embassy, where, after a ceremonial banquet, he spent the night.

attempting to adjust to his strange new duties: conferring with the trustees, meeting the officers of the university and the deans of the twenty graduate schools, having his own office moved from the second to the first floor of the Low Library in order, as he would later put it, that "both students and faculty might have direct and easy access to their president," prowling about the twenty-six-acre plant of the university, sometimes guided, sometimes footloose, always bemused. Accommodation did not come easily. The faculties of the university had, by and large, been aghast when Eisenhower's selection was announced—a man with no academic training or background and, in their view, a man without even a proper education; certainly a man of no intellectual attainment—but they were nonetheless quite prepared to welcome him with a generous heart. Frank D. Fackenthal, a kindly man who had been provost and acting president, and who had been one of those favored by the faculty committee to become president, was gracious and cooperative. "The general didn't feel the need of my help at all," Fackenthal later recalled. "The idea was that I would be upstairs in the old president's office, available, and I was—but the general never sent for me."

Academic people seemed to experience difficulty in getting to Eisenhower's office. The general had brought with him from Washington Kevin McCann, now retired from the army, as assistant to the president, and Major Robert Schulz as administrative aide. In Fackenthal's opinion this was "a tactical mistake." McCann and Schulz were "two delightful fellows, but they had no knowledge of academic affairs. . . . Their ability to make the wrong appointments, either for speaking or consultation, was very great. . . . They just didn't get the feel of the university."

Meanwhile Eisenhower was no slave to office routine. A month before he left Washington he had been invited south to play golf at Augusta National by William Robinson of the *New York Herald Tribune*. (They were now Bill and Ike.) There he had met some mighty good fellows— good golf companions, good bridge players—who would prove to be most loyal allies in the years ahead. One of the best was Clifford Roberts, a partner in the firm of Reynolds & Company, investment bankers. (They were soon Cliff and Ike.) On his last Tuesday at Fort Myer, April 27, Eisenhower had remembered to write Bill Robinson requesting that he arrange for a foursome at Blind Brook, a tolerably exclusive country club in Westchester County, north of New York City. Thereafter, on Wednesdays and Saturdays, Eisenhower regularly played golf with Bill Robinson, Cliff Roberts, and either Robert Woodruff of the Coca-Cola Company or W. Alton (Pete) Jones of Cities Service Oil Company. All good fellows. If the subject of politics was ever mentioned, on links or in locker room, it may be doubted that any partiality was expressed on behalf of the Democrats.

Certainly politics persisted as an item on Eisenhower's agenda. In a season filled with national political conventions the pressure was inevitable. Early in June the results of another poll were published: Eisenhower was still the first choice of voters of both parties. On June 7, when he officially took over as the thirteenth president of Columbia and greeted reporters in his office, he had to fend off the compulsory questions about politics ("I think I've said all I should") and attempt to guide the catechism back to Morningside Heights ("I'm not so sure of this [educational business]. At least there is one thing about it—I will work. If a fellow works hard, he can't go too far wrong"). But it was impossible to glue public attention to his professed concern for his post at Columbia. Mail flooded in upon him, pleading that he stand for President, swamping the university's postal facilities. Even granting that some of this torrent was artificially stimulated (some twenty thousand cards, letters, and telegrams were delivered in reponse to an appeal broadcast by another radio gossip, Walter Winchell), it was plain that Eisenhower was everywhere beloved, and that his was the only name that could astound the voters and fetch them to the polling places in great swarms.

How to account for this phenomenon? Politically, Eisenhower was still an enigma. Of the domestic issues perplexing the republic—atomic energy, civil liberties, fair employment practices, wage and price controls, farm price supports, the Taft-Hartley labor legislation, taxation—Eisenhower had spoken not a word. Nor had he so much as hinted as to whether he wore a Democratic label or a Republican one. No matter, the voters still yearned to make him their President. Why so?

A pair of social historians, Dorothy Burne Goebel and Julius Goebel, Jr., had suggested an answer in their essay *Generals in the White House* (1945), a study of American political behavior when the choice before the voters included a general. Their examination of the nine generals who had made it to the White House yielded a couple of useful generalizations. For the Goebels, the fuss over Eisenhower must have been like watching the precipitate in a test tube. Would he demonstrate the validity of what they had written? "To a greater or less extent," they had concluded, "every general who became President owed something to public anxiety that the place be filled by a personage. . . . In revolt against party maneuverings the public voice has turned to military chieftains because they have possessed reputation and have given promise of ideals beyond mere party. . . . In the face of enduring prejudice against the profession of arms the gage of virtue in civil office has been found in the belief that the general's service has been not for party but for country and thus for the people themselves."

No doubt about it, Eisenhower was a personage, and as for ideals, surely he was crammed to the brim with them. Further, he seemed to stand above mere party. Yet further, in 1948 the party maneuvers were so many outrageous subterfuges, ruptures, schisms, and angry caterwaulings, and the public was thoroughly sick of the whole uproar. Democrats had split off to left and right: one faction had tailed after Henry Wallace; another faction, the conservative southerners who would soon be called Dixiecrats, could not stomach Truman's program of civil rights for Negroes and instead chose to found a new party that would, they hoped, attract enough votes to throw the presidential election into the House of Representatives, where by exerting opportune leverage they could control the choice of a safe Democratic President. For their part, the Republicans were split down the middle: the division was between orthodoxy, as personified by Taft, and the soi-disant liberal eastern wing of the party, well financed, well organized, cool, confident, and led by the governor of New York, Thomas E. Dewey. (There were other Republican contenders—Stassen, General MacArthur, and Earl Warren, the governor of California—but they were of less account.)

In retrospect, it is little wonder that the voters cared not a whit whether Eisenhower was Democrat or Republican. Only he seemed not for party but for country and thus for the people. Ranged alongside him, Dewey, Truman, Taft, and the others were so many contentious pygmies. But Eisenhower, having abjured politics, was as like as not out at Blind Brook, concentrating on how best to pitch out of the rough.

The general was probably familiar with the Goebels' prognosis, and unquestionably some of his advisers had read it. (Their book, like his, was published by Doubleday.) The professional politicians may also be presumed to have studied it. At any rate a procession of politicos wended its way up Morningside Heights and into Eisenhower's office in the June days before the Republican convention. Senators and governors arrived by the dozen, most of them Democrats, each fearful for his preferment, each anxious that Eisenhower's name head his ticket. To each the personage grinned and shook his head: No. And daily the grin grew more forced. As the convention was gaveled to order in Philadelphia, Eisenhower lost more of his customary good humor. Had he not five months ago made it quite clear, quite conclusive that he "could not" accept high nomination to political office? Yet now, as the well-oiled Dewey machine moved smoothly toward victory, desperate Republicans working for Taft sought to stigmatize Dewey as the "can't win" candidate; all manner of stratagems were employed to impress Eisenhower into the holy crusade for orthodoxy. Presently Eisenhower refused to answer the telephone calls, read the telegrams, or receive the messengers dispatched from Philadelphia.

If the Republicans had not credited his firm no, he could scarcely censure the Democrats when in their turn they worked themselves into an even richer lather. Their plight, after all, appeared far bleaker. Democrats of every kidney saw Eisenhower as their savior: old-line bosses like Jake Garvey of Chicago and Frank Hague of Jersey City, big city mayors like William O'Dwyer of New York, such diverse southerners as the progressive Senator Claude Pepper of Florida and the conservative Senator Richard Russell of Georgia, two sons of the late President Roosevelt, reform Democrats, labor Democrats, reactionary Democrats, frightened Democrats: they scurried after a piper who had never piped them a note.

Their clamor may have afforded Eisenhower some mirth as he relaxed with his cronies in the locker room of Blind Brook or Deepdale; but in Washington Truman was not amused, he was dismayed by the mounting evidence of what looked like a potential stampede of Democratic delegates to Eisenhower. As the President, Truman had enough strength among those delegates to assure his nomination so long as Eisenhower's name was not presented to the convention. In that event, the hero could easily sweep all before him by acclamation. The silence from 60 Morningside Drive was unsettling: what was Eisenhower up to? Truman concluded he had best move swiftly to prompt a public renunciation from Eisenhower. With the President's approval, an amiable, rotund man, George E. Allen, was sent to New York on the double. Allen had been a kind of court jester in the past two administrations, and during the war Butcher had insinuated him into Eisenhower's circle of friends as well. He was superbly qualified as emissary, but he failed. He was brushed off. Eisenhower was more and more irritated by all the pressures, which he considered impertinences in view of his forthright declaration of January 23. At Truman's request, Secretary of the Army Royall undertook a second overture. Time was running out: Senator Pepper, the chief cheerleader atop the Eisenhower bandwagon, had already telegraphed the sixteen hundred delegates to the Democratic convention an invitation to a special caucus "to pick the ablest and strongest man available" for the party's nomination, one who would ensure "virtual election to the presidency." Everyone knew whom he meant. This foolish and melodramatic intrigue lent a certain urgency to Secretary Royall's telephone call and his consequent parley with Eisenhower. Almost simultaneously Pepper telegraphed Eisenhower to tell him his name would be offered to the delegates whether he consented or not. Eisenhower's temper flashed. The result was not one but two statements: in the first, released by the public relations bureau of the university, Eisenhower said, "I . . . could not accept nomination . . . or participate in a public political contest," and in the second, a reply to

Pepper, he slammed shut the door and locked it tight—"No matter under what terms, conditions, or premises a proposal might be couched, I would refuse to accept the nomination."

If Truman found comfort in these belated pronouncements, so also did some of the professional Republicans. These public-spirited citizens had been badly rattled by the possibility that the hero might somehow be seduced by their opponents. It was one thing to face Harry Truman, the uneasy champion of a splintered Democratic party, but to heave and strain against Eisenhower would, they knew, be an exercise in futility. Like Truman, they had elaborated various stratagems, just in case. One was ham-handed, the other quite elegant.

The first was a ruse from the familiar fetid cesspool that American politicians have for generations contentedly drawn upon. The word was passed—and furtively crept into print—that if Eisenhower were to succumb to Democratic temptations, he and his family would be reviled and abused in every blackguardly way. The Republicans would coax from the oily dirty sludge that lies at the bottom of all political activity a few of the filthier bubbles and explode them so that they would smear the hero and those he most loved. Did he comprehend the possibilities?

He did. For some little time Eisenhower had been aware that he was a central figure of at least one juicy story that had been making its imperishable rounds; friends (they had to be close friends) had deemed it necessary to tell him of another item that featured his wife. His celebrated self-starting temper was of no avail in respect of these tales. They hurt; surely they had contributed to his decision to withdraw from politics; but all things considered, the course dictated by wisdom was to ignore them.

Of General Eisenhower the story that had the liveliest currency was the one that coupled his name with that of Kay Summersby, alleging a long-continuing romantic attachment. In one variation the general was said to have planned to divorce his wife so that he might be free to marry Mrs. Summersby. The tale gathered sustenance from the fact that one of his closest wartime companions had indeed divorced his wife and subsequently married the woman with whom he had struck up an alliance overseas, and yet further sustenance from the fact that at least two high-ranking generals who had served under his command and were known to have been his close friends had been persistently and notoriously faithless to their wives at home. The fact of the Eisenhower-Summersby matter is that the whispers were not true. If those whispers ever had a purpose beyond idle malice, they have long since outlived it. They have, moreover, been sanctified by appearance in newsprint; it is a good bet they will be dully labored over the next few generations by candidates for a Ph.D. in history; they have indeed put on such muscle as they grow older that they will probably survive even the Last Trump.*

The tale to be spread about Mamie Eisenhower was that she suffered from alcoholism. It was equally false but more swinish. The best that can be said for it is that it was so palpably untrue that it was mercifully short-lived.

There was of course a more decorous way of achieving the same end, and the gentlemen of the Republican party no doubt hoped that no one would be obliged to turn his hand to the filth. Perhaps an intermediary could be found who would be able to assure himself and his coadjutors in the party that Eisenhower planned no such demented step as to pledge his incomparable prestige to the Democrats.

On the eve of the Democratic convention Eisenhower met and spent the evening with Edward J. Bermingham, an alumnus of Columbia and a man remarkable for his financial heft and acumen. They had much to talk about and perhaps a greater mutuality of interests than either of them had supposed before they met. Since Bermingham was to play a considerable part in Eisenhower's unfolding future—a part that has been too little noticed in the various authorized accounts of the general's career—it may be useful to have a closer look at him.

Bermingham was two or three years older than Eisenhower. He was a man very well known in his own rarefied circle but almost entirely unknown outside of it. Thus, while he was on terms of easy familiarity with the president or chairman of nearly every substantial bank and corporation west of the Appalachians, the editors of such standard references as *Who's Who in America* seemed never to have heard of him. After serving in the navy during the War of 1914–1918 Bermingham had joined William A. Read & Company, the Wall Street investment bankers. In 1921 he became a partner in the new firm Dillon, Read, and moved to Chicago to direct its affairs there. As a partner in Dillon, Read and later in Lehman Brothers he prospered. Having acquired an ample competence, he retired in 1940. He enjoyed a large company of friends; he owned commodious

---

* Remarks by the late President Truman, posthumously reported, served to revive once again the tale of an Eisenhower-Summersby intrigue. Once again there was gossip about letters allegedly exchanged between Eisenhower and General Marshall on the subject. Forrest C. Pogue, the executive director of the George C. Marshall Research Foundation in Arlington, Virginia, and the author of the definitive volumes of biography of Marshall, has written me that no such correspondence exists in the Marshall papers, and that in his many interviews with General Marshall no mention was ever made of any such matter.

My own belief is that no such correspondence ever existed, since neither man was likely ever to have written a letter on such a subject, even presuming (which I do not) that such a liaison ever existed.

apartments at fashionable addresses in Chicago and New York; he spent the summers on his ranch in Wyoming and the winters on his big farm in Alabama. He was active in political and financial affairs but it was one of his conceits never to accept a position that carried a title with it. Thus he could travel light and avoid unwelcome attention; thus he could work closely with and unofficially be a member of the executive committee of the Republican National Committee yet never be pestered by the questions of political reporters. In fine, Edward Bermingham was an invaluable man for Eisenhower to meet. The two men got along famously.

Presently Bermingham could lay to rest all the hobgoblins that had been fretting his Republican friends: General Eisenhower was safely and conclusively GOP material.

The president of Columbia was still unable, however, to devote himself to his diverse educational responsibilities. What was happening at home and abroad distracted him, and he was encapsulated in his mansion on Morningside Drive, cut off from the pulse and tempo of great affairs. No longer was his desk heaped high with a sheaf of cablegrams from all over the world, with top-secret plans elaborated to cope with this or that contingency. Only from the newspapers and an occasional telephone call to the Pentagon could he learn of the alarming succession of events that had begun with the Anglo-American agreement to integrate their zones of occupation in Germany and to postulate for this so-called Bizonia a federal German government, had continued with a plan to reform West German currency and to extend that reform to West Berlin, and had culminated in the Soviet determination of June 24 to halt all rail traffic between Berlin and the western zones. Now his old friend Lucius Clay was the military administrator on the spot, helping to shape and implementing the decisions taken by the commander in chief and Secretary of State Marshall. Now Eisenhower was out of it.

The United States, said Eisenhower on July 23, "must stand with absolute firmness in Berlin." (There was no evidence of any disposition to the contrary. Truman had nearly a month before issued orders for the massive airlift of supplies to West Berlin; by July 23 nearly four thousand tons of food, clothing, coal, and raw materials were daily airborne to the blockaded city.) At the time Eisenhower spoke to reporters at Governor Dewey's farm near Pawling, New York; they were naturally curious to know whether his conference with the Republican candidate for President would be crowned by Eisenhower's endorsement of Dewey. Eisenhower flashed his grin. "I have not identified myself with any political party," he said, and added, "I will not, at this time, identify myself with any political party."

412

To advise Dewey on U.S. policy in respect of Berlin, to hear occasionally of the teleconferences held among old friends sitting in Frankfurt, London, and Washington, to visit briefly with Beetle Smith when he was able to steal an hour from a hurried journey between Moscow and Washington—these were whiffs of battle smoke for the old warhorse. Before long Eisenhower was dictating anxious letters to Forrestal. On September 27:

> The news over the week end was completely depressing. . . . Frankly, the prospects look darker to me this Monday morning than they have yet and, goodness knows, we have had no really encouraging news since the fall of 1945. . . .
> . . . I believe that the time has come when everyone must begin to think in terms of his possible future duty and be as fully prepared for its performance as is possible.

What justification was there for such a gloomy view? Almost none. At the sessions of the United Nations in Paris, the U.S. and USSR were joined in debate chiefly for purposes of propaganda; elsewhere the horizon was clear. Even Forrestal, notoriously quick to take alarm, was in late September breathing easily. The conclusion is inescapable that Eisenhower, the president of Columbia, was apprehensive that he might have been tucked away and become Eisenhower, the man on the back shelf. Again on October 4, only eight days before he was formally to take the veil as president of Columbia at an impressive convocation on Morningside Heights, he wrote Forrestal that "the current situation [is] one of great gravity" and promised to be on tap in Washington for three or four days at the end of the month. In fact Eisenhower did travel to Washington. He was there on October 30, three days before election day; he visited the Chiefs of Staff; he told Forrestal he was still concerned about the state of world affairs. He may also have been curious about the election, but if so only to wonder how substantial would be the margin of Dewey's victory. "That was quite a day Tuesday," Forrestal wrote Eisenhower, and he was thinking of nothing but the astonishing election in which, in the teeth of all the seers, pundits, psephologists, polltakers, politicians, newspaper editors and reporters, betting commissioners, and other assorted experts, Truman had pulled off the greatest upset of the twentieth century, trounced Dewey, and put the Democrats back in power for another four years.

To a small but perceptive group of Americans, it was at once plain that the big winner in the presidential election of 1948 was Dwight D. Eisenhower. His way to the White House was now open and he could at once start running. He did so start. Furtively, to be sure, with no fanfare, everything on the q.t., but nevertheless he was running hard. Was Truman's victory decided at 9:30 A.M., eastern time, when the news was flashed that the state of Ohio was in the Democratic column? That same morning, in Chicago, Edward Bermingham sent Eisenhower a letter suggesting that he be the guest of honor at a dinner in Chicago to which would be invited a representative cross-section: the president of a railway, the Santa Fe, and presidents of two railway equipment companies, Pullman and Pullman Standard; the publishers of the three Chicago newspapers, John Knight of the *Chicago Daily News,* Colonel Robert (Bertie) McCormick of the *Chicago Tribune,* and Marshall Field of the *Chicago Sun-Times;* General Robert Wood, chairman of the board of directors of Sears Roebuck, and Sewell Avery, chairman of Montgomery Ward; the presidents of Swift and Armour, two of the biggest meat packing concerns; the chairman and president of the First National Bank; the president of Harris Trust & Savings; the president of the Northern Trust Company; officers and directors of International Harvester, the giant farm equipment company, and of Socony Vacuum, a petroleum company; and Robert Hutchins, president of the University of Chicago. Eisenhower at once accepted the invitation, which was only the first of many like it. On Thursday night, November 4, Winthrop Aldrich, president of the Chase Manhattan Bank, entertained him at an exclusive little dinner party at the Racquet & Tennis Club in Manhattan.

He was on his way.

Truman's success over Dewey was the classic example of what has been called Eisenhower luck. Without having lifted a finger, save to cast his own solitary vote for Dewey, Eisenhower found himself a leading candidate for the next presidential election. Dewey was henceforward out of contention; between Eisenhower and the Republican nomination the only considerable adversary was Senator Taft. Moreover, even if the evidence were not conclusive that Eisenhower discreetly seconded the efforts of those who wished him to run in 1952, even if it were true that Eisenhower, left alone, would have spurned presidential ambitions, the presumptive victory of Taft would have given Eisenhower's supporters the chance to appeal to his sense of duty: Taft as President was unthinkable, they would have argued, for as everybody knew Taft was an isolationist, and consequently his tenure in the White House would be a disaster for the nation and the free world, so called.

Was Taft in fact an isolationist? That is, did he advocate a policy that would have required the United States to withdraw into itself, stand aloof from political and economic entanglements with other countries, let the rest of the world go hang as it chose? Simply to raise the question may astonish those indoctrinated with the stereotyped view of Taft. The stereotype was exceedingly useful to that faction of the Republican party—the one led by Dewey and comprising many of the eastern financial figures who had customarily furnished much of the party's funds—which energetically urged substantial investments of American capital abroad. To stigmatize Taft as an isolationist was to weaken him in the opinion of those who imagined the United States was the logical world leader, virtuous, omnipotent, destined to confer upon societies everywhere the American way of life. For a variety of reasons, none of them very commendable, those who in the late 1940s shared this belief constituted a sizable constituency. The isolationist label was shrewd adversarial politics. But as it described Taft it was imprecise.

Senator Taft's views on the nation's foreign policy were, at best, inconsistent. In truth, foreign affairs did not greatly interest him. His preoccupation was rather with domestic affairs and particularly with fiscal policy. He had first been elected to the Senate in 1938, when every right-thinking Republican found himself staggered by the iniquities and follies of the New Deal, and it had been wholly natural for Taft to dedicate himself to the righteous work of smiting the New Deal wherever and whenever possible. That meant being passionately partisan. Taft was, moreover, a fundamentalist whose fundament was the Constitution. The Constitution! Where that noble document was concerned, no man was a stricter constructionist. The Constitution stood, not to be altered but to be conserved. Taft was conservatism incarnate: he honored caution, solvency, thrift, orthodoxy, order, stability, tradition.

For a man so intensely partisan, politics could rarely stop at the water's edge, as it was supposed to do when the nation's foreign policy was at issue. To Taft, a Democratic policy was automatically suspect. Further, he observed a tendency on the part of Democratic Presidents—Truman even more than Roosevelt—to behave as though foreign policy were the exclusive preserve of the President and his Department of State, to act as though the Congress existed only to place its stamp of approval on whatever the President deemed wise. For a man who reverenced the Constitution as did Taft, such a tendency threatened usurpation of congressional powers.

Taft had two sufficient reasons, then, to quarrel with American foreign policy as handed down by Democratic Presidents. In the result, he was collared with the reputation of an isolationist. His voting record often contradicted the reputation, but his stout contrariety to Democratic stratagems and his jealous insistence on the constitutional powers of the Congress affirmed it. Both propensities put him on a collision course with General Eisenhower, but any collision was well in the future and, as Taft saw it, if Eisenhower were truly a good Republican he would veer away in plenty of time.

General Eisenhower's schedule was uncomfortably crowded during 1949 and 1950; he had enough responsibilities to keep three vigorous men of sixty busy. He conscientiously tried to devote at least some time to Columbia; he was constantly on the move about the country, meeting and speaking with carefully chosen groups of industrial and financial leaders, permitting them to inspect him and discover that he was a paragon of formulary expression who could be relied upon to spout conventional Republican wisdom with a most beguiling bonhomie; in December 1948 he was appointed a consultant to Secretary of Defense Forrestal, and soon afterward the President asked him to act informally as chairman of the Joint Chiefs of Staff. Public appearances and speeches took further toll of his waking hours.

There was also the private life of a world figure caught up in a web of ambition, duty, and responsibility. General Eisenhower and his wife had abandoned their hopes of finding a house in the country, or even in the suburbs; they were reconciled to living in the mansion on Morningside Drive; but on Mamie Eisenhower's behalf the university had engaged an expensive interior decorator to temper the grandeur with some warmth and cheer. Still Eisenhower needed a private retreat. On the flat roof of the mansion stood a structure once used to house some part of its plumbing. This was cleared of clutter and filled with some of Eisenhower's comfortable old sticks of furniture deemed inappropriate for the mansion by its redecorator. Here the Eisenhowers could cut themselves off from the atrocious city, from Columbia, from politics, from the clamant world; here, as he put it, was "the one place where I could be myself."

It was here, too, that General Eisenhower explored in complete absorption the exacting problems confronting the amateur painter—for him more difficult than for most clumsy novices: his big strong hands, as he said, were "better suited to an ax handle than a tiny brush." And yet, as was to be expected, whatever he touched turned to gold: a few of his earliest daubs, offered at auction to benefit the National Urban League, fetched more than two thousand dollars apiece.

Of more moment in the general's private life was the fact that his small family had considerably grown. His son John, who had been vouchsafed a taste of wartime service, had while on postwar duty in Vienna met a young woman, Barbara Jean Thompson, like himself an army child, and they were married in June 1947. On March 31, 1948, General Eisenhower had become a grandfather, and the infant had become his namesake, Dwight David Eisenhower II. Naturally the general was tickled, naturally he proved a doting grandfather. Fourteen months later there was another child, Barbara Anne, and by the end of 1951 there would be a third, Susan Elaine; and so the general, and perhaps even more his wife, would be able to subside contentedly into place as grandparents, roles in which they found themselves thrust from the limelight, reduced to bit players, and restricted to onomatopoeic drivel. As always in such a circumstance, a pleasure.

Two of his three full-time pursuits could to some extent be combined, and one of them even used to mask the other. Thus, since Eisenhower, like any university president, had to consort with moneyed men in order to pass the hat, he could be adroitly manipulated to prove himself at the same time a worthy candidate of the Republican party. The device was not wholly effective. It was rather as if one of those magic cloaks of invisibility, so effective in fairy tales, had been draped about a man exposed to the matter-of-fact glare of twentieth-century publicity; and so, while the cloak concealed all it covered, it left exposed the man's legs, which were running fast toward the White House, and his head, which was Eisenhower's. In any event, Eisenhower's was a grueling regimen, the more so because of the demands on his time of official Washington.

At first the method of choice was to scamp the duties at Columbia. When the members of the University Council—the dean and one professor from each of the several colleges—gathered to meet with President Eisenhower for the first time in the fall of 1948, he greeted them genially, apologized for his necessary departure, and bade them farewell. After he had decamped they found before them, at each place around their table, a neatly mimeographed summary of the matters proposed for discussion, together with a brief account of the decision taken on each item. It was their introduction to the military method of handling academic affairs.

There were other university responsibilities that Eisenhower sought to avoid. An invitation to a meeting of the Association of American Universities, for example, went ignored. When the president of the association, Dr. Henry Wriston, who was also the president of Brown University, telephoned to remind him of the meeting, Eisenhower said he would send a deputy. Not so, Dr. Wriston told him. Eisenhower's temper flared briefly. "Who says I can't?" he demanded. "I say you can't," said Dr. Wriston gently, and explained that the rules of the association forbade deputies. Eisenhower grumbled, flew at the last moment by chartered airplane to Wisconsin for the conference, later acknowledged he had learned more about Columbia by his attendance than he could have done had he stayed in New York, and further displayed his inexperience by enthusiastically proposing two institutions as prospective members of the association. Dr. Wriston had the unpleasant duty of explaining that Eisenhower's nominations, being colleges, were not eligible for an association of universities. It was all most instructive.

But no matter how he tried to cut corners, reminders of his mortality teased and nagged. Late in March 1949, while he was busy with his multiple chores, Eisenhower was felled by one of the attacks that had freakishly beset him over the previous two or three decades. These episodes had been marked by similar symptoms: spasms of cramping pain in the midabdomen, a mild fever, malaise, and often an acute inflammation in the lower right quadrant of the abdomen quite as if he were suffering from appendicitis. Indeed, after making his own diagnosis, Eisenhower had in 1925 argued some surgeons into removing his perfectly blameless appendix. The attacks had persisted—occasional, isolated, capricious, lacking any apparent cause. On this occasion Eisenhower knew cursed well that he was sick. He took to his bed in the Hotel Statler in Washington and stayed there. His old friend and physician General Howard Snyder, suspecting some sort of enteritis (he was close: Eisenhower's ailment was a chronic terminal ileitis, which is also known as regional enteritis, or Crohn's disease), kept him in bed a few days on a diet of liquid foods, and then sent him south to Key West to rest and recuperate.

His constitutionally rugged good health returned in short order. By April 7 he was back among his friends at Augusta National, golfing, playing bridge, and thoroughly enjoying himself. He seized advantage of his brief illness to stay at Augusta for more than a month. His cronies there were struck by the fact that Eisenhower, who by habit had for years smoked four packs of cigarettes a day, had while at Key West quit, cold turkey. It was an impressive feat. Four packs, eighty cigarettes; say ten minutes to each cigarette: it meant that for more than thirteen hours in each day for years Eisenhower had kept at hand a smoking cigarette—and now, none? The good-natured kidding was inescapable. One friend clipped from a newspaper and mailed him the story of a convict who had besought the warden to lock him in solitary confinement for a few days so that he might break the habit of smoking; the plan had succeeded; next thing, so ran the story, the warden had considered having himself locked up in the same way and for the same reason.

The horseplay masked real concern among Eisenhower's most trusted advisers. He was, as his aides were uncomfortably aware, now nearly sixty years old, and even his robust vigor could not be trusted as eternal. He must be protected. For the sake of the country and, as one of his advisers wrote to another, for the sake of "the country's need for him—completely well, strong and alert—some time in the future," it was essential that Eisenhower's energies not be dissipated, that his hours be jealously secluded, his public appointments kept to a minimum. Kevin McCann and Bob Schulz were transformed into dragons guarding his door. Mere professors or deans of Columbia faculties were likely to be unceremoniously shunted aside; petitioners from off campus could expect to climb a steep and tortuous path. A cautionary tale of one such ascent has been told by Dr. Henry Wriston, who among his several hats and mortarboards wore one as president of the exceedingly prestigious Council on Foreign Relations. Dr. Wriston led a small delegation to Columbia to ask that General Eisenhower head a study group on relations with western Europe.* The study group would number perhaps twenty men, and it is a measure of the distinction of the Council on Foreign Relations that among them would be Hamilton Fish Armstrong, editor of the magazine *Foreign Affairs*; McGeorge Bundy; Allen Dulles; Philip Reed, chairman of General Electric; Jacob Viner and John H. Williams, two eminent academic economists; and Russell Leffingwell, a senior partner of J. P. Morgan & Company. The invitation to serve as chairman was considered an honor by the council. Eisenhower heard his visitors out, said he was much interested in their proposal, and suggested they clear it with his appointments secretary, Kevin McCann. In due course, McCann made an appointment with Dr. Wriston to discuss the matter over coffee at a midtown hotel. The discussion was protracted over what seemed to Dr. Wriston something like fifteen cups of coffee before at length McCann was ready to give his consent.

For Eisenhower to be involved with the work of the council was to introduce him into a circle of influential men who would be able to tell a great many other leading figures, shapers of opinion, of what account Eisenhower was as a leader and shaper himself. In his particular study group, moreover, one that addressed itself to the relations of the United States with the nations of western Europe, Eisenhower's performance was bound to be, and was, impressive. All this would be helpful in his discreet political spadework, but he could budget only so much time to the new effort. He declined to read the position papers prepared for the various members of his group, for like most military officers who have advanced beyond the grade of colonel, he preferred oral briefings. In practice, this meant that a staff member of the council, Percy Bidwell, would journey to Columbia with a briefcase full of papers and summarize them for the general one after another; later, in quite satisfactory fashion, Eisenhower would lead and control a discussion of them. And he controlled with a firm grip. When a young economist presumed to question his decision that a council paper should not be published, the general snapped: "Ap-

---

* The council's study groups were by no means merely drawing room debating societies; rather they were seedbeds of American foreign policy. From those study groups often emerged not only the analyses that led to basic decisions in foreign affairs but also the men who would carry out those decisions. John J. McCloy, a director of the council who served the government in several exalted posts during the war and after it, has recalled: "Whenever we needed a man, we thumbed through the roll of council members and put through a call to New York."

parently your hearing isn't very good. I said we would not publish it!"*

Besides McCann, the general's principal advisers during this time included his good friend Cliff Roberts, who had also agreed to take in hand his capital so that it might be judiciously invested; his more recent friend Bermingham (they would soon be Ike and Ed); Bill Robinson of the *Herald Tribune;* George Allen, who behind the façade of merriment and the endless flow of funny stories was an experienced and canny Mississippi politician; and Lucius Clay, who returned from Germany in the early summer of 1949. A few others would later be admitted to the inner circle, among them Sid Richardson of Fort Worth, one of the Texas oil multimillionaires, and Bill Burnham, a young investment banker whose access to financiers and industrialists all over the country would prove invaluable.

Two or three of these advisers undertook as well the general's education. Roberts and Bermingham both troubled to send Eisenhower illuminating, high-toned stuff, most of it having to do with economic subjects, especially taxation, and some of it being "forceful and clear" material, as Eisenhower gratefully acknowledged, that dealt with the menace of state socialism. This educational process would reach the point where one of his tutors would take exception to Eisenhower's characterization of the United States as "the chief exponent of the free system—of the dignity of the individual and of a capitalistic economy." The gravamen was against the last two words. The American economy, it was explained to Eisenhower, was poles apart from capitalism, which itself was a term "handily used by the Communists to damn us and all our works." The American economy was rather "an overall system of individual endeavor profitable to management, labor, and ownership, with vast numbers of labor among the stockholders and thus having ownership in their business. It would be well," the mentor counseled, "to find a synonym for capitalism." General Eisenhower proved docile. "Without any argument whatsoever," he replied, "I agree with your observation about 'capitalistic system.'" Henceforward the word "capitalism," adjudged indecent, would drop from sight and in its stead would emerge the more decorous "free enterprise."

Eisenhower's instruction in conservative finance and its semantic subtleties coincided with a time in American history distinguished by revulsion from everything associated with the Left. It was a time when terms like progressive, liberal, and socialist all became opprobrious epithets and were lumped, whenever possible, with the most scurrilous epithet of all, communist. In this time, too, there first emerged the slouching figure of Joe McCarthy, the Republican senator from Wisconsin, whose gross and

* The paper was later published, but not under the council's imprint.

scatter-shot assaults on communism would for a time submerge the Bill of Rights, jeopardize the health of the republic, and finally enable him to give his name to the era and to the odious behavior of which he was the most outrageous exponent.

Because the Republican McCarthy so swiftly became an eponym for this time in history, it has been less appreciated that the Democrat Truman had cleared the way for McCarthy's mischief. Badly jolted by the congressional elections of 1946—for the first time since 1928 the Republicans had won control of both Houses, largely by pledging to clean the communists out of Washington—Truman responded by issuing Executive Order 9806. This rescript established a temporary commission on employee loyalty and charged it with looking to "the removal . . . of any disloyal or subversive persons employed by the government" and with formulating "standards of loyalty so as to protect the government against the employment of disloyal or subversive persons." In this way a loyalty test was instituted, and at once disfigured American libertarian traditions. Four months later, in March 1947, Truman slapped out Executive Order 9835, which opened the way for any anonymous informer, whose identity and whose accusations would be withheld from those he accused, to smear the loyalty and destroy the livelihood of those employed by the government. All those employees (there were two million of them, with another five hundred thousand applying for jobs each year) had now to submit to a security check conducted by the FBI. The test of disloyalty was "membership in, affiliation with, or sympathetic association with . . . any . . . organization, association, movement, group or combination of persons, designated by the attorney general as totalitarian."

Predictably the attorney general's list of such organizations grew apace. Dissent was ever more often equated with subversion or disloyalty. The President having pointed the way, other patriots sprang up to sniff out sedition: the House Committee on Un-American Activities took on renewed vigor; a Senate subcommittee on internal security entered the lists, breathing fire; in many states, carbon copies of those committees were established; trade unions, public school systems, churches, and veterans' organizations appointed committees dedicated to the labeling of anything Left as sinister. Before long it was not necessary to prove anything about a citizen: simply to mention his name, to require him to deny, made him "controversial," and to be "controversial" was enough to be stigmatized, to be barred from many jobs, not for having done anything but only for having, on somebody's unchallengeable testimony, thought or said something that did not conform. Guilt, like disease in an epidemic, was carried by association. Friendships shriveled. The damage, psychic and material, was immeasurable: how to account the jobs lost in a time of full prosperity? the careers blasted? the deaths from coronary failure, crackup, despair? The orgy bred monstrous prodigies. "Tell me, Senator McCarthy, when did you discover communism?" "Oh, about two and a half months ago."

And so, on February 9, 1950, Senator Joe McCarthy told a Women's Republican Club meeting in Wheeling, West Virginia, that "I have here in my hand a list of two hundred and five [or eighty-one, or fifty-seven] that were known to the secretary of state as being members of the Communist party and who nevertheless are still working and shaping the policy of the State Department"—after which the red hunt took on all the symptoms of paranoia.

It is useful to compare Eisenhower's response to the national hysteria in April 1947, when he was still in uniform as chief of staff, and in 1950, after McCarthy had joined the chase. In April 1947 the hunt for Reds was still young; it was still far from attaining its finest frenzy. For some time a conspicuous quarry had been David E. Lilienthal, a public servant of distinction who, after several years as chairman of the Tennessee Valley Authority, had been nominated by President Truman to be chairman of the Atomic Energy Commission. His appointment requiring approval by the Senate, Lilienthal was the subject of aggressive inquiry from the last week of January until the second week of April, during the course of which he was accused by Senator Taft of being "soft on communism" and his family was slandered by sundry shadowy anti-Semitic outfits. The inquiry was, in the view of Senator Vandenberg, "a lynching bee"; for Lilienthal it was cruel and arduous. But his appointment was at length approved, and on April 19 he was a principal speaker at a banquet tendered by the American Society of Newspaper Editors. Later Lilienthal noted in his journal:

> General Eisenhower pushed his way toward me, giving me a knowing look, his head tilted forward in that characteristic way he has when he is serious. He shook my hand firmly. "I want to congratulate you on what you have said." Then, moving close and speaking in a low, intent voice, he said, "But what is more important I want you to know I am on your team—I mean I am on your team." I was flustered and murmured something about thanking him and saying I would be honored to be on his team. He looked at me closely with that "You know what I mean" look and said, "You can count on me."

Then it was June 1950. Senator McCarthy and company were in full cry, and no week went by without another victim pilloried, another reputation stained. This week the lightning struck, among others, an obscure economist in the Department of Commerce called Michael Lee. As had been their custom, the newspapers and weekly magazines panted after this latest victim; his name and picture appeared in *Time* magazine, and in the locker room of the Blind Brook Club, Ellis D. (Slats) Slater read with mounting indignation the account of Lee's alleged derelictions. Slater was a wealthy executive of one of the biggest distillery establishments in the nation, also a dedicated anticommunist, also one of General Eisenhower's friends. He appealed to Eisenhower: what can a man do, what *should* he do, to record his opposition to such as Lee? Without unduly hesitating over the distinction between allegation and proof of guilt, Eisenhower advised Slater to file his protest with his Republican senator. Slater agreed. He wrote a strong remonstrance about Lee to Senator Irving Ives. More sorely harassed than Lilienthal had been and lacking Lilienthal's powerful supporters, Lee was easily broken. He denied the accusations brought against him, and was later formally cleared of any charges of disloyalty, but evidently the proceeding depressed him: he quit the government service in the fall of the year.

An incident of perhaps no great importance, except as it shows the temper of the times and how some citizens adapted to that temper.

General Eisenhower's adaptability proves how smoothly he had transformed himself into a practical workaday politician. The point is made without in any way calling into question his honesty or his devotion to principle; rather the matter is simply one of his having honed his political sensibility to a reasonably sharp edge. Politicians quickly learn that their convictions on current issues must accurately reflect the popular temper on those issues, however flighty. In this case, as the nation had taken fright at the bugaboo of internal subversion, so had he. Similarly, when the nation began to quake at the menace of encroaching bolshevism abroad, so, effortlessly, did he, while at the same time persuading himself that he had not shifted his course by a single degree.

U.S. and USSR were by now both committed to the stately, portentous capers of the Cold War: each responded to the other's moves as if bent on proving that the other's worst fears were justified: the more the one urged its citizens to beware of the other's warlike intentions, the more promptly the other felt obliged to behave in the anticipated warlike fashion and the more snugly each nation fitted itself into the grotesque stereotype designed by the other.

The U.S. saw itself as champion of democracy and liberty. The U.S. had moved to shield Greece and Turkey from aggression or subversion—and had stifled freedom. The USSR saw itself as champion of all those ground down by imperialism, the last and most rapacious stage of capitalism. The USSR had moved to shield Bulgaria, Hungary, Rumania, Poland, and finally Czechoslovakia from imperialist incursions—and had strangled democracy. (Both powers had ignored the United Nations.) Naturally, in this climate of hostility, war scares abounded. In March 1948 General Clay had dispatched an ominous warning from Germany: ". . . within the last few weeks, I have felt a subtle change in Soviet attitudes . . . [war] may come with dramatic suddenness." This alarm had been stilled only after a feverish ten-day pother by all the proliferating federal agencies of intelligence and security, so called, which had resulted in the comforting assurance that the Soviets could probably not make war for another sixty days. A federal government so easily agitated was bound to excite in its turn reckless pugnacity at home and grave fears abroad. It had got to be customary—indeed, it had passed as rational—for officers of high rank, usually of the air force, to discuss an atomic onslaught against Russia. The preferred term for such a desolation was "preventive war." General George C. Kenny, commander of the Strategic Air Command; General Carl Spaatz, retired chief of staff of the air force; Lieutenant General James H. Doolittle, hero of the first bombing raid on Japan—these three, among others, publicly turned their attention to the advisability of such a prophylactic assault; and their opinions gathered force as awareness grew that the U.S. commanded air bases all along the perimeter of the USSR, and that a devastating mission was indeed feasible. General Eisenhower had not been happy with this propaganda. "I decry loose and sometimes gloating talk," he had said, "about the high degree of security implicit in a weapon that might destroy millions overnight." But the mischievous talk persisted.

American possession of the atomic bomb continued to govern, as well, American diplomacy. Shaken by the communist coup in Czechoslovakia in the spring of 1948, official Washington moved to form a military alliance for the defense of western Europe. Since it would fall to the lot of General Eisenhower to administer that alliance, it is worth a moment to take note of its genesis and early character.

The chief architect of the North Atlantic Treaty was Dean Acheson, the urbane and conservative lawyer who had in January 1949 succeeded General Marshall as secretary of state. Acheson had the bipartisan cooperation of Senator Vandenberg largely because he demonstrated himself to Vandenberg's satisfaction to be "totally anti-Soviet . . . so *completely* tough" in his dealings with the Russians as to rule out "any *chance at all*" for an agreement with them. The treaty negotiated by Acheson and a group of ambassadors from various European countries was signed in April by twelve nations—the United States, Canada, Britain, France, Belgium, the Netherlands, Luxembourg, Norway, Denmark, Iceland, Italy, and Portugal—which agreed that "an armed attack against one or more of them . . . shall be considered an attack against them all," but then promised that each would assist any other attacked only "by taking . . . such action as it deems necessary," and then modified even this vague commitment by stipulating that each would act only in accordance with its "constitutional processes." Those reservations gave the treaty a flimsy underpinning. Further, the inclusion of Portugal (and later of Greece and Turkey) made a mockery of the notion that it was a North Atlantic alliance of democratic nations; rather it gave rise to the conviction that any nation might join so long as it was anti-Soviet and could furnish airfields for speculative use against the USSR. Yet further, the hearings before the Senate Committee on Foreign Relations made it painfully obvious how unconventional would be the European defenses. Senator Bourke Hickenlooper, an Iowa Republican, inquired about mutual assistance to resist armed attack: was the U.S. "going to be expected to send substantial numbers of troops over there as a more or less permanent contribution to the development of [Europe's] capacity to resist?" "The answer to that question, Senator," Acheson retorted, "is a clear and absolute 'No.'" No American troops. Then who was to supply the manpower? Were the Germans to be ordered back into uniform? "We are very clear," said Acheson, "that the disarmament and demilitarization of Germany must be complete and absolute." No American troops, no German troops. But the other signatories to the treaty were still exhausted by the war; just beginning, thanks to the massive transfusions supplied under the Marshall Plan, to regain their vitality; in no shape to supply either manpower or armaments for the common defense. Then what would halt the Red Army from its widely heralded march to the English Channel? The American atomic weapons: they were the "sole means" of organizing a reasonable defense, as the French General André Beaufre acknowledged. When General Bradley, then chief of staff, visited Fontainebleau in 1949, the first question put to him by General de Lattre had to do with the availability of atomic weaponry. "Bradley's reply was favorable, and it was this that justified, so far as we [of the Western European Union] were concerned, the new Alliance."

Whether the alliance and the cumbersome, top-heavy military structure established to provide its dentures—the North Atlantic Treaty Organization, or NATO—were necessary and appropriate was most debatable. George Kennan, by this time the director of the policy planning staff of the Department of State, considered the project irrelevant at best. He did "not believe in the reality of a Soviet military threat to Western Europe," considered the "general preoccupation with military affairs [to be] to the detriment of economic recovery and of the necessity for seeking a peaceful solution to Europe's difficulties," and anticipated that the atomic diplomacy already in train would surely divide Europe into two armed camps and a frozen, exceedingly perilous Cold War. His analysis was sound, but since it did not lead to an advocacy of the mailed fist brandished in Stalin's face, it did not recommend itself to the cold warriors of Washington.

Another influential figure who opposed the North Atlantic Treaty was Senator Taft. His vote against ratification of the treaty would be held against him as his most culpably isolationist action, but in fact his opposition was antimilitarist: he saw the treaty as requiring the United States to tool up for the production and provision of armaments to the other eleven signatory nations, and so "with great regret" he set himself against it. (He was also opposed to the treaty because, as he wrote, "I felt it was contrary to the whole theory of the United Nations Charter.") His vote would be recalled three years later, when he wrestled with General Eisenhower for the favor of the national convention of the Republican party.

The Senate debate on ratification had scarcely been joined when Eisenhower was once again summoned to Washington, this time to lend his prestige to the cause of convincing the Congress that there should be broader cooperation with Britain and Canada in the field of atomic energy. Since the British and Canadians had, under the pressures of wartime, freely pooled their raw materials and their scientific and technical skills to harness the new force, any scheme to share the fruits so hard won seemed only reasonable, honorable, and minimally decent. As if that were not enough, the United States needed British cooperation if uranium ore for future explosives were to be steadily and surely supplied. But the depths to which an ill-humored Congress can sink are fathomless, and this particular Congress, elected in poisoned times, was more malevolent than most. For several weeks a joint congressional committee had been raking the Atomic Energy Commission with charges of "incredible mismanagement" and of coddling those who held "potentially subversive or otherwise objectionable views." In brief, no worse time could have been chosen for discussion of such a ticklish and capital matter. On the other hand, for the distracted Dean Acheson "there was not much time [left], good or bad."

On a hot and humid night there gathered at Blair House the President, Vice President Alben W. Barkley, Speaker Sam Rayburn, Acheson, Secretary of Defense Louis Johnson, Lilienthal, five senators, two representatives, General Eisenhower, and an assortment of lesser officials. As these notables assembled, a violent thunderstorm broke, drenching the forty or fifty correspondents who had gathered outside, full of wild surmise about a Cold War perhaps suddenly become hot.

Inside, a different sort of storm gradually developed. Acheson explained the need for a new agreement with the British, Lilienthal told of the

American need for raw materials, and Eisenhower, addressing himself to the military aspects of the matter, made an admirable statement on the need for good faith and mutual trust between British and Americans, and on how the unwarranted insistence on secrecy was already putting at hazard a vital partnership. At once the two Republican senators present erupted in dissent. Vandenberg, who preferred to be bipartisan only against the Russians, said he was "shocked." He deplored the way the U.S. kept on giving things away to the British and now proposed to give away "our" latest and most prized possession. He called upon Hickenlooper, "one of the best-informed men," and Hickenlooper roused himself for a stump speech: ". . . American people . . . opposed to giving away . . . We must protect our own security first and foremost . . . keep this vital secret to ourselves . . . we stand alone . . ."

Eisenhower was sitting at Hickenlooper's right, and his mobile face, always wonderfully expressive of his feelings, showed first a puzzled amusement, next consternation, and finally disgust. Scowling angrily, he broke in: "Do I have to begin by making a speech defending my Americanism?" Then he took sharp issue with Hickenlooper on the value of British friendship and the pitfalls of isolationism. "When it comes to the absolute necessity of this ally," he said, "I speak with some experience. But even leaving aside the matter of military necessity, we can't live alone in this world." He mentioned the American lack of such vital raw materials as tin and manganese. Hickenlooper, said Eisenhower, was crazy if he thought we could win a war by dropping an atomic bomb. Later Lilienthal noted in his journal that Eisenhower's rebuttal was a massacre.

The President's advisers met once again with congressional leaders six days later, on Wednesday, July 20, in a small room of the Capitol denoted 48G, for a conference described in the newspapers as "behind closed doors, and with window blinds drawn." The gesture toward security, however, was absurd: most of those who had attended the earlier meeting had, despite a presidential injunction to the contrary, already apprised the press of what was afoot, and the second meeting was attended by eight senators, six representatives, and all five members of the Atomic Energy Commission, a conclave as full of leaks as a colander. On this occasion Eisenhower sat between Lilienthal and Secretary Johnson, facing the congressmen. He was peppered with questions, and by more Republican senators—Eugene Milliken of Colorado and William F. Knowland of California were added to the strength—and he retreated in some confusion. "I'm just a soldier." Yes, all atomic weapons except a very few ought to be hoarded on our shores; no, he had not considered the grave implications of "giving away the secret." Knowland lost his temper and started to yell. More silkily, Milliken threatened to block any presidential action taken without congressional approval. All four Republican senators insisted that American secrets must be kept from the British.

Lilienthal left the meeting with Eisenhower. As they descended in a tiny elevator to the ground floor, Eisenhower seemed quite upset. "I never realized what a lot of cross-currents there are," he said. "I just don't know what all that sort of thing is about."

Next day (July 21, 1949) the Senate voted eighty-two to thirteen to ratify the North Atlantic Treaty, the first military pact ever to be concluded by the United States during peacetime. Two days later Truman sent the Congress a bill, the Mutual Defense Assistance Act of 1949, in which he asked for an appropriation of one billion four hundred and fifty million dollars to pay for the first year's costs of the pact, and to provide military assistance "to other nations whose increased ability to defend themselves against aggression is important to the national interest of the United States." Those "other nations," it developed, were Greece, Turkey, Iran, and, to the east of the Soviet Union, the Philippines and South Korea. One purpose of this "mutual defense," as was clear to the executive branch of the government if not to the Congress, was "to build up our own military industry." The inclusion of the Philippines and South Korea in the grand global design was striking: in the Philippines the need was to stamp out a stubborn native insurgency; in South Korea the need, in the summer of 1949, was more obscure, but in the spring of that year the Chinese Communist armies had completed the drubbing of Generalissimo Chiang Kai-shek's Nationalist government, which had retired from the mainland to the island of Formosa (Taiwan). In both South Korea and the Philippines, and elsewhere, there appeared a new military formation, the Military Advisory and Assistance Group (MAAG), which was to play an increasingly important part in the enforcement of Pax Americana.

What disturbed the Republican supporters of the Democratic policy was its cost. Vandenberg and John Foster Dulles (who was briefly a member of the Senate by virtue of an interim appointment made by Governor Dewey) were also alarmed by the broad powers assigned the President. "It's almost unbelievable in its grant of unlimited power to the Chief Executive," Vandenberg wrote his wife. "It would virtually make him the number one war lord of the earth." The issue was still decidedly in doubt when President Truman made public on September 23 an event of which he had been given a first and unconfirmed report three weeks earlier: "We have evidence that within recent weeks an atomic explosion occurred in the USSR." The Congress speedily agreed to appropriate the funds he had asked for.

The "explosion" had come at least two years earlier than expected. There was still a disposition to believe the Soviets incapable of such scientific and engineering accomplishment in such a brief time; hence the reference by the President to "an atomic explosion" rather than "a test of an atomic device." But the implications were clear, and mighty distasteful in Washington: the American monopoly of atomic destruction had vanished, and with it one system of Cold War diplomacy.

Anglo-American atomic cooperation fared no better. For a time it seemed that the Russian success would induce the requisite congressional blessings, but a case of espionage detected in British scientific circles sent the talks back into the limbo from which they had briefly emerged. The British were obliged to go their way alone, being refused American assistance even in the testing of their own first bomb.

Thus the way was left clear for the two great nuclear powers, each the champion of its intractable ideology, to confront each other.

While these weighty affairs were in train, General Eisenhower was concerned with more personal matters. He had returned to New York and then, as had become his custom, traveled with his wife to Denver to spend the month of August with her mother, Mrs. Doud, in her comfortable gray brick house set among maple trees in a staid well-to-do middle-class neighborhood. They all enjoyed this annual holiday. Mrs. Doud, her vivacity undimmed by the years, delighted in having Ike and Mamie under her roof; occasionally Mamie would join her mother for an evening at the dog races. For Eisenhower there was golf at the Cherry Hills Country Club and fishing in mountain streams on ranches owned by friends.

There was also, interchangeably, bridge to play and politics to talk with the friends and advisers who came west from Washington and New York. It was time to talk strategy, to devise plans for the presidential election of 1952, even to discuss what might be done about the congressional elections of 1950, to decide what role Eisenhower should play. Cliff Roberts, Bill Robinson, and George Allen were among those who visited him; the question of whether he should publicly identify himself as a Republican was much on their minds. At Eisenhower's request, Roberts assembled the arguments in favor of his declaring his party affiliation and reduced them to a memorandum based

. . . in part on the opinions and convictions of the thoughtful and patriotic citizens whose views have come to me. . . :

Under the guise of welfare legislation, those now in control of the Democratic Party are committed to socialistic doctrine. . . .

If the Democratic Party succeeds . . . in installing socialistic measures

429

and machinery, with clever political deceit, it will become impossible to replace the inevitable system of controls, except through dictatorship and subsequent revolution.

It is possible and, indeed probable, that between now and the time of the next Presidential election, the Democratic Party will complete the foundation of their socialistic program . . .

[Hence the] vital importance [of] the 1950 Congressional elections. Republican defeat . . . will give irresistible impetus to the further development of socialistic doctrine which the Presidential election in 1952 may be too late to arrest. . . .

To achieve the necessary strength in these Congressional elections, the Republican Party desperately needs . . . leadership . . . [Therefore] there is a strong feeling on my part that you should seriously consider joining the Republican Party at this time.

Bill Robinson, while agreeing that the Truman administration "is committed to Socialistic doctrines" and also fearful that a "sweeping Democratic victory" in the congressional elections "would . . . make this Nation a quasi Socialistic State, in a matter of months," nevertheless argued strongly against General Eisenhower's joining the Republican party "at this time." Such a step, Robinson urged, would encourage Democrats "to attack and discredit him at every turn," and would "undermine him with his faculty [at Columbia] which contains strong and leftish elements easily susceptible to sabotage." As if that were not dangerous enough, Robinson added, "Strong leftish elements in the student body could likewise be employed to harass and badger him and his [Columbia] administration."

Robinson's view, including his recommendation that Eisenhower "rally the large Independent vote for attack on the Administration's repudiation of the American doctrine," prevailed. The counsel was fuzzy, couched in imprecise generalizations, and studded with capitalized words like "Independent" and "American System"; it convinced. It ran parallel, too, to the thoughts exchanged in correspondence between Eisenhower and Bernard M. Baruch, the sage who had proffered advice to one President after another, sometimes on request. On the American political scene Baruch was for half a century a man of imposing reputation, which is to say, he imposed his reputation on one important official after another. With Eisenhower the ritual had proceeded in stately fashion: the note of congratulations on his appointment as chief of staff, the post-factum suggestion about who could have unsnarled the tangle of demobilization, the presentation of Baruch's private telephone number, the invitation to Hobcaw, his barony in South Carolina. By June of 1949 Eisenhower was expressing his concern about "the growing tendency of everyone to look

430

to the government for the cure of all social and economic ills" and "this constant increase in political control of local and individual affairs." Baruch agreed that here was "the central problem of our times" and suggested that Eisenhower put the savants at Columbia to work on it. He called it the "encroaching state," a phrase he credited to Eisenhower.

Much of this surfaced in the speech Eisernhower made on Labor Day to a convention of the American Bar Association in St. Louis. He staked out as his political ground "the middle way" where stood the "clear-sighted and the courageous . . . determined that we shall not lose our freedoms, either to the unbearable selfishness of vested interest [the ceremonial frown at the Right], or through the blindness of those who, protesting devotion to the public welfare [the deceitful Democrats, bent on installing socialism], falsely declare that only government can bring us happiness, security, and opportunity." Government, "especially the ever-expanding federal government," had to be watched sharply lest it "interfere more than is necessary in our daily lives." Above all, he said, what was needed was "more economic understanding and working arrangements that will bind labor and management . . . into a far tighter voluntary cooperative unit than we now have." Once again the apostle of unity, but now of a unity for increased productivity, a unity of labor and management. Class warfare? That was a falsehood preached by Karl Marx a century ago, and Marx, Eisenhower told the convention of the ABA, "could not imagine a great nation in which *there is no proletariat* [Eisenhower's emphasis], in which labor is the middle class he so much despised and hated." He added, reassuringly, that "the interests of labor and management in most situations are identical."

How much of this was the genuine, sure-to-God Ike Eisenhower it is hard to say, and the temptation is to load the blame for such kindergarten economics on well-intentioned advisers who were too slipshod to consult a good dictionary for the meaning of "proletariat." At any rate, his strategy was well defined. The middle way, the middle of the road, the "central position," as he put it in his speech at St. Louis, "in which are rooted the hopes and allegiance of the vast majority of our people"— this was the political territory claimed and cleared for Eisenhower by his advisers, and they would devote themselves to its cultivation for the next year or so.

That fall of 1949 in New York the plan was devised of an American Assembly, bringing together industrialists, financiers, lawyers, publishers, educators, government officials, and other such polished and seemly notables for a discussion of public affairs in reasonably undisturbed circumstances. In effect, this was the study group of the Council on Foreign Relations, inflated by inviting participants from all over the nation and then concentrated within a span of four or five days. A home for these discussions was found when Averell Harriman gave to Columbia the palatial country mansion his father had caused to be erected in the wooded hills back west of the Hudson. The eventual value of these assemblies, if any, was never estimated to be as great as the benefit to Eisenhower from raising the money to support them: most, if not all, of the wealthy businessmen who got the money up were fully aware they were promoting the prospect of his becoming President. There was a good deal of window dressing, but the aroma of politics hung over the whole enterprise, acrid and unmistakable.

Of more immediate moment to Eisenhower were his discreet meetings with Governor Dewey, after the second of which Dewey wrote Eisenhower a thank-you note at once guarded and explicit:

> . . . I enjoyed so much your hospitality last night and the delightful discussion we had.
> I do not desire to burden you on the subject we discussed but would like to have you feel that I am available, as are my friends.

At about that same time Bermingham wrote Eisenhower from Alabama, urging the importance to southern voters of the doctrine of states' rights, an issue just then commencing to inflame the heart of Dixie, and showing how, if adroitly managed, his candidacy could unloose the Democratic grip on the Solid South.

In December, Eisenhower traveled to Texas for a fortnight's visit with Sid Richardson, an interlude that was made to his order. Richardson was one of the luckier of the Texas oil operators. In 1935 he had discovered the fabulous Keystone Field in west Texas under which lay reserves of petroleum worth more than one billion dollars, and by the time he met Eisenhower, Uncle Sid was widely reputed to be worth about the same amount himself. Both men liked to hunt and fish, and Richardson owned an island in the Gulf of Mexico, San José, with splendid facilities for both amusements; the two men held similar views on intellectuals and talkative types generally (Richardson: "You ain't learnin' nothin' when you're talkin'"; Eisenhower: "An intellectual is a man who takes more words than is necessary to say more than he knows"); they got along together famously. Pausing in Fort Worth long enough to add Amon Carter to their company, they flew to Richardson's island to fish, shoot, and occasionally talk about politics, money, and oil. Since Eisenhower had been born in Texas, he was of course considered a Texan by every Texan, and his chances of carrying Texas in any presidential election were regarded as somewhat better than sure-pop; still, a little judicious politicking

432

with a pair of Texas multimillionaires could never go amiss. Back in New York, Eisenhower sent Richardson an Arabian carbine and a mounting so that he might have it ready to hand in his jeep when shooting birds on San José.

All proceeded smoothly. Bill Burnham arranged a dinner for Eisenhower with such other guests as the chairman of Standard Oil of New Jersey, the president of six other big oil corporations (Standard of California, Texaco, Socony-Vacuum, and the like), the executive vice president of J. P. Morgan & Company, the presidents of another ten assorted corporations, and a stray Vanderbilt. After dinner four of them—Burnham, the Morgan partner, the president of the Empire Trust Company, and the Vanderbilt—repaired with Eisenhower to 60 Morningside Drive for drinks and further conversation. The whole affair was, Eisenhower told Burnham, "a huge success."

Late in January 1950, Eisenhower visited Bermingham at his Alabama plantation ("We still must make a tough frontal attack on the Peppers and the Humphreys," Bermingham reminded Eisenhower), after which the general crossed over into Georgia to stay with Bob Woodruff of Coca-Cola at his Ichauway estate, where were kenneled seventy-five dogs of whom twenty-five or thirty were always in condition to hunt.

Then it was back to Columbia to resume the burdens of a university president. Another Republican aspirant was also an Ivy League educator: Harold Stassen was president of the University of Pennsylvania and shifting uneasily from foot to foot: should he once again proclaim his availability for the Republican nomination? In mid-April he was cautious. At dinner with Burnham in New York, Stassen stated his belief that Eisenhower's nomination in 1952 was inevitable and that the general should announce his candidacy pronto. Burnham was circumspect. "For his sake," he said, "I hope he never runs. For the sake of the country, I hope he does. I am sure he doesn't want the job—but I'm equally sure he's the only one who could win." Stassen's reaction to this play-acting was not recorded.

The end of the academic year was approaching. In his office in Low Library, President Eisenhower was handed the list of those who were to be awarded honorary degrees at the commencement exercises, a group of distinguished folk whom by custom he was expected to entertain at dinner. He was astonished to find on the list the name of Dr. Ralph Bunche, then the director of the Trusteeship Council of the United Nations. Now Eisenhower did not consider that he harbored racist ideas. He was quite sure he was no bigot. Yet he paused at Bunche's name: should a Negro (and his wife) be invited to his house for dinner? To be sure, he was a Nobel laureate, but might not some of his other guests be offended?

perhaps even outraged? It was difficult, but surely those who had voted to confer the degrees knew what they were about. (Later Eisenhower would tell an acquaintance that things went off very well and that the others at the dinner "made a point of seeking out the Bunches.")

His other affairs were more pressing. Burnham was arranging a series of luncheon parties—one with the presidents of the three biggest pharmaceutical houses, one with a small but illustrious group of Texans (men like H. L. Hunt, whose income was then estimated at two hundred thousand dollars a day; Robert Kleberg, the rancher; John H. Blaffer of Houston; and Edgar G. Tobin of San Antonio), and one with a dozen young New Yorkers marked as board chairmen of the future—and expeditions had been planned to Boston, where Robert Cutler of the Old Colony Trust Company was to bring together "a dozen gold-plated Boston magnates" to meet him, and to Minneapolis, where Harry A. Bullis, board chairman of General Mills, was to perform a like service. All these functions were private, of course, and all were put forward as occasions at which General Eisenhower would talk about Columbia and the mission of the university in combating "those paternalistic and collectivistic ideas which, if adopted, will accomplish . . . the collapse of self-government," but he was a dullard indeed who, after coming to meet the general, went away unaware that Eisenhower was an avid and assiduous candidate.

The fact being difficult to conceal, political correspondents were before long alert to it. "There is again much talk of General Eisenhower for President," Richard Rovere wrote at this time. "In fact, what might be called the second Eisenhower boom is under way." Rovere, after wondering what sort of President Eisenhower would make, observed, "We know surprisingly little about him, really." If by "we" Rovere meant the political writers and the generality of American voters, he was surely right; nevertheless, as he knew, that ignorance would count for little in the polling places, and in any case the uppermost cream of American voters was already learning at first hand all they needed to know of Eisenhower's ideology. The biggest worry facing Eisenhower's advisers was how to make sure the ardor of his admirers did not sufflate his boom too fast, too soon.

And then, on Sunday, June 25, 1950, events bustled politics temporarily into the wings.

When on the morning of June 25 the North Koreans launched an attack across the thirty-eighth parallel of north latitude, the artificial boundary separating the People's Democratic Republic of Korea (north) from the Republic of Korea (south), the official view as promulgated from Washington was that it was a "surprise attack." Enough facts about the curious circumstances that preceded the invasion have by now been published and assessed to make it evident that the attack was at least to some extent provoked by those—chiefly Chiang Kai-shek and Syngman Rhee—for whom a peaceful settlement in the Far East would have been disastrous. Chiang feared that the Chinese Communists would force him out of Taiwan (Formosa) and, further, would officially replace his Nationalist government in the United Nations, taking over his membership on the Security Council. Syngman Rhee had just been soundly trounced by the voters in the first free election in Korean history and now stood in danger of being ejected from office, perhaps exiled. Both men needed massive and immediate American support if they were to cling to their last handhold on power, yet both had been informed that their lands lay outside the "defensive perimeter" established by official American policy. Both men desperately needed an attack by the North Koreans so that American public opinion might be roused to change that policy.

Somebody initiated hostile actions along the thirty-eighth parallel. The North Koreans later said they had gone over to the offensive after repulsing three South Korean attacks. Major General Charles Willoughby, General MacArthur's chief of intelligence, would later speak of the "alleged 'surprise' of the North Korean invasion." At all events, North Korea was branded the aggressor by the Security Council of the United Nations, but as I. F. Stone has made clear after examining the pertinent documents, how the fighting began and which side started it has never been incontrovertibly established and probably never will be.

For General Eisenhower, once again removed from the inner councils of high strategy, the news was astonishing and at first dismaying, but after a time for reflection one might fairly conclude that no permanent damage had been done his long-range intentions. After all, when he came to offer himself to the voters, his surest strength would be his ability to cope with crisis: the sudden emergence of crisis could only remind the voters of who stood ready to serve them. Eisenhower's plans for the summer went unchanged. Once again he and his wife traveled to Denver; Burnham was pressed for suggestions about Eisenhower's Labor Day speech, the general stipulating that he wanted something other than merely "we must answer communist lies"; early in the autumn he agreed, at Baruch's insistence, to "meet with a group of distinguished men in a closed session for a discussion of security and mobilization problems."

The conference had apparently been called at the instigation of Stassen. Baruch spoke, a routine discourse on wartime inflation with which everyone agreed, and that was that. Eisenhower, unprepared, spoke spontaneously, at length, and most impressively. Henry Wriston of the Council on Foreign Relations said later, "I've never heard any public figure give as good an exposition of his general outlook. Many of the people who were there said, 'This is the man we want for President of the United States.'" So, in the precipitate of crisis, Eisenhower once again showed his happy proclivity for rising to the top.

He was, however, aware of the steady thrust and shift of forces that were bringing him, whether he wished it or no, back again to the inner circles where national policy was being decided—by Democrats. Those forces had been set in motion by debate on the question: Should the Germans be rearmed and invited to join the NATO forces against the hypothetical threat of an assault by the Red Army? It will be recalled that Secretary Acheson, queried in 1949 about the possible revival of German military capability, had flatly denied the possibility of such a thing. Again on June 5, 1950, Acheson had been unequivocal on the demilitarization of Germany. "There is no discussion of doing anything else," he had assured the members of the House Foreign Affairs Committee. "That is our policy and we have not raised it or revalued it." One day later it was made plain where the more fundamental aspects of U.S. foreign policy were decided—in the Pentagon. General Bradley said: "I do believe the defense of western Europe would be strengthened by the inclusion of Germany . . . great production facilities . . . very capable soldiers and airmen and sailors."

Army officers had in fact been devising plans for the rearming of Germany at least since November 1949, always under the watchful guidance of General Bradley, the chief of staff, and Lieutenant General Alfred Gruenther, the deputy chief of staff. Their plans had been approved by the Joint Chiefs on April 30. By August Gruenther had undertaken a hasty indoctrination of the State Department. (Acheson's conversion was easily achieved.) The Pentagon's able lobbyists had for some time been smoothly creating on Capitol Hill a climate favorable to the now familiar idea of arming a recent enemy against a recent ally.

In September the NATO Council was to meet in New York. By that time Gruenther and Bradley had got Acheson to agree to a "single package" in which were wrapped several valuable trinkets: the concept of an integrated multinational NATO army under an American supreme commander, the promise of more American troops, and German rearmament: take all or get none. A few days before the first session of the council, John J. McCloy, then American high commissioner in Germany, let it be known that in his opinion Germany could conceivably muster ten divisions for NATO. If the British foreign minister, Ernest Bevin, was unhappy about these well-planted hints, his French counterpart Robert Schuman was downright dismayed. France, so often overrun by its powerful neighbor, could not abide even whispers of German rearmament.

When Acheson formally apprised Bevin and Schuman of the American "single package" at a conference in his suite in the Waldorf Towers, one of his visitors ruefully characterized it as "the bomb in the Waldorf."

At this juncture General Marshall once again emerged from retirement, this time because of the sudden resignation of Louis Johnson as secretary of defense. Johnson's behavior, in Acheson's view, "had passed beyond the peculiar to the impossible."* Marshall's return to duty confronted Eisenhower with an exemplary model of service.

Naturally Eisenhower was familiar with all the infighting over German rearmament. Gruenther, the senior officer in the Pentagon most closely concerned, was one of Eisenhower's closest friends (and had been since the days in 1941 when he served as Eisenhower's deputy in the Third Army in Texas). Eisenhower had to be kept informed, even consulted on the best ways to wrap and seal the Pentagon's "single package," for President Truman had always had him in mind "as the logical man for [the] unique job" of supreme commander of NATO. Indeed, some of Eisenhower's closest political advisers, like Cliff Roberts, had for some time been privy to the secret that Eisenhower might be called to a "special military assignment."

But what if some of the European statesmen chose to reject the "single package"? And that, most emphatically, is what the French statesmen did, carrying with them the ministers of some of the smaller countries. Throughout the last fortnight of September the French steadfastly refused to accept even in principle the concept of German rearmament. The "single package" so neatly wrapped in Washington was coming unstuck in New York. What was worse, one of the most valuable trinkets in the package, the promise of Eisenhower as supreme commander of NATO forces, was about to burst out of its wrappings entirely.

On Sunday, October 15, in a televised interview on "Meet the Press," Governor Dewey of New York announced that he would never again be a candidate for President, but, he insisted in his well-modulated baritone, the Republican party had a peerless leader in General Dwight D. Eisenhower. The balloon had been loosed, the bandwagon set rolling. Reporters raced to telephones to inquire of General Eisenhower the answer to the secret of the decade. The general answered, in effect: Who, me? It was as though he had never heard of the White House, much less the presidency of the United States.

President Truman was not likely to be deceived by any amateurish clearings of the throat. On October 19 he dictated a note to Eisenhower,

* By a singular coincidence, that new cabinet position seemed to be proving fatal for its incumbent. Forrestal, the first secretary, fell to his death from a high hospital window. Johnson, the second, succumbed to a brain malady.

appending to it a handwritten postscript: "First time you are in town, I wish you'd come in and see me. If I send for you, we'll start the 'speculators' to work."

When Eisenhower reported to the White House on Saturday, October 28, he knew why he had been summoned and he knew, too, that the French had dug in their heels. He listened in silence as the President outlined the nature of the assignment he had in mind. Eisenhower replied that he would accept the post because he was a soldier who was called to duty, adding that he accepted the duty gladly because it was a job that very badly needed to be done. As he knew, however, he was accepting a mission that did not then exist. What odds the French would never agree to the rearming of Germany? The matter still called for adroit and lengthy negotiations. For the moment, Truman could only tell the defense ministers of the NATO countries what they already knew, that a senior American officer of highest rank would be available for the supreme command of NATO when circumstances smiled.

Eisenhower resumed his other quest. More travel, more speeches, more private dinners, more conversations with the wealthy and the well-placed, an exercise in political charm and affability: Houston on Friday, Dallas on Saturday, Oklahoma City on Sunday, and on Monday, November 13, a luncheon in a suite of private rooms of the Drake Hotel in Chicago, given by Bermingham. The host had assembled ten guests who tilted heavily to the right: they included General Robert E. Wood of Sears Roebuck; Sewell Avery of Montgomery Ward; Douglas Stuart, chairman of Quaker Oats; Harold Swift of Swift & Company; and John L. McCaffrey, president of International Harvester. "Kevin," Bermingham wrote to McCann, "you may query a couple of these names but I have definite reasons why each was asked."

Meanwhile, the French were promoting a plan of their own, one that called for German soldiers in modest numbers without requiring the rearmament of Germany. To Acheson it seemed to relegate Germany to a "second-class status," and he concluded that the American "single package" would have to be junked, and the concept of an American supreme commander linked instead to a unanimous agreement by the NATO nations on German participation "in principle." Only so, he considered, could the U.S. save face. General Marshall agreed. The whole matter was put over for disposition by the NATO ministers during their December meeting at Brussels.

Would the French yield? Nothing Eisenhower did could have any bearing on their decision; he kept his attention fixed on his private plans. Late in November he was invited to dinner by Clarence Dillon, the retired founder of Dillon, Read & Company. The guests included his son Douglas

Dillon; Russell Leffingwell, senior partner of J. P. Morgan & Company; John Schiff, senior partner of Kuhn, Loeb & Company; John D. Rockefeller, Jr.; Harvey Firestone; William Langley of Langley & Company; James C. Brady; Jeremiah Milbank; and Lord Brand, a British financier. Eisenhower found this august company plunged in gloom, for the day had brought, as Eisenhower noted, "the very worst news we had from Korea"—news of the disaster that had been visited on the troops ordered north to the Yalu by the manic MacArthur. It was Eisenhower's task to pluck up the spirits of the dinner party, to infect the company with his indomitable optimism. Here was a striking occasion: the Kansas farm boy so poor he had gone to school in hand-me-downs, the simple soldier confused by the cross-currents on Capitol Hill, called on to keep in countenance a clutch of the richest and most powerful men in the country.

The panic at the dinner party on November 28 was matched across the nation. Once again there was talk of preventive war. President Truman spoke so vividly at a press conference about use of the atom bomb that a "clarifying" statement had to be hastily issued denying that the rout of the Eighth Army in Korea had provoked any change in official reluctance to use the bomb. The British prime minister was flown across the Atlantic to confer with Truman. A flock of geese, flying in formation over Canada and observed by the early-warning radar system as they headed southeast (toward Washington!), excited orders in the Pentagon to ignore all telephone calls save those required in a defensive alert. All over the country, and especially in Washington, nerve fibers were stretched as taut as fiddle strings. On December 13 Truman proclaimed a national emergency.

A few days later the jitters had abated enough to permit Acheson and his aides to depart for Brussels. But the NATO ministers were in no better case: there was a general dread that war—worse than war, the final cataclysm—was imminent. The chief business before the council was to establish the NATO army, find the troops for it, and agree on a supreme commander. In France and elsewhere the widespread belief was that a deal had been struck: the French would agree "in principle" to incorporating German troops into the unified NATO force if General Eisenhower were appointed the supreme commander. In one pan of the scales, Eisenhower; balancing him in the other pan, the troops still hated and feared, the troops of an enemy recently defeated. It was a remarkable equilibrium.

Acheson flashed the word to Truman that the NATO Council unanimously approved the choice of General Eisenhower as supreme commander, and Truman promptly sought Eisenhower by telephone. He found him on the night of December 18 on a railroad siding at Bucyrus, Ohio, where he had paused to make a speech to some college students on his way west to Denver with his wife for the Christmas holidays.

439

Now his plans, great and small, were upset.

Unexpectedly back in New York, his name once again on the front pages of the newspapers, Eisenhower was driven to the rooms of the Council on Foreign Affairs and met at the door by its president Henry Wriston.

WRISTON: I don't think you're very happy.

EISENHOWER (*at the flash point of temper*): What do you know about it?

WRISTON: Nothing, except I always read between the lines in the newspapers, and I took a look at you.

EISENHOWER (*under control again, grinning*): No, I'm not happy.

Indeed he was not. He hated to leave the civilian life to which he had got accustomed and in which he had found himself surrounded by devoted courtiers, some of them merry, a few obsequious, all convinced of his distinction and personal eminence, all anxious to forward his ambition. But when Eisenhower heard the call of duty, he responded automatically, if reluctantly. While quite vexed at having had his long-range plans called into question, Eisenhower was on this December night at the Council on Foreign Relations immediately concerned by something else: he thought the command structure of NATO was all wrong. The roundabout conduits of authority—from him to the Joint Chiefs to the secretary of state to the various ministries of foreign affairs to the commanding officers of the armies of the various NATO member nations and so finally back to him—he found appalling.

WRISTON: Why not do something about it?

EISENHOWER: What could we do?

WRISTON: Send a memorandum to Mr. Truman.

EISENHOWER: Are you serious?

WRISTON: Yes. You've got a very distinguished group here.

And so he had—his study group. Taking a pad of yellow paper, Eisenhower busied himself with a memorandum on his proper relationship with the NATO governments. Allen Dulles telephoned the White House to make an appointment with Averell Harriman over the breakfast table next day. Eisenhower's notes were handed to a typist, and presently copies were passed round for collective analysis and criticism. At midnight Dulles hurried to catch the overnight sleeper to Washington, taking with him a memorandum for Truman recommending that General Eisenhower be sent abroad to visit each of the twelve NATO countries in an effort to clarify and rationalize his authority.

Back into uniform.

With the turn of the new year, 1951, Eisenhower was once again in the Pentagon. (The trustees of Columbia had agreed that he might go on indefinite leave of absence.) As a first step in reconstituting his staff for overseas duty he persuaded Bradley to assign him Gruenther as his chief of staff (besides being a first-rate administrator, Gruenther was very likely the best bridge player in the army). On Thursday, January 4, he and Gruenther spent several hours with Acheson being instructed in the problems of NATO. Acheson's indoctrination, apart from the standard doctrinal postures of the Cold War, was designed to clue the soldiers in on their role in Europe. The North Atlantic Treaty was more than military; it was "a means and a vehicle for closer political, economic, and security cooperation with western Europe." The supreme commander was to be "the embodiment of NATO . . . the constant and visible leader" of the unity and strength of western Europe. All this went down fairly well.

Once again in Europe. A whirlwind tour of inspection and consultation, during which the general mused on his political aspirations and how deep a dent had been put in them by this capricious tour of duty. He must, he decided, announce his "flat refusal to contemplate any political career at any time, including in [his statement] a request that all Americans recognize its unequivocal character."

He was twenty days away from the U.S., his homecoming airplane landing at an airfield near West Point on Saturday, January 27. For three days he secluded himself, working on his reports and on his statement rejecting all political ambition. First to the President, next to an informal gathering of congressmen, and finally in a televised speech to the public he declared his belief in the need for NATO and his confidence in its success. The whole performance was remindful of a candidate making a pitch for support, but Eisenhower insisted he sought only national unity in back of NATO.

His stand meant that he was aligning his considerable influence with the administration in what was known at the time as the Great Debate, and so, inevitably, he was headed toward a clash with Senator Taft. The issues in the debate were no small ones, although the disputants had some difficulty, then and later, in defining them with any precision. Indeed, those same issues would be revived and reargued in agonizing fashion a generation later, while Americans killed and were killed in Vietnam and Cambodia and Laos. Acheson said what was involved was "an assault by the bipartisan right upon the Administration's postwar foreign policy." Taft said: "The debates . . . had even more to do with the question of who shall determine policy than with policy itself. . . . The fundamental issue in the 'great debate,'" he added, "was, and is, whether the President shall decide when the United States shall go to war or whether the people of the United States shall make that decision." More temperately, Eisenhower saw the issue to be "the President's constitutional right, in peacetime, to deploy and dispose American forces according to his best judgment and without the specific approval of the Congress."

Taft grew hot when he considered how Truman had committed American troops to Korea without having first obtained the consent of the Congress. In the same way, he argued, summoning up wild and exotic place names, a President "could send troops to Tibet to resist Communist aggression or to Indochina or anywhere else in the world, without the slightest voice of Congress in the matter."

For his trouble, Taft was stigmatized and derided as an isolationist, but in his way he was moved by much the same sort of concern that had provoked Eisenhower to his European tour. Eisenhower had been anxious about his lines of authority as supreme commander. Similarly Taft insisted that for the President to commit American troops to an international army without the approval of the Congress was to act with improper authority; for the President to appoint Eisenhower the supreme commander of such an international army without submitting his plan to the Congress was disruptive of authority and usurped the powers of the Congress.

For his part, Eisenhower maintained a pretense of neutrality even though he "thought the President's rights were unchallengeable." He was, however, "vitally interested" that NATO should have the wholehearted support of all national leaders. He wished to be assured that both major political parties were dedicated to the concept of a collective defense against "possible Communist aggression"; if he were so convinced, he would publish his rejection of his political ambitions. With this in mind, one February night he invited Taft to come secretly to the Pentagon for a testing catechism. The two men met alone in Eisenhower's office, each wrestling with his ambitions and his principles. If Taft proved to be, in Eisenhower's opinion, an isolationist, then Eisenhower would destroy the statement of rejection he had so carefully elaborated; if Taft agreed with Eisenhower's view of collective security, then the way for Taft was broad and open to the White House.

Surely to no one's astonishment Taft flunked Eisenhower's test. George Allen was waiting near at hand to drive home with Eisenhower—the Eisenhowers were staying with the Allens while the general made his final arrangements—and on the way he was told some of the details. Taft had explained his concern over the constitutional questions raised by the President's taking action without the advice and consent of the Congress; he had given Eisenhower the impression he was too much interested in "cutting the President, or the Presidency, down to size"; impatient with what seemed to him the playing of politics, Eisenhower had dismissed these details and insisted on an answer regarding support of the "collective principle." What were details to one were principles to the other, and vice versa: the two could never agree.

Eisenhower destroyed the statement he had drafted. He was back in uniform, but he was very decidedly still in politics. In mid-February he and his wife left for Europe aboard the *Queen Elizabeth*. His valued political advisers were disposed variously:

Kevin McCann could obviously no longer serve as assistant to the president of Columbia. Looking about, Eisenhower had found that the trustees of Defiance, a small college in Ohio, were looking for a president; he had on November 6 sent them a warm recommendation of McCann. But selections of that kind are not made overnight: McCann went to Europe with the Eisenhowers.

William Burnham for a time thought of going too; the partners of his firm, F. S. Smithers & Company, had met to discuss the possibility in November and had approved the idea; but by the end of the year Burnham had reconsidered. Perhaps he had better, he suggested to Eisenhower, stay in the U.S. as "your unofficial 'eyes and ears.'" Eisenhower agreed. The possibility was raised that Burnham, an officer in the air force reserve, might be called to active duty. Eisenhower instructed Burnham to call Major Schulz, his aide, and tell him, as an order coming from Eisenhower, that he was not to go on active duty but was "to be starred by the Air Force and not to be called under any consideration without General Eisenhower first being notified."

Burnham was far too useful to be pre-empted by the air force. He had arranged for George Whitney, president of J. P. Morgan & Company, to send Eisenhower a weekly letter ("biased" but "frank") on current affairs as seen from Whitney's office at the corner of Wall Street and Broad Street. Burnham could report that Senator James (Red) Duff of Pennsylvania was visiting Eisenhower's friends in Texas and keeping the supple lines of communication open and well oiled. Burnham could confer with Stassen and later report that 70 percent of the Republican state and county chairmen across the country favored support of the NATO program and had confidence in Eisenhower, while 10 percent—"localized in the [*Chicago Tribune*] Iowa-Illinois belt"—were against NATO and Eisenhower because of isolationist ideas or because they suspected Eisenhower's actions *"are being dictated by* [the Truman] administration."

That rankled. It called for hasty disinfection by Eisenhower's friend on the Republican right, the man who was at home in the *Chicago Tribune* Iowa-Illinois belt.

Edward J. Bermingham had come to Washington from his farm near Midway, Alabama, to touch base with those congressmen in whom he routinely kept bright the flame of the true faith. He had lunched with the Alabama delegation and looked in on Representative Charles Halleck of Indiana, who had been Republican whip in the Eightieth Congress; Representative Leslie Arends of Illinois, the current Republican whip; Senator Kenneth Wherry of Nebraska, and others. He had warned Eisenhower that many of these men suspected the general's views on NATO to be carbon copies of those asserted by Truman and Acheson. In a letter to Bermingham drafted for his signature soon after he landed in Europe, Eisenhower hotly denied the imputation that "my acceptance of military duty [is] a 'joining of the Administration' and that . . . I not only participate in its policy-making, but I support all its foreign programs, possibly even, its domestic ones." You, he reminded Bermingham, "are quite well aware of the extreme degree in which I differ with some of our governmental foreign and domestic policies of the past years." He went on at great length to establish his sound conservative credentials, rashly winding up: "I would say this: If in ten years, all American troops stationed in Europe for national defense purposes have not been returned to the United States, then this whole [NATO] project will have failed."* Bermingham would presently be able to report that he had talked again with Arends and Halleck and had "softened them considerably."

At all events, Eisenhower's appointment to the Supreme Headquarters Allied Powers Europe (SHAPE) had served one most useful purpose: it had prevented the Eisenhower bandwagon from gathering headway too fast, too soon.

---

* More than twenty years later some 250,000 American troops were still stationed in Europe for national defense purposes.

CHAPTER FOUR

NATO and SHAPE

WHEN GENERAL AND MRS. EISENHOWER took up residence in the Trianon Palace Hotel at Versailles late in February 1951, the United States was a good country to be away from. The President, the secretary of state, the Joint Chiefs of Staff, the Central Intelligence Agency—in fine, all those who shaped the nation's foreign policy—were agreed that the Kremlin was plotting every move made by the North Koreans and by the Chinese, that the Soviets had a diabolical blueprint for world conquest, and that every step in their master plan was taken according to an inexorable timetable. Anyone who protested that the resolutely nationalist stand taken by Tito and Yugoslavia in opposition to the Kremlin proved that Stalin's reach had exceeded his grasp, and carried with it the clear portent that the Chinese communists would be similarly intransigent, was regarded as a fool or a knave, and perhaps a traitor as well. The President was at pains to alarm everyone within earshot by voicing his mistaken fears. "Our homes, our nation, all the things we believe in, are in great danger," Truman told his countrymen. "This danger has been created by the rulers of the Soviet Union." Some months before he had warned the Congress that the Russians had "the power to attack our cities in force," an assessment that was, to say the least, most dubious.

These chilling alarums from the watchtower quite naturally set many good citizens to acting irrationally. The President, having declared a national emergency, proceeded to put the country on a wartime footing, complete with control of prices, fix of wages, lid on production of items favored by civilians, and full steam up for the industrial production of armaments. A costly Civil Defense Administration was instituted and proved to be a great nuisance without achieving any discernible good. For many months to come the hideous scream of air raid sirens would assault the ears of New Yorkers, sounding warnings of unnecessary drills; there was talk of building underground shelters at a cost of several billions of dollars; many affluent landowners, lost in fantasies of imminent doom, in fact did have holes dug in their meadows to house their private lead-lined catacombs.

Eisenhower, while he professed the prevailing ideology,* and in fact had transformed himself into a pre-eminent cold warrior, nevertheless was luckily removed from the more sour and dispiriting aspects of the Cold War. In France he was once again a captain of the forces of freedom, glamorous as glimpsed from afar, commander of the armies of democracy, valiant paladin, warm and friendly, strong and confident, the Hero. Once again his countrymen, watching him from across the Atlantic, could equip him with various sets of opinions as they chose, making him liberal or reactionary, Democrat or Republican, whatever. The grin, the affable temperament, the bright blue eyes, the confident and purposeful set of head and shoulders, the vivid impression of candor and trustworthiness—all combined to make him the ideal surrogate.

It was impossible not to like him and difficult to imagine that one's beliefs and politics might not also be his.

His mission at NATO was an unusual one, presenting alike some attractive advantages and some insoluble problems. The problems included the forging of a truly integrated multinational army in which German soldiers would be co-equals. "An integration of forces had to be attained," the supreme commander wrote, adding, "Germany as a full-fledged member was vital to NATO. Indeed, until we could find a satisfactory arrangement for bringing a strong German contingent into our forces, our defense arrangements could not be called effective." Since in 1951 no man could have found any such satisfactory arrangement, NATO was quite certain to be of only limited effectiveness. Moreover, the command structure of NATO was clumsy, confused, and complex, nor, in the multinational nature of things, could it ever be properly rationalized.

---

* In his long letter of February 28 to Bermingham, Eisenhower had written:

We, as Americans, face a deadly danger for a very simple reason. Communism, both ruthless in purpose and insidious as to method, is using the traditional Imperialistic designs of Russia and the present physical strength of Asia and Eastern Europe to promote the Communistic objective of *world revolution and subsequent domination of all the earth* by the Communistic Party, centering in Moscow.

. . . [The U.S. is] the chief target of Communistic destructive purpose. . . .

Up to this point, I think there is no loyal American today who would disagree; the sole point of difference seems to be as to *how* we should go about the task we understand must be performed.

First and foremost, it is almost trite to say that our own country must remain solvent; that bankruptcy for us would be a tremendous, if not decisive, victory for the Kremlin. . . . I am sure that one thing worse than bankruptcy would be military defeat, yet it is my contention that *the only way we can achieve military success either in preventing war or in winning a war is through preserving the integrity of our economy and our financial structure.*

Eisenhower tried to improve matters by surrounding himself with his wartime comrades so that he might at least be frustrated among friends, but he had only indifferent success. On his way to Paris he stopped off in London and invited his old G-2, Major General Sir Kenneth Strong, and his former deputy G-3, General Sir John Whiteley, to meet him at Claridges for supper. He urged them to enlist again under the brave new banners of NATO, but both declined. In France he found that his deputy was to be Field Marshal Montgomery. Now sharing a more precise goal, the two men got along better, but SHAPE could never be the same as SHAEF.

At least his military assistants and aides were a buoy to his spirits. Kevin McCann had a desk near at hand. Also from the U.S. had come Colonel Paul T. (Pete) Carroll, who had been on his staff in the Pentagon, had helped with many of his speeches, and was to keep a tutelary eye on much of his political correspondence. Lieutenant Colonel Craig Cannon was back with him again, and Lieutenant Colonel Schulz, his personal aide, was still faithfully at heel. Perhaps most important, the engaging Colonel James Gault was back again in uniform, having in the meantime prospered as an investment banker in London. All these officers gave Eisenhower their devotion and unquestioning loyalty. They could provide advice, a smartly administered headquarters, a balanced checkbook, a smooth flow of appointed visitors, some laughter, occasional good companionship, and constant sympathetic support; but the problems of policy remained intractable, the questions of politics still vexed. Aides and assistants could only shelter him. The private Eisenhower was still a perplexed man, tugged by private conflicts and contradictions.

There were compensations. For one, he was cast in the gratifying role of the fearless underdog. The estimates of the number of Russian divisions commonly supposed to be poised ready to sweep across Germany and the Lowlands to the Channel ranged from one hundred and twenty-five to one hundred and seventy-five—and against this horde there were a mere twelve to fifteen divisions rallied by NATO. This ratio—ten or more to one—was satisfactory to patriots convinced that for Americans no combat is fair until they are faced by such odds; but with time and closer scrutiny the ratio shrank. Knowledgeable persons pointed out that the Soviet division is considerably smaller than the American one; moreover, the estimated number of such Red Army formations dwindled, the authorities belatedly confessed, to seventy-five, perhaps even less. Still, the Russians had a clear edge in manpower should they choose to push it.

Was there ever any real danger that the Red Army would march west? In the main the menace was a bugaboo, widely advertised to enlist public support for the Cold War. Those who feared a bolshevik onslaught had forgotten, if they had ever truly comprehended, the enormity of the devastation wrought in Russia by the Germans. The Nazis had ravaged a sweep of land that had been home for eighty-eight million Russians, in the process killing some fifteen million civilians and laying waste fifteen large cities, nearly two thousand towns, and some seventy thousand villages. Factories, railroads, bridges, power stations, collective farms, highways, coal mines, oil wells, dams, turbines, generators, houses and buildings of every kind had been destroyed. Livestock had been killed or carried away. Hospitals, medical centers, universities, museums, libraries, theaters, churches—all looted and wrecked. Such staggering destruction—which, as the historian D. F. Fleming has well said, cannot be intellectually grasped but only emotionally sensed—motivated the profound and powerful Soviet determination that never again should it come to pass. Hence the insistence that the countries of eastern Europe have governments friendly or, better, subservient to Moscow; hence the zest with which the vast estates of the Prussian Junkers, the seedbed of German militarism, had been carved up into small farms; hence the dread when, in the U.S., the demand grew that western Germany be rearmed and German troops added to the NATO army. If the Americans could not understand that dread, the French could, and reckoned it might provoke the Russians to strike in order to forestall such rearmament.

Eisenhower doubted that the Soviets would attack, but only because he doubted that the Politburo in the Kremlin would risk their "luxury apartments, [their] automobiles and planes, [their] retinue of servants . . . the wealth [they] enjoy" in a venture that would end in their defeat by allied armies, supported by guerrilla forces uprisen in all the sullen, resentful satellite nations.

At all events, Eisenhower was better off away from the U.S., where tempers had become so hateful that Senator William Jenner, Republican of Indiana, had called General of the Army George Marshall a "front man for traitors . . . a living lie . . . an errand boy, a front man, a stooge, or a co-conspirator for this administration's crazy assortment of collectivist cutthroat crackpots and Communist fellow-traveling appeasers"; away from the U.S., where he would surely have been embarrassed by being called as a witness in the splenetic Senate inquiry into "the Facts Surrounding the Relief of General of the Army Douglas MacArthur"; away from the U.S., where in the spring of 1951 the mood was compounded of anger, bitterness, frustration, and resentment.

On Monday, April 2, General Eisenhower took operational control of the NATO forces. SHAPE, his headquarters, was first housed in a hotel quite near L'Étoile in Paris; later it was removed to a cluster of buildings put up by French army engineers on a sixty-acre tract about twelve miles west of Paris, close to the suburban village of Rocquencourt. There his office was a large comfortable room, conventionally outfitted, in the one-story central structure. He and Mrs. Eisenhower dwelt in a substantial villa about four miles closer to Paris, near the village of Marnes-la-Coquette. The house was called Villa St. Pierre by the French, Quarters No. 1 by the American officers at SHAPE. It was one of four gathered in a neighborly group. Of the other three, Gruenther and his wife lived in one; Major General Howard Snyder, the medical officer, and his wife were in another; the third was divided into apartments for Schulz and Master Sergeant Leonard Dry, Eisenhower's orderly.

Except for tours of inspection, trips to confer with ministers or officers in other NATO countries, and afternoons of golf at the Morfontaine Club under the discreet guard of the French security police, Eisenhower stayed close to home or office. The American officers and their wives customarily entertained each other in groups of four or eight or twelve, meeting on the weekend for lunch and an afternoon of bridge for the men and canasta for the women, or sharing an early dinner and then perhaps watching the private screening of a Hollywood movie. They lived not so much in France as at an American army post that happened to have been set down among French-speaking people. Even their servants were American Negro GIs. A very few of the American SHAPE officers lived in Paris. One of these was Major Wilton B. (Jerry) Persons, one of Eisenhower's old friends. Frequently Mrs. Persons would telephone Mrs. Eisenhower. "Come in to town," Mrs. Persons would urge. "You're stuck way out there, why don't you come in here?" "Oh, it's more fun out here," Mrs. Eisenhower would say. Save to attend some rare official function, the Eisenhowers never left their garrison society to visit Paris, a few miles away. They were and they remained incurious about that city's enchantments.

Their exclusivity followed naturally from the fact that NATO (and consequently SHAPE) was developed by Americans to serve the uses of American foreign policy. Tlhe journalist John Gunther noted that of the two hundred and thirty-eight officers at SHAPE, more than one hundred were American.* Since another forty-odd officers were British, nearly two-thirds of the command were most comfortable speaking English, so perforce English became SHAPE's common tongue. English the language, and inevitably ever more American the military and administrative methods. As Dean Acheson had so felicitously put it, NATO was "a means

---

* Eisenhower told C. L. Sulzberger, chief foreign correspondent of the *New York Times,* that assignments to SHAPE were not to be considered plums, but rather thorns; as each nation had more officers chosen to serve at SHAPE, it gained not in prestige but rather in responsibility.

and a vehicle for closer political, economic, and security cooperation with western Europe."

NATO bore the stamp of Pax Americana, and SHAPE was its branding iron.

When he assumed his duties on April 2, 1951, General Eisenhower was sixty years old, a bit thicker through the middle but brimming with good health, as vigorous and energetic as a man twenty years younger, affable and easygoing as always with the correspondents sent overseas to visit and interview him, alert, talkative, relaxed, sunny of disposition, his mind fixed on two tasks: how to get the job of establishing SHAPE done well and quickly, and how to maintain a flexibility of choice in connection with the presidential election of 1952. Since the legend of his reluctance to strive for or to accept public office has settled and formed into a sort of sedimentary rock—indeed, has been sedulously burnished by those who take legends in charge—it warrants a priority.*

Still at the root of Eisenhower's dilemma over politics in 1951 were his own warring impulses, the precept and example of the respected George Marshall, and forty years of training in the army. The professional soldier, it had been drilled into him, abjures politics. Back in January 1947, when George Marshall had arrived in Washington to take up his duties as secretary of state, he had spoken to a throng of reporters in terms of flat finality. "I can never be considered as a candidate for public office," he had said. "I never could be drafted." He had raked them with his cool, level stare, adding: "I mean just what I said and not something else." The subject had never again been raised. But no matter how many times Eisenhower had tried to echo Marshall's statement, he had failed to convince. The reporters—whether by instinct or because others had tipped them the wink —consistently refused to credit his protestations.

With military tradition and the blunt precedent of Marshall to shunt him away from political aspiration, with the unequivocal caveat of Army Regulation 600-10.18 (". . . may accept nomination for public office, provided such nomination is tendered without direct or indirect activity or solicitation . . .") to warn him, Eisenhower had in effect had his strategy dictated: to seem never to seek office, to trust in an overwhelming demand that he consent to having office pressed upon him. That this strategy was flawed was soon apparent. His speeches while at Columbia had already suggested that he agreed with the ideas of Herbert Hoover and Robert

---

* Eisenhower himself would later say that the "turning point" in his attitude toward politics came on Tuesday, September 4, 1951, after a lengthy conversation with Senator Henry Cabot Lodge, Republican of Massachusetts. "For the first time," Eisenhower wrote later, "I had allowed the smallest break in a regular practice of returning a flat refusal to any kind of proposal that I become an active participant [in] politics." Of course it was the public Eisenhower who made that statement.

Taft more often than not, and he had confessed as much (off the record, of course) to at least one journalist; but a man widely known to hold such conservative views could scarcely expect an overwhelming popular outcry that he become President. Further, he was beginning to realize that he could not indefinitely hesitate, a diffident violet on a shady bank; soon he would have to seek office and seek it hard, or Robert Taft would have roped all the necessary delegates and have a comfortable majority of them tucked away.

It was therefore quite certain, since both army regulations and sound strategy required it, that Eisenhower would forthrightly spurn all temptations to become a professed candidate. It was equally certain that a numerous company of his nearest advisers would spring up to press his candidacy for him. Some of those committed to work for him Eisenhower could not control. They would propagandize and organize on his behalf no matter what he said or did. Others, however, and they included the most zealous of his advocates, would have ceased their labors in an instant if he had raised a finger. He never did. They kept up their strenuous politicking, much of it directly under his nose and some of it, one is obliged to conclude, at his instigation.

Kevin McCann left SHAPE to go to Defiance College in August 1951. The desk with his name on it remained in Eisenhower's outer office, however, and sure enough McCann was back at SHAPE by March 7, 1952, having in the meantime been actively politicking on behalf of Eisenhower in Ohio and writing the book, *Man from Abilene*, that would serve as Eisenhower's campaign biography.

William Burnham, having stayed in the U.S. for a time as Eisenhower's "eyes and ears," visited SHAPE in March 1951 and returned to spur the candidacy in Wall Street, Washington, and Texas, with special attention paid to influential journalists. In May, Burnham was back working at SHAPE as a civilian "economic analyst," ready to advise and to greet the more important and wealthier businessmen who flocked to Eisenhower's headquarters throughout 1951; he stayed on tap at SHAPE until November 20, 1951.

Edward Bermingham, ranging as was his custom back and forth across the U.S.—from Alabama to Washington to Chicago to Wyoming to Denver, Colorado, to Tulsa, Oklahoma, to New York City—and even sandwiching in a trip to Paris to see Eisenhower, was able to relay accurate political gossip and creative political advice. Bermingham was busily developing the 1951–1952 version of the Republican "southern strategy," working with Senator Karl Mundt, Republican of South Dakota, "on a plan for the realignment of the political parties of the North and South," one that he hoped would "set a new pattern for American politics." In brief, he hoped to have southern Democrats and northern Republicans agree on a conservative national ticket for President and Vice President. (His hopes cannot have been inordinately high, however, for he contemplated a Republican ticket in 1952 headed by Eisenhower for President and Mundt for Vice President.) Exploring the possibilities of his "southern strategy" with Mundt were Senators Owen Brewster, Republican of Maine, and Walter George and Richard Russell, Democrats of Georgia. Bermingham told both Brewster and Mundt that "unless the [Republican] Party definitely negatives the FEPC bill [for establishment of a Fair Employment Practices Commission] as a national issue and returns it to the states we are just fanning the air." He and Mundt hoped Eisenhower would announce that he was a Republican, or that he was not a Democrat, or at least that he "would not be available for the Democratic nomination." Without such an expression from Eisenhower, Bermingham feared that Taft would be nominated by default. But Eisenhower had decided it would be best to identify himself with "no faction, group, or party . . . even by so much as a sneeze."

William E. Robinson, as an executive of the *New York Herald Tribune*, was on terms of easy familiarity with newspaper publishers and editors; since 1948 he had been diligently promoting the Eisenhower cause with the Scripps-Howard, Hearst, Knight, and other newspaper chains and with publishers of the more widely circulated magazines as well. Political writers of syndicated columns—Walter Lippmann, Joseph Alsop, David Lawrence, Roscoe Drummond, Arthur Krock—were likewise cultivated, directly or indirectly. The propaganda, at first discreet and later clamant, became everyone's daily fare. Robinson found time to inspect some advance sheets of the late James Forrestal's diaries, excerpts from which were to be published by the *Herald Tribune,* and he noticed with concern that Eisenhower's aspirations to be President had been twice chronicled in 1947 by Forrestal: might these observations not prove embarrassing to Eisenhower in 1952? He wrote to SHAPE, calling the entries to Eisenhower's attention. The general's response was prompt: forget it.*

Clifford Roberts visited SHAPE and Eisenhower regularly throughout 1951. When the volunteer organization Citizens for Eisenhower was formed in the summer of 1951, Roberts was standing ready with an ample bankroll to finance it and also the host of Ike Clubs that sprang up overnight all over the country, like mushrooms after a summer rain. Roberts was assisted in this financing by others of Eisenhower's intimates from

* Eisenhower was thoroughly familiar with the Forrestal diaries. He had been sent the complete, unedited manuscripts by Clarence Dillon in September 1950, long before they were prepared for publication. His careful notes had been turned over to his aide, Schulz, and placed in his vault file.

Augusta National or Blind Brook—W. Alton (Pete) Jones, Ellis (Slats) Slater, L. B. (Bud) Maytag, and so on—and by Republican financiers—John Hay (Jock) Whitney and Sidney Weinberg of Goldman, Sachs, among many others—who sensed that at last the horse they were backing could win in a romp. Roberts was useful in other ways, too. Whenever Eisenhower found particularly provocative one of the weekly letters sent him by George Whitney, president of J. P. Morgan & Company, he would have a copy made for Roberts, consult with him about it, and then incorporate Roberts's comments in his reply to Whitney.

Milton Eisenhower, the general's youngest brother, had by 1951 left Kansas State College to become president of Pennsylvania State College, and the general sorely wanted his advice. By the end of May he was cautiously confiding to Milton some aspects of the dilemma that had him horned: "I do not mind telling you (for no repetition to anyone) that some of my friends have, in recent months, given me some anxious doubts as to the correctness of my confident assumption that I would never have any duty outside of uniform. . . . But I am clear as to one thing . . . I have no intention of voluntarily abandoning this critical duty unless I reach a conviction that an even larger *duty* compels me to do so. . . . I flatly stick to my resolution that I shall never *seek anything*." He coached his brother in the responses he might be called on to make to the avid politicians; none too soon, for before long Hugh Scott, a Republican congressman from Pennsylvania, and Harold Talbott, an executive of various corporations who had been the front man in raising funds for the campaigns of Wendell Willkie and Thomas Dewey, were both applying pressure on Milton in a Philadelphia hotel room. Milton told them he was opposed to his brother's entry into politics. "I can say positively," he asserted stoutly, following his brother's instructions, "that, so far as his personal inclinations are concerned, he has had and still has a violently negative attitude toward this political question." Talbott and Scott nodded. Yes, they agreed, it would be best to lie low for the next, say, ninety days; after that, the boom could start resounding. As the summer wore on, Milton had even greater cause for unhappiness: his name was being cited as authority by Scott and others, in the magazine *Newsweek* and elsewhere, to the effect that the general was a Republican, would respond to a draft, and so on. General Eisenhower, better informed than his brother, told him to relax. "Please quit worrying," he wrote Milton in September, "and don't forget your sense of humor." In October Robinson visited Milton at State College. They wrote to the general to suggest that they bring together six or eight of his "closest and most trusted friends" for an all-day secret session to discuss what he should do. For his part, Milton found himself in the position of urging his brother to stand for election. If the choice before the voters in 1952 were to be Truman or Taft, Milton argued, "any personal sacrifice on the part of any honest American citizen is wholly justified."

To General Eisenhower it was now plain that he must take steps to let one group of his advisers know what other groups of them had been up to. He had been appraised of the extensive organization on his behalf, reaching all the way to the Pacific northwest; Walter Williams of Seattle was already being mentioned as co-chairman of Citizens for Eisenhower. He knew, too, of the conversations between Lucius Clay and Governor Dewey. To his brother Milton he sent a hurried letter on October 31, enclosing a copy to be sent to Robinson: he was about to take plane for Washington; he would be at the suite reserved for him at the Statler; he planned to meet Lucius Clay there on the evening of Monday, November 5; could Milton be there too?

Lucius Clay, after retiring from the army, had been named chairman of the board of the Continental Can Company. He had close connections with men in industry and finance and also in the world of politics; he was known to be a close and longtime friend of Eisenhower. In the circumstance he had not been astonished to get a telephone call inviting him to come, late on a Saturday afternoon in October, to Governor Dewey's suite in the Roosevelt Hotel in Manhattan. Besides Dewey, the men present were Herbert Brownell, Jr., and J. Russell Sprague, two veteran Republican politicians bearing the ribbons and scars of the two presidential campaigns Dewey had fought and lost. These men had asked Clay: Would Eisenhower run? Clay had answered, Yes—*if*. Only *if* the nomination were positively assured him would he agree to accept it. (This was another way of saying what Eisenhower had already told his brother Milton: "I shall never *seek anything*.") That had been enough for Dewey, and the professional politicians had at once set about planning, organizing, hiring staff, finding office space, raising money.

When General Eisenhower, supreme commander of NATO forces, stepped off his airplane at Washington on Monday, November 5, there must have been at least a thousand American citizens who knew cursed well that he was a certain candidate for the Republican nomination for the presidency, and another ten million, to put it minimally, who would have hocked the family jewels if offered odds of one-to-ten that he would not run. Nevertheless, faithful to the ritual that only the man himself can say the word, a swarm of reporters clustered about him and sought to pry the word out of him. No use. The man dismissed as a boob at politics fielded every question and every insinuation, grinned, and went away to report to President Truman.

The President and Eisenhower talked for some little time. Having transacted their business about NATO and SHAPE, they turned to more momentous affairs. Truman, who could not be counted among the thousand citizens who knew for a certainty of Eisenhower's political plans, told him that the offer made in 1948 (Eisenhower as Democratic candidate for President, Truman stepping down to be candidate for Vice President) still held good in 1952, should Eisenhower elect to accept it. Eisenhower answered that such an offer presented him with difficulties, typical of which was his disagreement with the Democratic party on its policy toward labor. He indicated his distaste for the Wagner Act. The Democrats, he said, were not severe enough with labor. The two men nodded. They were quits with each other.*

Thereupon General Eisenhower was driven to the Statler Hotel, where he was received in his suite with much enthusiasm. He was in a world and at a time when everybody wanted him, sought him out, promised him whatever he wished: an exhilarating moment. Nothing novel; it had been like this since June of 1945, but still it was more intense now, twelve months before the next presidential election. Eisenhower could be forgiven if he experienced the inner glow that attends an awareness that your most influential acquaintances are determined on making you their chief.

Still, he was not entirely happy. With the prize within his grasp, he was beginning to think of reasons to spurn it, and so was his wife. Both in public and in private he grew more devious. At times the positions he took were flatly contradictory. He asked Lucius Clay to serve as intermediary with the professional politicians; back again at SHAPE he wrote Bermingham to ask if he would direct fund-raising efforts for his campaign; when Stassen visited him at SHAPE, their conversation was predicated on the assumption that Eisenhower would shortly be an avowed candidate for the Republican nomination.† Yet at the same time the general persisted in keeping secret his own political affiliation. When a foreign service officer came to SHAPE from Paris for a discussion of NATO affairs, Eisenhower

* The material in this paragraph is based upon the account by Arthur Krock (*Memoirs*, pp. 268–269), which was in turn based upon the testimony of William O. Douglas, then a justice of the Supreme Court. The account was later denied by both Truman and Eisenhower. Krock stands by his report, which he says was later "obliquely" confirmed by Eisenhower in private conversations.

† After their talk Stassen went back to his hotel in Paris, the Crillon, and wrote Eisenhower a long letter (eighteen pages of Crillon notepaper) in which he told Eisenhower of his political dreams, precisely and in detail. He proposed to run hard against Taft in the various primary contests but not simply as a stalking-horse for Eisenhower. He perceived three possibilities: Taft would whip Stassen, Stassen would take enough delegates from Taft so that Eisenhower could catch him, Stassen might win the nomination on his own; of these the second seemed most likely, in which case, Stassen wrote, "I am confident that you will be elected and will be a superb President and I will be very happy with this result."

told him: "I've just turned down forty thousand dollars for one word. . . . There was a fellow from *McCall's* [magazine] in here this morning, who offered me forty thousand dollars for a yes-or-no answer to the question, 'Are you a Republican?'" Eisenhower could take relish in the substantial mystification he had created out of the void; he could find a sardonic amusement in the way journalists salivated whenever he tinkled the bell; but he went further. To Cy Sulzberger, the foreign correspondent who had been his companion at golf and cards, he talked for more than an hour on December 11, privately, confidentially, and apparently with utmost candor, denying the evidence of everyone's eyes and ears, the evidence stacked in file folders just outside his office. From Sulzberger's notes:

He does *not* want to run for President. He has never wanted to run for that office. . . .

He has no intention of making any move to help those political leaders who are seeking to draft him as the Republican candidate. . . .

He is fully aware that there are many people who would like him to run for the Presidency, but . . . he does not intend to make any move in that direction, either covert or overt. . . . If the American people draft him as a candidate, he would respond to a call of duty, but he hopes this will not occur. He has no interest in politics . . .

. . . The politicians told him he would have to make some move pretty soon to give them a clue. He refused to do this. . . .

Eisenhower said that he would respond to a "call of duty" only if it were demonstrated by the country, forcing a convention to nominate him.

Sulzberger, most impressed with Eisenhower's "sincerity and fineness of character," on his departure asked the general for an inscribed photograph.

One consideration on Eisenhower's mind at this time was financial. Sid Richardson had earlier visited him at SHAPE and, besides agreeing to relay a message from Eisenhower to Senator Duff ("After I made my report to him from you," Richardson wrote Eisenhower, "I think the man wanted to kiss me"), had invited Eisenhower to join him in an offshore oil-drilling operation along the Louisiana coast. If the deal went through, if the well came in, if word of it got around—say, during the weeks just before the Republican convention—would he be smeared? would it cause a scandal? Already the old smears were circulating again—that Mamie Eisenhower was a dipsomaniac, that Eisenhower planned to divorce her and marry Kay Summersby, that Eisenhower's health was a ticklish proposition—and here was another possibility to be added, that Eisenhower had personally profited from his friendship with the Texas oil zillionaires and could no longer be trusted to make national policy in respect of petroleum on a detached and impartial basis.

Problems. Problems.

Once the professional politicians had been let into the arena, expedience became the formula. The amateur politicians, including Eisenhower's trusted friends and companions from Blind Brook and Augusta National, became at least as importunate as the professionals. Both groups chipped away at his obdurate public position, seeking to make it conform more precisely with what he had told them privately.

First came a flutter of cablegrams and letters filled with veiled references to such anonyms as "dependable friend," "prominent Texan," and "genial resident of Washington" (i.e., Lucius Clay, Sid Richardson, and George Allen). This was succeeded by a trip to SHAPE by Clifford Roberts and William Robinson for the purpose of convincing Eisenhower that he should publicly identify himself as a Republican. They arrived at Marnes-la-Coquette at about the same time as a letter from President Truman, who like every journalist in the U.S. desired Eisenhower to reveal the authoritative word: what were his political intentions? With Roberts and Robinson on hand to advise him, Eisenhower was able to fabricate a superbly ambiguous answer: he would not seek, although many pressed him to do so; the possibility of his political activity was "so remote as to be negligible," but on the other hand who can tell? Eisenhower was reluctant to move as far or as fast as his friends wished. In a letter he reminded Clay that he was still in uniform; once again he cited the pertinent army regulation.

The politicians could wait no longer. Henry Cabot Lodge, their chairman (for tactical reasons Dewey and Brownell had to lie low), made a swift trip to and from SHAPE; on January 6, 1952, he told reporters that Eisenhower in fact was a Republican, that he would accept the Republican nomination if it were offered him, and that he was aware of and in accord with the plans of his supporters. By going so far, Lodge had blundered. At SHAPE, Eisenhower exploded into one of his towering rages and dispatched a sharp cablegram of rebuke to Clay. Then, swallowing his choler, he handed the avid correspondents a prepared statement. He did not confirm that he was a Republican but only that Lodge had afforded "an accurate account of the general tenor of my Republican voting record." He did not say he would accept the Republican nomination but only that Lodge and his associates had the right "to place before me next July a duty that would transcend my present responsibility." He could not say that he approved what Lodge and the others were up to but only that "American citizens [may] organize in pursuit of their common convictions." To all these equivocations he subscribed one flat promise: "Under no circumstances will I ask for relief from this assignment in order to seek nomination for political office, and I shall not participate in the preconvention activities of others who may have such an intention with respect to me."

Alas! once in politics such promises are worthless.

As he sought to make clear, in letters to Bermingham and a few others, Eisenhower believed his statement should suffice "those who are trying to lay . . . a duty before me." "If these individuals are convinced," he added, still cross with Lodge, "that more than this is necessary from me, then this whole plan of theirs should be forthwith abandoned." But these hopes too would be frustrated.

The need was to demonstrate both to the candidate and to the Taft forces that a ground swell of public enchantment with Eisenhower was indeed running. Uncle Sid Richardson peeled a few banknotes from his roll. Madison Square Garden in New York City was hired for a midnight rally. A few celebrities served to pack the hall. The proceedings were filmed and a print handed to Jacqueline Cochran, a well-known aviator and wife of Floyd B. Odlum, a financier who had shown imagination in the manifold uses of the holding company. Amid a fanfare of publicity Miss Cochran flew the print across the Atlantic, and it was shown the general and his wife at a private screening in their living room—the sound and image of fifteen thousand people chanting, "We want Ike! We like Ike!"

By contrast, the flight to London of Clay, Richardson, and Allen in early February was made in relative secrecy. Eisenhower was in London, stopping at Jimmy Gault's town house, for the purpose of attending the funeral of George VI. Clay's mission was critical.

Clay knew what the politicians wanted, but it came as a rude shock to Eisenhower. Clay asked three questions: Would Eisenhower campaign if he were nominated? Would he campaign in order to win the nomination? Would he come back to the U.S. before the Republican convention to help his supporters?

Just forty days before, Eisenhower had publicly pledged he would do no such thing. His neck began to redden, an ominous sign.

Clay argued that he must agree. The Democrats had been in power for twenty years, and only Eisenhower could now unseat them.

Eisenhower lost his temper.

Clay insisted that to win the nomination was harder than to win the election. No matter what may have been promised Eisenhower before, he faced a bitter fight if he was to establish his leadership of the Republicans. Taft had already secured a frightening number of delegates—perhaps as many as four hundred and fifty of the six hundred and four necessary for nomination—and had another seventy or so wavering on the fence. Eisenhower must move at once or risk losing by default.

Here was the moment of decision. Did he want to be President or not? He could describe his conclusion as he chose—term it a call to a higher duty, a transcendent obligation—but rhetoric to one side he must now make up his mind. No help to lose his temper, no use to cuss politics and politicians; he must answer Clay's questions. It was like the exquisite pause before the first plunge into cold water.

He considered. Apart from his own conflicting emotions, he knew that back home many people were counting on him. Word of their activities had reached SHAPE daily, hourly. The chairman of the board of Standard Oil of California had resigned all his positions save one directorship in order to devote full time to the Eisenhower candidacy. From H. Jack Porter, a Houston oil operator, came news of the mighty struggle already joined in Texas, testing whether the delegates from that state would be committed to Taft or to Eisenhower. Paul Hoffman had gone on leave from the Ford Foundation to help organize Citizens for Eisenhower. The board chairman of General Mills was rallying support throughout Minnesota and neighboring states. These instances could be multiplied by the dozen.

At length Eisenhower nodded. Okay. Yes, he would campaign, he would fight for the nomination, he would return to the U.S. before the convention. He would go further: he would ask to be relieved of his command, he would resign his commission. (Necessary, in view of army regulations.) If he was in a fight, he had best get in it with both fists swinging.

Before they parted, Eisenhower and Clay discussed strategy. Clay wanted Eisenhower to come home in June. He also urged a trip to Abilene and a speech to the nation by radio and television. Quite naturally the politicians and image-makers were anxious that their candidate be identified as a Kansas Republican, a farm boy, the personification of all the sturdy American simplicities. Perhaps his speech might deal with peace, always an attractive theme, especially so when treated by a professional soldier.

Eisenhower was dubious about the value of an appearance in Abilene. He feared "a definite loss of sentimental interest" with no compensatory gain of "the so-called ammunition that the [political] workers need." But he went along with the idea, since "so many of my friends are perfectly certain they are right" about it. Both Clifford Roberts and William Robinson agreed the trip to Abilene would be valuable. Robinson, who was in New Hampshire busily preparing for the primary election of

March 11, scribbled an eighteen-page letter full of advice about Abilene and suggestions for the Abilene speech. But about Eisenhower's coming home to stay in June, he and Roberts were not so sure. "I'll talk to you about that one when I see you early in March," Roberts wrote Eisenhower.

On the night of the New Hampshire primary, Eisenhower played bridge with Roberts, Gruenther, and Sulzberger. The general ably feigned a lack of interest in the results. (He won a comfortable plurality: 46,661 votes to Taft's 35,838, with MacArthur trailing badly; these results had been accurately forecast by Clay and others among Eisenhower's advisers.)

The politicians had by this time taken firm control. When Clay arrived in Paris in mid-March, it was to tell Eisenhower he must return home no later than June 1. To quit SHAPE presented unusual difficulties: the outfit was in fact American and Eisenhower the choice of an American President, but SHAPE was legally the creature of fourteen allied governments (Greece and Turkey having been accommodated within NATO) and in consequence Eisenhower technically served fourteen masters. His first annual report to NATO was due on April 2; it presented a convenient occasion to request Truman for relief.

On April 11 Truman announced that Eisenhower's request for relief had been approved, to take effect on June 1. Now all was in the open: no longer needed anyone speculate.

Now, moreover, General Eisenhower was loose at last in the perilous byways of politics. Walter Lippmann noted the hazards in a letter to his old friend and associate in journalism, Herbert Bayard Swope:

> The thing that I have been worrying about in connection with Ike is his tendency to talk too much on too many subjects. Now, of course, he does this only privately, but once he takes off his uniform I am afraid he won't easily restrain himself.
>
> His great strength and his great value to the country lies . . . in that he stands for the big things about which there are really no violent issues. He must find some formula for not getting entangled in the little issues that are quite hot and full of politics.

This sound advice reached Eisenhower, perhaps forwarded by Swope, perhaps by Baruch, but too late, for already Eisenhower had got entangled in an issue that was indeed quite hot and full of politics. On March 24 Jack Porter, the oil operator in charge of capturing for Eisenhower the Republican delegates from Texas, had written to inquire about Eisenhower's views on the disposition of the petroleum deposits that lay under the continental shelf in the Gulf of Mexico and elsewhere—the offshore oil fields. The value of the deposits had been reckoned at one hundred billions of dollars at the prices then current. Who owned this immense wealth—the federal government or the proximate states? On the answer trembled the delicate price-supply balance crucial to the industry's control of petroleum. The cry of states' rights was duly raised, along with dire warnings of assaults upon free enterprise and socialist conspiracies to subvert the sanctity of private property. The "tidelands grab" by the Democrats in Washington, Porter urged Eisenhower, "is one of the major moves" in the campaign "to nationalize the oil industry."

On March 28 Eisenhower replied to Porter: "I agree with the principle that federal ownership in this case, as in others, is one that is calculated to bring about steady progress toward centralized ownership and control, a trend which I have bitterly opposed." Since at least one of every three of Eisenhower's wealthy supporters was either an oilman or an investment banker with heavy stakes in petroleum, the general's stand was scarcely astonishing. Nor can it be ascribed to his personal interest in an oil drilling venture (which had, by the way, come in a winner), for he had long since shown his conservative sponsors that his professed notions of political economy grew from the same predilections as their own.

Porter saw to it that Eisenhower's statement was properly publicized by releasing it to the biggest Texas newspapers. The timing was interesting: it was published a few days before the scheduled vote in the Senate on a bill to give the states title to all the offshore oil lands. (The bill was approved by the Congress and vetoed by President Truman; the Congress could not then muster enough votes to override the veto.) In this way Eisenhower found himself embroiled in a political squabble, but to no bad effect: his name was sweet with the states' rights crowd yet without stigma to those likely to regard the bill as a monstrous giveaway of the nation's natural resources. Still, the incident was cautionary. By the time Lippmann arrived at SHAPE to discuss European questions, Eisenhower was ready to act on his lesson. Lippmann, it was said, found him "vague and foggy" during their conversation.

In this testing time, besides supervising his remaining tasks at SHAPE, Eisenhower had to launch upon cram courses in the mysteries that would confront a President, everything from agriculture to wage and price controls. There was no want of advisers, but the advice was not always of a virginal purity. "It seems necessary to walk around some of the questions presented," he wrote his brother Milton, adding dryly, "I seem to sense a difference between a man's convictions and what he believes to be politically feasible."

All problems paled beside those of foreign policy, one of which, plainly enough, was administrative: who would be the secretary of state if Eisenhower were elected President? There is no evidence that Eisenhower concerned himself with the question at this early date, but other strong-willed men deemed it vital to make a case for or against the conspicuous candidate for the appointment.

John Foster Dulles, Eisenhower's senior by two years, tall, spare, stooped, melancholy of visage, dour, a man who gave the impression, as he hunched over a conference table, of being a glum and worldly turtle, was in every way prepared to be secretary of state. Over four generations his family, as he was fond of proclaiming, had served the Department of State, and two of his kin—a grandfather, John Foster, and an uncle by marriage, Robert Lansing—had actually been appointed secretary, the one by Benjamin Harrison and the other by Woodrow Wilson. He had himself, when a youth, been entrusted with various trivial diplomatic chores.

Further, religion and commerce had combined in Dulles to produce a man who was at once a Calvinist evangel and a shrewd casehardened man of affairs. A devout Presbyterian upbringing, with emphasis on the Bible and *Pilgrim's Progress,* replenished by a spiritual experience of remarkable intensity when he attended the Oxford Conference on Church and State in 1937, persuaded him, as he later wrote, "that there was no way to solve the great perplexing international problems except by bringing to bear upon them the force of Christianity," and led him by 1941 to become chairman of a Commission on a Just and Durable Peace which had been founded by the Federal Council of the Churches of Christ in America. He was zealous in the search "to find ways whereby the moral force of Christendom [might] make itself felt in the conduct of nations." In those same years he had used his redoubtable intellectual powers to become senior partner of Sullivan & Cromwell, a law firm with rooms in Wall Street, great prestige in financial circles, and a wide experience of negotiations on behalf of the biggest international cartels. He had a reputation as the world's most highly paid lawyer, membership on the directorates of an impressive set of corporations with international ramifications, and welcome access to financial leaders in all that part of the world still under the sway of capitalism; i.e., free enterprise.

Now Luke (XVI, 13) and Matthew (VI, 24) are agreed: "Ye cannot serve God and mammon." But Dulles had in these ways heeded the call of both, featly yoking them in the battle against atheistic communism wherever it might be found. One of the other texts he had studied was *Problems of Leninism* by J. V. Stalin, for a good lawyer must know the wiles and stratagems of his adversary; and some of his critics had been quick to point out that while collective security against Nazi Germany had never roused his enthusiasm, he could hardly wait to marshal a cordon of collective security against Russia.

True, he had enjoyed a brief isolationist phase before U.S. entry into the war. When the Japanese struck against China, when Hitler attacked first Poland, then the Low Countries and France, and finally Russia (that is to say, from 1937 to November 1941), Dulles counseled remaining aloof: "Only hysteria," he had said, "entertains the idea that Germany, Italy or Japan contemplates war against us." But by 1952 he was an outstanding elder statesman of the Republican party, recognized on all sides as its resident expert in foreign affairs. He had been a chief Republican architect of the U.S. wartime bipartisan foreign policy; a Republican critic of developments at the Dumbarton Oaks Conference in 1944, which laid the foundation for the United Nations; senior adviser to the U.S. delegation at the United Nations Conference in San Francisco (1945), where the structure of the U.N. was established; several times an American representative to the U.N. General Assembly; a Republican adviser at the meetings of foreign ministers at London in 1945, Moscow in 1947, and Paris in 1949; and the diplomatic hardhat who, overriding the protests of Russians, Indians, Burmese, Filipinos, Indonesians, and Netherlanders alike, drafted the peace treaty with Japan in 1951. What more appropriate than to cap that succession of achievements with an appointment as President Eisenhower's secretary of state soon after the elections in 1952?

One drawback was that Eisenhower knew Dulles only slightly. The situation, in early 1952, required the elegance of protocol. Dulles drafted two thoughtful memoranda on American conduct of foreign affairs and handed them to Eisenhower's designated intermediary, Lucius Clay. In one of them Dulles urged that the U.S. announce a policy of "retaliation," at a time and in a manner to be chosen by the U.S., in the event of any Soviet military aggression. Such an approach, he argued, would enable the U.S. to conserve its military power rather than expend it in costly defensive installations all over the world. Eisenhower was not entirely satisfied. On April 15 he wrote Dulles that he was disturbed by the possibilities of what he called "political aggression"—he had in mind the coup that had put Czechoslovakia within the Soviet sphere, but an internal shift of forces that upset the status quo anywhere outside that sphere would qualify—since the damage to "our resulting economic situation" would be as severe as if the aggression were by force. "To my mind," Eisenhower observed, "this is the case where the theory of 'retaliation' falls down."

Carefully clearing the details with Clay, Dulles arranged to meet Eisenhower at SHAPE on May 3. Very quickly they were Foster and Ike.

They conferred again in the next few days. Back in the U.S., Dulles conveyed to a few journalists an impression of dissatisfaction with Eisenhower: the general was not attending to his homework, he pushed aside the memoranda given him about foreign affairs and at night preferred to relax with his tales of the Wild West. Toward Eisenhower, however, Dulles behaved with a wary deference. He wrote on May 20:

> The most interesting development has been a call I had from Bob Taft, who asked me to talk with him . . . Anticipating what he had in mind, I talked the situation over with Herb Brownell and Lucius Clay and we agreed that I should, if possible, try and shape the discussions so as to promote the foreign policy plank in the Republican platform which would avoid an open battle between the so-called "isolationist" wing and the so-called "internationalist" wing, and also avoid the possible risk of a plank being adopted on which it would be difficult for you to run.
>
> When I saw Taft he bid for my support or at least "neutrality," saying that he believed that we could work together on foreign policy. I said that it was my intention to come out in public support of you. . . .
>
> Taft then expressed the thought that I might attempt to prepare a draft [of the plank] on behalf of both you and him. . . .
>
> Immediately on my return I got in touch with Lucius and Herb Brownell, who seemed gratified at the way the situation had developed. However, I wanted you personally to know and approve . . .
>
> I do not want any possible doubt in your mind as to where I stand. As soon as I returned from Paris I gave Herb Brownell my unqualified "proxy."

Dulles so could present himself as the only man to have the confidence of both factions of the Republican party. Assuredly nothing now stood in the way of his climactic appointment?

Or was there something? In May 1952, before Eisenhower left Europe for Washington, he had a visit from an old friend and wartime comrade, Anthony Eden, once again in office as foreign secretary. An exchange of good wishes: perhaps they would once again be working closely together. Eden felt obliged to go further. Should Eisenhower become President, Eden expressed the hope that Dulles would not be appointed his secretary of state, "because," he said, "I do not think I would be able to work with him." This remarkable request was based upon a British mistrust of Dulles that had its roots in the negotiation of the Japanese peace treaty: Dulles had, in the British view, violated an undertaking he had made with Herbert Morrison, foreign secretary for the Labour government; Eden was not quite ready, as Morrison decidedly was, to consider Dulles's action a calculated duplicity, but he unquestionably found most trying

Dulles's self-righteousness and his disregard "for the consequences of his own words."

As to Eden's entreaty, Eisenhower kept his own counsel.

It was getting time to leave, to head for home, to take up the strange challenges of a new sort of public life. Last-minute suggestions were streaming in on every hand. Here was a letter from Roy Roberts, president of the *Kansas City Star*, with advice about the scheduled speech at Abilene: "Be yourself. Write your own speech, give your own views, and be yourself." This sound advice Eisenhower turned over to Kevin McCann, who was to draft the Abilene speech. Here was a note from Bill Robinson: he had got a half-dozen experienced reporters—John Gunther, Marquis Childs, Peter Edson of Scripps-Howard, Roscoe Drummond, James Reston, and Bert Andrews—to draw up a list of good tough questions, questions calculated to embarrass or discomfit Eisenhower, so that the fledgling candidate might prepare himself for the free-swinging press conferences in which he might soon be baited, cornered and trapped.

If the prospect made Eisenhower uneasy, there was one consolation: on May 27 the foreign ministers of France, Italy, the Benelux countries, and West Germany signed the accord that created the European Defense Community (EDC). The treaty still had to be ratified by the various governments, but at last it seemed that West German soldiers were to be added to NATO's strength. Eisenhower's mission at SHAPE had moved appreciably closer to the point where it might be described as a success.

CHAPTER FIVE

The Plunge

EVENTS ON EISENHOWER'S RETURN on June 1 had been planned to fit into a becoming pattern, but after a certain point they took an erratic downward plunge.

The report to the commander in chief. More a courtesy call than a formal presentment, the visit was an amicable prelude to a political brawl the make-believe nature of which Eisenhower imperfectly understood. Truman had imagined that the world hero was a Democrat; certainly he had hoped he was. Now, as the two men confronted each other, the President knew the general would be a partisan opponent, and a formidable one. Strong handshake, vivid blue eyes, wide friendly grin; even without his uniform this man would walk off with votes in boxcar lots. The talk turned to politics and its propensity for subsisting in the gutter. Eisenhower grumbled about the nasty rumors once again making the rounds, the slanders about him and his wife. Truman nodded sympathetically and asked about them. With distaste, Eisenhower synopsized the worst of them. Professional politician contemplated professional soldier with an amused compassion. "If that's all it is, Ike," said Harry Truman, "then you can just figure you're lucky."

The first press conference. What for a lesser man would have been an act of cowardice was for Eisenhower a stroke of prudence: with the connivance of the secretary of defense, reporters were summoned to the Pentagon to meet a candidate who, being still in uniform and within military environs, could decline to answer questions on other than military matters. Later the general was mustered out of the army at a ceremony held on the Pentagon steps, but he was able to slip out of Washington without again facing the press corps. The journalists were frustrated and cross, but Eisenhower had won a postponement of a few days during which he could observe, listen, and get a sense of the national temper.

The triumphal return to the scenes of his childhood. Since Joseph McConnell, president of the National Broadcasting Company (and a Blind Brooker), had decided that Eisenhower's big speech at Abilene qualified as a "public service," the facilities of radio and television could be offered without a drain upon Eisenhower's campaign funds. To have the necessary cables and electronic gadgetry run in from Omaha, Nebraska, cost some sixty thousand dollars, but the other networks blithely engaged to share the expense. The entire visit to Abilene proceeded under the unblinking gaze of an enormous apparatus of publicity. On June 4 the candidate came by private airplane to Kansas City and by private train to Abilene, with cameras recording each stage of the journey. A ceremony to dedicate his boyhood home as a shrine, a ceremony to lay the cornerstone of what would be the Eisenhower Museum close by, a parade of floats and high school bands in honor of the homecome hero, who sat with his wife and a group of friends atop the marquee of the Sunflower Hotel, Abilene's premier structure. The climax was to have been an address delivered to a vast throng—twenty to forty thousand people gathered in the town park, according to the promoters' fond expectation—and broadcast nationwide by radio and television. The speech itself was intended as the first of a series in which Eisenhower would make known his views on the problems then perplexing the republic. It had been happily envisaged as the kickoff of his romp to the White House. In the event, it was more like the knell for a funeral cortège. A sudden heavy rainstorm kept the crowds at home and turned the park into a quagmire. On the television screen Eisenhower loomed and diminished, the shadowy picture of an old man reading, in stumbling and uncertain fashion, a dull and gassy speech to a display of empty seats. The hand of the amateur was everywhere evident.

In New York the professionals, gazing impassively at the televised catastrophe, determined on prompt remedial action. Abilene had been a mistake. Since he had already been provided time to study all embarrassing questions, the candidate might be trusted to conduct a televised press conference there, but he must then come back to New York and take up residence at Columbia so that various restoratives might be applied to his public image. The Republican convention was little more than five weeks away. Taft had the irreproachable Republican record and the Republican program calculated to fetch a convention of orthodox Republican traditionalists who were panting, after twenty long parched years, for the lush green pastures of patronage and power. To offset Taft's undeniable magnetism, buttressed by perfervid loyalties, there was only Eisenhower's popularity and personality. The imperious need, then, was to hog-tie as many Republican delegates as possible and expose them, close up, to the furnace of that personality—the hearty handclasp, the bright blue eyes, the grin—while encouraging the candidate to expatiate, pianissimo, on his political beliefs. At least in Abilene he had met a random assortment of delegates from a half-dozen midwestern states. Now procedures must be organized, regularized, systematized.

None of this was what the candidate had hoped for or been led to expect. Where now the dreams of being nominated by the acclamation of both major parties? Where now the proud pledge, "I flatly stick to my resolution that I shall never *seek anything*"? Later, in tranquillity, he would recall of this anxious time that he "had no burning ambition to win the nomination"; he would even look back on the disastrous speech at Abilene as "a good statement of sound progressive Republican doctrine"; but in truth Eisenhower lusted after both nomination and election, and his eight days at Morningside Heights—a blur of appointments and conferences with new faces, of telephone calls from strange voices, all urgent and immediate—were charged with a mounting concern that tested his natural sunny optimism. For the first time he began to comprehend that he might lose the nomination to Senator Taft. That would indeed, for a world hero, be a humiliating experience.

Eight days in New York was long enough. City and state were too firmly associated in the Republican mind with Governor Dewey—the "me-too" candidate who had, in the vengeful view of Taft's adherents, twice led the

GOP to defeat—for Eisenhower to linger there. It was decided he should remove his headquarters to Denver. He had met delegates from a number of eastern states; he could resume the practice in the West. Whether or not it was by design, it was useful for Eisenhower in these interviews to confine himself to such platitudes as "A bankrupt America is a defenseless America," for in that way he could seem to remain above politics, uncommitted; he could be, as Marquis Childs neatly put it, "a clean slate on which each citizen could write his own hopes and aspirations." No harm was done by this approach, for privily Eisenhower had long since made clear his general attitudes and specific doctrinal convictions to selected figures in the business community.*

The prickly fact remained, as the time of the convention approached, that Taft had many more pledged delegates than did Eisenhower; indeed, the senator's more sanguine supporters were claiming first-ballot votes only sixteen short of the six hundred and four needed to carry off the nomination. Their assertion was blather, designed as a retort to the charge, effectively broadcast by the Lodge-Dewey-Brownell faction, that Taft could never win a national election; but unquestionably Taft could count as many as five hundred and thirty committed delegates, which was fully one hundred more than those listed as safely in Eisenhower's column. The general's managers were faced with the task, then, of somehow rustling sixty or seventy of Taft's delegates and stampeding them into Eisenhower's corral. Their scheme was matured by the end of June and would afford a foretaste of the candidate's future campaign strategy.

The scheme was based on what was termed a moral issue, a "straight-out issue of right and wrong" in Eisenhower's words, the dispute over accreditation of some seventy delegates to the convention—seventeen

---

* For example, H. Jack Porter, Eisenhower's lieutenant in the struggle for Republican delegates in Texas, had on February 14 sent the general a memorandum on various issues; to wit: on civil rights, an effort to obtain the northern Negro vote would result in the loss of the southern vote; on states' rights, support them, and forget about any Fair Employment Practices Commission; on labor legislation, collective bargaining is all very well, but the Taft-Hartley Act must not be tinkered with; on federal spending, it should be curtailed, and so should taxes; on the national debt, it should be reduced and the budget balanced; on public housing, private capital should be encouraged to do the job; the executive has got too big and powerful, it now subordinates the Congress, it must be checked and restrained. To this Eisenhower had answered: "The presentation you make . . . is, of course, generally parallel with my own thinking on the subjects you mention."

For another example, Floyd B. Odlum on February 20 had mailed Eisenhower a lengthy screed on taxation in which, among other things, he characterized the federal income tax as "the worst of all wrong things" because it had opened the door to all sorts of mischievous changes in the socioeconomic structure of the republic. It destroyed initiative; it was confiscatory. Eisenhower warmly agreed. "In essence, I have believed," he wrote Odlum, "and in fact have been preaching for some years, the doctrine you are supporting."

from Georgia, thirteen from Louisiana, and, most conspicuously, thirty-eight from Texas. The Republican party in the South, as every practicing politician knew, was more a convenience for the dispensation of patronage than a political party. The patronage apparatus had for some years belonged to Taft, and so by common consent had the southern delegates. In May the Eisenhower faction, subsidized by the petroleum plutocracy, rallied throngs of Texans—presumably Democrats until quite recently—in the Republican county conventions and handed the Taft faction a sound drubbing. But at the state convention at Mineral Wells on May 27 the Republican national committeeman, a Taft chattel, summarily excluded the Eisenhower delegates on the grounds they were bogus Republicans, and qualified only Taft supporters.

Eisenhower's managers at once struck attitudes of shock, incredulity, and righteous horror. The whole thing, they cried, was "a steal." And since they had carefully alerted newspapers, wire services, magazines, radio, and television to the impending uproar, the way was cleared for Eisenhower to step forward as the champion of Integrity and the Summum Bonum to do battle against the dark forces of Evil. As the national convention was gaveled to order, the circumstance was readymade for the merchandisers, the public relations wizards, the experts of motivational research. An amendment in the rules of the convention designed to favor the Eisenhower faction was guilefully dubbed the "fair play" amendment, and the epithet was popularized by all the political reporters. Broadsides were emblazoned with scare headlines, THE EYES OF TEXAS, and the delegates were warned THE REPUBLICAN PARTY WILL WIN IN NOVEMBER ONLY IF IT COMES TO THE VOTERS WITH CLEAN HANDS. Eisenhower pickets paraded inside and outside the convention hall flourishing signs that read, THOU SHALT NOT STEAL. In confusion, the Taft faction sought a compromise. (Eisenhower, a man familiar with conciliation, was understood to approve the Taft offer. "Swell," he was heard to say.) But Senator Lodge rejected it on the grounds that one cannot compromise a moral issue. By the time that issue came before the convention the nation had been persuaded that Taft and his supporters were bent on political mischief of an unprecedented enormity; the delegates, a majority of whom unquestionably favored Taft, felt obliged to reject the Taft compromise and seat the Eisenhower delegates, and so they did, by a decisive vote, 658–548.

After that it remained only to tally the votes on the first ballot. Taft's forces had been routed by the moral issue. It was plain to every competent observer that a majority of the delegates preferred Taft; it was plain they hated Dewey and had no great love for the man they regarded as Dewey's me-too internationalist candidate ("Phewey on Eisenhewey" was the snarl of some Taft adherents); it was even evident that nearly half of New York State's ninety-six delegates would have voted for Taft had not Governor Dewey threatened the mutinous with summary reprisals. Taft was simply no match. He could never prevail against such a cold and remorseless adversary.

Did the celebrated Case of the Stolen Texas Delegates have any merit? The truth is, not much. After a dispassionate study, a group of political scientists concluded, "there was little reason to consider either convention [whether of Taft or of Eisenhower delegates] *wholly* representative of Texas Republicans." But their judgment came two years later and ignored the practical aspects of the matter. By then the dust was settled and all rancors had been forgotten. By then Eisenhower was President and Taft was beyond caring about the moral issue, for he was dead.

During the tedious struggles, the duplicities, the hubbub and vulgarity of the convention, the candidate withheld himself, relatively serene. He had hoped to remain aloof in Denver, surveying the scramble with an austere and arctic detachment, but he had at length permitted himself to be argued into taking up residence in Chicago at the Blackstone Hotel, comfortably removed from the steaming, sweating press of politicians packed into the stockyards amphitheater, where the mercury stood well above one hundred degrees. He suffered himself to be exposed to more delegates—two adjoining suites were provided him at the Blackstone so that he might shuttle back and forth between delegations, distributing equitable doses of his formidable charm; anon he met with his chief lieutenants, anon the leaders of uncommitted delegations were vouchsafed an audience with him. He conferred with Dulles about those paragraphs in the party platform that dealt with foreign policy and he stipulated revisions, but more, it would seem, to remind all concerned as to whose was the controlling word on that policy than to make changes of substance.

He remained at his command post as he had done since 1942, remote, insulated, sheltered by a dedicated and competent staff. Others strove, sweltered, waited without, queued up to crowd into elevators, scurried here and there, were snubbed, plotted, lied, went without sleep, drank too much bad booze, fought for taxicabs, flirted, cheered and whistled, hurried, sat bored for hours on end, paraded, wrangled, and shouted themselves hoarse; General Eisenhower stayed cool in his hotel suite, emerging only for such obligatory rituals as the Sunday morning attendance at divine worship. When Cyrus Sulzberger dropped in for a chat, once again, as if someone had pressed a button, Eisenhower insisted that he was not "running for" or "seeking" public office. (This time Sulzberger eyed him fishily. "I don't think he means this quite as sincerely as he did . . . some months ago," Sulzberger confided to his journal.) Because others were clearly visible—Governor Dewey smiling toothily on the floor of the convention, in command of the New York delegation; Governor Sherman Adams of New Hampshire, floor manager of the Eisenhower forces; Senator Lodge, tall, handsome, assured; Herbert Brownell darting about, whispering to chairmen of delegations; General Lucius Clay, emerging now and again from his suite at the Blackstone to give an order—the notion took root that Eisenhower was merely a pawn, a figurehead, a fellow who knew nothing of the mysteries of politics, who was docile and obedient to the powerful will of others. If he was aware of these whispers, he did nothing to dispel them: he was far too wise in the ways of winning and holding men's loyalties to trouble himself over such trivial gossip. Why should he care? If things went well, that was good; if things went poorly, he would have ample time to apportion the blame or even, should it seem advisable, to assume the responsibility himself.

When he chose, he could flick on his television set and gaze at the proceedings within the amphitheater—the reverent reception accorded Herbert Hoover; the appearance, heralded but flatulent, of his old commander Douglas MacArthur; the booing of Governor Dewey; the frenzied demonstration touched off when the chairman introduced "Wisconsin's fighting marine," a man attacked for exposing the traitors in our government," Senator Joe McCarthy—and he could even get glimpses of the rallies being staged in his honor all around Chicago, complete with torchlight parades, leggy Eisenhowerettes in specially designed frocks, Fred Waring's band, and eight big barrage balloons swinging aloft in the glare of huge searchlights.*

Certainly Eisenhower's television set played to an attentive audience on the morning of Friday, July 11. His four brothers were watching with him, as were Cliff Roberts, Bill Robinson, Lucius Clay, Harold Talbott, a couple of senators, and a few other friends. (Mrs. Eisenhower was confined to bed in her room with an infected tooth, and attended by her

* The advance man who organized these demonstrations was Arthur Gray, Jr., yet another of the Wall Street investment bankers (Gray was on leave from Kuhn, Loeb & Company) risen like the sword of the Lord and of Gideon to do battle for Eisenhower and against the encroachments of creeping socialism. Gray, whose title during the Eisenhower crusade was chairman for special events of Citizens for Eisenhower, had been sent to Chicago a few weeks before the Republicans gathered there, with instructions to change the atmosphere, which was oppressively Old Guard and pro-Taft. So hostile was Chicago to Eisenhower, Gray observed later, that bankers would cancel the loan applications of any citizen wearing an "I Like Ike" button on his lapel. The melody of choice at an Eisenhower rally, Gray added, was "The Sunshine of Your Smile."

mother and by General Snyder.) At the end of the first ballot, Eisenhower stood nine votes short of victory:

Eisenhower	595
Taft	500
Warren	81
Stassen	20

Harold Stassen, eternally hopeful, saw a chink of light at the end of the long tunnel: a deadlock imminent, perhaps persisting through a second and third ballot, and then—why not?—the stampede to Stassen. Nineteen of Minnesota's twenty-eight votes had been cast for him as the state's somewhat shopworn "favorite son," but the chairman of the Minnesota delegation, Senator Edward Thye, was prepared. His agents were posted at the elbow of the chairman of the convention, Representative Joe Martin of Massachusetts; he had but to signal and he would be recognized. Stassen pleaded No! but Thye was resolute. "No one could disagree," he said later, "because it was that simple." He raised his arm. Martin recognized Minnesota. The nineteen votes were shifted to Eisenhower's column. Mission accomplished.

After the moment of elation in the general's suite and the abrupt, awkward journey (just a walk across the street but every step contested by dense throngs of people) to Taft's headquarters so that the victorious might pay his respects to the defeated, there remained one question to be resolved. The running mate. The candidate for Vice President. How best to balance the ticket?

Good politicians anticipate such a question by providing several possible answers and then measuring each possibility against the demands of the moment when the decision must finally be taken. Eisenhower's managers, always assuming their man would win in July, had recognized some months earlier that Republican rancors would best be assuaged by seconding the general with one identified as a solid-core right-wing anticommunist conservative. Richard M. Nixon, a jowly, beetle-browed senator from California, fitted that bill of particulars precisely, and he offered other advantages. He was relatively young (thirty-nine); he was earnest, ambitious, and industrious; he was committed to no others, being only and always for himself; the part he had played while a member of the House Committee on Un-American Activities in the conviction of Alger Hiss for perjury had given him what was, in those bilious times, an enviable renown. Further, since he was from California, he could prove helpful in thwarting any embarrassing initiatives by Governor Earl Warren, who might aspire, like Stassen, to be a compromise candidate in the event of an Eisenhower-Taft deadlock. And if Nixon's technique for winning elections revealed a relish for gouging an opponent's jugular and a total lack of scruple as to how he gouged it, perhaps he might put those traits to positive use both before and after Eisenhower's nomination.

Dewey had been in touch with Nixon as early as May, while Eisenhower was still at SHAPE. To an ambitious young man, Dewey's proposal had been most gratifying. And yet the approach laid Nixon under a subtle constraint, obliging him to engage in some deft footwork. Very delicately he had to undermine Governor Warren's position as "favorite son" while yet seeming to honor his own pledge to support Warren. Moreover, he knew that Dewey, Brownell, and the other Eisenhower lieutenants would be eyeing him narrowly to see how he rose to the occasion they had presented him with. Politicians admire proof of performance. What Nixon did and how he did it provoked Warren and his associates to an implacable and enduring hostility; many of them would forever consider Nixon's name roughly synonymous with "treachery."

In discussions of the vice-presidency with Eisenhower, Nixon's name was pressed early and regularly. It came to be mentioned with growing respect. Especially as he reflected on McCarthy's unbridled assault against communists in government, Eisenhower perceived that above all he had better have a running mate with an unimpeachable record of anticommunism. (McCarthy had at last presumed to vilify even General George Marshall, as revered a figure as could be found on the American landscape. Marshall was, McCarthy had said, part of "a conspiracy so immense, an infamy so black, as to dwarf any in the history of man," and Marshall would, McCarthy had added, "sell his grandmother for any advantage." As these libels had been heaped upon each other, interest in Eisenhower's reaction to them had grown more intense, and not least among Eisenhower's military comrades.) On Wednesday night, July 9, Brownell dined with Eisenhower, and Nixon was a chief topic. By this time Nixon was at the top of Eisenhower's private list of candidates, and the general authorized Brownell to seek a ratification of Nixon by Republican leaders. Some two dozen Republican elders were assembled in a parlor of the Hilton Hotel and, after a desultory consideration of other names, they voted their unanimous but unenthusiastic endorsement of Nixon. He may be said to have been the choice of Dewey and Brownell, accepted with a cursory shrug by Eisenhower.

Senator McCarthy gave the Republican party ticket his blessing next day. Reporters intercepted him as he emerged from General Eisenhower's rooms at the Blackstone. "Are you pleased with the ticket, Senator?" he was asked, and he answered, "I think Dick Nixon will make a fine Vice President."

There elapsed between Republican nomination and national election an interval of a bit more than sixteen weeks. An imperishable American tradition requires that at a minimum the last eight weeks of the campaign be crammed with alarums and hairbreadth escapes in the night, with dark deeds and gallant heroics, with grim pursuits and gorgeous pratfalls; in short, that it be a stirring and high-toned melodrama staged by a master of low farce. In every particular the campaign of 1952 met the test; it proved diverting to the most fastidious.

More consequential, however, was the fact that the campaign proved exceedingly educational. Many misapprehensions were corrected. The press and the more discerning of the electorate learned things about Eisenhower they would earlier have dismissed as inconceivable, and for his part Eisenhower came to understand how far less gently journalists handle a political candidate than they do a supreme commander. On both sides the process of education began very quickly, no doubt spurred by the nomination of Adlai Stevenson, governor of Illinois, to oppose General Eisenhower in the run for the White House.

Stevenson, a man as old as the century, was physically unimpressive —balding, a trifle paunchy. He had been truly reluctant to accept the nomination; more, he had actively resisted his selection. Later Eisenhower's public relations specialists would cleverly stigmatize Stevenson as hesitant, indecisive, a Hamlet, but the reasons for his disinclination were many and obvious. He was relatively unknown, had little experience of politics, no wide acquaintance even among Democrats, no manager, no staff, and very little money. He was being asked to run against a national hero, a world figure, a man with limitless financial backing and the support of most of the country's newspapers. Further, he would have to run against all the hostilities, frustrations, and exasperations that had accumulated during the twenty years the Democrats had held power—what was epitomized by Republican orators in the snarled phrase "the mess in Washington." He was uncomfortably aware that the most reliable private polls showed that Eisenhower would attract about 65 percent of the popular vote. He was, and he knew it, little more than a sacrificial goat.

Yet Stevenson was a man of wit and elegance, of intellectual clarity and good sense, of high style and buoyancy, a man blessed with a serene confidence. He had early shown a disconcerting ability to prick and deflate his great adversary. Eisenhower, in accepting his party's nomination, had announced he would lead a "crusade for freedom in America," the first goal of which would be "to sweep from offices" the Democratic administration.

It was a presumptuous pose, inflated with the self-righteous morality that was to become an Eisenhower hallmark, and Stevenson had promptly retorted that he would conduct not "a crusade to exterminate the opposing party, as our opponents seem to prefer," but rather a campaign to inspire "a people whose destiny is leadership . . . of a world in ferment." Eisenhower, after a ten-day sojourn fishing for trout in a creek high on the western slope of the Rockies, returned refreshed to Denver and addressed himself to the tasks of the campaign. Before long he was making speeches on domestic policy. "The great problem of America today," he said, "is to take that straight road down the middle," steering clear of the reactionary Right and radical Left. This was no more than the standard maneuver to establish identity with the vast majority of the electorate, but coming from a man who had yet to repudiate the reactionary Right within the Republican party (e.g., Senator Jenner and Senator McCarthy, who had slandered General Marshall), it did not impose on Stevenson, who made pointed references to "those who favor what has been described as the middle-of-the-gutter approach." In short, quite a few Americans found Stevenson doing precisely what they had hoped and expected of Eisenhower, and a little thrill ran along the nerve ends of the political experts. It seemed just barely possible that there might yet be a race worth watching.

Meantime the question of Eisenhower's attitude toward Jenner and McCarthy nagged. Why would the hero-candidate not instinctively leap to the defense of George Marshall, so respected a man, so helpful in forwarding Eisenhower's own glorious career, and now so meanly maligned? To be sure, one could argue that Marshall needed no defense, that it was time Eisenhower stood clear of Marshall's shadow, that unity of the Republican party was paramount, but such propositions paled alongside considerations of honor and loyalty. The question was sure to be raised at his first Denver press conference; indeed, one journalist, Murray Kempton, touched by what he imagined to be the general's political innocence, was careful to forewarn Eisenhower by putting his press secretary, James C. Hagerty, on notice of his intention. "General," Kempton duly inquired, "what do you think of those people who call General Marshall a living lie?" Now one of Eisenhower's favorite rules of conduct, as he had confided to intimates, was: Never lose your temper, except intentionally. On this occasion his performance deserved high marks. He jumped to his feet. His face flushed. His voice was choked and angry. How dare anyone say such a thing about "a perfect example of patriotism and loyal service to the United States"? He could himself scarcely abide in the same room with anyone who would utter such wickedness. He shook a trembling finger at Kempton. His words, sharp with outrage, exploded around Kempton, who suddenly sensed that throughout Eisenhower's outburst of wrath Senator Jenner's name had never been mentioned. A few minutes later Hagerty led Kempton over to Eisenhower for an introduction. The performance was over, forgotten. The general smiled his wonderful warm smile.

To much the same group of reporters, at about that same time, Eisenhower undertook to explain why despite all his protests to the contrary he had at length been induced to run for the presidency. His single motive, he declared, had been to keep the isolationist Taft out of the White House. He maintained it would be disastrous to relinquish the direction of American foreign policy to a man of Taft's pinched and narrow Weltanschauung.* Apparently Eisenhower imagined his blunt talk would be kept off the record—an impossible notion during a hotly contested election campaign. His language, little of it flattering to Taft, was widely reported and so found its way to Murray Bay in Quebec, where for two or three generations the Taft family had enjoyed a summer retreat. Here Senator Taft had come at the end of July to contemplate the wreckage, as he considered it to be, of the Republican party. Eisenhower's reported remarks seemed to confirm his worst fears: the general approved the foreign policy of the Democrats; he was another me-too candidate like Governor Dewey before him; no matter who was elected the Republican party had been shattered. Senator Taft—Mr. Republican—shrouded himself in a profound silence.

The senator's silence was deafening at the Hotel Commodore in Manhattan, where Eisenhower's campaign headquarters had been established. If the Republican party was not shattered, Eisenhower's managers were compelled to conclude that it was sorely riven, and that the substantial fraction of it still loyal to Taft (a fraction that might, despite the convention, be larger than one-half) was bruised and resentful. One could speak slightingly of the Old Guard, but could the Republicans win a national election without it? "Until Bob Taft blows the bugle," the Republican national committeeman from Indiana was heard to say, "a lot of us aren't going to fight in the army." Here was the general, but where were the troops?

A political writer, Ed Lahey of the *Chicago Daily News*, known to have Taft's confidence, visited the senator at Murray Bay and his first dispatch manifested the gravity of the situation. "General Eisenhower's chances of winning the support of Senator Taft of Ohio," Lahey wrote, "are about zero." He went on to detail the conditions of Taft's support,

* Later it would suit Eisenhower's convenience to insist that his sole motive for seeking the presidency was to spare the nation four more years of Truman, that if he could have known Adlai Stevenson would be the Democratic candidate he would never have got into politics. This explanation, like the one naming Taft, may be dismissed as an attempt to embroider the legend that the general did not long to be President.

if any: no reprisals against Taft supporters in any new Republican administration, no tampering with the substance of the Taft-Hartley Act, and "*finally,*" Lahey reported, shifting into italic gear, "*Senator Taft would like to see General Eisenhower talking like a Republican and acting like a man running for President.*"

These ominous strictures were underscored by the lukewarm reception accorded Eisenhower at a convention of the American Legion (his speech was interrupted ten times by applause; in contrast Stevenson spoke far more forthrightly and was interrupted by cheers twenty-five times) and by a scathing editorial blazoned on the front page of nineteen newspapers of the Scripps-Howard chain, one of the earliest and most ardent of Eisenhower's supporters. "Ike is running like a dry creek," the editorial scolded. He seemed "just another 'me-too' candidate," he must "come out swinging," he must "hit hard, [and if] he doesn't, he might as well concede defeat."

"Right after Labor Day, I'll really start swinging," Eisenhower promised a deputation of worried politicians on August 28. He was nettled. He knew best his physical stamina, his reserves of energy. He resented having others tell him how to conduct such affairs. He had estimated he could campaign under a full head of steam for eight weeks. He had reached that decision in Denver, yet now here in New York the politicians were getting apprehensive. They were like so many armchair generals, criticizing the course of a military campaign, who had never smelled gunpowder.

In any event, it was essential that he meet with Senator Taft, and as soon as possible. Even as his stamp of final approval was given the plans for strategy in the campaign, an invitation that the senator meet with the general in New York was sped on its way.

Republican strategy, quite naturally, was focused on Eisenhower's unprecedented popularity. Plans for the campaign had first been presented to the candidate and his chief advisers early in August by Robert Humphreys, director of public relations for the Republican National Committee. Eisenhower had listened without comment, but later he complained to Sherman Adams, who had signed on for the campaign as his chief of staff. "All they talked about was how they would win on my popularity," he had growled. "Nobody said I had a brain in my head."

As the strategy had been further developed, the flavor of public relations had grown ever more pungent. In the East, an outfit of bright young people who called themselves the Eisenhower-Nixon Research Service was already engaged in the contrivance of various cunning theses, e.g., that Stevenson was Truman's "captive candidate," powerless to mop up the mess in Washington or to stem the onward creep of socialism. On the

West Coast, the firm of Whitaker and Baxter, which boasted more than twenty years' experience at packaging and merchandising political candidates, had been retained for more of the same; presently billboards would appear along the California freeways proclaiming "Faith in God and country; that's Eisenhower—how about you?" The Kudner Agency had earlier been appointed by the Republican National Committee; now, on September 4, there appeared Ben Duffy, a jaunty outsize leprechaun, the president of Batten, Barton, Durstine & Osborn, to take personal charge of all televison and radio on behalf of Eisenhower. Duffy got the general to exchange his steel-rimmed spectacles for horn-rimmed ones; Duffy gentled him into permitting his chops to be smeared with the cosmetics appropriate to television; in a dozen ways Duffy (as he later acknowledged to a reporter from *Tide,* the trade magazine of advertising) concentrated on the merchandising of Eisenhower's frankness, honesty, and integrity, on his sincere and wholesome address.

Apart from "I Like Ike," the issues of the campaign had been epitomized in the snappy formula K_1C_2 coined by Senator Mundt, co-chairman of the Republican speakers' bureau. K_1 stood for Korean War, a calamity to be charged against the Democrats, and C_2 the allegations that Corruption and Communism had fouled the federal government and so produced the mess in Washington. Beyond that, the only essential Republican tactic was to ensure party unity, unquestioning and outspoken.

The matter of party unity proved disconcerting to Eisenhower's admirers. They had assumed he was the Hero who towered above the political arena; they had imagined he was of the "liberal" or "progressive" persuasion within the Republican party. In short, they had made him over into their own image of him. Their awakening began on Tuesday, September 9, and three days later it was complete. "What's happened to Ike?" they asked each other in dismay, when in truth the only change was in the depth of their own perception.

On that Tuesday, Eisenhower joined Senator Jenner on a platform at Indianapolis and called for election of the Republican ticket "from top to bottom." He thus directly urged the re-election of Jenner, who had called General Marshall "an eager front man for traitors" and "a living lie." Much applause; Eisenhower raised his arms in acknowledgment; suddenly Jenner sprang forward to seize Eisenhower's hand and clutch it aloft in triumph, and so composed a striking display for the photographers.

Three days later Eisenhower interrupted his campaign swing to confer with Senator Taft at his home on Morningside Heights. From their two-hour conversation Taft emerged with a lengthy statement—a manifesto of orthodox Republican doctrine, in effect an ultimatum—which Taft had earlier prepared and as to which, he complacently told the assembled reporters, he and Eisenhower were "in full agreement." On every salient aspect of domestic policy—a drastic reduction of federal spending, a curb on executive power, elimination of federal controls, firm restrictions on labor unions, "liberty against creeping socialization"—Eisenhower agreed with Taft's guidelines. Even as to foreign policy Taft purred that "our differences are differences of degree."

This affecting demonstration of harmony grievously distressed some elements among the Republicans and afforded the Democrats occasion for derision. "It looks," commented Adlai Stevenson, "as if Taft lost the nomination but won the nominee." In Oregon, Senator Wayne Morse, a Republican, announced he had withdrawn his support of Eisenhower and would instead vote for Stevenson. The defection of some Republicans and more independents had been anticipated and discounted in advance; far more valuable was the strength of the new bond between Eisenhower and Taft—between, indeed, the Dewey wing of the party and the Old Guard who, devoted as they were to Taft and much as they detested Dewey, would now support Eisenhower's candidacy vocally, actively, and financially. Taft had blown the bugle: the general would now find many more troops falling in. The Democrats gleefully labeled the affair the "surrender of Morningside Heights." Taft and the Old Guard, rejoicing, could agree. Perhaps only Eisenhower and his most intimate advisers recognized that no surrender was possible where no discernible doctrinal difference had ever existed.

At all events, it was as well the Republican party could present a unified front to the nation, for an event without parallel for foolishness even in the annals of American politics, an episode compounded about equally of absurdity and gooey bathos, was about to burst upon the heedless populace, threatening the Republicans with woe, whipping the campaign into a proper frenzy, and for the first time in his unwonted role of political leader presenting Dwight Eisenhower with a decision of some gravity. This was the celebrated Case of the Nixon Fund.

On Monday, September 15, the candidate was aboard his campaign train, absorbed in his odd new trade. Most of his hours were spent in his special Pullman, the last of eighteen or twenty cars that comprised what some public relations witling had dubbed the "Look Ahead, Neighbor" Special. His car was equipped with galley and dining area (for twelve, at a pinch); compartments for him, his wife, her mother, his servant, his wife's maid, and General Snyder; a shower-bath; a small lounge in which were fitted a half-dozen overstuffed chairs and a sofa; and the railed platform from which, at whistle stops, the candidate addressed the crowds come to greet him. In the cars just ahead were his chief aides: Governor Adams, Senators Fred Seaton and Frank Carlson, Bobby Cutler, Jerry Persons, Jim Hagerty, Gabriel Hauge, Tom Stephens; his secretary, Ann Whitman; Congressman Leonard Hall, charged with coordinating the candidate's activities with those of the Republican National Committee; and the three or four dozen others who were needed, part-time or full-time, to keep the microcosm functioning. Ahead, too, were the dining car, a headquarters car for the press, and four or five dozen members of the press corps.

Self-centered, preoccupied, indifferent to the world around him except as it reacted to him and what he had to say, the candidate was borne through Indiana, Illinois, Minnesota, Iowa, Nebraska. His speeches were improving and so was his delivery of them. Back in New York, the main speeches were now planned and scheduled by a board of strategy including Brownell, Stassen, and C. D. Jackson, a senior executive of Time, Inc., the publishing house; they were drafted by Emmet J. Hughes, a senior editor of *Life*, and teletyped to the candidate's train; Cutler and Hauge tinkered with them further; so did the candidate.

The fact was, however, that the voters did not much care what Eisenhower had to say. They greatly admired him, everywhere they poured into the streets to catch a glimpse of him, they were delighted to cheer him (and Mrs. Eisenhower, too); but the political reporters noticed that after they had seen and cheered him, as like as not they would turn around and go home, unwilling to tarry while he lambasted the Democrats. Their apathy was not astonishing: political scientists have grown weary documenting the lack of interest in politics of the American electorate. In the words of one study that focused particularly on the campaign of 1952: "In the electorate as a whole the level of attention to politics is so low that what the public is exposed to must be highly visible—even stark—if it is to have an impact on opinion."

Curiously, in view of the strenuous efforts of Senator McCarthy and others, including Nixon, to inflate the bugaboo of internal subversion, the issue of domestic communism had scarcely any impact on public opinion. Corruption proved far more fetching as an irritant, and quite soon one or other of the public relations experts had characterized Truman's as the "scandal-a-day" administration; thereafter, both Eishehower and Nixon sanctimoniously labored the matter, indignation over "wickedness in government" being an easy emotion for Eisenhower to summon up.

In this placid landscape of earnest Republican endeavor there exploded on Thursday, September 18, the story that would provide a highly visible —even stark—issue, one that would galvanize the electorate and provide for the discriminating a memory that would yield sardonic mirth for at least a generation. SECRET NIXON FUND, shouted the *New York Post*, lowering its voice only slightly to add, SECRET RICH MEN'S TRUST FUND KEEPS NIXON IN STYLE FAR BEYOND HIS SALARY. If the article depending from these scareheads was anticlimactic, the facts were nonetheless embarrassing for the Republicans. Seventy-six wealthy Californians had forked out contributions to build a sum in excess of eighteen thousand dollars which had been disbursed on Nixon's account for stationery, printing, travel and hotel expenses for Nixon and his wife, and his office expenses in Washington.*

In Washington, both Democratic and Republican national committees leaped to action: the Democrats to demand that Eisenhower boot Nixon off the ticket, the Republicans to holler foul and "left-wing smear." As other newspapers took up the hue and cry, their correspondents aboard Eisenhower's campaign train pressed for a statement from the candidate, a response, a comment, anything. At first Hagerty was lofty. "We never comment on a *New York Post* story," he said. Later, hounded by the reporters, he would say only that Eisenhower had no statement to issue. Quite naturally, the silence hatched rumors: yes, Nixon would walk the plank; William Knowland, the senior senator from California, would replace him; Knowland had already been summoned by telephone and would join the train at St. Louis. The "Look Ahead, Neighbor" Special had become a pressure cooker.

In truth, Eisenhower knew nothing of the *Post* story nor of the rumors. His managers had decided not to disturb him until after his speech on farm policy at Omaha. Their man, they reckoned, was too new to rough-and-tumble politics to be entrusted with a decision.

The rumors were remarkably accurate. There was indeed a disposition to dump Nixon, especially in New York. Here were the men closest to Eisenhower, those whom he most trusted, men like Lucius Clay and Bill Robinson, who felt a responsibility for having got Eisenhower into this scandalous muddle; men like Dewey and Lodge, who appreciated the need to protect unscathed an invaluable Republican property. These men were furious with Nixon; his accursed fund had jeopardized a Republican victory. Adams and Brownell, after conferring by telephone, separately called

---

* This is not the place for an examination of the Nixon fund, nor of why it was deemed necessary to augment the $87,000 he was paid in salary and expenses by the taxpayers. Sympathetic analyses have been supplied by Earl Mazo, Garry Wills, and Nixon himself which purport to explain why, for example, Nixon's financial agent could rake in contributions from bankers, real estate speculators, and executives of petroleum companies, yet stoutly reject the idea of contributions by members of a labor union since, as he put it, "A labor union is a special interest."

We are here concerned with how Eisenhower conducted himself in an unforeseen and unwelcome situation.

Senator Knowland, who was on holiday in Hawaii, and instructed him to join Eisenhower's train immediately. Every contingency had to be anticipated.

Eisenhower was informed of the fund early Friday morning. He was reliably reported to be "staggered and shaken." Where now his Crusade? How to maintain his moral posture? On his immediate schedule were two important speeches, in Kansas City on Friday and in St. Louis on Saturday; in each it was proposed he take great swipes at corruption and the "mess in Washington"; how now? "Let's find out the facts before I shoot my mouth off," he said. He instructed Sherman Adams to get hold of Paul Hoffman at his home outside Los Angeles and have him retain reputable lawyers and accountants to make an immediate investigation of the fund. He scribbled a message to Nixon ("I suggest immediate publication . . . of all documentary evidence . . . Any delay will . . . arouse additional doubt or suspicion") and instructed Seaton to transmit it to Nixon or his campaign manager Murray Chotiner. A brief statement was issued giving Nixon rather vague and conjectural support. Should he call Nixon himself? He decided not: better to keep the affair at arm's length and dispose of it on the staff level. ("Our train schedules today," he wrote in the message given Seaton for Nixon, "seemingly prevent a telephone conversation but you know I am ready to consult with you . . . whenever . . . physically possible.")

The campaign train moved on. Across the nation the political commentators for press and television rejoiced: the fund was a splendid morsel, more succulent than any they could have imagined. For Eisenhower it was an affliction, and his sleeping hours grew briefer, his waking hours more encumbered. Somewhere in Missouri the train ground to a halt at a whistle-stop and the candidate, flanked by a handful of local politicians, made his way to the rear platform for one of the brief talks that he spouted by rote.* Suddenly he was called away to take a telephone call: Lucius Clay from New York with the latest word of Nixon. Opinion was hardening. Bill Robinson, publisher of the *Herald Tribune,* voice of the eastern Republicans, had told Clay his next edition would carry an editorial terming the fund "ill-advised" and calling for Nixon's withdrawal from the ticket and his submission to a determination of the facts "in the light of General Eisenhower's unsurpassed fairness of mind." Brownell had conducted a survey on the question of dumping Nixon; most approved the

---

* He had committed to memory two recitals for such occasions. In one, the egg lecture, he professed to be scandalized by the idea that an egg, a blameless chicken egg, was the target of no less than one hundred taxes—it's time for a change! In the other he held aloft a conveniently notched two-by-four as the symbol of one dollar and then struck two pieces off it to show what was left of the dollar's purchasing power after twenty years of Roosevelt and Truman—it's time for a change!

idea; Brownell would report the results to Eisenhower in person as soon as he could.

A gloom settled over the campaign train, aggravated by the passengers' sense of isolation from the world of affairs. Letters and telegrams were delivered at every train stop; Hagerty told the reporters that about half called for Nixon's dismissal. That he would make such an announcement revealed how close the party elders were to a decision. The reporters polled themselves: they stood forty to two for dumping Nixon, but they believed the bucket of whitewash was ready, with Eisenhower about to apply the brush. In these circumstances it was decided that Eisenhower should meet informally with the reporters, it being understood that what he said would not be quoted or attributed to him—an impossible injunction. He strode forward to the press car. Equivocal smiles all around; beer was poured. A first question: "Do you consider the Nixon thing a closed incident?" Eisenhower frowned and shook his head. "By no means," he said. He had been told of the fund only the day before, he observed, and he confessed he had been greatly disturbed. He knew Nixon little and only briefly, but he seemed the sort of young leader that was wanted; he could not believe Nixon was involved in anything crooked or unethical, but Nixon must prove it. "Of what avail is it," demanded Eisenhower rhetorically, "for us to carry on this Crusade against this business of what has been going on in Washington if we ourselves aren't as clean as a hound's tooth?"

The reporters now had all they needed. Nixon must prove himself clean as a hound's tooth, thus the tenor of their copy; and when word of this reached the Nixon entourage in Portland, Oregon, every man jack of them was as furious with Eisenhower as Eisenhower's managers were with Nixon. A curious turn for the leader celebrated as the emollient master of reconciliation.

Still Eisenhower did not telephone Nixon. No train schedules interfered now: the general had reached St. Louis Saturday evening and would not leave until late Sunday night; Nixon was at his hotel in Portland, waiting; no call from Eisenhower. There was word at Nixon's hotel switchboard that Sherman Adams had called, but at Nixon's request Chotiner returned the call to say that Nixon would talk to no one but Eisenhower.

It was now quite plain that Eisenhower and the men around him wished Nixon to bow out. That was the unmistakable sense of all the heavy hints dropped ever since Friday night, when the early edition of the *Herald Tribune* had been published. Nixon had comprehended every hint, but by Saturday night it was equally plain that Nixon and the men around him had decided that he would not jump and, if pushed, would fight for his political life. He would refuse to acknowledge any impropriety in his unorthodox fund; he would defy the Hero.

By Sunday the hints were open appeals, with nothing concealed save the general. First a three-hundred-word telegram from Stassen (". . . I have regretfully reached a conclusion . . . I should frankly tell you . . . imperative . . . withdraw as running-mate . . . deeply regret . . . best wishes . . ."), then in the late afternoon a telephone call from Governor Dewey with a suggestion that Nixon go on television and let the American people decide: "If you stay on it isn't blamed on Ike, and if you get off it isn't blamed on Ike. All the fellows here in New York agree with me." Obviously Ike, the man of "unsurpassed fairness of mind," had decided that no matter what happened he must not be blamed. Nixon told Dewey he would consider the idea of a television appearance. In due course Chotiner telephoned Arthur Summerfield, the chairman of the National Committee and the strongest (if not the only) Nixon advocate on the Eisenhower train, to ask how such a broadcast would be financed. Funds had earlier been allocated for two broadcasts by the vice-presidential candidate, but was Nixon to be that candidate? Who could say? Talk of the broadcast sputtered into silence.

The hours ticked away. Was Eisenhower waiting for Nixon to call him? At last—it was after 11 P.M. in St. Louis, after 10 P.M. in Portland—a call was put through: Eisenhower to Nixon.

"Hello, General."

"Hello, Dick."

An exchange of small talk, the opening skirmish in a game of cross-continental poker played by a pair of experts for exceedingly high stakes. Nixon knew Eisenhower rather better than Eisenhower knew Nixon: Nixon knew Eisenhower had been the supreme commander, the general who won the war; knew that "even as a candidate he was accorded the respect, honor, and awe that only a President usually receives"; knew that despite "his great capacity for friendliness, he also had a quality of reserve which, at least subconsciously, tended to make a visitor feel like a junior officer coming in to see the commanding general." Eisenhower knew of Nixon little more than that he had been a lieutenant commander in the navy and later an anticommunist congressman. He did not even know Nixon's age.

With great circumspection, Nixon opened the passage. If the general and the Republican National Committee so decided, he said, he would offer to withdraw.

"You know," said Eisenhower, "this is an awfully hard thing for me to decide. I have come to the conclusion that you are the one who has to decide what to do. After all . . . if the impression got around that you got off the ticket because I forced you to get off, it is going to be very bad. On the other hand, if I issue a statement now backing you up, in effect people will accuse me of condoning wrongdoing."

Nixon said he would be happy to make the decision, but first the public, and the general too, should be able to hear "my side of the story."

Oh, said Eisenhower hastily, although his friends disagreed as to whether Nixon should stay on the ticket, all were of accord that he must have a chance to tell his story to the country. "I don't," he went on, "want to be in the position of condemning an innocent man. I think you ought to go on a nationwide television program and tell them everything there is to tell, everything you can remember since the day you entered public life."

"General," Nixon asked, "do you think after the television program that an announcement could then be made one way or another?"

Eisenhower equivocated.

With the experience of six years in California politics behind him, Nixon ventured to lecture the general, to warn him against "those people around you who don't know a damn thing about it."

"We will have to wait three or four days after the television show," Eisenhower insisted, "to see what the effect of the program is."

"General," said Nixon, "the great trouble here is the indecision." Then he added sternly, "There comes a time in politics when you have to pee or get off the pot."

But Eisenhower would not yield. It was essential that he retain control of the options.*

At once Eisenhower passed the word that money for the broadcast must be made available. By midnight the money had been found and arrangements completed. Ben Duffy of BBD&O set about hitching together a network of sixty-four NBC television stations, one hundred and ninety-four CBS radio stations, and almost all the five hundred and sixty radio stations of the Mutual Broadcasting System for Nixon's use on the next Tuesday night.

The campaign train moved on to Cincinnati, where on Monday night Eisenhower was to speak on a subject dear to the hearts of orthodox Republicans—the folly and disaster of Democratic policy in the Far East and how it brought about the loss of China to the communists and led to the war in Korea. The speech was a pretty specimen of distortion and partisan politics, doing violence to a policy initially shaped by General

* Three wide-eyed witnesses were on hand to overhear Nixon's remarkably brash admonition as quoted above—Chotiner; James Bassett, the press secretary; and William Rogers, a Washington lawyer and old friend. This account draws heavily on the admirable researches of Stewart Alsop in his *Nixon and Rockefeller: A Double Portrait.* Garry Wills, another close student of the episode, has it that Nixon said not "pee" but "piss," but these scholiastic variations are not vital.

Marshall when Eisenhower himself was chief of staff of the army, and descending to the device of misquoting a former associate; but it attracted little attention, for it was shouldered aside by speculation about Nixon's upcoming speech.

The premise that candidates for President and Vice President always cooperate closely during a campaign, and the corollary that the latter always yields to the former, were alike exploded on Tuesday, September 23, 1952. As the hour of the broadcast approached (it was 6:30 P.M. in Los Angeles, 9:30 P.M. in New York and Cleveland) Eisenhower's managers sought vainly to instruct Nixon and, failing that, at least to obtain advance knowledge of what he proposed to say. Nixon and his managers coldly refused to work in any kind of concert.

On the Tuesday, Eisenhower whistlestopped through Ohio, from Cincinnati north to Cleveland. As usual, local politicians clambered aboard, were photographed with the candidate, their faces contorted by immense smiles, and departed. One such was Representative Charles Halleck, a regular in the Taft organization who, like Taft, was determined that Nixon should not be forced off the ticket. He noted when Eisenhower's friend Bill Robinson jumped aboard the train and was at once ushered back to Eisenhower's sanctuary in the last car: bad news for Nixon. As quickly as possible he got hold of Summerfield, who was then at Republican headquarters in Washington, and sounded the alarm. Summerfield in turn called Robert Humphreys, the public relations man, and told him, "We have got to get to Cleveland immediately." Halleck, recalling later the events of that day, would say, "Humphreys and Summerfield and Halleck really worked on that one."

Early in the evening the train pulled in at Cleveland, and the candidate withdrew to a hotel to restore his tissues. There was a conference by telephone with his New York headquarters. With less than two hours to go before the broadcast, Governor Dewey placed a call to Nixon in Los Angeles. The call came at, to put it moderately, an inconvenient moment for Nixon, but that was not Dewey's concern. Two of Nixon's aides sought to block the call, but at length Dewey reported to Nixon: "There has just been a meeting of all of Eisenhower's top advisers. They have asked me to tell you that . . . at the conclusion of the broadcast tonight you should submit your resignation to Eisenhower." Nixon was stunned. Was this Eisenhower's order? Dewey declined to say so directly, but broadly hinted that he spoke for Eisenhower. "What," he asked, "shall I tell them you are going to do?" Nixon refused to say. Tell them, he rasped, to listen to the broadcast.

In Cleveland it was about 8 P.M. when Humphreys was summoned to Eisenhower's hotel room. The general lay sprawled on his bed, pillows propping his head. Sherman Adams stood on one side, General Jerry Persons on the other. Persons told Humphreys of the latest rumor going around, that Mrs. Nixon had paid ten thousand dollars in cash to have the new Nixon house in Washington redecorated. Humphreys stoutly denied it. He had seen the house within the fortnight, he said, furnished only with couches and draperies fetched from California. Eisenhower listened intently and said little.

An hour to go till the broadcast. Would Nixon do as Dewey had bidden him? What was he going to say? Not to know was intolerable. At Eisenhower's instruction Adams telephoned Chotiner to ask if Nixon was going to tender his resignation as requested. "Sherm," Chotiner answered, "if you want to know what's going to be said, you do what I'm going to do. You sit in front of the television and listen."

At the municipal auditorium a great throng gathered to watch the televised Nixon and later to hear Eisenhower in person. Three flights up, in the manager's office, a television set stood in a corner. In front of it on a small couch sat Eisenhower and his wife; on a chair next to him sat Bill Robinson. Adams, Summerfield, Hagerty, and another two dozen aides crowded the room behind them—a predominantly hostile audience. In his big hands Eisenhower held a block of paper and a pencil. He tapped the pencil rhythmically on the pad—an old habit. A hush as the broadcast began.

To be properly relished, the speech must be appraised by two different measures—what it said to its total audience and what it said to Dwight Eisenhower. By the first measure it was cunning, expertly contrived, artfully emotional, an effective paradigm of the wiles of public relations. It deserved a review by *Variety*, the hard-boiled weekly arbiter of show business, and it got one: "a slick production . . . parlaying all the schmaltz and human interest of the 'Just Plain Bill'–'Our Gal Sunday' genre of weepers." By the second measure it was an extraordinarily bold act of defiance, and not an inflection of it was lost on Eisenhower, at whom it was directed. The people with him were affected by Nixon's performance, some quite openly dabbing their tearful eyes with handkerchiefs. Not Eisenhower. He gazed intently, his pencil tap-tap-tapping. Twice he jabbed his pad with his pencil, the second time so sharply he shattered the lead. The first jab came when Nixon said:

"I would suggest that under the circumstances both Mr. Sparkman [John J. Sparkman of Alabama was the Democratic candidate for Vice President] and Mr. Stevenson should come before the American people, as I have, and make a complete statement as to their financial history. If they don't it will be an admission that they have something to hide. And I think you will agree with me.

"Because, remember, a man who's to be President and a man who's to be Vice President must have the confidence of all the people."

The clear implication was that Eisenhower, too, should make a complete financial statement, lest people think he had "something to hide." Nixon had gone so far as to mention gifts—the dog Checkers—but Eisenhower would find awkward any listing of gifts. His second jab, the one that broke the pencil, came toward the end of Nixon's performance:

"And now, finally, I know that you wonder whether or not I am going to stay on the Republican ticket or resign. Let me say this: I don't believe that I ought to quit, because I am not a quitter. . . .

"But the decision, my friends, is not mine. I would do nothing that would harm the possibilities of Dwight Eisenhower to become President of the United States. And for that reason I am submitting *to the Republican National Committee* tonight through this television broadcast *the decision it is theirs to make.* . . . [Stab, splinter.] Wire and write *the Republican National Committee* whether you think I should stay or whether you think I should get off. And whatever *their decision* is, I will abide by it." (Italics added.)

From this moment on Nixon would be known as Tricky Dick. His maneuver was superb: the Republican National Committee was comprised of men like him, party men, regulars, men like Summerfield and Karl Mundt who had voted for Eisenhower while never swerving from their devotion to Taft: now the decision was theirs, not Eisenhower's. The general might command a few starry-eyed Citizens for Eisenhower-Nixon, but soon he would be surrounded and overborne by Republican troops of the line, the Old Guard.

Or would he? Superficially, Nixon had scored a triumph. "Well, Arthur," Eisenhower said to Summerfield, "you sure got your money's worth." Downstairs in the auditorium the crowd, led by another Taft stalwart, Representative George Bender, was chanting, "We want Nixon! We want Nixon!" Eisenhower had in hand a speech deploring inflation; plainly it would have to be jettisoned. Ben Duffy and a few other wordsmiths went with Eisenhower into a room apart to rough out some notes. Duffy, for one, was prepared. Earlier that day he had been reached by Bruce Barton, an elder statesman of BBD&O, who had been in a state of advanced excitement. "Ben," Barton had said, "tonight will make history. This will be the turning point of the campaign. The general must be expertly stage-managed and when he speaks, it must be with the understanding and the mercy and the faith of God. My suggestion is that . . . at the conclusion of Nixon's speech . . . the general come out with the following memo in his own handwriting: 'I have seen many brave men perform brave duties. . . . But I do not think I have ever known a braver act than I witnessed tonight, when a young private marine, lifted suddenly on to the height of national prominence, marched up to the TV screen and bared his soul . . .'" There had been a great deal more, and much of it funnier, but Duffy and the others had scant time to catch Eisenhower's ear. The general, much preoccupied and little press-agented, marched out to greet the crowd: "I have seen many brave men in tough situations. [*Applause*] I have never seen anyone come through in better fashion than Senator Nixon did tonight [*Applause*]."

So much for the amenities. Now the general addressed himself to Nixon's insubordination. The chain of command had to be made unmistakably clear. He spoke to the crowd in Cleveland, but his words were darts directed at the National Committee and at Nixon. He had not yet made up his mind, he said, whether Nixon would remain on the ticket, adding: "It is obvious that I have to have something more than one single presentation, necessarily limited to thirty minutes, the time allowed Senator Nixon. I am not going to be swayed by my idea of what will get the most votes. . . . I am going to say: Do I myself believe this man is the kind of man America would like to have for its Vice President?" He then read from the telegram he had sent Nixon: "While *technically* no decision rests with me, you and I know the realities of the situation require a pronouncement which the public considers decisive. *My personal decision* is going to be based on personal conclusions. I would most appreciate it if you can fly to see me *at once*. Tomorrow evening I will be at Wheeling, West Virginia." (Italics added.)

Such a telegram was tantamount to a command, and to make it public was to serve notice on Nixon that any further disobedience would be considered lese majesty. But in Los Angeles Nixon and his staff, splashing in the wave of congratulatory telegrams and telephone calls from all over the country, were in a state of gleeful excitement bordering on euphoria. Before Eisenhower's telegram could be delivered, partial word of it came over a news wire as a bulletin, and once again Nixon concluded he was being badly used. A display of temper was quickly curbed, but he remained defiant. When he was handed the full text of Eisenhower's telegram, with its bidding to a conference in West Virginia, Nixon retorted that he would resume his campaign tour. "Will be in Washington Sunday and will be delighted to confer with you at your convenience any time thereafter," he wired Eisenhower. That was not independence, it was insolence. Relations between the two traveling groups had plumbed their depth.

A flurry of telephone calls followed. Eisenhower wanted Nixon delivered in West Virginia, as ordered; Nixon demanded assurances of a full-throated endorsement with no further catechism. For one, retreat from a previously prepared position; for the other, loss of face. Each man yielded something, but it was significant that when Eisenhower greeted Nixon on the airfield at Wheeling the next night it was with the precise note of condescension. "You're my boy," he said.

The unseemly episode left its scars. The association of the two principals was lastingly tainted: neither would ever wholly trust the other again. More immediately, there was the matter of Eisenhower's financial declaration. It had to be wrung from him. First Hagerty announced, on his behalf, that Eisenhower would make a statement of his finances "later on," but Eisenhower himself, at a subsequent off-the-record press conference, said he would do no such thing. When his refusal inevitably found its way into print, he was obliged to change his mind and invite public attention to the extraordinary relief he had enjoyed from taxation on the swollen fee paid him for his memoir of his wartime command.

After the episode of the Nixon fund, however, Eisenhower's election was a virtual certainty. A candidate who could convert such an episode into a rededication of his crusade against corruption could ignore any further vicissitudes. Eisenhower could agree to strike from the text of his speech at Milwaukee, Wisconsin—home state of the baleful Senator McCarthy—the paragraph that paid tribute to General Marshall and defended him against the slanders of McCarthy, a paragraph that Eisenhower had himself suggested, but while his irresolution would amaze and alarm his admirers, it may be doubted that the weakness cost him a single vote.

In any case, assisted by the ministrations of his speech writers and his public relations adepts, Eisenhower went rolling through October on the crest of a surge of public affection. On Friday, October 24—late enough in the campaign, as Emmet Hughes has pointed out, "to assure a high level of popular attention, yet not so late as to invite criticism as a last-minute device"—Eisenhower delivered his speech (written by Hughes) on the sharpest issue of the campaign, pledging that if elected, "I shall go to Korea," and declaring it was his "goal" to end the war there. In the final days of the campaign came a blizzard of ten-second films produced for television (the soundtrack was used for radio spots), too simple-minded to be called simplistic, in which an actor or actress cast as a typical voter put a question and General Eisenhower, wise, kindly, avuncular, decisive, batted it out of the ballpark:

VOICE: Mr. Eisenhower, what about the high cost of living?

EISENHOWER: My wife, Mamie, worries about the same thing. I tell her it's our job to change that on November 4th.

VOICE: Mr. Eisenhower, can you bring taxes down?

EISENHOWER: Yes. We will work to cut billions in Washington spending, and bring your taxes down.

VOICE: General, the Democrats are telling me I never had it so good.

EISENHOWER: Can that be true when America is billions in debt, when prices have doubled, when taxes break our backs, and we are still fighting in Korea? It is tragic. It is time for a change.

VOICE: General, just how bad is waste in Washington?

EISENHOWER: How bad? Recently, just one government bureau actually lost four hundred million dollars and not even the FBI can find it. It's *really* time for a change.

None of this was much more than terminal ritual. Truman, fiercely campaigning on behalf of Stevenson, could say of the Hero he had for four years wooed to lead the Democratic party, "Why, this fellow don't know any more about politics than a pig knows about Sunday," but the absurdity registered only as an amusing comment by a politician about to become a has-been. Eisenhower had said this and that about farm policy, defense policy, and foreign policy, about national economic policy, taxation, the national debt, and peace and prosperity—no matter, no one save Stevenson's staff had paid much attention. Stevenson had pledged to "talk sense to the American people," but at the end it mattered more that Ike and Mamie could lift their voices in a heartfelt performance of "God Bless America," for in American politics the gimmick has at least for a generation counted for more than good sense.

Recalling how they had been embarrassed by their predictions of the 1948 election, the psephologists approached the 1952 election with ludicrous circumspection. "Outcome Highly Uncertain," said the newspapers on the eve of election day. On Wednesday morning, beguiled by the number of votes cast (which proved chiefly that the U.S. had grown more populous), the newspapers were talking of the greatest Republican landslide of the century.*

It was an unusual day. Across the country were men and women in their forties, citizens of substance, who had never before voted for a winner in a presidential election. It was a day of jubilation, a day when it seemed as if the well-heeled exurban commuters might build bonfires

---

* Eisenhower tallied 33,936,252 votes to Stevenson's 27,314,992, a margin of a trifle less than 11 percent. By contrast, Theodore Roosevelt, Harding, Coolidge, and Hoover defeated their Democratic rivals by margins of 20, 28, 30, and 18 percent respectively.

in the aisles of their trains to celebrate their unaccustomed political triumph. Not since 1920 had the Republicans experienced the joy of booting the Democratic rascals out of office, not since 1932 had the Republicans been in office themselves. Like Ike? These prosperous citizens would have delighted to kiss the ground he walked upon.

Another glance at the returns showed that Eisenhower's smashing victory—442 electoral votes to 89 for Stevenson; all but nine states in the Republican column; precincts of the big industrial centers of the North and states of the solidly Democratic South alike swung to Eisenhower—was nonetheless a curious one. It was almost wholly personal. The Congress was Republican, but only by the slenderest of margins: less than a dozen votes in the House and only one in the Senate. (Before long Senator Wayne Morse would formally shift his allegiance to the Democrats, leaving the edge in the Senate to be determined by the Vice President's solitary tie-breaking vote.) This scant advantage was, to the sharp eye, a portent—a little cloud, like a man's hand—that before long the Republican heaven would be black with clouds and wind unless somehow Eisenhower could impart some of his personal magic to his fellow Republicans.

Musing on these and other matters, the President-elect departed with his wife for Augusta, Georgia, and a holiday of golf and bridge.

Awaiting the Eisenhowers was a warm welcome within the heavy steel fencing and the high dense shrubbery surrounding the Augusta National Golf Club.

The club was then, and has remained, one of the most exclusive establishments of its kind in the United States, and the word "exclusive" must here be taken in all its most select senses. The club's governors excluded, were snobbishly aloof, barred entrance, admitted only a socially restricted membership, and complacently ignored requests that they change their ways. Furthermore, whenever its most celebrated member approached its precincts, the club became at once even more exclusive: even its other members desisted from inviting guests when Eisenhower chose to be in residence. It was, indeed, comfortably like the officers' clubs Eisenhower had known during his long military career, with the difference that here only general officers were admitted. Augusta National had less than three hundred members. They were white, predominantly Anglo-Saxon, Protestant, wealthy, conservative, like-minded; most of them businessmen from New York, Detroit, Cleveland, San Francisco, Washington; withdrawn in their enclave, paying little heed to Georgia and its ways, save that of course they punctiliously observed the local custom of racial segregation. As at an army club, the atmosphere was masculine. There was even a uniform—the club's emerald-green blazer, worn over gray flannel trousers.

On this visit, as before, the Eisenhowers used the cottage belonging to Robert T. (Bobby) Jones, the immortal of golf who in retirement had been a founder of Augusta National and was still the club's president. (Subsequently the couple would stay at what was demurely referred to as "Mamie's cabin," a big three-story country house built and furnished for them by the club at a cost of about one hundred and fifty thousand dollars; it stands among pine trees not far from the tenth tee of the golf course.)

It is easy to see why Eisenhower found Augusta National an agreeable place to visit. Apart from the companionship of men whom he found congenial (jolly, extroverted men with nicknames like Slats and Pete and Schooie), apart from the warm afternoons of golf and the cool evenings of bridge, Augusta National had always enabled him to slide smoothly from public rigor to private relaxation—blessed relief. Until November 1952. On this visit, when first he stepped into the sparkling morning sunlight and sauntered happily with his friends to the first tee, he found, besides his foursome and their caddies, a quartet of unsmiling men in felt hats and topcoats, absurdly out of place. The Secret Service. No budging them. The four golfers, their four caddies, and their four custodians moved self-consciously down the fairway. (In time the agents would appear in more appropriate plumage, but they would be ever at hand.)

Privacy, Eisenhower recognized, would be harder than ever to come by, and the private Eisenhower would have very few minutes left in the day.

In the ten weeks before he was to be inaugurated, Eisenhower faced three chief tasks: selection of the men (and the two or three token women) who would administer the government under his directon; planning the orderly transfer of government from the Democrats to the Republicans; and honoring the pledge to go to Korea—a pledge that had been so couched as to leave the impression that he would personally end the savage, senseless killing in that embittered land. The first task—selection of his cabinet—he deputed to two trusted advisers; the transfer of government was initiated by Truman and rather sullenly affirmed by Eisenhower; and to end the fighting in Korea would of course require the months of delicate, protracted diplomacy that had been disrupted by Eisenhower's politicking.

The advisers charged with the selection of the cabinet were Lucius Clay and Herbert Brownell, who on the one hand were urged to pay little heed to any advice from Republican party leaders but on the other hand were privily counseled to discuss their nominations with Thomas E. Coleman, one of Senator Taft's closest advisers and also, conveniently, the Republican national committeeman from Wisconsin, Senator Mc-

Carthy's state. It was plain that the principal members of the cabinet must be the secretaries of state, the treasury, and defense; as matters turned out, Clay was paramount in the selection of two, maybe of all three.

For secretary of state Foster Dulles was plainly the leading candidate, but there were others. For example, Eisenhower had known and admired John J. (Jack) McCloy since 1942. (Besides, for what they were worth, Eisenhower may have recalled the cautionary entreaties of Anthony Eden against Dulles.) Clay, however, argued that Dulles was the most satisfactory choice to Taft, and by the end of the campaign the matter had been settled. Sherman Adams would later assert that once the selection had been made, Dulles told Eisenhower: "With my understanding of the intricate relationships between the peoples of the world and your sensitiveness to the political considerations involved, we will make the most successful team in history."*

Clay found his choices for both secretary of the treasury and secretary of defense at a meeting of the Business Advisory Council at Sea Island, off the coast of Georgia. (Members of the council, an appendage of the Department of Commerce, are an elite who run the nation's biggest enterprises.) First he tapped Charles E. Wilson, president of General Motors, to run the Pentagon. Wilson, a big, bluff, pompous man, was reputed to be the highest-paid executive in American industry ($201,000 a year in salary, $380,000 in bonuses), so he was a natural choice for an administration that proposed to represent business and industry. Next day Clay sought out George M. Humphrey, president of M. A. Hanna & Company, a Cleveland conglomerate with subsidiary fingers in everything from iron ore and steel production to plastics and banking. The two had met in October 1948, when Humphrey had come to Germany as chairman of a commission to determine which German factories should not be dismantled under the war reparations program; the brief encounter seemed scarcely a sufficient recommendation. "Lucius," Humphrey complained, "why in the devil did you ever think of me?" In fact, Humphrey had been suggested to Clay by Sidney Weinberg of Goldman, Sachs, a man who for twenty years had been equipping the federal government with executives committed to a sound fiscal policy. Eisenhower had never set an eye on Humphrey—had in all likelihood never even heard of him—before being told he was to be secretary of the treasury, but the two men got along famously from the first moment they met, when the balding Humphrey,

---

* Something about this quoted remark—perhaps its complacency?—grated on those around Eisenhower. In February 1969 General Schulz wrote me that it was not "wholly correct." Rather, Dulles had said to Eisenhower: "With my long diplomatic experience in the world and your personal friendship with the great majority of the free world leaders—we ought to do all right."

cheerful and assured, strode into Eisenhower's temporary office in the Commodore Hotel and Eisenhower greeted him with, "Well, George, I see you part your hair the same way I do." According to a sturdy yarn that circulated at the time, Humphrey stipulated only one condition for his acceptance of the post. "If anyone talks to you about money," he is said to have instructed Eisenhower, "you tell him to go see George," and Eisenhower was tickled to agree. Such an arrangement spared Eisenhower any worry about what he had referred to during the campaign as "the Federal Reserve Bank and all that stuff."

Eisenhower's readiness to appoint to positions of great power men whom he knew little or not at all should not astonish. The men had been screened by trusted lieutenants: for him it was left only to weld them into his team. The team! Who knew better how to train, to organize, and, having delicately fitted together its components, to lead a team to victory? Or, better, to inspire a team to a triumphant crusade? So in NATO, in SHAPE, in SHAEF and AFHQ; so, reaching far back to the hazy past when he had coached football players at half-forgotten army posts, back all the way to the plebes at West Point. The team! To guide and direct it was what came most naturally to him.

In the meantime, while still his team was being mustered, the President-elect responded to the President's invitation to familiarize himself with the problems he would soon be inheriting. On Tuesday, November 18, Eisenhower arrived in Washington from Augusta. Half a million people cheered him in the streets of the capital. He was due at the White House at 2 P.M.; he appeared five minutes early, accompanied by Joseph M. Dodge, a Detroit banker appointed a week before as his "personal liaison" with the director of the Bureau of the Budget, and with Senator Henry Cabot Lodge, who was to be his "personal liaison" with all other departments and agencies of government.*

This want of careful planning and preparation—by a political party that had been out of power for twenty years, a party that was, moreover, now headed by a man celebrated for his painstaking attention to every imaginable contingency—is incomprehensible except on the supposition that Eisenhower had been so unsettled by the cannonades and the drumfire of the political campaign that he had lost all perspective. "No individual," Eisenhower wrote later, "can be completely or fully prepared for undertaking the responsibilities of the Presidency"; yet when President Truman

* By statute the budget for fiscal 1954, which with indifference alike to logic and common sense would run from July 1, 1953, to June 30, 1954, was required to be presented to Congress before January 15, 1953. Attention had to be paid beforehand, since only five days would elapse between the statutory limit for submission of the budget message by the outgoing administration and the inauguration of the incoming one.

earnestly attempted that preparation, Eisenhower's response was grudging.

Truman and his chief advisers—Acheson of State, John W. Snyder of Treasury, Robert A. Lovett of Defense, and Harriman, the Mutual Security administrator—had spent long hours reducing to explicable form at least the most pressing of Eisenhower's future tasks: debate in the United Nations on the Korean armistice; disposition of the Anglo-Iranian dispute over petroleum; problems confronting the European Defense Community, which were presumably close to the heart of the man who had so recently held the sword of SHAPE at NATO's gate; the question of the war being conducted by the French against the Vietnamese in Indochina, a war in which the United States was already involved to the extent of having assumed "between one-third and one-half of the financial burden." The list was long and chock-a-block with intractable items. Was this why Truman found Eisenhower "unsmiling" and "tense"? Acheson has recalled that Eisenhower "seemed embarrassed and reluctant to be with us—wary, withdrawn, and taciturn to the point of surliness." Truman would remember Eisenhower's "frozen grimness," and wonder whether "in the heat of partisan politics" the President-elect "had gotten a badly distorted version of the true facts" about the world to whose center stage he had once again come. Truman and Eisenhower, once so affable with each other, now circled each other stiff-legged and watchful.

At all events, it was not one of Eisenhower's happier times. At the root of his display of petulance was an incident of the campaign, his invocation of the war in Korea for what Truman considered "partisan political purposes." Truman could "never understand how a responsible military man, fully familiar with the extreme delicacy of our negotiations to end hostilities, could use this tragedy for political advantage." At the time of Eisenhower's pledge, "I shall go to Korea," Truman had denounced it as demagogic; the day after the election he sent Eisenhower a telegram of congratulations, adding that his presidential airplane was at Eisenhower's disposal "if you still desire to go to Korea." Eisenhower retorted tartly that "for [his] planned trip to Korea" he would use any available transport plane.

Against this chilly background the two men met, chaffered suspiciously, and took their leave of each other.

More appointments to the President-elect's cabinet followed. Douglas McKay, a wealthy automobile salesman from Oregon and a long-time Republican politician who shared Eisenhower's misgivings about publicly owned electric power systems, was named secretary of the interior; next day Brownell was nominated to be attorney general and Stassen to be Mutual Security administrator. In succeeding days there were always new names to make front-page headlines. It was clear that Jim Hagerty was masterfully managing the news, though not yet clear why he did so piecemeal, releasing the names like a fisherman dribbling chum: Ezra Taft Benson as secretary of agriculture, Sherman Adams as assistant to the President, Summerfield as postmaster general, Mrs. Oveta Culp Hobby as Federal Security administrator, Lodge as representative to the United Nations, Sinclair Weeks as secretary of commerce, and finally Martin P. Durkin as secretary of labor. It was a cabinet of no particular distinction. Only one selection was at all astonishing: Durkin, the prospective secretary of labor, was president of the United Association of Journeymen Plumbers and Steamfitters, a Democrat, and an outspoken opponent of the Taft-Hartley Act. (When told of the nomination, Taft snorted, "Incredible!") Yet it was a cabinet calculated to put in good humor the substantial, conservative businessmen of the nation—"nine millionaires and a plumber," according to the quip current in Washington at the time.*

Suddenly the reason for Hagerty's measured disclosure of these and other appointments was manifest: the entire procedure had been a cover, an exercise in security to conceal the fact that for several days General Eisenhower and his party had been first bound for Korea and then touring that bleak and desolated land.

The war in Korea—to that point the most infuriating and hateful conflict in U.S. history, the war that had forever tarnished the reputation of Eisenhower's former chief Douglas MacArthur—the war in Korea had by December 1952 come to stalemate. North Koreans, whether or not provoked, had rolled across the thirty-eighth parallel; Americans, supported by contingents from others of the United Nations, had pushed them back all the way to the Yalu River, threatening China; "volunteers" of the Chinese Red Army had swept the U.N. troops well back into South Korea; thereupon caution had seized both adversaries and, despite the discharge of invective and polemic from either side, they had settled down to defensive warfare, once again roughly along the thirty-eighth parallel. As early as March 1951, President Truman had attempted to initiate negotiations toward a cease-fire, a truce, an armistice; but MacArthur, in an extraordinary display of his overweening presumption, had promptly torpedoed the effort by announcing his own proposal for a cease-fire, one the Chinese were sure to reject out of hand. (Truman endured still another act of such

---

* Like most wisecracks, this one was imprecise. Benson, for one, was no millionaire. He compensated by supplying a full measure of spiritual wealth, for he was one of the Council of Twelve who governed the Church of Jesus Christ of Latter-Day Saints, more commonly known as the Mormons. ". . . we've got to deal with spiritual matters," Eisenhower reminded Benson. "I feel your church connection," he added, sliding easily into a more commercial idiom, "is a distinct asset."

insubordination before at length dismissing MacArthur.) Truce negotiations had finally been launched in July 1951, but without a cease-fire; the slaughter had continued unabated; American casualties would rise from slightly more than seventy-five thousand when negotiations were begun to more than one hundred and fifty thousand by the time they were completed—about twelve thousand American dead, or five hundred deaths a month because of American insistence on fighting while negotiations toward an armistice dragged on.

On his arrival in Korea, Eisenhower was once again the five-star general and only incidentally the President-elect. He conferred briefly with old comrades: Mark Clark, commanding general in the Far East, and James Van Fleet, a classmate at West Point, now commanding the U.S. Eighth Army. He was able to visit his son John, a field officer of the 15th Infantry, a division then deployed in the front lines. To an officer as experienced as Eisenhower it was obvious that "in view of the strength of the positions the enemy had developed . . . any frontal attack would present great difficulties." Syngman Rhee, the puppet president of South Korea, was full of fierce threats about how his troops would drive all the communists off the peninsula and back into China. MacArthur had earlier given Rhee his pledge to unify North and South Korea and so achieve *"the future stability of the continent of Asia."* Rhee's vaporings did not impose on Eisenhower, nor did MacArthur's italics and antiquated notions of how the Oriental would submissively follow "aggressive, resolute and dynamic leadership." MacArthur hankered to blockade China and bomb Manchuria. Eisenhower saw the matter with a colder eye:

> At this time—December 1952—it had been tacitly accepted by both sides . . . that we were fighting defensively and would take no risks of turning the conflict into a global war. . . . My conclusion as I left Korea was that we could not stand forever on a static front and continue to accept casualties without any visible results. Small attacks on small hills would not end this war.

Yet plainly the war had to be ended. One of the chief reasons for Eisenhower's electoral victory had been the widespread conviction that the Hero would be able to extricate the nation from the war. He had been given what amounted to a mandate to end the intolerable conflict: any way he wanted, but end it.

Trying to end a war is a spirited game that any number can play. On December 5, the day Eisenhower's airplane headed homeward east from Seoul, halfway round the globe in New York City his old commander General MacArthur was the principal speaker at a festive session of the

National Association of Manufacturers. MacArthur had conceived, he said, "a clear and definite solution to the Korean conflict," one that entailed no "danger of provoking universal conflict." At once beset by reporters, MacArthur declined to reveal his solution, but rather loftily acknowledged that if the President-elect were interested he would discuss it at that level.

For MacArthur again to inject himself into the Korean question served as a reminder that Asia and the Pacific had been the scene of his heroics just as Europe and the Atlantic had been that of Eisenhower's. Superficially their wartime rivalry had been one of prestige, a contest for headlines and space on the front pages of the newspapers; but in reality they had waged a struggle for strategic primacy: which theater should be accorded priority and in consequence the essential troops, weapons, and ships to transport them? The debate had persisted after the war and become a thesis of Cold War doctrine. While General MacArthur had been directing the Korean War, General Eisenhower had been spurring NATO to rearm Europe; each had been anxious about his share of the wealth sluiced out by the Pentagon. By an inevitable alchemy their rivalry had been transmuted into politics: as soon as MacArthur had recognized that his own chances of preferment were negligible he supported the efforts of Senator Taft to carry off the Republican nomination: anything to stop Eisenhower. Once they had been four-star general and major, then each was five-star general, now one would soon be commander in chief, but the other would have no joy on the day.

Eisenhower was told of MacArthur's speech to the NAM when he was aboard the cruiser *Helena*, to which he had transferred at Guam. Some of his party advised him to ignore the overture. He had best not get involved with one so demonstrably jealous. Eisenhower disagreed. What mischief could come of talking with MacArthur? At least, his advisers counseled, keep his response to the invitation private. Again Eisenhower disagreed. He radioed MacArthur he was "looking forward to informal meetings" to gain "the full benefit of your thinking and experience," and he instructed Hagerty to give his message to the press.

On leaving Korea, Eisenhower had been bone-weary and showed it. Once aboard the *Helena*, however, his buoyancy and confidence were soon restored. Brownell and Charles Wilson of his prospective cabinet and Hagerty and General Jerry Persons of his staff had accompanied him to Korea; they were still with him, and at Wake Island others joined the party—Foster Dulles, George Humphrey, and Douglas McKay of the proposed cabinet; Joseph Dodge, who would be director of the Bureau of the Budget; General Lucius Clay, trusted crony and essential adviser; and Emmet Hughes, now officially an administrative assistant, at hand to draft statements and speeches. Now was the time to start weaving these various threads into one harmonious fabric.

For their frequent meetings they had a formidable agenda, but despite the portentous bulletins issued by Hagerty from "the epic mid-Pacific conference," not much was accomplished. Aboard the *Helena* and later, ashore at Pearl Harbor, there was general discussion of "how best to combat Soviet-dominated Communism throughout the world" and especially in Asia, but conclusions were tentative and sketchy. The most decisive result of the conversations was to attract the attention of the exalted tourists to Admiral Arthur W. Radford, who was then CINCPAC (commander in chief, Pacific). Radford was an obstinate sailor who nevertheless had the good sense to be pliable when he found himself at odds with his superiors. (Eisenhower quickly sized him up as "extremely useful . . . a man of tough conviction who would . . . time and again modify his views.") More important, Radford believed that Asia, not Europe, would be the premier battleground of the Cold War, and this attitude precisely dovetailed with the political requirements of the moment. A dominant chord of Republican dogma was that the accursed Roosevelt and the accursed Truman had for too long favored the needs of Europe while ignoring those of Asia; per corollary, the Joint Chiefs of Staff and especially their chairman, General Omar Bradley, carried the ineradicable taint of commitment to Truman's policies and therefore, in the view of Senator Taft and other Republican paladins, should be dumped as hastily as possible. The suspicion of complicity with Truman's malpractices clouded even Eisenhower's lustrous reputation: how better to exonerate himself than by appointing as chairman of the Joint Chiefs one who, like Radford, symbolized a shift of strategic emphasis? The matter was worth thought.

Two-day stopover in Hawaii. Golf on the links beside the sea at the Kanehoe Marine Air Station. Airplane to California and on to New York. "We face an enemy," Eisenhower told reporters, "whom we cannot hope to impress by words, however eloquent, but only by deeds—executed under circumstances of our own choosing." Two men in particular hoped to influence the nature of those deeds—Douglas MacArthur and Winston Churchill.

The MacArthur solution to the Korean War was to threaten its immediate and cataclysmic expansion: an ultimatum that if the Chinese did not at once do thus and so, the U.S. would drop atomic bombs on targets within China. When Eisenhower rejected this advice MacArthur went away bristling. Later, in the circle of a few intimates, he spoke bitterly. "The trouble with Eisenhower," he said, "is that he doesn't have the guts to make a policy decision. He never did have the guts and he never will."

Next came Winston Churchill, at seventy-eight once again H.M. Prime Minister, now concerned lest the new American government might provoke a bigger war in the Far East by loosing the troops of Generalissimo Chiang Kai-shek—trained and equipped by Americans—against the armies on the Chinese mainland. Even mention of the redoubtable Churchill rattled the Republican elders: was he come with British enchantments to ensnare Eisenhower as he had earlier seduced Roosevelt? A group of apprehensive Republican senators wrung from Eisenhower an assurance that he would make no commitments to Churchill during his visit. Accordingly, Eisenhower was at pains to remind Churchill of the potential mischief if the impression got abroad—or took hold in the United States Senate—that the United States and United Kingdom might be forming some sort of special alliance. But for a time talk of "unleashing Chiang Kai-shek" was muted.

A week or so before his inauguration as the nation's thirty-fourth President, Eisenhower presided over two lengthy meetings of the men and women, still polite strangers to each other, who would soon be governing the country under his direction. It was unprecedented—a kind of preview, as it were, of his administration; a gathering of his proposed cabinet and principal executive assistants; a shakedown; another stage of Eisenhower's continuing effort to forge unity and make a team.

The meetings were held in a large formal chamber of the Commodore Hotel—gray, green, and gold—and the first began with a prayer by Ezra Benson, the Mormon elder soon to be secretary of agriculture. This token of spiritual propriety having been spread on the record, the company sat down to lunch in the sunshine of Eisenhower's bonhomie. Afterward the President-elect read to his guests the most recent draft of his inaugural address, and when he had finished they burst into spontaneous applause. "I think it is wonderful," said Charley Wilson, the big white-haired corporation executive; "I am in favor of flying the flag pretty high." His enthusiasm was representative. Not only the prospective cabinet secretaries but also the men who had been assembled by Sherman Adams to function as Eisenhower's staff officers—all were infected by the obviously earnest demeanor of the remarkably likable man who was their leader. His performance could seem humble (and might more precisely be described as shy) but his personal magnetism was a mighty constant.

Yet Eisenhower was restive, "because," as he said, "here is this thing going out to probably one of the greatest audiences that has ever heard a speech. It is going in the papers. Here are thousands out in front of us." Other hundreds of thousands were waiting all around the world, some in chancelleries, some at shortwave receivers, some with headphones adjusted to secret radio transmitters, for, as Eisenhower was aware, his first speech was sure to be regarded as a momentous passage of the Cold War, and some in his vast audience would be fearful lest it might signal the approach of holocaust.

The talk around the luncheon table wandered. There was discussion of what sort of hats the men should wear to the inauguration, of how long the parade would last and when it should start, of when the cabinet officers should be sworn in and who might attend that ceremony.

Eisenhower returned to the subject of his speech. He was undertaking, he believed, a spiritual crusade, and he felt the need to identify "the fellow plowing a row of corn or driving a taxi" with his crusade. Did his speech accomplish that purpose?

Never a man to neglect a phrase, Charley Wilson exclaimed, "You flew the flag! It was wonderful!"

There were few substantive suggestions. The talk drifted away once again. Next day most of the discussion focused on the need to end the wage and price controls imposed by Truman because of the Korean War and on the fond Republican dream of a balanced budget and a consequent reduction of taxes.

Still Eisenhower was fretful about his speech, and even less than three days before he was to deliver it spoke of junking the draft so painfully elaborated and starting afresh with a completely new version. To Emmet Hughes, his sympathetic collaborator during those last days, it seemed clear that Eisenhower was "humbled, awed, a little troubled" by his imminent investiture. He was still fussing with the typescript, still interlineating changes on Sunday, January 18, while at the Pennsylvania Station a crew held ready his six-car special train. At length, an hour late, he stepped aboard his private car. Mrs. Eisenhower was with him, and their son John, ordered home from Korea for the ceremony by President Truman, with their daughter-in-law.

South and west through repellent industrial landscape lightly mantled by sooty snow, a special train of the Pennsylvania Railroad Company carried Dwight David Eisenhower toward the culmination of his career.

A robust man three months past his sixty-second birthday, blessed with vigor and vitality: who walked with springing step, hard and fit, weighing little more than he had as an athlete at West Point forty years before; whose clear fair skin flushed sanguine with laughter or anger or sudden excited interest; whose intensely blue eyes, unless of course he grinned, were his most arresting particularity.

A man in whom the habit of command was so deeply ingrained that he rarely found himself called upon to exercise it; who had cultivated, instead, the knack of leading men effortlessly—by being quick with praise and quick to take responsibility for mishaps, skilled in the delegation of responsibility, ready to seek advice and to absorb it, and willing to move more than halfway toward compromise, at least in unimportant matters.

A man whose combined shrewdness, ease of manner, and self-control were so smoothly geared as to give the impression of wisdom; who considered himself a masterful judge of men and had often proven that ability; who, years before, had come to appreciate that he should make only those decisions that could not be made by others, but should then make them "in clean-cut fashion and on his own responsibility"; who never moved directly, on his own, when the same ends could be fashioned indirectly through the efforts of others; industrious yet facile, cautious yet swift; content to let others presume him stupid and lazy so long as his goals were achieved. A man canny and precise in his mental processes, observant, retentive, with a puissant will to win.

For all these reasons—and others, such as his apparent candor and sincerity, his accomplished simplicity and modesty—the man traveling to Washington in business car number 90 of the Pennsylvania Railroad seemed the hope of the nation, the more especially since he was to take office at a time when the war in Korea was dragging on through its third year, the national budget was deep in deficit, and the western alliance (the nations of NATO and their dependencies) was bleeding from wounds in Iran and Indochina, while at home the American ethos as loftily expressed in the Declaration of Independence was being coldly and persistently trampled. Who, if not a Hero like Eisenhower, could right these wrongs?

And yet . . .

The train, only slowing as it rumbled through Trenton, Philadelphia, Chester, Wilmington, clattered down a clear track, no stops: steady clickety course to Washington, fetching the President-elect to his ultimate pedestal.

. . . there were misgivings, too, about Eisenhower's prospects as President.

For example, when had he ever harbored an original idea? An idea conceived and thought through by himself, unbeholden to his hardworking and devoted staff? An idea under any rubric of human activity, political, social, economic, or even military? If he could do such a thing, he had as yet given no evidence of it. Nowhere in his speeches or letters or other writings could there be found an idea that was not worn out and obsolete before he was born.

Such a lack of independent thinking was, taken by itself, not crippling or even necessarily distressing: one must, after all, turn back as far as James Madison to find a President for whom creative intellection was not a burden. But even more than his recent predecessors, Eisenhower had seemed a weathercock, shifting with every deep current of popular passion. A case in point was his professed estimate of the Soviet Union—chilly back in the early 1930s, benevolent during the war and for a couple of years after it (an episode deftly expunged from the record as a bit of nonhistory), and at last arctic as the propaganda of the Cold War became the articles of a patriot's faith. In short, he had seemed less leader than trimmer, and in view of the problems looming within and without the republic, this was not cause for complacency.

Moreover, there was the highly specialized character of Eisenhower's career. For forty years he had been a soldier, a man largely withdrawn from the struggles and vicissitudes of society, sheltered within a professional cadre that held its own in high esteem and gazed with a withering indifference at most of those outside it. His life had been articulated and circumscribed by the chain of command, a phrase which is not metaphor but precise description. The soldier lives by commands; he learns to execute; as he rises along the chain of command, he does so because he is an able executive. Eisenhower had proved himself an executive of superior attainments: delegating decision, decentralizing responsibility, taking pride in being self-effacing and in constantly giving credit to others until the action had become an involuntary reflex. The executive leads by getting others to do what must be done. The procedure is unexceptionable within a chain of command where all are bent in one direction, as toward victory in war. Associates can be selected with one chief criterion in mind: teamwork, cooperation, unity. Victory in war is, to be sure, a hideously confused task, involving dissension and conflict at every step—over strategy, tactics, personnel, weapons, supply, training, morale, objectives, the nature of the enemy, the value of an ally, and a myriad other matters —but still, when contrasted with the labyrinthine perplexities involved in administering and governing a modern industrial nation, the conduct of warfare is trivially simple.

Now, as Chief Executive, Eisenhower would have to harness a team of associates—Republican politicians, elite technicians, ambitious roosters, civil service bureaucrats, opportunists, palpable frauds, and others at the public trough—who would be enthusiastically pulling toward a dozen contrary objectives. His closest associates, the men whose advice he most trusted, more often than not were valued because they had achieved success in a commercial society, but whether this was a reliable measure for excellence in government remained to be seen. Could a group of self-made millionaires be led to do what was needed by a genial President in whose concept of leadership a self-effacing indirection was rated higher than any other weapon in the political arsenal?

The challenge promised to provoke a lively interest.

The six-car Eisenhower train pulled into Washington on a siding one hundred yards from Union Station, so that the family might transfer to limousines in welcome seclusion. They were driven to a private entrance of the Statler Hotel, then lifted to their special accommodations on the top floor.

God was now invoked, less as a deity than as a political weapon and promotional device.

It can be safely assumed that so far as Dwight Eisenhower was concerned, the recourse at this juncture to religion and religiosity was, on the whole, reverent. To be sure, he had for years been notably indifferent to the outward and visible aspects of worship; Sunday had more often found him on a golf course than in a church; he had no very firm grasp of theology, nor even a loose one; but the evidence is clear that the religious training of his childhood in Abilene had left an indelible, if fuzzy, mark. What is more, he believed that as President he should set a respectable example. Regular worship is respectable; ergo, he should change the habits of a lifetime and join the membership of some respectable church. For whatever reasons (his wife's family were Presbyterians; at least seven of his predecessors had belonged to that sect) he had added himself to the strength of the National Presbyterian Church in Washington. A special service was to be conducted there by its pastor, the Reverend Edward L. R. Elson, on the morning of Tuesday, January 20, immediately before the ceremony of inauguration.*

Meanwhile, on Sunday, carpenters were working overtime constructing for the inaugural parade what was known as "God's Float," a name that the float's ingenious designers hoped would be celebrated throughout the world. It was the last float to have been thought of; it would be first in the order of march. It would be emblazoned with two slogans, "In God We Trust" and "Freedom of Worship"; it was to feature an edifice purporting to be a place of worship, carefully nondenominational. Of this curiosity, the editor of an Episcopalian journal would later write: "Standing for all religions, it had the symbols of none, and it looked like

---

* Elson, elated by this distinguished accession to his parish, wrote later that "through his personal conduct and expression [Eisenhower] has become the focal point of a moral resurgence and spiritual awakening of national proportions." Elson's report of this resurgence and awakening coincided with a "Back to God" crusade conducted by the American Legion and launched by Eisenhower.

nothing whatsoever in Heaven above, or in the earth beneath, except possibly an oversized model of a deformed molar left over from some dental exhibit."

God's Float had, however, a value transcending its absurdity: it was a symbol of Eisenhower's anticommunist crusade, of moral and spiritual superiority to the godless Russians. It was a way of piously proclaiming, God is on our side. For years Eisenhower had struggled in one way or another to put this notion into words. He had declared that one of the two cornerstones of the American democracy was "a deep and abiding religious faith."* He had defined democracy as "a political expression of a deep and abiding religion." To a congress of the World Council of Churches he had urged the need for "A *deeply felt* religion." Throughout his recent political campaign he had contended that America's strength lay in its "spiritual values," and as for God being on the side of America, he had maintained that "the Almighty takes a definite and direct interest day by day in the progress of this nation." In Eisenhower's view, "spiritual weapons" would forever be "our country's most powerful resource, in peace or in war"; surely they would prevail over the atheist hordes poised to the east. Religion was something that resisted precise definition but could nevertheless be *"deeply felt."* And it was respectable.

"Religion," as Eisenhower put it later, "was one of the thoughts I had been mulling over for several weeks." And so, after his unwonted attendance at church on Tuesday morning, he found himself wondering if the nation "were not getting too secular." Pondering the matter, he decided to write a little prayer that would preface his inaugural address. The effort took him five or ten minutes. It had none of the poetic magic that suffuses Christian ceremony with beauty; rather it suggested George F. Babbitt before a session of the local Rotary: "Almighty God, as we stand here at this moment, my future associates in the Executive branch of government join me in beseeching . . ." No matter; it sparkled with the earnest sincerity that was Eisenhower's own personal magic.

Whether or not by divine intervention, a shaft of sunlight gleamed through the low clouds and off the patches of grimy snow, as Dwight David Eisenhower took the oath and became the thirty-fourth President of the United States. First his little prayer, and then he was into his initial Cold War pronouncement as President:

". . . We sense with all our faculties that forces of good and evil are massed and armed and opposed as rarely before in history. . . .

"At such a time in history, we who are free must proclaim anew our faith. . . .

* The other cornerstone was free enterprise.

506

"The enemies of this faith know no god but force, no devotion but its use. They tutor men in treason. They feed upon the hunger of others. Whatever defies them, they torture, especially the truth.

"Here, then, is joined no argument between slightly different philosophies. This conflict strikes directly at the faith of our fathers and the lives of our sons. . . .

"Freedom is pitted against slavery; lightness against the dark."

Who so craven as to stand aside when good was arrayed against evil, and lightness was challenging the dark? The clarion was unmistakable, and it called to war.

PART FIVE

COLD WARRIOR

CHAPTER ONE

New President: Old Problems

Fiscal policy . . . Vietnam . . . Iran . . . McCarthy . . . The
Rosenbergs . . . The "national interest" . . . National security
. . . and a new administration in Washington.

ON THE CHILLY MORNING in the middle of the twentieth century when
Dwight David Eisenhower was ushered into an oval room in the west
wing of the White House (January 21, 1953), the presidency of the
United States presented many familiar aspects of precedence and prestige.
But in its crucial characteristics it was so strange and new compared with
the presidency twenty years before, when last a Republican had held it,
as to be almost unrecognizable. Superficially, some of the changes could be
ascribed to the two Democratic Presidents who had held the office during
those twenty years, but far more profound forces had been at work, almost
making it seem that the presidency had been plucked up by the four ele-
mentals, whirled about, dashed to bits, and reassembled haphazard. The
world had undergone violent alterations (with still other paroxysms impending), and it followed that the presidency, now in some ways the most
powerful position in the new changed world, had been similarly transformed.

Most of Eisenhower's memories of how Washington operated, stemming
from the days when he had been a staff officer in the War Department,
were either misleading or irrelevant. Back in that tranquil age of Republican ascendancy, White House, Congress, and Supreme Court had all
been confidently and comfortably fixed within the dispensation of the
GOP. No more; nor for any of the eight years of Eisenhower's administrations. During six of those eight years, while Eisenhower would survive a
moderately severe cardiac occlusion, a major abdominal operation for
terminal ileitis, and a cerebral angiospasm—in short, while he survived
assaults on his heart, his guts, and his brain—he would be obliged to
coquet with a Democratic Congress in order to have his legislative pro-

gram enacted; and he would find the nation's noblest aspirations most unexpectedly, even exasperatingly, sustained by a Supreme Court whose chief justice was, to his embarrassment, his own responsibility, and whose members were far from being (as once had been the case) overwhelmingly conservative. Eisenhower's constituency, whether narrowly regarded as limited to Republicans, or more broadly as comprehending the nation as a whole and even a large part of the world, was tangled and complicated. His various constituents would press him toward diverse and contradictory goals. The time of a comfortable consensus comfortably congregated was no more.

At first the President's own party was only fitfully responsive to his leadership, seeming more to heed the counsel of Senator Taft or even that of the unruly Senator McCarthy; moreover, the President had been quick to appreciate that the Republicans "did not look upon the results of the election as the threshold of opportunity; rather it was the end of a long and searing drought, and they were at last reveling again in luxurious patronage." So long as Taft lived (he died on July 31, 1953), Eisenhower deemed him a valued lieutenant. Taft's successor as leader of the Republican majority in the Senate, William Knowland of California, had little of Taft's ability and less of his influence. Eisenhower considered him "cumbersome," a notably mild judgment in view of Knowland's persistent interference in Far Eastern foreign policy. (Knowland was derisively nicknamed by his colleagues "the senator from Formosa.") The President fancied the Republican leaders in the House of Representatives were more malleable, more easily persuaded to become members of the team.

In the Senate, on the Democratic side of the aisle, was to be found a singular personage, a handful for any President and particularly for a Republican as unseasoned in partisan politics as Eisenhower. This was the newly elected minority leader—majority leader after 1954—the wily, willful, and ambitious Lyndon Baines Johnson. The Democrats were in as striking disarray as the Republicans, if not more so, but Johnson was a consummate politician who knew what power was, what it was made of, and how to use it. After eight years in the White House, Eisenhower would be able to point to precious few laws enacted without the consent and active support of the senator from Texas. The questions could be seriously debated: Who governed the nation? Which was the more responsible party?

There were other disturbing changes—administrative, technological, political, military—of more or less importance. A minor vexation was the attitude of the Washington press corps. While still in uniform Eisenhower had got accustomed to correspondents who were part of the team, congenial, respectful, well disposed to him and his objectives, cheerfully cooperative; yet during the recent campaign the reporters on his train had shown their marked preference for Stevenson. That had been hard for Eisenhower to forget. At first the new President had no need for the benevolence of the press corps. After all, the publishers of some 80 percent of the country's daily newspapers had supported his election, and at least 60 percent of the country's citizens, according to polls, approved the way he was managing his first administration. In these circumstances it was a courageous journalist who filed copy critical of the beloved Hero. "I don't think," a Washington columnist remarked in October 1953, "our readers are ready for critical reporting yet." Such restraint could not long endure. Indeed, at a press conference only a week or so later Eisenhower would be hard pressed by a roomful of inexorable inquisitors who put him thoroughly out of temper.* After a year of experience of the Washington press corps, the President dictated a reflective memorandum about the reporters for what he termed his diary.† They were, he judged, "far from being as important as they themselves consider, but" they had to be placated, a tiresome chore. They had, he believed, little sense of humor. They took themselves more seriously than they did their job—in Eisenhower's view, a cardinal error. When it came to human mentality, Eisenhower had his own taxonomic system: some minds were interested in ideas, some in facts and things, some in personalities and gossip. Taking one with another, journalists seemed to him to fit only in that last category. He rated Roscoe Drummond of the *New York Herald Tribune* and Arthur Krock of the *New York Times* the best of a pesky lot.

Television was another of the strange new prodigies afflicting the presidency, and as it asserted its grip on its audience the deceptions of show business and entertainment began to outweigh debated issues as the political realities of substance. Television was better suited to display Eisenhower's merits than was the press. It was flawed: the ministrations of neither BBD&O nor Robert Montgomery, the aging juvenile of movies turned director of television, could keep the camera from distorting the ruddy glow of Eisenhower's complexion to a ghastly gray, nor the lights from flashing off his spectacles when he read a speech; yet the searching eye of the medium faithfully reported Eisenhower's warmth and candor

---

* See pages 603–604.
† Into Eisenhower's "diary" went memoranda he dictated to his secretary, Mrs. Ann Whitman, either for his own records or to be sent to close associates; letters to old friends; notes of telephone conversations deemed important; and so on. Some were filed in folders marked "Diary," some in folders marked "Personal Diary." Still others were squirreled away in less accessible crannies, under seal, to be kept secret until a certain future date. In any case, Eisenhower was constantly attentive to the needs of successive generations of historians and managed, whether or not deliberately, to supply ammunition for each of the quarrelsome schools of historiography.

and sincerity. The worst of it was that the several public relations adepts of the new administration perceived, in the conjunction of Eisenhower and television, a gorgeous opportunity for merchandising the new, improved, better-packaged Republican enlightenment. Early on, C. D. Jackson, the tall and urbane Time-Life executive who had signed on as the President's special assistant in psychological warfare, was heard to say, "We will merchandise the hell out of the Eisenhower program," and sure enough, before long the *Wall Street Journal* was reporting that "Eisenhower & Co. have opened a new sales department right in the White House. The new division of the Republican Administration is headed by a man President Eisenhower privately calls 'the greatest salesman in the world'—the Seattle mortgage banker, Walter Williams."

This was the man who had been co-chairman of Citizens for Eisenhower during the campaign; he was now undersecretary of commerce, eager "to 'sell' the President's policies to the public—and tout his achievements." Salesmanship was desirable, for as a White House aide explained to the *Journal's* reporter: "We all suddenly realized we were busy manufacturing a product down here, but nobody was selling it." President Eisenhower obviously approved of these commercial projects, for he helped to plan, rehearsed, and on June 3, 1953, starred in a BBD&O television production, an unprecedented report to the nation featuring four members of his cabinet. It was a plausible entertainment, full of homespun. "One of our best shows," Ben Duffy of BBD&O said proudly. To connoisseurs, the format of the show was a familiar one. A columnist for an advertising trade magazine commented:

> Undoubtedly the most effective commercial of the month was the President's TV appearance . . . It closely followed the pattern of an agency new-business solicitation. The President let each department head, armed with slides, present the story of his branch of the business. Then he wrapped the whole thing up in a masterful manner and asked for the order. As a TV salesman, we think you will agree, Dwight Eisenhower has few peers.

But press-agentry, television hokum, partisan politics, even the rumblings of the seditionist Senator McCarthy—these were unconsidered trifles when ranged alongside the somber, intractable problems besetting the presidency at mid-century.

First and last, those problems engendered a climate of crisis in which emergency came to be commonplace and serenity a phantom. No sooner could one crisis be perceived, appraised, and challenged by a task force of experts than another would bob up to distract, and then another, and another. Perhaps the most exasperating dilemmas to confront the Eisenhower administration in its early months were three.

ONE: How to strike a proper balance between a military policy sufficient to brandish the nation's mailed fist, and so ensure the national defense, and a fiscal policy that would entail a balanced budget, decreased taxes, reduced public debt, and vastly diminished federal costs, and so protect the national economy.

President Eisenhower believed the two policies were one. "The relationship," he said, "between military and economic strength is intimate and indivisible." This was no new notion. It will be recalled that he had underlined his words when in February 1951 he had written his friend Bermingham: *the only way we can achieve military success . . . is through preserving the integrity of our economy and our financial structure.*

The difficulty was that defense was so costly, the more so since those who manufactured the weapons had to be guaranteed a handsome profit for their enterprise lest they lose interest and turn to the manufacture of other things, such as plowshares. Of the budget for fiscal year 1954, inherited from Truman, nearly 60 percent, amounting to more than forty-six billions of dollars, was earmarked for defense. Defense? Defense against whom? Iran? Laos? Guatemala? No: as everybody knew, it was the Soviet Union or, perhaps better, the malign forces of international communism. But since nothing is worse than a vague adversary, better it be the Soviet Union, with headquarters of evil in the Kremlin; erstwhile ally, latterly by common consent accepted as bloodthirsty and implacable enemy. Witnesses vied with each other to testify to the country's mortal danger and to the urgent need for an expanded defense. Americans, Foster Dulles warned, were caught up in "an irreconcilable conflict."

Although the event had not yet been officially acknowledged, on November 1, 1952, a hydrogen bomb had been "successfully" exploded, for the first time in history, at the Eniwetok Proving Grounds in the Pacific. The force of the blast, which obliterated an island, was estimated to be the equivalent of three million tons of TNT, or one hundred and fifty times as powerful as the explosion that destroyed Hiroshima. Operational control of such a device would have seemed sufficient defense against any threatened attack on the U.S., but air force officials in the Pentagon were not satisfied. A group of eminent scientists, cerebrating under the auspices of the air force, had produced a top-secret study, the Lincoln Report.*

* The name came from the Lincoln Laboratory, near Boston, established in the early 1950s for the study of radar detection, early warning devices, and other like matters bearing on continental defense.

Excerpts from this study—dealing with Soviet progress in the development of guided missiles and other sophisticated weapons, and suggesting the imminent vulnerability of the U.S. to attack—were thoughtfully circulated among selected congressional leaders, with the predictable result that the hon. gentlemen were chilled with dread and fortified in their convictions as cold warriors. More to the point, they were primed to approve federal expenditures for defense above the levels recommended in Truman's final budget—even a few among them who, as members of the Republican Old Guard, were fanatic about a balanced budget.

It followed that Eisenhower, no matter which course he chose, was certain to be assailed. If he presumed to slice the Truman budget he was endangering the nation's security—nay, its very existence. If he failed to slice that budget he was a traitor to Republican principles, to sound fiscal policy, and to his own campaign rhetoric. He sought a compromise and was jumped from both sides. He thought to shave the Truman budget for FY 1954 and postpone any ultimate decision on military strategy until he would be called on to frame his own budget for FY 1955. In effect, as his critics were swift to point out, this course was not change of strategy but evasion of it; in Congress voices were raised demanding whether strategy was deciding the budget or Republican insistence on a balanced budget was deciding strategy. At Eisenhower's direction a little more than five billion dollars was lopped off the military budget. The Joint Chiefs of Staff, having in mind the alarming reports received from the CIA and elsewhere of the growing Soviet nuclear capability, coupled with the surmised Soviet progress in rocketry and long-range missiles, promptly objected. The cuts, they warned, "would seriously endanger national security"; indeed, any cuts at all, they insisted, were "beyond the dictates of national prudence."

Eisenhower did not share their misgivings. To him the Soviet Union was "a backward civilization with a second-rate production plant."

By the end of April the President was ready to expound his budget estimates to a group of Republican congressional leaders, among whom of course was Taft. Eisenhower's proposals, despite a soothing exegesis by his budget director and his secretary of the treasury, could not be disguised: the unpalatable truth was that massive sums were still to be spent on the military, that deficits yawned in the months ahead, that the first Republican budget would be out of whack. In the cabinet chamber where the meeting was held, Taft sat at an angle across the table from Eisenhower, his dismay palpable. When he spoke his voice was harsh and angry. "The one primary thing we promised the American people," he rasped, glaring at Eisenhower, "was reduction of expenditures. Now you're taking us down the same road Truman traveled. You haven't moved an inch from the Truman program. It's a repudiation of everything we promised in the campaign." Taft chiefly deplored the huge sums spent for arms. He put no confidence in recommendations made by the Joint Chiefs and he said as much bluntly. Nor did the advice of the National Security Council carry much weight with him. He made a flat prediction: if the budget were not reduced, the Republicans would lose control of both houses of Congress in the elections of 1954.

Eisenhower was steaming. He hunched forward to retort to Taft as angrily as the senator had spoken, but some alert associates quickly intervened to break the tension with inconsequential chatter. Given a few moments, Eisenhower cooled off and, when he spoke, measured his words. In a low-pitched, even tone he reviewed global strategy: the need to keep Europe strong, to block the Russians from the Middle East and its rich reserves of oil, to protect Southeast Asia from communist incursions, to maintain a show of American strength everywhere. But, he agreed, he must take hold of the upward curve of expenditures and bend it down. While this effort was in train he must have authority to spend the money needed to defend the national security. Whether or no that security was truly in jeopardy, Eisenhower's was the word that ruled. Taft's prediction would be fulfilled, but none would argue the Republicans lost control of the Congress solely because Eisenhower's budget for FY 1954 was unbalanced.

Meanwhile the President's first exasperating dilemma went unresolved.

TWO: How to resolve the impossible contradiction of a foreign policy which required on the one hand sustaining the health and vigor of two chief European allies, Britain and France, yet which prescribed on the other hand the penetration by American interests of former British and French colonies or spheres of influence, ostensibly in order to keep the wealth of those former dependencies safe for capital investment.

Britain is the closest ally of the United States, France its oldest. These two nations had held, before the War of 1939–1945, the world's two greatest colonial empires; those empires had made them rich and had conferred upon them the glories and prerogatives of world powers. But during the war and after it their colonies had slipped from their grasp; one by one their principalities had shrugged off the imperial harness; their spheres of influence had shrunk. British Empire became British Commonwealth, French Empire became French Union.

Yet there were evident differences between the two, grown more obvious over the years. The extraordinary mix of commercial brigandage, hypocrisy, self-assurance, pugnacity, sagacious foresight, and dumb luck that had during the seventeenth and eighteenth centuries produced the British

Empire, by 1953 still boasted vast resources of manpower, vital raw materials, and such strategic strongpoints and trading posts as (from west to east) Gibraltar, Malta, Cyprus, Aden, Singapore, Hong Kong. The Commonwealth existed as a cohesive force largely because its member nations —the United Kingdom, Canada, Australia, New Zealand, South Africa, India, Pakistan, Ceylon—derived more temporary benefit than mischief from their association.

In contrast, the French Union lacked cohesion and economic development. Its members—especially those of North Africa and Indochina—were restive if not rebellious. They sought freedom and the control of their own destinies. If France were to hold her place as a world power, she felt obliged to forge the French Union into a viable political entity. Her leaders believed that the U.S. should recognize this need and assist France in maintaining her global status. The French premier in early 1953 was René Mayer, and he made it clear when he left Paris for Washington to talk with Eisenhower that if the government of the U.S. wanted France to play an effective part in the future of Europe, U.S. aid for French commitments overseas was indispensable. In short, if the U.S. wanted France as a stout anti-Soviet partner in Europe, the U.S. must help France quell rebellion in Vietnam.

As an exercise in logic, this line of argument was admirable, but it failed to fetch Eisenhower. When military commander of NATO, Eisenhower had unavailingly sought to persuade the French "to interpret, publicly, their Far Eastern war effort in terms of freedom versus communism," a course that would have entailed an unequivocal renunciation by the French of any colonial ambitions in Indochina. That, in the French view, was silly. They wanted rather to re-establish their authority in one of the most beautiful and richest parts of their empire. Any attempt to paste the anticommunist label on their struggle against the Viet Minh seemed absurd, for the decision to take up arms had been made by a government of which the French communists were part. To Eisenhower and Dulles, as to Truman and Acheson before them, the anticommunist nature of the conflict was nevertheless clear. Only under a banner with an anticommunist device could American support for the French military effort be approved by Congress. Immediately after his inauguration Eisenhower set about devising plans to strengthen the French forces in Vietnam "politically and militarily."

Thus meddlesome and confused, leaving the French resentful, American policy toward Vietnam moved into higher gear.

A similar question clamoring for the President's attention when he took office was posed by the petroleum of Iran. This came about because the government of Iran, after years of growing dissatisfaction with the Anglo-Iranian Oil Company, had on May 1, 1951, nationalized the Iranian oil fields and the entire Iranian oil industry. To anyone wondering why an American President should be concerned with what seemed the internal affair of an impoverished Middle Eastern country, the answer was not far to seek. For a thousand miles Iran and the Soviet Union share a common border; moreover, before the nationalization, Anglo-Iranian had been producing about half the crude oil and natural gas that flowed from the world's most abundant reserves.

Anglo-Iranian was controlled by the British government, which owned 56 percent of the company's stock; it had for more than forty years enjoyed a monopoly of the country's oil deposits. For the British, the arrangement had been most gratifying: in 1950, the last year of operation before nationalization, profits had amounted to nearly two hundred million pounds sterling, of which more than fifty million pounds went to the British government in taxes. For the Iranians, the arrangement was humiliating: the government was paid in that year only sixteen million pounds, or less than one-third what the British government pocketed in taxes alone; the Iranian workers at the refinery at Abadan, the biggest in the world, were wretchedly paid, treated with contempt, barred from the company's hospitals, swimming pools, restaurants, and buses, and excluded (save for a token few) from training or advancement within the company. Anglo-Iranian also sought to keep Iran from using its own oil to launch any industrial enterprises based on oil: Iranian oil was dearer in Iran than in Britain, being sold at a profit of 500 percent. It was more sensible for an Iranian who wanted oil to import it from the Soviet Union than to buy what had come up from the ground under his own feet. The guiding British policy was: extract, exploit, export. Bahman Nirumand, a young Iranian intellectual, wrote in 1967:

> In this light, it is understandable that . . . nationalization of the oil industry signified national liberation from the century of British tutelage. . . . the national aspect outweighed the economic one. . . .
>
> This fact cannot be overemphasized, [nor can] the fact that the country, its freedom of action, and its capacity for development were actually sold for money which the people never enjoyed and practically never saw. It was not Iran that profited by the oil deal, but Britain (and a few Iranians) into whose pockets and accounts in foreign banks the money flowed. It is natural, therefore, that most of the protests . . . came from the people, rather than from politicians, and were aimed against British domination rather than the Anglo-Iranian Oil Company.

"Into this state of affairs," as Anthony Eden would have it, "erupted Dr. Musaddiq."* Sir Anthony, a man of uncommon physical beauty, was pleased to regard Mohammed Mossadegh as a figure of fun, "the first bit of real meat to come the way of the cartoonists since the war. 'Old Mossy,'" Eden would amusedly recall, "with his pyjamas and iron bedstead." Even Eisenhower, ordinarily so loath to speak ill of anybody, would write of "a semi-invalid who, often clad in pajamas in public, carried on a fanatical campaign, with tears and fainting fits and street mobs of followers." This laughingstock, the butt of so much cruel ridicule, was the premier of a sovereign state, elected to his post by a large majority of the Majlis (the Iranian parliament) to administer legislation passed unanimously by both houses of the Majlis which nationalized Iran's only wealth. Iran's? To Eden it was "a very valuable British asset."

Anglo-Iranian, creature as it was of the British government, was also, together with Standard Oil of New Jersey and Royal Dutch Shell, one of the three giants of the international oil cartel. Nationalization by Iran provoked from the cartel a predictable retort: a boycott of all Iranian oil.† The cartel at once increased the flow of oil elsewhere in the Middle East, to maintain the sensitive price-supply balance.‡ Simultaneously, the officers of several American oil companies glimpsed that the time was ripe to insinuate a wedge into Britain's preferential position in Iran and so collapse it. Various initiatives were extended to Mossadegh, who in 1952 was still tolerated in the U.S., even treated with a kind of gingerly respect. Of these, the most intriguing was the mission to Iran undertaken in August 1952 by Pete Jones, Eisenhower's jovial friend and companion and chairman of the board of Cities Service Oil Company. Jones arrived in Teheran at the personal invitation of Mossadegh; he was much impressed

---

* The name of the Iranian premier has been transliterated from Arabic to our own alphabet in at least a half-dozen ways. In this work the attempt has been to follow the various spellings as they appear within quoted remarks, and otherwise to follow the spelling most generally accepted in the United States (Mohammed Mossadegh) despite the authority of Sir Anthony Eden, who specialized in Oriental languages at Oxford, making Persian his main one and Arabic his second one.

† Eisenhower, in an unusual burst of plain speaking, bluntly stated that the boycott was instituted by the "British government, supported by the governments of the West." Here was an admission, perhaps inadvertent, of how intimately interwoven are the public governments of the voters and the private governments of petroleum.

‡ In Iraq, where ownership of oil was shared by Anglo-Iranian, Shell, the Compagnie Française des Pétroles, Jersey Standard, and Mobil Oil, the annual output went from 6.7 million tons in 1950 to 19 million tons in 1952; in Kuwait, where the concession was jointly shared by Anglo-Iranian and Gulf Oil, output went from 17 million tons to 37 million tons; in Saudi Arabia, where four American companies—Jersey Standard, Mobil Oil, Texaco, and Standard of California—operated jointly as the Arabian American Oil Company (Aramco), output rose from 27 million tons to 40.8 million tons.

with conditions at the deserted refineries of Abadan. "The free world knows," he said, "the Iranians can manage their own oil industry and operate the refinery." He concluded an agreement to operate the industry under an Iranian board of directors. (*Praise be to Allah, Lord of the Worlds, the Beneficent, the Merciful.*) The deal fell through. (*They think to beguile Allah and those who believe, and they beguile none save themselves; but they perceive not.*) Jones had nevertheless thrust his own company into the Iranian tangle in such fashion that he hoped to be taken into account in any subsequent division of the spoils. (*In their hearts is a disease, and Allah increaseth their disease. A painful doom is theirs because they lie.*)

Now Eisenhower was President, and the American oil executives, men of patience, considered that most of their objectives had been achieved. Mossadegh, they imagined, was ready to sign with them a contract to establish a consortium of oil companies which would substitute for the hated Anglo-Iranian. Of the consortium, the American share would be at the least 40 percent. The British share would be considerably reduced, but such are the fortunes of war. At least the Russians would be shut out and Iran, although still impoverished, would be integrated within the sphere of American influence. Iran would remain part of the free world, so called. (*And when it is said unto them: Make not mischief in the earth, they say: We are peacemakers only. Are not they indeed the mischief-makers? But they perceive not.*)

THREE: How to preserve the nation's internal security and at the same time safeguard civil liberty. To put the matter another way, how to frame and enforce tests of a citizen's loyalty, or of the risk he might pose to the nation's security, without seeming to curb expression of dissent from national policies, without doing violence to the Bill of Rights—and without apparently taking leave of one's senses. Parallel to this dilemma ran another: how to conduct in secret the vital affairs of an open society.

Even before his electoral triumph, Eisenhower had assumed the prescribed stance against the disloyal—which in 1952 meant communists and those alleged to be communists, those who were supposed to prefer the USSR to the USA. In more than a score of campaign speeches he had trotted out the communist issue, not neglecting to accuse the Democrats of "a toleration of men who take papers from our secret files and pass them on dark streets to spies from Moscow." Since he was committed to a purge of subversive federal employees to the number, it was said, of several thousand, it followed naturally that the whole grisly affair would be raised at the first meeting of his cabinet. His cabinet officers agreed that it would not suffice for those who wished to serve in the Eisenhower administration merely to demonstrate that there was no "reasonable doubt" as to their "loyalty"; they must make a positive showing that their employment would serve "the interests of national security." Only so, Eisenhower believed, could he "close this gap in our defenses."

None of this had much to do with reality. While the nation was coursing in full cry after the Reds, fevers ran high and were characterized by delirium, confusion, tremors, and vivid hallucinations. It was a nightmare world. As Richard Rovere has pointed out, the fact was replaced by its symbol ("I have a document here . . .") and transformed into the Multiple Untruth. It was the world of McCarthyism.

In the early months of 1953 Senator Joe McCarthy was at or near the apogee of his raucous career. Senator Taft, the majority leader, imagined he had tucked McCarthy away where he could do no mischief: Taft had found him a berth as chairman of the Senate Committee on Government Operations, which had for its bailiwick the administrative efficiency and fiscal probity of the various executive agencies. To expect McCarthy would subside to such a demure task was fatuous. Swiftly he plucked forth his committee's permanent subcommittee on investigations, twisted it to fit his bent, appointed himself its chairman, and forthwith began to rake the State Department with his investigative artillery.

Eisenhower was puzzled and dismayed. Within ten days of his inauguration there had been mounted no less than ten separate investigations of the State Department alone; some of these had, to be sure, been instituted by his own Republican administration, and he considered that only if these should fail of their purpose might a Republican congressman then step in. If he was wrong, what had become of teamwork? His deportment toward McCarthy had always been punctiliously correct, not to say craven. His postelection letter of congratulations ("I look forward to working closely with you in carrying out the responsibilities [the people] have entrusted to us") had gone to McCarthy as to other Republican victors, yet McCarthy was acting like an adversary, quite as though a Democratic President were still in the White House. What was more, McCarthy obviously had terrified the other Republican leaders. Here was Taft, for example, telling a national television audience that McCarthy's investigations were "very helpful and constructive," and here was Foster Dulles approving "any disclosures resulting from congressional inquiries that will help make" the State Department "more competent, loyal, and secure." Meantime the investigations had drawn a hailstorm of angry criticism from sundry associations of irreproachable respectability. Yet Eisenhower held his tongue.

In truth, McCarthy had slight cause to linger over his scattershot inquiries into the State Department, for on February 25 one of the businessmen recruited to staff the new Republican dispensation—Donald B. Lourie, formerly president of the Quaker Oats Company, who had been appointed undersecretary of state for administration—chose R. W. Scott McLeod to run the department's bureau of security and consular affairs. McLeod, a former FBI agent and briefly an assistant to the crustaceous Senator Styles Bridges of New Hampshire, was a deplorable selection and demonstrated for the nth time the folly of placing businessmen of political innocence in posts of political responsibility. McLeod was also McCarthy's henchman and eager instrument. In short order he made clear what he had in store for the forty thousand State Department employees who had suddenly been placed under his jurisdiction: he proposed "to clean out the State Department, and also to smooth the way for Republican-directed congressional committees to make a record against former Secretary of State Dean Acheson's administration." The shambles McCarthy had commenced to make of the State Department was relentlessly aggravated by McLeod. This former police agent, wholly without experience of foreign affairs, laid about him with an axe, paying particular heed to the foreign service officers, upon whom the secretary of state must depend for information and professional advice. A good eyewitness account of the disaster was filed by Louis Halle:

> For approximately a year McLeod had a free hand with the American career service. It was during this year that blackmail, intimidation, and other pressures of a similar character were used to their fullest. The highly trained professional corps was decimated, demeaned, and demoralized; the whole apparatus through which the foreign relations of the United States had to be conducted was, in large measure, wrecked.

Proof of these charges, were any needed, was afforded by the report of a select commission (the Secretary of State's Public Committee on Personnel) which revealed that not a single junior foreign service officer was appointed from 1952 to 1954. There can be no doubt that the loyalty-security programs worked severe damage to the morale of the foreign service.

Most if not all of this lamentable business was known to President Eisenhower. Occasionally he would discuss the morale of the foreign service and the State Department at a cabinet meeting, or with Secretary Dulles. To his constituency, however, he stayed mum.

In no way could the President hold himself aloof from the cries of the red-hunters. They assailed him from all sides. Had some godforsaken subversive painted murals in a substation of the San Francisco post office? The President must needs take notice of the allegation and address a memorandum to the postmaster general. Did Senator Arthur V. Watkins (Republican, Utah) dispatch to the White House a crazed constituent brimful of psychotic alarums about red plots? The President found it necessary to pass the lunatic along to the appropriate deputies of the secretaries of state and defense. Did some citizen attest that he knew a man (a big real estate operator) who knew a man (a big Russian operator) who had enough clout to dictate strategy to Molotov? This nonsense too must be forked over to Foster Dulles and presently channeled through the conduits of Foggy Bottom.

But together with these incidents, to which the President of the United States gravely turned his attention during his first weeks in office, there was another matter, cut from the same piece of cloth, that would linger long on the conscience of the nation. This was the case of Julius and Ethel Rosenberg, a young married couple, parents of two boys.

When Eisenhower was inaugurated, the Rosenbergs had already been convicted of having conspired to deliver to Soviet agents sketches of atomic weapons. (Their acts of espionage were said to have taken place in 1944 and 1945, so it could not be argued that they had trafficked with an enemy.) They were under sentence of death—the first, indeed the only citizens ever to be so convicted and sentenced during peacetime. An appeal for executive clemency, ducked by Truman in the last days of his administration, awaited Eisenhower's decision.* If he had chosen to look for them, Eisenhower could have found any number of justifications for intervention. The case against the Rosenbergs was a dubious one, based almost entirely on the evidence of witnesses whose reliability was questionable, since they were accomplices in the crimes alleged, with ample motives for lying; scientists familiar with the technical aspects of the designs allegedly pilfered were skeptical of the testimony; many eminent persons, including Albert Einstein and Pope Pius XII, had urged clemency; in western Europe and particularly in France voices had been raised in protest against what seemed a savage punishment; why, asked scores of American citizens (their pleas flooding in to the White House at the rate of fifteen thousand a week), why must the Rosenbergs die? Why could their sentences not at least be commuted to life imprisonment?

In the political climate of 1953, with McCarthyism running at full tide and most of the nation's newspapers howling for the blood of "A-spies," as the Rosenbergs could be conveniently labeled, only the most resolute and compassionate leader, one disdainful of the mob, could have withstood the deep passions and vengeful hatreds loosed by the trial and the verdict

* Truman had, however, commuted the death sentences of two Nazi spies, caught after they had been landed on the coast of Maine from a Nazi submarine, during wartime.

of guilt. The popular conviction was that, were it not for the Rosenbergs, the Soviet Union could never—at least never so soon—have developed atomic weapons; hence all the woes of the republic could be laid at their door. The Rosenbergs, whether innocent or guilty, came opportune to the nation's need. Judge Irving R. Kaufman, before sentencing them in April 1951, had seized the chance to lecture them:

"I consider your crime worse than murder. . . . I believe your conduct in putting into the hands of the Russians the A-bomb years before our best scientists predicted Russia would perfect the bomb has already caused, in my opinion, the Communist aggression in Korea, with the resultant casualties exceeding fifty thousand and who knows but that millions more of innocent people may pay the price of your treason. . . .

". . . this diabolical conspiracy to destroy a God-fearing nation . . .

"It is not in my power, Julius and Ethel Rosenberg, to forgive you. Only the Lord can find mercy for what you have done.

". . . you are hereby sentenced to . . . death, and . . . you shall be executed according to law."

According to law, Judge Kaufman was the only jurist who could pronounce the sentence, nor could any other jurist, whether of appellate court or even Supreme Court, countermand it. Their writ was limited to correcting any errors of law; they decided there were none. The only man who could upset the sentence was the President of the United States.

Eisenhower had no doubt of the Rosenbergs' guilt, and if a doubt had ever edged up to nudge him, Attorney General Brownell was ready to show him evidence "that wasn't usable in court" to prove the Rosenbergs were "the head and center of . . . the *prime* espionage ring in the country." But Eisenhower never required such a boost. In rejecting the appeal for clemency he showed that he had familiarized himself with Judge Kaufman's homily:

"[Their] crime . . . far exceeds that of the taking of the life of another citizen; it involves the deliberate betrayal of the entire nation and could very well result in the death of many, many thousands of innocent citizens. [They] have in fact betrayed the cause of freedom for which free men are fighting and dying at this very hour. . . .

". . . I have determined . . . my duty . . . not to set aside the verdict. . . ."

It would seem that the most powerful argument prompting the President was one he characterized as statecraft: the psychological effect throughout the world if he were to tamper with the decision of the judiciary. "My only concern," he told his cabinet on June 19, 1953, "is in the area of statecraft—the *effect* of the action." In his own judgment, there would be a significant adverse reaction abroad if he were to mitigate

Judge Kaufman's sentence. The impression would gain currency, he believed, that American democracy was unable to take a definite action in a clear-cut case. Since western Europe on balance favored clemency, one must look farther east to identify the effect of the action, the statecraft, that Eisenhower had in mind. He was concerned mainly with the Russians. A few days before the Rosenbergs were executed he wrote to Clyde Miller, whom he had known as a member of the faculty of Columbia's Teachers College, of "the known convictions of Communist leaders that free governments—and especially the American government—are notoriously weak and fearful and that consequently subversive and other kinds of activity can be conducted against them with no real fear of dire punishment on the part of the perpetrator."

Whether or no the communist leaders held such "known convictions," Eisenhower believed they did. Further, he deemed it necessary to serve notice on the Russians that while he was President the American government would sternly suppress espionage and subversion. Even though she was a woman, Mrs. Rosenberg must be executed, Eisenhower wrote his son, for if her sentence were commuted "from here on the Soviets would simply recruit their spies from among women."

And so the Rosenbergs were electrocuted, first Julius and then Ethel, in the early evening of Friday, June 19, 1953. That was the day after their fourteenth wedding anniversary, and a careful few minutes before sundown, when their Sabbath would begin.

The affair troubled Eisenhower. He confessed as much to his cabinet, telling them on the Friday that he could not remember a time in his life when he felt more in need of help from someone much more powerful than he. But it was a matter of security.

Security is a ticklish business, not least because it diminishes as the apparatus designed to ensure it extravagates. (Security officers, presiding over a proliferating bureaucracy and exchanging bulging files of malicious gossip, were solidly entrenched in most government agencies and departments by the spring of 1953.) Perhaps because he was a soldier and had spent forty years of his life engaged in professional tasks that were better conducted away from the public gaze, Eisenhower found the tricky contradictions of security in a democratic republic harder to resolve than other men might have done; perhaps he did as well as his predecessor and his successor. One can note that secrecy, the politics of evasion, and the use of security officers to supervise transactions of all kinds were all customary procedure for Eisenhower. When in the first weeks of his presidency the undersecretary of state, his old friend and comrade Beetle Smith, suggested that the men charged with a comprehensive overhaul of basic foreign policy might best be sequestered at the National War College while they tinkered with their tasks, since such an arrangement would "keep them out of everybody's hair and avoid publicity," Eisenhower agreed. He had already commented, of the procedure for reviewing foreign policy, "Sounds to me like a conspiracy! But not a bad one." The practice of concealing from the voters of the republic their most important affairs had by that time an illustrious tradition. The historian Oscar Handlin has written: "From the outbreak of the Spanish civil war onward there was a transparent lack of candor in what the people were told." No doubt a diligent researcher could turn up earlier examples of equally perspicuous mystifications, but from 1953 onward the clouds appreciably thickened, culminating in what would come to be known as "the credibility gap."

As part of his valiant effort to unscramble security and civil liberty, Eisenhower gave courteous ear to the Socialist party leader Norman Thomas. Like many thoughtful people at the time, Thomas was disturbed by the proneness to treat dissimilar political and social viewpoints as one. In particular, he was dismayed by the confusion of socialists with communists. Not so, he argued: a right-wing socialist is a "liberal-conservative," which is to say, a middle-of-the-roader. Eisenhower was impressed. Three days later he took the matter up with his cabinet, remarking that he was disposed to credit the loyalty of socialists and could see no reason to bar them from the less sensitive jobs. Yet Scott McLeod, security officer of the State Department, had written Thomas that he would oust any socialist. Eisenhower quoted Thomas as reporting a dictum then making the rounds that "McCarthy runs McLeod and McLeod runs Dulles." Dulles was not amused. The Socialist party, he reminded the President, equated capitalism with warmongering in its platform. But the President insisted the term "socialist" covered a lot of ground, spreading over even to the right of center.

Still he worried about the matter, at length suggesting to Brownell that a cutoff date be arbitrarily fixed: friendliness toward the Soviets before that date would be regarded as unobjectionable, but after it any who sympathized with or propagandized for the Soviets must be considered "either very stupid or very dangerous." For such a cutoff date he proposed the blockade of Berlin (June 1948) and reminded Brownell that "any American could have been excused for statements or actions favorable to the Soviets during the war and *even as late as 1948*." (The emphasis is Eisenhower's.) He thus allowed a generous leeway: his own strictures on the Soviet Union had not been unmistakable until 1947. Finally, returning once again to the basic dilemma, he added, "we must search out some positive way to put ourselves on the side of individual right and liberty as well as on the side of fighting Communism to the death."

Nothing much happened as a result of this memorandum. The dilemma remained, its alternatives in stubborn opposition. The salient action taken by the new administration served only to hone the contradiction between those alternatives. This was President Eisenhower's Executive Order 10450, issued in May 1953 to supplant President Truman's Executive Order 9835 of March 1947. The basic standard affecting federal employment was hardened from a barrier if there were "reasonable grounds . . . for belief" of disloyalty, to hiring only when "clearly consistent with . . . national security"; it was extended from the eleven agencies deemed "sensitive," to the entire federal establishment (and thence, by imitation, to much of private industry); the criteria which gave substance to the standard were likewise significantly expanded by the addition of a sweeping paragraph that listed a great variety of disqualifications having little or nothing to do with loyalty but giving every zealous security officer license to heed mischievous gossip. (The first clause of this paragraph drew the line at: "Any behavior, activities, or associations which tend to show that the individual is not reliable or trustworthy.")

Of the three most vexing problems confronting the new administration, then, the first—military policy versus fiscal policy—was, in the beginning, evaded; the second—support for the U.S.'s two principal allies as against appropriation of their richest assets—was fumbled; the third—security or civil liberty—was exacerbated.

These problems, apart from their intractability, shared other attributes. If there had been no international communist conspiracy—real or imagined, it made no difference—the first and third problems would have vanished and the second could have been handled much more forthrightly. In the event, all three were blamed on the Cold War with the Soviet Union; all fed hatreds on this side of the well-advertised iron curtain. Further, all three problems were inherited from the previous administration and so could be ascribed to Harry Truman by any Republican rhetors not overly inflamed by a passion for the truth.

To blame Harry Truman for what he bequeathed to Dwight Eisenhower was as impertinent as to blame Dwight Eisenhower for pursuing fundamentally the same foreign policy as had Harry Truman. Each man honored the same set of national values. Each called upon advisers who had been cast in the same mold. (Some of them, to the shame and scandal of the Republican Old Guard, were the same men.) Each fixed his eyes on the same objectives as illumined by the same interpretation of the national interest.

Just what is "the national interest"? The question is not easily answered, for the concept depends much on time and circumstance and even more on the particular bias of the individual using the phrase. Statesmen clam up, citing the responsibility of it; patriots spit fire, invoking it; we wage wars halfway round the world to defend it; yet earnest attempts to define the thing seem fated to wing off into vague formulations of political and philosophical ideals. Thus a foreign service officer, in a semi-official essay on American foreign policy, has suggested that the national interest would best be served by "a world environment that permits and encourages our development as a people and as a nation." By way of illustration, the writer noted President Wilson's call to war in April 1917, in which he proclaimed, "The world must be made safe for democracy." Was that celebrated dictum, as often charged, so much idealist claptrap? No, said the foreign service officer; to the contrary, it was a realistic expression of the American conviction that "a German victory would not result in the kind of world that would best promote our own national interests." The reasoning is circular, but no more so than in most discussions of the national interest.

Another stab at a definition has been made by the staff of the Brookings Institution in studies financed by the Rockefeller Foundation and the Carnegie Corporation. Here one can glimpse the social scientist at work, industriously fuzzing the matter behind a façade of (to use one of his favorite phrases) complex variables:

> The *national interest* [voice is that of Institution, sustained by Foundation and Corporation] may be defined as the general and continuing end for which a nation acts. It embraces such matters as the need of a society for security against aggression, the desirability to a society of developing higher standards of living, and the maintenance of favorable conditions of stability both domestically and internationally. . . . security and well-being . . . changing social habits and values . . .
> . . . The *national interest* exists and is a fact that cannot be defined out of existence. . . .
> To summarize: the *national interest* is what a nation feels to be essential to its security and well-being . . .

Something of economic theory has crept in; something reminiscent of what Dean Acheson, then an assistant secretary of state, told a congressional committee in November 1944:

> We cannot go through another ten years like the ten years at the end of the 'twenties and the beginning of the 'thirties, without having the most far-reaching consequences upon our economic and social systems. . . .
> When we look at that problem, we may say it is a problem of markets. You don't have a problem of production. The United States has unlimited creative energy. The important thing is markets. We have got to see that what the country produces is used and is sold under financial arrangements

which make its production possible. . . . we must look to foreign markets. . . .

. . . The first thing that I want to bring out is that we need these markets for the output of the United States. If I am wrong about that, then all the argument falls by the wayside, but my contention is that we cannot have full employment and prosperity in the United States without the foreign markets.

In 1944, then, the nation's security and well-being cried out for foreign markets. Eight years later a presidential commission had sniffed out another need: the U.S., which for many years had produced more raw materials than were domestically consumed, by mid-century had converted that surplus into a deficit; after 1950 U.S. industry devoured 10 percent more raw materials than were domestically produced. President Eisenhower, in his first inaugural address, acknowledged both these needs:

We know . . . that we are linked to all free peoples not merely by a noble idea but by a simple need. No free people can for long cling to any privilege or enjoy any safety in economic solitude. For all our own material might, even we need markets in the world for the surpluses of our farms and our factories. Equally, we need for these same farms and factories vital materials and products of distant lands. . . .

Markets. Raw materials. The shape of "the national interest" looms through the mists of ideological cant and begins to grow more distinct.*
There was, though, no point in dressing the national interest in such drab and commercial garb. National enthusiasm rises in response to gaudier, more emotional stimuli. President Truman had sounded the tonic note, anticommunism, when he unfurled his Truman Doctrine: "a frank recognition that totalitarian regimes imposed on free peoples, by direct or indirect aggression, undermine the foundations of international peace and hence the security of the United States." Truman had gone on to say: "I believe that it must be the policy of the United States to support free peoples who are resisting attempted subjugation by armed minorities or by outside pressures." Under this formula was developed the policy of con-

---

* In the thinking of men who manage the big international corporations, the shape and purpose of the national interest grew steadily clearer with the passage of the years. By April 1964, for example, the treasurer of the General Electric Company could say: "Thus, our search for profits places us squarely in line with the national policy of stepping up international trade as a means of strengthening the free world in the Cold War confrontation with Communism." Six months later the company's president would tell an audience of businessmen: "I suggest we will perceive: that overriding both the common purposes and cross-purposes of business and government, there is a broader pattern—a 'consensus' if you will, where public and private interest come together, cooperate, interact and become the national interest."

tainment, the purpose of which was to ensure that the international communist conspiracy (real or imagined) could not wrest any more real estate from the free world, to reserve markets and raw materials for the security and well-being of the U.S., to keep the free world in status quo.

The label "free world," a noble conceit which at first glance might have seemed merely a burst from the artillery of Cold War propaganda, was in truth an accurate phrase. Not only were there relative freedoms west of the iron curtain—of speech, assembly, press, religion, and the like—which were not uniformly honored east of it, but there was also one absolute freedom, and it was decisive: the freedom to invest capital and to use capital funds for profit in international commerce. Just as this absolute freedom was exclusively the privilege of the free world, so it was also the most cherished and the most savagely defended. Freedom of speech, assembly, or press could go by the board in Greece or Guatemala, in the Congo or Iran, but the freedom of capital to travel about unencumbered was sacrosanct.

At all events, when Eisenhower assumed the presidency, he was obliged —by the demagoguery of McCarthy, by his own campaign promises—to be more anticommunist than Truman. It was no easy matter, but he accepted the challenge cheerfully.

How the new President would tackle his responsibilities was a question that, first and last, never troubled the vast majority of his constituents. What was to worry about? Eisenhower, after all, had been a supreme commander, trained to shoulder awesome duties, to take fearful decisions; he was accomplished in guiding men of hostile persuasions to united effort and triumphant concord. Few if any Presidents had taken office with anything like his superlative talents and hard-won experience as a leader.

Yet would that experience count for much now that he was a politician and a statesman? Obviously the nature of his tasks was quite different. Truman, a far less exalted soldier but a far more practiced politician, thought he knew the answer. Richard E. Neustadt reported:

> In the early summer of 1952, before the heat of the campaign, President Truman used to contemplate the problems of the General-become-President should Eisenhower win the forthcoming election. "He'll sit here," Truman would remark (tapping his desk for emphasis), "and he'll say, 'Do this! Do that!' *And nothing will happen.* Poor Ike—it won't be a bit like the army. He'll find it very frustrating."

Even earlier, Truman had ruefully taken the measure of presidential power. "I sit here all day," he had said, "trying to persuade people to do the things they ought to have sense enough to do without my persuading them. . . . That's all the powers of the President amount to."

But of course Eisenhower also was committed to the concept of leadership by persuasion, and always had been, from the time when first he had studied how best to get things done. Early in his first term, indeed, he lectured an associate on leadership. Striding back and forth in his oval office, clenching his big right fist and churning it round against the palm of his big left hand (one of his pet isometrics), the President worried the matter of his relations with the Congress: whether or not he should publicly chastise a few of the more recalcitrant congressmen so as to bend them to his will. "Now, look," he said, "I happen to *know* a little about leadership. I've had to work with a lot of nations, for that matter, at odds with each other. And I tell you this: you do not *lead* by hitting people over the head. Any damn fool can do that, but it's usually called 'assault'—not 'leadership.' . . . I'll tell you what leadership is. It's *persuasion*—and *conciliation*—and *education*—and *patience*. It's long, slow, tough work. That's the only kind of leadership I know—or believe in—or will practice."

The exercise of presidential initiatives to badger a balky Congress is usually self-defeating, and in any case Eisenhower entered office determined not to use any such strategy. He was, he liked to say, a "Constitutional President," by which he meant to suggest that unlike his two Democratic predecessors, he honored the traditional separation of powers and had only respect for the legislative branch of government. Moreover, he stood ready to lay on his esteem thick and sticky, with a trowel. At an early meeting of his cabinet he urged all hands to be silent in the face of the hostile sniping from the Congress. Everything would simmer down, the President was confident, if only no rancors were tossed on the fire. The Republicans who made up the slender congressional majority, he insisted rather wistfully, would soon learn that they could remain in power, responsible for government, only by effective teamwork with the executive. Harmony with the Congress! In pursuit of it he invited every last member of it—more than five hundred men and women—to a series of luncheons at the White House and ladled out copious doses of his potent charm. Alas! the Old Guard was immune. To Eisenhower's hot indignation, during 1953 the Democrats were needed no less than fifty-eight times to succor the administration, "their votes providing the margin of victory when Republican defections or absences imperiled the happy glow."

Just as Eisenhower had anticipated friction with the Congress, so he looked forward to the smooth function of his executive branch of government. Possibly not at once; but he was confident, who had long experience of a staff operation, that he could shift into close gear the men and women chosen for him by his trusted advisers and within a reasonable period of time have them working efficiently together. He reckoned that they would comport themselves properly with the Senate (which could approve or reject his cabinet appointments), with their subordinates in their various departments, and with him. On each count he would find he was somewhere wrong.

First, however, the White House staff had to be indoctrinated and adapted to its new ways.

The kingpin of that staff was Governor Sherman Adams, who had resigned his responsibilities in New Hampshire and was now adorned with a spanking new title, Assistant to the President. Adams had at once been dubbed Eisenhower's chief of staff, as though he were comparable in influence to Beetle Smith at SHAEF or Al Gruenther at SHAPE. He was no such thing, nor even close to it; but his responsibilities were so vague and general that journalists fell into the habit of referring to him as the Assistant President; and in Washington, where rumors have been known to circulate, the impression grew that while Eisenhower relaxed and golfed at Augusta or Palm Springs, Adams was in fact the President.

Adams's own view of his job was wryly disparaging: it was "scrubbing the administrative and political back stairs" at the White House. Eisenhower, he recalled, had told him: "I need somebody to be my assistant in running my office. I'd like you to continue on at my right hand, just as you've been in the campaign. You would be associated with me more closely than anybody else in the government." His responsibilities were never precisely defined; they were "implied rather than stated." "Eisenhower," Adams decided, "simply expected me to manage a staff that would boil down, simplify and expedite the urgent business that had to be brought to his personal attention and to keep as much work of secondary importance as possible off his desk."

In practice, Adams was to be the man who said no on Eisenhower's behalf. He said no to cabinet secretaries and to congressmen, to journalists and to jobhunters; he said no short and sharp, without troubling to be polite about it; and so he would come to be warmly detested on the Hill, in the National Press Club, at Republican National Headquarters, and elsewhere across the country.

And Eisenhower, for whom Adams said no, remained universally beloved. It was a useful association.

The staff over whom Adams would preside numbered, at the outset, about two dozen. In order to avoid the invidious distinctions of protocol, it may be best to list the more important among them in alphabetical order:

Paul T. (Pete) Carroll, at the time a brigadier general, was staff secretary, charged with the proper routing of all paperwork (mail, memoranda, reports, and the like) and serving as liaison with those departments and agencies concerned with national security. We have met General Carroll before, when he was an aide to Eisenhower in the Pentagon and later at SHAPE; after his sudden death in September 1954, his place was filled by Colonel Andrew J. Goodpaster.

Robert (Bobby) Cutler was special assistant for national security affairs, which meant that he served as secretary of the National Security Council and chairman of its Planning Board.

James C. Hagerty was press secretary.

Gabriel Hauge was an administrative assistant who advised the President on economic matters and wrote an occasional speech.

Emmet Hughes was an administrative assistant who signed on solely as a speech writer.

C. D. Jackson was a special assistant on matters having to do with Cold War propaganda and psychological warfare. He was also a member of a commission on Cold War strategy headed by an investment banker, William H. Jackson (no relation), whose activities were shadowy, even clandestine. C. D. Jackson lasted a little more than a year and was replaced by Nelson Rockefeller, whose subsequent departure left the post vacant.

Major General Wilton B. (Jerry) Persons was at first a special assistant in charge of congressional relations, a job for which he was superbly qualified by reason of his many years as chief lobbyist for the army. After a few months, however, he was promoted to deputy assistant to the President, and an administrative aide to the late Senator Taft, Jack Martin, was put in charge of liaison with the Congress.

Maxwell Rabb, who had been Senator Lodge's administrative aide until Lodge was defeated in his bid for re-election by a wealthy young congressman, John F. Kennedy, moved into the White House and presently became secretary to the cabinet, a newly created office.

Bernard M. Shanley, a New Jersey attorney who had been active in Republican politics on behalf of Harold Stassen, became special counsel.

Thomas E. Stephens, a shrewd and entertaining politician from Dewey's entourage, became appointments secretary.

Charles F. Willis, Jr., a co-founder of Citizens for Eisenhower in 1952, was rewarded with a job as assistant to Adams, with the Herculean task of cleaning the bureaucratic stables of those Democrats not protected by civil service regulations and replacing them with honest Republicans.

This assortment of professional soldiers, investment bankers, journalists, and lawyer-politicians is an instructive one. Signally absent were those to whom Eisenhower had been most attentive in the months before he had proclaimed his availability as a Republican candidate for President.

None of the men whose advice and support had been crucial to him was a member of his new official family.*

The duties of his new staff served to suggest part of the President's exacting routine. On Mondays (usually) a meeting with the legislative leaders, chaperoned by Jerry Persons. On Wednesdays (usually) a press conference under the tutelage of Jim Hagerty. On Thursdays a three-hour session of the National Security Council, debating an agenda prepared by Bobby Cutler. On Fridays a three-hour cabinet meeting, more informally staged by Max Rabb. All these were occasions for persuasion and conciliation.

The meeting of the National Security Council was by all odds President Eisenhower's favorite official function. As early as April 23 he was telling the legislative leaders: "More and more, we find that the central body in making policy is the NSC. Its sessions are long, bitter, and tough. Out of that sort of discussion we're trying to hammer policy." What kind of policy? Only the most recondite, topmost secret policy, policy that scarcely anybody was permitted to know anything about, policy that even some of those who squirmed into the NSC's council chamber might never be told about. Bobby Cutler, the official guardian of these dark secrets, was, like every healthy schoolboy, enchanted by the cloaked and mysterious atmosphere surrounding the affairs of the NSC. He noted with satisfaction how Foster Dulles, dismayed by a meeting "too largely attended," would direct "a knowing look at me across the table" and then "clam up," refusing to discuss sensitive matters when "more than a certain number of persons" had been admitted to the chamber. Cutler (and Eisenhower, too) tried valiantly to control the number round the NSC table, but as the President's evident interest in NSC affairs mounted, so also the outside pressure mounted to get inside. (The members of the NSC, as defined by statute, were the President, the Vice President, the secretaries of state and defense, the director of civil defense mobilization, the chairman of the Joint Chiefs of Staff, and the director of the CIA. Eisenhower invited, as

---

* To be sure, Carroll had been privy to much of Eisenhower's political hocus-pocus in France, as had Persons, but neither of these men had been numbered among his intimate advisers.

Clifford Roberts and William Robinson remained his friends and golfing companions, but circumspect, in the middle distance. Ed Bermingham was occasionally invited to dine with the President at the White House; no more than that. William Burnham succumbed to leukemia a few days before Eisenhower's first inauguration. Kevin McCann returned to Defiance College in Ohio, but he was ever on call and often on duty in the White House as crony, speech writer, and general handyman. General Lucius Clay and Governor Dewey continued as advisers, but by the back door. Only Milton Eisenhower, the President's younger brother ("He's got all the brains in the family"), would later take an official presidential assignment.

The faithful Robert Schulz, by 1953 a lieutenant colonel, was of course still at heel as military aide, as loyal and deferential as ever.

well, the secretary of the treasury and the director of the budget; a few others were admitted on an ad hoc basis.) To be added to that select strength was like coming up with the Holy Grail. After too many had wangled their entry and matters "too sensitive for more general exposure" were to be discussed, Eisenhower would have to bid Cutler bring a carefully chosen half-dozen into his oval office following the NSC meeting. My, to be one of that half-dozen!

In plain fact, the NSC assessed and evaluated policy in respect of a single nation (Iran, say, or Guatemala), of a region (the Middle East, perhaps, or Indochina), or of a discrete subject (the European Defense Community or the technological capability to develop long-range missiles). Its role was advisory only: its members might unanimously recommend a course of action, but the President, if he chose, could decide otherwise. Even if its recommendations had never been accepted, however, the NSC, as Eisenhower saw it, was engaged in two salutary exercises: its members, by continuously planning policy, were accustoming themselves to working together on hard problems; and further, by systematically reviewing every aspect of national policy, the NSC was providing insurance against the sudden crisis that might unexpectedly erupt somewhere. Eisenhower himself was happily occupied with what he liked to do best: the orderly process of reasoning and analysis that is represented in the commander's estimate of a situation.

In short, under Eisenhower the NSC became an exclusive think-tank, affording primary instruction in applications of the theory of games as developed by the mathematicians John von Neumann and Otto Morgenstern, and simultaneously caressing the ego-structures of those who were permitted to participate regularly.

In contrast, cabinet meetings were attended by more than twice as many government officials as shared in NSC meetings; the matters discussed were rarely considered critical; and most important, the cabinet officials too often conducted themselves like contentious heads of rival departments rather than like statesmen who were members of a corporate body. It was plain that if Eisenhower was to get his cabinet officers working together harmoniously, he had his conciliatory work cut out for him.

Individually, many of the cabinet officers likewise proved abrasive (or stupid) in one way or another, especially at first. "Engine Charley" Wilson, who had been promoted from president of General Motors to secretary of defense, managed to provoke the most hilarious rumpus even before the new administration had been sworn in. General Motors held a sizable share of the contracts let by the Pentagon, and awaiting action by the new secretary was an application by GM for an increase in profits on its contracts. Further, Wilson owned shares of GM stock worth two and one-half million dollars and stood to collect over the next four years another six hundred thousand dollars from bonuses and other fiduciary arrangements, he having stipulated he would do nothing inimical to GM's interests during that time. But since 1863 it has been illegal (according to Section 434, Title 18 of the U.S. Code) for an official "directly or indirectly interested in the pecuniary profits" of a corporation to transact business with it "as an officer or agent" of the government. Predictably, the members of the Senate Armed Services Committee found these facts, taken together, arresting. Wilson could not agree. He was asked whether there might not conceivably be a conflict of interest for him, who now stood to profit personally from decisions he would be making as secretary. His answer almost reconciled the Democrats to their loss of the 1952 elections. "I cannot conceive of [a conflict]," said Charley Wilson, "because for years I thought what was good for our country was good for General Motors, and vice versa." If the remark meant anything, it meant that he confused General Motors with the general welfare, and the country promptly greeted this notion with a Bronx cheer. Wilson was puzzled and angered. "I really feel you are giving me quite a pushing around," he told that courteous gentleman Richard Russell of Georgia, one of the senators who questioned him. When the senators withheld their approval of his nomination, Wilson turned sullen. He prepared a statement saying he refused to sell his GM stock; the Senate could take him as he was or leave him. He had not come to Washington to cheat or thieve, he said. Senatorial approval was a matter of indifference to him. Forced sale of his stock would cost him a ton in taxes.

To protect the Eisenhower administration from starting off with a slapstick whacked athwart its vast expanse of britches, Senator Leverett Saltonstall, chairman of the Armed Services Committee, scurried to Wilson's hotel suite to reason sweetly with him. No dice. Wilson was adamant. Sorrowing, Saltonstall withdrew. Late that afternoon (it was Wednesday, January 21, the day after Eisenhower's inauguration) Jerry Persons summoned Saltonstall to the White House. Wilson was with the President, relaxed and affable, having just gulped down an immense draft of the patented Elixir Eisenhoverii. "It's all over," said Persons, smiling upon his return from the President's office. "The issue is all decided. Wilson's going to sell all his stock."

Persons spoke too soon. Wilson may have decided, but there was a complete echelon of Pentagon officials one step down from him—Roger M. Kyes, his deputy secretary, also from General Motors; Robert T. Stevens, whose textile firm made uniforms for the army and who was slated to be secretary of the army; Harold M. Talbott, designated as secretary of the air force; and Robert B. Anderson, a Texas oilman nominated as secretary of the navy—who were all caught up in the same conflict of interest. Anderson had powerful friends aplenty in the Senate, but as for the others, Persons noted privately on Friday, January 23: "Going is rough." He was convinced "we will never get Talbott or Stevens unless they are willing to dispose of their holdings as Wilson is going to do." But after another ten days of prayer and meditation, all officials had agreed to divest themselves of their noxious securities.

Eisenhower was sorely vexed by the episode. He foresaw a day when Presidents would be able to enlist only "business failures, political hacks, and New Deal lawyers" for government service. But he put a brave face on it. It was, he told Adams, the first test of the administration's ability to distinguish right from wrong; whether he believed the test had been passed with high marks was not clear.

Foster Dulles was the next cabinet officer to get off on the wrong foot. The occasion was his first speech as secretary of state, and like all his speeches it had been studied and approved in advance by Eisenhower. Although apparently concerned with a major shift of strategy in the nation's foreign policy (from containment of the Soviets to liberation of the "enslaved" nations of eastern Europe), the speech was in truth addressed to domestic politics, to winning for the administration and in particular for the secretary of state the reputation of being more fearlessly anticommunist than Truman or Acheson. On this score the speech deserves closer examination, which it will get.* For the moment, however, it is necessary only to point out that by scornfully denigrating the efforts of his predecessor, Dulles succeeded in angering and embittering a great many of the career officers in the State Department, so much so, indeed, that he was constrained to assemble the personnel of the department out of doors, in the grounds back of the department's block of buildings, for a pep rally. Here he managed to make matters worse by informing his new associates that he expected them to display "positive loyalty." His injunction alienated particularly the foreign service officers who, as Chip Bohlen would recall, did not relish being "treated as suspect characters." Dulles was then flown to Europe to talk with the British and French foreign ministers, who had also been disaffected by Dulles's speech.

Another cabinet officer to get embroiled with his departmental subordinates was Sinclair Weeks, the secretary of commerce, and once again the administration was shown to be curiously insensitive when the matter at issue was a businessman's profits. The manufacturer of a substance enigmatically yclept AD–X_2, alleged to prolong the life of a storage battery, had for five years wailed that official approval of his miraculous additive had been withheld because of sinister practices within the National Bu-

* See pages 548–552.

reau of Standards, a part of the Department of Commerce. No less than twenty-four senators applied pressure on Dr. Allen V. Astin, director of the bureau, but since the bureau's tests had established that AD–X2 was worthless goo, Dr. Astin said no. His ouster was demanded by a Senate committee, and a week later Secretary Weeks swung the axe. Dr. Astin, he said had not been sufficiently responsive to "the play of the market-place." Two days later President Eisenhower—faced with a choice between his own secretary of commerce and some obscure scientist appointed by the Democrats—announced his confidence in Weeks and his belief that Weeks had been neither arbitrary nor unjust in giving Astin the boot. To fire a government scientist, however, is akin to stirring up a hornet's nest with a footrule. In short order four hundred scientists and other employees of the bureau had threatened to resign, any number of learned societies had filed angry protests, Dr. Detlev Bronk, president of the National Academy of Sciences, had urged that Dr. Astin's ouster be revoked, and in the White House President Eisenhower, sadly wagging his head, had agreed. A decent four-month interval, during which the journalists could be distracted by other abominations, and Dr. Astin was quietly reinstated.

Other cabinet officers had other like problems, but only one found it possible to resist the President's smooth conciliatory skills. This was the secretary of labor, Martin Durkin, who provided the only instance, as Eisenhower put it, "of failure to achieve a meeting of minds between me and any principal subordinate."

As Adams had perceived, the appointment of Durkin "was an experiment doomed from the start to failure." The fault was Eisenhower's. He had imagined he could pluck from the ranks of labor an official who would be his principal adviser on matters affecting labor and would also act as his lightning rod in case of any thunderstorms along the labor-management front. Durkin, he hoped, would shield him from strikes, officials of the CIO or AFL, John L. Lewis, squabbles over the Taft-Hartley law, and other such distasteful reminders of the struggle to spread it around more equitably. He discounted the certainty that a man like Durkin, plunked down among a Humphrey, a Weeks, a Wilson, and a Dulles, would instinctively pat his pocket to make sure his wallet was safe and thereafter map strategy for the impending sessions of collective bargaining.

Everything about Durkin's appointment was wrong, and idiotic as well. Every other secretary as a matter of course found his undersecretary and assistant secretaries on a list of brass-collar Republicans, but to fill the administrative positions in Durkin's department was "an ordeal." Weeks, as secretary of commerce, could feel "he had a responsibility to protect the interests of business and industrial management in the formulation of the administration's labor policies," and no one would turn a hair, but let Durkin seek to protect the interests of organized labor and he was anathematized. "It seemed to me," Eisenhower wrote later, "that [Durkin] kept thinking of himself as an employee of a labor union, serving in the cabinet merely on an interim basis while on vacation from his true work." How did Eisenhower imagine that Humphrey or Wilson or Weeks regarded his service in the cabinet?

The wonder is that Durkin persevered for eight months. He resigned when, as he said, officials of the administration, including President Eisenhower, broke their agreement to work for changes in the Taft-Hartley law. At his next press conference the President commented icily that it was hard to break an agreement that had never been made.

Eisenhower remained unshaken in his conviction that he must be patient and conciliatory in order to weld his chief lieutenants into an effective team. One of his aides, Emmet Hughes, who had resigned his job after eight months and gone to Europe as a correspondent for *Life*, continued to worry about Eisenhower and the Republicans, about what they were doing and, even more, what they were not doing. Late in November Hughes presumed to send Eisenhower a long letter in which, tactfully, he warned that the appearance (at least from Rome) was that the Eisenhower administration was indecisive: "Good will and virtuous intent, yes," Hughes wrote. "Bold deed and solid achievement, no." The President's answer came swift and cordial. He emphasized, much as he had done to Mountbatten in September 1943, the urgent need to build a confident, harmonious staff. He recalled how he had followed the same course at the War Department in 1942, in North Africa in 1943, in London and later in Brittany in 1944: ignoring the impatient clamor for quick engagement with the enemy, insisting on first assembling and training a strong team. Over the long haul, Eisenhower maintained, this course was vastly preferable to isolated victories. His cabinet was improving, he told Hughes, citing how even George Humphrey, the arch-conservative, had "fairly glowed" as he exulted after a recent cabinet meeting over the expanded housing program and the increased unemployment insurance.

Until his principal subordinates were better schooled in his ways, Eisenhower was content to settle for good will and virtuous intent, and to postpone any reach for bold deed and solid achievement. Criticism that he was doing little or nothing he ignored.

An obvious drawback to a smoothly functioning, highly organized staff system, one in which much important work is delegated to trusted associates, is that the chief executive may soon appear to be a puppet, an amiable fathead going through a few ceremonial motions, a figure of fun.

Another drawback is that an efficient staff of devoted and admiring functionaries can blanket a Chief Executive so warmly within their protective cocoon that he may never glimpse how tragic problems are emerging to menace the health of the republic; at the least they can blunt his awareness of those problems and distract him from any useful consideration of them by pressing upon him more familiar crises and entreating his undivided concentration.

To take up first the latter of these possibilities, both the subject of much speculation by the growing tribe of Eisenhower's critics at the time and later, there can be no question that there existed in the early 1950s, alongside the intractable dilemmas described earlier, several domestic concerns of weight and substance. Among these were the decay of the cities, the gloomy plight of educational techniques and facilities, the fast-paced waste and rapine of natural resources (soon to be subsumed under the fashionable term ecology), the condition of American Negroes (who would presently prefer to be called blacks), American Indians and Mexican-Americans, and the proliferation of the human species. If Eisenhower did little or nothing about these testing tasks, if his celebrated program of highway building served to exacerbate a couple of them, it cannot be said that they were not drawn to his attention. First and last they kept intruding but were simply ticketed with a low priority except as they happened to coincide with the needs of the Cold War. In short, Eisenhower brushed them aside much as most of his successors in office have done.

As to whether Eisenhower was a figurehead rather than an active President, the evidence, it must be admitted, is impressive. Here at home was Sherman Adams, busily riding herd on the thousand and one matters of housekeeping, administration, congressional liaison, staff organization, politics, patronage, and interdepartmental infighting that have traditionally preoccupied Presidents; and there, darting about the world, signing treaties, chaffering with heads of state, lining up military bases all around the rim of the Soviet Union, and supervising the Cold War with one hand while petrifying the nation's foreign policy with the other, was Foster Dulles. What was left for Eisenhower to do?

Thus the appearances, but they were as usual deceptive.

In the early months of his administration, while he was coaching and training his team, Eisenhower threw himself into the process of government if not with exhilaration, at least with an enormous curiosity and a zest to tackle a new kind of challenge. Almost at once there were signs, however, that he had decided his new challenge was not so new to him, after all.* As soon as he decently could he resumed the tested routines of

* On the evening of his first day at work, he noted: "My first full day at the President's Desk. Plenty of worries and difficult problems. . . . The result is that today

541

AFHQ and SHAEF and SHAPE, withdrawing whenever possible behind official spokesmen, emerging only for press conferences and occasional public appearances, which he regarded with a cold eye as a distasteful duty. Increasingly, as his confidence in his chief lieutenants grew, he relinquished to them more responsibility. "A President who doesn't know how to decentralize," Eisenhower said, "will be weighed down with details and won't have time to deal with the big issues." Adams was given and took more power as the Cerberus at the President's gate. "Anybody who had legitimate business of sufficient importance to occupy the attention of the President got in," Adams said later; "those that didn't didn't. I knew the difference."

Business of sufficient importance. Adams knew what was meant by the phrase, and what was excluded by it. There were areas of the President's job in which, quite simply, Eisenhower took no interest. They bored him. Often he did not trouble to keep himself even sketchily informed about them, and his ignorance of them, snappishly admitted, was as often on display at his press conferences. Close observers concluded that in general what bored him were the domestic affairs of the republic, whereas he maintained a firm control over its foreign affairs. The analysis was imprecise, for he ignored some aspects of foreign affairs and worried extravagantly about some domestic concerns. It is more accurate to say that Eisenhower kept a sharp eye on all matters that touched on what he thought of as the national security; but anything on the "civilian side"—the phrase is that used by Colonel Goodpaster, Eisenhower's staff secretary after September 1954, to describe the business of the departments of labor, commerce, agriculture, and health, education, and welfare—was likely to get short shrift.

Yet Dulles was so painfully visible as he hustled around the world on his righteous mission of confounding international communism that some found it hard to believe that the President had much more to do with the national security than to rubber-stamp—or occasionally veto—the initiatives planned and mounted by the learned and patriotic secretary of state. Those who were disenchanted by Dulles's rigid adversarial posture, who could not believe that Eisenhower, so likable, so warmly responsive to any friendly overture, so pliant, so accommodating, would ever share Dulles's harsh Calvinistic view of world rivalries, sought to picture a President amenable to a détente with the Soviet Union but imprisoned by the

just seems like a continuation of all I've been doing since July '41—even before that." Once again Eisenhower had an eye cocked on the historians for whom that note had been written. His hasty reflection was either presumptuous or carefully planned, but in either event it was symptomatic of the temper of a man who had for ten years been surrounded by deference, timeserving, and instant obedience.

dogmas of his secretary of state, barred from achieving his dream—everybody's dream—of world peace. This notion was, for anyone able to separate wish from fact, plainly bunk, but it flourished early and late. In the summer of 1953, when Eisenhower was sojourning at his summer White House in Denver (and trying to find time for golf, bridge, and fishing), Dulles was flown west from Washington for a conference with his chief that lasted several hours. The newspapers were duly filled with cautious speculation about the widening gap between President and secretary of state which had culminated in Dulles being summoned to Denver so that Eisenhower could personally chastise him. Eisenhower was sardonically amused by these tales; in a lengthy memorandum of instructions he sent to Dulles he included a paragraph of reassurance, lest Dulles imagine the newspaper talk had any basis in fact.

The truth is that Dulles did Eisenhower's bidding in matters of high policy, and also served as the convenient butt for any criticism of that policy so that Eisenhower's avuncular image might be preserved.

And what of the private Eisenhower, the man customarily concealed behind image and public persona?

Anon glimpses of the private Eisenhower were vouchsafed—more frequently than they had been when he was in uniform and could exercise closer control of them, less frequently than was the case with Democratic predecessors—and those glimpses had the predictable effect, especially since they were so craftily doled out by the masterful Jim Hagerty. The vast majority of American voters were vastly delighted by the glimpses given them, and so they were confirmed in their abiding affection for the Hero; a small but articulate minority (eggheads, media manipulators, intellectuals, and other suchlike un-Americans) were confirmed in their view of Eisenhower as a dull and trivial fellow, on a par with Warren Gamaliel Harding. The more Eisenhower took command of the middle, that invaluable reach of American politics that lies betwixt the odious extremes of Left and Right, the more he took command of the voters; and his every private distraction from the cares of office plucked a voluptuous chord to stir the Great American Middle. Golf, bridge, trout fishing, romping with one's grandchildren, cookouts on a charcoal grill, moving to a new house in the country, paperback westerns, hand-painted oil paintings, stag dinners—it would be hard to compile a list of innocent pleasures and relaxations that would more surely fetch and tickle the electorate. There was something here for everyone, and nothing to turn off any but the crabbed and high-toned intelligentsia. More, what was glimpsed of his private behavior, supplementing his public comportment, restored a certain dignity to the presidency that had been threatened by Truman's gaudy shirts, worn when he was at Key West; by Truman's vivid language when referring to the columnist Drew Pearson; by Truman's fits of pique, as when he reacted to criticism of his daughter Margaret's singing.

Some of Eisenhower's private recreations warrant a word of comment.

Golf. That the President's passion for this diabolical pastime was pure and intense is beyond question. In evidence, there is an affecting paragraph entered in his "diary" on a Saturday, February 7, 1953, by his secretary Ann Whitman: "Today the President wanted to play golf very very badly. He awoke to a cold and drizzly rain. He peered at the sky frequently during the morning, and finally after another excursion out to the porch, announced, 'Sometimes I feel so sorry for myself I could cry!' With which he arranged a bridge game, whereupon the sun came out. A truly unfair set of things." In every way he showed that he would much rather be on the links than in the White House; indeed, he had a driving range installed within it and a practice putting green just outside it, and on any sunny day when he could not escape to Burning Tree, the posh golf club of upper-crust Washington, he could be found pitching golf balls on the south lawn of the White House just outside his own oval office. His addiction to the game, so well publicized, was unquestionably a factor in lifting its popularity and bringing it within the grasp of every truck-driver and ethnic hardhat with Waspish pretensions.

Bridge. The close circle of friends he had formed at Augusta National and Blind Brook were also his favorite choices for a rubber of bridge; they remained his private cronies during his years as President. They had to pass the test of Mamie Eisenhower's approval, for as one of them told a reporter: "Mamie wants her soldier boy around, and Ike likes to be around her. So when you play bridge, you play at Ike's place. He doesn't go out with the boys at night." They also had to be responsive to his beck, but they were all men who could afford to drop everything and fly a few thousand miles when he felt like a few rubbers of bridge. When he itched to play cards in Denver, Cliff Roberts and Slats Slater would fly west from New York and Freeman Gosden, the Amos of the old "Amos 'n' Andy" radio show, would fly east from Los Angeles. Occasionally the whim would seize Eisenhower in more distant places. Once he was in Rambouillet, outside Paris, when he thought to take a short holiday at Culzean Castle in Scotland. (The Scots had given him the rights to that castle during his lifetime.) Ignoring the position of the sun in the sky, Eisenhower telephoned Bill Robinson in New York (where it was well after 2 A.M.) and invited him to Culzean for bridge. "Without a moment's hesitation" Robinson and Pete Jones accepted Eisenhower's suggestion, arriving, as the President observed, "slightly worse for wear," despite having contrived to catch a nap during their transatlantic flight. Eisenhower's ambassador to the Court of St. James's, Jock Whitney, was summoned from London to make a fourth.

Moving to a new house in the country. Taking up residence in the White House was a frustration for Mamie Eisenhower. She knew it was temporary. Once again, as for so many times in her thirty-six married years, she was in someone else's house, she was unable to feather her own nest. This time, however, there was something she could do about it.

In 1950, when Eisenhower was still at Columbia, George Allen had told him of the farm he had bought near Gettysburg, and his wife Mary had told Mamie of the stone farmhouse she planned to remodel. That kind of talk was a powerful temptation, and Mamie had succumbed. The Eisenhowers soon bought a fairly substantial farm (about one hundred and ninety acres) not far from the battlefield at Gettysburg. On it were the usual farm structures—an ancient and decrepit house, some barns and sheds. In 1953 Mamie decided to have the house restored. Her dreams proved impossible of fulfillment: the thing had to be torn down and a new structure built to replace it. By the time the Eisenhowers were finished they had a modern and costly farm complete with big new barns, landscaping, a herd of Black Angus cattle, and such trinkets as a radio-equipped tractor, the whole worth more than a half-million dollars. The financing was complex and involved a little help from Eisenhower's friends. Capital was supplied by Pete Jones of Cities Service, B. C. (Billy) Byars of Tyler, Texas, a rancher and oilman, and George Allen. These three agreed to operate the farm, paying its costs and collecting its conjectural profits; but officials of the Internal Revenue Service, after turning up no evidence that the three had tried very hard to make the farm a profitable venture, ruled that the capital funds could not be deducted as business expenses but must be accounted as an outright gift. Those funds, constantly replenished, were also used to pay the salary of the farm's manager, General Arthur S. Nevins, another old friend who had been chief of SHAEF's G-3 in 1945.

The main house was built to specifications sketched out by Mamie Eisenhower, who disdained the assistance of an architect. She knew what she wanted, and if when it was finished it was "not completely convenient," if new walls had occasionally to be torn down because she had forgotten "a detail or two" like central air conditioning or the proper placement of electric wiring, no matter, because she was happily if expensively at work building the first home she and Ike had ever had.

The President and his lady began using the farm for weekends and holidays sometime in 1954; it was their home long before they left the White House.

Stag dinners. In mid-April 1953, Eisenhower got the idea of inviting

"American citizens, normally outside of government service" to visit the White House for "a simple stag dinner" and "a chat over general conditions." The dinners, usually for a dozen or perhaps as many as sixteen guests, began in June and were considered an immediate success, at least by the Republican National Committee. Attendance at once became, in some circles, a status symbol of immense value; before long Leonard Hall, chairman of the National Committee, began to insist on inserting two or three names in the list for each dinner to pay off old political debts or run up new political credits. Since others than Eisenhower were involved in selecting his guests, conclusions about the guest list cannot be entirely watertight. For example, it is unlikely that Eisenhower invited many of the two dozen politicians who showed up over the course of the first thirty-eight of his stag dinners. But his hand is evident in the striking character of the guest list: more than half were bankers, industrialists, oilmen, merchant princes, chairmen of the boards of great corporations—the men whose opinions he most valued and with whom he got along most easily. For every hundred businessmen an artist would be roped in, or a composer or a physicist or an architect or a journalist, as a bit of yeast for the great wad of dough. A few of the reverend clergy managed inclusion, and a half-dozen labor leaders, and a few college presidents, but by and large these bean feasts were laid on for men of commercial substance. Eisenhower gave every evidence of enjoying them.

One flaw was at once apparent: they were stag. The Republican ladies squawked, and so shrilly that the President was obliged to arrange some special breakfasts for ladies only. At these affairs Eisenhower talked little and listened, or so it was said, a great deal.

It will have been observed that much of this range of activities, launched as private entertainments, inevitably grew more and more public, and hence became astutely managed for public relations value. Thus, while the President was not permitted by his watchdogs to show up for the Masters Tournament at Augusta National, he would play each year's winner a well-publicized round of golf on the day after the tournament, in what amounted to a command performance. Again, beginning in 1954 the President's Christmas card would be a reproduction of one of his own oil paintings, and to be on his Christmas list was of course a much prized honor. (The canvases for his paintings were prepared by a competent craftsman, usually an army private who before being drafted had been a professional illustrator or art designer. Down in the bowels of the White House this anonymous soldier would sketch with charcoal the subject the President wanted to paint, taking care to draw his outline just so, for the President was fussy about such things, sometimes requiring that the nose for one of his portraits be at dead center of the canvas.)

But all his activities, whether private, semiprivate, or public, served remarkably to endear Eisenhower to his countrymen. As the Hero was gradually transmuted into the Cold Warrior, he had well-nigh solid support in whatever he did, with more often than not no questions asked. This blind trust stands as an extraordinary testimonial to his celebrity as a supreme commander and to the potency of his charm, his celebrated grin, and his conspicuous candor, so much a part of his public persona. Is there a suggestion here that Dwight D. Eisenhower was not truly candid? not always truthfully direct with his countrymen? The testimony of close and careful observers differs, depending on whether they were his critics or his confederates. Richard H. Rovere, a perceptive and discriminating critic, wrote of Eisenhower in December 1955 this simple, declarative statement: "The President is not a devious man." Richard M. Nixon, Eisenhower's shrewd and perceptive confederate, wrote of him in 1961: "He was a far more complex and devious man than most people realized, and in the best sense of those words."

Here is a charming contradiction. Perhaps, to resolve it, the best course is to examine the Cold Warrior at work and make our own determination. It is plain that Eisenhower, so constantly apprehensive of the judgments of history, in many ways sought to secure his own glittering space in the American pantheon, and not least as victorious Cold Warrior. "The United States never lost a soldier or a foot of ground in my administration," he once proudly said. "We kept the peace," he pointed out. "People ask how it happened—by God, it didn't just happen, I'll tell you that."

During Eisenhower's years as President, however, the United States was acting as the world's cop, assuming protective responsibility not only for its own citizens but, such was the reach of its covetous embrace, for every country in the free world. Did that responsibility not in some way extend to the soldiers and ground lost by other nations of the free world? The question must be studied.

At all events, the Cold Warrior would be gratefully honored because he kept his countrymen at peace for eight relatively prosperous years. When Eisenhower settled to his tasks, the two most pressing, it seemed to him, were Korea and Vietnam. In Korea the killing persisted; an end to it was essential. As to Vietnam, in Eisenhower's remarkable recollection of the matter the conflict was "subject to misinterpretation and an American support for the French . . . could not achieve unanimous domestic approval." Nevertheless, plans were at once devised to strengthen the French imperial power in Vietnam. No Americans would be involved—yet.

As we shall find, there were other problems posed by the Cold War.

CHAPTER TWO

Education in Crisis

Suffering McCarthyism . . . Containment or rollback . . . The Bricker amendment . . . The death of Stalin . . . Peace for Korea . . . Counterrevolution in Iran . . . The Supreme Court and the Negroes.

WHILE THEY ARE BEING FOMENTED, all wars, whether hot or cold, show the same characteristics. Hatreds are pumped up, lies broadcast, protests throttled. Thus are achieved a high morale and a national unity. Immemorially, reaching back to the kindergarten of the species, one side incarnates good while those opposed are evil. (As President Eisenhower had proclaimed, "Freedom is pitted against slavery; lightness against the dark.") The warrior's avowed aim must always be unexceptionable, and of all aims the noblest is peace. Peace for our time, peace with honor, peace with justice, peace with prosperity, peace indivisible, peace everlasting. Thus having established unassailable rectitude, the warrior can manipulate unnoticed his more dishonorable devices.

First it was essential to fix the official view of international affairs, the one that could be taken up and expounded by all right-thinking editors and commentators, that could subsequently be embroidered and fashioned by State Department spokesmen as occasion demanded, the view that would drive from the marketplace all others as being dangerously defective and possibly treasonable. The task of defining this official view was deputed to Foster Dulles. The learned advocate had read a few of the published works of Lenin and Stalin and so knew better than most their wicked wiles. What was more, Dulles's forensic strength was as the strength of ten, because his heart was pure as a presbyter's. He had his brief ready by nightfall of January 27, 1953, his sixth day in office, and as usual it had been studied and approved by the President. It was the official policy of the new administration, and the nation would be more or less stuck with it for the next eight years. Indeed, its end is not yet, for it became an integral part of the republic's conventional wisdom, almost impossible to shuck off.

The Dulles address, grave and portentous, was broadcast on both television and radio, with the television audience being given glimpses of a map that showed what Dulles described as the "area which the Russian communists completely dominate," one that reached six thousand miles from the Elbe in the west to the Taiwan Strait in the east. Stalin, said Dulles, had designs on Japan "with its great industrial power," and he showed on the map how Japan would "be within the communist pincers" if the Reds won all of Korea. Stalin lusted for Indochina, Thailand, and Burma, for they comprised "the rice bowl of Asia" on which both Japan and India depended for food. Stalin had told Hitler in 1940 that the Middle East, with its rich oil reserves, was "the center of Soviet aspirations." Stalin was scheming in Africa "to arouse the native people against the western Europeans who still have political control" there and who count on the raw materials of Africa for their domestic prosperity. In brief, said Dulles, the "Soviet communists are carrying out a policy which they call encirclement" and which had as its ultimate objective, of course, the gobbling up of the United States. Once they had "completed their encirclement of the United States," Dulles warned, they would "be ready for what Stalin has called the decisive blow against us with the odds overwhelmingly in their favor." Opposed to this "deadly serious" threat was an American foreign policy characterized by Dulles as one of "openness, simplicity, and righteousness." To those being held "captive" beyond the iron curtain, Dulles promised that "you can count on us."

Parts of this speech were woefully misinformed, parts were plainly dishonest, most of it was addressed solely to domestic political favor. The notion that the Chinese communists slavishly followed the dictates of Moscow was a misconception that enthralled Dulles for several years; conceivably if he had heeded the counsel of those foreign service officers who were more familiar than he with the course of Chinese affairs over the previous two decades he might have saved himself the embarrassment of ignorance publicly displayed, but those counselors had been effectively silenced by the attacks upon them by Senator McCarthy and his cohorts, and by the timorous acquiescence of Dulles and Eisenhower in those attacks. Discussion of the statements attributed by Dulles to Stalin is difficult; since the secretary never disclosed the source of them, one cannot say where was fancy bred, or in the heart or in the head. But it was when he came to the matter of "encirclement" that Dulles did greatest violence to the facts known to him and to Eisenhower—and to the Russians.

Who had whom encircled? The U.S. had air bases in Britain, Morocco, Libya, Saudi Arabia, Turkey, the Philippines, and Okinawa, as well as in Alaska and within its own continental limits, and from any of these bases atomic bombs could be delivered on targets within the Soviet Union. Further, plans were being mooted to establish such bases in Norway and in Spain.* Yet further, the U.S. had a military alliance (NATO) with Canada, Iceland, and twelve European nations, and talks would soon begin looking to military aid for and cooperation with the nations signatory to the Baghdad Pact, and other talks would result in a military alliance (SEATO) embracing Pakistan, Thailand, the Philippines, and Australia, and yielding still another air base, in Pakistan. Finally, the U.S. was supplying arms, military hardware, and money to the French fighting in Indochina, and U.S. soldiers and U.S. military aircraft were installed in Korea and Japan, ready for action. The ring around Russia was firm and complete. When Dulles spoke of a Russian encirclement of the United States, then, he was not using the language in its customary sense.

Talk of liberating those held "captive" beyond the iron curtain was likewise removed from reality, so far removed indeed that it soon began to excite alarm of another widespread war. As was noted earlier, Dulles's speech was composed primarily for domestic consumption, to remind Americans (and particularly those whose families had immigrated from eastern European lands) that Eisenhower, Dulles, and the Republicans generally condemned the doctrine of mere containment of communism as being supine, as being—in the words of the Republican platform, devised by Dulles and approved by Eisenhower—"negative, futile and immoral." But could not such a pledge be airily dismissed as bait to trap voters? No, for only the day before Dulles's speech the President had sharply asserted to the Republican congressional leaders his "uncompromising" intention to redeem all pledges of platform and campaign. Moreover, a week later Eisenhower announced that the U.S. Seventh Fleet, which by Truman's order had been patrolling the Taiwan Strait like a cop on his beat, would henceforth forbid only forays by the Chinese communists against Taiwan but would ignore any hostile action mounted

* A base in Norway presented difficulties because her constitution explicitly prohibits an establishment of foreign soldiers on her soil. In a memorandum of March 3 to Dulles, Eisenhower would suggest that "she might get away with it [if it] could be made to appear a completely *defensive* step." In other words, he advised Dulles, try the device of NATO. "I would talk NATO a lot more," Eisenhower added, "than I would a strategic air base."
A few weeks later the President would lament to Republican legislative leaders the question of Spanish bases. How to get them? A treaty with Spain did not seem feasible, he observed, because it would provoke an ideological debate. Had the legislative leaders any ideas? They did, and soon U.S. air bases in Spain would be operative.

"Have A Care, Sir."

from *Herblock's Here and Now* (Simon & Schuster, 1955)

by Chiang Kai-shek's troops against the Chinese mainland. No longer, said President Eisenhower, was there "any logic or sense" in restraining Chiang.

The decision—widely hailed as "unleashing" Chiang—was a curious exercise in befuddlement. Eisenhower seemed content to disguise his actual intentions from all kinds of people. His allies, particularly Eden of Britain and Prime Minister Jawaharlal Nehru of India, were confused and indignant, the more so when rumors, carefully let slip and nourished by figures within the White House, led to speculation that the U.S. was considering a naval blockade of China. Congressmen were likewise confused, as were expert political commentators and, quite naturally, the American people. Presumably the decision was designed to unsettle the Chinese communists, whose armies still stood in Korea, but they had the advantage of having taken Chiang's measure and so were not likely to be frightened by the threat. After close scrutiny, Eisenhower's order could be seen to have changed nothing. The Seventh Fleet had for some time been assisting Chiang's forces in their nuisance raids anyway. In effect, the cop on the beat had switched the red stoplight to green, but the traffic was too decrepit (or too timid) to do much more than inch across the roadway. Very slowly two solid facts emerged.

ONE: Chiang had been "unleashed" not because he could do any great damage to the People's Republic of China (all his troops could inflict no more than the most superficial of flesh wounds), but because the Eisenhower administration was obliged to unleash him in order to silence the China lobby, a combination of Old Guard Republicans, wealthy importers, and magnates of the publishing business.

TWO: The Eisenhower administration was in any case engaged in a comprehensive study of national security and foreign policy which would lead to adoption of a reasonable facsimile of the Truman policy of containment. Talk of liberation would persist, the about-face would never be publicly acknowledged, but the broad lines of policy would be the same as those developed by the Truman administration.*

* They *had* to be the same, Robert R. Bowie has said, "because fundamentally those basic lines of policy, in terms of security, of economic interests, of relations with allies and relations with the Soviet Union and relations in the Far East, were the product of the external conditions, as they were perceived, and the American sense of its interests, which really weren't partisan." Bowie added: "There wasn't anywhere near as much room for maneuver as some campaign oratory might have suggested." Bowie was director of the Policy Planning Staff of the State Department from 1953 to 1957, representing the State Department on the Planning Board of the National Security Council.

The comprehensive study, protracted through six months of laborious deliberation, engaging the talents of more than two dozen highly qualified officials, and winding up just about where it had begun, was a phenomenon to delight the most captious. It was dubbed Operation Solarium because it was in that room of the White House that

Long before this study was fairly afoot, events had conspired to lead the new administration into the footsteps of the old. Some of the problems were inherited ones; but even the new problems prompted familiar partisan reactions from the Republican congressmen, whose twenty years in opposition had in effect programmed them to strike automatic postures of antagonism when confronted by any proposal from an occupant of the White House. But all the problems vexing the republic—the persistent war in Korea, Iran, Suez, trade with China, Vietnam, Burmese resentment of the behavior of those of Chiang's soldiers who had sought refuge in Burma, the appointment of a new American ambassador to the Soviet Union, the struggle to repudiate the "secret agreements" allegedly contracted with the Russians by the perfidious Democrats, the growing clamor for a constitutional amendment that would strip the President of his power to make treaties, even the speculative questions posed by the death of Joseph Stalin—all these were dwarfed during the first months of Eisenhower's presidency by the destructive impact of Senator Joe McCarthy on the domestic tranquillity of the republic and on the conduct of the republic's business abroad both with its allies and with its adversaries.

It seemed curious at the time, it seems curious in retrospect, that the Hero, the former supreme commander, the beloved President of the United States, could have suffered McCarthy so long after their paths first crossed. To be sure, a number of Eisenhower's wealthiest sponsors, the Texas oil peerage, also admired and supported McCarthy, and Eisenhower was dutifully striving to be at least as anticommunist as McCarthy —but suavely, more genteelly. There was, however, nothing in McCarthy's slambang reckless deportment, nothing in his cruel hounding of the innocent or foolish, nothing in his gross vulgarity, nothing in his aimless, almost wholly unorganized sedition, nothing in the way he flouted the law and ravaged the truth, nothing in his short-lived, ignorant, essentially unproductive career that Dwight Eisenhower could approve, nothing indeed that would not repel and disgust him. Why then, when at any time the President could have withered McCarthy with a glance, a gesture, a word, why, when McCarthy was tumultuously wrecking the foreign service, demoralizing the State Department, keelhauling the International Information Agency and its subsidiary Voice of America, when he was making the United States at once a laughingstock among its detractors and an object of fear and contempt among its allies, why in the name of reason did Eisenhower not flick a finger and squash him?

President Eisenhower approved the project, personally nominating some of the participants. (He naturally inclined to suggest army officers whose intellectual prowess had impressed him.)

Opportunities abounded. The ladies and gentlemen of the press, having in the first place inflated McCarthy and McCarthyism, now earnestly desired to bring him low; they proffered the President at nearly every one of his press conferences a motive and a circumstance for the coup de grâce. Within the White House every second presidential assistant urged him to seize the moment. Without, as each shameful week inched along, more of the citizenry despaired. By a delectable irony many of those citizens (and not a few of them of a heretical, even communist persuasion) had voted for Eisenhower rather than Stevenson precisely because they imagined that only a hard-boiled Republican President would be able to cope with the likes of McCarthy. But Eisenhower did nothing.

The pattern had been set long before when, during the campaign, Eisenhower had chosen to delete from a speech to be delivered in Wisconsin—McCarthy's home state—a brief paragraph of tribute to General Marshall, whom McCarthy had vilified as a dupe of the communists and a traitor. From all accounts of that distressing episode, Eisenhower had cut the paragraph on the anxious recommendation of the professional politicians; some accounts would have it that Eisenhower submitted only after irritable snorts. The politicians in question were plainly scared of McCarthy: scared of what he might charge against Eisenhower if Eisenhower were publicly to dispute McCarthy's opinion of Marshall on McCarthy's turf. The politicians had got into the habit of tugging the forelock whenever McCarthy swaggered past, for he had a reputation (whether or not deserved) of having personally ended the political careers of no less than eight United States senators. Might not such a baleful champion sway the national accounting of votes even for a presidential candidate? If McCarthy could destroy the usefulness of a Marshall, as he had done, what price his assault on an Eisenhower? The entreaties of the politicians had, at all events, been firmly embedded within seemly rationalizations, among which were: the unity of the Republican party must be preserved; we are guests in the state of Wisconsin and when in Wisconsin should be gracious to its junior senator; and, most beguiling of all, Eisenhower's "deep feeling concerning General Marshall's outstanding character and achievements" might, if expressed aloud, "be inadvertently embarrassing [to] General Marshall."

Having chosen to ignore McCarthy, Eisenhower had at once been attacked for having surrendered to him. The attacks put his back up. He was not used to such contumacy. In the previous decade he had grown accustomed to deference and respect from those around him, to associates who instantly stood up when he entered a room and remained at easy attention until he had seated himself. To be charged with capitulation to

McCarthy angered him deeply. Equally profoundly did the attacks shape his attitude toward McCarthy in the first months of his presidency.*

Once in the White House, Eisenhower persevered in publicly ignoring McCarthy while privately taking refuge in other admirable rationalizations. Thus: the President should not demean his office by engaging in controversy with McCarthy. ("I will not get in the gutter with that guy," he once angrily told C. D. Jackson.) Thus: the President should not meddle in what was properly the internal business of the Senate, which alone could discipline or censure one of its own. Thus: Eisenhower grew increasingly bitter with the press, with those writers, editors, and publishers who had accorded McCarthy the headlines that had earlier given him prestige and power and now grew insistent that Eisenhower topple McCarthy. (The President waxed so fond of this sophistry that he kept searching for an editorial writer or television commentator who agreed with him. At length he found one: an obscure radio announcer, Virgil Pinkley, whose voice was broadcast into the air over Los Angeles and environs. Proudly Eisenhower cited him in letters to friends as a cogent authority.)

But if the President yearned to smite McCarthy down, he gave no sign. If he desired other senators to close ranks and censure the senator from Wisconsin, he dropped no hint, direct or indirect, to any Republican senator who might have organized such a scheme. (Vice President Nixon, who as a senator had been a member in good standing of McCarthy's gang, was detailed by the administration to keep a restraining hand on McCarthy's coattails, but no other effort to block his course has ever been recorded.) If the President believed that the press, or television, should have been encouraged to demolish the man he accused them of having exalted, he lifted no finger to assist the process. (It is true that one month after Edward R. Murrow of the Columbia Broadcasting System produced a television program which focused on McCarthy's career a cold and critical eye, Eisenhower did confide to his press conference that he regarded Murrow as a friend.)

President Eisenhower, then, did about as little as could possibly be done to shield the republic from McCarthy's mischief. One is tempted to agree with Richard Rovere's sorrowing judgment that Eisenhower was McCarthy's captive, held as nearly captive for the first two years of his

* As candidate, Eisenhower had wished to avoid any encounter with McCarthy in Wisconsin and had instructed his staff to steer clear of the state. Someone had blundered. A tour through Wisconsin had been scheduled. "This occasioned," Eisenhower wrote later, "the sharpest flareup I can recall between my staff and I during the entire campaign." Eisenhower could have kept his temper. In November he carried Wisconsin by 979,744 to 622,175, while McCarthy, proven the weakest man on the Republican ticket, carried the state by only 870,444 to 731,402.

first term as any President of the United States has ever been held. Consider only the first months of 1953. Apart from dictating the dismissal of the State Department's ranking experts on China, McCarthy forced the resignation of two successive directors of the International Information Administration, caused the death by suicide of a wholly innocent radio engineer who feared one of McCarthy's well-publicized investigations, and dispatched to Europe a pair of preposterous emissaries, Roy Cohn and G. David Schine, respectively the chief counsel and the chief consultant of his investigative committee, allegedly to inquire into subversion in American agencies overseas but in effect to transfigure the image of the republic into something at once farcical and shameful. For some little time the nation was convulsed by McCarthy's charges, usually spread across the front pages of the newspapers in beetling black headlines, that the State Department had given shelfspace, in libraries maintained abroad, to some thirty thousand books by communist authors, and by the consequent rowdydow over the removal (and even the burning) of the offensive books, most of which had been written by authors of excellent repute.*
When the President nominated Charles Bohlen to be ambassador to the Soviet Union, McCarthy commenced to rumble ominously. He growled that to call Bohlen a "security risk" was "putting it too weak." Dulles should be put "under oath," since his earlier statements on Bohlen appeared "to be completely untrue." Senator Taft had little use for Bohlen, but he exercised his considerable influence to get the appointment approved in order to protect the President's prestige. He also warned the White House: no more appointments to which McCarthy might object.†
But it was the essence of the McCarthy caper to move from one disruption to another: presently he announced that he had negotiated an agreement with Greek shipowners that purportedly blocked trade with China, North Korea, and the far eastern ports of the Soviet Union. By what authority did a junior senator from Wisconsin "negotiate" such "agreements"? Quite clearly he was usurping the powers and responsibilities of the President and the Department of State, but no matter, for Vice President Nixon, operating coolly, arranged a luncheon for McCarthy and Dulles from

* Among the authors pilloried was a historian, Foster Rhea Dulles, a cousin to the secretary of state. "Why," demanded the secretary petulantly, "have they got my cousin on that list?" But of course he knew the answer, or at least suspected it: the right wing of the Republican party was seeking to force his resignation.
† To this Dulles would surely have added a fervent amen. The Bohlen episode did not show the secretary at his best. "I couldn't stand another Alger Hiss," he told Bohlen. (Dulles had nominated Hiss to the Carnegie Endowment for International Peace *after* he had been shown some inconclusive FBI gossip about Hiss.) On their way to Capitol Hill for a hearing on Bohlen's appointment, Dulles requested Bohlen that he not permit the photographers to take pictures of them together. Bohlen judged that Dulles feared a right-wing campaign against him.

which the secretary of state emerged to give his blessing to McCarthy's mischief as being "in the national interest."*

In short, Senator McCarthy was able to disorder matters so as to persuade a great many Americans first, that Senator McCarthy stood like a lion at the gates of the city, defending it against all nefarious enemies, and second, that President Eisenhower lay snoozing in his tent, boots off, heedless, captive.

The first of these foolish notions was dead by mid-1954. The second persists today, largely because President Eisenhower was an exceptionally astute man who perceived that he could accomplish a great deal, and a great deal more easily, the more he was able to work in the shade, away from the glare of public attention.

Let Senator McCarthy have his headlines: President Eisenhower was busily at work on the battlements of the free world. To the devil with popular applause; he would confidently await the judgment of history.

As to Joe McCarthy then, there were two contradictory views. The civil libertarians, those who reverenced the Bill of Rights, most journalists and editors, and the intellectuals generally considered him a scandal and a plague, and impatiently awaited his summary execution by the man best fitted for the job—President Eisenhower. From the White House the angle of vision differed. In truth, President Eisenhower had precious little time to squander on McCarthy, for matters of greater substance demanded his attention. These matters overlapped, as many as five at a time competing for his consideration; and the way he addressed himself to them sometimes revealed an appalling contrariety between what was publicly professed and what was privately undertaken—a defect common to all statesmen of the Cold War. Although these matters were often indissolubly intermingled, they are better treated separately.

The Bricker Amendment (January 7, 1953–February 26, 1954)

Senator John Bricker, Republican of Ohio, was an ornament of the Grand Old Party's isolationist right wing, tall, amiable, and blessed with a luxurious crest of wavy white hair, regular features, a dignified carriage, and a comfortable vacuity behind a broad blank frontal bone. He stood in a direct line of such Republican politicians, reaching back to the martyred Warren Gamaliel Harding. He was a former governor of Ohio, a pillar of the Young Men's Christian Association, a Mason (thirty-third

---

* If further evidence were needed of the protean character of the "national interest," that statement of Secretary Dulles surely affords it.

degree), a member of the Ancient Arabic Order of Nobles of the Mystic Shrine, and a principal spokesman in the Senate of the Pennsylvania Railroad. In common with many other Republican senators (and most of the southern Democrats) Bricker had fumed over the way in which Democratic Presidents had for years worked their will with the nation's foreign policy while according to the Senate only the most casual of acknowledgments. Teheran! Yalta! Potsdam! Those were words, despite the paucity of esses, to be hissed. Secret pacts! The United Nations! A cabal, scheming to supplant states' rights and the national sovereignty with a Declaration of Human Rights elaborated by a commission whose chairman had been—who else?—Eleanor Roosevelt.

On those ample foundations was erected the platform for the last hurrah of the isolationists.

The Bricker amendment was born January 7, 1953, and christened, for parliamentary purposes, Senate Joint Resolution 1. It was sponsored by Bricker and sixty-two other senators; it was backed by the American Medical Association, the United States Chamber of Commerce, the Daughters of the American Revolution, an impressive fraction of the American Bar Association, something called the Committee for Constitutional Government, the American Legion, the Veterans of Foreign Wars, and an ad hoc sodality called the Vigilant Women for the Bricker Amendment, which would later present to the Senate a petition bearing, it was claimed, five hundred thousand signatures. What had exercised these patriots was their dread that one day someone might wake up to count the Constitution (or some other jewel in the crown of the republic) and find it missing, spirited away, perhaps to the USSR, by treaty or presidential agreement. Bricker warned, in one characteristic harumph, of the danger of "socialism by treaty." Lest this happen, the Bricker resolution proposed a constitutional amendment that would (1) give the Congress "power to regulate all Executive and other agreements with any foreign power or international organization," and (2) require that a "treaty shall become effective as internal law in the United States only through legislation which would be valid in the absence of a treaty." To adopt such an amendment would take the approval of two-thirds of the Senate (well-nigh guaranteed by the number of senators sponsoring the resolution) and of the House (where it could probably have been whooped through overnight), and a ratification by the legislatures of thirty-six states (no hard thing, considering the temper of the times).

Had it been so approved and ratified, no question about it, the amendment would have severely cramped the republic in its destined role as global gendarme.

The man most concerned was Foster Dulles, who was already spinning his webs of alliance all over the world. At once he perceived that Bricker was lumbering straight into those webs and would inevitably tear them all apart. More, he recognized how the amendment would impair a number of useful presidential prerogatives, "notably," as he reminded Sherman Adams, "[the disposition of] U.S. troops abroad." To make things worse, the unhappy Dulles had made a public record of his belief that "treaty law can override the Constitution." "Treaties," he had further argued, "can take powers away from Congress and give them to the President; they can take powers from the state and give them to . . . some international body, and they can cut across the rights given the people by the . . . Bill of Rights." Just what Bricker maintained: it was as though Dulles had prepared the brief for the prosecution. Useless for Dulles to protest that he had voiced those warnings while a Democratic President was in the White House, busily concocting executive agreements with scantest reference to the Congress (or to the people), for he was now advising a Republican President how best he might travel the same path. His position was, then, untenable, and he was obliged to scramble nimbly, to call upon his redoubtable skills of advocacy, to claim that what he had plainly said nonetheless did not accurately reflect what he believed, to plead that treaties and executive agreements were not so bad after all, and that to pinion the President (and his secretary of state) in the conduct of foreign affairs would be a grave danger to the republic. Far better to give Eisenhower (and Dulles) a free hand to rally the spiritual and military forces of the free world for a crusade against communism, details to be filled in as necessary or when convenient.

Everything about the debate over the Bricker amendment vexed Eisenhower sorely. At first he missed the point, believing that if the Constitution were to be changed at all it should be by domestic amendment rather than by foreign treaty, and had to be shown how Bricker's amendment would disrupt his presidential powers. Next he essayed his own patented formula of assuagement and conciliation: he invited Bricker into his oval office and applied the old oil, sometimes solo, sometimes in duet with Dulles, at least once in trio, with Brownell. None of this did much good. For his part, Bricker began to assume that Eisenhower was veering round to support of the amendment, but Dulles stood always at hand, determined to quash any compromise.

Eisenhower was next plaintive. The Bricker amendment was "a damn thorn in our side." Still, because of his passion not to offend anybody in the Congress, he kept the matter as an item on his agenda for cabinet meetings, seeking a way to avert "a head-on collision over this darn thing."

Did Bricker simply want "something big in public with his name on it"? Could they perhaps form a commission to study the matter and so give it a decent burial? After three months of this inconclusive palaver, Eisenhower had at last made up his mind that he was opposed to the amendment, but even after six months he was still reluctant to urge any Republican senators to join him in opposition. An exchange at a cabinet meeting, July 17, 1953:

DULLES: We just have to make up our minds and stop being fuzzy on this.

EISENHOWER: I haven't been fuzzy about this. There was nothing fuzzy in what I told Bricker. I said we'd go just so far and no further.

DULLES: I know, sir, but you haven't told anybody else.

Meanwhile Taft died, and was replaced as leader of the Republican majority by William Knowland, who supported some sort of Bricker amendment. But the first session of the Eighty-third Congress was adjourned in early August; the President had managed at least to postpone any vote, any decision.

While the Congress was in recess, the issue was more sharply drawn. Bricker was quite certain to press for a vote on his amendment, and it had to be his version, not diluted, the purposes clear. For his part, Eisenhower was now uncomfortably aware that his leadership of a nation that had assumed hegemony of the free world—the world of free enterprise, the capitalistic world—was under attack and that he must with every weapon at his command seek to scotch that attack. Too long he had dawdled. Already Walter Lippmann, the most thoughtful spokesman of those who believed the United States should seize world hegemony, was warning of the "crisis" that had been precipitated by the "abdication of the powers of the executive and the usurpation of Congress." Always sanguine, always confident, Eisenhower sought to relieve the pressure by resorting to quips. When Bricker rejected a last attempt to compromise, Eisenhower observed tartly that the senator's advisers seemed resolved "to save the United States from Eleanor Roosevelt," and a few days later he passed along a feeble witticism then going the rounds to the effect that the Constitution was being demolished "brick by brick by Bricker." But the pressure intensified.

On January 25, 1954, Eisenhower was at last moved to address the Senate leadership in unmistakable terms. "I am unalterably opposed," he wrote Knowland, "to the Bricker amendment," and he added:

Adoption of the Bricker amendment in its present form by the Senate would be notice to our friends as well as our enemies abroad that our country intends to withdraw from its leadership in world affairs. The inevitable reaction would be of major proportion. It would impair our hopes and plans for peace and for the successful achievement of the important international matters now under discussion.

The important international matters then under discussion—what might they have been in late January 1954? The bloody war in the jungles of Vietnam? The parliamentary struggles over the European Defense Community? The tug-of-war over Egypt's demands that the British withdraw from Aden and from the vicinity of the Suez Canal? All these were sufficiently absorbing, and there were others, none of them of the kind that a wise American President would care to leave to the Senate or to the people. Democracy, too, has its limits.

In evidence, here on the President's desk lay a letter from his older brother Edgar, a letter brimming over with anger because the President had not had the sense to approve the Bricker amendment forthwith. Dwight dispatched a stinging reproof to Edgar; he put his stamp of approval on the decision of Sherman Adams to give the boot to the chairman of the President's Commission on Intergovernmental Relationships, Clarence E. Manion, an erstwhile dean of the law school of Notre Dame University and a cosseted minion of the extreme right wing of the Republican party who had been touring the country urging passage of the Bricker amendment; he telephoned a few senators, soliciting their support of his posture; he awaited the Senate's pleasure.

The vote was taken late in February. The Bricker amendment was rejected fifty to forty-four, but by that time all the forces of isolation had regrouped behind the respected Walter George of Georgia, a far more resourceful opponent than Bricker. In the vote on the George substitute, the Republican leader Knowland voted aye (to oppose, as he said, "a dangerous tendency toward executive encroachment on legislative powers") and so did the Democratic leader Lyndon B. Johnson ("because all my people in Texas want it"). There were ninety senators present. Sixty of them constituted the prescribed two-thirds majority. Sixty votes were cast for the George amendment, but at the last moment a ninety-first senator slipped into the chamber to vote nay, and so the amendment died. The ninety-first senator was a Democrat, and his timely intercession led to speculation that the whole affair had been stage-managed by the wily Lyndon Johnson.

In his turn Johnson would have occasion to be thankful that the George substitute had been defeated, but in February 1954 it was Eisenhower who rejoiced.

The Death of Stalin and a Few Repercussions (February 2–July 27, 1953)

In his first message on the State of the Union, President Eisenhower announced he would invite the Congress "to join in an appropriate resolution making clear that this government recognizes no kind of commitment contained in secret understandings of the past with foreign governments which permit [the enslavement of any people]." Ostensibly such a resolution was part of foreign policy in the Cold War, designed to put the Soviet Union on notice that a stern and righteous government now headed the forces of anticommunism. Actually, as attested by the storm of Republican applause that greeted Eisenhower's remark, the resolution was partisan domestic politics, inflammatory and cynical. It was an exercise in demonology, based on assumptions that were accepted Republican dogma of the time: that the Democrats had—it was an instance of their "twenty years of treason"—made secret agreements at Yalta and Potsdam that betrayed into slavery the peoples of eastern Europe, that in effect the Democrats had conspired with the communists to build a communist empire. The Republicans had pledged in their campaign to "repudiate all . . . secret understandings such as those of Yalta"; now in power, Eisenhower wished to redeem that pledge, but no one could find any secret agreements to repudiate. At a press conference Eisenhower was obliged to acknowledge that no secret agreements had been discovered.

Still, some sort of resolution had to be submitted to the Congress, and Eisenhower found himself exquisitely impaled: if he repudiated the agreements of Yalta and Potsdam, and inferentially the policies of Roosevelt and Truman, he would infuriate the Democrats, the sturdiest supporters of his own foreign policies; if he failed to repudiate those agreements and did not specifically mention Yalta, he would enrage most of the Republicans and find himself the architect of a rupture within his own party.

At length Eisenhower decided what the resolution should say and personally drafted much of its language. It bristled with Cold War rhetoric (". . . subjugated to the captivity of Soviet despotism . . . domination of a totalitarian imperialism . . . forcible absorption . . . aggressive despotism . . .") but avoided any mention of Yalta or Potsdam and eschewed the word "repudiation." How could one repudiate what did not exist? His draft was unveiled at a meeting of the Republican legislative leaders on February 16. Dulles noted with satisfaction that it might cause "a little indigestion" behind the "iron curtain" and would help allay the fears of the enslaved that the United States was abandoning them to their fate. The Republican congressmen listened in stony silence.

Events marched in predictable fashion. The resolution was sent to the Congress. It was hailed by Democrats and denounced by Republicans. Dulles and Eisenhower both argued the need for unanimity of support if the resolution were to be effective. The Republicans snorted and, using their slight majority, on March 3 rammed through the Senate Foreign Relations Committee an amendment that warned of the possible "invalidity" of any agreements made with the Russians. The Democrats promptly announced they would fight that amendment on the floor of the Senate. Lyndon Johnson gleefully predicted that he would protect the President's prestige "before the country and the world."

The stage was set for a splendid brawl.

At this moment, most courteously, Stalin died. All hands fetched an immense sigh of relief and at once consigned the resolution to oblivion.

The death of Stalin! What a moment for speculation, by cold warriors the world around! The syllogism ran like this: (1) All dictatorships collapse upon the death of the dictator (e.g., Nazi Germany and fascist Italy); (2) the Union of Soviet Socialist Republics is a dictatorship; (3) ergo, the USSR will now collapse.

But the syllogism was flawed.

The President was told of the gravity of Stalin's illness when he woke at 6:30 A.M. on Wednesday, March 4. He was told that advisers were awaiting him in his office—C. D. Jackson, Jim Hagerty, Bobby Cutler, and Allen Dulles, Foster's younger brother, who had been appointed director of the CIA. The day was chill and wet. The President was cross when he joined the others an hour later: as he knew, his day was already crowded with urgent business, and now *this*. "Well," he demanded, "what do you think we can do about *this?*"

What, indeed? The world was in an anguish of dread over the imminent possibility of a nuclear Armageddon; in Korea bloody warfare was still in train; Eisenhower the Hero, only six weeks in office as President, stood at the head of all the forces of the free world, arrayed against the forces of darkness, and at this moment his evil adversary, the man reputed to rule an empire that stretched from the Baltic to the Sea of Japan, lay dying in the Kremlin. What to do? This was big stuff, end-of-an-era stuff, and the four advisers were tense with excitement and self-importance. All across the land Americans would be thankful, when soon they heard the news, that Eisenhower, the man trained to command and accustomed to great decisions, was their President in the White House. He would know what to do. He was a man of peace, everybody knew he was, and he would know how to achieve it.

What concerned Eisenhower, in this testing moment, was the lack of staffwork. At least since 1946, he complained, officials of the State Department and the Psychological Strategy Board had been gabbling about what might happen when power in the Kremlin shifted to new hands. But were there any plans? any studies? any course charted for the government to follow? He knew of none. Another charge to be laid against his predecessors, against the "mess in Washington." The lack of planning proved the value of Bobby Cutler's work with the NSC, and of C. D. Jackson's schemes of psychological warfare. How could Eisenhower decide what must be done when no plans had been devised for his approval?

In the event, the President and his advisers spent a couple of hours scribbling and then picking holes in a series of drafts of a likely statement for the occasion. Foster Dulles arrived to argue that no statement at all be issued. The group moved into the cabinet chamber to join the NSC, scheduled to meet that morning, and after another couple of hours a statement was released. It spoke for the American people to "all the people of the USSR . . . the children of the same God who is the Father of all peoples everywhere." Stalin was not mentioned by name. The statement was in effect a prayer, not for Stalin's recovery, but for intercession by the Almighty to bring the world "peace and comradeship." Directed as it was to a society whose constitution proclaimed atheism to be national policy, the prayerful statement was obviously also Cold War cant. It was followed by stiff, chilly "official condolences" after news of Stalin's death had been broadcast.

But no overtures of peace came from the White House.

They came instead from the Kremlin.

Rather than preside over the collapse of their government Stalin's successors, even as they busied themselves with their internecine struggles for hierarchical preferment, at once made it clear that they sought peace. Peace—or at least a détente—wherever in the world there was tension. Georgi Malenkov, the chubby politician who first and briefly was vested with Stalin's power, announced on March 15 in a speech to the Supreme Soviet: "At the present time there is no disputed or unresolved question that cannot be settled peacefully by mutual agreement of the interested countries." He added: "This applies to our relations with all states, including the United States of America," and his declaration was roundly cheered by the deputies. On the face of it, Eisenhower could scarcely have expected more, short of an engraved invitation, if he had truly desired to seek a peaceful accommodation with the Soviet Union. But in the spring of 1953 the security managers of the free world were wary of any talk of peace, and at once they began to intone their melancholy litany of reasons for avoiding any parleys with the Russians. "Nothing that has happened, or which seems to me likely to happen," said Foster Dulles, "has changed the basic situation of danger in which we stand." Malenkov, said a great many statesmen, must back up his "words" with peaceful "acts"—that is, he must make concessions of substance even before approaching the negotiation table. If the Russians say they want something, it necessarily follows that we must refuse it. We dare not launch negotiations until we are a great deal stronger. The Russian overtures are a deceitful trick, designed to get us to lower our guard, slow up or even stop our program of rearmament, and abort the European Defense Community. The Soviet peace offensive is "nothing but a pipedream."

So Malenkov's proposal went unanswered. (President Eisenhower observed that the United States had received no direct communication from the Kremlin.)

But the Russian peace offensive, so called, could not be wholly ignored. Given the intensity of the yearning for peace the world over, given the volatile mix of politics in the U.S. and the increasingly sullen temper of the British, the French, and those other allies whose support the U.S. was anxious to keep safe, it was plainly necessary to acknowledge the thrust for peace, even if possible to eclipse it. That task fell to the leader of the free world and he accepted it easily. It was essentially a staff procedure. Sherman Adams correlated a suitable audience and date for a speech on foreign policy—a meeting of the American Society of Newspaper Editors on April 16, a month in the future; Emmet Hughes was summoned and, after some preliminary conversation with the President ("The excitement of the man and the moment was," for Hughes, "contagious and stirring"), set to work drafting the speech; in consultation with C. D. Jackson, various functionaries in the State Department set about organizing the complex machinery for having the speech broadcast and reprinted in dozens of different languages. The speech itself evolved through more than a score of drafts and was in danger of succumbing to "the ambushes of policy debate and bureaucratic scrutiny." Dulles was leery of it, questioning the need of a speech entirely. Churchill, while hailing the text, counseled postponement. Once Eisenhower himself suggested scrapping it. All this was routine.

A few days before the speech was to be delivered the President was flown to Augusta National for some golf and relaxation. The night before its scheduled delivery he suffered another attack of his chronic ileitis (it was officially described as food poisoning, since his physicians had yet to make the proper diagnosis), and the next morning he was still in pain. Back in Washington for the ASNE luncheon, he was in worse pain than ever. On his feet to speak, his big hands tensely gripping the lectern, he was aware that he was sweating heavily and having chills. He was dizzy, he feared he might faint. His voice got slack and, toward the end of his paper, he was skipping sentences. Only iron resolve kept him going. He plowed through to a finish and even, after a brief rest, went on to Griffith Stadium to throw out the traditional first ball for the opening of the American League's baseball season. Then it was back to Augusta National, where once again he demonstrated his remarkable physical resilience: for the first time since his inauguration he shot a round of golf in less than ninety and on April 19 trounced Senator Taft by carding an eighty-six. In the clubhouse and later at Mamie's Cabin he could further rejoice because his speech had everywhere been hailed as evidence that the United States was once again assuming firm leadership of the free world and (less cause for celebration) because his speech was regarded as proof that the tenor of American foreign policy was the same under Eisenhower as under Truman.

The speech itself was a superior example of Cold War propaganda and should be placed in the context of that tension. One week before its delivery Dr. Konrad Adenauer, the seventy-seven-year-old chancellor of the West German Republic, had completed a state visit in Washington; he had warned the Senate Foreign Relations Committee to beware of Russian overtures, grimly declaring, "We must be prepared for the worst"; he and Eisenhower had joined in a communiqué in which they called on the Russians to allow free elections in East Germany and to liberate German war prisoners still in the USSR; the U.S. had pledged to supply West Germany with military equipment. Joe McCarthy's ineffable adjutants Roy Cohn and G. David Schine were at this time galloping around Europe, laboring to focus American attention on the menace of Soviet bolshevism.* Because in Korea the negotiations for an armistice seemed to be making hopeful progress, seventy-eight-year-old Syngman Rhee sent Eisenhower a protest "drastic in tone and extreme in its terms," threatening to sabotage any peace agreement. Rhee's expostulation was seconded from Taiwan by Generalissimo Chiang Kai-shek, both messages arriving just before Eisenhower was to make his major address on the chances for peace. No matter what he said, the belligerent pressures at home and from abroad remained constant, locking him into the martial posture of the Cold Warrior. What he said, stripped of the rhetoric he professed to disdain, was plain enough: if the Russians truly sought a general détente,

* In this season the red scare spread, increased in virulence, and plumbed new depths of absurdity. The management of a professional baseball team traditionally known as the Cincinnati Reds announced in all gravity that henceforth they would prefer to be called the Cincinnati Redlegs.

they should (1) sign the peace treaty with Austria, (2) release the "thousands of prisoners still held from World War II," (3) conclude "an honorable armistice in Korea" (the Russians had of course consistently denied responsibility for the warfare there), (4) agree to "a free and united Germany, with a government based upon free and secret elections," and (5) concede "the full independence of the East European nations." In return, the United States would agree to discuss how to reduce "the burden of armaments," any limitations and prohibitions to be enforced by "a practical system of inspection under the United Nations." In Eisenhower's view, he had pointed the path to "a golden age of freedom and peace." If the Russians did not exactly tumble over themselves to accept this approach, they did on April 25 give over the entire front page of Pravda to their reply, rejecting "preliminary demands" but repeating that they stood ready for "serious businesslike discussions of disputed problems both by means of direct talk and also in necessary cases within the framework of the UN." But in the White House nobody picked up the telephone.

Meanwhile the Korean War had stood in bloody stalemate, with the ground combatants and (except for Rhee) the statesmen on both sides thoroughly sick of it. Only the elite technicians of the U.S. Air Force, who flew bombing missions or at ultrasonic speeds strafed the countryside beneath them, still hankered for the experience, the promotions, and the extra pay that went with combat duty; only their morale still bubbled high. For a number of reasons the war was grinding to a halt. President Eisenhower knew his countrymen were anxious to have done with it; so was he. In February, at his orders, word had been discreetly passed that if the truce negotiations did not begin to show results, a few atomic weapons might, to use the jargon of the military, be wasted. The hint may or may not have been effective; President Eisenhower believed it was. An outstanding obstacle to final settlement was the disposition of war prisoners, with the U.S. steadfastly rejecting the concept of involuntary repatriation. (The issue was made to appear more ideological than it really was; in fact the prison camps of South Korea held many South Korean civilians, some indiscriminately seized during sweeps conducted to halt guerrilla activity, some who had chosen imprisonment as preferable to the struggle for existence in the wartorn land, and these people obviously wished to stay home.) When the U.S. commander late in February offered to exchange sick and wounded prisoners in accordance with the terms of the Geneva Convention of 1949, the truce negotiations were joggled off dead center. Once again, however, it was the death of Stalin that afforded the circumstance decisive to settlement of the war.

Chou En-lai, premier and foreign minister of the People's Republic of China, had traveled to Moscow for Stalin's funeral. There was opportunity to discuss with the new Russian leaders a revision of policy as to the Korean War. By the end of March, with Chou back in Peking, the Communists had announced proposals for resumption of the truce talks and repatriation of war prisoners "in accordance with the stipulations of the 1949 Geneva Convention." In turn Eisenhower had voiced a cautious optimism, and so had provoked the obduracy of Rhee, noted above. The truce negotiations had progressed, but because of Rhee they had once again commenced to sputter and stall. In Washington, Secretary Dulles used a background interview (a device to make public a debatable shift of foreign policy without identifying the responsible spokesman) to suggest that the U.S. would make peace in Korea if the Communists would agree to a boundary far north of the existing battlefront, giving South Korea about four thousand square miles of new territory. Rhee promptly denounced the proposal, and Senator Taft declared that any settlement based on a divided Korea would be "unsatisfactory," suggesting that nothing less than total surrender by the North Koreans would serve the purposes of the free world. Peking called attention to the "reluctance" of the U.S. to expedite the truce talks.

Early in May President Eisenhower convened a meeting of senior advisers in the White House to take stock. He had already told reporters at a news conference on April 23 that "there can be no real peace in Korea that ignores the other and broader problems in Asia." He had in mind the insurrection of the Viet Minh against the French in Indochina. On the same day, across the ocean in Paris, Foster Dulles had warned the ministers assembled for a meeting of NATO of "the carefully planned and prepared offensive which has now been launched in Laos. . . . We must assume," Dulles had added, "the continuance of hostilities in Indochina."* So any peace in Asia had to comprehend not one but two sets

---

* Dulles had also noted that the Indochinese hostilities were "a struggle in which the United States is also participating—very delightfully from a financial and end-item standpoint . . ." His paper to the NATO ministers had included the delightful financial figures:

Shipments of end-items		Offshore procurement contracts	
Fiscal 1951	$900 million		
1952	1,100 million	Fiscal 1952	$640 million
1953	3,000 million	Fiscal 1953	1,300 million
1954	3,600 million	Fiscal 1954	1,500 million
	(anticipated)		(anticipated)

End-items are commodities manufactured in the United States and sold to clients abroad. Offshore procurement describes commodities manufactured abroad under contract for use or purchase by the United States. Both phrases are Pentagon jargon.

of hostilities. (Three, if the insurrection against the British in Malaya is counted.) Quite apart from Rhee's determination to subvert any viable truce, there was the suggestion by the Chinese that they might seek, instead of the bipartisan truce talks to settle the dispute over prisoners of war, a multinational political conference. Of the two, the Chinese plan seemed the greater obstacle. All present at the session in the White House agreed with Eisenhower that the Reds were stalling and that their suggestion "should be flatly rejected." How to bring them swiftly to heel?

On May 10 and 11 U.S. bombers attacked the hydroelectric power plants on the Yalu River, the frontier between Manchuria and Korea. There were very few military objectives left in North Korea in 1953; a couple of years before, Major General Emmett O'Donnell, Jr., commander of the Far Eastern Bomber Command, had told the Senate Armed Services Committee: "I would say that the entire, almost the entire Korean peninsula is just a terrible mess. Everything is destroyed. There is nothing standing worthy of the name." To be sure, there were a score or more of irrigation dams, behind which was stored most of the water needed to produce the rice for North Korea, but the destruction of such irrigation dams had, as all military leaders everywhere well knew, been stigmatized as a war crime by the Nuremberg Tribunal. (Only the Nazis had ever ventured such an outrage, in Holland in 1944 and 1945.) Beginning on May 13, U.S. airplanes attacked five of those dams. Soon reconnaissance aircraft could photograph the havoc: the first flood had devastated twenty-seven miles of valley farmland.

Whether or not those bombs convinced, the Communist negotiators met U.N. objections, and the truce talks resumed under a full head of steam, leaving only the bellicose Syngman Rhee plunged in gloom.

Whose was the decision to destroy those irrigation dams? The responsibility—in the chain of command which Eisenhower throughout his career had so effectively fought to keep plain and clear—lay with the commander in chief, the President. But the decision itself: did it come from the commander in chief of United Nations forces in Korea, General Mark Clark? from his immediate superiors, the Joint Chiefs of Staff? or from a more exalted perch? The record is cloudy. Clark himself later wrote (obscurely, through the good offices of a ghost) of his authorization "from Washington . . . to carry on the war in new ways never yet tried in Korea," but it is not certain which came first, the authorization or the bombed dams, nor from whom the authorization issued. All those certainties lie locked under seal of the utmost secrecy, perhaps never to be discovered. Only the man of ultimate responsibility is known.

Even as the decision was being put into effect, around the world in London Sir Winston Churchill, having lost patience with the American refusal to initiate steps toward a détente, had taken matters personally in charge, with the magniloquence for which he was celebrated. Ever since Eisenhower's election Churchill had been seeking to establish with him the same easy intimacy he had enjoyed with Roosevelt, but with a signal lack of success. Eisenhower had none of Roosevelt's bravura, and it was exceedingly unlikely that Dulles would ever encourage him to adopt such a style. Churchill had been kept at arm's length. Early in March he had pressed for a conference of (reading from left to right) Stalin, himself, and Eisenhower, but the President had declined and then Stalin had died. Now ten weeks had passed and Churchill considered such a meeting to be even more urgent. "If there is not at the summit of nations," he told the Commons, "the will to win the greatest prize and greatest honor offered to mankind, doom-laden responsibility will fall upon those who now possess the power to decide." It was a reproof addressed to those who were "frightened" of informal meetings unless they could be assured in advance that positive agreements would result, a stern rebuke of Eisenhower and Dulles. Reaction to Churchill's speech was sharply divided. In Britain it excited enthusiastic approval, in Europe warm sympathy and interest, in the Soviet Union a cordial endorsement. On the other hand, the upper slopes of official Washington were ice-crusted. Harold Macmillan, then a minister in Churchill's cabinet, attended a party at which some of the staff of the American embassy expressed "alarm and almost indignation" over Churchill's speech. In Washington, reactions were as hasty and intemperate. Churchill, said Senator Knowland, was inciting "a Far Eastern Munich." The State Department, with Eisenhower's approval, issued a frosty statement commending Churchill's "high purpose" but demanding that the Russians provide "concrete evidence" that a high-level conference "would promote positive results" by first agreeing to a truce in Korea and a peace treaty for Austria. At his press conference of May 14 Eisenhower coldly rejected a summit conference. "I see nothing that you could really point to as definite evidence of good faith [on the part of the Russians]," he said.

But if Eisenhower did not choose to take part in a summit conference *with* the Russians, and so attempt an accommodation in the Cold War, less than a week later he was hurriedly scheduling a summit conference *without* the Russians, and the motive for his abrupt change of plans goes a long way to define more precisely what the President intended when he evoked a golden age of peace. For his motive in summoning the leaders of Britain and France into conference was to salvage the European Defense Community, an apparatus the Russians and many others feared as a provocation to war.

EDC was what Eisenhower, as supreme commander of SHAPE, had

labored to promote throughout western Europe. EDC was the device by which twelve or fifteen divisions of German troops could be marshaled, trained, armed, and put at the disposal of NATO. For what purpose? Ostensibly to oppose Russian aggression, but no responsible statesman could be found who seriously credited that threat as a real one. Meanwhile, the specter of another German army risen so soon from the bloody ashes of a war less than ten years old, the echo of der Stechschritt pounding on the cobbles and pave of cities from Minsk to Marseille, the nightmare memory of jackboot and Stuka, of Schutzstaffel and swastika—all these set the flesh acrawl in every land that had been invaded by the Nazi. Close observers could not decide where apprehension cut deeper, in the Soviet Union or in France. President Eisenhower had few if any compunctions about arousing alarm in the Soviet Union, but France was another matter.

For the men in the Kremlin, still struggling in the wake of Stalin's death to fix their hierarchical order, the most effective way of forestalling EDC —and the menace of a new German army—was to raise the possibility of a unity of East and West Germany. As early as March 31, 1953, they had announced (through General Vasily Chuikov, chairman of the Soviet Control Commission in Berlin) that "reunification of the country" would be "wholly and fully" in accord with Soviet wishes. (No response from the U.S.) Later the East German parliament had appealed to the British House of Commons for a conference of U.S., U.K., USSR, and France to achieve reunification. On April 24 the West German Bundesrat had refused to ratify the treaty establishing EDC; the rejection had been effected by the Social Democrats, who had argued that without EDC a unified Germany was still possible. Meanwhile, sweeping changes were afoot in East Germany, instigated by one faction within the Kremlin and promoted to enhance the possibilities of unification. The first steps were taken toward abolition of military control within the Soviet zone; the process of socialization was pushed aside; rumors circulated of credits to be extended by the state bank to promote private enterprise. The government of the United States could scarcely have been unaware of this ferment, for its webwork of intelligence agents reaching eastward from Berlin was far too well organized. At some level, however, intelligence was divorced from operations and even from contingency planning, for any rational use of intelligence would inevitably have led to negotiations with the Russians, and the logic of U.S. strategy dictated that the pressures of the Cold War be inexorably applied—especially at this moment, when conflict in the Kremlin might yet demonstrate the validity of the syllogism based on the death of Stalin.* By mid-May the West German Bundestag had ratified EDC and approval by the Bundesrat seemed assured. Only action by the French National Assembly was lacking.

On Wednesday afternoon, May 20, President Eisenhower thrust behind him the frets of a balanced budget and an adequate schedule of military procurement, the problems raised by Operation Solarium, the tensions of the Cold War, the difficulties of putting a halt to the war in Korea, and the caterwaulings of Senator McCarthy. For a few hours all this would, he hoped, be forgotten while he played a round of golf at Burning Tree.

Since he was naturally a cheerful and optimistic man, the President was confident that at least one of his problems might resolve itself. EDC, for example. The French premier, René Mayer, and foreign minister, Georges Bidault, had visited him in Washington a few weeks earlier; he had taken them for a jaunt down the Potomac on the presidential yacht, the *Williamsburg;* not a pleasure trip, strictly business, with the ambassadors to Washington from Vietnam and Cambodia holding themselves ready for consultation as required; lengthy negotiations, during which the President had agreed to help the French quell the insurrection in Indochina with massive transfusions of American arms and American money. (Presently word circulated in Washington that plans had been formulated to win the war in Indochina within two years.) In return for American military assistance in Vietnam, the President had sought assurances from the French on EDC. To be sure, Bidault had talked "on both sides of the question," but surely he recognized how vital to the free world was EDC?

---

* While the disposition in Washington was to move slowly or not at all, so also did it follow that Adenauer of West Germany and Walter Ulbricht of East Germany would resist unification of their divided zones. Adenauer was the leader of the Christian Democratic Union, a middle-class, right-wing political party that attracted the nascent industrial and commercial interests of West Germany; his ties to the U.S. were well established (his half-American wife was cousin to the wives of Lewis Douglas and John J. McCloy); the will of the United States ran parallel to his own. Ulbricht, boss of the German Socialist Unity party, was a thoroughgoing doctrinaire, zealously determined to hold power in rigid, dogmatic fashion and equally determined to resist any adversary, even a contrary faction in the Kremlin. Both Adenauer and Ulbricht would have been superseded, had Germany been unified in 1953.

Ulbricht countered the tentative Russian gestures toward unification by making it seem that the higher norms of production which he had espoused were tied in with the process of socialization, suddenly slighted by the Russians. The workers, who had wanted less toil and more socialism, were all at once confronted with more toil and less socialism. On June 15 they threatened a general strike in Berlin unless the hated higher standards of production were revoked; two days later riots broke out all over the Soviet zone of Germany, carefully fanned by radio programs broadcast from transmitters financed by the CIA; the Red Army promptly and bloodily intervened; and two weeks later President Eisenhower would permit himself some sardonic observations about "the workers' paradise" and how the "repressions of tyranny finally result[ed] in spontaneous revolt."

After all, the whole idea of EDC had been a French one—invented by René Pleven, the French premier back in October 1950.

At all events, on this soft May afternoon Eisenhower was happy to forget the whole thing. Out of his presidential duds, into some comfortable old clothes. Golf.

The President was on the back nine when he was interrupted by Bobby Cutler and Pete Carroll. They bore an urgent cable from Douglas Dillon, his ambassador in Paris, a message freighted with alarm. It seemed that René Mayer desperately needed an immediate meeting of the Big Three —U.S., U.K., and France—to shore up his waning prestige with the French Assembly. Indeed, already it might be too late to save EDC.

No more golf on this warm Wednesday.

By 6 P.M. Eisenhower, Cutler, and Carroll were in the President's oval office. C. D. Jackson joined them, and Beetle Smith, and other senior officials. (Foster Dulles was on a junket to the Near East.) Yes, to save EDC they had best book a meeting "at the summit"; perhaps the attendant fanfare would sway some votes in the Assembly. Transatlantic telephone call to Churchill, a distasteful task for Eisenhower, for some thought— and the President was one of them—that Churchill's dramatic speech nine days before, praying for peace, had been a mischief and had encouraged those among the French who wished to delay ratification of EDC. On the telephone a protracted gabble as to whether the captains of the free world should meet in Presque Isle, Maine, as Eisenhower preferred, or in Bermuda, as Churchill insisted. At length the two agreed to meet with René Mayer in Bermuda in mid-June, "to develop common viewpoints . . . on the many problems that must be solved cooperatively so that the cause of world peace may be advanced."

Eisenhower might as well have completed his round of golf. If the meeting had ever been held, there could have been no common viewpoint on the war in Vietnam, for René Mayer had already told General Henri Navarre, the French commander who had devised the plan which, it was hoped, would rout the Viet Minh, that France must seek a "sortie honorable" from Indochina; but American strategists would not agree until after at least another twenty years of bitter fighting that the time had come to talk of honorable withdrawals. Nor could the discrepant viewpoints on EDC have been composed. Indeed, Mayer's government collapsed the very next day, or as soon as the premier let it be known that he proposed to begin a debate on EDC in the National Assembly. During the next five weeks, four different aspirants would attempt to form a government and each would fail because of EDC, which came to be known along the Quai d'Orsay as the "cadavre dans le placard"—the corpse in the cupboard; in the meantime the Bermuda conference was postponed again and again, pending the selection of a premier to represent France. The fifth hopeful, Joseph Laniel, a dour Norman conservative who won a vote of confidence on June 27, was able to do so only by virtue of a remarkably discreet ministerial statement that suggested he meant to keep the corpse on ice and well hidden. By that time the Bermuda conference had been indefinitely postponed for quite another reason: on June 23 Churchill had suffered a second stroke; his condition steadily deteriorated; by June 27 the end seemed near; he rallied, but it was plain that he could attend no conferences at the summit for several months.

The protracted failure of the French to form a government, a shift to the Left in Italy strong enough to threaten the coalition government of Alcide de Gasperi, the strained relations between the U.S. and Britain—these were developments to test the free world's alliance, and they were all the effects of the thaw that followed upon Stalin's death. Macmillan noted in his journal: "It looks as if Europe was breaking up under Malenkov's sunshine. Stalin's icy blasts kept it together." Even as he wrote, Anglo-American friendship was being more sorely tested, in the Near East.

There remained the war in Korea, and the closer it inched toward eventual armistice the more obstreperous were those who would be happy with nothing less than a crushing defeat of the North Koreans and the Chinese who had come to their aid. They comprised a notably fractious and essentially negative company. Rhee was their ranking ideologue, and their number included American generals who could not abide the thought that they would go down in history as commanders of troops who had not conquered the gooks, and right-wing Republicans who could not forget that their platform in 1952 had assailed the Democrats Truman and Acheson for "ignominious bartering with our enemies," yet who now glumly witnessed the Republicans Eisenhower and Dulles doing precisely the same thing. Anything that would have torpedoed an armistice would have delighted these men. From May 25 onward the South Koreans boycotted the armistice negotiations; when on June 8 the biggest roadblock to peace —repatriation of war prisoners—was surmounted, Rhee at once organized street demonstrations in Seoul against the truce; on June 17 Rhee again raised objections to the entire procedure of peacemaking, in a long letter to Eisenhower full of fearful alarm; and the next day he capped all his earlier disruptions by ordering the guards to turn loose more than twenty-seven thousand inmates of South Korean prisons, thus effectively demolishing the agreement on war prisoners that had been so painfully constructed.

Reaction to this demented exploit varied widely, separating the prudent from the reckless. When Dulles was waked around 2 A.M. by a conscientious duty officer at the State Department and told of what Rhee had done, he was consternated. He had warily acquainted various Asian statesmen—Nehru of India was the most recent—of U.S. determination to use atomic weapons unless an armistice could be contracted without undue difficulty. Now, because of Rhee, the armistice was in grave jeopardy. What if the other side were forthwith to cancel further negotiations on the reasonable grounds that the United States was unable to honor any agreements to which the South Koreans were party? Would atomic weapons remain an item on the agenda? In short, could Rhee's aberration precipitate the holocaust? Dulles decided to telephone the President, although what Eisenhower could do about the matter at 2 A.M. was at best conjectural. The news likewise disturbed the President, but he was able to resume his slumber. The two men met later that morning to canvass the situation. It was disconcerting, but much depended on the exercise of good sense by the accursed Communists.

Rhee's action was viewed with sympathy by General James Van Fleet, former commander of the U.S. Eighth Army in Korea and Eisenhower's West Point classmate, and by General Mark Clark, commander in chief of U.N. forces on the scene. (Clark had already urged the Joint Chiefs in Washington to permit Rhee to release those prisoners of war who were not to be repatriated, and to release them "without further screening or explanations," which was essentially what Rhee had done. Clark was now obliged to lodge severe complaints with Rhee.) In Washington, Senator McCarthy went further. He said that "freedom-loving people throughout the world should applaud" what Rhee had done. His statement called to mind one of the catchwords of that paranoid time, "Better dead than red."

The President was of course aware of these pressures (and of others, like the swell of protest over the imminent execution of the Rosenbergs, and the explosion of tension in East Germany, both of which were in train at this same time), but he also fully recognized that the need of the moment was to get Rhee behaving properly before he could make matters, if possible, even worse. What, for example, if Rhee were to pull the South Korean troops out of the line? They manned two-thirds of the front: if they were abruptly pulled back, the Americans and the other U.N. forces could be easily overrun. Or what if Rhee were to order the South Koreans to attack, and so effectively scuttle the truce? Eisenhower on June 18 cabled a stern rebuke to Rhee, warning him that he must "immediately and unequivocally" accept the authority of the U.N. command or—what? There was little room for maneuver. Eisenhower could only lamely threaten that he would "effect another arrangement." Next day he was constrained to remind his cabinet that the principal enemy in Korea was, despite appearances, still in the north.

An assistant secretary of state, Walter Robertson, was dispatched to Korea to bridle Rhee. He succeeded, but only after promising Rhee well-nigh everything the old man could think of as conditions for his good behavior: a mutual security pact, hundreds of millions of dollars in food and outright economic aid, an agreement that the U.S. would join South Korea in shunning the political conference scheduled to follow the armistice if that conference did not promptly agree to South Korean demands, and other concessions, some in treasure, some in prestige. He might have got still others, but on July 9 the Communists launched a sharp offensive against that part of the line held by the South Koreans, pushing forward several miles along a broad front. Those losses served to remind Rhee of his vulnerability if he tried to go it alone, and on July 11 he publicly promised his support for the armistice.

Rhee's tactics had cost the U.S. dearly. (U.S. arms were then suffering more than a thousand casualties a week, and as Clark would recall, "the maddening part of it was that we had been virtually in complete agreement . . . on the truce terms" when Rhee released the prisoners.) He had protracted the war for forty days and Eisenhower had rewarded him with valuable concessions. If Truman and Acheson had dared to offer a truce like the one now to be signed the Republican howls would have been savage; as it was, the right-wing Republicans were sharp in their dispraise of Eisenhower and Dulles. Senator Knowland was asked, "Is this a truce with honor that we are about to get?" and he answered, "I don't believe so."

As the time appointed for the signing of the truce documents approached, Eisenhower's usual confidence and optimism deserted him. He was to hear on Sunday night, July 26 (Washington time), of the signing; on the preceding Friday and Saturday nights he departed from his custom by staying up till long after midnight, talking with friends. He labored over the statement he planned to broadcast as soon as the truce was signed. He telephoned Hagerty to ask whether he should conclude his message with a sentence pinched from Lincoln's second inaugural address ("With malice toward none, with charity for all . . ."). Hagerty approved. Eisenhower added it. Still he fretted. Republican orators would one day point proudly to the peace in Korea as a chief, perhaps *the* chief achievement of Eisenhower's first six months in office; once again a Republican had plucked the nation from a bloody shambles into which it had been plunged by the Democrats. Though he would make the same boast, Eisenhower knew better.

Word from Panmunjom reached the White House at 9:38 P.M., and at 10 P.M. the President was speaking to the country by radio and television. "My fellow citizens: Tonight we greet, with prayers of thanksgiving . . . an armistice . . . the cost of repelling aggression . . . incalculable . . .

paid in terms of tragedy . . . to prove once again that only courage and sacrifice can keep freedom alive upon the earth . . . widows . . . orphans . . . veterans who bear disabling wounds . . . valorous armies of the Republic of Korea . . . inspired by President Syngman Rhee . . . carnage of war . . . must be vigilant . . . free peoples one step nearer to their goal of a world at peace. . . ."

Someone had given the order to bomb the irrigation dams at Toksan, Chasan, Kuwonga, and Toksang. Someone had authorized what he knew to be a war crime.

Next day the President dictated to his secretary of state a memorandum on Korea. It was full of ideas about assistance to that ravaged land. Four days later the President sent similar memoranda to his secretary of defense and to his Mutual Security administrator.

"He'll sit here," Truman would remark (tapping his desk for emphasis), "and he'll say, 'Do this! Do that!' *And nothing will happen.* Poor Ike—it won't be a bit like the army. He'll find it very frustrating."

On September 30 the President, who had then been back in Washington from his summer holiday for about three weeks, sent memoranda to his secretary of state, his secretary of defense, and his Mutual Security administrator reminding them of his earlier memoranda, now two months old, and praying them to inform him of action taken.

Nothing happened. The secretary of state was busy with other affairs, and so was the secretary of defense, and so was the Mutual Security administrator. Korea was in the past.

Suez (I) and Iran (March 4, 1953—August 5, 1954)

Anthony Eden, once again the British foreign minister, arrived in Washington in early March, simultaneously with the word of Stalin's mortal illness. He had come, as he explained later, "mainly to discuss economic matters," and sure enough, presently Jim Hagerty began to hand out press releases having to do with the convertibility of pounds into dollars within fixed limits of fluctuation, current trade accounts as against accumulated sterling debts, and other such arcane matters which would be printed, if at all, somewhere back in the financial pages of the newspapers. But in fact Eden had more pressing affairs on his mind, which were not deemed suitable for public contemplation. The communiqué issued following his conversations with Eisenhower and Dulles "said little, as is usual with such documents."

The statesmen were concerned with the Middle East. Their conversations, pursued for nearly ten days, were exceedingly delicate for both parties, since the principal item on the agenda (although of course it was never cited as such) was the passage of imperium, the transfer of responsibility from Britain to the United States for the care and feeding of that strategically vital region of the world. Under the crust of that region lay the greatest part of the world's known deposits of petroleum; through one end of it had been carved the Suez Canal, for seventy years a British preserve and an essential link to the wealth of India and other British colonial possessions; it was chiefly inhabited by Arabs but now suddenly cradled as well the vibrant and squalling infant state of Israel. The exchange of imperium in this region would be no easy matter.

As recently as 1950 British leaders had fancied that Britain "was still a Great Power" in the Middle East, but events had swiftly punctured the illusion. First in May 1951 came the Iranian decision to nationalize the oil fields, installations, and refineries of Anglo-Iranian Oil, then in October the summary expulsion from Iran of all Anglo-Iranian's British employees, under shaming circumstances.* Only a week after the departure of the British from Abadan, the Egyptian prime minister denounced the twenty-year Anglo-Egyptian treaty of friendship and alliance, which still had five years to run. This latter development was in Eden's view "more forbidding" than any of the setbacks in Iran, not least because the Egyptians would shortly be demanding expulsion of the British from the vast military base along the banks of the Suez Canal—a base three miles wide and sixty-five miles long, comprising workshops, stores of munitions and supplies, hospitals, airfields, encampments, and all the gear to sustain and equip an army of eighty thousand troops. Because of these events, the British balance of export-import payments began calamitously to slump, and a government fell, and as Churchill once again became Her Majesty's first minister Britain began to sense that the days of her imperial glory, with all its appurtenances of wealth and power and leisure and cultivation, were in eclipse.

With the passing months the nationalist ferment throughout the Arab world seethed, taking on a strong antimonarchist flavor. Farouk, the obese, corrupt, and profligate king of Egypt, was forced to abdicate in July 1952 when a group of army officers headed by Major General Mohammed Naguib staged a successful coup d'état. And the day Eden arrived in Washington was the fourth day of violent rioting in Teheran, the violence

---

* "It is difficult," Harold Macmillan wrote in his diary at the time, "to conceive any procedure more calculated to destroy the last vestige of British prestige."

capping weeks of tension as Premier Mossadegh sought to assert his authority over the young shah of Iran, Mohammed Reza Pahlevi.*

Upon Eden's arrival, Eisenhower at once plunged into a discussion of the Middle East. He was, Eden noted, "extremely worried about the position in Iran." The President remarked that the American ambassador, Loy Henderson, had so far committed himself in support of the shah that Mossadegh might well request his recall; in any event, it might be necessary to replace Henderson with an envoy who was "less compromised." Despite Henderson's open intervention on behalf of the shah, Eisenhower still believed Mossadegh to be "the only hope for the West in Iran." When Dulles observed that Mossadegh was certain to reject the most recent Anglo-American proposals to resolve the dispute over oil, the President said there was a man in whom the Iranians had confidence, his good friend Pete Jones of Cities Service; he could be sent to Iran with authority to get the oil flowing again. That would be far better than permitting Soviet Russia to gain a foothold in Iran. If that happened, Eisenhower feared either the loss of Middle Eastern petroleum reserves or the threat of another world war. Eden was skeptical, but reported to Churchill that Eisenhower "seemed obsessed by the fear of a communist Iran."

The conversations proceeded, but at one remove from the President's office. Bedell Smith got involved in them, lending them the expertise of a man who had recently had charge of the CIA; Eden was impressed with Smith's "deft and ingenious" contributions to the discussion. The Americans persisted in dreading that Mossadegh would somehow associate himself with the Russians. Eden was dubious, arguing that Iranian policy was rather to play off the great powers one against the other; but the Americans, trapped in their anticommunist myopia (a condition to which Senator McCarthy was still making signal contributions), could not be diverted. In the end there was agreement: to find, as Eden delicately phrased it, "alternatives to Musaddiq."

"The difficulty of this situation," Eden telegraphed to Churchill, "remains that the Americans are perpetually eager to do something. The President repeated this several times." It was a difficulty that Eden would perceive again, coupled with "a desire to reach a quick solution at almost any cost and . . . a pathetic belief that, once agreement was reached, all would be well." He would also detect "an apparent disinclination by the United States Government to take second place even in an area where

---

* Eisenhower chose to refer to Mohammed Reza as the "constitutional monarch" of Iran, a phrase suggesting dynastic tradition and juridical stability. In fact, the young man was the son of Reza Khan, a Cossack soldier who in the early 1920s had muscled his way from the ministry of war to a military dictatorship, finally being named shah and seizing the ancient Peacock Throne. His fellow feeling for Hitler had led in 1941 to his ouster and exile, his young son becoming shah in his stead.

primary responsibility was not theirs," but on this score one must take into account the natural sensitivities of a proud power in the process of being unceremoniously demoted to juniority.

Eden's other chief concerns were the British base along the Suez Canal and, in general, the arrangements for a Middle Eastern defense organization. Eisenhower promptly agreed that the maintenance of the base was mandatory, that for the British to abandon the canal zone before a strong defense establishment had been guaranteed was unthinkable. "In contrast to Dulles," Eden advised Churchill, Eisenhower "was clear and firm on this point." Once again Eisenhower asked Eden to take up the details with Dulles; once again the conversations were continued at a lower level. What was in dispute was (as between the British and the Egyptians) how quickly and completely the British would depart from Egyptian soil and (as between the Americans and the British) how best to come to terms with the Egyptians. The British earnestly desired their devoted allies to join with them, act together, agree on policy as it affected Egypt and the Middle East. "The President could not have been more friendly," Eden noted, but there were troublesome differences, and as the months dragged on those differences widened from cracks to chasms. To Eisenhower (at the time and as he blandly recalled these matters years later), the only point at issue was the propriety of American participation in discussions of the British presence on Egyptian soil unless the Egyptians wished the United States to participate and invited them so to do. In short, purely a matter of protocol. To Eden, to Churchill, and to other ministers of the Tory government, Eisenhower's seemly diffidence was eyewash. They appreciated (as no doubt so did the President and his advisers) that Egypt desperately wanted American military and economic assistance, and that in consequence to wangle an invitation from General Naguib would be a simple matter. Soon the British realized that other, more invidious influences were at work. American policy in the Middle East, the British reluctantly recognized, was based on the conviction that Britain was a colonial oppressor of sinister cast; the Americans believed, if the stock of the United States were not to slump sharply on the Middle Eastern exchange, they must keep the British at arm's length.

How had this come about? It was based on advice given Eisenhower by Dulles, advice which in turn derived from a sympathetic interpretation of Arab nationalist ambitions, deduced by Dulles from the reports of veteran American diplomats assigned to posts in the Middle East. Of these, the American ambassador to Egypt, Jefferson Caffrey, may be regarded as representative. Caffrey was a respected career officer of the foreign service who had been in Cairo since 1949; he had skillfully kept open his lines of communication to the successive leaders of Egypt while retaining his concern for the plight of the masses of wretched Egyptian fellahin. The British mistrusted him; for his part he believed the sooner the British were out of Egypt, the better off the Egyptians would be.

Dulles visited the Middle East, Pakistan, and India on a hurried three-week tour during May. His trip started off with a gorgeous example of the sort of blunder that got the State Department so disliked around the world during President Eisenhower's two administrations. The mixup began with the notion that Dulles present, on Eisenhower's behalf, a gift to the king of Saudi Arabia, a man who controlled the disposition of an incalculable wealth of petroleum. A brief pause ensued while various anonymous desk officers in the department reconsidered. No, they at length decided, no: better the gift were tendered General Naguib as a leading figure of the Muslim world. To Eisenhower the message was relayed (someone along the line having apparently been stricken with a head cold) that an appropriate gift from one celebrated warrior to another might be a gold revolver. The suggestion baffled the President. Gold revolver? What, he asked his secretary Ann Whitman, what is a gold revolver? Ordnance not being her field of special competence, Mrs. Whitman shrugged dubiously. In his turn the President shrugged. By gold revolver, he decided, the Department must have meant a revolver with a gold inscription plate—to hell with it, let them do what they want. The gold revolver, it developed a few days later, was a *Colt,* a Colt .38, and the gift, when it was finally presented, was the worst of diplomatic gaffes: the British were outraged, considering it symbolic of an American intention to arm the Egyptians despite any agreement to the contrary reached with the British.

On Dulles's return, he jotted down his "Conclusions on Trip," which were duly passed along to the President. His memorandum included some memorable comments:

> British position rapidly deteriorating, probably to the point of non-repair . . . we find an intense distrust and dislike for the British . . . no respect for the French as a political force . . . United States position also not good . . . [This last was attributed to the American policy of friendly support for Israel, and to the tendency of the Arabs to associate the U.S. with British and French "colonial and imperialistic policies."]
>
> . . . Also, almost entire area caught in fanatical revolutionary spirit that causes countries to magnify their pro[b]lems and depreciate soviet threat. . . .
>
> . . . Efforts by the U.S., which by natural inclination and self interest finds itself somewhat in the middle between the British and Near Eastern positions, are increasingly resented by British. They interpret our policy

as one which in fact hastens their loss of prestige in area. To some extent, regardless of efforts to the contrary on our part, this may be true. . . .

Such reflections did not conduce to American eagerness to be allied with the British in negotiations over the Suez Canal base. Churchill was vexed and let Eisenhower know as much. By mid-June Eisenhower's ambassador in London, Winthrop Aldrich, was telegraphing to report that Churchill feared the President might in his turn be nettled, since his last two messages to Eisenhower had gone unanswered. The prime minister urgently suggested that the proposed Bermuda conference be held without further delays. (The French were still attempting to form a government.) But Eisenhower was more reluctant than ever to meet with the British alone; he instructed Dulles to have Aldrich advise Churchill to resume negotiations with the Egyptians, and further to explain to Aldrich that while the Americans had earnestly sought to build a Middle East Defense Organization akin to NATO, they had now ruefully shelved the plan as impractical. A few days later the whole matter was postponed indefinitely when Churchill suffered his stroke.

The question of the military base along the banks of the Suez Canal was left in abeyance. Throughout 1953 British soldiers were waylaid by Egyptian extremists, some kidnapped, others killed. The policies of the great powers could not be suitably reconciled.

The policies of the United States and Britain as regards Iran were more easily composed. Once Eden had recognized that the solution involved American participation in the exploitation of Iranian oil resources, discussions had moved forward amicably. ("The Americans," Eden had noted, "were properly reluctant to appear in the role of securing commercial interests for themselves.")

It is appropriate to preface an account of the solution in Iran with a text. It is taken from President Eisenhower's celebrated address to the American Society of Newspaper Editors, delivered at the Statler Hotel in Washington on April 16, 1953, and broadcast to the nation by means of radio and television:

"Any nation's right to a form of government and an economic system of its own choosing is *inalienable*.

". . . Any nation's attempt to dictate to other nations their form of government is *indefensible*."

It will be recalled that early in March, Eden, Dulles, Beetle Smith, and others had agreed to look for "alternatives to Musaddiq." By the time the President spoke at the Statler, the search for alternatives was well under way. The suitable studies were in train, the suitable intelligence being assessed. Mossadegh, it appeared, had won the enmity of large landowners (several of whom held seats in the Iranian senate) because he had announced plans for a sweeping land reform; he had disaffected several general officers of the Iranian army; he had antagonized Ayatollah Kashani, a mullah who, as speaker of the Majlis, had led the most extreme nationalists. The ground looked to be well cultivated and admirably provided with the basic necessities for a swift, smooth coup d'état. Indeed, already at least one abortive putsch had been staged by a tribal princeling in the south of the country, and there had followed isolated acts of terrorism, most of them giving evidence of a bizarre if rather grisly imagination. A majority of the Majlis supported Mossadegh, but his opposition, growing in confidence, was able to convert it into an instrument of obstruction. Even the strong man to unite the opposition was not lacking; he was an army officer, a hard case called Fazollah Zahedi. A caviling critic would have found in General Zahedi, considered purely as a champion of the free world's interests, one or two trifling flaws. He had been a Nazi collaborator during the war and had been imprisoned for those sympathies when Iran was occupied by the British and Russians. He still harbored an intense antipathy for the Russians, which was appropriate, but also for the British, which was regrettable. More to the point, however, he enjoyed the support of those Americans involved in ironing the wrinkles out of Iranian affairs.

Late in May, when his nation's hardships began to seem insupportable, Mossadegh appealed to President Eisenhower for help, pleading that the boycott of Iranian oil imposed by Anglo-Iranian and faithfully maintained by the international oil cartel was still further impoverishing an already wretched people. (In Iran at this time infant mortality was five hundred of every one thousand live births.) Iran had the oil, but since she had no technicians, no markets, and no transportation, she had no revenues. "We are of course grateful," Mossadegh wrote, "for the aid heretofore granted Iran by the Government of the United States." Iran had been among the first to receive U.S. aid under President Truman's Point Four program—one million dollars in FY 1951, raised to twenty-three million in each of the last two years of Truman's administration. Now the axe had fallen. "For example," Mossadegh indicated, "the Export-Import Bank which was to have advanced Iran twenty-five million dollars for use in the sphere of agriculture did not do so because of unwarranted outside interference. . . . I invite Your Excellency's sympathetic and responsive attention to the present dangerous situation of Iran . . ."

The appeal might have been more tactful. The hint of possible Iranian recourse to the Soviet Union might have been dropped. At all events, President Eisenhower waited a month and a day and then, in an eight-hundred-word letter, said no. The United States, he made clear, stood behind Anglo-Iranian in its boycott of Iranian oil. If Iran wished to improve its economy, the answer lay in reaching a "reasonable agreement" with the British "whereby the large-scale marketing of Iranian oil would be resumed." In short, no.

Meanwhile, Mossadegh had had some success in selling petroleum to Italy and, even more significant, to Japan. Such commerce made the boycott look unexpectedly shaky. When Mossadegh elected as well to deal more forthrightly with his opposition in the Majlis, he handed Washington the pretext it had been waiting for. Yielding to the pressure of his own National Front Party, Mossadegh announced that he would "place the question of dissolution or continuance of the Majlis before the people for decision." The people, the ultimate sovereign, would decide the question by referendum: on August 3 in Teheran, on August 10 in the provinces. The result was an overwhelming popular mandate for Mossadegh— something on the order of 98 percent.

When the vote in Teheran was tallied, President Eisenhower was in Seattle to speak to a conference of governors. The spread of communist influence in Asia and the Middle East was much on his mind. He spoke of Indochina and Indonesia, both vital to the security of the United States. "Iran," he added, "is in a weakened condition. I believe I read in the paper this morning that Mossadegh's move toward getting rid of his parliament has been supported and of course he was in that move supported by the Tudeh, which is the Communist Party of Iran.* All of that weakening position around there is very ominous for the United States . . . somewhere along the line, this must be blocked. It must be blocked now. . . ."

Blocked now. Two or three days later Brigadier General Norman Schwarzkopf turned up in Teheran. In the 1940s Schwarzkopf, who had once commanded the New Jersey state police, had been assigned the job of training police troops for the shah; he was back now, he said, "just to see old friends again." Zahedi was one of his old friends and, by coincidence, Zahedi picked this time to drop from sight. He went into hiding in, it was suspected, the U.S. embassy. Schwarzkopf's arrival rattled Mos-

---

* The Persian word "tudeh" means "in the hills." It appears to have been adopted as a name by the Iranian Communist party at the time that party was outlawed a few years earlier. At this critical time in Iranian affairs, the Iranian Communist party was, in the view of at least one competent observer, "totally paralyzed by its pronounced dependence on the Soviet Union." Four months earlier, Mossadegh had himself ordered the jailing of many Tudeh leaders; and even now, in August, he could not bring himself to collaborate with the Tudeh initiatives. The Tudeh, however, pressed its support upon him.

sadegh's adherents. An editor of a Teheran newspaper commented: "Grave danger threatens our country. Eisenhower's words are not empty threats; they are already being turned into deeds. . . . The conference with the Shah of General Schwarzkopf, who is in the CIA, is not without significance . . . and is certainly not an accident." Schwarzkopf provoked the alarm, but the CIA agent in charge was Kermit (Kim) Roosevelt, a grandson of President Theodore Roosevelt. Kim Roosevelt had slipped into Teheran unnoticed several days earlier, and had promptly stitched together a small team of conspirators—CIA men from the embassy and trusted Iranian intelligence operatives.

The director of the CIA, Allen Dulles, had taken plane to Switzerland to supervise the conspiracy personally; Loy Henderson met him for a discussion of last-minute procedures. The hour approached.

On Thursday, August 13, the shah signed a rescript dismissing Mossadegh and naming Zahedi as premier. Confusion. The shah and his queen had withdrawn to his summer palace on the Caspian Sea; it would seem the conspirators had hoped to arrest Mossadegh and transport him there too. Delays. At length at 1 A.M. on Sunday, August 16, the commander of the shah's bodyguard, Colonel Nassiri, appeared at Mossadegh's residence to deliver the decree. Nassiri headed an armed party and found the house guarded by government troops. Dismay, disorder, a skirmish. Nassiri was arrested. The nocturnal conspiracy had failed. The shah and his queen fled the country to Baghdad and thence to Rome.

Ambassador Henderson cabled a report to Washington on Monday: the shah believed Mossadegh "absolutely mad and insanely jealous, like a tiger who springs upon any living thing that it sees moving about him." As for the shah, he needed a job; he had a large family but no money; he dreamed of coming to the U.S.; his morale was low. "An American" had assured him Zahedi could not fail in his intrigue, but he had failed, all had failed.

President Eisenhower was in Denver on a summer holiday. Henderson's cable was delivered to him, together with a memorandum from Beetle Smith. The plan had failed, Smith wrote, because the Iranian army generals had vacillated for three long days. Now, said Smith, we may "have to snuggle up to Mosadeq if we're going to save anything . . . I daresay this means a little added difficulty with the British."

But all was not yet lost.

Basically, to stage an effective counterrevolution, two ingredients were required: the support of the army and a willing mob. So far the army had been loyal to Mossadegh. It had been trained and equipped by the United States, though, and there was much the Pentagon could do to swing it back of the conspiracy. Major General George C. Stewart, director of the Office of Military Assistance, Department of Defense, later testified:

> . . . when this crisis came on and the thing was about to collapse, we violated our normal criteria and among the other things we did, we provided the army immediately [with supplies] on an emergency basis. . . . [We] created an atmosphere in which they could support the Shah. . . . The guns that they had in their hands, the trucks that they rode in, the armored cars that they drove through the streets, and the radio communications that permitted their control, were all furnished through the military defense assistance program. . . . had it not been for this program, a government unfriendly to the United States probably would now be in power.

As for the willing mob, such a commodity was easily purchased in Teheran, and at a reasonable price. One authority has it that Kim Roosevelt's Iranian agents emptied the athletic clubs and steam rooms of Teheran, producing a pride of weight-lifters, gymnasts, wrestlers, and assorted musclemen who paraded through the bazaars braying pro-shah slogans and gathering great crowds along their way. Another authority speaks of "a lumpenproletarian mob, armed with knives and clubs," moving on the center of the city. There is here no essential discord. All agree the uprising brought riots, terror, violence, bloodshed, death. As to the cost, accounts vary. One careful analyst cites the sum of nineteen million dollars as the expense to the American taxpayers for ousting Mossadegh from the office to which he had been elected. Another expert cites evidence adduced at the subsequent trial of Mossadegh showing that on August 18 American agents had cashed "check No. 703,352 of the Melli Iran Bank made out in the sum of $390,000 to Edward G. Donally for 32,643,000 rials," in order to have plenty of Iranian currency available. The sum seems not to have been sufficient, for trustworthy witnesses recall taxi drivers and chauffeurs who flourished dollar bills, their payment for fetching the mob here and there, to demonstrate on demand.

A tank bearing General Zahedi rumbled up to Mossadegh's house and its cannon demolished the structure. The premier surrendered to police a day or two later. The shah nerved himself to return to his homeland on August 22.

President Eisenhower had been kept informed of these developments, and he was content. He was officially notified of the success of the operation on August 21 by Lieutenant General Charles P. Cabell, USAF, deputy director of the CIA. Presently Beetle Smith passed along a memorandum conspicuously unsigned and undated, urging the President that it was "worth your reading." (Presumably the memorandum came from Kim Roosevelt.) Two sentences are worth quoting: "The Shah is a new man. For the first time, he believes in himself because he feels that he is King of his people's choice and not by arbitrary decision of a foreign power."

No question about it, President Eisenhower was hugely delighted. He cabled his congratulations and best wishes both to the shah and to the new premier, General Zahedi. He promised Zahedi "sympathetic consideration" of his request for "immediate financial aid" and on September 5 sent him forty-five million dollars.

On September 23 President Eisenhower, in an unpublicized ceremony, awarded to Kermit Roosevelt the National Security Medal.

On October 8 the President dictated an entry for his "Personal Diary." "The things we did [in Iran]," he wrote, "were 'covert,'" and he went on to acknowledge that the United States would have been embarrassed if the part played by its agents in the conspiracy had been publicly known. He added that "our agent there, a member of the CIA, worked intelligently, courageously and tirelessly. I listened to his detailed report and it seemed more like a dime novel than an historical fact."

With the access to power of General Zahedi, changes occurred. Newspapers were suppressed, printshops raided and shuttered, books confiscated, censorship instituted, prominent editors and other journalists jailed and in some cases killed. Mossadegh's ministers and members of the National Front were arrested, as were thousands of their supporters. Mossadegh himself was sentenced by a military court to three years in solitary confinement; his foreign minister was executed; his minister of justice had his eyes gouged out, and he died in jail. Countless communists were executed; many army officers met the same fate. At the University of Teheran students and faculty grew accustomed to sudden nocturnal arrests; on at least one occasion police agents shot unarmed students to death.

Of conditions by the end of 1953, Eisenhower wrote: "For the first time in three years Iran was quiet—and still free."

The most important of the changes in Iran concerned the exploitation of petroleum resources. What had to be done was to arrange compensation for Anglo-Iranian, form a consortium of international oil companies, insert the American companies into the midst of that consortium, guarantee the American companies a free and clear passage through the tortuous channels of American antitrust legislation, and gradually reabsorb the flow of Iranian oil into the world market without upsetting the delicate balance of price and supply. All this called for heroic work, and the hero who stepped forward to make a miracle was Herbert Hoover, Jr., son of the former Republican President, a geological engineer who earlier had advised the Iranian government on the development and production of its oil. Hoover was named special petroleum adviser to Secretary Dulles.

(Dulles perfectly understood the complexity of the negotiations, for the law firm of which he had been senior partner—Sullivan & Cromwell— had long been counsel for both Anglo-Iranian and Standard Oil of New Jersey.) There was at first some slight difficulty when it was learned in London that someone in the State Department had conceived the idea of forming one big American company which would buy out Anglo-Iranian and take over the entire concession. If the step was proposed as a means of sidestepping the antitrust laws, it failed, for the American oil companies rejected it and the British likewise quickly expressed their concern. In the end the National Security Council, with President Eisenhower in the chair, summoned up the magic phrase "national interest" and recommended that American participation in the consortium not make the companies liable to prosecution. The Department of Justice produced the necessary ruling. The five American international giants—Jersey Standard, Mobil, Texaco, Gulf, and Standard of California—got 40 percent of the concern developed to operate the nationalized industry on behalf of the Iranian government; Anglo-Iranian (it is now called British Petroleum) was able to retain 40 percent; Royal Dutch Shell (of which the British government owns a substantial part) was given 14 percent; and the Compagnie Française des Pétroles got 6 percent. Iran was to share equally with the consortium in the profits. Complaints from representatives of American companies which had failed to get a slice of the pie were at first coldly dismissed with the comment that such dissent only served the interests of international communism; when the outcries persisted, the five big companies yielded 5 percent to be divided among some eight lesser companies, and all concerned relaxed, having reduced the risk of charges that the Iranian settlement served the interests of the international oil cartel.

The settlement was to be signed in August 1954, and for his reward Hoover was to be named undersecretary of state, succeeding Beetle Smith. While Iranian production of petroleum was gradually increased and fitted into the world's markets, at a rate that would not jeopardize world prices, the United States government (the American taxpayers) would shovel something in the neighborhood of a quarter of a billion dollars into Iran to keep the military dictatorship solvent and stable. In effect, the United States government would supply a generous subsidy to more than a dozen American oil corporations so that they might restrict and control production in Iran.

None of this was astonishing. More than a dozen American oil corporations and their officers had generously helped to elect the President in the White House. All parties agreed in their commitment to freedom, anticommunism, and the American way of life.

Civil Rights (I) (January 20, 1953–May 17, 1954)

On taking office, Dwight Eisenhower presided over more than one hundred and fifty-six million Americans. Of these some sixteen million, a little more than 10 percent, were Negroes.* For two hundred years or more the Negroes had struggled to free themselves from slavery and from something even more pernicious—the belief, widely held by white Americans, passed along to their children, and so poisoning the ethos of American society, that Negroes are brutish creatures forever shackled by racial taints into a condition of moral and intellectual inferiority. Two Democratic Presidents had for a generation exerted a degree of leadership to end these prejudices, but the powerful influence of the southern Democrats, entrenched by seniority in their consequential congressional posts and appreciably abetted by their conservative Republican friends of the North, had served to interdict any substantial legislative remedy. The pressure of the Negroes and their white allies against the reactionary coalition of southern Democrats and northern Republicans mounted in the postwar years. How could it be otherwise? Negroes had fought for the United States. Were equality of employment, housing, education, the vote, the right to share in the profits accruing from exploitation of the postwar world still to be denied them? Young Negroes, hard of fist and tough of resolution, would be damned if they would continue to accept second-class citizenship.

President Eisenhower, once supreme commander of so many Negro soldiers, was not unaware of the pressure. What he underestimated was the intensity of it and the reaction to it, and how they were impelling the nation toward tragedy. Nor did he at first appreciate that the struggle for civil rights was not simply a domestic issue but an international one, compromising the moral posture of his administration and American leadership of the free world in the Cold War.

The question of how best a President should handle the matter, so intimately affecting one in ten of the nation's citizens and to some extent contaminating the humane impulses of the other nine in ten, has never been satisfactorily answered. As for Eisenhower, procedure began with what he called his "philosophy on this subject." It went like this: "I believe that political or economic power to enforce segregation based on race, color, or creed is morally wrong and should by all practicable and reasonable

* The term of choice in the 1950s was still Negro. Not until late in the next decade would preference shift to the term black, and since it would be inaccurate to exercise the preference retroactively, the term Negro will be used here.

means be abolished as soon as possible. . . . There must be no second-class citizens in this country." To this can be added, from his first message on the state of the union: "I believe with all my heart that our vigilant guarding of these [civil] rights is a sacred obligation binding upon every citizen. . . . We know that discrimination against minorities persists . . . This fact makes all the more vital the fighting of these wrongs by each individual, in every station of life, in his every deed."

In line with his reluctance to offend the Congress, the President proposed to restrict his every deed to the authority of his own office, by ending segregation in the District of Columbia, including the federal government, and also segregation in the armed forces. Having declared his intentions, Eisenhower entrusted the workaday details to his staff and turned his attention elsewhere.

Some of his staff procrastinated. Some were in any case unwilling to lift a finger to end discrimination. In general they were agreed that the President was an essentially decent man, that he had proclaimed an essentially decent goal, that he had set an essentially decent example for the rest of the nation, and that there the matter might rest. At this time there were no Negroes on the White House executive staff. (There never had been, under any President.) Directly after Eisenhower's election, however, a Negro had been invited by Governor Adams to join "the team." He was E. Frederic Morrow, a lawyer with twelve years' experience as field secretary for the National Association for the Advancement of Colored People (NAACP), who had been given leave from the job he then held with the Columbia Broadcasting System to join Eisenhower's campaign train. Adams told Morrow that both he and Eisenhower wanted him with them in Washington, and a letter from Adams confirmed the offer. Maxwell Rabb, one of Adams's assistants, advised Morrow to quit his CBS job, and he did, but then for several months while Morrow spent his savings, and Rabb let Morrow's telephone calls go unanswered, and the White House complacently neglected the persistent pressures of the Negro minority, nothing happened. Six months after Morrow had been told to resign his job at CBS, he was told by Bernard Shanley that there was "nothing available for [him] in the White House." It says much about the temper of the President's associates that Eisenhower would later tell Morrow of "a threat that the President's staff would walk out in a body the day [Morrow] walked into the White House."*

---

* Morrow was at last appointed an administrative assistant in July 1955. He found the other members of the staff cold but correct. Most of the stenographers in the White House pool (all white) at first flatly refused to work for a black man, but there were one or two who gave the others a proper example. More than three years later Morrow was officially administered his oath of office. That was on January 27, 1959, and President Eisenhower, who usually attended such ceremonies, was ab-

Before turning to an account of how the President and his staff handled the problem of civil rights, it may be useful to recall something of Eisenhower's childhood and career, considered particularly as they helped to shape his feelings and beliefs about Negroes.

In Abilene, when Eisenhower was growing up there, he used to play black man, or crack the whip, or shinny. "Our games at that time always seemed to involve running," his brother Edgar said later. "It is only a happy boy that does those things." None of the children who happily played black man was a Negro, though, for no Negro families lived in Abilene. Likewise when he went to West Point, Eisenhower found himself amid white men exclusively; then and in the years that followed, the friendships he formed like as not were with southern officers, and he slipped easily into their habits of speech and thought. Thus in a letter to his son, sent from North Africa in February 1943, he would write: "I . . . find myself living in a comfortable house, nicely heated, and staffed by Mickey [McKeogh] and a group of darkies that take gorgeous care of me." (The term "darky" was one specifically proscribed in a War Department booklet issued in 1942 to help officers command their troops more effectively.) Nevertheless, in Britain, in North Africa, and later in France, Eisenhower was at pains to ensure that the treatment of Negro troops and white troops was evenhanded. When the Allies needed tens of thousands of riflemen to carry out Eisenhower's plan for a major counterattack in the Ardennes, it was suggested that Eisenhower invite the Negro troops in the supply services to volunteer for the infantry and fight in the same command with white troops. He agreed. He had a circular drafted in which he pledged Negro volunteers they would be assigned for service in infantry units without regard to color or race. Beetle Smith, when he saw the circular, at once sent Eisenhower a sharp note characterizing it as "most dangerous . . . in regard to negro relations" and in violation of the War Department policy of segregating blacks from white troops. Eisenhower conceded that he would prefer not to "run counter to regs in a time like this" and personally rewrote the circular (Negro volunteers were segregated into platoons commanded by white officers and white noncoms). In April 1948, while Eisenhower was president at Columbia and also serving an occasional chairman of the Joint Chiefs of Staff, he was invited to testify before the Senate Committee on the Armed Services on a bill calling for both a military draft and universal military training. Eisenhower supported both proposals, but the senators took him afield in their questioning. They wanted his views on segregation in the army and

---

sent. "The White House," Morrow noted in his journal, "is a little embarrassed about me."

what the army was doing about it. He recommended all-Negro platoons within larger white formations. ". . . if you make a complete amalgamation," he said, "the Negro is going to be relegated to the minor jobs, and he is never going to get his promotion . . . because the competition is too tough." A regional conference of the NAACP was in session at the time, and the delegates reacted promptly and angrily. Their resolution charged Eisenhower with virtually endorsing racial segregation.*

In short, like the vast majority of Americans, Dwight Eisenhower was a man who had lived most of his life almost completely insulated from his black fellow citizens; his prejudices about Negroes, like those of most white Americans, were rooted more in intellectual laziness than in positive conviction; unlike most Americans, Dwight Eisenhower was goaded by conscience to give play to his best impulses, and those impulses, nourished by the religious training of his childhood and youth, were sturdy.

During the first weeks of his administration, President Eisenhower was reminded of the problem chiefly at his press conferences by Alice Dunnigan, a reporter for the Associated Negro Press. Whenever she was recognized by the President, Mrs. Dunnigan stood ready with questions about segregation in schools on army posts (quickly corrected) or about the Committee on Government Contract Compliance, a group named by Truman for the purpose of eliminating discrimination by companies which held contracts with the government (Eisenhower promised action very soon; sixteen weeks later he appointed a new committee). But after the press conference of May 28 Mrs. Dunnigan found it difficult to catch the President's eye.

By coincidence, one week later, on June 4, a front-page story in the *Washington Evening Star* touched off a pother in the White House. Whether deliberately or no, the President displayed his temper, with the result that the staff at once sprang into belated activity. The newspaper story that had provoked the President was based on a telegram sent him by Representative Adam Clayton Powell, Jr., Democrat of New York. Powell had made public his telegram, for he feared that otherwise it might never have reached the President's desk. The burden of Powell's telegram was that Eisenhower's avowed policy of ending segregation in the federal establishment was being flouted by his subordinates in the army and navy, the Veterans Administration, and the Department of Health, Education and Welfare. "The hour has arrived," Powell told the President, "for you

* Some years later Eisenhower was still troubled by the testimony he had given that day. He told Frederic Morrow that before appearing on Capitol Hill, he had made it his business to seek advice from old friends in the Pentagon as to what he should say. Subsequently, when he recalled whose advice he had solicited, he realized that every one of them had been officers whose roots were in the Deep South.

to decisively assert your integrity. You cannot continue to stand between two opposite moral poles."

The temptation to answer Powell by calling him a liar was strong, and one or two White House aides were eager to succumb to it; luckily for Eisenhower it was resisted, for Powell's case, if not airtight, was substantial. Adams's assistant Max Rabb was now designated the man in charge of minority affairs (no one had earlier been assigned such a specific responsibility) and instructed to decontaminate the area forthwith. A veteran at mollifying indignant congressmen, Rabb adroitly placated Powell with flattery and promises, and persuaded the secretary of the navy, Robert Anderson, a native of Texas, to order an end to segregation on navy bases in Norfolk, Virginia, and Charleston, South Carolina.

Rabb's quick footwork had won for the administration time and room for maneuver.

Meanwhile, responsive to the spirit of the times, the Supreme Court had moved decisively against discriminatory practices. An opinion in early June that opened restaurants in the District of Columbia to well-behaved and respectable patrons no matter what their race or color was unanimously endorsed. On that same "decision Monday," though, the court reserved decision on five actions that challenged the constitutionality of segregation in the public schools. The justices wanted more time for reflection and study; they wanted, as well, a brief from the attorney general that would include his opinion on the intent of the Fourteenth Amendment to the Constitution (". . . No State shall make or enforce any law which shall abridge the privileges . . . of citizens of the United States . . . nor deny to any person . . . the equal protection of the laws"). The request presented the administration with a splendid opportunity to register the weight of its influence in the scales of justice, but the President was not entirely happy with the invitation.

When the Eighty-third Congress adjourned on August 4, the President could turn his thoughts to a brief holiday in Colorado. His Democratic adversaries, being out of office and hence separated from the public trough, would have it that he was too long and too often on holiday. They sought to create the illusion of a President preoccupied with golf rather than with affairs of state, a man more off than on the job. Perhaps such criticism was merely uninformed. We have already noted how closely in touch he had been, while in Colorado, with the violent changes in Iran; mention has been made of how Dulles was brought west to confer with him at length on security policies of a most solemn character (these included the dangerous reliance on "nonconventional weapons," and the need to abate that emphasis; the disposition of U.S. forces abroad and the risk of suddenly recalling them, even though they were an irritant in the lands where they were stationed; the desirability of renewing efforts to relax world tensions, perhaps to begin with "mutual withdrawals of Red Army Forces and of United States Forces"; and the advisability of better informing the public of the destructive potential of atomic and hydrogen bombs). The President used this holiday, as well, to do some hard thinking about segregation, discrimination, and associated matters. A couple of days before he was flown to Denver he had given a radio report on what was called the "Achievements of the Administration." "We have used the power of the federal government," he had claimed, "to combat and erase racial discrimination and segregation—so that no man of any color or creed will *ever* be able to cry, 'This is not a free land.'" Others, hearing those brave words, had not been convinced. An editorial in the *Washington Post* had seized on the President's assertion with the comment that "relatively little has been done" to guarantee equality of opportunity. Rabb had taken a marked copy of the newspaper to Eisenhower's desk. "Mr. President," he had said, "someday they will eat their words." The President had grunted. "We'll see," he said.

In his temporary offices in the administration building at Lowry Air Force Base near Denver, Eisenhower considered the problem. He was aware that the Democrats had got a lot of mileage out of the issue. He wanted to collar a good part of the Negro vote, but he knew it would not be easy. The course of his calculations can be charted with some precision.

On Thursday, August 13, he announced through Jim Hagerty the formation of a President's Committee on Government Contracts to replace Truman's Committee on Government Contract Compliance. New name, new members, new aims. Vice President Nixon would be chairman, to emphasize its prospective status; the vice chairman would be a Negro attorney, J. Ernest Wilkins (later to be appointed assistant secretary of labor). Eisenhower himself added to the committee a southerner, John Minor Wisdom, who was the GOP national committeeman from Louisiana. And while Truman's committee had been advisory and honorary, Eisenhower's was to be given power to enforce his policy of ending discrimination in the hiring policies of any company under contract to the federal government—a vast if conjectural commitment.

On Friday, August 14, he wrote a lengthy letter to his old friend James F. Byrnes, who after having held a succession of powerful posts in various Democratic administrations had retired to sulk as governor of South Carolina. From that eminence Byrnes had proclaimed his apostasy from the Democratic party and his warm approval of Eisenhower and the Republicans. Now Eisenhower wrote Byrnes that he had been puzzling over the question of segregation in the schools and the larger question of equal opportunity. He believed that those who insisted that reform could be brought about only by federal laws and federal police power were mistaken. His oath of office, Eisenhower argued, reinforced his own convictions that he was obliged to weed out discriminations within the area of federal responsibility. Would Byrnes not perhaps get in touch with those governors of southern states who agreed that to cooperate with the federal government was a Good Thing?

Byrnes's reply was sour and grudging. Yes, he agreed that pupils in the schools of the Charleston Navy Yard should not be segregated as were those in the public schools of South Carolina, but no, he could not agree with the President's recent order forcing compliance on private companies that did business with the government. It smacked to Byrnes of a Fair Employment Practices Committee, and he reminded the President that it was because of Democratic advocacy of FEPC that he himself had publicly embraced Eisenhower in 1952. He considered that a presidential order backed by the purchasing power of the federal government was a Bad Thing. If Eisenhower wanted an FEPC, at least he should have it legislated by the Congress, not enact it by executive fiat.

On Wednesday, August 19, even before he had digested Governor Byrnes's retort, Eisenhower was busy dictating for his diary a private memorandum on the "Responsibility of the Attorney General to provide a factual brief on the segregation of pupils in primary schools." The President was against it. He felt that such a brief, especially as it involved the attorney general's opinion on the intent of the Fourteenth Amendment, was properly the responsibility of the Supreme Court itself, and one which the court should neither abdicate nor evade.

On Wednesday, August 19, so long as he was on the subject, the President dictated another memorandum for the record, this one on "Party organization in the southern states." Question had been raised whether a committee of southern Republican politicians chaired by John Minor Wisdom of New Orleans was to be formal or informal. No matter, urged the President (who was so constantly charged with a lack of interest in Republican party affairs), no matter; what signified was that Leonard Hall, recently elected GOP national chairman, should at least establish how best Republicans might prosper in the South.

To prosper, to get votes: there was the rub, for how could the Republicans hope to highjack a healthy share of the Negro vote up North and at the same time prosper down South, where a constituency existed solely at the pleasure of the dominant whites? It was the old dilemma of principle versus expediency. The President wavered but then grasped the nettle firmly.

On Friday, September 4, he sent a letter to Nixon, enclosing his correspondence with Jimmy Byrnes. "No man is discharging his full duty," he wrote Nixon, "if he does nothing in the presence of injustice, even though these matters might not be suitable ones for punitive legislation." He still preferred example and persuasion to the force of law; he would rather establish "criteria that are dictated by decency and fairness." He advised Nixon to issue a statement of intentions as soon as possible to disarm critics like Byrnes wherever they might be, North or South. In short, he counseled Nixon to do it for him.

Suddenly chance presented the President with another surrogate. On September 8 the chief justice of the Supreme Court, Fred Vinson, died suddenly of a heart attack, and within three weeks Eisenhower had appointed Governor Earl Warren of California in his stead.

The choice provoked a mixed reaction, one that can best be suggested by the fact that Eisenhower's brother Edgar assailed the appointment as a surrender to the Left while Eisenhower's brother Milton reported he had heard Warren was the nominee of reactionaries. To Edgar the President wrote: "From the very beginning of my acquaintanceship with [Warren], I had him in mind for an appointment to the high court—although, of course, I never anticipated an early vacancy in the chief justice position. . . . Well—here is a man of national stature, of unimpeachable integrity, of middle-of-the-road views, and with a splendid record during his years in active law work." To Milton the President wrote that Warren was "very definitely a liberal-conservative; he represents the kind of political, economic, and social thinking that I believe we need on the Supreme Court." It was absurd, he added, to think that reactionaries had recommended him.

The President was dismayed by the mixed reception, and also by the rumors that came to him that he was simply paying off a political debt. If those rumors had reached him, he knew, they must also have reached Warren and so have robbed the prospective chief justice of his joy in the occasion. Eisenhower let off steam by dictating a memorandum to be entered in his private diary. He had, he said, at once ruled Dewey out of consideration for the post both because he was too political and because he was obviously Eisenhower's political sponsor. But there was "no possibility of charging that [Warren's] appointment was made as payment for a political debt," since Warren had not released his delegates at the national convention until after Eisenhower's nomination had been a certainty. Eisenhower believed Warren would "restore the prestige of the Court." Moreover, he pledged that when Warren's confirmation came up before the Senate in January: "If the Republicans as a body should try to repudiate him, I shall leave the Republican Party and try to organize an intelligent group of Independents, no matter how small."

Warren's recess appointment enabled him to join the court immediately and take part in the work of the autumn session. In November the attorney general filed a brief amicus curiae, as he had been requested to do; he argued strongly that the Fourteenth Amendment forbade racial segregation in public schools and that the Supreme Court was empowered to resolve the issue; in December an assistant attorney general, J. Lee Rankin, joined lawyers of the NAACP to argue the case before the court.

In January 1954 Eisenhower sent Warren's nomination to the Senate. For several weeks it was delayed in the Committee on the Judiciary; it was confirmed on March 1 by a voice vote without opposition.

The chief justice sent the President a note on March 19 to express his thanks for the appointment. Four days later the President replied warmly, in his own hand. "I congratulate the nation," he wrote, "which is so fortunate as to have such a dedicated, able and devoted public servant." And week after week, on "decision Monday," the press room of the Supreme Court building filled with larger numbers of reporters awaiting an opinion in the case of *Brown* vs. *Board of Education of Topeka, Kansas* and associated cases involving the public school systems of Delaware, South Carolina, Virginia, and the District of Columbia. For fifty-eight years the rule of law had been that the Fourteenth Amendment was not violated if Negro children were provided "separate but equal" facilities for education; on the basis of that rule seventeen southern and border states (and the District of Columbia) had compelled segregation in their public school systems, while four others (Kansas was one) had permitted segregation.

On Monday, May 17, 1954, it was clear that something extraordinary was afoot. Rather than being told to wait for the court's opinions to be handed them in the press room, as was the custom, the reporters were ushered into the august marble court chamber to hear an opinion read by the chief justice himself, "in a firm, clear voice and with expression." The lofty hall was hushed, the audience tense, as the chief justice approached the nub of the court's unanimous opinion. "We come then," he said, "to the question presented: Does segregation of children in public schools solely on the basis of race, even though the physical facilities and other 'tangible' factors may be equal, deprive the children of the minority group of equal educational opportunities?" An infinitesimal pause. "We believe," said the chief justice, "that it does." One of the reporters present, I. F. Stone, wrote that it "was all one could do to keep from cheering, and a few of us were moved to tears." Stone singled out one sentence from the lengthy opinion. "To separate them [Negro children]," said the chief justice, "from others of a similar age and qualifications solely because of their race generates a feeling of inferiority as to their status in the community that may affect their hearts and minds in a way unlikely ever to be undone." Specifically, as to the fifty-eight-year-old rule of law, the court decreed: "Separate educational facilities are inherently unequal . . . segregation is a denial of the equal protection of the laws."

Reversal of the rule of law stunned most of the politicians and newspaper editors of the South. Reversal stunned President Eisenhower, too. He had sworn to uphold the Constitution, and he recognized that the justices of the Supreme Court were the acknowledged interpreters of the Constitution, and he could never forget that the chief justice was his man, and yet—he personally thought the decision was wrong, and he was not persuaded by the reasoning that had convinced the nine justices of the Supreme Court. Before long he would be characterizing his nomination of Earl Warren as "the biggest damfool mistake I ever made," a more abrupt turnabout than was usual even for Eisenhower. His immediate reaction was glum. The day after the court's astonishing decision he summoned the commissioners of the District of Columbia to the White House and urged them to see to it that Washington set an example for the rest of the country in the integration of the pupils in public schools. A day later, to the reporters at his press conference, he said simply: "The Supreme Court has spoken and I am sworn to uphold the constitutional processes in this country; and I will obey."

The soldier had been given his orders. Whether he approved them or not was irrelevant. He would obey.

CHAPTER THREE

Exacerbation of Crisis

Still suffering McCarthyism . . . Harry Dexter White, J. Robert Oppenheimer, and the great Red hunt . . . The nuclear deterrent . . . Festering Vietnam . . . EDC and the "agonizing reappraisal" . . . "Massive retaliation" . . . The domino theory . . . Counterrevolution in Guatemala . . . SEATO.

ONE THING AND ANOTHER—the Bricker amendment, the propaganda battles with the Soviet Union in the Cold War, Suez, Iran, the settlement in Korea, EDC, the riots in East Germany, the war in Indochina, the execution of the Rosenbergs, the protracted debate over a proper policy for military expenditures as against the need to reduce the budget, the emergence of Red China as a world power, the insistent civil rights pressures—these were some of the matters that provided President Eisenhower with a convenient justification for disregarding the troublesome behavior of Senator Joe McCarthy. No matter how flamboyantly that eponym for the gritty anxieties of the time seemed to bestride the world's affairs, the President was concerned with tasks that seemed to him graver and more demanding of his attention. Nor does the list cited above by any means exhaust the catalogue of his troubles during the first months of his administration. In July 1953 the American economy had begun to sag into a recession of the kind that was guaranteed to disconcert a Republican President who could recall the days of Herbert Hoover; by April 1954 trade union leaders were demanding more forthright action by the federal government, and Eisenhower was talking about how the nation had reached the point of no return. Moreover, and even more painful, the government of the USSR had announced on August 20 (while Eisenhower was on his "working vacation" in Colorado) that a hydrogen bomb had been exploded experimentally, and the Atomic Energy Commission had at once confirmed that a Russian thermonuclear device had indeed been tested eight days earlier. The President remarked at a press conference: "Now, the knowledge that they have this bomb is, of course, an acute one for the Defense Department. I should say that it is a fact that is probably causing each of us more earnest study—you might say almost prayerful study—than any other thing that has occurred lately."

But no matter how exacting or how endless the problems that challenged the President, it was not always possible to ignore McCarthy and McCarthyism. Sometimes the President would be dragged into a turmoil McCarthy had precipitated; sometimes he or one of his lieutenants would be driven to act or speak in order to show how the administration was more effective than McCarthy at throttling subversion; sometimes members of his staff, impatient with the President's refusal to flatten McCarthy, would maneuver him into an apparently adversarial position; once, almost inadvertently, Eisenhower himself seemed for a moment to tilt a lance at McCarthy.

This last incident occurred on the campus of Dartmouth College in June 1953, when the president spoke informally at commencement exercises. At the time confusion was at its height over the policies of the International Information Administration and the libraries it maintained overseas to acquaint foreigners with the United States. Books by distinguished authors alleged to be communists were being removed from shelves, proscribed, hidden or burned, replaced, and generally shuffled about in dutiful response to McCarthy's vague but ominous charges. At first Foster Dulles issued no directive; when at length he did it was at once withdrawn for a series of revisions. "We were all working in the dark," said an IIA official later, "and making fools of ourselves." Around the world arose a shrill protest against McCarthy, against the burning of books. At Dartmouth, Eisenhower said:

"Don't join the book burners! Don't think you are going to conceal faults by concealing evidence that they ever existed. . . .

"How will we defeat communism unless we know what it is . . . ?

"And we have got to fight it with something better, not try to conceal the thinking of our own people. They are part of America. And even if they think ideas that are contrary to ours, their right to say them, their right to record them, and their right to have them at places where they are accessible to others is unquestioned, or it isn't America."

Clear enough; but three days later the President compounded confusion by first telling his press conference, "I just do not believe in suppressing ideas," and then adding, ". . . if the State Department is burning a book which is an open appeal to everybody in those foreign countries to be a Communist, then . . . they can do as they please to get rid of them"—which, while muddled as to syntax, was plainly a sanction of book burning in certain circumstances. Further, he refused to say that he had intended to criticize McCarthy. Yet at his next press conference he was provoked when a reporter insisted that he had expressed approval of burning some books.

A couple of weeks later, a half dozen of the President's senior aides got caught up in a grotesque two-day intrigue designed to discredit McCarthy because a newcomer to the senator's staff had written an article for an obscure right-wing magazine in which he had charged that the "largest single group supporting the Communist apparatus in the United States today is composed of Protestant clergymen." To dissent from such nonsense was about as difficult as to protest the pox, but nevertheless his senior aides congratulated each other once they had got the President's signature on a message of complaint.

The full measure of the administration's sensitivity to McCarthyism began to be taken in the fall of 1953. At a cabinet meeting late in September, Summerfield and Brownell—perhaps thinking of the off-year elections due in five weeks—raised the question of making a public announcement of the number of cases disposed under Eisenhower's Executive Order 10450, the one establishing his new improved program of security. Nixon chimed in: a public announcement would be invaluable, since the issue of communism had caused so much anxiety during the campaign of 1952.* In October the cabinet agreed: publish the current results of

* It had done no such thing (see page 480).

the security program, to show evidence of progress by the Republicans in ousting undesirable persons from the government service. On October 23 (ten days before election day) Hagerty announced on behalf of the President that in the first four months of Eisenhower's security program one thousand four hundred and fifty-six persons had been dropped from the federal payroll and all but five of these, it was said, were holdovers from the Truman administration.

One thousand four hundred and fifty-six *spies? Communists?* Well, no, Hagerty had not exactly said *that*. On the other hand, he had not said they were *not* all spies or communists. The matter was left in the air. Whatever they were they had been "separated" from the federal establishment by Eisenhower, not by Truman; by the Republicans, not the Democrats. Before long, here came Senator McCarthy to talk on a nationwide network of television and radio stations about "one thousand four hundred and fifty-six Truman holdovers who were all security risks," for what might one expect from "a discredited politician" whose administration had been "crawling with communists"?

The controversy generated by Hagerty's release rapidly became known as "the numbers game." The rules were that Democrats denounced and Republicans reproachfully testified to the truth of, and the White House kept cautiously hedging. Meanwhile the Democrats won most of the off-year elections, which may have proved this or that but did not noticeably disturb Eisenhower. "I have lost skirmishes before," he told the reporters, and they laughed.

That was on Wednesday, November 4, the day after the elections. On Monday, November 2, the day before the elections, Brownell had told Eisenhower of another matter he believed should be made public. Someone in the Department of Justice (most likely someone in the FBI) had handed him a file that purported to show there had been subversive activity in the Truman administration and, further, that high-ranking officials in the White House had been aware of it. Brownell particularly implicated a former assistant secretary of the treasury, Harry Dexter White, whom Truman had later appointed executive director of the International Monetary Fund. The evidence against White was so clear, Brownell told the President, that he considered it his duty to make it public.

White? Harry Dexter White? Had Eisenhower ever heard of him? His associates had always been struck with the fact of Dwight Eisenhower's accurate and retentive memory, and particularly by his ability to recall names, dates, historical events. Eisenhower had met Harry Dexter White. He had lunched with him and Henry Morgenthau in June 1944, and while no busy man can be expected to remember every casual acquaintance he has met during a crowded decade, that lunch had been a special occasion, at which had first been discussed what later came to be called the Morgenthau Plan for a punitive treatment of postwar Germany. It had been said, indeed, that Eisenhower was the man who had inspired the Morgenthau Plan, and many of his friends, anxious to keep his image bright amid the gathering shadows of the Cold War, apprehensive of how such tales might dim his prospects for the presidency, had been at pains to deny that Eisenhower was in any way associated with the Morgenthau Plan. No, they had said; no, it was Harry Dexter White who had conceived that scheme. At all events, it seems likely that White's name was known to Eisenhower.

On Thursday, November 5, the President telephoned the attorney general. Yes, said Brownell, he proposed to make his public pronouncement on the case of Harry Dexter White next day in Chicago, in a speech to the Executives Club. Brownell had already gone through the proper channels. He had checked his speech with Jim Hagerty.

Who was Harry Dexter White? He was a scholarly economist and expert on fiscal affairs. Together with Maynard Keynes of Britain he had negotiated (1942–1944) the monetary agreements signed at Bretton Woods, New Hampshire, and had planned for the United Nations the International Monetary Fund and the International Bank for Reconstruction and Development (the World Bank). Later (1945) the same two men had concluded a comprehensive agreement on proposals for the expansion of world trade, including the establishment of an International Trade Organization. In short, White and Keynes had collaborated to design the structure of postwar capitalism that would keep the free world fiscally integrated until the whole thing came unstuck in August 1971. The structure he had helped to devise would endure for a quarter-century —no mean monument.

In 1947 White had resigned his position with the International Monetary Fund because of ailing health. He was then fifty-five years old; he had a cardiac condition.

In 1948 White had been accused of espionage by two confessed traitors —Whittaker Chambers and Elizabeth Bentley—both of whom had earned a reputation for paltering with the truth. In March 1948 White had testified before a federal grand jury, which later refused to indict him. On August 13 he had denied to the House Committee on Un-American Activities that he had ever been a communist or had ever been involved in espionage. On August 16 White had collapsed and died of cardiac failure.

On Friday, November 6, 1953, Herbert Brownell said to the Executives Club, in part: "Harry Dexter White was a Russian spy. He smuggled secret documents to Russian agents for transmission to Moscow. Harry Dexter White was known to be a Communist spy by the very people who appointed him to the most sensitive and most important position he ever held in government service." He added that the FBI had sent a report on White's "espionage activities" to the White House; that Truman had nevertheless nominated White to the International Monetary Fund; that a second FBI report had been prepared "for delivery to the President" but that "the Senate Banking and Currency Committee was permitted to recommend White's appointment . . . in ignorance of the report," and that "the Senate itself was allowed to confirm White . . . without . . . being informed that White was a spy."

It is difficult to conceive of a graver charge—in effect, one lodged by a President of the United States against his immediate predecessor. Harry Truman had never backed away from a political brawl, and he waded into this one swinging wildly. On Tuesday the ugly affair was given an uglier twist when Harold Velde, the congressman who had become chairman of the House Committee on Un-American Activities, presumed to issue a subpoena which was served on Truman during the latter's visit to New York. Eisenhower had not expected that development and, not least because he was quick to appreciate how the action might cause a revulsion of the public mood to his own damage, he strongly disapproved. At 9:15 the next morning he once again telephoned Brownell, to make clear that he deplored the serving of a subpoena on Truman. The President had one other tidbit for the attorney general. Brownell had not specifically said that Truman had personally seen the FBI reports, only that they had been sent to the White House "for delivery to the President." But now Eisenhower had knowledge of that final step: the evening before, Dulles had informed him that a search of State Department files had showed that, yes, the report on White had in fact reached Truman's desk and attention.

The President then turned his attention to a routine, the briefing by Hagerty and others of his staff on questions that might be raised by reporters at his press conference, scheduled for 10 A.M. in the Executive Office Building. One subject for questions dwarfed all others. The occasion afforded one last opportunity, if it were necessary, for someone to remind Eisenhower of his acquaintanceship with White. Then, fifteen minutes late, the quick walk from the White House to the building across the street.

One hundred and seventy-five reporters were on hand for this twentieth of the President's press conferences. Only nineteen minutes had passed before Eisenhower abruptly strode out. Those nineteen minutes were electric with tension and a wholly uncustomary hostility. Twice the transcript notes that there was [Laughter], but each time the laughter was derisive. There was time to put twenty questions; eighteen of them had to do with Brownell's charges.

The President was never asked anything directly about White. Twice he volunteered references to White, as follows: ". . . a man named White, a man whom I had never met, didn't know anything about. . . . [The attorney general] did mention the word 'White' although as I say I didn't know who White was." A third reference to White bobbed up when the President gave his account of the events leading up to Brownell's speech. By this time Eisenhower was quite angry. He said: "Ladies and gentlemen, I am going to answer my last question right now on this subject for this morning, at least. I told you exactly, Mr. Brownell . . . reported to me . . . evidence that there had been subversive action in which high Government officials were aware of it; he gave me the name as Mr. White, and he . . . said, 'Certainly, I am not going to be a party to concealing this,' is the way he explained it to me. I said, 'You have to follow your own conscience as to your duty.' Now that is exactly what I knew about it."

The reporters showed their distaste for the entire affair (one of them characterized it as "pretty squalid"), but they pressed the President closely. Was the FBI report justified in calling White a spy when a grand jury had refused to credit the FBI evidence? The President refused to comment. Should Brownell have impugned the loyalty of a former President? The President pounced. "You said Mr. Brownell impugned the loyalty of a President. I don't know—certainly he never told me—that he said that the President of the United States ever saw the papers. He said they went to the White House. Now, that is all he ever told me, and I think you have made a mistake." Who had made a mistake? The President was asked about the propriety of an attorney general offering information from the files of the FBI to a luncheon club in Chicago rather than to a grand jury or a committee of the Congress. The President brushed the question aside. He was asked whether it was proper for a man never indicted by a grand jury and now dead to be characterized by the attorney general as a spy, and for the attorney general further to accuse a former President of harboring that man. "I am not either a judge nor am I an accomplished lawyer," the President replied. "I have my own ideas . . . but . . . the attorney general is here to answer it himself. Let him answer it." Mr. Leviero, of the *New York Times*: "He has refused to answer the questions, you see." [*Laughter*]

In short, a stormy nineteen minutes. A week later, when the first question addressed to him concerned "the Harry Dexter White case," the President was sharp: "I should like to make clear, ladies and gentlemen, that so far as this case itself is concerned, I haven't another single word to say about it, certainly not at this time, and don't intend to open my mouth about it." Once burned.

The hubbub over Harry Dexter White abated, but there was more to come.

On Saturday night, November 7, when the clatter over the White affair had long since been sounded fortemente and was rapidly approaching its fortissimo, a thirty-three-year-old lawyer named William Liscum Borden, an executive of the Westinghouse Corporation (in the division that had contracted to supply nuclear reactor engines for submarines) who had formerly been executive director of the Joint Congressional Committee on Atomic Energy, mailed two letters, having taken care to have them registered so that they would surely reach their intended recipients. One letter was addressed to J. Edgar Hoover at the FBI; the other, which contained a copy of the first, was addressed to the chairman of the Joint Congressional Committee on Atomic Energy.

In his letters Borden stated his "own exhaustively considered opinion, based upon years of study of the available classified evidence, that more probably than not, J. Robert Oppenheimer is an agent of the Soviet Union."

Oppenheimer? The man who had ushered in the atomic age? Oppenheimer a Soviet agent?

The charge, so shocking when it was made public in April 1954, was old stuff to government officials responsible for the "security" of the nation. Most of the particulars in the bill presented by young Borden were so ancient as to be virtually antediluvian, to wit: Oppenheimer had joined many left-wing organizations before the war; his wife had formerly been married to a member of the Communist party and had once been a member herself; until 1941 his younger brother and his sister-in-law had also been members of the party; Oppenheimer himself had contributed money to the Communist party (more accurately, he had made contributions, as he supposed, through the party to various "causes," principally that of the Spanish loyalists). Not only were these items old stuff, some of them were widely known, even broadcast and proudly boasted. Considered within the context of their time, they were evidence of an essentially quixotic rebellion against the ineffectiveness of government in the 1930s. Yanked out of context and considered for the first time during the time of McCarthyism in the Cold War, they could seem heinous. The timing of Borden's letter about Oppenheimer was everything.

Everybody whose business it was to know about Oppenheimer's political past knew about it. J. Edgar Hoover knew of it. Major General Leslie Groves, the army officer who had supervised the nuclear weapons laboratory at Los Alamos, knew of it. The Atomic Energy commissioners knew of it. Those of their subordinates who were concerned with security knew of it. All those men knew also of a conversation, obscure in detail, in which a friend of Oppenheimer's was alleged to have raised the subject of transmitting secret technical information to the Russians. (Oppenheimer had himself reported the conversation, but only after a delay of eight months, and then not wholly truthfully.) All those men also knew that Oppenheimer had recruited for work at Los Alamos and elsewhere throughout the Manhattan Project several scientists who were believed to have been communists or sympathetic to the Communist party, just as they knew of the circumstances that had required such recruitment, and of the substantial contributions those recruits had made to the development of nuclear weapons. A small army of security agents had kept Oppenheimer under surveillance for more than eleven years: they had tapped his telephones, they had monitored his homes and his offices with electronic devices, they had opened his mail, they had shadowed him day and night: the fruits of their painstaking labors comprised a stack of reports more than fifty inches thick.* In 1947 most of this voluminous file had been meticulously reviewed by the Atomic Energy commissioners and they had unanimously voted Oppenheimer a clearance so that he might become chairman of the General Advisory Committee to the commission. One of the five commissioners giving approval was Lewis L. Strauss, a man of markedly conservative views whose concern over security matters was conspicuous even in the age of McCarthyism.

As chairman of the GAC, Oppenheimer had opposed the all-out effort to develop the hydrogen bomb—the Super, as it was known in AEC circles—but his dissent had scarcely been exceptional. In October 1949 the GAC had been convened to advise as to whether the United States should undertake an intensive effort to construct the new weapon—twenty times?—one hundred times?—nobody knew how many times more terrible than the one that had demolished Hiroshima or the one that had crisped Nagasaki. The GAC members present (Fermi, Rabi, Conant of Harvard, DuBridge of CalTech, and other distinguished scientists and engineers) had, to Oppenheimer's astonishment, unanimously expressed a reluctance for the United States to "take the initiative at that time in an all-out program" to develop such a weapon.

Borden's accusatory letter, however, had singled Oppenheimer out as the man who had been "remarkably instrumental in influencing" the military and the AEC "to suspend H-bomb development" from 1946 to 1950 (when President Truman had ordered a crash program) and who had thereafter "worked tirelessly . . . to retard the United States H-bomb program." Oppenheimer had never made a secret of his objections to the hydrogen bomb (about which, in any case, he had written Conant in the fall of 1949, "It would be folly to oppose the exploration of this weapon.

* The target of this extraordinary vigilance was of course aware of it. Later Oppenheimer would comment acidly, "The government paid far more to tap my telephone than they ever paid me at Los Alamos."

We have always known it had to be done, and it does have to be done . . . But that we become committed to it as the way to save the country and the peace appears to me full of dangers"), but his views, however anguished and ambiguous, would seem in retrospect remarkably restrained and thoughtful.

At all events, Borden's letter contained no new evidence, no item of information that had not been officially known and for years officially recognized. What was new was the timing. The letter was delivered while the fuss over the White affair was still at its height, and the President's reaction to Borden's stale charges must be judged in that context.

First the FBI. The copious file on Oppenheimer was reduced to a summary one inch thick and, covered by copies of Borden's letter, distributed to the President, to the secretary of defense, the chairman of the AEC. The summary was dated Friday, November 27, 1953, and reached the three men the next Monday. It came as news to Eisenhower and Wilson; both men were shocked. The chairman of the AEC by then was Lewis Strauss, appointed by Eisenhower six months before; to him the summary covered familiar ground. He ordered that it be circulated among the other four AEC commissioners.

Meanwhile Robert Oppenheimer had returned to theoretical physics. Since 1947 he had been director of the Institute for Advanced Studies at Princeton (the post had been offered him by one of the trustees of the institute, a trustee who chanced to be Lewis Strauss), and in September 1952 he had resigned as chairman of the GAC. He had, though, been tendered and had accepted a contract as a consultant to the AEC, and that contract would not expire until June 1954. (His services as a consultant were requested only twice in the period from September 1952 to December 1953, when Borden's letter reached Eisenhower's desk.) Because of that contract Robert Oppenheimer still held his "Q" clearance—the kind that permitted access to matters of the highest secrecy. Because of that "Q" clearance President Eisenhower faced a decision.

As usual, there were options. One: the President could request (or demand) a formal hearing on the charges against Oppenheimer. Two: the President (or some other official acting on his behalf) could require Oppenheimer's resignation, and accept it swiftly and discreetly or accompany its acceptance with the customary exchange of formal public correspondence. Three: the President could do nothing at all, simply let Oppenheimer's contract expire without again consulting him in any AEC business. To the physicists and other scientists outraged by what was done to Oppenheimer, the man who had made such a tremendous contribution to his country's might, this last course would later seem the best one, indeed the only decent one. At Oppenheimer's hearing, I. I. Rabi would voice that outrage with passion:

"In other words, there he was. He is a consultant, and if you don't want to consult the guy, you don't consult him, period. Why you have to then proceed to suspend clearance and go through all this sort of thing—he is only there when called—and that is all there is to it. So it didn't seem to me the sort of thing that called for this kind of proceeding at all against a man who had accomplished what Dr. Oppenheimer had accomplished. . . . We have an A-bomb . . . and what more do you want—mermaids?"

But to President Eisenhower and his advisers, the second and third options were not attractive. With some agitation Charley Wilson told the President he had been informed that Senator McCarthy knew of the report on Oppenheimer sent round by the FBI; he could stir up a fearful mess. If McCarthy did not know of it yet, he soon would, for Borden's letter to the FBI had gone also to the Joint Congressional Committee on Atomic Energy and hence would soon be available to members of both houses of Congress in both parties. If only in self-defense, then, the President had to cancel the option of letting Oppenheimer's contract run to expiry. Even a request that Oppenheimer resign would be considered dangerously flabby, the more so after the harsh criticism recently visited on Truman by the Eisenhower administration. How excoriate Truman for his laxity toward alleged communist spies while giving houseroom at the AEC to one alleged to be "an agent of the Soviet Union"?

In the late afternoon of Thursday, December 3, these and other aspects of the matter were canvassed in the President's oval office by Eisenhower, Brownell, Wilson, Bobby Cutler, and Arthur Flemming, director of the Office of Defense Mobilization. Jerry Persons, retired army officer and Eisenhower's trusted crony, listened closely but said little. Since the responsible agency was the AEC, those assembled agreed that Strauss should be summoned. He was. Upon his arrival the President inquired whether the AEC had conducted an investigation of the charges against Oppenheimer, as required by his Executive Order 10450. No hearing, said Strauss, had yet been held, but the President's Executive Order would in due course be applied to all AEC personnel, including those who, like Oppenheimer, were contract consultants. Thereupon Eisenhower directed that there be "a full examination" into the charges, and that in the meantime a "blank wall" be placed between Oppenheimer and all government operations.

His advisers having dispersed, the President dictated for the record a memorandum to Brownell. He had, he informed his attorney general, "directed the heads of departments and agencies . . . to place a blank wall between Oppenheimer and all areas of our government operations, whether . . . sensitive . . . or otherwise."

Out went the President's directive, to the AEC, the CIA, the Pentagon, officers of the army, navy, and air force all over the world, bureaucrats high and low, and, along the alert federal grapevine, dozens of government officials who, strictly speaking, had no "need to know." Out it went, spreading a stain.

Was it necessary for "security"? Or was it a necessary act of cruelty, undertaken in the name of "security" but more precisely dictated by the precedent established in the affair of Harry Dexter White? What was accomplished by placing a "blank wall" between the secrets and the man who had done so much to devise them? Eisenhower himself answered those questions in part. After dictating the memorandum to Brownell, a copy of which would be inserted in his "diary," he withdrew into the deeper recesses of his reticence and dictated a memorandum for his "personal diary," the notes for which were subsequently burned by Mrs. Whitman. Here he acknowledged (it was like talking to himself) that to bar Oppenheimer from the secrets of the AEC was not merely to lock a stable door after a horse had maybe been stolen, "it would be more like trying to find a door for a burned-down stable." In short, Eisenhower recognized that he had achieved nothing for the sake of "security," he had only protected his administration from the likes of McCarthy by sacrificing the good repute of a scientist whose usefulness was in any event terminated.

In the months and years that followed the hearing and the announcement that his judges had found Oppenheimer loyal and unusually discreet with secrets but had nonetheless ruled that he was a "security risk," no longer to be trusted by the government he had served so well, his devoted associates and the scientific community generally were disposed to single out three men as chiefly responsible for what they considered a national disgrace: Lewis Strauss, chairman of the AEC; Gordon Gray, chairman of the Personnel Security Board; and Edward Teller, the physicist usually credited with developing a practicable hydrogen bomb. Strauss, the word went, had hated Oppenheimer since the day in June 1949 when the physicist had publicly ridiculed Strauss's apprehensions about the shipment of radioisotopes to friendly countries abroad;* Strauss's motives, Oppenheimer's friends insisted, were purely vengeful; in any case there can be no question but that Strauss, who was to be Oppenheimer's chief appellate judge, was also his hostile adversary both during the proceedings

---

* David Lilienthal, at the time the chairman of the AEC, would long remember his impression of Strauss on that occasion: "There was a look of hatred . . . that you don't see very often in a man's face."

"Who's Being Walled Off From What?"

from *Herblock's Here and Now* (Simon & Schuster, 1955)

before the Personnel Security Board and later. At the outset of Oppenheimer's hearing, Gray had announced that "this proceeding is an inquiry, and not in the nature of a trial," but thereafter—by attitude, procedure, ruling, and otherwise—Gray behaved more like a man presiding over a star chamber tribunal. Teller, whose own security clearance had been granted him in 1942 only after Oppenheimer had interceded on his behalf, testified at the hearing: "If it is a question of [his] wisdom and judgment, as demonstrated by [his] actions since 1945, then I would say one would be wiser not to grant [Dr. Oppenheimer] clearance," and as a result would suffer the obloquy and ostracism visited on him by many of his fellow scientists.

Ten years would pass, almost to the day, after President Eisenhower's "blank wall" directive before another President would make partial amends to Oppenheimer for the injury done him. On December 2, 1963, Lyndon Johnson (acting for John Kennedy, who had been assassinated ten days before) conferred on Oppenheimer the Fermi award—a citation, a gold medal, and a check for fifty thousand dollars—"on behalf of . . . the people of the United States."

In the atmosphere of the White House, incidents like the White affair and the Oppenheimer affair were so much deplorable static, distracting the President from the business of statecraft. To his budget of serious problems already cited, three others must now be added. Nuclear warfare. A summit meeting with Churchill. Vietnam.

The possibility of nuclear annihilation, everyone's waking nightmare during the 1950s, dismayed Eisenhower, especially after he assumed the burdens of the presidency. As a soldier, he appreciated more vividly than any bellicose civilian the frightfulness of nuclear weaponry. Yet as a soldier, he had helped to lock the nation into the atomic arms race.* In short, Eisenhower embodied the chilling paradox of the new weapons: the United States must maintain its nuclear arms superiority in order to bargain from strength, but the United States dare not permit a nuclear arms race lest the planet be riven by some ghastly mischance.

In the early months of his presidency he had pondered that arms race with Lewis Strauss, then his special assistant for atomic energy affairs, but to no avail. On July 2 Strauss was sworn as chairman of the AEC,

---

* As chief of staff, General Eisenhower had strongly supported the so-called Baruch Plan for international control of atomic energy, which was conceived in 1946 and at once became an instrument of Cold War rhetoric. It included clauses that would make it repugnant to the Soviet Union, but its American sponsors insisted that it must be ratified in its entirety or there would be no international controls. As President, Eisenhower continued to support the Baruch Plan while he professed to believe it would serve the Russians' self-interest.

and after the ceremony Eisenhower walked him over to the bay window of the oval office. The two men stood looking out toward the Mall and the Washington Monument, and Eisenhower said: "Lewis, let us be certain about *this*. My chief concern and your first assignment is to find some new approach to the *dis*arming of atomic energy. . . . The world simply must not go on living in the fear of the terrible consequences of nuclear war." Strauss was not sanguine. The President added: "Meanwhile, we have to continue to keep our lead in weapons development. I am counting on you for that, too." Halt the arms race but keep the U.S. ahead in nuclear weaponry.

Meanwhile a top-secret study, the Lincoln Report (see page 515), had reached the National Security Council. Here were set down, for the guidance and instruction of the men who were to make national security policy, an assessment of the possibilities of an atomic onslaught by the Soviet Union and an appraisal of the defenses of the North American continent against such an attack. (The study had been prepared by a panel of eminent scientists, one of whom was Robert Oppenheimer.) The moral was plain: war had become too dangerous for humanity. The people should be better informed of the nature of the awful new weapons.

Acting on the advice of the NSC, the President had told C. D. Jackson to prepare a candid speech about nuclear warfare. Several drafts were composed. None had satisfied Eisenhower. He was not content with an inventory of destruction; he wanted somehow to strike an affirmative note. He took this concern to Denver for his "vacation," and the report, four days later, of a Russian test with thermonuclear reaction spurred his concern. He discussed what he should say with those of his advisers who visited him in Colorado. (His comments to Foster Dulles ran like this: Our people must know what A-bombs and H-bombs can do; once this information is spread abroad, if the men of the Kremlin still decline international controls, the assumption must be that they propose aggression; therefore the U.S. must stand ready to reply at once with still greater violence; such a deterrent capability will be so costly as to raise the threat that we will be driven to dictatorship or war; therefore, should we now consider whether we should *initiate* war? At all events, any policy of increased military preparation requires an informed public opinion.) On his flight east to attend the funeral of Chief Justice Vinson, the President had an idea. He mentioned it to Bobby Cutler, and a memorandum went at once to Jackson and Strauss:

> In discussing with the President this morning the action taken at the [National Security] Council yesterday . . . the President suggested that

you might consider the following proposal which he did not think anyone had yet thought of. . . .

Suppose the United States and the Soviets were to turn over to the United Nations, for peaceful uses, X kilograms of fissionable material . . .

BOBBY

Jackson did nothing about the suggestion,* and for a week or so neither did Strauss. The AEC chairman, an exceedingly suspicious man, feared that fissionable material—uranium—contributed by the U.S. might be pilfered by the USSR, but once he had developed a plan to block such brigandage, he was ready with a memorandum of his own that went to the President, Dulles, Jackson, and the Joint Chiefs of Staff. The suggestion was now enveloped in the bureaucratic process, where its weight would be reduced, its face lifted, and its image otherwise primped. As it began its journey through channels, the President scribbled a note in his own hand:

The mere discovery by men of nature's principle of nuclear fission is of itself no possible danger to mankind. . . . The danger confronting us, therefore, is to be examined from two aspects: the first of these is comprehension of the extent of the destructive power now transportable in a single bomb; the second is determination of the objectives and purposes of the men or nations to whom this destructive force is available.

At about this time Churchill, recovered from his stroke, once again began to press for a meeting at the summit. Several matters bothered him— the protracted negotiations over prisoners of war in Korea; the deteriorating position of the United Kingdom in the Middle East; the storage of some atomic bombs in England, to be dropped by British bombers in the event of war; the vexatious question of Trieste, claimed since the end of the war with equal ardor and justice by both Italy and Yugoslavia—and Churchill considered they were better discussed face to face, as he had done with Roosevelt. Moreover, he was still anxious to arrive at a détente with the Soviet Union, so that he who had been anathematized as a war-

* Bedell Smith, at this time still undersecretary of state, was one of those who would later say that the suggestion had in fact originated "in the brain of C. D. Jackson." Smith would go on to characterize Jackson: "Fellow who throws off a lot of ideas; one or two of them sometimes are good. But nothing but an idea, a good thing to say. The administration needed to say something about atomic energy; why not this?"

Like presidential speeches, presidential ideas and suggestions more often than not are bastards, fathered by some other man. Their breeding is less important than their efficacy, and an idea is always more likely to prove efficacious when the President's name is attached to it.

monger might be remembered in history as the great peacemaker, and to win a détente he needed to make use of Britain's "special relationship" with the U.S. On October 7 he urged by cablegram a meeting as soon as possible—perhaps in the Azores? perhaps without the French?

But the President was not yet ready for a tête-à-tête with Churchill and at once replied that October was impossible and that the French must in any event be included.

During this time Trieste had been simmering on the back of the stove, and so had Vietnam. Trieste seemed more of a problem for the U.S. than in fact it was, for experienced European diplomatists had the matter in hand and might well have straightened it out sooner than they did, had it not been for the Americans. The dispute involved the Istrian peninsula, at the head of the Adriatic, and the city which was its principal port. Centuries ago a possession of the Venetian republic, Trieste had passed into the hands of the Hapsburgs and by them had been incorporated into the Austro-Hungarian empire; after the War of 1914–1918 it had been presented, as an award for picking the victors in advance, to Italy; and similarly after the War of 1939–1945 it had been demanded as recompense by Yugoslavia. Over the generations the people inhabiting the peninsula had been inextricably intermingled and, thanks to marriage and other Christian sacraments, had come to hate each other. Italians, Croats, Slovenes, south Slavs of all kinds; fascist, royalist, republican, communist; fisherman, peasant, shopkeeper, clerk; the mix had bubbled and boiled, and its solution was murky. By 1948 Trieste and the land around it had become a token in the Cold War, divided into two zones, with American and British troops occupying the one that included the port and Yugoslav troops patrolling the other. To the governments of the U.S., U.K., and France it had seemed expedient to propose that both zones be turned over to Italy. But in the summer of 1948 Yugoslavia had been expelled from the bloc of "communist" nations for being too nationalist, and suddenly it was important to find an equitable solution. In September 1953 British and Americans agreed that the best plan was simply to impose a settlement: one zone to Italy, the other to Yugoslavia, Italy to make free the port facilities of Trieste, both parties to guarantee proper treatment of minorities. The plan would work only if a public announcement were made that the solution was imposed and final; the firmer the better, said the British. "What," Eisenhower asked Foster Dulles on September 30, "are we doing about the Trieste affair?" The two men conferred. They agreed that the Anglo-American statement should not be too categorical. They would go no further than to speak of their "hope that the measures being taken will lead to a final peaceful solution." In Eden's view this language was "a serious weakening of the proposals," and he was proved right when the Italian premier greeted word of the plan with the comment that it in no way prejudiced Italy's claim to both zones. Marshal Tito forthwith closed the frontier, called up reserves, moved warships, and appealed to the U.N. The Italians ordered reinforcements to their side of the frontier. President Eisenhower instructed units of the U.S. Sixth Fleet to proceed to the Adriatic. Riots broke out in Belgrade and Rome. Blood was spilled in the streets of Trieste. Anti-British demonstrations raged on both sides of the Adriatic. Then all at once the entire matter was discreetly removed into the diplomatic underground in London, where the parties to the dispute could smooth out their disagreements in civil discourse. And they did.

Vietnam would not be so easily composed.

Vietnam was different. Vietnam was the irremediable wound of the Cold War. Vietnam supplied Eisenhower with his most urgent motive for insisting on a French presence at any meeting at the summit. In October 1953 the President still hoped that he would be able to persuade France to adopt his policy as to Vietnam. The governments of France and the United States held contrary views, and events were driving them further apart, but still Eisenhower hoped. His policy was a patchwork of questionable assumption, inconsistency, and internal contradiction, but policy in France had likewise proved shaky as her ministers were shuffled about and especially as the war in Vietnam was protracted into a condition of inevitability; and so the President kept hope: perhaps Pax Americana might yet prevail.

In retrospect, it is useful to review the underpinnings of Dwight Eisenhower's policy in respect of Vietnam.

ASSUMPTION: That the Viet Minh—(more properly the Viet Nam Doc Lap Dong Minh Hoi (League for the Independence of Vietnam)—was a gang of hard-core communist revolutionaries acting at the bidding of their communist masters in Peking and Moscow. Beginning with the OSS operatives who had worked side by side with Viet Minh agents against the Japanese back in 1944, there were many American officials who knew that assumption was false, knew the Viet Minh was a coalition of nationalist Vietnamese political groupings, formed and led by the Indochinese Communist party but representing a broad spectrum of Vietnamese opinion. Ho Chi Minh, who was the Viet Minh's first secretary general and was declared premier of Indochina by the French in 1946, was known to be a communist, but in the fall of 1948 a study made by a group of American intelligence experts (attached to the Office of Intelligence and Research of the Department of State) found no evidence that Ho Chi Minh took his orders from Moscow. "If there is a Moscow-directed conspiracy in Southeast Asia, Indochina is an anomaly so far," said the report filed by the office's evaluation section. Nevertheless, it suited American policy to deny the patriotic and nationalist character of the Viet Minh; to Eisenhower, "Ho Chi Minh was, of course, a hard-core Communist, while the Vietminh, the forces under his command, were supported by the Chinese Communists in the north," and the war "was in fact a clear case of freedom defending itself from Communist aggression."

INCONSISTENCY: In August, only a few days after the United States had negotiated an armistice in Korea, the National Security Council recommended, and the President approved, the thesis that "under present conditions any negotiated settlement [in Vietnam] would mean the eventual loss to Communism not only of Indochina but of the whole of Southeast Asia." The NSC paper added: "The loss of Indochina would be critical to the security of the U.S." These notions, thus transformed into U.S. national policy, were in collision with French opinion, but Eisenhower moved to circumvent that opinion by sharply increasing military aid. Early in October he dictated a note for his personal diary: "We have engaged to help . . . on a very major scale in Indochina in return for which France has irrevo[c]ably promised" to give the associated states their independence and to support EDC. The President estimated that about one billion dollars would be spent in 1954 for military aid to France. (Ultimately one billion one hundred million dollars would be allocated for such aid, which would pay for an estimated 78 percent of the costs of the war.) But the French people were increasingly troubled by the war and, responsive to their temper, the French National Assembly on October 28 adopted a resolution demanding that the government of Joseph Laniel "do everything possible to achieve a general peace in Asia by negotiations." For his part, Laniel pledged "in the clearest and most categorical fashion" that "France . . . like the United States in Korea, would be happy to welcome a diplomatic solution of the conflict." In Washington the administration sensed the first hints of alarm. If an Indochinese victory—viz., a communist victory—were to be averted, the war would have to be internationalized.

CONTRADICTION: On the one hand the U.S. pressed the French to internationalize the conflict by permitting an American military mission to train Vietnamese soldiers in the use of American weapons and by taking advice on tactics and strategy from American officers, but on the other hand the American commander in chief rejected suggestions of intervention by U.S. forces either on the ground or in the air. The French were loath to yield control of their war, now more than seven years old. Pride and the demands of prestige are enormously inflated once national honor is involved. The Americans had needed only autochthonous help to quell the Hukbalahap insurgency in the Philippines; the British were handling the insurrection in Malaya without pressing the panic button; surely the French could do the same against the Viet Minh? So, as Eisenhower observed, the French clung to "their exclusive responsibility" and would accept American aid only if they might use it "according to their fixed political and military policies." The President was obliged to put his trust in the plan devised by General Henri Navarre. Early in November Vice President Nixon bobbed up in Hanoi, dispatched by Eisenhower to urge a more robust martial effort against the Viet Minh; a negotiated truce, Nixon warned, "would place people who want freedom and independence in perpetual bondage." Presently the Mutual Security administrator, Harold Stassen, would assure Republican legislative leaders that thanks to the Navarre Plan, Indochina would be pacified by 1955. Indeed, at times the plan seemed to be working fairly well: announcement was made that on November 20 a Viet Minh stronghold had been seized, a fortified town far back in northwestern Vietnam, a place with one of those names that sound so strange to western ears. The French commander announced that he would hold the base instead of destroying it, for he thought well of its strategic value. It was called Dien Bien Phu.

At all events, the time was overripe for the meeting at the summit that Churchill had three times proposed. When his fourth urgent request was cabled to the President on November 5, it was answered the next day by a cable from Eisenhower suggesting possible dates for a meeting in Bermuda. A day later all was agreed: a four-day conference early in December. Eisenhower closed the exchange on November 9 by observing that a recent Soviet note took serious exception to the bilateral and trilateral meetings favored by the foreign ministers of the United States, the United Kingdom, and France. (The Soviets argued that where the peace of the world was concerned, China and the USSR should be invited to participate.) The Bermuda Conference would, Eisenhower surmised, in itself afford the best retort to the Soviet note.

Four days later (in the midst of the clamor over the Harry Dexter White case) Eisenhower and his wife took train for Canada, on the eve of her fifty-seventh birthday, for a state visit to Ottawa. Henry Cabot Lodge, his ambassador to the United Nations, went along and on the way suggested that an excellent forum for the President's proposed speech on the peaceful uses of fissionable material would be the General Assembly of the United Nations. The President agreed. After the inevitable staffwork, it was arranged that Dag Hammarskjöld, secretary general of the U.N., would issue his invitation only after Eisenhower had been able to show a draft of the speech to Churchill in Bermuda.

Before the President could devote himself to any questions that might arise in Bermuda, other perplexities confronted him. Advice to an ambassador: Clare Boothe Luce, his envoy to Italy, wished to know what the United States could do to keep the communists from taking over; the President wrote her that the CIA might well be planning to invest some "risk" capital, how much he would leave to Allen Dulles to decide. (Then a memorandum to Beetle Smith in the State Department to explain that he must be roundabout with Mrs. Luce and "hope that she would get the point.") A two-hour session with his secretaries of state, the treasury, and defense: it was agreed that production of nuclear weapons would facilitate a reduction of armed forces, especially those of the army, and so make possible a reduced budget in fiscal 1955. (The decision taken during those two hours would later be labeled with a gibe, "More bang for a buck.") On politics: the President dictated a long reflective memorandum to Leonard Hall, chairman of the Republican National Committee, probing, recommending various steps to enhance Republican prospects, his tone confident and assertive, that of an executive assigning tasks to a none-too-bright subordinate; later another memorandum went to Hall, Adams, Lodge, Summerfield, and Tom Stephens on the need for better Republican press-agentry. (This was dictated while the lumps raised by the Harry Dexter White case were still tender.) On civil rights: the President sent a letter to Governor Byrnes that showed a greater concern for states' rights than for the Negroes. (The school segregation cases were then sub judice of the Supreme Court.) On security: the President had just time before his departure for Bermuda to place "a blank wall" between Oppenheimer and all areas of government operations. He was then running on a tight schedule, every minute appointed, hundreds of people at home and abroad awaiting his convenience; but his temper was sweet, his smile warm, the wave of his hand encompassing as he mounted the steps to his presidential airplane.

Over the long comfortable weekend at the Mid-Ocean Club in Tucker's Town, the statesmen, hidden away by barbed wire from the curious, protected by bristling echelons of troops with bayonets and security guards armed to the teeth, met regularly, talked much, and accomplished almost nothing. There was precious little they could agree on. Their single most important understanding was a negative one: they managed to ignore Ho Chi Minh's offer to negotiate a truce in Vietnam. (The offer was first made on November 29 by cablegram to the Paris correspondent of a Swedish newspaper; the official French reaction was that the message was "full of propaganda" and could not be considered unless formally transmitted.) At Bermuda the French were plunged in an unhappy predicament. Laniel, the premier, fell sick (he was running an alarming six degrees of fever according to a note that Jackson passed to Dulles), and Bidault, the foreign minister, who privately deemed EDC an urgent necessity and was strongly opposed to any negotiations with the Viet Minh, found himself, as spokesman for the government, obliged to present quite other views. For their part Eisenhower and Dulles flatly opposed negotiations and wanted nothing more earnestly of France than ratification of EDC.

Another matter, closely associated with the first, offered the three powers another opportunity for agreement. For some months they had been delicately fencing with the Soviets over the question of a meeting of foreign ministers, and at length on November 26 the Russians had approved the proposal, serving notice that when they met they would ask for a five-power conference, to include China. The condition had presented the three western powers with an excuse, should they have chosen, to reject any parley whatsoever; "this is, of course," Eisenhower had told the press in Washington, "one subject that must be studied very thoroughly"; and indeed it was, for the three foreign ministers had quite different reasons for undertaking any conversations with the Russians. Eden wanted to negotiate a general European settlement, one that would include a satisfactory solution of the question of Germany and of how that nation might be reunified. Bidault was convinced the French government would never ratify EDC without first attempting to negotiate such a settlement; he further imagined that at a five-power conference he might take advantage of confusion within the "communist bloc" to make a satisfactory arrangement on Indochina. Dulles dreaded any four-power conference that might lead to an encounter with China, but he recognized that as a result of the armistice in Korea such a meeting was mandated; at the least he hoped to ensure that Indochina would never find a place on the agenda, lest it lead to a negotiation for an armistice in Southeast Asia as well. Meanwhile the essential task was French ratification of EDC. Dulles suspected the Russians had agreed to a meeting of foreign ministers only to force postponement of that ratification. Any meeting, he insisted, must start soon and be quickly concluded. The three powers agreed to meet in Berlin as early in January as the Russians could make it.

France, Dulles argued, must ratify EDC in February; otherwise he could no longer give assurance of congressional support for NATO.

For the rest, the Bermuda Conference was a rehearsal of a Cold War theme with variations. Churchill urged a "new look" at East-West relations, with particular emphasis on trade with and travel in the countries behind the "iron curtain"; Eisenhower and Dulles took note of the suggestion. There was an exchange on the use of the monstrous new weapons now ready to hand. Dulles observed that if the Communists broke the armistice in Korea, the United States would attack Chinese bases with the "most effective" weapons; Eden deplored U.S. bellicosity, warned that it might lead to general war, and indicated that Her Majesty's government would support neither the use of atomic weapons nor a blockade of China; Eisenhower rejoined that the U.S. would consult with its allies but would not "as a matter of principle, in all circumstances" exclude the possibility of using nuclear weapons; Churchill reminded everyone that the USSR had "never yet made any public declaration that they would engage in atomic warfare," and he considered that it would be folly to provoke them into such a declaration.

On the Monday, Eisenhower dictated a lengthy memorandum in which he particularly bewailed the presence of the crowds of reporters. They robbed the occasion of its intimate informality, they led the statesmen (or their advisers) to make talk which was aimed at their "home constituencies." In brief, they seduced a modicum of statecraft out into the open, where it might be examined by just anybody, and so be suffused with embarrassment. It was too bad.

On the Tuesday, the President and his party took plane for New York. Aloft, all was business: revision of the last draft of the speech, typing in outsize type of Eisenhower's reading copy, mimeographing of the several dozen copies needed for U.N. dignitaries and press; men like Dulles and Strauss preoccupied with unwonted clerical tasks, the President an amused observer. And that afternoon the speech, stage-managed with consummate care, even to the point of a coded message to Moscow bidding Ambassador Bohlen impress upon Molotov the lofty import of the President's message to the U.N.

Eisenhower's project, as shaped and transmuted at the hands of a half-dozen cautious staff assistants and fearful advisers, wound up as a proposal that the United States and the Soviet Union each contribute from its nuclear stockpile enough fissionable materials to create an international supply to be used for peaceful purposes—"agriculture, medicine, and . . . abundant electrical energy in the power-starved areas of the world." Yielding to rhetoric, the President pledged "before you—and therefore before the world—[this government's] determination to help solve the fearful atomic dilemma—to devote its entire heart and mind to find the way by which the miraculous inventiveness of man shall not be dedicated to his death, but consecrated to his life."

The General Assembly of the United Nations rose to its feet and cheered and applauded for nearly a minute; the Soviet delegation joined in the celebration. Viewed solely as an exercise in psychological warfare, it was an unmixed triumph. There stood the United States—as personified by the simple, noble, sincere advocate of peace and international amity, Dwight D. Eisenhower, shyly grinning and bobbing his head to acknowledge the applause—urging that the fearful thing be "taken out of the hands of the soldiers [and] put into the hands of those who will know how to strip its military casing and adapt it to the arts of peace." In a time of somber dread of holocaust, Eisenhower's offer was good tidings of great joy. The greeting given it by Madame Pandit, the president of the Assembly (and Nehru's sister), was representative: "It was an historic occasion. . . . The speech *assumed* coexistence in the world. It was conciliatory in every way." The world turned its gaze upon Moscow. How would the Kremlin respond to this generous overture?

But in Cold Wartime, an offer to one's adversary is likely to be less than openhearted, and so it was with Eisenhower's. The CIA had formed a tolerably accurate estimate of the quantity of fissionable materials the Soviets had on hand, and as Eisenhower would later write: "Our technical experts assured me that even if Russia agreed to cooperate in [the] plan . . . the United States could afford to reduce its atomic stockpile by two or three times the amount the Russians might contribute, and *still improve our relative position.*" (Emphasis added.) Since it was reasonable to assume that the men in the Kremlin also knew how to count, those familiar with the problem were not sanguine that much had been done to brake the atomic arms race. Lewis Strauss was privately asked what would happen if the Russians accepted the proposal; the question appeared to stump him.

The Russians did not accept the proposal. They again called for a complete prohibition of all nuclear weapons as a necessary precondition of international control of armaments, a step the American military could of course never consider since it would entail yielding a clear strategic advantage.

So much for taking the bomb "out of the hands of the soldiers."

Once again in the White House, the President summoned his secretary of state for another discussion of their most tantalizing objective, EDC. Dulles was due in Paris in a day or so for a session of the NATO Council, and he wished to administer a deliberate shock to French public opinion on the question. Now, he said, was the time; and Eisenhower, whose affection for the French had never been overmastering, agreed. Dulles spread out the pages of a paper he proposed to read the NATO Council. It was stern stuff. Further procrastination by France, Italy, and the smaller Benelux countries—but his strictures were aimed chiefly at France—in forging a political, economic, and military unity of western Europe would compel "an agonizing reappraisal" of United States policy. Too harsh? Too peremptory? No, the President did not think so. He approved.

Then Dulles was gone and the President was left to contend with his domestic afflictions. Among these was Senator Joe McCarthy, who had presumed to take issue with the leader of his party, with the President; who had gone so far indeed as to attack the President's policies, foreign and domestic; who had invited "every American who feels as I do about this [British] blood trade with a mortal enemy [China] to write or wire the President . . . so he can be properly guided" and had thus loosed a downpour of some fifty thousand letters and telegrams on the White House. To his associates the President continued to insist that he would ignore McCarthy, and that remained his professed posture; but McCarthy's destructive energy kept pressing the President (and his senior associates) to further contaminations of the civil liberties of the republic and its sovereign citizens. As the senator persevered in his baleful scrutiny of the foreign service and especially of those officers who had served in China, as his wandering attention was attracted to the army and the possibility that here too were harbored sinister malefactors, the President deemed it expedient to refer now and again to the number of "security risks" detected, collared, and dismissed from government service by the Argus-eyed monitors of his so-called security program. In December the number was one thousand four hundred and fifty-six; soon it would be swollen by 50 percent.

There is some evidence that Eisenhower may occasionally have been disgusted by these tasks. By mid-December he was looking forward to a day when he would be free of the presidency and all its responsibilities. No second term for him, he wrote his brother Milton: ". . . if ever . . . I should show any signs of yielding . . . please call in the psychiatrist—or even better the sheriff." A few days later he went so far as to list the men he believed would make the best candidate for the Republicans in 1956: his brother Milton, if only he were not an Eisenhower, would have been ideal; as matters stood, the President endorsed (in this order) Lodge, Nixon, Brownell, Stassen, Deputy Attorney General William P. Rogers, Secretary of the Army Robert Stevens, Halleck, Senator Charles Potter of Michigan, Senator Barry Goldwater of Arizona, and (possibly) Knowland.*

So long as McCarthy and his investigations dominated the domestic scene, clouds of rancor and suspicion would hug the American landscape, and so long President Eisenhower and his associates would vie with McCarthy at the business of hunting down the reds. (This was known at

* It is likely that if he had waited only a few months, Eisenhower would have drawn a shorter list. Their behavior in connection with McCarthy's impending caper might have eliminated two, perhaps four, of these possible candidates. On the other hand, in view of Eisenhower's pronounced penchant for compromise, perhaps not.

the time as "grabbing the Commie issue away from Joe.") It seemed the thing to do. It was thought to pay lavish political dividends, and small matter if it also served to pollute the wellsprings of liberty a trifle. Consequently some of it was larded into the President's 1954 message to the Congress on the state of the union. There were, said Eisenhower, more than two thousand two hundred citizens who had been "separated from the Federal government," all security risks of one kind or another, nature of risk unspecified. "Our national security demands," he went on, ". . . investigation . . . evaluation of derogatory information . . . I shall recommend . . . additional funds . . . to speed these important procedures."

Taking one thing with another, the state of the union, in the President's opinion, was good. "Much for which we may be thankful," he said, "has happened during the past year." He cast a selective glance around the horizon and found something for everyone: the war ended in Korea, the nation "most prosperous," inflation curbed, taxes down, cost of armaments "less oppressive . . . yet we are militarily stronger every day," and segregation "on the way out." Abroad, "heartening political victories" in Iran won "by the forces of stability and freedom," and "behind the iron curtain . . . signs that tyranny is in trouble." It was like a strong hand gently rocking the cradle. "There has been in fact," the President argued, "a great strategic change in the world during the past year. That precious intangible, the initiative, is becoming ours. Our policy, not limited to mere reaction against crises provoked by others, is free to develop along lines of our choice, not only abroad, but also at home."

Whence this remarkable confidence, bordering on complacency? If a soldier-statesman have only one perceived enemy (say, the Soviet Union) and if he imagine that all other potential aggressors (China, the Viet Minh, other insurgent forces wherever in the world) act only at the bidding of the first as part of a "world Communist conspiracy," to seize the initiative may seem feasible; to postulate the various options available to one's foe and, pursuant to the terms of von Neumann's theory of games, to interdict them follows as the next logical step. Some process of that sort had been in train ever since the spring of 1953, when Eisenhower had authorized Operation Solarium. The policy paper elaborated by that study, designated NSC 162, had been discussed by the NSC during October and gradually had led to what came to be known as the "new look" at American defensive strategy: an increased dependence on tactical nuclear weapons and strategic airpower as the chief deterrent to aggression. The "new look," as specified in NSC 162/2, was later characterized by one academic authority as "a major landmark in the movement of policy away from the idea that a future war would be like World War II." However that may be, the decision taken by the President on November 11 after consultation with his secretaries of state, treasury, and defense, formed the underpinning for the bolder and more truculent attitude struck in public by the secretary of state. First had come Dulles's statement to the NATO Council in Paris, repeated next day at a gathering of newspaper correspondents, that the United States would have to undertake "an agonizing reappraisal" of its foreign policy if France failed to ratify EDC. (The French press had at once angrily retorted that Dulles's warning was "brutal.") Next, five days after Eisenhower's message on the state of the union, Dulles unveiled in a speech to the Council on Foreign Relations in New York what he called a "new concept of collective security." It was, he said, based "primarily upon a great capacity to retaliate [against aggression], instantly, by means and at places of our choosing." Elsewhere in his remarks he referred to a "deterrent of massive retaliatory power," and presently into the language had come a new phrase—"massive retaliation."

Its critics found a number of points to complain about in this speech: it seemed to suggest that the United States meant to reply "instantly" (without pausing to consult either with the Congress or with friendly allies) to every local conflict, wherever and involving whomever, by dropping thermonuclear bombs. On both sides of the Atlantic the speech aroused alarm, and Dulles was reproached. The President should have shared any blame, for almost certainly he submitted a draft of Dulles's speech to careful study and revision, but censuring Eisenhower was still almost unheard of. It went generally unnoticed that the President had five days earlier used similar language to warn that "we and our allies have and will maintain a massive capability to strike back [against aggression]."*

Of more interest is the fact that on two widely separated fronts the United States was already preparing to assume the initiative, not merely with words, but with military muscle. One was Vietnam, the other was Guatemala. Curiously, in both these theaters of Cold War, American involvement would reach a high pitch of intensity just as the attention of the American public was unprecedentedly fastened on its television screens, where was unfolding the lurid melodrama of Joe McCarthy versus the United States Army. Since it has not been mentioned before in these pages, perhaps an account of these confused and intertwined affairs should begin with a glance at Guatemala.

* Louis Halle has written (*The Cold War As History*, p. 281) that Dulles showed his speech in advance of its delivery to one person only, a lawyer new to the State Department. If Eisenhower did not also see it, the occasion was truly exceptional. At all events, the President saw no need to alter any of the emphases of Dulles's speech next morning when he met reporters at his press conference. Dulles would himself clarify some of the ambiguities of his speech two months later in an appearance before the Senate Foreign Relations Committee.

The land is one of forests and sierras and rocky plateaus, and also of coastal slopes where on great plantations are grown bananas and coffee and cotton. Most of the people are Indians, wretchedly poor, illiterate; peasants; descendants of the dazzling Mayan culture, the greatest of the Western Hemisphere until the Spanish conquistadors came with gunpowder and the cross of Christianity. Few people can have been deeper in the toils of exploitation in 1944 than those Indians. Speaking either very little Spanish or none at all, they comprised a cheap and helpless labor force, at the mercy of their masters, the ladinos.* The Indian was treated by the ladino with contempt, cheated of his wages and in the length and conditions of his employment, forbidden the right to organize a trade union, humiliated as in turn the ladino was humiliated by the gringo, the North American. The gringo's power in 1944 was symbolized by the United Fruit Company—owner of hundreds of square miles of land, major stockholder in the country's railroad, and employer of forced labor. United Fruit was accustomed to regard Guatemala as its fief; to control it, the company depended upon General Jorge Ubico, a brutal despot who proudly compared himself to Hitler.

For a wonder, the dictator was overthrown in 1944 by an uprising of students led by a revolutionary junta that included two young army officers—Javier Araña and Jacobo Arbenz Guzmán—and an influential businessman, Guillermo Toriello. Under the auspices of this junta an election was held in December 1944 that brought to office a schoolteacher, Juan José Arévalo, who drew better than 86 percent of the votes cast. Arévalo promptly undertook to reform the economy and improve the miserable existence of the Indians. For example, forced labor was abolished and the minimum wage was raised to twenty-six cents a day. Predictably, those first tentative steps were assailed by employers as being "communistic." There was more direct opposition: export of bananas by United Fruit, which had accounted for 41 percent of the Guatemalan foreign exchange, dropped 80 percent within four years; the steamship line W. R. Grace and Pan American Airlines ceased their promotion of tourism; several petroleum companies put a halt to their prospecting; the World Bank, responsive to the State Department, withheld loans; the Mutual Security Administration cut off all military assistance. At the end of his term in office President Arévalo disclosed that his administration had been obliged to quell no less than thirty-two attempts to overthrow it, all allegedly incited by United Fruit. The American ambassador was

* As an adjective "ladino" means sly, crafty. As a noun it is used by North Americans to describe a Spanish-speaking person of mixed Spanish and Indian descent, a mestizo. In Guatemala the term covers both the mestizo and the white man.

asked to leave the country after he had sought to provoke unrest by publicly charging "persecution of American business."

In March 1951 Arbenz, who had served in Arévalo's government as minister of defense, took office as president. The revolution was seven years old and widely welcomed. Arbenz had got twice the number of votes of all other candidates. There were a new constitution, legislation for social security, an extensive program of education, a sturdy trade union movement protected by a labor code. Impressive evidence of the revolution's vigor would later be cited in an economic study of twelve Latin American republics for the nine-year period 1945–1953. Despite an annual increase in population of 3 percent, Guatemala scored the highest annual increase in national income per capita—8.5 percent. (The other countries in the survey were Argentina, Brazil, Chile, Colombia, Cuba, the Dominican Republic, Ecuador, Mexico, Panama, Peru, and Venezuela.)

Arbenz had pledged agrarian reform; in June 1952 the law enacting it was approved by the congress. This law provided for expropriation of idle lands, and in March 1953 the Arbenz government did something quite remarkable: it expropriated two hundred and thirty-four thousand acres of uncultivated land on the Pacific slope belonging to United Fruit. The indemnity offered was six hundred thousand dollars in 3 percent twenty-five-year bonds; the amount was based on the value set on the land one year before, for tax purposes, by the company itself, and the terms of payment were the same as those offered to and accepted by scores of other owners whose undeveloped land had been similarly dispossessed. Unacceptable, said the United Fruit spokesman; the company demanded compensation of just less than sixteen million dollars, and the State Department chimed in to say that the amount demanded was precisely what was due under international law. The dispute was still at issue when the Arbenz government announced its intention of expropriating an additional one hundred and seventy-three thousand acres of idle land owned by United Fruit, this tract on the Caribbean slope.

Rash behavior. What was worse, Arbenz had accepted the advice of communists and had indeed welcomed their participation in his government. Not many; no ministers; only some bureaucrats having to do with education, social security, and agrarian reform; carefully removed from such fields of force and authority as the police or the army; in no way approaching the influence of the Communist parties of France or Italy. No matter: the presence of only one communist was all that was needed to simplify matters enormously for the Eisenhower administration. Intervention in the affairs of a sovereign state was not merely permissible; in the sullen climate of the 1950s it was mandatory. Kenneth Redmond, president of United Fruit, was reported to have put it succinctly, if privately: "From here on out it's not a matter of the people of Guatemala against the United Fruit Company; the question is going to be Communism against the right of property, the life and security of the Western Hemisphere." Eisenhower and his advisers would sound the same keynote, allegro. The official State Department document would later charge that Arbenz had accepted the communists as "an authentic domestic political party and not as part of the worldwide Soviet Communist conspiracy." The real issue, Foster Dulles would say, was "Communist imperialism," and he would warn that Guatemala might have been picked out to become the Red bastion menacing the Panama Canal (seven hundred miles to the southeast).

At all events, the decision was taken late in 1953 to organize a counter-revolution in Guatemala. The job was delegated to Allen Dulles and the CIA. As a first step, a little team was organized to operate on signals from the varsity team that Eisenhower was coaching from the White House. The lesser team was a squad of sure-footed ambassadors to the Central American states and a rather larger number of resourceful CIA agents. There was John E. (Jack) Peurifoy, recently home from Greece, where he had efficiently employed the Truman Doctrine to stifle the insurgents; he was now selected by the CIA to be Eisenhower's ambassador to Guatemala, a fresh meadow for his peculiar talents. As for the rest, Whiting Willauer, ambassador to Honduras, would later sketch the picture with broad strokes for a Senate committee:

Q. Mr. Ambassador, was there something of a team in working to overthrow the Arbenz government in Guatemala . . . ?

WILLAUER: There was a team.

Q. Jack Peurifoy was down there?

WILLAUER: Yes, Jack was on the team over in Guatemala; that is the principal man, and we had . . . Ambassador Robert Hill, in Costa Rica . . . and we had Ambassador Tom Whelan in Nicaragua, where a lot of the activities were going. And, of course, there were a number of CIA operatives in the picture . . . the CIA was helping to equip and train the anti-Communist revolutionary forces.

The second step was the selection of a proper cat's-paw—the man around whom dissident Guatemalans might be expected to rally and who would carry out the orders given him. A former executive of United Fruit, one Walter Turnbull, suggested Miguel Ydígoras Fuentes, who had lost the 1950 election to Arbenz and had retired into exile in San Salvador;

here two CIA agents called on him, offering assistance to overthrow Arbenz. When Ydígoras asked what they would expect in return, they were forthright: Ydígoras was "to favor the United Fruit Company and the International Railways of Central America [a subsidiary of United Fruit]; to destroy the railroad workers labor union . . . to establish a strong-arm government, on the style of Ubico [and] to pay back every cent that was invested in the undertaking." Ydígoras rejected the offer.

Next the CIA turned up a colonel, Carlos Castillo Armas, a ferret-faced graduate of the Army Command and General Staff School at Fort Leavenworth who had led an abortive right-wing coup back in 1950. He proved amenable, and was placed at the head of a band of mercenaries scraped together by the CIA and mustered for training across the border in Honduras. Already the plot had a code name, El Diablo, and the more or less covert support of Anastasio Somoza, the dictator of Nicaragua. (The CIA had assembled a few P–47 Thunderbolts and C–47 transports at Managua International Airport; their pilots were Americans recruited by the CIA.)

Little of this had escaped the attention of the Guatemalan government. In mid-January 1954 Guillermo Toriello, one of the junta that had overthrown Ubico, and who had more recently been the Guatemalan ambassador in Washington, called on Bedell Smith at the State Department to pay his respects on the occasion of his departure for home. The visit moved Smith to send the President a memorandum, since in any case it was time to bring him abreast of current developments in Guatemala. Smith spoke of Toriello, "who has represented the fellow-traveling Government of President Arbenz in Washington for a year." Toriello, he said, had "tried to convince" him "that 'Guatemalan Communists are different,' that they are without real influence in his Government, and that Guatemala is the victim of a slanderous press campaign inspired by American companies and State Department officials privately interested in them."*

"The facts," Smith continued, "are otherwise." He went on to give the President a handy résumé of the official administration dogma on Guatemala: "Guatemalan Communists control the national labor organizations; lead major Government political parties; advise the President on high policy; occupy key positions in the Government radio, press, agrarian reform, social security and other agencies; and freely use combined Gov-

---

* What Toriello had in mind was obvious and also widely known: that as counsel to United Fruit, Foster Dulles had drawn the contracts ("leprous" contracts, as they were called by Latin Americans) that turned over whole departments of Guatemala to United Fruit; that Allen Dulles had formerly been president of the company; that John Moors Cabot, then Assistant Secretary of State for Inter-American Affairs, had substantial holdings in United Fruit securities. Bedell Smith himself, after his retirement from government service, took a seat on the board of directors of United Fruit.

ernment and Communist facilities to disseminate floods of Communist and anti-United States propaganda. The Guatemalan Government has abundantly proved its Communist sympathies and toleration of Communist activities. . . . Guatemalan Communists are in fact disciplined agents of international Communism." Smith went on to speak of the "merciless hounding of American companies there by tax and labor demands, strikes, and, in the case of the United Fruit Company, inadequately compensated seizures of land under a Communist-administered Agrarian Reform Law," but he had dictated nearly one full page (the limit imposed for most communications directed to the President) so he closed with an anticlimactic assurance that journalists and prominent senators and congressmen of both parties were concerned about events in this Latin land grown suddenly shadowy behind an alleged iron curtain.

At the end of January Arbenz's aides published correspondence between Castillo Armas and Ydígoras that proved the existence of a plot to overthrow the government of Guatemala and that showed how the "government of the North" had concocted the plot and was even then pushing its execution. It was like a cry for help, lifted across the Western Hemisphere. It went ignored. No questions were put to the President about Guatemala at his press conferences then or for the next three months.

The other two matters—American involvement in Indochina and the downfall of Senator McCarthy—then gathering momentum were likewise in the hands of presidential deputies and being directed along lines that Eisenhower would subsequently approve.

First as to McCarthy. The senator was on another of his rampages of harassment—fulminating now at the army and its secretary, Robert T. Stevens; thunderously investigating one of its installations, Fort Monmouth in New Jersey; savaging an honorable general in unparalleled terms of abuse—and had managed to demoralize the army as he had earlier the foreign service. All deplorably in character; but now there were signs that McCarthy would soon be bent on assailing the President himself, accusing him of being "soft on communism." The evidence abounded. Any investigator needed only look back to the time after V-E Day when the supreme commander was still faithful to the precepts that had served to conquer the Nazis. Unity and amity with the Soviet Union, cooperation with those German communists who had fought against Hitler during the war from their underground, stern measures against those who had collaborated with the Nazis, an unwary attitude toward certain Americans in military government who could never have been appointed to positions of trust by, say, the Eisenhower who commanded SHAPE—so unscrupulous an investigator as Joe McCarthy could have minced a man who had held such views; the "evidence" added up, after all, to an even more hideous picture than that presented with telling effect by anonymous witnesses before the loyalty and security boards of President Eisenhower's own administration.

Sherman Adams was informed of McCarthy's ominous schemes by at least one apprehensive journalist, and the story would later be confirmed in a letter sent the President by his brother Milton. Senator Stuart Symington, a Democrat of Missouri, was Milton Eisenhower's informant; he had learned of some inflammatory allegations in the files of the McCarthy committee that would, he said, be damaging not only to Eisenhower but also to the Dulles brothers. (Symington apparently imagined that President Eisenhower might use his authority with the Republican leadership of the Senate to have McCarthy deposed from his chairmanship, a forlorn hope.)

Sherman Adams was plainly alarmed. McCarthy's "challenge of the prerogatives of the executive branch," Adams wrote later, was "unmistakable and serious." He perceived that the Republican party could be split asunder if McCarthy were given more rein. "Henry Cabot Lodge suggested that it was high time for the administration to take a more thoughtful look at the situation." Indeed it was. Adams pledged to the journalist Joseph Alsop that "the White House now meant to fight McCarthy without giving or asking quarter," but at the same time the role the White House played in any collision with McCarthy had to be concealed lest the President be clipped by flying debris. A meeting was held in the attorney general's office: Brownell, his deputy William Rogers, Adams, Lodge, the army's general counsel John Adams, and Jerry Morgan, the President's special counsel. A plan was devised to expose some of McCarthy's less appetizing provocations to the glare of publicity, and the lawyers discussed the preparation of a memorandum that would define the limit beyond which the executive branch would not accept interrogation by committees of the Congress. Assuredly there was here no ringing defiance of the demagogue, but at least some clerks had dug in their heels and even thrown up an earthwork. It was meek enough, but it was a start.

Word of the meeting spread through Washington, arousing McCarthy's lively suspicions. He telephoned the White House to request an appointment with the President, but his call was never returned. Soon it was forgotten, for his staff had turned up another unfortunate victim, this time an obscure army dentist whose routine promotion from captain to major McCarthy would characterize as "the key to the deliberate Communist infiltration of our armed forces."

For his part, President Eisenhower was preoccupied with the French and Indochina, too much so to be distracted by the antics of Senator McCarthy and his callow assistant. From at least three directions Eisenhower was getting top-drawer advice about the Viet Minh and how they might be checked; to ponder the messages that streamed across his desk from Berlin, Saigon, and the Pentagon was enough to demand all his concentration, but the struggle over the Bricker amendment was then at full tide, and if he were overborne on that issue his hopes of conducting a rational foreign policy in the Cold War would be impaired. For the President, McCarthy could be only something remote, occasionally glimpsed in a newspaper headline, the mention of whom at a cabinet meeting or a press conference warranted a sharp rebuke.

Foster Dulles was in Berlin attending a conference of foreign ministers; in Saigon was Lieutenant General John W. (Iron Mike) O'Daniel, sent there by Eisenhower to appraise the French military effort against the Viet Minh; and meeting regularly, usually in the Pentagon, was a Special Committee—Roger Kyes, deputy secretary of defense; Bedell Smith, undersecretary of state; Admiral Radford, chairman of the Joint Chiefs; Allen Dulles of the CIA of course; and three or four lesser military lights— appointed by the President to advise him on United States policy regarding Indochina. The matter, then, was well staffed and the President might be confident that the reports regularly handed him represented the best judgment of his most trusted counselors. Eisenhower's intelligence—cold, unhurried, precise—fitted the reports into what he hoped would be a resistless pattern and led him to his unemotional decisions.

What the President wanted, what he was striving for in the first months of 1954, was to imbue the French with the will to win in Vietnam; to ensure that they had enough Vietnamese troops to do the job by persuading the French to issue an unequivocal pledge of Indochinese independence from colonial controls; and to convince them of the need to ratify the treaty that would establish EDC, or, to put the matter as it seemed to the French, to convince a people who had been twice within one generation ravaged by German invasions that Russia, not Germany, was their more menacing enemy. In the late winter and early spring of 1954 the President was chiefly trying to keep the French from negotiating a settlement in Indochina, to keep them fighting effectively against the Viet Minh. Right or wrong, he was of a mind that the only alternative if the French retired from the field was for American military power to take up the challenge. Perhaps he believed the war should go on because, as he wrote (and as his critics have been at pains to remind us he wrote), the loss of Vietnam would have meant "the loss of valuable deposits of tin and prodigious supplies of rubber and rice." Perhaps it was because he could not abide "the surrender of millions to Communist enslavement." Perhaps he dared yield to no further encroachment of communism on the free world because he feared the consequent howls from the McCarthys and Knowlands of his own Republican right wing.* The President's instant motive, whether simple or complex, is neither crucial nor relevant. It is enough to report what he was asked to do and what he did.

In January the French asked the United States to supply them with four hundred mechanics trained in the maintenance of B–26 and C–47 aircraft. The request was referred to the Special Committee. Smith suggested sending two hundred air force mechanics. Kyes wondered if that were not a first step along the road to outright intervention by U.S. combat forces. Smith scouted the notion, but argued that victory in Indochina was so vital he would support intervention by U.S. air and naval forces. Radford agreed. Kyes thought the matter important enough to warrant its being taken to the highest level. (The French also wanted some pilots, but that request could be arranged directly with the CIA, which was operating an airline in the Far East.) It was agreed that Smith would carry the committee's recommendations to the President. One of these was that General O'Daniel be designated chief of the U.S. Military Advisory and Assistance Group (MAAG) in Vietnam, another that the air force technicians be assigned to this group and used only at bases where they would be secure from combat or capture.

The President was disposed to treat the question of the air force personnel cautiously. He invited congressional leaders of both parties to the White House for exploratory discussion. Sure enough, it developed that even such senators as Russell of Georgia and Stennis of Mississippi had misgivings about committing U.S. servicemen to Indochina. Would that not open the door to further U.S. involvement? The President gave reassurances but, in the way such things happen word of congressional qualms got out and traveled all the way to Berlin, to the conference of foreign ministers, where Bidault, already arguing that the war in Indochina be brought to the negotiation table for a political settlement, grew more insistent than ever.

The Berlin Conference (January 25–February 18, 1954) had been getting nowhere. To the western three—Dulles, Eden, Bidault—the "German question," the second point on their agenda, meant the unification of East and West Germany, but to Molotov it meant the problem of achieving European security, which in turn meant the junking of EDC, an instrument he feared was aimed against the Soviet Union. The third point on the agenda, a treaty of peace with Austria, was lost in the same muddle.

* Eisenhower confided to his good friend Gruenther that "Knowland has no foreign policy except to develop high blood pressure whenever he mentions the words 'Red China.' "

If the conference was to achieve anything, it must be on the first point, "Measures for reducing international tension and convening a five-power conference," and since that involved inviting Red China to take a hand in settling world problems, Dulles was dead set against it. Eden, however, perceived a gleam of hope: perhaps Molotov would be content with, and Dulles could be persuaded to accept, a five-power conference limited to discussion of Far Eastern problems. Bidault would be relieved, for a settlement of the war with the Viet Minh might then somehow be arranged.

Meanwhile, despite senatorial uneasiness, the air force technicians had already left for Vietnam. The President spoke of the matter with less than candor. He was asked if American technicians were servicing American bombers in Indochina. "I couldn't say whether they are or not," he answered, "but we do have a military mission. One of their jobs is instructing in air as well as the rest of the things." Later, when told a member of the Senate Armed Services Committee feared "we are inching our way into war in Indochina," and that the committee had not been informed "of the sending of additional technicians," the President flushed with anger. He insisted the Congress was kept informed. "There is no attempt here," he said, "to carry on the affairs of America in a darkened room."

It was on that same day that Eisenhower cabled Dulles instructions on the need to keep the French from relaxing their war effort:

> There is no ground whatsoever for assuming we intend to reverse or ignore U.S. commitments made to French. Those commitments were based upon assumptions that French would act comprehensively and vigorously in prosecuting war; and their commitment in this regard is as binding as is ours in providing additional money and equipment. . . .
>
> General O'Daniel's most recent report is more encouraging than given to you through French sources. . . . To summarize, administration has no intention of evading its pledges in the area providing the French performance measures up to the promises made by them as basis for requesting our increased help.

But the French demanded a conference with Indochina included on the agenda, and Dulles could do no more than reject China as one of the five governments acting as host. (The British resolved that dilemma by suggesting that there be no conveners, no convened, but simply a gathering of interested parties.) A place was set, Geneva, and a day to begin, April 26. Western unity was in shards. The French people wanted an end to the war, the British government held that French forces should at least stand fast in order to preserve a negotiating position at Geneva, and only the United States clung to the conviction that the war should go on until the

Viet Minh had been smashed. Eisenhower's leadership of the free world had sustained a reverse, whether an irreversible one the next weeks would show.

On his return to Washington, Foster Dulles scarcely had time to report to the nation about the conference in Berlin—the West had won "one hundred percent of what we wanted" on Far Eastern issues, he said, and "No informed observers believe that we were outmaneuvered at Berlin" —before he had to leave for Caracas, Venezuela, for the tenth Inter-American Conference. (The President had not been on hand to greet Dulles on his arrival from Berlin. After a weekend of quail shooting at George Humphrey's plantation in Georgia, the President had been flown to Palm Springs, in the California desert, for six days of golf and reflection on the unpleasant turn of events abroad.) Dulles had a job of work at Caracas: he had to lay the juridical groundwork for the coup d'état against Guatemala, the coup which his brother Allen's CIA subordinates had already for some little time been organizing. His job had also been organized for him: while he was in Berlin, Bedell Smith had got the Operations Coordinating Board (a kind of potting shed for the National Security Council) "to work to prepare a black book for Caracas"—a compendium of the sins and errors into which Guatemala had been led by its social-democratic revolution, and a vade mecum of tactical procedures at the conference.

The secretary's job was not a hard one. Representatives of twenty of the American republics, so called, were on hand (Costa Rica sent no delegation as a protest against the dictatorship in Venezuela, the host government), and all of them were clients of the United States and consequently eager to solicit the benevolence of the administration of which Foster Dulles was such a distinguished luminary. Votes in favor of resolutions proposed by Dulles would, then, be easy to find. Votes in favor of a resolution addressed against the ferment in Guatemala would be even easier in a company that included the agents of such bravos as Somoza of Nicaragua, Batista of Cuba, Trujillo of the Dominican Republic, Pérez Jiménez of Venezuela, Rojas Pinilla of Colombia, and Odría of Peru. Dulles's key resolution argued that "the domination or control of the political institutions of any American State by the international communist movement, extending to this hemisphere the political system of an extra-continental power, would constitute a threat to the sovereignty and political independence of the American States," and called for "appropriate action" against an "intervention in American affairs."

To Foster Dulles the truth of this assertion was as self-evident as the splendid raiment worn by Hans Christian Andersen's emperor, but as far as Guillermo Toriello could see, the emperor was as naked as a jaybird, and he said as much. (Dulles was heavily amused by Toriello, who was "so innocent" as to ask, "What is international communism?") The Dulles resolution, said Toriello, was no more than "the internationalization of McCarthyism," and so touched off a debate in which he got more applause than did Dulles. Applause, but not votes; not when next day a voter might be praying for economic assistance. After the debate, during which the U.S. successfully fended off all attempts to amend the resolution, it was carried by a vote of seventeen to one—Argentina and Mexico abstained, and only Guatemala voted nay. A Uruguayan delegate said: "We contributed our approval without enthusiasm, without optimism, without joy, and without the feeling that we were contributing to a constructive measure."

The resolution was adopted on March 13, 1954. The conference had two more weeks to run, but Dulles at once left Caracas for Washington, his job done. Leadership of the U.S. delegation was turned over to Henry F. Holland, then assistant secretary of state for inter-American affairs.

In Washington, meanwhile, the President had come as close to rebuking McCarthy as he had ever done. The proximate causes for his unusual behavior were McCarthy's slashing attack on an army general who had been decorated for gallantry in combat and McCarthy's public humiliation of Robert T. Stevens, secretary of the army. (In London, the *Times* had commented acidly of this affair: "Senator McCarthy achieved today what General Burgoyne and General Cornwallis never achieved—the surrender of the American Army.") At last Eisenhower was stung into a calculated reproof. He did not mention the senator by name, his phrases had little bite ("queasily worded," one correspondent wrote, and another commented, "pretty feeble, and . . . a very long time coming"), but there was no mistaking his target, and he even drew a diagram for bringing McCarthy low: ". . . it is the responsibility of the Congress to see to it that its procedures are proper and fair . . . I expect the Republican membership . . . to assume the primary responsibility . . . since they are the majority party and, therefore, control the committees." McCarthy was prompt to retort. "Apparently," he said, in his gravelly voice, "the President and I now agree on the necessity of getting rid of Communists." As if to emphasize his insolence, he later announced that he was withdrawing the word "now," lest it cause some "misinterpretation."

In fact the President was in a poor way to criticize McCarthy, for his administration had been aping the devices of McCarthyism all on its own. More numbers had been published, purporting to show how diligent Eisenhower's team had been in ferreting out subversives. For weeks the press had been seeking to establish some certainties about the twenty-two hundred security risks the President had proudly mentioned in his message on the state of the union: who were they? how many were spies, if any? At last some figures were announced, but they failed to convince because they would not stand still. A scorecard was needed for what disgusted critics now called the "numbers racket":

Date Announced	"Security" Dismissals	"Subversives"
March 1	2,244	355
March 2	2,427	383
March 4	2,429	422

McCarthy had reason to giggle. His own staff could not have done better.*

Curiously, now that McCarthy and McCarthyism were about to burst, like some spectacular nova, into a dazzling notoriety that would keep Americans by the millions nailed in front of their television sets for one hundred and eighty-seven hours, spread over eight weeks from April 22

---

* Later that month the President found time to raise questions of his own bearing on the subject of communists in government. He sent a memorandum to his attorney general to inquire: Had any congressional committees turned up any alleged subversive who could be indicted? Specifically, had the McCarthy committee found any who could be indicted? Had any been uncovered by the various executive commissions appointed under his loyalty-security program? In short, what were the undisputed facts?

Undisputed facts remained hard to come by. Throughout 1955 Philip Young, chairman of the Civil Service Commission, would produce sets of figures dealing with dismissals and resignations. Here they are, with annotations:

Date Announced	"Security" Dismissals	"Security" Resignations
January 3, 1955	3,002	5,006

These figures Eisenhower would later cite in *Mandate for Change*, page 315, quite as though they were final. Young's report added that of the 3,002 dismissed, 2,096 were "subversives," in the sense that their dossiers included information of "subversive activities, subversive associations, or membership in subversive organizations." It need be said only that a "subversive organization" was one which the attorney general chose to add to a list of such. His criteria were both arbitrary and flexible.

July 28	3,432	5,447

At this point, Commissioner Young remarked that the job "is done."

September 26	3,614	5,696
September 29	3,586	5,684

The later figures represented a "correction."

November 28	3,685	5,920

By this time the procedure had run out of steam and was getting a very poor press. A couple of weeks later the counsel of a Senate subcommittee which had been inquiring into these figures and whatever methods were used to arrive at them announced that he had checked the 3,586 "security" dismissals of September 29 and had found that all but 342 of them had been dismissed for reasons having nothing to do with security. Thereafter the whole shameful business was swept under the carpet.

to June 17, President Eisenhower could all but banish the senator from his mind and concentrate on seizing the initiative in the Cold War. Occasionally, to be sure, McCarthy would intrude, like a recurrent hiccup. Very early during the course of the televised army-McCarthy hearings, Senator Charles Potter, a Republican of Michigan, was invited to come privily to the White House in order to acquaint the President with what was going on. If one is to credit Potter's later account of his visit with Eisenhower (and this is hard, for his book is marred by errors of all kinds), the President was utterly unaware that Robert Stevens, the man who had been selected to serve as his secretary of the army, had taken the stand that day (April 22) to testify; nor did he know how his old friend and comrade Bedell Smith had fared as a witness. By May 11 the hearings had taken a turn that once again forced them on Eisenhower's attention: Stevens wished to provide the committee conducting the hearings with the names of all the officers who had been involved in the promotion and, subsequently, the honorable discharge from the army of the dental officer who had been singled out by McCarthy as the symbol of communist conspiracy among the military; General Matthew B. Ridgway, the army's chief of staff, was violently opposed to any such procedure; now the problem had been bucked up to the commander in chief for a decision. Eisenhower wanted the case handled on its merits. "Of these," he confided to his personal diary, "I know nothing. I have not followed the hearings either in the press or by television or radio." (In Vietnam, the insurgent Viet Minh had just succeeded in capturing Dien Bien Phu, he needed every available moment to consult with his advisers on the nation's proper next step, yet he must turn aside to deal with the case of an army dentist.) Eisenhower's first inclination was to tell the army "to provide every possible bit of information," but more prudent counsel prevailed. On May 13 (and, to drive the point home, again, and this time publicly, on May 17) the President directed the secretary of defense to instruct all employees of the defense establishment that they were not to testify about any of their "conversations or communications" dealing with "official matters" nor to produce any "documents or reproductions" concerning such matters. At once McCarthy protested that this presidential order was an "iron curtain," adding darkly, "I don't think the President is responsible. I don't think his judgment is that bad." The defiance was scarcely noticed. Following the President's tentative, belated criticism of McCarthy, the ranks of his deputies had implacably closed. Soon the senator would be squashed flat.

A striking feature of the two chief initiatives taken by the U.S. in 1954 was the extent to which the affairs of America were carried on, if not in a darkened room, at least with as much secrecy as could be maintained, and with a great deal more secrecy than seems compatible with an open society. Always, to be sure, the President was at pains to acquaint leading congressmen with the broad aspects (if not the crucial details) of his strategy; but the people, the sovereign in the republic, knew next to nothing of what was planned by their own government, of the war that at least twice was almost launched, of the paramilitary steps short of war that were actively pushed, or of the liberties stifled, the lives ended, the legal government toppled, the corrupt dictatorship instituted in its stead—always in the name of the free world. Indeed, much of what was done in secrecy then is still secret now. But the outlines have come clear.

Rationalization of American policy was plain enough. A group of men —honorable, intelligent, experienced—sitting together regularly as members of the National Security Council, had reached a reasoned conviction that the nationalist insurgencies the world around would bring not independence for their peoples but only a slavery more wretched than the colonial dependency they sought to overthrow. In short, what seemed patriotic insurrections were truly dangerous revolutions that threatened to carry rich, populous lands out of the "free world" and into the orbit of the "communist bloc." What had already taken place in China must not be permitted to take place elsewhere, and especially not in Indochina.

Shortly before his press conference of April 7, the President scribbled some notes on what was presently to become celebrated as the "falling domino" principle. Sure enough, a reporter obliged by putting a remarkably opportune question:

Q: Mr. President, would you mind commenting on the strategic importance of Indochina to the free world? I think there has been, across the country, some lack of understanding on just what it means to us.

THE PRESIDENT: . . . First of all, you have the specific value of a locality in its production of materials that the world needs.

Then you have the possibility that many human beings pass under a dictatorship that is inimical to the free world.

Finally, you have . . . what you would call the "falling domino" principle. You have a row of dominos set up, you knock over the first one, and what will happen to the last one is the certainty that it will go over very quickly. . . .

Now . . . two of the items from this particular area that the world uses are tin and tungsten. . . . There are others, of course, the rubber plantations and so on.

Then . . . Asia, after all, has already lost some 450 million of its peoples to the Communist dictatorship, and we simply can't afford greater losses.

But when we come to the possible sequence of events, the loss of Indochina, of Burma, of Thailand, of the [Malay] Peninsula, and Indonesia following, now you begin to talk about areas that not only multiply the disadvantages that you would suffer through loss of materials, sources of materials, but now you are talking really about millions and millions and millions of people.

Finally, the geographical position achieved . . . turns the . . . island defensive chain of Japan, Formosa, of the Philippines and to the southward; it moves in to threaten Australia and New Zealand.

It takes away, in its economic aspects, that region that Japan must have as a trading area or Japan, in turn, will have only one place in the world to go—that is, toward the Communist areas in order to live.

So, the possible consequences . . . are just incalculable to the free world.

The metaphor of the falling dominoes had been used by others; it is safe to assume it had for some months been a favorite of the men of the National Security Council. Those like-minded men were agreed that the forces of the free world must take their stand and fight to defeat what they perceived as communist aggression in Indochina. They recognized that, as Eisenhower would acknowledge, "the mass of the population supported the enemy," and that "it was inevitable that the French should find it impossible to retain the loyalty of their Vietnamese troops," but neither of these considerations shook their conviction that the Viet Minh had to be militarily defeated.

The U.S. stood alone, and what is more, President Eisenhower knew it.

As for the French, General Paul Ely, their army chief of staff, had visited Washington in March and had specifically told Foster Dulles that "in the mind of the French government and the French command, a military solution of the Indochinese conflict did not seem possible within reasonable terms and at a tolerable price, and that it was advisable to find a political solution to the problem." Next Anthony Eden cabled the British ambassador in Washington to say that while "We fully share United States desire to see Indochina preserved from communism . . . we feel it would be unrealistic not to face the possibility that the conditions for a favorable solution in Indochina may no longer exist." Those views had duly been communicated to Foster Dulles and Bedell Smith, and by them carried to the White House.

Was there a satisfactory political solution? Sir Roger Makins, the British ambassador, suggested the possibility of dividing Vietnam by partition. Smith rejoined that the United States (viz., the National Security Council) had already carefully studied such an idea but had decided it would lead to communist domination of Southeast Asia (the "falling domino" principle) and had therefore rejected it.

Dilemma. "Even if others were reluctant to act," Eisenhower wrote, "we could not afford to sit on the sidelines and do nothing." Yet he felt strongly that the U.S. should intervene in Indochina only as one of a co-alition of free nations. The memory of the hateful war in Korea was still fresh; to end it had been one of the few achievements of his young ad-ministration; would the Congress concur in the need to send American troops to fight in another Asian war, one even farther from home than Korea? Would the people? Plainly what was needed was a cram course in the desperate plight of Indochina. Such a curriculum appears to have been assigned by the National Security Council, for its leading members hopped to it with a will. The President's reference to the "falling domino" principle can be considered to have opened the campaign of enlighten-ment, and thereafter for a week or ten days there followed a spate of speeches by the President, the secretary of state, Admiral Radford, the Vice President, and others—all subtly hinting of U.S. intervention. Coming as it did only a fortnight before the scheduled conference at Geneva, where political settlement of the fighting in Vietnam was on the agenda, this pro-gram of agitation and propaganda was the more remarkable. Perhaps the most energetic pedagogue was Foster Dulles. He conducted what in Richard Rovere's view "must undoubtedly [have been] one of the boldest campaigns of political suasion ever undertaken by an American states-man"—lectures and briefings for congressmen, journalists, radio and tele-vision entertainers, molders of opinion down to the humblest level—all designed to warn of the impending disaster in Indochina should the U.S. not at once don battle dress.

While this organized effort was at its height, Eisenhower quietly slipped away for a few days of rest and golf at Augusta National. He had been scheduled to address a meeting of the American Society of Newspaper Editors on April 16, but the date conflicted with his cherished custom of playing a round of golf with the winner of the Masters Tournament (that year his friend Ben Hogan was to defend his title but lose in a playoff), so a month earlier he had asked the Vice President to fill in for him. Nixon agreed. Speaking off the record, Nixon said: ". . . if in order to avoid further communist expansion in Asia and particularly in Indochina . . . we must take the risk now by putting American boys in, I believe that the executive branch has to [do] it, and I personally would support such a decision." Correspondents of newspapers in London and Paris identified Nixon as the source of these inflammatory remarks. The storm of angry congressional protests that followed showed how strong was the popular revulsion from any American involvement in the war. Another approach would have to be found.

A possibility already sounded with the French General Ely was Operation Vulture, Admiral Radford's pet scheme: sixty B–29s (the so-called Flying Fortresses) to be flown from bases in the Philippines and, accompanied by one hundred and fifty navy attack bombers from the carriers *Essex* and *Boxer,* to bomb Viet Minh positions around beleaguered Dien Bien Phu: one heavy raid to rescue the threatened garrison. Radford's heart was set on Operation Vulture, and since Ely had heard Eisenhower instruct the admiral to give priority to every French request made with the purpose of lifting the siege of Dien Bien Phu, he quite naturally reported to Premier Laniel in Paris his firm impression that the Americans would, if the French requested it, launch a strike against the Viet Minh forces investing the fortress.

Radford had also sought to peddle his Vulture to a small group of congressional leaders. He and Dulles had spent more than an hour at the President's behest lecturing the leaders of both Houses and of both parties on the crisis in Vietnam; what was wanted, they said, was a joint resolution approved by both Houses permitting the President to use American air and naval power in Indochina. But once the legislators learned that Dulles and Radford (and Eisenhower) were proposing that the U.S. proceed with Vulture on its own, without allies, they had refused their support. No joint resolution, they had told Dulles, unless Britain, Australia, New Zealand, and the free nations of Southeast Asia were involved as well in helping the French. And Eisenhower, apprised of this congressional reluctance, found himself bound to agree.

Even as Dulles and Radford were telling the President of the congressional reaction to his request for a joint resolution, across the Atlantic in Matignon, a small town near the coast of Brittany, a meeting had been convened of a French war council: to his country house Laniel had summoned Paul Reynaud, Bidault, Pleven, and Generals Juin and Ely. Also present was an officer dispatched from Hanoi by General Navarre to report that the fortress of Dien Bien Phu could be saved only by a bombardment laid down by American aviation—in short, by Operation Vulture. The moment had come, the moment pledged Ely by Admiral Radford, the chairman of the American Joint Chiefs of Staff. With the consent of his war council, Laniel sent to Paris for the American ambassador, Douglas Dillon, to present him with an official request for the air attack described by Radford. Dillon assured Laniel he would transmit the request to Washington, but in the same breath expressed his doubts that any action would be undertaken without the consent of the Congress and the active cooperation of the other interested powers, especially those of the British Commonwealth. Laniel nodded. He understood. So much for Ely's "impression bien nette" of Radford's assurance.

Encoded cables sped back and forth. Early Monday came Dulles's reply: ". . . it is not repeat not possible for U.S. to commit belligerent acts in Indochina without full political understanding with France and other countries. . . . U.S. is doing everything possible . . . to prepare public . . . action is impossible except on coalition basis . . . U.S. [will] do everything short of belligerency."

Bidault understood. Laniel understood. But the American refusal rankled.

Another swift effort had to be made to bring Britain round to the Eisenhower-Dulles policy. Eisenhower wrote Churchill a long letter urging a coalition of nations (U.S., U.K., France, Australia, New Zealand, Thailand, the Philippines, the Associated States of Indochina), reminding Churchill that the failure to halt Hirohito, Hitler, and Mussolini "in unity and in time" had brought "many years of stark tragedy and desperate peril," and suggesting there was something to be learned from that historical analogy.* Dulles followed the letter in a few days to attempt personal suasion, but he found Eden "determined [not to] be hustled into injudicious military decisions" and leery of proclaiming any defensive coalitions just before going to the conference table at Geneva. Eden welcomed the idea of a coalition for the collective defense of Southeast Asia, but he argued the need to invite India and Burma to join; any indication that India might be included, however, left Dulles aghast. (India was neutralist in the Cold War, and in Dulles's Manichaean view neutralism was as bad as communism.) The matter was left in abeyance.

On his return to Washington, though, Dulles at once set about convening an informal group to plan the collective defense of Southeast Asia, and for that purpose he invited the ambassadors of only those nations which Eisenhower had listed in his letter to Churchill—no India, no Burma. To keep the arrangements within his control, Dulles had word of them released to the press. In London, Eden was furious. His cold diplomatic language described Dulles's action as "entirely contrary to the spirit of our agreement." It was all most unfortunate, even if it had happened, as Eisenhower charitably put it, "possibly through misunderstanding." So stern were the protests filed by the British ambassador that

---

* The reminder was presumptuous. Few Englishmen knew better than Churchill the folly of having permitted Hitler his aggressions in Europe, Mussolini his in North Africa, and Hirohito his in China; few Englishmen had more bitterly opposed the policy of appeasement in the 1930s. On the other hand, Eisenhower's secretary of state had viewed with equanimity the Japanese invasion of Manchuria and Hitler's reoccupation of the Rhineland.

Dulles was constrained to change the character of the meeting to a general preparation for the negotiations at Geneva. But British animosities were not soothed.

Nevertheless, the foundations had been laid for the South-East Asia Treaty Organization (SEATO), which is what the President and his secretary of state had been aiming for. Another concern, since they reposed confidence neither in the French nor in the structure of any government for Vietnam that might be devised at Geneva, was to find a strong anticommunist Vietnamese patriot of some experience and, if possible, of some ability as well—a man who could emerge as premier of the South Vietnam that now appeared to be an inevitable outcome of the Geneva settlement. There was such a man and he had been resident in the United States for some little time. His name was Ngo Dinh Diem. He claimed to be the descendant of mandarins (this was a vanity, and untrue); he had been a functionary in the French colonial government, rising to the ministerial level; he had shunned collaboration with the Japanese during the war; he had a reputation for probity; most important, he was a devout Roman Catholic and a militant anticommunist. With these credentials, Diem had easily formed liaisons with influential figures in Washington, with Francis Cardinal Spellman in New York, within academic circles, and among liberals who had been frightened by McCarthyism into extravagantly anticommunist attitudes. He had gradually acquired a most intriguing set of sponsors, and it followed that he had attracted the attention of the CIA. To his many inviting qualities could now be added yet another: he was available. In May 1953 he departed for Belgium and thence to Paris, where he might more conveniently be in touch with the plump, indolent emperor of Vietnam, Bao Dai. The one a French puppet, the other assumed to be an American one; for a short time their strings could be pulled in concert.

Secretary Dulles, proudly taking note that he had clocked one hundred and four thousand miles (believed to set a new record for travel by a cabinet member during the first fifteen months in office) in his search for peace, was flown to Paris once again on April 20 for a meeting of the NATO Council, convened on the eve of the fateful Geneva Conference. He planned to consult with Eden and Bidault. He planned also to call upon Bao Dai, with a view to persuading him to go back to Vietnam with Ngo Dinh Diem and command the struggle to hold back the communist tides.

Objectively, pressures were mounting, for the defenders of Dien Bien Phu had been pushed to their limit, and the fate of that remote fastness had come to symbolize the fate of all Indochina. Bad enough that Truman had "lost" China, now Eisenhower was about to "lose" Indochina—unless Foster Dulles, by adroit footwork, could make it seem otherwise.

A cablegram from General Navarre on April 23 stated he saw only two alternatives: Operation Vulture or a request for a cease-fire. Bidault showed the message to Dulles. By Bidault's later account, Dulles asked: "What if we were to give you two atomic bombs?" Since such weapons would incinerate defenders and attackers alike, the answer to the question was not hard to predict; yet by rejecting the offer the French would shoulder another share of the responsibility for "losing" Indochina. Dulles cabled Eisenhower an "eyes only" message advising of Navarre's latest request for intervention by U.S. B–29s, and added: "Bidault gives the impression of a man close to the breaking point. . . . He is obviously exhausted and is confused and rambling in his talk."

It remained for Dulles to make the British seem also to be responsible for the "loss" of Indochina or, as Eisenhower would later put the matter, "to bring the British position into the clear." On Saturday, April 24, Dulles and Admiral Radford met with Eden. Surrender of Dien Bien Phu, they suggested, would be followed by collapse of French resistance throughout Indochina and perhaps also by a general Vietnamese uprising against the French; what was needed was a dramatic gesture of Anglo-American support. The Congress was more likely to authorize intervention if the British would at least offer token assistance, perhaps the dispatch of some RAF units from Malaya to Hanoi. The U.S. would undertake to internationalize the conflict if only the British would lend a hand.

Personally, Eden doubted both the military and the political merits of this scheme, but he undertook to call a special meeting of the British cabinet to discuss them. Amid the mounting concern of British press and public, the cabinet met the next day, Sunday. Churchill shared Eden's opinion. As he saw it, the British were being asked to assist in deceiving the American Congress into consenting to a military operation of dubious value, one which might well provoke a major war. The cabinet unanimously agreed: "We are not prepared to give any undertaking now, in advance of the Geneva conference, concerning United Kingdom military action in Indo-China."

Meanwhile, in his White House office, the President had been reviewing the stream of top-secret messages from Dulles in Paris and from foreign service officers and embassies around the world. Robert McClintock in Saigon, for example, sent word that Navarre was now ready to sue for peace unless the U.S. would agree to commit troops and so internationalize the war. Yet Dulles reported that Eden feared U.S. intervention might lead to a third world war. The talk of a cease-fire was no longer limited simply to Dien Bien Phu; now it was of a cease-fire for all Vietnam. From Australia and New Zealand came reports that the governments of those countries might join in a collective action if it were proposed by the U.S.; if true, this meant that two Commonwealth nations were edging away from British policy. "A very tough one for us," mused the President, "but I think I would go along with the idea." On this Sunday he and Dulles exchanged several cablegrams, and presently Dulles proposed an immediate public statement to be jointly issued by the governments of the U.S., U.K., France, the Philippines, and the Associated States of Indochina, declaring their common purpose to check further communist advances in Southeast Asia and to use "eventual military means" to that end. Word of the scheme was brought to Eden; he was further told that President Eisenhower would seek congressional approval of a bombing strike by American naval aircraft if the British would consent to join in the public statement. Once again Churchill summoned his cabinet into emergency session. Should the United Kingdom support direct American intervention in Vietnam and, very likely, later American attacks on the Chinese mainland? The cabinet decided not, and instructed Eden so to inform Dulles and Bidault when he should see them on his way to Geneva.

In Washington, Eisenhower was "disappointed." In Paris, Dulles could reflect that the United States had taken a firm stand as the strong bulwark against communist encroachment, while the British had seemed hesitant and timorous. The press would be discreetly informed.

And so, under the most melancholy of auspices, with the three principal western allies mistrustful each of the others, the Geneva Conference was called to order. Foster Dulles refused to acknowledge the presence of Chou En-lai of China; similarly Georges Bidault ignored Pham Van Dong, the Viet Minh minister of foreign affairs. The statesmen set about to make a peace.

In Washington, the President was scheduled to meet with the Republican legislative leaders. It was a fit time to acquaint the congressmen with the situation in Guatemala, to foreshadow the stirring events soon to take place there. "There are some things which we are doing now," read the memorandum drafted for the meeting, "consistent with the anticommunist resolution adopted at Caracas." Accurate information was required, evidence "that would convince the minds of reasonable men" of the communist penetration of Guatemalan political institutions. Once it could be shown that "the international communist organization has achieved domination and control of these political institutions, we must be prepared to invoke the consultative procedure contemplated by the Rio Treaty" to consider the threat to the peace of the Americas.

No need to go into much more detail.

Later that day the President dictated a letter to his old friend General Gruenther at SHAPE outside Paris. His thoughts had turned once more to Vietnam and to the battles the French were fighting there. A sad and somber conflict. What was lacking was spirit; the French need, Eisenhower wrote, "A new and inspirational leader—and I do *not* mean one that is 6 feet 5 and who considers himself to be . . . the offspring of Clemenceau and Jeanne d'Arc." Eisenhower deplored the inability of the French to make up their minds that the Russians were more to be feared than the Germans. At all events, the problem of the moment was how best to stop communist advances in Southeast Asia.

On May 7 the French garrison at Dien Bien Phu surrendered to the Viet Minh. Dulles, who had determined to show his disapproval of any cease-fire agreement by turning his back on the conference that might negotiate it, had already left Geneva and was in Washington. When news of the collapse of Dien Bien Phu reached the White House, Dulles came to the President's office and the two men were closeted with Cutler, the special assistant for national security affairs. Eisenhower spent some time revising the draft of a radio-television speech Dulles was to make that night; he wanted some easily memorable phrases in it, such as, "The United States will never start a war" or "Only the Congress can declare war."* Next the President decided that if certain provisions were agreed to by France, the U.S. government should and would seek authority from the Congress "to intervene with combat forces." The stipulations included a concession of "genuine freedom" to the Indochinese states and an agreement that the U.S. would assume the "major responsibility" for training Vietnamese troops and "share responsibility for military planning." No longer was British involvement a precondition. Dulles engaged to convey to the French the President's views.

When the Laniel government gave the American offer a reserved welcome, Eisenhower, after conferring with Dulles, Radford, and Secretary of Defense Wilson, directed Dulles to draft a resolution that the President could present to a joint session of the Congress requesting authority to commit American troops in Vietnam. Once again the U.S. was balanced

* The United States might have to undertake "serious commitments" to help defend Southeast Asia, the secretary would declare that night, but the President would authorize no "military action" without congressional approval. "Only the Congress can declare war," the secretary would say.

on the knife's edge: contingency planning was being sped by both State Department and Pentagon: the diplomatic latticework, the rigging of a complex military machine. In Geneva, Eden, struggling to patch together a cease-fire, was dismayed to learn, belatedly and from reports in the press, of what his friends and allies were up to.

While the conditions of American intervention were still being mooted by the French, while the community of U.S. intelligence was estimating the chances were fifty-fifty that American intervention would in its turn precipitate an armed intervention by the People's Republic of China, Foster Dulles telephoned Eisenhower to talk about the traffic of tankers transporting petroleum to China. U.S. aircraft, as both men knew, did reconnaissance over the Taiwan Strait and subsequently their information was relayed to Chiang Kai-shek's officers in Taipei; the Chinese Nationalists then attempted to search suspicious ships and seize their cargoes. The U.S., Dulles commented, was similarly searching ships bound for Guatemala; "it's a little illegal, but no one so far has picked it up." Chiang's officers assumed that U.S. reconnaissance indicated acquiescence in their behavior. Since August 1953 two Polish ships had thus been intercepted; for various reasons other efforts had failed. Now three Soviet tankers carrying thirty thousand tons of fuel for jet airplanes were bound for Chinese ports. Should Chiang's men be told of them? Eisenhower gave permission to inform Taipei about the oncoming Soviet tankers, but he added he did not wish to urge that the ships be intercepted.

The comparable U.S. reconnaissance in the Caribbean was not watertight. In mid-May the Swedish ship Alfhem, chartered by a British firm and carrying a cargo of small arms and ammunition manufactured by Skoda in Czechoslovakia, put in to Puerto Barrios. From the Guatemalan point of view, a routine circumstance: for several years the Guatemalan government had sought to purchase arms, first from the United States, then elsewhere; refused on all sides of the free world and uncomfortably aware of the imminent putsch organized by the CIA, President Arbenz had at last sent an old friend, Major Alfonso Martínez, to shop behind the iron curtain; he had purchased ten million dollars' worth of arms; recognizing that the shipment would be seized by the United States in the absence of ordinary precautions, the purchaser had given instructions to ensure delivery. All normal and satisfactory.

The view from Washington was quite different. To reporters Dulles spoke with "gravity" of a "massive shipment of arms from behind the Iron Curtain" and wondered "why, if the operation was an aboveboard and honorable one, all of its details were so masked." The U.S. already enjoyed an arms-aid agreement with Nicaragua; on May 17 negotiations were hastily initiated with Honduras for the same sort of pact; the crinkly papers having been duly signed three days later, U.S. Air Force Globemaster airplanes began at once shuttling back and forth transporting rifles, machine guns, and ammunition to the two countries. Everyone involved was confident these arms would quickly become equipment for Castillo Armas and his scruffy band of CIA-trained mercenaries. On May 20 the U.S. blocked shipment from Hamburg of a small cargo of antiaircraft shells ordered by Guatemala. On May 26 U.S. authorities halted a French freighter in the Panama Canal and confiscated a shipment of rifles consigned to El Salvador but suspected to be slated for delivery to Guatemala. Finally, the U.S. Navy was ordered to institute what amounted to a blockade of the Guatemalan coast. Ambassadors in Washington were informed that suspicious vessels were to be searched, with the consent of the governments involved if time permitted. At least three friendly governments protested the U.S. restriction. The French rejected the U.S. request and the Dutch strongly objected to the search of a freighter at San Juan, Puerto Rico. Nor were the British agreeable. It seemed to Anthony Eden that the American fears of a communist take-over in Guatemala were "exaggerated," nor could he possibly "acquiesce in forcible action against British ships on the high seas." Nevertheless, Dulles insisted that if necessary the U.S. Navy would stop and search even a British ship. As for the rule of law, he made clear his belief that the exigencies of the Cold War required revision of the traditional rules or their flexible application. For Eden, such talk was "worrying," but as an experienced diplomatist he set about finding a way to preserve Anglo-American unity that would at the same time maintain the freedom of the seas.

The French still finding Eisenhower's stipulated preconditions imperfect, the question of American intervention in Vietnam remained open. The Joint Chiefs of Staff, most of whom contemplated any American involvement in Indochina with a fishy eye, sent a memorandum to Secretary of Defense Wilson in which they advised that "from the point of view of the United States, with reference to the Far East as a whole, *Indochina is devoid of decisive military objectives and the allocation of more than token* U.S. armed forces *in Indochina would be a serious diversion of* limited U.S. capabilities." Whether or not the Chinese intervened, the Joint Chiefs recommended that the disposition of U.S. forces be limited to "air and naval support directed from outside Indochina," with atomic weapons being used if "militarily advantageous."

At Geneva the conference seeking an armistice in Vietnam proceeded slowly, almost imperceptibly, leading Eisenhower to conclude that the communists were deliberately stalling the negotiations to gain military advantage. On the other hand, Eden and other delegates were persuaded that it was the Americans who were working to block negotiations, even to wreck the conference. Indeed, Eisenhower had lost all patience. On June 10 he cabled Bedell Smith, the undersecretary of state then heading the American delegation, to suggest that he delegate leadership to someone of lesser rank and come home. Conversations with the French over the possibilities of U.S. intervention were likewise stalemated. In the National Assembly the temper of the French deputies was daily hardening against the policy of the Laniel government. The leader of the opposition, Pierre Mendès-France, called for a radical transformation of that policy "to make sure that France's aim is not the intervention of the United States, but an honorable end of the terrible conflict which has lasted for eight years." Two days later, on June 12, the Assembly refused the Laniel government a vote of confidence in its Indochinese policy. The government fell.

With the tides running strongly against his own policy, President Eisenhower concluded that the U.S. must end any substantive participation in the Geneva Conference. He now instructed Bedell Smith to come home, only stopping off in Paris so that he might pay a call upon Mendès-France, who was to be the next French premier.

On Tuesday, June 15, Foster Dulles informed the French ambassador, Henri Bonnet, that the time for American intervention had run out.

On the same Tuesday, Dulles charged the Guatemalan government with conducting a "reign of terror" against those who sought to rid the country of procommunist elements. That government, aware of the coup d'état about to be launched, had responded by arresting several right-wing leaders and suspending civil rights during the "crisis." Ferdinand Schupp, who had been attached to the U.S. embassy in Guatemala with the title of deputy chief of the USAF mission, abruptly fled the country with a former chief of the Guatemalan air force; the two men landed their small airplane in El Salvador; they had taken flight to join the CIA's small air force.

The next day, in the second floor dining room of the White House, the President took breakfast with a small group of his paramount advisers: Foster and Allen Dulles, Charles Wilson, representatives of the Joint Chiefs. Allen Dulles reviewed the CIA plans, due to be set in motion in a couple of days. Eisenhower listened attentively, then glanced at the men around the table. "Are you sure this is going to succeed?" he asked. His advisers were confident. "I want all of you to be damn good and sure you succeed," he said. "I'm prepared to take any steps that are necessary to see that it succeeds. When you commit the flag, you commit it to win."

On Thursday, in Paris, the Emperor Bao Dai yielded to pressure and nominated Ngo Dinh Diem to be prime minister of whatever kind of non-communist Vietnam might emerge from the negotiations at Geneva.

Later that same day, in Washington, the army-McCarthy hearings finally came to an end, with Senator Potter, much to his own astonishment, joining the Democrats on McCarthy's subcommittee to form an anti-McCarthy majority.*

Early Friday morning the CIA's P–47s dropped bombs on San José, a town on the west coast of Guatemala which was an air and naval base. With morning light Castillo Armas, driven in a shabby station wagon, crossed the border from Honduras at the head of his so-called army of liberation; the nondescript force moved up the road a few miles and made camp. Army units pinned them down; they showed little zeal to fight. The only real pugnacity in evidence was that of the American mercenaries hired to pilot the P–47s, but they encountered heavy antiaircraft fire, and one was shot full of holes while at least one other was forced to crash-land. The "war of liberation" was stuttering to a stop. On Sunday, June 20, at the suggestion of Allen Dulles a memorandum from the CIA agent in charge of the putsch was delivered to Eisenhower. The substance of the message was this:

> All depends on the Guatemalan army. If it remains loyal, Castillo Armas will be defeated. No other elements of the population will join Armas. Army officers are hesitant. They believe more justification is needed for them to defect. Overflights of Armas aircraft are drawing heavy ack-ack. No evidence of bombing thus far. Much evidence that the Guatemalan government may arm the students and the labor organizations. The Guardia Civil [police] are thought to be under communist influence. There is no confirmation that San José or Puerto Barrios have fallen. Armas depends on an internal uprising. His "army" numbers three hundred but, counting the dissidents who might later join him, it may total more than six hundred. They are equipped with rifles, sub-machine guns, and fifty-mm. mortars, none of U.S. manufacture. The whole effort is psychological: a few airplanes, a great deal of radio to create an *impression*. Deception and timing are all-important. If no latent resistance has been stimulated within the next twenty-four hours, the assumption must be that Castillo Armas will have failed.

Meanwhile a spokesman at the State Department had announced: "The department has no evidence . . . that this is anything other than a revolt

* The diverting story of how Potter's press secretary, a veteran newspaperman named Thomas McIntyre, managed to finagle Potter into an anti-McCarthy stance was told by Richard Rovere in the *New York Review* of October 28, 1965.

of Guatemalans against the government." In the United Nations the American member of the Security Council, Ambassador Henry Cabot Lodge, sang the same sweet melody: ". . . the information available to the United States thus far strongly suggests that the situation does not involve aggression but is a matter of Guatemalans against Guatemalans." Not by accident, the putsch had been planned for the month when Lodge would be sitting as president of the Security Council and would thus be in a position to short-circuit any appeals from Guatemala to the United Nations. So much he featly did. With an able assist from the French and British members, who gallantly abstained from voting, Lodge succeeded in keeping a request by Guatemala for action on its behalf from even being inscribed on the agenda.

A smoothly functioning team; but at least once Eisenhower's senior aides disagreed and had to take their dispute to the highest level. On the afternoon of Tuesday, June 22, the Dulles brothers came to the President's office together with Henry Holland, the assistant secretary of state for inter-American affairs. At issue was the matter of the CIA's little air force. Allen Dulles wanted immediate replacements for the aircraft lost. Holland was strongly opposed. He dreaded the angry reaction against the U.S. throughout Latin America once it were known, as it surely would be, that the gringo had again brazenly intervened. Hands off, said Holland. Too late, said Allen Dulles; we are committed, we must support Castillo Armas.

"What do you think Castillo's chances would be," the President asked his CIA chief, "without the aircraft?"

"About zero," Dulles said.

"Suppose we supply the aircraft. What would the chances be then?"

"About twenty percent."

The President considered. On the one hand, the ancient charge of U.S. intervention in the Caribbean, so damaging throughout Latin America. On the other hand, the chance to help an anticommunist faction, a course of action that would uphold the Caracas resolution and might win a skirmish in the Cold War. (And it would restore the dominance of U.S. commercial interests.) His duty, Eisenhower wrote later, was clear. He would order two P–51 fighter-bombers south to Nicaragua.

The meeting broke up. Eisenhower walked to the door with Allen Dulles and, with a grin, said, "Allen, that figure of twenty percent was persuasive. Showed you'd thought the thing through realistically. If you'd said ninety percent, I'd have had a tougher decision, but you seemed to be honest."

Dulles returned the grin. "Mr. President," he said, "when I saw Henry

[Holland] walk in your office with three big law books under his arm, I knew he'd lost his case already." The two men laughed.*

In less rarefied circles, amusement was restrained. On Friday, June 25, President Arbenz instructed the chief of his armed forces, his friend Colonel Carlos Enrique Díaz, to arm the students, the trade unions, and the political parties of the coalition that had elected him. So, he believed, his government could protect itself not only from the invaders but against dissident elements in the army. (Army officers had begun to show signs of disloyalty, a natural result of their dissatisfaction with "civilismo," the policy of the Arbenz government to prize loose the army's traditional grip on the nation's political life.) But Colonel Díaz reported on Saturday that other officers refused to obey the order to arm the civilians. On Sunday Toriello, the foreign minister, met with Peurifoy, the American ambassador, and offered to resign but urged that Arbenz be kept in office. Not enough. Later that day Arbenz resigned and a junta headed by Colonel Díaz took command. On Monday Díaz told Peurifoy he would outlaw the Guatemalan Communist party. Not enough. Díaz was marched out at gunpoint and an adequately reactionary officer, Colonel Elfego Monzon, took command. Enough. The "war of liberation" had reached a satisfactory climax.

On June 30 Foster Dulles spoke to the United States by radio and television. The "evil purpose of the Kremlin" to find "nesting places" in the Americas had, he said, been thwarted. "Led by Colonel Castillo Armas, patriots arose in Guatemala to challenge the communist leadership—and to change it. Thus the situation is being cured by the Guatemalans themselves."

Looking back reflectively on this episode, Eisenhower would recall "the disaffection of the Guatemalan armed forces and the population as a whole with the tyrannical regime of Arbenz. . . . The rest of Latin America was not in the least displeased. . . . Castillo Armas . . . proved to be far more than a mere rebel; he was a farseeing and able statesman. . . . he enjoyed the devotion of his people."

And now a look at the aftermath of Eisenhower's putsch in Guatemala. The junta, as its first act, disfranchised the "illiterate masses," some 70 percent of the people, including nearly all the Indians; all constitutional guarantees were suspended; the Congress was dissolved; agrarian reform was suspended, the lands expropriated from United Fruit were restored,

---

* To preserve some vestige of U.S. anonymity the P-51s were transferred to Nicaragua, whose ambassador in Washington had first to "buy" them. David Wise and Thomas B. Ross, in *The Invisible Government,* their study of the CIA, wrote that the transaction involved "some interesting financial legerdemain." Money changed hands, but "it was CIA money that paid for [the airplanes]."

and eight hundred thousand acres of land were taken from the peasants and handed back to the latifundios, the big landowners; the subsoil of almost half the country was deeded over to speculators in petroleum for future exploitation; legislation guaranteeing rights to workers and their unions was repealed; a penal law against communism established a committee for defense which met in secret and could declare anyone a communist, with no right of appeal; those named were arrested, those arrested could expect death; within four months the committee had registered seventy-two thousand communists and sympathizers.

The wave of repression provoked even a rebellion within the regular army. An "audacious and criminal" scheme inspired by communists, said Castillo Armas, after it had been quelled.

Eisenhower would speak of the "thundering majority" given Castillo Armas in the election a few months later. His phrase was an understatement. The "free election" was strictly a "sí o no" proposition, with 485,693 ballots being counted as sí and 400 as no, which works out at 99.9 percent, a splendid testimonial to "a farseeing and able statesman."

There can be little doubt that President Eisenhower's policy toward little Guatemala—an impoverished land about the size of the state of Tennessee—was to some extent shaped and hardened by the course of events in Indochina and by the difficult negotiations at Geneva. The administration was under constant pressure, exerted by the influential "China Lobby" and others, lest it approve any concessions to the communists at Geneva and so seem to yield to the bugaboo of appeasement. The mood of the Congress on this score was apparent late in June when the House of Representatives attached to a foreign aid bill a rider which stipulated that none of the funds appropriated "shall be used on behalf of governments which are committed by treaty to maintain Communist rule over any defined territory of Asia"—and passed the rider by a vote of three hundred and ninety to none. It was aimed at Britain, France, or any power that might presume to conclude a treaty of nonaggression with communists. In that sultry climate, made more oppressive when Lyndon Johnson introduced a Senate resolution (approved sixty-nine to one) denouncing "communist penetration of the Western Hemisphere [as] external aggression," he would have been foolhardy indeed who was less than pugnacious toward the Arbenz regime. (Johnson's resolution was introduced only hours before the meeting at which the President decided to dispatch two fighter-bombers south to help Castillo Armas.)

Bedell Smith had returned to Washington a day earlier, his tough old soldier's face fixed and grim, his guts lacerated by ulcers, a forbidding symbol of stubborn anticommunism. He had reported to Eisenhower on his interview with Mendès-France: the determination to end the fighting as quickly as possible, the earnest request that the U.S. restrain Ngo Dinh Diem (whom Mendès obviously took to be the Eisenhower administration's creature) from sabotaging any truce the French might reach with the Viet Minh.

Diem had already departed for Saigon to face the frustrating task of creating some sort of order out of the postwar chaos. Soon he would encounter Colonel Edward Lansdale, USAF, who had been seconded to the CIA and ordered to Vietnam some months before to head a team of experts in counterguerrilla warfare; his team, called the Saigon Military Mission, had been instructed "to undertake paramilitary operations against the enemy and to wage political-psychological warfare." It is clear that even before Eisenhower had got involved in the protracted discussions first with the British and later with the French on the question of U.S. intervention, he had concluded that U.S. interests would best be served by establishing a small, experienced force of U.S. specialists on the scene, a team that would be ready to take advantage of whatever situation developed. Lansdale, whose exploits against the Hukbalahap insurgents in the Philippines almost matched his subsequent celebrity, was the CIA agent who would now become one of Diem's most trusted advisers.

Churchill and Eden followed Smith to Washington with the purpose, as Eden saw it, of persuading Eisenhower "at least to give the French a chance of reaching a settlement at Geneva within the next few weeks." But nothing had happened to shake the President's conviction that any negotiated settlement in Indochina would endanger the security of the United States (hence Lansdale's undercover mission to Saigon and his hurried concoction of "dirty" tricks for use against the Viet Minh); Eisenhower and Dulles hoped only for a settlement on the least objectionable terms; the President was determined that neither Dulles nor Smith should be party to further Geneva negotiations, and that the United States should not be signatory to any instrument making concessions to the Communists. President and secretary of state were already directing their energies toward an anticommunist alliance in Southeast Asia, while the British were as bent on postponing talk of any such treaty until after the work at Geneva was completed.

During Churchill's brief visit the Vice President was out around the country, being useful to the Republican party after his own fashion, preparing the ground for the off-year elections that fall, charging the Democrats with being "soft on communism," blaming Truman and Acheson for the "loss" of China and the current crisis in Southeast Asia, keeping in character. There were signs that the Democrats, wearying of the profitless competition as to which party could cut the more anticommunist figure, had grown resentful of rubbish like Nixon's mechanical recitations ("McCarthyism in a white collar," quipped Adlai Stevenson.)

Eisenhower, too, was troubled. On Monday, June 28, he sent Nixon a reproachful note scolding him for his attacks on Acheson and other Democrats at a time when he, Eisenhower, was attempting to forge a bipartisan foreign policy. But two days later, at his press conference, the President took a quite opposite stand. Asked if Nixon's charges spoke for the administration, reminded that Sam Rayburn, the minority leader in the House, had rumbled that if Nixon made more speeches along the same line there might not be any bipartisan foreign policy, Eisenhower refused to criticize "my Vice President." ". . . you can normally take it," he added, "when he talks, he is talking pretty much the language of this administration. . . . I wouldn't try to excommunicate him from this party if I were you."

During a televised press conference in Washington, Churchill had alluded to his persistent desire for a meeting at the summit—at this time himself, Eisenhower, and Malenkov—and had observed that it "might be a great help." He had spoken of making "a real good try" at establishing "peaceful coexistence" with the Russians, so preferable to the "doom-laden" current state of affairs. Asked about the idea later, Eisenhower kept it at arm's length—not actually rejecting it but showing no pleasure whatever in it. "If there is any proof of the other side that they will keep their agreements," he said, as if describing the wildest of improbabilities, "I think we would be, all of us, quite content to do almost anything."

Back again in London, Churchill returned to the scheme in what was the first of an exchange of messages with Eisenhower. He had been in touch with Molotov, he said, his tone enthusiastic; perhaps the conversation would lead to an Anglo-Soviet meeting, after which . . .

Eisenhower's reply was indifferent. We wish you well, he indicated, but the affair is your responsibility.

Churchill was irked by Eisenhower's evident want of interest. He recalled that he had been urging such a meeting since May 4, 1953—fourteen months past—and still the President hung back. Much good might come of it, Churchill insisted: for example, a growing hostility between the USSR and the Chinese communists.

Eisenhower had only one point to make in reply: the United Kingdom should, as the United States had done, take a firm stand against Red China.

Churchill stubbornly persevered, a man talking in an empty room. His third message was answered a couple of weeks later: in an "eyes only" letter Eisenhower wrote that he had no confidence in Churchill's proposed meeting with Malenkov; he proposed instead that Churchill make a masterly speech against colonialism, suggesting that the fires of nationalism might be channeled and turned against the Soviet Union.

The President having reconsidered, Bedell Smith was sent back to Geneva at the last moment, restoring the U.S. delegation to something more than "observers." Not much more: Smith took no active part in the closing negotiations, but rather remained in his private rooms, isolate, nursing his gastric ulcers and his lumbago, his manner curt, his temper short. On July 21 the Final Declaration was signed by France and by the Viet Minh; a statement of U.S. policy was announced by Smith at the final session:

> . . . my Government is not prepared to join in a declaration such as is submitted. However, the United States makes this unilateral declaration . . . .
> (i) it will refrain from the threat or the use of force to disturb [the agreements and declaration]; and
> (ii) it would view any renewal of the aggression in violation of the aforesaid agreements with great concern and as seriously threatening international peace and security.

As for the general elections designed to unite the divided land, elections scheduled according to paragraph 7 of the Final Declaration to be held in July 1956, Smith pledged:

> . . . my government wishes to make clear . . . :
> In the case of nations now divided against their will, we shall continue to seek unity through free elections supervised by the United Nations . . .
> . . . the United States . . . will not join in an arrangement which would hinder this. Nothing in its declaration . . . is intended to or does indicate any departure from this traditional position.

Thus the public profession. But on July 7 Foster Dulles had argued that the United States should work to delay any elections and to demand the kind of guarantees of electoral procedures that the Communists could be expected to reject. Further, Dulles instructed Smith by secret cablegram: "Since undoubtedly true that elections might eventually mean unification Vietnam under Ho Chi Minh, this makes it all more important they should be only held as long after cease-fire agreement as possible and in conditions free from intimidation to give democratic elements best chance."

It should also be noted, in connection with paragraph (i) above, that Colonel Lansdale's Saigon Military Mission, acting under instructions from Washington, was already busily planning the use of force to disturb and disrupt the Final Agreement. Its original orders had been modified, but they still included preparation of "the means for undertaking paramilitary operations" in North Vietnam.

On July 30 a Republican senator, Ralph Flanders of Vermont, introduced a resolution, S.R. 301, to censure Senator McCarthy, listing as his reasons McCarthy's contempt for the Senate, his habitual misconduct, and his "habitual contempt for people." During the debate that raged over the next three or four days, Flanders was treated in extraordinary fashion: snubbed and rebuffed by some of his colleagues, by others pursued and implored to change his mind. At least two members of Eisenhower's cabinet, Flanders would later recall, "were very much disturbed," and one of these "told me what was the universal opinion among the conservatives, that I was ruining the Republican party, and again asked me to be reasonable." Knowland, too, the majority leader, attempted at a small dinner party to bring the Vermonter round. McCarthy was still deemed a doughty campaigner by the right wing of the Republican party; they looked to him to smite the Democratic opposition, especially in the midwestern states, and so lead the GOP to triumph in the off-year congressional elections. But more powerful forces were privately stirring—in the cloakrooms, at unpublicized gatherings of the Senate leadership—and late on August 2 the Senate approved a substitute motion: that a select committee be appointed to consider the charges against McCarthy.

Some apprehension was evident that the committee was only a convenient device for perpetuating McCarthy in his destructive career, but in fact the inner circle of the Senate, the conservative coalition of southern Democrats and senior Republicans that controlled the life of the upper House, had reached its wintry, collective decision: McCarthy had become more trouble than he was worth, McCarthy delendum est.

The President kept his attention focused on the developments in Indochina.

As he knew, most of the governments that had hammered out the settlement at Geneva regarded their work as effective: the war in Vietnam was ended; the French would stay to shore up Bao Dai's regime, now to be administered by Diem; their presence would ensure the elections in 1956, peacefully and properly conducted. For his part, the President had a poor opinion of the settlement, and so did his chief advisers. The National Security Council characterized it as a "disaster," and believed it marked "a major forward stride of Communism which may lead to the loss of Southeast Asia." If Communism was to be stopped, a strong South Vietnamese government backed by a tough South Vietnamese army was essential; but the national intelligence estimate handed Eisenhower on August 3 held that neither the French nor the Vietnamese were a good bet to establish such a government even with U.S. support, and the prediction was that conditions would get steadily worse. Under those circumstances, U.S. military aid would be wasted. The Joint Chiefs warned the President: "It is hopeless to expect a U.S. military training mission to achieve success unless the nation concerned is able effectively to perform those governmental functions essential to the successful raising and maintenance of armed forces." Moreover, any U.S. military effort was sharply limited by the Geneva agreements: American forces were supposed not to exceed the number present in Vietnam when the armistice was signed—three hundred and forty-two officers and enlisted men.

Truly, in President Eisenhower's view, a disaster.

No matter: he had been confronted by disastrous situations before; it was likely that he would heed on this occasion the adviser who argued a resolute course of action despite the odds against it. Foster Dulles urged that the Diem regime, while "far from strong or stable," could best be buttressed by a program of military training. Invigorated by his stout anti-communist zeal, the staff of the National Security Council prepared a "Review of U.S. Policy in the Far East" which embodied three proposals, military, economic, and political: the U.S. would cooperate with the French military "only so far as necessary to build up indigenous forces able to provide internal security"; the U.S. would supply funds directly to the Vietnamese, shunting the French off from "the levers of command"; the U.S. would support Premier Diem but encourage him to tinker with the kind of representative democracy that had served the United States so well.

On Friday, August 20, amid a last-minute rush of business, the President gave this NSC paper his approval. The authors of the two-and-a-half-million-word "History of U.S. Decision-Making Process on Vietnam Policy," the vast work commonly known as the Pentagon Papers, would later write of that particular decision: "American policy toward post-Geneva Vietnam was drawn." The United States had replaced France and had assumed France's burden in the defense of Southeast Asia against communism. "The available record," the authors of the Pentagon Papers went on, "does not indicate any rebuttal" of the warnings carefully entered by both the National Intelligence Board and the Joint Chiefs of Staff. "What it does indicate is that the U.S. decided to gamble with very limited resources because the political gains seemed well worth a limited risk."

One cannot be sure, even at so near a remove from the events of that August 1954, that President Eisenhower's cold, clear, exact intelligence was moving with its customary precision. He was exhausted. Sherman Adams has spoken of the "spells of depression" Eisenhower experienced that summer. Ann Whitman, his personal secretary, agreed with Adams that "he was being faced with too many vexing problems that either had no solution or that required great personal concentration before making decisions for which he alone was responsible."

At all events, on Saturday, August 21, the President left Washington for a working vacation in the Colorado mountains. He would enjoy precious few days of complete relaxation, for he had already committed himself to sundry speaking engagements and ceremonial presidential appearances, and the inexorable press of world affairs was ever present. Back briefly in Washington to address an American Legion convention at the end of the month, he was flown west once again on August 30 in his presidential airplane, the *Columbine*; his companions included Herbert Hoover, Jr., recently returned from the protracted negotiations to settle the dispute over Iranian petroleum, and Sherman Adams. Late in the day he came to Des Moines and paused for an address at the Iowa State Fair. Once again he was downcast, for earlier that day had come word that after three years of promises and postponements, the French National Assembly had finally and firmly rejected the European Defense Community (EDC). It was, said Secretary of State Dulles in Washington, a "tragedy." He and the President had had ample advance notice of the vote, but precognition did not mitigate the bitterness of the defeat. In Des Moines the President looked out over a grandstand filled with prosperous Iowa farm families, made a couple of small pleasantries, launched into an abecedarian discussion of "our relations with the world," raised the question "Why must we have friends?" and so came to what lay heavy on his mind—the "major setback . . . serious setback," the rejection of EDC. At once his natural buoyancy came to his rescue:

"When we have our setbacks we are disappointed. But we must not be discouraged.

"America has never quit in something that was good for herself, and the world.

"We will not quit now. We shall never do so. . . .

"We need not despair. We must not.

"And so, the opportunity to say some of these things to you this evening, at the very moment when this one setback has occurred, makes me feel better.

"You inspire me, I assure you—because when I see America represented like this, how can you be fainthearted? It can't be done."

The ovation given him was the last swallow of the President's bracing tonic. Feeling once again his cheerful self, he traveled on to Denver. He would have four days before being buffeted by still another crisis.

CHAPTER FOUR

Protecting the Status Quo

The Chinese offshore islands . . . The unleashing of Chiang . . . The balance of nuclear terror . . . Radioactive fallout . . . West Germany joins NATO . . . Disarmament? . . . The leashing of Chiang.

IN THE EVENING of Friday, September 3, a message from the Pentagon was handed the President at his temporary White House in Denver; for several hours the Chinese had been raking with artillery fire an island called Quemoy, just off the coast of China in a position to command the port of Amoy. Once again U.S. citizens would be obliged to dip deep into another apprehensive lesson in political geography.

In December 1949, when Chiang Kai-shek fled the Chinese mainland to take refuge on Taiwan, one hundred and thirty miles away in the China Sea, he had shipped ahead China's gold bullion and her foreign exchange, and it was his intention to send to Taiwan as well the troops of his defeated Nationalist armies. (The Taiwanese wanted no part of Chiang or his troops, but they were not consulted.) Not all Chiang's troops, however, made the crossing. Some, having defected, stayed in China. Others, a scattered ragtag, seized the string of islands that dotted the coast from Amoy three or four hundred miles north to Shanghai. They established themselves as piratical bosses of a couple of dozen of these—the Tachens, far to the north of Taiwan; the Matsus, some rocky outcrops off the port of Foochow; and Quemoy, the biggest of the lot, which had been the home of several thousand farmers and fisherfolk. The troops had no legal right to these offshore islands, only the precarious right of seizure: once dislodged, they were finished. Juridical right to the Pescadores, another group of islands farther out in Taiwan Strait, and to Taiwan itself, had been vested in the Republic of China by decision of the Allied heads of government at their meetings in Cairo, Yalta, and Potsdam. Now, as a result of the civil war, there were two Republics of China: the victorious People's Republic of China, sovereign on the mainland, and Chiang's defeated Republic of China, clinging to a shadow of sovereignty on Taiwan. Which was the true Republic of China?

Late in 1949 Republican leaders, spurred by the "China Lobby," had clamored for some sort of American protectorate over Taiwan; at least, argued Senators Taft and Knowland and former President Hoover, use the U.S. Navy to shield the island from the communists. To Dean Acheson, then secretary of state, such maneuvers seemed like "toying with the mousetrap," and President Truman agreed. In January 1950 Truman declared without qualification that the U.S. government regarded Taiwan as Chinese territory, that the U.S. "has no desire to . . . establish military bases on Formosa [Taiwan] at this time," nor would the U.S. "provide military aid or advice to Chinese forces on Formosa [Taiwan]."

Less than six months later the war in Korea brought a revision of that policy: Truman instructed the Seventh Fleet to protect Taiwan but at the same time counseled Chiang to desist from any military provocations against the mainland.

With the inauguration of Eisenhower came further changes of policy. The much publicized "unleashing of Chiang," almost at once belittled by all administration spokesmen, was the tip of the iceberg; below the surface, concealed from press and public, a wide range of activities—espionage, sabotage, guerrilla raids, clandestine military operations conducted by land, air, and sea—had been steadily going forward, supported by ever greater allocations of U.S. funds and equipment. By the late summer of 1954 those operations had enough substance and continuity to be called a war. In Washington the combatants were called Chinats (Chiang's Nationalist troops) and Chicoms (the armed forces of the Chinese People's Republic), and while U.S. involvement in the struggle was covert, U.S. officers were training, advising, and all but leading Chiang's troops in their operations. A complex of military airfields had been constructed. The Civil Air Transport, ostensibly a Chinat commercial airline, was "a CIA proprietary" already engaged in flights over China. Western Enterprises, Inc., another CIA outfit, was extensive enough to maintain its own housing development, post exchange, and social clubs at Taipei. In general, the Americans had as their mission the incitement of Chinat belligerence against the Chicoms.

In this campaign of harassment, the offshore islands were of critical importance. They were vulnerable, to be sure, almost impossible to hold against a determined assault; but so long as they were controlled by the Chinats they were invaluable as bases for guerrilla raids, as sites for radar installations that could probe into the mysterious mainland, and as a means of disrupting Chicom communications along the entire eastern coast. Moreover, to hold them poised a threat of expanded military activity, perhaps even of an invasion; that threat held Chicom troops posted to the coastal provinces and so restricted their activity elsewhere—in Indochina, for example, or in Korea, or peacefully tilling their own fields. In the event, there were skirmishes, forays by both sides to take prisoners for intelligence reasons, and at last, on September 3, the bombardment of Quemoy, in the course of which two U.S. army officers attached to MAAG in Taipei were killed.

The question had been put to President Eisenhower: What policy should the United States adopt? Specifically, should the United States intervene to keep the Chinese People's Republic from asserting its claim to territory which was clearly its own?

The President could phrase the matter quite differently. He could say: The Chinese communist government is an interloper, not recognized by the U.S. as the rightful government of China, not recognized by the world community as fit to be a member of the United Nations, without legitimate claim to the offshore islands or indeed to the mainland territory of China itself. Without doubt that kind of assertion would have been cheered to the echo by the "China Lobby" and such of its spokesmen as Knowland, the "senator from Formosa," but it would also have isolated the United States and marked its government for the derision and dismay of its allies. The choice confronting the President was more limited—actually having to do only with his policy as to those offshore islands—but the danger that his decision would invite the alienation of his country's allies was quite as great.

Meanwhile his chief adviser on the conduct of his foreign policy was himself in the Far East. Foster Dulles was in Manila collecting signatures on his Southeast Asian collective defense treaty, the SEATO pact, from Australia, Britain, France, New Zealand, Pakistan, the Philippines, Thailand, and the U.S.—a treaty signed by only one nation (Thailand) of Southeast Asia and only two others (Pakistan and the Philippines) of any part of Asia. Inescapably, SEATO would seem to the world another instance of the white man's burden, an arrangement undertaken for the Asians whether they wanted it or no. But SEATO was the best that Foster Dulles could contrive, under pressure, to supply a juridical basis for the protection the U.S. meant to extend to Indochina. The SEATO treaty was accompanied by a Pacific Charter designed to abort any complaints that SEATO was just another exercise in colonial domination, but unhappily Dulles insisted on referring to the treaty as an "Asiatic Monroe Doctrine," a phrase not calculated to attract such Southeast Asian states as India, Ceylon, Burma, and Indonesia.

Then, alerted by his President, Secretary Dulles hustled to Taipei to confer with Chiang (the generalissimo was assured he did not "stand alone" against communist aggression; the U.S. would not be "intimidated" by any intensified military activity) and then to talk briefly ("very usefully") with Japanese Premier Shigeru Yoshida before at last taking plane for Denver to report to Eisenhower.

The President had called a special meeting of the National Security Council for Sunday, September 12, to discuss "the place of the U.S. in . . . the western Pacific." It would be the first occasion of an NSC meeting outside Washington.

Pending the secretary's arrival, Eisenhower could ponder advice from other trusted lieutenants. His Joint Chiefs, for instance: he was informed that only Ridgway, then army chief of staff, believed the U.S. should make no commitment to defend the offshore islands. The others—Twining of the air force, Carney of the navy, and their chairman, Admiral Radford —were agreed that loss of the islands would deal such a devastating blow to the morale of Chiang's forces that the U.S. should alter its policy and commit its military might as a shield for at least ten of the islands, those considered to be essential outposts. The Chiefs were unanimous that the U.S. could defend Taiwan without regard to the offshore islands and that Chiang's men could not hold the offshore islands without U.S. assistance; three of the four senior officers wanted the President to extend the shield across the Taiwan Strait, right to China's doorstep.

The CIA agreed, stopping short of any recommendations. A CIA report dated September 9 estimated that the offshore islands could easily be captured and that Taiwan itself would fall fairly quickly unless the U.S. intervened.

It was, as Secretary Dulles observed after his arrival, a "horrible dilemma." At the Sunday meeting of the NSC, Radford pressed his bellicose thesis: the offshore islands were militarily valuable; hence the U.S. should not only defend them but should carry the war to the mainland by helping the Chinats to bomb the Chicom troop concentrations now suspected to be preparing an assault on Taiwan. The President would have none of this. He pointed out that Radford was no longer talking of "a limited, brush-fire war" over Quemoy but of an all-inclusive conflict. "If we attack China," Eisenhower emphasized, "we're not going to impose limits on our military actions, as in Korea." His meaning was clear: an attack on China would be a war of nuclear weapons, a general war, and "if we get into

663

a general war, the logical enemy will be Russia, not China, and we'll have to strike there."

Dulles suggested a solution. Since the aim was to block the capture of the offshore islands without committing the U.S. to defend them, the proper course was to persuade an ally to take the matter before the U.N. Security Council with a view to obtaining a resolution for a cease-fire in the Taiwan Strait. And if the Soviet Union were to veto such a resolution? No matter: either way the United States stood to gain.

Eisenhower liked the idea. Presently Dulles would be in London; he could broach the plan to Eden.

It would seem that at least at the highest level, the Eisenhower administration had somewhat shifted its strategic concepts. From neither the President nor his secretary of state had come any talk of "massive retaliation." To be sure, the moral and legal grounds for such a retaliation against the Chinese were shaky, but that consideration had not dissuaded them from the irregular seizure and search of ships in the Caribbean, or from engineering counterrevolutions against two legitimate governments, or from striving to undermine the Geneva negotiations to end a war. Rather the reason for the shift seems to have been the character of nuclear weapons. The nature of those weapons, still far from fully comprehended today and much less so then, put in question their suitability as a deterrent against aggression and as a means for keeping peace in the world. Since these speculations reach to the roots of Dwight Eisenhower's policies as a Cold Warrior, they warrant an exploration, one that will take us back several months for a reflective look at events the meaning of which would be incomprehensible for another several years to even the wisest of scientists. Even today those events are, for many scientists, the occasion for intolerant controversy.

> The widespread and growing fear of radioactive fallout from nuclear tests was, according to the best authorities, unreasoning; but it was real.
> —Dwight D. Eisenhower

On March 1, 1954, the first of the so-called Castle series of thermonuclear tests was exploded near Eniwetok in the Marshall Islands. It was, Lewis Strauss reported, "a stupendous blast in the megaton range"—later estimated to have been equivalent to twelve to twenty-two megatons of TNT, perhaps as much as one thousand times more powerful than the A-bombs dropped on Japan in 1945. This was the experimental "three-stage" bomb: the FFF weapon, fission-fusion-fission, yielding twice as much destructive energy as its designers had reckoned it would. The fallout of radioactive particles from the blast was likewise much greater than had been anticipated. Nearly four hundred persons were unexpectedly exposed to radiation; most of these were Marshall Islanders, a few were American servicemen, but the most seriously affected were twenty-three Japanese fishermen whose trawler, although some one hundred and twenty miles away, had been strewn with a litter of radioactive ashes.

Word of the disaster horrified the world. Here was further evidence of the pernicious potency of these weapons. Atomic energy and atomic weapons were facts of life, but more to the point they were facts of death. Almost at once Strauss and various spokesmen of the AEC commenced to issue statements designed to soothe the public alarm. An American physician, director of the U.S. Atomic Bomb Casualty Commission in Hiroshima, inspected the twenty-three Japanese fishermen after they had reached their home port two weeks later and subsequently announced that they would recover within a month. (They were sick of an uncommon medical entity, radiation sickness. One died five months later; all the others were still confined to hospital two years later.) Radioactive fallout, said Strauss, would soon drop harmlessly into the ocean; there was no danger of its being carried to the United States or other inhabited areas. (Poisonous isotopes from the blast were identified in rain falling on Japan, in the lubricants of an Indian airplane, in winds over Australia, and falling to earth as far away as Europe.)

The bland reassurances released by official spokesmen in and out of the AEC were not disingenuous. They were simply uninformed. Relatively little was known in 1954 about the effects on the human embryo and on the infant of bombardment by low-level radiation. On the other hand, the scientists in the AEC division of biology and medicine might have been more anxiously inquisitive about those effects. Nature had long since supplied them with a wealth of clues. Whatever the reason (perhaps the pressures of the "national interest"? the great national malaise of anti-communism? a lack of impetus to explore?), most biologists, geneticists, and public health specialists were slow to follow those clues to see where they might lead. Reassurances multiplied. A study produced by the National Academy of Sciences, the most prestigious of authorities, stated: "Thus far except for some tragic accidents affecting small numbers of people, the biological damage from peacetime activities (including the testing of atomic weapons) has been essentially negligible."

Later, as evidence accumulated of the dangers from fallout, as awareness grew that the wound was inward, unfelt and unseen, most often the lot of an infant or one not yet born nor even conceived, as strange new terms like strontium 90 and iodine 131 worked their way into the language, as questions were raised about the clear and significant increase in the incidence of leukemia and other malignant diseases, especially among young children, as the debate over the wisdom or folly of continuing nuclear tests waxed more intense, the President of the United States would necessarily take a limited view of the matter. Whatever information he was given came from his appointed advisers, Strauss and the other commissioners of the AEC, men whose primary duty was to maintain the nuclear superiority of the United States. In the event, President Eisenhower would put his high repute at the service of the AEC's misleading certitudes. Comforting statements about fallout would issue from the White House.

But Eisenhower had been greatly concerned by the reports of the first Castle shot, the one that had blighted the Japanese fishermen, and his concern was shared by many of his allies overseas and by religious leaders the world around. The British were particularly alarmed. In the press and in the Commons throughout April the matter most fiercely discussed was that of atomic holocaust, the more so since, as Churchill acknowledged in the course of the debate, the British Isles were "a bull's-eye target" for annihilation by H-bomb. (The debate coincided with Dulles's strenuous efforts to maneuver Britain into a commitment to help avert the impending surrender of Dien Bien Phu.) In his Easter message broadcast April 18 Pope Pius XII included the remonstrance that "peace cannot consist of an exasperating and costly relationship of reciprocal terror."

When Churchill visited Washington with Eden in June (at about the same time the putsch in Guatemala was getting under way) he had used the occasion to impress once again on Eisenhower his deep aversion to use of the hydrogen bomb. His misgivings were the livelier because of what one could assume to be settled U.S. strategic policy: at a restricted meeting of foreign ministers in April, Foster Dulles had urged the use of atomic weapons, like conventional weapons, "whenever and wherever it would be of advantage to do so." Churchill's strictures reawakened Eisenhower's concern.

Not unexpectedly, Anthony Eden showed a disposition to avoid any atomic warfare over Quemoy and the Matsus when, late in September, Foster Dulles mentioned the matter to him. Eden was a great deal more receptive to the idea of referring the problem to the U.N. through the Security Council.

Quite apparently, the doctrine of "massive retaliation" was dead and even its younger brother, "selective retaliation," seemed peaked and drawn. By the fall of 1954 something very like atomic stalemate looked to have become the strategy of necessity, and that impression gained much in vigor after the President returned to Washington from Denver. In rapid-fire order Eisenhower made three speeches—the first extemporaneous, the other carefully drafted and revised—and those listening closely could conclude that the United States had shifted gears and was now operating under a revised strategic concept.

On October 19, the President to a gathering of foreign service officers and State Department personnel: "Since the advent of nuclear weapons, it seems clear that there is no longer any alternative to peace, if there is to be a happy and well world."

On October 20, to a convocation at Trinity College, in Connecticut: "We have arrived at that point, my friends, when war does not present the possibility of victory or defeat. War would present to us only the alternatives in degrees of destruction. There could be no truly successful outcome."

That night, to an American Jewish tercentenary dinner in New York City: "The major new factor in the world today . . . is the rapid development in military weapons—weapons that in total war would threaten catastrophe."

These cool, temperate remarks did not, however, relax world tension. On both sides of the iron curtain suspicion and fear had flourished too rankly and for too long a time to disappear because of a few words spoken in realistic acknowledgment of the balance of terror. More to the point, there were those whose patriotic resolve was to cultivate the rancors that luxuriated alike in the U.S. and USSR. The Cold War continued unabated.

Having reached an understanding with Eden on the matter of the Chinese offshore islands (New Zealand would be asked to submit the question of a cease-fire to the U.N. Security Council), Foster Dulles could switch his overview from East to West and inspect, with mixed feelings, Eden's attempts to find a wholesome substitute for the late lamented EDC, done in by the French Assembly a scant month before. President Eisenhower had puzzled to find an approach toward such a substitute and had sent his ideas to the State Department; steps had been taken to develop the President's suggestions; none of these efforts was as well conceived as Eden's. Lazing in his bath on a summer Sunday morning, Eden had been struck with the notion that twelve divisions of West German troops might yet be added to NATO's strength, France might yet reconsider and sanction an armed German force-in-being, European unity might yet be advanced, by means of a patchwork formula based on the Brussels Treaty of 1948.* His thought was simply to bring Italy and West Germany into the pact, expanding it into a mutual defense agreement for all western

* The Brussels Treaty was a fifty-year compact pledging mutual military aid in the event of attack; its signatories were Britain, France, Belgium, the Netherlands, and Luxembourg.

Europe and affording at the same time a framework for closer political cooperation. A "brilliant and statesmanlike British initiative," said Dulles in public; in private he complained the Brussels Treaty had no supranational features. By this he meant that both President Eisenhower and he had hoped the device of the European Defense Community (EDC) might have led to some sort of federation of European states, perhaps even a United States of Europe. That concept had been dangled before the Congress, where xenophobia was endemic; to reflect that the Old World was at last going to wise up and emulate the New had flattered many a congressman, and a great many more had been fetched by the corollary proposition that a United States of Europe would be able to stand on its own feet and would require no more huge subsidies from the U.S. Treasury.

But if Eden's solution lacked supranational features, it was still the best available for bringing West German troops into NATO. It was uncluttered, it would work. A nine-power conference in London quickly agreed on the main provisions: the Brussels Treaty organization to admit West Germany and Italy, to take a new name (Western European Union), and to establish controls over armaments; West Germany to be recognized as a sovereign state, the German Federal Republic, to be accepted as a member of NATO, and to be encouraged to muster an army of some five hundred thousand men and to build an air force of thirteen hundred airplanes. In a separate protocol, Adenauer pledged that the new state would not manufacture atomic, bacteriological, or chemical weapons, guided missiles, tanks or their major components, long-range bombers, or large warships.

Three weeks later, on October 23, the foreign ministers of fifteen nations met in Paris to give formal approval to these arrangements. Less than ten years after V-E Day, the more populous and industrialized sector of Germany was once again becoming a military power.

Here was a development of inestimable importance in the Cold War, brought about with astonishing speed. The Russians' greatest dread had been the rearming of western Germany. They had opposed EDC for that reason. Now came the Western European Union, deliberately devised to restore Germany as a military and perhaps irredentist threat. Before WEU there had been a balance of terror; uncomfortable to be sure, but still a balance. The equilibrium was now upset. The Russians had only a few months for diplomatic maneuver before the German army would be a force-in-being, a fact.

The conference in London had been, said Foster Dulles, "without doubt one of the great conferences of all time." The Paris accords, said Eisenhower, were the "beginning of a new era for Europe" and they had "brought us measurably nearer to world stability and peace."

The Russians at once pressed for a meeting of four foreign ministers—Dulles, Eden, Mendès-France, and Molotov—to consider the reunification of Germany, the withdrawal of all armies of occupation, and the advisability of a conference on the peace and security of Europe.

No, said Churchill; no, not "at this particular stage."

No, said Eisenhower; no, not until the U.S. was satisfied the Soviet Union truly wished to discuss steps toward peace.

The Political and Security Committee of the General Assembly of the United Nations voted unanimously that its subcommittee on disarmament be instructed to resume its deliberations. The subcommittee was composed of representatives from five nations—the United States, United Kingdom, France, Canada, and the Soviet Union—and these powers joined in supporting the resolution. Nobody entertained any considerable hope that this subcommittee would take even a first step toward disarmament. Western statesmen would demand a foolproof system of inspection predicated on their avowed conviction that the Russians were not to be trusted, and the Russians would refuse to permit any system of inspection by hostile foreigners. Nothing would happen. Disarmament would remain an illusion.

On November 1, 1954, the day before the Republicans lost control of both houses of Congress, Chinese aircraft bombed the Tachen Islands; later in the day Chinese artillery bombarded other offshore islands nearby. These events, commonplace incidents of the nuisance war protracted by Chiang and his American overseers, provided Eisenhower's advisers with an opportunity to lock him deeper in his policy toward China. The President's position was further complicated three weeks later when the Chinese announced in a radio broadcast from Peking that they had captured, tried, and sentenced thirteen Americans and a number of Chinese nationalist counterrevolutionaries. Of the Americans, eleven were air force personnel, two were civilians; all were convicted of espionage and sentenced to terms ranging from four years to life. Vigorous U.S. protests were at once mounted. The charges were "trumped up," said a spokesman for the State Department; they were "utterly false," said the Pentagon's functionary. A curious inclination to treat the case of the civilians separately from that of the airmen was soon apparent in the official U.S. attitude: the airplane carrying the air force officers and men had been shot down over China while hostilities in Korea were still in train, and so it could be argued that they were subject to the terms of the armistice agreement covering prisoners of war; the two civilians, on the other hand, were CIA agents, and State Department officials might argue that their detention "furnishes further proof of the Chinese Communist regime's disregard for accepted practices of international conduct," Dulles might declaim that the Chinese "outrage the elemental decencies of international conduct," but the fact remained that the two men had accepted the dangerous CIA assignment of organizing and training teams of counterrevolutionary Chinese and they had been caught while trying to drop supplies to their teams of saboteurs in the northeastern provinces of China.

Knowland, the "senator from Formosa" who was also the Republican leader in the Senate, was outraged. In direct defiance of the express admonitions of the President, Knowland demanded on the floor of the Senate that the U.S. Navy blockade the coast of China "until these Americans are released." Senators Joe McCarthy and William Jenner queued up to second Knowland's outburst.

Eisenhower was pursuing a more delicate course, one that was imperiled by Knowland's clumsy pugnacity. Dulles's idea of having the "war" submitted to the U.N. Security Council by a friendly ally, with a view to obtaining a cease-fire, was no longer the preferred approach, not because the government of New Zealand was any less willing to undertake the assignment but because Chiang Kai-shek disapproved. He feared that once the Security Council got involved it would go further and rule that Taiwan was properly a province of the People's Republic of China and, worse, that the People's Republic should be seated as the permanent member of the Security Council in place of his own makeshift government. In vain did Dulles assure the generalissimo the United States would never permit the Security Council to engage in such absurdities; Chiang was obdurate. Eisenhower and Dulles concluded they had better reinforce their position with a device of questionable legality, a mutual defense treaty with Chiang's shadow Republic of China.

Negotiation of the treaty was taken in hand by Dulles and George Yeh, Chiang's shadow foreign minister, early in October. By November 23 Dulles could send the President a memorandum reporting that the treaty (by which the two governments pledged themselves to "maintain and develop their individual and collective capacity to resist armed attack and Communist subversive activities") covered only Taiwan and the Pescadores, and that Chiang's government agreed that "the use of force from either of these areas . . . will be a matter of joint agreement," and further that the offshore islands would not be additionally fortified from Taiwan without the consent of the U.S. In short, Chiang was once again on a short tether. (The treaty also provided that the mutual pledges could by common consent be extended to other areas; e.g., the offshore islands.)

Dulles was confident the treaty gave assurance that if any war erupted over the offshore islands, the U.S., not Chiang, would be responsible. That was all to the good, but the treaty spawned other problems, not the least of which was: How could it be a treaty at all, when the Supreme Court had held that a treaty is "primarily a compact between independent nations"? Chiang's shadow government represented no independent and sovereign nation. On Taiwan Chiang and his followers were at best guests, more strictly trespassers, but they had no ghost of a legal claim to the island. Dulles knew this, and no doubt he also knew that the character of the instrument he had negotiated would be sharply questioned once it was submitted to the Senate for the advice and consent constitutionally required of that body. Perhaps Dulles and Eisenhower anticipated that the very act of concluding the compact with Chiang would per se endow his regime with a substance of legitimacy. Perhaps they considered they were only making a military alliance. Perhaps they hoped somehow to extricate themselves from their "horrible dilemma." At all events they knew that dubious as their treaty might be, in the anticommunist climate of 1955 it would go speedily through the Senate, with the new Democratic majority competing with the Republican right wing as to who might better extol it.

Meanwhile, State Department and White House continued to cooperate closely. On December 18 Herbert Hoover, Jr., (now the undersecretary, nominated to the post as a reward for his part in satisfactorily settling the Anglo-American division of Iranian oil) sent Eisenhower a memorandum apprising him that two days later Yeh would wait upon him to request that he announce the U.S. would give Chiang logistic support for the defense of the offshore islands. Hoover suggested that the President base his response on a recent NSC recommendation (NSC 5429/4), which read:

> For the present, seek to preserve, through United Nations action, the status quo of the Nationalist-held off-shore islands; and, without committing U.S. forces except as militarily desirable in the event of Chinese Communist attack on Formosa [Taiwan] and the Pescadores, provide to the Chinese Nationalist forces military equipment and training to assist them to defend such off-shore islands, using Formosa [Taiwan] as a base.

But Eisenhower decided that any announcement of logistic support would unjustifiably extend the compass of the treaty, or alliance; and he took occasion to warn Yeh and, through him, Chiang that it would be a military error to deploy still more troops on the small, exceedingly vulnerable offshore islands. In effect, the President was applying to Chiang's tether some cautionary tugs.

All these developments—the treaty negotiated with Yeh, the conversation with Yeh in which Eisenhower clamped the brakes on any extension of the treaty, the efforts to keep alive New Zealand's initiative toward a cease-fire, the diplomatic steps taken to free the captured airmen, the muffling of Senator Knowland and the confusion of the "China Lobby" —all were addressed to the safekeeping of the status quo. First and last, the preservation of that condition was Dwight Eisenhower's driving purpose in life. He might, indeed, be most appropriately enshrined as the President of the Status Quo, that wondrous land more day-before-yesterday than today, land of Model Ts and simple honor, of long lazy afternoons at the ball park, of savings in the bank and a wholesome gross national product, that never-never land of heart's desire, that land for which Dwight Eisenhower stood as the friendly, smiling symbol; honest, sincere, honorable, decent; the beloved Hero.

To his oval office, command headquarters of his global struggle to conserve the status quo, came messages from the heads of states allied with the U.S., reports from his senior advisers, questions deemed to be of such moment as to warrant his personal decision. Not too many of these last reached him. His staff system functioned smartly, insulating him from the exigent trivia of the presidency and from a great deal that was by no means trivial. Adams deflected the politicians on the Hill, Nixon assumed the job of political campaigning, Humphrey sweated to get the national economy purring in high gear, others of cabinet rank—Benson, Brownell, Mrs. Hobby, McKay, Mitchell, Weeks—labored to keep the domestic departments of government operating efficiently. The President, what time he was not relaxing with friends over a game of bridge or golf, concentrated on the great questions of the Cold War, on defending the status quo. He had fixed ideas about the nature of the problems that should be brought to him for decision and a vast impatience with those that he believed should be dealt with by a subordinate. He had once, while still president of Columbia, defined the matter with jocular brutality. "In the army as a general," he told an acquaintance, "I'd shoot a major for not making some of the decisions that at Columbia the president of the university has to make." As President of the United States he could order his affairs to his own satisfaction, leaving himself time for—

A conversation with his old friend Lucius Clay, who arrived to launch the crusade to convince Eisenhower he should stand for President again in 1956. The mid-term elections had been sufficient evidence that without his name on the ticket the Republican party was impotent. The GOP must be revitalized, Clay argued, and Eisenhower alone could do the job. The President listened and reserved his decision.

His correspondence with Churchill. The prime minister wrote to reassure the President about Red China, to dismiss that nation as a potential warmaker. The Chinese, Churchill reminded Eisenhower, had no chrome, no nickel, and very little aluminum, copper, and manganese; only tungsten, of the metals vital to ordnance. More important, Churchill considered the time ripe for a meeting at the summit. On both counts Eisenhower disagreed: he wanted no meeting of leading statesmen, and he feared the Chinese might go to war whether they had the necessary resources or no.

His last brush with Joe McCarthy. The Senate voted censure of McCarthy on December 2, and all at once the demagogue was finished. The power to terrify others had gone out of him. At the White House the reaction was not behindhand. Eisenhower had a date to play golf two days later with Prescott Bush, a Republican senator from Connecticut, but rain fell and Bush instead called Sherman Adams to urge that he get the President to send for Senator Arthur Watkins—chairman of the select committee that had recommended censure of McCarthy—and "give him a good pat on the back." "Will do," said Adams. Before noon Watkins was in Eisenhower's oval office. Hagerty told reporters that Eisenhower had "congratulated the senator on the splendid job he did" and so begot a front-page story for all the Sunday newspapers. (Eisenhower had not intended that Hagerty tell the press of Watkins's visit; he even scolded Hagerty, but not, Hagerty surmised, as though he meant it.) On the Tuesday McCarthy snarled that Eisenhower was soft on communism; he apologized for having supported Eisenhower's election. Too late. Now when Eisenhower ignored him, it would at last be appropriate.

His daily reports from Foster Dulles, who was in Paris in mid-December for the NATO meetings. The critical business at those conclaves concerned nuclear weapons: talk of an Air Defense Technical Center to be established at The Hague as an adjunct to SHAPE; discussion of M.C. 48, a secret paper reflecting, said Dulles, "the unanimous opinion of the military advisers, the military council, as to the best means . . . the only effective means, of providing a defense of Western Europe"; in short, nuclear ordnance. Their discussion made clear that the NATO ministers reluctantly agreed their soldiers and airmen must incorporate the terrible weapons in their plans, but the ministers also displayed a becoming concern for public opinion: what would the people think, when word of those plans got abroad? Still, as Dulles argued, the weapons "would assure the reality of a successful defense and an avoidance of what we all, under present conditions, must dread, that is, the necessity of a liberation, which in fact would leave very little to be liberated."

So, as everyone preferred to believe, those armaments were only to maintain the status quo.

But the Chinese found intolerable a status quo that robbed them of what was rightfully theirs and, moreover, converted their possessions into a means by which mischief-makers might visit them with harm.

The Tachen Islands, more than two hundred miles north of Taiwan, were occupied by a full division of Chiang's troops; another island to the north, Ichiang, was held by another couple of thousand of Chiang's soldiers. American officers were also on hand as advisers, training specialists, and intelligence experts. On January 10, 1955, Chinese airplanes bombed the Tachens, inflicting what Chiang's radio reported as "considerable" damage. On January 18 Chinese troops, transported in motorized junks, swarmed up the beaches of Ichiang and in two hours overwhelmed the occupation forces.

The island was "of no particular importance," Dulles told a press conference. Surely Eisenhower agreed with that judgment, but he was as always careful to leave himself ample room for maneuver. The "small islands . . . now under attack," he told his own press conference next day, on January 19, were not "essential" to the defense of Taiwan; even the Tachens were not "a vital element" in that defense; nevertheless the Tachens "are of value, there is no denying that, they are of value as an outpost, an additional point for observation"; if the U.N. were to try to arrange a cease-fire, "it might be a good thing." In short, the U.S. might find it necessary to defend the offshore islands, or it might not; who could say?

Any war fought nine thousand miles away is less dolorous than one fought on one's own doorstep. In this case the issues were so unreal, so faraway, that a threat of war to dispute them was the more shocking. The objectives for which men were fighting and dying were so obscure that the CIA had found it advisable to have scholars research and write a descriptive analysis of the offshore islands, to illustrate their report with maps and photographs, to have it privately printed and bound as a pamphlet, and to give the pamphlet a restricted circulation within what had come to be known in Washington as the intelligence community. One copy had been delivered to the White House, its cover bearing a scribbled message from Allen Dulles to Moaney, the President's valet, instructing him to place it on the President's night table.

Thursday, January 20, was a day for a session of the National Security Council. It was plain, as Eisenhower wrote later, that "the time had come to draw the line," that is, to tell the Chinese which of their possessions they might safely reclaim, and which they might attempt to reclaim at their peril. In short, the enemies of China (both Chinese and American) were with impunity to post military establishments on islands within sight of the mainland and announce in advance their intention. Further, this was to be done under the rubric: We are keeping the peace. "I believed," Eisenhower wrote later, "the Korean War had resulted, partially at least, from the mistaken Communist notion that under no circumstances would the United States move to the assistance of the Korean Republic. I resolved that this time no uncertainty about our commitment to defend [Taiwan] should invite a major Chinese Communist attack."

But the line to be drawn would include more Chinese territory than Taiwan. For, as Dulles observed on that Thursday morning, ". . . we all agree that we cannot permit the Communists to seize *all* the offshore islands." The Tachens might be evacuated, but Quemoy and the Matsus should be held, as well Taiwan and the Pescadores. President Eisenhower, again noting the serious psychological consequences (to the morale of Chiang's defeated armies) if Quemoy and the Matsus were to be abandoned, ordered plans for this revised policy (evacuation of the Tachens) to be begun.

A part of these plans was the drafting of a special message to the Congress on United States policy for the defense of Taiwan, and a difference of opinion quickly arose within the administration as to what the President should say in his message. Once again the two admirals among the Joint Chiefs resisted withdrawal from any of the offshore islands. Carney, the chief of naval operations, was particularly opposed: evacuation of the Tachens, he insisted, would be far more difficult than either defending them or reinforcing them. He acknowledged that Chiang's troops could not defend them without U.S. help; in fine, he foresaw work ahead for the U.S. Seventh Fleet. The President was not impressed. Asked how long it would take to evacuate the Tachens, Carney and Radford reckoned two weeks. In the judgment of the CIA, the Chinese Communists would not harass such an operation. Foster Dulles predicted the Nationalist forces on the islands would surrender if they were left to shift for themselves. The draft of the President's message was somewhat tempered to eliminate emphasis on withdrawal, but what Eisenhower wanted said would be said.

His message was delivered on January 24. It was designed as a warning to the Chinese, but it served as well to alarm a great many Americans. "In the interest of peace," the President declared, "the United States must remove any doubt regarding our readiness to fight, if necessary, to preserve the vital stake of the free world in a free [Taiwan], and to engage in whatever operations may be required to carry out that purpose." Those operations included a tutelary eye on "closely related localities," undefined but clearly intending Quemoy and the Matsus. Specifically, the President desired the Congress to approve a joint resolution authorizing him to take certain steps which as commander in chief he was already constitutionally empowered to take. "Eisenhower," said Senator Wayne Morse of Oregon, "is passing the buck," and a great many congressmen, including the Speaker of the House, Sam Rayburn of Texas, were notably unhappy to be asked to share the responsibility for the risks of a war in Taiwan Strait, risks that only a few men in the executive branch could reasonably assess. But Eisenhower wanted a display of national unity, and he got it swiftly when the joint resolution (entitled Public Law 4) was passed by the Senate 85 to 3, and by the House 410 to 3. In effect, the Congress approved Eisenhower's three-tiered strategy of evacuating the Tachens, warning the Chinese against massing troops and aircraft in Fukien province opposite Taiwan, and pinning Chiang to his island fortress.

The show of unity, as the President knew, was hollow. Not only were a number of congressmen distressed by the way they had been constrained to share responsibility for a decision they believed was the President's alone, the people had also testified to their misgivings. Of the hundreds of letters mailed to the White House in the wake of the President's special message, opposition to intervention in Taiwan Strait ran a trifle more than three to one over support of Chiang. (The letters were examined for evidence of concerted propaganda; none was found.) A few of the correspondents wanted the matter referred to the U.N., but that possibility was ruled out when Chou En-lai rejected an invitation to discuss New Zealand's proposal of a cease-fire except on the condition that Chiang's representative be "driven out from the Security Council" and China's permanent seat on the council given to the People's Republic of China. Only then, Chou declared, could the U.N. properly consider the "acts of aggression" and "intervention in China's internal affairs" of which the U.S. was guilty. His reply was brushed aside. It was "a very bellicose statement," said President Eisenhower; Chou's "abrupt rejection" of the invitation, said a spokesman at the State Department, was a "further flouting of the U.N."

The affair had now been accorded the status of a crisis, at least by the press, and in this crisis whatever restraint was apparent was being exercised by the Chinese and, rather shakily, by President Eisenhower. Chiang and several of Eisenhower's advisers were hell-bent for immediate confrontation, blockade of China, preventive war, and the like. Two factors chiefly lent the crisis a more perilous aspect than was warranted. First, there were those in Washington who, as Eisenhower wrote Churchill, were "violent in their efforts to get us to take a much stronger, even a truculent position" toward the Chinese, and among them were some of the President's military advisers and the leader of his party in the Senate; their clatter worked to confuse even his warmest admirers, leaving in question whether he did in fact have a policy and, if so, what that policy was. Second, the President and his secretary of state consistently misread the Chinese intentions and their capabilities, descrying a threat of war where there were only aggrieved complaints about U.S. meddling and apprehensions of outright U.S. aggression. Their misreading followed logically from their belief that, as Dulles phrased it, "International Communism uses the power of Russia and now of Mainland China to pursue its goal of world domination." They saw the war in Korea, the insurgency in Indochina, and the Chinese determination to reclaim their island territories as carefully timed components of one cunning master plan, deliberately probing the defenses of the free world and very likely conceived by those arch conspirators "the men in the Kremlin."* Thus Eisenhower would write of how "it seemed probable that the Soviet Union would do all it could to get the United States bogged down in a debilitating war with Communist China"; he would write Churchill of his belief that "international Communism [might] penetrate the island barrier in the Western Pacific and thus be in a position to threaten the Philippines and Indonesia immediately and directly"; and he would warn Churchill that what the Chinese "are really interested in is Formosa [Taiwan]—and later on Japan." Churchill argued in vain against these ideas; in vain he attempted to persuade the President to disentangle his policy by returning Quemoy and the Matsus to China. Eisenhower detected here a whiff of appeasement. He glimpsed another Munich. In short, so long as the commander in chief was under constant pressure from the radical right wing of his own party and was at the same time soberly convinced that the Chinese government proposed to pounce upon its neighbors south and east, so long the crisis in the Taiwan Strait would remain explosive.

On Saturday, January 29, Eisenhower issued instructions in the business of evacuating the Tachens: if the operation were attacked by Chinese aircraft, the commander of the Pacific Fleet, Admiral Felix Stump, was authorized to counterattack but ordered not to carry the action back to the Chinese bases unless such "hot pursuit" was deemed essential. Stump was instructed to exercise restraint.

There was a hitch. Chiang's Kuomintang commanders would not, in their turn, give approval for the departure from the Tachens until Chiang had been sent an explicit assurance by Washington that the U.S. would

* While Dulles could perceive these three separate proceedings as orchestrated into one continuous and sinister schema directed against the United States, he could at the same time instruct the chiefs of U.S. missions to some fifteen Pacific countries in "the broad strategy which underlies our desire to maintain at least a potential of three fronts against the Chinese Communists if they should commit open aggression —the one in Korea, the one in [Taiwan], and the one in Indochina."

commit its forces to defend Quemoy and the Matsus—a guarantee that exceeded the terms of the treaty still before the Senate.

On Monday, January 31, another conference at the White House: prolonged discussion; at length the President indicated he would authorize the use of U.S. forces to defend the offshore islands. No announcement of this critical decision. Chiang was told, but otherwise it was kept secret. Chiang was also told of administration efforts to hasten the Senate's approval of the treaty.

Evacuation began on February 4 and was completed without incident a week later.

Plainly "the men in the Kremlin" had been at no pains to get the U.S. "bogged down in a debilitating war" with China. The leaders of the Soviet Union were preoccupied with a shift of power. Malenkov was replaced as premier by Nikolai Bulganin, a suave, soft-spoken man of fifty-nine; and the stocky, ebullient, sixty-year-old Nikita Khrushchev, who had for sixteen months past been the secretary general of the Communist party's Central Committee, now caught the world's wondering attention as he stepped forward to become the most powerful figure in the Soviet government. He did not fit the mold.

Eisenhower volunteered a comment: "We know, of course, when any major change of that kind takes place, that it does express dissatisfaction with what has been going on internally." To the contrary, it was dissatisfaction with what had been going on *externally* that led to the shuffle of leading officials within the Soviet Union.

Most of the Kuomintang soldiers from the Tachens were to be assigned to reinforce the defenses of Quemoy and the Matsus; those islands remained in dispute, a possible provocation of more serious conflict. The government of the United States had made a commitment to protect them—or had it? On February 9, 1955, the Senate voted sixty-four to six to approve for ratification the treaty of defense negotiated with George Yeh, Chiang's so-called foreign minister. The next day Yeh paid calls upon Dulles and Walter Robertson, assistant secretary for Far Eastern affairs, prior to taking his formal leave; later he told reporters the United States would "defend all the related positions and localities which are deemed important to the defense of Formosa [Taiwan] and the Pescadores." He was asked if the pledge affected Quemoy and the Matsus. "Of course," said Yeh, and added that the pledge covered "all the offshore islands." This precipitated a flurry of semantic confusion, after which Yeh issued another statement: the defense of the offshore islands was a "possibility," a matter "for the United States to decide."

Foster Dulles, following a speech in which he referred to the shift in the Russian leadership as "despotic disarray" and proclaimed, of the Taiwan crisis, that "We dare not relax, because the moment of relaxation is the moment of peril," departed for the Far East to instruct the ministers of SEATO in the "cruel, despotic nature of Communist rule." In Bangkok, as the SEATO conference closed, Dulles professed himself satisfied with the results. The phrase "international communism," he pointed out to correspondents, had been included in the final communiqué. "Now we have made the words respectable here," he said. A week later he was with Chiang Kai-shek on Taiwan, carrying out Eisenhower's instructions to put an unmistakable limit on U.S. responsibility for the offshore islands. Authority to use the armed forces of the U.S. outside the area defined in the treaty, Dulles told Chiang, was to be left to the President of the United States; there could be no further commitment for the defense of Quemoy and the Matsus. The secretary also suggested that Chiang patiently await the inevitable schisms that would soon sunder the communist leadership of China. Chiang agreed. For his part, he desired the U.S. to resist admission of China to the United Nations. Dulles protested that he did not know how he could more firmly have opposed that eventuality; Chiang laughed and agreed. On the chances of a cease-fire supervised by the U.N., Chiang insisted he would never approve such an arrangement; Dulles urged that he not instruct his representative on the Security Council to cast a veto against a cease-fire but rather leave the matter to be rejected by the Soviet Union.

The world watched nervously the secretary's trip through Southeast Asia and back by way of Taiwan, speculating as to whether at the end of it would come a relaxation of tensions or a loosing of atomic bombs. Allies of the United States grew increasingly apprehensive despite zealous evangelism by both Eisenhower and Dulles. During a long conversation at Bangkok, Dulles sought to persuade Eden of U.S. restraint and moral rectitude; no use; twelve days later, in a speech to the Commons, Eden called on the Kuomintang to hand the offshore islands back to China. On his own return, Dulles was more bellicose than ever. On March 8 he broadcast by radio and television a martial report to the nation, one that bristled with warnings of "military challenge" and threats of "new and powerful weapons of precision, which can utterly destroy military targets without endangering unrelated civilian centers." Two days later he reported in even more somber terms to the National Security Council. "I believe there is at least an even chance that the United States will have to go to war," Dulles told the NSC, assembled for its regular weekly meeting on Thursday, March 10. "If we defend Quemoy and Matsu," he contended, "we'll have to use atomic weapons. They alone will be effective against the mainland airfields."

President Eisenhower agreed.*

Dulles was prey to one misgiving: how much stomach for fighting had Chiang's troops? If they were attacked, would they resist?

Eisenhower was displeased. "The United States," he remarked, "cannot possibly save the Nationalists if they don't want to be saved." Dulles's doubt put the problem "in a different light."

Once again Radford moved to inspirit the warhawks. The morale of Chiang's troops, he asserted, depended on their hope of fighting for their homeland, and to keep that hope alive they must be allowed to fasten their grip on Quemoy and the Matsus. And if war came—

If war came, President Eisenhower interjected, it would be recognized as a war the United States had never sought.

The next day the Dulles brothers, Bobby Cutler, three of the four chiefs of staff (Admiral Carney was in the Far East, whence came reports that "U.S. military leaders" had predicted a general war might be "only weeks away"), and Colonel Goodpaster, Eisenhower's staff secretary, met with the President to assess Chiang's capacity to resist without active American help. Eisenhower decided to send Goodpaster to Pearl Harbor, where he might confer with Admiral Stump and get a first hand military estimate of the problem. On March 15 Goodpaster was back in the White House to tell the President that the next ten days—March 15 to 25—were the time of greatest peril; the Kuomintang defenses were still under construction; a sudden amphibious assault on the Matsus might succeed. No attack was expected, however, in less than four weeks.

President and secretary of state greeted this report by using the ten-day period of greatest danger to make statements presumably designed to be cautionary but in effect inflammatory. On Tuesday, March 15, Secretary Dulles told his press conference that in the event of war in the Far East the U.S. would probably use tactical atomic weapons. On Wednesday the President was asked about that forecast, and he answered:

"Now, in any combat where these things can be used on strictly military targets and for strictly military purposes, I see no reason why they shouldn't be used just exactly as you would use a bullet or anything else.

"I believe the great question about these things comes when you begin

---

* At this same time Karl Rankin, the experienced U.S. ambassador in Taipei, was explaining to C. L. Sulzberger of the *New York Times* how weak in logistics were the Chinese. While on Taiwan the Kuomintang had airfields for jet aircraft and pipelines to pump fuel for them, the Chinese had as yet no effective air bases in Fukien province (across Taiwan Strait), no railways near the coast, and only a few inferior roads over which to truck fuel once their airfields were built.

to get into those areas where you cannot make sure that you are operating merely against military targets. But with that one qualification, I would say, yes, of course they would be used."

On Friday Dulles was in Ottawa with the doleful message that China was taking dead aim at Taiwan and that Japan was next on the Chinese agenda. On Sunday, back in New York, Dulles warned that the United States might again be obliged to "forego peace in order to secure the blessings of liberty," and the next day, in still another speech, he was more specific. The Chinese, he declared, were "an acute and imminent threat," they were "dizzy with success," they were pursuing a course of "aggressive fanaticism" which he likened to that of Hitler. They were "more dangerous and provocative of war" even than the Soviets.

The American reaction to the fusillade of ominous exhortation was numbed and bemused.* When President Eisenhower was being briefed preparatory to his press conference on Wednesday, March 23, his press secretary Jim Hagerty relayed to him "a frantic plea" just received from the State Department, become suddenly sensitive to that public reaction:

> "Mr. President," he said, "some of the people in the State Department say that the Formosa Strait situation is so delicate that no matter what question you get on it, you shouldn't say anything at all."
> I could see the point of this advice. But I didn't take it.
> "Don't worry, Jim," I told him as we went out the door of my office, "if that question comes up, I'll just confuse them."

Sure enough, in one hundred and fifty well-chosen words of muddled syntax and contrary significations, the President indeed confused and silenced —at least on the matter of the Taiwan crisis—the two hundred and eleven correspondents who attended his press conference that day.

As the ten-day period of greatest tension inched closer to its conclusion, other voices entered the debate. On Thursday, March 24, Lester Pearson, the Canadian secretary of external affairs, told the Parliament in Ottawa that while Canada "could not stand aloof" from a war that threatened the existence of the U.S., "I do not consider a conflict over the possession of those Chinese coastal islands, Quemoy and the Matsus, to be such a situation." One by one the closest allies of the United States were cutting themselves clear of what they regarded as an impossible business.

That evening the warhawks around the President took a remarkably imprudent step. Admiral Carney, chief of naval operations, invited to

---

* A poll taken by George Gallup's psephological outfit showed that only 10 percent of Americans knew who occupied the offshore islands and only 14 percent knew even approximately how close those islands were to the mainland.

dinner a group of Washington correspondents and gave them a background briefing, speaking, as he imagined, off the record. (Later Carney would repudiate his remarks, but his guests had made careful notes which they were ready to offer in rebuttal.) Carney said the Chinese "probably will initiate an attack on Matsu in mid-April. The significance of the timing is that it would tie in with the Afro-Asian conference in Bandung. . . . The all-out attack on Quemoy would be some weeks later . . ." His briefing confirmed what had been generally believed in Washington but never actually published: that at least some of the President's military advisers were pressing Eisenhower "to destroy Red China's military potential and thus end its expansionist tendencies."*

Word that it was Admiral Carney, one of his chiefs of staff, who had so rashly insinuated his views to a group of journalists might have sent President Eisenhower into one of his celebrated rages; but he reacted with cold and terminal decision, recognizing that the axe had better fall without haste. He moved deliberately. On Saturday, March 26, the day after Carney's indiscretions had made headlines in newspapers across the country and had once again sent anxieties to a feverish peak, Eisenhower dictated (with one eye cocked on the record of history) another of those notes for his diary:

> Lately there has been a very definite feeling among the members of the cabinet, often openly expressed, that within a month we will actually be fighting in the Formosa Straits. It is, of course, entirely possible that this is true, because the Red Chinese appear to be completely reckless, arrogant, possibly overconfident, and completely indifferent to human losses.
>
> Nevertheless, I believe hostilities are not so imminent . . .
>
> I have so often been through these periods of strain that I have become accustomed to the fact that most of the calamities that we anticipate really never occur.

A couple of days later the President planted a story of his own, using Jim Hagerty for his purpose. Carney's prediction, Hagerty told another gathering of journalists, was the "parochial" opinion of one of the armed services and should not be confused with the facts of the matter. On March 30 at his press conference, Eisenhower stepped on Carney's evalua-

* The Bandung Conference, sponsored by Burma, Ceylon, India, Indonesia, and Pakistan, was to bring together the representatives of twenty-nine nations of Africa and Asia for a week (April 18–24) to discuss the economic and social development of the two continents and tackle such problems as colonialism, racialism, and national sovereignty. With casual indifference to the concerns of the great white powers, the sponsors had invited China but *not* Chiang's shadow government. Delegates to the conference spoke for one billion four hundred million black, brown, and yellow people, more than half the population of the world.

tion of the crisis once again. He was asked if the admiral would be reprimanded for his remarks. "Not by me," retorted the President. Of course not: two echelons in the chain of command intervened between commander in chief and chief of naval operations, and one reason for the existence of those echelons is to enable the delegation to a subordinate of a distasteful task. Charles Wilson, secretary of defense, issued an order directing that all military personnel must henceforth submit for clearance all speeches, press releases, and "other information" intended for publication.*

Carney's briefing, thanks to the press, had a tonic effect: it made evident the existence of a "war party," so called at once by the redoubtable Lyndon Johnson, and by him identified with the right-wing Republicans; once exposed to the glare of public scrutiny, it shriveled. The President's restraining hand grew firmer as public and congressional pressures for a rational diplomacy intensified. Those pressures had made it quite clear that the United States could no longer engage to commit its armed might to defend the coastal islands held by the Kuomintang. Two luncheon sessions with congressional leaders at the end of March confirmed the President in his renewed resolution. Although its echoes would still rumble and mutter for some time, the thunderstorm over Quemoy and the Matsus had now passed.

While Chou En-lai was telling the delegates to the Bandung Conference that the Chinese had come there "to seek unity and not to quarrel," President Eisenhower was dispatching a mission to Chiang Kai-shek in an effort to extricate the United States from the unpleasant dilemma into which his policy had plunged it. On the one hand, he risked involvement without allies in a nuclear war over a half-dozen coastal islands that had no conceivable claim on U.S. "national interest" except as their possession contributed to the morale of Chiang's Kuomintang armies; on the other hand, he must if possible persuade Chiang to withdraw the bulk of his forces from those islands and convert them "from precarious symbols of Chinese Nationalist prestige into strongly defended, workable outposts."

In Bandung, the contrast between Chou and the caricature of the Chinese openly given credence by Eisenhower and Dulles was positively embarrassing to the United States. "Reckless, arrogant, possibly overconfident"? "An acute and imminent threat"? On the contrary, Chou

---

* Late in May 1955, when Eisenhower nominated Radford to another term as chairman of the Joint Chiefs and Twining to another term as air force chief of staff, Carney was quietly replaced as chief of naval operations. Matthew Ridgway, who had long been critical of the policies of the Joint Chiefs but had been consistently outvoted, had earlier requested retirement as army chief of staff.

showed self-possession, maturity, willingness to conciliate, friendliness, and an easy, relaxed self-confidence. An impressive performance, capped on April 23 when he declared the Chinese government "willing to sit down . . . with the United States government to discuss the question of relaxing tension in the Far East."

The offer caught the Eisenhower administration flat-footed. The President had only just returned from his annual spring junket to Augusta, following the Masters Tournament; Foster Dulles was away for a five-day rest at his retreat on Duck Island in Lake Ontario; the assistant secretary of state for Far Eastern affairs, Walter Robertson, was one of Eisenhower's emissaries to Chiang Kai-shek (the other was Admiral Radford); the man left in charge at Foggy Bottom was the undersecretary, Herbert Hoover, Jr., a man trained as a geologist and petrochemical engineer but weak in experience of diplomacy. The answer to Chou framed under Hoover's direction (and approved by President Eisenhower over the telephone from his Gettysburg farm) imposed a number of prerequisites to any negotiations, as evidence of Chinese sincerity, and observed that "of course the United States would insist on Free China participating as an equal in any discussions" of the Taiwan Strait.

The next day, in Taipei, George Yeh declared that his government could "never sit at the same table" with the Red Chinese. As matters stood, that statement effectively blocked negotiations between China and the United States. Yeh then welcomed Eisenhower's two emissaries, Robertson and Admiral Radford, and the conversations with Chiang were ready to begin.

Eisenhower's instructions were exacting. Robertson and Radford were to try "to induce the generalissimo to propose some solution to the Formosa-Quemoy-Matsu problem that will be acceptable both to him and to us"—a solution "that will neither commit the United States to go to war in defense of the offshore islands nor will constitute an implied repudiation of the generalissimo" by the Eisenhower administration. The President had a solution, but he wanted Chiang to volunteer it. The President wanted Chiang to suggest redeployment of his troops; he hoped for at least a partial evacuation and in return he was willing to promise Chiang he would maintain on Taiwan substantial U.S. forces, including marines and an air wing. In his conversations with Chiang, Robertson was authorized to go further: if Chiang would agree to evacuate Quemoy and the Matsus, the United States would then, to guarantee the defense of Taiwan, undertake to interdict all sea lanes from Swatow north to Wenchow, five hundred miles of Chinese coastline, the entire western shore of Taiwan Strait. But, as Robertson reported to the State Department in a lengthy message, Chiang resisted any further evacuation. He had pulled out of the Tachens, but he was determined to defend Quemoy and the Matsus—unaided if necessary. He judged that the President must have revised his policy, since Eisenhower no longer stood ready to aid in their defense as he had pledged he would do in his message of January 31. Radford acknowledged the President had changed his mind. Chiang voiced concern about the psychological effect throughout Asia once word had spread that the United States had privily reneged its commitment. Yeh argued that to lose the islands in battle would do less harm to Kuomintang morale than to evacuate them without a fight. (In the margin of the message, at this point, Eisenhower scribbled, "I agree.") Robertson urged that the proposed interdiction of sea lanes would offer a stouter defense of Taiwan than could the coastal islands, but Chiang, after withdrawing briefly to consult with his singular wife, returned to insist that the islands were now a symbol and their abandonment would injure the prestige of the United States. Robertson here saw fit to dispute the idea that the U.S. and its President had reneged a pledge. Not so, he declared; the course of the affair, he insisted, had run thus: Before the decision to evacuate the Tachens had been taken, Eisenhower had determined there would be no public announcement of the U.S. commitment to defend Quemoy and the Matsus, although under the circumstances at that time the U.S. would have come to their defense; Foster Dulles had emphasized that the U.S. commitment was a unilateral one, always contingent on changing circumstances; on January 31, to be sure, the President had confirmed to Chiang the U.S. readiness to defend the islands; since then, however, pressures both congressional and popular had mounted; circumstances had altered; as matters now stood, the United States could not help defend the islands, for that policy lacked a united national will. Eisenhower would continue to espouse Chiang's cause and, if the generalissimo chose, would at once furnish evidence of his increased support.

But Chiang was unable to volunteer the solution to the President's dilemma that Eisenhower had hoped for, and on the whole Eisenhower could find no fault with his reluctance.

His emissaries to Taiwan having failed, Eisenhower realized that he must reconsider Chou's offer to discuss the disputes between the United States and China. Back from Duck Island, Dulles let the door to negotiations open a crack at his news conference, and Eisenhower admitted to reporters that the U.S. might, after all, "talk to the Chi-Coms" without Chiang's shadow government being present. "Now, if we overstated the case [in the first reply to Chou's offer], well," Eisenhower conceded, "that was to that extent an error in terminology."

To Senator Knowland, the "China Lobby," and the desperate war party generally, this was a bitter setback. There was even talk that Knowland might resign as minority leader in protest against the possibility of conversations with the Chinese. Negotiations to reduce the tension had, indeed, already begun: V. K. Krishna Menon, the Indian diplomat who acted as Nehru's representative in foreign affairs, had gone to Peking to discuss the release of American airmen held prisoner in China, and on May 30 he would announce the scheduled release of the first four—combat fliers who had been captured during the Korean War. A kind of de facto cease-fire had by common consent intervened in the Taiwan Strait. Krishna Menon pursued his efforts—in London, in Ottawa, at the U.N. in New York, and at last in Washington, where he talked with Eisenhower, Dulles, and Nixon. Eisenhower was uncharacteristically disobliging with the Indian ("Krishna Menon is a menace and a boor," he noted in his diary) and he twice rejected the suggestion of any negotiations over the U.S. prisoners, insisting that only after they had been released could conversations begin.

Krishna Menon's perseverance succeeded. The eleven fliers condemned as spies were released on July 31. On August 1 talks commenced on the ambassadorial level between the Chinese and the Americans exploring the release of the American CIA agents (prognosis: dubious) and the repatriation of the several thousand Chinese who had come to the U.S. as students in the 1940s but had found their return home difficult and in many cases impossible (they had been restrained by the U.S.; prognosis: fair).

The first crisis over Taiwan had been contained.

During the time Dwight Eisenhower was President and for at least another decade after it, a remarkable fixity of popular opinion about Eisenhower and his secretary of state would be evident, a general disposition to hold Eisenhower innocent and to blame Dulles for what often seemed a most disagreeable foreign policy. On every hand Eisenhower was praised as a reasonable man, a man of accommodation, the wonderfully pacific commander in chief, the five-star general who waged peace more energetically than he had waged war—and who had waged war more successfully? Dulles, to the contrary, was rigid; he was the dour, stubborn ideologue; vain, doctrinaire, narrow, harsh, legalistic, self-righteous. Eisenhower had amiable instincts; Dulles smothered them. Eisenhower's smile was radiant; the corners of Dulles's mouth turned down, incised, as in a death mask. Oh! (ran the common prayer of the day, often enough bursting into print) if only Eisenhower and not Dulles were devising American foreign policy! The prayer, like so many another, was illusory.

The error was the familiar human one of confusing the contents of the package with its wrapper, of assuming that the face a man turns to the world is an accurate guide to his temper. That man with the pinched and sour visage: he dreams of torts and misdemeanors; he casts about for ways to deceive or to revenge himself on his neighbors. His compeer, whose good humor gleams and caresses all around him, is manifestly a good man. How can he abide his associate? Why has he not chosen a more sympathetic companion? Getting down to cases, why did the bonhomous Eisenhower not select a chief adviser on foreign affairs—a secretary of state—whose ideas were more compatible with his own? Why did the President permit his secretary of state to shape and administer a foreign policy that more than once almost transformed Cold War into nuclear holocaust, and so provoked apprehensions to excruciating pitch? Thus the error—fertilized and cultivated by journalists and editorial cartoonists —that the President was only a rubber stamp for the plans and decisions of the wily Dulles. Nor, it must be noted, was Dulles at any particular pains to correct the error. He collaborated in the preparation of articles, published in journals of wide circulation, designed to display his sagacity and primacy in statecraft.

The facts are more prosaic. As President, Eisenhower was constitutionally charged with the conduct of foreign relations, and he knew it. That a man with the habit of command so well ingrained in him should turn over to another so grave a responsibility is simply inconceivable. Eisenhower did not. His method of command remained substantially as he had elaborated it over the last dozen years and more, a staff operation: the National Security Council and its satellite Planning Board and Operations Coordinating Board explored the problems of the day, and on each problem or program canvassed the views of the federal departments and agencies concerned; examined and cross-examined specialists; drafted discussion papers; searched for alternatives, for disagreements; defined contingencies; agreed on recommendations and submitted them for debate by the President and his senior advisers; and so at last arrived at a consensus, on which the President might (or might not) scribble his initials in approval.

In this process, Foster Dulles was the President's most trusted adviser. When a problem became a crisis (as too often happened) the two men consulted constantly. "There were so many telephone calls," Eisenhower later recalled, "that you just didn't attempt to keep track of the number. . . . We'd be in close touch all the time. I suppose some days eight or ten times." The two men held well-nigh identical opinions about the demands on foreign policy of the Cold War; point by point their minds met in familiar agreement, and on familiar grounds, for Eisenhower responded to Dulles's "very strong faith in moral law," his constant search for "what was right, and what conformed to the principles of human behavior as we'd like to believe them and see them." "Not only were our relations very close and cordial," Eisenhower would recall, "but on top of that I always regarded him *as an assistant* and an associate with whom I could talk things out very easily, digging in all of their various facets and tangents and then—when finally a decision was made, I could count on him to execute them. [Emphasis supplied.]"

For his part, Dulles was careful to obtain Eisenhower's approval of his plans, speeches, often even of his statements to the press. He understood he was secretary of state at the pleasure of the President; he remembered how his uncle Robert Lansing, by an excess of independence, had forfeited the trust of President Woodrow Wilson; he kept his lines of communication to his own President open and smooth with regular use.

As between the two men, there was no illusion. Eisenhower was paramount. First and last the foreign policy of the United States, so widely attributed to Dulles, bore the stamp of Dwight Eisenhower, and it was not a rubber stamp.

CHAPTER FIVE

Thaw in the Cold War

Disarmament: the U.S. proposals accepted by the USSR and withdrawn by the U.S. . . . A conference at the summit in Geneva . . . The "spirit of Geneva" . . . Summer months in Colorado . . . Eisenhower sustains a heart attack.

ONE OF THE POINTS on which Eisenhower and Dulles agreed was the undesirability of a conference involving the U.S. and USSR—the meeting at the summit so long and so earnestly sought by Churchill. One reason for their reluctance was the hostility and suspicion of right-wing Republicans concerning the wartime agreements made with the Soviets at Teheran, Yalta, and Potsdam. At those conferences, so ran the familiar charge, the Democrats had contrived the "sellout" of Poland and China to the communists; what might go next, at another such conference? Nonetheless, pressures at home and abroad mounted steadily for a summit meeting.

Another reason that Eisenhower and Dulles gave for their hesitance was the need to deal from "positions of strength." Not so much strength of arms (there was a glut of weapons on hand, although of course new weapons systems were always in short supply); rather, Eisenhower spoke of the strength to come from a "material, intellectual, and spiritual community of interests among the free world," a unity that he and Dulles reckoned was one attribute of the monolith of international communism. That monolith might be more imagined than real, but before he parleyed with its spokesmen, Eisenhower felt the need of a comparable "solidity of communion and partnership" back of him as the leader of the free world.

The reason most often advanced, though, was the lack of "tangible evidence of Soviet sincerity," the absence of "actual deeds giving some indication of a Communist readiness to negotiate constructively." When Eisenhower gave examples of the sort of deeds he had in mind, as like as not he would cite a matter that might be achieved at the negotiation table but was not likely to be yielded as a precondition to negotiations.

None of these reasons satisfied the generality of mankind, weary of living under a constant threat of destruction. On April 5, 1955, Anthony Eden succeeded Churchill as Britain's prime minister; Eden at once called for a general election so that he might feel he had the country's support, and during the campaign he called for a summit meeting. The French prime minister, now Edgar Faure, had already done the same. It began to seem that Eisenhower and Dulles were the only two in the world who were opposed.

Certainly the Russians were keenly in favor of a meeting of the Big Four. The time was approaching when pursuant to the Paris accords of 1954, West Germany would achieve its national sovereignty and join NATO, with leave to muster an army and build an air force, and the Soviet Union's new leaders were unlimbering new policies calculated to avert what they perceived as a threat of preventive war against them. Less than three weeks after Khrushchev and Bulganin had taken the reins of the Soviet government, negotiations were initiated with Austria to conclude a state treaty (viz., a peace treaty): Soviet occupation troops would be withdrawn if the Austrian government would agree to join no military coalition such as NATO, and to permit no foreign military bases on Austrian territory. On the same day—it was February 25, when Dulles was in Bangkok for his SEATO meetings—the Soviet representative joined diplomats of Britain, Canada, France, and the U.S. in London to begin their discussions of disarmament, nuclear and conventional—the discussions that everyone expected would be futile.

Both these matters—an Austrian state treaty and disarmament—had been often cited by President Eisenhower as the sort of thing ("deeds, not words") which alone he would consider as evidence that the Soviets were "sincere" in their desire for a diminution of world tensions. Plainly, the Kremlin was up to something. But the world was distracted by the crisis over Quemoy and the Matsus.

On April 19 the USSR proposed that the foreign ministers of the Big Four meet "in the nearest future" in Vienna to conclude a treaty "for the restoration of an independent, democratic Austria." Here was unmistakable evidence of the "sincerity" Eisenhower and Dulles had demanded. It was embarrassing. Eisenhower would recall how, soon afterward, Dulles walked into the President's office ". . . and he grinned rather ruefully and he said, 'Well, I think we've had it.' And I said, 'Yes, I can see that; I knew you were going to say that.'"

But perhaps, after all, there was still a way to avert the meeting at the summit. Perhaps Dulles could persuade the British and French to settle instead for a meeting of foreign ministers. He tried. In Paris on May 7 for a meeting of the NATO Council, Dulles spread the word that "the President of the United States cannot spend a lot of time arguing" the matters at issue. "That is the reason why he has a secretary of state," Dulles insisted, "to relieve him of that task, because he has many other tasks, including the broad lines of foreign policy. He cannot negotiate details." To no avail: the demand for a summit meeting was universal. Eisenhower realized that unless he complied he would be marked as "senselessly stubborn." Once West Germany had formally become the Federal Republic of Germany and joined NATO, the governments of Britain, France, and the U.S. sent identical notes to the USSR proposing a meeting of the heads of the four governments "to remove sources of conflict between us." The note was released to the press with appropriate fanfare and so managed to crowd off the front pages of the newspapers an event of even more striking importance. This was the stunning reversal of Soviet policy on disarmament, embodied in the proposals suddenly submitted on May 10 to the five-nation subcommittee of the U.N. committee on disarmament meeting in London.

The Russian turnabout was a thunderbolt. It caught the other delegates quite unawares. For France, Jules Moch said, "The whole thing looks too good to be true." To the British delegate the western "policy of patience" appeared to have "achieved this welcome dividend," and he pointed out that the western proposals had been "largely, and in some cases entirely," incorporated in the Soviet draft. The U.S. delegate, James J. Wadsworth, said he was "gratified to find that the concepts which we have put forward over a considerable length of time, and which we have repeated many times during the past two months, have been accepted in

690

a large measure by the Soviet Union." The Russian delegate, Jacob Malik, had presented a paper that disemboweled the western position. For years western spokesmen had complained that the Soviet Union wanted only to abolish nuclear weapons (while refusing to permit the apparatus of inspection by which such an abolition could be enforced) but said nothing about their own overwhelming preponderance in conventional armies and armaments. Now the Russians accepted the western limitations on the size of armies, accepted the western rate of reduction of both conventional and nuclear armaments, and accepted the institution of one international agency to control the various ways to make war. This agency, according to the Russian proposal, would maintain a staff of inspectors who would be permanent residents of all signatory states. They would enjoy, "within the bounds of the control functions they exercise, unimpeded access at all times to all objects of control," including "records relating to the budgetary appropriations of States for military needs." Further, they would assume the "rights and powers to exercise control, including inspection on a continuing basis, to the extent necessary to insure" that the proposed treaty would function. The Russians went so far as to stipulate the location of "control posts" at large seaports, at railway junctions, on the big autobahns, and at airfields.

By any test, the Russian proposal was a most encouraging step toward an end to the demented arms race, so costly, so ominous. Of course the diplomatists eagerly pursued the unexpected Soviet offer? No.

On May 11, the day after the proposal had been tendered, Eisenhower held his regular weekly press conference:

Q: Mr. President, I wonder if you have had an opportunity to see a report on the latest Soviet disarmament plan.

THE PRESIDENT: On what?

Q: On what has been described as the recent Soviet disarmament plan submitted to the summit.

THE PRESIDENT: You mean the one submitted through the Disarmament Commission in London?

Q: Yes, sir.

THE PRESIDENT: Well, I have just had a chance to glance at it.

Q: Do you care to comment on it, sir?

THE PRESIDENT: No, not at the moment. The whole question is so confused. It has still some of the elements they have always had in it. They

691

want to get rid of one kind; we would like to get rid of everything. It is something that has to be studied before you can really comment on it.

On May 18, despite Malik's desire to continue negotiations looking toward a treaty on disarmament, the western delegates demanded a recess to allow time to study the Soviet proposals further. It was a curious request, since those proposals had followed so closely the earlier drafts submitted by the British and French as to suggest, as one American journalist wrote, that they had been "plagiarized." But four votes always count more than one, and so the talks were postponed, not to be resumed until fifteen weeks later. President Eisenhower would not publicly revert to the subject until his press conference of July 6, when he was asked whether the United States would not "have to move away somewhat from the concept of total drastic disarmament"—the declared objective of U.S. policy since April 1952—"toward a sort of standoff." The President's answer showed how far the U.S. had shifted its ground on the question of inspection:

"I wouldn't want to have anything I now say taken as authoritative, for the simple reason that the more one studies intensively this problem of disarmament, the more he finds himself in a squirrel's cage. . . .

"Now, when we come down to it, every kind of scheme of, let us say, leveling off, as I understand your meaning—standby, where you are now—or actually reducing, everything comes back, as I see it, to acceptable methods of enforcement.

"How do you enforce such things? This brings us instantly to the question of examinations, of inspections.

"Now, one way to approach this problem is what would we, in the United States—suppose we took a vote of this body today or we started as a committee of the whole to study it, what kind of inspection are we ready to accept? Are we ready to open up every one of our factories, every place where something might be going on that could be inimical to the interests of somebody else?"

In short, when the iron curtain was pulled up, a red, white, and blue curtain quite as formidable was hastily rolled down.

It is entirely possible that the leaders of the Soviet Union made their proposal only after they had judged it would be rejected. If this is the case, they had taken a page from the American book of Cold War strategy. At all events, the Soviets had already devised a plan for use whether or not negotiations for disarmament fell through: on May 14, in Warsaw, they signed a treaty of mutual defense with seven nations of Eastern Europe. The text of this treaty (called the Warsaw Pact) declared that a "remilitarized" West Germany "increases the danger of a new war and creates a threat to the national security of peace-loving states."

And on the same day the Russians accepted the western invitation to a summit meeting.

Neither President nor secretary of state had much appetite for the meeting now definitely scheduled. Dulles's misgivings were perhaps a shade keener than Eisenhower's; certainly his public acknowledgment that the summit had now appeared on the horizon was grumpier. (He saw "danger"; Eisenhower discounted it.) But both men moved purposefully to prepare for the occasion: aides were summoned and set to drafting "position papers" on every conceivable issue that might reach the summit.

Disarmament was such an issue, but one that called for special handling. There were many crannies in the federal superstructure into which it might have been tucked—the Planning Board of the National Security Council, for example, now in the charge of Dillon Anderson, a high-powered Houston lawyer and banker who had replaced Bobby Cutler as Eisenhower's special assistant for national security affairs, or the Policy Planning Staff of the State Department, directed by Robert Bowie. On the face of it, the logical cubbyhole for disarmament was in the office of Harold Stassen, who on March 19 had been appointed Eisenhower's special assistant for disarmament, a post of cabinet level that had been at once nicknamed secretary of peace.* It says much for the prospects of disarmament, seriously considered as an objective of the Eisenhower administration, that the project ended up in the hands of the President's special assistant for Cold War strategy, Nelson Rockefeller.

Every sign pointed to the urgent need for an American initiative on disarmament that would effectively blanket the embarrassing Russian proposals of May 10. In June, when he arrived in San Francisco to share in the celebration of the U.N.'s tenth birthday, Molotov inconveniently dwelt on those proposals once again. "It is up to the U.S.A. and other western powers to make the next move" on disarmament, Molotov declared; the USSR had "accepted in full their proposal" regarding conventional arms and armies, so there could now be "no reason to put off a settlement of the problem of atomic weapons." What was needed was a scheme by which the U.S. could maintain its clear nuclear superiority and

---

* Finding a spot for Stassen had become something of a problem. As director of the Mutual Security Administration he had been responsible for developing and allocating foreign aid, a task that too often encroached on the responsibilities of the State Department—or so at least Foster Dulles believed. A bureaucratic shuffle that made Stassen the Foreign Operations administrator was no help. Once Eisenhower sent Dulles a memorandum on Stassen and "his possible use in the State Department." Eisenhower assured Dulles that Stassen was "quite ready and willing to do anything that we ask . . . in any capacity that we deem desirable." But Dulles was not to be moved.

yet present to the world the image of a peaceful, smiling land. It was not an easy ruse to pull off. Rockefeller assembled a panel of surefire dependable experts, found them working space in the Marine Corps base at Quantico, Virginia, wound them up, and set them to whirring. Out of this earnest endeavor came an idea for aerial surveys to enforce any agreements on disarmament; nothing new, but perhaps, if accompanied by a suggestion for the exchange of "a complete blueprint of [all] military establishments . . . from one end of [both] countries to the other," it might serve to muffle the thunder of the Russian proposals. When this notion was presented to him, Eisenhower was enthusiastic. It met one exceedingly important requirement: the Russians were sure to reject it. Every passage in the five-power U.N. negotiations over the past months and years guaranteed so much. And yet it was bound to have wide public appeal.*

On June 13 the statesmen had agreed to meet in Geneva on July 18: a little more than a month in which to prepare for the summit, for what was regarded as at least a caesura in the Cold War and might, with skillful management, prove to be a more lasting accommodation. The Soviets seemed to be pursuing a generous and lenitive course; might this mean there was, after all, no such animal as international communism, bent on world dominion? They were talking of something called "peaceful coexistence"; could they be trusted? Eisenhower and Dulles refused to believe it. Dulles, while welcoming the "liberation" of Austria, saw "a new set of dangers": "the wolf has put on a new set of sheep's clothing, and while it is better to have a sheep's clothing on than a bear's clothing on, because sheep don't have claws, I think the policy remains the same." Eisenhower, only a trifle more optimistic, considered the new Russian approach merely "a tactical change," without "concrete evidence" of any "real easing of tensions." Both men were convinced it was essential that the free world be vigilant. As it happened, two proceedings had earlier been planned, which came pat to their hand as reminders that the world was in a fearful predicament. Both were military exercises, with appropriately military code names: Operation Alert and Operation Carte Blanche; both were calculated to scare the wits out of the general populace.

Operation Alert was an exercise staged by the Office of Defense Mobilization over three days, June 15 to 17. According to the scenario, the U.S. had been subjected to a sudden devastating nuclear attack: fifty-three cities across the continent had been destroyed or so severely damaged that their populations were in terrified flight; six cities in Alaska, Hawaii,

* In March 1965, when he was questioned on this point, Eisenhower was emphatic. "We knew the Soviets wouldn't accept it," he said; "we were sure of that."

694

"*Yes, We'll Be There, Rain and Shine.*"

from *Herblock's Here and Now* (Simon & Schuster, 1955)

Puerto Rico, and the Panama Canal Zone had also been hit; uncounted millions were dead, and vast clouds of radioactive fallout billowed over the whole country. Early on June 15 the President and fifteen thousand federal employees fled from Washington to take shelter in thirty-odd secret emergency headquarters, some as much as three hundred miles away. Eisenhower and his staff were driven in limousines up into the Catoctin Mountains to Camp David. On his way Eisenhower signed a simulated proclamation of martial law in the simulated national emergency. The Wednesday-to-Friday afforded him a welcome respite from Washington; he had more time than usual to practice chip shots and concentrate on the putting green. On the Friday night he addressed the nation by radio and television from a simulated "underground Pentagon," seizing the occasion to appeal directly to the public for "your support" in getting the Congress to approve a bill authorizing military reserves, essential for the "security and safety" of the U.S. "Trained men will be needed," he said, "on the spot at the time the disaster occurs." Disaster? The administrator of civil defense, Val Peterson, corroborated the disaster. It was presumed, he said, that the "casualties" of the attack numbered fourteen million seven hundred and fifty thousand. Another four million or so had been saved by the simulated evacuation of thirty-five cities. The President remarked that his "deepest impression" had been that "the most devout daily prayers . . . should be uttered in the supplication that this kind of disaster never comes to the United States." Amen.

For Operation Carte Blanche the scenarists moved overseas. A simulated war was staged June 20 to June 28 between Northland (northwest Germany, Holland, and Belgium) and Southland (southern Germany and eastern France), during which a total of three hundred and thirty-five atomic bombs were "dropped" within forty-eight hours. The stated purpose of this demented exercise was to warn the Soviet Union of NATO's nuclear capability (perfectly timed, only three weeks before the heads of government would convene at Geneva) and to reassure West Germany that NATO, by using tactical nuclear weapons, could successfully defend German territory. To this end, the exercise was well publicized, West German journalists being flown all about the "play" area in NATO aircraft. The net effect was devastating to the planners, the scenarists, the Cold Warriors. The exercise demonstrated conclusively that tactical nuclear warfare, which had been endorsed by Radford and Dulles and even by Eisenhower, would reduce the lands it was designed to protect to so much "radioactive rubble."

By Friday, July 1, four position papers had been prepared. The first set forth the goals the United States hoped to achieve in Geneva; the second set forth (in the order of their presumed importance) the goals the U.S. imagined the USSR hoped to achieve; the third and fourth were the U.S. estimates of what chance each power had of achieving its goals. (In this exercise in political science, France and the United Kingdom, the other two parties to the conference at the summit, had apparently no goals deemed worthy of special consideration.) Taken together, the four papers afford a schematic apprehension of the mentality of the men charged with planning U.S. policy in the Cold War as of July 1955. No less interesting were the estimates of U.S. planners as to how their British and French allies would align themselves on the various matters at issue.

The goals the United States had charted have an endearing, wistful quality. The first three objectives were: a unified Germany, militarized and safely within NATO; European security, by which was meant fewer Soviet troops stationed in central Europe and a relaxed Soviet grip on the countries of eastern Europe; and a leveling and control of armaments, with the United States retaining an unchallenged superiority of and supervision over nuclear weapons. The likelihood of Soviet concurrence in any of these was nil.

Nine Soviet goals were listed. The most important was presumed to be a recognition by the western powers of the "moral and social equality" of the Soviet Union. If this objective were attained, it was feared, the Soviet Union could more easily maintain its hold on its satellites, neutralism in the Cold War would be encouraged, and the tensions tormenting the world would be seen as coming not from opposing principles but merely from rivalry between two great powers. The Soviets were expected to do too well in realizing this goal; President Eisenhower could minimize their progress "by avoiding social meetings where he will be photographed with Bulganin, Khrushchev, etc., and by maintaining an austere countenance." The United States was opposed to all nine Russian goals, the British were thought to oppose six of them, the French only two. Both the British and French actually supported the fourth and seventh goals on the list—freer trade with the "communist" bloc, and recognition of China as a great power and her promotion into what would then become the Big Five. The Americans thus faced an uphill job if they were to keep the Cold War in the freezer.

As he made ready for his journey to Geneva, President Eisenhower had every reason for confidence and optimism. For some months he had been floundering about in a welter of unpleasant domestic vexations of the sort that would have done serious mischief to almost any other President, yet he had survived them all unscathed. He was held in higher public esteem than ever. His frets had been mostly on what his staff secretary, Colonel Goodpaster, called the civilian side—affairs having nothing to do with national security. The sorry muddle over the vaccine developed to prevent poliomyelitis was one such, and it was compounded by the ineptitude of Oveta Culp Hobby, the wealthy Texan whom Eisenhower had appointed secretary of health, education and welfare. Another was the prolonged fuss involving the Tennessee Valley Authority (TVA), the Atomic Energy Commission (AEC), the city of Memphis, and a pair of privately owned public utility corporations. (This commotion was known as the Dixon-Yates affair, taking its name from the presidents of the two utilities involved.) Here the difficulty was one of conflict of interest, with an investment banker, Adolphe Wenzell, having been retained by the Bureau of the Budget as a consultant on the Dixon-Yates contract to build a steam plant in Memphis for the AEC, while he was also serving as vice president of the First Boston Corporation, the banking house which was to arrange the profitable financing for the steam plant. Over the spring of 1955 the President spoke too much and too hastily of Wenzell, the Dixon-Yates contract, and the TVA, revealing that he knew next to nothing of a business which threatened to impugn the integrity of his administration. More and more often as he spoke in press conference, the veins in his neck and forehead swelled and throbbed, telltale signal that his temper was dangerously close to the surface.*

Yet in July, when he was about to take plane for Geneva, President Eisenhower could reflect that according to the Gallup poll only 16 percent of his fellow citizens could find any reason whatsoever to be dissatisfied with the record of his administration. On the Hill, the Senate backed him almost unanimously. The foreign affairs of the republic were his to order as he chose, with no strong voice heard from any quarter to gainsay him.

The authority of his position was impressive. It was, indeed, unassailable.

During his last hour in the White House before leaving to board his presidential airplane, *Columbine III*, Eisenhower showed why he was so highly esteemed by so many Americans. He spoke to the nation by radio and television—Foster Dulles had strongly urged against his making a speech, but Eisenhower knew better—about his journey to Geneva and

---

* On July 11 the President ordered the Dixon-Yates contract canceled. He had been informed the city of Memphis would build its own power plant. "Philosophically," he noted in his diary, "a great victory for the administration." Several months later the AEC announced that no cancellation fees would be paid the Dixon-Yates combine on the ground that Wenzell's conflict-of-interest rendered the contract illegal. Dixon-Yates sued. The Supreme Court in January 1961 held that the contract was not valid because of Wenzell's dual status.

Mrs. Hobby resigned her cabinet post on July 13. In accepting her resignation, Eisenhower said that it marked "a sad day for the administration."

why he was making it. He spoke of establishing "a spirit and attitude." "If we can change the spirit in which these conferences are conducted," he said, "we will have taken the greatest step toward peace . . . that has ever been taken in the history of mankind." Whether or not inadvertently, he had with a phrase created something that would be known as "the spirit of Geneva." He went on: ". . . the common desire for peace is something that is a terrific force in this world and to which I believe all political leaders in the world are beginning to respond. They must recognize it." His conclusion, couched in simple phrases and spoken with his matchless mix of earnest sincerity and winning warmth, was a great plucking of strings.

"The free world lives under one religion or another. It believes in a divine power. It believes in a supreme being. . . . Now it is natural for a people steeped in a religious civilization, when they come to moments of great importance—maybe even crises such as now we face—to turn to the divine power that each has in his own heart, for guidance, for wisdom, for some help in doing the thing that is honorable, that is right.

"I have no doubt that tonight throughout this country and indeed throughout the free world, that such prayers are ascending. This is a mighty force, and it brings me to the thought that through prayer we could also achieve a very definite and practical result at this very moment.

"Suppose on the next sabbath day observed by each of our religions, Americans, one hundred and sixty-five million of us, went to our accustomed places of worship, and, crowding those places, asked for help, and by so doing demonstrated to all the world the sincerity and depth of our aspirations for peace. This would be a mighty force. None could then say that we preserve armament because we want to. We preserve it because we must."

On the next sabbath, whether in their places of worship or in more profane precincts, Americans could reflect that their President was a good man.

The conference at the summit, said Eden, upon its conclusion, "has given this simple message to the whole world: it has reduced the dangers of war." The world wanted nothing more. If there were no substantive accords on the grave matters at issue between capitalist West and socialist East, no matter; if Germany stayed divided, if disarmament remained an uneasy dream, if the security of Europe was still conjectural, with its countries split betwixt NATO and the Warsaw Pact, no matter—so long as the great powers capable of destroying all humanity within an hour or two had met, confronted each other, and agreed that war between them was an impossibility. So much they had done. Status quo was desirable. Coexistence, all agreed, was not only feasible, it was essential. No one had seriously anticipated more.

At his first meeting in Geneva, within a few hours of his arrival, Eisenhower was advised by his secretary of state that he should remind Prime Minister Eden and Premier Faure of the ground rules for the Conférence à Quatre: they were not to attempt to settle matters of substance but only seek to explore the "approaches" by which progress might be made toward resolution of the many difficult problems confronting the world. The President was not entirely happy with these restrictions. He had been much impressed by the conciliatory statements made by Bulganin only the day before and he wanted the Russians to be given every opportunity, in the same cordial and reasonable terms, to come to concrete discussions of the issues dividing the world.

The President's role was a complicated one, with many conflicting mandates, and Eisenhower was uncomfortably aware of his own limitations. Yet at the same time he had an exhilarating sense of mission: what could be more exalting than the pursuit of peace? And perhaps it might be closer than anyone had reckoned.

The four statesmen were to meet as the heads of their governments, but Eisenhower was also a head of state, and that fact set him apart from the others. Wherever he moved he was surrounded by cumbersome security forces: helicopters circled about his airplane as it landed, unsmiling Secret Service men moved at a dogtrot alongside his limousine as it rolled through the streets of Geneva. The comparison with the carefree Russians, driven about in open touring cars, with no fanfare and not even a police escort, excited some unflattering comment among the Europeans. At earlier conferences of the sort, a good deal of informal and reciprocal entertaining had been the custom, with private discussions over the dinner table and during the later evening making a contribution to the general harmony of nations. But President Eisenhower, apart from appearing at a formal dinner for all delegations given by the president of the Swiss republic, took all his meals at Creux de Genthod, the villa on Lake Geneva supplied him by a Swiss manufacturer of perfumes. Other delegations were invited to dine with him, but unlike the others he accepted no hospitality in exchange; on the night the Russians came, they left directly after the coffee. The President was under some constraint. He envied those who, like Eden, were at ease in two or three foreign tongues and so could usually find a way to talk informally even with the Russians, and without the awkward interposition of an interpreter. Further, there was the complexity of some of the problems and the stubborn intractability of others. They were too much, he knew, for any one man; they called for the patience, experience, and skill of a considerable staff; at most, he could only guide and be guided by his advisers. Yet further, he knew of his own relative inexperience: he could recall how he had sent Bedell Smith to tackle the delicate diplomatic chaffering of wartime, even the negotiations leading to the surrender of the Nazi armies. To bargain with foreign adversaries across a conference table was not his field of special competence. What he did best—with warm strong handclasp, friendly grin, amiable demeanor, and air of earnest simplicity—was bring others to accommodate, to conciliate, to put faith in his unswerving devotion to duty. Just now, that duty was the peace of the world.

With his exuberant optimism, President Eisenhower had glimpsed at least a possibility of the peace everybody yearned for. Perhaps, with his talk of "a terrific force . . . to which I believe all political leaders . . . are beginning to respond," he had convinced himself. At all events, he came to Geneva accompanied by his wife, who hated airplane travel; his son, who thoughtfully played Scrabble with his mother during the flight, to distract her from her fears; his personal secretary, Ann Whitman; his staff secretary, Colonel Goodpaster; and his nine officially designated consultants—Foster Dulles, Dillon Anderson, Jim Hagerty, and a half-dozen top-echelon functionaries of the State Department. Still other special assistants and senior advisers—Stassen, Rockefeller, Radford, Gruenther, and Robert Anderson, the deputy secretary of defense—were sequestered in the wings, awaiting their summons to center stage should the time be ripe.

Eisenhower could perceive signs of a "deep longing for peace" on every hand, even in the behavior of the crowds he saw lining the streets of Geneva.* Under the circumstances, for Eisenhower to wipe off his smile and replace it with "an austere countenance," as requested by the State Department, was a flat impossibility. Acting with his natural friendliness, he greeted the Russians—the entire official delegation: Bulganin, Khrushchev, Zhukov, Molotov, Gromyko, Zarubin, Malik, Vinogradov, Troyanovsky—at the Palais des Nations before the first formal meeting of the conference. With Marshal Zhukov, the warrior who had been his friend and comrade in postwar Berlin, and who was now the Soviet minister of defense, he lingered several minutes, trading reminiscence. In his turn, Khrushchev confided to the President that Zhukov, by coming to Geneva to join in the conference, had been obliged to miss his daughter's wedding. After the first session Eisenhower again made it his business to join the Russians for another cordial chat. One of them ventured to remark that such personal encounters were useful. Eisenhower warmly agreed. Without personal contacts, he observed, you might imagine someone was

* Competent observers reported that few of the citizens of Geneva showed any interest whatever in the four statesmen. None of them could draw "more than a handful of gawkers" into the streets.

fourteen feet high, with horns and a tail. The Russians rocked with laughter.

That Monday night, July 18, was the occasion for Eisenhower's receiving a half-dozen of the Russian delegation for dinner at his villa. Once again the evening proceeded amicably. With thoughtful courtesy Eisenhower had managed to rustle up a pair of gifts for Zhukov's daughter—a portable radio, then a contrivance still in considerable demand, and a pen-and-ink desk set inscribed, "From the President of the United States, July 1955"—and his gesture was gratefully acknowledged. Over the after-dinner coffee Eisenhower remarked that he hoped to talk further with Zhukov about their experiences of war—but only of the war that was past, not of any future war. (In an aside to Ambassador Bohlen, Zhukov inquired whether the President was suggesting a private interview; if so, he would arrange to suit the President's convenience.) In another exchange Bulganin, speaking of Foster Dulles, who was also present, mentioned that he showed a degree of understanding of the USSR, and Khrushchev, to make clear that Bulganin had intended polite disparagement, not praise, added that Dulles had never visited their country. Eisenhower promptly asked why they did not invite Dulles for an excursion. But the subject was not pursued.

On Wednesday, July 20, Zhukov was back in Eisenhower's villa for a private luncheon. (The only others present were the interpreters, Bohlen and Troyanovsky.) Once again the two old soldiers swapped stories of the days when they had commanded vast and victorious armies. Then they turned to the Cold War.

Zhukov spoke at length of the USSR policies. They were, he insisted, pacific and nonaggressive in character. He swore to it. His country, he said vehemently, did not want war.

Eisenhower answered that all his experience of Zhukov in Berlin led him to believe his old friend; he believed him now.

Zhukov acknowledged that the USSR was well armed, but he repeated that his country had no hostile intentions. Arms were necessary, he said. How could it be otherwise, in the face of the NATO bases in Europe? The Soviets were absolutely determined there should be no repetition of invasion from the West, as in 1941. He appealed for détente. The only reason he had come to Geneva, he added, was to urge improved relations between the U.S. and USSR.*

* The night before, the Russians had been guests of the British at dinner. In the course of their discussions Bulganin told Eden categorically that it was not possible for his government to agree to the immediate reunification of Germany. Later, Eden wrote: "As I reflected upon our conversation later that night, I felt that there was a genuine streak in what I had been told. The West, and in particular the United States, has never clearly understood the terrible significance of the German invasion

Eisenhower observed that fear and distrust flourished on both sides; they were emotions difficult to dispel. After the war, he recalled, the U.S. had demobilized its armies and then found itself subjected to pressures. As examples he cited the Greek insurgency, with support coming from Bulgaria and Yugoslavia; the blockade of Berlin; the experience of Chiang Kai-shek, attacked and then routed by communists; finally, and worst of all, the war in Korea. (All plotted by the ogre of international communism, although President Eisenhower did not use the phrase.) These instances were bad enough, but now, on top of them, came the armaments race.

Zhukov suggested that a way to begin to relax tensions would be to call a halt to polemic and invective between the nations.

Eisenhower pointed out that he could control neither the Congress nor the press.

Zhukov spoke of the intentions of their two governments: if both desired that tensions be relaxed, surely that would be helpful. He urged an end to rival blocs of nations and called instead for alliances.

If one may judge from what he subsequently wrote about this conversation, Eisenhower had decided that Zhukov was merely parroting arguments that had been earlier presented to the conference by the Soviet delegation. However that may be, the range of subjects the two men discussed now widened. Inspection, Eisenhower inquired, inspection to determine the facts of disarmament? Why not? Zhukov rejoined, and why not also reduce the size of armies? Eisenhower agreed. Zhukov denied that the USSR interfered in the domestic policies of other nations. Eisenhower replied that he was glad to hear it. Zhukov declared his government would prove it, or at least would sign a convention pledging noninterference. A moment later he spoke in support of the Chinese arguments in respect of Taiwan and of membership in the United Nations. By the time Eisenhower raised the question of the prisoners of war still held in the Soviet Union, the two men had plainly reached the end of their road. Eisenhower

for Russia. A nation of eighty million had invaded a nation of one hundred and sixty million, devastated its western provinces and almost reached its capital. The Russian people could never forget this. They had no Atlantic between them and Germany, not even a Channel. They would not run such risks again. . . . Russians have long memories, they would be feckless not to take precautions."

At breakfast the next morning, Wednesday, Eden and his foreign minister Harold Macmillan told Eisenhower and Dulles of their evening with the Russians, of how their guests had been cordial, abstemious, well-behaved. After hearing Eden's report, Eisenhower declared that the Russians were either communist zealots or power-mad dictators: the question was, how to deal with them if they were zealots? how to deal with them if they were dictators? On the answer to those questions, he suggested, depended correct western policy.

had been given a memorandum by Dulles alleging the detention of more than two hundred thousand German, Italian, and Japanese prisoners; a few hundred Austrians, Dutch, and Spanish were also believed held somewhere in Russia, as were even a few Danes, Belgians, and Norwegians. Zhukov said that Eisenhower's figures were much exaggerated.

President Eisenhower was troubled by the conversation. Zhukov was changed; he was "a subdued and worried man." "He's not the man I used to know," the President told Mrs. Whitman. "He's been well trained for this performance." Apparently it never occurred to him that Zhukov could say the same of him, and with as much truth. The world was also greatly altered in the ten years since 1945; if President Eisenhower and Marshal Zhukov had *not* changed, that fact would have caused agitated comment. What reason had Zhukov not to be worried? Who knew better than the Soviet minister of defense the terrible power for destruction that in ten years had darkened the world? If Zhukov were not "a subdued and worried man" he would have been a fair candidate for the booby hatch.

Later on that same Wednesday, President Eisenhower turned his attention to what he would subsequently describe as "the most effective proposal of the conference"; to wit, his own proposal for mutual overflight by the U.S. and USSR of each other's country as a technique of inspection, what came to be known as the "open skies" plan. For this purpose he was joined by the advisers who had been charged with disinfecting the proposal and scrutinizing it for possible flaws—Rockefeller, Stassen, Admiral Radford, General Gruenther, and Deputy Secretary of Defense Anderson. Also on hand were Dulles, Dillon Anderson, Assistant Secretary of State Livingston Merchant, and Colonel Goodpaster. A gathering of star-spangled men, dedicated to the dream of disarmament. The moment called for a striking, dramatic gesture, one that would catch the imagination of the world and bathe the United States in a lambent glow, revealing it to be the mighty apostle of peace. On the first two substantive issues before the conference —reunification of Germany and European security—the debate had been friendly but had led to stalemate. As to the third, disarmament, the initiative had been seized by the Russians; the need was to retrieve it. Stassen read the draft of a "Statement by President Eisenhower on the Subject of Disarmament." In the discussion that followed the President decided he would make the open skies proposal. He observed that in his opinion, since the Russians already knew "the location of most of our installations, mutual agreements for such overflights would undoubtedly benefit us more than the Russians, because we know very little about their installations." For the proposal to have proper impact, no word of it could be let slip. It was agreed that the President would decide later whether to interpolate the open skies scheme into his opening general statement or to hold it in reserve until after Bulganin had spoken.

The proposal was divulged, indeed, amid theatrics flamboyant enough to satisfy the most finical of De Milles. On the spur the President had decided to unveil his scheme forthwith. He stopped reading, removed his spectacles, turned to the Russians, and spoke from memory: ". . . have been searching my heart and mind . . . convince everyone of the great sincerity of the United States . . . should address myself for a moment principally to the delegates from the Soviet Union . . . new and terrible weapons . . . surprise attack . . . give each other a complete blueprint of our military establishments . . . facilities for aerial photography . . . all the pictures you choose . . . thus lessening danger and relaxing tension . . . quest for peace . . . the statesman's most exacting duty . . ." Just as he reached the end of his earnest delivery, the lights in the lofty chamber of the Palais des Nations winked out: a sudden storm had swept up, unsuspected by those sitting attentive, cut off from the world by devices that muffled sound and frigerated the imprisoned air.

In the abrupt gloom Eisenhower said: "I didn't know I'd put out the lights with that speech." The remark won a laugh from the three dozen men clustered about the hollow square of tables.

Presently the delegates adjourned to the cocktail lounge. To Eden, the Russians "poured scorn" on Eisenhower's proposal. To Eisenhower, Khrushchev smiled and shook his head: No. But the scheme was not officially rejected.

"Most spectacular," Eisenhower wrote later, "in the eyes of the press and the public, had been our opportunity to demonstrate to the world, in the open skies proposal, the dedication of the United States to world peace and disarmament and our sincerity in offering a concrete way in which we would participate." No question the proposal was a spectacular victory for the Cold Warriors who specialized in what they called the "p" factor—the psychological implications of an act, a gesture. But during the 1950s the word "sincere" had become a pejorative, associated with the seductive wiles of Madison Avenue, and it is of interest that Robert Donovan would report, of Rockefeller's experts impaneled at Quantico, that they "gave careful study to trends of public opinion in Europe" as they formulated their open skies scheme. Not disarmament was their objective so much as public opinion. And in Geneva, when the proposal was dramatically unfurled, Richard Rovere would remark that "it seemed only a gimmick, and there was a good deal of hilarity on the subject of Batten, Barton, Durstine & Osborn's intervention in world affairs."

"This has been an historic meeting," said the President, speaking at the final conference session on July 23. "It has been on the whole a good week." No agreement on any issue; every perplexity passed along to the foreign ministers for them to dispute in October; but nevertheless the President could note that "the prospects of a lasting peace with justice, well-being, and broader freedom, are brighter. The dangers of the overwhelming tragedy of modern war are less." This generous estimate was short-lived. Rockefeller, the special assistant for Cold War strategy, and Dulles, the secretary of state, both analyzed the conference and were disturbed by what they found. They agreed it had been the occasion of a smashing personal triumph for the President—everybody had liked Ike; and after he came home the American people had given him a vote of unprecedented confidence: 79 percent approval in the Gallup poll—but the "spirit of Geneva" presented some grave problems for the future of U.S. foreign policy. Rockefeller raised the question: Could NATO continue as "the core of U.S.-European policy"? The difficulty was that in the face of the apparent détente at Geneva and the consequent elation of public opinion in western Europe, official circles in London, Paris, Brussels, and Amsterdam had got jittery. Peace seemed to be looming, and the thought of it brought uncertainty and apprehension. Might the U.S. now pull its troops out of Europe? Dulles's analysis was more elaborate. "The unconcealed anxiety of Soviet rulers to obtain a 'relaxing' of tension," he judged, was owing to their economic compulsions, to their need for "at least a temporary period when they could meet more fully the craving of their people for better living conditions." The summit meeting had been unavoidable, but "Geneva has certainly created problems for the free nations." The fear that held their alliance together had abated; their sense of moral superiority had been blurred. Plainly the Soviets had achieved substantial gains toward what was presumed to be their most cherished goal—a western concession of Soviet "moral and social equality." This was to be deplored, but it had been anticipated. On the other hand nothing had happened to justify any relaxation of vigilance. The Cold War had not moderated. Copies of this statement of post-Geneva policy went to the White House and to all U.S. chiefs of mission; the paper was also shown the British ambassador.

The "spirit of Geneva" had been given its notice.

President Eisenhower came home to find his administration scorched by a scandal involving Harold Talbott, his old friend and occasional companion at the bridge table. Talbott was an experienced fund raiser for the Republicans who had been rewarded with an appointment as secretary of the air force. He had subsequently written letters on air force stationery to solicit business for a firm of industrial engineers in which he had retained a special partnership, and from which indeed he drew a share of profits amounting to more than sixty-five thousand dollars a year; he had been so careless as to help obtain lucrative contracts with concerns doing business with the Department of Defense. This was clearly a no-no. The President had no choice: he accepted his friend's resignation.

Eisenhower was mettlesome and irritable, impatient for the Congress to adjourn so that he might escape to Denver and the Rocky Mountains. The first session of the Eighty-fourth Congress expired early in August. As soon as he had attended to the bills awaiting his disposition and given instructions for the next round of talks on disarmament, Eisenhower hurried west. Denver, ah! and two days later he was high on the western slope of the Rockies, fishing the St. Louis Creek on Byer's Peak Ranch with his old friend Aksel Nielsen.

The next six weeks were on the whole the least onerous Dwight Eisenhower experienced as President. After five days of trout fishing in mountain streams he returned to Denver, where most of his days were spent at the Cherry Hills Country Club playing eighteen, twenty-seven, even thirty-six holes of golf a day. His physician and old friend, General Howard Snyder, told a reporter, "Eddie, if that fellow couldn't play golf, I'd have a nut on my hands." (His bag of golf clubs and several boxes of balls were standard accessories wherever Eisenhower went. Even at Geneva he had spent a part of every day whacking golf balls about, enduring the occasional interruptions as "security" messages were handed him from trouble spots roundabout the world.) When the weather was foul, he had his paints; he would work from photographs or rough drawings supplied him by one of his staff. In the evenings there was bridge, stag, at his suite in the Brown Palace Hotel, and he never lacked companions. The pleasant round of his days was seldom broken. Once he had to travel east to survey the extraordinary damage done along the Atlantic coast by a particularly destructive hurricane; and on the same trip, in an address to the American Bar Association, he was able to take some of the bloom off the "spirit of Geneva." Again, he had to take time out for a certain amount of politicking, as when he spoke at a breakfast gathering of the forty-eight Republican state chairmen.

Politics for the Republicans looked like velvet in the late summer of 1955, always assuming that President Eisenhower would run for a second term. Everyone agreed he was a shoo-in, and the proof was that no Democrat was challenging Adlai Stevenson's right to run and once again be obliterated. What could be said against Eisenhower's candidacy? Farm prices were sharply down, to be sure, but that was blamed upon Ezra Benson, the much beleaguered secretary of agriculture; no onus attached to the President. Again, Eisenhower had pledged in 1952 to balance the budget and reduce the public debt, to reverse the harum-scarum fiscal policies of the Democrats. In fact, he had done no such thing (the public debt had risen by more than eight billion dollars, and in three peacetime years the deficit in the budget had totaled more than nine billion), but in a time of general prosperity the voters would shrug such fiscal incomprehensibilities into oblivion. The danger of a recession was long gone, Eisenhower's patient amiability had effectively smothered the opposition within his own party, why should a Republican not rejoice?

Eisenhower needed no man to explain to him his benefits. Those who regarded him as an innocent in politics to the contrary notwithstanding, he knew exactly what he was about. For years he had appreciated the value of telling one man this and another man that. He knew precisely why he should keep his own counsel and, in this jungle of overgrown promises and tangled loyalties, why he must protect his options. He recognized how sorely he was wanted by others, and how far he must test their reliability in order to keep his own highroad free of snares and mines. Fairly frequently he had told one or other of his associates he preferred to serve only one term; as often he had been urged to reconsider. By September the pressures were growing for him to declare himself, yes or no. In Washington it was held that his holiday was deliberately prolonged so that he might make up his mind. Of all his associates, his decision meant most to Richard Nixon, the man who stood next in line of succession. Nixon traveled to Denver in early September and found the President "particularly testy, easily irritated, and on edge." He refused to discuss politics. He was in Colorado, he said, to fish and play golf. (Later Nixon told reporters he was "more optimistic" than ever that the President would run again.) When the forty-eight GOP state chairmen came to Denver, Eisenhower had for them a sensible warning, one which within the fortnight would acquire the eerie quality of prophecy.

"We don't believe for a minute," he said, "that the Republican party is so lacking in inspiration, high-quality personnel, and leadership that we are dependent on one man. We don't believe it for a minute.

"Now as long as we have a man in the leadership position, why of course, as a party, we are going to be loyal, we are going to help in the fight.

"But humans are frail—and they are mortal. Finally, you never pin your flag so tightly to one mast that if a ship sinks you cannot rip it off and nail it to another. It is sometimes good to remember that."

That was on Saturday morning, September 10. Four days earlier the President had been routinely informed that his special assistant on disarmament, Harold Stassen, acting on his instructions, had withdrawn all the proposals so long supported by the U.S. with exemplary zeal and tenacity. No longer was the U.S. government attracted by the concept of inspection and control of nuclear arms—indeed, of any arms. The clear implication was that the U.S. was developing a new weapons system, one that required the cloak of secrecy.

One other event that took place while the President was in Denver must be mentioned, for although he knew little of it at the time, its consequences were to snowball and considerably embarrass him in the next few years. On August 28 a fourteen-year-old Negro boy, Emmett Till, who had gone south from Chicago to visit his uncle in Mississippi, was abducted by three white men, cruelly beaten, and murdered. Three days later his body was taken from the Tallahatchie River. Two men conclusively identified as his kidnappers were charged with the crime, tried, and acquitted by an all-white jury. The killing outraged the nation and in particular its Negro citizens. For six generations those citizens had patiently waited for an approximation of justice. They would wait a little longer, but time was running out.

More golf. Another few days of trout fishing. On Friday, September 23, back to Denver; a couple of hours' work in the forenoon, then out to Cherry Hills for eighteen holes of golf, a lunch of chopped beef with big slices of raw onion, and another nine holes of golf. Thrice the President was summoned from the course by the demands of the telephone. The second call came from Dulles, seeking approval of a letter to the Russians about their plan for arms inspection, but the first and third calls were from officious operators displaying more zeal than good sense: no one was on the line to talk to the President. After the third call he went into a towering rage—the worst display of temper his friend and physician Howard Snyder had ever seen. Home at length in his mother-in-law's house, Eisenhower spent an hour or so before dinner at his easel. George and Mary Allen, old friends and latterly neighbors in Gettysburg, joined Mrs. Doud and the Eisenhowers for a dinner of roast lamb. A comfortable, pleasant evening, with laughter and relaxation, as always with Allen. The President went to bed around 10 P.M.

A little more than four hours later, early on Saturday morning, the President suffered a coronary thrombosis. A blood clot had got stuck in an artery feeding the anterior wall of his heart and had blocked the supply of blood to that part of the heart muscle. The attack was first described as "mild," but the cardiologist subsequently summoned from Boston, Dr. Paul Dudley White, termed the coronary "neither mild nor serious [but] moderate." Words had to be selected with great care, for much hung in the balance—the Republican party's primacy, of course, and control of the White House; apart from that, for a few, merely their profits and the stability of their investments, but some were persuaded that nothing less was involved than the life of the republic and the peace of the world.

Meanwhile Dwight Eisenhower rested quietly in Fitzsimons General Hospital, a military institution a few miles from Denver. An oxygen tent covered him. A team of physicians kept constant vigil.

How to measure the gravity of the crisis? The President of the United States, the leader of the free world, lay stricken. He might recover within a few weeks, he might die in the next moment, he might be confined to his sickroom for months—possibly even to the end of his term in office. Who then would exercise presidential power? According to the Constitution, "In case of . . . the President['s] inability to discharge the powers and duties of the said office, the same shall devolve on the Vice President," but nothing was said of what would happen should the President regain his ability to discharge the powers and duties of his office. When earlier Presidents had been comparably disabled—James A. Garfield by an assassin's bullet, Woodrow Wilson by a cerebral stroke—and had remained for several months in no condition to head the state, in neither case had a Vice President assumed presidential power. In this case a remarkable set of coincidental circumstances seemed to suggest that the crisis might likewise be resolved by resolutely pretending that in fact there was no crisis. The Congress was not in session; no high office requiring presidential appointment was vacant; no urgent business demanded the attention of the government; for a wonder, no critical conflict seemed to vex the world at the moment; the Cold War, thanks to the "spirit of Geneva," was temporarily in thaw. It was a time of torpor, as it had been for six weeks past while Eisenhower had been strenuously relaxing on golf course and at bridge table. The federal government was in estivation. Sherman Adams, Herbert Brownell, and Harold Stassen were all out of the country, Jim Hagerty was on holiday, Foster Dulles was in New York for a meeting of the U.N. General Assembly, George Humphrey was out of town. The only important government figure in or near Washington was the Vice President, Richard Nixon. The gravity of the crisis brought him, as he later put it, to "a momentary state of shock." He was conscious of "a tremendous responsibility . . . like a great physical weight." He realized, instinctively conjuring up a phrase hallowed by right-wing Republican usage, he was only "one heartbeat from the Presidency."

Nixon was by no means the only Republican to have glimpsed that terminal possibility. If he was momentarily in a state of shock, so were Dulles, Adams, Humphrey, Hagerty, Brownell, and a great many others whose high offices were held only at the pleasure of the President. At first, while still numbed by news of the heart attack, Hagerty had an-

Eisenhower's victory at the Republican convention in July 1952 left Robert A. Taft, "Mr. Republican" to his supporters, plunged in gloom.

Eisenhower considers his running mate, Richard M. Nixon. A few days later, word of Nixon's highly unorthodox income, supplied by California businessmen, would wi public interest in the campaign.

GOP politicians beam as Eisenhower shakes hands with Senator Joe McCarthy. Earlier Eisenhower had endorsed McCarthy's bid for re-election.

Dwight D. Eisenhower takes the oath as President of the United States on January 20, 1953. Harry S. Truman stands, left; Nixon awaits his turn, right.

How to promote the administration: The President makes his sales pitch on television, assisted by four members of his cabinet — Attorney General Herbert Brownell, Secretary of Agriculture Ezra Taft Benson, Secretary of HEW Mrs. Oveta Culp Hobby, and Secretary of the Treasury George Humphrey.

In June 1954 Prime Minister Churchill and Foreign Secretary Anthony Eden (right) traveled to Washington to confer with the President and Secretary of State John Foster Dulles (left).

At last, in the summer of 1955, the President and Dulles met at the summit in Geneva with the Russians. From left: Nikolai Bulganin, USSR; Eisenhower, U S.; Edgar Faure, France; and Eden, Britain.

On October 25, 1955, the President is wheeled to the sun deck at Fitzsimons Army Hospital in Denver. On his shirt was stitched the message, "Much better, thanks."

The President is off for a turkey shoot with his host, George Humphrey, at Thomasville, Georgia. Soon he will announce his candidacy for re-elction in 1956.

In September 1956 the President sauntered with Mrs. Eisenhower in the garden of their new house in Gettysburg. Overseas the Suez crisis was coming to its ominous climax.

In the Oval Office at the White House, Foster Dulles confers with the President on the explosive affairs in Hungary and the Middle East. It is October 30, 1956.

The President holds a press conference in June 1957. His problems with his budget and his legislation on behalf of civil rights tested him sorely during that summer.

Following his minor cerebral spasm in November 1957, the President deliberately set himself the test of properly participating in the NATO conference at Paris in December. Here he is flanked by Prime Minister Harold Macmillan, at his right, and Paul-Henri Spaak, the NATO Secretary-General, at his left.

Late in August 1958 the President was often photographed playing golf on the links at Newport. But at home the conflict over civil rights for Negroes was more clamorous than ever, and abroad the Chinese were once again threatening to assert their rights to their offshore islands.

The President's "historic" meeting with Negro leaders. From left, Lester Granger, Martin Luther King, Jr., E. Frederick Morrow, the President, A. Philip Randolph, Attorney General William P. Rogers, Rocco Siciliano, and Roy Wilkins.

In March 1959 the President met with Congressional leaders — Charles Halleck, Everett Dirksen, Sam Rayburn, Lyndon B. Johnson, and Nixon — to brief them on the status of the crisis over Berlin. In the rear are Allen Dulles of the CIA, Secretary of State Christian Herter, and Secretary of Defense Neil McElroy.

Foster Dulles, dying of cancer, was still Eisenhower's special consultant in May 1959 when the President and the former prime minister visited him at Walter Reed Hospital.

When Khrushchev's airplane landed in Washington, Eisenhower's visage was grim. By the time the two men reached Camp David, the President's buoyant good humor had once again taken command.

The summit in collapse. While de Gaulle was distressed and Macmillan bitterly disappointed, Eisenhower was able to maintain his composure. The capture of the U-2 and its pilot kept the Cold War on ice.

Presidential power is about to pass from the oldest man to hold the office to the youngest ever elected. They conferred twice together before Kennedy's inauguration.

Two old warriors urge the nation to fight more fiercely in Vietnam. Generals Eisenhower and Bradley before the television cameras in November 1967.

The funeral services for Dwight Eisenhower were held in the National Cathedral in Washington on April 1, 1969.

Abilene, Kansas, April 2, 1969. The casket of former President Eisenhower is carried to its final resting place.

nounced that the attorney general, who was on holiday in Spain, had been asked to return to formulate an opinion as to the possible need for delegating some or all of the President's powers to the Vice President. (That was on Monday, September 26, and on the New York Stock Exchange the Dow-Jones industrial average tumbled 31.89 points, the sharpest drop recorded since the panic of October 29, 1929.) Brownell took plane in Madrid that same day. While he was airborne, caution and reason reasserted themselves; all talk of legal opinions about constitutional prerogatives was stilled; to the perceptive Richard Rovere the abrupt reversal could "only suggest that all of the men around Mr. Eisenhower [did] not wish to take any step that could result in giving Mr. Nixon greater authority or even in giving Mr. Nixon the impression that greater authority was soon to be his."

Directly or indirectly, President Eisenhower was responsible for the reversal of policy by the men around him. Whether or not he actually instructed Hagerty to discourage Brownell from any study of the constitutional questions involved is not important; what matters is that on Hagerty's arrival in Denver, General Snyder informed him of the President's wishes: "Tell Jim to take over and make the decisions and handle the story." Hagerty, quickly aware of the rumors flying about (as for instance of a power struggle between Nixon and Adams for control of the government) lost little time. Having established that Eisenhower's remarkable vitality had persuaded Dr. White to consider his patient's chances for complete recovery "reasonably good," and further that the President would be well enough to confer with his advisers after another couple of weeks, Hagerty recommended that all consideration of a delegation of Eisenhower's duties to Nixon be dropped. In Washington, Humphrey, Adams, Brownell, and others had independently reached the same conclusion. If there was any disposition to enhance the Vice President's style and status, it was promptly and firmly checked. At the meeting of the National Security Council on Thursday, September 29, it was decided that Brownell should be asked to draft a statement on the conduct of the government in the weeks ahead; this statement of procedure was to be referred to the cabinet at its meeting the next day and, if approved by them, was to be released to the press. Brownell's proposal fixed Nixon in his formulary routine as prescribed by Eisenhower: he should continue to preside over NSC and cabinet meetings as long as the President was out of town. Further, Brownell contemplated that "Governor Sherman Adams, the Assistant to the President, will leave for Denver today and will be available there, in consultation with the President's physicians, whenever it may later become appropriate to present any matters to the President."

Was this procedure, Nixon inquired, necessary? He had rather thought that Governor Adams would remain in charge of the White House during Eisenhower's absence. No, said Foster Dulles, Governor Adams was the proper selection as liaison with the sick President, he alone should decide all questions and administer all matters of government business coming to and from the President. Speaking, as Adams recalled, "firmly and emphatically," Dulles recited the arguments in favor of Brownell's proposal, closing with the proposition that Adams was recognized nationally as the public figure most closely identified with the President. Nixon quickly agreed. He seconded Dulles's remarks.

Next day Adams was in Denver. Despite the urgent counsel of the right-wing Republicans, as represented by Senator Styles Bridges, Nixon had "let the White House clique take command."

The President rested quietly, the wound in his heart healing, the oxygen tent removed now for several hours at a time, the physicians still vigilant.

Hagerty was in control. His task was a delicate one, and he executed it with consummate professional skill. His task was not merely the technical one of moving information about a sixty-five-year-old sick man to an affectionate and apprehensive constituency around the world but also, even more important, the metaphorical one of creating a credible image of the strong leader taking control of his party, his state, and the forces of the free world. Hagerty was obliged to modulate gently from the invalid to the President who could succeed himself in office if he chose to, and could guide the destinies of the republic for another four years. Hagerty was equal to both aspects of his task.

The first phase involved an invasion of the President's cherished privacy, down to the most intimate detail. Later, when he learned how specific those details had been (they included the nature and rate of his bowel movements), Eisenhower was aghast; but in fact Hagerty's bulletins, issued three times a day and supplemented by fortnightly reports by Dr. White, only followed Eisenhower's own instructions that nothing be concealed. (And those bulletins were devoured with enormous interest by the public.) The bulletins also provided a glimpse of the President's middle-brow tastes in music (he listened to recorded performances of "Clair de Lune," "Flirtation Waltz," "To a Wild Rose," medleys from *The Student Prince* and *The Merry Widow, Songs My Mother Taught Me,* "Drink to Me Only with Thine Eyes," and the like). Word was forthcoming of the first book he read (Conan Doyle's *Sir Nigel*) and of how he worked crossword puzzles cut from the newspapers. He was not permitted to read the newspapers lest he be upset by them. His health mended apace.

The second phase proceeded with the artful production of Hagerty's masterpiece. One by one the senior members of his administration were brought to Denver, ushered into the President's hospital room for unvarying half-hour bedside interviews, escorted from Fitzsimons General to Lowry Air Force Base for a press conference with the assembled reporters, and there encouraged to play variations on the theme of the President's grasp of complex matters both foreign and domestic. Occasionally there were slips, to be sure, as when Hagerty was observed to supply a member of the cabinet with a prepared statement on the President's physical appearance before the secretary had been admitted to the President's room, or when Dulles rather tactlessly disclosed that the President knew nothing of the crisis in French affairs provoked by the troubles in Algeria, but the bungles were rare, and they were lost in the steady stream of reassuring news items expertly sluiced from Denver.

The President walked from Fitzsimons General Hospital on Friday, November 11, just less than six weeks after he had been stricken. In Washington, gathered to greet him and his wife at National Airport were the Vice President, the cabinet, the diplomatic corps, and other dignitaries. The welcome was televised to the country. Quite evidently the President was restored to good health. Even though he would spend only the weekend in Washington, retiring for further convalescence at his Gettysburg farm, it was clear that matters were, or very soon would be, back to normal. In proof, on Saturday Eisenhower appeared on the back lawn of the White House to take a few practice swings with his golf clubs. In further proof, jokes began to make the rounds, the surest American evidence that all was once again sliding into the familiar routine. Back in 1953 the joke had been:

A: Hey, can you imagine? What if Ike died and we got Nixon as President!
B: Yeah, but what if Adams died, and we got stuck with Ike!

Now, in November 1955, the current joke had Nixon greeting Eisenhower in front of the Capitol with a hearty slap on the back. "Welcome back, Mr. President," he says. "I'll race you to the top of the steps!"

All was well again.

CHAPTER SIX

An End and a Beginning Amidst Crisis

A second term for Eisenhower? For Nixon, too? . . . Eisen-
hower's ileitis . . . Turbulence in the Middle East . . . and
behind the iron curtain . . . Revolt in Hungary and a war over
Suez . . . The Eisenhower Doctrine . . . The battle of the
budget . . . and for civil rights . . . Little Rock . . . Sputnik
. . . Eisenhower's cerebral occlusion.

IF THE EISENHOWER ADMINISTRATION had followed the pattern of most presidential terms, its record would in the main have been complete by, say, the end of August 1955, when the Eighty-fourth Congress had gone home to lick its wounds and make ready for its last session, when the executive branch could have undertaken the retrospective job of surveying nearly three years of accomplishment or failure and have begun to whet its rhetoric of pride or of justification. There would have remained only one major and one minor problem: Would Dwight Eisenhower be a candidate for re-election? And if so, would he be satisfied to retain Richard Nixon on the ticket as his running mate? All administration planning, once those questions had been answered, could be addressed to the correction or the concealment of past error and the celebration, under bright lights, of all available triumphs. Even the fruitless meeting of the foreign ministers, convened to attempt a disposition of the problems left unsettled at the summit, had the quality of an interval, denoting an end to one phase of the Cold War and the beginning of another, perhaps less ominous.

The pattern of past presidencies was not, however, a guide to the exigent present. Almost as soon as Eisenhower had announced that yes, he would run again, his decision was put in question by another siege of sickness, capped by a major surgical operation. Now, surely, he would declare himself out of the running? No, rather the ailment and the surgery would both be airily dismissed as of no importance. The worrying problem of Nixon, too, went unresolved for many weeks. Even after the campaign had been joined and its issues fairly well defined, it very nearly

714

came unstuck when the mismanagement by Dulles of a Cold War ruckus in the Near East intervened. In the event, that affair clinched the election for Eisenhower. These diverse occurrences combined to tickle the interest of the electorate. And underneath them, largely ignored, seethed the resentment of the Negroes. Besides Emmett Till, murdered in Mississippi, there was young Autherine Lucy, the first Negro student at the University of Alabama, who was barred by white racists from sitting in her classes, and there was Mrs. Rosa Parks, the seamstress who was reviled, arrested, and found guilty of refusing to give up her seat when some white people climbed on a bus in Montgomery, Alabama. The reverberations of those incidents of race hatred, and another hundred score less publicized, moved the nation ever closer to the edge of violent upheaval.

The circumstances of Eisenhower's decision to stand for re-election were remarkably similar to those that obtained in the winter of 1951–1952. The show of reluctance, the hesitation, the period of protracted vacillation, the rumors, the elaborate machinery constructed to fashion a verdict—all these were reminiscent of the days before Eisenhower was mustered out of the army. The men organized to influence the decision were familiar; so too were the arguments marshaled to persuade. Even the assurance his friends demanded of him, that he would not "pull the rug out from under them" while they were busy with their preliminary organization, was, he realized, "exactly the phrase" the same men had used in 1951.

As in 1951, Lucius Clay was fugleman of the group determined to draft and elect Eisenhower. As in 1951, Eisenhower never said him nay. Clay's wooing had begun right after the 1954 elections had been won by the Democrats (see page 672), and he never relaxed. The heart attack, so far from discouraging him, led him only to redouble his efforts. Now he had as well a medical argument: retirement to inactivity for a man who had led such a strenuous life would be fatal. Eisenhower's physicians agreed. The National Citizens for Eisenhower, the extra-Republican campaign device of 1952, was reconstituted; all Ike's old friends rallied round—William Robinson, Cliff Roberts, the oil men and the railroad men, W. Alton (Pete) Jones and Fred Gurley, the politicians, industrialists, and bankers, Tom Dewey, Paul Hoffman, Walter Williams, Dan Thornton—and it was plain that Eisenhower intended to pull no rug out from under any of them.

In mid-January, 1956, Eisenhower invited a dozen of his closest associates to the White House for an informal dinner and a carefully planned discussion. He wanted frank judgments as to whether or not he should run, from Brownell, Leonard Hall, Foster Dulles, Lodge, Adams, Persons, Humphrey, Summerfield, Hagerty, Howard Pyle, Tom Stephens, and his brother Milton. The other eleven might argue pro or con, he told them;

his brother would summarize the arguments on either side. To what purpose this charade? Save for his brother, every manjack was beholden to the Eisenhower administration: five were members of his cabinet, five were on his staff, and one was chairman of the Republican National Committee. Who aside from Stephens, the semiprofessional jester, would do otherwise than supply earnest reasons for another four years of the blessed status quo? (Stephens pleaded for Eisenhower's early announcement as a courtesy to the other candidates, of whom, he said, he was one [Laughter].) The others gravely discharged their obligation. Eisenhower as gravely thanked them all and kept his own counsel. In mid-February his physicians, after examining X-ray plates, told the President his heart was sound. Dr. White told reporters he would vote for Eisenhower, should he be a candidate. Promptly Eisenhower was flown south for ten days of quail shooting and golf on George Humphrey's Georgia plantation. On February 25 he was flown back to Washington. His mind was made up. His family knew of his decision. Lucius Clay was invited to the White House; he was told of it. So were Adams, Hagerty, Persons, Nixon, and one or two others. The reporters were told at his news conference of February 29: his decision was "positive, that is, affirmative."

The first question put to Eisenhower after he had made his decision public was his pleasure about his running mate. Poor Nixon! The heir apparent was in a most lamentable plight. Still "a heartbeat away from the Presidency," he must needs watch his every word and gesture, indeed edit his every thought, lest by some sudden expectant grin, some telltale gleam in his eye, he seem to suggest the ineffable. He had to school himself to stalk about stiff-legged, stony-faced, now and again permitting himself the frosty grimace that passed for a smile of welcome. Too exultant a smile might be taken for his anticipation of an impending Eisenhower heart attack. He must heartily second all efforts to persuade his chief to run again; yet simple common sense dictated that he cling, by whatever perilous handholds, to his position as the man who might, the man who would, the man who must become President—if.

But did Eisenhower want Nixon as his Vice President a second time around? It is quite certain that Eisenhower maneuvered in gingerly fashion to edge Nixon off the ticket even before he had publicly made known his own decision to run again. To move forthrightly against him would have been impolitic, for Nixon was a darling of the Republican right wing, the more so since McCarthy had been tumbled into oblivion. In Eisenhower's view, nevertheless, Nixon had some shortcomings. For one, he was not much liked. The polls consistently showed him running behind Stevenson in the so-called "trial heats" staged from time to time by Gallup or some other psephologist; some polls had even shown that Nixon did not lead all other possible Republican candidates. To Nixon, Eisenhower termed these results "most disappointing," and he added, "We might have to initiate a crash program for building you up." These comments must have been sufficiently humiliating (Nixon bridled at having to be humble in Eisenhower's presence), but Eisenhower was concerned with something else as well: Was Nixon of presidential stature? Had he sufficient administrative experience? How good an executive was he? Certainly he had had limited experience of major responsibilities, handled on his own, and so, beginning in late December 1955, Eisenhower had urged him to think seriously of stepping down from the vice-presidency and accepting instead a post in the cabinet—not Justice, nor State, but any other he wanted; why not Defense? "You should," Eisenhower told him, "make a searching survey of the probable advantages and disadvantages to yourself and to the party before you give me an answer."

But Nixon did not take seriously the idea of a post in the cabinet, nor is it hard to see why he dismissed it. A Vice President is elected by the people to a four-year incumbency; the job may be a joke, but when the President is a man in his late sixties with a history of cardiac damage, the only way is up. A cabinet secretary, on the other hand, holds his job at the will of the President; if he does poorly—or is made to seem to have done poorly, a relatively simple matter in the dense underbrush of bureaucracy—the only way is down and out. When the subject came up again (Nixon has said it came up "at five or six of our private conversations, usually in a casual way"), Nixon at last began to take it seriously. Indeed, he did some "private agonizing" about it and quickly decided that what was afoot was a plot to dump him. "It seemed to me," he wrote later, "that it was like the fund controversy all over again."

In truth, as Nixon well knew, Eisenhower had for some time been beating the bushes for promising young Republicans and had done his best to give them what he called "political visibility"—by which he meant appointing them to positions of trust and nudging them out on the Republican banquet circuit to make speeches and exhibit their profile, their wife and children, and any other seductive political assets. He could think of seven "able administrators and leaders," but the list, as Nixon must also have reckoned, included few who could conceivably have been remodeled into serious rivals.*

* Eisenhower's list was headed by Robert Anderson, a Texan who had first been his secretary of the navy and next his deputy secretary of defense, and who would later be named his secretary of the treasury. He was a man of no political experience who had no taste for politics. Others were Brownell and Lodge, neither of whom would have been satisfactory to the Taft wing of the party; General Gruenther, still commander of SHAPE; Lucius Clay, suspected by many of being a Democrat; Gabriel

The fact was that Nixon stood alone as a nationally known candidate. He had his drawbacks, but the competition was not even in the starting blocks. Still Eisenhower temporized. He had urged the Vice President to decide his own future and he was fortified in his view of Nixon's prospects by the opinions of many trusted advisers, including the president of J. P. Morgan & Company. He hotly denied to reporters that there was any disposition to "dump" Nixon; he declared, "The only thing I have asked him to do is to chart out his own course, and tell me what he would like to do." Nixon interpreted the remark as a rebuff and was about to announce that he would not be a candidate in 1956, but Hall, the GOP chairman, dissuaded him. Eisenhower was not, said Hall, obliquely suggesting he would prefer someone else, and he added that Nixon was wrong to judge Eisenhower's statements as if the President were a political sophisticate—which says much about Hall's perspicacity.

Eisenhower wanted Nixon to dance somewhere in the cotillion; Nixon, proud but bashful, wanted to be invited to lead it. The ludicrous flirtation, transcendent in its triviality, wore on week after week until, late in April, Hall asked Nixon to unbend for the good of the party. Some more "intense soul-searching," and at last Nixon called on the President to say that he would be honored to . . . But Eisenhower at once sent for Jim Hagerty and instructed him to take Nixon to the reporters so that he might make the announcement himself. Hagerty was authorized to say that the President was "delighted."

And there, with luck, the matter might have rested, but unhappily the President's health was once again endangered, and the fact served to remind nervous people of the actuarial tables; that is, of how the one who was Vice President in 1957 might well be President before 1960. On the night of June 7–8 Eisenhower suffered another attack of the chronic ileitis that had troubled him for so many years but had never been precisely diagnosed. This time, when his distress persisted, he was taken to Walter Reed Hospital. Between three and five o'clock on Saturday morning, June 9, he underwent an emergency operation.* It was, no question about it, major surgery; Governor Adams has told of how he was informed that the chances were six or eight to one against the recovery from such an operation of a patient as old as Eisenhower. The surgeon who gave Adams those worrying tidings surely reckoned without Eisenhower's robust phys-

---

Hauge, Eisenhower's personal haruspex as to economics but a babe in the political arena; and Eisenhower's brother Milton.

* Technically, the operation was an ileo-transverse-colostomy: the diseased section of the ileum (in Eisenhower's case, about ten inches) was surgically bypassed and the healthy intestine connected by incision to the right side of the transverse of the large intestine.

ical constitution. Responsive to the needs of the moment—the Republican national convention was only two months away—the President recuperated quickly, was said to be working five hours a day by mid-June, once again convalesced at Gettysburg, and was back in the White House on July 15. Len Hall confidently told reporters: "It's Eisenhower and Nixon. That's it." The Democrats chafed in futility. Here was Eisenhower, who in all reason should have acknowledged he was an elderly valetudinarian and should have been propped up in a rocking chair with a shawl to protect him against drafts, being portrayed by his press secretary as some kind of natural force, puissant and tireless. A "Hagerty curtain" had been drawn to conceal the truth about Eisenhower's health, complained a Democratic senator, who went on to pay tribute to "one of the most masterful suppressions of the facts ever put across by the advertising techniques of Madison Avenue." Independent voters and even some Republicans were likewise concerned, if the private soundings taken by agents of Harold Stassen were to be trusted. On July 20 Stassen told the President of his surveys: Nixon's name on the ticket would cost the Republicans at least 6 percent of the electorate; the margin would certainly result in the loss of congressional seats, quite possibly enough of them to ensure continued Democratic control of the Congress. Stassen suggested that Eisenhower might replace Nixon with Christian Herter, the governor of Massachusetts, who had run well in the private polls. There was nothing in the world to keep Eisenhower, had he chosen to, from telling Stassen that his mind was made up, that he wanted Nixon for his running mate. Unquestionably Stassen would at once have shelved his private surveys. But Eisenhower said nothing of the kind. Later he would rather lamely maintain that he was so preoccupied with last-minute cares before traveling to Panama to attend a meeting of the Presidents of the Americas (he left by airplane the next day) that he had had time only to be astonished by Stassen's attitude and to tell him that he was of course "free" to do as he chose about the nomination of a candidate for the Vice Presidency. In the event, when Stassen announced his advocacy of Herter over Nixon ("I am confident," Stassen said to the reporters, "that if the . . . convention nominates . . . Herter for Vice President, President Eisenhower will be pleased to have him on the ticket"), the reaction of the Republican professionals, and especially of the hard-shell right wing, was so vehement and so hostile that Stassen's campaign soon collapsed. (One month after the November elections Eisenhower would nominate Herter to succeed Herbert Hoover, Jr., as undersecretary of state.) It was the classic Eisenhoverian formula: to allow some other to loose a trial balloon and then, if it were shot down in flames, to turn, palms upspread and jaw unhinged, the picture of wondering innocence.

Politics were the distraction in 1956, and considerable bitterness was added, most noticeably in the southern states, over racial injustice.

In Montgomery, Alabama, cradle of the old Confederacy, because of affronts to Negroes on the public buses, a boycott of the municipal transportation system was called by Protestant clergymen; it spread to other southern cities. To the unreconstructed whites such behavior smacked of insurrection. The times called for a leader of courage and principle, and in Montgomery there emerged a young Baptist minister, Martin Luther King. The battle cry of King's cohorts was nonviolence. Angry white politicians retorted with a call to "take up our shotguns." In Washington J. Edgar Hoover, director of the FBI, perceived the sinister influence of the Communist party. All over the South White Citizens' Councils were being formed, with members taking a pledge to oppose integration and the "Communist theory of one world, one race." Investigative reporters estimated three hundred chapters with nearly eighty thousand members in Mississippi alone, and more than sixty chapters with another fifty thousand members in Alabama. Director Hoover had found only one hundred and twenty-seven such chapters throughout the South; the White Citizens' Councils, Hoover told the cabinet early in March, "either could control the rising tensions or become the medium through which tensions might manifest themselves." To this close reasoning Hoover added that the sale of firearms had suspiciously increased in the South, as much as 400 percent in one community.

Rather than step forward as a leader Eisenhower chose to retire into the reflection that he was President of all the people and not of only one group of them. To the left and to the right of him were the extremists: the Negroes who demanded equal treatment, and the whites who denied it with violence and disorder. This left for him the vast, perdurable constituency of the center: those who automatically profess to believe the self-evident truth that all men are created equal but do little about it, preferring to live and let live. Thus when he was asked what he proposed to do about the rioting at the University of Alabama provoked by the admission of its first Negro student, he spoke of the defiance of law "that all of us deplore" but added, addressing himself to his constituency: "I would certainly hope that we could avoid any interference with anybody else as long as that state, from its governor on down, will do its best to straighten it out." In short, the federal government would not interfere with the states if the state officials would only do their undefined best. So in February of an election year. And when it was pointed out to him that the legislatures of four southern states (Georgia, Mississippi, South Carolina, and Virginia) had passed resolutions of interposition declaring that the Supreme Court's decision outlawing segregation in the public schools had no force and effect in their states, and he was asked about the role of the federal government in the enforcement of the Supreme Court's decision, President Eisenhower wagged his head. "I expect that we are going to make progress," he said, "and the Supreme Court itself said it does not expect revolutionary action suddenly executed. We will make progress," the President said, "and I am not going to attempt to tell them how it is going to be done."

With the beginning of the second school year since the Supreme Court had called for the integration "with all deliberate speed" of the public school system, more demonstrations were mounted against Negro children seeking to attend schools in Tennessee, Kentucky, and Texas. (In the deep South no attempts were yet made to break the crust of ancient custom.) In private President Eisenhower expressed himself vividly and bluntly. To Emmet Hughes, once again on the team as a speech writer, he was vehement. "I am convinced," he declared, "that the Supreme Court decision set *back* progress in the South *at least fifteen years*. . . . It's all very well to talk about school integration—you may also be talking about social *dis*integration. Feelings are deep on this, especially where children are involved. . . . And the fellow who tells me that you can do these things by *force* is just plain *nuts*." [Emphasis supplied by Hughes.] In public he again singled out for his disapproval the "extremists on both sides" and proceeded with a revealing definition of those extremists. "The South is full of people of good will," he said, "but they are not the ones we now hear. We hear the people that are adamant and are so filled with prejudice that they even resort to violence; and the same way on the other side of the thing, the people who want to have the whole matter settled today. This is a question of leading and training and teaching people, and it takes some time, unfortunately."

Once again, the counsel the Negro people had heard for more than a century: You want your rights too fast, you want them today; you are getting too aggressive, too surly; why aren't you more grateful for what the reasonable white people have granted you? Moderation! These things take time. We must proceed gradually.

Since, speaking for the Democrats, Adlai Stevenson had also said, "We must proceed gradually, not upsetting habits or traditions that are older than the republic," it was plain that most Negro children would have at least another year to wait until their public education would be as good as that of white children. Another year as second-class children. Indeed, the whole issue of civil rights was laid away among camphor balls, and there it would remain, combustible.

Whether he handled his political affairs expertly or indifferently was for Eisenhower largely irrelevant. Politics was not his métier. For him politics was not a task to be undertaken but an instinctive reflex of his subtle and calculating nature. In his view the business of the President was the world and the position of the United States in it. He found his positive satisfaction when he turned from domestic chores to the challenge of ordering world affairs.

The character of the Cold War was much changed since 1953. The President could confidently recite a list of "advances" he perceived "all over the world"—in Indochina, Korea, Iran, Trieste, Austria, Guatemala; a "taint of colonialism" removed here, "communism" or a "communistic" party repelled there—triumphs for none of which he would have disdained the credit, but he had been too intimately involved in the crises, the conflicts, and the rivalry fully to comprehend the nature of the change. Further, he was in an election year, always a time for the truth, the whole truth, to step shyly into the background.

The change was fundamental. In Europe the contending parties had agreed, since there were no grounds for agreement, that the lines drawn would be held firm: no unification of Germany; the opposing armies of NATO and Warsaw Pact shuffled about as might or must be; disarmament in limbo; intelligence agents tunneling underground from both sides; fog of suspicion hugging the landscape east and west; combat confined within the clandestine scope of CIA and KGB, or whatever might be the most convenient set of initial letters: the deadlock that went under the name of "peaceful coexistence." In the weeks that followed Geneva, while Eisenhower first bustled about on his energetic vacation and later lay hushed and still in hospital, Foster Dulles had been cogitating the shifting pressures and tensions of the Cold War. He had attentively followed the peregrinations of Khrushchev and Bulganin through Burma, India, and Afghanistan, noting the technical assistance offered, the trade agreements concluded. To escape the quarantine imposed by the free world, the USSR was plainly turning south and southeast to the lands formerly parts of colonial empires. By December 1955, Dulles had formulated his fears at a meeting of NATO ministers in Paris: international communism, he warned, was planning "indirect" swipes at "the Near and Middle East and South Asia," and especially at the petroleum reserves so "essential to the industrial life of Western Europe." By one of the ironies of Cold War dynamics, the Soviet thrust that had alarmed Dulles was a predictable response to western initiatives in the region.

As NATO had been designed to contain the Soviet Union from the Baltic to the eastern end of the Mediterranean, so SEATO had been slapped together to contain any communist threat from the Philippines west to Pakistan. This had left a gap of nearly three thousand miles between Turkey and Pakistan. SEATO was a fragile barrier at best, and to reflect that NATO's flank might be turned in the Middle East, endangering the wealth of petroleum, was cause for alarm. How to plug the gap? Since the early 1950s the British and Americans had been seeking to establish some sort of military alliance—a Middle East Treaty Organization? a Central Treaty Organization?—but in vain. No METO, no CENTRO could be assembled to link NATO and SEATO. The roots of the difficulty were tangled and tough: most of the states in the region were Arab, newly emerged into national independence and brimming with hostility toward those who had so long kept them subjugated as colonial possessions, or trust territories, or mandates; moreover, there was one state in the region, Israel, that was hated and reviled by all the others. If Israel were to be invited to join METO or CENTRO, no Arab state would sign on. If only Arab states were to join, excluding Israel, the United States could join only with difficulty, for the United States had a special relationship toward Israel—banker, tutor, protector, busybody—in short, a thoroughly familial kinship. There was the Arab League, the association of Arab states formed in 1945 with British blessings, but the glue that kept the league together was the Arab hatred of imperialism. The most hated of the imperialists, of course, were precisely the British and French.* So the Arabs, alienated and suspicious, were bound to regard any effort by the British or French to forge a METO or a CENTRO as a plot to keep alive European influence in the Middle East; the United States they identified as the power ambitious to succeed Britain and France as imperator of the region. As for Israel, Arab leaders came to consider her, as Gamal Abdel Nasser phrased it, only "one of the outcomes of imperialism," one of

* The British had moved in to dominate the Middle East as the Ottoman Empire slowly collapsed: first Egypt (1882) and the Sudan (1899); then, after the war of 1914–1918, Iraq, Palestine, and Jordan; British influence was unrivaled throughout Arabia. France had gradually taken over the countries of North Africa from the Turk —Algeria (1847), Tunisia (1881), and Morocco (1912)—either by conquest or as "protector"; in 1920 France had assumed as well the mandate over Syria and Lebanon. Of the other Arab states, Libya and Yemen had been dismissed as too desolate for profitable exploitation. The British still in 1956 controlled a number of small but exceedingly wealthy sheikdoms, sultanates, and other protectorates carved out along the southern and eastern edges of the Arabian peninsula, but most of the Arab states had by then won their independence. The fierce rebellion of the Algerian Arabs against the French was actually raging at this time.

As Egypt had been the first of these states to come under British control, so she was the last to achieve her freedom. The reason for Britain's sticky fingers was the Suez Canal, a waterway wholly within Egyptian territory and under Egyptian sovereignty. Not until 1954 did the British government, responsive to sympathetic but firm pressure by the Eisenhower administration, sign an Anglo-Egyptian treaty and agree to withdraw British troops from the canal zone. The last soldiers were to leave by June 1956.

the pawns in "the great force that throws around the whole region a fatal seige." Egypt refused Israeli ships passage through the Suez Canal, since the two countries were technically at war with each other.

At length, early in 1955, with clandestine British encouragement, a first step toward a regional military alliance had been taken by the only Arab leader whose sympathies were dependably with the British—Nuri es-Said, the premier of Iraq. Nuri held office thanks to British support, and he had dreamed of making Baghdad rather than Cairo the core and axis of the Arab world. In Baghdad on February 24, 1955, he made a treaty of mutual cooperation with Turkey and invited other states with interests in the area to join if they wished. In the circumstances, Washington and London both rejoiced: here at last was the framework for a solid military bulwark reaching through what Dulles had called the "northern tier" of countries bordering on the Soviet Union, from Turkey of NATO to Pakistan of SEATO. International communism, one might suppose, had been more straitly contained and, sure enough, from Moscow came a growl about "the intrigues of aggressive circles in the United States and their associates close to the borders of the USSR." At this time Khrushchev had only just emerged as boss of the Soviet collective leadership. His attention was riveted on the menace of a West Germany rearmed and added to the strength of NATO; he had time for no more than a glance at the Middle East. Dulles and Eden could pleasurably contemplate the prospect of other Arab nations in due course subscribing to the Baghdad Pact. But only four days after the signing of it an event occurred that would crush all hopes of Arab unity with the West in the Cold War and would, to the contrary, prepare the ground for the most treacherous of the crises President Eisenhower would be called on to resolve during his years in the White House.

On the night of Monday, February 28, two platoons of Israeli paratroopers, acting on the orders of David Ben Gurion, who had only the week before returned from retirement to take the post of minister of defense, struck suddenly at an Egyptian army encampment on the northern outskirts of Gaza, ambushed its reinforcements, killed thirty-eight persons including civilians and at least one child, and summarily ended whatever hopes had lingered for peace between Arab and Israeli.

The savagery of the Gaza raid provoked widespread disgust and indignation. At the U.N. the Security Council unanimously condemned it. The U.S. delegate, James J. Wadsworth, termed it "indefensible," the more so because it had followed upon a period of relative peace and stability. Everything had been quiet, and what is more, Nasser had been given "assurances from the United States and the United Kingdom that everything would remain quiet." Those assurances had been urged upon Nasser by U.S. and U.K. officials to justify their refusal to sell him arms. Eisenhower in particular was anxious to avoid any suggestion of an arms race in the Middle East; he liked to cite the Tripartite Declaration of 1950, by the terms of which Britain, France, and the U.S. had agreed to consult each other to ensure that any arms sold either to Israelis or Arabs would be limited and kept in balance.

The Gaza raid, though, had taught Nasser that his restraint, his pacifism, and his policy of economic and social development in Egypt were positive dangers in view of Israel's bellicose behavior. Late on the night of the raid, once he had concluded that it was not, despite his fears, the first engagement of a general Israeli onslaught, Nasser decided he must once again appeal to the U.S. for arms. Egypt was short of everything: she had only "six serviceable planes; about thirty others were grounded for lack of spare parts; Britain had stopped deliveries. . . . [Her] tank ammunition would last for a one-hour battle. . . . 60 percent of [her] tanks were in need of major repairs. [Her] artillery was in the same deplorable state." On March 10 Nasser had made a special request for arms to the U.S. ambassador, Henry Byroade; his bid was duly relayed to the State Department, and when it reached Eisenhower's desk in the White House the President was astonished. "Why," he had exclaimed, "this is peanuts!" But despite the obvious defensive character of the arms sought, the Eisenhower administration had been reluctant to meet the request. Earlier, on March 6, Nasser had arranged with Syria and Saudi Arabia to recommend to all Arab states a common military and economic alliance; but only Yemen would later accept the invitation.

The lines had been drawn, and as in a stately dance the powers had begun to circle, bow, clasp hands, disengage, smile, nod, and seek another partner to resume the round. The United Kingdom consented to join the Baghdad Pact. The United States bowed and withdrew, despite urgent entreaties, from any formal commitment; President Eisenhower would go no further than to post a military mission to Baghdad and to cooperate with but not to become a member of the Pact. Nasser, after amicable conversations first with Marshal Tito and next with Pandit Nehru, following which he had put his name to a communiqué that condemned "military alliances and power entanglements that heighten tension," had traveled to the conference at Bandung, where he was warmly welcomed and was introduced to the powerful temptations of neutralism. If he could not purchase his desperately needed arms in the West, he would look to the East.

At a diplomatic reception in Cairo on the evening of May 18, Nasser took the Soviet ambassador to one side and put a quiet question: "We want to have arms from you; what will be your answer?" After three days the ambassador, Daniel Solod, had an answer from the Kremlin for Nasser: the matter could be arranged. Negotiations began, but they moved slowly.

Chiefly the talks dragged because Nasser still harbored hopes he might buy arms from Britain or the United States. His army was familiar with western armaments, had trained with them, had flown western aircraft. Moreover, there was the impediment of communism. So even as the talks with the Russians (and the Czechoslovaks, who had been brought in partly to mask the Russian presence, partly as true associates) proceeded cautiously, Nasser was careful to apprise the Americans in general terms of his course. On June 9 he told Ambassador Byroade what he was up to, at the same time hinting he would prefer arms from the U.S. The State Department responded with an invitation to submit a schedule of Egyptian military requirements. Nasser complied on June 30. Nothing happened. In Washington everyone was busy preparing for the meeting at the summit in Geneva.

During the Geneva Conference, indeed, the British and Americans found time to worry together about the Middle East. Eden and Macmillan met with Eisenhower and Dulles on Wednesday, July 20, 1955, for breakfast—at what was, at least for Macmillan, "the unconscionable hour of 8:30 A.M."—and Dulles reported that Egypt had requested arms of the U.S. He suggested that if the U.S. did not supply them, Egypt might turn to the USSR. Eden expressed his doubts the Soviets would sell arms to Egypt. (All the Arab states were admirably anticommunist.) The talk turned instead to methods of supplying British tanks to Iraq at American expense. Plainly the western statesmen thought Nasser was bluffing.

On July 31 Nasser dispatched an inquiry to Washington through diplomatic channels: What action had been taken on his schedule of requested armaments? When after three weeks he had no reply, Nasser and the Egyptian revolutionary junta took their decision. On the night of Thursday, August 25, the fedayeen* crossed into Israel to initiate a campaign of terrorist reprisals for terrorist acts, the most recent links in an endless chain of vengeance reaching back at least to Genesis 16-21, to the days of Ishmael and Isaac. And on that same August 25 the Egyptians resolved to accept Russian military hardware.

The Baghdad Pact, designed to contain and frustrate international communism, had instead brought the Soviets leapfrogging into the heartland of Arab nationalism.

Rumors of the arms deal were widely published toward the end of August, and on August 30 Dulles took official notice of them. The papers

---

* The singular form of this Arabic word has come to mean a commando, but it has a long usage as one who stands ready to sacrifice himself for his country.

were signed probably on September 24, which was also the day President Eisenhower was stricken by a coronary occlusion.

It will be recalled that when first his aides were apprehensively adjusting to the fearful news that the President had suffered a heart attack—none yet knew how severe—they had congratulated themselves on the "spirit of Geneva," on the fact that for a wonder there was at the moment no Cold War crisis on the horizon. Not, however, all his aides. For one, Foster Dulles knew better. He had refused to credit the CIA reports of the Soviet-Egyptian arms deal until mid-September; on September 20, encountering Molotov at the United Nations, he had complained of a "violation of the spirit of Geneva," but Molotov dismissed it as a purely commercial transaction; to Macmillan, also in New York for the U.N. meetings, the deal was "a new and sinister element [in] this already complicated tangle of confusion." Wasting no time on sour reflections over his earlier and unfounded complacency, Dulles now scrambled to avert disaster. Nasser had too long been ignored; now, too late, he would be ardently wooed. Kermit Roosevelt, the CIA operative who had so smoothly managed the coup d'état in Iran and who was also Nasser's personal friend, was hurriedly dispatched to Cairo with instructions to advise Nasser how foolish he would be to buy arms from the Soviets. Roosevelt reckoned the deal was already an accomplished fact, but he took plane to Cairo anyway. On his heels came George V. Allen, assistant secretary of state for Near Eastern and African affairs, bearing what was widely reported to be an ultimatum from Dulles to Nasser.

Clearly, if the United States had a policy toward Nasser, it was in flux, and the same could be said of United States policy toward Middle Eastern affairs generally.* The pressing need of the moment was for a leader who could guide a team of expert advisers through "a Middle Eastern tangle of conflicting considerations, one with so few possibilities of being resolved that it had to be lived with rather than settled." The leader was President Eisenhower. The words just quoted are his. But he lay still in bed in Fitzsimons General Hospital, under an oxygen tent, and it was left for his

---

* After the brief, violent war over the Suez in the fall of 1956, a subcommittee of the Senate committees on foreign affairs and on the armed services conducted an exhaustive study of United States policy in the Middle East. The chairman of this subcommittee, Senator William Fulbright, observed in 1957: "I have been impressed with the difficulty of determining what our policy was in the Middle East during these last three or four years. I am unable to find any consistent theme or principle involved in our attitude toward Egypt. At one moment we seemed to encourage Nasser and at another to thwart him without any compelling reason for such shifts being evident, at least to me. Such rapid changes of attitudes were, I am sure, confusing to our allies and friends as well as to our enemies."

team of expert advisers and assistants to determine whether, unguided, they could shape and control the crisis.

As Roosevelt had surmised, his mission to Nasser was fruitless. The arms deal was formally announced in Cairo on Tuesday, September 27. Allen arrived on September 30, and in four days was able at least to restore a friendly atmosphere for civilized discourse between the two nations.

Meanwhile the Baghdad Pact had been adding strength: Pakistan had signed on September 23 (Iran followed suit on October 11). Since this meant that on paper the Soviet southwestern border had been sealed, Dulles was gratified. He had always placed reliance in such pieces of paper, representing, as he hoped they would, the pledge of the governments subscribing. The British still pressed the United States to join the pact, but Dulles steadfastly refused until the Palestine question—that is, the Arab-Israeli dispute—could be settled. This was grit in the gears of the Anglo-American alliance; and other signs of friction were working their way to the surface, sprouting from what Macmillan was to call the "seeds of strife."

The seeds had put down roots in the sandy soil of the Middle East, and the roots reached down into the rich deposits of oil beneath. ONE: An armed clash in October between Saudi Arabian troops and Arab troops led by British officers at a point along a disputed border of the sultanate of Muscat and Oman. At issue, because of the oil underneath, was an obscure oasis called Buraimi. Word reached Eden that Dulles had termed this clash a British act of aggression, basing his charge on "Public opinion in Saudi Arabia." In that absolute monarchy, the only public opinion was the private opinion of officials of the Arabian-American Oil Company (Aramco) and their royal client King Saud. The incident sharpened the hostility between Dulles and Eden. TWO: The revenues paid Saud by Aramco, which in November were on the order of twenty-three million dollars a month. Saud spread much of this money around—especially in Jordan, but in Lebanon, Syria, and Iraq as well—to arouse opposition to the Baghdad Pact. In Eden's view, "American, that is Aramco, money was being spent on a lavish scale to abet communism in the Middle East"; he deplored the disposition of the U.S. government to regard the payments as a purely commercial transaction. THREE: The Tripartite Declaration of 1950. Eden wanted armed force visibly deployed in the area to show that the U.S., U.K., and France meant what they had said about violations of the Arab-Israeli frontiers, but at the time—January 1956—Eisenhower was reluctant to take such action without congressional authorization.*

---

* Six months later a warship of the U.S. Sixth Fleet would be loaded with arms and stationed in the Mediterranean, ready to succor any nation that might be attacked. This gesture of impartiality was short-lived. The vessel was soon withdrawn.

Eisenhower was by then warily resuming his presidential duties and gauging how much damage had been done the cherished Anglo-American amity.

The damage was symptomatic and imperfectly understood. The key fact of Middle Eastern polity was the collapse of British influence, long since foreseen by Dulles. He had postulated that phenomenon so beloved of political scientists, a power vacuum, and had anticipated that the United States must move in, if possible without offending the British, or forfeit the Middle East to the Soviets. (The Arabs vainly protested the notion of a vacuum in the Middle East, contending that they could manage their own affairs without interference by foreign powers.) But throughout the winter of 1955–1956, while the concept of British empire was crumbling and U.S. economic and political dominion was aggressively being asserted, collision was inevitable and abrasive. In the path of the crunch, marked for destruction, stood the elegant figure of Anthony Eden.

During this time, while Eisenhower's health was slowly mending, Eden's was deteriorating. It is significant that in the months that saw the Suez crisis gradually aggravated, the premier statesmen of the free world should have been functioning at considerably less than their best ability. Dulles, too, was impaired; he would fetch up in hospital a few months later for a lengthy operation to excise some malignancies. Eden's ailment was in his bile duct: after three operations the duct had been patched with plastic, but he was still subject to unpredictable bouts of fever and he was prone to be liverish, hot-tempered, and impatient. This susceptibility, customarily concealed under his dapper demeanor, was most apparent in his attitude toward Nasser. Thus, after an ill-advised British attempt to get Jordan to join the Baghdad Pact had led to the fall of three successive Jordanian governments, riots in Amman, and violence to British and American government property on both sides of the Jordan River, Eden was inclined to blame the Arab animosity on Nasser; when in March 1956 King Hussein of Jordan dismissed Sir John Bagot Glubb, his long-time British adviser and commander of the crack Arab Legion, Eden was infuriated. Anthony Nutting, who was Eden's undersecretary of state for foreign affairs, has recalled how Eden shouted at him: "What's all this nonsense about isolating Nasser or neutralizing him, as you call it? I want him destroyed, can't you understand?" And when Nutting urged that Eden, before toppling Nasser, should have in mind an alternative, a more amenable man to succeed him, so as to avoid anarchy in Egypt, Eden shouted in reply: "But I don't want an alternative, and I don't give a damn if there's anarchy and chaos in Egypt." Eden's startling behavior appears to have been at least in part pathological. Nutting spoke of a "metamorphosis . . . due to sickness and to the poison from a damaged bile duct, which was eating away at his whole system." As the Suez crisis reached its climax, Eden would be in "a state of acute intoxication," in the technical sense of that word.

Against that dispiriting background negotiations to contract for Anglo-American assistance in the construction of the High Aswan Dam were taken in hand.

That enormous engineering project, the dream nearest to Nasser's heart, would make possible irrigation for new farmland and electric power for industrialization. In fine, the High Dam at Aswan was expected to pluck Egypt from wretched poverty and bring the land economic independence and security.

A few days after the formal announcement of the Soviet arms deal, while rumors were still circulating that the Russians were offering to finance and build the great dam as well, Nasser proved himself a true-blue neutralist. His ambassador in Washington, Ahmed Hussein, informed Dulles that his government would rather accept such aid from the U.S. than from the USSR, even though American terms were expected to be much stiffer. To Dulles, fearful lest the Soviets might be moving to fill the "power vacuum" in the Middle East, Hussein's visit was welcome indeed. A week later engineers from the World Bank—more properly the International Bank for Reconstruction and Development, a specialized agency of the United Nations, dominated by U.S. capital funds and having as its president a U.S. banker, Eugene Black—were in Cairo to explore further the feasibility of the project. By the end of November discussions involving the Egyptian minister of finance, officials of the World Bank, British ambassador Sir Roger Makins, and Herbert Hoover, Jr., undersecretary of state, were under way in Washington.

The time was propitious. Eden, his rage at Nasser still in the future, had launched a diplomatic endeavor for compromise of the disputed Arab-Israeli boundaries.* Foster Dulles likewise had in mind a scheme, even more ambitious, for bringing peace to the hate-riven Holy Land, and he offered it for inspection at a meeting of the National Security Council at Camp David on December 8, 1955. In brief, the scheme involved U.S. approval of the joint agreement that had been elaborated to

---

* A month later another Israeli raid, once again meticulously mounted and dispatched by Ben Gurion, this time into Syria, effectively shattered any prospects for Eden's peace initiative. Ironically, the raid also disrupted an Israeli military mission to Washington. Moshe Sharett, then the Israeli foreign minister, was on the point of closing a deal by which the U.S. would equip Israel with four squadrons of F–86 jet aircraft and other armaments when news of the fifty-six Syrians slain by Israeli soldiers was published around the world, precipitating what Abba Eban, then Israeli ambassador to the U.S., later called "an appalling international situation."

finance the construction of the High Dam, and a secret U.S. mission to the Middle East to inspire a peace settlement by Arabs and Israelis—one that would dispel the fears that each had of the other, remedy the plight of the hundreds of thousands of Arabs who had been uprooted from their homes in Palestine, and establish fixed permanent boundaries. Dulles recommended, the other NSC members debated, it was left to President Eisenhower to decide.

As to the peace mission there could be no disagreement but only a question as to who would be charged with the delicate task. The financing of the dam was more closely scrutinized. The U.S. was to allocate fifty-six million dollars; fourteen million more was to come from Britain; the World Bank was to lend two hundred million, contingent on an understanding that the governments of the U.S. and Britain would "consider sympathetically . . . further support" amounting to another one hundred and thirty million dollars, spread over a period of fifteen years. The wisdom of such a long-term commitment was questioned. The strength of the likely and continuing opposition—legislators from cotton-growing states, wary of stiffer Egyptian competition in the world markets; legislators with constituencies emotionally identified with Israel—was analyzed. The question was canvassed as to whether Nasser, as a so-called neutralist, was playing off West against East in order to get the better of each. (This presumed tactic was characterized as "blackmail.") But Dulles argued strongly in favor of the project, and Eden was at the time known to favor it, so the President decided the United States should proceed as planned. The Anglo-American offer to assist Egypt to build the High Dam was announced on December 16.

To conduct the ticklish negotiations with Nasser and Ben Gurion, Eisenhower selected Robert B. Anderson, the Texas oilman who would soon lead his list of possible substitutes for Nixon as a candidate for Vice President. Anderson left for Tel Aviv on January 9, 1956, and for a time he was busily and secretly engaged in the Middle East, shuttling back and forth between Cairo and Tel Aviv.

At some point in December or January, Anderson's secret mission was somehow yoked—in the minds of at least some of the few men who knew of it—with the decision to help pay the costs of the High Dam; that is, a few American officials at the highest level came to understand that Anglo-American financial aid would be forthcoming only if Anderson's mission succeeded. It failed. Ben Gurion, by then once again prime minister, demanded that any negotiations be conducted directly with Nasser and in public. In the explosive Arab political world, especially after the Israeli raid on Syria, those terms were impossible for Nasser to meet. Whether Ben Gurion deliberately imposed conditions he knew

Nasser could not satisfy is of some interest but not so crucial to Eisenhower's future perplexities as this fact: unknown to Anderson, Ben Gurion during this very time was urging his cabinet to approve General Moshe Dayan's war plan to conquer the eastern stretch of the Sinai peninsula.

At all events, during the early months of 1956 the American commitment to the High Dam at Aswan steadily lost support in influential circles, while those opposed to such assistance gained in number and in confidence. And so the Suez crisis inevitably inched closer.

In February 1956, Eugene Black, president of the World Bank, returned to Washington from Cairo, having reached substantial agreement with Nasser on the fiscal aspects of the project. Black had yet to realize that U.S. interest in the Aswan High Dam was curdling. As Sherman Adams would recall, of the atmosphere in Washington at this time: ". . . any attempt to give aid to the Arabs always met with opposition behind the scenes in Washington, where . . . alert representatives of the many well-organized pro-Israel lobbies . . . were always effective and influential in the Capitol. Consideration for the great body of private opinion in the United States favoring Israel was a large factor in every government decision on the Middle East." When Dulles discussed the financial arrangements with congressional leaders, he found them recalcitrant. He was constrained to remind them that the underlying U.S. motivation derived from the Cold War, that the U.S. was competing with the Soviet Union for the loyalties of the Arab world. Eisenhower ruefully observed that the Soviets were able to vie with the United States in capital investment and industrial technology, America's long suits. "This shows the advantages a dictatorship possesses," said the President, "in being able to choose its own ground and then moving very fast."

This was an overestimation of the Soviet Union's power and cunning, based on a misconception of the character of its government. At the time, mid-February, Khrushchev had just delivered a lengthy report to a closed session of the twentieth Congress of the Soviet Communist Party. An attempt was made to keep his speech secret, but before long it was known to include a detailed and comprehensive indictment of Stalin, complete with a grim bill of particulars—the murders, purges, and other crimes he had committed against socialism and against his party. This speech, as word of it spread through the Soviet Union and the countries of eastern Europe—a process considerably assisted by the CIA and its several powerful radio transmitters—caused a great shudder of horror from Berlin to Peking.

A brave dream of the future had been shattered by the sordid deeds of the past. In revulsion, the peoples of eastern Europe—Communist party members foremost among them—began to ponder rebellion. Their ideas would coalesce into action in synchrony with the approaching Suez crisis.

After substantial agreement had been reached in February on the Anglo-American offer of aid, Nasser sent notes to Washington and London requesting changes in the conditions attached to the offer. Weeks, then months, passed, but no answer was sent him.

The project was in a kind of cold storage. Was it on? was it off? No one knew for sure. Decision was in suspension, slowly drifting, waiting for something to happen, an event that would show either that the High Dam was worth fighting for in Congress or that support for it should be scrapped. Suspicion was sown that Nasser was dickering with the Soviets. On April 3 Dulles scoffed at the idea. To his press conference he insisted that Nasser had not repudiated "ties with the West" or accepted "anything like vassalage to the Soviet Union." Rather, he said, Nasser was "actuated . . . by a desire to maintain the genuine independence" of the Arab world. Late that month Nasser was handed a new worry: during a visit to England, Khrushchev had suddenly suggested the possibility of an arms embargo on the Middle East if it could be arranged through the U.N. To Nasser, that meant that if he were to get the arms he regarded as vital to Egyptian security he might have to deal with a nation not affiliated with the U.N. On May 16 the government of Egypt announced establishment of diplomatic relations with China.

If this was not the event for which Eisenhower and Dulles had been waiting, it would serve as an excuse for an event. Recognition of China was, after all, something less than earth-shaking. Britain had done so years before, and so had Israel. But to the "China Lobby" it was perfidy. Overnight the pressure against U.S. aid for the High Dam enormously intensified. A State Department spokesman acknowledged that U.S.-Egyptian relations were to be reviewed. At his press conference Dulles said that the recognition of China was "an action that we regret." Eisenhower chimed in next day by saying, "Well, of course, we think that Egypt was mistaken."

The incident provoked a reconsideration of neutrality in a world split, as Eisenhower and Dulles believed, by a Manichaean conflict between the forces of freedom and those of godless international communism. On June 6 Eisenhower delivered himself of a little homily on the subject to his press conference, but even though he and Dulles had discussed the matter at some length, what he said and what Dulles said a few days later came out so scrambled that they managed to confuse and alarm both allies and neutrals. What Eisenhower said seemed to suggest that Egypt might after all be granted funds for her dam:

"If you are waging peace, you can't be too particular sometimes about the special attitudes that different countries take. We were a young country once, and our whole policy for the first one hundred and fifty years was, we were neutral. We constantly asserted we were neutral in the wars of the world and wars of Europe and its antagonisms.

"Now, today there are certain nations that say they are neutral. This doesn't necessarily mean what it is so often interpreted to mean, neutral as between right and wrong or decency and indecency.

"They are using the term 'neutral' with respect to attachment to military alliances. And may I point out that I cannot see that that is always to the disadvantage of such a country as ours. . . .

"If [a nation] has announced its military association with another great power, things could happen to it, difficulties along its borders, and people would say, 'Good enough for it. They asked for it.'"

This was uncomfortably remindful of George Washington's celebrated plea that the United States beware of "entangling alliances"—odd counsel indeed, coming from the man, who, as military commander and President, had led the nation into compacts of collective defense with forty-two other nations. Further, he seemed to be saying that if his smaller and weaker allies should get into trouble with the Soviet Union for entering into a military association with the United States, people would shrug and say, "Serves them right. They asked for it." Dismay. Dulles scurried to the White House. A hasty conference. A clarifying statement: "The President does believe that . . . special conditions [may] justify political neutrality but . . . no nation has the right to be indifferent to the fate of another. . . . The President does not believe that association for mutual security with the United States will involve any country in added danger, but on the contrary, will provide added security."

Then Dulles made matters worse by proclaiming that neutrality had "increasingly become an obsolete conception and, except under very exceptional circumstances, it is an immoral and shortsighted conception."

Everything was now in a proper muddle and, to compound the confusion, on June 8 President Eisenhower was carried to Walter Reed Hospital for major surgery to correct his ailing intestine. For the next five weeks he would be absent from the levers of control; other men would cogitate and decide whether or not the United States should throw its weight in the scales on behalf of the High Dam. In particular George Humphrey, secretary of the treasury, made known his considerable misgivings. None could have been more influential. At length, on Friday, July 13, President Eisenhower was driven to Camp David for an NSC meeting.

It is fitting that the repudiation of the U.S. obligation to help Egypt build its High Dam should have come, anticlimactic, at the end of a protracted time of uncertainty. Dulles, who had first recommended the project, now announced his reversal. The recognition of China, a second big arms deal with the Soviet Union, the rumor that the new Russian foreign minister, Dmitri Shepilov, had made a tempting offer to help finance the dam—this was evidence to demonstrate that the proffer of U.S. aid for the dam had failed to keep Nasser from swinging further into the Soviet orbit. The U.S. proposal should therefore be withdrawn. Humphrey and others of the NSC who had never thought well of the idea expressed relief. In reaching his decision, President Eisenhower could reflect, in that election year, that many in both houses of the Congress were stubbornly opposed to U.S. aid for the dam. He knew also that the premiers of Britain, France, and Israel opposed it. He took the decision to renege.

Now came the Egyptian ambassador, back from Cairo with word that Nasser had dropped his request for changes in the terms of the offer: he was prepared to accept it as it stood. Hussein was received by Dulles on Thursday, July 19, and told that the U.S. government was no longer interested in the project. The British canceled their part of the agreement the next day.

In international affairs the style with which a thing is done can be as important as the thing itself. In this case the style appeared to be that of a deliberate slap in the face—or so Nasser believed, and said. In his view the worst part was the statement released to the press by the State Department, with its impeachment of Egypt's economic resources and of her financial reliability. Eisenhower had examined the statement before it was released. "I looked at it," he acknowledged later, "and it seemed all right and I said, 'All right. Go ahead.'"

The timing of the rejection was striking. The world's three leading spokesmen for neutrality in the Cold War—Tito, Nehru, Nasser—were conferring on the Adriatic island of Brioni over July 18 and 19; they were expected to issue a communiqué inviting other uncommitted nations to join them in a neutralist bloc (they did not); thus a dramatic action announced by the United States on July 19 would have psychological impact on the unaligned nations, the more so if that action answered the question as posed by Dulles: "Do nations which play both sides get better treatment than nations which are stalwart and work with us?" In short, repudiation of the American obligation was Cold Warfare. The slap in the face was calculated.

Nobody seems to have conjectured how Nasser might retort to the cancellation. Everybody involved assumed he would be angry and hurt; some few evidently hoped the rebuff might topple him from power; but Americans as well as British and French were consternated when on July 26 Nasser nationalized the Suez Canal Company.

The Suez crisis was now at hand. The world tended to blame "that awful Nasser" for the crisis or, if the provocative cancellation of the High Dam was recalled, the world tended to blame "that awful Dulles." But if any single decision can be said to have precipitated Nasser's nationalization of the canal, that decision was taken by Dwight Eisenhower, who later said: "I have never doubted the wisdom of canceling our offer."*

The Suez Canal was built, controlled, and operated by a private stock company, the Compagnie Universelle du Canal Maritime de Suez, which after a two-for-one stock split in 1924 was capitalized at eight hundred thousand shares having a par value of a trifle more than eighty dollars each. Of the company's thirty-two directors, sixteen were French, nine British, and five Egyptian; one was Dutch and one American. Forty-four percent of the stock, by far the biggest single holding, belonged to the British government. Roughly another 44 percent was privately held by various French institutions and individuals. The balance was owned by individuals of other nationalities. The company was profitable: its income in 1955 was reported to be nearly ninety-nine million dollars, and more than thirty million was distributed in dividends. (The Egyptian government was by ancient covenant paid about five million dollars.) Shares changed hands on the Bourse in Paris at better than three hundred dollars apiece in 1955: by July 1956 their value had somewhat depreciated but was rising once again.

The canal was of course far more valuable than the company, especially to a maritime nation like Britain. For the first half of the century the British had looked upon the canal as essential to their empire—the lifeline to India and the Orient—and it was an attitude they would not lightly toss aside. Still in the 1950s the canal was invaluable to their commerce. Roughly one-third of the ships to transit the canal in 1955 had been British; most of those ships were oil tankers; two-thirds of Britain's crude oil imports passed through the canal.

In these circumstances it was quite natural for the British to be emotional about a canal they had come to regard as their own, for Eden to say, as he did when he heard of Nasser's decree of nationalization: "The Egyptian has his thumb on our windpipe." What was not natural, what

* Dulles wrote Eisenhower a letter that Eisenhower approvingly cited, in which Dulles alleged: "Nasser has . . . said that he planned for nearly two years to seize the Suez Canal Company, but was waiting for a good occasion." Dulles added that Nasser had pressed for the U.S. decision on assistance for the High Dam, "and I suspect he did so in order to create the 'occasion' for which he said he was looking." This is an instance of the proclivity of western statesmen for attributing to Nasser statements he had never made. Close students of Nasser's political career and achievement know of no such statement on nationalization or seizure of the canal. See Kennett Love, *Suez: The Twice-Fought War*, pages 159–160, 320–321, 361, and elsewhere.

would indeed be impossible to justify, was for Eden and the French premier, Guy Mollet, to leap upon Nasser's wholly legal, wholly proper decree as though it were an act of international brigandage, for the British and French governments to use it as an excuse to make war.

President Eisenhower was back in the White House when Nasser issued the decree, back from the trip to Panama he had undertaken to show the country he had recovered from his operation. His health was improved, no question about it; but to an old friend who had not seen him in a year or more the changes would at once have been apparent. He was pale. He was thin. His clothes hung on him as though they had been cut for a bigger man. Along with his weight he had lost some of his buoyancy and assertive self-confidence. C. L. Sulzberger noticed these things, and spoke to the President's physician, General Snyder. "He's regained five pounds from his minimum," said Snyder. "These things go slowly." And Mamie Eisenhower reminded Sulzberger that with the ileitis behind him, Ike would be able once again to eat the chili and other spicy Mexican dishes he fancied.

On the morning of Friday, July 27, the President was at his desk early to study the cables from Andrew Foster, chargé d'affaires in London, from Eden, and from Douglas Dillon, the ambassador in Paris. He read, too, a translation of Nasser's long speech authorizing the nationalization of the Suez Canal. Later he summoned Allen Dulles, Undersecretary of State Hoover, and his staff secretary, Colonel Goodpaster. (Foster Dulles was still in South America.) In the afternoon came another cable from Eden.

The messages from overseas were hot, but Eisenhower, who had experienced his share of sudden, dismaying emergencies, was cool. He noted that Eden was already contemplating military action—"force," as Eden put it, "to bring Nasser to his senses"—and that the British Chiefs of Staff had already been instructed to prepare military plans. Eisenhower thought of these as "contingency" plans, but to Eden they were war plans and no mistake. His officers had told him about two months would be needed to mount an invasion; he would call for a partial mobilization on Thursday, August 2. He was making ready. As Eisenhower had rather expected, the French were "even more emotional" than the British; their foreign minister, Christian Pineau, like Premier Guy Mollet a socialist, compared Nasser to Hitler and wanted prompt military action to topple him.

The President had a number of objections to these hotheaded expediencies masquerading as policy. He questioned the assumption that Nasser had "unilaterally flouted a solemn treaty." He doubted the validity of Eden's assertion that the Egyptians lacked the technical ability to operate the canal efficiently.* Most important, he opposed the use of force as unjustified and as potentially destructive of the United Nations. The British and French had almost automatically dismissed any recourse to the United Nations as time-wasting and in any case futile, since a sensible solution stood in danger of being blocked by a Soviet veto in the Security Council.

At all events, inasmuch as Eden had requested an immediate meeting of the United States, the United Kingdom, and France to discuss the emergency at the "ministerial level," Eisenhower decided to send Robert Murphy to London straightway. Murphy was deputy undersecretary of state and was, as well, long acquainted with a number of the senior ministers of Eden's government and particularly with Harold Macmillan, once his counterpart as political adviser to AFHQ and now chancellor of the exchequer. The President's instructions were calm. Murphy was "to see what it's all about." He was to encourage a dispassionate assessment of the affair and to discourage impulsive armed action. "Just go over and hold the fort," the President told Murphy.

On his first evening in London, Murphy dined amicably with Macmillan and Field Marshal Lord Alexander, another old friend from the days of campaigns in North Africa. All was gracious, dignity and tradition palpable, the after-dinner brandy "admirable," the circumstances pat for disclosure of an eighteenth-century strategy. Macmillan was quite frank about British intentions to send an expedition, since "Nasser has to be chased out of Egypt" and British authority re-established; Alexander was equally candid about British war plans and his approval of them. Murphy thought all this "made good sense" and he reported it fully to the President. Two days later he relayed two "most secret" messages—from Eden and Macmillan—emphasizing that the British government had decided to "break Nasser" without further delay. "It seems," Macmillan noted in his journal on that Tuesday, July 31, "that we have succeeded in thoroughly alarming Murphy. He must have reported in the sense which we wanted, and Foster Dulles is now coming over post-haste. This is a very good development."

A good development to Macmillan, the most bellicose of Eden's ministers, but for Eisenhower a glum and depressing development, one that plunged him into despondency. True, Foster Dulles had taken plane for London and on only two hours' notice; true, at last the United States was taking seriously the Suez crisis and the extent to which that crisis was

---

* Here Eisenhower could draw on his personal experience as an army officer. Thirty years earlier he had studied the operations of the Panama Canal, a far more complex mechanism, and he was satisfied that no great technical competence was required to operate the Egyptian canal. The British disparagement of the "Gyppos" was merely the British lion of imperialism twitching its tail, and Eisenhower recognized it as such.

bringing the whole world closer to the ultimate disaster; but Eisenhower was sad, for he perceived more clearly than his old friends in Whitehall how profound was the schism now sundering a strong alliance. On Wednesday, August 1, Macmillan and Dulles talked for an hour. The Suez crisis, Macmillan argued as plainly as he could, was "a question not of honour only but survival." Later he wrote with satisfaction in his journal: "I think he [Dulles] was quite alarmed; for he had hoped to find me less extreme, I think. We *must* keep the Americans really frightened. They must not be allowed any illusion. Then they will help us to get what we want, without the necessity for force."

It is hard to imagine a grosser miscalculation of the American temper, and specifically of Dwight Eisenhower's nature, and more specifically of President Eisenhower's likely reactions during an election year. The fact that these miscalculations were made by a responsible and experienced British minister who knew Dwight Eisenhower fairly well and who was, moreover, by inheritance himself partly American raises the miscalculations to heights of scarcely credible folly.

There now ensued three months of carefully wrought schemes and diplomatic conferences; misunderstandings, deceptions, and prevarications; entanglements over legal niceties and confusions over semantic imprecisions; compromises, threats, and secret conspiracies; espionage, apprehensive transatlantic telephone conversations, armed clashes, votes and vetoes at the United Nations, and finally a haughty silence—all sliding by against the noisy background of a U.S. presidential campaign. The hectic activity masked and muddled one central dispute—would Eden make war against Nasser in the face of Eisenhower's stubborn contrariety? —and that dispute, in turn, was the veneer concealing another: whose influence, British or American, would endure in the Middle East?

Oil had been uppermost in President Eisenhower's mind when first he studied the implications of Nasser's unexpected nationalization of the canal company—oil, for without it NATO would be crippled; oil, for without it the economic security of all western Europe would be at hazard; oil, for without it much of American finance capital, at home and overseas, would be endangered. These reflections had led the President to a germinal notion for resolving the crisis: since Egypt could not be faulted for exercising her power of eminent domain over a waterway that lay under her sovereignty, perhaps the canal might be internationalized, by treaty, with Egypt's sovereign consent. Might not other nations then step in to guarantee freedom of traffic by all nations? On his return from Lima, Dulles at once appreciated the possibilities of the scheme—one sure to appeal to a lawyer—and it was thereafter in one form or another at the heart of every American attempt to deflect warfare.

First an international conference—kill time, cool off the hotheads. Invite those eight nations signatory to the Convention of Constantinople of 1888,* and those others whose shipping most often used or depended upon the canal: Australia, Ceylon, Denmark, Ethiopia, West Germany, Greece, India, Indonesia, Iran, Japan, New Zealand, Norway, Pakistan, Portugal, Sweden, and the United States. It will be seen that the list was heavily weighted in favor of the western powers and their allies and client states. Only one, the Soviet Union, was of the so-called Soviet bloc; four others—Ceylon, Egypt, India, Indonesia—were considered "neutrals."

Egypt and Greece refused to attend the conference, and sure enough, the voting on matters of substance was eighteen to four. But even before the representatives of the twenty-two nations had gathered in London, Eisenhower and Dulles deemed it prudent to refer their plans to the federal government's Foreign Petroleum Supply Committee (FPSC). Since the FPSC was comprised of senior executives of the international colossi of petroleum—Jersey Standard, Texas, Mobil, Standard of California, Gulf, Sinclair, Getty, and so on, and such of their subsidiaries as Aramco, Caltex, and Creole—it was well that its members know of the administration's concern for the supply and distribution of petroleum if the canal should be blocked or the Middle Eastern pipeline facilities disrupted. On August 14 Secretary Dulles told them "what line he expected to take at the London Conference." Their interests, although generally sympathetic with those of their British associates in the international oil cartel, were by no means identical with them. The widest divergence was in attitudes toward the canal itself. To the British the canal was vital; without it their tankers would have to journey round Africa, a route from the Persian Gulf two-thirds again as long and even costlier in time. To the Americans the canal was a convenience, no more; and for a striking reason the men of the big international companies could actually regard the loss of traffic through the canal as a blessing. Their reason arose from a long-smoldering conflict within the American petroleum industry over imports. The dispute pitted the independent oil producers against the international titans whose imports of cheap crude from Venezuela and the Middle East threatened the profits, even the survival, of the domestic producers. In the summer of 1956 the oil wells of Texas, for example, were closed down fifteen

* The Convention of 1888 was a mechanism by which the rambunctious European powers of the time prized loose Britain's military grip on the canal by neutralizing it and guaranteeing the right of transit to all nations. The signatories were nine: Austria–Hungary (the Hapsburg monarchy), Britain, France, Germany, Italy, the Netherlands, the Ottoman Empire, Russia, and Spain. The world having somewhat changed since 1888 (even Constantinople had become Istanbul), these nine were a rather different eight: Britain, Egypt, France, the Netherlands, Italy, Spain, Turkey, and the USSR.

days a month, with the regulatory state commission permitting only some eighteen barrels a day to be drawn from each well. "The torrent of foreign oil," said the chairman of the Texas commission, "robs Texas of her oil market" and of nearly a million dollars a day. Price cuts impended. From the states along the Gulf and those in the midcontinent arose a howl that was the more piteous because it was raised in an election year. Hearings were held by Arthur S. Flemming, director of the Office of Defense Mobilization, who concluded he must certify to the President that the national security was threatened by the rising influx of foreign crude. But their imports were most profitable for the giant international concerns; they wanted no federal regulation. Then fortuitously there erupted the Suez crisis. It silenced the domestic oil producers. They would have to wait for another day, when no emergency threatened to unsettle the world's supply of petroleum.

When Secretary Dulles met with the FPSC he was concerned with problems of supply and distribution, and he was also at pains to let the committee know that the Eisenhower administration would oppose any nationalization by the Arab states of concessions granted to American oil companies. Such assets, he indicated, were *"impressed with international interest,"* and if there was a takeover it "should call for international intervention." The members of the FPSC gratefully responded by constituting themselves members of a new organism, the Middle East Emergency Committee (MEEC), ready to study the needs for supply of foreign petroleum and to advise on how to meet the needs. The administration and the American members of the oil cartel had thus defined and agreed upon the most important aspect of the Suez crisis: no measure, least of all one of force, should be taken that might further excite the nationalist fevers of the Arab world.

Dulles thereafter guided the London Conference to an attempt to persuade Nasser to internationalize the canal. The effort was predestined to failure when Robert Menzies, the Australian premier, was entrusted with leadership of the deputation of five statesmen that traveled to Cairo to wait upon Nasser. Before his selection Menzies had broadcast a speech over the BBC in which he flatly asserted: "We cannot accept either the legality or the morality of what Nasser has done." He antagonized Nasser, and most of the Egyptians with whom he had dealings considered him boorish and offensive. To the astonishment of no one the mission failed, and Menzies was quick to blame President Eisenhower for the failure. Nasser had firmly rejected international controls on Wednesday, September 5; that same day Eisenhower told his press conference that "the United States is committed to a peaceful solution of this problem." Later Menzies wrote that the next day Nasser's "whole attitude had stiffened" because he had read in the Egyptian newspapers a statement of U.S. policy "which said, in headlines, that 'there must be no use of force' . . . From that time on," Menzies added, "Nasser felt he was through the period of danger." In this questionable account of what had transpired Menzies quoted what Eisenhower actually had said at his press conference one week earlier, to wit: ". . . we are determined to exhaust every possible, every feasible method of peaceful settlement. . . . We are committed to a peaceful settlement of this dispute, nothing else."*

In truth, President Eisenhower was disturbed and coldly angered by the mounting evidence that the British and French were bent on making war against Nasser no matter how forthcoming and reasonable the efforts to find a peaceful solution. On September 2 he had again warned Eden against "the use of force or the threat of force," adding, "I must tell you frankly that American public opinion flatly rejects the thought of using force," and on September 8 he reiterated those counsels even more firmly. Eisenhower would have been a great deal angrier had he known how far advanced were the plans for the invasion of Egypt. The military preparations were already buttoned up; D-day was set for September 15, with the invasion fleet leaving Malta on September 9; the soldiers and sailors and airmen were poised to take off on September 8 when Eden at the last minute postponed their operation. The delay came about because once again the United States had leaned its great weight against Eden's policy. Foster Dulles had devised a new scheme.

The President's firm and consistent opposition to their use of force first puzzled, then dismayed his friends in Britain, for they had thought to find him stalwart at their side. His allies in France, more matter-of-fact, less affected by sentiment and nostalgia, regarded Suez as only another front in their war against Nasser and Arab nationalism; they were already fighting in Algeria, now they meant to fight in Egypt as well, and Eisenhower's policies were to them of less account. As the British ministers reluctantly recognized Eisenhower's disapproval of their schemes, they succumbed to the temptation of blaming U.S. hostility on Foster Dulles: he had a hold on Eisenhower, or perhaps Eisenhower simply left to Dulles the formulation of national policy, but at all events Dulles became the symbol of their opposition. Eden had for some time been in the habit of referring to Dulles

* On September 14, on his way back to Australia, Menzies stopped off in Washington, where he is reported to have been quite as insolent to Eisenhower as he had earlier been to Nasser. He is quoted as having said to the President that his (Eisenhower's) statement to the press "had pulled the rug clean out from under his [Menzies's] feet." Eisenhower is then supposed to have retorted: "What can I do? This is a democratic country!" To which Menzies is said to have replied that the task of a President is to be a leader. This tale is reported by Hugh Thomas in his book *Suez* (Harper & Row, 1967), page 72, on the authority of "a senior officer."

as "that terrible man." Dulles now obliged by supplying Eden with instances of behavior that Eden would condemn as devious or ambiguous or deceitful.

Dulles's new scheme was for establishment of an outfit to be called the Suez Canal Users Association (SCUA). President Eisenhower regarded it as a device "for collective bargaining with Nasser . . . and for mutual assistance if the Canal and the Middle East pipeline should become wholly or partially blocked." Eden saw SCUA quite differently. As he told a tumultuous session of the Commons on September 12, SCUA would "help prepare the way for a permanent system" of control over the canal. SCUA would "employ pilots" to convoy its members' ships, collecting dues from them at rates to be determined by SCUA, and paying to Egypt only what SCUA deemed "appropriate" for the "facilities provided by her." If Egypt interfered with SCUA, Eden made clear, the British government would feel free to take further steps "through the United Nations or by other means."

As word reached Washington of the stormy debate in the Commons, one in which members of the Labour party had emphasized their rancorous opposition to Eden's warlike stance, both Eisenhower and Dulles were perturbed. Dulles was reported to have described Eden's speech as "gunboat diplomacy." He framed a statement describing SCUA and its purposes; the President read it carefully and approved it. Next day Dulles gave to a press conference this considerably more restrained interpretation of SCUA: "The idea that this is a program . . . designed to impose some regime on Egypt is fantastic," he said, adding, in answer to a question, "We do not intend to shoot our way through [the canal]. It may be we have the right to do it but we don't intend to do it as far as the United States is concerned."

Eden felt betrayed. Dulles's statement seemed to him "an advertisement to Nasser that he could reject the project with impunity." "Such cynicism towards allies," Eden wrote in his memoirs, "destroys true partnership. It leaves only the choice of parting, or a master and vassal relationship in foreign policy. . . . American torpedoing of their own plan on the first day of launching it, left no alternative but to use force or acquiesce in Nasser's triumph."

Two days before Dulles issued his statement, Eden and Mollet had privily decided to instruct the Suez Canal Company to order all its non-Egyptian personnel off the job on the night of September 14–15. The expected paralysis of the canal following the walkout of the pilots had originally been planned as the pretext for armed Anglo-French seizure of Suez, with D-day falling on September 15. Two hundred and five pilots had been employed by the company back on July 26. One hundred and fifteen of them were either British or French; only forty were Egyptian. (Of the others, most were Dutch and Scandinavian.) When the foreign pilots walked out, their job was faultlessly handled by seventy Egyptians and eleven experienced Greeks, whose government had declined to yield to the company's pressure. First Eden had fancied that nationalization of the canal company would afford an excuse for invasion, but the canal had continued to function smoothly; next he had imagined that once the experienced European pilots had departed, the Egyptians would find the task too much for them, yet still the canal was operated smoothly. "As it soon turned out," President Eisenhower would observe, "not only were the Egyptian officials and workmen competent to operate the Canal, but they soon proved that they could do so under conditions of increased traffic and with increased efficiency. . . . The assumption upon which the Users Association was largely based proved groundless. Furthermore, any thought of using force, under those circumstances, was almost ridiculous."

For Eden, most embarrassing. He had divided Britain from her alliance with the United States and, what was worse, he would now have to find some other pretext for war or else "acquiesce in Nasser's triumph."

No head of state nor minister reposed much hope in SCUA—not Dulles, not Eden, not Mollet or Pineau (who called it a scheme "pour noyer le poisson," to drown fish), not even Eisenhower, most sanguine of statesmen. It was left, though, to Dulles to drive the last nail in SCUA's coffin. Once again the occasion was a press conference. He was asked for a comment on the widespread reports of a split—between the United States on the one hand, and Britain and France on the other—over SCUA and the decision in London to establish it. His answer, slightly tidied up by State Department functionaries, touched first on SCUA: "There is talk about the 'teeth' being pulled out of it. There were never 'teeth' in it, if that means the use of force." The remark was certain to anger Eden and may well have been calculated to do so, for Dulles was vexed with the British: they had without prior consultation joined with the French in a formal request to the Security Council of the United Nations for the question of Suez to be placed on its agenda, and Dulles considered this simply asking for trouble. Next he turned to the more fundamental "difference in our approach to this problem of the Suez Canal." This difference was, as Dulles saw it, "the so-called problem of colonialism. Now there," said the secretary of state, "the United States plays a somewhat independent role" while "the shift from colonialism to independence . . . is in process" —a period of time that he was so rash as to estimate at fifty years. "I believe the role of the United States," the secretary went on, "is to see that that process moves forward in a constructive evolutionary way and does not either come to a halt or take a violent revolutionary turn . . .

744

I suspect that the United States will . . . try to aid that process, without identifying itself one hundred percent either with the so-called colonial powers or with the powers which are primarily and uniquely concerned with the problem of getting their independence as rapidly as possible."

Since, as noted above, this homily from Dulles had been carefully revised within the State Department, and, if precedent counts for anything, had been previously discussed with the President, it may be accepted as United States doctrine as of October 2, 1956, precisely five weeks before the day set for a national election. It was a doctrine that infuriated Eden and most of his Tory government, a doctrine that brought Anglo-American relations to an all-time low for the twentieth century, a doctrine—it does not seem too much to say—that served to push Britain further on her course toward collusion with France and Israel to make war on Egypt.

During this time when the alliance to which he had devoted much of his professional life was coming apart at the seams, President Eisenhower was distracted by the demands of domestic politics. At first he had contemplated making no more than five or six major campaign speeches, most of them televised addresses from Washington, but the Republican politicians clamored to get him out on the hustings, if possible to campaign in closely contested states where it was hoped some of his magic might magically be absorbed by the despondent Republican candidates, but in any case to display to the voters his restored bloom of health. In early October the GOP professionals began to experience their idiosyncratic twinges of doubt: their private polls showed a shift in voting patterns suggesting that many of those who had voted for Ike in 1952 were forsaking him in 1956. Could it be true? A two-day swing through the Pacific Northwest was suddenly tacked on to his campaign schedule and as suddenly expanded to a four-day tour that reached south to Los Angeles. As always, the President took obvious and genuine delight in the great welcoming roars of the crowds gathered to hear him. As usual, his private comments on the "mob"—"they don't want to think, they just want to yowl" —were cold and sardonic. He recognized the importance of his rolling up as big a majority as he could so that his influence with the Congress would be substantial despite the limitation on his incumbency, yet he begrudged every minute spent away from his office while dire events were impending overseas. "After all," he told his press conference one day early in October, "I have got a job here to do, and this [campaigning] isn't like establishing a summer headquarters in Denver or even staying a week in Augusta. There you can take your staff and you can operate just as effectively as you can here. But when you're out campaigning . . ."

When you are out campaigning, you cannot be abreast of developments that were, during all October, tumbling over each other, uncontrolled, an avalanche overwhelming the rigid frontiers of the Cold War. But if he had been at his desk, with intelligence reports crowding in on him hourly, President Eisenhower would still not have known how gravely the situation in the Middle East was deteriorating, and even if he had known what his allies were conspiring to do it is questionable whether he could by mid-October, have deflected them from their course.

Unknown to Washington and its corps of intelligence agents, the Israelis and the French had been—each government for its different reasons —for some time complicitous in their schemes of war against Nasser. In violation of the Tripartite Declaration of 1950, the French supply of arms to Israel was in full flood by the summer of 1956—jet aircraft, tanks, cannon and howitzers, half-tracks and trucks, rocket launchers, radar equipment—all the sinews of modern conventional warfare. On October 2, the day Dulles spoke about U.S. attitudes toward colonialism, General Dayan in Tel Aviv instructed his general staff that their tentative date for an Israeli invasion of the Sinai was October 20.

On Friday, October 5, the foreign ministers of the powers involved in the crisis gathered in New York to begin three days of debate at the Security Council. Dulles wanted to know why Selwyn Lloyd and Pineau had insisted on bringing the Suez crisis before the U.N.—was it to find a peaceful solution? or were they bent on war? They expressed their doubt that a peaceful solution could be found unless Nasser chose to yield and so permit redress of western grievances in the Middle East. Dulles disagreed vehemently. Basing his arguments on the warning letters Eisenhower had recently sent to Eden, he urged that an unnecessary resort to force was sure to make enemies for the West throughout Africa, Asia, and the Arab world.*

The debate at the U.N. was largely window dressing. Dag Hammarskjöld, dedicated to making the U.N. live up to the expectations of it, called Lloyd and Pineau to private talks with the Egyptian foreign minister, Mahmoud Fawzi (the first instance of direct negotiations since the canal company had been nationalized), and presently the conversations appeared to have been singularly promising. Lloyd dictated what came to be known as the Six Principles, Hammarskjöld wrote them down, and to everyone's astonishment Fawzi accepted them (transit through the canal

---

* As the crisis came to climax, Eden's health suffered. He told one of his advisers he had regular recourse to amphetamine pills. On this same Friday, while visiting his wife in hospital, he had a sudden bout of fever, chills and ague, and lost consciousness. He was put to bed with a temperature of 106° and kept in hospital over the weekend. But he went back to 10 Downing Street on the Monday.

without discrimination, overt or covert; the sovereignty of Egypt to be respected; operation of the canal to be insulated from the politics of any country; tolls and charges to be decided by agreement between Egypt and the users; a fair proportion of the dues to be used for development of the canal; disputes to be settled by arbitration). But the British and French had not come to the U.N. save to make what Robert Murphy called a "courtesy gesture," and as Murphy and his State Department colleagues would presently appreciate, the British and French "knew their military schedule would be disarranged if they became entangled in drawn-out procedures in New York." That would never do. Egyptian acceptance of the Six Principles made their case most awkward. Worse, President Eisenhower had broadcast the glad tidings on television, at the outset of a political broadcast—"the best announcement," he said, that "I could possibly make to America tonight." He went on:

"The progress made in the settlement of the Suez dispute this afternoon at the United Nations is most gratifying. Egypt, Britain, and France have met through their foreign ministers, and agreed on a set of principles on which to negotiate; and it looks like here is a very great crisis that is behind us. I don't mean to say that we are completely out of the woods, but I talked to the secretary of state just before I came over here tonight and I will tell you that in both his heart and mine at least, there is a very great prayer of thanksgiving."

So much for American domestic politics.

Rather than get involved in negotiations that might lead to an unsatisfactory peaceful solution, Lloyd and Pineau attached to their Six Principles a rider that added, as President Eisenhower would observe, "a note of belligerence." More, the rider was sure to make the Six Principles unpalatable to Nasser, for it embedded them in the obsolete proposals made by Menzies and in the equally obsolete scheme for SCUA, which Nasser had already rejected. Lest Lloyd find himself somehow snarled in further pacific overtures, Eden bid him take plane at once for consultations in London.

Indeed, Eden had much to consult about. Mollet had handed him a plan for the perfect pretext—airtight and waterproof—for the war against Nasser they had both been pining for.

The French scheme was one of synthesis. Together with the British they had planned an armada—Operation Musketeer—which had been first scheduled for September 15, then postponed four days, then a week, then another twelve days to October 8, then indefinitely delayed. The French had also equipped the Israelis with the armament for another invasion— Operation Kadesh—which Dayan had tentatively scheduled to begin October 20. The trick was to combine the two and synchronize them. This would not be easy, for the Israelis, in order to give deception to their mobilization southwest against Egypt, had mounted a series of slashing raids to the east against Jordan, and the British were pledged by treaty to defend Jordan against such attacks. Dayan had himself taken a hand in the raid of October 10 on Qalqilya—the biggest military action since the Palestine war—in which some fifty Jordanians had been killed while the Israelis had lost eighteen dead, with another half a hundred wounded. King Hussein had requested the British commander in the Middle East to honor his nation's pledge by ordering the RAF into action against the Israeli aircraft strafing Jordanians inside Jordan. (There was no Jordanian aviation.) Only what Eden later called "a wise and rapid exchange of cautionary messages on the spot" prevented an eerie brawl: British airplanes allied with Jordan attacking Israeli airplanes provided by France, which was allied with Britain to attack Egypt, Jordan's ally. Such was the logic of Middle Eastern politics.

The idea of combining the two operations was presented to Eden on October 14 by two French emissaries who met with Eden at Chequers, the prime minister's country house outside London. The plan called for Israel to attack Egypt across the Sinai toward the canal; Britain and France then to issue an ultimatum calling on the combatants—Israel and Egypt— to pull their troops back from the canal, ostensibly so that an Anglo-French occupation force might protect the canal from the ravages of war. Thus, on the pretext of being peacemakers, the two powers could intervene and control the canal. Eden, scarcely able to conceal his excitement, told the emissaries he would send Anthony Nutting, his undersecretary of state for foreign affairs, to Paris in two days with his answer. Nutting had been present while the emissaries were unfolding the scheme, and he was shocked by it. He perceived that Britain would be at one stroke in violation of the U.N. Charter, the Tripartite Declaration of 1950, and the treaty with Egypt of 1954; further, he sensed how such an action could snowball —the commonwealth in disarray, a powerful ally incensed, British interests in the Arab world devastated, the vital flow of petroleum halted—and these reflections led him to conclude he would resign if "this sordid conspiracy" were consummated. Eden and his senior ministers scouted these gloomy forebodings. They saw instead a more chilling alternative, "to surrender altogether," as Macmillan put it, "not only the Canal, but Western prestige in the Middle East," which in turn would lead to "Pan-Arabism, dominated by Communism, and the right flank of Europe turned. . . . unthinkable."

Eden determined to give his consent to the French scheme in person. He and Lloyd took plane to Paris at dusk on Tuesday, October 16. He likewise resolved not to apprise his American allies of his decision. He wished to show that Britain was still a power capable of bold and independent achievement, and besides he was convinced that "it was idle to hope for effective action by the United States." His senior ministers agreed. In Macmillan's view, the President "seemed unable to make up his mind. I sometimes felt," Macmillan would recall, "that both he and Dulles had lost their nerve and really believed that, if we were to act strongly, the Russians would intervene and the Third World War be launched. None of us at home had any such fears."

Eisenhower and Dulles had lost neither their nerve nor their wits. Both were sadly aware that their oldest and closest allies were mistrustful of them, but Eisenhower, canny and experienced, had seen to it that what the director of the CIA called "the tradecraft of intelligence" was ready to supplement or substitute for the friendly exchange of information among allies. When the British blackout went into effect—it seems to have been ordered on October 14—the President had available a superb instrument of espionage, the CIA's most recent and most secret contrivance, a high-altitude jet-powered glider, the U-2. Photographs showed the Israeli mobilization and proved too that Israel had at least sixty late-model Mystères—French fighter planes—although the French had told the U.S. of only twelve. In short, the French had violated the Tripartite Declaration of 1950, and the Israelis were about to make war.

Late on Monday, October 15, the President conferred with Foster Dulles, Colonel Goodpaster, and one or two others about this disquieting information. They swallowed the Israeli deception whole. They judged that Ben Gurion meant to attack Jordan, perhaps to seize the territory west of the River Jordan. Dulles remarked that in a few minutes he was to see Abba Eban, the Israeli ambassador, who had been summoned home for consultation. This presented Eisenhower with the opportunity of sending, by way of Eban, a blunt personal message to Ben Gurion. Eisenhower instructed Dulles to tell Eban: "You go out and tell Ben Gurion if any of his moves are being made because he thinks we will in effect have to support him just because we're going to have an election, you tell him first, that I don't give a damn whether I'm re-elected, and secondly, that we're going to do exactly what we've been saying [i.e., oppose the use of force], and that's that!" To Dulles the President added, "Foster, you must not soften this thing and put it in diplomatic language. This has got to be absolutely my words."

Already Eisenhower had heeded the advice of the Middle East Emergency Committee—the group of executives of the big international oil companies—and had authorized the director of defense mobilization to grant generous subsidies and mortgage insurance for the construction of big sixty-thousand-ton tankers "up to the total called for by the government's full emergency requirements." No matter what happened to the Suez Canal, the big oil companies would feel no pinch.

Early on Tuesday morning, October 16, the President took off on a five-day campaign tour of the Far West.

It is pleasant to conjecture as to what might have happened had the Eisenhower administration included a staff astrologer—always presuming, of course, that the President would have placed his reliance in that curious discipline. It was a season of portents and calamities. There were floods in India, landslides in Colombia, avalanches in the Himalayas. In Cambodia bubonic plague raged. An emerald of champion size was found but shattered during attempts to dislodge it from the quartz in which it was embedded. In Moscow Khrushchev assured U.S. Ambassador Bohlen that a solution to the Suez crisis would be found; he commended the U.S. government on its constructive and serious policy. All at once—Eisenhower being still preoccupied with domestic politics—the portents grew more ominous. And they came in clusters.

On Friday, October 19, while Eisenhower was campaigning in southern California:

From Paris Ambassador Dillon reported that an old friend, a cabinet minister, had unofficially told him of the French-British-Israeli plan for collusive war against Egypt (but his dates were wrong). Fresh sheaves of photographs taken from ten or twelve miles above Israel and Cyprus arrived, to be studied by CIA photoreconnaissance experts. CIA agents noted, on Cyprus, the military stores in the crowded harbor. From Warsaw came word that Wladyslaw Gomulka, who had been arrested and imprisoned in 1951 as a Titoist (i.e., a traitor to Stalinist "socialism"), had been freed and invited to take his former post on the central committee of the Polish Communist party; Khrushchev, who had headed a delegation of Soviet officials to Warsaw, was reported to have protested, fulminated, but at length withdrawn to Moscow. What did this portend for the success of the well-advertised U.S. policy of a rollback of international communism? A sudden heavy traffic in encoded radio signals exchanged by Paris, Algiers, and Tel Aviv was observed, and the most acute brains in the secretive National Security Agency were at once set to work to break the codes.

It was plain enough that most of these portents were of war; plain, too, that the others were of turbulent change behind the iron curtain. After his special airplane had landed at Denver on Saturday, Eisenhower spoke vaguely of Suez and of Poland: ". . . differing opinions between friends of ours . . . a critical situation . . . [and then] these captive peoples . . . Our hearts go out to them . . . if we keep strong our confidence, and above all our faith in . . . our country and our God, we will win through."

Around the world in Israel, Ben Gurion addressed a letter on this Saturday to Eisenhower. He had decided he had better keep alive the deception about Jordan, and he wrote that "the entry of Iraqi forces into Jordan," referring to an aborted display of arms by Nuri es-Said, the Iraqi strong man, "would be the first step in the disruption of the *status quo*." Israel could scarcely remain indifferent to these threats, he added, and asked that the President use his influence in the "appropriate capitals" to thwart them.

The next day, back in Washington, Eisenhower learned of the elections in Jordan that had brought to the parliament of that country a majority solidly committed to Arab nationalism, men who preferred Nasser's ideas to the alliance with Britain, who comprised what Eisenhower called an "anti-Western majority."

On Monday, October 22, all considerations of Suez and the Middle East were swept aside by the news from Hungary. The anti-Stalinist spirit had spread quickly across the border from Poland, and far more fervently. Eisenhower would later tell how from 8:36 A.M. till 6:17 P.M. he was at the center of no less than twenty-three conferences and ". . . practically all had to do with subjects directly or indirectly related to the developing Hungarian crisis."

One of Eisenhower's more remarkable talents—attested alike by his admirers and his critics—was his ability to turn without confusion or perplexity from one problem to another wholly different problem, giving each in turn his undistracted concentration. That ability was to be tested during the twenty-three conferences of this crowded Monday as never before or after in his time as President. At one moment he was the protector of peace, firm and sure; at the next he was Cold Warrior, speculating as to how he might provoke "centrifugal, disruptive currents" in the countries of eastern Europe. In short, how to keep the lid on the Middle East yet help to blow it off Hungary—and invest these contradictory procedures in the garb of one consistent national policy without seeming absurd.

As if two major sources of international tension were not enough for the world to tolerate at one time, Guy Mollet's minister of war chose this moment to issue orders for the capture of an airplane which had been chartered by Morocco and was carrying, under the protection of King Mohammed V, five Algerian nationalist leaders including Ahmed Ben Bella* to a conference in Tunisia. By a ruse the airplane was brought

* Ben Bella was the man who six years later would be released from jail to become premier of the newly independent state of Algeria.

down in Algiers and the five FLN chiefs seized and jailed. The immediate and predictable result of this folly ("We are dishonored!" cried the French president, René Coty, when he heard of it) was fury throughout the Arab world—European shops plundered in Tunis, the French consulate in Jerusalem burned, scores of Europeans slaughtered in Morocco, and strikes and riots all along the southern shore of the Mediterranean.

On this same Monday, his journey shrouded in utmost secrecy, Premier David Ben Gurion was flown from Israel to Villacoublay, an airport on the fringes of Paris. He had come to secure final agreement on the salient features of the conspiracy against Egypt.

But it was chiefly to Hungary that President Eisenhower now turned his thoughts.

The people of Hungary had some harsh goads driving them to rebel, more political than economic. They were obliged to support a costly military apparatus that gobbled too greedy a share of their national resources; a ruthless and ubiquitous secret police employed all manner of terror, bribery, and torture; the tyranny of Matyas Rákosi was supplanted, after Stalin's death and at the direction of Moscow, by the relatively compassionate regime of Imre Nagy, but Khrushchev blundered by reinstating Rákosi and keeping him in power for eighteen months. He had been ousted once again in July 1956, but memories of the happier days under Nagy clung, to be kindled by word of the successful accession of Gomulka in Poland. Meanwhile a wide diffusion of educational opportunity had waked a whole generation to the challenge of strange new ideas. In effect the country was a crate of inflammable explosives, needing only the tiniest of sparks to flare up and burst.

All this served to remind Eisenhower of the pledges he had made four years before, when first he ran for the presidency. "The American conscience," he had declared in August 1952, "can never know peace until these [enslaved] people are restored again to being masters of their own fate," and he had gone on to promise that "never shall we desist in our aid to every man and woman of those shackled lands . . . who is dedicated to the liberation of his fellows." A month later he had been more specific. He spoke of using "every political, every economic, every psychological tactic" to keep alive the spirit of freedom "in the nations conquered by communism." "Thus," he had pledged, "we shall help each captive nation to maintain an outward strain against its Moscow bond." But he had emphasized that his program was "the farthest thing from an act of war." An act, only, of Cold War.

In practice, these pledges had been honored by an incessant bombardment of the countries of eastern Europe with propaganda broadcast over the twenty-eight transmitters of Radio Free Europe.* For years this torrent of exhortation had persisted: communism was wicked, life was better and happier in the West, let freedom ring . . . And now the fruit of those years of effort; "now," as Eisenhower could note with satisfaction, "there were chains breaking in Poland and Hungary." The character of the propaganda loosed by RFE was of course determined by the CIA, and one may safely assume that on occasion it was discussed at the highest level. At all events, though the subject is still concealed under various seals of secrecy, it is not hard to trace the tenets of official dogma until they are transformed into gobbets of torn and bloody flesh. Thus:

On Monday, October 22, the students and faculties of three universities march in the streets of Budapest calling for Imre Nagy as premier. On Tuesday night Nagy is named premier, but the demonstrations continue, exciting the secret police to fire on the crowds. Rioting, ugly in temper, erupts: the great brute of force, having tasted blood, thirsts for more. Red Army soldiers, summoned by Nagy's predecessor, are blamed upon Nagy. Violence and bloodshed increase, due chiefly to the secret police. On the following Monday, after a week of revolt, announcement is made that the Soviet troops are to be withdrawn from Budapest, and on Tuesday, October 30, from the Kremlin is issued a statement of capital importance—"one of the most significant," says Allen Dulles, "to come out of the Soviet Union since the end of World War Two." The Soviet Union holds forth the objective of a "great commonwealth of Socialist nations" which can be constructed "only on the principle of full equality, respect for territorial integrity, state independence and sovereignty and noninterference in the domestic affairs of one another." The Soviet Union admits "downright mistakes," and questions whether Soviet troops should remain "on the territory of Hungary." The Soviet Union acknowledges the justice of the position taken by the working people of Hungary in demanding the elimination of "serious shortcomings in the field of economic construction," and in requiring more consumers' goods and less bureaucracy. In Budapest the statement is hailed as a victory for the forces of democratic socialism.

But meanwhile, back in Washington, Foster Dulles has been examining the cables from overseas with an expectant eye. On Saturday, October 27, he reports to the President that the Hungarian revolt is widespread. "The Nagy government in Hungary," he says, "includes a number of 'bad' people, associated with the Molotov school, and will have difficulty in attracting support."

---

* General Eisenhower had in 1950 launched the fund drive of the Crusade for Freedom to raise money for RFE. The directors of the parent organization included Allen Dulles, later director of the CIA, and C. D. Jackson, who served for a time as Eisenhower's special assistant for psychological warfare.

Word of these assumptions spreads quickly. Officials of the United Nations take note that the U.S. delegation, headed by Henry Cabot Lodge, is "active in the corridors . . . but active not in support of the Nagy government, but against it. American aides would insistently tell one that Nagy was just as bad a communist as Khrushchev, that the whole dispute was just a falling out of thieves, that the Nagy representatives at the United Nations had an appalling communist record and so on." And on Monday, October 29, word of the U.S. propaganda line having reached the Munich headquarters of Radio Free Europe, the transmitters are aimed toward Hungary to carry a vehement campaign against Nagy—"a campaign that had," in the judgment of a Hungarian communist writer who broke with his party during the rebellion and fled to Paris, "a fatal effect on all that followed." Nagy's government is characterized as a Trojan horse, and the rebels are exhorted to fight on: "Do not hang your weapons on the wall," cries the RFE broadcaster. "Not a lump of coal, not a drop of gasoline for the Budapest government, until [the ministries of] Interior and Defense are in your control."

For several reasons—not least the importunate prodding of Radio Free Europe—the nature of the revolution is altered. It swings from left to right. To the more authoritarian men in the Kremlin, this is anathema. Their pressures force a reversal of the earlier and amazing accommodation; fresh divisions of Red Army troops pour over the borders into Hungary. Nagy protests this violation of the Warsaw Pact. He is deposed and flees for shelter within the Yugoslav embassy. Soviet tanks and artillery rumble into Budapest. In the next few days more than thirty thousand Hungarians and seven thousand Red Army soldiers are killed. Scores of thousands of Hungarians take flight into Austria. The revolution is crushed.

In the corridors of the United Nations, the same members of the U.S. delegation who a fortnight before had vilified Nagy and his colleagues now mourned them as heroes and martyrs.

Anna Kethly, sixty-seven, the president of the Hungarian Social Democratic party, had been appointed delegate to the United Nations by the Nagy regime before it was overthrown. A refugee in Brussels, Miss Kethly charged in November that Radio Free Europe had "gravely sinned by making the Hungarian people believe that Western aid was coming when no such aid was planned."

At a press conference President Eisenhower was reminded by a reporter that Vice President Nixon had said on October 29 that the uprisings in Poland and Hungary had proved how right was the "liberation position" of the Eisenhower administration. He was asked, "in view of the latest developments," precisely what was that liberation position. "We have never asked," said the President, "for a people to rise up against a ruthless military force. . . . we simply insist upon the right of all people to be free to live under governments of their own choosing."

Someone in the United States had been happily inspired to call the Hungarian rebels the "freedom fighters." No matter whether the epithet was strictly accurate, it fitted into the "liberation position" of the Eisenhower administration. Back in October, after the day when he had devoted twenty-three conferences to the developing Hungarian crisis, President Eisenhower had found it necessary to devote more of his time to his other urgent affairs. On Tuesday, October 23, for example, he was obliged to acknowledge that his Democratic rival for the presidency, Adlai Stevenson, had successfully hit upon a campaign issue and had managed to puff it up so big that it demanded an answer. The issue in question was the testing of hydrogen bombs—the "super"—and Stevenson, for the best of reasons,* wanted it stopped and wanted the United States to take the lead in stopping it. Behind him quickly rallied a glittering array of scientists with unexceptionable credentials, men whom Eisenhower would later disparage with quotation marks—he would write of how "misleading statements . . . by partisans, on the advice of their 'experts,' nearly drowned the sober and largely contrary testimony . . . given by the Atomic Energy Commission and the National Academy of Sciences." Eisenhower was damned if he would let "that monkey"—his favorite counterword for Stevenson—decoy him into answering in a speech; other Republicans did that, a whole battery of them, from Nixon ("playing dangerous politics with American security") and Dewey and Wilson and Brownell to Foster Dulles, who spoke loftily of "those who are not fully conversant with the details of the problem, which have to remain to some extent confidential." Eisenhower would content himself with authorizing a statement ex cathedra, and for that purpose he summoned Dulles and Lewis Strauss to advise on the substance, and Emmet Hughes, back again as his special assistant on speeches and campaign strategy, to help shape the text.

The net effect of all these Republican orations and lucubrations was to demonstrate the obvious, for posterity if not for the voters of 1956: how any activity, no matter how lethal or how foolish, may be made to seem essential and prudent if only it is justified by the necessities of Cold War. Time has shown how wrong was Strauss about the character of the fallout from the tests of 1954 at Eniwetok; he was just as wrong about all

---

* Stevenson argued: first, tests to improve a weapon already powerful enough to "destroy the largest city in the world" were supererogatory; second, since the testing anywhere of such a weapon could be quickly detected, no inspection was required; third, "these tests themselves may cause the human race unmeasured damage."

the other tests.* Eisenhower was unhappy with his advice, once wheeling on him and exploding, "My God, we simply have to figure a way out of this situation. There's just no point in talking about 'winning' a nuclear war." He wanted some new proposals from Strauss, who had none. At length the President sourly approved the release of a reassuring statement: "The continuance of . . . H-bomb testing—by the most sober and responsible scientific judgment—does not imperil the health of humanity. . . . We must continue—until properly safeguarded international agreements can be reached—to develop our strength in the most advanced weapons—for the sake of our own national safety, for the sake of all free nations, for the sake of peace itself."

Folly. All over the world the silent mortal wounds would go on being inflicted, untraced, scarcely noticed save by those few who examine the gradual shifts in the statistics of death rates—an increase in this column, a diminution in that one. And in the 1950s, few dared to suggest that some of the growing number of those who contracted cancer formed part of the casualty lists of the Cold War.

The reasssuring statement was handed to reporters on Wednesday, October 24. Early that same day Eisenhower was told of the resignation of Sir Walter Monckton as Eden's minister of defense because he believed Eden's scheme for war against Egypt to be "a great blunder." It is a measure of how ill-informed Eisenhower was of his closest ally's affairs that he learned of the event fully thirteen days after the fact of it, and then only because someone dropped a remark at a cocktail party.

Wednesday, October 24. In two weeks the demands of the political campaign would have dissipated; in two weeks, saving some hideous mischance, Eisenhower would be triumphantly returned to office and with a greater majority of votes than in 1952.

Wednesday, October 24. On that day, in the Paris suburb of Sèvres, the articles of conspiracy were signed on behalf of the governments of Britain, France, and Israel. Ben Gurion had demanded a British signature on the document to ensure that the British would live up to their undertakings. The text of the ultimatum that the British and French were to issue, once

* Strauss wrote that the Marshall Islanders had been "placed under continuous and competent [medical] supervision" and that he was informed by the medical staff that "they anticipated no illnesses." A medical check in 1957, Strauss wrote confidently, showed "no deaths"; those exposed to radiation were "found to be in good health." In short, as Strauss believed, radiation was of no account and the tests should be, with proper precautions, continued. Nevertheless, the radiation from those tests had marked some of those Islanders for sure death. Sentence had been passed, execution would follow more slowly. One death from leukemia, unmistakably linked to the tests, was reported as long as eighteen years later; the victim had been an infant one year old when first exposed.

the Israeli troops had approached the canal zone, had been agreed upon. Plans were at last complete.

President Eisenhower now found himself in a very odd dilemma. He knew in a general way about the imminent hostilities; he desired to abort them, and surely he had the power to do so—but precisely what was to be stopped? and when? and where? and how could he stop whatever it was without characterizing his friends and allies as liars?

At this juncture the governments of Egypt, Jordan, and Syria announced that they had agreed to pool their military strength, and in the event of war with Israel would place their armies under Egyptian command. Ben Gurion seized upon this announcement as proof that Israel was in "direct and immediate danger."

In Washington the obligations of the presidential campaign intruded on Eisenhower, but his chief anxiety, dwarfing even the alarms over Hungary, arose from the mounting tension in the Middle East and the threat it posed to the essential flow of petroleum. Just offstage, the oil company executives of the Middle East Emergency Committee were likewise watchful and concerned. Eisenhower was, though, still also obsessed by the menace of international communism. At the regular meeting of the NSC on Friday there was much speculation about the men in the Kremlin. Allen Dulles reported that recently Khrushchev had been observed at a reception in Moscow and never had he looked so grim. "His days," said Dulles, "may well be numbered." Around the table cabinet officers and military chiefs stirred and pondered. These were dangerous times. The President warned that the Soviet Union, its grip on Poland and Hungary having been loosened, "might be tempted to resort to extreme measures, even to start a world war." His colleagues were grave. "This possibility," said the President, "we must watch with the utmost care." They then turned back to the Middle East.

To know that momentous events impended and yet be ignorant of their thrust and even their schedule was intolerable, the more so since they seemed to have been stirred up by old friends and close allies. What the hell was going on? Eisenhower decided he must address himself to Ben Gurion, since the Israeli mobilization was now plainly well advanced, with no corresponding activity in the Arab countries neighboring. The President's cabled message was dispatched at 12:25 P.M. on Saturday, 7:25 P.M. in Tel Aviv: "I renew the plea," Eisenhower said, in unmistakably monitory terms, "that there be no forcible initiative on the part of your government which would endanger the peace and the growing friendship between our two countries." He was then driven to Walter Reed Hospital for the physical examination deemed advisable by the Republican politicians so that the voters might be reassured, with the election only ten days away, that he was bursting with good health.

What else could be done by the chief executive of the most powerful nation on earth? From the hospital he instructed Foster Dulles to summon Abba Eban, the Israeli ambassador, and question him closely as to what the Israeli mobilization portended. He sent orders overseas to Winthrop Aldrich, his ambassador in London, to question British ministers to the same end. Amid all the tests and X rays at Walter Reed, taking time from the series of wheelchair excursions back and forth along hospital corridors —"Israel and barium make quite a combination," he commented acidly —he cabled Ben Gurion another admonition, making clear he would invoke the Tripartite Declaration, which bound the U.S., Britain, and France to squash any violation of the Egyptian-Israeli frontiers. In view of what he already knew, this second message would seem to have been his careful way of placing his government unequivocally on the record. He also authorized the State Department to advise any Americans "who are not performing essential functions" to leave the Middle East "as a matter of prudence." The Sixth Fleet steamed eastward to take these citizens aboard.

Eban told Dulles he knew nothing of what was going on in Israel save for the routine defensive precautions against the murderous raids by the fedayeen, presumably from Jordan.* In London, on Sunday night, Aldrich had Selwyn Lloyd to dinner at the embassy in Grosvenor Square. Aldrich asked specifically whether Israel planned to attack Egypt. Lloyd answered that he had no information on the matter. Aldrich pressed him, remarking that Washington had intelligence of such an assault. Lloyd insisted he knew nothing of it. Britain, said Lloyd, was more disquieted by the possibility of an attack on Jordan. These lies having been duly pronounced, Aldrich could only relay to Washington his lively suspicions.

"I just can't believe it," Eisenhower said that night, of the hints that the British might have joined the French in supporting Israel's belligerence. "I can't believe they would be so stupid . . ."

Another few hours, and Dayan would be visiting the room where Ben Gurion lay sick—another statesman ill as the Suez crisis came to climax —abed with four degrees of fever from a respiratory infection he had picked up at Sèvres. Ben Gurion was composing his reply to Eisenhower's cables. Later, in the last hours before he ordered his troops into action,

* The careful records kept by the United Nations Truce Supervision Organization show that from January 1, 1955, to September 30, 1956—roughly the period from Ben Gurion's resumption of leadership as minister of defense to the Israeli-French collusion against Egypt—border incidents had resulted in the death of one hundred and twenty-one Israelis as against four hundred and ninety-six Arabs, a ratio of roughly one to four.

Dayan would permit himself some scoffing comments on the "sterility" of U.S. policy and the "hollowness" of Eisenhower's two cabled warnings. They showed, Dayan wrote in his diary, that Eisenhower "thinks the imminent conflict is likely to erupt between Israel and Jordan and that Britain and France will cooperate with him in preventing this. How uninformed he is of the situation!"

Quite true: the diplomatic courtesies required of Eisenhower that he seem uninformed.

On Monday morning, October 29, while he was airborne for a campaign speech in Miami, Eisenhower was uninformed that Israeli paratroops screened by French Air Force Mystères had been dropped into the Sinai thirty miles east of Suez. He was still uninformed that other Israeli task forces were poised to knife west and south into Egypt. He did not yet know that hostilities had begun.

News of the invasion traveled slowly. The Sinai was a rocky waste, inhabited chiefly by Bedouins; Israeli raids were commonplace, and perhaps this was only another such, probing somewhat deeper than usual. Journalists in London did not learn of it for six hours; Eisenhower was not told of it till his airplane landed at Richmond, Virginia, a few minutes before 6 P.M., fully eight hours later.

Now at last he knew the target and the timing. Now the problem had been presented. He issued instructions as to who should await him at the White House to discuss what had to be done, and then, imperturbable, he went ahead with his last campaign speech of the day.

The Dulles brothers, Hoover of State, Wilson of Defense, Admiral Radford, and two or three others had been assembled by Colonel Goodpaster when the President's automobile slid up to the back entrance of the White House in the evening gloom. The time for surprises was past. Eisenhower had only to make sure his chief aides were agreed on what he had in all likelihood already decided to do: insist upon an immediate cease-fire. First, as to the Israelis. "All right, Foster," Eisenhower would later recall instructing his secretary of state, "you tell 'em that, goddamn it, we're going to apply sanctions, we're going to the United Nations, we're going to do everything that there is so we can stop this thing." Next, as to the British and French. This was trickier. In its broad design collusion was obvious enough, and even its details were beginning to come clear, but to an experienced soldier like Eisenhower it "looked clumsy." He still did not know the timetable of the operation, but he recognized an intervention that was political and for that reason lacking in military efficiency. Despite what he had learned of the complicity at least of the French, he was obliged to assume that the British proposed to honor their obligations under the Tri-

759

partite Declaration. It seemed therefore routine to summon the British chargé d'affaires, J. E. Coulson, and acquaint him with U.S. intentions to invoke the declaration. "We will stick to our undertaking," the President told Coulson. That meant, if necessary, the use of military force. "Would the United States not first go to the Security Council?" Coulson inquired. "We plan to get to the United Nations the first thing in the morning," said Eisenhower shortly. "When the door opens. Before the USSR gets there."

The cease-fire Eisenhower was determined to put through took eight days to realize. It was achieved by means of remorseless pressures coldly exerted by the President on a British government the leaders of which were his ancient friends and comrades. During those eight days, despite occasional provocations, the President remembered the injunctions of his physicians and kept his temper—with only one or two lapses.

The first day, Tuesday, October 30, was the worst. It began with the arrival of Ben Gurion's answer to Eisenhower's warnings, a deceptive and evasive answer in which he spoke of the "ring of steel" that Nasser had forged around Israel, apparently unaware that the President had sharp eyes in the skies above Israel and her neighbors, quite able to perceive where the steel was and where it was pointed. As the day wore on, Eisenhower and Eden exchanged several cabled messages, with growing asperity on both sides. In the process the President learned that the British considered the Tripartite Declaration to be "ancient history" and "without current validity." It was not from Eden, though, that Eisenhower learned of the deceptive ultimatums issued by the governments of Britain and France ostensibly to bring to an end the hostilities that had not yet reached the canal zone. He learned of that development from the news tickers. It was an unforgivable affront. For a friend and ally to send lengthy messages across the ocean without so much as hinting at the grave step he was about to take, a step in violation of a shared responsibility and taken at the very time when the matter was under consideration by the Security Council of the United Nations, was certain to turn Eisenhower's amiability to flint. The air in his oval office, they said, became briefly a blue haze, and by the empathic process that operates around a well-loved personage, presently the indignation among the members of his staff was palpable enough, said one of them, "to suffocate the White House." The President was very angry, but it was a carefully frigerated wrath. From that moment Eden's ambitions were destined to go smash.

Nor were matters improved when, in the Security Council chamber, the resolution offered by Lodge, which called for an immediate cease-fire and required "all members" to "refrain from the use of force or threat of force in the area," was vetoed by Britain and France—the first veto by Britain in the history of the U.N. The same such vetoes, a few minutes later, likewise defeated a somewhat milder Soviet resolution that also sought a cease-fire.

For Eisenhower—as for the MEEC—the notion of a western nation athwart the Suez Canal by force, by strength of arms, was a nightmare. It was sure to rouse further the fevers of nationalism among the Arabs, and then—more nationalization of oil fields, pipelines sabotaged, NATO immobilized, and just when chains were snapping in Poland and Hungary. It was too bad of the British and French; folly; it must be stopped. Beginning on Wednesday, the last day of October, there was an increased sale of sterling, absorbed by the Bank of England; this led to further sharp selling and speculation. Men, munitions, and money are needed to wage a war. Britain had the men and the munitions. In September, her gold and dollar reserves had begun to melt. They dwindled faster in October. Early in November they began to drain away at a frightening rate. "This cost of war," Eisenhower would later observe, straight-faced, "was not irrelevant."

On that Wednesday the President broadcast a report to the people—not political, he insisted, simply an assessment of his search for peace in a time when violent change had come to Hungary and the Middle East. A first draft of his speech had been prepared by Foster Dulles and sent to the White House in mid-afternoon, but it was unsatisfactory. The President quickly sketched to Emmet Hughes the outline for a fresh approach; Hughes rushed to work with two secretaries in the cabinet room; Dulles came over to review the fresh typescript—to Hughes's eye he was "ashen gray, heavy-lidded, strained"; under great time pressure they strove to complete a final draft. In the White House press room, cater-cornered across the west wing, the news tickers chattered, feeding out their running accounts of the air raids then in progress by British bombers on Cairo and the airfields near the city. On the lawn off to the south the President relaxed by hitting golf balls in the pale autumnal sunlight. The broadcast was to begin at 7 P.M. Fifteen minutes before the hour the President, freshly dressed, joined Hughes in the cabinet room, taking the speech from him page by page. Four minutes before broadcast time he accepted the last page with a grin: "Boy, this is taking it right off the stove, isn't it?" Before the television cameras he was calm and self-assured: ". . . it is—and it will remain—the dedicated purpose of your government to do all in its power to localize the fighting and to end the conflict. . . . In the past the United Nations has proved able to find a way to end bloodshed. We believe it can and that it will do so again."

About noon on Thursday, November 1, Nasser spoke with the U.S. ambassador, Raymond A. Hare. He asked Hare to tell President Eisenhower that Egypt was under attack by Israel, Britain, and France, and that he was asking for the help of the United States. It was then about

5 A.M. in Washington. Nasser later told of an exchange of messages. "Then they [presumably the U.S. State Department] asked me: 'Are you asking our help in order to ask the Russians if we refuse?' I told them: 'I haven't asked the Russians.'" Nasser got his answer from Washington the next day. It was "that of course America cannot go to war against their allies but that they will do all they can to solve the problem in the United Nations—supporting the United Nations." Nasser was disappointed—at first.

In Washington the President had indeed resolved to pursue the demand for a cease-fire at the United Nations, with the difference that the U.S. resolution would this time be offered before the General Assembly, the Security Council having been hobbled by the Anglo-French vetoes. "It is nothing less than tragic," said Foster Dulles, of the schism now separating the U.S. from her allies. But as the President, once more on the campaign trail, said that night in a speech in Philadelphia, "we cannot and we will not condone armed aggression—no matter who the attacker, and no matter who the victim. We cannot—in the world, any more than in our own nation—subscribe to one law for the weak, another law for the strong . . . There can be only one law—or there will be no peace."

The debate at the United Nations lasted late into the night, with Dulles personally presenting the case for the U.S. resolution. The President wanted a vote taken as soon as possible, so Dulles kept his post at the General Assembly, faithfully maintaining the pressure. The vote came at 2 A.M. on Friday, and the U.S. resolution was carried sixty-five to five, only New Zealand and Australia joining the conspirators in opposing it.

Sometime during the same night Syrian army engineers destroyed three pumping stations of the pipelines of the Iraq Petroleum Company, which was owned by a consortium of British, French, and American oil interests. Those pipelines had a capacity of five hundred thousand barrels a day— no longer. Earlier on Thursday, British bombers had sunk the *Akka*— she was an old surplus U.S. Army LST—which the Egyptians had loaded with cement and maneuvered in such fashion as to block the canal if sunk. So Eden's scheme to protect the canal from the ravages of war was thwarted by his own bombers. No more petroleum through Suez.

On Friday evening, while playing backgammon with his wife at their home near the Washington Cathedral, Foster Dulles experienced pains that led him to be hospitalized in Walter Reed. There, next morning, in a long operation, an adenocarcinoma was found and a section of his large intestine removed.

The weekend was the time of Eisenhower's great frustration. The leadership of the Soviet Union, having painfully wrangled through the necessary debates, had concluded that they must reverse their astonishing statement of October 30 projecting a "socialist commonwealth," and were moving to crush the Hungarian revolution. Simultaneously the western alliance was riven by the insistence of the British and French on hastening their collusive invasion of Egypt. The Anglo-French armada—one hundred warships and troop transports—was nearing the Egyptian coast even as a half-dozen armored divisions of the Red Army were clattering toward Budapest. As a shield to blunt these two aggressive thrusts the President of the United States had whatever moral strength could be summoned up by the United Nations—an organization which in the postwar years had at the insistence of the great powers been converted from a potential guardian of global peace into their docile creature.

Now the matter of Hungary was to come before the Security Council of the U.N., and Lodge had been armed with another resolution, one that bid the Soviet Union "desist forthwith from any form of intervention." The President was informed that Britain and France wished to be associated with the U.S. resolution. Absurd! said the President on Saturday, but the next day he observed that if the British would only countermand their invasion of Egypt, they would be welcome as co-sponsors of the resolution. No chance: Eden was bent on Nasser's destruction: "If we draw back now," he cabled Eisenhower, "everything will go up in flames in the Middle East," and he spoke of the invasion as a "police action." Haste was needed because of the outcries of protest from all over the world, not least in London and in the House of Commons itself, so the colluders had instructed the military to drop paratroopers at the northern end of the canal a day ahead of the amphibious invasion. Word of the drop—at dawn of Monday, November 5—awaited Eisenhower at his desk and confirmed him in his resolve to halt the violence.

The banks and exchanges being once again open, the brisk selling of sterling was resumed around the world, driving the pound further down. Most of the heavy trading was in New York, and this provoked speculation as to whether the attack on the British reserves had come on cue from George Humphrey, secretary of the treasury, or perhaps from an even higher level. At least Humphrey was well informed of developments, and so was the President.

The only pipeline functioning was that of the Trans-Arabian Pipe Line Company (TAPline), from Saudi Arabia to Lebanon, with a capacity of three hundred and twenty thousand barrels a day. TAPline was owned by four American firms—Jersey Standard, Socony Mobil, Texaco, and Standard of California—but King Saud's royal displeasure would have been incurred if any crude oil from his country were to find its way to Britain or France. No petroleum could be carried through the canal. What Eden had called a "police action" bid fair to deprive Europe and NATO of essential petroleum.

These considerations were at the top of the agenda in Eisenhower's office at mid-morning. Hoover confirmed that TAPline alone was carrying oil. NATO's supply, he said, was in jeopardy. Eisenhower issued instructions about heavy tankers and the fleet oilers of the U.S. Navy. Go slow, he directed, with help for the British and French. A question was raised about the Soviet Union: were they likely to send armed forces into Syria? Eisenhower shook his head. The airfields were inferior, he said. But Allen Dulles should be asked to send U-2s on a perfunctory mission of verification.

Later that day the President was handed a message that occasioned another brief, abrupt explosion of temper. The message was from Bulganin, and what momentarily enraged Eisenhower was that the Russian, so recently involved in the bloody suppression of Hungarian rebels, was proposing the "joint and immediate use" of American and Soviet air and naval forces to "crush the aggressors and restore peace" in the Middle East—"backed by a United Nations decision." "If this war is not stopped," Bulganin argued, "it is fraught with danger and can grow into a third world war."

Once again icily calm, the President summoned a group of advisers—Hoover and Herman Phleger from the State Department among them, filling in for the hospitalized Foster Dulles—and swiftly drafted a public statement in lieu of a formal reply. Bulganin's proposal was "unthinkable"; it was "an obvious attempt to divert world opinion from the Hungarian tragedy"; any Russian intervention in the Middle East would be immediately met with determined opposition by the United States.

That night Bulganin sent stern warnings to Israel, Britain, and France. Toward Eden he brandished rockets presumably armed with atomic warheads. Of Mollet, a socialist, he demanded an explanation as to how the precepts of socialism could be squared with the waging of an "open colonial war." Ben Gurion he admonished that Israel was "sowing a hatred . . . among the peoples of the East . . . which puts in jeopardy the very existence of Israel as a state." Those messages were broadcast from Radio Moscow even as the President was conferring with his aides on the statement he proposed to release to the press and radio. Once again, as so often in the course of the Cold War, ordinary citizens cringed, wondering in which dark night death might come unannounced, pouncing sudden and, they hoped, as painless as the wink of an eye.

The effect of Bulganin's warnings on the resolution of the crisis is debatable, but they seem certainly to have been a ponderable factor. Eden, confronted by disunity within his own cabinet (one senior and two junior ministers had already resigned, and others were said to be contemplating the step), was sorely troubled and very weary. Late that night he telephoned Mollet at least twice, first to discuss Bulganin's messages, later to recommend that their two governments agree to a cease-fire. Mollet wished assurances from the highest possible level in Washington—from President Eisenhower himself if that could be arranged—that the United States would respond if the Russians attacked the British and French invasion forces in Egypt, which was well beyond the NATO area.

At the time Mollet was putting these questions to Douglas Dillon, the American ambassador in Paris, the President was in the White House library talking on a closed television circuit to a group of his supporters in Boston. It was election eve. He had one last televised speech to make in the last minutes before midnight. These were only formal gestures. He wanted to win the election, of course, and with a thumping majority, and he expected he probably would; but he proposed to waste no energy on worry or agitated conjecture about its outcome.

On that election eve he was, as well, exerting all the pressures he could on the three aggressors. Economic sanctions on Israel would have been, in the closing days of the election campaign, far too risky, but there were other inducements available. Golda Meir was then Israel's foreign minister, and it was known that she was anxious to abide by the General Assembly demand for a cease-fire. As for Britain, her gold reserves had fallen within a week by one hundred million pounds (almost two hundred and eighty million dollars) and in New York on that Monday sterling had been offered for sale in huge blocks; later Eden would reckon that the run on the pound had reached "a speed which threatened disaster to our whole economic position." Nor was Eisenhower in any hurry to respond to Mollet's urgent petitions for a U.S. military shield covering the Middle East as well as the lands guaranteed by NATO. In short, the screws had been turned about as far as they could go.

On Tuesday morning, election day, the chief candidate was at his desk early, to learn that British and French assault troops had landed at the northern end of the canal. Presently Allen Dulles arrived, together with Hoover and a few others, bringing the latest intelligence reports: the Soviets seemed to be up to something, just what was not clear. Once again the President authorized Dulles to send the U-2s over Syria and Israel, but, he added, *not* over the Soviet Union. "If the Soviets should attack Britain and France directly," he said, "we would of course be in a major war." The United States would, he went on, take military action even though the Congress was not in session to vote its approval of such a course. The prospect of Soviet intervention raised additional questions. If Russian aircraft were found to have landed on Syrian airfields, should the British and French not take steps to destroy them? The President thought so, and he wanted as well to find out if the U.S. Sixth Fleet was equipped with atomic antisubmarine weapons. There were other measures to be looked to so that the nation might be militarily ready for action: he directed that they be attended to at once.

Rumors that fed alarm were abroad over Washington. Murphy would recall a staff meeting in the State Department at which an eminent official —not, Murphy noted smugly, a foreign service officer—exclaimed, "We must stop this before we are all burned to a crisp!" As the rumors spread along the bureaucratic grapevine, Eisenhower's precautions may have contributed to the sense of dismay in the capital, but the commander in chief was himself calm and wary. He was satisfied that the Russians neither wanted a general war nor, for geographical reasons, were in a position to start one. In mid-morning his wife and he were driven the eighty miles to Gettysburg to vote.

In Britain that day Macmillan told the cabinet he could "not any more be responsible for Her Majesty's exchequer" unless a cease-fire were ordered. He had made a last attempt to relieve the pressure on the pound by requesting a transfer of money from the International Monetary Fund. The request was, as he later put it, "referred to Washington," by which he meant that the directors of the Fund would not permit Britain to withdraw her quota of the Fund's capitalization without the approval of the U.S. government. (In virtue of its preponderant share of the Fund's capitalization, the voice of the U.S. director was decisive in such a transaction.) U.S. approval, Macmillan had been told, was conditional upon British agreement to the cease-fire. It was the final turn of the screw.

President Eisenhower returned to Washington by helicopter about noon. He was met by Colonel Goodpaster, who brought him news of Eden's capitulation.

Back in the White House, he listened as Radford read off a list of twenty or thirty steps recommended by the Joint Chiefs to achieve a military alert. He commented, questioned, glanced at intelligence reports, suggested, issued instructions—but his mind was elsewhere, in London, where Eden had at last come to terms.

A new transatlantic cable had that day been put into service. The President required that he speak to the prime minister. Presently he was told that his call had been put through. "Hello," he said. "Anthony." He listened. "This is a very clear connection," he said. "First of all, I can't tell you how pleased we are that you found it possible to accept the cease-fire—having landed." They discussed the mechanics of the United Nations caretaking force that was to be sent to Egypt to guard the peace. Eden hoped Americans would be included in the force, but Eisenhower wanted "none of the great nations in it," because "I am afraid," he said, "the Red boy is going to demand the lion's share." Eden was on his way to report his decision to the Commons. "If I survive here tonight," he said, "I will call you tomorrow. How are things going with you?" "Oh," said the President carelessly, "we have given our whole thought to Hungary and the Middle East. I don't give a damn how the election goes. I guess it will be all right."

The cease-fire began at midnight, Greenwich time.

The nation elected Eisenhower to a second term as President; more than 57 percent of the voters preferred him to Stevenson. But the Democrats retained control of both Houses of the Congress.

The shooting had been stopped, and without question it was President Dwight Eisenhower who had stopped it. But the Suez crisis remained.

The problem was to pull the Middle East back into approximately the status quo ante; that is, to get the British, French, and Israeli troops out of Egypt and to get the canal and the pipelines back into operation. In turn, this meant that the United States, through the agency of the United Nations, had to make the three allies disgorge the fruits of their military victory, in order to demonstrate for all the world to see that to make war is bad policy. Disgorge: it was the word Foster Dulles had used more than three months before when he had told Eden that Nasser must be made to "disgorge" the Suez Canal. A vivid word; Eden would later reproachfully recall that it "rang in my ears for months," while the United States government was bidding him to cease and desist from the use of force. It had not been intended as programmatic when Dulles blurted it; rather, as his associates in the State Department had observed, Dulles was given to sudden exclamations of an explosive kind, usually to relieve the tensions of a difficult discussion. "Perhaps," as Robert Murphy conjectured, "Dulles wanted to show some sympathy, which I am certain he felt, for our allies' indignation about Nasser." An unfortunate impulse for a secretary of state; unfortunate, too, that Eden had not been schooled to recognize it and discount it as such.

At all events, Eisenhower had now to work—through his deputies and through the United Nations—to force the British, French, and Israelis to disgorge. What had their spasm of violence accomplished? At least three lessons were writ large for the pages of history:

ONE: The state of Israel, which had been born in the Promised Land—the land, as the bitter jest had it, too often promised—was a full-fledged modern state, come to stay, and quite ready to demonstrate her sovereignty with a first-rate fighting force, tough, well led, well trained, well equipped, and superbly opportunist.

TWO: It was a fact, as Harold Macmillan had recognized, "that France and Britain, even acting together, could no longer impose their will." To Macmillan that fact was alarming: "Never before in history had Western

Europe proved so weak." The world had changed. Power had spurted out of its traditional grooves, spurted and skidded away, to follow the beck of the rich and strong, the cruel and destructive.

THREE: The way lay open for the United States to assert that her national interests demanded peace and stability throughout the Middle East and, per corollary, that the Soviet Union should keep hands off. In short, the attempt would be made to congeal the complexities of Middle Eastern politics into the rigid postures of the Cold War.

These lessons—self-evident, incontrovertible—nevertheless carried within them odd contradictions. While it was true that Britain and France could no longer even in concert impose their will on the course of international affairs, Britain alone could exercise a restraint amounting to veto on the schemes of her stronger, richer ally, as two years before in Indochina, as a year before in respect to Quemoy and Matsu. And while it was plain to Eisenhower that the time had come for the United States to press her dominion in the Middle East, the Congress might withhold approval of his ventures there if at the same time he presumptuously compelled Britain and France and especially Israel to disgorge their military conquests.

All this, as the devoted Sherman Adams perceived, "placed Eisenhower in an embarrassing and worried dilemma." He was anxious to mend the shattered Anglo-American alliance, of which his career was, he knew, a symbol, and the obvious way to go about it was to succor Britain's straitened economy with massive transfusions of cash and credit, and at once to replenish her supply of petroleum, now disrupted by her ill-advised adventure at Suez. But he would not authorize those actions, not yet, not while hostile troops still occupied Egyptian soil. The United Nations had voted sixty-five to one (Israel alone opposed; Britain, France, and eight others abstained) to order the invaders out, and until they complied the President was determined to withhold his hand.

Eden was dismayed. He had not foreseen that "the United States Government would harden against us on almost every point and become harsher after the cease-fire than before." In vain he sought an escape from the net of economic sanctions; in vain Harold Caccia, the new British ambassador in Washington, appealed to George Humphrey to relax the iron controls clamped down on the International Monetary Fund. Humphrey made it clear that Britain would get not a penny till her soldiers were out of Egypt. Pineau was in Washington, incognito, conferring privily with Allen Dulles and Admiral Radford at the French embassy: could the Americans not be made to realize the terrible threat of a Russian presence in the Near East and the Middle East? the meaning of all the Russian armaments sent to Nasser and captured by the Israelis? the menace of communist fingers reaching out to snatch the vast resources of oil? But still President Eisenhower withheld his hand.

The President's moral posture—his insistence on principle, on support for the United Nations, against armed aggression, and on one law alike for the strong and weak—particularly exasperated his allies, who were quick to perceive its inconsistencies. One law? But if sanctions were to be invoked against those who had warred on Egypt, why not against those who had warred on Hungary? If Eisenhower condemned aggression "no matter who the attacker, and no matter who the victim," how justify the CIA-supported aggression against Guatemala? and how justify Lodge's tactics to prevent that aggression even being placed on the agenda of the U.N. Security Council? "When this point was put to the United States officials," Eden noted acidly, "they had no answer."

U.S. policy thus was manifestly hypocritical. The *New York Times* commenced an editorial article by quoting Matthew VII, 5: "Thou hypocrite, first cast out the beam out of thine own eye; and then shalt thou see clearly to cast out the mote out of thy brother's eye." Britain announced on November 20 a program of compulsory rationing of fuel oil and gasoline; France had already done the same, as had Sweden, Norway, Denmark, Italy, and Turkey. At a reception in Moscow, Khrushchev surveyed the Suez affair and the splintered western alliance with satisfaction. The invasion of Suez had been, he observed, a "hopeless attempt to restore lost colonial bastions." Warming to his theme, he declared: "History is on our side," and addressing himself specifically to the capitalists of the world, he predicted, "We will bury you." In Britain, in France, throughout western Europe, animosities were roused against the United States. Pineau expressed French "bitterness." In London more than one hundred Tory members of Parliament deplored U.S. policy as "gravely endangering the Atlantic alliance."

Eisenhower was unmoved. By November 26 he had at last been able to get away for a holiday at Augusta National; the next day he issued a statement from his temporary White House: the "differences" which had arisen "from a particular international incident . . . in no way should be construed as a weakening or disrupting of the great bonds" that united the U.S., Britain, France, and other allies. The NATO alliance, he added, was still "a basic and indispensable element of American defense alliances."

A suitably decorous statement, but just before the President had left for Augusta, Herbert Hoover, Jr., had insistently relayed to him from the State Department the growing European sense of betrayal, the European suspicion that the U.S. government was using the Suez affair as a device to buttress American oil companies in the Middle East at the expense of their British colleagues within the international oil cartel. Indeed, some observers had long since concluded that it was not hypocrisy, but rather oil, that had supplied the motive power for U.S. policy throughout the Suez crisis. Yet the Middle East Emergency Committee, the group composed of executives of the fifteen biggest American companies with international interests, had for some time been in suspension, adjourned sine die. Most of the industry, according to a memorandum circulated within the Socony Mobil Company, had been "strongly urging that MEEC be reactivated," but the Eisenhower administration had "simply refused." This could only have meant that the oil industry was engaged in an internecine war, and so it was: the integrated, internationalized titans importing crude from Venezuela and elsewhere, so that it might be profitably refined within the United States, arrayed against the domestic oil producers, who still sought federal controls on the imports so that—the supply being sensibly limited —the price of their own crude might once again soar. Certainly one consideration influencing the President was the fear that should he seem too eager to bail the British and French out of their predicament, American oil interests in the Middle East would be jeopardized.

Timing was everything, a delicate matter: move slow, and so keep the friendship of the Arabs; but not too slow, lest the NATO alliance collapse. Gauge the pressures most carefully: reports of rationing, long-range forecasts of winter weather in Europe, statistics on closings of European factories and refineries, dwindling of gold reserves in European central banks. So ticklish the test, so equivocal the response.

By Wednesday, November 28, the pressures in Britain were close to bursting. Eden, exhausted, had withdrawn to Jamaica at the urgent suggestion of his physicians; in his absence Selwyn Lloyd, it was agreed, would announce to the Commons on Monday, December 3, the withdrawal of British and French forces from Suez without delay. Since the Conservative government would need in advance some scrap of good news to palliate this confession of defeat, Eisenhower concluded that the U.S. should publicly implement the plan, developed months before by MEEC, by which five hundred thousand barrels of oil would be daily shipped to Europe. The presidential directive was pronounced on Friday, November 30.

The Suez crisis now began to abate. But still it simmered, now and again it bubbled to a low boil, for the Israelis had yet to agree to be dislodged from the land they had conquered in Sinai and in the Gaza Strip. For Eisenhower to convince Ben Gurion that war was bad policy would be hard. Their national interests differed.

With British and French influence in the Middle East down the drain, President Eisenhower had concluded that the United States must fill what all around him called a "power vacuum." While he sojourned at Augusta, his staff experts of the State Department and National Security Council sweated to shape a plan to safeguard the U.S. national interests (viz., the oil) and to block any venturesome exploit in the region by the Soviet Union. Speed was essential. The Baghdad Pact was in shards. Its one Arab member, Iraq, threatened to boycott any session attended by its strongest member, Britain. The U.S. had to work fast to repair the damage.

Once again, most of the supervisory load would necessarily be shouldered by Eisenhower. Foster Dulles, after leaving hospital in mid-November, had spent a couple of weeks recuperating in the sunshine at Key West. He conferred briefly with Eisenhower at Augusta on his return north to Washington, but his instant concern was the annual meeting of the NATO Council in Paris, where he would be called upon to parley with Lloyd and Pineau for the first time since the collusive invasion of Egypt. As if that were not sufficiently chilling a prospect, the chief business before the NATO Council was to be a report by a committee of three —the foreign ministers of Canada, Italy, and Norway, designated intramurally as the Three Wise Men—which raised the questions, "Should NATO recognize itself as a frankly anti-Soviet alliance or should it work ultimately for a détente?" and "Should there be a restatement of the aims of the alliance in the context of competitive coexistence?"—questions that seemed to suggest the Cold War itself was approaching an amicable settlement. Was it possible? Dulles had been studying the matter, jotting down his thoughts as the basis for a paper he would read to the NATO Council. There was a double standard in the world (he had often discussed it with Eisenhower): one set of values for the free world, another for international communism. "The U.S. feels however that we do not need to contemplate that this double standard will go on forever. . . . Soviet despotism will become unable to go on living by standards that decent people despise. Thus we can look forward to an end of the dangerous division of the world." His physicians had suggested he need not dread a recurrence of the cancer that had hospitalized him.

Nor, in Dulles's absence overseas, could another senior officer supervise the formulation of U.S. policy in the Middle East. Hoover was resigning as undersecretary of state and his successor, Christian Herter, would be for some time familiarizing himself with his new duties. Middle East policy—what would come to be known as the Eisenhower Doctrine—remained the President's task.

Not that Eisenhower, during his holiday, was not preoccupied with other grave matters of state. Of these, the most intractable was the nation's budget for the fiscal year 1958, the budget he would have to send to Capitol Hill for congressional approval even before he was inaugurated for his second term. He was not satisfied with the budget, for which he was ultimately responsible; he thought it called for the spending of too much money, it offended his strong sense of fiscal conservatism, but he was stuck with it. For the first time in a year when the country was at peace the President would be calling for expenditures of more than seventy billion dollars—in fact, of nearly seventy-two billion.* Most of the increase in this budget was due to the cost of weapons and other military gear, and to the inflation which in two years had driven the cost of those items up 18 percent. On December 7 Secretary Wilson and other officials of the Department of Defense were summoned to Augusta to justify their demands; Percival Brundage, director of the Bureau of the Budget, came too, eager to slice two and one-half billion dollars from the Pentagon's proposals. Eisenhower had to decide which figure, Budget's or Pentagon's, would go into his final budget. An official of the Bureau of the Budget has observed that when Eisenhower was faced with budgetary problems, a "careful balancing of political alternatives and political considerations was very much in the forefront of his mind. . . . His political instincts were of a very high order." So on this occasion. He knew how military chiefs and service secretaries fought for fatter appropriations, heedless of the inflationary pressures they created; he knew, as he would tell the Republican leaders three weeks later, "This country can choke itself to death piling up military expenditures just as surely as it can defeat itself by not spending enough for protection." But on this Friday, in the office fitted for him above the professional's shop at Augusta National, the President thought twice. His political instincts told him that at a time of Cold War with international communism, the Democrats would interpret any economies achieved at the expense of the nation's defense as proof of a Republican disposition to disregard the sinister schemes of the Kremlin. The logic of Cold War propaganda admitted of no other conclusion. McCarthy had grown fearsome on the strength of it. Democrats and Republicans still cynically vied for votes by each claiming to be more anticommunist than the other. In that climate Eisenhower could afford to yield the Democrats no advantage. He decided in favor of the spender, Wilson, and against the economizer, Brundage.

If one may judge from his odd preparations, the President was aware that he had at least one and probably two or three major quarrels upcom-

---

* The budget for FY 1958 estimated expenditures of $71,807,000,000 and receipts of $73,620,000,000. Hence for the third straight year there would be a balanced budget and a surplus, anticipating a reduction of taxes. Unhappily, estimates were one thing, realities another. In fact, expenditures for FY 1958 would reach $71,936,000,000 while receipts, owing to a business recession, would be only $69,116,000,000—not the last of Eisenhower's deficit-burdened years.

ing with the Eighty-fifth Congress. On the last day of 1956 he invited to the White House the Republican leaders; on the first day of 1957 he brought together congressional leaders of both parties. On one level he was showing them that these holidays, traditionally given over to the excessive consumption of wines and spirits and the consequent recovery, were to him just another routine Monday and Tuesday, all in the week's work; on another level he was proselytizing, dead serious, for a legislative program that he recognized, better than most, was endangered by the fact of his being the first President to come up against the Twenty-second Amendment to the Constitution ("No person shall be elected to the office of the President more than twice"). The Senate, he knew, was bristling with Democratic statesmen each persuaded of the blessings that would be secured for the republic once he were elected President. The list of candidates, encouraged by Eisenhower's failure to transmit his personal magic to other Republicans, included Adlai Stevenson, by now a quadrennial blossom, Senators Humphrey of Minnesota, Kefauver of Tennessee, Kennedy of Massachusetts, Symington of Missouri, Johnson of Texas, and no doubt a few others bashfully awaiting destiny's trump. His shifting dependence on these men and their occasional supporters would afford the President a stern test in pragmatic politics.

On Monday, December 31, and again on Tuesday, January 1, the President cited, with differing emphases, the three issues which he expected would have political impact in the months ahead. The evidence indicates that he did not accurately fathom how they would affect the political ambitions of his congressional adversaries nor even how they would interrelate with each other against the continuing background of the Cold War. The three were: the Eisenhower Doctrine in the Middle East, the budget, and civil rights.

"The existing vacuum in the Middle East," Eisenhower told the leaders of both parties on the Tuesday, "must be filled by the United States before it is filled by Russia." He wanted the Congress, as its first order of business, to approve his plan: special economic aid and military assistance, to include the armed forces of the U.S., to repel any threat by international communism against a Middle Eastern country. But the congressmen were in no hurry. They listened, asked questions, and went away unconvinced.

The President tried again that Saturday before a joint session of the Congress, but failed to impress large numbers of influential personages. Once again Arab leaders derided the notion of a power vacuum in their region which they could not cozily fill themselves; Arab nationalism, the heads of state of Egypt, Syria, Saudi Arabia, and Jordan insisted, was "the sole basis on which Arab policy could be formulated." In short, said Nasser and the others to Eisenhower, do us a favor, keep out. To Dean Acheson, the Eisenhower Doctrine was "vague . . . not a statement of policy, but an invitation to devise one . . . not very useful." Foster Dulles went up the Hill again and again to warn against "communist aggression" and "Soviet imperialism." Without favorable action by the Congress on the Eisenhower Doctrine the Middle East would be "lost," and there was "a very great likelihood" that American soldiers would have to be sent there to fight and die. The aggression he presaged was "the most serious threat we have faced over the last ten years." But the senators had heard these ominous forebodings from Dulles for four years; now they were weary of them. Now they kept him testifying for six days. At times he flushed with anger. At times, stung by questions that seemed to impugn both his ability and his probity, perhaps aware that the senators' mail was running heavily against the Eisenhower Doctrine, with much of it aimed at him, his voice rose shrill and harsh. At length, his composure badly frayed, he blurted another of those shattering remarks that so ill became a secretary of state. Asked about the possibility of concerting the Eisenhower Doctrine with Britain and France, he answered, "If I were an American boy . . . I'd rather not have a French and British soldier beside me, one on my right and one on my left." State Department spokesmen were hard at it for the next twenty-four hours putting out disclaimers, corrections, explanations, and apologies. President Eisenhower found it necessary to say he had "no reason whatsoever" for changing his opinion that Foster Dulles was the greatest secretary of state in the modern era.

The Democratic Senate methodically set to work to whittle the Eisenhower Doctrine—more formally, Senate Joint Resolution 19—down to manageable size. Dulles objected, but only as a matter of record. Along straight party lines, the Eisenhower administration was overruled; the blank check it had requested was refused. The President's appeal for specific authorization to use the armed forces of the U.S. was denied; instead, U.S. readiness to use its armed forces if requested to do so was affirmed, so long as such use "shall be consonant [with] treaty obligations" and with the charter of the United Nations. The Senate also insisted that the executive branch should not evade its own responsibility: the U.S. "is prepared" to send troops if the President "determines the necessity thereof." Debate on the resolution dragged on.

Echoes of the Suez crisis resounded. The oil lift to western Europe was going poorly; there were reports in February 1957 that Britain was down to two weeks' supply; the French and British ambassadors both addressed formal appeals to the State Department. President Eisenhower was disturbed. "We must not allow Europe to go flat on its back for the want of oil," he said, "if the oil can be provided." If "conference and argument" did not convince the oil companies, then the government "would have to move in . . . some other direction"—a veiled threat of federal controls. He had many good friends in the oil industry, but they could be exasperating. "Business in its pricing policies," he had urged, "should avoid unnecessary price increases especially at a time like the present," when inflationary pressures were at work. His friends in the oil industry had responded to this appeal by raising the price of crude by thirty-five to forty cents a barrel—an estimated annual cost to the consumer of one billion dollars, including at least eighty-five million dollars to the defense establishment. Asked about these price hikes, the President showed concern. "I wasn't merely asking them to be altruistic," he said. "Their own long-term good is involved, and I am asking them merely to act as enlightened Americans. Now, unless this happens, the United States has to move in with so-called controls of some kind, and when we begin to control prices," he said sadly, "it is not the America we know."*

The most resonant echo of Suez, however, came from Israel, and its din threatened any congressional approval of the Eisenhower Doctrine.

While Britain and France had unconditionally withdrawn their troops from Egypt, Israeli soldiers remained, dug in, in the Gaza Strip on the Mediterranean and at Sharm al-Sheikh on the southern tip of the Sinai. As for the Strip, Ben Gurion would withdraw his troops only if Israel might keep control of civil administration and police power; the hundreds of thousands of Palestinian refugees who crowded the Strip constituted a problem which could perhaps be solved through the good offices of the United Nations. As for the troops at Sharm al-Sheikh, they would be withdrawn once Israel was guaranteed passage for shipping in the Gulf of Aqaba to Elath, Israel's southern port.† Here the matter rested throughout January, the U.N. demanding Israel's prompt and unconditional withdrawal, Ben Gurion and the Israeli Knesset stubbornly refusing, and Nasser as stubbornly rejecting all efforts to clear the canal until the last Israeli should have withdrawn from Egypt.

Ben Gurion saw Israel embattled against "the Soviet Union . . . the entire United Nations Organization, and in the first place . . . the government of the United States." Superficially, the struggle was sparked by the

* The Suez crisis was profitable to the oil industry. Several companies reported the highest quarterly profits in their history for the first quarter of 1957; profits of the five biggest were up 18.6 percent over those for the first quarter of 1956.

† The latter condition presented a nice point in international law. The Gulf of Aqaba between Egypt and Saudi Arabia narrows at its southern end to form the Strait of Tiran, only six miles wide. Assuming the three-mile territorial limit, the Strait of Tiran could not be regarded as international waters. Farther north the gulf widens and washes the coast of both Israel and Jordan; here, clearly, it is an international water. By precedent in international law, any vessel may navigate territorial waters when it is headed for international waters, *if* a state of belligerency does not exist. In 1957 such a state of belligerence still existed between Israel and Egypt.

question as to whether the U.N. (and the U.S.) would invoke economic sanctions to oblige Israel to comply with the several U.N. resolutions demanding immediate withdrawal of her troops; but underlying the dispute over sanction was Oil, to lose which would set off a chain of unpleasant changes that, as President Eisenhower had already told the Congress, "would have the most adverse, if not disastrous, effect upon our own nation's economic life and political prospects." Oil: the state of Israel, surrounded by countries rich in that resource, was denied it by all of them. The Soviet Union had ended its exports of oil to Israel after the attack on Egypt; American companies likewise refused to supply Israel lest their sensitive arrangements with the Arabs be strained.

So Ben Gurion stood fast, and Nasser stood fast, and in their gleaming new headquarters by Turtle Bay in New York City the members of the U.N. General Assembly voted a sixth resolution bidding Israel to quit Egypt.

At this time King Saud of Arabia arrived in the United States on a state visit, at the explicit behest of President Eisenhower. The advent of few other mortals could have more embittered the state of Israel, American Jews, and libertarians wherever. Saud was a despot. As Keeper of the Holy Places of Islam—Mecca, chiefly, and Medina—Saud was a principal spokesman for the Moslem world, and also a chief patron of the brisk slave trade that flourished in the Hejaz. Throughout his absolute monarchy the various forms of Christian worship were discouraged or suppressed, and Jews were strictly barred. The Arabian American Oil Company (Aramco) routinely examined its personnel to make sure that no Jew might inadvertently be found working in Arabia; in deference to what Dulles termed Saud's "idiosyncrasies," the State Department similarly screened out Jewish foreign service officers, interdicted Jewish servicemen headed for the big air base at Dhahran, and suspiciously inspected the passports of all U.S. citizens traveling to Arabia.

All this was, to be sure, deplorable, but President Eisenhower had a Cold War to fight and believed that Saud would be a useful ally; "he at least professed anti-Communism," the President observed, and so several weeks earlier he had issued instructions that Saud be accorded a systematic beauty treatment by the various federal organs of propaganda and enlightenment, looking to an attempt to supplant Nasser as leader of the Arab world. To little effect: when Saud arrived in New York City on January 29, 1957, the mayor turned his back. Saud, said Mayor Robert Wagner, "is not the kind of person we want to officially recognize in New York City." But Eisenhower had escort ships of the U.S. Navy sent down the bay to greet the despot, and Henry Cabot Lodge was there with sundry U.N. officials and Arab dignitaries, and when next day Saud was flown to Washington he was greeted at the airport by President Eisenhower personally—the first time a foreign notability had ever been so honored —and he found the avenues of the city thronged by government employees who had been granted extra time for lunch to mark the occasion. There was a formal dinner at the White House—white ties and tailcoats, robes and hoods—attended by the chief executives of Aramco and of its four corporate owners (Jersey Standard, Socony Mobil, Texaco, and Standard of California) and by a press of interested investment bankers. Thus the power of Oil, not to overlook the strategic significance of the fifty-million-dollar air base the U.S. had built at Dhahran.

Saud was duly impressed. He spoke kindly of the Eisenhower Doctrine. The king did not, however, have a vote in the United States Senate, and that body cared neither for Saud nor for the glittering entertainments provided him by the President. It seemed to both the majority leader, the Honorable Lyndon Johnson, and the minority leader, the Honorable William Knowland, that the United States was showing signs of joining those who wished to smite Israel with economic sanctions, and both men grew restive. From Florida, where he was on holiday, Johnson sent a letter to Foster Dulles bidding him "instruct" the U.S. delegation at the U.N. "to oppose with all its skill" any sanctions against Israel and even any vote on such sanctions. Knowland threatened to resign his office as U.S. delegate to the General Assembly if sanctions were imposed on Israel.

Dulles was too preoccupied with his diplomatic traffic with Ben Gurion to answer Johnson's letter with the respectful dispatch expected by that sensitive legislator. On the same day Johnson dictated his letter, Dulles had handed an aide-mémoire to the Israeli ambassador, Abba Eban. It promised U.S. influence to block raids by the fedayeen from the Gaza Strip and U.S. influence to guarantee "free and innocent passage" for the vessels of all nations through the Gulf of Aqaba; would Israel then not withdraw her troops? Four days later Ben Gurion's answer was handed Dulles: it was still no. On Saturday, February 16, Senator Johnson returned from Florida and was outraged to find that Dulles had not answered his letter. Indeed, Dulles was not even in town. He had left with Cabot Lodge for Thomasville, Georgia, where George Humphrey had a plantation. The President had been there for eight days shooting quail, playing golf, taking it easy, thinking of this and that.*

* Earlier that winter the Reverend Martin Luther King had sent Eisenhower an urgent appeal to come South and speak out, offer moral leadership on the issue of racial integration in the public schools. King's letter was given to Governor Adams, who showed it to Brownell. The two men agreed that such an effort by Eisenhower "could not possibly bring any constructive results." King was disappointed. Eisenhower, asked on February 6 why such a speech would not be possible, said: "Well, . . . I have a pretty good and sizable agenda on my desk every day, and as you

Dulles and Lodge discussed Ben Gurion's refusal with Eisenhower and Humphrey for perhaps ninety minutes. Dulles felt strongly that the U.S. must stand for sanctions against Israel. If not, the Arab nations would conclude that U.S. policy was controlled by the Jews; they would gravitate toward the Soviet Union, and the Eisenhower Doctrine would fall before it had been established. Lodge believed that without the doctrine the way was open for war. Eisenhower preferred, if there were to be sanctions against Israel, that both public and private assistance be cut off. Humphrey, after checking with Treasury officials, reckoned that Israel realized, from private gifts and purchases of Israeli bonds, about one hundred million dollars a year. It was a thorny problem in politics. At the very least the responsibility must be shared with the Democratic leaders.

But the Democratic leaders, many of them intent on their plans for the campaign of 1960, were notably reluctant to share the burden. They would not go south to Thomasville to talk with the President, they would not instead accept a conference with Dulles in Washington, they insisted the President come north to meet with them. On February 19 Eisenhower cut short his holiday and was flown north. That same day Johnson found his letter to Dulles reprinted in New York and Chicago newspapers. His letter —ignored, unanswered, and now leaked to the press. In a cold fury the majority leader called into session the Senate Democratic Policy Committee and had his arguments against penalties to Israel sanctified as party dogma.

The meeting early next morning at the White House—the President, Nixon, Dulles, Lodge, six staff members, and more than a score of congressional leaders—was tense and frosty. Adams noticed Senator Johnson turn and look at Senator Russell "with a determined expression which seemed to say that he was not going to yield an inch." Knowland was equally determined. Why should sanctions be invoked against a little country like Israel for failing to comply with a U.N. resolution, when no sanctions had been voted against a great power like Russia despite the U.N. resolution condemning the bloody repression of rebellion in Hungary?

Hungary: mention of that country evoked once again the embarrassing specter of the 1952 campaign, when the Republicans had spurned the Truman policy of containment as "immoral" and had bravely spoken of liberating those enslaved behind the "iron curtain." The Eisenhower administration, though, had settled for a far less ambitious course of action. It had done, as Eisenhower said, "the only thing it could": welcomed to

---

know, I insist on going for a bit of recreation every once in a while . . . Now, I have just got as much as I can do for the moment. And . . . I have expressed myself on this subject so often in the South, in the North, wherever I have been, that I don't know what another speech would do about the thing right now."

Two days later he left for a twelve-day rest in Thomasville.

the U.S. as many Hungarian refugees as possible, and scored appropriate propaganda points in the Cold War. Nixon had been sent to Austria to make more propaganda. Eventually homes and jobs had been found for more than twenty thousand refugees.*

When Knowland raised the question of sanctions against Russia, however, Cabot Lodge withered his notion with one brief mortuary comment. "The U.N.," said Lodge, "will never vote for sanctions against either Russia or the United States."

Congressional concurrence in Eisenhower's policy of invoking sanctions against Israel could not be obtained. It was too unpopular. Senator Russell bid him shoulder the burden alone. "America has either one voice or none," said Sam Rayburn, speaker of the House, "and that voice is the voice of the President—whether everybody agrees with him or not."

Johnson, still without experience of the weight of such loneliness, was quick to tell the reporters waiting in the White House press room, "Our views have not changed."

At the U.N. the pressures multiplied for a quick vote on sanctions. By letter and cablegram to Ben Gurion, Eisenhower applied his own pressures. That his decision had been taken was quite clear. American Jewish leaders, invited to Washington, listened to urgent appeals by Dulles.

And meanwhile, action on the Eisenhower Doctrine was in abeyance. If Eisenhower persevered in supporting sanctions against "the little state," Johnson had it within his power to gut the doctrine. The issue was never drawn. On March 1 Golda Meir, the Israeli foreign minister, pledged the U.N. that her country contemplated "full and prompt withdrawal" of troops from the Gaza Strip and the Sharm al-Sheikh area of the Sinai.

The last Israeli troops moved out as U.N. Emergency Forces moved in, on March 6.

The Senate approved the joint resolution, the Eisenhower Doctrine, on March 5 and the President signed it on March 9.

On March 29 a convoy of nine freighters passed through the Suez Canal. The Suez crisis, which dated from July 19, 1956, when Foster Dulles had turned his thumbs down on U.S. aid to Egypt to build the

---

* The project had not been greeted in the U.S. with universal good will. American Negroes, for instance, reflecting that charity begins at home, found themselves wondering why comparable zeal had never been harnessed to find proper homes and jobs for as many American-born Negroes. Why, if it came to that, did the Vice President, rather than going such a long way to Austria, not simply catch a plane for Mississippi? Why, when the President visited Thomasville, Georgia, did he not look about him as he was driven to Humphrey's plantation? So the Cold War backfired.

The disparaging epithet "Hunky" has long served in the U.S. as the offensive label for a Hungarian; it is of some interest that the term "Honkie," as used by militant blacks against whites generally, had its provenance at the time of the campaign for Hungarian Refugee Relief.

High Dam at Aswan, was dead at last, aged eight months and ten days. If there had been a winner, it was the Eisenhower administration, now firmly lodged as presumptive protector of the Middle East—that is, of the Oil—but what protection was needed, or would be accounted helpful, still awaited proof.

As the Suez crisis subsided, Eisenhower took up the task of knitting together the raveled Anglo-American alliance. He and Dulles met at Bermuda with Harold Macmillan, the new British prime minister, and Selwyn Lloyd, still the foreign minister, for conversations over a long weekend, March 20 to 24. The talks were overdue. Anti-American sentiments were widespread in Britain, nor had Macmillan himself troubled to conceal his chilly view that U.S. policy had been confusing, vacillating, lacking in logic, and wounding to U.S. allies.

Eisenhower arrived in Bermuda tanned and relaxed after a six-day cruise in the Bahamas aboard a U.S. warship. He was looking forward to the conference—once again at the Mid-Ocean Club—for Macmillan was an old friend from their days in North Africa, and besides he meant to get in some golf. He had made ready some agreements for prompt public announcement—the U.S. decisions to collaborate more actively with the nations signatory to the Baghdad Pact and to deploy a number of intermediate-range ballistic missiles (IRBMs) in Britain on sites manned by British personnel—but many other matters needed ventilation if the two powers were once more to be as friendly as formerly.

As to Suez, there was little room for agreement since the British were still bitter over Nasser. When it came to the oil of the Middle East there was, in Eisenhower's subsequent phrase, "some very plain talk," for the Americans had manifestly usurped what had been an exceedingly lucrative British preserve. The British still controlled the oil under Kuwait, a rich pool, but their reach to grasp the oasis of Buraimi, reckoned another rich resource, was disputed by Saud of Arabia, and hence by his American partners in Aramco, and hence by the U.S. government. More plain talk.

Other matters variously vexed President and prime minister. Eisenhower complained about the way the French and British press were "continuing to abuse the U.S. and U.S. personalities," and he wondered why a discreet control might not be exercised. (Privately, Dulles observed that the British press had made "particularly vicious and coordinated attacks on President Eisenhower personally.") Macmillan feared that the governments of countries newly liberated from colonial status (he mentioned Cambodia and Ghana as examples) would join the Soviet bloc in voting on issues of importance at the U.N. He suggested the advisability of reducing the status of the U.N. while elevating that of the regional bodies such as the

Organization of American States. Passing on to the larger question of colonialism, he objected to the far-flung campaign of propaganda on the issue, a pressure "to which the United States was contributing." Eisenhower spoke at length of how to persuade peoples of the benefits to them of staying within the established framework, of promising that "in time" they would have freedom of choice, and of how, "if the choice to stay were made attractive," there should be no unrest. He pointed to Puerto Rico as an example of this benign approach. Dulles spoke of the strategic importance of certain areas, of "our present intention to stay on in Okinawa," and "of the importance of holding the present anti-Communist positions, insular and peninsular, around the Communist land mass." No dissent was voiced.

The statesmen were content. Apart from their plain talk, they had reestablished a warm rapport.

The second of the three issues the President had singled out for attention on New Year's Day was his seventy-two-billion-dollar budget. As has been noted, its size dismayed him. It called for spending at an alarming rate. Further, he assumed as an article of Republican faith that a Congress controlled by Democrats—those notoriously free and easy spenders —would force appropriations up ever higher and so make his budget even more dangerous for the nation's economy. He approached the ominous thing as if it were booby-trapped and loudly ticking.

It was frequently charged while still he was President, and even more often afterward, that as chief executive Eisenhower was indecisive, hesitant, equivocal, bumbling, vague, contradictory, and weak. To find instances of his firm, decisive action on unpopular issues is not hard; Sherman Adams has cited Eisenhower's "unhesitating" support of sanctions against Israel as "one of the most courageous decisions" he took while President. But anyone seeking an example of his shiftless inconsistency need look no further than upon what came to be called the Battle of the Budget: from January 16, 1957, when he delivered the budget message to the Congress, to September 3, when with acrid memories of the first session of the Eighty-fifth Congress still hot within him he signed the last appropriations bill. He never acted more ineffectually. He never gave his domestic critics better grounds for derision.

His budget was submitted, and on the same day his secretary of the treasury held a press conference. The President had recommended "a carefully balanced budget . . . well adapted to the needs of the present and the future." George Humphrey flung it down and danced upon it. "I would deplore the day," said Humphrey, "that we thought we couldn't even reduce expenditures of this terrific amount." He went on to lament "the terrific tax we are taking out of this country," and to add, "If we don't [reduce expenditures], over a long period of time, I will predict that you will have a depression that will curl your hair." It was a hasty statement, ill-considered, difficult to quote at once accurately and intelligibly since its syntax was so unkempt;* its economics were, to say the least, dubious; no matter, the last few words, about "a depression that will curl your hair," were pre-eminently quotable and, on the news wires of a dozen press associations, sped round the world with the implication that the President of the United States and his secretary of the treasury had squared off against each other.

This was a misapprehension, as was the notion that the size of the budget meant Eisenhower had deserted fiscal conservatism to embrace the "new Republicanism." A slogan which already in 1957 had lost its sheen while still it resisted precise definition, new Republicanism, or modern Republicanism, was a coinage of Arthur Larson, a secondary figure in the Eisenhower administration. Larson had written a book, *A Republican Looks at His Party,* which had a fleeting vogue in 1956. On election night, in Eisenhower's moment of triumph, when he stood, arms upraised in victory, before a crowd of ecstatic Republicans in the ballroom of the Sheraton-Park Hotel in Washington, he had once again invoked that slogan. "I think," he had crowed, "that modern Republicanism has now proved itself. (Cheers.) And America has approved of modern Republicanism." (Wild cheering, prolonged applause.) Of course America had done no such thing; she had pronounced her contradictory approval of Ike Eisenhower and the Democratic party; modern Republicanism was still an unknown quantity. But Old Guard Republicans sourly examining the seventy-two-billion-dollar budget were led to conclude that this New Deal–Fair Deal economics was the modern Republicanism.

The President hastened to disabuse them. He agreed with Humphrey, he assured the large throng of reporters at his next press conference; had himself edited and approved the memorandum that had formed the basis of Humphrey's prepared remarks; agreed with Humphrey that the budget should be cut wherever possible; went even further, saying: "If they can, I think if Congress can, its committees, it is their duty to do it." It was an extraordinary spectacle: the President and the secretary of the treasury throwing to the wolves the meticulous planning of months.

* Compare, for instance, the efforts made by Eisenhower at page 127 of *Waging Peace* and by Richard E. Neustadt in *Presidential Power,* John Wiley & Sons, 1960, page 66. Nathaniel R. Howard, editor, *The Basic Papers of George Humphrey, 1953–1957,* The Western Reserve Historical Society, 1965, seems to have used a version that had been dry-cleaned and pressed since it had been uttered.

"Who Gave Him The Do-It-Yourself Kit?"

from *Herblock's Special for Today* (Simon & Schuster, 1958)

With relish the wolves gathered to do their duty. A ribald rivalry popped up between Democrats and Republicans: which party could more effectively portray themselves to the voters and taxpayers as the champions of economy? We can cut at least two billion, said Knowland; three, said Senator Styles Bridges, Republican; six or even six and one-half, said Senator Harry Byrd, Democrat. All grinned. All ravened.

Belatedly the President recognized his error, but to rectify it required him to speak with two tongues. He must be frugal, but he must also protect his budget. The consequence was that when the President spoke on the subject he would seem to contradict what he had said the week before; every firm sentence was likely to be crippled by a qualification. A federal budget is not often a subject that will rouse the citizenry—too vague, too remote—but in the late winter of 1957 it caught the national attention. Congressional mail was heavy with protests against spending and prayers for tax relief. There was evidence that this chorus of dissent had been artfully orchestrated, but few congressmen troubled to identify the source of inspiration. By mid-March the Democratic majority in the House, together with ten Republicans, voted a sardonic resolution "respectfully" requesting Eisenhower "to indicate the places and amounts in his budget where he thinks substantial reductions may be best made." The Democrats were easily winning the economy championship.

Eisenhower's dander was up, but his range for counterattack was limited. He sent off a letter to the Speaker of the House claiming that during his first term he had reduced the federal civilian work force by "almost a quarter of a million," that the tax cut of 1954 had "saved our people almost twenty-five billion dollars in taxes," and that "we have in prospect three balanced budgets in a row." The accuracy of these boasts was questionable, and in any event he knew what to expect as a retort: Sure, but what have you done for us this year? Public pressures against his budget were incessant. In Boston a mock "tea party" was staged so that Senator Byrd might assail "taxation without representation." As logic it was vacant but as propaganda it made a flock of headlines.

With lupine courtesy Senator Johnson welcomed to a hearing of his appropriations subcommittee the new director of the U.S. Information Agency, Arthur Larson. "We look to you," Johnson purred to Larson, "as the distinguished author and spokesman for your party to enlighten us." Modern Republicanism was about to be bathed in vitriol. Of the seven Republicans on Johnson's subcommittee, most were of the Old Guard; only one stood ready to succor the unhappy Larson. A month before, Larson had been so ill-advised as to mount an attack on the party of Roosevelt and Truman. "Throughout the New and Fair Deals," he said, "this country was in the grip of a somewhat alien philosophy, imported from Europe."

Eisenhower no doubt agreed, but he was far too sensible to say as much within the hearing of reporters. The day after Larson's speech the House subtracted nearly 30 percent of USIA's appropriation. Under Johnson's leadership the Senate would slice it by another fifteen million dollars. "I just say it is a mistake," said Eisenhower, exercising iron control; ". . . the tools to wage peace . . . I think it is a mistake to cut as seriously as these people have." But he would wait until he had left the White House before he found it safe to characterize the cuts as an "irresponsible diminution of an agency on the front line in the cold war," and to acknowledge how "profoundly" he wished the Congress had been controlled by his own party.

The President took his fight for the budget to the people on May 14. His televised speech was vague and ineffectual. The next day at his press conference he was reminded that more Democrats than Republicans were supporting his program; did he intend to "punish those Republicans who are not supporting your program or reward those who do support you?" But of course the Republican who most forthrightly opposed his program was Senator Knowland of California, the minority leader; Eisenhower was obliged once again to equivocate. "I don't think it is the function of a President of the United States," he said, "to punish anybody for voting what he believes."

In the end the Battle of the Budget resulted in four billion dollars clipped from the administration's budget. As is customary, some of those funds were likely to be restored during the second session of the Congress. Economies are generally transacted while everyone is watching; when the taxpayers nod, by tradition the funds that have been cut are restored. In this case, as will presently be noted, the Russian sputnik was destined to galvanize the Congress into spending vast funds they had never before dreamed of. They would restore what they had cut, they would authorize further billions. Nevertheless, at the time, in the summer of 1957, President Eisenhower suffered a well-deserved drubbing. It was, as Adams acknowledged, "a serious and disturbing defeat for him," and one he would learn much from. Never again would he make the same mistakes about his budget.

The third major issue prompted by the President on New Year's Day, civil rights, afforded a classic instance of partisan politics at work. The program the President proposed was a modest one, far less ambitious than the legislation urged by Truman in 1948, and he spoke of it with appropriately modest sentiments. The President told the Congress he was "proud of the progress our people are making in mutual understanding—the chief buttress of human and civil rights," and he observed that "we are moving closer to the goal of fair and equal treatment of citizens without regard to race or color," but, these pieties to one side, the issue was political to a degree.

Eisenhower was fresh from an election in which he had made substantial gains among Negro voters. He had proposed identical legislation in that election year only to watch, without astonishment, as the southern Democrats in the Senate smoothly consigned it to certain death and burial in committee. To propose enactment of the same legislation again in 1957 was to assume that the Democratic leadership of the Congress would once again be angrily splintered, northern liberals against southern reactionaries; the Republicans could then take center stage as defenders of the public weal, reasonable and united, and so gain even further support among the Negroes. To enhance this Republican prospect, the leaders of the Democratic majority in both Houses were Texans, viz., southerners, who could be expected to lead the fight against any civil rights legislation; one of them, Lyndon Johnson, was a candidate for the presidential nomination in 1960 and so could be expected to do himself irreparable damage in any bruising battle with the northern liberals. To take Johnson out of the fray in 1960 would appreciably improve the chances of the Republican candidate, presumably Nixon. So the Republican fantasy, in the winter and spring of 1957.

To the Democrats in general and to Johnson in particular the politics of civil rights had a quite different aspect. Johnson perceived all the snares laid for him by Brownell and the other Republican politicians; he perceived, as well, that by guiding some sort of civil rights program through the Senate he might be able to convert it from Eisenhower's bill to Johnson's bill and, in the process, alter his national image from Johnson the Texas southerner to Johnson the Texas westerner and so on to Johnson the national healer of wounds and master architect of Democratic destinies. But to achieve such a success, he would have to devise a bill so bland that the southerners would not fight it to the last ditch yet with enough bite in it to attract the support of the northerners.

These contrary schemes got their first test of strength late in June when the civil rights bill passed by the House reached the Senate. By a six-vote margin the Senate kept the bill out of committee and scheduled it for debate on the floor—a clear if narrow victory for the Republicans. The next day, by a seven-vote margin, the Senate passed a bill that authorized the building by the federal government of a single dam at Hells Canyon near the Idaho-Oregon border. The Eisenhower administration had strenuously opposed the Hells Canyon project, preferring three smaller dams, privately financed. The issue was low-rate public power versus private power, costlier for the consumer. Put another way, the issue was "creeping socialism" versus a "giveaway of natural resources." To Republican politicians study-ing the voting pattern on these two Senate bills, it seemed obvious that a vile Democratic deal had been arranged: in exchange for a handful of votes by "self-styled liberals" from the Pacific Northwest to bottle up the civil rights bill, at least five southern senators had switched their allegiance and voted for public power.

The truth lay one level deeper. The Republicans, by lining up almost solidly to keep the civil rights bill out of committee, had broken their an-cient alliance with the southern Democrats. With artful forethought Lyndon Johnson had moved swiftly to weld a new alliance of southern and western Democrats, one that would help hold the party together dur-ing the divisive debate on civil rights.

The debate—it lasted, with interruptions, from July 8 to August 7—was marked by one sweeping change in the administration's bill and one damaging amendment to it. President Eisenhower's tactics during the de-bate were confusing, erratic, and equivocal. The one Negro administrative officer on his staff, Frederic Morrow, considered the President's behavior "shocking." Certainly the President bore a major responsibility for the way his own bill was disemboweled.

The sweeping change in the bill was the elimination of its Part III, which empowered the attorney general, on his own initiative, to seek in-junctions against violations of any civil right—the right, say, to ride on a public bus, or drink a cup of coffee at a public lunch counter, or use a public restroom, or get a fair shake in a lawcourt, or vote in an election, or send children to an unsegregated public school. In short, Part III was designed to end the discriminations of Jim Crow. To Senator Richard Russell of Georgia, Part III was "most cunningly designed and contrived" to give the attorney general power to use "our military forces to destroy the system of separation of the races . . . at the point of a bayonet." At his press conference of July 3, the President was asked to comment on Russell's objections.

THE PRESIDENT: Well, I would say this. Naturally, I am not a lawyer and I don't participate in drawing up the exact language of proposals. I know what the objective was that I was seeking, which was to prevent anybody illegally from interfering with any individual's right to vote, if that individual were qualified under the proper laws of his state, and so on. . . .

Q: Mr. President, in the light of that, would you be willing to see the bill written so that it specifically dealt with the question of right to vote rather than implementing the Supreme Court decision on the integration of the schools?

THE PRESIDENT: Well, I would not want to answer this in detail, because I was reading part of that bill this morning, and there were certain phrases I didn't completely understand. So, before I made any more remarks on that, I would want to talk to the attorney general and see exactly what they do mean.

These stumbling admissions of ignorance about a premier measure among those sponsored by his administration, a measure drafted within his Department of Justice, were noted with chagrin by those senators still struggling to salvage Part III. They were also noted by the wily Johnson, who thereupon encouraged Senator Russell to discuss his objections with the President personally. During their long talk, the President assured Russell that "the overriding provision of the bill that [he] wanted set down in law [was] the citizen's right to vote." Up on the Hill a stubborn fight on behalf of Part III was still being waged, but the heart went out of it after the President's press conference of July 17. The first question touched on his authority, under Part III, to use federal troops to enforce the integration of public schools in the South.

THE PRESIDENT: . . . I can't imagine any set of circumstances that would ever induce me to send federal troops . . . into any area to enforce the orders of a federal court, because I believe that common sense of America will never require it. . . . I would never believe that it would be a wise thing to do in this country.

In ten weeks such a set of circumstances would arise and the President would ruefully reflect on his presumption. On this Wednesday morning in July another question dealt with the amendment to gut Part III, the amendment "which would take out of the bill all injunctive power except to deal directly with the right to vote." How would the President regard such a bill?

THE PRESIDENT: Well, I think the voting right is something that should be emphasized. If in every locality every person . . . is permitted to vote, he has got a means of taking care of himself and his group, his class. He has got a means of getting what he wants in democratic government, and that is the one on which I place the greatest emphasis.

The right to vote is surely one of the proudest privileges of a constitutional democracy. The President was a reasonably well-informed man; he had himself sojourned in the South, often for extended periods of time; he was well aware that it was a one-party region, where Republicans were eyed as some kind of monstrosity. Had it escaped his attention that the right to vote in the South, where rival candidates in a Democratic primary vied with each other in demagogic appeals to racism, was worth next to nothing? Did he knowingly place "the greatest emphasis" on something he knew to be worthless? Had he any idea how many Americans—black and white—would be murdered in the South before the right to vote would mean anything? There was a final exchange at this press conference that served to nail Part III of the civil rights bill in its coffin:

Q: . . . are you convinced that it would be a wise extension of federal power at this stage to permit the attorney general to bring suits on his own motion, to enforce school integration in the South?

THE PRESIDENT: Well, no; I have—as a matter of fact, as you state it that way, on his own motion, without any request from local authorities, I suppose is what you are talking about.

Q: Yes, sir. I think that this is what the bill would do, Part III.

THE PRESIDENT: Well, in that, we will see what they agree on. . . . I personally believe if you try to go too far too fast in laws in this delicate field that has involved the emotions of so many millions of Americans, you are making a mistake. . . . you cause trouble rather than benefit.

One week later the Senate stripped Part III, fifty-two votes to thirty-eight. The government was left with authority to act only against violations of voting rights. "This," wrote Eisenhower in retrospect, "was a blow."

Lyndon Johnson planned to weaken the bill still further—that is, bring it still further toward acceptance by the southern senators—by amending it so as to require a trial by jury in the event a federal court found someone in willful disobedience of its order to refrain from violation of a citizen's voting rights. On that score the President was unequivocally opposed, and with good reason. To interpose a jury trial between a federal judge and his legal orders would fatally impair the right to vote, for how often would a southern jury convict a southern white man in a case alleging violation of a black man's civil rights? Moreover, the amendment as drafted would also weaken the whole web of federal law, since it would call in question the enforcement of dozens of federal statutes. But Johnson found the necessary votes, and the amendment was passed by a nine-vote margin.

789

Eisenhower and Brownell were both bitterly disappointed. What had happened was remote from what had been conjectured a few months earlier. It now seemed there would be no Civil Rights Act of 1957; certainly there had been no filibuster by southern senators nor even a loud angry dispute among the Democrats. The only chance of salvaging the bill lay with the House: if its leaders would refuse to accept the Senate's version of the legislation, perhaps an acceptable compromise might still be elaborated. But Speaker Sam Rayburn was for accepting the Senate bill unaltered. Nevertheless, delicate negotiations were undertaken. Carefully solicited by White House strategists, letters and telegrams from Negro leaders began to arrive urging the President to veto the "phony" civil rights bill. Each protest, as it arrived, was as carefully relayed to the press by Hagerty and his assistants; a lively propaganda was presently in full swing. Meanwhile the House Republicans bayed "Sellout" at the Senate. No bill at all, said Joe Martin, the House minority leader, would be "infinitely better" than the Senate version.

A compromise emerged. The objectionable jury trial amendment was limited to actions resulting from infringements of the right to vote, and further limited by the stipulation that in the absence of a jury trial, a federal judge might impose no harsher penalty than ninety days' imprisonment and a fine of three hundred dollars. Johnson was apprehensive that his southern colleagues might filibuster against even that concession. He reasoned further with his friends. On a Friday afternoon, August 23, he called the President. "I can get [Senator] Ervin [of North Carolina] and the others to agree to a compromise of three hundred dollars and forty-five days," he said. After calling Knowland and Martin, Eisenhower told Johnson the suggestion was acceptable. He went further. He complimented Johnson on his successful negotiation of the solution.

The Civil Rights Act of 1957, the first such legislation since 1875— was it Eisenhower's or Johnson's triumph? was it a triumph at all?—was passed and sent to the White House by the Congress on August 29, 1957.

Eisenhower was peevish and weary.

The grinding, protracted struggles with the Democratic-controlled Congress in which he had, he knew, not done as well as he should have; the implacable inflationary pressures in the economy, of which he had been reminded at his last press conference by a reporter who complained of the prices of everything going up a cent or two, up a dime, up a quarter; in London the disarmament talks hopelessly snarled, and now the Russian announcement that they had successfully test-fired an intercontinental ballistic missile; the special election in Wisconsin to fill the seat

"What! My Administration Influenced By Money?"

from *Herblock's Special for Today* (Simon & Schuster, 1958)

of Joe McCarthy, who had died in the spring, won handily by a Democrat. To make matters still worse, uncomfortable questions were being put, exploring the custom of his administration to give preference to the well-heeled, the longheaded men of business. Just recently Eisenhower's appointment of an ambassador to Ceylon had been challenged: the man selected was unfamiliar with the name of Ceylon's prime minister, but at least he had contributed large sums of money to GOP campaigns. There seemed no end to the President's troubles.

Since July he had been planning to get away for a long holiday by the sea, at Newport, Rhode Island. He and Mamie would take over an admiral's quarters on Coaster's Harbor Island, in Narragansett Bay. He grudged every minute away from the Newport Naval Station. He would fish, he would golf, he would relax; by God, he would relax and forget his troubles.

Even the Eisenhower Doctrine, the enactment of which he had called "the legislative process at its best," had turned out to breed problems one after another, the latest of them an immediate affliction and one that he could not discuss freely.

First, in April, there had been a bargain-basement dust-up in Jordan, which had at once been diagnosed in Washington as "trouble . . . instigated by Communists." It began with a quarrel between the young King Hussein and his premier, Suleiman al-Nabulsi, the one seeking closer friendship with the United States, the other striving to achieve Arab unity and maintain his small country's neutrality betwixt U.S. and USSR. There ensued a bewildering shuffle of short-lived governments in Jordan, with army officers swept about as in a revolving door. The king, falling easily into the habit of his more sophisticated contemporaries, remembered to charge a "communist plot." International communism, he declared, had inspired "efforts to destroy my country." Instantly two aircraft carriers, a battleship, two cruisers, twenty-four destroyers, and two submarines—the main strength of the U.S. Sixth Fleet—plowed east across the Mediterranean. Eisenhower announced that the "independence and integrity" of Jordan were "vital to the national interest of the United States and to world peace." The tumult died away. A stable Jordanian government took charge. But Hussein insisted that Jordan was "not interested" in any alliance based upon the Eisenhower Doctrine. In which case, what was the Sixth Fleet doing, idling about off the coast of Lebanon and Syria? The fleet was withdrawn. A costly journey to and fro, to no fruitful purpose.

Syria was the present vexation. For some months CIA agents had been on the prowl in and around Syria, casting about for a way to establish a government that would readily invoke the Eisenhower Doctrine and thus give the U.S. an opportunity to use her influence as had been done in Turkey, Iraq, and Iran. The need was imperative, if only because of the pipelines that carried Iraqi oil through Syria to the sea, and could so easily be sabotaged. The Syrian government, however, had turned instead to the Soviet Union to purchase arms; in Damascus it was feared the Eisenhower Doctrine was a new western imperialism conveniently disguised as protection against communism. In August the Syrians had found, they said, evidence to confirm their fears: "an American plot to overthrow Syria's present regime." They had expelled three Americans, a military attaché, a vice consul, a secretary for political affairs; the last of these they had described as an "expert on coups d'état" who had got his training in Iran and Guatemala.* In Washington the inevitable retort came from Foster Dulles; the Syrian leaders "seem to be influenced," he said, "by international communism." "The suspicion was strong," Eisenhower would recall, "that the Communists had taken control of the government." Intolerable. Once again the Sixth Fleet had been ordered to the eastern Mediterranean; U.S. aircraft were flown from Europe to the U.S. base at Adana, Turkey. Next the President privily assigned Loy Henderson, a foreign service officer with experience of the Near East, to canvass Syria's neighbors and determine whether they were disposed to take direct military action against the threat of a communist regime in Syria. After discussions with the leaders of Turkey, Lebanon, Iraq, and Jordan, Henderson returned on September 4 solemn and portentous. The situation in Syria, he announced on his arrival, could have "serious effects upon the security of the whole free world."

The President was impatient. He would talk to Henderson at Newport; he would not wait to receive his report at the White House.

As if these demands on his flagging attention were not enough, he was informed on Tuesday, September 3, that the governor of Arkansas, a man named Orval Faubus, had ordered units of the Arkansas National Guard to throw a cordon around Central High School in Little Rock, ostensibly to "preserve peace and good order," actually to exclude from the school nine Negro children who had been chosen to assist at its integration. It was as though someone—Faubus? the Negroes? the Supreme Court?— had conspired to thwart the President's blessed chance to relax. He was sure to be asked about the affair at his press conference. He called the attorney general. Later, sure enough, the questions came. What did he think about it? What did he plan to do about it? Patience.

* One presumably impartial witness, Patrick Seale, writing under the auspices of the Royal Institute of International Affairs, has observed that the evidence presented by the Syrians to back up their charges is "hard to dismiss as fabrications."

THE PRESIDENT: . . . Now, time and again a number of people—I, among them—have argued that you cannot change people's hearts merely by laws. . . . The Supreme Court . . . pointed out the emotional difficulties that would be encountered by Negroes if given equal but separate schools, and I think probably their reasoning was correct, at least I have no quarrel with it.

But there are very strong emotions on the other side, people that see a picture of mongrelization of the race, they call it. They are very strong emotions, and we are going to whip this thing in the long run by Americans being true to themselves and not merely by law.

His thoughts turned to his imminent holiday and to his wife, just back from hospital after twenty-four days of recuperation following an operation. They would be flown to Quonset Point Naval Station the next morning. Already he was sniffing the salt air off the sea.

By Wednesday Eisenhower's remarkable buoyancy had once again asserted itself. He brimmed over with his characteristic ebullience. "Never did I feel so good on the first two hours of getting away from Washington," he said as he arrived in Rhode Island.

The links of the Newport Country Club stretched before him, rolls and folds of green, pockets of white sand, an exhilarating challenge.

Three days later the President was back in the White House. He had to confer with Brownell on this accursed business at Little Rock. Since he was in Washington, he could confer as well with Foster Dulles and Loy Henderson on Syria and the Middle East. But he would stay only one day in Washington.

As to Syria and her neighbors in the Middle East, the showing made to Eisenhower was alarming. Henderson reported a fear throughout the region that the Soviet Union might try to overthrow one government after another, using the crisis in Syria as a precedent. Apprehension was sharpest in Lebanon, where the premier, Camille Chamoun, doubted he could continue to endorse a policy of amity with the U.S. "more than three to six months if something were not done to remove a Soviet-dominated Syrian regime." The President acted swiftly and decisively. He ordered accelerated delivery of U.S. arms to Jordan, Lebanon, Turkey, and Iraq. It was done at once. Within two days, eight USAF transport planes carrying jeeps, machine guns, recoilless rifles, and ammunition had landed in Jordan; other planes were bound for the other countries. The President authorized the secretary of state to issue a statement on his behalf, an expression of hope that "the international communists would not push the

Syrians into any acts of aggression against her neighbors." Throughout the Middle East there was a wild surmise: What next?

As to the Little Rock affair, the facts were quite as alarming. The governor of one state had defied the order of a federal court; the governors of other states had extravagantly praised his defiance, inviting his contemptuous behavior to spread like a contagion over the republic.* Violence was already abroad; mobs were gathering, obedient to the summons of professional bigots; in Alabama the Ku Klux Klan had seized a feebleminded Negro, tortured him, castrated him, and left him bleeding by a roadside as a warning to all presumptuous integrationists. The President moved with circumspection. The federal court in Little Rock was inquiring into Governor Faubus's failure to comply with its order. It was best to be patient. No statement. No precipitate action. The President went back to Rhode Island.

The contrast between his firm resolution on the Syrian situation and his caution as to Little Rock was striking. Strength in the Cold War six thousand miles away; prudence and a soft word at home. Yet the condition of Negroes at home was certain to be thrust into the Cold War. Indeed, the Syrian affair was all at once deflated, and rather absurdly, while the ruckus in Little Rock grew steadily uglier and spread into other southern states.

In the Middle East it was suddenly apparent that despite Henderson's gloomy appreciation, none of the Arab states was much concerned about Syria's internal politics. Unlike Dulles and Henderson, the Arab leaders were able to distinguish Arab nationalism from communism.† Even the Lebanese announced they would fight beside Syria against an attack "from whatever quarter." In Cairo, Nasser declared the U.S. had created an "artificial uproar" over Syria. Hussein of Jordan pointedly left for a holiday in Italy. Saud of Arabia complained that American concern was "exaggerated." The Arabs were united—against the Eisenhower Doctrine. At the very least, American prestige in the Middle East had suffered a solid wallop.

American prestige was also involved at Little Rock. A world audience watched, horrified and incredulous, as white men and women reviled, spat

* The praise came from governors of states in the Deep South. A survey showed that after more than three years since the Supreme Court had ordered integration of the public schools "with all deliberate speed," seven states of the Old Confederacy had made no move whatever. The seven were Alabama, Florida, Georgia, Louisiana, Mississippi, South Carolina, and Virginia.
† Before very long the Syrian government, having decided the time was propitious, moved to outlaw and dissolve the Syrian Communist party. The action put an end, at least temporarily, to the American illusion that the Syrian government was a pawn of the Kremlin.

upon, and threatened Negro children going to school in the capital city of an American state. Analysis of press reaction around the world was duly called to the President's attention: in Switzerland, sober dismay; London more sorrowful than critical; the Netherlands harshly unfavorable; Paris newspapers filled with quotations from American newspapers criticizing Eisenhower's apparent apathy; Tokyo's judgment, a disgrace. On Monday, September 9, an elementary school in Nashville, Tennessee, just built at a cost of five hundred thousand dollars, stood ready to receive three hundred and eighty-eight white children and one Negro child. That night it was virtually destroyed by an explosion of dynamite. Seven Ku Klux Klansmen were arrested. Hagerty, the President's press secretary, told reporters that Eisenhower "thought it was a terrible thing." Hagerty's wizardry with the press was beginning to fray: pictures kept appearing that showed the President teeing off, or sitting in his golf cart, or grinning on the eighteenth green. On other pages of the newspapers were the stories of Negro clergymen beaten by mobs. Eisenhower was shown relaxing by the sea.

On that same Monday, September 9, the President signed the Civil Rights Act of 1957.

In this business of Little Rock, as in the protracted struggle over that legislation, a salient consideration, one that was certain to flaw the outcome whatever it might be, was that only white men were involved in the process of formulating a decision that intimately concerned Negroes. The President was the creature of his rearing, training, education, associations, friendships—as we all are of ours; and in his case, as we have seen, all had been and still was lily-white. In consequence he had scant comprehension of the dimensions of the problem of race in the United States, but on the other hand he had a high regard for and proven confidence in his own ability to take hold of a problem and solve it. The question of chief interest on this occasion was: what kind of wrong hold would he get on the problem?

On Wednesday Sherman Adams called the President to tell him that Faubus would like to meet him to talk the matter over. Faubus would send a telegram requesting an interview; how did that strike the President? Adams was bound to say that Brownell urged the President not to encourage the telegram. The President spoke of other, related matters: "they," he said, apparently referring to the growing host of his critics, "they" failed to take into account the seethe of anger in the South. He was reluctant, he said, to interfere with the governor's responsibilities. At length he said that if Faubus honestly wanted to talk, it was okay with him, any time, any place.

Next the President had a call put in to Brownell. To his attorney general the President spoke of Faubus's proposed telegram. Faubus should make it clear, the President stipulated, that "any good citizen will comply with the proper order of a federal court." He complained that the whole United States seemed to think the President had a right to walk in and simply say, "Disperse—we're going to have Negroes in the high schools, and so on," and it would be done. But that was not so. He reminded Brownell of states' rights, and of the governor's right to call out the National Guard to preserve law and order. Brownell agreed. The President repeated his instructions as to what Faubus should say in his telegram, and rang off.

The language required of Faubus actually read: "It is certainly my intention to comply with the order . . . by the district court." What Faubus wired instead was: "It is certainly my desire to comply with the order . . . consistent with my [constitutional] responsibilities," which was quite a different formulation. The President raised no objection, but his single condition for receiving the governor had not been accommodated.

Faubus came to Newport on Saturday. For twenty minutes he and the President talked alone and measured each other; then they joined Brownell, Adams, and others for a discussion that lasted more than an hour. As with the altered phrases in Faubus's telegram, which the President had chosen to ignore, a fuzziness developed in the conversation: the President imagined the governor had agreed to go home to Little Rock and change his orders to the National Guard so that the militia would "continue to preserve order but allow the Negro children to attend Central High School." Perhaps Faubus had agreed to do so, but the statement he later issued to reporters was silent on the point. The troops stayed at their stations, their orders unchanged. The Negro children stayed away from the school.

Eisenhower was outraged. The word went out that he believed he had been double-crossed. Further, and perhaps even more heinous, Faubus had failed to pay proper respect to the office of President of the United States.

On the following Friday, September 20, Ronald Davies, the federal judge sitting in Little Rock, declared: "It is very clear . . . that the plan of integration adopted by the Little Rock school board and approved by this court and the Court of Appeals . . . has been thwarted by the governor of Arkansas by the use of the national guard. It is equally demonstrated . . . that there would have been no violence in carrying out the plan of integration . . ." Judge Davies thereupon enjoined Faubus and the officers of the National Guard from any further interference with the integration. The troops were withdrawn later that day. At last the governor had done something Eisenhower could approve. Now he might postpone his own decision for two or three days. Already Brownell was reminding him that, soon or late, he might have to order army troops to Little Rock. Eisenhower brushed the thought away. To move troops might spread violence. He was loath even to consider it. He spoke bitterly of Faubus's broken promise. If the Negro children were admitted to the school, he asked, was there a legal way for the governor to close the school entirely? Brownell promised to look into the question. The President feared that Faubus and other southern governors might abolish public schools entirely. He groaned. Well, at least he had got the weekend free.

On Monday, September 23, from all over Little Rock there assembled a mob, goaded by the White Citizens' Council and by Governor Faubus, determined to bar the door of Central High School to the Negro children. City and state police put up barricades. The mob, distracted by the appearance of four Negro reporters, whirled about, beating anyone whose skin was colored. During the confusion the Negro children slipped unnoticed into the school. A handful of white children, recent adepts in bigotry, left in protest, apprising the mob of what had happened. Hysterical white women commenced to scream, "The niggers are in our school!" and the riot was on. It lasted three hours and resulted in the departure of the Negro children at noon, under heavy police escort.

Eleven A.M. in Newport. Eisenhower was on his way to the country club when an urgent telephone call from Brownell fetched him back. Now he was faced with the need for another crisp decision.

Across the South the consensus was that Faubus had been right to call out the guard and, further, that the rioting vindicated his sound judgment. He was a folk hero. To the contrary, Eisenhower, whose popularity and prestige had never stood higher than at his second inaugural eight months before, had lost considerable ground, especially in the South.*

As of Monday afternoon, the governor of Arkansas seemed to have outmaneuvered the President, especially since Eisenhower had so recently gone on record as being against the idea of sending federal troops anywhere to enforce the orders of a federal court. As this notion gathered strength, so did dismay at the picture of the President disporting himself on the golf links of Newport while a full-fledged crisis in race relations was raging elsewhere in the republic. Even his trusted friend Al Gruenther, now retired from the command of NATO and resident in Washington, wrote him to urge that he return at once to the White House. Eisenhower irritably disagreed; he retorted to Gruenther:

* According to the Gallup poll in January 1957, 79 percent of Americans approved the way Eisenhower was doing his job; by early October—after his eventual decision at Little Rock—only 64 percent approved his action, and in the South 53 percent thought he had been wrong while a scant 36 percent approved the course he had taken.

The White House office is wherever the President happens to be. To rush back to Washington every time an incident of a serious character arose would be a confession that a change of scenery is truly a "vacation" for the President and is not merely a change of his working locale. This is untrue. I have never been away from Washington when the important problems did not follow me and the necessity for making the decisions remain with me. . . .

. . . The great need is to act calmly, deliberately, and giving every offender opportunity to cease his defiance of Federal law . . .

Nevertheless, the President was sensitive about his public image and about public reactions to what he hoped was his private behavior. After many telephone calls had been exchanged with the attorney general about the proclamation and the statement the President was to issue about events at Little Rock, Eisenhower asked Brownell for advice about his behavior: should he stay in his office? steer clear of the country club? Brownell suggested he should follow his normal routine and avoid the appearance of being frozen.

The proclamation of Monday evening commanded "all persons" obstructing integration in Little Rock "to cease and desist therefrom and to disperse forthwith." The stately clump of this official jargon failed to impress the rabble that hastened from hundreds of miles around to demonstrate in Little Rock on Tuesday. Their arrival hastened the decision that had impended ever since the rioting began the day before. Eisenhower had two telephone conversations with Brownell on Tuesday morning, the second to discuss the frantic appeal for help from Woodrow Wilson Mann, the mayor of Little Rock. At 11:45 A.M. Knowland called to ask if the President would be coming back to Washington. "No," said Eisenhower, and then bethought himself. "Well," he said, "I might." At 12:08 P.M. he decided to sign the order to federalize the Arkansas National Guard and send regular army troops to Little Rock. He was, an aide reported, "deeply troubled." At 12:15 P.M. he called the army chief of staff, General Maxwell Taylor, and after mooting with him the preferability of using the guard or the army, decided on the army. Taylor agreed: paratroopers of the 101st Airborne were flown from Fort Campbell, Kentucky, to be replaced by units of the guard as they were made ready. At 12:47 P.M. the President instructed his secretary, Mrs. Whitman, that they would leave for Washington at 3:30 P.M. He was in wretched spirits.

Back in the White House, the President was shown another recent survey of world press reaction. Predictably, the Soviet propaganda mill was busily churning out a combination of slanted facts and wicked fancy. According to a report of the U.S. Information Service, "News photographs were particularly damaging to U.S. prestige." USIS officials feared a serious adverse public reaction abroad if further violence erupted at Little Rock. The President was properly concerned.

So what had gone wrong? Had he erred? He spoke to the country on Tuesday night, he spoke of "demogogic extremists," of "disorderly mobs," of "violent opposition." He mentioned the decision of the Supreme Court that had outlawed segregated public schools; he asserted, "Our personal opinions about the decision have no bearing on the matter of enforcement"; he emphasized his own ties to the South and his many southern friends; he dwelt on the legal, the constitutional aspects of his action, and surely they were sound. Yet he was excoriated by men for whom he had the deepest respect—Senator Richard Russell of Georgia, for instance, the courtly leader of the southern conservatives and longtime ally of the Republican conservatives of the North—they were accusing him of issuing "orders to mix the races."

"Few times in my life," Eisenhower wrote Russell, "have I felt as saddened as when . . ."

He must erase the impression that he had sent troops to Little Rock for the sake of the Negro school children or to help achieve integration. No! He had done so to oblige obedience to the order of a federal court, no more.

". . . the obligations of my office required me to order the use of force within a state to carry out the decisions of a federal court. . . ."

Here was the contradiction, the essence of what was wrong with Eisenhower's grasp of the tragic problem. First he had temporized, as if hoping the problem might somehow take care of itself or be resolved by an intervention of providence; next he had maintained that "you cannot change people's hearts merely by laws," and still had refused his leadership despite repeated appeals by the southern Negroes most sorely beset; now at length he had been forced to put his reliance on what he had earlier scorned, the law of the matter. Now he must hope that by enforcing the law with troops he might somehow control the explosive emotions he might have contained earlier in the year by forthright authority of his own persuasive personality. He could not have it both ways, first disparaging the law but declining to win men's hearts, then invoking the law and backing it with bayonets. His ambition had been to unite the country, to reconcile opposing factions by calling upon a vigorous and growing Center. But on this issue the Center was divided. Indeed, Eisenhower could himself no longer properly define that Center. For some months those of his aides concerned with racial and minority problems had been pressing him to give audience to a small group of Negro leaders. Now he argued he could not receive the Negroes because if he did he would have to give equal time to the leaders of the Ku Klux Klan. So it seemed to the President: the Negroes forming one extreme, the KKK the other, and himself holding a Center that had swerved far off center.

In Little Rock the high school was again open and the Negro children were at last in attendance. Nothing had been permanently settled. The troops would stand guard over Central High School throughout the school year, Faubus would solicit and be given a state law to close the school next fall, the issue would once again wind through the courts. Emancipation awaited a President more deeply stirred by the denial of human rights.

This President was obsessed by problems he was certain were of greater gravity than the inequality of a small fraction of his fellow citizens.

On Friday, October 4, the Soviet Union lifted into orbit an artificial satellite, the first in history. They called it "Sputnik," a word whimsically translated as "fellow traveler." Their news agency, Tass, presently reported that Sputnik weighed one hundred and eighty-four pounds, that it was zipping around the earth at approximately eight thousand miles an hour at an altitude of five hundred and sixty miles. Its course was polar (counterclockwise north–south–north), and as the earth revolved, its satellite passed over different countries of the world, sending back continuous radio signals from two transmitters.

Of the many conceivable reactions to the news of this event, Americans seem chiefly to have experienced either of two. First: unfeigned delight at the astonishing and unexpected leap into space. This exultant emotion, swiftly suppressed, was harbored only by the naïve. Second: profound gloom suffused with fear; the United States, ever victorious, destined by God to be the world's most powerful nation, blessed with an economic and political system of superlative merit, whose people were masters of a matchless technology, had all at once plummeted to second place, yielding primacy to a herd of hopelessly backward peasants. This despair possessed every patriot and cold warrior: If the Reds could put a sputnik aloft, surely they could send intercontinental ballistic missiles winging anywhere they chose? drop hydrogen warheads wherever? rule the world?

No, for at least two good reasons. The technology of orbiting a satellite was and is markedly different from that of delivering on target an ICBM; even more important, there was substantial doubt that the Soviets had any considerable number of ICBMs to launch even had they wished to do so. In August they had announced the successful test-firing of an ICBM; four days later Pentagon spokesmen had imperturbably reported that the USSR had launched at least four and probably six ICBMs in a series of tests two months earlier. (This marked a small underground war between opposing intelligence services: the U.S., cool and disdainful, was reminding the USSR that huge U.S. electronic grids—the "billboard" radar installations in northern Turkey—were quite able to monitor and track any Soviet missiles for three thousand miles or more.) Those tests had suggested to U.S. analysts that the Soviet missiles were still appreciably short of readiness for use. "The big thing to remember," Eisenhower had told his press conference on September 3, "is that a mere tested vehicle is a long ways from actual production."

Nevertheless, the Soviet sputnik was a most impressive scientific feat. As if to show it had been no fluke, on November 2 the Russians hoisted another satellite, six times as heavy as the first one, into an orbit more than a thousand miles in space. To American scientists the weight of the first sputnik had been "fantastic," for the satellite they planned to launch weighed less than twenty-two pounds.* Now came a second sputnik with a payload of more than half a ton, indicating that Soviet science had developed rocket propulsion fuels well beyond current U.S. capability.

The scientific facts demonstrated one towering political fact: the postulates that had guided Dulles—and Eisenhower—in the Cold War stood exposed as flimsy and hazardous. Dulles, for example, had predicted that "under the pressure of faith and hope and peaceful works, the rigid, top-heavy and overextended structure of Communist rule could readily come into a state of collapse." The policy of "containment" had been replaced, at least rhetorically, by the policy of "rollback," which in practice had once again become the policy of "containment." The pressure of faith and hope and peaceful works had been buttressed by the pressure of economic and social boycott and by the pressure of military bases in a menacing ring of steel that girdled the landmass from Berlin to the China Sea— to what end? Since 1950 the Soviet economy had flourished (in 1950–1957 the Soviet gross national product was up better than 7 percent annually, a rate of increase nearly 50 percent greater than that of the U.S.) and quite obviously so had Soviet science. It was a time when Americans glumly surveyed the roster of those scientists who had vouchsafed them a fleeting monopoly of nuclear power: Einstein (German), Fermi (Italian), von Neumann (Hungarian), Teller (Hungarian), Szilard (Hungarian), Bohr (Danish), and Oppenheimer (American but booted out in disgrace by the Eisenhower administration). The entire American educational system might have to be restructured in order to train more American children in the scientific disciplines.

* More embarrassment attended the first American effort on December 6. After much fanfare of publicity, the rocket vehicle which was expected to lift a three-pound satellite into orbit from Cape Canaveral, Florida, instead exploded on its launching pad and the brave attempt fizzled.

These fancies, so disconcerting to American cold warriors, spawned criticism, most of it aimed at Secretary Dulles but a good bit of it splashing on the President as well. To begin with there was stern disapproval of the slighting tone used by Eisenhower and officials of his administration when they came to speak of the Soviet achievement. Thus, after the first sputnik had been lifted aloft, the President spoke of how "they say they have put one small ball in the air," and Sherman Adams airily dismissed the need to engage in "an outer-space basketball game." Editorial writers and newspaper columnists at once unlimbered the word "complacency" and gave it a thorough workout.

To some extent, complacency was the wrong charge. It is true that the spectacular Russian ventures into space prodded the President to take some specific steps—the appointment of Dr. James Killian, president of the Massachusetts Institute of Technology, as a special assistant for science and technology; the transfer of a panel of scientists from the Office of Defense Mobilization to more immediate reference as advisers to the President; some administrative safeguards to keep the production of military missiles from being snarled in interservice rivalries—that he might otherwise have never considered, as it is also true that those steps were little more than a fresh approach to the flow chart of responsibilities within the executive branch. But the National Security Council had under constant review whatever clues to Soviet weaponry might have been netted by the various agencies of intelligence. The U–2, that remarkable instrument of high-altitude espionage, was already engaged in flights over Soviet territory —detected by Soviet radar but still far beyond reach of Soviet ground-to-air missiles—with the result that within the CIA and the White House a few trustworthy souls were able to draw reasonably accurate conclusions about the development of the Soviet ability to make war. The Soviet inclination to make war was of course another matter entirely, and any attempt to define that x factor was likely to yield only a character analysis of the man making the attempt.

In addition to these tools, the President was in the habit of nominating to advisory panels various citizens of blameless background who could independently study the facts available and, from the varying standpoints of their special competences, collaborate to produce reports that could be set against the conclusions already reached by the NSC. In this way the President could from time to time consult an impartial jury of experts, as insurance lest his own advisers might have led him astray or inclined him to overlook a possibility, good or bad.

Thus in April 1957 Eisenhower had appointed a group of citizens who collectively bore a crushing title: the Security Resources Panel of the Science Advisory Committee of the Office of Defense Mobilization; and this group's findings came to be known as the Gaither Report, taking its name from the chairman, Rowan Gaither, who was then the chairman of the Ford Foundation. The Gaither Report was a tolerably lurid forty-page warning entitled "Deterrence and Survival in the Nuclear Age." It afforded a fair example of how cold warriors and the tensions of the Cold War could interact to give the unwary an agonizing attack of the jitters. William C. Foster of the Olin Mathieson Chemical Corporation, who was a director of the Gaither panel, was widely quoted as saying, of his weeks of work on the report: "I felt as though I were spending ten hours a day staring straight into hell."*

With guidance by men like Foster, the Gaither Report was sure to take a doleful view of the future. "We have found no evidence," the report declared, "in Russian foreign and military policy since 1945 to refute the conclusion that USSR intentions are expansionist, and that her great efforts to build military power go beyond any concepts of Soviet defense."

This was to say: what in the hands of the U.S. we think of as deterrent, in the hands of the USSR we regard as aggressive. Since in the USSR the military experts took a mirror view of the problem, the chances for disarmament or détente were, in late 1957, nil.

The Gaither Report stated that the Russians were superior to the Americans in weapons technology. All evidence "clearly indicates an increasing threat which may become critical in 1959 or early 1960." The civil defense precautions undertaken by the U.S. in 1957 "will not give adequate assurance of protection to the civil population," therefore some twenty-five billion dollars should be spent to build shelters all over the nation. "The current vulnerability of SAC [Strategic Air Command] to surprise attack during a period of lessened world tension (i.e., a time when SAC is not on a SAC 'alert' status), and the threat posed to SAC by the prospects of an early Russian ICBM capability, call for prompt remedial action." Another nineteen billion dollars, making forty-four billions in all, should be spent on improved weaponry. It was, as the phrase goes, as American as apple pie: incomprehensibly vast sums of money to be spent on security, and little time wasted on the quality of what was to be made secure.

A good many of these dire predictions found their way into the hands of one enterprising reporter or another. President Eisenhower had reckoned they would; what he had not imagined was that his careful efforts to guard

* Foster had served under President Truman as deputy secretary of defense, so he was no stranger to the Cold War and could scarcely be accounted an impartial expert. He was later to help light a balefire to alert the republic to the danger it faced from Soviet and scientific achievements. Foster would go so far as to deliver a speech which was interpreted as advocating preventive war.

against any dreadful eventualities would be turned against him, and the Gaither Report he had requested used as evidence of his complacency, simply because he was not ready to accept all its recommendations without demur or investigation.

A great holler went up in the press. President Eisenhower was neither prepared to act upon the vital warnings of the Gaither panel nor willing to let the country know how desperate was its plight if those warnings were not heeded.

For months now the President had been the target of increasingly hostile criticism: he had botched the fight over his budget, he had suffered his own civil rights legislation to be emasculated, he had refused his leadership in the intensified racial crisis, he had permitted the Soviet Union to intrude its influence in the Middle East, Little Rock was his fault, inflation was undermining the economy, he had stood by while the Soviet Union outstripped the U.S. in the conquest of space, the country stood in deadly peril, but he blandly denied the public's right even to be informed of the emergency.

Worst of his delinquencies were the sputniks. The sputniks had inflicted the deepest wounds in the American ego, so deep indeed that the President had decided even before the second satellite was lifted that he must invite Prime Minister Macmillan to Washington, in the hope that the visible Anglo-American unity might serve to soothe the national alarms. Macmillan was urged to cook up some excuse for his visit—a lecture, an honorary degree—lest the reason for his arrival be too obvious. Perhaps never did a state conference go so smoothly: all had been tidily composed beforehand: collaboration on weapons, on nuclear energy, on missiles.*
The British were under no illusions as to the cause of this sudden rush of friendship. "The President," Macmillan observed, "is under severe attack for [the] first time. Foster [Dulles] is under still more severe attack. His policies are said to have failed everywhere. . . . The President . . . complained a good deal about 'politicians' and the attacks upon himself. (This is a new experience for him. Up to now, he has been immune.)"

Next Eisenhower had sought to reassure the nation with a series of televised speeches on science and defense, the subjects of the moment. Four speeches were scheduled. Two were delivered. They were pedestrian efforts. At a time when a disillusioned people were being plied with gaudier tailfins on more expensive automobiles as compensation for the sputniks whirling about in space, it was not enough for the President to say: "We want adequate security. We want no more than adequacy. But we will accept nothing less. My friends, it has always been my faith that eventual

---

* Macmillan noted in his journal: "I could hardly believe my ears—such rapid progress, to be publicly announced."

triumph of decency and freedom and right in this world is inevitable." Not enough. None of the phrases reverberated, and the voice had warmth but no spirit, no urgency.

Early in November the Gallup poll reported that only 57 percent of his fellow citizens had confidence in the way Eisenhower was running the country—a comfortable majority, but down 22 percent from January. There had been confidence at least in his grasp of military affairs. It was shaken.

Over Sunday and Monday, November 10 and 11, the President was given a complete physical examination at Walter Reed Army Hospital. His condition was pronounced "excellent."

From Friday, November 15, to Thursday, November 21, the President relaxed at Augusta National, working a little, golfing regularly. There had been fewer press conferences than usual; reporters got the impression the President was withdrawn, secluded within a circle of his intimate cronies. All that was known was that he planned another of his science and security speeches, to be delivered in Cleveland toward the end of the month, and that in December he was to attend a session of the NATO Council in Paris. Jim Hagerty was already in Paris to prepare the ground.

The drumfire of criticism continued unabated.

On Monday, November 25, the President was driven to Washington National Airport to greet the king of Morocco, Mohammed V, come on a state visit. The day was cold and damp. Back in the White House for what had become a customary midday rest, he was shaken by a chill, a thing of no importance. Having rested and lightly lunched, the President strolled to his oval office to take up again the routine affairs of state.

At his desk he sensed a sudden and strange dizziness. He had just suffered his third serious illness in twenty-six months—what was carefully not described as a "stroke," but rather as a "cerebral occlusion." The President of the United States could not hold his pen, nor pick up a piece of paper, nor speak a coherent sentence. He was almost completely helpless. He was at length able to ring for his secretary, the devoted Ann Whitman.

CHAPTER SEVEN

Policing the Globe

Tension in the Middle East . . . and in Venezuela . . . Intervention in Lebanon . . . The exit of Sherman Adams . . . Once again, the Chinese offshore islands . . . The Democrats gain in Congress.

A MONDAY AFTERNOON. Nothing pressing on the President's agenda until that night, a state dinner to honor Mohammed V.

Mrs. Whitman quick to answer her summons, quick to appreciate that something dreadful was afoot. The President talking gibberish. She must not panic, no; but where was his physician, General Snyder? or his staff secretary, General Goodpaster? Bells pushed. Snyder was away from his office, but Goodpaster came swiftly in and as swiftly took command. Within seconds the President was on his feet, Goodpaster's hand steady on his elbow, and he was being guided to his bedroom in the Executive Mansion.

No pain. No difficulty in walking. Just a whirling perplexity, and the aphasia—saying something and hearing it come out silly—and the bewilderment.

Soon in bed. The physician on hand. Asleep.

Once again his loyal staff—what the right-wing Republicans liked to call the palace guard—were shaken and dismayed. No need to remind them of what the President had told his press conference twenty months before: "I have said, unless I felt absolutely up to the performance of the duties of the President, the second that I didn't, I would no longer be there in the job or I wouldn't be available for the job." He regarded those words as a pledge to the American people. It was inconceivable that he would hedge. What then was to be done? What ailed him? What of the state dinner that night? What to say to the press? Why was Hagerty in Paris when he was needed here? (A cablegram was sent to Hagerty bidding him hasten home.)

The President slept.

Mamie Eisenhower's distress was quite naturally keener than that of the White House staff, but private and personal. Her son John had been summoned and joined her in her bedroom, next door to the President's. The two sat waiting, apprehensive, wondering what might be wrong, how grave, whether permanent.

In mid-afternoon General Snyder arrived with several other army physicians to find out. For an hour or more they tested, prodded, examined, questioned, and at length conferred privately. Clearly it was a cardio-vascular accident of some sort, but which? a hemorrhage? a thrombosis? an embolism? Those words would needlessly alarm; they hit upon the word "spasm"—a minor "spasm," they agreed, and so informed the President. That it was relatively minor was already becoming obvious. Eisenhower was speaking more clearly, his mind was active, his temper was character-istically short, and his robust vitality was odds-on to warrant him a swift recovery. Still—no one could be sure. The attending physicians nodded, agreed they must bring in two or three neurologists for consultation, and departed. The President, once again alone, drowsed.

Meanwhile, word was spreading and leaving more men aghast. Mrs. Whitman told Governor Adams. "The President has gone back to the house," she said. "Just now he gave up and went home. I can't imagine what's wrong with him." Adams telephoned Nixon's office on Capitol Hill: he wanted the Vice President ready in case he were needed.

More hasty agitated conferences: General Snyder with Mrs. Eisenhower and John, Governor Adams in and out, General Goodpaster ready at hand. In the room adjoining, the President was awake and within him was stirring the stimulus that drove him most powerfully—his sense of duty. He had, he recalled, to be host that night to Mohammed of Morocco. He pulled himself together, slipped a dressing gown over his pajamas, stuck his feet into slippers, and padded casually into his wife's room. Odds were he imagined those in the room would be happy to see him, for he had his big cheerful smile on his face when he shuffled in. Doctor, wife, and son were alike consternated, and a lively dispute at once erupted, three against one, with Governor Adams presently joining the majority. Eisenhower, his words tumbling out thick and twisted, insisted he meant to attend the state dinner as planned. Faced with opposition, he flushed, grew stubborn, then abruptly swung around and was understood to splutter, "If I cannot attend to my duties, I am simply going to give up this job. Now that's all there is to it." He was gone.

Nixon replaced the President at dinner that night, but Mrs. Eisen-hower, poised and gracious, was the hostess as usual. The White House reporters were told only that the President had suffered a "chill."

Early the next morning Nixon, Foster Dulles, and a half-dozen other senior officials gathered in Adams's office. In their ignorance of Eisenhower's condition, they were even more concerned than they had been two years before at the time of his heart attack. Nervous, apprehensive, their inclination was to fix upon someone to blame for their plight and the President's. They had not far to seek. His critics were culpable. The unhappy President had been "deeply wounded by the attacks upon him." The notion that the President never read the newspapers was absurd; of course he read them, and had "suffered deeply under recent criticism—and this [his stroke] was the result."

Thus his loyal and devoted associates closed ranks around their stricken chief.

Upstairs in the Executive Mansion another team of physicians—mainly neurologists—was deploying another battery of tests. They came downstairs to Nixon and the others with good news and bad. Eisenhower was not seriously afflicted by his stroke, but who could tell when he might not be felled by another one—graver, more damaging? For Nixon, sobering intelligence. He had already been told by Adams, "You may be President in the next twenty-four hours." Now he was told that Eisenhower should have sixty days of complete rest lest his volatile blood pressure once again start to surge up. It was proposed, and Nixon agreed, that he substitute for the President at the NATO meeting now only twenty days away. This was to reckon without their host.

Eisenhower, after experiencing frustration and a flash of temper when he found he was still unable to put the words he wanted on his tongue, had reconciled himself to a day away from his desk. But he meant to get to work soon—he would tackle government business on a limited scale on Wednesday—and he was determined to attend the NATO meeting. He regarded the Paris conference as a test: if he were able to travel to Paris and participate actively in the proceedings, he would have proved to his own satisfaction that he could continue to function as President; if he fell short of that goal, he would resign.

Such a step, while without precedent in American history, would not have come as a staggering shock at the time. In fact, many persons—politicians like Senator Wayne Morse, and editors of newspapers and magazines—were forthrightly urging Eisenhower to resign. Even those who damned Nixon as an odious liability joined the chorus. The alternative, it was believed, was to maintain in power a figurehead behind whom sinister forces schemed unseen. So eminent a commentator as Walter Lippmann recommended that Eisenhower delegate his powers to Nixon for the period of his convalescence. His many protestations to the contrary notwithstanding, Eisenhower attended closely to these editorial counsels; they angered him, and they confirmed him in his determination to put himself to the trial. Rather than rest, as he had been bidden by his physicians, he deliberately stepped up his activity during the fortnight before he would be leaving for Paris.

Not least of his preoccupations was the budget for the fiscal year 1959, which had to be clinched and made ready to send to the Congress in early January 1958. After his experiences with its predecessor earlier in the year, Eisenhower was in no mood for "modern Republicanism." He moved without hesitation toward accelerated spending on military programs, advanced weapons systems, and space age projects; without compunction he authorized "curtailments, revisions, or eliminations of certain present civil programs, and deferments of previously recommended new programs." In short, he turned his back upon school and hospital construction, welfare, urban development, housing, and other civil needs, but he approved a peacetime record for spending on military hardware at home and military assistance abroad.*

Eisenhower's knotty sessions with his budget director, Percival Brundage, struck familiar chords in the President's memory, reminding him of recent ordeals. And now, as he began to look forward to his trip to Paris for the NATO Council, other echoes of the past began to resound: in the United States but even more insistently in the countries of western Europe a clamor was raised for another session at the summit. Why was there no accommodation in the Cold War? Why no attempt to make a reasonable settlement with the Soviet Union? Why—as the danger of Soviet ICBMs grew greater; as the United States government contemplated for reply only a generous distribution of her own IRBMs, offering to scatter them on NATO bases from Norway to Turkey; as fearful talk of ballistic missiles and anti-ballistic missiles filled the newspapers; as the whole demented structure of devastation grew more menacing—why in tophet could the statesmen not attain a more hopeful coexistence?

On the eve of the NATO conference the Russians suggested a meeting at the summit to seek an accord on disarmament, an immediate ban on all nuclear weapons tests, to last at least two years, and the demilitarization of central Europe. Dulles dismissed the idea on the grounds that the Russians were not to be trusted. "Our experience," he wrote in an article for the magazine *Life*, "demonstrates that the governments dominated by international communism practice Lenin's dictum, 'Promises are like pie crusts, made to be broken.'" Prime Minister Nehru of India made a public appeal

---

* His budget for FY 1959 projected expenditures of $73.9 billion and receipts of $74.4 billion, yielding a modest surplus. In fact, for that twelvemonth, expenditures topped $80.3 billion and receipts were only $67.9 billion, leaving a substantial deficit and a nation of patient taxpayers whose postal rates were also raised.

to Eisenhower "to stop all nuclear test explosions and thus to show to the world that [you] are determined to end this menace." Eisenhower rejected the appeal. It was, he cabled Nehru, "a sacrifice which we could not in prudence accept." The U.S. government had once again retreated behind the slogan: Never negotiate save from a position of strength.

"The NATO meeting," Eisenhower later concluded, "was a success." If this judgment was limited to his personal achievement, it was sound: he was welcomed in Paris by cheering scores of thousands; on all sides his gallantry in attending the meeting so soon after his illness was acknowledged; even his request for thirty seconds of prayerful meditation after the last session won respectful assent, with traces of amusement for the most part repressed; he had passed his self-imposed test with colors flying. But as far as U.S. policy was concerned, the NATO meeting could not be accounted a success. One ally after another insisted on negotiations with the Soviets before any deployment of nuclear missiles would be permitted. They made abundantly clear the European determination to seek an abatement of the Cold War. Dulles might stubbornly sustain old enmities by poking the embers of an outworn ideology, he might succeed in twice inserting the phrase "international communism" into the final communiqué, but the Norwegians, Danes, Dutch, Canadians, even the Germans were tiring of his intransigent refusal to seek an accommodation of nuclear rivalries.

Back in the U.S., Eisenhower and Dulles appeared together on television to report to the nation—two elderly men on a shadowy screen, speaking tiredly of their readiness "to make any conceivable effort . . . to reduce world tensions" and of how the Soviets had "failed to inspire confidence in free men." But they failed themselves to lift hearts, to inspire confidence.

The President's second term had three years to run. In many ways those years would seem like a rerun of his first five years. The same crises would recur, having only the comfort of familiarity. The same frozen confrontations—the Middle East, Quemoy and Matsu, Little Rock, Berlin, racial tension, Vietnam, disarmament, pleas for meetings at the summit—would reappear like ducks in a shooting gallery. And as the old problems bobbed up again, their monotony relieved only by the emergence of a few new ones, criticism of the Eisenhower administration would wax. Hopeful Democrats would seize upon all kinds of issues, most of them, like the so-called "missile gap," fabricated from whole cloth. President Eisenhower would take refuge from criticism in the consolation that his elaborate technique of staff planning—involving the cabinet, NSC, and occasional advisory commissions—was sufficient to fend off each crisis as it appeared.

One fresh aspect was the presence of new faces round his council tables. Of his four most senior cabinet officers, three had departed by January 1958: George Humphrey of Treasury, replaced by Robert Anderson; "Engine Charley" Wilson of Defense, replaced by another businessman, Neil McElroy, formerly president of Procter & Gamble, a manufactory of soaps and detergents; and Herbert Brownell, the attorney general, succeeded by his deputy William Rogers, a close friend of Vice President Nixon. The only one left of the top four cabinet officers was Foster Dulles, and he was resented, mistrusted, and disliked as never before, drawing fire alike abroad and at home. The rumors of his impending resignation were heard on every hand; they were printed in the newspapers.

"Trash," said the President angrily when he was told of them, and he went on to praise Dulles as "the wisest, most dedicated man that I know."

Loyalty is a highly prized virtue, but Foster Dulles was an exceedingly unpopular man and to stand at his side was risky. Further, the economic "recession" was getting worse and even beginning to feel like a full-fledged depression. More men were out of work. Farm prices were skidding. More hard questions were being asked about the President's frequent trips south to play golf. What with one thing and another, in the late winter of 1958 Dwight Eisenhower's popularity, as measured by the polls, was never so sickly.

On April 30 the President was asked a question about Indonesia. "The prime minister of Indonesia calls on the United States for a clear effort to prevent the United States citizens from aiding the rebels. He claims Americans are flying rebel planes. What is your reaction to that, sir?"

The question had been expected.

The republic of Indonesia, despite its independence won in 1949, was still seeking to dislodge the Dutch from West Irian, the western half of the island of New Guinea. Late in 1957 President Achmed Sukarno had warned of economic retaliation if the Dutch rejected a peaceful solution of the dispute; in December the government had authorized strikes against Dutch-owned enterprises and seizure of Dutch banks and commercial interests. In Paris the NATO Council had viewed these "serious events . . . with concern." Four giant American oil companies (Jersey Standard, Socony Mobil, Texaco, and Standard of California) operated oil fields in Indonesia, so naturally the U.S. government was likewise concerned.

By a striking coincidence, a group of Indonesian rebels had materialized in January 1958 declaring its intention of saving the republic from Sukarno and the communists. Asked about this rebellion in February, Foster Dulles told reporters it was "primarily an internal problem," but that quite naturally the U.S. would look with favor upon an Indonesian government "which is constitutional and which reflects the real interest" of the people. He doubted the Muslim people of the republic would ever settle for "a communist-dominated government."

For a time in March and April the rebels were able to field military units of some substance; they had named a government of sorts; they had backing from some external source, for foreign aircraft conducted nuisance raids against Sukarno's troops and dropped small arms to the rebels. "We are pursuing what I trust is a correct course from the point of view of international law," Dulles told the House Foreign Affairs Committee. "And we are not intervening in the internal affairs of this country." When the air raids persisted, the Indonesian premier, Djuanda Kartawidjaja, voiced his accusations against "United States and Taiwan adventurers."

So when he was asked the question, the President expected it.

THE PRESIDENT: I had a discussion about this one this morning, and I can say this only: when it comes to an intrastate difficulty anywhere, our policy is one of careful neutrality and proper deportment all the way through so as not to be taking sides where it is none of our business.

Now, on the other hand, every rebellion that I have ever heard of has its soldiers of fortune . . . people going out looking for a good fight and getting into it sometimes in the hope of pay, and sometimes just for the heck of the thing. . . .

As I say, we will unquestionably assure the prime minister, through the State Department, that our deportment will continue to be correct.

This answer was not true. Indeed, an aura of improbability shimmers all around it, as when the President used the chilly phrase "intrastate difficulty" to describe a bloody rebellion fomented by counterrevolutionaries, as though he were wondering whether or not it fell within the jurisdiction of the Interstate Commerce Commission. The untruth blanketed a wide expanse of time and space, too, for the President was declaring that his administration would never interfere in the internal affairs of another sovereign state. This was rhetorical flummery, as evidenced by past, present, and future actions of his administration; but so long as his fellow citizens were persuaded he was protecting the nation from the dangers of international communism no one would blow the whistle on him.

As for the present the CIA had recruited American fliers to pilot B–26s and ferry other aircraft in and out of an airstrip in the North Celebes in support of the rebels trying to overthrow Sukarno. As their base of operations the CIA fliers used Clark Field, a U.S. Air Force base near Manila in the Philippines. Every detail of their activities was necessarily kept most secret. Any allegations about their mission was routinely denied. Nothing might ever have been known of it save for one mishap: one of the B–26s was shot down and its pilot, Allen Lawrence Pope, was captured by the Indonesian army—eighteen days after the President had spoken airily of "soldiers of fortune." The diary, documents, and identification papers Pope carried were sufficient proof of his respect for "careful neutrality and proper deportment."

A remarkable turnabout of U.S. policy followed. Within five days of Pope's capture—even before the Indonesian army had made public any word of his capture—the sale to Indonesia of thirty-seven thousand tons of rice was approved by the State Department, and licenses were granted for the export to Indonesia of a shipment of small arms and nearly one million dollars' worth of aircraft and radio parts.

This commerce was hastily authorized despite some deplorable remarks by Sukarno. The president of Indonesia predicted "the fall of capitalism and imperialism" as "an historical certainty." He foresaw a "new era" of "socialism and the brotherhood of man." Those "who cannot understand or [who] oppose the trend of the times," he said, "will be destroyed." Not the sort of comment to commend him to Eisenhower or to Dulles.

While the President was with one finger, so to say, maintaining a careful neutrality and proper deportment in the internal affairs of Indonesia, he was plunging with both hands into the internal affairs of Lebanon.

In 1958 Lebanese politics were unusual: it was nominally one of the Arab countries and a member of the Arab League; but a slim majority of its people were Christian—Maronite Catholic—and this odd mix had resulted in an odd political pattern. President, foreign minister, and commander in chief of the army were traditionally Christian; prime minister and speaker of the legislature were Muslim. The compromise had been comfortably adjusted for nearly a generation. He who tinkered with it risked disruption, even chaos.

Following the brief war over Suez in 1956, the delicate balance had been jeopardized by an influx of Arab refugees from Palestine. In the early spring of 1958 it was finally upset by Camille Chamoun, president of Lebanon, when word got about that he favored an amendment of the Lebanese constitution which would permit him an unprecedented second term. To the Lebanese people this was intolerable. Eisenhower might believe Chamoun "the ablest of the Lebanese politicians," but in Lebanon the list of his transgressions was lengthy and growing. Arab nationalists considered him too closely allied with the great western powers. Lebanon alone in the Middle East had accepted the Eisenhower Doctrine. It was whispered that Chamoun owed his election to the CIA. He had manipulated the parliamentary elections in 1957 so expertly as almost to eliminate all parliamentary opposition.* And now Chamoun would amend the constitution to perpetuate himself in office? Rebellion erupted. Armed mobs rioted. In Tripoli and Beirut, USIS libraries were sacked and burned. Leaders of the opposition warned that violence would continue until "the dictatorial power of Camille Chamoun falls." From the U.S. ambassador in Beirut came an urgent cablegram. Chamoun wished to know "what our actions would be if he were to request our assistance."

President Eisenhower shared with Dulles a "deep-seated conviction that the Communists were principally responsible for the trouble [in Lebanon], and that President Chamoun was motivated only by a strong feeling of patriotism." Eisenhower cleared time to consult with the Dulles brothers and a few other advisers on Tuesday, May 13. The meeting turned out to be held, as Eisenhower would recall it, "in a climate of impatience" because of a unanimous belief on the part of those in his oval office that Chamoun's alarm had been touched off by still another communist provocation. As the President and his advisers surveyed the globe, they fancied they could identify all sorts of initiatives by international communism—Foster Dulles preferred to capitalize the initial letters of those words, as if to make of them a malediction—contrived in the Kremlin and cunningly designed to undermine the free world. In Eisenhower's subsequent view, "the Soviets were pushing everywhere, stirring up trouble in Venezuela, Indonesia, and Burma, not to mention the Middle East." As if deliberately to exasperate, at the same time from the Kremlin came urgent invitations, publicly promoted, to attain a peaceful coexistence. Thus the Soviets announced a unilateral suspension of nuclear weapons tests, appealing to the U.S. to follow suit, but the U.S. dismissed the offer as propaganda and went on testing.

Here was a nice instance of the danger of succumbing to an obsession. Because of the Cold War the perception of the President and his senior advisers was focused on one grievance to the exclusion of all others. Communism—or better, international communism—took the blame for violent disorders, riots, even rebellions, that were more properly attributable to the ferment of nationalism, or to failures of U.S. foreign policy, or to other causes more obscure and more complex. One root of Indonesia's troubles, for example, was parochial. Sukarno, who was in a good position to judge, later maintained the rebels were partly motivated by a separatism based on the economic rivalry between Sumatra and Java, the two richest islands of the republic; anticommunism was an afterthought, adopted when

---

* Even Foster Dulles had professed concern at the remarkable outcome of those elections. They seemed to have been too efficiently managed.

the rebels recognized that external aid would be given them only if they brandished a banner bearing that brave device. The troubles in Burma derived from a purely local struggle to find which elements of the coalition that had ended colonial rule would hold power in the new independence. Venezuela was another matter. What happened in Burma or Indonesia went generally unnoticed in the West, but what was happening on that very day in Venezuela would make outsize headlines all across the United States.

In Eisenhower's office the discussion of Lebanon and the Middle East droned on. Radio stations in Cairo and Damascus were broadcasting encouragement to the Lebanese rebels: this seemed a sign that the new United Arab Republic—the alliance of Egypt and Syria, proclaimed in February—might be up to some mischief. Was it communist-inspired? Perhaps not; but in any case it would be wise to take military precautions. The Sixth Fleet was once again ordered to take up station at the eastern end of the Mediterranean. A shipment of small arms and ammunition was expedited for delivery to Lebanon. Some light tanks must be found and sent as well. As for troops, no; not yet; intervention by U.S. troops must be regarded as a last resort, and Chamoun must be so informed.

The senior advisers dispersed to carry out their various instructions. The President was left alone for a few moments to reflect on the world's many troubles—including that in Algeria, where right-wing French army officers were in revolt against the latest French government, and were demanding the return to power of Eisenhower's wartime comrade Charles de Gaulle. Presently he was called on the telephone. Christian Herter, the undersecretary of state, was on the wire to tell him that mobs were rioting in Caracas, Venezuela, that Vice President Richard Nixon and other members of his party had been attacked, and that word from the embassy at Caracas indicated the situation appeared to be confused if not actually hazardous.

Venezuela. Had international communism struck again?

Nixon was on the last leg of a jaunt that had taken him, at Eisenhower's request, to eight South American countries. He was a man who conscientiously sought out confrontations with adversaries, real or fancied, and in 1958 confrontations were not hard to arrange in Latin America. After cantankerous public dialogues in Argentina and Peru, he was amply forewarned that a visit to Caracas might prove perilous. Characteristically, he plunged ahead. His earlier experiences afforded a reasonably accurate prognosis of what was bothering a good many Latin Americans about their rich and powerful neighbor to the north: they resented United States intervention in Guatemala, they objected to the practice of the Eisenhower administration of rewarding dictators like Odría of Peru and Pérez Jiménez of Venezuela with gauds and honors, and they were increasingly aware that for every U.S. dollar invested in Latin America nearly three dollars were taken out—by what one observer has called "the policy of the suction pump."

Caracas, in May 1958, was a risky spot for a ranking U.S. official. Less than four months before, a revolutionary junta had expelled the despot, and, as it was learned that he had run up short-term debts of more than one billion dollars, as the Venezuelan financial crisis deepened, as unemployment rose and poverty spread like an epidemic, sullen fury gripped the populace. They hated the memory of Pérez Jiménez, they hated all those who had helped keep him in power. His policies had been warmly endorsed by Foster Dulles and George Humphrey, Eisenhower's most trusted ministers. Now here came Eisenhower's Vice President. Caracas had its welcome ready.

Hostility was evident at Maiquetía, where Nixon's airplane put down, and again in the working-class suburbs of Caracas, where people shook their fists at the passing motorcade. In the city the limousines were caught in a traffic jam, and an angry mob surged around them, hurling curses, rotten eggs, rocks, and brickbats. The windows of the automobiles were shattered. For a few seconds the lives of the Nixons were in real danger. Then by great good luck the chauffeur of the leading limousine glimpsed a chink of daylight. He raced his engine hard ahead, and the motorcade sped out and away from the mob. The whole horrifying affair was at once blamed on the communists.

Plainly the Caracas mobs had not been enraged by Nixon and his wife as private individuals. Rather they had been ready to assail an official who happened to be the symbol of the United States of North America, the Yanqui, the gringo. The temptation was strong to prattle instead of how international communism had conspired to mount the outrageous attack and of how the whole affair fitted into a pattern. Indeed, at his press conference next day, Wednesday, May 14, the President would wag his head and gravely speak of "a sort of pattern around the world—in Burma, in Jakarta, in South America, other places—that looks like there is some kind of concerted idea and plan . . . in this particular case, there was a pattern."

Unquestionably communists were involved in the Caracas rioting and they may even have taken a leading part. (It is the professed desire of communists, seldom realized, to form the vanguard of the proletariat.) Just as certainly the riots would have occurred if there had been no communists anywhere in the hemisphere. But the notion that U.S. policy might have been at the root of the ugly incident was too unpalatable. At least in public it was dismissed.

As soon as he heard of the rioting and the threat to the Vice President and his party, President Eisenhower ordered two companies of paratroopers to Puerto Rico and two companies of marines to the U.S. naval base at Guantánamo, Cuba—a thousand U.S. troops ready to take and hold Maiquetía airport, on the Caribbean near Caracas, if the Venezuelan army could not control the situation. Officially the troops would be used only if the Venezuelan government requested their help; in fact, they were poised for more forthright action. Happily, the mob's frenzy was exhausted. The Nixons took plane for Puerto Rico on Tuesday.

Twice in one day—first in Lebanon, later in Caracas—Eisenhower had been called upon to act as a commander in chief. Weapons in one direction, troops in another. It was like old times.

"Maybe I should be digging out my uniforms," he told his wife that evening, "to see whether they still fit."

The Cold Warrior could in any case seek to capitalize on the exhibition of Latin American resentment. Nixon was asked to delay his arrival in Washington so that a proper welcome for the homecoming hero could be arranged. President Eisenhower was at the National Airport on Wednesday morning, together with the entire cabinet and leaders of the Congress from both parties. There were fifteen thousand people in the crowd, as Nixon told the story. As Eisenhower later told it, one hundred thousand turned out. Anyway, a good crowd was there.

In Washington a rueful re-examination of policy toward Latin America was now belatedly undertaken. After a difficult gestation there would at length emerge an Inter-American Development Bank, a device that had been twice aborted, in 1955 and again in 1957, by officials of the Treasury Department.

The angry boil in the Middle East seemed also to be simmering down. Chamoun persisted in protests to the Security Council of the U.N. that Egypt and Syria were instigating rebellion in Lebanon, and Eisenhower had no doubt the accusations were true; but most of the Lebanese unrest was owing to Chamoun himself and his maneuvers to wangle himself a second term as president. The patriarch of the Maronite Catholic Church blamed Chamoun for the rebellion and further for the threat of religious warfare between Christians and Muslims. He recommended that Chamoun be retired from the presidency and replaced by General Fuad Shehab, commander of the army. The patriarch was at pains to deny that the Lebanese disorders were provoked either by communists or by Egypt and Syria. But he changed no minds in Washington.

The world being for the moment relatively untroubled, the President considered that Foster Dulles might profitably visit the new French premier, Charles de Gaulle. For the last six months Dulles had been darting to and fro around the world—to Baghdad, to Manila for a meeting of SEATO, to Copenhagen, Berlin, and Paris on NATO business—and everywhere he had busily propagandized against the idea of negotiating with the Russians at the summit.* Perhaps de Gaulle, too, might need to be converted to anti-summitry. At all events, Dulles looked forward to conferring with the new French premier. He could be no worse than his predecessors and might be a distinct improvement.

The Dulles-de Gaulle interview might better have never been held. Dulles was most concerned with trying to convince the French they should not seek to become an independent atomic power. He had prepared an offer, scrupulously sanitized by Lewis Strauss of the AEC, the Defense Department, and all the senior American officials of NATO: "The United States is prepared to undertake to maintain nuclear weapons in France, of a character and quantity, and at locations, recommended by the appropriate NATO authorities and approved by France and the United States, for use by qualified French and United States forces in the event of an armed attack." This was not at all what de Gaulle had in mind. He had already determined that France must acquire her own means of deterrence and that she must be extricated from a "NATO under American command" so that she might more easily bring about a détente with Russia "followed by understanding and cooperation." But such a policy was certain to scandalize Foster Dulles. Even in respect of the Middle East, Dulles blundered. The cynosure of the moment was Lebanon, a land which for many years had been under French governance; inevitably de Gaulle took a special interest in the course of Lebanese affairs. Dulles assured him that the United States would take no momentous decision in that region without first consulting him.

The conversations began on July 4, giving Dulles the chance to tender de Gaulle a deft acknowledgment of the United States debt to France in

* One of his arguments was that at such a summit conference Eisenhower might "make statements that are misleading and give the impression that the Cold War is ended when in reality it is not." One of the foundation stones of Dulles's policy was fear. He worried that the "free" nations might no longer fear international communism, that they might relax and make peace. "Our democratic representative forms of government," he warned at a SEATO meeting in March, "cannot take the measures necessary to protect the free world, to have adequate defense, to help each other, unless our peoples feel a very real sense of danger. . . . That, and that alone, is the source of the authority which we require to make ourselves safe and secure and to work with and help each other."

the struggle for independence. They ended the next day with Dulles's question, "A summit meeting?" which he answered himself by saying, "Deceptive and divisive." It was not clear whether de Gaulle agreed with this judgment.

On the night of Sunday, July 13, swift and terrible events occurred in the ancient city of Baghdad, capital of Iraq. Moving boldly and encountering no opposition, a group of young Iraqi army officers converged on the royal palace and—the palace guards resistlessly joining them—slew the young king, Faisal, and his uncle Abdul Illah, the crown prince and former regent. There remained the pro-western premier, Nuri es-Said, seventy years old, who owed his position to his ancient friendship with the British and his concessions to the Iraq Petroleum Company. Disguising himself in a woman's robes and yashmak, he fled. He was found next day and torn to pieces by a delirious mob. It was reliably reported that Nuri's own aide-de-camp gave him the coup de grâce.

Who in Iraq opposed this sudden convulsion? As it turned out, very few, if any. It was the logical end to a regime that had survived for thirty years by mercilessly exploiting a wretched people. It was also the end to the government of the only Arab state signatory to the Baghdad Pact, and so it represented a grave defeat for the western powers. "This was the country," as Eisenhower would put it, "that we were counting on heavily as a bulwark of stability and progress in the region."

The CIA had been caught napping. Only one advance hint of the coup d'état had been picked up by its agents, and that one had been disregarded.

Word that an Iraqi republic had been established by a brigadier general named Abdul Karim el-Kassem reached Washington before dawn on Monday the 14th and at once stirred the Eisenhower administration into action. In the State Department, in the Pentagon, at CIA headquarters, in the White House, anxious men scrambled to acquaint themselves with the somber turn of events. One difficulty was that Iraq cannot be conveniently approached by troops from any direction; another was that there was no Iraqi official who could be relied upon to lead a counterrevolution; a third was the uncertainty as to whether the coup might not have been planned by Nasser and his UAR Arab nationalists, with the idea of proceeding to further uprisings in Jordan and Lebanon. What Eisenhower feared was "a complete elimination of Western influence in the Middle East"—which, being translated, meant the loss to the West of the fabulous wealth of Middle Eastern petroleum.

The President was at his desk by 7:30 A.M. that Monday; he was determined, even before his advisers began to gather, that the United States must take vigorous action—not in Iraq, where the trouble had erupted, but in Lebanon, since the president of that small country had by good luck already requested U.S. intervention. An NSC meeting was scheduled that morning with an agenda of routine matters; it was adjourned a few minutes before 11 A.M. for the extraordinary conference in the President's office. The Vice President was there; the two Dulles brothers; Robert Anderson from Treasury; two senior officers from the Defense Department; General Nathan Twining, chairman of the Joint Chiefs of Staff; General Persons and General Goodpaster of the White House staff; Bobby Cutler, back again as Eisenhower's special assistant for national security affairs; and Gordon Gray, who was soon to take Cutler's place. As usual, Allen Dulles spoke first, giving an intelligence briefing, assisted by two technicians who had come armed with maps and charts. The CIA assessment was antagonistic to Nasser, although as Dulles said, "We have no information as yet that Nasser himself is behind the coup." The CIA director spoke of Jordan—"King Hussein has also been the target of a plot"—and of Lebanon—"President Chamoun is alarmed"—and his assistants began to furl their maps and charts.

There was a team of U.N. observers in Lebanon, but they were given short shrift on this Monday morning. United States national interests were involved; the U.N. could wait.

The observant Cutler decided that the President was the most relaxed man in the room. As he watched him lolling comfortably in his swiveled armchair, Cutler perceived that Eisenhower already knew exactly what he planned to do. Once Allen Dulles was finished, the time had come to act. The President turned to Twining. Foster Dulles intervened: "Mr. President, would you wish to hear my political appreciation?" The President showed some embarrassment. "Go ahead, Foster," he said; "please." For some minutes the secretary of state spoke, estimating Soviet reactions to possible U.S. intervention in the Middle East, Egyptian reactions, reactions elsewhere in the world. The Arab countries would be resentful, Britain would have to do thus and so, the U.S. would have to beef up its military forces at Dhahran in Saudi Arabia. He mentioned Syria, the Suez, Kuwait; the pipelines, the canal, oil. He was careful and inclusive.

After a courteous acknowledgment the President turned once again to Twining with questions about the Sixth Fleet, the marines, the C–119s and C–124s that could be used to transport reinforcements, the jet fighters and fighter-bombers that could be dispatched; how many and how quickly. Now two professionals were talking quietly and knowledgeably, of Camp Lejeune and Donaldson Air Force Base, of Myrtle Beach and Augsburg, West Germany. A question for General Persons: "Jerry, how soon can you assemble the legislative leaders?" a question for Foster Dulles: "Where is

Lodge? Shouldn't he present our position to the U.N.?" Then back to Twining.

"How soon can you start, Nate?"

"Fifteen minutes after I get back to the Pentagon, sir."

"Sure?"

"Positive, sir."

"Well, what are we waiting for?"

The marines landed in Lebanon next day, considerably astonishing the sunbathers and ice cream vendors on the peaceful beaches of that country.

As a soldierly performance it was impressive. As a political performance it was dubious. The congressional leaders, when told of what was afoot, had no relish for the scheme. Speaker Sam Rayburn warned of U.S. involvement in a purely local conflict. Senator William Fulbright bluntly challenged the assumption that the Lebanese crisis had been provoked by communists.* None of the more influential congressmen voiced approval of intervention; several were puzzled by the decision to put troops in Lebanon after a government had been overthrown in Iraq. But the President clearly had the necessary authority to take the step.

Eisenhower's plan dismayed the British as well. Macmillan took sardonic note of the present policy, so marked a change from what he characterized as the "almost hysterical outbursts over Suez" in 1956; but he feared the effects that might follow on the U.S. intervention—damage to the oil installations at Tripoli, to the pipelines through Syria, to the massive oil production at Kuwait on the Persian Gulf. "Our sterling oil might dry up," Macmillan noted in his diary on July 14, "and what real guarantee had we from [the] U.S.?" At the end of that long day in Washington, the President telephoned Macmillan. The prime minister too had received nervous messages from Chamoun and from King Hussein of Jordan— "the two little chaps," as Macmillan called them—and the President now informed him of the U.S. decision, and that the Sixth Fleet was already approaching Beirut. Macmillan said, "You are doing a Suez on me." Eisenhower laughed, Macmillan laughed, they laughed together; Macmillan did not record how much of this laughter was hollow. But Macmillan was still alarmed: he wanted Eisenhower's assurance that the United States would not pull out of Lebanon and abandon the British, should they meanwhile have sent troops to help Hussein. In fact, Britain flew twenty-five hundred paratroops to Amman on Thursday, July 17.

* Fulbright was of course bang right. When Robert Murphy, the deputy undersecretary of state, reached Lebanon a few days later he was able to satisfy himself quickly that "Communism was playing no direct or substantial part in the insurrection."

The new French premier got no telephone call from the White House, nor had the American ambassador a report for the Quai d'Orsay before the marines had landed. De Gaulle, recalling Dulles's word given ten days before, was offended. What had happened to the Big Three? Was it now the Big Two? or just the Big One?

Reaction throughout the Middle East was angry and hostile—so much so that Robert Murphy would be sent winging to Beirut on Wednesday, July 16, to soothe Arab alarms and calm Arab fevers.

Considerable interest attached to the response of the Soviet Union to the display of U.S. armed might so near her southern borders. It was, as Eisenhower had surmised it would be, a restrained response, limited to words. The U.S. was guilty of "an open act of aggression" and a "direct act of war and piracy." The U.N. should "curb aggression" and "protect the national independence of the Arab states which have fallen victim to an unprovoked attack." All this was patently propaganda, an automatic reflex. Perhaps the sliest comment came from the Soviet delegate to the U.N., who observed that he detected "an acute smell of oil" as the troops moved across the Lebanese beaches.

What had President Eisenhower hoped to accomplish by his swift flexing of U.S. military muscle? Even before the marines landed, Chamoun had recognized the futility of his seeking a second presidential term. Apart from Chamoun and the members of his cabinet, almost no one in Lebanon wanted the U.S. to intervene. Indeed, the speaker of the Lebanese legislature had been quick to protest that intervention, both to Eisenhower and to the Security Council of the U.N.; and Lebanese troops very nearly fired on their self-proclaimed protectors. The official word in Washington was that after the coup in Iraq, Lebanon was desperate, it was in turmoil, its people were on the edge of panic. But these frightful tales were belied by the languid perplexity, approaching torpor, of the people on the beaches as the marines waded in, clad in full battle dress. Chamoun himself was scarcely a credible ally. By the time Murphy reached his official residence in Beirut, Chamoun was a wreck of a man who for sixty-seven days past had not dared look out of a window, much less step out of doors. The U.S. ambassador told Murphy he thought Chamoun might actually have lost his sanity. In any case, General Shehab would replace Chamoun as president on July 31.

What then was the purpose of the intervention? President Eisenhower of course had a great deal to say on the matter: a statement issued by Hagerty on July 15 as the first contingent of marines was landing, at 9 A.M. Washington time: a special message to the Congress, sent to the Hill later that day; and finally a televised statement broadcast to the people that night. He spoke of "highly organized" plots in Iraq and Jordan; of civil strife in "Lebanon, that little country," strife "actively fomented by Soviet and Cairo broadcasts"—a neat coupling of Nasser with the Kremlin; of how marines had been landed "to protect American lives" and to assist Lebanon to preserve its independence; of how the "pattern of conquest" in "tiny Lebanon" called for the same procedures employed by the communists in Greece in 1947, by the communists when they "took over Czechoslovakia in 1948," when they "took over the mainland of China in 1949," and when they "attempted to take over Korea and Indochina, beginning in 1950." "Lebanon," he said, "was selected to become a victim" of that same communist pattern. He spoke of ideals that "serve the cause of peace, security and well-being, not only for us, but for all men everywhere."

So much for the ostensible purpose, the "cover" story, the conditioned reflex of U.S. propaganda in the Cold War.

In the event, nothing much happened. The last U.S. troops were withdrawn from Lebanon after one hundred and two days of being stationed in the country; the operation was later estimated to have cost the U.S. taxpayers two hundred million dollars. Eisenhower, in analyzing the Cold War operation, wrote:

> . . . the problem was to select the least objectionable of several possible courses of action. . . . the question was whether it would be better to incur the deep resentment of nearly all the Arab World (and some of the rest of the Free World) and in doing so to risk general war with the Soviet Union or to do something worse—which was to do nothing.

This analysis is less interesting for what it says than for its vast silences. A military commander of Eisenhower's experience would scarcely have been satisfied with only two possible courses of action; indeed, he spoke of "several" but mentioned only two, one vague, the other negative. While it has never been officially acknowledged, and may never be, one contingency about which Eisenhower was mum was certainly considered, planned, hoped for, even perhaps counted upon—but at last regretfully abandoned. This was forcible counterrevolution in Iraq and the reestablishment in Baghdad of a government satisfactory to the western powers and to the international oil companies. Signs of this contingent planning bob up at every hand.

There was, to begin with, the strength of the forces sent in allegedly to protect U.S. citizens and shore up the shaky Lebanese independence: three weeks after the first landings, those forces were swollen to more than one hundred and fourteen thousand combat-ready troops, an army considerably larger than the Lebanese army and packing a far greater punch—

the U.S. troops came equipped with atomic howitzers. But the force in Lebanon by no means exhausted the total. In addition there was a Marine Corps regimental combat team, summoned from Okinawa, which had taken up station in the Persian Gulf to "guard against a possible Iraqi move into Kuwait." What had this to do with the protection of U.S. citizens, or the independence of Lebanon? A tactical air task force was also moved from western Europe to what Eisenhower described as "our" base at Adana, Turkey; these aircraft were equipped with thermonuclear weapons. Was such an armada necessary to put down a small number of Arab dissidents in Lebanon? President Eisenhower also instructed General Twining to use—subject to Eisenhower's personal approval—"*whatever* means might become necessary to prevent any unfriendly forces from moving into Kuwait." (The emphasis was Eisenhower's, and it was thermonuclear.) Later, Eisenhower would calmly observe, "In the state of tension then existing, these measures would probably bring us no closer to general war than we were already."

In Washington, the men charged with protecting the national interest had been stung by the Iraqi coup. At least forty-five million dollars' worth of U.S. military assistance had fallen into the hands of the new Iraqi republic. What was worse, that revolutionary government now knew of the secret military plans of the nations which had been members of the Baghdad Pact, and if they chose, the new Iraqi leaders might turn those secrets over to Nasser or even to Khrushchev. Yet worse, there were the top-secret plans Nuri had been cooking up to use the Iraqi army for mischief in Syria; Nasser would be able to make much of those plans in radio broadcasts all over the Middle East. Or, presuming that the new Iraqi government headed by Premier Kassem was merely nationalist, it might take steps to nationalize the Iraq Petroleum Company—and while this would most nearly affect the British, Jersey Standard and Socony Mobil were also partners in the company. Nationalization of such a property, Dulles had long since pledged the oil company executives, would surely lead to intervention (see page 741).

In these circumstances, it is not astonishing that the U.S. ambassador in Baghdad was advised by the State Department that the marines being landed in Lebanon might be used to help "loyal" Iraqi troops to restore a proper government in Iraq. The marines might well have been used for such a purpose if any Iraqi could have been found who cared to challenge the coup. None could be found; Kassem made no precipitate move to nationalize the petroleum; the Soviet Union concluded its military maneuvers in the south of Russia; the General Assembly of the U.N. unanimously approved an Arab resolution instructing Hammarskjöld to arrange for

825

"the early withdrawal of the foreign [U.S. and British] troops" from Lebanon and Jordan.

Another crisis provoked, another crisis endured. The strain of it had cost the President: he had spent "anxious hours"; he was very tense; his state of health worried his old friend and physician Howard Snyder, who examined him every day at about noon—"He might blow a valve again," Snyder confided to a White House visitor, one of Eisenhower's close acquaintances. Nor was the President the only American exhausted by the constant recurrence of crisis, by a foreign policy calculated to keep the citizenry on edge and fearful of what each new day might bring.

Nor would matters soon improve.

With the off-year congressional elections impending, three other problems chiefly plagued the President: revelations of the improper conduct of his trusted deputy Sherman Adams; the nagging question of civil rights and more particularly of the racial integration of the public schools, including once again the high school in Little Rock; and the threat of another global crisis, this one precipitated by the renewed efforts of China to re-establish control of her offshore islands, the Quemoy and Matsu groups.

The Adams affair was the most vexing for the President. To observers both inside the White House and out of it, the affair was simply incomprehensible. Adams, the paragon of rectitude and integrity, the man who had ordered Harold Talbott to resign as secretary of the air force when it developed that Talbott had got tangled in a conflict of interest, whose reputation for selfless efficiency and for homespun virtues like thrift, industry, and piety was unmatched, whose very presence in the White House was reproachful proof that the Republicans had cleaned up the Democratic "mess in Washington"—Sherman Adams, chilly exemplar of Yankee incorruptibility, had been shown to have accepted the payment of more than two thousand dollars' worth of hotel bills in three cities and the gifts of an Oriental carpet and—eye-popping symbol of debauched profligacy—a coat woven from the costly wool of the exotic vicuña. Worse, he had accepted this largess from a manufacturer of woollens, Bernard Goldfine, whose occasional difficulties with the Federal Trade Commission had resulted in telephone calls to that regulatory agency from Adams—from Adams, of whom it was said (incorrectly) that he was second only to Eisenhower in political wallop.

From the moment these startling facts were spread on the record of the House Committee on Legislative Oversight, the outcome for Adams was certain. He was out. As Eisenhower's naysayer he had acquired too many enemies—all the Republican right wing, who wrongly suspected he exerted a liberal sway over the President; most of the press corps, disenchanted by his brusque manner; and, of crucial importance, the Republican campaign contributors, who rightly feared the effect of Adams's lapse of judgment on the congressional elections. The only remaining question concerned Eisenhower's behavior toward his fallen angel. Eisenhower's attitude compelled attention because of the reports that he had himself accepted gifts worth hundreds of thousands of dollars. What kind of double standard of political morality might apply?

Eisenhower prepared a brief statement, read it to a few staff members, including Adams, and several times revised it. His confidence grew that the statement would, as Adams said later, "end, once and for all time, the speculation about whether I would remain . . . in the White House." The President read his statement on June 18 to the two hundred and fifty-seven reporters who crowded the Indian Treaty Room for his press conference. It began with a disarming acknowledgment of the ancient political custom of gift giving; "a gift," he said, "is not necessarily a bribe. One is evil, the other is a tangible expression of friendship. . . ." He continued:

"The circumstances surrounding the innocent receipt by a public official of any gift are therefore important, so that the public may clearly distinguish between innocent and guilty action. Among those circumstances are the character and reputation of the individual, the record of his subsequent actions, and evidence of intent or lack of intent to exert undue influence."

So much for the general practice of accepting valuable gifts. The character and reputation of the most eminent recipient, the President of the United States, were beyond question. He could address himself to the character and reputation of his loyal assistant: "I personally like Governor Adams. I admire his abilities. I respect him because of his personal and official integrity. I need him."

For Eisenhower, that was the end of it. But the pack baying at Adams's heels was not to be diverted, and the statement—or at least three little words of it—seemed only to confirm what the growing number of the President's critics had asserted for years; that Ike was a figurehead, that Dulles ran the nation's foreign affairs and Adams its domestic affairs while Eisenhower amiably sauntered back and forth between golf course and bridge table.

The howling for Adams grew shriller. It was painful. The President delegated the Vice President to keep a watchful eye on the situation. Nixon's relations with Adams were "not close, not unfriendly, but just correct." He and the chairman of the Republican National Committee—by now Meade Alcorn—took quiet soundings of Republican sentiment within the Congress and among the state organizations. By August 28

Alcorn was ready to tell Eisenhower of the overwhelming conviction that Adams must go. Eisenhower assigned to Alcorn the unpleasant task of giving Adams the verdict. Adams had left for a fishing holiday in Canada; by the time a telephone call reached him, Eisenhower too had left for his holiday, again in Newport. As was his wont when faced with a disagreeable responsibility, Eisenhower declined to request Adams's resignation but hoped instead that Adams could be got to volunteer it. This course was repugnant to Adams since it was not his "nature to run in the face of adversity," but he was loyal to the last. He quit.

Behind him he left a mounting swell of criticism of Eisenhower: either the President should summarily have dismissed his principal assistant for his bad judgment in a conflict of interest or he should have displayed a stubborn fidelity to a valued chief of staff. Instead, he had vacillated.

The recurrent affliction of civil rights pestered the President over much those same three months. His trials began on Monday, June 23, with what was for Fred Morrow a historic occasion, for it was the President's first face-to-face encounter with Negro leaders since he had taken office sixty-five months before. The leaders were four: Dr. Martin Luther King, president of the Southern Leadership Conference; A. Philip Randolph, president of the Brotherhood of Sleeping Car Porters and an AFL–CIO vice president; Lester Granger of the National Urban League; and Roy Wilkins of the NAACP. Rogers, the attorney general, attended the meeting.

It was "pleasant," Morrow noted later, but "nothing much was accomplished." The Negroes came prepared with suggestions for a nine-point program which was essentially a set of guidelines by which Eisenhower might take belated leadership on an issue that was, they knew, already dangerously explosive. The President listened attentively. The appointment, set for thirty minutes, stretched out almost twice as long. Then photographers were summoned and everyone affixed ceremonial expressions.

Dr. King had requested the meeting. After it was over he had a comment for Morrow: he thought Eisenhower a nice fellow but far from being able to grasp the gravity of the situation.

Two days earlier, a federal judge had granted the Little Rock school board a stay of two and a half years before starting to integrate the public schools there. This action was reversed by the circuit court of appeals on August 18. The school board then appealed to the Supreme Court, which met in special term on August 28 to take the case sub judice. Additional arguments were heard on September 11. Next day the Court unanimously ordered immediate resumption of integration of the schools in Little Rock; the Court unanimously reaffirmed this order on September 29.

The effect of this protracted litigation was to present the President with a fistful of opportunities to lead, to guide, to inspire, to teach, to win the hearts of his fellow citizens over to an appreciation of the noble words with which Thomas Jefferson had starred the Declaration of Independence. Throughout these three months the President was meeting journalists at press conferences; he could have presented them with statements or simply awaited their questions in order to assume the leadership so desperately needed. He refused every opportunity. What was worse, in view of the warnings of crisis ahead—which were to be tragically confirmed— the President actually gave comfort to those who complained the Supreme Court's rule was too abrupt and coercive. At his press conference of August 27, on the eve of the Supreme Court's special term to consider the tangled case of Little Rock school integration, the President admitted he might have told friends in private that he thought integration should proceed more slowly.*

The evidence is that during these months of public wrangle the President was a troubled man. His impulses were at war with his associations, past and present. "Civil rights in the Eisenhower administration," said Fred Morrow, who was in many ways the most competent witness, "was handled like a bad dream, or like something that's not very nice, and you shield yourself from it as long as you possibly can, because it just shouldn't be." During 1958 the struggle against civil rights resulted in bombs being touched off all over the South—there were at least four dozen such explosions—and by October the bigots were bombing synagogues as well as schools. In Atlanta an attack on a Reform Jewish institution called The Temple caused two hundred thousand dollars' worth of damage and followed similar dynamitings in Miami, Jacksonville, and Birmingham. The man who boasted of bombing The Temple in Atlanta identified himself as "General Gordon of the Confederate underground."

In his outrage over this incident, Eisenhower gave a hint of the travail the country's racial conflict was causing him. "From babyhood," he told a press conference, "I was raised to respect the word 'Confederate'—very highly, I might add—and for hoodlums such as these to describe themselves as any part or any relation to the Confederacy of the mid-nineteenth century is, to my mind, a complete insult to the word."

His veneration for the Confederacy helped deter the President from giving the leadership the nation needed.

* Four years after the Supreme Court order to provide equal educational opportunities for all children and to do so with all deliberate speed, the same seven southern states (see note, page 795) had still taken no step toward integration and planned none; in three other states—Arkansas, North Carolina, and Tennessee—a total of two hundred and seventy Negro children had been placed in classes with white children.

"And All This Time I Was Hoping You'd Speak Up."
from *Herblock's Special for Today* (Simon & Schuster, 1958)

The squabble over the Chinese offshore islands began just before Eisenhower left for his summer holiday at Newport—the Colorado Rockies had again been forbidden him by his physicians—and lasted until just before the congressional elections, no doubt making a modest contribution to the results of that vote. The squabble found the Eisenhower administration in an untenable position which, by maladroit diplomacy, was transformed into an intolerable dilemma, one that could apparently be resolved only by nuclear catastrophe or Chinese restraint. Happily, the government of Mao Tse-tung and Chou En-lai was, as in the earlier wrangle over these same islands, a great deal more sensible and even-tempered than the government of Dwight Eisenhower and Foster Dulles. In retrospect, it is plain that Eisenhower and Dulles were playing a game of deception; that Eisenhower never intended to permit the use of nuclear weapons, no matter how "clean" they might be; that he was engaged in an exercise of flimflam designed to frigerate a Chinese quarrel without himself losing face. While Eisenhower and Dulles were playing their game, the rest of the country might be bewildered, fearful, even unruly, but they nevertheless could not be acquainted with the great secrets which perhaps might put their lives at hazard.

The news that the Chinese had begun to shell Quemoy and the smaller Tan Islands lying even closer to shore could not have astonished the President. Like as not, if he had been Mao's military commander in the region, he would have done the same; it was the only soldierly procedure possible. Quemoy and the Tans were so many fishbones stuck in the throat of Amoy harbor; using them as bases, Generalissimo Chiang Kai-shek and the Kuomintang armed forces could disrupt the maritime traffic along China's east coast. Chiang was, moreover, one of the dwindling few who still imagined that the Eisenhower-Dulles policy of "rollback" was more than political rhetoric: he kept writing Eisenhower that he could establish beachheads on the mainland, the time for rebellion was ripe, he wanted of the U.S. only logistical support, when might his invasion begin? Each of these bubbles was duly punctured by Eisenhower. Meanwhile, against Eisenhower's wishes and advice, Chiang steadily reinforced the island outposts until by August some one hundred thousand troops—his best—were deployed on them. The Chinese naturally considered these armies a provocation. Shelling of the islands and of vessels supplying them from Taiwan was intensified.

The President, pausing only to order elements of the Sixth Fleet from the Mediterranean to join the Seventh Fleet in Taiwan Strait, took wing for the golf links at Newport.

On Thursday, September 4, the bombardment of Quemoy still continuing, Foster Dulles arrived at Newport to confer with the President. He brought with him a memorandum that set forth the collective apprehensions of the State Department, the Joint Chiefs of Staff, and the secretary of defense: the Chicoms, backed by the Soviets, were reckoned to be poised to "liberate" Taiwan, with the Philippines and Japan next on their schedule of conquest; Quemoy and the Matsus were seen as the first bite; the Chicoms would move against Quemoy if they assumed the U.S. would stand aloof, but if they thought the U.S. would intervene, perhaps with nuclear weapons, they would likely withdraw as they had in 1955; loss of Quemoy would breach the perimeter defense of the Far East, with Japan swinging into the Sino-Soviet orbit and Okinawa untenable; if nuclear weapons were involved, a wave of revulsion against the U.S. would surely follow, peaking in Japan; but if the U.S. should intervene she must not lose.

For a couple of hours the President mooted this bleak estimate with Dulles, Goodpaster, and Captain E. P. (Pete) Aurand, his naval aide. At length Eisenhower and Dulles set to work on a statement to be issued by the President and designed to discourage any Chinese effort to reclaim Quemoy. Presently Eisenhower wearied of the task. No, he told Dulles; *you* issue the statement, saying that it has my approval, and then depending on what kind of reception it gets I can follow it up on Saturday.

Later, after Eisenhower had sped off for more golf, Dulles appeared before reporters—not as secretary of state, speaking not for attribution; only as a "briefing officer," a transparent disguise that would conceal him for perhaps thirty minutes—and told them that "we would not wait until the situation was desperate before we acted" to protect Quemoy and Matsu. Further, he said, any attempt by the Chinese to establish their control of the islands "would be a crude violation of the principles upon which world order is based, namely, that no country should use armed force to seize new territory."

This assertion turned logic inside out. Anyone with eyes to look at a map could see that "these wretched offshore islands," to use Harold Macmillan's irritable phrase, were as much a part of the mainland as is, say, Staten Island in New York harbor or San Juan Island in Seattle harbor; indeed, Dulles acknowledged as much next day to the British ambassador. Force was not threatened "to seize new territory," but to reclaim what was patently part of the Chinese People's Republic. Logic, on the other hand, had no part to play in a game of bluff and threat, which was what China and the U.S. were engaged upon.

To bluff effectively, one must seem to be backed by a united people and an enthusiastic set of allies. The U.S. had neither. Any number of dismayed critics sprang up to protest Dulles's Newport statement—senators, newspaper editors, influential clergymen—of whom the most scath-

Convoy

from *Herblock's Special for Today* (Simon & Schuster, 1958)

ing was Dean Acheson, himself the chief architect of the policy of containment. The decision taken by Eisenhower and Dulles was, Acheson said, "horrendous." The government had been maneuvered by Chiang "into a situation of which it has lost control"; the attitude struck by Eisenhower and Dulles was that "nothing will be done to extricate ourselves from this position during periods of quiet, and that nothing can be done about it in times of crisis. This is an attitude which ought not to be tolerated."

It was soon evident that, overseas, most U.S. allies felt the same. Dulles cabled Macmillan that he and the President hoped "to *stop* the threatened invasion" but if Quemoy were attacked, the U.S. would intervene. He doubted whether such an intervention could be effective "without at least some use of atomic weapons; I hope no more than small air bursts without fallout. . . . an unpleasant prospect, but one I think we must face up to." (Dulles was at this time seventy years old, the allotted Biblical span.) Macmillan, as he studied this message, felt "somewhat depressed." He replied that "public opinion will not be easy to steer." Speaking for the United Kingdom and the Commonwealth countries, he warned that "None of them will support, wholeheartedly, the U.S. position." He reminded Dulles that in 1955 Churchill had written Eisenhower: ". . . a war to keep the coastal islands for Chiang would not be defensible here."

The U.S. bluff was plainly in danger. President Eisenhower regretfully bagged his golf clubs and returned to Washington to exhort the nation by radio and television.

Even allowing for the partisan, Cold Wartime character of his speech, the President's sophistries were regrettable. Taking advantage of the general ignorance of the geography of the area, he placed Quemoy vaguely "in the Formosa Straits." Of the armies massed on the island, of its use as a base from which to molest Chinese shipping, he said nothing. He spoke of "naked force" being used "for aggressive purposes." The bombardment of Quemoy he characterized as the first step in "an ambitious plan of armed conquest. This plan," he said, trotting out a refurbished version of the old domino theory, "would liquidate all of the free world positions in the Western Pacific area and bring them under captive governments . . . hostile to the United States and the free world. Thus the Chinese and Russian Communists would come to dominate at least the western half of the now friendly Pacific Ocean." If the U.S. did not resist this "armed aggression," if she submitted to threats, she would be vainly attempting to appease "ruthless despots." Appeasement, Munich, Mussolini, Hitler—they were all dusted off and depended from Quemoy, spectral warnings of what would surely happen if the Chinese were allowed to take possession of their island. "There is not going to be any appeasement," the President promised.

As in 1955, Eisenhower had been under pressure from his military officers to be more bellicose, even to delegate to the U.S. commanders in the area his authority as commander in chief to commit U.S. forces to action. He reserved that power, and as in 1955, his officers came to agree that perhaps the Kuomintang troops should after all be withdrawn from Quemoy. By mid-September the administration was in a quandary: how firm was the leash on the stubborn Chiang? and could it be used to tug his armies back to Taiwan? It was clear that the nation was decidedly reluctant to make an issue of Quemoy: while in 1954 the White House mail had run three to one against U.S. intervention, now in 1958 a count of the thousands of letters flooding the White House and State Department showed fully four to one against.

When news of this response to the President's speech was published in the *New York Times,* the interventionist stalwarts of the administration were outraged. "Sabotage," cried Nixon, and demanded to know why "the weight of the mail rather than the weight of the evidence" should determine U.S. foreign policy.

But at a level above the Vice President's indignation, the decision had already been taken to relax the tension. The President had privily apprised the British that he would not permit the use of tactical atomic weapons in a limited operation like deterrence. With an election impending it was incumbent on the President to brake the hotheads. The obedient Dulles withdrew a trifle from the brink. Chiang's deployment of troops was "rather foolish," he told reporters, and he put stress on the chances for "a cease-fire in the area." Eisenhower, who had already described Quemoy as "a thorn in the side of peace," now began to emphasize that it was "so close to the mainland"; of Quemoy and Matsu, he said, "fundamentally anyone can see that the two islands as of themselves, as two pieces of territory, are not greatly vital to Formosa." The domino theory had collapsed. Like an expiring sigh, the hot air was leaking out of the crisis. The Air Force generals were satisfied: they had observed under combat conditions their newest toy—the air-to-air missile called the sidewinder—and it had performed with venomous efficiency, taking out several Chinese MIG–17s. The admirals were content: the various LSTs and LSDs given the Kuomintang to land supplies on Quemoy were proving satisfactory. Both the Chinese People's Republic and the United States had, throughout the time of threats and bluff, kept an escape hatch available; now they were content to slide through it; away from the world's apprehensive gaze their ambassadors began, in Warsaw, the patient diplomatic business of picking up the pieces and fitting them together again.

The shelling ceased. The U.S. Seventh Fleet ceased its convoy activities and kept its distance. Once again something approximating peace settled over Taiwan Strait.

The President wanted Dulles to talk face-to-face with Chiang, to give the U.S. leash on him a few admonitory tugs, since by now it was obvious that an attack by his troops on China would not be supported by the U.S. or her allies. The secretary's airplane, flying a polar route, landed near Fairbanks, Alaska, at 10:15 A.M. on Monday, October 20. There he was handed a message from the CIA: the shelling of Quemoy, suspended when U.S. warships ended their escort operations, had been resumed (a U.S. destroyer had again provided convoy). Dulles was sufficiently disturbed by the news to telephone Eisenhower at the White House, where it was then 5:30 A.M. Should he go on to Taipei or turn back to Washington? The President instructed him to go on and to convince Chiang to avoid any further provocative acts. After three days of talks, Chiang pledged not to use military forces against the Chinese People's Republic. The leash was still firm. The shelling of Quemoy once again became desultory and at length was halted altogether. But the crisis had dragged on almost until election day.

The elections were, for the Republicans, a disaster. The Democrats picked up thirteen seats in the Senate and forty-nine seats in the House. Not for a generation had they dominated the Congress so completely. The President, asked about the landslide defeat, was bitter. "The United States did give me," he recalled, "a majority of I think well over nine million votes. Here, only two years later, there is a complete reversal; and yet I don't see where there is anything that these people consciously want the administration to do differently."

The Vice President's private analysis attributed the rout to the sputnik, the recession, and the scandal over Sherman Adams.

Neither man gave any weight to the administration's conduct of the Cold War—the reluctance to sit down with the Russians; the refusal to suspend tests of nuclear weapons and the attendant fallout of radioactive poisons; the persistent policy of containment, carried to preposterous and often terrifying lengths; the foreign policy that so often left the United States marooned, her allies uncertain and ambivalent. But if the polls both before and after the election could be trusted, the achievement of a stable peace motivated more voters than any other issue.

CHAPTER EIGHT

Collapse of a Policy

Crisis over Berlin . . . Pressures for another conference at the summit . . . Dulles dies . . . Khrushchev's visit . . . Personal diplomacy by the public Eisenhower . . . The summit scheduled for Paris . . . The U-2 and the summit toppled . . . Repudiated by Japan . . . Outbursts in Indochina . . . in Cuba . . . in the Congo . . . U.S. gold reserves dwindle . . . The Democrats regain the White House.

DURING THE 1950s the men who controlled the national security postulated an "international communism" centered in the Kremlin and directed by a handful of faceless figures who followed the dictates of a revolutionary firebrand named Lenin. International communism was assumed to be an ideology, a religion, a way of life; it was also a worldwide conspiracy. Its determined adherents were bent on global conquest, presumably by force and violence. They planned to subvert and then overthrow "all we hold dear"—more specifically, liberty, democracy, free enterprise, and the like. Worship would be replaced by godless atheism, liberty and democracy by slavery and a ruthless despotism, free enterprise and private property by a bleak totalitarianism under which all would be owned and controlled by the state. International communism was a monolith, having at its command vast armies united by their ambition to rule the world. Dissent, so it was believed, did not exist—at least not for long. The dictator spoke: hundreds of millions marched, a juggernaut.

In this view of the world, international communism—or a small executive committee of international communist strategists—had a master plan for encompassing the downfall of the free world. The plan prescribed an incessant probing of the free world's defenses, testing where they might be weakest and there mounting an energetic aggression. So far in 1958 a series of these probes had been identified and promptly rebuffed or contained, in Indonesia, Burma, Venezuela, Lebanon, and at Quemoy; so far the forces of freedom had proved valiant and resolute. But international communism never relaxed its efforts. Suddenly in November it struck again, this time at Berlin.

Eisenhower would make it seem a sudden crisis. Khrushchev, he wrote, with one pronouncement "transformed the city of Berlin, which had remained relatively quiet for more than nine years, into a tinderbox."

His advisers in the Department of State saw nothing sudden about the crisis. Eleanor Dulles, Foster's younger sister, who was a ranking officer of the department's Office of German Affairs, observed that "Khrushchev had brought to a climax what had been for many months a prime objective, that is, to push the western powers out of the city and make way for a possible surge of Soviet troops toward the Rhine."

What had provoked these alarms was Khrushchev's announcement on November 10 that the time had come for the occupying forces to withdraw from Berlin, transferring their control of the city to the sovereignty of the German Democratic Republic (GDR); i.e., the East German "puppet." A few days later a long Russian note to the western powers formalized the proposal. The USSR considered null and void the compacts made at Potsdam for the occupation of Berlin; that part of the city occupied by the western powers (West Berlin) should become "an independent political entity—a free city," which would be demilitarized; guarantees of freedom of access and of communications to West Berlin should be negotiated with the GDR; if agreement were not reached within six months, the functions of the Soviet authorities would be turned over to the GDR, which would then control the access routes to Berlin.

These proposals were of course flatly unacceptable to the western powers, none of which had so much as recognized the existence of the GDR as a sovereign state, much less stood ready to negotiate with it. To Eisenhower, the Soviet disavowal of the Potsdam compacts on Berlin was further proof that "international agreements, historically considered by us as sacred, are regarded in Communist doctrine and in practice to be mere scraps of paper."

But in the Soviet view the western powers had already violated those pacts. At Potsdam the wartime allies had agreed, inter alia, "to prevent the revival or reorganization of German militarism and Nazism." Yet the western powers, and notably the United States, had encouraged the militarization of the Federal Republic of Germany (West Germany), going so far as to supply West German troops with hundreds of IRBMs of a type (the Matador) that could be fitted with nuclear warheads. Thanks to the U.S., West Germany was building an army with thermonuclear punch. The commander in chief of NATO's ground forces, central front, was General Hans Speidel, formerly Rommel's chief of staff; and at SHAPE reporters noticed the German officers were once again wearing their battle ribbons, although out of consideration for their present allies, they wore only those ribbons won on the eastern front. The Soviets could be forgiven for fearing that this militarist Gemütlichkeit presaged more than the defensive posture assumed by NATO.

West Berlin presented a special problem for the Russians. There, one hundred and ten miles within the GDR, the western powers maintained, by Soviet estimates, more than one hundred espionage organizations, not to mention the several radio stations and other organisms for propaganda. There, primed by huge subventions from the U.S. treasury, the western sectors of the city glistened with all the seductions of a prosperous capitalism while the eastern sector, drab and disciplined, offered only a shabby contrast. Each year some three hundred thousand Germans fled the GDR seeking the comforts and relative freedoms of West Germany. West Berlin, said Khrushchev, was a "kind of cancerous tumor." Surgery was indicated.

Stiff diplomatic notes were exchanged. Threats of martial force rattled back and forth, each side pointing an accusing finger at the other. By the turn of the year the Berlin crisis was angrily inflamed.

As the year turned, and while the eyes of the world were focused on Berlin, there occurred close to the nation's doorstep a most improbable event, a revolution. A band of young guerrilleros—a few hundred students and peasants, led by a handful of romantics who had been holed up in the Sierra Maestra on the southeastern edge of Cuba—in the last weeks of 1958 summoned up an irresistible momentum and, moving steadily westward across the island, gathering strength as they proceeded, they deflated the Cuban army, put the dictator Batista to flight, and entered Havana in triumph on January 1, 1959. Their leader, Fidel Castro, thirty-one years old, bearded like most of his followers—they were dubbed "los barbudos"—arrived on Thursday, January 8, to take power and be tendered a wild and hysterical welcome.

What of Castro's politics? Had the dictator been overthrown by a communist? Was the Cuban revolution part of international communism's master plan?

On November 23, 1958, the U.S. ambassador to Cuba, Earl E. T. Smith, told Robert Murphy, the deputy undersecretary of state, that "the Castro movement is infiltrated and controlled by the Communists." On December 3 Kenneth Redmond, president of the United Fruit Company, alerted Foster Dulles that the company's sugar crop was endangered by Castro and his rebels; in just this way, four years before, Dulles had learned of what was afoot in Guatemala. Eisenhower was of course aware of the growing strength of the rebellion. Back in June, Castro's brother

Raul had led a band of guerrilleros who kidnapped twenty-seven U.S. sailors and marines outside the U.S. naval base at Guantánamo, in consequence of which the admirals in Washington had pressed for "an immediate intervention . . . of divisional size"; but before long the servicemen had been released with no more damage than ruffled sensibilities. In late December the CIA for the first time warned the President that "Communists and other extreme radicals [would] probably participate in the government" if Castro's rebellion succeeded. Eisenhower was wroth. Why had Allen Dulles's agents taken so long to sound the alarm?

But as the new year came in, everyone's attention was fixed on Berlin.

In early January 1959 the President and his advisers concluded that the Soviets seriously proposed to turn over control of the access routes to Berlin to the East Germans—in Washington's view an action tantamount to blockading those routes. (Secretary Dulles had earlier suggested the possibility of dealing with the East Germans as "agents" of the Soviet Union, but Adenauer was so distressed by what seemed a faint presentiment of future recognition of a sovereign East Germany that Dulles hastily reaffirmed his customary rigidity.) Already one U.S. Army truck column had been delayed several hours at a checkpoint west of Berlin; already General Lauris Norstad, in command of NATO forces, and the U.S. Chiefs of Staff had shown a combative disposition; already Eisenhower had been obliged to order restraint. Studying the Soviet notes, the President decided that Khrushchev was speaking in at least "the tone of an ultimatum." On May 27—six months from the date of the Soviet note that mentioned a delay to last that long—the western powers might discover that West Berlin could be approached only by coming to terms with the East Germans. An unthinkable condition.

By mid-January the U.S. government had determined, rather than yield its rights in Berlin, to accept the risk of general war.*

In an atmosphere of mutual recrimination, in which the threats bandied back and forth involved ICBMs and IRBMs which without warning could turn populous countrysides into radioactive wastelands, those trapped between the two great nuclear powers were naturally the most apprehensive. The British felt particularly exposed and vulnerable. Many of them questioned their government's acceptance of U.S. missiles and their emplacements within the British Isles, a decision that made of them a first-round target. Before long a lively propaganda was in full swing, led

---

* Treaties concluded after V-E day gave the United States unmistakable rights to be in Berlin, but no instrument had ever been drafted to confer rights to travel to and from the city. General Clay and Marshal Zhukov had made a verbal agreement, that was all.

by an organization called the Campaign for Nuclear Disarmament (CND), to which an array of distinguished artists, scientists, professionals, and clergymen lent their prestige and their imaginative energies. The objectives of CND, articulated with bravura, were to persuade Britain to divest herself of her nuclear weaponry and to quit her nuclear alliance with the U.S. In West Germany, much the same sort of campaign proved vexatious to the government in Bonn. Harold Macmillan, sensitive to the political character of the dissent in Britain, had been mooting—there was to be a general election later that year—what good might come of it if he were to visit Moscow. He recognized that in the hostile climate of the time such an initiative would be "rather a startling and almost sensational event," he suspected that Dulles and Eisenhower would view any such journey with dismay, but still he judged that a readiness to talk reasonably with the Russians could not come amiss.

Eisenhower and Dulles were indeed concerned, but they appreciated the political overtones of Macmillan's travels. Nevertheless it was of urgent importance that the western alliance confer, if only to agree upon the broad lines of contingency planning in the face of the Berlin crisis. It was plain that Dulles must undertake another transatlantic journey—to London, Paris, Bonn—taking with him a generous supply of his most persuasive proprietaries.

The secretary's task was not simplified by the recent collapse of two special conferences called in Geneva for the purpose of relaxing world tensions, the Conference on the Prevention of Surprise Attacks and the Conference on the Discontinuance of Nuclear Weapons Tests. Responsibility for the failure of both was at least shared by the U.S. government. The U.S. delegates to the surprise attack conference were given less than one month to do their homework, scarcely enough to acquaint themselves with the questions that might be raised, much less with the reasons for the answers their government would insist they make. So woefully unprepared was the delegation that the government had not even provided the funds to defray the expenses of the several scientists required as advisers; a private foundation did. The test ban conference failed even more wretchedly, recalling (see page 690) the time in May 1955 when the Soviet Union had suddenly accepted western proposals for general and nuclear disarmament only to have the United States as suddenly withdraw "all of its . . . substantive" commitments on the subject. In this case—after scientists from both sides of the "iron curtain" had agreed that a test ban could be effectively policed, after Eisenhower had reacted to this good news by announcing that the U.S. would temporarily halt its testing program, after substantial progress had been made in the drafting of a test ban treaty—a startling statement was issued by the White House. On

January 5, the same day the conference met to resume its work on the treaty, Eisenhower announced that "new data . . . indicate that it is more difficult to identify underground explosions than had previously been believed." In short, the rules of the game had been changed while the game was still going on. The effect of Eisenhower's announcement was to split the scientific community (some of the American scientists negotiating at Geneva challenged the "new data" reported by Eisenhower) and to mark the United States government as an exceedingly sharp customer. The "new data" may have satisfied those (like Dr. Edward Teller, the Air Force generals, and some of the AEC commissioners) who valiantly resisted any test ban, but they made Dulles's work harder: if the U.S. could be charged with bad faith in the test ban conference, how fully could she be trusted in the negotiations to resolve the Berlin crisis?

Dulles came to London on February 4, to 10 Downing Street after dinner that night, and Macmillan was "shocked at his appearance." He was in fact already a dying man, though he did not yet know it: the cancer which had been treated surgically two years before had metastisized and was already beyond therapy. From shock Macmillan proceeded to astonishment —Dulles, he found, was far more accommodating than had been his wont, far more flexible. "He seemed to be ready to discuss new ideas." Even more astonishing, the man who had labored for a year to demolish the idea of a summit meeting now "quite firmly" introduced a plan for such a meeting "to which the President would come," for the following May.

As for the squabble over Berlin, because of which the U.S. government was ready to risk a general war, Dulles learned that neither in London nor in Paris did the statesmen greatly care whether a Russian sergeant or an East German sergeant stamped the passes or punched the railway tickets of those bound for West Berlin. Certainly the distinction was no reason for war. Only Adenauer in Bonn, because of his obsession against any recognition of the GDR, saw the matter in the same light as did Eisenhower and Dulles.

More stiff notes were sent back and forth. Dulles came home, issued a statement ("We do not accept . . . We are resolved . . ."), and on February 10 was taken to hospital—"the most valuable man in foreign affairs that I have ever known," said the President. "America needs him and I think each one of us needs him." A few days later, following the fateful operation, Eisenhower was asked about the possibility of Dulles's resignation.

"I feel this way about Secretary Dulles," he answered. "The doctors have assured me there is nothing in his disease that is going to touch his heart and his head, and that is what we want.

"I am constitutionally responsible for conducting the foreign affairs of

842

the United States, and the man who has been my closest associate, certainly my principal assistant, and on whom all the responsibility for details has been resting, my closest friend and confidant in this whole business, is Secretary Dulles. I know of no man—in my knowledge—in the world that has equaled his wisdom and his knowledge in this whole complicated business.

"Therefore, as long as Secretary Dulles believes that he is in shape to carry on, he is exactly the person I want."

With Dulles in hospital and Macmillan gone to Moscow, Eisenhower took time to reflect on the question: Will the Soviets go through with their threat to leave East Germany on May 27 and abandon their responsibilities with respect to Berlin? It was vital to avoid any miscalculation or muddle. With three months left before the Soviet deadline, he dictated a memorandum listing the considerations he deemed important: how best to keep the Congress apprised of developments; how to react to Soviet ultimatums, if any; how to count on the Congress to react swiftly, in an emergency; how to keep his stratagems secret; how to warn the American people of impending danger without alarming them; how best to coordinate his contingency planning with NATO and especially with the governments of Britain, West Germany, and France (the U.N. was here ignored). He sent this memorandum to Gordon Gray, his special assistant for national security affairs, with instructions to have a paper dealing with these questions prepared for the National Security Council. The Joint Chiefs of Staff had long since prepared, revised, updated, and polished the bulky, detailed sheaf of papers that charted the possible military actions required.

It would be imprecise to say that these exercises were irrelevant. Any prudent governor must allow for the mischance that his best plans will go bust, when he will have to be ready with a second-best possibly entailing warfare. But at the time—the end of February 1959—it was crystal clear to those who had heard or read with any care the Soviet statements on the issue of Berlin that what Khrushchev wanted was not war or anything close to it, that what he wanted was a summit conference. He wanted to talk with Eisenhower. The Germans—West and East—might be present during the conversations as observers; Macmillan and de Gaulle might participate, no matter; but the chiefs of the two nuclear giants must sit down together and talk sensibly together. So much was essential.

Eisenhower was stubbornly opposed to the idea. He preferred his way, the staff way, a procedure that set as a prerequisite a fruitful session at the foreign minister level. Against a summit meeting there was what he termed "a very great psychological reason: when the people of the world understand there is going to be a head of state or a head of government summit conference, they expect something to come out of it; and a feeling of pessimism and, in a way, hopelessness, I think, would be increased if you entered such a meeting and then nothing real came out of it, as indeed was the case at Geneva. . . . I think it would be a very grave mistake to go to a summit conference unless there was some kind of preparation so that you could know the world could recognize the progress made."

Curiously, Khrushchev was at the time saying very much the same to Macmillan. The prime minister reported Khrushchev's opinion to be, "If a summit meeting failed, it would be worse than no meeting." Macmillan and Khrushchev discussed how to combine a summit meeting with meetings of foreign ministers or other specialists, how to devise a procedure most likely to yield results. A Russian note to the western powers proposed a summit conference but conceded the possibility of an earlier meeting of foreign ministers. On Eisenhower's instructions, the U.S. draft of a suggested reply accepted the ministerial meeting but simply ignored the summit conference.

Out of these contrarieties there appeared to emerge a stalemate, but in truth the Berlin crisis was disappearing, or evolving, into a labyrinthine ceremony in which the statesmen fumbled and groped for a formula that would enable the mistrustful U.S.A. and the suspicious USSR to contrive a brief encounter. At the end of the labyrinth, improbably enough, was a twelve-day visit by Khrushchev to the United States, one that was resented and only grudgingly made possible by Eisenhower.

The confused preliminaries to the Khrushchev visit ended in an unprecedented muddle. A chief difficulty lay with Eisenhower, whose antipathy toward the Russians and any premature meeting with them led him to be by turns deaf to what his allies were telling him, inconsistent in his attitudes toward his allies and his advisers, and slipshod in his dealings with his deputies in the State Department. Such behavior was uncharacteristic. It can be explained (not excused; Eisenhower had no patience with excuses, least of all for his own mistakes) by the concurrence of two events, each of which affected him deeply.

The first event was the rejection by the Senate of his nomination of Lewis Strauss to be secretary of commerce. Strauss had made some important enemies during his tenure as chairman of the Atomic Energy Commission; he was a stiff-necked conservative; he was remembered as the architect of Oppenheimer's downfall and so had antagonized the scientific community; he was a vain and haughty man who took no pains to be urbane. Nevertheless, he would surely have been confirmed—a President's choice for his cabinet is given virtually automatic approval; not in thirty-four years had one been rejected—if such senators as Lyndon Johnson and

John Kennedy had not had their hands outstretched for the prize of the presidency in 1960. On June 19, after twelve wearing weeks, Strauss was rejected by a vote of forty-nine to forty-six. Eisenhower had fought hard to win his confirmation. The defeat was a severe rebuff to Eisenhower. "Shocking," he wrote to a friend, "and shameful."

The second event, more disturbing, more wearing, more melancholy, was the death on May 24, after fourteen weeks of wasting disease, of John Foster Dulles, Eisenhower's most trusted associate. Macmillan, who had noted in his journal that he was "quite convinced that we can have no effective negotiation with anyone but Khrushchev," and that the West "ought therefore to propose, right away, a summit meeting," had arrived in Washington on Thursday, March 19, and the next day was taken by the President to Dulles's suite of rooms at Walter Reed Hospital. Dulles was already emaciated. "He was *against* almost everything," Macmillan observed. "He was strongly against the idea of a *summit;* he did not much like the foreign ministers' meeting. . . . I felt that his illness had made his mind more rigid and reverting to very fixed concepts. I felt also sorry for the President." Over that weekend Eisenhower and Macmillan wrangled with some heat over their reply to the Soviet note and over the question of a summit meeting, but the President, distracted perhaps by Dulles's illness, perhaps by his determination not to be "dragooned" up to the summit, somehow failed to grasp how urgent was Macmillan's advocacy of an early conference with Khrushchev.

Late in May statesmen gathered from all over Europe to attend Dulles's funeral. The foreign ministers adjourned their conference in Geneva to come. At one moment Eisenhower was full of admiration for Adenauer because the German chancellor "proposed nothing new," because of his rigid attitude toward the Soviets; at the next moment he lectured the four foreign ministers—and particularly Andrei Gromyko—on the need for flexibility in their negotiations. The President was apparently unaware of this inconsistency. He was still intent on fending off a meeting at the summit with Khrushchev, unless, as he kept insisting, the foreign ministers were able first to make "progress" at Geneva. It began to seem that his price for a summit meeting was prior concessions of substance by the Russians at the foreign minister level.

As spring wore into summer, the situation as to summitry was stuck: Khrushchev wanted to talk with Eisenhower, but the foreign ministers at Geneva were making no progress—in Eisenhower's phrase, "they seem to be off to a very slow start"—so Eisenhower was in no hurry to talk to Khrushchev. On July 7 Khrushchev told a group of American state governors who were visiting Moscow that if he and Eisenhower were to exchange visits to each other's countries it would be "a useful thing." When he was asked about the idea, the President was able to restrain his enthusiasm. There were "many questions, very serious," he said, "very tough questions to settle." He had said he would go anywhere, meet anyone, walk that extra mile for peace; nothing was more important than peace; he waged peace constantly. But first there must be "progress"; not words, but actions—actions to prove that the untrustworthy Soviets could be trusted, anyway a little. He chose not to talk with Khrushchev.

One step down the deputies exchanged equable visits. Frol Kozlov, a member of the Soviet presidium, a first deputy premier, one of the "men in the Kremlin," came to the U.S., traveled about, traded banter with politicians, inspected steel mills and automobile plants, and opened a Soviet trade exhibit in the New York Coliseum; Vice President Nixon was scheduled to go to Moscow to open a corresponding U.S. exhibit, after which he hoped to travel about as had Kozlov. Now Khrushchev was angling for a comparable exchange by the heads of government.

Well, said a few State Department experts, why not? Why not treat the Russians with a dose of Eisenhower's incomparable charm? Ike was well known there, much admired, a symbol of the alliance against Hitler; if he were to move freely among the peoples of the Soviet Union he would be irresistible. Robert Murphy prepared the recommendation that Eisenhower make an offer to Khrushchev—more precisely, accept Khrushchev's offer—of an exchange of visits. Eisenhower agreed, "very reluctantly," said Murphy, and all at once the train was off the rails. Murphy imagined that Eisenhower, by sheer dint of personality, would crumble the walls of Soviet hostility. Eisenhower imagined that his invitation to Khrushchev was conditional upon "such progress" by the foreign ministers "as would justify a meeting of the four heads of government." The President supposed that Murphy, in handing the letter of invitation to Kozlov for transmission to Khrushchev, would make clear its conditional character. Murphy instead thought of Eisenhower's triumphal tour of the Soviet Union and of how it would belie "the monotonous Soviet diet of official distortion and misrepresentation regarding the United States."

The invitation was accepted with alacrity.

Eisenhower was displeased to receive a report from Christian Herter (who had succeeded Dulles as secretary of state) saying that the foreign ministers' conference continued in stalemate, and to learn from Murphy that the conditions for Khrushchev's visit had not been made clear. He was now stuck with an unwelcome guest—"a most unpleasant experience"—without having got in return any countervailing concession from the Soviets. Khrushchev had what he wanted; Eisenhower had only impotent fury. No use to bark at Murphy and the other State Department officers.

The President had to lump it. The failure was his: he had not issued unmistakable instructions.

"Prospects for . . . easing world tensions now seemed to lay," as President Eisenhower would put it, "in direct contacts between the heads of governments."

On August 3 he called a special press conference to confirm "one of the worst kept secrets of a long time," that he and Khrushchev proposed to exchange visits within the next couple of months. The scheme was at once subjected to a barrage of angry criticism. The incessant propaganda of the Cold War had made patriotism synonymous with anticommunism; to invite Khrushchev was to invite His Satanic Majesty. One senator called it "a national disgrace." A Roman Catholic prelate asserted it was "like opening our frontiers to the enemy in a military war." Labor leaders, prominent liberal thinkers, educators, newspaper editors, ex-Presidents—for one reason or another, all those who traditionally scamper into print vied with each other to proclaim their outrage. President Eisenhower had his hands full asserting his leadership on behalf of what threatened to become a disaster area.

Nor was the exchange of visits any more popular abroad. Chancellor Adenauer was aghast—was this the sort of thing to be expected now that his old friend Dulles was dead?—and President de Gaulle was equally disturbed. Eisenhower undertook to reassure his apprehensive allies by promising to confer with them before entertaining Khrushchev. His journey to Europe was also announced on August 3. But was this sudden flurry of personal diplomacy not a reversal of the Dulles policy? Not at all, said President Eisenhower at an extraordinary press conference called in a gymnasium next door to his temporary White House office in the Gettysburg postoffice. "This is far from a reversal," the President insisted. The invitation to Khrushchev had often been discussed with Dulles; nothing new, all in order.

But for the President to plunge into personal diplomacy was of course quite new, and recognized as such by Dulles's old associates in the State Department. Their testimony is explicit. Robert Bowie, chief of the department's policy planning staff, has said that the President "was less cautious [than Dulles], or less constrained about exploring ways which might offer some means of breaking out of [a rigid] set of relationships." Livingston Merchant, a deputy undersecretary who was one of Dulles's closest advisers, recalled Eisenhower saying, "Foster rather discouraged me from traveling too much, and he was right. He used to tell me . . . that I had . . . a unique position as President of the United States, and that I should not either wear myself out, or debase this [position] . . . by traveling

847

too much; that this was a bank account which should be saved for the big capital investments, and not drawn on idly, frivolously."

More than usually sensitive to the mood of the country, the President felt, in the late summer of 1959, that the moment had come for a big capital investment of his unique prestige. Harry Truman had criticized him for damaging that prestige by going about the world, especially to Russia. "I get a little bit weary," Eisenhower retorted, "about people that just say, 'Well, this would be a terrible blow to Presidential prestige,' or any other prestige. We are talking about the human race and what's going to happen to it." He left for Europe early in the morning on August 26.

Bonn. The exuberant crowds lining the road to the U.S. embassy at Bad Godesburg numbered more than three hundred thousand—twice the population of Bonn—an outpouring sufficient to persuade Adenauer of the popular support for Eisenhower's forthright diplomacy with the Soviets.

London. The occasion was a renewal of old friendships rather than a contest of political wills. Eisenhower was host at a dinner for his wartime comrades, an affair which could have been placed off limits to all ranks below field marshal, admiral, and air marshal without appreciably diminishing the roster of guests. On Monday evening, August 31, he and the prime minister spoke extemporaneously on televison from Number 10 Downing Street to the largest audience assembled since the queen's coronation. "I always have wanted a summit meeting," said Macmillan. "Well, Harold," said Eisenhower, "when we are talking about peace, we are talking about . . . the imperative of our time. . . . I think people want peace so much that one of these days governments had better get out of the way and let them have it."

Paris. Once again enormous crowds turned out to cheer the President. ("How many," Eisenhower asked de Gaulle, "along the route this morning?" "At least a million," de Gaulle told him. "I did not expect half as many," said Eisenhower, deeply moved.) In truth, Eisenhower had not looked forward to the encounter with de Gaulle. Despite their public protestations of amity, neither man liked the other.* To make matters worse, their views on policy differed sharply. De Gaulle disputed the American assumption that "whether in the realm of security, economics, finance, science, technology, or anything else, the fundamental if not the sole reality was that of America." He disputed the fixed idea of an ideological struggle

---

* "I have the liveliest feelings of friendship for General Eisenhower," de Gaulle told an American journalist, David Schoenbrun. "He is honest and good." The French president then fetched a deep sigh and added: "Men can have friends. Statesmen cannot." Thus the public de Gaulle. In private he spoke with more asperity. Discussing the three leaders—Eisenhower, Khrushchev, and Macmillan—with whom he would soon be meeting at the summit, he said of the first two, "Ce sont des cons," and he dismissed the third with a wave of disdain.

between freedom and international communism, perceiving instead a clash of traditional national interests. "After what has happened to Russia during the two world wars," he asked Eisenhower, "do you believe that a Peter the Great would have settled the matter of frontiers and territories any differently from Stalin?" Already he had pulled the French Navy out of NATO; already he had forbidden the emplacement of U.S. nuclear weapons on French soil unless he held the power of veto over their use, a decision that had obliged NATO to shift several fighter squadrons armed with nuclear weapons from France to Germany; already he had pressed to have the German General Speidel ousted from his NATO command in France; already he was driving to equip France with her own nuclear deterrent. When Eisenhower argued that France could never afford to approach nuclear parity with the Soviet Union, de Gaulle observed that for a French deterrent to be effective, "it is enough to be able to kill the enemy once, even if he possesses the means to kill us ten times over," thereby neatly deflating the insanity of the U.S.–USSR arms race. This bizarre deviation from Cold War norms was attributed to de Gaulle's mystical commitment to the "grandeur of France," a pathetic posturing, wholly divorced from reality, perhaps pathological. In the U.S. he was derided. A more accurate assessment would come in a later time.

For a few days Eisenhower relaxed with friends at Culzean Castle in Ayrshire (see page 544). He was home in the White House on Monday, September 7, to make sure that all was ready for his inconvenient guest.

Most of the housekeeping had been taken care of by Murphy and the Soviet ambassador, Mikhail Menshikov. Their negotiations were complex, embracing schedule, itinerary, security, public and private entertainments, details of coverage by the press and other media, lists of prominent persons to be invited to attend the various functions, and the like. Vice President Nixon, freshly back from the Soviet Union, where he had engaged in a much publicized debate with Khrushchev, had conscientiously drawn up a list of recommendations on how Khrushchev should be treated: aggressively, argumentatively, keeping him on the defensive. Eisenhower chose to ignore these suggestions and even to countermand them. Pointedly, he assigned Cabot Lodge as Khrushchev's constant companion during the visit, thereby ensuring Lodge a great deal of excellent exposure to the voters and denying it to Nixon, a slight that did not pass unnoticed, with the next presidential campaign just in the offing. Murphy and Menshikov also settled the financial aspects of the exchange of visits: the United States would pay the expenses of Khrushchev's twelve days in this country, the USSR would assume the costs of Eisenhower's Russian travels.

A few days before Khrushchev's arrival, Lyndon Johnson sent a memorandum to Eisenhower on the need for national political unity while his guest was in the U.S. (To ensure that it reach the right people, this memorandum went from Johnson to the Texas oilman, Bob Anderson, who was then secretary of the treasury, to Eisenhower, and then for action to Eisenhower's new chief of staff, General Persons.) The issues likely to divide the nation, said Johnson, included labor-management disputes and civil rights. For the duration of Khrushchev's visit, the President and the congressional leaders agreed, truce would be declared on these touchy matters. (Nothing could be done about the fact that a half-million steelworkers were already on strike.) United, Democrats and Republicans could together fix upon Khrushchev a chilly gaze.

To the generality, unaware of the bungling that had led to Khrushchev's visit, it had seemed that President Eisenhower was taking the lead in thawing the Cold War, and this impression had been confirmed by the reports of what he had said abroad, especially in London. His demeanor upon Khrushchev's arrival in Washington was, then, perplexing. The Russian's smile as he stepped from his airplane was a dazzling burst of good-fellowship. By contrast Eisenhower seemed glum, almost sulky—most unusual.

Three days before, the Soviets had launched a large rocket toward the moon, hitting it within eighty-four seconds of the estimated time of arrival. "This was a noteworthy feat," Eisenhower observed, "but the propaganda purpose of the timing was blatant." Khrushchev presented Eisenhower with a small model of the projectile. "This seemed, at first, a strange gift," Eisenhower would recall, "but it then occurred to me that quite possibly the man was completely sincere." In this renitent spirit he sat down to his first conversation with his guest.*

In the President's oval office were Nixon, Herter, Lodge, and two or three others. Khrushchev was accompanied by Gromyko, Menshikov, and two others. Eisenhower began by outlining the subjects that he would like to discuss, later and thoroughly, at Camp David. Some of the subjects were irritants, like the matter of Berlin and the more recent problem of Laos. (On September 4 the Laotian government had formally requested the U.N. to "dispatch . . . an emergency force" to halt an alleged aggression by rebels allegedly equipped and supported by the North Vietnamese

---

* Khrushchev had brought other gifts: a shotgun, a malachite jewel box for Mrs. Eisenhower (a museum piece, said Lewis Strauss after inspecting it, worth at least five thousand dollars), twelve jars of caviar (turned over to the Secret Service to be analyzed), bottles of vodka and wine, an album of phonograph records, and an elk's head.

communists. The next day the State Department accused China and the USSR of having plotted with North Vietnam to provoke the crisis in Laos.) Other subjects—trade, cultural exchanges, a reduction of hostile propaganda—were more constructive. Where would Khrushchev like to begin?

Khrushchev agreed with the President's agenda; he wished to add to it only the question of disarmament.

Eisenhower was in complete accord.

Khrushchev remarked that he wished to present the views of his government. "We believe that you do not want war," he said, "and we assume that you also believe this about us."

Eisenhower answered that nothing could be achieved by mutual suicide.

The main thing, said Khrushchev, was to establish trust; to stop supposing that while one or other of us was saying one thing, he was thinking something else. Trust, mutual trust—there was no other way. If we approach each other in the expectation that the other's economic and political system will be overturned, we will be in trouble. Let history judge which system is better and meantime live in peace as good neighbors.

Right, said Eisenhower. Now, how do we clear away the underbrush so as to establish mutual trust? As one instance of the sort of thing that bred mistrust, he mentioned the Communist party in the United States, a subversive group, he said, controlled and directed by Moscow, dispensing Moscow's propaganda. That makes Americans fearful and tense, it leads to witch-hunts as in the days of Senator McCarthy (I've read about that, Khrushchev interjected), and so, the President resumed, we must proceed step by step. The first step is Berlin. The United States has a responsibility in Berlin, and there should be no unilateral action taken by the Soviets there. Other steps will follow.

Speaking of propaganda, said Khrushchev, he had read the text of Vice President Nixon's most recent speeches on his way across the Atlantic. They were *not* calculated to reduce tensions and soothe tempers, *not* designed to bring a better atmosphere. If—

Nixon here interrupted. There ensued a brief wrangle which was cut short by the President. Let's talk about propaganda, Eisenhower said firmly, but let's not talk propaganda among ourselves. Why not, he suggested, trade a half-hour television program, back and forth, once a month?

Khrushchev was reminded that he had agreed to a proposal, made by Eric Johnston, for an exchange of filmed speeches by himself and Eisenhower, but the U.S. had dropped the idea.

Eisenhower said he would look into it.

Reflecting on his crowded schedule over the next ten days, Khrushchev confessed he had not realized how hard-pressed he would be. He might need some help.

You mean, asked Eisenhower, you'd like me to make one of your speeches for you?

Khrushchev chuckled. Not possible, he said. Then he told of how, when he was touring the United Kingdom, one city after another, and had finally protested to Eden that he needed sleep, Eden had told him he might skip an English city along his way, but if he presumed to slight a Scottish city there was danger Scotland might quit the empire.

Everyone smiled politely. Eisenhower suggested a ride in his helicopter, for a bird's-eye view of Washington.

Fine, said Khrushchev, but first a quick review. About the American Communist party: it was *not* controlled by Moscow. As for Berlin, the question was of a treaty to end the state of war with Germany. Good: let us exchange views. The USSR, he said, has no plan for unilateral action in Berlin, although, he added slyly, the U.S. had taken unilateral action in Japan, where "we were deprived of rights we should have had." In conclusion, he agreed that now, after fourteen years, the German question must be settled.

The meeting stood adjourned. The photographers were ushered in. After pictures were taken, the President and the premier were left alone with their interpreters for a few minutes of relatively private conversation.

Eisenhower had hoped to turn this occasion to account by persuading Khrushchev of his "priceless opportunity to go down in history as one of the truly great statesmen of all time . . . if he would use the power of his position in the furtherance of disarmament, relaxation of tensions, and support of peace." In the event, his remarks were obviously sincere and earnest; even in the transcript they have the authentic ring of Eisenhower at his best, his unaffected candor, his warmth, his goodness of spirit, his idealism. It was a moving appeal. Possibly some of its impact was lost in the translation, but Khrushchev seemed to have been affected by it. The difficulty lay in its underlying assumption, which was wrong. Eisenhower spoke of his own power—constitutionally circumscribed, confined to but one nation, limited in time to but sixteen more months—and contrasted it to Khrushchev's, which he imagined to be absolute, reaching throughout the "communist bloc" and indeed, by reason of the ubiquitous communist parties, into the "free world" as well. Khrushchev of course knew better. The alliance of the USSR and the People's Republic of China was already severely strained. His trip to the U.S. would weaken it further. Nor was his own tenure in office anything like so certain as Eisenhower supposed. Of these matters he said nothing. He contented himself with responding that while the USSR also wanted peace, the goal could not be achieved by the desires of one side only. He emphasized that he believed in Eisenhower personally and in his good will. If both sides showed good will and determination, he said, all problems could be settled.

Eisenhower said he prayed this would come to pass.

There followed the helicopter ride over Washington.

For the next ten days Khrushchev and his party (his wife, his son, his two married daughters, and one son-in-law accompanied him) were largely on their own. Cabot Lodge was their constant escort, of course, and they were always surrounded by security officers and trailed by journalists, officials of both countries, and throngs of the curious, but in general it was Khrushchev's show. He encountered various sets of representatives of the American people; by turns he experienced hostility, reserve, heckling, provocation, friendliness, and suspicion; he succeeded at least in demonstrating that he was a stubborn, resourceful, shrewd, thin-skinned, affable, and fallible human being, a vast improvement over the stereotype of Cold War propaganda. (His unassuming wife was on every hand acknowledged an amiable, grandmotherly soul.)

Eisenhower did little to smooth their way. At his press conference on Thursday, September 17, Khrushchev's first day away from Washington, the President was asked whether some Americans, noting Khrushchev's "apparent conviction and sincerity . . . his friendliness, warmth of personality [might not] get the idea, well, he is a pretty good fellow after all, and perhaps insidiously their general feeling of opposition to the whole idea of communism might become weak . . . ?" Eisenhower rejected the idea. "I think the American public," he said, "is strong enough to see and hear this man or any other man, and capable of making their own decisions. . . . I do not believe that master debaters or great appearances of sincerity or anything else are going to fool the American people long."

Extensive reports on the journey about the country were filed each day by Lodge, affording the President a running commentary on whatever was on the premier's mind. On the crowds that turned out to see him in New York: "Those who have never seen a camel will always come to see one." During the flight to Los Angeles Khrushchev asserted that he had read many of Allen Dulles's intelligence reports; he mentioned a letter the shah of Iran had written to Eisenhower, the Turkish military plans, and so on. On the Fox lot in Hollywood he was vexed by the attempts to get him to pose with starlets for what Lodge characterized as "low-grade publicity pictures." Khrushchev noticed how one press agent tried to make a dancer lift her skirt while being photographed with him. "This, he thought, was in very poor taste," Lodge reported. That night, at a banquet in Los Angeles, Mayor Norris Poulson was constrained to prove his stanch anticommunism. He recalled Khrushchev's celebrated boast, "We shall bury you" (see page 769), and proceeded to pluck it out of context. "You shall not bury us," Poulson proudly proclaimed, "but if challenged, we shall fight to the death." It was Khrushchev's second encounter that day with Poulson; earlier the mayor had welcomed him to Los Angeles with one curt sentence. Lodge, forewarned of Poulson's dinner speech, had got him to tone it down, but it still affronted Khrushchev. The premier raced through his prepared text and then turned on Poulson with icy wrath. The sense of his remark about burial, he said, should be quite clear within its context; he had been referring to the inevitabilities of history, not challenging to war. "I trust," he said, "that even mayors read the newspapers." And then, while his audience sat in an awful hush, Khrushchev said: "It is a question of war or peace between our countries, a question of life or death for the peoples. . . . If you think the Cold War is profitable to you, then go ahead." The room was silent. "I can go," said Khrushchev, "and I don't know when, if ever, another Russian Soviet premier will visit your country." At this point, a reporter noted, "the fright in the hall was a tangible and present thing." But Khrushchev's anger was controlled. His tone relaxed, he cracked a joke or two, and sat down. Behind the scenes Gromyko spoke shortly to Lodge: the provocations, he said, had been organized; perhaps the day in Pittsburgh should be canceled; indeed, perhaps the premier should cancel his trip entirely and return at once to Washington. Lodge applied his smoothest diplomatic wiles to mend the wounds.

Freeman Gosden, one of the President's cronies, sent him a message saying that his friends in Los Angeles had decided their town would be the one at which the Russians would aim their first ICBM. In the White House there was some uncertainty whether or not Gosden had intended this only as a quip.

"Now I begin to understand some of President Eisenhower's problems," Khrushchev told Lodge as they traveled north to San Francisco. "Now I realize his difficulties better. He is surrounded by certain elements who want to prevent a normalization of relations with the Soviet Union." Lodge protested that when it came to foreign affairs Eisenhower was "surrounded" by nobody but Herter and himself, but the premier had formed his own judgment.

"This city of San Francisco has charmed me!" Khrushchev announced a day later. Thereafter the trip was relaxed and carefree, the crowds in Iowa and in Pittsburgh responding to his geniality and gusto with ever warmer friendliness.

There remained an abbreviated weekend at Camp David, during which President and premier held a series of conversations—calmly, dispassionately, no raised voices—on a wide range of subjects. On arms limitation (they agreed it was "a most important problem," the arms race was both costly and dangerous; they could agree on no way of tackling the problem); on Eisenhower's trip to the USSR (they agreed—or rather, Eisenhower's grandchildren decided—that the President and his family would make their visit in late May or June); on the Far East (they agreed to disagree); on a nonaggression pact (Gromyko proposed it, Herter countered with an offer of a consular treaty, and both ideas were shelved); on trade (they agreed that if political tensions could be relaxed perhaps the American laws forbidding trade with the Soviet Union might be repealed); on cultural exchanges (they agreed to expand them); on a summit conference (Eisenhower would attend no such conference so long as there was any threat of duress over West Berlin); on Berlin and Germany—and here, on the issue that nearly a year before had precipitated an alarming crisis, the issue that had caused the gravest apprehensions, cost so many hours of contingency planning, and for a time threatened to splinter the western alliance, here at last a change appeared in the substantive positions of the two opposed superpowers.

Or at least a change was said to have appeared. So tiny was it, so elusive, that it was less a change of substance than a face-saving formula devised to permit Eisenhower to agree to a summit conference without seeming to have abandoned his previous posture of disdainful refusal. On the issue of Berlin there was scant room for maneuver. Months before his visit to the U.S., Khrushchev had denied issuing any ultimatum over Berlin. He had declared that May 27 was no absolute deadline for the transfer of Soviet controls to the GDR, and had conceded that the western allies had lawful rights for their stay in Berlin. What was left for Moscow and Washington to disagree about? Only the right of the USSR to make a peace with the GDR, one effect of which might be to require the western powers to deal with the East Germans, whom they did not recognize, in order to keep West Berlin supplied. Having made a peace with West Germany, the U.S. could scarcely deny the right of the USSR to make a peace with East Germany; the possible consequences of that peace were, however, indigestible.

The difficulty lay in the stubborn contrarieties of the Cold War. Khrushchev had said he would definitely sign the peace treaty; Eisenhower had as definitely said he would never negotiate under duress, at the threat of force. They had spoken, they would never retreat. Yet Khrushchev wanted a summit conference; and for his part Eisenhower, after acknowledging that the problem of Berlin—"a free city, sitting inside a Communist country"—was "an abnormal situation," had come to realize that if he wished to make an agreement with the Soviets he was "almost compelled" to do it on the summit level. To wriggle out from under this confrontation, Eisenhower would claim that Khrushchev had made a vital concession: he had agreed not to insist on signing his peace treaty with the GDR within a stated period of time, and so had restored the question of Berlin to its serene status of the year before.

Even if Khrushchev had agreed to such a thing, it was meaningless, for he could at his pleasure clap a time limit back again on his proposal. But Eisenhower's secretary of state specifically denied, on October 6, that the Soviet determination to make a peace treaty with East Germany had in any way been affected by the conversations at Camp David. The change of substance, visible only under a magnifying glass, was that negotiations on the status of Berlin must be resumed, "that no time limit should be set on them, but that they must not be delayed indefinitely."

In effect, Soviet diplomacy had achieved its goal. There would be a meeting at the summit, and Eisenhower was now as much persuaded of its necessity as had been Macmillan before him. The two principals emerged from Camp David, as one reporter put it, "not only smiling but apparently in genuine friendliness." Little wonder that Khrushchev in his farewell address, televised to the American people, spoke of the Cold War as of some unpleasant memory, fixed in the past. "Goodbye, good luck, friends!" cried Khrushchev, speaking in English, smiling with benign kindliness. Eisenhower too basked in the sunshine of the world's regard. In Britain an influential journalist wrote: "Mr. Eisenhower brought honor to himself, dignity to his office, distinction to his nation, and hope to the cause of peace. He has never enjoyed more public respect than he does now, nor has he ever deserved it so much."

The only western leader now out of step was de Gaulle. The French president wanted no summit conference until he had caught up with the other heads of government. Khrushchev had visited Britain and the U.S.; he must visit France too. Britain, the U.S., and the USSR were all nuclear powers which had tested and possessed nuclear weapons; France must achieve, if not parity, at least her atomic independence. Then it would be time to think of summit conferences. On October 21 the French government urged a postponement until the spring of 1960, citing the same argument (the need for "an effective reduction of tension") so often used by Eisenhower and Foster Dulles. Eisenhower was nettled. His leadership of the free world was challenged, and by one whom he did not count among his favorites. Besides, his time in office was running out. He wanted to leave, as his monument, a solid foundation for an enduring world peace. A détente had begun to emerge at Camp David; the time to foster it was now, not next spring. But de Gaulle moved at his own pace: the first French atomic bomb could not be tested before February, and he announced that Khrushchev would be visiting France in March; no summit until April or May. Eisenhower had no choice but to accede to de Gaulle's wishes. At the end of the year a date was finally set for what was described as the first in a series of summit conferences to seek the solution of major disputes. The four heads of state would meet in Paris on May 16, 1960.

Once again distinction must be drawn between the public and the private Eisenhower, those two quite different, even contradictory inhabitants of the same beguiling fleshly envelope.

During the months of waiting for the summit conference—made possible as a result of American blunders and Russian persistence, and then vexatiously postponed—the public Eisenhower was highly visible, promoting good will, journeying from one continent to another, Europe, Asia, Africa, South America, everywhere acclaimed the soldier-statesman, the tireless crusader for the shining goal of peace, the hero. On the eve of his first trip, speaking from his office by television to the American people, the President said: "I hope to make this truth clear—that, on all this earth, not anywhere does our nation seek territory, selfish gain, or unfair advantage for itself. I hope all can understand that beyond her shores, as at home, America aspires only to promote human happiness, justly achieved."

There were in his address the obligatory references to "predatory force . . . aggression, subversion, and penetration . . . a world sorely troubled by atheistic imperialism," but the emphasis was on reducing world tensions, on peace and mutual cooperation. In sum—" 'Peace and friendship, in freedom.' This, I think, is America's real message to the world."

And who better than Dwight Eisenhower to deliver that message? Wherever he went—from Italy around the world to India and back to Tunisia and Morocco; later in Argentina, Brazil, and Chile—the people came out in their hundreds of thousands to hail him and, unmistakably, to roar their approval of his proclaimed policy of peace.

The private Eisenhower was confronted by subtler tasks that required a less agreeable policy. In Taiwan, in Laos, in Thailand, Tibet, Pakistan, Iraq, and Turkey—that is to say, all along the southern border of what was wrongly assumed to be the Sino-Soviet bloc—the treasure and the military might of the United States had been deployed for purposes anything but peaceful, although they were understood to serve the U.S. national interests. Depending on local circumstance, the activities involved espionage, subversion, attempts to stir up rebellion, the training and equipping of national armies, or the overthrow or vassalage of national governments. Nor of course were these activities limited to Asia and the Middle East.

The shift from public to private and back again was smoothly accommodated. Thus on December 23, the day after his return from his first journey abroad, the President conferred with Douglas Dillon, now the undersecretary of state, Allen Dulles of the CIA, and General Goodpaster, his staff secretary. Two anticommunist factions were disputing control of the government of Laos and, Dillon warned, there was danger of a coup d'état. (The State Department backed the leader of one faction.) Allen Dulles emphasized that the two quarreling factions must be got to patch up their differences before elections should be held. (The CIA station chief in Laos backed the leader of the other faction.) Already nearly three hundred million dollars' worth of military equipment had been sluiced into the peaceable land; the Eisenhower administration was determined at any cost to convert Laos into a bastion of freedom and a bulwark against communism. Both contrary factions were now armed to the teeth with U.S. weapons and in consequence so was the Pathet Lao—the guerrilla bands, presumably led by communists, which had with monotonous success organized the villagers northward along the banks of the Mekong River. Eisenhower approved the course of action outlined by Dillon. Before long the first in a series of coups d'état would once again provoke bloodshed.

That night the President lighted the national Christmas tree at ceremonies on the Ellipse, back of the White House. The ceremonies were conducted by something called the Pageant of Peace.

Again, when he returned from his second trip, the one to South America, the President was able to slip easily from public to private role to deal with the most pressing of his Latin American problems, the revolution in Cuba. The question of what to do about Castro had vexed the Eisenhower administration for fourteen months. For one thing, was he or was he not a communist? In the summer of 1959 a report jointly prepared by the sundry intelligence agencies insisted that yes, he was "pro-Communist and his advisers [were] either Communist or pro-Communist." Yet by November General Charles Cabell, still deputy director of the CIA, firmly told a Senate committee that "Castro is not a Communist . . . It is questionable whether the Communists desire to recruit Castro . . . that they could do so if they wished or that he would be susceptible to Communist discipline if he joined." Nevertheless, the continuing expropriation of land owned by U.S. investors caused complaint, and before long the President was being urged by Vice President Nixon and by the Chiefs of Staff to encompass Castro's downfall by organizing a counterrevolution within Cuba, presumably to be led by CIA agents. In early March, while the President was in South America, a French freighter laden with seventy-six tons of Belgian rifles and grenades exploded in Havana harbor, killing scores and injuring hundreds of Cuban dock workers. Was it sabotage? Had it been instigated by the U.S. or, as seemed more likely, by Cuban exiles in Florida? If so, it was never proven, although a Belgian expert later alleged sabotage. At all events, Castro charged U.S. complicity.

On March 7, 1960, Eisenhower was back in the White House. At his next press conference, on March 16, the President spoke of Cuba in amiable terms. "We are friendly with the Cuban people," he said, "and we want to get the kind of understanding with their government that will make mutual progress feasible." So the public Eisenhower.

On the next day, March 17, the President privily ordered the CIA to organize, arm, and train Cuban exiles, looking toward a possible armed assault upon the Caribbean island. Their staging area would be in Guatemala, a country with which the CIA was familiar.

And still the opportunities for the public Eisenhower and the private Eisenhower to operate at cross-purposes were not exhausted.

On his first good-will tour, in December 1959, Eisenhower had stopped overnight in Turkey and spent the next couple of days in Pakistan. As he well knew, both these countries had a special usefulness for the United States: each had permitted the installation of air bases and surveillance by highly sophisticated electronic gear. Both bases—at Incirlik near the southern coast of Turkey, and at Peshawar in the hot dry valley below the Khyber Pass in Pakistan—were spy centers. From both bases were flown the U–2, the high-altitude jet-powered glider nicknamed "the black lady of espionage" by the Soviets. The U–2s had been flying into Soviet airspace for four years, photographing the land below, the factories, the airfields, the defenses, the railways, the ICBM launching sites, stripping bare the secrets of Soviet technology and of the Soviet ability to attack or retaliate against attack.

A risky business, and the President was fully aware of the perils. He personally authorized the U–2 missions, not individually but as a series of two or three flights to be undertaken within a specified period of time as weather permitted. After several such approvals, "Well, boys," Eisenhower had said, "I'll tell you one thing. Some day one of these machines is going to be caught and then we're going to have a storm." Foster Dulles had disagreed. He contended the Russians would never protest the flights, since to do so would entail the humiliating admission that their skies had been repeatedly invaded while below they could only fume in impotent frustration. Further, Allen Dulles had assured the President that a U–2 pilot would never be taken alive. Nevertheless, Eisenhower anticipated the possibility of mischance. As Gordon Gray, his special assistant for security affairs, has said, "It was recognized that some day there might be an accident if we continued to use this device."

During 1959 and the early months of 1960 fewer overflights were scheduled than before, perhaps reflecting prudence in the face of possible détente. In any case, the U–2 was obsolescent: the time was not far off when it would be superseded by the Samos satellite. Two overflights, however, were authorized for the month of April—by the private Eisenhower. The reasons for his decision have as yet not been fully elucidated. The risks by April 1960 were graver than ever: the President's board of consultants on foreign intelligence activities is known to have been concerned that the Soviets had developed, or were approaching the development of, a capability to strike with rocketry at the U–2. On the other hand, the memory was still fresh of how the Japanese had sent diplomats early in December 1941 to parley in Washington: might the Russians similarly be planning a nuclear Pearl Harbor?

Whatever the logic (or illogic) of it, the first flight took place on Saturday, April 9, without event. The second flight was scheduled for Thursday, April 28, to go from Peshawar in Pakistan north and west across the Soviet Union to an airfield at Bodö in Norway. Because of bad weather it was twice postponed and at length rescheduled for Sunday, May 1— beyond the limit of the original dispensation. The pilot was ready for takeoff at 6 A.M.; after he had waited many minutes, sweltering in his cumbersome pressurized suit and helmet, he was told that mission command still lacked the coded approval from Washington—an unprecedented procedural rupture. The pilot imagined his flight would surely be canceled, but at 6:20 A.M. the signal came that he was cleared for takeoff.

At that moment the summit conference, awaited with sanguine expectation the world around, was cleared for smashup.

The affair of the U–2—piloted by Francis Gary Powers, who was employed by the CIA at a wage of thirty thousand dollars a year; shot down near Sverdlovsk, an industrial center near the center of the Soviet Union, on May Day, a premier holiday in that country—plunged the Eisenhower administration into what was by any test its most embarrassing predicament, a carnival of foolishness, a parade of lies and blunders and self-deceptions that led the government of the United States, for the first time in its history, to the humiliating admission that it had knowingly lied and that it was guilty of espionage and of having deliberately violated the territory of another sovereign power.

For an administration schooled to move smoothly along staff-regulated grooves, the mess was a painful instance of egg on the face. Much if not all of the mess might have been avoided if the President had reposed less confidence in the conviction of the CIA (in which the Pentagon concurred) that the U–2 was so fragile it would virtually disintegrate if subjected to any unusual stress—say, the near-miss of a bursting rocket. After falling nearly fifteen miles to impact, the spy gear in the airplane would scarcely yield the Soviets any priceless secrets. "Self-destroying mechanisms were built in." As for the unfortunate pilot, he too would be conveniently silenced: when the U-2 disintegrated at that height, the pressurized equipment and oxygen hoses would become a deathtrap. "What the hell," said one close presidential aide, "they were paying 'em thirty grand." So firmly rooted was the belief in these assumptions that the President would say of the pictures released by the Soviets of the U-2 wreckage: ". . . we know that they were not, or we believe we know that they are not pictures of the plane that was downed."

But of course the plane was shot down; its pilot, owing to a combination of fluky circumstances, survived his plane's disability and his remarkable tumble through space; and in due course the President's assumptions about the U-2 were likewise shot down. The disconcerting proof would be produced by the Russians only after several days, during which the government of the United States found itself tangled in one lie after another, and finally had to confess the self-evident.

A fortnight intervened between the downing of the U-2 and the meeting at the summit, a painful time. The President was busy with speeches. He signed bills, including another civil rights bill which was not much of an improvement over the earlier act. He issued a Mother's Day proclamation. He presided over an extraordinary meeting of the National Security Council held, because of a civil defense exercise, in a highly secret mountain retreat outside the capital. He managed to squeeze in several rounds of golf. He opened an AFL–CIO trade exhibit at the National Guard Armory in Washington (". . . as we help our brother," he said, "we make this a more peaceful, a more prosperous, all in all a better world . . . and materially we all profit . . . by cooperation among nations"). But always near the front of his mind was the reflection that his hope of helping to build a sure foundation for a lasting peace was all but shattered. He remained calm.

On the evening of Sunday, May 8, the President conferred with Herter and one or two others. He had determined to shoulder responsibility for the U-2 mission. The statement issued by the State Department the next day was, in one salient respect, deliberately fuzzy: it said nothing about terminating surveillance by U-2s. Eisenhower had instructed the CIA that such flights were not to be resumed, but he was damned if he would say so publicly. This was certain to anger Khrushchev, as was the argument in Herter's statement that U.S. espionage was mandatory, since the Soviet Union persisted in maintaining a "closed society" from which at any moment a devastating surprise attack might be launched against the free world. Indeed, Khrushchev at once flung this argument aside with contempt: ". . . it is not the burglar who is guilty, but the owner of the house he broke into, because he locked it, thereby compelling the burglar to break in. But this is a philosophy of thieves and bandits!"

Ordinarily the President's departure for a conference as important as the one in Paris would have been the occasion for fanfare—an appearance on television, a speech to the nation, a gathering of august personages to bid him farewell. These celebrations were canceled. Eisenhower was grim as he boarded his big airplane. A drizzle of rain was falling as his presidential jet thrust up and eastward.

If the affair of the U-2 caused Eisenhower any dismay in the two weeks before the meeting at the summit, it was trivial when set alongside the discomfiture of Khrushchev. For three years the Soviet premier had been seeking détente with the U.S.; now, within three days, the Central Committee of the Communist party's presidium experienced an upheaval that appreciably weakened his political position. Now, to regain support, perhaps even to survive, he must jeopardize the summit conference he had so ardently solicited. But that Eisenhower knew of Khrushchev's domestic difficulties may be doubted.

Khrushchev, the aggrieved party, was the first of the foreign heads of government to reach Paris. Presently he sent a memorandum to de Gaulle expressing his outrage over the violation of Soviet airspace and specifying the conditions Eisenhower would have to meet if Khrushchev were to attend the summit meeting: the President would be obliged to denounce the U-2 flights, announce they had been discontinued, publicly apologize on behalf of the United States, and "pass severe judgment" upon those responsible. His memorandum proceeded with accusations of "perfidy." The likelihood of Eisenhower's concurring in these requirements was nil. The damage had already been done in Washington by the flood of statements, first mendacious, later contradictory, at last stiffly honorable, but all ill-advised, since one by one they blocked every path by which an adversary might have found an escape from an intolerable situation and one, moreover, for which Washington was primarily responsible.

Macmillan arrived in Paris "full of apprehension" on Sunday morning, May 15; Eisenhower a little later. That afternoon the two met with Adenauer and de Gaulle at the Elysée Palace. The four statesmen made an attempt to discuss the agenda of the summit meeting, but all were too much distracted by its imminent abortion. "I don't know about anybody else," Eisenhower observed, "but I myself am getting older." "You don't look it," said de Gaulle. They agreed that the summit was now in grave danger. Eisenhower remarked that Khrushchev might try to put him in the dock. "I hope," said the President, "that no one is under the illusion that I'm going to crawl on my knees to Khrushchev." De Gaulle smiled. "No one is under that illusion," he said.

Macmillan left to keep an appointment requested by Khrushchev. The Soviet premier gave Macmillan the impression that he regarded the discord narrowly, as an affair of honor between himself and Eisenhower: "He said that his *friend* (bitterly repeated again and again) his friend Eisenhower had betrayed him. . . . he was obviously incensed by the statements made by Herter and Eisenhower . . . which he thought aggravated their offense."

Meanwhile Eisenhower was meeting with Herter and a battery of advisers from the State Department. He wondered whether the U.S. ought perhaps to torpedo the summit conference without waiting for the USSR to do so. There was talk of the emotional, even pathological reactions of the Russians about their frontiers, as though they were somehow different from the nationalist reactions of other sovereign states. But what to do now? How far to go, to soothe the Soviet sensibilities? The President was urged to do nothing, say nothing, that might compromise the Samos, the spy satellite then being developed. "I'll renounce the U–2," Eisenhower declared. "Its use is at an end, as far as I'm concerned." This was less a concession than a recognition of the realities.

At 6 P.M. there was another meeting at the Elysée—Eisenhower, de Gaulle, and Macmillan, accompanied only by translators. Eisenhower wondered why he alone had not been sought out by Khrushchev. Macmillan reported that Khrushchev was waiting to hear from Eisenhower. Macmillan had also concluded that Khrushchev's posture of the moment was dictated by his need for political support at home. Eisenhower thereupon launched into as much of an act of contrition as he was ever likely to make. He had, he said, never contended the U–2 flights were proper; they were distasteful, disagreeable, and illegal; but he was damned if he was going to be the only one at the summit to raise his hand and promise never again to do what everybody else was doing, particularly when hundreds of Soviet spies were, he conjectured, at work in the United States. He would not pledge not to take measures to ensure the safety of the American people. "However," he added, "the U–2 is now almost obsolete."

The three men turned to a general discussion of disarmament, Berlin, and such other problems. As they rose to leave, de Gaulle mentioned Khrushchev's threat to attack bases from which U–2s penetrated the Soviet Union. Eisenhower paused. "Rockets," he remarked, "can travel in two directions."

Despite this routine bravado, the affair of the U–2 visibly impaired the ring of military bases wrought by the U.S. around the USSR and China.

Diplomatic notes of protest went from Moscow to the governments of Norway, Pakistan, and Turkey; from those governments in turn notes of protest were sent to Washington; and in the wake of the muted assurances given its allies by the Eisenhower administration, it was apparent that neutralism in the Cold War was moving from strength to strength. Notwithstanding U.S. attempts to reverse the decision, the government of Pakistan would at the first opportunity cancel the lease on the U.S. base at Peshawar. In Turkey the government of Premier Menderes, as repressive a tyranny as any in the "free world," would be overthrown on May 27. There would be rioting in Japan in protest against the known presence of U-2s in that country, and the U.S. would be obliged to send a note to Tokyo pledging they would not be used on "intelligence . . . missions." The whole question of U.S. bases in Britain would again be hotly debated and the treaties governing their use reviewed and revised.

These cautionary events lay, however, in the future. Just now, on the eve of the first session of the eagerly anticipated summit, all was gloom and foreboding. The record of blunders and ineptitude by Eisenhower and his principal advisers had been, for nearly a fortnight, remarkable; still they managed, in the last few hours left to them, to contrive richer foolishness. So long did the President keep mum on his decision to halt U-2 activity over and along the borders of the Soviet Union that his silence can only be interpreted as deliberate and provocative: Soviet sovereignty had been invaded, the President had proclaimed his justification of the violations, the only permissible inference was that he meant to persist in them. The challenge was without precedent in the history of nations, and none could have been more galling to a sovereign power. The tactic may have been considered shrewd poker, but it caused mischief among the most devoted of U.S. allies, and it removed whatever chance remained to salvage the disrupted summit.

Further foolishness: on this Sunday night in Paris, with the first gathering at the summit only hours away, Thomas Gates, the boss of the Pentagon, the Philadelphia investment banker chosen by Eisenhower to be secretary of defense, ordered the military might of the United States to the alert. All around the globe, soldiers, sailors, and airmen moved to battle stations.

The order for combat readiness and communications alert came from Gates himself, on duty at the Ritz in Paris, shortly after midnight, Paris time. It was 6 P.M. in Washington, 3 P.M. on the West Coast. Obedient, if a trifle bewildered, the Pentagon transmitted the orders. The duty officers were uncertain how urgent was the alert (they could choose from a range numbered one to five, depending on danger; they hit upon number three, the safe median between a practice drill and a shooting war) and Gates stayed in command, first at the Ritz and later, in the dark hours before dawn, in a front room of the U.S. ambassador's residence. No subsequent congressional inquiry could find Thomas Gates to have been a drowsy sentinel on the ramparts of the free world. (The alert was canceled about ten hours later, after word of it had thoroughly alarmed a great many apprehensive citizens across the country.)

Macmillan had been asked to take breakfast with Eisenhower (at the early hour he deplored, 8 A.M.) and he found the President "depressed and uncertain." Others were laboring apart on a draft of a statement for the opening session. When the text was produced, Macmillan thought it *"not very good and much too truculent."* Herter and others from the State Department, arguments, great confusion, a distasteful proceeding—"the Americans," Macmillan noted, "in considerable disarray." But at last a phrase was inserted declaring the U-2 flights "suspended . . . and not to be resumed."

At the Elysée, de Gaulle had arranged for a large circular table to be placed in an elegant saloon one flight up. Here Khrushchev would sit at his left hand, Macmillan at his right, and the President across from him. Khrushchev was the first to arrive, Eisenhower the last; the two men disregarded each other. Eisenhower had earlier arranged with de Gaulle to recognize him first so that he might reply to the notes Khrushchev had handed Macmillan and de Gaulle. But after de Gaulle's brief and dignified remarks of welcome:

KHRUSHCHEV: I would like the floor.

EISENHOWER: I would also like to make a short statement.

De Gaulle was in the course of recognizing Eisenhower when:

KHRUSHCHEV: I was first to ask for the floor and I would like my request to be granted.

De Gaulle glanced at Eisenhower. The President nodded. Khrushchev was recognized. He rose and read a fifteen-minute statement which, due to the obligatory translations, took three times as long. It was, said Eisenhower later, "a long diatribe." To Macmillan it was "a mixture of abuse, vitriolic and offensive, and legal argument," but in any case it "was a most unpleasant performance." To de Gaulle, more dispassionate, it was "a statement similar to the one he had read to me the day before." However he may have spoken, Khrushchev made clear that Eisenhower would not be welcome in the Soviet Union and that no useful purpose would be served by convoking another meeting at the summit for another six or eight months, or until after Eisenhower's second term as President should have expired.

After that, nothing was left save the obsequies. Khrushchev would hold press conferences for his self-justification, in the course of which he would alienate most of those who had been earlier convinced of the merit of his position. The leaders of the three western powers would gather to contrive how, by means of adroit publicity, they might shift the blame for the foundered conference upon the shoulders of Khrushchev.

On Wednesday, May 18, an unsmiling Eisenhower lunched with de Gaulle at the Elysée, his last formal duty of the agonizing four-day wrangle. As they bade each other farewell, de Gaulle proved himself once again equal to the occasion. "With us it is easy," he reminded his ancient comrade; "you and I are tied together by history."

There followed a brief visit with Antonio Salazar, the aging dictator of Portugal. This was required of the President, since he had earlier visited Generalissimo Francisco Franco, the dictator of Spain; his advisers had warned him that Salazar, whose government was after all an ally in NATO, might be affronted if he were not extended a comparable diplomatic courtesy.

The Hero came home on Friday, May 20. His airplane touched down at Andrews Air Force Base in mid-afternoon. A large throng of dignitaries cheered him as he stepped to the tarmac. His tearful wife embraced him.

What followed was instructive. The President of the United States was home from an international fiasco for which his government stood solely responsible. What de Gaulle called "this . . . absurdly ill-timed violation of Soviet airspace," what had suffused Macmillan with a "disappointment amounting almost to despair," had smashed all hopes of a détente and revived the chilling fears of the Cold War. Dwight Eisenhower's credibility had been mauled at home and abroad. In lying about the U–2, his government had sought to deceive the Soviets but had succeeded only in misleading Americans and betraying the cause of peace. Yet along the way from airport to White House more than two hundred thousand of his countrymen massed to cheer him, and as he was driven down Pennsylvania Avenue, overhead a great banner proclaimed, "Thank you, Mr. President." It was like a triumphal return from a great victory. National confidence in Eisenhower's leadership, as measured by the Gallup poll, was up.

Less than six months were left before the people would select his successor. In just eight months he would at last have retired. Time was running out on Eisenhower's much publicized search for peace with justice.

The catalogue of Eisenhower's achievements in those last eight months does not impress.

The materials with which to make peace—at home between the Negroes and the dominant whites, or abroad in the Cold War—were in short supply, and the time during which they might have been fabricated was gone. The major share of the President's attention, as had always been the case, was devoted to foreign affairs, but the distractions of politics in this election year were more clamorous than usual, and it cannot be said that Eisenhower's contributions toward a Republican triumph were without flaw.

The latest white-Negro confrontation had arisen from a new kind of clash in the long struggle for equal rights. The arena chosen was the public lunch counter in bus stations, chain stores, and the like. Negroes had always been refused service at such counters, and not only in the South. Now they demanded service, and when they were ignored patiently continued to sit, thus giving the language a new word—sit-in. The sit-in demonstrations began in North Carolina in early February 1960; college students invented them and after forming a Student Non-Violent Coordinating Committee (SNCC) made of them a zestful political action across the land. The Associated Press reported that more than a thousand of these nonviolent protestors had been arrested within seven weeks of the first sit-in, but they could not be deterred from flourishing their splendid new weapon. The President was asked whether he approved of this passive resistance to segregation; did he see the demonstrations "as manifestations of moral courage . . . ?" "I know about these as they come just briefly to my attention," he answered, holding them off at arm's length; but, he added, if a person should seek his rights "in a perfectly legal way, then I don't see any reason why he shouldn't do it." Eisenhower would never warm the sit-ins with the sunshine of his smile, he would never perceive that for him, leadership against segregation was a moral imperative in the United States of the 1950s and 1960s.

The President was personally concerned only as Cold Warrior. Once home from the collapsed summit at Paris, he concentrated his attention on another good-will tour, another journey to seek "peace and friendship, in freedom." He would travel to what he termed the "bastions of the Free World in the Far East"; that is, the client states of the U.S. military dispensation—the Philippines, South Korea, Taiwan, Okinawa—and perhaps Japan as well.

Perhaps Japan; but perhaps not, for as Eisenhower would assert, "the

Communists, having canceled the trip to the Soviet Union, set about to disrupt this one also." Indeed, the President was persuaded that "once more what we were up against [was] international Communism." The trip to Japan was canceled, because, as Eisenhower saw it, of "persisting demonstrations staged by both labor federations and student organizations . . . surly, noisy mobs, consisting partly, as we later learned, of paid demonstrators . . . Viewed from any angle, this was a Communist victory."

The account is distorted. It magnifies an almost irrelevant coincidence out of all proportion. The rioting was directed against a new Japanese-American security treaty, and only incidentally against President Eisenhower's visit. Sloppy staff work, particularly within the State Department, resulted in a schedule for his Far Eastern trip that would have brought him to Tokyo during the time of greatest turbulence against ratification of the treaty. Some of the violence might have been deflected in his direction, but only as he was a symbol of the militarist policy opposed by a great many Japanese—many more than "the Communists and extreme left-wing Socialists" he later singled out for blame. They were protesting U.S. military bases in Japan, which might be used against China or in support of Chiang or for U-2 flights. They had begun voicing their opposition back in November 1959; in January they had tried to bar the premier, Nobusuke Kishi, from taking plane to Washington to sign the treaty; by the end of May snake-dancing demonstrations involving more than two million Japanese were convulsing the country. They demanded Japanese neutrality in the Cold War, Kishi's resignation, dissolution of the Diet, and, almost as an afterthought, the cancellation of Eisenhower's visit.

On his return to Washington, the President found it necessary to defend his administration's foreign policy and to assert the success of his tour to the Far East. His argument relied on the fancied responses of his adversaries: "One clear proof of the value, to us, of these visits is the intensity of the opposition the Communists have developed against them."

Back in the White House, Eisenhower found the vexatious question of Cuba once again surfacing. The scheme for military operations was by late June well in hand: anti-Castro volunteers were being recruited by the CIA, with the main force being trained in Guatemala and others being schooled at a special U.S. Army establishment in Panama. On Great Swan Island—a small outcrop in the Caribbean about four hundred miles due south of Cuba—the CIA had constructed a fifty-kilowatt radio station and since May had been directing at Cuba a comprehensive anti-Castro propaganda. In a general way the Cuban government knew about these enterprises. As early as April a seaborne invasion from Guatemala had been forecast, and before long the United Fruit Company had been linked to the conspiracy. (In fact, a former president of United Fruit was also president of the shadowy corporation ostensibly operating Radio Swan, the CIA transmitter on Great Swan; Cuba did not start protesting that "counterrevolutionary radio station, supported by U.S. dollars," until June.)

Still the Eisenhower administration had not taken the obvious step and moved to cripple the Cuban economy by slicing the quota of imported sugar.* There were good reasons to postpone decision, to move with restraint, even to refrain entirely from tinkering with the sugar quota. Other Latin American countries, it was feared, would at once accuse the U.S. of economic aggression: per corollary, it was possible that Castro, whose control of Cuba was still insecure, might welcome such aggression by the "colossus of the North" as a means of ensuring his grip. Some advice given Eisenhower on this score is pertinent: if the quota were to be canceled, he was told, the funds freed (estimated at between one hundred million and one hundred and fifty million dollars a year) should at once be directly allocated to projects for the economic development of other Latin American countries, with an attendant fanfare of publicity.

Still the administration hesitated. Later, when Castro had frankly espoused friendship with the Soviet Union, Eisenhower would be criticized for want of "imagination," failure to identify the forces of social revolution rising all over the world, inability to channel those democratic tides into harmony with U.S. national interests. This would be to criticize the administration for inability to alter its fundamental character: men whose objective is to preserve the status quo cannot fairly be faulted for resisting social change.

The logic of the revolution put an end to Washington's forbearance. Castro had determined to remove Cuba from the list of one-crop countries: his government had arranged for the purchase of some thirty new factories—even a steel plant—from the Soviet Union, and Russian petroleum had begun to arrive in April. In all likelihood the U.S. would never have fostered that kind of Cuban economic development; at all events, Castro never asked and the Eisenhower administration never proffered. Toward the end of May three oil refineries in Cuba—Standard Oil, Texaco, and Shell—were asked to process a small amount of Russian crude. They were said to be reluctantly ready to consent to the request when Robert Anderson, the secretary of the treasury, pressed them to re-

* At the time sugar accounted for about 30 percent of national income and about 80 percent of Cuban exports. Since so many other economic activities were dovetailed into the sugar industry, one may safely conclude that the industry was dominant in the nation's economy.

fuse. Some U.S. property—hotels, sugar cane farmland—had already been expropriated, and on June 22, while Eisenhower was on his way home from the Far East, Herter, testifying in secret, asked the House Committee on Agriculture to report favorably a bill authorizing Eisenhower to end the sugar quota. Despite the earnest advice of Philip Bonsal, the latest U.S. ambassador to Havana, the administration's policy of "patience and tolerance" was at an end.

Castro reacted with a predictable denunciation. He charged the "Yankee imperialists" with economic aggression; he warned that if they tried to "force us to surrender by hunger," he would seize all "Yankee property down to the nails of their shoes." The Texaco refinery was seized on June 29, those of Shell and Standard on July 1.

Authority to cut the sugar quota was bustled through the Congress in extraordinary fashion. The Senate version of the bill and the House version—both passed unanimously—were in sharp conflict, and a compromise was not reached until early Sunday morning, July 3, after an all-night wrangle. Congress and President alike were ruefully surveying the effects of having ignored the realities of Latin America for too many years, and wondering whether this provoking revolution of Castro's might not perhaps become an embarrassment suitable for export. Belatedly the President had commenced to worry about "our future course of action—a course which included both cooperation against dictatorships and cooperation for economic and social progress." Perhaps the status quo might be inched along a bit. What was needed, the President reflected, were "new policies that would reach the seat of the trouble, the seething unrest of the people, but without causing bloodshed and more suppression."

In this spirit the President proclaimed on July 6 that "with the most genuine regret" he was reducing Cuba's sugar quota by seven hundred thousand tons, substantially all that was left for the balance of 1960. "This action," he observed as he signed the proclamation, "amounts to economic sanctions against Cuba. Now we must look ahead to other moves —economic, diplomatic, strategic."

On the same day he met with advisers to ponder U.S. aid "to show Latin America that the United States wanted to raise the standards of living of *all* her peoples." From the discussion there presently emerged a plan to ask the Congress for six hundred million dollars—one hundred million for repair of damage done by earthquakes in Chile, five hundred million "for a better way of life for the individual citizens of . . . Latin America." The authorization was enacted by Congress on September 8.

In the meantime, secretly, the President had earmarked thirteen million dollars for military action by Cuban counterrevolutionaries against Cuba.

These matters had scarcely been arranged when another East-West confrontation began to develop in the heart of Africa.

The Belgian Congo, a vast tract of land (larger than Texas and Alaska together) which for many years had been the personal property of the king of the Belgians, in late 1959 was unexpectedly agitated by riots. A National Congolese Movement, headed by the militant thirty-four-year-old Patrice Lumumba, wanted freedom, not when the Belgians chose to confer it but right away. Lumumba was jailed, but the Belgians were obliged to release him and allow him to join with other Congolese in a conference at Brussels, at which it was agreed to give the big colony its independence on June 30, 1960. In a preliminary general election Lumumba's supporters won the biggest share of seats in the National Assembly, and he was named premier.

The infant state was woefully unprepared for self-government; there were, moreover, powerful interests abroad which were bent upon maintaining their grip on the Congo's wealth. (In the province of Katanga, rich deposits of copper, cobalt, gold, silver, and—of special value in the atomic age—uranium had attracted capital investment from Belgium, Britain, and France.) These two elements, inexperience on the one hand and covetous commerce on the other, blended naturally to produce turmoil. In Katanga, a pliable Congolese named Moise Tshombe accepted Belgian support, hired Belgian mercenaries with income from the Union Minière du Haut Katanga, and announced secession of the province from the republic. Elsewhere the Force Publique, a black constabulary, rebelled against its white officers, ushering in a period of pillage and rapine that sent many white residents of the Congo in fearful flight to Europe.

Lumumba was able to halt the violence for a time by the expedient of dismissing the Belgian officers and promoting all ranks of the Force Publique one step, but soon the looting and disorder began again. Thereupon the Belgian government intervened with paratroops "to protect her interests." On July 10 Lumumba appealed to the U.N. for military assistance, "not to restore [the] internal situation in [the] Congo but rather to protect the national territory against [an] act of aggression . . . by Belgian metropolitan troops." Four days later the Security Council of the U.N. approved the request. The leaders of the Congo were aware that at the time the U.N. was unlikely to take any substantive action without U.S. approval, and further that Belgium was an ally of the U.S.; Lumumba and the Congo president, Joseph Kasavubu, joined in sending a cable to Khrushchev asking him "to watch hourly over the situation" in view of the threat "from Belgium and certain Western countries supporting Belgium's conspiracy against our independence." Khrushchev was happy to oblige. His response spoke of "criminal actions" and the Soviet determination to oppose them. Once again protests began to speed back and forth between Washington and Moscow. The propaganda of the Cold War was once again inflamed. U.N. troops from six or seven African nations were on patrol in the Congo by July 16. Soviet aircraft (Ilyushin-14 civil transports) and technicians were on hand in the Congo a month later. A U.S. attack aircraft carrier was stationed at the mouth of the Congo River. In London, Macmillan was uneasily comparing the summer of 1960 with that of 1914: "Now Congo," he noted, "may play the role of Serbia."

To President Eisenhower and his advisers the blame was easy to fix: Lumumba was responsible. Later, in his memoirs, Eisenhower would show as on a fever chart the swift rise of his angry contempt for Lumumba. On June 30 he was "the radical and unstable Congolese prime minister," but within two weeks "we were . . . convinced [he] was a Soviet tool," and by the first week of September he was "a Communist sympathizer if not a member of the Party."

The time had come for a change. Kasavubu was "a man of . . . moderation"; he could be relied upon. Joseph Mobutu, chief of staff of the Congolese armed forces, had been selected by the CIA for a leading role. With CIA support he would before long be ready for his own coup d'état. Meanwhile, there was Dag Hammarskjöld, the U.N. secretary-general, whose advisers—members of the so-called Congo Club—were dependable men, Americans either by birth or by naturalization. Ralph Bunche, Heinrich Weischoff, Henry Labouisse, Andrew Cordier—at one time or another each would be on hand. A few necessary precautions: close down the airports in Leopoldville, Stanleyville, Luluabourg, and other Congolese centers, and forbid the landing or takeoff of any but U.N. planes; seize control of the Leopoldville radio transmitter; pay the Congolese forces with U.N. funds, giving credit for this largess to Mobutu. By September 6, all was done. Next, arrest Lumumba. He would be cut off from his supporters in Stanleyville; if all were managed well, he would be toppled from political power and, from Washington's point of view, a good thing.

"Reviewed as a whole," Eisenhower would recall, "the Congo crisis represented a forward step in the influence of the United Nations."

In the fall of the year, the headquarters of the United Nations in New York was briefly to become the cockpit of the Cold War, with the world's statesmen taking turns, each in his fashion, at trying to win the world's good opinion. To New York came an unprecedented swarm of commanding figures—Khrushchev, Macmillan, Nehru, Nasser, Tito, Sukarno of Indonesia, Nkrumah of Ghana, Gomulka of Poland, Castro of Cuba, Diefenbaker of Canada, Kadar of Hungary, Prince Norodom Sihanouk of Cambodia, King Hussein of Jordan, Menzies of Australia, Touré of

Guinea, Golda Meir of Israel; heads of state, heads of government, foreign ministers—and for various reasons they presented President Eisenhower with some unprecedented problems.

There was the need for protecting the persons of these visitors. The more objectionable of them, men like Khrushchev, Castro, and Kadar, could be ordered confined to the island of Manhattan and their protests ignored; but the question of adequate security was plainly going to be troublesome and might well endure until Christmas.

There was the irritating possibility that Khrushchev might maneuver somehow to contrive another summit meeting, or that the leaders of the neutral nations—Nehru, Nasser, Tito, and others—might publicly urge one. Eisenhower wanted no part of such an affair, and he was ready to go to considerable lengths to avoid it. (Khrushchev was quite as cool to the idea.)

There was the question of his own participation in the proceedings. His first inclination had been to address the General Assembly late, not soon, so that he could shape his speech with an eye to the character of earlier debate. On reflection, he decided to speak on the first day—avoid argument, set tone, preserve dignity. His speech was lofty and righteous, calling for noninterference in the African countries' internal affairs, economic assistance for them, and support for their educational efforts. Later, during Eisenhower's conversations with some of the visiting statesmen, Nasser expressed disapproval of the U.N. action in closing the Congo airfields to all other aviation. The step, Nasser said, had shaken the confidence of the "entire world" in the U.N. Eisenhower thought his remonstrance exaggerated, but there is evidence the administration was concerned about the mounting Afro-Asian dismay at the overthrow of Lumumba and the way it had been done.

Finally, to trouble the President further, there was the possible effect on the election campaign, then reaching a critical stage, of some Cold War brawl at the U.N. He was aware that the U-2 affair had been wounding to the Republican posture as the party of peace with justice; another such affair might prove fatal for Richard Nixon.

"All we want out of Ike is for him to handle Khrushchev at the U.N. and not let things blow up there. That's *all*." So, to the journalist Theodore White, spoke one of Nixon's inner circle of political advisers early in September, when the polls showed Nixon leading the Democratic candidate, John F. Kennedy, and all was confidence in the Nixon camp.

In truth, there was a constraint among the leading Republicans. The Vice President's campaign directors were angered by an early lapse of Eisenhower's. Months before the conventions had chosen the two candi-

"A Little Bit Closer—Not Too Close—Smile—That's It."

from *Straight Herblock* (Simon & Schuster, 1964)

dates, Nixon had concluded that Kennedy "was most likely to be nominated and would be the hardest to beat." His own strongest asset was his
experience—eight years in the highest councils of government, regular
attendance at meetings of the cabinet and National Security Council, presumed participation in the discussions that preceded the capital decisions
of the Cold War—from the start Republican oratory concentrated on
this theme. The question had come up at Eisenhower's press conference
on August 24. One reporter asked the President "to tell us some of the big
decisions that Mr. Nixon has participated in," and the President had observed that "no one participates in the decisions . . . no one can make a
decision except me if it is in the national executive areas." Another
reporter inquired further into the process:

Q: We understand that the power of decision is entirely yours, Mr. President. I just wondered if you could give us an example of a major idea
of his [Nixon's] that you had adopted in that role, as the decider and
final—

THE PRESIDENT: If you give me a week, I might think of one. I don't remember.

The remark delighted the Democrats and produced a flurry of headlines
across the country.

Later Eisenhower would loyally insist that "Dick Nixon has the broadest and deepest preparation and experience of any man I know," but the
damage was done. Nixon acknowledged that the earlier remark "was to
plague me the rest of the campaign," and do mischief "to one of my
strongest campaign themes and assets—my experience as Vice President."

After so many years in Eisenhower's shadow, Nixon was at last in a
position to make the decisions—at least for the campaign. The two men
had discussed Eisenhower's participation and Eisenhower had argued that
since Nixon must establish himself as the new leader of the party, it would
be well if he, Eisenhower, stood aside in the early weeks, lest he diminish
Nixon's image. Nixon left with the impression that Eisenhower would
pick his own time to join in the politicking. That impression would be disputed by members of the White House staff.

At all events, as Kennedy's attacks on the Eisenhower administration
mounted, while Nixon persisted in a low-keyed defense, the President
fretted. He felt that Nixon's counterattack should have more sting. On
October 1 he sent Nixon a letter saying as much, advising that Nixon's
campaign "should be more hard-hitting—not necessarily in terms of personal attack but in urgent support of our own plans, programs and candi-

dates." Eisenhower realized that the record of his eight years as President was the paramount issue in the November elections; Kennedy's talk of a "new frontier" and of the need to get the country moving again, as though for eight years it had been stagnating in the shallows, was intolerable. The charges that U.S. prestige abroad had slumped—charges amply sustained by USIA surveys of opinion in western Europe, the Far East, and Latin America—were particularly galling. In mid-October the President left Washington on a nine-day tour of the country, with speeches to be delivered in Detroit, St. Paul–Minneapolis, San Francisco, and Houston. The excursion was billed as "nonpolitical," but at every stop he lambasted Democratic "fear-mongering" and the "wails" of "misguided people." From Palm Springs, where he had paused two or three days for golf, he announced that he was about to start fighting hard for Nixon and Lodge. Republicans everywhere took heart. All the polls showed the election to be a close one; surely once Eisenhower had put his matchless appeal to work for Nixon, counting the votes would be a formality.

No doubt about it, Eisenhower's intervention in the last ten days of the campaign gave Nixon's chances a dramatic boost. Eisenhower's way with crowds was always remarkable, and in the fall of 1960 that magic was more powerful than ever because the crowds sensed he was making a kind of farewell appearance. Of course he was angry, too—angry at the slurs of the Democrats and angry in defense of his eight years of stewardship—but no matter, he was good old Ike; up from poverty to the pinnacles of power and renown, yet still everyone's next-door neighbor; just folks, yet still a Hero. So when he appeared on the hustings, pink-cheeked and vigorous, the crowds roared their affection for him—in Philadelphia, New York, Cleveland, Pittsburgh. But their affection was a non-negotiable item. The voters loved Dwight Eisenhower, not Richard Nixon. On November 8, despite all Eisenhower could do, by the narrowest of margins the voters repudiated the Republicans. What if the President had hit the trail sooner? What if he had visited Illinois, so narrowly lost? Or Texas? Or Michigan?

The defeat of Nixon and Lodge was, for Eisenhower, the bitterest of disappointments. It meant a rebuff for the President and his eight years of leadership. It meant a defeat as his fifty years of service to the republic came to a full stop.

Just after noon on Wednesday, November 9, Nixon telephoned the White House from California. The President "could not hide his own crushing disappointment." Nixon had "never heard him sound more depressed." At this point their accounts somewhat differ. As the President recalled the matter, Nixon angrily complained, "We were robbed," and went on to report frauds in Cook County, Illinois (which embraces Chicago, the fief of Mayor Richard Daley, a Democrat), and in several counties of Texas; the President then said: "I heard something about that, Dick, and you probably were robbed. But please don't ever say so out loud because if you do you'll be finished politically forever." Nixon's recollection was that Eisenhower "still had lots of fight left: he had heard early reports of fraud charges and [he] urged me to do everything possible to check them out."

Whatever the two men said, they both realized that to challenge the count of votes would be disruptive, wrong, impossible. It was time, Eisenhower recognized, "to begin winding up our affairs and preparing to turn the reins of government over to my successor."*

On that same Wednesday the President was flown south for thirteen days of golf at Augusta National and a fourteenth day of quail shooting with Pete Jones on the latter's Georgia plantation.

Back in early February, the President had appointed a Commission on National Goals and charged it with developing "a broad outline of national objectives and programs for the next decade and longer." This heavyweight project, conceived in a happier time when Eisenhower fancied he could foresee a comfortable Republican vista stretching into the middle distance, had been entrusted to a group of thinkers led by Henry Wriston, Eisenhower's old friend from the Council on Foreign Relations. Not long after Eisenhower had returned from his sojourn at Augusta National, Wriston turned up at the White House with his associates to deliver the commission's report. The group was shepherded to the steps of the White House for photographers.

Across Pennsylvania Avenue a reviewing stand was being constructed, token of a new President's inauguration. Amid the clatter of hammers, Eisenhower, Wriston, and the others posed for photographs. Eisenhower waved a hand toward the activity across the way. "Look, Henry," he said; "it's like being in the death cell and watching them put up the scaffold."

A man long accustomed to the exercise of great power feels more keenly the deprivation of it than one who has used it briefly. Even a man who has served a few months in the White House, in a post of no great importance, gets a little drunk in virtue of his proximity to power; becomes addicted; and suffers withdrawal symptoms when his time comes to depart. As with others, so with Eisenhower. More so, since for nearly twenty years he had had only to crook a finger to work his will with a vast apparatus of authority. Sherman Adams had the impression, when he

* Thruston Morton, chairman of the Republican National Committee, actually pressed the charges of fraud, but in the crucial state of Illinois the board of elections (four Republicans and one Democrat) unanimously rejected the charges.

visited the President at Newport in the summer of 1960, that Eisenhower "was leaving the presidency with some reluctance and that he would miss it." He was a conscientious man and the tasks he had set himself were unfinished.

Six weeks left.

The national economy was in recession. Unemployment was increasing: by the time he left office there would be some five and one-half million unemployed, more than 8 percent of the labor force. A serious deficit in the balance of international payments had led to an alarming erosion of gold reserves. Both these were matters calling for active intervention by the President. As for the first, Eisenhower was not unduly agitated. "Although intermittent declines in economic activity persist as a problem in our enterprise system," he would observe in his annual message on the State of the Union, "recent downturns have been moderate and of short duration. There is, however, little room for complacency. Currently our economy is operating at high levels, but unemployment rates are higher than any of us would like, and chronic pockets of high unemployment persist."

The second of these matters, however, the imbalance of payments, was grave, involving as it did confidence in the dollar on the part of the international financial community. The value of U.S. gold reserves had slipped below eighteen billion dollars for the first time since the War of 1939–1945; the total demands that could hypothetically have been presented for claim against the U.S. Treasury exceeded that sum. Gold was necessary to keep the dollar strong. The dollar had become the chief international currency; it was the symbol of financial supremacy. A strong dollar was necessary to assert U.S. leadership and control of the "free world." As gold drained away, so did the dollar's strength and so did U.S. supremacy. Pax Americana was proving expensive. The cost of military dominion was threatening U.S. economic dominion. This was a novel dilemma in 1960, one not previously faced by the guardians of U.S. national interests.

The President took steps to acquaint his successor of these sobering facts. The "young whippersnapper," as Eisenhower was understood to have referred to Kennedy, came to the White House on December 6, and Eisenhower was favorably impressed by his ready grasp of the complexities of statecraft. They were to meet again on Thursday, January 19—the day before Kennedy's inauguration—for a last recital of the problems that were Eisenhower's legacy. The world was still a handful of nettles for any man of a mind to impose Pax Americana:

THE CONGO. This locus of crisis was deemed stable enough to warrant exclusion from the Eisenhower-Kennedy agenda. Yet Congolese affairs were in violent turmoil. Despite widespread popular support, Lumumba had been arrested by soldiers under the command of Mobutu (the CIA's man) and on January 17 had been secretly flown from Leopoldville to Elizabethville, capital of the secessionist province of Katanga. This abduction delivered Lumumba into the hands of Moise Tshombe, who took his orders from the Belgians, and effectively sealed his death warrant. Indeed, the Congolese leader was murdered on the night of January 17, two days before Eisenhower's second meeting with Kennedy.

None of this was known two days later in the White House. Not until mid-February, when Lumumba's death could no longer be concealed, would a deceitful account of it be circulated, but the falsehoods failed to convince. Among the emerging African nations the U.S. was already in ill repute, since the controlling hand of the Eisenhower administration was seen behind Lumumba's downfall and death; word that he had been murdered, as later attested by a U.N. commission, caused such a wave of revulsion among Africans and American Negroes that U.S. policy toward the Congo would have to be significantly altered.

By then Dwight Eisenhower was far removed from responsibility.

CUBA. Economic warfare between Cuba and the U.S. had been briskly escalated in the last months of 1960. In mid-October Eisenhower had forbidden any U.S. exports to Cuba, excepting only some medical supplies. The Cuban government had retorted by nationalizing some five hundred private enterprises—banks, sugar mills, distilleries, hotels, insurance companies, cinemas, textile mills, stores—most of them owned by U.S. concerns. In mid-December Eisenhower canceled the Cuban sugar quota for the first quarter of 1961.

Castro was by now convinced the U.S. planned an invasion of Cuba during the last days of the Eisenhower administration. He ordered a general mobilization. His apprehensions were quite comprehensible: the CIA scheme of an invasion of Cuba was well advanced, and word of the CIA training camps in Guatemala had been widely published. Kennedy had been told of the CIA's military dreams by mid-November, and since they followed closely what he had himself advocated during the presidential campaign only a month before, he could scarcely instruct the CIA now to cease and desist. Plans for the assault on Cuban beaches proceeded, gathering their own momentum in the absence of orders to the contrary.

Any unrest in Central America was automatically interpreted by the State Department as evidence that Castro was exporting his communist subversion across the Caribbean. It is a sign of the jitters in Washington that an abortive uprising against the repressive government of Guatemala should have so alarmed Eisenhower that he sent U.S. naval units and aircraft to patrol the Guatemalan coast. Meanwhile he hoped a leader of the Cuban exiles could be selected and recognized as head of the legal government of Cuba, if possible before Kennedy's inauguration.

Castro, prey to his own jitters, decided on January 2 that the U.S. embassy and consulate in Havana were overstaffed, probably with espionage agents; U.S. personnel, he decided, should be limited to eleven persons. His note making this demand was delivered to the State Department at 1:20 A.M. on January 3, in the view of well-conducted diplomats an insufferable discourtesy. Secretary Herter sent a memorandum to Eisenhower later that morning recommending termination of relations with Cuba. Eisenhower at once agreed.

On January 19 Eisenhower told Kennedy it was "the policy of this government" to support "to the utmost" any forces opposed to Castro. The business of "helping train anti-Castro forces in Guatemala," Eisenhower urged, should be "continued and accelerated."

Whether this was the counsel of wisdom, from an experienced soldier to a young and exhilarated President-elect, would soon be determined. For his part, Castro saw the new Kennedy administration as offering "a little hope of humanity for peace" and declared himself ready to resume diplomatic relations with the United States.

The CIA's schemes, now matured and gathering speed, would end for a time the chances for peace in the Caribbean.

INDOCHINA. Cuba, the Congo, Berlin, the U–2, Lebanon, Suez—these affairs had obscured Indochina and had, during Eisenhower's second term, distracted the attention of his senior advisers from the intriguing perplexities of jungle warfare. While they were elsewhere engaged, the governments of both South Vietnam and Laos had come unstuck.

In Saigon, the regime of Ngo Dinh Diem had halted agrarian reform, jailed political rivals, become ever more despotic, spurned the national elections stipulated by the Geneva Agreements of 1954, and in consequence had steadily disaffected larger segments of the population. The Eisenhower administration had poured huge sums of money into the country for the purpose, as Eisenhower wrote Diem in 1954, of "developing and maintaining a strong, viable state, capable of resisting attempted subversion or aggression through military means." Economic and military aid in the next five years amounted to more than one and one-half billion dollars. What these generous sums bought, first and last, was corruption. By 1960 a national intelligence estimate would predict that "dissatisfaction and discontent with the [Diem] government will probably continue to rise [and] will almost certainly in time cause the collapse of Diem's regime."

Yet Eisenhower was more alarmed over the situation in Laos. The government of that unhappy land had been convulsed by at least a half-dozen coups d'état since the time in December 1959 when Eisenhower had hoped (see page 857) by decisive U.S. aid to stabilize Laos as a bastion of freedom. His choice had fallen upon an ambitious, reliably right-wing army officer named Phoumi Nosavan; the prime minister was the serene and patient Prince Souvanna Phouma, anticommunist but neutralist, who desired above all that his country should be at peace; to his left was his younger half-brother, Prince Souphanouvong, the energetic leader of the Pathet Lao. Souvanna sought to establish a coalition government embracing all elements. His half-brother was willing, but not Phoumi, who, backed by the CIA and the U.S. generals, first agreed to join the coalition but then, having been supplied with U.S. artillery and shells, assaulted the capital, Vientiane, and drove Souvanna Phouma into refuge in Cambodia.

Eisenhower, who always preferred to deal with a legally constituted government, was now in quandary. Souvanna Phouma was incontestably the legitimate premier, yet he was also "an accomplice . . . of the Communist Pathet Lao." Meanwhile another prince, Boun Oum, had appeared on the scene as head of a provisional government, "one to which," Eisenhower would gratefully testify, "we could give open support." On the last day of 1960 he issued instructions to, among others, General Charles Cabell, deputy director of the CIA, and General Lyman Lemnitzer, then chairman of the Joint Chiefs of Staff. "For the moment," said the President, "here's what we must do: Induce Souvanna Phouma to resign as prime minister and if possible persuade him to leave Cambodia and depart for France. Get Boun Oum to allow the [Laotian] national assembly to approve his government. . . . [Let] Khrushchev know that . . . we are moving our forces to assure, if necessary, that the legitimate government of Laos will not be destroyed, and that if a major war comes, the United States will not be caught napping."

As his officers rose to leave, the President added: "We cannot let Laos fall to the communists even if we have to fight—with our allies or without them."

That was the quagmire Eisenhower would bequeath to Kennedy on January 20. Boun Oum's government was already appealing for help against what was said to be an invasion by North Vietnamese and possibly also Red Chinese troops (a month later Boun Oum would admit at a press conference that the talk of invasion had been a lie, told so as to encourage foreign support) and Eisenhower was determined that his last days as President would not be marred by a sudden successful communist aggression. "The United States lost no foot of the Free World to Communist aggression" during his eight years in office; that would be his boast and he meant to keep it unsullied. When he spoke to Kennedy, the day before the inauguration, he revived in all solemnity the old domino theory of how the fall of Laos would mean the subsequent fall of Cambodia, South Vietnam, Thailand, Burma—all Southeast Asia. He had tried to alert the governments of Britain and France to the danger but had been unable to win their consent to the invoking of the SEATO treaty. "Our unilateral intervention," the President told the President-elect, "would be our last desperate hope in the event we're unable to prevail upon the other signatories to join us."

The time was approaching to pack it in. He had already made his Farewell Address, a ceremony for which, as he was aware, the precedent had been vouchsafed him by the nation's first soldier President. The address had been in the process of composition for some weeks. His speech writer for the occasion, Malcolm Moos, was a young political scientist who had been drafted from the faculty of the Johns Hopkins University. Moos had used a phrase—"the military-industrial complex"—that had riveted the President's attention. Apt phrase to describe what was certainly a real and growing danger in American society: he would use it. There was another threat already visible in early 1961, to mention which would do him honor: "we must avoid," he would warn, "the impulse to live only for today, plundering, for our own ease and convenience, the precious resources of tomorrow." But his chief aspiration remained "a peace guaranteed by the binding force of mutual respect and love."

As those were the last words of his Farewell Address, so he would desire to be remembered by his contemporaries and by history, as the soldier who fought for peace.

Then the morning of Friday, January 20; the ride in crisp brilliant sunshine along avenues lately covered by a fall of snow; the oldest man to hold the office accompanying the youngest ever to assume it; the father-figure, a benevolent smile on his lips, hearing in the shouts of the crowds a new exultant note for Kennedy but still as well the warm vibrant note of deep affection for Ike, the note that would never be muted. And after the ceremony, after the prayers and the recitation by the old poet and the inaugural speech by the new President, Dwight and Mamie Eisenhower could steal away, for the first time in so many years no longer the cynosure (but still discreetly guarded by Secret Service agents), to be driven to the F Street Club where the official family of the Eisenhower administration—cabinet ministers, heads of other government agencies, and their wives—were guests of Mr. and Mrs. Lewis Strauss at a luncheon that was, if not festive, at least relaxed and pleasant.

Then Gettysburg and the farm and what remained of life.

PART SIX

WHAT REMAINED OF LIFE

DWIGHT EISENHOWER was then seventy years old, held by most of his fellow citizens in warmest affection, behind him a life as full of achievement as any man could dream of, but still no rest ahead. The demands on his time were incessant. All kinds of people wanted all kinds of things of him, most often his prestige conferred upon one scheme or another. Scholars and journalists waited upon him, and boy scouts, Republican politicians, publishers, TV network executives, college students, and other seekers after truth or power or wealth—the routine file of those for whom it is more blessed to receive than to give, and in such strength that he still required a sturdy hedge of loyal aides to protect him. Retirement? "Well," said Eisenhower, a year after he had left the White House, "my wife thinks it's nothing but a word in the dictionary. I think I've more demands made upon me than I've ever had in my life." The only appreciable advantage was that public notice was no longer taken of how many hours he spent playing golf or relaxing in other ways.

Yet he was still firmly in public life, and there were some tasks that only he could shoulder. One of these was to be the patriarch and sage of the Republican party, a burden at once honorary, inescapable, irksome, and gratifying. Another, his chiefest personal responsibility, was to make a record of his eight years as President, to compose for the future a seemly portrait of Eisenhower the statesman.

Commercial considerations played no part in his literary labors; he was under no compulsion to hustle a dollar. Apart from his substantial and well-invested capital, he had twenty-five thousand dollars a year from a presidential pension and another fifty thousand a year to meet the expenses of his private and public affairs. By act of the Congress he had been restored to the rank and quality of general of the army, a status that conferred on him the services of an officer and a few enlisted men, and that gave to him and Mamie free transportation and free medical and hospital care. No financial worries gnawed at him.

Office space was found when the president of Gettysburg College obligingly relinquished his commodious residence, set on one corner of the college campus. Down into the basement of this house went rows of file cabinets laden with the most private of Eisenhower's presidential papers. (The bulk of his papers would be removed to the Eisenhower Library in Kansas.) Some of the rooms on the ground floor became offices for the men who would help in the compilation of his record as President; Eisenhower's own office was one flight up, with rooms for other aides. Kevin McCann was still on hand, and Bob Schulz; for a time Ann Whitman stayed on as his personal secretary; from the White House staff came William Ewald to do the necessary research among the papers. The general's son John was entrusted with the task of organizing the records so that all would be ready as needed. His brother Milton, by now president of the Johns Hopkins University, was available for discussion and editorial suggestions. Doubleday was once again to be his publisher; the firm assigned a young editor, Sam Vaughan, who would for several years keep an eye on a project that would eventually beget four books.

As an author, Eisenhower remained exceptional. He would be paid in the ordinary way, by royalties—not again would he be privileged to have loopholes tunneled through the tax laws for his exclusive benefit, as with *Crusade in Europe*—yet he was no ordinary writer toiling in lonely concentration. His books were staff constructions: they were planned and shaped in committee, other hands drafted typescript, and Eisenhower's hand in the finished product was chiefly editorial, applied to striking out and interlineating as he searched for the satisfactory phrase.

Much of the work proceeded while he was otherwise and elsewhere occupied. Apart from his well-earned hours of leisure, he had engaged with CBS News to film for television a series of conversations—first at Gettysburg, later at Palm Springs in the California desert, along the beaches of Normandy to commemorate the twentieth anniversary of D-day, in Abilene and at West Point as he reminisced about his childhood and young manhood—for him a lucrative undertaking, but not one that enabled him to give undivided attention to writing his books. He was further distracted by the importunities of his constant visitors and by the way his successor was conducting the nation's affairs.

For power to have passed from the oldest to the youngest meant above all a change in the style of the presidency. The contrast was vivid; it tempted instant historians to suggest that the succession marked the end of an era. Nothing so portentous: the Cold War was unabated, but the new young President would speak, in his inaugural address, of how "the torch has been passed to a new generation of Americans," and at least on the surface the nation's affairs had indeed been taken in charge by a group of men remarkably unlike their predecessors. Kennedy and his circle of advisers were younger; they seemed also to be more receptive to ideas, less stodgy, less doggedly committed to the status quo. The atmosphere of substance and dignity that had permeated the White House under Eisenhower was dissipated; something twinkled; Kennedy introduced panache, and his wife Jacqueline chic. Instead of Eisenhower's stag dinners, paralyzed with propriety, there were under Kennedy formal dinners like the one honoring the American Nobel laureates, a distinguished company of literary figures, mathematicians, physicists, biologists, and peacemakers. Instead of entertainments by Fred Waring's Pennsylvanians, there were concerts by Pablo Casals.

Those changes, it is safe to say, left Eisenhower calm, but others were certain to disturb him. Kennedy chose to let lapse the regular meetings of the National Security Council and to convene its members only after crisis had flared; regrettable. His fiscal policies were likewise deplorable, the more so since Douglas Dillon, a man Eisenhower had once briefly considered as a Republican candidate for President, was Kennedy's secretary of the treasury. Presumably Dillon acquiesced in the Keynesian notions of deficit financing and an unbalanced budget. To Eisenhower such ideas were anathema.

Before long he was publicly denouncing "overzealous central agencies" and the "mania" to "dominate rather than serve local government," but what really roused him was Democratic spending. At first he kept his complaints private, but even then he was sure he would have to air them in public. "What else can I do? I put a stop to the New Deal–Fair Deal spending spree only to see the same mania come back just as strong under this present bunch. I have no choice but to try to stop it again. To do otherwise would be a dereliction of duty . . ." Duty. He had been heeding its call for as long as he could remember, no way to break the habit. He waited only until he was asked to speak at a Republican fund-raising dinner and then he decried the Kennedy administration as "obviously . . . floundering . . . in the surging financial, fiscal, and economic currents of our times." The Democrats were hostile to business. The Democrats cared nothing for the balanced budget.

But, having been there, Eisenhower would not criticize the new President for his calamitous ventures as Cold Warrior. The thumping that Kennedy's policy sustained at the Bay of Pigs passed without a word of censure from Eisenhower, with nothing save Eisenhower's nimble leaps to sidestep attempts to pin the responsibility for the CIA's schemes on him. He resolutely refused to make political capital of the alarming confrontation that developed when the Soviets sought to exploit Cuba as a base for their nuclear missiles. First and last, he preferred to level his Republican guns at domestic targets.

Fittingly, for a man scandalized by the pace of change as the world he had known slipped into the shadows, those domestic targets abounded. Kennedy's "strenuous efforts" to increase the power of the executive branch were, Eisenhower said at the first news conference he granted after leaving the White House, "a threat to our liberties." On the social scene matters were even more wicked. When he came to Abilene to dedicate the Eisenhower Library, he wagged his head over the decline in "our concept of beauty and decency and morality"; over the use by theater and film producers and publishers of books and magazines of "vulgarity, sensuality, indeed downright filth, to sell their wares"; over the sort of painting "that looks like a broken-down tin lizzie loaded with paint has been driven over it." The times they were a-changing. In the early 1960s a type of dance called the twist enjoyed a brief vogue; maybe it was all right, said Eisenhower, but it did reveal "some kind of change in our standards."

Apart from taking pokes at the Democrats and deploring the decay of moral principles, Eisenhower was from time to time called upon to beat back attacks on the probity of his stewardship. He could afford to ignore the revelation that the founder of the John Birch Society, an outfit on the outermost extreme of the Right, considered him a knowing tool of the communists; but on a more rational level of discourse the Senate had been pressing an investigation into the stockpiling in the 1950s of various commodities deemed vital for strategic reasons, and suspicions of sinful profits from these transactions had got abroad, with George Humphrey's name attached. Eisenhower held a press conference in Cleveland to rally the righteous to Humphrey's defense. He found any suggestion of Humphrey's dishonesty so incredible that he had recourse to a remarkable metaphor. "If Secretary Humphrey ever did a dishonest thing in his life," said Eisenhower, "I'm ready to mount the cross and you can put the nails and spear in me."

Taking one thing with another, the old warrior's round of days was reasonably serene, leaving him ample opportunity for satisfied reflection on his attainments. He was kept busy but not too busy. There was always something requiring his participation in the days ahead—the dedication of the John Foster Dulles Airport near Washington; a visit with Harry Truman at Independence, to patch up the spat provoked ten years before during the 1952 campaign; a speech to the National Association of Manufacturers, or for the opening of the George Marshall Library at the Virginia Military Institute; more solemn occasions, like the funeral of Sam

"Well, Now, The Way I Look At It,
I Don't Think I Ought To—Uh—Get Involved."

from *Straight Herblock* (Simon & Schuster, 1964)

Rayburn or that of Eleanor Roosevelt: or perhaps the acceptance of yet another redundant award—and his life was comfortable. Now he was the country squire on his Gettysburg farm. In the winters he and Mamie traveled to Palm Springs, where they had many friends, and always in the proper season they would arrive at Augusta National for two or three weeks spent within the circle of his most trusted friends.

The only discernible flaw in this Eden was duty, and most especially his duty to the Republican party when the next presidential election began to loom large ahead. As its chief and elder sage, naturally he was bound to head the GOP in its every endeavor to turn the rascally Democrats out and restore the nation to its proper governors. He lent himself to this task without demur. He gathered a hundred Republicans at a picnic on his farm for a discussion of their party's chances in 1964; he presided over another group of Republican leaders come to Hershey, Pennsylvania, for a conference on the same tempting subject. Who would carry the Republican standard in 1964? Evidently not Nixon: his run in 1960 had won him too many aggrieved critics. His chance would come only if the two leading candidates—Barry Goldwater and Nelson Rockefeller—might somehow contrive to battle to a stalemate.

Neither Goldwater nor Rockefeller was a man Eisenhower would have chosen to lead the party. (Nor was Nixon, for that matter.) His preferences, as they had been in 1960, as they had been for Vice President in 1956, were Robert B. Anderson, the conservative Texan who had served as Eisenhower's secretary of the treasury, Lucius Clay, Al Gruenther, or his brother Milton. The difficulty with Goldwater was that he was one of the right-wing primitives of the party, hostile to the eastern financiers who had so long controlled it, often hostile even to the Eisenhower administration (he once called it "a dime-store New Deal"). The difficulty with Rockefeller went back to 1960, when in Rockefeller's effort to wrest the nomination from Nixon he had seemed to suggest that military defense was dangerously skimped during the 1950s; to Eisenhower this was unforgivable contumacy. Further, Rockefeller had jeopardized his own political allure by divorcing his wife of thirty-one years and marrying a woman who was herself divorced. In New York the Republican leaders who had won Eisenhower the nomination in 1952—Clay, Brownell, and others—wanted at all costs to avert a struggle between Goldwater and Rockefeller that would tear the party asunder and hand the presidency again to Kennedy and the Democrats almost unchallenged. In their view, only Eisenhower could save the party from such a senseless conflict. He should name the new candidate whom he would support and he should assume active leadership in that candidate's behalf. Instead, Eisenhower released a list of ten eminent Republicans whose names, he suggested, might be added to those of Goldwater and Rockefeller for the party's debate and ultimate decision.

On Thursday, November 21, 1963, Eisenhower arrived in New York on ceremonial business. His old friends—Clay, Brownell, and the others—had arranged to meet with him on the following Saturday for the conversation they hoped would end with the selection of Eisenhower's chosen candidate.

On Friday, November 22, all political plans were scrambled by the assassination of President Kennedy. All at once Lyndon Johnson was President, and everything had changed in the maneuvering for political precedence in 1964. The new President wished to talk to the old one, and so Eisenhower took plane for Washington and seized the occasion to lecture Johnson on the need for reduced spending and a smaller deficit.

While Eisenhower would cheerfully encourage a sudden President who happened to be a Democrat, he was as determined as ever to supplant him with a Republican—but which Republican? Henry Cabot Lodge? In August Lodge had accepted the post of U.S. ambassador in Saigon; in November Eisenhower urged him to come home and run for President. Lodge did indeed return to Washington for a time, and he spoke at length with Eisenhower, who wanted him to become the "commonsense" candidate. Was Lodge then Eisenhower's choice? So it must have seemed to all good Republicans when the conversation between the two men was reported on the front page of the *New York Times*, but a few days later, on his way west to Palm Springs, Eisenhower had his private car shunted to a siding in the railroad yards at Harrisburg so that he and Mamie might have to dinner the personable young Republican governor of Pennsylvania, William Scranton, and his attractive wife Mary. The Scrantons and Eisenhowers were together for five hours; word of this, too, found its way into print, and of how the general had pressed the governor to make a run for the presidency. Did that mean that Scranton was, after all, Eisenhower's choice?

Lodge went back to Vietnam, Scranton kept his own counsel, and Eisenhower traveled to the California desert, where from the Eldorado Country Club he could watch Rockefeller and Goldwater scramble for the nomination. What Eisenhower desired was an open convention of the Republicans, come July, with three or four contestants for the party to choose from, each defining how his policies differed from those of the others. So the American system works, according to the primers that deal with civics, and so Eisenhower hoped it would work in 1964.

Meanwhile, in the real world, Goldwater's political mechanics were busily assembling delegates from the southern and western states, and although he fared badly in the early primary elections, the number of delegates committed to him steadily grew.

Late in May 1964, Eisenhower having returned to Gettysburg, he was persuaded by his friends on the *New York Herald Tribune* to describe his notion of the best kind of Republican candidate. The formula he devised, which was published on the eve of the primary in California, appeared tailor-made to fit Rockefeller. The strategy seemed plain to the watchful political haruspices: Rockefeller was to wallop Goldwater in the primaries, Goldwater's pledged delegates would wallop Rockefeller at the convention, and the party elders would then be free to select the candidate who could lead a united party against the Democrats. But to everyone's astonishment, Goldwater by the narrowest of margins won the voting in California and so disposed of Rockefeller. Since Goldwater's nomination was widely regarded as promising a devastating Republican defeat, the question was now posed: How to stop him?

Eisenhower telephoned Scranton. The governor of Pennsylvania motored to Gettysburg on Saturday, June 6, and conferred at length with the party's acknowledged chieftain. Eisenhower was dismayed by the prospect of Goldwater's nomination. He and Scranton spent some time assessing the effect of it on local, state, and national elections; the prognosis was gloomy. Clearly, if Goldwater was to be stopped, the time had come for firm and decisive action. When Scranton left he took with him the impression that Eisenhower wanted him to declare his candidacy and would publicly support his effort. Scranton was due in Cleveland the next day for the annual conference of governors; he was scheduled to appear on a television program, *Face the Nation*. "I'll be watching," Eisenhower assured him.

That evening the word was carried across the country that Eisenhower had at last chosen his candidate. On Sunday morning the news was on every newspaper's front page. That news disturbed George Humphrey, of whose counsel Eisenhower had a high opinion. Humphrey thought well of Goldwater. By telephone to Gettysburg he applied pressure to dissuade the general from support of any other candidate. When Scranton arrived at his hotel in Cleveland on Sunday morning, he was given a message to telephone Eisenhower. He was concerned, the general said, lest perhaps some misunderstanding had been born of their talk the day before. All the newspapers were full of a story that he was supporting Scranton for the presidency, but he wanted no part of a "cabal"—Eisenhower's word, perhaps suggested by Humphrey—against Goldwater. If Scranton declared his candidacy, he was on his own.

Thus the latest in the series of Eisenhower's vacillations. After the convention he would say: "I was never trained in politics; I came in laterally, at the top. In the service, when a man gives you his word, his word is binding. In politics, you never know." On this Sunday, June 7, it was Scranton who was bewildered.

On Monday Eisenhower in his turn traveled to Cleveland, to address the governors' conference. There he began to realize the lamentable effect of his contradictory conversations with Scranton, an impression that would soon be confirmed by his brother Milton.

Meanwhile, in Washington, the Senate had begun to vote on another, stronger civil rights bill, and Goldwater, as senator from Arizona, was voting for amendments designed to cripple the bill. (A few days later he would be one of the few Republicans to vote against the bill itself.) That the presumptive nominee of the Republican party for the presidency should be a champion of a racist, segregationist policy was bitter for Eisenhower. Something must be done, and straightway. He telephoned Governor Scranton in Harrisburg to ask if he had heard the news of Goldwater's vote. Indeed Scranton had heard. "Frankly," he said, "I'm sick about it." "Bill," said Eisenhower, "I feel even worse than that." He was furious with Goldwater. He hoped Scranton would run and run hard for the presidency. He was sending two aides—Malcolm Moos and Robert Merriam—to Harrisburg, to impress on Scranton how serious was his concern. Later, Eisenhower talked with reporters. He would not be a party to any stop-Goldwater campaign, he said, but he felt strongly that the GOP wanted a candidate who unmistakably favored civil rights for Negroes; and further, he had serious reservations about Goldwater's ability to conduct a proper foreign policy. The next day, Friday, June 12, he issued a formal statement: "A free, fair, and active competition among party personalities . . . is good for the health and vigor of the party . . . I welcome the entry of Governor Scranton, whom I have long admired, into the contest."

The effect of these belated equivocations on Goldwater's candidacy was nil. Eisenhower had only acquired a reputation for bumbling, meddlesome ineffectuality.

More followed at the convention in San Francisco. Scranton's supporters would draft a resolution—on civil rights, or on the question of control over nuclear weapons—and Eisenhower would first seem to approve it, only later to repudiate it. The general was neutral. He desired to conserve his influence. He had accepted a commission to be a commentator on the proceedings for the American Broadcasting Company's television network, a chore that principally required his being available for an occasional interview before ABC cameras. On Thursday, July 16, after the delegates had finished their biggest job, he pledged to "do my best to support" Goldwater, manfully gulping the distasteful medicine.

That night Goldwater, in his acceptance speech, trumpeted his celebrated proposition—*"Extremism in the defense of liberty is no vice! . . . Moderation in the pursuit of justice is no virtue!"*—which at bottom flouted Eisenhower's cherished convictions and precepts. Still the general's comment was muted. Goldwater's dictum, he observed, "would seem to say that the end always justifies the means." He added, "The whole American system refutes that idea."

The Goldwater nomination, far more conclusively than the Kennedy election, slammed the lid on the Eisenhower era. In August attempts were made to cobble the divisions within the party. Eisenhower said he was now "satisfied" with Goldwater as a candidate, but his enthusiasm was manifestly under wraps. He could never gladly associate himself with a man whose slogan was "A choice, not an echo." His fears were confirmed by the humiliating election. The worst trouncing ever suffered by a presidential candidate at the polls gave Eisenhower one further duty—to help mop up the shambles.

In December, General Eisenhower assisted at the surgery required to keep the Republican party from shuddering into final coma. Together with Nixon he got Goldwater to agree on a new chairman for the Republican National Committee, a professional capable of stanching the party's wounds. Then, so far as it is ever possible for a former President to withdraw from politics, Eisenhower withdrew. His big hands ached more often with arthritis; he was more often deprived of his great pleasure, to try again to negotiate the golf course at Atlanta in less than eighty strokes. He was still mettlesome and possessed of unusual physical vigor, but he was seventy-four years old. Surely duty should make no further demands on him.

His memoirs of the White House years were now being published, and like most autobiographical works they suffered from a measure of complacency. All autobiographies are based on the assumption that the author is a remarkable fellow with a remarkable story to tell, or else why tell it? Eisenhower was assuredly a remarkable fellow with a remarkable story to tell, but his chosen method of telling it involved the collaboration of other, less remarkable fellows who were concerned that Eisenhower should tell only those things that would bathe him in an indulgent light and preserve him for posterity as a President of superlative gifts and immaculate attainment. For this reason and others, Eisenhower's memoirs failed to find favor with their critics. The first volume, *Mandate for Change*, disappointed because it offered no surprises. It was too predictable. "The man, like his book, is a bore," one reviewer snapped, and another complained that all the storms and misfortunes of Eisenhower's first term in the White

House had "a way of coming out rosy." In exceptionally short order the hero was being more coldly scrutinized, an uncommon experience. His second volume, *Waging Peace,* is an appreciably better book than the first, yet its critics were even more scathing. "The deficiencies of the memoir," Oscar Handlin wrote, "reflect Ike's unwillingness to contemplate the possibility that he might have been wrong at any point." Henry Kissinger, a man who had yet to achieve more than parochial renown, also found fault: "[Eisenhower sees] the global turmoil entirely in terms of the East-West conflict . . . opaque . . ." And in the most widely read of reviews the judgment was "plodding . . . satisfied, bland . . . evasive and generally dull."

But if among the literati there was a disposition to sneer at Eisenhower's accounting of his past labors, he was still in demand as a fount of wisdom and experience. Journalists constantly sought his opinion of the successive crises racking the republic. When in April 1965 President Johnson dispatched twenty-three thousand marines and airborne troops on the crude, hasty, and ill-considered intervention in the Dominican Republic—an intervention that throttled a popular democratic revolt against a repressive and brutal junta, an intervention deceitfully justified by Johnson on the grounds that the rebellion had been "taken over and really seized . . . [by] a band of Communist conspirators"—he was harshly criticized by any number of influential journals in the U.S. and abroad, especially in Latin America, and he was bitterly assailed by Senator Fulbright, chairman of the Senate Foreign Relations Committee. Not so by Eisenhower. The general called the intervention "a sensible thing." "I have nothing to criticize," he said, adding, "Communists only respect force."

On the domestic scene, the Negroes had at last lost their patience. They had practiced civil disobedience in the spring of 1963 in hostile Birmingham, and had at once been savaged by snarling police dogs and knocked about by firehoses spurting water with the force of jackhammers. Nonetheless their demonstrations leapfrogged across the South, then west to Sacramento and north to Detroit, New York, Philadelphia, and Chicago—more than seven hundred and fifty demonstrations tallied by the Department of Justice in the ten weeks following the first affray in Birmingham—unmistakable evidence that the Negroes were bent on asserting their rights as citizens of the United States. The Civil Rights Act of 1964 helped, but not much. The temper of those demonstrations could be traced to the frustrations the Negroes had experienced for generations, most recently at the hands of the Eisenhower administration. At first, so long as they were directed by Martin Luther King, the doctrine of nonviolence prevailed and the tactic was civil disobedience to rouse the conscience of the community against injustice. By 1965, the conscience of the community being still somnolent, the blacks had taken to the streets of the cities and put parts of Los Angeles and Chicago to the torch. At a press conference in mid-August, General Eisenhower searched, as before, for the safe Center between extremes. "I believe the United States," he said, "has been becoming atmosphered, you might say, in a policy of lawlessness. If we like a law, we obey it. If we don't, we are told, 'You can disobey it.'" But it would take more than Eisenhower's disapproval to scuttle the practice of civil disobedience.

At that press conference or another assembled at about the same time, General Eisenhower gave his blessing to President Johnson's most recent escalation of the war in Vietnam.* "I support the President on Vietnam," said Eisenhower, presumably referring to Johnson's announced policy of raising U.S. fighting strength in South Vietnam from seventy-five thousand to one hundred and twenty-five thousand. Eisenhower was no doubt familiar with all Johnson's decisions, and in detail, for his former staff secretary, Andrew Goodpaster, was then assistant to the chairman of the Joint Chiefs of Staff, and the two men were frequently in touch.

In early October, President and ex-President spent an hour together. They had the buildup of troops in Vietnam to discuss and, more pressing, the fact that in a couple of days Johnson would be driven to Bethesda Naval Hospital for gall bladder surgery. Johnson wanted hints from an old hand as to how to handle the press and public relations of a term in hospital while President. (The bulletins after Johnson's surgery and during his painful convalescence were uniformly cheerful.) What the two men said about Vietnam has not been disclosed, if it ever will be, but what happened after their conversation is plain enough: the buildup of U.S. troops proceeded, the number of airplane flights for hostile purposes steadily mounted, and the list of targets for bombers (excluding the Hanoi-Haiphong area and the approaches to the Chinese border) lengthened. The only change came in the stated purpose of Rolling Thunder, from an attempt "to break the will of Vietnam" to an attempt to block or reduce the passage of men and supplies from north to south.

With great satisfaction, Eisenhower in November withdrew to Augusta, Georgia, for another of his sojourns at Augusta National. His wife was

* On February 1, 1964, Johnson authorized Operation Plan 34–A, a program of clandestine warfare against North Vietnam, without congressional approval. On February 13, 1965, he authorized Rolling Thunder, the sustained bombing of North Vietnam. (Planning of this operation was actively under way during the presidential campaign of 1964, while Johnson was deriding Goldwater for advocating full-scale air attacks on North Vietnam.) On April 1, 1965, Johnson decided to use American ground troops for offensive action in South Vietnam; he kept this decision secret. Four months later he authorized the deployment of forty-four battalions, comprising nearly two hundred thousand troops; the full force of this decision was likewise concealed from the public.

with him. They took up residence in Mamie's Cottage, the commodious white green-shuttered country house near the tenth tee on the golf course, and settled down for what they expected would be an unmarred holiday.

On November 9, 1965, General Eisenhower suffered his second heart attack, a myocardial infarction like the first. On November 11, when he was in hospital, he sustained his third attack. He was flown to Walter Reed for protracted treatment and convalescence.

When a man of seventy-five has survived three heart attacks, it might be assumed that he would be tempted to take it easy. But Eisenhower had always led an active life and he was not willing to change. He watched his diet, regretfully forswearing all kinds of cheeses, to which he was partial, but keeping outdoor exercise and especially golf on his agenda. By the end of January 1966 he was up and about and giving tongue to his support of Johnson's war policies and in particular to the renewal of air raids on North Vietnam. (The raids had been suspended for thirty-seven days.) The hiatus in the bombing had never been endorsed by the Joint Chiefs, and Eisenhower declared on January 31 that to have done other than resume the bombing would have "given sanctuary" to aggressors. Thereupon he quit his hospital.

His days were as full as ever. He was finishing work on another memoir, the anecdotal *At Ease*, which would be accorded a far warmer reception than its predecessors—"serves admirably to flesh out and give life to the image of one of the most durable popular heroes of our time," wrote the reviewer in the *New York Times*—and anon he was occupied with the plans and prospectus for a small college of liberal arts which would bear his name. This institution was close to his heart. He and the film comedian Bob Hope posed for photographs, each man in the act of aiming a shovel into the earth at Seneca Falls, N.Y., for the ceremony known as breaking ground. In May it was back to hospital again, for his arthritis was once again hampering his golf and he had been told of new therapeutic procedures that might mitigate the pain in his gnarled joints.

The private Eisenhowers had a celebration that summer—their golden anniversary—which inevitably became public. On July 1 they were able to enjoy the occasion quietly with family and a few friends; the public aspects of it included a "national tribute" with Bob Hope and Robert B. Anderson, the oil man, as cochairmen of a campaign to collect tax-deductible donations looking toward the foundation of Eisenhower College. "For a beloved leader," the cochairmen declared, "there can be no finer tribute, no more cherished gift."

In that same week the Seventh Air Force began bomb strikes against North Vietnam's oil storage facilities and her supplies of petroleum, oil, and lubricants (P.O.L. in the military shorthand). "Official Washington," an analyst in the Pentagon reported, "reacted with mild jubilation to the reported success of the P.O.L. strikes and took satisfaction in the relatively mild reaction of the international community to the escalation."

By that time the war in Vietnam had poisoned the life of the republic. Public outcry against the administration's conduct of the war was reinforced by public disgust and disillusionment with the purposes of the war. Hundreds of thousands of young men had been taken to fight in a land about which they knew next to nothing, against a people they knew less, for reasons that were at best obscure. Other young men were reaching the difficult decision that they must refuse to heed the call to join the army. Some burned their draft cards, others quit the country, still others went to jail rather than serve in a hateful war. Their elders, when they were not protesting the war and demanding its summary settlement, were insisting on a reallocation of national priorities and citing with dismay the lengthy list of grave problems—the blighted cities, the foul air, the inequitable sharing of the nation's wealth, the decay of civil liberties, the injustices visited on the blacks, the decline of education, the plague of automobiles and the spread of concrete to carry them, the rotten quality of life and its conditions—that hourly grew worse due to the insatiable demands of the military and the industries required to satisfy them; in short, due to the demands of what that wise old soldier Eisenhower had warned against, to wit, the "military-industrial complex." Indeed, Eisenhower's words appeared again and again on the placards borne by the immense throngs that rallied to protest the war and demand an end of it. Other placards in those demonstrations bore the words he had extemporized over British television: "I think people want peace so much that one of these days governments had better get out of the way and let them have it."

And what of Eisenhower in this time? Did he heed the outcry? Did he recall what he had said yesterday, and the day before? Pentagon analysts identified three schools of thought in official Washington in the fall of 1966: the "disillusioned doves," led by Secretary of Defense Robert McNamara, who sought to limit and reduce the war; the military faction, who argued for the deployment of more troops and a wider, brisker war; and President Johnson and his senior advisers in White House and State Department, who attempted to blaze a trail between the other two. Like a good soldier, General Eisenhower put his considerable influence at the disposal of the Joint Chiefs and the commander in Vietnam, General William Westmoreland. In December 1966, upon emerging from his third visit to Walter Reed Medical Center within the year (he had been hospitalized this time for gall bladder surgery), Eisenhower announced that he knew U.S. bombing operations in North Vietnam were "aimed exclusively at military targets." Since on that same day Harrison Salisbury had published his eyewitness accounts of the destruction of peaceful villages (complete with their inhabitants) up to fifty miles away from the military targets around Hanoi, General Eisenhower was constrained to observe that "unfortunately, there are some civilians around these targets," and to add, "Is there any place in the world where there are not civilians?"

In the spring of 1967 the debate among Johnson's senior advisers sharpened, with the Joint Chiefs calling for two hundred thousand more troops in Vietnam (to a total of more than six hundred and seventy thousand) and an extension of the ground war into Laos, Cambodia, and perhaps North Vietnam. To the contrary, McNamara urged that the air war be braked and Westmoreland given no more than thirty thousand additional troops. McNamara worried over the way the war had polarized the country, "with seeds of the worst split in our people in more than a century." On this score, the Joint Chiefs saw no cause for concern. In July a compromise was reached: Westmoreland's troops would be boosted by fifty-five thousand, to a total of five hundred and twenty-five thousand, and Johnson authorized the bombing of more fixed targets, all within the previously forbidden zones close around Hanoi and Haiphong. The military still suffering frustration, General Eisenhower on July 15 assailed what he called a "war of gradualism," and pressed the Congress to declare war against North Vietnam. That war, he said, "should be given first priority. Other goals, however attractive, should take second place." By October he was ready to declare he would "take any action to win." Asked specifically if he would draw the line at the use of nuclear weapons, he replied: "I would not automatically preclude anything. When you appeal to force to carry out the policies of America abroad there is no court above you."*

And in November, as the surge of protest against the war mounted ever higher, General Eisenhower made one more effort to swing opinion around in favor of it. To Gettysburg he invited his ancient comrade General Bradley; the two would sit before the television cameras on Friday, November 24, and on the following Tuesday, the tape having been

* Thomas E. Dewey, who was present when Eisenhower spoke so freely about the possibility of holocaust, was quick to clarify the statement. Eisenhower simply meant, said Dewey, "that you don't inform the enemy on what you intend to do." Two weeks later, at his birthday celebration in Gettysburg, Eisenhower laughed to scorn the idea of using nuclear weapons in Vietnam. "This is silly," he said. Nonetheless, he kept alive the possibility of using them against the Chinese communists, advice unpleasantly reminiscent of the Air Force general who had been eager to "nuke the Chinks."

carefully edited, it would be broadcast by CBS as a special "news" program. Bradley was amenable. He had accepted a post as cochairman of a short-lived outfit called the Citizens Committee for Peace with Freedom in Vietnam (Eisenhower and Truman were both members), the purpose of which seemed to be to oppose any settlement of the war short of total military triumph. For the requirements of this program Eisenhower spoke more belligerently than ever before. After Bradley had defined the object of his committee as to help the American people understand the war—"and when they understand it, they will be for it, we think"—Eisenhower took over to argue the chances for military victory. "This respecting of boundary lines on the map," he said. "I think you can overdo it." He suggested a foray into North Vietnam "either from the sea or from the hills. . . . I would be for what we call 'hot pursuit' "—in the air or on the ground, into Cambodia or Laos—"it wouldn't bother me." He was asked: into China? "Yes," he replied. And that, with a cursory dismissal of the " 'kooks' and 'hippies' and all the rest that are talking about surrendering," was that.

That night General and Mrs. Eisenhower left in their private railroad car, bound for their cottage near the golf course at Palm Desert, California. His freedom to play golf would be limited—his arthritis and other ailments had hindered such joys for nearly two years—and his affairs pursued him. An office had been cleared for him near Indio, on the ranch owned by Floyd Odlum and Jacqueline Cochran; here he talked with the reporters who still followed him about, met with other visitors, and contended with the inevitable flood of correspondence.

He was now confronted with another presidential campaign, one in which the capital issue was certain to be Vietnam, and the response of the voters to it decisive. His own attitude toward it was fixed and unyielding. Sixteen years before, when he was a candidate for the presidency, Americans were fighting and dying in another Asian war, and he had then declared: "The first task of a new administration will be to review and re-examine every course of action open to us with one goal in view: to bring the Korean war to an early and honorable end. . . . For this task a wholly new administration is necessary. . . . The old administration cannot be expected to repair what it failed to prevent."

He had added that in his search for an early peace, he would go to Korea. Now, when the nation was racked by bitter debate over the war in Vietnam, he said: "I don't regard myself as a missionary, and I don't want to convert anybody. But if any Republican or Democrat suggests that we pull out of Vietnam and turn our backs on the more than thirteen thousand Americans who died in the cause of freedom there, they will have me to contend with. That's one of the few things that would start me off on a series of stump speeches across the nation."

Whether intentionally or not, Eisenhower seemed to have foreclosed the chance for a Republican candidate to do what he himself had done sixteen years before: bring an odious war to a swift and honorable end.

In the early spring of 1968 General Eisenhower was, saving only President Johnson, quite the most zealous in exhorting the nation to martial unity. The spectacle of discord depressed and distressed him. "The current raucous confrontation," he wrote, in an angry sermon published by the *Reader's Digest*, "goes far beyond honorable dissent. . . . it is rebellion, and it verges on treason. . . . *I will not personally support any peace-at-any-price candidate who advocates capitulation and the abandonment of South Vietnam.*" He would surely have persevered in these strictures except that after playing a round of golf in desert heat that rose into the nineties, he suffered a fourth myocardial infarction. That was on Monday, April 29. He and Mamie had planned to leave Palm Springs a week later.

For a couple of weeks General Eisenhower lay in hospital at March Air Force Base, much of the time under intensive care in the cardiac unit. Specialists were flown from Washington to supervise the medical examinations and treatment. At length he was deemed fit enough to be flown east to Walter Reed Hospital in Bethesda. He was carried to a suite of rooms on the third floor, his wife took up residence in rooms close at hand, and he entered upon what was presumed to be a period of convalescence and recuperation.

News of Eisenhower's brittle condition set in train various hasty improvisations and pushed other projects to urgent completion. The general's career as a man of letters, for example, was visibly reaching the end of the line. His last productions required immediate attention. His final book was hurriedly assembled for the presses. This was called *In Review: Pictures I've Kept*, and consisted of an album of photographs set in a text drawn from the books he had earlier published. Kevin McCann spit on his hands and drafted a series of brief articles which, after they had been somewhat revised by Eisenhower, would appear in the *Reader's Digest* under Eisenhower's byline. In the houses of at least three other publishers the finishing touches were put to what in the trade are called tombstone biographies. Other affecting signs of the general's conjectured departure could be detected. The Scott Paper Company, for one instance, offered for sale rolls of "softly scented" toilet paper in polymerized wrappers; in exchange for two such wrappers and the sum of one dollar and fifty cents, the firm of Brown & Bigelow engaged to send a portfolio of reproductions of four of Eisenhower's paintings, the general's royalties from the transaction having been assigned to Eisenhower College. In Washington the Bureau of Printing and Engraving was already equipped with the plates needed to produce commemorative postage stamps. On Capitol Hill sundry congressmen canvassed plans for suitable memorials: perhaps to rename the interstate highway system in his honor? And every day brought to Walter Reed dozens, scores, sometimes hundreds of letters mailed from every state of the union, each of them a missive of good cheer for the general and most of them attesting that daily prayers were being offered for his swift recovery. Very evidently Dwight Eisenhower was still one of the most beloved mortals on earth.

For the central figure bedded down amid all this concern and tension, a man trained over fifty years or more to face facts, the signs and portents were plain enough. His constitution was still rugged, even after incessant and frequently punishing performance for nearly seventy-eight years, and he might be laced up tight and so kept mobile yet a while, but he was too sensible a patient to count on it.

At all events, there was more behind him than before him and ample opportunity, as his days in hospital wheeled slowly by, to look back and reflect. As he knew, a good deal of reflection had already been done on his years in the White House, some of it by college professors, much of it uninformed, and very little of it flattering. Doubtless the college professors were Democrats and full of depravity, but Kevin McCann was already composing a draft of an article that might scold some sense into them. Eisenhower knew cursed well his record of achievement had more heft and substance than its critics were acknowledging. He dared hope that history would gentle him.

Surely the singular fact about Dwight Eisenhower is that he should in his fifty-second year, after a time of frustration and the performance of unsung tasks of small consequence, have found himself so placed that for twenty years the story of his career would approximate the history of the world. An unheralded soldier, he would command the mighty armies that invaded North Africa and then Europe, closed the ring around Nazi Germany, and so helped vanquish the forces of fascism. With no experience of statecraft, he would lead the most powerful nation on earth and, while waging a perilous Cold War, nevertheless for eight years keep his countrymen secure and at peace. Here are two enduring accomplishments, either of which is sure to keep his name lustrous for as long as history may be recorded. They are the achievements that bulk biggest to anyone looking back over Eisenhower's career. Eisenhower himself considered them his greatest achievements; he was disposed to believe that of the two his wartime contribution to the triumph over Nazi Germany was perhaps of more historic consequence even than his keeping the peace for eight years as President.

It is fit that Eisenhower should have ranked his martial accomplishment over the pacific one he achieved as a statesman. The estimate acknowledged that he had devoted his mature years to his soldierly profession, years of rehearsal that were crowned with the command so coveted by officers senior to him and more widely experienced in military affairs. To have been named supreme commander of the Allied Expeditionary Force was the supreme climax of a professional career; to have led that force to victory was his highest aspiration come true. Any subsequent exploit would necessarily seem somehow anticlimactic.

Manifestly, Eisenhower's was a splendid share in the triumph over fascism. If he was not the only officer who could have led the Allied force in the West, he was assuredly the best one available, and the armies and armadas he commanded had accomplished their mission with dispatch and with a flourish. If it cannot be persuasively argued that the western Allies were predominant in vanquishing the Nazi legions, they were nonetheless crucial to that end. In the event, Eisenhower was the winning symbol of Allied might, and victory conferred upon him an imperishable renown. (Soldiers lose battles or cities; generals win them.) His victory ensured that history would wink at his occasional lapses. The friction with his more temperamental officers would be forgotten, and the indecision that robbed his armies of their steady supply of matériel, and the political wrangles that now and then distracted him from his principal task—victory would drop a veil over those details.

The character of the victory was exceptional. To have knitted contrary military customs and traditions into a firm international alliance, to have prized loose the grip on Europe of the Nazi storm trooper, to have ended the terror that desolated so much of the world, to have put a stop to the crimes and seized many of the criminals, to have conquered the scourge of fascism—here, surely, was reason for what Churchill called "the greatest outburst of joy in the history of mankind." And Eisenhower, as the symbol of that joy, was become a world figure. Now, as he lay still in hospital, he could when he chose summon from his memory the message Marshall had sent him the day after V-E Day:

> . . . the greatest victory in the history of warfare. . . . outstanding success . . . You have met and successfully disposed of every conceivable difficulty . . . you have been selfless in your actions, always sound and tolerant in your judgments and altogether admirable in the courage and wisdom of your military decisions.
>
> You have made history, great history for the good of mankind . . .

His fellow citizens were warmly agreed. Bursting with pride and gratitude, they had delighted to honor him in any way he chose.

Eisenhower's opportunity to achieve the second of his great feats, then, followed directly from the accomplishment of his first. If the Nazis had won the War of 1939–1945, if the mighty force commanded by Eisenhower had been defeated, the U.S. presidency would have become a bauble of no very great consequence and his countrymen would never have elected him their chief magistrate.

And then he had been elected President.

"The United States never lost a soldier or a foot of ground in my administration," Eisenhower said later. "We kept the peace. People asked how it happened—by God, it didn't just happen, I'll tell you that."

The observation epitomizes Eisenhower's proud and prudent record in the conduct of foreign affairs, and if it seems a negative achievement one need only reflect on the foreign policy of the three Presidents who followed him in office and consider the cost in treasure and blood authorized by them. Perhaps the salient aspect of Eisenhower's success in his pacific regime is that it was brought about—and likely could only have been brought about—by a professional soldier, an experienced military commander. It has been earlier remarked that one of the pervasive doubts about Eisenhower as he assumed the presidency in 1953 was precisely whether it was wise to entrust to a soldier the governance of such a mighty and potentially bellicose power, yet in retrospect it is clear that only a man trained to command and accustomed to obedience could have safely conducted the affairs of the nation during the perils of the Cold War during the 1950s.

Of that, more anon. For the moment it will suffice to take note of the paradoxical verdict on Eisenhower as he left the White House in 1961: he was at once the most popular and the most criticized American of the day. The judgment reflected on the one hand the general satisfaction with Eisenhower's domestic policies, and on the other the growing disenchantment over his failure to reach an accommodation with the Soviet Union in the Cold War.

In his own opinion, Eisenhower's foremost domestic achievement was something intangible, "an atmosphere of greater serenity and mutual confidence," as he put it; the reaffirmation of the dignity of his office; the establishment of a national unity. It is certainly true that after twenty years of Democratic government the country was divided and cantankerous, and neither Truman nor the war in Korea was a source of unity; but it is hard to find evidence that the blessings listed above were specifically singled out and purposefully pursued as goals. Even Eisenhower spoke of them in gingerly fashion. "If the conclusion that [they were] brought about as the efforts of this administration is correct," he said, "then I think that's a very great accomplishment." If, as is more likely, they simply happened along the way, as fruits of his sunny personality, the accomplishment is still a notable one.

A survey of the domestic scene after his eight years in office does not disclose many impressive successes, and more than a few of those are negative. Thus, Eisenhower did *not* raze the constructions of the New Deal and Fair Deal but even reinforced some of them; he did *not* preside over the country during a terrible economic depression; he did *not* (as some had feared he might) follow McCarthy's example by doing serious mischief to the civil liberties of the republic. The forty-eight states became fifty while he was President. A few overdue adjustments within the executive branch of government were effected. The St. Lawrence Seaway, a project long bruited, was at last put into operation. His crowning domestic achievement was the interstate highway system, what has been called "the most mouth-watering pork-barrel device ever conceived," forty-one thousand miles of highways as originally authorized, and since expanded. Eisenhower was quite proud of this project. Because of it there would be, as he wrote, "avenues of escape for persons living in big cities threatened by aerial attack." "More than any single action by the government since the end of the war," he mused, "this one would change the face of America with straightaways, cloverleaf turns, bridges, and elongated parkways. Its impact on the American economy," he concluded, "was beyond calculation." On that score, at least, he was bang right.

Of greater consequence during Eisenhower's presidency were the two issues that could be termed the moral imperatives: McCarthyism and racial injustice. In neither case did Eisenhower exert his awesome political resources to inspire, to lead. In neither case did he take the initiative. Less than two years after he had taken office, to be sure, McCarthy was a spent force; the question remains whether Eisenhower, by forthrightly opposing him, might not in those years have shielded the republic from much injury, both at home and abroad. His refusal to exercise his authority against racial injustice likewise raises a question. His inertia was plain, and wounding alike to the Negroes and to the self-respect of the whole country; but argument can be made that he best maintained his authority by not stepping too far ahead of the multitude of his followers. In short, as a politician Eisenhower appreciated the risk of staking his high repute on such a contentious cause.

The Supreme Court which did so much to loose and channel the flood of Negro aspirations was essentially an Eisenhower court. It would be angrily anathematized as a Warren court by diehard racists, and Eisenhower often remarked that he considered his appointment of Warren to the court "the biggest damfool mistake I ever made," just as many scholars of American jurisprudence believe the appointment one of the best in the court's history. The fact remains that during his eight years Eisenhower appointed a chief justice and four associate justices, and all—excepting one whose tenure was quite brief—subsequently served the court and the nation with distinction. If the President's appointments in the executive branch had been as distinguished by excellence as his appointments to the bench, his administration might itself have excelled more often in the performance of its domestic duties.

In 1968, though, these considerations weighed not at all on most of his fellow citizens in their judgment of Eisenhower. To them he was a good man, a decent man, wholly admirable, to be trusted. They recalled his governance as agreeable: he had kept America strong and prosperous; he had not tinkered too much with her innards; he had not experimented, as his predecessors had done; he had not changed and unsettled; he had stood as a symbol of America's generous and helpful spirit, of her resolute courage, of her God-fearing rectitude; he had labored to keep the peace. Already a deceptive nostalgia was welling up for the 1950s. There had been no rioting in the streets while Eisenhower was President, no divisive war in Vietnam, no throngs of barefoot youngsters who let their hair grow to their shoulders and chanted, "We shall overcome," no massive demonstrations for peace gathered before the main entrance to the Pentagon itself, no frightening violence and lawlessness. There had been no thought of assassination in the 1950s, yet already in the early spring of 1968 Martin Luther King had been slain, his murder touching off a wave of angry rioting in more than a hundred cities, with troops summoned to quell the disorders, and thousands of persons arrested, and thirty-nine dead. Little wonder that Eisenhower's presidency was remembered with affection, that the prayers of the faithful were with him now that he was confined to hospital, convalescent.

Yet, as noted earlier, Eisenhower had also been widely criticized at the time he was leaving office, and in the years that followed the criticism had mounted.

In the view of his critics, Eisenhower had badly misgauged the character of the Cold War. He had swallowed whole the domino theory, the premise that international communism was a monolith bent on world conquest, and the Manichaean concept of a conflict between good and evil. He had confused nationalist struggles for independence with conspiracies by the Kremlin to subvert the "free world."

In some part these miscalculations were owing to the circumstances of

Eisenhower's election in 1952. He had believed he was obliged to be more anticommunist than Truman. He had concurred in the mistrust of the twenty years of Democratic stewardship, the more so lest his own part in those years be held against him. He had appointed as his chief assistants— Dulles, Humphrey, Wilson—men of the Republican right, and when their consensus had made even more inflexible the sterile policy of Cold War he intervened only to block the terminal aspects of that policy. He had thus found himself imprisoned within a strategy that often cut the U.S. off from its traditional allies. The slambang mischief of Senator Joe Mc-Carthy had invigorated that strategy as it had demoralized the foreign service, and so made more difficult the task of perceiving the nature of the adversary. The persistent notion of a Sino-Soviet bloc in the face of the mountains of evidence belying it was still another error conceived during the campaign of 1952, and one that was thereafter lovingly cultivated by the "China Lobby" and such reliable right-wing Republicans as Knowland.

Some of Eisenhower's critics have argued that he preferred to follow the consensus of his advisers rather than seize the initiative in innovative fashion, because consensus was his "operating style," based on his years of experience as a staff officer and as a commander served by a staff. This fails to take into account Eisenhower's own carefully formulated opinions, elaborated over the years and tempered in wide-ranging discussions with his most intimate friends especially after he was out of uniform. In no way can the Cold Warrior be divorced from his Cold War policies of the 1950s. They were his quite as much as they were those of his advisers.

"The United States never lost a soldier or a foot of ground in my administration. We kept the peace. People ask how it happened—by God, it didn't just happen, I'll tell you that."

Eisenhower has the credit for ending the war in Korea, and it may be that he deserves it, although details of that unsatisfactory settlement are still obscure. Perhaps the threat of the use of nuclear weapons sufficed to convince the North Koreans and Chinese to conclude a truce; perhaps the decision to bomb the dikes and dams of North Korean valleys, with the consequent danger of widespread starvation, was the cruel argument that convinced: the full story cannot be told until an account of events as seen from the other side can be assessed. Eisenhower has taken the credit for blocking attempts by international communism to snatch Guatemala and Iran; but eloquent testimony from those lands persuades that, rather, the menace of communism was only a device manipulated for the purpose of overthrowing elected governments that were seeking to improve the lot of peoples long exploited by their oppressors. The military adventure in Lebanon was plainly undertaken to protect valuable investments in

Middle Eastern petroleum and only peripherally, if at all, to discourage an alleged takeover by communists.

The two clamorous crises provoked by the dispute over the Chinese off-shore islands occupied by Chiang Kai-shek's troops offer an excellent instance of how Eisenhower kept the peace. On each occasion he was under intense pressure to go to war, pressure exerted by an impressive assortment of advisers and clients—Foster Dulles and various State Department officials, most of the Joint Chiefs, Chiang himself, the "China Lobby," influential congressmen—but he would go no further than to supply Chiang with a great deal of military equipment and give his approval to the CIA's persistent efforts to foment trouble along China's borders. He was deterred from direct intervention, of course, by the outspoken opposition of his Atlantic allies, but that opposition merely afforded him an argument to reinforce his own conviction.

Similarly in the case of Indochina, Eisenhower was able to use the refusal of Britain to join in any intervention as a welcome confirmation of his own decision—taken despite the advice of Foster Dulles and Admiral Radford to the contrary—to reject French appeals for help to save Dienbienphu. He said no to the use of nuclear weapons; he said no to the use of ground troops unless they marched in with British and Asian allies. Likewise the decisions to make massive commitments of military and financial aid to the puppet government in Saigon were Eisenhower's, as were the decisions to authorize hostile acts, "dirty tricks," acts of war against the Viet Minh undertaken by Americans under the direction of Americans.

Responsibility for the attack on Cuba at the Bay of Pigs was shouldered by Kennedy, but it was Eisenhower who had ordered that the attack be prepared, just as the operation was carried out under the purview of officials—Allen Dulles, General Lyman Lemnitzer, and others—who were completing what they had begun at Eisenhower's instigation.

"The United States never lost a soldier or a foot of ground in my administration." If what Eisenhower meant was the blood of an American soldier fighting in an American war, or a foot of American soil, he was right. If, on the other hand, Eisenhower was speaking in his capacity as leader of the free world in the Cold War, then he overlooked the successful Cuban revolution which, during his administration, led to the "loss" of that country; he overlooked as well the men encouraged by U.S. propaganda to take up arms against the government of Hungary, the men shot down in aircraft that had—deliberately or no—crossed the borders of the Soviet Union, the men lost in the long secret warfare waged along the eastern and southern borders of China, the adventurers recruited by the CIA and lost on missions that may have taken them anywhere from Albania to Zanzibar.

He forgot, too, those of all ages and all lands who died and those who may still die because of the radiation they sustained during the testing of nuclear weapons, before scientists had learned what they now know about those baleful devices.

In short, the Eisenhower years of peace were a troubled and often bloody time during which, in unaccustomed secrecy imposed for reasons of "national security," the United States was being schooled to behave like a global imperial power. The trouble was stirred and the blood was spilled to protect the status quo. Taking one thing with another, the status quo is not one of the more rousing causes for which man can be brought to fighting pitch. There was in it plenty to defend but little that aspired to extend the frontiers of humanity, little that dared, nothing new, only a vast wealth to protect. Fafnir was never a heroic creature.

At all events, just as Eisenhower had to his credit two splendid achievements, so he was aware of his one surpassing failure: his inability to establish the basis for an enduring accommodation with the Soviet Union, his inability to win peace for the world. Of the five men elected President during the Cold War and before he died, Eisenhower was the one who might have seized that prize, the one whose authority and matchless qualities of leadership might have won for mankind that greatest boon. He failed, and his failure was the measure by which he lost the claim to true greatness. Since he was always his own severest judge, it is likely he harbored the bitter knowledge of it during the summer of 1968.

As he lay in hospital, politics attracted most of Eisenhower's attention. It was an exceptional election year, and a sadly confusing one. By the end of March, Lyndon Johnson had accepted the fact that his conduct of the war in Vietnam had left him politically toxic. He had withdrawn his name from consideration. Robert Kennedy, younger brother of the assassinated President, had since March been running hard for the Democratic nomination, and his candidacy vexed Eisenhower. He seemed to be a "peace" candidate, and he was doing well in the primaries. Still, he faced strong opposition within his party, and this boded well for the Republicans, but whom would they choose? Not Romney, surely, nor Rockefeller; then John Lindsay? Charles Percy? Ronald Reagan? Nixon, perhaps?

Eisenhower's grandson David was engaged to marry Nixon's younger daughter Julie. That dynastic alliance would seem to have clinched Eisenhower's endorsement of Nixon, but an embarrassment intruded. At a news conference the year before, the general had been asked to name his preference for the Republican candidacy; he had spoken of the many men he admired and respected; he mentioned Rockefeller, Romney, Percy, Reagan; other names tumbled off his tongue, and then, as he paused, awaiting another question, at his side Mamie had plucked at his sleeve and loudly whispered, "You forgot Dick!" "Oh, yes," said Eisenhower quickly. "Dick Nixon—a fine American, splendid candidate." What was it that always seemed to tangle his tongue when it came to Nixon?

Suddenly the election year was confused by yet another tragedy. An assassin slew Robert Kennedy, an incredible event for a nation that had begun to envision him as the best and fitting choice to follow his murdered brother to the White House. Another episode of the accursed violence that dogged the republic. News of the shocking business was given Eisenhower carefully, lest it upset his convalescence.

Late in the evening of June 15, while he was strolling slowly about his suite of rooms, Eisenhower suffered another attack—his fifth, once again a myocardial infarct. Once again he was put under intensive care. His physicians reported cardiac irregularities—extrasystoles—but added they were responding to therapy. The attack was a mild one; thirty days after it he was permitted other visitors than members of his family, and one of the first he received was Nixon. The two men chatted together for nearly an hour. Nixon was confident. He was fairly sure he had the votes he would need at the convention in Miami. His organization was running efficiently and smoothly. For his part, Eisenhower saw no Democratic challenger whom Nixon could not handily defeat. To withhold his endorsement could only injure Nixon's chances of nomination. Eisenhower said he would call a brief news conference in a day or two to make his announcement.

On Thursday, July 18, a half-dozen reporters gathered in the east lounge of Eisenhower's suite at Walter Reed. The general arrived in a wheelchair; he stepped from it and walked the last six or seven steps to a desk. He was wearing a blue dressing gown; on the breast pocket had been stitched the words "Feeling great again," but his appearance belied them. He was thin, some twenty pounds lighter than the man the reporters remembered. He read his endorsement of Nixon. He said he hoped the statement would lay to rest the persistent notion that he had never particularly admired Nixon. "This is a mere misapprehension," said the public Eisenhower.

On August 5 he read a message that was taped for transmission to the Republican convention; later he could watch his image on his television set. How old he looked, and frail! No matter: he was in high spirits, very enthusiastic about the thunder of cheers given him by the convention delegates.

The next day, Tuesday, he was slammed by another infarction, and this sixth was a massive one.

Ten days later the old warrior sustained a seventh attack, not an infarction like the first six but a ventricular fibrillation which was described as very grave. At least four times he had to be treated with electric shock to restore a normal cardiac rhythm; each time he lost consciousness; once or twice his physicians despaired of his life; each time he rallied.

At this juncture, with bulletins on Eisenhower's health appearing daily in the newspapers, a spokesman for Walter Reed Army Hospital disclosed that at least twenty persons who said their health was good had telephoned the medical center to offer their hearts for transplant into General Eisenhower. "Nothing," wrote an editor of the *New York Times*, "is more telling of the esteem in which Dwight D. Eisenhower is held . . . the willingness of so many Americans to give up their lives . . ." but the quixotic idea was rejected. A new heart would count for little. The general's recovery continued, though, and, said the surgeon general of the army, it approached "the proportions of a miracle. . . . the prayers of millions of his friends . . ." By August 29 he was off the critical list.

President Johnson had already proclaimed the week of October 13 as "Salute to Eisenhower Week." On October 14 the general would be seventy-eight years old. On the eve, telegrams were arriving in bundles, and cards and letters filled dozens of postal bags. His nurses and attendants were preparing their own celebration for their patient. On the day, at a signal, one of his nurses raised a window of his bedroom and outside the United States Army Band and Chorus struck up a "Happy birthday, General Eisenhower, happy birthday to you," following with "Army Blue," "The Yellow Rose of Texas," and "The Caissons Go Rolling Along." The general was wheeled to the window and he waved a small flag with five white stars on a field of red. His wife was beside him, applauding the band, tears standing in her eyes. Before long a nurse lowered the window.

The weeks passed. Word was brought the patient that Nixon had been elected President. The patient lay quiet, surrounded by his nurses and physicians, his wife still at hand, bulletins occasionally being issued. ". . . has spent a comfortable day. . . . It has been determined that surgery will be performed . . . to relieve the intestinal obstruction . . . Mrs. Eisenhower has visited him frequently . . . He asked for his glasses and read for a brief period this afternoon. . . . His progress is little short of remarkable." He developed pneumonia. He was "generally weaker." He was being "treated vigorously . . ." He was very weak. "He is resting comfortably and his spirits are good." He suffered a temporary congestive heart failure. ". . . progressively weaker . . . sleeping for brief periods . . . impossible to predict . . . no appreciable improvement."

A little after noon on Friday, March 28, 1969, Dwight Eisenhower died.

There was no anguish, no shock, and little weeping. An American hero was dead, but only after a long life filled with honors and affection, only as the sun sets after a long and dazzling day. The old warrior was at last at peace.

Flags were lowered to half-staff.

The nation had paid out its sorrow slowly, over the weeks while Eisenhower lay moribund. Now all but the private grief was spent. During those weeks the plans long since carefully prepared had been reviewed and finally approved—good staffwork. Now from all over the world the dignitaries were gathering—kings, princes, and potentates, chiefs of state and heads of government, prime ministers and presidents, generals and admirals—the pomp and panoply of seventy-five sovereign nations come to Washington for the solemn ceremony.

In the first days the statesmen were in the forefront. President Nixon spoke the eulogy. With the widow's approval he related what she had said were the dying warrior's last words: "I've always loved my wife. I've always loved my children. I've always loved my grandchildren. I've always loved my country."

In his celebrated Guildhall address after V-E Day, General Eisenhower had said: "I come from the heart of America." Now, as he had planned it, he was to be taken back there again, back to what he had called "the most beautiful region under God's blue sky."

The army took over from the politicians. Eisenhower's body lay in an eighty-dollar military coffin, clad in his army uniform complete with the trim jacket he had made famous. His flag-draped casket was placed in a railroad car of a funeral train with black crepe drawn across its windows. In the last car of the train—the same private car that General and Mrs. Eisenhower had used to travel back and forth between Gettysburg and Palm Springs—the family traveled, in seclusion. Forty hours from Washington to Abilene.

Forty hours to come full circle on the journey that had begun fifty-eight years before, when the rawboned farm boy left to try his luck at West Point. First and last that luck had been remarkably good, but it had been fortified first and last by an unquenchable optimism, a growing comprehension of how to get others to do what he wanted done, and an infinite capacity for winning affection. These qualities had been informed by a cold, exact, dispassionate intelligence.

Now, over his bier in Abilene, the Fifth Army band played "Ruffles and Flourishes" and "Hail to the Chief." Dwight Eisenhower was home.

"IT'S IKE HIMSELF. PASS THE WORD."

Notes

Works are generally cited in brief form; for full titles and authors' names see the Bibliography (pages 962–968). The following abbreviations are used:

BB Mss.   The Papers of Bernard Baruch, Princeton University.

DDE   Dwight David Eisenhower (see Bibliography for his works cited).

DDE-A   Matter in DDE Library, Abilene, Kansas (General Services Administration, National Archives).

DDE-G   Matter in DDE files, Gettysburg.

DOHC   Dulles Oral History Collection, Princeton University.

EP   *The Papers of Dwight David Eisenhower: The War Years* ed. Alfred P. Chandler, Jr. (5 vols.) The Johns Hopkins University Press 1970.

FonF   *Facts on File.*

JF Mss.   The Papers of James Forrestal, Princeton University.

JFD Mss.   The Papers of John Foster Dulles, "Conference Dossiers," category IX. Princeton University.

OHRO   Oral History Research Office, Columbia University.

PPs   *Public Papers of the Presidents: Dwight D. Eisenhower* (8 vols.) United States Government Printing Office 1960–1961.

ONE

APOTHEOSIS

1. Victory

4   Titles of documents: Strong 275.
4   "To save German": Dönitz 437.
4   "A separate and partial": ibid. 450.
5   "The decision as to when": DDE to War Department, cited Truman I 205.
5   "To continue to make a front": ibid.
6   "The brute issues": Churchill, cited Ismay 367.
6   "Communist intrigues": ibid.
6   "Attitude becomes more": ibid.
6   "Has no business": Brooke's diary, cited Bryant II 441.
7   "Keep in touch": Summersby 242.
7   "Lonely and pathetic": ibid.
7   "The principal": Middleton *N.Y. Times* May 6, 1945.
7   "The greatest military": Zhukov, cited Butcher 845.
7   "The most brilliant": Hatch, quote from jacket.
9   "Do you understand . . . faithfully": Summersby 243.
9   Original mss. of DDE's two messages on the German surrender are in DDE-A.
10 "From the outset": Ismay 258.
10 "To give some immediate": Hopkins memorandum, cited Sherwood 883.
11n. *Correspondence* between heads of government, US, UK, USSR, 209.
12 "Strictly military": R. Murphy 270.
12 "But the big blue folder": ibid., and author's conversation with Murphy.
13 "A rare lapse": R. Murphy 270.
13 "A godsend": from jacket of *Eisenhower's Six Great Decisions* by W. B. Smith.
13 "Without the slightest sign": Summersby 243.
13 "No gaiety, no joking": ibid.
13 "The last four days": Butcher 836.
14 "The signal for the": Churchill VI 548.

2. The Victors Measure Each Other

15 "General Ike and his": Butcher 852.
15 "German problems should be": cited Truman I 301.
16 "Could be interpreted only": R. Murphy 273.
16 "Were trying to create a rift": ibid.
16 "Abandonment of this enormous": Churchill VI 601.
16 "Barbarous Asiatics": Montgomery *Memoirs* 319.
16 "I view with profound": Churchill VI 603.
16n. "An iron curtain is": ibid. 573.

16n. "Should be recognized": Dutt letter to editor, *New Statesman* Oct. 25, 1968.
18 "Ike said he felt": Butcher 855.
18 "Finish the job": *N.Y. Times* June 5, 1945.
18 "The public expressions": Sherwood 899, 909.
18 "A Red wave": *N.Y. Times* June 6, 1945.
18 "The Soviet Union is": ibid.
19 "It is a tremendous honor": ibid.
19 "The odor of death": R. Murphy 289.
20 "Affable and soldierly appearing": DDE *Crusade* 435.
20 "I asked to see": Montgomery *Memoirs* 336.
20 "Did the trick": ibid.
20 "The divergent views": Montgomery *Memoirs* 338.
20 "All this looked a bit": ibid.
20 "View was that we could not": ibid.
20 "Began to look deliberate": DDE *Crusade* 436.
20 "The unexplained lack": Clay 22.
20 "What's going on here?" R. Murphy 289.
20n. Titles: Clay 450–51.
21 "I shall arrest you": ibid.
21 "To stay as long as he": DDE *Crusade* 437.
22n. See Clay 26.
23 The toasts: Butcher 861–62.
23 "Held nothing but bright": DDE *Crusade* 438.

3. Adoration

23 "Britain, the U.S. and Russia": *N.Y. Times* June 12, 1945.
23 "Are very friendly": ibid.
23 "Heartwarming": ibid.
24 "Ike, good old Ike": DDE *At Ease* 299.
24 "Good morning, sir. I see": Butcher 863.
24 "Earned in the blood": DDE *At Ease* 388–89.
24 "Alone, but unconquered": ibid.
25 "Those damn Frogs": see for example EP #592.
25 "We know very well": Treuenfels 19.
26 "Satisfactory but not spectacular": Butcher 866.
26 "There has been a considerable": *N.Y. Times* June 16, 1945.
27 "Thought it a mistake": Sherwood 914.
27 "The quicker the maximum": *N.Y. Times* June 16, 1945.
28 "Oh, God, it's swell": *N.Y. Times* June 19, 1945.
28 "Stand up, so they can": Butcher 869.
28 "Drive slowly. Avoid": ibid.
28 "A Kansas farm boy": *N.Y. Times* June 20, 1945.
28 "I'm only a simple soldier": *N.Y. Times* June 22, 1945.
28 "But I don't suppose that Congress": *N.Y. Times* June 21, 1945.
28 "This man is absolutely a natural": Arthur Burns interview, OHRO.
29 "I stand before the elected": *Congressional Record* June 18, 1945.
29 "Hello, Mother, how are you?": *N.Y. Times* June 21, 1945.
29 "I do not believe it": ibid.
29 "Oh boy, I'm glad to be": ibid.
30 "I am in the federal service and": ibid. June 22.

TWO

OBSCURITY

1. The Background

35   "Too weak . . . what little cash": DDE *At Ease* 31.
36   "As a mechanic-engineer": Kornitzer 14.

2. Abilene

37   "A very small, dead place": Lyon 49.
37   "At this writing, Hell is": Lyon 59.
37   "Entrancing": DDE *At Ease* 88.
38   "He was just another average chap . . . regular guy": F. T. Miller 73–83 passim; Davis 84–85.
38   "Religious teaching . . . hard work and thrift": Kornitzer 55.
38n. "This was a good way": ibid. 32–33.
39   "We never dared to stay out": ibid. 52.
39   "Seemed a mansion": DDE *At Ease* 72.
40   "It made us scrappers": Davis 73.
40   "Any time anybody walked on us": Kornitzer 48.
40   "They'd make us feel like beggars": Davis 73.
40   "Never suffered this way": DDE *At Ease* 70.
40n. "If we were poor": ibid. 36.
42   "Either the school at Annapolis, or": letters to Bristow in Eisenhower Museum.
42   "Nineteen years of age this fall": ibid.

3. West Point

43   "The officer corps became the mirror": Huntington *Soldier* 227.
43   Since both notions . . . a southern accent: see Janowitz 79–103, especially 83.
44   "Where else can I get": DDE *At Ease* 4.
44   "It would be difficult to overemphasize": DDE *At Ease* 7.
44n. Report of the Superintendent, USMA, 1922, 7–8, cited Janowitz 133.
45   "One of the most promising": *N.Y. Times,* cited Davis 136.
45   "It was a bitter blow": Hatch 44.
45   "No disappointment in his later life": Davis 140.
45   "End of my career as an active": DDE *At Ease* 16.
45   "To have been outstanding in athletics": Janowitz 135.
46   "We saw in Eisenhower": F. T. Miller 149–50.
46   "Born to command": DDE *At Ease* 26.
46   "Ultimately the United States would be": F. T. Miller 146.
46   "A terrible rage against this barbarity": Hatch 58.
46   "Eagerly expressed his own desire": F. T. Miller 146.
46   "Such a war would be righteous": Hatch 59.
47   "The four-year course, however, simply was not": Huntington *Soldier* 295. Janowitz 218–19.

48   "Military traditionalism implies": Janowitz 22.

48   "Integrity, courage, self-confidence, and": DDE speech June 4, 1952, at laying of cornerstone, Eisenhower Museum.

4. Need to Excel

49   "That nebulous region": DDE *At Ease* 131.

49   "In those days the man stayed": ibid. 126.

50   "It would please me . . . Yes, sir": ibid. 122.

50   "A vivacious and attractive girl": ibid. 113.

51   "The decision was to perform": ibid. 118.

51   "Couple of days": ibid.

52   "Organizational ability": ibid. 137.

53   "My mood was black": ibid.

5. Between Wars

54f.   "Pacifism and its bedfellow": MacArthur 90.

56   "Goddammit, my guns are ivory-handled": Ayer 73.

56   "Too weighty, unwieldy and cumbersome . . . engine of destruction": DDE "Tank" 453–58.

57   "I was told that my ideas": DDE *At Ease* 173.

59   "Life with General Conner was": ibid. 187.

60   "I never knew exactly how Ike felt": Mary Ellen Murphy interview with Mrs. Fox Conner, 1952.

60   "You mean I should *vamp* him?": ibid.

60   "You bawled me out and I thank you": ibid.

61   "No matter what orders you receive": DDE *At Ease* 199.

61   "An exceptionally efficient officer": ibid.

61   "A watershed in my life": ibid. 200.

61   "To identify and train those officers": Janowitz 139.

61   "Graduation there was thought to be": DDE *At Ease* 201.

61   "You will probably fail": ibid.

62   "You are far better trained": ibid.

63   "The one more or less invisible figure": ibid. 187.

64   "Splendid service . . . devotion to duty": C. Osborne 31.

64   "Every officer . . . anxious to do": DDE *At Ease* 205.

64   "The officer had to establish": Janowitz 145.

65   "Most of the time people were": Mary Ellen Murphy interview with Kate Hughes, 1952.

65n.   "His favorite song": F. T. Miller 119.

66   "Please don't go until you've met": *Army Times* Editors 5.

68   "Joint Resolution to promote peace and": U.S. War Policies Commission Hearings, Parts 1–3, 1931.

68   Testimony on profits: ibid. 131, 558. For cooler views of alleged profiteering see ibid. 687–700, 735–55.

69   "What it is claimed is the investment": ibid. 382.

69   "Liberal intelligentsia": Huntington *Soldier* 310–11.

69f.   All other quotes by DDE from "War Policies" 489.

70   "In time of war the nation": U.S. War Policies Commission Hearings, Parts 1–3, 88–89, 112–113.

71   "To draft statements, reports, and letters": DDE *At Ease* 213.

71   "He was a peculiar fellow . . . He had a *brain*": DDE interview with author, Aug. 1967.

71f.   Re bonus marchers: Weaver 18 et seq.

72   "Aggressive . . . lawless . . . an ever-present": Report of Chief of Staff to the Secretary of War on the employment of Federal troops, Aug. 15, 1932. This report was probably drafted by DDE.
72   "A considerable" . . . "communists and persons . . .": Hoover statement and order from Hurley to MacArthur, both July 28, 1932, both cited by Weaver.
73   On DDE during bonus march, see Drew Pearson syndicated column, Sept. 28, 1957.
73   "Free to object": DDE *At Ease* 216.
73   "Incipient revolution in the air . . . focus of the world today": Remarks by MacArthur, July 28, 1932. Transcript attached as appendix to Report of Chief of Staff to the Secretary of War, Aug. 15, 1932.
73   "A few brickbats, stones and": Report of Chief of Staff to the Secretary of War, Aug. 15, 1932. On what reporters reported, see Weaver.
73n. *Time* Aug. 8, 1932; and see Farago 89.
75   "All that night, lights burned": Pogue *Marshall* I 276.
76   "Approximately three hundred thousand men": Annual Report of the Chief of Staff for fiscal 1933, cited Davis 234. The report was drafted by Major DDE.
76   "Valuable training in mobilization": ibid.
76   "The greatest social experiment": Pogue *Marshall* I 280.
76   "The best antidote for mental stagnation": ibid. 311.
76   "The most instructive service I have ever had": ibid.
76   "Gross waste . . . downright corruption": Sherwood 55.
76   Table: figures cited MacArthur 99.
77   "But it seemed that some of the aging": Sherwood 76.
77   "Visionaries": ibid. 11–12.
77   "He was a patriotic American unafraid": DDE *At Ease* 213.
77n. Ibid. 76.
78   "If a man cannot find satisfaction": *Infantry Journal* XLIII 237–38; cited Huntington *Soldier* 310.
79   "If sufficient men, munitions, and money": MacArthur 102.
79   "Set a meager pay scale": DDE *At Ease* 221.
79   "An army of 30 divisions, supported": McCann 96.
79   "A military adequate to deal": DDE *At Ease* 225.
80   "He never reached his desk . . . home again": ibid. 228.
80   "Your success . . . my own judgment": cited McCann 94–95.
81   "Probably no one has had more, tougher . . . hell": DDE interview with author, Aug. 1967.
81f. "I didn't like it . . . and let's let it go at that": ibid.; see also *At Ease* 225–26.
82   "Now *that's* the time": author's interview, Aug. 1967.
82   "It is the evil things that we shall be": Neville Chamberlain, speech broadcast Sept. 3, 1939.
82   "We have been listening": DDE letter, cited McCann 52–53.

6. With Troops

83   "The War Department policy": DDE letter to Gerow, ibid. 26.
84   "Have you learned to tie": DDE *At Ease* 236.
84   "Never had in any one stretch": DDE to Gerow, cited McCann 21.
84   "I need you in War Plans": DDE *At Ease* 238.
85   "A man possessing broad vision": Pogue *Marshall* II 163.
86   "Live with mud, malaria": DDE to Gerow, cited McCann 32.
86   "The brilliant planning": Pogue *Marshall* II 162.
86   "Colonel Eisenhower . . . conceived and directed": Drew Pearson and Robert Allen, cited McCann 33.
86   "The chief says for you to hop": DDE *At Ease* 245.

THREE

THE GROWING BURDEN OF COMMAND

1. To the War Department

89 "Had no clear idea": DDE *Crusade* 15.
89 "Fragmentary and obscure": ibid.
92 "War Department had given no": Catton 115.
92 "I don't think there should be": Truman to Nelson, cited Catton 118.
92 "Nearly fifteen times as great": Truman I 171.
92 "If it hadn't been for taxes": ibid. 178.
93 "So as to permit use of forces": Joint Planning Committee to Joint Army & Navy Board, Dec. 21, 1940, "National Defense Policy for the U.S."; cited Pogue *Marshall* II 127.
94 "What should be our": DDE *Crusade* 18.
95 "The most essential thing now": memo from Marshall and Stark to President, Nov. 27, 1941, cited Matloff and Snell 79.
95 "Important that this troop": ibid.
95 "Precipitance of military action": ibid.
95 Assistance to the Far East: EP #1.
96 "General, it will be a long time": DDE *Crusade* 21–22.
96 "I agree with you": ibid. 22.

2. An Eye to the East

98 "As rapidly as possible": Matloff and Snell 8.
98 "The Army would defend the": ibid. 45.
98n. "For Christ's sake": T. H. White *Stilwell* 27.
99 "The yielding of the Philippines": MacArthur to Marshall, cited EP #33 note 1.
99 "We have at least four-fifths": Churchill III 611.
99 "Ships! Ships! All we": EP #53.
100 "Entirely unjustifiable": EP #33 note 1.
100 "There is here a keen": EP #33.
100 "Incidentally General Eisenhower in WPD": EP #69.
101 "American help cannot or will not": Sayre to Roosevelt, cited Stimson and Bundy 397–98.
101 "Since I have no air or sea protection": MacArthur to Marshall, cited ibid. 398.
102 "We can't do this at all": Pogue *Marshall* II 247.
102 "To arrange for the capitulation": EP #122.
103 "You are directed to make": EP #143.
103 "Message to MacA was approved": EP #145.

3. An Eye to the West

104 "The War Department is just like": T. H. White *Stilwell* 19.
105 "It's hard as hell to find anybody": ibid. 27.
105 "Methods of Co-operation between . . . intelligent command": EP #22.
105f. "There must be one man in command": Sherwood 455.
106 "A supreme commander . . . government": EP #23.

106 "The purpose of these rigid restrictions": ibid.
106 "The Japanese machine was working with": Churchill IV 136.
106 "Wavell never had a chance": DDE *Crusade* 29.
106 "We are no longer single, but married": Churchill III 686.
107 "It would, I think, be fatal": cited Bryant I 235.
107 "The whole scheme . . . wild and half-baked": ibid. 236.
107n. "The region Malaya-Australia": EP #24.
108 "We've got to go to Europe and fight": EP #73.
108 "Went to Bill Somervell this A.M.": EP #80.
109 "Eisenhower, I must have assistants": DDE address, dedication of George C. Marshall Research Library, May 23, 1964; cited Pogue *Marshall* II 337.
109n. "The old gag about 'they shall' ": T. H. White *Stilwell* 30–31.
110 "Tom Handy and I stick to our ideas": EP #88.
110 "More tired-looking than I'd ever": McKeogh and Lockridge 21.
110n. "Of analytical mind and a certain": DDE *Crusade* 31.
111 "The Navy wants to take all": EP #129.
111 "We've got to go on a harassing": EP #134.
111 "A minimum of one month and a": cited Sherwood 303–304.
111 "Was not alone in thinking": Ismay 225.
111 "The first phase, involving the occupation": Sherwood 304.
111 "It is . . . no exaggeration": cited Gwyer 93.
112 "The Russia of Stalin will be erased": Sherwood 305.
112 "Maximum promise of . . . to assist Russia": EP #160.
112 *"We must"* keep on sending: EP #162.
113 "Was the most likely place where": R. Murphy 84.
113 "He initiated it, he kept it going": ibid.
113 "The reasoning is without validity": EP #162.
114 "An academic study and should": cited Matloff and Snell I 176.
114 "Gradually some of the people with": EP #185.
115 "I have felt terribly. I should": EP #189.
115 "My father was buried": EP #190.
116 "I want you to know": Pogue *Marshall* II 338 and DDE *At Ease* 248–49.
117 "My part in winning the war": ibid.
117 "I was startled . . . I looked at it": DDE *At Ease* 249. See also Cline 108.
118 "Urgent ratholes": Stimson diary, cited Pogue *Marshall* II 304.
118 "To attack our principal enemy": EP #207.
119 "Hold for me. GCM": EP #207 note 1.
119 "Off on the wildest kind of": Stimson and Bundy, 416–17.
119 "Single end . . . an attack, by combined forces": Matloff and Snell 185.
120 "A pleasant and easy man": cited Bryant I 285.
120 "May be a good fighting man": Sherwood 523.
120 "Momentous meeting": Brooke, cited Bryant I 286.
120 "No hesitation in cordially accepting": Churchill IV 317.
120 "Entire agreement . . . with all": Matloff and Snell 189.
120 "In principle": ibid.
120 "Our two nations are resolved": Churchill IV 321.
120 "Many if not most . . . reservations": Matloff and Snell 189.
121 "Much disturbed": EP #233.
121 "I spent much time": Truscott 21–22.
121 "He looks fine. I hope that": EP #254.
122 "The first good news for the United Nations": Sherwood 542.
122 "At variance with the long-standing": Matloff and Snell 190.
122 "Very precarious . . . nothing but token forces . . . drastically reduced . . . the simple fact": Matloff and Snell 204, 207, 214, 222n.
122 "Would have the enthusiastic": MacArthur to Marshall, cited Matloff and Snell 215–16.
123 "Negotiations . . . which may lead": Catton 106–107.
123 "Bolero is *supposed* to have the approval": EP #278.
124 "The failure of top officials": *Industrial Mobilization for War,* U.S. Government Printing Office, nd; cited Sherwood 554.
124 "It will be carried out with": EP #236.
124 "A good many craft of the smallest": Matloff and Snell 192.
125 "This morning I attended a committee": EP #280.

125   *"Type of officer to serve as"*: EP #292.
126   "The Pershing of this war": McKeogh and Lockridge 24.
127   "A decisive type . . . who appears to be": EP #318.
127   "Who's smoking . . . I don't permit": Mark Clark *Calculated Risk* 18–19.
127   "Essential": EP #318.
127   "Who would you name . . . across the table from you": EP #318; see also DDE *Crusade* 66–67.
127   "Conditions in England and the need . . . experience and knowledge . . . the secretary of war": Arnold 315.
128   "Should be Ike": ibid.
128   "I believe it highly desirable": EP #325.
128   "I certainly do want to read": DDE *Crusade* 50.
129   "The C/S told me": EP #328.
129   "The C/S says I'm the guy": EP #333.
129   "I had to work by influence and": Churchill IV 324.
129n. Mark Clark *Calculated Risk* 20.
130   "Had faith in the power of the": ibid. 322.
130   "The power of Great Britain and": ibid. 335.
130   "All preparations are proceeding": ibid. 340.
130   "To explain to you": ibid.
130   "We must never let GYMNAST": ibid.
130   "Inevitable sometime in 1942": Sherwood 569.
130   "Yes": ibid. 563.
130   "In the course of": ibid. 577.
131   "Margin between success or failure": cited Matloff and Snell 237.
131   "Though they think it may be": ibid.
131   "Time for us to do": EP #331 note 2.
132   "He was dressed in his zip-suit": Bryant I 322.
132   "There was general agreement": EP #344.
132   "So-called 'sacrifice' operation": EP #344 note 3.
132   "Possibility, at least of": ibid.
132   "We must be ready": ibid.
132   "Doubtful as to what P.M. and": Brooke diary, cited Bryant 325.
133   "We hold strongly to the view": Churchill IV 381–82.
133   "Very upset": Brooke, cited Bryant I 328.
133   "A bit peevish": ibid.
134   "The leader in a democracy": cited Pogue *Marshall* II 330.
134f. "If disaster is to be expected . . . to directly or indirectly": Matloff and Snell 242.
135   "Critically weakened": ibid. 186.
135   "Greatest battle of attrition": Alan Clark 264.
135   Diary excerpts cited ibid. 254.
136n. "Somewhat worried about our": *Goebbels* 262.
136n. "[Our soldiers in North Africa] retarded": ibid. 360.
137n. "If we see that Germany": *N.Y. Times* June 24, 1941.
138   "I've got to have someone": Davis 303.
138   "First deliberate attempt by the": DDE *Crusade* 51.
138   "Day of the Dupes": Gwyer 627–28.
139   "Operations in Western Europe in 1942": Matloff and Snell 243–44.
139   "Persuade by accomplishment rather than": EP #353.

4. Second Front in 1942?

140   "Mickey . . . this looks exactly like": McKeogh and Lockridge 30.
140   "I feel as though I'm living in": Davis 314.
141   "An excellent demonstration of the art": cited Davis 310.
141   "Ike had made a grand impression": Butcher 21.
141   "After watching Ike deal with the press": ibid. 20.
141   "No one but a Sunday School teacher": ibid. 14.
141   "It is a rather lonely life I lead": EP #390.
141   "Quite astonished": EP #377.

143 "Practically incommunicado": EP #358.
143 "There seems to be": EP #358.
143 "Am somewhat uncertain": EP #367.
143n. "The best alternative . . . as possible": Matloff and Snell 244.
144 "The British Staff and Prime Minister": EP #370.
144 "Very stirred up": Stimson and Bundy 424.
144 "Finally and definitely . . . the enemy in 1942": FDR memo, cited Sherwood 603–605.
144 "In my mind [an invasion of France in]": Brooke, cited Bryant I 343.
145 "The belief of this headquarters . . . assistance": EP #379.
145 "I personally estimate": ibid.
145 "Russia is the great . . . this eventuality": EP #381.
147 "Very suspicious . . . that Marshall was trying": cited Bryant I 342.
147 "There is an atmosphere of": EP #384.
147 "The last few days have been": EP #387.
147 "Four months, with an absolute . . . we should attempt the job . . . whole-hearted cooperation": ibid.
147 "Missed the point that after": cited Bryant I 342–43.
147 "Well, I hardly know where to": Butcher 29.
147n. "Believed that an operation": Truscott 49.
148 "Churchill's warnings that the Channel": Sherwood 591.
148 "Repeated assertion . . . as to the disastrous": Stimson and Bundy, 432.
148 "So many tales have been published": Churchill III 655–57.
148n. "For the first time . . . astonished": EP #513.
148n. "Discouraging, discouraging": Butcher 119.
149 "Was based upon nationalistic": DDE *Crusade* 71.
149 "The crash program, the head-on": Gwyer 350–51.
149 "In the military as in": Churchill III 673.
149 "Elaborately fortified . . . the finest . . . absolutely red": Ismay 297.
150 "As a combined U.K.-U.S.": EP #389.
150 "The least harmful": Pogue *Marshall* II 346.
150 "A great joy": Churchill IV 448.
152 "Visibly withering": R. Murphy 206.
153 "The United States delighting in": de Gaulle *Unity* 83.

5. Torch

154 "Not a first-class fighting force": EP #389.
155 "We are here only to listen": Butcher 49.
155 "Whether or not we should discuss": Matloff and Snell 294.
155 "The most trying of my life": EP #484.
156 "Entirely upon political factors": EP #473.
156 "The risks of the projected operation": ibid.
157 "Something of a quite desperate": ibid.
157 "Sailing a dangerous political sea": ibid.
157 "Hurrah!" "O.K., full blast": Churchill IV 543.
157 "Very glum . . . a great many . . . how it was our intention . . . May God prosper": Churchill IV 478, 486, 481.
158 "November 8, sixty": Butcher 95.
158 "You are about my oldest friend": EP #157 note.
158n. "Are the British really": Churchill IV 465.
159 "A major crisis . . . satisfactory performance": EP #502.
159 "Skillful and determined": de Gaulle *Unity* 15.
160 "Nobody ever pays attention to": Murphy 121.
160 "All resistance movements within": Memo of conversations between OSS representative and Fighting French in London, Sept. 3–10, 1942, cited Langer 297.
161 "The French as a people had": Langer 174.
161 "A peculiar form of French": Churchill IV 640.
162 "With a kind of horrified": Murphy 123.
162 "Fantastically inadequate": ibid.

183 "I have lost all our fighting ships and": Churchill IV 620.
183 "The tribes . . . In Morocco alone . . . quiet": EP #622.
183 "The Kingpin is honest . . . of several days": ibid.
184 "Superb distribution of emphasis": Sherwood 651.
184 "A moral and sentimental character": Churchill IV 629.
184 "Anything for the battle, but": ibid. 631.
184 "I do understand your resentment": Mark Clark *Calculated Risk* 112.
185 "Displays of French military style": Pendar 122–23.
185 "Unfeasible . . . had to be turned": Daugherty and Janowitz 298.
185 "The resistance movements in all the occupied": Lockhart 213.
185 "I have requested the liberation of all": FDR, cited Sherwood 654.
186 "So we who tried to defend America": Carroll 72–73.
186 "Since this operation started": EP #641.
186 "The sooner I can get rid of all these": EP #673.
186 "Not set up any . . . merely required . . . the region": EP #641.
186 "We had no legal or other right . . . choosing": DDE *Crusade* 108.
186 "Such a resort to Nazi methods": ibid. 130.
187 "Heads must roll, Murphy": R. Murphy 173.
187n. "I attempted to force Giraud": EP #644.
188 "Soft-gloving snakes in our midst": Pyle 54.
188 "A mistake . . . command decision": R. Murphy 169, 168.
188 "To enter into any 'protocol' ": EP #696 note 1.
188 "A cagier diplomat": EP #723.
188 "Eisenhower . . . was far too much immersed": cited Bryant I 430.
189 "International diplomatic problems": EP #734 note 3.
189 "Last night forty American tanks": Ciano 548.
190 "Kingpin notified and will arrive": EP #736.
191 "During the period of active hostilities": EP #725.
191n. "It would have been easy to finish": Liebling *Road Back* 228.
192 "And not one of them accepted": Liebling *Road Back* 231.
192 "One complication was the age-old": DDE *Crusade* 128.
194 "Pleased to see you . . . he's a fine guy": Macmillan II 220–21.
195 "A grave error": ibid. 222.
195 "No objections": R. Murphy 182.
195 "Peyrouton's [appointment] . . . has been received": EP #777.

7. Victory in Africa

196n. "For some time we despaired": Ian Jacob, ms. diary entry Jan. 13, 1943.
197f. "Was of a general air of . . . on the Commander-in-Chief": ibid. Dec. 30, 1942.
198 "As a sort of deputy": EP #775.
198 "So confident of my complete familiarity": EP #765.
199 "A real bad one . . . in no way . . . operations": cited Bryant I 448, 447.
199 "Had so laboriously planned": EP #777.
199 "Held on a very short lead": Howe 354.
199 "Ike seems jittery": Sherwood 676.
199 "Standing to attention like a Roman": Macmillan II 245.
199 "I feel very strongly": EP #755 note 2.
199 "Of course carry out . . . and retirement": ibid.
200 "Ike's foul frame of mind": Butcher 233.
200 "Controlling certain strategic": DDE *Crusade* 136.
200 "Optimism and buoyancy": ibid.
200 "Blurted out . . . most miraculous": ibid. 137.
200 "I told him his neck": Butcher 243.
201 "I have tentatively come": EP #775.
201 "Could not help flattering": cited Bryant I 454–55.
201 "Delay action on Patton": EP #779 note 1.
202 "Rich organizational experience": EP #705.
203 "There will probably be": EP #810.
203 "Best if the American": FDR to Churchill, cited Churchill IV 725.

204 "Particular types of intelligence": EP #832.
204 "Eyes and ears" "brains, tact, and": EP #816.
205 "What a godsend it was": EP #899.
205 "Tales home to the boss": Bradley 32.
205 "Goddam spies running around": ibid. 45.
206 "He is too valuable": Butcher 247–48.
207 "After all, four or four and a half": ibid. 251.
207 "Alarmed" "exploded": Bradley 56–57.
208 "I could not believe that": ibid. 58.
208 "To avoid being branded": ibid.
208 "Future employment . . . campaign approaches": EP #906.
208 "All I have is actual": Patton to Marshall, cited Howe 573.
208 "Forward troops have been": cited Bradley 62.
209 "It is . . . assumed . . . should cease": ibid. 62–63.
209 "Deeply concerned": Tedder 411.
209 "Quite mad and very . . . country since the 17th": Patton, cited Bradley 63.
210 "To be stripped down": EP #906.
210 "Aroused a fear in my mind": EP #945 note 1.
210n. "The American gives up": cited Howe 582.
212 "The southern portion of your": EP #947.
213 "At no time, perhaps, in the whole": Macmillan II 320–21.
213 "A goddam waste of time": Farago 262.
214 "Many attractive features . . . penetrated": EP #949.
215 "There, General, are the fruits": Macmillan II 325.

8. Soldier in Politics

216 "Well-armed and fully organized": Tedder 428.
216 "The operation offers scant": EP #942 note 1.
216 "It is perfectly clear . . . in the last degree": ibid.
216 "We have told the Russians . . . I cannot imagine": Tedder 429–30.
216 "Operation Husky will be prosecuted": EP #942.
216 "Quickly decided that it would": Montgomery Memoirs 157.
216 "Be allowed to make . . . own Army": ibid. 158.
217 "Little brigade-groups all over": Tedder 434.
217n. "The one quality that can be": EP #1062.
218n. "Always shrunk from the thought": Matloff 127.
218n. "First objective . . . could be made": Churchill IV 791, 793.
218n. "A decisive invasion of": Matloff 133.
219 "Remote oasis": de Gaulle Unity 104.
219 "Every movement, every part": ibid. 105.
220 "Three different times . . . He talks persistently": Butcher 316.
220 "I am quite certain": cited Bryant I 519.
221 "Glad . . . He said . . . sustain in Italy": DDE Crusade 167, 168; see also Churchill IV 818.
221 "Heart lay in an invasion . . . a mere convenience": Matloff 153.
222 "Very passionately . . . gladly . . . rather than throw away": Churchill IV 826.
222 "On the momentum": Alexander, cited Churchill IV 827.
222 "Post-Husky would be in": Matloff 155.
222 "The local political mess": EP #1075.
223 "Keep the position fluid": Sherwood 721.
223 "The right and duty . . . their regular Government": Woodward British Foreign Policy; cited Macmillan II 257.
223 "Completely unacceptable . . . quite impossible . . . unpardonable": ibid. 258, 260.
224 "The military command . . . of their duties": de Gaulle Unity 109.
225 "I want to give you . . . you and I want": Churchill V 173–74.
225 "The committee . . . Military Commander-in-Chief": cited de Gaulle Unity 112.
226 "Calculated outburst . . . shrouded in sorrow": de Gaulle Unity 117–18.
226 "Seriously jeopardize the safety": EP #1054 note 1.
226n. "In a most amiable": EP #1054.
227 "Was in excellent form . . . well-chosen phrases": Macmillan II 345.

227 "We will not tolerate . . . approved by you": EP #1057 note 1.
227n. "My two strongest and ablest": EP #1075.
228 "Oh, yes . . . advise me to do": Macmillan 347.
228 "In the public press . . . no definite action": EP #1057.
228 "Reactionary, old-fashioned . . . whatsoever": EP #1069.
228 "Stupid and vacillating": Macmillan II 346.
228 "I am here . . . in my charge": de Gaulle *Unity* 119.
229 "Was almost insulting . . . by fundamental distrust": Macmillan II 348.
229 "The organization of the French": de Gaulle *Unity* 119.
229 "The necessity of dictatorial": EP #1064.
229 "A definite victory": EP #1070 note 5.
229 "De Gaulle has definitely lost . . . impotency": EP #1069.
229 "I am quite sure . . . losing ground": EP #1075.
230 "I feel as if my stomach": Butcher 343.
230 "Like a football coach who is pleased": ibid. 340.

9. The "Soft" Underbelly

231 "The operation will proceed": EP #1104.
231 "If I use this . . . They treat me . . . that's what I is": Gunther *Eisenhower* 154.
232 "Of course, anybody can draw": ibid.
232 "The American commander-in-chief of the": ibid. 155.
232 "General, to go down into folklore": ibid. 156.
232n. "Actually dared": ibid. 156. But see also Gunther, "With Eisenhower in Sicily."
233 "I am particularly pleased that": EP #1051.
233 "The fate of Sicily must be": cited Blumenson 78–79.
234 "Not tremendously excited" . . . "find out about it later": Sherwood 742.
234 "Let us consult together": Churchill V 55.
235 "Was in a state of considerable": Macmillan II 372.
235 "A firm policy of joint": EP #812.
235 For the exchanges between the two governments, see Coles and Weinberg 160–68.
235 "There should be no senior partner": EP #812 note 3.
236 "Only in the event that the Italian": EP #1138.
236 "That they could be immediately broadcast": EP #1139.
236 "In no event should our officers": cited Churchill V 55.
236 "Speaking broadly, it is quite right": EP #1164 note 1.
236 "Poor Eisenhower is getting": Macmillan II 375.
236 "What has me worried . . . is the": EP #1147.
237 "There are some contentious people here": Churchill V 64.
237 "My position is that once Mussolini": ibid.
237 "Beginning to get rather rattled . . . conceivable point": Macmillan II 377.
237 "Turned Red overnight . . . which had to be . . . Fascism in Italy is extinct": Churchill V 99.
239 "Enemy resistance will be very great": Montgomery *Memoirs* 161.
239 "If this was so I did not": EP #1168.
239 "As much as his nervous temperament": Butcher 386.
240 "Sicilian phase . . . rapidly to a close . . . succeeding in evacuating . . . light equipment": EP #1185.
241 "Giving Patton a jacking up": Butcher 390.
241 "If this thing ever gets out": Farago 343.
241 "That no move be made . . . in AVALANCHE": EP #1187.
242 "We never for a single instant forget": EP #1188.
242 "It will land us in all sorts of": EP #1187 note 1.
242 "Depend upon the decency": EP #1187.
243 "Dear General Patton: This personal": EP #1190.
243 "I clearly understand": EP #1190.
243 "To determine . . . the extent": DDE *Crusade* 181.
243 "Moreover, it is acutely distressing": EP #1190.
244 "But nevertheless if there is": ibid.
244 "No letter that I have been called upon": ibid.

245   "Brilliant success": EP #1191 note 1.
245   "If I am correctly informed": cited Butcher 393.
246   "A formidable document": Macmillan II 384, 375.
246   "A crooked deal": R. Murphy 216.
246f. "Passive assistance . . . It is these factors": EP #1213.
247   "Far more frightened of the German": EP #1221.
248   "Main object": CCS 319/5, Aug. 24, 1943, cited Matloff 227.
248   "Seeking every honorable avenue": Wedemeyer memo Aug. 24, 1943; cited Cline 298.
248n. "Over 32 Brigadier Generals and": EP #1236 note 1.
249   "Well aware that no one except": EP #1223.
249   "A small political attack": EP #1226 note 1.
249   "Two of your least trained divisions": EP #1226.
250   "Long ago . . . conflicting commercial": EP #1210.
250   "Honest opinion for what it may": EP #1233.
250   "I do not see how": ibid.
251   "In this emergency": Macmillan II 390.
251   "Any place any time": EP #1228.
252   "Ammunition, supplies and a few": EP #1232.
253   "Due to changes in the situation": EP #1244 note 1.
253   "Whether or not . . . we should proceed": ibid.
254   "I intend to broadcast the existence": EP #1244.
254   "I . . . have determined *not* to accept": EP #1245.
255   "He could not overlook the": Strong 160.
255   "Badoglio has gummed up the works": Bradley 166.
255   "This is General Dwight D. . . . United Nations": EP #1243 note 4.
256   "To play a little poker": EP #1262.
256   "To keep the enemy upset . . . reasonable time": EP #1246.
257   "Big worry": EP #1262.
257   "Be pleased to inform their lordships": cited Butcher 416.
258   "We will have no truck with fascism": Sherwood 742.
258   "We will permit no vestige of": ibid.
258   "The Italian campaign showed": Carroll 185.
258   "Hates fascism and the Germans": EP #1299.
259   "Electioneering for Roosevelt": Butcher 377.
259   "With Parkinsonian proliferation": Macmillan II 453.
260   "There could be no doubt . . . disregarded her now": de Gaulle *Unity* 143.
260n. "Was like a red rag to a bull": Macmillan II 558.
261   "Tense but not unexpected": EP #1251.
262   "The situation has arisen which we": EP #1255.
262   "In reasonably good shape": EP #1271.
262   "The logical and inevitable choice": Butcher 421.
264   "Should have . . . Joint Chiefs of Staff": Arnold 456.
264   "The most acute difference I ever": Churchill V 224.
264   "Worked himself . . . anything else": Brooke, cited Bryant II 51.
265   "It is personally distressing to me": EP #1327.
265   "Remained aloof": Butcher 431.
265   "Expressed a great hope that you": Deane's letter to Marshall, cited Matloff 278 note 22.
266   "It was his idea that General Marshall": minutes of meeting, President and Joint Chiefs, Nov. 15, 1943; cited Matloff 338–39.
266   "The hottest one yet": Butcher 442.
266   "That the original proposal would go": EP #1408.
267   "Ike was embarrassed": Butcher 446.
267   "General Marshall remained completely": DDE *Crusade* 196.
267   "I hate to lose General Marshall": Butcher 446.
267   "You and I know the name of": The quoted remark is combined from DDE *Crusade* 197 and Sherwood 770.
268   "A fortunate beneficiary of": Butcher 452.
268   "A football quarterback who has been": ibid.
269   "Who will command it? . . . Then nothing will": Sherwood 787; Matloff 363.
269   "When will the commander in chief": Sherwood 791.
269   "He made it against": ibid. 802.

269   "I feel I could not sleep at night": ibid. 803.
269   "From the President to Marshal Stalin": DDE *Crusade* 208.

10. Command of Overlord

270   "Well, Ike, you are going to command": ibid. 207.
270   "For the first time, we now feel": Butcher 454.
270   "I am deeply appreciative of your": EP #1410.
271   "I discovered, as I had expected": Brooke, cited Bryant II 115.
271   "Although extremely able, are somewhat": EP #1701.
271   "Somebody like Hodges or Simpson": EP #1426.
272   "I would want Patton": EP #1423.
272   "A bad mistake . . . by my ablest": ibid.
273   "Had by a separate route": Churchill V 428.
273   "The situation appears to me": EP #1373.
273   "Friends in fact, in spirit, and": Declaration of Teheran.
274   "OVERLORD and ANVIL are the supreme": CCS 426 1, Dec. 6, 1943, cited Bryant II 107.
274   "Disastrous . . . at least two divisions": Churchill V 429.
274   "Designed to enable Rome": ibid. 432.
274   "With Eisenhower and all his high": ibid. 436–47.
274   "A hazardous enterprise on the Italian": ibid. 440.
274   "I had hoped that we were hurling a wildcat": ibid. 488.
275   "A risky affair . . . the attack would not . . . careful consideration . . . a force of several strong . . . landing craft would be needed": DDE *Crusade* 212–13.
275   "Active, knowledgeable, fact-armed": Churchill V 441.
275n.   "Entirely aside from OVERLORD-ANVIL": EP #1473.
276   "I am profoundly disturbed": EP #1425.
276   "Unprintable": Macmillan II 441, 443.
276   "Directed to take no action": EP #1425 note 2.
277   "Good": ibid. note 4.
277   "A love fest": Butcher 473.
277   "I must have your help . . . Splendid!": de Gaulle *Unity* 216–17.
278   "You will be under terrific strain": EP #1450 note 8.
280   "It is obvious that strong and positive": EP #1483.
281   "On the pitfalls to avoid": EP #1256 note 1.
281   "True basis . . . selflessness . . . must each have . . . in no sense of . . . *the utmost* . . . seek and absorb . . . All of us are human . . . has very definite executive responsibilities": EP #1256.
282   "Must cease at once . . . all British": EP #1427.
282   "Was one of the luckiest . . . everything was going well": Duncan Emrich, *Folklore on the American Land*, Little Brown 1972, p. 153.
283   "Rather well acquainted": EP #1248.
283   "The selection of Eisenhower": cited Bryant II 106.
284   "Every obstacle must be": EP #1497.
284   "I entirely agree with the": cited Bryant II 140.
285   "The destinies of two great empires": Harrison 68.
285   "Localitis . . . had warped": EP #1531 note 3.
285   "Eisenhower sees the situation": cited Bryant II 152.
285   "To allot enough landing craft": Ambrose *Supreme Commander* 361.
286   "The really important war": cited Ambrose *Supreme Commander* 363. See also EP #1539 note 2.
286   "To take alarm . . . really worried . . . I very much fear . . . irremediable cleavage": Tedder 508–509.
286n.   "To secure the progressive": cited Tedder 503.
287   "Simply have to go home": Butcher 498.
287   "The responsibility for supervision": EP #1577 note 1.
287   "If a satisfactory answer is not": EP #1601.
287   "Amen": EP #1601 note 9.
287   "Took rather a grave . . . be injured": Churchill V 528.

287 "Our chances for success . . . grossly exaggerated": EP #1630.
288 "The French railway system is": cited Tedder 535.
288 "Transportation system was on the point": Harrison 224.
288 "The bonus from resistance was of a size": Foot 387.
288 "To prove critical in the": Harrison 230.
289 "The most stringent observance": EP #1563.
289 "As soon after the 15th of April": EP #1636.
290 "Since it is the evident destiny": cited Farago 417.
290 "I have grown so weary": EP #1657.
291 "You simply will not guard your tongue": EP #1659.
291 "The work of God. His will": cited Farago 423.
291 "An unnecessary luxuriousness": EP #1688.
292 "I think, at times, I get . . . my theater too long": EP #1587.
292 "As soon after June 6": EP #1587 note 1.
293 "I've seen him sit in the shade": *American Heritage* Editors 55.
293 "Especially careful" and list of items: EP #1559.
294 "Statements derogatory . . . once a month thereafter": EP #1567.
294 "Especially watchful to see that": EP #1602.
294 "Their attitude to women": Ferguson and Fitzgerald *Studies in the Social Services* 97–98; cited Calder 311.
294 "Must aim at the restoration": Eden *Reckoning* 461.
294 "Will give us more authority": cited Gabriel Kolko 72.
295 "We are going to need very badly": EP #1601.
295 "Where, when and how . . . consult": Coles and Weinberg 667–68.
295 "France, who brought freedom to the world": cited Pogue *Supreme Command* 145.
296 "Strictly on a military basis . . . thoroughly cooperative": EP #1653.
296 "Calculated insult": de Gaulle *Unity* 224.
296 "In order that arrangements": EP #1675.
296 "The limitations under which": EP #1681.
297 "In French cipher, if necessary": ibid.
297 "Deal with him direct . . . groups": ibid.
297 "I request that this matter": ibid.
297 "I do *not* desire that Eisenhower": EP #1691 note 1.
297 "The strain is telling on him": Butcher 539.
298 "No real director of thought": Brooke, cited Bryant II 189–90.
298 "To military matters and . . . I think I should tell you . . . for de Gaulle": EP #1691.
299 "I must freely admit": cited Harrison 136–37.
     Weisung 51: Harrison, Appendix D, 464–67.
300 "Began to insist strongly": Harrison 259.
301 "Must go on": EP #1720.
301 "Weather forecasts while still indefinite": EP #1728.
301 "The smell of victory": DDE *At Ease* 275.
302 "Weather prospects . . . are rather favorable": EP #1731.
302 "The whole thing . . . a rather sorry mess . . . hazard . . . weather . . . unpredictable . . . unless . . . in the weather": EP #1732.
304 "The French authority which": de Gaulle *Unity* 229.
304 "C'est de la fausse monnaie": Nicolson II 377.
304 "Chancy": Tedder 545.
304 "I am quite positive that": ibid. 546.
305 "Seemed to be traveling": DDE *Crusade* 250.
305 "Okay. Let's go": Ambrose *Supreme Commander* 417.

11. Victory in Europe

306 "I have as yet no information": EP #1737.
307 "General plan . . . carefully outlined": DDE *Crusade* 229.
307 "I doubt that there has ever been": W. B. Smith *Decisions* 157.
308 "Looked sick and tired out . . . at any cost": Speidel, cited Harrison 412–13.
308 "Let's, for God's sake, keep our eyes": Tedder 582.

309 "Knock about a bit down there": Bradley 241.
309 "I thoroughly believe you are going": EP #1759.
309 "The immediate task of this Army": cited DDE *Crusade* 260.
309 "Whenever there is any legitimate": EP #1774.
309 "Blitz attack of VIII Corps goes in": EP #1774 note 2.
309n. "The enemy is extraordinarily nervous": cited Tedder 571.
310 "It was refreshing to hear": Tedder 563.
310 "I know the bocage country well": ibid.
310 "Ike is considerably . . . Monty's attack": Butcher 594–95.
310 "Tell Montgomery tactfully": Tedder 557.
310 "We must use all possible energy": EP #1807.
310 "To set my eastern flank alight": EP #1813 note 1.
310 "Will continue without a halt": ibid.
310 "My whole eastern flank will burst": EP #1826 note 1.
310 "Brilliant stroke which will knock loose": EP #1826.
310 "The heaviest and most concentrated air attack": Pogue *Supreme Command* 188–89.
311 "Was spending his reputation": Bradley 325–26.
311 "The feeling that existed against me": Montgomery *Memoirs* 233.
311 "It was always very clear to me": ibid. 235.
311 "It is quite clear that Ike": cited Bryant II 244.
311 "To put all his cards on the table . . . he is evidently a little shy": ibid.
312 "Well, I'll tell you. Montgomery": author's interview with DDE, Aug. 1967.
312 "The line that we actually held": DDE *Crusade* 267.
313 "Too 'soft' in his relations": Tedder 570.
313 "Bleak and sterile . . . winning the other": Churchill VI 719, 721.
313 "I am impressed by Eisenhower's statement": ibid. 723.
313 "Deeply grieved . . . dazzling possibilities . . . fall naturally into his control": Ehrman V 356.
313 "I always think of my early geometry": ibid.
313 "At the earliest possible date": ibid. 357.
313 "An impression must be made": ibid. 361.
314 "Some point or other . . . along the Brittany": Churchill VI 67.
314 "If the intercepts are right": Butcher 630.
314 "In every form of the . . . limp": ibid. 634–35.
314 "Big, strong, and dominating": EP #1892.
314 "So obviously stirred, upset": ibid.
315 "Lay down the mantle of my": cited Butcher 639.
315 "Might have altered the whole": Macmillan II 511.
316 "Thus were sown the seeds . . . generation": ibid.
316 "A most important operation in Greece": EP #1932.
316 "Scraped everything available": EP #1932 note 4.
317 "What I think is that we should": Fred Smith.
317 "There must be no room . . . supported": Most of the Eisenhower quotes in this paragraph are from DDE *Crusade* 287; the others are in Fred Smith.
318 "The center of strategy and the stake": de Gaulle *Unity* 291.
318 "Qualified to exercise the administration": cited ibid. 247.
319 "Without a trace of difficulty": ibid. 295.
319 "A group of individuals who call . . . Liberty": memorandum of de Gaulle talk with Forrestal Aug. 18, 1944, JF Mss., box 38.
319 "Rather premature arrival": EP #1896.
320 "To silence or set aside": de Gaulle *Unity* 291.
320 "To open the route to Paris": cited Gabriel Kolko 89.
320 "The conduct of operations is your": de Gaulle *Unity* 297.
321 "It looks now as if we'd be compelled": EP #1908.
321 "I rushed in there Sunday morning": EP #1925.
321 "The Allies transferred nothing because": de Gaulle *Unity* 319.
322 "Did not hide . . . dissatisfied": ibid.
322 "As a show of force . . . firmly": DDE *Crusade* 297.
322 "All in favor of maintaining order": EP #1988.
322 "So strong and so well armed that": ibid.
323 "Enemy resistance on the entire": EP #1933.
323 "In France, the German front has": cited Ehrman V 399–401.
323 "Militarily the war is won": cited Butcher 657.

323   "Make peace, you fools": cited Ehrman V 342–43.

324   "One can already foresee": ibid. 401–402.

324   "Eisenhower's new plan": cited Bryant II 262.

324   "A broad front strategy . . . a very lofty perch": Montgomery *Memoirs* 241.

325   "In the first place, I have always been": EP #1900.

326   "Exploit our success by . . . crossing": EP #1935.

326   "From the beginning of this campaign": EP #1936.

326   "Usual caution": ibid.

326   "This forced Patton, to the southeast": ibid.

326   "The most momentous error of the war": *N.Y. Times* Nov. 8, 1970.

326   Montgomery's censure: Montgomery *Memoirs* 255–56.

327   "We are stretched to the absolute limit": EP #1953.

327   "A fantastic idea . . . based merely on": ibid.

328   "Until after the development of Antwerp": SHAEF Planning Draft, May 30, 1944; cited Charles B. MacDonald "The Decision to Launch Operation MARKET-GARDEN" in Greenfield *Command Decisions* 439.

328   "Had not the capacity he needed . . . the use of Antwerp": Eden *Reckoning* 468–69.

328   "We will be opening the ports of Havre": EP #1935.

328   "Steady, Monty! You can't": Wilmot 488–89.

329   "Explained to Montgomery . . . our need": DDE *Crusade* 306.

329   "This point was . . . ever mentioned": Montgomery *Memoirs* 259.

329   "The need to gain the use of Antwerp": Tedder 590.

329   "Monty seems unimpressed by necessity": cited Summersby 169–70.

330   "I feel that Monty's strategy": cited Bryant II 291–92.

331   "We have succeeded even beyond": EP #1968.

331   "It is heavy going": EP #1994.

331   "We have facing us now one of our": EP #2023.

331   "I am quite sure that the Combined": EP #2063.

332   "A bloody revolution": cited Gabriel Kolko 97.

333   "To achieve success, the tactical battle": EP #1979 notes 1, 3.

333   "Marshall listened, but said little": Montgomery *Memoirs* 254.

333   "You will hear *no* more on the subject": ibid. 284.

333   "Eisenhower completely fails": cited Bryant II 334.

333   "He has never commanded anything": ibid.

333   "In view of the American preponderance": ibid. 335.

333   "The major effort must be directed": ibid. 337.

333   "Begin putting forward the above proposals": ibid. 339.

333   "There is no doubt he . . . to Ike myself": ibid. 343.

334   "Worried and ill at ease": ibid.

334   "We have . . . failed; and we": ibid. 344–45.

334   "We want no one else": ibid. 345.

334   "There can be no question of": EP #2154.

335   "I personally regard the whole thing": cited Bryant II 349.

335   "Did not want anybody": ibid. 346.

335   "Unfit to win the war": ibid.

335   "Accused Ike of violating principles": ibid. 352.

336   "We are getting fearfully stretched": EP #1993.

336   "More than a mere local attack": EP #2198.

337   "The present situation is to be regarded": DDE *Crusade* 350.

337   "Forty-eight hours": Strong 221.

337   "It was a difficult moment": ibid. 225.

337   "I'd question whether . . . to do": Bradley 476.

338   "Great confusion and . . . tight grip": cited Bryant II 358.

338   "Was glum and scarcely spoke": Strong 226.

338   "Well, Brad, those are my orders": ibid.

338   "He was very excited . . . before he finished": cited Bryant II 360.

339   "What made me really mad": Strong 226.

339   "By rushing out from his fixed": EP #2195.

340   "Essential . . . obtain from the Russians": EP #2190.

340   "Now that you have been placed": EP #2193.

340   "Like Christ come to cleanse": cited Bryant II 361.

340   "Resist this chance to tweak": Bradley 477–78.

340 "There were no reserves anywhere": cited Bryant II 361.
340 "Hodges is the quiet reticent type": EP #2194.
341 "To discuss the western front": EP #2201 note 1.
343 "[About the] articles in certain London": cited DDE *Crusade* 356.
343 "No longer work in essential harmony": de Guingand *Generals* 107.
343 "Since the Americans were the stronger . . . have to go": ibid. 109.
343 "I think we had better . . . too late": ibid. 108.
343 "Really tired and worried": ibid.
344 "Stunned . . . several other things which I": ibid. 108–109.
344 "What an incredibly lucky . . . disastrous": ibid. 109.
344 "I've just come from SHAEF": ibid. 111.
344 "Dear Ike . . . understand you are": ibid. 112.
345 "Of the serious reverse he had just": cited Bryant II 375.
345 "The battle in the west is very . . . as urgent": Churchill VI 278–79.
345 The weather is at present . . . our allies: cited ibid. 279.
346 "One major thrust . . . overwhelming strength": EP #2232 note 1.
346 "You may assure the Combined Chiefs": EP #2268.
346 "Strong enough . . . Goddammit it": Summersby 218–19 and Ambrose *Supreme Commander* 586.
347 "Double attack . . . might soon become": cited Bryant II 398.
348 "Hot dog, Courtney . . . his mind is up north": Bradley 511–13.
348 "Brad, that's wonderful . . . bridgehead": Butcher 768.
349 "I was consulted by Eisenhower . . . in the north": cited Bryant II 429n.
349 "Cutting off the Ruhr . . . history of warfare": George C. Marshall, *Biennial Report of the Chief of Staff, U.S. Army, to the Secretary of War* (1945). That year being exceptional, it was published by Simon and Schuster, 1945.
351 Question and answer: cited Butcher 707.
351 Question and answer: ibid. 784, 788.
351 Question and answer: ibid. 788.
352 "Never have I seen such wonderful": Summersby 226.
352 "Pretty stiff price to pay": Bradley 535.
353 "From all that had been previously": cited Bryant II 441.
353 "An almost static role": Churchill VI 461.
353 "A terrible mistake": cited Bryant II 447.
353 "Why should we not cross the Elbe": Churchill VI 463.
354 "Upset Eisenhower quite a bit": SHAEF diary, cited Ambrose *Supreme Commander* 637.
354 "My plan is simple and aims": EP #2378.
354 "I have not changed any plan": EP #2381.
354 "To expend military resources": DDE to Melvin Laird, Sept. 12, 1961; DDE-A; cited Gabriel Kolko 374.
354 "The importance of entering Berlin": Churchill VI 467.
355 "In all history there has never been": Warlimont 487–88.
355 "Our own initiative": Allen Dulles *Secret Surrender* 51.
356 "In this instance, the Soviet government": cited Churchill VI 442.
356 "Much upset, and seemed deeply stirred": ibid. 442–43.
356 "No political implications . . . between us": ibid. 447–48.
356 "In a state of almost violent unrest": EP #2061.
356 "The economic future of Europe": Pogue *Supreme Command* 439.
357 "Now we should begin . . . sound economic conditions": cited Forrestal 38–40.
357 "May I suggest that information": EP #2049.
358 "To testify at first hand about": DDE *Crusade* 409.
358 "Only our spearheads": EP #2416.
358n. "With some of Mr. Roosevelt's": ibid. 409–10.
359 "It would seem that the western allies": Churchill VI 515–16.
360 "To discuss action . . . occupation areas": cited Bryant II 450.
360 "Remarkable political advantages": cited Ambrose *Supreme Commander* 653.
360 "Personally and aside from all": ibid. 653–54.
361 "I shall *not* attempt any move": EP #2462.

FOUR

WILL HE? WON'T HE?

1. Military Governor

368   "Want it! He wants it so bad": Author's interview with Sir Ian Jacob.
369   "Thank the Lord that will not": R. Murphy 257.
370   "Silly . . . the most intelligent": *N.Y. Times* Sept. 20, 1945.
370   "Failure to grasp the realities": Clay 18.
370   "This thing was assembled": R. Murphy 281.
370   "The charge which was placed": Churchill VI 675.
371   "Might well put us in a position": cited Truman I 87.
371   "Master card . . . with such big stakes": Stimson diary May 15, 1945; cited Alperowitz *Atomic Diplomacy* 98.
371   "At the earliest possible moment": Churchill VI 559.
371   "Incredible pressure": Atomic Energy Commission, Oppenheimer hearings, 31; cited Alperowitz *Atomic Diplomacy* 101.
371   "Babies satisfactorily born": cited Churchill VI 637.
371   "Vivid detailed accounts . . . in the President's manner": R. Murphy 307, 306.
372   "If you insist on doing this or": cited Bryant II 478.
372   "Capable of eliminating all the Russian": ibid. 478.
372   "Delivery of the bomb . . . etc.": ibid.
372   "He never asked a question": cited Churchill VI 670.
373   "In such a way as to insure": DDE *Crusade* 442.
373   "That the total sum of reparations": Byrnes 29.
373   "A basis for discussion": ibid.
373   "In the termination of lend-lease": DDE *Crusade* 442.
373n. "Unfortunate and even brutal": cited Sherwood 894.
374   "Deprecated the Red Army's": DDE *Crusade* 442.
374   "Conscious of a feeling of depression": DDE *Mandate* 312.
374n. "Force is the only thing the Russians": Truman I 412.
375   "Merely personal and immediate": DDE *Crusade* 443.
375   "As horrible and destructive": ibid.
375   "Deeply perturbed . . . almost angrily": DDE *Mandate* 313.
375   "Special bomb . . . as soon as weather": Truman I 420.
375   "This is the greatest thing in history": ibid. 421.
375   "A common understanding and common": DDE *Crusade* 459.
376   "A genuine atmosphere of . . . benign and . . . spirit of amity": *N.Y. Times* Aug. 14, 1945.
376   "I see nothing . . . a few crackpots": ibid. Aug. 15.
377   "Before the atom bomb . . . insecure again": Snow 360–61.
377   "A joyous shout of approval": DDE *Crusade* 465.
377   "Mutual desire for friendship": Clay 49.
378   "During the months of August, September": DDE *Crusade* 444.
378   "There is widespread anxiety": cited Truman I 523.
378   "Our possession of the secret": ibid. 524.
378f. "About our relations . . . humanitarian purposes": Stimson and Bundy 642–46.
379   "His standing in the near future": Butcher 852.
380   "We appear to be treating": Harrison's report, quoted *N.Y. Times* Sept. 30, 1945.
380   "Opposition to the faithful execution": cited Farago 816.
381   "Lies . . . some so-called investigators . . . saw": DDE *Crusade* 440.
381   "To get the smell of shit": author's interview with Lichine; see also Ayer 248.
381   "Beloved naughty boy": author's interview with Lichine.
381   "No more revolutionary than the first": Ayer 246.
382   "I love war and responsibility and": cited Farago 797.

382 "Reactionaries! . . . Do you want a lot of . . . I don't know anything . . . The Nazi thing . . . election fight": *N.Y. Times* Sept. 23, 1945.
383 "It was the first time I ever": Summersby 278.
383 "Nothing to apologize for . . . camps . . . in splendid shape . . . few months ago": *N.Y. Times* Oct. 1, 1945.

2. Chief of Staff

385 "A political genius": Wills 118.
386 "The preservation of . . . way of life": Testimony, House Military Affairs Committee, Nov. 15, 1945.
386 "Let us name a couple . . . friendship with the United States": ibid.
387 "I am sure of . . . virtue out of necessity": ibid.
388 "Members of the Regular Army": Army Regulations 600–6b(1).
388 "I love that man . . . the sun rises": Cutler *Rest* 264.
389 "For whom there is no military need": *N.Y. Times* Jan. 10, 1946.
390 "Too much form and too little": DDE campaign speech, Baltimore, Sept. 1952.
390 "Which I believe is beyond the capacity": *N.Y. Times* Nov. 17, 1945.
390 "Which I believe is . . . its use could be based . . . would have authority . . . become impotent": Forrestal testimony, Senate Committee on Military Affairs; cited Rogow 217.
391 "I expect each of you": ibid. 284.
392 "It was exactly the kind of": Forrestal 136.
392 Text of telegram: Kennan I 547–559.
392 "Required reading for hundreds": ibid. 195.
392 "Moral support to the Russian cause": ibid. 133.
392 "Exactly like one of those primers": ibid. 294.
392 "Spoken in a conversational tone": *N.Y. Times* Feb. 10, 1946.
392 Text of Stalin's speech: ibid.
393 "The declaration of World War III": Forrestal 134–35.
393 Text of Churchill's speech: *N.Y. Times* March 6, 1946.
393 "Organized international cooperation": Treuenfels 85–86.
394 "I'm tired of babying": Truman I 552.
394 "Well, Mac . . . see you again": *N.Y. Times* May 11, 1946.
394 "Quick as dinner . . . for the presidency": DDE, author's interview, Aug. 1967.
395 "There is no possibility of my": *N.Y. Times* Sept. 29, 1946.
395 "I haven't the effrontery": ibid. July 5, 1947.
396 "A country place somewhere . . . my headquarters": DDE to Capt. Everett Hazlett, July 19, 1947; DDE-A.
397 "Money alone had no temptation": DDE *At Ease* 324.
397 "Don is collaborating with the": DDE to Joseph E. Davies, Dec. 31, 1947; DDE-A personal file.
397 "This had been common practice": DDE *At Ease* 326.
398 "Could you imagine me in such": DDE to Thomas Watson, April 2, 1948; in Eisenhower Project, Johns Hopkins University.
398 "Actually, it was General . . . who launched": Fred Smith.
400 "Were not impressed . . . heckling": Krock 283.
401 "Put the pressure . . . force of government": Fulton Lewis, Jr., cited Childs 104–105.
402 "A terrific popular pressure . . . than a miracle": DDE to Milton Eisenhower, Oct. 18, 1947; cited McCann 144.
402 "I still don't believe . . . realistic about it": McCann 147.
402 "Politics is a profession": DDE *At Ease* 335.
402 "I am not available for . . . tendered me": cited McCann 148–51.

406 "Both students and faculty might have": DDE *At Ease* 342.

406 "The general didn't . . . for me . . . tactical mistake . . . of the university": Frank D. Fackenthal interview, OHRO.

407 "I think I've said . . . I'm not so sure": *N.Y. Times* June 8, 1948.

407 "To a greater or less extent . . . people themselves": Goebel and Goebel 267–68.

409 "To pick the ablest and strongest": cited Phillips 210–11.

410 "No matter under what terms": *N.Y. Times* July 10, 1948.

412 "Must stand with absolute firmness . . . I have not identified . . . any political party": ibid. July 24.

413 "The news over the weekend . . . as is possible": DDE to Forrestal, Sept. 27, 1948; JF Mss.

413 "The current situation": ibid. Oct. 4, 1948.

413 "That was quite a day Tuesday": ibid. Nov. 5, 1948.

416 "The one place . . . be myself": DDE *At Ease* 340.

416 "Better suited to an ax handle": ibid. 341.

417 "Who says I can't?" "*I* say . . .": Henry Wriston interview, OHRO.

418 "The country's need for him": McCann to Bermingham, Mar. 30, 1949; DDE-A personal file.

419 "Apparently your hearing isn't": Henry Wriston interview, OHRO.

419n. "Whenever we needed a man": cited Kraft "School."

420 "Forceful and clear": DDE to Bermingham, Dec. 3, 1948; DDE-A personal file.

420 "The chief exponent of": ibid. Feb. 28, 1951.

420 "Handily used by the communists": Bermingham to DDE, April 14, 1951; ibid.

420 "Without any argument whatsoever": DDE to Bermingham, April 20, 1951; ibid.

422 "Tell me, Senator McCarthy": cited Rovere *McCarthy* 55.

422 "I have here in my hand . . . State Department": ibid. 124–25.

422 "Soft on communism": cited LaFeber 59.

422 "A lynching bee": cited Lilienthal II 166.

422 "General Eisenhower pushed . . . count on me": ibid. 170.

424 "Within the last few weeks": Forrestal 387.

424 "I decry loose and sometimes": cited Fleming 398.

424 "Totally anti-Soviet and": Vandenberg 485.

424 "An armed attack against": NATO Pact, cited LaFeber 76–77.

425 "Going to be expected . . . No": Acheson 285.

425 "We are very clear": cited LaFeber 77.

425 "Sole means": Beaufre 24.

425 "Bradley's reply was favorable": ibid. 25.

425 "Not believe in the reality of": Kennan I 464, 410.

426 "With great regret": cited Acheson 286.

426 "I felt it was contrary": Taft 89.

426 "Incredible mismanagement": *N.Y. Times* May 23, 1949.

426 "Potentially subversive or": Lilienthal II 531.

426 "There was not much time": Acheson 316.

427 "Shocked . . . our . . . one of the best-informed": Lilienthal II 543–48.

427 "American people . . . opposed to giving away . . . we stand alone": ibid. 547–48.

427 "Do I have to begin . . . alone in this world": ibid.

427 "I'm just a soldier . . . giving away": ibid. 550–51.

428 "I never realized what a lot of": ibid. 552.

428 "To other nations whose increased": cited Phillips 269.

428 "To build up our own military": memorandum of Foreign Assistance Coordinating Committee, June 22, 1949; cited LaFeber 78.

428 "It's almost unbelievable . . . warlord of the earth": Vandenberg 503–504.

428 "We have evidence that within": Truman II 307.

429f. "In part on the opinions . . . repudiation of the American doctrine": All quotes are from a seven-page report comprising two memoranda, both in Roberts folder, DDE-A personal file. Letter to author from Clifford Roberts, Oct. 22, 1971; affirmed authorship.

430 "The growing tendency of everyone": DDE to Baruch, June 8, 1949; BB Mss.

431 "The central problem . . . encroaching state": Baruch to DDE, June 22, 1949; ibid.

431 "Middle way . . . than we now have": speech to American Bar Association, Sept. 5, 1949; cited DDE *Mandate* 11–12.

431 "Could not imagine . . . majority of our people": same speech, cited by McCann 181–82.

432 "I enjoyed so much . . . as are my friends": Thomas E. Dewey to DDE, Dec. 23, 1949; DDE-A Personal File.

432 "You ain't learnin' nothin' ' ": cited Bainbridge 223.

432 "An intellectual is a man who": cited Goldman 291.

433 "A huge success": DDE to Burnham, Jan. 16, 1950; DDE-A Personal File.

433 "We must still make a tough": Bermingham to DDE, Feb. 7, 1950; ibid.

433 "For his sake . . . I hope he never": Burnham to DDE, April 19, 1950; ibid.

434 "Made a point of seeking out": Sulzberger *Candles* 649.

434 "A dozen gold-plated": Cutler *Rest* 264.

434 "Those paternalistic and collectivistic": from a letter sent over DDE's signature to dozens of prominent citizens in 1950; DDE-A Personal File.

434 "There is again much talk of . . . little about him, really": Rovere *Affairs of State* 3, 6. The piece from which the quote is taken first appeared in *Harper's* May 1950.

434 "Surprise attack": Department of State, Publication 3922, Far Eastern Series 34, July 20, 1950, iii.

435 "Alleged 'surprise' of the North Korean": Willoughby "The Truth About Korea," *Cosmopolitan* Dec. 1951; cited Stone *Hidden History* 60.

435 "We must answer communist lies": DDE to Burnham, Aug. 21, 1950; DDE-A Personal File.

435 "Meet with a group of distinguished": DDE to Baruch, Sept. 16, 1950; BB Mss.

435 "I've never heard any public figure": Henry Wriston interview, OHRO.

436 "There is no discussion of . . . revalued it": Acheson 436.

436 "I do believe the defense . . . and sailors": cited ibid.

436 "Single package": Lawrence W. Martin, "The American Decision to Rearm Germany," in Stein 645–660.

437 "Had passed beyond the peculiar": Acheson 441.

437 "As the logical man": Truman II 257.

437 "Special military assignment": Roberts to DDE, Oct. 21, 1950; DDE-A Personal File.

438 "First time you are in town": Truman II 257.

438 "Kevin, you may query": Bermingham to McCann, Nov. 9, 1950; DDE-A Personal File.

438 "Second-class status" . . . "In principle": Acheson 458–59.

439 "The very worst news we had": DDE to Bermingham, Dec. 12, 1950; DDE-A Personal File.

440 "I don't think you're . . . I'm not happy": Henry Wriston interview, OHRO.

440 "Why not do . . . distinguished group here": ibid.

441 "A means and a vehicle . . . visible leader": Acheson 493–94.

441 "Flat refusal to contemplate": DDE *Mandate* 13.

441 "An assault by the bipartisan": Acheson 491.

442 "The debates . . . had even more to do . . . that decision.": Taft 21–22.

442 "The President's constitutional right": DDE *Mandate* 13.

442 "Could send troops to Tibet": Taft 33.

442 "Thought the President's rights . . . aggression": DDE *Mandate* 13.

443 "Cutting the President": ibid. 13–14.

443 "Your unofficial 'eyes and ears' ": Burnham to DDE, Dec. 27, 1950; DDE-A Personal File.

443 "To be starred by the Air Force": memorandum of telephone call, Burnham to Schulz, in Burnham folder, ibid.

443 "Biased . . . frank": Burnham to Eisenhower, Feb. 23, 1951; DDE-A Personal File.

443 "Localized in the . . . belt": ibid.

443 *"Are being dictated by"*: ibid.

444 "My acceptance of . . . domestic ones . . . I would say this . . . will have failed": DDE to Bermingham, Feb. 28, 1951; DDE-A Personal File.

444 "Softened them considerably": Bermingham to DDE, April 14, 1951; ibid.

445 "Our homes, our nation, all the things": Truman speech; cited Halle 241.

445 "The power to attack our cities": ibid.

446 "An integration of forces": DDE *Mandate* 15.

446n. DDE letter to Bermingham, Feb. 28, 1951; DDE-A Personal File.

448 "Luxury apartments . . . the wealth [they] enjoy": cited McCann 217.

448 "Front man for traitors . . . appeasers": 96 *Congressional Record,* 81st Congress, 2nd Session, 14914–7.

449 "Come in to town . . . out here": Mary Ellen Murphy interview with Mrs. Persons, July 1952.

449 "A means and a vehicle": Acheson 493.

450 "I can never be . . . something else": *N.Y. Times* Jan. 22, 1949.

450n. "For the first time": DDE *Mandate* 18.

451 "On a plan for the realignment": Bermingham to DDE, May 4, 1951; DDE-A Personal File.

452 "Unless the . . . Party definitely": Bermingham to DDE, July 1951 (undated); ibid.

452 "Would not be available": Bermingham to DDE, Sept. 9, 1951; ibid.

452 "No faction, group or": DDE to Bermingham, Sept. 24, 1951; ibid.

453 "I do not mind telling you": DDE to Milton Eisenhower, May 30, 1951; Eisenhower Project, Johns Hopkins University.

453 "I can say positively": Milton Eisenhower to DDE, June 18, 1951; ibid.

453 "Please quit worrying": DDE to Milton Eisenhower, Sept. 20, 1951; ibid.

453 "Closest and most trusted," "any personal sacrifice": Milton Eisenhower to DDE, Oct. 20, 1951; ibid.

455n. "I am confident": Stassen to DDE, Dec. 15, 1951; DDE-A Personal File.

456 "I've just turned down forty": Theodore Achilles interview, DOHC.

456 "He does *not* . . . nominate him": Sulzberger *Candles* 700–705.

456 "After I made my . . . kiss me": Richardson to DDE, Dec. 1, 1951; DDE-A Personal File.

457 "Dependable . . . of Washington": cablegram, Roberts and Robinson to DDE, Dec. 18, 1951; ibid.

457 "So remote as to be": DDE *Mandate* 19.

457 "An accurate account . . . respect to me": *N.Y. Times* Jan. 8, 1952.

458 "Those who are . . . abandoned": DDE to Bermingham, Jan. 7, 1952, DDE-A Personal File.

458f. Based on Lucius Clay interview, OHRO.

459 "A definite loss . . . they are right": DDE to Roberts, Feb. 19, 1952; DDE-A Personal File.

460 "I'll talk to you": Roberts to DDE, Feb. 19, 1952; ibid.

460 "The thing that . . . full of politics": Lippmann to Swope, Mar. 27, 1952 (in Wilton Persons folder); ibid.

461 "Tidelands grab is one . . . oil industry": Porter to DDE, Mar. 24, 1952; ibid.

461 "I agree with the principle": DDE to Porter, Mar. 28, 1952; ibid.

461 "Vague and foggy": Sulzberger *Candles* 742.

461 "It seems necessary to walk": DDE to Milton Eisenhower, April 4, 1952; Eisenhower Project, Johns Hopkins University.

462 "That there was no way to solve": cited Rovere *Affairs of State* 59.

462 "To find ways whereby": ibid.

463 "Only hysteria entertains": ibid. 58.

463 "Political aggression . . . 'retaliation' falls down": DDE to J. F. Dulles, April 15, 1952; DDE-A Personal File.

464 "The most interesting . . . unqualified 'proxy' ": Dulles to DDE, May 20, 1952; ibid.

464 "Because . . . work with him": Drummond and Coblentz 165; see also DDE *Mandate* 142.

465 "For the consequences": Eden *Full Circle* 64.

465 "Be yourself . . . be yourself": Roy Roberts to DDE, May 5, 1952; DDE-A Personal File.

466   "If that's all it is . . . lucky": Childs 134.
467   "Had no burning . . . Republican doctrine": DDE *Mandate* 34, 35.
468   "A bankrupt America is": ibid. 37.
468   "A clean slate on which": Childs 145.
468   "Straight-out issue of": cited Pusey 19.
468n.   "The presentation you make": DDE to Porter, Feb. 20, 1952; DDE-A Personal File.
468n.   "The worst of all wrong": Odlum to DDE, Feb. 20, 1952; ibid.
468n.   "In essence I have believed": DDE to Odlum, Feb. 29, 1952; ibid.
469   THE REPUBLICAN PARTY WILL WIN: Cutler *Rest* 270.
469   THOU SHALT NOT STEAL: W. S. White 177.
469   "Swell": ibid. 176.
469   "Phewey on Eisenhewey": cited Rovere *Affairs of State* 24.
470   "There was little reason": David and others 53.
470   "Running for . . . some months ago": Sulzberger *Candles* 768.
471   "Wisconsin's fighting marine . . . exposing the traitors": cited Rovere *McCarthy* 180.
471n.   Based on Arthur Gray interview, OHRO.
472   "No one could disagree": Edward Thye interview, OHRO.
473   "A conspiracy so immense": cited Goldman 213.
473   "Sell his grandmother": cited Rovere *McCarthy* 178–79.
473   "Are you pleased . . . a fine Vice President": ibid. 181.
474   "Crusade for freedom": DDE acceptance speech, *N.Y. Times* July 12, 1952.
475   "A crusade to exterminate": Adlai Stevenson acceptance speech, *N.Y. Times* July 27, 1952.
475   "The great problem of America": cited Goldman 220.
475   "Those who favor what has": ibid. 223.
475   "General, what do you think": Kempton.
475   Never lose your temper: Adams 22.
475   "A perfect example of": Kempton.
476   "Until Bob Taft blows": cited Goldman 221.
476f.   "General Eisenhower's chances . . . *running for President*": cited W. S. White 186–87.
477   "Ike is running like a dry": *N.Y. World-Telegram and Sun* Aug. 25, 1952.
477   "Right after Labor Day": DDE *Mandate* 55.
477   "All they talked about": Adams 20.
478   "Faith in God and country": cited W. L. Miller 19.
478   "What's happened to Ike": See, for example, Joseph C. Harsch.
478   "From top to bottom": DDE speech Sept. 9, 1952; FonF XII 288.
479   "In full agreement . . . differences of degree": W. S. White 187–91.
479   "It looks as if Taft lost": FonF XII 296.
480   "In the electorate as a whole": Campbell and others 60.
481   "We never comment on a": Mazo 101.
481n.   "A labor union is a special": cited Richard Donovan.
482   "Staggered and shaken": Hughes 38.
482   "Let's find out the facts": Cutler *Rest* 284.
482   "I suggest immediate publication": cited Cutler *Rest* 285.
482   "Our train schedules": ibid.
482   "Ill-advised . . . fairness of mind": *N.Y. Herald Tribune* Sept. 20, 1952.
483   "Do you consider . . . hound's tooth": Mazo 107–108.
484   "Imperative . . . best wishes": cited ibid. 108–109.
484   "If you stay on . . . agree with me": Nixon 99.
484   "Hello, General . . . is the indecision": ibid. 99–100.
484   "Even as a candidate . . . receives . . . commanding general": ibid. 76.
485   "My side of the story": Stewart Alsop 62–63.
485   "Those people around you": ibid. 63.
485   "General, the great trouble here": ibid.
485n.   "Piss": Wills 104.

486 "We have got to get": Mazo 113.
486 "Humphreys . . . worked on that one": Charles Halleck interview, OHRO.
486 "There has just been a meeting . . . going to do": Nixon 110.
487 "Sherm, if you want to know": Mazo 113.
487 "A slick production . . . genre of weepers": *Variety* Sept. 24, 1952.
487 "I would suggest that . . . all the people": cited Wills 108.
488 "And now, finally, I know . . . abide by it": Nixon 117.
488 "Well, Arthur, you sure got your": DDE *Mandate* 68.
488 "We want Nixon! We": Goldman 230 and Mazo 119.
488 "Ben, tonight will make history": Teletype, Barton to Duffy, Barton Papers, Wisconsin State Historical Society.
489 "I have seen many brave men": cited Goldman 230.
489 "It is obvious . . . Vice President?" cited Wills 111.
489 "While technically . . . West Virginia": ibid. 112.
489 "Will be in Washington . . . any time thereafter": Mazo 120.
490 "You're my boy": ibid. 121.
490 "Later on": FonF XII 312, 330.
490 "To assure a high level": Hughes 33.
490 "I shall go to Korea": *N.Y. Times* Oct. 25, 1952.
490 VOICE: Mr. Eisenhower, what about . . . It's *really* time for a change: cited W. L. Miller 60–61; see also Charles Boswell, unpublished MS biography of Ben Duffy, 341.
491 "Why, this fellow don't know": cited Rovere *Affairs of State* 72.
491 "Outcome Highly Uncertain": *N.Y. Times* Nov. 3, 1952.
494 "With my understanding": Adams 89.
494 "Lucius, why in the devil": Pusey 54; and Lucius Clay interview, OHRO.
494n. "With my long diplomatic": Schulz to author, Feb. 11, 1969.
495 "Well, George, I see": Childs 167 and Pusey 55.
495 "If anyone talks to you": Childs 167; and see Goldman 241.
495 "The Federal Reserve Bank and": Rovere *Affairs of State* 41.
495 "Can be completely or fully": DDE *Mandate* 28.
496 "Between one-third and one-half": Truman II 519.
496 "Unsmiling . . . tense": ibid. 514.
496 "Seemed embarrassed and": Acheson 706.
496 "Frozen . . . in the heat . . . true facts": Truman II 521.
496 "Partisan political . . . never understand . . . political advantage": ibid. 501.
496 "If you still desire": ibid. 505.
497 "Incredible!": DDE *Mandate* 91.
497n. "We've got to deal with spiritual . . . distinct asset": Benson 12.
498 "In view of the strength": DDE *Mandate* 94–95.
498 *"The future stability"*: cited Gunther *MacArthur* 169.
498 "Aggressive, resolute, and dynamic": MacArthur, *N.Y. Times* Aug. 29, 1950; cited Fleming 612.
498 "At this time—December 1952—it": DDE *Mandate* 95.
499 "A clear and definite solution": cited R. J. Donovan 19.
499 "Looking forward . . . and experience": ibid. 20.
500 "The epic mid-Pacific . . . throughout the world": cited Hughes 49, 50.
500 "Extremely useful . . . modify his views": DDE *Mandate* 96.
500 "We face an enemy": ibid. 97.
500 "The trouble with Eisenhower": Edmund G. Love to author.
501 "I think it is wonderful . . . the flag pretty high": R. J. Donovan 3.
501 "Because here is this thing": ibid.
502 "The fellow plowing": ibid. 9.
502 "You flew the flag": ibid.
502 "Humbled, awed": Hughes 53.
503 "In clean-cut fashion and on his": EP #1256.
505 "Standing for all religious . . . dental exhibit": *Episcopal Church News,* cited W. L. Miller 43–44.
505n. "Through his personal conduct": Elson 48, cited W. L. Miller 19.
506 "A deep and abiding religious": DDE speech, Dec. 3, 1946; cited Kornitzer 143.
506 "A political expression of": DDE speech, 1948; ibid.
506 "A *deeply felt* religion": DDE speech, cited W. L. Miller 19.
506 "Spiritual values": DDE speech, June 1952; ibid. 33.
506 "The Almighty takes a definite": ibid. 34.

506   "Spiritual weapons . . . or in war": ibid. 45.
506   "Religion was one of the thoughts": DDE *Mandate* 100.
506   "Were not getting too secular": ibid.
506   "Almighty God, as we stand here": PPs 1953, 1.
506   "We sense with all our . . . the dark": ibid. 1–4.

FIVE

COLD WARRIOR

1. New President: Old Problems

512   "Did not look upon . . . luxurious patronage": DDE to Emmet Hughes, Dec. 10, 1953; DDE-G.
512   "Cumbersome": private DDE memorandum, Jan. 18, 1954, in personal diary; DDE-G.
513   "I don't think our readers": cited Anderson 180.
513   "Far from being as important": personal diary Jan. 18, 1954; DDE-G.
514   "We will merchandise the hell": cited Neustadt 98.
514   "Eisenhower & Co. have opened": cited W. L. Miller 69.
514   "To 'sell' the President's policies": ibid.
514   "We all suddenly realized": ibid. 71.
514   "One of our best shows": ibid. 69.
514   "Undoubtedly the most effective": Bill Tyler in *Advertising Agency,* ibid. 70–71.
515   "The relationship between military": DDE *Mandate* 446.
515   "An irreconcilable conflict": U.S. Congress, Senate Committee on Foreign Relations, 83d Congress, 1st Session, Nomination of John Foster Dulles, Secretary of State-designate, Jan. 15, 1953, 11.
516   "Would seriously endanger . . . prudence": Huntington *Common Defense* 70–71.
516   "A backward civilization": DDE to William H. Draper, Jr., Mar. 16, 1953; DDE-G.
516   "The one primary thing": R. J. Donovan 109; and DDE-G, Staff Notes 1953 folder.
518   "To interpret, publicly, their Far Eastern": DDE *Mandate* 109.
518   "Politically and militarily": ibid.
519   "In this light it is understandable . . . Oil Company": Nirumand 46–47.
520   "Into this state of affairs . . . iron bedstead": Eden *Full Circle* 193, 198.
520   "A semi-invalid . . . mobs of followers": DDE *Mandate* 159.
520   "A very valuable British asset": Eden *Full Circle* 201.
520n.   "British government, supported by": DDE *Mandate* 159–60.
521   "The free world knows the Iranians": *N.Y. Times* Aug. 29, 1952; cited Nirumand 71.
521   Italicized quotes are from the Koran, in seriatim: Sûrah I, 1–2, Sûrah II, 9, 10, 11–12.
521   "A toleration of men who take": DDE speech, San Antonio, Texas, Oct. 14, 1952.
522   "Reasonable doubt . . . loyalty . . . of national security": R. J. Donovan 286.
522   "Close this gap": DDE *Mandate* 308.
522   "I have a document here": Rovere *McCarthy* 167–68.
522   "I look forward to working closely": DDE to McCarthy, Nov. 12, 1952; DDE-G.
522   "Very helpful and constructive": FonF XIII 83.
522   "Any disclosures resulting . . . loyal and secure": ibid.
523   "To clean out the State Department": Des Moines (Iowa) *Sunday Register* Mar. 15, 1953; cited Halle 273.
523   "For approximately a year . . . in large measure, wrecked": Halle 273.
525   "I consider your crime . . . according to law": cited Schneir 170–71.
525   "That wasn't usable . . . ring in the country": cited Hughes 80.
525   "[Their] crime . . . far exceeds . . . set aside the verdict": PPs 1953, 40–41.
525   "My only concern is in": cited Hughes 80.
526   "The known convictions of Communist": DDE to Miller, June 10, 1953; DDE-G.
526   "From here on the Soviets": DDE to John S. D. Eisenhower, June 16, 1953; cited DDE *Mandate* 225.
527   "Keep them out of everybody's hair": Cutler *Rest* 309.

527   "Sounds to me like a . . . good one": ibid.
527   "From the outbreak of the Spanish": Handlin.
527   "McCarthy runs McLeod and": cited R. J. Donovan 171.
527   "Either very stupid or very": DDE memo to Brownell, Nov. 4, 1953; DDE-G.
527   "Any American could have been . . . fighting Communism to the death": ibid.
528   "Clearly consistent with . . . national security . . . sensitive . . . Any behavior,
       activities . . . reliable or trustworthy": For a discussion of Executive Order 10450
       and its effect on employment practices, see Brown, especially chapter 2.
529   "A world environment . . . A German victory . . . our own national interests":
       Wanamaker 11.
529   "The *national interest* may be defined . . . its security and well-being": Brookings
       Institution 399–401.
529   "We cannot go through another ten years": Acheson, Hearings before the special
       subcommittee on Post-War Economic Policy and Planning, H.R., 78th Congress,
       2nd session; cited Williams 235–36.
530   "We know . . . that we are linked . . . distant lands": PPs 1953, 4.
530   "A frank recognition that totalitarian": Truman, address to the Congress, March
       12, 1947; cited Jones 272.
530   "I believe that it must . . . outside pressures": ibid.
530n. "Thus, our search for profits": speech, John Lockton, April 22, 1964: cited Magdoff
       196.
530n. "I suggest we will perceive": speech, Fred J. Borch, Nov. 9, 1964; ibid.
531   "In the early summer of 1952": Neustadt 9.
531   "I sit here all day, trying to persuade": ibid. 9–10.
532   "Now, look . . . I happen to *know*": Hughes 124.
532   "Their votes providing the margin": *Congressional Quarterly Almanac;* cited
       R. J. Donovan 151.
533   "Scrubbing the administrative": Adams 75.
533   "I need somebody to be my": ibid. 1.
533   "Implied rather than stated": ibid. 50.
533   "Eisenhower simply expected me": ibid.
535   "More and more, we find that": notes of legislative leaders' meeting, April 23,
       1953; DDE-G.
535   "Too largely attended . . . a knowing look . . . clam up . . . more than a certain":
       Cutler *Rest* 298.
536   "Too sensitive for more general": ibid. 306.
537   "I cannot conceive of": hearings on Wilson's nomination before Senate Armed
       Services Committee, cited R. J. Donovan 25.
537   "I really feel you are giving me": cited DDE *Mandate* 110.
537   "It's all over. The issue": Leverett Saltonstall interview, OHRO.
538   "Going is rough": DDE-A, Official File.
538   "We will never get": ibid.
538   "Business failures, political hacks": DDE diary; cited *Mandate* 111.
538   "Treated as suspect characters": Charles Bohlen interview, DOHC.
539   "The play of the marketplace": cited Rovere *Affairs of State* 124.
539   "Of failure to achieve a meeting": DDE *Mandate* 199.
539   "Was an experiment doomed": Adams 62.
539   "An ordeal": ibid. 57.
539   "He had a responsibility": ibid. 303.
540   "It seemed to me": DDE *Mandate* 198.
540   "Good will and virtuous": Hughes 160.
540   "Fairly glowed": DDE to Hughes, Dec. 10, 1953, in DDE diary, Dec. 1953;
       DDE-G.
541n. "My first full day": cited DDE *Mandate* 112.
542   "A President who doesn't know": cited Patrick Anderson 135.
542   "Anybody who had legitimate business": ibid. 153.
542   "Civilian side . . . insecurity affairs": Andrew Goodpaster interview, OHRO.
544   "Today the President wanted": DDE diary, Feb. 7, 1953; DDE-G.
544   "Mamie wants her soldier boy . . . at night": Knebel 57.
544   "Without a moment's hesitation . . . slightly worse": DDE *Waging Peace* 431.
       SHAEF's G–3 in 1945: Pearson and Anderson 432–33.
545   "Not completely convenient . . . a detail or two": DDE *At Ease* 359.
546   "American citizens . . . general conditions": DDE-A, Official File 101–B-1.

547   "The President is not a devious man": Rovere *Affairs of State* 342.
547   "He was a far more complex and devious": Nixon 161.
547   "The United States never lost a soldier": Patrick Anderson 179.
547   "Subject to misinterpretation": DDE *Mandate* 104.

2. *Education in Crisis*

549   "Area which the Russian . . . you can count on us": Dulles speech, Jan. 27, 1953; much of it cited Halle 233–34, much in FonF XIII 25.
550   "Uncompromising": DDE *Mandate* 195.
550n. "She might get away": DDE memo to J. F. Dulles, Mar. 3, 1953, DDE diary; DDE-G.
552   "Any logic or sense": PPs 1953, 17.
552n. "Because fundamentally . . . have suggested": Robert R. Bowie interview, OHRO.
554   "Deep feeling concerning . . . General Marshall": DDE *Mandate* 318.
555   "I will not get in the gutter": R. J. Donovan 249.
555n. "This occasioned the sharpest": DDE *Mandate* 317.
556   "Security risk . . . too weak": cited R. J. Donovan 88.
556   "Under oath . . . completely untrue": ibid. 87.
556n. "Why have they got my cousin": Merson 3B; abridged from *The Reporter* Oct. 7, 1954.
556n. "I couldn't stand another": Charles Bohlen interview, DOHC.
557   "In the national interest": Rovere *McCarthy* 34.
558   "Socialism by treaty": cited DDE *Mandate* 278.
558   "Power to regulate . . . etc.": Bricker Amendment, ibid. 594.
559   "Notably . . . U.S. troops abroad": cited Adams 105.
559   "Treaty law can . . . Bill of Rights": cited DDE *Mandate* 279–80.
559   "A damn thorn": cited Hughes 142.
559   "A head-on collision": ibid. 143.
560   "Something big in public": ibid.
560   "We just have to make up . . . told anybody else": cited Hughes 144, including note.
560   "Crisis . . . abdication . . . usurpation": Lippmann; cited Goldman 258.
560   "To save the United States": cited Adams 108.
560   "Brick by brick by Bricker": cited R. J. Donovan 241.
560   "I am unalterably opposed": ibid. 239.
561   "A dangerous tendency": ibid. 242.
561   "Because all my people": cited Hughes 144.
562   "To join in an appropriate": PPs 1953, 13–14.
562   "Repudiate all . . . secret": Republican platform 1952; cited R. J. Donovan 47.
562   "Subjugated to . . . aggressive despotism": FonF XIII 59.
562   "A little indigestion": notes of legislative leaders' meeting, Feb. 16, 1953; DDE-G.
563   "Before the country and the world": cited Evans and Novak 66.
563   "Well, what do you think": Cutler *Rest* 321.
564   "All the people of the USSR": PPs 1953, 75.
564   "At the present time there is no": cited LaFeber 144.
565   "Nothing that has happened": Dulles news conference, April 3, 1953; cited FonF XIII 105, 81.
565   "Nothing but a pipedream": Adenauer *Memoirs;* cited Kolko and Kolko 689.
565   "The excitement of the man": Hughes 104.
565   "The ambushes of policy debate": ibid. 107.
566   "We must be prepared": Hearing, U.S. Senate Committee on Foreign Relations, April 9, 1953.
566   "Drastic in tone and extreme": DDE *Mandate* 182.
567   "Thousands of prisoners . . . honorable . . . free and united . . . freedom and peace": PPs 1953, 184–88.
567   "Preliminary demands . . . of the UN": FonF XIII 130.
568   "In accordance with the stipulations": ibid. 97.
568   "Reluctance": ibid. 114.
568   "There can be no real peace": PPs 1953, 201.

568 "The carefully planned and prepared . . . in Indochina": JFD Mss., box 475.
568n. "A struggle in which": JFD Mss., box 475.
569 "Should be flatly rejected": DDE *Mandate* 183.
569 "I would say . . . worthy of the name": Senate Committee on Armed Services, hearing on the military situation in the Far East, 3075; cited Kolko and Kolko 616.
569 Twenty-seven miles of valley farmland: see Bibliography, anonymous entry, "Attack on Irrigation Dams" 40.
569 "From Washington . . . to carry on the war": Mark Clark *Danube* 267.
570 "If there is not at the summit of nations": FonF XIII 150.
570 "Alarm and almost indignation": Macmillan III, 511.
570 "A Far Eastern Munich": FonF XIII 150.
570 "High purpose . . . positive results": ibid.
570 "I see nothing that you could": PPs 1953, 285.
571 "Reunification . . . fully": FonF XIII 99.
572 "On both sides of the question": DDE *Mandate* 168.
572n. "The workers' paradise . . . revolt": PPs 1953, 463.
573 "To develop common viewpoints": PPs 1953, 326.
573 "Sortie honorable": Navarre *Agonie de l'Indochine* 3; cited Fontaine II, 102.
574 "It looks as if Europe was": Macmillan III, 513.
574 "Ignominious bartering with": Republican platform 1952.
575 "Without further screening or": Mark Clark *Danube* 265.
575 "Freedom-loving people throughout": FonF XIII 201.
575 "Immediately and unequivocally": DDE *Mandate* 186.
576 "The maddening part": Mark Clark *Danube* 288.
576 "Is this a truce": cited R. J. Donovan 126.
576 "My fellow citizens . . . world at peace": PPs 1953, 520–22.
577 "He'll sit here": Neustadt 9.
577 "Mainly to discuss economic": Eden *Full Circle* 211.
578 "Said little, as is usual": ibid. 252.
578 "Was still a Great Power": Macmillan III, 140.
578 "More forbidding": Eden *Full Circle* 226.
578n. "It is difficult": Macmillan III, 349.
579 "Extremely worried about": Eden to Churchill; cited Eden *Full Circle* 212.
579 "Less compromised . . . only hope . . . communist Iran": ibid.
579 "Deft and ingenious": Eden *Full Circle* 213.
579 "Alternatives to Musaddiq": ibid.
579 "The difficulty of this situation": Eden to Churchill; cited Eden *Full Circle* 213.
579 "A desire to reach a quick . . . and apparent disinclination": Eden *Full Circle* 256.
579n. "Constitutional monarch": DDE *Mandate* 161.
580 "In contrast to Dulles": Eden to Churchill; cited Eden *Full Circle* 249.
580 "The President could not": Eden *Full Circle* 250.
581 Gold revolver DDE diary, May 26, 1953; DDE-G.
581 "British position . . . rapidly . . . may be true": Dulles memorandum, "Conclusion on Trip," JFD Mss., box 475.
582 "The Americans were properly reluctant": Eden *Full Circle* 202.
583 "We are of course grateful . . . present dangerous situation of Iran": PPs 1953, note to #129, 485–86.
584 "Reasonable agreement . . . resumed": PPs 1953, 483.
584 "Place the question of dissolution": Nirumand 82.
584 "Iran is in a . . . blocked now": PPs 1953, 541.
584 "Just to see old friends": Wise and Ross *Invisible Government* 112.
584n. "Totally paralyzed by": Nirumand 87.
585 "Grave danger threatens": *Teheran Daily News* Aug. 9, 1953; cited Nirumand 84–85.
585 "Absolutely mad . . . moving about him": Henderson cable, Aug. 17, 1953; DDE-G, Iran folder.
585 "Have to snuggle up to Mosadeq": Smith memorandum to DDE; ibid.
586 "When this crisis came on . . . be in power": Hearings on the Mutual Security Act of 1954 before the House Committee on Foreign Affairs, 83d Congress, 2nd Session, 503, 569–70; cited Engler 206.
586 "A lumpenproletarian mob, armed": Nirumand 87.
586 "Check No. 703,352 of the Melli Iran Bank": *Le Monde* Sept. 17, 1953; cited Nirumand 87.

586 "Worth your reading": C. P. Cabell to DDE, Aug. 21, 1953; DDE-G.
586 "The Shah is a new man . . . foreign power": CIA memo; DDE-G.
587 "Sympathetic consideration": PPs 1953, 580–81.
587 "The things we did . . . an historical fact": DDE personal diary, Oct. 8, 1953; DDE-G.
587 "For the first time in three years": DDE *Mandate* 166.
589 "Philosophy on this subject. I believe": ibid. 234.
590 "I believe with all my heart": PPs 1953, 30.
590 "Nothing available": Morrow 12.
590 "A threat that the President's": E. Frederic Morrow interview, OHRO.
591 "Our games at that time": Kornitzer 253.
591 "I find myself living in a comfortable": EP #850.
591 "Most dangerous . . . in regard to negro": Ambrose *Supreme Commander* 560.
591 "Run counter to regs": ibid.
591n. "The White House is a little": Morrow 275.
592 "If you make a complete amalgamation": Hearings before the Senate Committee on Armed Services, 80th Congress, 2nd Session, 996.
592 "The hour has arrived": cited R. J. Donovan 156.
592n. Morrow interview with author. See also Morrow interview, OHRO.
593 "Nonconventional . . . mutual withdrawals": DDE memo to J. F. Dulles, Sept. 8, 1963, in DDE diary; DDE-G.
594 "We have used the power": PPs 1953, 556.
594 "Relatively little has been done": cited R. J. Donovan 154.
594 "Mr. President, someday . . . We'll see": ibid.
595 "No man is discharging": DDE to Nixon, in DDE diary; DDE-G.
596 "From the very beginning . . . law work": DDE to Edgar Eisenhower, Oct. 1953, in DDE diary; DDE-G.
596 "Very definitely a liberal-conservative": DDE to Milton Eisenhower, Oct. 9, 1953, in DDE diary; DDE-G.
596 "No possibility of charging": DDE personal diary, October 8, 1953; DDE-G.
597 "I congratulate the nation": DDE to Warren, Mar. 23, 1954; DDE-A.
597 "In a firm, clear voice . . . of the laws": Stone *Fifties* 61. Supreme Court opinion cited by Stone.
598 "The biggest damfool mistake": cited Fred Rodell, *N.Y. Times Magazine* July 28, 1968, and by Stephen Ambrose to author in a report of Ambrose interview with DDE.
598 "The Supreme Court has spoken": PPs 1954, 491.

3. Exacerbation of Crisis

599 "Now, the knowledge that they": PPs 1953, 617.
600 "We were all working in the dark": Merson.
600 "Don't join the book burners": PPs 1953, 415.
600 "I just do not believe": PPs 1953, 427.
600 "Largest single group supporting": Matthews.
601 "One thousand four hundred and": FonF XIII 394.
601 "I have lost skirmishes before": PPs 1953, 738.
602 "Harry Dexter White was a": cited R. J. Donovan 178–79.
603 "At 9:15 the next morning": Phone call from DDE to Brownell: DDE-G, folder marked Phone Calls, July–December 1953; Nov. 11, 1953.
604 All quoted remarks on page 603 and through "[*Laughter*]" on page 604 are from PPs 1953, 757–65.
604 "I should like to make clear": ibid. 781.
605 "Own exhaustively considered opinion": In the Matter of J. Robert Oppenheimer: Transcript of Hearing Before Personnel Security Board, Washington, April 12, 1954, through May 6, 1954; cited Stern 1.
606 "Take the initiative at that time": ibid. 145.
606 "Remarkably instrumental": cited Stern 218–19.
606 "It would be folly to oppose": ibid. 141.
606n. "The government paid far more": Stern 113.

608 "In other words, there he was": Transcript of Oppenheimer Hearings 465–70; cited Bernstein 156.

608 "A full examination . . . blank wall": DDE *Mandate* 311.

608 "Directed the heads of departments": DDE diary, Dec. 3, 1953; DDE-G.

609 "It would be more like trying to find": DDE personal diary, Dec. 3, 1953; DDE-G.

609n. "There was a look of hatred": Lilienthal III, 522.

611 "This proceeding is an inquiry": cited Stern 263.

611 "If it is a question of . . . clearance": ibid. 339.

611 "On behalf of . . . the people": cited Stern 464.

612 "Lewis, let us be certain . . . that, too": Strauss 336–37.

612 "In discussing with the President": cited R. J. Donovan 185–86.

613 "The mere discovery by men": DDE diary, Sept. 28, 1953; DDE-G.

613n. "In the brain of . . . why not this": Lilienthal III 593.

614 "What . . . are we doing about the Trieste affair": DDE diary Sept. 30; DDE-G.

614 "Hope that the measures being taken": cited Eden *Full Circle* 183.

614 "A serious weakening of": ibid.

615 "If there is a Moscow-directed conspiracy": *Pentagon Papers* 8.

616 "Ho Chi Minh was, of course, a hard-core": DDE *Mandate* 335–36.

616 "Under present conditions . . . security of the U.S.": *Pentagon Papers* 10.

616 "We have engaged to help": DDE personal diary, Oct. 8, 1953; DDE-G.

616 "Do everything possible to achieve": FonF XIII 355.

616 "In the clearest and most categorical fashion": cited Cooper 87.

617 "Their exclusive responsibility . . . policies": DDE *Mandate* 337.

617 "Would place people who want freedom": FonF XIII 368.

618 "Hope that she would get the point": DDE diary, Nov. 7, 1953; DDE-G.

618 "Full of propaganda": FonF XIII 403.

619 "This is, of course . . . one subject": PPs 1953, 803.

619 "New look": DDE-G, Bermuda-Miscellaneous folder.

620 "Most effective" . . . "as a matter of principle" . . . "has never yet made . . . atomic warfare": U.K. Bermuda Minutes, Dec. 7, 1953; DDE-G.

620 "Home constituencies": DDE-G, Bermuda-Miscellaneous folder.

620 "Agriculture, medicine, and . . . areas of the world . . . to his life": PPs 1953, 821–22.

621 "Taken out of the hands of the": PPs 1953, 820.

621 "It was an historic occasion": Lilienthal III 445.

621 "Our technical experts assured me": DDE *Mandate* 254.

621 "An agonizing reappraisal": See Eden *Full Circle* 57.

622 "Every American who feels as I": FonF XIII 412.

622 "If ever . . . I should show any signs": DDE to Milton Eisenhower, Dec. 11, 1953, in DDE diary; DDE-G.

623 "Grabbing the Commie issue": See, for example, Joseph and Stewart Alsop 222.

623 "Separated from the Federal . . . but also at home": PPs 1954, 12, 7–8.

623 "World Communist conspiracy": ibid. 8.

623 "A major landmark": Huntington *Common Defense* 74.

624 "Brutal": cited in David Schoenbrun cable to Edward R. Murrow of CBS; copy in JFD Mss., box 475 (Paris NATO trip).

624 "New concept of collective security . . . massive retaliatory power": J. F. Dulles speech, Jan. 12, 1954; cited R. J. Donovan 326.

624 "We and our allies have and will": PPs 1954, 10.

625 "Communistic": Schneider *Communism in Guatemala* 21f n.; cited Horowitz *Yalta* 166.

626 "Persecution of American business": *N.Y. Times* June 27, 1950; cited Barnet 230.

626 An economic study of twelve Latin American republics: *Latin American Highlights,* The Chase National Bank, Sept. 1956; cited Horowitz *Yalta* 178–79.

627 "From here on out it's not a matter": Guillermo Toriello *La Batalla de Guatemala;* cited Galeano 52.

627 "An authentic domestic political party": U.S. Department of State, *Intervention of International Communism in Guatemala,* USGPO 1954, 8–9; cited Barnet 231.

627 "Communist imperialism": Same paper, 32, cited Horowitz *Yalta* 179.

627 Q: Mr. Ambassador . . . Willauer . . . revolutionary forces: Hearings, Part 13, 865–66, Senate Internal Security Subcommittee, 87th Congress, 1st Session; testimony by Whiting Willauer, July 27, 1961; cited Wise and Ross *Invisible Government* 167–68.

628 "To favor the United Fruit Company": Fuentes 49–50.
628 "Who has represented the fellow-traveling": W. B. Smith memo to DDE January 15, 1954; DDE-G, Guatemala folder.
628 "The facts are otherwise . . . Agrarian Reform Law": ibid.
629 "Government of the North": FonF XIV 46.
629 "Soft on communism": Joseph and Stewart Alsop 228.
630 "Challenge of the prerogatives": Adams 143.
630 "The White House now meant": Joseph and Stewart Alsop 228.
630 "The key to the deliberate Communist": Rovere *McCarthy* 39.
631 "The loss of valuable deposits": DDE *Mandate* 333.
631 "The surrender of millions": ibid.
632n. "Knowland has no foreign": DDE to Gruenther, July 2, 1954; in his diary, DDE-G.
633 "I couldn't say whether they": PPs 1954, 226.
633 "We are inching our way . . . darkened room": PPs 1954, 254.
633 "There is no ground . . . increased help": cited DDE *Mandate* 343–44.
634 "One hundred percent of what . . . No informed observers": FonF XIV 57.
634 "To work to prepare a black book": C. D. Jackson to J. F. Dulles, Feb. 26, 1954; JFD Mss., box 477.
634 "The domination or control . . . American affairs": From USDS paper cited in note for page 627, cited Horowitz, *Yalta* 169–70; see also FonF XIV 85–86.
635 "So innocent . . . What is international communism?": Dulles statement, Caracas Conference, March 8, 1954; JFD Mss., box 477.
635 "The internationalization of McCarthyism": Philip B. Taylor, Jr., "The Guatemala Affair," *American Political Science Review* Sept. 1956, 971; cited Horowitz *Yalta* 170.
635 "We contributed our approval without": *N.Y. Times* March 16, 1954; ibid. 171.
635 "Senator McCarthy achieved today": *The Times* of London; cited Rovere *McCarthy* 31.
635 "Queasily worded": Stone *Fifties* 62.
635 "Pretty feeble, and": Rovere *Affairs of State* 188.
635 "It is the responsibility of the Congress": PPs 1954, 291.
635 "Apparently the President and I": FonF XIV 68 and note.
636 March 1 data: *N.Y. Times* March 2, 1954.
636 March 2 data: ibid. March 3.
636 March 4 data: ibid. March 5.
636n. All data from FonF XV 5, 266, 321, 329, 394, and 425.
637 Had fared as a witness: Potter 13–23. An invaluable corrective of this work has been afforded by Richard Rovere, *"The Untold Story of McCarthy's Fall,"* 3–5.
637 "Of these I know nothing": personal diary, May 11, 1954; DDE-G.
637 "To provide every possible bit": ibid.
637 "Conversations . . . official . . . reproductions": DDE diary entries May 13 and May 17, 1954; DDE-G.
637 "Iron curtain . . . I don't think the President": FonF XIV 166.
638 "Mr. President, would you mind . . . to the free world": PPs 1954, 382–83.
639 "The mass of the population . . . Vietnamese troops": DDE *Mandate* 372.
639 "In the mind of the French . . . to the problem": Paul Ely *Mémoires* 65; cited Fontaine II, 108.
639 "We fully share United States . . . no longer exist": cited Eden *Full Circle* 91–92.
640 "Even if others were reluctant": DDE *Mandate* 358.
640 "Must undoubtedly . . . one of the boldest": Rovere *Affairs of State* 193.
640 "If in order to avoid further": cited R. J. Donovan 266.
642 "Impression bien nette": Fontaine II, 108.
642 "It is not repeat not . . . short of belligerency": Dulles to Dillon, *Pentagon Papers* 39–40.
642 "In unity and in time . . . desperate peril": cited DDE *Mandate* 347.
642 "Determined . . . military decisions": Eden *Full Circle* 93.
642 "Entirely contrary to the spirit": ibid. 98.
642 "Possibly through misunderstanding": DDE *Mandate* 349.
644 "What if we were to give you": Georges Bidault *D'une résistance à l'autre* 918; cited Fontaine II, 114.
644 "Bidault gives the impression": Dulles cablegram to DDE, April 23, 1954, in DDE diary; DDE-G. Also cited DDE *Mandate* 350.
644 "To bring the British position": DDE *Mandate* 351.

644 "We are not prepared to give": cited Eden *Full Circle* 105.

645 "A very tough one for us": DDE personal diary, April 27, 1954; DDE-G.

645 "Eventual military means": cited Eden *Full Circle* 106.

645 "Disappointed": DDE *Mandate* 351.

645 "There are some things . . . Caracas": DDE diary memo, April 1954; DDE-G.

645f. "The international communist . . . Rio Treaty": Notes of legislative leaders' meeting, April 26, 1954; DDE-G.

646 "A new and inspirational leader": DDE to Gruenther, April 26, 1954, DDE personal diary; DDE-G.

646 "The United States will never . . . can declare war": Cutler memorandum, *Pentagon Papers* 41.

646 "To intervene with . . . for military planning": *Pentagon Papers* 41.

646n. "Serious commitments . . . the Congress": FonF XIV 154.

647 "It's a little illegal, but": DDE and J. F. Dulles telephone conversation, noted in DDE personal diary, May 1954; DDE-G.

647 "Gravity . . . massive shipment . . . so masked": U.S. State Department paper on Guatemala (see note for page 627; cited Horowitz *Yalta* 171, 173.

648 "Exaggerated . . . acquiesce . . . on the high seas": Eden *Full Circle* 134–35.

648 "Worrying": ibid. 135.

648 "From the point of view . . . militarily advantageous": *Pentagon Papers* 44–46.

649 "To make sure that France's aim": cited Cooper 90.

649 "Reign of terror": FonF XIV 198.

649 "Are you sure . . . commit it to win": *Newsweek* March 4, 1963; see also Wise and Ross *Invisible Government* 176.

650 "All depends on the Guatemalan army . . . will have failed": memorandum to DDE, June 20, 1954; DDE-G, Guatemala folder.

650 "The department has no evidence": cited Wise and Ross *Invisible Government* 176.

651 "The information available . . . against Guatemalans": USDS paper on Guatemala (see note for page 627) 14.

651 "What do you think . . . his case already": DDE *Mandate* 425–26. DDE speech, Booksellers' Association, June 10, 1963; cited Wise and Ross 166–67.

652 "Evil purpose of the Kremlin . . . Guatemalans themselves": cited Wise and Ross 180–81.

652 "The disaffection of . . . devotion of his people": DDE *Mandate* 426.

652n. Wise and Ross 178.

653 "Audacious and criminal": FonF XIV 270.

653 "Thundering majority . . . a far-seeing and able statesman": DDE *Mandate* 426.

653 "Shall be used on behalf . . . of Asia": FonF XIV 215.

653 "Communist penetration of the": cited Evans and Novak 77.

654 "To undertake paramilitary": *Pentagon Papers* 54.

654 "At least to give the French": Eden *Full Circle* 131.

655 "McCarthyism in a white collar": FonF XIV 227.

655 He sent Nixon a reproachful note: DDE diary, June 28, 1954; DDE-G.

655 "You can normally take . . . if I were you": PPs 1954, 611–14.

655 "A real good try . . . doom-laden": FonF XIV 214.

655 "If there is any proof": PPs 1954, 612.

656 Text of Smith's statement cited in *Pentagon Papers* 52–53.

656 "Since undoubtedly true": ibid. 22.

657 "The means for undertaking": ibid. 54.

657 "Habitual contempt for people": FonF XIV 260.

657 "Were very much disturbed . . . reasonable": Senator Ralph Flanders interview, OHRO.

657 "Disaster . . . loss of Southeast Asia": *Pentagon Papers* 14.

658 "It is hopeless": ibid.

658 "Far from strong or stable": ibid. 15.

658 "Only so far as necessary . . . the levers": ibid.

658 "American policy toward . . . a limited risk": ibid.

659 "Spells of depression . . . alone was responsible": Adams 128.

659 "Tragedy": ibid. 125.

659 "Our relations with . . . major setback . . . It can't be done": PPs 1954, 787–91.

661   "Toying with the mousetrap": Acheson 350.
661   "Has no desire . . . Chinese forces on": cited ibid. 351.
661   "A CIA proprietary": *Pentagon Papers* 137.
662   "Asiatic Monroe Doctrine": FonF XIV 297.
663   "Stand alone . . . intimidated . . . the place of the U.S. in . . . the western Pacific": ibid. 305.
663   "Horrible dilemma . . . a limited, brush-fire . . . as in Korea . . . we'll have to strike there": DDE *Mandate* 463–64.
664   "The widespread . . . but it was real": ibid. 474.
664   "A stupendous blast in the": FonF XIV 98.
665   "Thus far except for some tragic": National Academy of Sciences, "A Report to the Public"; cited Strauss 415.
666   "A bull's-eye target": Winston Churchill; cited Fleming 683.
666   "Peace cannot consist of an": Pius XII; ibid.
666   "Whenever and wherever it would be": J. F. Dulles "talking paper" prepared for use April 23, 1954; JFD Mss., box 477.
667   "Since the advent": PPs 1954, 915.
667   "We have arrived at that": ibid. 917.
667   "The major new factor": ibid. 922.
668   "Brilliant and statesmanlike": cited Eden *Full Circle* 162.
668   Supranational: ibid.
668   "Without doubt one of the great": FonF XIV 329.
668   "Beginning of . . . stability and peace": ibid. 354.
669   "At this particular stage": ibid. 355.
669   "Trumped up . . . utterly false": cited Wise and Ross *Invisible Government* 107.
669   "Furnishes further proof": ibid. 108.
670   "Outrage the elemental . . . conduct": FonF XIV 397.
670   "Until these Americans": ibid.
670   "Maintain and develop . . . use of force . . . joint agreement": J. F. Dulles to DDE, Nov. 23, 1954; DDE-G, Formosa 1952–1957 folder.
671   "Primarily a compact": cited Rovere *Affairs of State* 254.
671   "For the present, seek to": Hoover memo to DDE, Dec. 18, 1954; DDE-G, Formosa folder.
672   "In the army as a general": Luther Evans interview, OHRO.
673   "Give him a good pat on the back." "Will do": Senator Prescott Bush interview, OHRO; see also Ann Whitman memo for DDE files; DDE-G, McCarthy folder.
673   "The unanimous opinion . . . would assure . . . be liberated": JFD Mss., box 478 (NATO meeting, Dec. 14–20, 1954).
674   "Considerable": FonF XV 9.
674   "Of no particular importance": *N.Y. Times* Jan. 19, 1955.
674   "Small islands . . . a good thing": PPs 1955, 186–87.
674   One copy had been delivered: CIA pamphlet in Formosa folder, DDE-G.
674   "The time had come": DDE *Mandate* 466.
675   "I believed . . . Communist attack": ibid. 467.
675   "We all agree that we cannot": cited ibid.
675   "In the interest of peace . . . related localities": PPs 1955, 210, 209.
676   "Eisenhower is passing the buck": cited R. J. Donovan 305.
676   "Driven out from . . . internal affairs": FonF XV 43.
676   "A very bellicose": PPs 1955, 262.
676   "Abrupt rejection": FonF XV 43.
676   "Violent in their efforts": cited DDE *Mandate* 470.
677   "International Communism uses the power": Dulles to closed session of SEATO, Bangkok, Feb. 21, 1955; JFD Mss., box 478.
677   "It seemed probable that the Soviet Union": DDE *Mandate* 469.
677   "International Communism . . . later in Japan": DDE to Churchill, Feb. 1955; cited ibid. 470, 473.
677   "Hot pursuit": Jan. 29, 1955, memo DDE-G, Formosa folder.

677n. "The broad strategy which": Dulles in Manila, Mar. 2, 1955; JFD Mss., box 478.
678 "We know, of course, when": PPs 1955, 252.
678 "Defend all . . . the Pescadores . . . for the United States to decide": FonF XV 49; and see Fleming 712.
679 "Despotic disarray . . . moment of peril": *N.Y. Times* Feb. 17, 1955.
679 "Cruel, despotic nature": JFD Mss., box 478.
679 "Now we have made the words": cited Sulzberger *Giants* 136.
679 "Military challenge . . . civilian centers": FonF XV 73.
679 "I believe there is . . . mainland airfields": cited DDE, *Mandate* 476.
680 "The United States cannot": ibid.
680 "U.S. military leaders . . . only weeks away": FonF XV 73.
680 "Now, in any combat . . . would be used": PPs 1955, 332.
681 "Forego peace . . . of liberty": FonF XV 91.
681 "An acute and imminent threat": *N.Y. Times* Mar. 22, 1955.
681 "A frantic plea . . . just confuse them": DDE *Mandate* 477–78.
681 "Could not stand aloof . . . situation": FonF XV 98–99.
682 "Probably will initiate . . . expansionist tendencies": *N.Y. Times* Mar. 25, 1955, and see FonF XV 98, 106.
682 "Lately there has been . . . never occur": DDE diary, Mar. 26, 1955; DDE-G, cited DDE *Mandate* 478–79.
682 "Parochial": FonF XV 98.
683 "Not by me": PPs 1955, 374.
683 "War party": FonF XV 98; and see Evans and Novak 171.
683 "To seek unity and not to": FonF XV 130.
683 "From precarious symbols of": DDE *Mandate* 481.
684 "Willing to sit down": FonF XV 137.
684 "Of course the United States would insist": ibid.
684 "Never sit at the same table": ibid.
684 "To induce the Generalissimo": cited DDE *Mandate* 481.
685 "I agree": DDE on Robertson cablegram to Dulles April 25, 1955; DDE-G, Formosa folder.
685 "Talk to the Chi-Coms . . . error in terminology": PPs 1955, 427, 428.
686 "Krishna Menon is a menace": DDE diary, July 14, 1955; DDE-G.
687 "There were so many . . . them and see them": DDE interview, DOHC.
688 "Not only . . . execute them": ibid.

5. Thaw in the Cold War

689 "Material, intellectual . . . free world": PPs 1955, 483.
689 "Tangible evidence of . . . actual deeds": DDE *Mandate* 505.
690 "In the nearest future . . . democratic Austria": FonF XV 129.
690 "And he grinned . . . 'to say that' ": DDE interview, DOHC.
690 "The President of the . . . negotiate details": press conference, May 7, 1955; JFD Mss., box 478.
690 "Senselessly stubborn": DDE *Mandate* 506.
690 "To remove sources": FonF XV 158.
690f. "The whole thing looks . . . policy of patience . . . accepted . . . by the Soviet Union . . . necessary to insure . . . control posts": The quotes, most from Philip Noel-Baker, *The Arms Race,* Oceana Publications, 1959, are cited in Stone *Polemics and Prophecies* 264–271.
691 "Mr. President, I wonder . . . comment on it": PPs 1955, 497–98.
692 "Plagiarized": Beal 298.
692 "Have to move . . . standoff . . . I wouldn't . . . somebody else": PPs 1955, 676.
692 "Remilitarized . . . peace-loving states": FonF XV 167.
693 "Danger": ibid. 166.
693 "It is up to the U.S.A. . . . weapons": FonF XV 205.
693n. "His possible use": DDE to Dulles, Mar. 10, 1954, in DDE diary; DDE-G.
694 "A complete blueprint": PPs 1955, 715.
694 "Liberation . . . the wolf . . . the same": press conference, May 15, 1955; JFD Mss., box 478.

694   "A tactical change . . . tensions": DDE *Mandate* 506.
694n.   "We knew the Soviets": DDE interview, DOHC.
696   "Your support . . . disaster occurs": FonF XV 207.
696   "Deepest impression . . . United States": ibid. 208.
696   "Radioactive rubble": Kissinger 291–94.
697   Nine Soviet goals were listed: All papers in JFD Mss., box 478.
698n.   "Philosophically, a great": DDE diary, July 14, 1955; DDE-G.
698n.   "A sad day": FonF XV 232.
699   "A spirit and . . . because we must": PPs 1955, 704–705.
699   "Has given this simple": cited Eden *Full Circle* 311.
700   "Approaches": notes of meeting July 16, 1955, 8:30 P.M.; DDE-G.
701   "Deep longing for peace": DDE *Mandate* 513.
701n.   "More than a handful": Rovere *Affairs of State* 277.
702n.   "As I reflected . . . precautions": Eden *Full Circle* 301–302.
703   Instead for alliances: Zhukov-Eisenhower talk from Bohlen's notes; DDE-G.
704   "A subdued and worried": DDE to Mrs. Whitman; DDE-G, Geneva Notes.
704   "The most effective proposal": DDE *Mandate* 519.
704   "The location of most": notes of meeting, July 20, 1955, 6 P.M.; DDE-G.
705   "Have been searching . . . exacting duty": PPs 1955, 715–16.
705   "I didn't know . . .": DDE-G, Geneva Notes.
705   "Poured scorn": Eden *Full Circle* 304.
705   "Most spectacular in the eyes": DDE *Mandate* 529.
705   "Gave careful study": R. J. Donovan 345.
705   "It seemed only a gimmick": Rovere *Affairs of State* 290.
705   "This has been an historic": PPs 1955, 722.
706   "The core of U.S.-European": Rockefeller report; DDE-G.
706   "The unconcealed anxiety . . . social equality": Dulles statement, box 478.
707   "Eddie, if that fellow": Interview, Edward Folliard, OHRO.
708   "Particularly testy": Nixon 153.
708   "More optimistic": FonF XV 296.
708   "We don't believe for a minute": PPs 1955, 816.
709   "Mild . . . neither mild nor": cited R. J. Donovan 366; and see FonF XV 333–34.
710   "In case of . . . the President's": U.S. Constitution, Article II, Section 1, Para. 5.
710   "A momentary state . . . weight": Nixon 132–33.
711   "Only suggest that all . . . soon to be his": Rovere *Affairs of State* 322.
711   "Tell Jim to take over": cited R. J. Donovan 367.
711   "Governor Sherman Adams . . . the President": cited Adams 186.
712   "Firmly and emphatically": ibid.
712   "Let the White House clique": cited Nixon 149.

6. *An End and a Beginning Amidst Crisis*

715   "Exactly the phrase": DDE diary; cited DDE *Mandate* 568.
716   "Positive, that is, affirmative": PPs 1956, 266.
717   "Most disappointing . . . building you up": cited Nixon 158, 159.
717   "You should make a searching": DDE *Waging Peace* 7.
717   "At five or six of our": Nixon 160.
717   "Private agonizing": ibid.
717   "It seemed to me that it was": ibid. 164.
717   "Political visibility": DDE *Waging Peace* 7.
717   "Able administrators and": ibid.
718   "The only thing I had asked": PPs 1956, 287.
718   "Intense soul-searching": Nixon 166.
718   "Delighted": FonF XVI 144.
719   "It's Eisenhower and Nixon": ibid. 237.
719   "Hagerty curtain . . . Madison Avenue": ibid. 244.
719   "Free": DDE *Waging Peace* 10.
719   "I am confident": FonF XVI 244.
720   "Take up our shotguns": ibid. 68.
720   "Either could control the rising": cited R. J. Donovan 390.

720   "That all of us deplore . . . straighten it out": PPs 1956, 234.
721   "I expect that we are going to": ibid. 270.
721   "I am convinced . . . just plain *nuts*": cited Hughes 201.
721   "Extremists on both . . . some time, unfortunately": PPs 1956, 736–37.
721   "We must proceed gradually": Stevenson speech, Los Angeles, Feb. 7, 1956; cited Cochran 269.
722   "Advances . . . all over the world": PPs 1956, 738–39.
722   "Indirect . . . Near and Middle . . . Western Europe": Dulles at NATO meeting, Paris, Dec. 15, 1955; JFD Mss.
723   "One of the outcomes . . . fatal siege": cited Barnet 134.
724   "The intrigues of aggressive": cited Love 235.
724   "Indefensible": ibid. 85.
724   "Assurances from the United States": Love 84.
725   "Six serviceable planes . . . deplorable state": Salah Salem; cited Seale 205.
725   "Why, this is peanuts!": Love 88.
725   "Military alliances and . . . heighten tension": cited ibid. 225.
725   "We want to have arms": ibid.
726   "The unconscionable hour": Macmillan III 619.
727   "Violation of the spirit": cited Love 282.
727   "A new and sinister element": Macmillan III 635.
727   "A Middle Eastern tangle": DDE *Waging Peace* 28.
727n. "I have been impressed . . . our enemies": cited Love 279.
728   "Seeds of strife": Macmillan III 629.
728   "Public opinion in Saudi Arabia": cited Eden *Full Circle* 335.
728   "American, that is Aramco": ibid. 343.
729   "What's all this nonsense": Nutting 34–35.
729   "But I don't want an alternative . . . in Egypt": ibid.
729   "Metamorphosis . . . his whole system": ibid. 33.
730   "A state of acute": Thomas *Suez* 100.
730n. "An appalling international situation": cited Love 114.
731   "Consider . . . further support": Love 303.
732   "Any attempt to give aid": Adams 247–48.
732   "This shows the advantages": cited ibid. 248.
733   "Ties with the West . . . genuine independence": cited Love 293.
733   "An action that we regret": FonF XVI 167.
733   "Well, of course, we think": PPs 1956, 522.
734   "If you are waging peace . . . asked for it": ibid. 554–55.
734   "The President does believe": ibid. 556.
734   "Increasingly become an obsolete": Dulles speech, Iowa State University, June 9, 1956.
735   "I looked at it . . . 'Go ahead' ": Eisenhower interview, DOHC.
735   "Do nations which play both": Dulles press conference, Apr. 2, 1957.
736   "I have never doubted the wisdom": DDE *Waging Peace* 33.
736   "The Egyptian has his thumb": cited Thomas *Suez* 31.
736n. "Nasser has . . . said . . . was looking": ibid. 34n.
737   "He's regained five pounds": Sulzberger *Giants* 319, 322.
737   "Force . . . to bring Nasser": Eden to DDE, July 27, 1956; DDE-G.
737   "Contingency": DDE *Waging Peace* 37.
737   "Even more emotional": ibid. 36.
737   "Unilaterally flouted a solemn": ibid. 38.
738   "To see what it's all about": cited R. Murphy 422.
738   "Just go over and hold the fort": ibid.
738   "Admirable": R. Murphy 423.
738   "Nasser has to be chased": cited ibid. 424.
738   "Made good sense": R. Murphy 424.
738   "Break Nasser": cited DDE *Waging Peace* 40.
738   "It seems that we have succeeded": Macmillan IV 105.
739   "A question not of honour . . . for force": ibid. 106.
740   "What line he expected to": notes of a Socony Mobil official; cited Engler 236.
741   "The torrent of foreign oil": ibid. 231.
741   *"Impressed with international"*: notes of a Socony Mobil official; ibid. 237.
741   "We cannot accept either the": cited Love 402.
741   "The United States is committed": PPs 1956, 737.

741   "Whole attitude had . . . of danger": cited Love 417.
742   "We are determined to exhaust": PPs 1956, 720.
742   "The use of force or": cited DDE *Waging Peace* 667.
743   "That terrible man": Drummond and Coblentz 162.
743   "For collective bargaining with Nasser": DDE *Waging Peace* 51.
743   "Help prepare the way . . . other means" FonF XVI 305; see also Eden *Full Circle* 482.
743   "Gunboat diplomacy": FonF XVI 305.
743   "The idea that this . . . is concerned": cited DDE *Waging Peace* 674; see also Eden *Full Circle* 483.
743   "An advertisement to Nasser . . . triumph": ibid. 483–84.
744   "As it soon turned out . . . ridiculous": DDE *Waging Peace* 51.
744   "Pour noyer le poisson": cited Love 438.
744   "There is talk about the 'teeth' . . . as rapidly as possible": *Bulletin* of the Department of State, 1956, 577 et seq., cited Finer 293, 288–89.
745   "Mob . . . they just want to yowl": Hughes 193.
745   "After all, I have got a job here": PPs 1956, 885.
747   "Courtesy gesture": R. Murphy 432.
747   "Knew their military schedule": ibid.
747   "The best announcement I could . . . thanksgiving": PPs 1956, 903.
747   "A note of belligerence": DDE *Waging Peace* 55.
748   "A wise and rapid exchange": Eden *Full Circle* 512.
748   "This sordid conspiracy": Nutting 90–97, 14.
748   "To surrender altogether . . . unthinkable": Macmillan IV 149.
749   "It was idle to hope for": Eden *Full Circle* 519.
749   "Seemed unable to make up . . . such fears": Macmillan IV 148.
749   "The tradecraft of intelligence": Allen Dulles *Craft* 6.
749   "You go out and tell Ben Gurion . . . my words": cited Love 454.
750   "Up to the total called for": PPs 1956, 901.
750   "Differing opinions between friends": ibid. 980–81.
751   "The entry of Iraqi forces": cited Love 460.
751   "Anti-Western majority": DDE *Waging Peace* 60.
751   "Centrifugal, disruptive": ibid. 65.
752   "We are dishonored": Tournoux *Sécrets* 116; cited Love 456.
752   "The American conscience . . . of his fellows": *N.Y. Times* Aug. 26, 1952; cited Fleming 806.
752   "Every political . . . an act of war": *N.Y. Times* Sept. 22, 1952; ibid. 807.
753   "Now there were chains breaking": DDE *Waging Peace* 68.
753   "One of the most significant": cited ibid. 79.
753   "Great commonwealth . . . economic construction": cited Fleming 799.
753   "The Nagy government in Hungary": cited DDE *Waging Peace* 69.
754   "Active in the corridors . . . and so on": Conor Cruise O'Brien in *Writers and Politics;* cited Horowitz *Yalta* 289.
754   "A campaign that had a fatal": Tibor Meray *Thirteen Days That Shook the Kremlin* 98; cited Fleming 810.
754   "Do not hang your weapons": Radio Free Europe; ibid.
754   "Gravely sinned . . . aid was planned": FonF XVI 404.
754   "Liberation position . . . their own choosing": PPs 1956, 1100–1101.
755   "Misleading statements . . . of Sciences": DDE *Waging Peace* 475.
755   "Playing dangerous politics with": FonF XVI 340–41.
755   "Those who are not fully": ibid.
755n.   "Destroy the largest . . . unmeasured damage": Stevenson speech, Chicago, Oct. 15, 1956; FonF XVI 349.
756   "My God, we simply have to figure": Hughes 203.
756   "The continuance of . . . H-bomb . . . for the sake of peace itself": PPs 1956, 1000, 1002.
756   "A great blunder": cited DDE *Waging Peace* 64.
756n.   "Placed under continuous and competent . . . good health": Strauss 412–13.
756n.   One death from leukemia: *N.Y. Times* Nov. 21, 1972.
757   "Direct and immediate danger": *Waging Peace* 66.
757   "His days may well be numbered": ibid. 67.
757   "Might be tempted . . . utmost care": ibid.
757   "I renew the plea": cited Love 473.

758   "Israel and barium make": cited Hughes 212.
758   "Who are not performing": cited DDE *Waging Peace* 70.
758   "I just can't believe it": cited Hughes 212.
759   "Sterility . . . hollowness . . . uninformed . . . of the situation!": Dayan diary; cited Love 475–76.
759   "All right, Foster, you tell 'em": ibid. 503.
759   "Looked clumsy": DDE interview, DOHC.
760   "We will stick to our undertaking": DDE *Waging Peace* 73.
760   "Ring of steel": cited ibid. 74.
760   "Ancient history . . . without current validity": ibid. 75.
760   "To suffocate the White House": Hughes 218.
760   "All members . . . in the area": FonF XVI 354.
761   "This cost of war was not": DDE *Waging Peace* 92n.
761   "Ashen gray, heavy-lidded": Hughes 220.
761   "Boy, this is taking it": ibid. 221.
761   "It is—and it will remain": PPs 1956, 1065.
762   "Then they asked me . . . the United Nations": Love 557.
762   "It is nothing less than tragic": cited DDE *Waging Peace* 83.
762   "We cannot and we will not": PPs 1956, 1072.
763   "Desist forthwith from any": FonF XVI 365.
763   Absurd! said the President: DDE diary and staff memoranda, meetings of Nov. 3 and 4, 1956; DDE-G.
763   "If we draw back now": Eden to DDE, cited in DDE *Waging Peace* 88 and Love 578.
764   "Joint and immediate . . . third world war": FonF XVI 364; and see DDE *Waging Peace* 89.
764   "Unthinkable . . . an obvious": cited Hughes 223.
764   "Open colonial war . . . sowing a hatred": cited Love 610–11.
765   "A speed which threatened disaster": Eden *Full Circle* 556.
765   "If the Soviets should attack": DDE diary and staff memoranda, Nov. 6, 1956; DDE-G.
766   "We must stop this before": R. Murphy 435.
766   "Not any more be responsible": cited Thomas *Suez* 146.
766   "Referred to Washington": Macmillan IV 164.
766   "Hello . . . Anthony . . . be all right": cited in part DDE *Waging Peace* 92; in most part Love, 627–28.
767   "Disgorge . . . rang in my ears": Eden *Full Circle* 437.
767   "Perhaps Dulles wanted to show": R. Murphy 430.
767   "That France and Britain, even": Macmillan IV 198.
768   "Placed Eisenhower in an": Adams 261.
768   "The United States Government": Eden *Full Circle* 561.
769   "When this point was put": ibid. 566.
769   "Thou hypocrite, first": *N.Y. Times* Dec. 3, 1956; cited Finer 460.
769   "Hopeless attempt . . . bury you": FonF XVI 386.
769   "Gravely endangering": ibid. 393.
769   "Differences . . . defense alliances": ibid. 394.
770   "Strongly urging . . . refused": cited Engler 262.
771   "Should NATO recognize itself": paper, June 8, 1956, from Department of External Affairs, Ottawa; JFD Mss., box 480.
771   "The U.S. feels however that": Dulles memorandum, Dec. 9, 1956; ibid.
772   "Careful balancing of political alternatives": Roger W. Jones interview, OHRO.
772   "This country can . . . for protection": cited Adams 364.
773   "The existing vacuum": cited DDE *Waging Peace* 178.
773   "The sole basis on which": FonF XVII 18.
774   "Vague . . . not a statement of": ibid. 10.
774   "Communist aggression . . . the most serious threat . . . If I were an American boy . . . on my left": ibid. 10, 11, 26.
774   "No reason whatsoever": PPs 1957, 101.
774   "Shall be consonant . . . necessity thereof": FonF XVII 45.
774   "We must not allow Europe": PPs 1957, 125.
775   "Business in its pricing policies": ibid. 20.
775   "I wasn't merely asking . . . America we know": ibid. 127.
775   "The Soviet Union . . . the United States": Ben Gurion 151.

776 "Would have the most adverse": PPs 1957, 9.
776 "Idiosyncrasies": cited Engler 257.
776 "He at least professed": DDE *Waging Peace* 116.
776 "Is not the kind of person": FonF XVII 27.
777 "Instruct . . . to oppose": cited Evans and Novak 178.
777 "Free and innocent": cited DDE *Waging Peace* 684.
777n. "Could not possibly bring": Adams 340.
777n. "Well, I have a pretty good": PPs 1957, 131.
778 "With a determined expression": Adams 281.
778 "The only thing it could": DDE *Waging Peace* 89.
779 "The U.N. will never vote": cited Adams 284.
779 "America has either one": ibid. 285.
779 "Our views have not changed": ibid.
779 "Full and prompt withdrawal": FonF XVII 69.
780 "Some very plain talk": DDE *Waging Peace* 123.
780 "Continuing to abuse the U.S. and": memo of talks of March 20, 1957, Bermuda Conference; JFD Mss., box 481.
780 "Particularly vicious and": ibid.
781 "To which the United States was": ibid.
781 "In time . . . if the choice": ibid.
781 "Our present intention . . . land mass": ibid.
781 "Unhesitating . . . one of the most courageous": Adams 276.
781 "A carefully balanced budget": PPs 1957, 59.
781 "I would deplore the day": Sources in note, below quote.
782 "I think that modern Republicanism": PPs 1956, 1090.
782 "If they can, I think if": PPs 1957, 74.
784 "Respectfully . . . to indicate the places": FonF XVII 80.
784 "Almost a quarter of a . . . in a row": PPs 1957, 303.
784 "We look to you . . . to enlighten us": cited Evans and Novak 186.
784 "Throughout the New and Fair Deals": ibid. 185.
785 "I just say it is a mistake": PPs 1957, 361–62.
785 "Irresponsible diminution": DDE *Waging Peace* 138.
785 "Punish those Republicans . . . ? I don't think": PPs 1957, 353.
785 "A serious and disturbing": Adams 380.
785 "Proud of the progress our people": PPs 1957, 23.
787 "Shocking": Morrow 165.
787 "Most cunningly . . . a bayonet": FonF XVII 212.
787 "Well, I would say this . . . they do mean": PPs 1957, 521.
788 "The overriding provision": DDE *Waging Peace* 156.
788 "I can't imagine any set": PPs 1957, 546.
788 "Well, I think . . . greatest emphasis": ibid. 547.
789 "Are you convinced . . . than benefit": ibid. 555–56.
789 "This was a blow": DDE *Waging Peace* 158.
790 "Infinitely better": FonF XVII 276.
790 "I can get Ervin and the others": cited DDE *Waging Peace* 161.
792 "The legislative process at its best": PPs 1957, 641.
792 "Trouble . . . instigated by Communists": DDE *Waging Peace* 194.
792 "Efforts to destroy my country": FonF XVII 130.
792 "Independence and integrity": ibid. 137.
792 "Not interested": ibid.
793 "An American plot to overthrow": ibid. 258.
793 "Expert on coups d'état": ibid.
793 "Seem to be influenced by": FonF XVII 276.
793 "Serious effects upon the security": ibid. 282.
793 "Preserve peace and good order": FonF XVII 293.
793n. "Hard to dismiss": Seale 293.
794 ". . . Now, time and again . . . merely by law": PPs 1957, 640, 646.
794 "Never did I feel so good": ibid. 657.
794 "More than three to six": DDE *Waging Peace* 202.
794 "The international communists": FonF XVII 289.
795 "From whatever quarter": ibid. 297.
795 "Artificial uproar": ibid.
795 "Exaggerated": ibid.

796   "Thought it was a terrible thing": *N.Y. Times;* cited Stone *Fifties* 207.
796   "They . . . they": Telephone calls, Sept. 1957; DDE-G.
797   "Any good citizen will comply": ibid.
797   "It is certainly my intention . . ." "It is certainly my desire": cited DDE *Waging Peace* 166; see also PPs 1957, 674n.
797   "Continue to preserve order but": DDE dictation, Sept. 1957; DDE-G.
797   "It is very clear . . . that the plan": cited DDE *Waging Peace* 167.
798   "The niggers are in our school!": FonF XVII 308–309.
799   "The White House office is wherever": DDE dictation, Sept. 1957; DDE-G.
799   "All persons . . . to cease and desist": Proclamation No. 3024.
799   "No. Well, I might": phone calls; DDE-G.
799   "Deeply troubled": Adams 354.
799   "News photographs were particularly damaging": Toner notes, Sept. 24, 1957; DDE-G.
800   "Demagogic extremists . . . Our personal opinions": PPs 1957, 689–94.
800   "Orders to mix the races": cited DDE *Waging Peace* 173.
800   "Few times in my life . . . of a federal court": Sept. 26, 1957; DDE-G, Little Rock folder.
802   "The big thing to remember": PPs 1957, 640.
802   "Fantastic": FonF XVII 321.
802   "Under the pressure of faith and hope": J. F. Dulles *War or Peace;* cited Drummond and Coblentz 184.
803   "They say they have put": PPs 1957, 724.
803   "An outer-space basketball game": FonF XVII 331.
804   "I felt as though I were spending": J. and S. Alsop 362.
804   "We have found no evidence": *N.Y. Times* Jan. 20, 1973.
804   "Clearly indicates an increasing threat . . . prompt remedial action": ibid.
805   "The President is under severe . . . immune": ibid. 320–21.
805   "We want adequate security . . . inevitable": PPs 1957, 816.
805n. "I could hardly believe my ears": Macmillan IV 322.
806   "Excellent": FonF XVII 366.

7. *Policing the Globe*

807   "I have said, unless I felt": PPs 1956, 291–92.
808   "The President has gone back": cited Adams 195.
808   "If I cannot attend to my duties": ibid. 197.
809   "Deeply wounded by the attacks": Charles Murphy "The White House Since Sputnik," 232.
809   "Suffered deeply under recent criticism": Larson *Eisenhower* 147.
809   "You may be President in": Nixon 171.
810   "Curtailments, revisions, or eliminations": PPs 1958, 18.
810   "Our experience demonstrates": Dulles in *Life,* Dec. 16, 1957; cited FonF XVII 401.
810   "To stop all nuclear test explosions": PPs 1957, 834n.
811   "A sacrifice which we could not": ibid. 833.
811   "The NATO meeting was a success": DDE *Waging Peace* 232.
811   "To make any conceivable effort": PPs 1957, 849.
812   "Trash . . . the wisest": PPs 1958, 97.
812   "The prime minister of Indonesia": ibid. 357–58.
812   "Serious events . . . with concern": FonF XVII 409.
812   "Primarily an internal problem": FonF XVIII 50.
813   "We are pursuing what I trust": cited Wise and Ross *Invisible Government* 140.
813   "I had a discussion . . . to be correct": PPs 1958, 358.
814   "The fall of capitalism . . . destroyed": FonF XVIII 139.
814   "The ablest of the Lebanese": DDE *Waging Peace* 266.
815   "The dictatorial power of": FonF XVIII 154.
815   "What our actions would be if he": cited DDE *Waging Peace* 266.
815   "A deep-seated conviction that": DDE *Waging Peace* 266.
815   "In a climate of impatience": ibid.

815   "The Soviets were pushing everywhere": ibid.
817   "The policy of the suction pump": Kirk 214–21. Data on U.S. investments in Latin America and on the income from those investments appears in *Balance of Payments Statistical Supplement* of the Department of Commerce, rev. ed. Washington 1963, and is summarized by Magdoff 98.
817   "A sort of pattern around the world": PPs 1958, 395, 398.
818   "Maybe I should be digging": DDE *Waging Peace* 519.
819   "The United States is prepared to undertake": Dulles, notes for talk with de Gaulle, July 3–6, 1958; JFD Mss., box 482.
819   "NATO under American command": de Gaulle *Memoirs of Hope* 202.
819n.   "Make statements that are": Dulles to Far East chiefs of mission, Mar. 14, 1958; ibid., box 481.
819n.   "Our democratic representative forms of government": Dulles to SEATO Conference, Mar. 12, 1958; ibid.
820   "A summit meeting?": Dulles notes for talk with de Gaulle, July 3–6, 1958; JFD Mss., box 482.
820   "This was the country": DDE *Waging Peace* 269.
820   The CIA had been caught: Allen Dulles 155, 84.
820   "A complete elimination of Western": DDE *Waging Peace* 269.
821   "We have no information . . . the coup": cited DDE ibid. 270.
821   "King Hussein . . . President Chamoun": ibid.
821   "Mr. President, would you wish": Cutler *Rest* 363.
821   "Jerry, how soon . . . How soon . . . ? What are we waiting for?": cited ibid. 363–64.
822   "Almost hysterical outbursts": Macmillan IV 511.
822   "Our sterling oil . . . from the U.S.": ibid. 512.
822   "The two little chaps": cited DDE *Waging Peace* 273.
822   "You are doing a Suez on me": Macmillan IV 512.
822n.   "Communism was playing": R. Murphy 450.
823   "An open act of aggression . . . unprovoked attack": FonF XVIII 226.
823   "An acute smell of oil": *N.Y. Times* July 16, 1958; cited Engler 264.
823   The U.S. ambassador told Murphy: R. Murphy cable to secretary of state; DDE-G, Lebanon folder.
823f.   "Highly organized . . . actively fomented . . . tiny Lebanon . . . a victim . . . all men everywhere": PPs 1958, 553–57.
824   "The problem was to select . . . to do nothing": DDE *Waging Peace* 274.
825   "Guard against a possible Iraqi": ibid. 278.
825   *"Whatever* means might become": ibid.
825   "In the state of tension then existing": ibid.
825   "Loyal": Jack Anderson dispatch from Baghdad; cited Fleming 922n.
826   "The early withdrawal of the foreign": FonF XVIII 274.
826   "Anxious hours": DDE *Waging Peace* 289.
826   "He might blow a valve again": Sulzberger *Giants* 501.
827   "End, once and for all time": Adams 446.
827   "A gift is not necessarily . . . under influence": PPs 1958, 479.
827   "I personally like . . . I need him": ibid.
827   "Not close, not unfriendly": Mazo 176.
828   "Nature to run in the face": FonF XVIII 307.
828   "Pleasant . . . nothing much": Morrow 233, and E. Frederic Morrow interview, OHRO.
829   "Civil rights in . . . it just shouldn't be": Morrow interview, OHRO.
829   "General Gordon of the Confederate": FonF XVIII 332.
829   "From babyhood I was raised": PPs 1958, 742.
832   A memorandum that set forth the collective: memo, Sept. 4, 1958; DDE-G, Formosa 1958–1961 folder.
832   For a couple of hours the President mooted: memo of conference, 10:30 A.M., Sept. 4, 1958; ibid.
832   "We would not wait until the situation": FonF XVIII 289.
832   "These wretched offshore islands": Macmillan IV 546.
834   "Horrendous . . . to be tolerated": FonF XVIII 290; and see Fleming 934.
834   "To *stop* the threatened": cited Macmillan IV 546.
834   "Without at least some use": cited ibid. 548.
834   "Somewhat depressed": Macmillan IV 546.

834   "Public opinion will not be easy": cited ibid. 549.
834   "None of them will support": ibid. 548.
834   "A war to keep the coastal": ibid. 549.
834   "In the Formosa Straits . . . to be any appeasement": PPs 1958, 694–700.
835   "Sabotage": Mazo 177.
835   "Rather foolish": FonF XVIII 313.
835   "So close to . . . not greatly vital to Formosa": PPs 1958, 718.
836   "The United States did give me": ibid. 831–32.

8. Collapse of a Policy

838   "Transformed the city of Berlin": DDE *Waging Peace* 329.
838   "Khrushchev had brought to a climax": Eleanor Dulles 213.
838   "An independent political entity": FonF XVIII 361.
838   "International agreements, historically": PPs 1959, 6.
839   "Kind of cancerous tumor": FonF XVIII 389.
839   "The Castro movement is infiltrated": Earl Smith 161.
840   "An immediate intervention": R. Murphy 411.
840   "Communists and other extreme": cited DDE *Waging Peace* 521.
840   "The tone of an ultimatum": ibid. 334.
841   "Rather a startling and almost": Macmillan IV 559.
842   "New data . . . indicate that it is more difficult": FonF XIX 1–2.
842   "Shocked at his appearance": Macmillan IV 587.
842   "He seemed to be ready": ibid. 588.
842   "We do not accept . . . We are resolved": FonF XIX 49.
842   "The most valuable man . . . needs him": PPs 1959, 168–69.
842   "I feel this way . . . person I want": ibid. 191–92.
843   He dictated a memorandum: memo Feb. 27, 1959; DDE-G, Berlin Paper folder.
843   "A very great psychological reason": PPs 1959, 210–11.
844   "If a summit . . . worse than no meeting": cited Macmillan IV 625–26.
845   "Shocking and shameful": DDE to Joseph Dodge, July 6, 1959; DDE-A.
845   "Quite convinced that we can have no": Macmillan IV 636.
845   "He was *against* . . . for the President": ibid. 644.
845   "Proposed nothing new": DDE *Waging Peace* 397.
845   "They seem to be off to a very": PPs 1959, 527.
845   "A useful thing": FonF XIX 222.
846   "Many questions, very serious . . . very tough": PPs 1959, 507, 508.
846   "Very reluctantly": R. Murphy 488.
846   "Such progress . . . as would justify": DDE *Waging Peace* 406.
846   "The monotonous Soviet diet of": R. Murphy 487.
846   "A most unpleasant experience": DDE *Waging Peace* 407.
847   "Prospects for . . . easing world tensions": ibid. 412.
847   "One of the worst kept secrets": PPs 1959, 560.
847   "A national disgrace": FonF XIX 246.
847   "Like opening our frontiers": ibid. 279.
847   "This is far from a reversal": PPs 1959, 581.
847   "Was less cautious, or less constrained": Robert R. Bowie interview, OHRO.
847   "Foster rather discouraged me": Livingston Merchant interview, OHRO.
848   "I get a little bit weary": PPs 1959, 593.
848   "I always have wanted . . . let them have it": PPs 1959, 622, 623, 625.
848   "How many . . . along the route": de Gaulle *Memoirs of Hope* 210.
848   "Whether in the realm of": de Gaulle *Memoirs of Hope* 211.
848n. "I have the liveliest feelings of": cited Tournoux *La Tragédie* 327.
848n. "Ce sont des cons": ibid. 256.
849   "After what has happened": ibid. 212.
849   "It is enough to be able": ibid. 215.
850   "This was a noteworthy feat": DDE *Waging Peace* 434.
850   "This seemed, at first, a strange": ibid. 435.
850   "Dispatch . . . an emergency force": FonF XIX 285.
851f. Notes of formal conversation, 3:30 P.M., Sept. 15, 1959; DDE-G.

852f. Notes of private talk, 5 P.M. Sept. 15, 1959; ibid.
853   "Apparent conviction and sincerity . . . I think the American . . . the American people long": PPs 1959, 666.
853   Lodge reports on trip; DDE-G.
854   "The fright in the hall was a tangible": John Osborne 42.
854f. Notes of Camp David talks; DDE-G.
855   "A free city . . . an abnormal situation": PPs 1959, 698.
855   "Almost compelled": ibid. 737.
856   "That no time limit should be": Khrushchev interview with Tass, Sept. 29, 1959; cited Fleming 976.
856   "Not only smiling but": Stone *Fifties* 290.
856   "Mr. Eisenhower brought honor to": Max Freedman in *Manchester Guardian* Oct. 1, 1959; cited Fleming 987.
856   "An effective reduction of tension": FonF XIX 333.
857   "I hope to make this truth clear": PPs 1959, 795.
857   "Predatory force . . . aggression": ibid. 797.
857   "Peace and friendship, in freedom": ibid. 799.
858   "Pro-Communist and his advisers": Thomas *Cuba* 1231.
858   "Castro is not a Communist": ibid. 1249.
859   "We are friendly with the Cuban": PPs 1960, 300.
859   "Well, boys, I'll tell you one thing": DDE interview, DOHP.
859   "It was recognized that some day": Gray to author.
861   "Self-destroying mechanisms were built in": DDE *Waging Peace* 547.
861   "What the hell, they were paying": Confidential source.
861   "We know that they were not": PPs 1960, 412.
861   "As we help our brother, we": ibid. 400.
862   "It is not the burglar who is guilty, but": cited Wise and Ross *U-2 Affair* 129.
862   "Pass severe judgment . . . perfidy": cited DDE *Waging Peace* 553.
862   "Full of apprehension": Macmillan V 202.
862   "I don't know about anybody else . . . under that illusion": notes of meeting, 2:30 P.M., May 15, 1960; DDE-G, Paris meetings folder.
863   "He said that his *friend*": Macmillan V 202–203.
863   "I'll renounce the U-2": notes of meeting, 4:30 P.M., May 15, 1960; DDE-G, Paris meetings folder.
863   "However, the U-2 is now almost": notes of meeting, 6 P.M.; ibid.
863   "Rockets can travel in two": ibid.
864   "Intelligence . . . missions": FonF XX 158.
865   "Depressed and . . . in considerable disarray": Macmillan V 204.
865   "Suspended . . . and not": cited ibid. 205.
865   "Khrushchev: I would like . . . be granted": notes of meeting, May 16, 1960; DDE-G, Paris meetings folder.
865   "A long diatribe": DDE *Waging Peace* 555.
865   "A mixture of abuse": Macmillan V 205.
865   "A statement similar to the one": de Gaulle *Memoirs of Hope* 250.
866   "With us it is easy; you and I": notes of May 18, 1960; DDE-G, Paris meetings folder.
866   "This . . . absurdly ill-timed violation": de Gaulle *Memoirs of Hope* 247.
866   "Disappointment amounting almost": Macmillan V 213.
867   "As manifestations of moral . . . shouldn't do it": PPs 1960, 294.
867   "Bastions of the Free World in the": DDE *Waging Peace* 561.
867f. "The Communists, having canceled": ibid.
868   "Once more what we were up against": ibid. 563.
868   "Persisting demonstrations staged by": ibid. 561.
868   "Viewed from any angle, this was": ibid. 563.
868   "The Communists and extreme left-wing Socialists": ibid. 561.
868   "One clear proof of the value": PPs 1960, 533.
869   "Counterrevolutionary radio station": Wise and Ross *Invisible Government* 331.
869   Want of "imagination," failure to identify: See, for example, Szulc 131 and Schlesinger *Thousand Days* 222.
870   "Yankee imperialists . . . nails of their shoes": FonF XX 222.
870   "Our future course of action": DDE *Waging Peace* 536.
870   "New policies that would reach": ibid. 537.
870   "With the most genuine regret": PPs 1960–61, 563.

870 "This action amounts to economic": cited DDE *Waging Peace* 535.
870 "To show Latin America that the United States": ibid. 536.
870 "For a better way of life for the individual": ibid. 537.
871 "To protect her interests": ibid. 574.
871 "Not to restore . . . by Belgian metropolitan troops": FonF XX 241.
871 "To watch hourly over the situation": ibid. 255.
872 "Now Congo may play the role": Macmillan V 265.
872 "The radical and unstable Congolese": DDE *Waging Peace* 573.
872 "We were . . . convinced . . . was a Soviet": ibid. 574.
872 "A Communist sympathizer if not a": ibid. 575.
872 "A man of . . . moderation": 573.
872 "Reviewed as a whole, the Congo crisis": ibid. 576.
873 "Entire world": cited ibid. 584.
873 "All we want out of Ike is": T. H. White, *Making of the President 1960* 309.
875 "Was most likely to be nominated": Nixon 305.
875 "To tell us some of the . . . I don't remember": PPs 1960, 652–53.
875 "Dick Nixon has the broadest": PPs 1960, 736.
875 "Was to plague me": Nixon 339.
875 "To one of my strongest": ibid.
875 "Should be more hard-hitting . . . and candidates": cited DDE *Waging Peace* 599.
876 "Fear-mongering . . . misguided people": PPs 1960, 779, 789.
876 "Could not hide . . . more depressed": Nixon 395.
876 "We were robbed . . . I heard something about that, Dick . . . finished politically forever": *N.Y. Times* April 6, 1969, 1, 32.
877 "Still had lots of fight left": Nixon 395.
877 "To begin winding up our affairs": DDE *Waging Peace* 603.
877 "A broad outline . . . decade and longer": FonF XX 47.
877 "Look, Henry, it's like": Henry Wriston interview, OHRO.
878 "Was leaving the presidency": Adams 453.
878 "Although intermittent declines in": PPs 1960–61, 921.
878 "Young whippersnapper": Schlesinger *Thousand Days* 126.
880 "The policy of this government": ibid. 164.
880 "A little hope of humanity": FonF XXI 29.
880 "Developing and maintaining a strong": PPs 1954, 949.
880 "Dissatisfaction and discontent": *Pentagon Papers* 3.
881 "An accomplice . . . of the Communist": DDE *Waging Peace* 608.
881 "One to which we could give": ibid. 609.
881 "For the moment . . . or without them": cited ibid. 610.
881 "The United States lost no foot": DDE *Waging Peace* 624.
882 "Our unilateral intervention": cited Clifford 604.
882 "We must avoid the impulse to live": PPs 1960–61, 1039.
882 "A peace guaranteed by the binding": ibid. 1040.

SIX

WHAT REMAINED OF LIFE

885 "Well, my wife thinks it's nothing": CBS Reports, Eisenhower on the Presidency, Part II, Nov. 23, 1961, 1.
887 "Overzealous central agencies . . . mania . . . dominate": FonF XXI 273.
887 "What else can I do? I put a stop": *N.Y. Times* Oct. 14, 1961.
887 "Obviously floundering": FonF XXII 217.
888 "Strenuous efforts . . . a threat to our": ibid. 156.
888 "Our concept of beauty . . . in our standards": ibid. 204.
888 "If Secretary Humphrey ever": ibid. 180.
890 "A dime-store New Deal": cited T. H. White *Making of the President 1964* 109.
891 "Commonsense" candidate: *N.Y. Times* Dec. 8, 1963.

892   The formula he devised: *N.Y. Herald Tribune,* May 25, 1964.
892   "I'll be watching": Scranton to author, June 1973.
892   "Cabal": ibid.
892   "I was never trained in politics . . . you never know": cited T. H. White *Making of the President 1964* 73.
893   "Frankly, I'm sick about it": Scranton to author, June 1973.
893   "A free, fair, and active competition": FonF XXIV 194.
893   "Do my best to support": ibid. 235.
894   "Would seem to say that the end": ibid. 236.
894   "Satisfied": ibid. 262.
894   "The man, like his book": Kirstein.
895   "A way of coming out rosy": James Reston *N.Y. Times Book Review* Nov. 10, 1963.
895   "The deficiencies of the memoir . . . wrong at any point": Handlin in *Atlantic,* Oct. 1965.
895   "The global turmoil entirely in terms of": Kissinger in *Book Week,* Oct. 17, 1965.
895   "Taken over and really seized": Johnson speech, May 2, 1965; cited Evans and Novak 522.
895   "A sensible thing . . . I have nothing to criticize": FonF XXV 171.
896   "I believe the United States has been becoming": ibid. 295.
896   "I support the President on Vietnam": FonF XXV 297.
896   "To break the will of Vietnam": See *Pentagon Papers* 468.
897   "Given sanctuary": FonF XXVI 27.
897   "Serves admirably to flesh out": *N.Y. Times Book Review,* June 18, 1967.
898   "Official Washington reacted with mild": *Pentagon Papers* 480.
898   "Disillusioned doves" led by: ibid. 511.
899   "Aimed exclusively at military targets . . . unfortunately, there are some civilians": *N.Y. Times* Dec. 28, 1966.
899   "With seeds of the worst split": *Pentagon Papers* 535.
899   "War of gradualism . . . should be given": *N.Y. Times* July 22, 1967.
899   "Take any action . . . court above you": ibid. Oct. 4, 1967.
899n. "That you don't inform the enemy": ibid.
899n. "This is silly": cited Larson *Eisenhower* 174.
900   "And when they understand it . . . are talking about surrendering": CBS News Special, Nov. 28, 1967.
900   "The first task of a new administration": DDE speech, Detroit, Oct. 24, 1952.
901   "The current raucous confrontation . . . *of South Vietnam*": *Reader's Digest,* April 1968, 49–53.
902   He was disposed to believe that of the two: See R. L. Tobin 29.
903   "The greatest victory in the history . . . the good of mankind": cited Ambrose 667.
904   "The United States never lost a soldier": cited Anderson 179.
904   He was at once the most popular and the most criticized American: James Reston in *N.Y. Times* Jan. 19, 1961, 20.
904   "An atmosphere of greater serenity": CBS Reports, Eisenhower on the Presidency, Part I, Oct. 12, 1961.
904   "If the conclusion that . . . great accomplishment": ibid.
905   "The most mouth-watering pork-barrel": Denison and Tomlinson.
905   "Avenues of escape . . . beyond calculation": DDE *Mandate* 501, 548–49.
905f. "The biggest damfool mistake": Sources cited at p. 598.
909   He was aware of his one surpassing failure: R. L. Tobin 29–30.
910   "You forgot Dick!" "Oh, yes": Leo 95; see also *N.Y. Times* July 19, 1968.
910   "This is a mere misapprehension": *N.Y. Times,* ibid.
911   "Nothing is more telling of the esteem": ibid. Aug. 21, 1968.
911   "The proportions of a miracle": AP dispatch, Oct. 13, 1968.
911   "Has spent a comfortable . . . no appreciable improvement": bulletins published in *N.Y. Times,* February and March, passim.
912   "I've always loved my wife": *N.Y. Times* Mar. 31, 1969.

Bibliography

Acheson, Dean, *Present at the Creation,* Norton 1969.

Adams, Sherman, *First-Hand Report,* Harper 1961.

Albertson, Dean, ed., *Eisenhower As President,* Hill and Wang 1963.

Allen, George, *Presidents Who Have Known Me,* Simon & Schuster 1960.

Alperowitz, Gar, *Atomic Diplomacy: Hiroshima and Potsdam,* Vintage 1965.
    Cold War Essays, Doubleday Anchor 1970.

Alsop, Joseph and Stewart, *The Reporter's Trade,* Reynal 1958.

Alsop, Stewart, *Nixon and Rockefeller: A Double Portrait,* Doubleday 1960.

Ambrose, Stephen E., *Eisenhower and Berlin, 1945,* Norton 1967.
    The Supreme Commander, Doubleday 1970.

American Heritage, Editors of, *Eisenhower, American Hero,* American Heritage Publishing 1969.

Anderson, Dillon, "The President and National Security," *Atlantic,* January 1956.

Anderson, Patrick, *The President's Men,* Doubleday 1968.

(Anonymous) "The Attack on the Irrigation Dams in North Korea," *Air University Quarterly,* 6, Winter 1953–54.
    "What Goes On at Ike's Dinners," *U.S. News & World Report,* February 4, 1955.

Aptheker, Herbert, *American Foreign Policy and the Cold War,* New Century 1962.

Army Times, Editors of, *The Challenge and the Triumph: The Story of General Dwight D. Eisenhower,* Putnam 1966.

Arnold, H. H., *Global Mission,* Harper 1949.

Ayer, Fred, Jr., *Before the Colors Fade: Portrait of a Soldier, George S. Patton, Jr.,* Houghton Mifflin 1964.

Bainbridge, John, *The Super-Americans,* Doubleday 1961.

Barnet, Richard J., *Intervention and Revolution,* Meridian 1968.

Beal, John Robinson, *John Foster Dulles,* Harper & Row 1957.

Beaufre, André, *NATO and Europe,* Knopf 1966.

Ben Gurion, David, *Israel: Years of Challenge,* Holt, Rinehart & Winston 1963.

Benson, Ezra Taft, *Crossfire,* Doubleday 1962.

Bernstein, Jeremy, "O Crucified Jove," *The New Yorker,* May 10, 1969.

Bethe, Hans, "The Case for Ending Nuclear Tests," *Atlantic,* August 1960.

Bidwell, Percy, *Raw Materials,* Harper 1958.

Blumenson, Martin, *Sicily: Whose Victory?,* Ballantine 1968.

Bradley, Omar N., *A Soldier's Story,* Holt 1951.

Brookings Institution, *Major Problems of United States Foreign Policy, 1954* (Washington), 1954.

Brown, Ralph S., Jr., *Loyalty and Security,* Yale University Press, 1958.

Bryant, Arthur, *A History of the War Years Based on the Diaries of Field-Marshal Lord Alanbrooke:* Volume I *The Turn of the Tide,* Doubleday 1957; Volume II *Victory in the West,* Collins 1959.

Butcher, Harry, *My Three Years with Eisenhower,* Simon & Schuster 1946.

Butler, J. R. M., *Grand Strategy* Volume II (September 1939–June 1941) and Volume III (June 1941–August 1942) Part II, in *A History of the Second World War*, ed. J. R. M. Butler, Her Majesty's Stationery Office; Volume II 1957, Volume III 1964.

Byrnes, James F., *Speaking Frankly*, Harper 1947.

Calder, Angus, *The People's War*, Pantheon 1969.

Campbell, Angus, Philip E. Converse, Warren E. Miller, and Donald E. Stokes, *The American Voter*, Wiley 1960.

Carroll, Wallace, *Persuade or Perish*, Houghton Mifflin 1948.

Catton, Bruce, *The War Lords of Washington*, Harcourt Brace 1948.

Chandler, Alfred P., Jr., ed., *The Papers of Dwight David Eisenhower: The War Years*, 5 vols., The Johns Hopkins Press 1970.

Childs, Marquis, *Eisenhower, Captive Hero*, Harcourt Brace 1958.

Churchill, Winston S., *The Second World War* (Houghton Mifflin): Volume III *The Grand Alliance*, 1950; Volume IV *The Hinge of Fate*, 1950; Volume V *Closing the Ring*, 1951; Volume VI *Triumph and Tragedy*, 1953.

Ciano, Galeazzo, *The Ciano Diaries*, ed. Hugh Gibson, Doubleday 1946.

Clark, Alan, *Barbarossa*, Penguin 1966.

Clark, Mark, *Calculated Risk*, Harper 1950.
　　　From the Danube to the Yalu, Harper 1954.

Clay, Lucius D., *Decision in Germany*, Doubleday 1950.

Clifford, Clark M., "A Viet Nam Reappraisal," *Foreign Affairs*, July 1969.

Cline, Ray S., *Washington Command Post: The Operations Division*, Department of the Army 1951.

Cochran, Bert, *Adlai Stevenson*, Funk & Wagnalls 1969.

Coles, Harry L., and Albert K. Weinberg, *Civil Affairs: Soldiers Become Governors*, Department of the Army 1964.

Conner, Virginia, *What Father Forbad*, Dorrance 1951.

Cook, Fred J., *The Warfare State*, Macmillan 1962.
　　　"The CIA," *The Nation*, Vol. 192, p. 529.

Cooper, Chester L., *The Lost Crusade*, Dodd, Mead 1970.

Correspondence Between the Chairman of the Council of Ministers of the USSR and the Presidents of the U.S. and the Prime Ministers of Great Britain During the Great Patriotic War of 1941–1945, Foreign Language Publishing House, Moscow, 1957.

Crankshaw, Edward, ed., *Khrushchev Remembers*, Bantam 1971.

Cutler, Robert, *No Time for Rest*, Little, Brown 1966.
　　　"The Development of the N.S.C.," *Foreign Affairs*, April 1956.

Daugherty, William E., and Morris Janowitz, *A Psychological Warfare Casebook*, The Johns Hopkins Press 1958.

David, Paul T., and others, *Presidential Nominating Politics in 1952*, The Johns Hopkins Press 1954.

Davis, Kenneth S., *Soldier of Democracy*, Doubleday Doran 1945.

Deane, John R., *The Strange Alliance*, Viking 1947.

de Guingand, Francis, *Operation Victory*, Hodder & Stoughton 1947.
　　　Generals at War, Hodder & Stoughton 1964.

Denison, George, and Kenneth Y. Tomlinson, "Let's Put Brakes on the Highway Lobby," *Reader's Digest*, May 1969.

Donovan, Richard, "Birth of a Salesman," *The Reporter*, October 14, 1952.

Donovan, Robert J., *Eisenhower: The Inside Story*, Harper 1956.

Dönitz, Karl, *Memoirs*, Hillary 1958.

Drummond, Roscoe, and Gaston Coblentz, *Duel at the Brink*, Doubleday 1960.

Dulles, Allen, *The Craft of Intelligence*, Harper & Row 1963.
　　　The Secret Surrender, Harper & Row 1966.

Dulles, Eleanor Lansing, *John Foster Dulles: The Last Year*, Harcourt, Brace & World 1963.

Dulles, John Foster, "Policy for Security and Peace," *Foreign Affairs*, April 1954.

Eden, Anthony, *The Reckoning*, Houghton Mifflin 1965.

 Full Circle, Cassell 1960.

Ehrlich, Blake, *Resistance: France*, Little, Brown 1965.

Ehrman, John, *Grand Strategy* Volumes V (August 1943–September 1944) and VI (October 1944–August 1945), in *A History of the Second World War*, ed. J. R. M. Butler, Her Majesty's Stationery Office; both volumes 1956.

Eisenhower, Dwight D., "A Tank Discussion," *Infantry Journal*, November 1920.

 "War Policies," *Infantry Journal*, November–December 1931.

 Crusade in Europe, Doubleday, 1948.

 Mandate for Change, Doubleday 1963.

 Waging Peace, Doubleday 1965.

 At Ease, Doubleday 1967.

 "Let's Close Ranks on the Home Front," *Reader's Digest*, April 1968.

 (*See also* Chandler.)

Eisenhower, Milton S., *The Wine Is Bitter*, Doubleday 1963.

Elson, Edward L. R., *America's Spiritual Recovery*, Revell 1954.

Engler, Robert, *The Politics of Oil*, University of Chicago Press 1961.

Evans, Rowland, and Robert Novak, *Lyndon B. Johnson*, New American Library 1966.

Farago, Ladislas, *Patton*, Ivan Obolensky 1964.

Finer, Herman, *Dulles Over Suez*, Quadrangle 1964.

Finney, John W., "The Long Trial of John Paton Davies," *New York Times Magazine*, August 31, 1969.

Fleming, D. F., *The Cold War and Its Origins*, 2 vols., Doubleday 1961.

Fontaine, André, *Histoire de la Guerre Froide*, 2 vols., Fayard 1965–7.

Foot, Michael R. D., *SOE in France 1940–1944*, Her Majesty's Stationery Office 1966.

Forrestal, James, *The Forrestal Diaries*, ed. Walter Millis, Viking 1951.

Fuentes, Miguel Ydigoras, *My War with Communism*, Prentice-Hall 1963.

Galeano, Eduardo, *Guatemala: Occupied Country*, Monthly Review Press 1969.

Garland, Albert N., and Howard M. Smyth, *Sicily and the Surrender of Italy*, Department of the Army 1965.

Gaulle, Charles de, *War Memoirs* Volume II, *Unity*, Weidenfeld & Nicolson 1959.

 Memoirs of Hope, Simon & Schuster 1971.

Goebbels, Paul Josef, *The Goebbels Diaries*, ed. Louis P. Lochner, The Infantry Journal Press and Doubleday 1948.

Goebel, Dorothy Burns, and Julius Goebel, Jr., *Generals in the White House*, Doubleday 1945.

Goldman, Eric F., *The Crucial Decade—and After*, Vintage 1960.

Graebner, Norman A., "Eisenhower's Popular Leadership," *Current History*, October 1960.

Gray, Robert Keith, *Eighteen Acres Under Glass*, Doubleday 1962.

Greenfield, Kent Roberts, ed. *Command Decisions*, Department of the Army 1960.

Greenfield, Kent Roberts, and Stetson Conn, eds., see *United States Army in World War II*.

Gunther, John, "With Eisenhower in Sicily," *Collier's*, September 25, 1943.

 The Riddle of MacArthur, Harper 1951.

 Eisenhower: The Man and the Symbol, Harper 1952.

Gwyer, J. M. A., *Grand Strategy* Volume III (June 1941–August 1942) Part I, in *A History of the Second World War*, ed. J. R. M. Butler, Her Majesty's Stationery Office 1964.

Hadley, Arthur T., *The Nation's Safety and Arms Control*, Viking 1961.

Halle, Louis J., *The Cold War As History*, Colophon Books, Harper and Row 1971.

Handlin, Oscar, "Do the Voters Want Moderation?" *Commentary*, September 1956.

Harkness, Richard and Gladys, "The Mysterious Doings of CIA," *Saturday Evening Post,* November 6, 1954.

Harrison, Gordon A., *Cross-Channel Attack,* Department of the Army 1951.

Harsch, Joseph C., "What's Happened to Ike?" *The Reporter,* October 28, 1952.

Hatch, Alden, *General Ike,* Holt 1944.

Herz, Martin F., *Beginnings of the Cold War,* McGraw-Hill 1969.

History of the Second World War, A, ed. J. R. M. Butler, United Kingdom Military Series, Her Majesty's Stationery Office; Volumes II, III, V and VI of *Grand Strategy,* see entries at Butler, Ehrman, and Gwyer.

Horowitz, David, *From Yalta to Vietnam,* Penguin 1967.

—— ed., *Containment and Revolution,* Anthony Blond 1967.

Howe, George F., *Northwest Africa,* Department of the Army 1957.

Hughes, Emmet John, *The Ordeal of Power,* Atheneum 1963.

Huntington, Samuel P., *The Soldier and the State,* Harvard University Press 1957.

—— *The Common Defense,* Columbia University Press 1961.

Hyman, Sidney, "The Failure of the Eisenhower Presidency," *The Progressive,* May 1960.

Ingersoll, Ralph, *Top Secret,* Harcourt Brace 1946.

Ismay, Hastings, *Memoirs,* Heinemann 1960.

Janowitz, Morris, *The Professional Soldier,* Free Press of Glencoe 1960.

Jones, Joseph M., *The Fifteen Weeks,* Harbinger Books, Harcourt Brace Jovanovich 1964.

Jungk, Robert, *Brighter Than a Thousand Suns,* Harcourt Brace 1958.

Kempton, Murray, "The Underestimation of Dwight D. Eisenhower," *Esquire,* September 1967.

Kennan, George E., *Memoirs,* Little, Brown: Volume I, *1925–1950,* 1967; Volume II, *1950–1963* 1972.

Kirk, Betty, "Policy of the Suction Pump," *The Nation,* October 5, 1957.

Kirkpatrick, Ivone, *Mussolini,* Avon 1968.

Kirstein, G. G., "Crusade in America," *The Nation,* November 23, 1963.

Kissinger, Henry A., *Nuclear Weapons and Foreign Policy,* Harper 1957.

Knebel, Fletcher, "Ike's Cronies," *Look* June 1954.

Knoll, Erwin, "The Oil Lobby Is Not Depleted," *New York Times Magazine,* March 8, 1970.

Kolko, Gabriel, *The Politics of War,* Random House 1968.

Kolko, Joyce and Gabriel, *The Limits of Power,* Harper & Row 1972.

Kornitzer, Bela, *The Great American Heritage,* Farrar, Straus & Cudahy 1955.

Kraft, Joseph, "School for Statesmen," *Harper's,* July 1958.

Krock, Arthur, *Memoirs,* Funk & Wagnalls 1968.

LaFeber, Walter, *America, Russia, and the Cold War 1945–1966,* Wiley 1967.

Langer, William L., *Our Vichy Gamble,* Norton 1966.

Larson, Arthur, *A Republican Looks at His Party,* Harper 1956.

—— *Eisenhower, the President Nobody Knew,* Popular Library 1968.

Leo, John, "Dwight David Eisenhower: Ranking an Ex-President," *Commonweal,* April 11, 1969.

Liebling, A. J., *The Road Back to Paris,* Doubleday Doran 1944.

—— *Mollie,* Ballantine 1964.

Lilienthal, David, *Journals* (Harper & Row): Volume II *The Atomic Energy Years,* 1965; Volume III *Venturesome Years,* 1967.

Lockhart, Robert H. Bruce, *Comes the Reckoning,* Putnam 1947.

Love, Kennett, *Suez: The Twice-Fought War,* McGraw-Hill 1969.

Lyon, Peter, *The Wild Wild West,* Funk & Wagnalls 1969.

MacArthur, Douglas, *Reminiscences,* McGraw-Hill 1965.

Macmillan, Harold, *Memoirs:* Volume II *Blast of War,* Macmillan (London) 1967; Volume III *Tides of Fortune,* Harper 1969; Volume IV *Riding the Storm,* Harper 1971; Volume V *Pointing the Way,* Macmillan (London) 1972.

Magdoff, Harry, *The Age of Imperialism,* Monthly Review Press 1969.

Marshall, Katherine Tupper, *Together,* Tupper and Love 1946.

Matloff, Maurice, *Strategic Planning for Coalition Warfare, 1943–1944,* Department of the Army 1959.

Matloff, Maurice, and Edwin M. Snell, *Strategic Planning for Coalition Warfare, 1941–1942,* Department of the Army 1953.

Matthews, J. B., "Reds and Our Churches," *American Mercury,* July 1953.

Mazo, Earl, *Richard Nixon,* Avon 1960.

McCann, Kevin, *Man from Abilene,* Doubleday 1952.

McKeogh, Michael, and Richard Lockridge, *Sergeant Mickey and General Ike,* Putnam 1946.

Merson, Martin, "A Businessman Gets the Business," *Washington Post & Times Herald,* October 10, 1954.

Miller, Francis Trevelyan, *Eisenhower: Man and Soldier,* Winston 1944.

Miller, William Lee, *Piety Along the Potomac,* Houghton Mifflin 1964.

Montgomery, Bernard, *Memoirs,* World 1958.

    An Appeal to Sanity, World 1960.

Morgenthau, Hans J., "The Decline and Fall of American Foreign Policy," *New Republic,* December 10, 17, 1956.

    "Arguing About the Cold War," *Encounter,* May 1967.

Morrow, E. Frederic, *Black Man in the White House,* Coward-McCann 1963.

Murphy, Charles J. V., "Eisenhower's White House," *Fortune,* July 1953.

    "The Eisenhower Shift," *Fortune,* January, February, March, and April 1956.

    "The Budget and Eisenhower," *Fortune,* July 1957.

    "The White House Since Sputnik," *Fortune,* January 1958.

Murphy, Robert, *Diplomat Among Warriors,* Pyramid Books 1965.

Neustadt, Richard E., *Presidential Power,* Wiley 1960.

Nicolson, Harold, *Diaries and Letters,* Volume II, Atheneum 1967.

Nirumand, Bahman, *Iran, the New Imperialism in Action,* Monthly Review Press 1969.

Nixon, Richard M., *Six Crises,* Doubleday 1962.

Nutting, Anthony, *No End of a Lesson,* Potter 1967.

O'Brien, Conor Cruise, "The Congo: A Balance Sheet," *New Left Review,* May-June 1965.

Osborne, Charles, ed., *Ike: A Pictorial Biography,* Time-Life Books 1969.

Osborne, John, "Final Image," *Life,* October 5, 1959.

Parmet, Herbert S., *Eisenhower and the American Crusades,* Macmillan 1972.

Pearson, Drew, and Jack Anderson, *The Case Against Congress,* Simon & Schuster 1968.

Pendar, Kenneth, *Adventure in Diplomacy,* Cassell 1966.

Pentagon Papers, see Neil Sheehan.

Phillips, Cabell, *The Truman Presidency,* Macmillan 1966.

Pogue, Forrest C., *The Supreme Command,* Department of the Army 1954.

    George C. Marshall (Viking): Volume I *Education of a General,* 1963; Volume II *Ordeal and Hope,* 1966.

Potter, Charles E., *Days of Shame,* Coward-McCann 1965.

Powers, Francis Gary, *Operation Overflight,* Holt Rinehart & Winston 1970.

Public Papers of the Presidents, 1953 to 1960–1961, 8 vols., U.S. Government Printing Office 1960–61.

Pusey, Merlo, *Eisenhower the President,* Macmillan 1956.

Pyle, Ernie, *Here Is Your War,* Holt 1943.

Raskin, Marcus G., and Bernard B. Fall, eds., *The Viet-Nam Reader,* Vintage 1965.

Roberts, Chalmers, "The Day We Didn't Go to War," *The Reporter,* September 14, 1954.

Robichon, Jacques, "Les Alliés Débarquaient en Afrique," *Historia,* November 1967.

Rogow, Arnold A., *James Forrestal,* Macmillan 1963.

Rostow, Walt W., *The United States in the World Arena*, Harper 1960.

Rovere, Richard, *Affairs of State: The Eisenhower Years*, Farrar, Straus & Cudahy 1956.

    "Eisenhower Over the Shoulder," *American Scholar*, Spring 1962.

    "The Untold Story of McCarthy's Fall," *New York Review*, October 28, 1965.

    Senator Joe McCarthy, Meridian 1960.

Rundell, Walter, Jr., *Black Market Money: The Collapse of U.S. Military Control*, Louisiana University Press 1964.

Scheer, Robert, and Warren Hinckle, "The 'Vietnam Lobby,'" *Ramparts*, July 1965.

Schlesinger, Arthur M., Jr., *A Thousand Days: John F. Kennedy in the White House*, Houghton Mifflin 1965.

    "Origins of the Cold War," *Foreign Affairs*, October 1967.

Schneir, Walter and Miriam, *Invitation to an Inquest*, Doubleday 1965.

Scott, Peter Dale, "Laos: The Story Nixon Won't Tell," *New York Review*, April 9, 1970.

Seale, Patrick, *The Struggle for Syria*, Oxford University Press 1965.

Seide, Ray, "How I Selected Westerns, Bought Socks, and Prepared Paintings for President Eisenhower," *Esquire*, March 1962.

Shannon, William V., "Eisenhower As President," *Commentary*, November 1958.

Sheehan, Neil, Hedrick Smith, E. W. Kenworthy, and Fox Butterfield, *The Pentagon Papers*, Bantam 1971.

Shepley, James, "How Dulles Averted War," *Life*, January 16, 1956.

Sherwood, Robert, *Roosevelt and Hopkins*, Harper 1948.

Smith, Earl E. T., *The Fourth Floor*, Random House 1962.

Smith, Fred, "The Rise and Fall of the Morgenthau Plan," *United Nations World*, March 1947.

Smith, Merriman, *Meet Mister Eisenhower*, Harper 1954.

Smith, W. Bedell, *My Three Years in Moscow*, Lippincott 1950.

    Eisenhower's Six Great Decisions, Longmans Green 1956.

Snow, Edgar, *Journey to the Beginning*, Random House 1958.

Steel, Ronald, *Pax Americana*, Compass Books, Viking 1968.

Stein, Harold, ed., *American Civil-Military Decisions*, University of Alabama Press 1963.

Stern, Philip M., *The Oppenheimer Case*, Harper & Row 1969.

Stimson, Henry, and McGeorge Bundy, *On Active Service*, Harper 1948.

Stone, I. F., *The Hidden History of the Korean War*, Monthly Review Press 1952.

    The Haunted Fifties, Random House 1963.

    Polemics and Prophecies, 1967–1970, Random House 1970.

Strauss, Lewis L., *Men and Decisions*, Doubleday 1962.

Strong, Kenneth, *Intelligence at the Top*, Doubleday 1969.

Sulzberger, Cyrus L., *A Long Row of Candles*, Macmillan 1969.

    The Last of the Giants, Macmillan 1970.

Summersby, Kay, *Eisenhower Was My Boss*, Prentice-Hall 1948.

Szulc, Tad, *The Winds of Revolution*, Praeger 1963.

Taft, Robert A., *A Foreign Policy for Americans*, Doubleday 1951.

Tatu, Michael, *Power in the Kremlin*, Viking 1969.

Taylor, Maxwell D., *The Uncertain Trumpet*, Harper 1960.

Tedder, Arthur, *With Prejudice*, Little, Brown 1966.

Thomas, Hugh, *Suez*, Harper & Row 1967.

    Cuba, Harper & Row 1971.

Tobin, James, "The Eisenhower Economy and National Security: Defense, Dollars, and Doctrines," *Yale Review*, March 1958.

Tobin, Richard L., "Dwight D. Eisenhower: What I Have Learned," *Saturday Review*, September 10, 1966.

Toland, John, *The Last 100 Days*, Bantam 1967.

Tournoux, Jean-Raymond, *Sécrets d'État*, Plon 1961.
    La Tragédie du Général, Plon 1967.
Treuenfels, Rudolph, ed., *Eisenhower Speaks*, Farrar, Straus 1948.
Truman, Harry S., *Memoirs* (Doubleday): Volume I *Year of Decisions*, 1955. Volume II *Years of Trial and Hope*, 1956.
Truscott, Lucian K., Jr., *Command Missions*, Dutton 1954.
Tully, Andrew, "Ike's Bunkered Haven," *Collier's*, August 5, 1955.
United States Army in World War II, The, ed. Kent Roberts Greenfield and Stetson Conn, Department of the Army; see entries under Cline (1951), Coles and Weinberg (1964), Garland and Smyth (1965), Harrison (1951), Howe (1957), Matloff (1959), Matloff and Snell (1953), Pogue (1954).
Vandenberg, Arthur, Jr., ed., *Private Papers of Arthur Vandenberg*, Houghton Mifflin 1952.
Wanamaker, Temple, *American Foreign Policy Today*, Bantam Matrix 1964.
Warlimont, Walter, *Inside Hitler's Headquarters*, Praeger 1964.
Waugh, Evelyn, *Unconditional Surrender*, Chapman & Hall 1961.
Weaver, John D., "Bonus March," *American Heritage*, June 1963.
Werth, Alexander, *Russia at War*, Dutton 1964.
White, Theodore H., *Making of the President 1960*, Atheneum 1961.
    Making of the President 1964, Atheneum 1965.
    ed., *The Stilwell Papers*, Sloane 1948.
White, William S., *The Taft Story*, Harper 1954.
Williams, William Appleman, *The Tragedy of American Diplomacy*, Dell 1962.
Wills, Garry, *Nixon Agonistes*, Houghton Mifflin 1970.
Wilmot, Chester, *The Struggle for Europe*, Collins 1952.
Wise, David, and Thomas B. Ross, *The U-2 Affair*, Random House 1962.
    The Invisible Government, Random House 1964.
Ziemke, Earl F., *Stalingrad to Berlin*, Army Historical Series, ed. Stetson Conn, Department of the Army 1968.

Index

censorship, Eisenhower's use of, 188, 290, 296

Central Intelligence Agency (CIA), 114n, 390, 563, 621, 632, 722, 727, 732, 753, 858, 908; Iranian coup, 585; 587; Guatemalan operation, 627–628, 634, 649–651; and Vietnam, 643, 654; in China, 661, 663, 669, 674, 675, 686, 908; in Suez crisis, 749–750; in Syria, 792; Indonesian operation, 812–815; in Lebanon, 814–815, 820–821; Cuban counterrevolution, 858–859, 868, 870, 879, 887. See also U-2's

Ceylon, 110, 111

Chambers, General William E., 278

Chamoun, Camille, 794, 814–815, 818, 823

Chatel, Yves, 180

Chiang Kai-shek, Generalissimo, 109, 115, 266, 389, 394, 428, 435, 501, 552, 566, 647, 660–663, 669–671, 676–680, 683–685, 831, 834, 836, 908

China: alliance with, 193; Communist-Nationalist conflict, 389, 435, 660; Communist victory, 428, 485; relation to Soviet Union, 445, 459, 676–677, 852, 907; McCarthy's effect on policy toward, 549, 556; Nationalists backed by U.S., 550–552; and Korean truce, 568; conferences with, 617, 619, 633; Soviet oil to, 647; U.S. policy toward, 656, 660–661, 670, 676–687; offshore islands crisis, 660–664, 669–671, 674–675, 831–836, 908; U.S. prisoners, 669, 686; Eisenhower and, 672–686. See also Chiang Kai-shek; Chou En-lai; Korean War

China "lobby," 653, 661–662, 672, 685, 733, 907

China-Burma-India theater of war, 109, 115. See also Stilwell

Chotiner, Murray, 482, 483, 485n, 487

Chou En-lai, 568, 645, 676, 683, 685

Churchill, Prime Minister Winston, 12, 99, 161, 199, 278, 279, 303, 332, 642n, 666, 672, 677; attitude toward Soviet Union, 6, 15, 354–355, 359; and Eisenhower, 6, 138, 143, 156, 197, 264, 282, 335, 569–570, 613–614; German surrender and occupation, 14, 19; postwar policy, 15, 313–316, 356; in wartime, 106–107, 107n, 113, 114, 119, 120, 129–135, 138, 144–148, 155–157, 170, 181, 184, 191, 201, 203, 216, 218–222, 248, 262–275, 283, 286–287, 303, 324, 345–347; French policy, 220, 223, 227, 276–277, 296; Italian policy, 234–237, 242, 244, 246, 260n; on Berlin capture, 353–354, 358, 359; at Potsdam, 370–374; and Cold War, 393, 447, 565; promotes summit conference, 570, 573–574, 655, 688; Suez crisis, 578–582; Bermuda Conference, 617–619; Southeast Asia issue, 641–645 passim, 654

Citizens for Eisenhower, 452, 454, 459, 471n, 514

civil liberties, 521, 527, 622, 905

civil rights, 773; Truman program, 408; and Eisenhower, 433, 468, 541, 589–599, 720–721, 777n–778n, 786–790, 796, 800, 828–829, 905; racial injustice, 720–721, 795, 796, 829; 1957 act, 785–790, 796; Little Rock crisis, 793–801; Eisenhower meets leaders, 828; sit-ins, 867; civil disobedience, 895. See also school integration

Civilian Conservation Corps (CCC), 74–76

Clay, General Lucius, 19–21, 22n, 370, 372, 376, 377, 383, 399, 412, 420, 424, 672, 717n, 84on; political background, 369; and Eisenhower's presidential campaigns, 454–460, 463–464, 471, 481, 482, 715, 716; presidential adviser, 493, 499, 535n

Cohn, Roy, 556, 566. See also McCarthy, Senator Joseph

Cold War, 114n, 398, 667; prelude, 15, 22, 133, 137, 350; basis, 214, 373n, 499; formulation of policy, 318; Eisenhower and, 351, 404, 404n, 412–413, 446, 500, 504, 547, 672, 687, 906; begins, 393; U.S.-U.S.S.R. positions, 423–426; U.S. policy, 499–500, 648, 692, 724, 802; relation to fiscal policy,

831; Berlin crisis, 840, 842; death, 845; on U-2's, 859. *See also* foreign affairs

Dunnigan, Alice, 592

Durkin, Secretary of Labor Martin P., 497, 539–540

Eaker, General Ira, 250

Eban, Abba, 730n, 749, 758, 777

Eberstadt, Ferdinand, 390

Eddy, General Manton, 206n, 212

Eden, Sir Anthony, 6, 167, 223, 236, 240, 242, 286, 294, 464, 494, 520, 552, 577, 582, 614, 619, 632; and Southeast Asia, 639, 643–644, 654; and U.S. Caribbean policy, 648; and China, 666; European mutual defense, 667–668; as prime minister, 689; Soviet negotiations and, 689; on four-power conference, 699; linguistic skill, 700; supports U.S.S.R., 702n–703n; and Middle East, 724, 726, 728–731; conflict with John Foster Dulles, 728, 742–745; Suez crisis, 729, 736–748, 756, 760, 762–770; illness, 729–730, 746n

Egypt, 189, 578, 580–581, 723n, 724–749, 752, 757–769, 773–775, 779, 816

Eichelberger, General Robert, 250

Eisenhower, Arthur (brother), 29, 34, 41, 279

Eisenhower, Barbara Anne (granddaughter), 416

Eisenhower, Barbara Jean Thompson (daughter-in-law), 416, 502

Eisenhower, David (father), 33–36, 38–39, 41, 74, 115–116

Eisenhower, Dwight David

PERSONAL: as hero, 7–8, 14, 23–30, 33, 143, 182, 365–366, 446, 547, 876; appearance and characteristics, 8, 62, 74–75, 93, 121, 140–142, 159, 182, 194, 227, 254, 280, 311, 328, 365, 475, 737; background, 33–41, 505; sports, interest in, 41, 45, 49, 207, 543–544, 546, 640, 707, 780, 827; West Point, 42–48; prewar army service, 46–86; marriage, 51; children, 57–59, 60 (*see also* Eisenhower,

John); friendships, 64, 92; relaxation, means of, 157, 207, 232, 278–279, 282, 492–493, 543–546, 593–594; writing, 179, 202, 396–398, 403, 490, 513n, 885–886, 894, 897, 901; leadership, views on, 202n, 217; his own leadership, 222, 280–283, 367, 502–504, 532, 780, 912; habits, 230, 418; health, 233, 238–239, 418, 456, 565–566, 709–713, 714, 715, 718, 727, 734, 761, 806–810, 898–900, 901, 909–911; and public, 282, 332, 543, 885; nickname, 282; finances, 291, 396–398, 420, 456, 490, 885; tastes, 291–292, 330, 416; painting, 416, 546, 707, 901; contrast between private and public self, 365–369, 857–858; economics, views on, 446n, 468n, 515, 530; religion, views on, 497n, 505–507, 699; bridge, fondness for, 544; retirement, 885–911; death, 911–912

IN WARTIME: in War Plans Division of War Department, 86–125, 141; commanding general, ETO, 126–133, 137–150; commands North African expedition, 153–215, 263, 280; rumors of dismissal, 181, 200–201; Sicily campaign, 215–222, 229–240, 263; Italian campaign, 221–222, 237–238, 251–257, 260–263, 268, 275–276, 280, 281; negotiates for Italy's surrender, 233–238, 240–247, 250–261; rumored appointment as chief of staff, 248–250, 262–267; appointed supreme commander AEF (SHAEF), 270; analysis of military career, 902–903

POSTWAR: 15–23; military governor, Occupation, 30, 365, 367–384; chief of staff, 381, 384–403, 404, 486; president of Columbia University, 395–398, 403–406, 411, 412, 416, 417, 430, 434, 441; commands NATO forces (SHAPE), 437–448, 459–460, 466, 499, 570

PRESIDENCY: supported for presidential nomination, 8, 28–30, 368, 380, 388, 394–402, 407–420, 429–438, 443–444, 450–468; press support for, 452; nomination, campaign and election,

foreign affairs, U.S.: Eisenhower on, 29; Eisenhower's position, 356, 476; 1945 policy, 356–357, 377–379, 388; Taft and, 414–415; 1951 policy, 445; "massive retaliation," 463, 624, 664; 1952 policy, 517; "containment," 531, 538, 550, 552, 778, 802, 837; and anticommunism, 530–531, 549–552, 562–565, 568, 579, 584, 615, 619–620, 622–629, 632, 634, 637–643, 647–648, 651–654, 657, 662, 671, 677–678, 689, 694–696, 702, 703n, 728, 733, 757, 771, 773, 776, 781, 792, 802, 810–811, 815, 816, 817, 820–822, 837, 839–840, 868, 879, 881; liberation of satellite nations, 538, 549–552, 563, 567, 753, 754, 778–779; affected by McCarthyism, 549, 553; encirclement, 549–550; congressional versus presidential power in, 558–562; Soviet peace offers, 564–567; summit conferences, 570, 619, 634, 654–655, 668, 688–691, 693, 810, 836, 842–845, 855–857, 866; secrecy, 638; "falling domino" theory, 638–639, 834, 881, 906; bipartisan policy, 655; Eisenhower's influence, 686–688, 690, 697, 739; "position of strength," 689, 810; post-Geneva policy, 706; based on fear, 819, 826, 831; "status quo" character, 868

foreign service, effect of McCarthyism on, 522–523, 554, 622

Formosa. *See* Taiwan

Forrestal, Secretary of Defense James, 319–320, 356, 379, 390–393, 404n, 413, 416, 437n, 452

Fort Myer, 110, 137, 139, 266n, 388

Fort Sam Houston, 49–51, 86, 110

Foster, William C., 804

France, 66, 582; Eisenhower and, 25–26, 172, 178–179, 260, 295, 350, 621; Vichy government, 108–109, 113–114, 151–152, 152n, 159–161, 163–165, 168, 174n, 176, 179–181, 184, 192–195 *passim*, 224, 277, 298, 304; reentry into war, 113; U.S. policy toward, 152, 159, 199, 222–223, 295–298; liberation, 191; unified under de Gaulle, 219; southern, invasion,

269, 273–274, 284–285, 313–316, 322; communists in, 277, 319–321, 626; preinvasion preparation, 286–287; preinvasion political situation, 290, 294–298, 303; 1944 Allied campaign in, 307–315, 319, 322–324; liberation of Paris, 318–322; Dulles policy toward, 621; signs SEATO treaty, 662; war against Egypt, 745–751, 757–768; Algerian revolt, 752, 816; anti-U.S. policy, 819; and nuclear weapons, 849, 856. *See also* de Gaulle, General Charles; invasion, cross-Channel; North Africa; Resistance, French; Vietnam

Franck, Professor James, 372

Fredendall, General Lloyd P., 158, 178, 185, 205

French Committee on National Liberation, 225, 228–229, 260, 276–277, 294–298, 318

French National Committee, 188, 219, 224, 225

French West Africa, 113, 188, 192

Fulbright, Senator William, 727n, 822

Funston, Major General Frederick, 49

Gaither Report, 804–805

Gale, General Humfrey, 328

Gardiner, Colonel William, 253

Gasperi, Alcide de, 574

Gates, Thomas, 864

Gault, Colonel James, 19, 291, 292, 360, 367, 447

Geneva conferences: *1954*, 633, 640, 643–649, 653, 654, 656–658 *passim*, 664, 880; *1955*, 694–706, 726

George VI, King, 226–227, 458

George, Senator Walter, 452, 561

Georges, General Alphonse, 224n

German Democratic Republic (GDR), 838–839, 855. *See also* Germany

German Federal Republic, 668, 690, 838. *See also* Germany

Germany: surrender, 3–14, 355; Eisenhower's attitude toward, 15, 23, 194; occupation of, 16–23, 279, 317, 356; defeat in Russia, 135–136; occupation of Italy, 233–234, 236; bombing, 286; treasure, 357; economy and industry,

Jackson, C. D., 480, 514, 534, 563–565, 573, 612–613, 753n

Jacob, General Ian, 196–197

Japan, 17, 21, 94, 96, 97, 100, 106, 108, 123, 361, 374–375, 377, 550, 639, 864, 867

Jenner, Senator William, 448, 475, 478, 670

Jews, in North Africa (1942), 153, 174n, 184, 192, 195; in occupied Germany, 379–381, 382–384. See also Israel

Jodl, General Gustave, 3–5, 9, 11, 136

John Birch Society, 888

Johnson, Lyndon B., 512, 561, 563, 611, 653, 683, 773, 777–779, 784, 786, 788, 789, 844, 891, 895–896, 901, 909

Johnston, Eric, 851

Joint Chiefs of Staff, U.S., 17, 108, 264, 265, 273, 283, 416, 500, 648, 658, 663, 683n, 843, 898. See also Combined Chiefs

Joint Staff Mission, 107

Jones, W. Alton, 406, 453, 520, 545, 579, 715

Jordan, 729, 748, 751, 757–759, 773, 792–794, 822

Juin, General Alphonse, 174, 176, 198, 641

JUPITER, 130

Kansas City, 28

Kasserine Pass, 198, 202n, 203–205, 210

Kaufman, Judge Irving, 525–526

Kempton, Murray, 475–476

Kennan, George, 392

Kennedy, John F., 534, 611, 773, 845, 873–876, 878–882, 890, 908; Eisenhower's opinion of, 887–888

Kenney, General George, 250, 424

Kesselring, Field Marshal Albert, 261–263

Keynes, John Maynard, 317

Khrushchev, Nikita, 750, 848n; comes to power, 678, 689, 724; at Geneva Conference, 701–702; in Asia, 722; destalinization speech, 732; and revolt of satellites, 750–751, 757; on Suez, 769; Berlin crisis, 838–839, 842; U.S. visit,

844–847, 849–856; on U-2 incident, 861–865; political problems, 862; at Paris Conference, 862; anti-Eisenhower speech, 865; attends UN, 872–873

Killian, Dr. James, 803

King, Admiral Ernest J., 102, 106, 119, 138, 144–154, 198, 264–267 passim, 307, 374

King, Reverend Martin Luther, 720, 895, 906; and Eisenhower, 777n–778n, 828

Kleberg, Robert, 434

Kluge, Field Marshal Gunther, 323

Knowland, Senator William, 427, 481, 512, 560–561, 570, 576, 622, 632n, 657, 661, 662, 670, 672, 685, 777–779, 784, 785, 907

Knox, Frank, 119, 263

Koenig, General Pierre, 296, 318, 321

Korea, 552; U.S. air bases, 550

Korean War, 434–435, 439; campaign issue (1952), 478; Eisenhower and armistice, 490, 493, 496–499, 907; truce, 566–570, 574–577; cause (Eisenhower's view), 675. See also Rhee, Syngman

Kozlov, Frol, 846

Krishna Menon, V. K., 686

Krock, Arthur, 452, 455n, 513

Krueger, General Walter, 85

Kyes, Roger M., 537, 631, 632

La Guardia, Fiorello, 68, 259

labor: Eisenhower and, 455, 468n, 479, 539, 540; management and, unity of, 431

Lahey, Ed, 476–477

landing craft, 108–109, 119, 124–125, 130, 218, 231, 261, 273–274, 278, 283–284

Langley, William, 439

Laniel, Joseph, 574, 616, 618, 641, 642, 649

Lansdale, Colonel Edward, 654, 656

Laos, 441, 568, 851, 857, 880–882

Larson, Arthur, 782, 784

Latin America, 816, 817. See also individual countries

Lattre de Tassigny, General Jean de, 17, 20, 425

11, 15n, 16, 17, 20–22, 158n, 197–
198, 207, 216–218, 231, 237, 239,
240, 247, 251, 262, 271, 278, 284,
292, 303, 304–307, 348–349, 350;
conflict with Eisenhower, 127, 220,
271, 309–311, 324–345, 347, 352–
354, 447
Montgomery, Alabama, 715, 720
Moos, Malcolm, 882, 893
Morgan, Lieutenant General Frederick
E., 26, 278
Morgan, Jerry, 630
Morgenthau, Secretary of Treasury
Henry, Jr., 316–317, 379, 601
Morgenthau Plan, 23, 317, 398, 602
Morocco, 113, 153, 163, 170n, 171, 178,
179, 182, 184, 198, 249, 366, 550,
752
Morrow, E. Frederic, 589, 590n–591n,
787, 828–829
Moseley, General George Van Horn, 67,
71, 77
Mossadegh, Mohammed, 520–521, 579–
587
Mountbatten, Admiral Lord Louis, 121,
126–130, 146n, 264, 281, 288
Mueller, Merrill, 245
MULBERRY, prefabricated invasion ports,
288
Mundt, Senator Karl, 451, 478, 488
Murphy, Robert, 19–21, 236, 247, 277,
371, 382–383, 766, 822n, 823; Eisen-
hower political adviser on Germany,
12, 16, 369; on North Africa, 113,
152n, 159–171, 173–176, 180, 182–
183, 187–188, 192, 195, 223, 226n,
227n, 228; and Suez crisis, 738, 767;
arranges Khrushchev visit, 846, 849
Murrow, Edward R., 141, 368n, 555
Muscatelli, M., 192, 195
Mussolini, Benito, 5, 211, 233–235, 237,
258
Mutual Defense Assistance Act, 428
My Three Years with Eisenhower
(Butcher), 397

Naguib, General Mohammed, 578, 580
Nagy, Imre, 752–754
Naples, 257, 262, 263, 299
Nasser, Gamal Abdel, 723–743, 760–

763, 767, 775, 776, 780, 795, 820,
825, 872–873
National Association for the Advancement of Colored People (NAACP),
590, 592, 597
National Citizens for Eisenhower, 715
National Defense Act of 1920, 55, 67
National Draft Eisenhower League, 401–
403
National Intelligence Board, 658
"national interest," 210, 214, 297, 367,
528–530, 557, 588, 683, 768, 770
national security, 515–517, 521–522,
526–528, 530, 542–543, 552, 600,
609, 612, 741, 805, 837, 909
National Security Council (NSC), 534–
536, 564, 588, 612, 616, 623, 634,
638, 639, 658, 687, 693, 711, 750,
803, 843, 887
Navarre, General Henri, 573, 617, 641,
644
navy. See U.S. Navy
Nazism, 165, 192. See also denazification; Germany; Hitler, Adolf
Negroes: attacks on, 709, 715; and Hungarian refugees, 779n; and Congo
crisis, 878–879. See also civil rights;
school integration
Nehru, Prime Minister Jawaharlal, 552,
575, 735, 810, 876
Nelson, Donald, 91–92
Netherlands, 148, 298, 308, 326, 329,
424, 569, 648
Netherlands East Indies, 96, 102, 107,
113n. See also Indonesia
Nevins, General Arthur S., 545
New Deal, 74–77, 91
New Guinea, 107
Ngo Dinh Diem, 643, 650, 654, 657,
880
Nicolson, Harold, 163, 304
Nicaragua, 627, 647
Nirumand, Bahman, 519
Nixon, Richard M., 600, 622, 713, 779,
812, 827, 894; vice-presidential nomi-
nee, 473; campaign fund case, 479–
490; on Eisenhower, 547; and Mc-
Carthy, 555, 556; and civil rights,
594–596; and Vietnam, 617, 640; anti-
communist speeches, 655; usefulness as

vice president, 672; and second term, 708, 714, 716–719; position during Eisenhower's illnesses, 711, 808–809; attacked in Venezuela, 817–818; Moscow visit, 846; and Khrushchev, 851; Cuban stand, 858; defeat in 1960 presidential election, 873–877; Eisenhower's opinion of, 890, 910; delivers Eisenhower eulogy, 912

Noguès, Auguste, 163, 178–179, 183, 188, 190, 224–226, 382

Normandy, battle for, 307–314, 318. *See also* invasion, cross-Channel

Norstad, General Lauris, 840

North Africa: expedition (GYMNAST, TORCH), 18, 25, 99, 113–114, 120, 130–135, 136n, 138–139, 143n, 146–147, 148n, 150–214, 230, 239; political aspects, 150–154, 156–188, 190–195, 199–200, 215, 219, 223–229; American occupation, 250; postwar discontent, 518

North Atlantic Treaty, 424–429, 441

North Altantic Treaty Organization (NATO), 425, 550, 571, 619, 763–764; basic principles and command, 436–440, 465; Eisenhower as supreme commander (SHAPE), 436–449, 459–460, 465, 499, 570–571; effectiveness, 446; U.S. domination of, 450, 460; West German membership, 667–668, 689–690, 838–839; and nuclear weapons, 673; opposes Warsaw Pact countries, 699, 722; Soviet view of, 702; Eisenhower reaffirms, 769; aims discussed, 771; seeks Cold War abatement, 810–811; French sentiment against, 819, 849

Norway, 84, 130, 148, 298, 424, 550, 864

nuclear power: bombs, 10, 301, 370–379, 381, 387, 606; German scientists, 359, 385; Eisenhower and, 375, 377, 666; diplomatic use, 424–425, 429, 619–620, 623–624; Allied cooperation, 426; Russian success, 428–429, 515–516, 599; and Korea, 439; H-bomb, 515, 755; relation to air bases, 550; threatened use in Korea, 567, 575, 907; controls and disarmament, 593,

611–613, 620–621, 689–690, 708–709, 810, 841; and armed forces reduction, 618; peaceful uses, 617, 620; proposed for Vietnam, 644, 648; effects of, 664–666, 756n, 836, 909; fear of, 666–667; contemplated use, 669, 673, 679–680, 765–766, 825, 834, 899; and NATO, 673, 696–697; attack exercises, 694–696; H-bomb testing, 755–756, 836, 841–842; scientists, 802; French policy, 848, 856. *See also* espionage; Oppenheimer, J. Robert

Nuri es-Said, 724, 751, 820

Nutting, Anthony, 729–730, 748

Nye, General Archibald, 126

O'Daniel, General John W., 631–633

Odlum, Floyd B., 458, 468n, 900

Odlum, Jacqueline Cochran, 458, 900

Office of Strategic Services (OSS), 114, 114n, 160, 318

Office of War Information (OWI), 114n, 186, 187

oil, 102, 822, 825; Middle East, U.S. and Soviet attempts to control, 295, 404n, 496, 517, 518–519; Eisenhower's involvement with, 456, 460–461; companies, and government, 519, 520n, 774; U.S. dominates, 587–588; Soviet interest in, 722; effect of Suez crisis, 739–741, 750, 757, 761–763, 768–769, 774, 775n, 779; and Arab-Israeli war, 776; effect on U.S. policy, 777, 793, 812, 820, 907–908

"Open Skies" proposal, 704–705

Operation Alert, 694

Operation Carte Blanche, 694–696

Oppenheimer, J. Robert, 371, 605–612, 802, 844

Oran, 99, 156–158, 176–178, 185, 188

Ord, Major James, 79–81

Organization of American States, 781

OVERLORD. *See* invasion, cross-Channel

Pacific Charter, 662

Pacific Theater of Operations, 19, 94–95, 100, 114, 122–123, 279; European theater emphasized, 93, 98, 107–108, 111, 112–113, 118, 249; combined command, 105–106; troop redeployment to, 361

Price, Colonel Xenophon, 64
prisoners, Axis, 213, 214, 348, 349; U.S.
  in Soviet Union, 703
propaganda. *See* psychological warfare
Psychological Strategy Board, 564
psychological warfare (propaganda),
  118, 185–186, 236, 258, 564, 620,
  705
public and press relations, 26, 86, 141,
  179, 187, 203, 231–232, 246, 259,
  280, 291, 351, 388, 465–467, 472–
  514, 555, 618, 619, 798
Pucheu, Pierre, 276
Pyle, Ernie, 188
Pyle, Howard, 715

Quemoy. *See* China: offshore islands
  crisis
Quezon, Manuel, 78–82, 101–102

Rabb, Maxwell, 534, 590, 593–594
Radford, Admiral Arthur W., 500, 631,
  632, 640–642, 644, 646, 663, 675,
  680, 683n, 684–685, 701, 704, 759,
  766, 768
Radio Free Europe, 753–754
radioactive fallout, 664–665, 756n, 836,
  909. *See also* nuclear power
Ramsay, Admiral Sir Bertram, 271, 303,
  304, 306, 332
Randolph, A. Philip, 828
Rankin, J. Lee, 597
Rankin, Karl, 680n
Rayburn, Representative Sam (Speaker
  of the House), 426, 655, 676, 779,
  790, 822
Redmond, Kenneth, 626
Reed, Philip, 419
refugees (DPs), 379–384
reparations, German, 317, 373
Republican party, 70, 249, 426; and
  Eisenhower, 351, 368, 392, 399–402,
  409–412, 415, 417, 429–430, 437,
  444, 450, 452–459, 466–470, 532,
  708; John Foster Dulles as elder statesman of, 463–464; 1952 convention,
  469–474; campaign, 474–492; during
  Eisenhower's administration, 511–512,
  516–517, 574, 576, 688; and Mc-
  Carthy, 522–523, 554, 630; and Ei-

senhower's foreign policy, 562; civil
  rights stand, 595; "new Republican-
  ism," 782; Eisenhower as elder states-
  man of, 885, 888–894
Resistance, French, 159–162, 163, 169,
  173–175, 182, 185, 187, 191, 191n,
  192, 218, 219, 229, 276, 277, 288,
  295, 297, 315, 318, 320–321
Reston, James, 465
Reynaud, Paul, 641
Reynolds, Quentin, 245
Reza, Pahlevi, Shah Mohammed, 579
Rhee, Syngman, 435, 498, 566, 567–
  569, 574–577
Ribbentrop, Joachim von, 112
Richardson, Sid, 420, 432, 456–458
Richberg, Donald, 397
Ridgway, General Matthew, 90, 109–
  110, 255, 637, 663, 683n
Roberts, Clifford, 406, 420, 429, 437,
  452, 457, 459, 471, 535n, 544, 715
Roberts, Roy, 465
Robertson, Walter, 576, 678, 684–685
Robinson, William, 397, 406, 420, 429–
  430, 452–454, 457, 459, 465, 471,
  481, 482, 486, 535n, 544, 715
Rockefeller, John D., Jr., 439
Rockefeller, Nelson, 534, 693, 701, 704,
  705, 890–892
Rogers, William, 485n, 622, 812, 828
Rol, Colonel, 321
Rome, 222, 240, 247, 252, 255–257 *passim*, 262, 263, 270, 273–274, 300. *See
  also* Italy
Rommel, Field Marshal Erwin, 108, 114,
  165, 203–204, 300, 308
Rooks, General Lowell, 16
Roosevelt, Franklin D., 10, 74, 75, 85,
  91, 93, 95–96, 97, 101, 114, 119, 313;
  early war strategy, 100, 102–103, 106,
  113–116; and North African campaign, 113, 120, 130–133, 138, 155,
  157, 181, 184–185, 191, 199–201,
  203; French policy, 152–153, 159,
  199–200, 215, 222–229, 276–277,
  295, 297–298, 304, 318–319; and Eisenhower, 199–200, 248, 266–267,
  282; Italian policy, 234–237, 244,
  246, 260n, 274; on fascism, 258; selection of invasion commander, 262–270;

confers with Eisenhower, 279; British distrust of, 293; postwar policy, 350; death, 358n; Yalta terms, 373
Roosevelt, Kermit, 585–586, 727–728
Rosenberg, Julius and Ethel, 524–526, 575
ROUNDUP (cross-Channel plan), 119, 121–125, 127, 129, 134, 144, 146n, 148n
Rovere, Richard, 434, 522, 547, 555, 640, 705
Royall, Kenneth, 399, 404n, 409
Ruhr, 325–326, 349–351, 352, 354, 356–357, 373
Rumania, 6, 323, 423
Rundstedt, Field Marshal Gerd von, 299–300, 308, 323, 351
Russell, Senator Richard B., 239, 409, 452, 537, 632, 779, 787, 800
Russia. See Soviet Union
Ryder, General Charles W., 158, 175n, 176–177, 212

Salazar, Antonio, 866
Salerno (AVALANCHE), 237, 240–241, 246, 247, 251–256, 261, 273, 281, 286
Samos satellite, 860, 863
Sardinia, 221–222
Saud, King, 728, 763, 776, 780, 795
Saudi Arabia, 550, 728, 773
Sayre, Francis B., 101–102
Schiff, John, 439
Schine, G. David, 556, 566. See also McCarthy, Senator Joseph
school integration, 593–598, 618, 720–721, 786–787, 793–801, 828. See also civil rights
Schulz, General Robert L., 388, 406, 418, 447, 449, 494
Schuman, Robert, 436
Schupp, Ferdinand, 649
Schwarzkopf, General Norman, 584
Scott, Senator Hugh, 453
Scranton, Governor William, 891–893
second front. See invasion, cross-Channel
Secret Service, 493
selective service, 85, 93
Sforza, Count Carlo, 259, 260n
Shanley, Bernard M., 534, 590

Sherwood, Robert, 148, 181, 184, 200, 234
SHINGLE. See Anzio
Sicily, invasion of (HUSKY), 200, 202, 208, 211, 215–222, 226, 227, 229–233, 239–240
Simpson, General William, 271, 331, 340
Singapore, 103, 108
Slater, Ellis D., 423, 454, 544
SLEDGEHAMMER (1942 cross-Channel plan), 119, 121–126, 129–132, 134–136, 143–147
Smith, Earl E. T., 839
Smith, Fred, 316–317, 398
Smith, General Walter Bedell, 637; and German surrender, 3–4, 9, 12–13, 701; as Eisenhower's chief of staff, 13, 138, 145, 157, 160n, 228, 265, 270–271; and Eisenhower, 227n, 346, 368, 388; in wartime, 245–247, 250–251, 253, 272–273, 275, 277, 278, 284, 310, 323, 335–340, 342–344; and State Department, 579, 582, 585–586, 626–629, 631, 634, 639, 649, 653, 656
Snyder, General Howard, 418, 449, 707, 711, 737, 807–808, 826
Sokolovsky, General Vassily, 19
Somervell, General Brehon B., 108, 109n, 250
Soong, T. V., 109, 115
South America, 109, 857–858. See also names of countries
Southeast Asia. See Asia
Southeast Asia Treaty Organization (SEATO), 550, 641–643, 662, 679, 722–724, 882
Souvanna Phouma, Prince, 881
Soviet Union (Russia): and German surrender, 4–6, 10–13; conflict with Allies, 6, 10, 16; Eisenhower and, 10, 11, 13, 17–27, 96, 111–114, 387, 392–393, 398, 504, 527, 909; entry into war against Japan, 96, 97, 361, 373–375; war against Germany, 108, 111–112, 119n, 129, 131, 135–136, 149, 221, 268, 299–300, 323, 345, 350, 351, 353–355, 359, 447–448, 702n–703n; and second front, 122–123, 129, 133, 135, 145–147, 149, 269, 302;

987

wartime alliance, 193, 339–341; link with U.S. troops, 353–354, 360; Anglo-American opposition, 354; nuclear bomb in relation to, 372; postwar relations with U.S. and Britain, 371–374, 387; Eisenhower visits, 375–377; and China, 445, 549, 676–677; and encirclement, 445–448, 550; seeks improved world relations, 564–573, 697, 700–706; urges summit conferences, 617–619, 632–633; rejects nuclear controls, 620–621; fears German rearmament, 668, 702n; leadership change, 678; disarmament offer, 691–692; Eastern European defense post, 692; interest in Asia and Africa, 722; Egyptian arms deal, 724–727, 730, 733; effect of satellite revolts, 751–753, 757; and Suez crisis, 764; space program, 785, 801–802; economy, 802; spied on, by U.S., 803; accuses U.S. of aggression, 822. *See also* Berlin; Cold War; communists; post war power. *See also* Khrushchev *and* Stalin

Spaatz, General Carl A., 144, 250, 282, 286–287, 336, 424

space program, 785, 801–805

Spain, U.S. air bases in, 550

Special Operations Executive, 174

Spiedel, General Hans, 308, 838, 849

Sprague, J. Russell, 454

Sputnik, 785, 801–802, 805

Stagg, Group Captain J. M., 301–303, 304–305

Stalin, Josef, 6, 10, 11n, 17, 18, 27, 97, 157, 266, 268–269, 341, 345, 350, 353, 360, 370–372, 376, 392, 462, 549, 553, 562–568, 572, 574, 732

Stalingrad, 135–136, 214

Stark, Admiral Harold R., 91, 95, 102, 106

Stassen, Harold, 403, 408, 433, 435, 443, 455, 472, 484, 496, 622, 693, 701, 704, 708, 710, 719

State Department. *See* U.S. State Department

states' rights, 618, 797

Stephens, Thomas E., 534, 715–716

Stettinius, Secretary of State Edward R., 357

Stevens, Secretary of the Army Robert T., 537, 622, 629, 635–637

Stevenson, Adlai E., 474–475, 476n, 477, 479, 491–492, 655, 707, 716, 755, 767, 773

Stewart, General George C., 586

Stilwell, General Joseph W., 90, 98n, 109, 115, 122, 250

Stimson, Secretary of War Henry, 96, 102, 106, 109, 111, 112, 118–120, 138, 148, 269, 371, 374, 378–379

Strauss, Lewis L., 606–613, 620, 665–666, 755, 819, 844, 882

Streett, General St. Clair, 117, 117n

Strong, General Kenneth W. D., 3–5, 9, 204, 239, 240–242 *passim*, 245–247, 253, 255, 275, 336–339, 447

Stuart, Douglas, 438

Stump, Admiral Felix, 677, 680

Stuttgart, 6, 359–360

Suez Canal, 315; crisis, 577–578, 580, 582, 723n, 730, 732, 736–746, 748–751, 756–770, 774, 775n, 779–780

Sukarno, Achmed, 812–815, 872

Sulzberger, Cyrus, 456, 460, 470, 737

Summerall, General Charles, 67

Summerfield, Arthur, 484, 486, 488, 497, 600

Summersby, Kay, 7–8, 13, 19, 22, 128, 138, 157, 162, 207, 292, 330, 352, 360, 411n, 456

SUPER-GYMNAST (North African invasion), 113–114

Supreme Court. *See* U.S. Supreme Court

Supreme Headquarters Allied Powers Europe (SHAPE), 447–450. *See also* North Atlantic Treaty Organization

Swift, Harold, 438

Swope, Herbert Bayard, 460

Symington, Senator Stuart, 630, 773

Syria, 151, 165, 200, 730n, 757, 765, 773, 792–795, 816

Taft, Senator Robert, 400–401, 408, 414–415, 426, 441–442, 450–451, 455n, 460, 464, 467–470, 472–473, 476–479, 486, 488, 493, 497, 500, 512, 516, 522, 556, 560, 566, 568, 661

and, 512, 532; and Vietnam, 646; position on Chinese islands, 675–676; and Middle East situation, 773–775; budget battle, 781–785; and civil rights, 785–790. *See also* House Committee on Un-American Activities; House Military Affairs Committee

U.S. Forces in the European Theater (USFET), 365

U.S. Military Academy (West Point), 42–48, 110, 116

U.S. Military Advisory and Assistance Group (MAAG), 632

U.S. Navy, 390; Department of, 104, 106, 121, 155, 285

U.S. State Department, 118, 250, 422; investigation of, 522–523, 553, 556; and John Foster Dulles, 538; international opinion, 581. *See also* individual secretaries of state

U.S. Supreme Court: Eisenhower and, 512; civil rights, 593, 595–598, 721, 828

U.S. War Department, 27, 49–50, 55, 82, 84–85, 93, 104, 110, 112, 232, 238; Eisenhower at, 67–77, 86–125, 141; Operations Division (OPD), 97, 118–119, 134, 264, 388–389

universal military training, 27, 385–388 *passim,* 390

V-1 and V-2 rockets, 308, 309, 312, 326, 358

Van Fleet, General James, 90, 498, 575

Vandenberg, Senator Arthur, 400, 424, 427, 428

Vaughan, Sam, 886

Velde, Harold, 603

Venezuela, 815–818

Vichy France. *See* France

Victor Emmanuel, King, 233–235, 252, 253, 257–260

Vietnam (Indochina), 109, 200, 441; U.S. involvement in, 496, 518, 547, 550, 568, 572–573, 615–619, 624, 630–633, 638–650, 654, 657–658, 880, 896–900, 908; French defeat, 616, 637, 641, 644–646, 654–658, 666; peace offers, 618; elections, 656, 880; U.S. policy, 658

Viner, Jacob, 419

Vishinsky, Andrei, 20–21

Voice of America, 553

Wadsworth, James J., 724

Wagner Act, 455

Wainwright, General Jonathan, 103

Walker, Walton, 49

War Department. *See* U.S. War Department

War Plans Division, 84–85, 94, 96–97, 100, 108, 109, 112, 114

War Policies Commission, 69

War Production Board, 91

Warren, Chief Justice Earl, 408, 472, 473, 512, 596–597, 905; civil rights stand, 597–598

Warsaw Pact, 692, 699, 722

Watson, Thomas J., 29, 395–396, 398

Wavell, General Sir Archibald, 106

Waugh, Evelyn, 163

weather, influence on military operations, 231, 301–302, 304–305

Wedemeyer, Colonel Albert C., 126, 248

Weeks, Secretary of Commerce Sinclair, 497, 539–540

Weinberg, Sidney, 453, 494

Welles, Sumner, 102, 195

West Point. *See* U.S. Military Academy

Western European Union, 668

Western Task Force, 158, 163, 217

Westmoreland, General William, 898

Weygand, General Maxime, 152n, 159, 165

Wheeler, Senator Burton K., 18

Wherry, Senator Kenneth, 444

White, Harry Dexter, 317, 601–604, 609, 617–618

White, Dr. Paul Dudley, 709, 716

Whiteley, General John F. M., 336–339, 341, 447

Whitman, Ann, 480, 581, 609, 659, 701, 799, 805–808, 886

Whitney, George, 443, 453

Whitney, John Hay, 453, 545

Wickersham, General Cornelius, 369

Wilkins, J. Ernest, 594

Wilkins, Roy, 828

Willauer, Whiting, 627

Williams, John H., 419

Acknowledgments

I met General Eisenhower through the kindness of Samuel S. Vaughan, of Doubleday & Company. The general offered me access to his files in Gettysburg, a dispensation later given effect by his son, John S. D. Eisenhower, who was also helpful in other ways. Kevin McCann and Robert Schulz of the general's staff were always obliging. Mrs. Joyce Mehring's familiarity with the files was an essential benefit.

Mrs. Mary Ellen Murphy made available to me her notes of interviews with several of General and Mrs. Eisenhower's friends and associates. Charles Boswell loaned me the typescript of his biography of the late Ben Duffy, and other source materials.

I am especially indebted to librarians. At the Eisenhower Library in Abilene to Dr. John Wickman, Roland W. Doty, Jr., and George Curtis; at the Eisenhower Project of the Johns Hopkins University to Dr. Alfred Chandler, Michael Stewart, and Mrs. Elizabeth Smith; at Princeton University to Alexander Clark and Mrs. Wanda Randall; at Columbia University to Louis M. Starr and Mrs. Elizabeth Mason; to Miss Helen Ruskell and the staff of the New York Society Library; to Mrs. Ellin Roberts and the staff of the Woodstock Library; and to the Mid-Hudson Library System.

Stephen E. Ambrose read the early part of my typescript and made useful suggestions. Harry Sions, my friend and editor, offered ceaseless encouragement.

Finally, for a sustenance beyond reckoning, I have to thank Jane D. Lyon.